UNDERSTANDING PSYCHOLOGY

Fifth Edition

UNDERSTANDING PSYCHOLOGY

Fifth Edition

Sandra Scarr
University of Virginia

James Vander Zanden
Ohio State University

RANDOM HOUSE

New York

CHAPTER-OPENING PAINTING CREDITS

Chapter 1: From *Understanding Psychology*, 4th ed., by Sandra Scarr and James Vander Zanden, Random House, 1984. **Chapter 2:** Hirshhorn Museum and Sculpture Garden, Smithsonian Institution. **Chapter 3:** Private collection; courtesy of Allan Stone Gallery. **Chapter 4:** Collection, Byron Meyer. **Chapter 5:** Gift of the Semmes Foundation, McNay Art Museum, San Antonio, Texas. **Chapter 6:** Collection, The Museum of Modern Art, New York. **Chapter 7:** Courtesy of Fischbach Gallery. **Chapter 8:** Collection, The Museum of Modern Art, New York; Mrs. Simon Guggenheim Fund. **Chapter 9:** Courtesy of Hammer Galleries, New York. **Chapter 10:** Rose Art Museum, Brandeis University, Waltham, Massachusetts; gift of Anita Kahn, New York; photo by Herb Gallagher. **Chapter 11:** The Chrysler Museum, Norfolk, Virginia; gift of Walter P. Chrysler, Jr. **Chapter 12:** Hirshhorn Museum and Sculpture Garden, Smithsonian Institution. **Chapter 13:** Private collection; photo by Malcolm Varon. **Chapter 14:** Albright-Knox Gallery, Buffalo, New York; gift of Seymour H. Knox; © The Buffalo Fine Arts Academy 1979. **Chapter 15:** © Rod MacKillop; photo, Jerald Melberg Gallery, Charlotte, North Carolina. **Chapter 16:** Collection of Paul Jacques Schupf, Hamilton, New York; photo courtesy of Marlborough Gallery, New York.

Library of Congress Cataloging in Publication Data

Scarr, Sandra.
    Understanding psychology.

    Includes bibliographies and indexes.
    1. Psychology. I. Vander Zanden, James Wilfrid. II. Title.
BF121.S324   1987   150   86–26263
ISBN 0–394–35958–5

Manufactured in the United States of America

Cover design: Lawrence R. Didona

Preface

Although this is the Fifth Edition of *Understanding Psychology*, it is in fact the second edition that we have written. In the Fourth Edition—our first—we took what had been a very brief, basic text and amplified its coverage. With the publication of this edition, we finally feel the book is truly *ours*. In it we have sought to make the scientific enterprise that is psychology as absorbing for students as it is for us.

Some of our colleagues hold a pessimistic belief that students today are interested only in simple, factual information that can be directly applied to their everyday lives. This view causes us great concern. In our many years of teaching experience at public and private universities, we have known undergraduates in all their variety—from the freshman who grew up on a farm to the street-smart urbanite, from the older woman returning to college to the child genius. They are all different, but their interest in studying psychology is not. And what they want most from their introduction to psychology is not just personally applicable information, but an intelligent and interesting course that describes human behavior in all its remarkable complexity.

We feel that even at the introductory level, students deserve the opportunity to think about what we know, and still do not know, in psychology. Accordingly, in this text we do not gloss over uncertainties in knowledge; nor do we try to appear authoritative where knowledge is lacking. Rather, we present controversies in ways that students can ponder. Thus, *Understanding Psychology*, Fifth Edition, offers students a way to think critically about information in the social and biological sciences, to understand what kinds of questions psychological research can and cannot answer, and to grasp how one can and cannot get reliable answers to these questions. The advantage of this approach is that students learn to become *critical consumers* of information in newspapers, television, and other media. Long after the facts of introductory psychology have become dim memories, students will remember how to evaluate "research" reported in the media.

We also believe that students deserve an account of the "big picture" of human behavior, and so the interaction between biology and experience is an important theme in this book. Without harping on physiological details, we continually remind the reader that we are all biological organisms—members of the human species—with distinctive developmental patterns and likely courses of behavior. We also express respect for individual differences and hope that students will come to understand the ways in which each of us becomes both human and unique. In sum, our approach has been to explain human behavior by integrating biological and social perspectives and showing their relationships. This *interactive* approach is not only intrinsically important for students to understand but also serves the pedagogical purpose of linking and clarifying what would otherwise be a confusing array of topics ranging from neurons to social groups.

Organization

For the instructor, *Understanding Psychology*, Fifth Edition, offers a logical and appealing way to organize the introductory course. In the first chapter we introduce students to the field of psychology: its history, theories, and research methods. Thereafter, our interactive theme shapes the organization of the book.

In Part One we look at the biological bases of behavior, from brain physiology to consciousness to the drives and emotions which motivate our behavior. Part Two examines the systems by which the organism receives and processes information: from sensation and perception to learning, memory, and thought, intelligence and creativity. In Part Three we look at the individual in the social environment: how we interact with one another and how we behave in groups. The two life-span chapters of Part Four review the biological to social spectrum from a developmental point of view. After this survey of human behavior and development, Part Five focuses on the individual personality: what makes each of us unique, how we fare under everyday stress, how and why disturbance and breakdown occur, and, finally, the possible forms of intervention and change.

We believe that this is a logical and understandable way to present introductory psychology, one that other textbooks too seldom follow. You may feel free to read the chapters in a different sequence, since each does stand on its own, but we hope that you will find the logic of the book's organization compelling.

Highlights of the Fifth Edition

Our main objective for this edition was to strengthen the biology/experience theme as a framework for the book. We also set ourselves four additional goals:

1. To *solidify coverage* in those topic areas pointed out by reviewers of the Fourth Edition.

We have added an entirely new chapter, "Health and Stress" (Chapter 14), focusing on the physiological and psychological effects of stress and on ways of coping with stress in everyday life. New sections on aggression and the biochemical foundations of emotions have been incorporated into Chapter 3; a discussion of Sternberg's model on levels of intelligence has been added to Chapter 8; and male/female gender issues have been elaborated upon in the development chapters. These are just a few of the ways in which we have revised the text to enhance and tie together even more closely the book's coverage of an expansive body of empirical knowledge, theoretical views, and contemporary controversies.

2. To *update the text* with recent studies, new findings, current issues, and, occasionally, a new perspective on an old issue.

Having kept a close eye on the field's publications and an ear to the thoughts and criticisms of reviewers and colleagues, we are confident that *Understanding Psychology* is more up-to-date than ever. New research on left- and right-handedness, updated coverage of psychoactive drugs, especially the use and abuse of cocaine and PCP, and a report on attempts to replicate human vision in robots for both industrial and military use represent the kind of up-to-the-minute coverage we have added. Relevant major issues now being brought to our attention by the media and other sources are highlighted. They include such nationwide dilemmas as teenage pregnancy, the AIDS epidemic, and the homeless mentally ill.

Finally, we have remained aware of the changing views coming from the field on many issues, and we have tried to incorporate these new perspectives in *Understanding Psychology*. Perhaps one of the least expected is the revised attitude toward research on extrasensory perception. As the last edition noted,

the field had closed the door, in many ways, on this research. But because of new findings that cannot be ignored, we point out in our chapter on perception that the profession is taking another look at ESP.

3. To *enhance the book's appeal to students* with carefully chosen, improved applications and new introductory sketches in each chapter that will whet the students' natural curiosity.

The *applications* serve several useful purposes. First, they make the text more interesting to read because students can relate to them actively. Second, they facilitate learning because they make the task of studying more enjoyable. Thus, we present a wealth of interesting applications that offer useful information and sound advice on such concerns as understanding the motivational problems behind eating disorders, quitting smoking, fighting insomnia, meditating, improving study habits (plus a section devoted specifically to studying for exams), choosing a day-care center, and handling stress on the job. These applications, plus many others, are presented throughout the book, both in the text itself and in boxed inserts. Whether relevant or not to the individual student's immediate personal needs, we believe they can only reinforce full understanding of the related theories.

The new *sketches* that introduce each chapter are designed to pique the reader's interest by using real-world examples to illustrate the concepts about to be presented. For instance, we draw the student into the chapter on personality with a fascinating sketch of how the Behavioral Science Unit of the FBI pieces together detailed personality profiles of murderers by studying photographs of the murder scene and autopsy reports. At the beginning of the chapter on memory and thought we talk about Russian psychologist Alexander R. Luria's findings about a newspaper reporter who showed incredible mnemonic skills. Students may have heard of people like this reporter, but our guess is that they are unaware that such people's unusual ability severely impairs their thought patterns. We believe that students will be compelled to read on so as to find out why.

4. To *strengthen the pedagogical apparatus* both in the text and in the student supplements.

As in past editions, we have included such reinforcing aids as an outline of contents at the beginning of each chapter, end-of-chapter summaries, end-of-chapter lists of page-referenced key terms, and annotated lists of suggested readings. We bring to the new edition *definitions and pronunciation guides* for key terms at the bottoms of the pages on which the key terms are introduced. We feel these pedagogical aids will help focus students in their reading of the chapter and so will facilitate learning. Along with the Student Self-Tutor that accompanies the book, we believe the apparatus provides a solid support base for student readers.

We should also mention an important goal our publisher set out to achieve in the new edition. Although *Understanding Psychology* has always been a beautiful book, we were not totally pleased with the quality of the illustrations in previous editions. So we asked Random House to revise the art program, with particular attention to the anatomical drawings in Chapters 2 and 5. The results are even better than we had hoped for. The *new illustrations* that enhance this edition are brighter and clearer—more functional and more fun to look at.

Acknowledgments

Four specialists helped us incorporate the solid research coverage in the Fourth Edition that remains the foundation of the Fifth Edition. We thank, again, Jeffrey Wack, Timothy McNamara, Kathleen McCartney, and Roni Beth Tower.

We want to thank the wonderful people at Random House who continue to give an enormous amount of time, care, and attention to this book: Laurel Miller, our trustworthy project editor on the Fourth and Fifth Editions; Cecilia Gardner, who efficiently guided this edition through copyediting and production; Kathy Bendo, our resourceful photo editor; Barbara Salz, the photo researcher; John Lennard, who designed this lovely book; Jennifer Brett, who oversaw the production process; Alison Husting, our developmental editor, who coordinated the reviewing process; Rochelle Diogenes, our supplements editor, who developed the ancillary materials; and Marie Trupia, whose administrative assistance helped us all. Our special thanks go once again to senior editor Mary Falcon, who was responsible for our initial involvement with this book and has guided us through two editions.

A number of academic reviewers of the Fourth and Fifth Editions gave us valuable help in reaching our goal of making psychology understandable, enjoyable, and exciting for all students:

Seymour Baron, Kent State University
Glenn Baskett, Tuskegee Institute
Paul Bronstein, University of Michigan, Flint
Parnell Cephus, Jefferson State Junior College
William Chase, Joliet Junior College
David Cohen, California State College at Bakersfield
Jerry Counce, University of Kentucky
Winifred Curtis, Community College of Rhode Island
Stephen Davis, Emporia Kansas State University
Donna Duffy, Middlesex Community College
William Dwyer, Memphis State University
Mary Ellen Edwards, Edison Community College
Thomas Edwards, CUNY—Medgar Evers College
Victor Fields, Montgomery College
Victor Garlock, Cayuga Community College
Barbara Goebel, Illinois State University
Ellen Huft, Glendale Community College
Roger Humm, Ball State University
Morton Isaacs, Rochester Institute of Technology
Timothy Lehmann, Valencia Community College
Joseph Mangenello, Gloucester Community College
Al Mayer, Portland Community College
Carol Moore, University of Michigan, Flint
Joel Morogovsky, Brookdale Community College
Gary Naseth, Oregon Institute of Technology
William Ogden, Garland Community College
Carol Pandey, Los Angeles Pierce College
Pat Ryan, Tompkins-Cortland Community College
Gary Schaumburg, Cerritos Community College
Dean Schroeder, Laramie County Community College
Alan Schultz, Prince Georges Community College
Jack Shilkret, Anne Arundel Community College
Fred Shima, California State College at Dominguez Hills
Adolph Streng, Jr., Eastfield College
Vivian Travis, Winthrop College
Valerie Vogel, State University of New York College at Buffalo
Charles Waugh, University of Maine
Thomas Weatherly, De Kalb Community College
James Windes, Northern Arizona University

Sandra Scarr
James Vander Zanden

Note to the Instructor

To provide a total learning and testing system, a number of ancillaries have been developed around *Understanding Psychology*. Among them are the *Student Self-Tutor*, the *Exercise and Practice Exam Book*, and the *Test Bank*, all originally developed by National Evaluation Systems, Inc. (NES), an educational research firm that ranks among the nation's foremost experts in testing. For the Fifth Edition, these aids have been revised and, in our opinion, greatly enhanced by Larry Nucci of the University of Illinois at Chicago, Paul Rosenfeld, and Darren Newtson and Diana Julian of the University of Virginia.

We believe that the *Student Self-Tutor*, the *Exercise and Practice Exam Book*, and the *Test Bank*, together with the *Instructor's Manual*, color transparencies and slides, films, computerized activities, test generator programs, and customized testing service that are available, will be invaluable to your students —and to you.

Student Self-Tutor

In the 1950s, a technique for effective studying, known as SQ3R, was developed. SQ3R is an abbreviation for a five-step approach to studying *any* subject: Survey, Question, Read, Recite, and Review. Using this method, students break information into manageable chunks—either chapters or sections of a chapter—and actively process it.

SQ3R operates as follows. First the student *surveys* the chapter or section, looking at headings, illustrations, and the summary, to get an idea of the topics that are covered and the relative importance of each. In the second step the student turns each of the headings into one or more *questions* to stimulate his or her curiosity about the subject matter. Next the student *reads* the chapter or section. In the fourth step, the student *recites* aloud as much of the material as he or she can recall. Finally, the student *reviews* the information, noting what he or she has omitted or misunderstood during recitation and rereading those passages.

Today there is a renewed interest in SQ3R among psychology instructors, and a number of authors have incorporated some of its elements into introductory psychology textbooks. We advocate SQ3R and think that authors who have used it in their texts have taken a step in the right direction. However, to students who are assigned a textbook that includes SQ3R features but who choose not to use them, the features may prove distracting and actually impede learning. In addition, *in its ideal form, SQ3R is a process in which the student must actively participate.* (To convince students how important it is to participate in their own learning, we ask them to imagine how fit they would become if they merely *watched* Jane Fonda work out!) To include SQ3R in a textbook is to return the student to a more passive role and is therefore somewhat self-defeating.

The final reason for not including SQ3R in a textbook—and perhaps the most compelling one—is that the most effective means of studying is to spend most of one's study time on recitation—and, of course, recitation cannot be incorporated into a textbook.

Thus we have decided to offer students a separate SQ3R workbook, called the *Student Self-Tutor (SST)*, which is packaged *free* with the text. The SST has sixteen chapters, which correspond to the chapters in the text. It is to be kept open next to the text and used in tandem with the student's first reading of each chapter.

For each chapter, the *SST* includes:

- "Survey," which provides an overview of the chapter

The *SST* is then broken down into text chapter sections and proceeds with the Q-R-R-R steps of the study method. For each chapter section, the *SST* includes:

- "Question," which asks the student to consider several questions suggested by the section headings

- "Read," which directs the student to the appropriate pages in the text

- "Recite," which presents the learning objectives to be covered in the recitation as well as reminders (printed in italics) to check against. (These are the same learning objectives that are keyed to test questions in the student's *Exercise and Practice Exam Book* and the *Test Bank*.)

- "Review," which provides conceptual and factual questions to test comprehension

If, after completing the Q-R-R-R steps for a section, the student is satisfied with his or her mastery, he or she can go on to the next section. If not, the three Rs should be repeated.

There are real advantages to using the *SST:*

- It is easy and enjoyable to use. Most important, the very act of using it creates the cognitive involvement that students need for learning.

- It provides a complete SQ3R system, including— and *stressing*—recitation, the most important step in the process.

- It is not a distracting element in the textbook. Although students are required to read the text, they can ignore the *SST* if they like.

In the following "Note to the Student," we urge students to give the *SST* a try. If they faithfully perform the SQ3R steps—especially the recitation part—mastery is practically unavoidable. If they merely read the *SST* sections as they read the text, an increase in learning will still occur. Moreover, not only will they increase their mastery and enjoyment of introductory psychology, but they will learn a study technique that can be used to master any written material.

Exercise and Practice Exam Book

Unlike the *SST*, the *Exercise and Practice Exam Book* (*EPEB*) is to be studied after a chapter has been read and before midterms and finals. New to this edition is a self-assessment component that, like the *SST*, actively engages students. After completing each chapter, students can score their own exercises according to subject area or type of knowledge (conceptual or factual) tested. In this way they can evaluate their own strengths and weaknesses and

develop a personalized study strategy. For each chapter of the text, the *EPEB* includes:

- Learning objectives from the "Recite" section of the *SST*, which alert students to their goals in studying the chapter

- A chapter outline, which helps students refresh their recollections of the broad concepts covered in the chapter

- Crossword puzzles, acrostics, visual mnemonic devices, matching terms, and definitions, which reinforce students' memories and are easy, enjoyable, and effective activities

- Two practice multiple-choice exams, of twenty questions each, containing both factual and conceptual items, which are keyed to learning objectives and to specific pages in the text

Test Bank

The *Test Bank*, prepared by Darren Newtson and Diana Julian at the University of Virginia, consists of 140 multiple-choice questions per chapter. Approximately half of these are conceptual, and half involve factual knowledge. These questions are keyed to learning objectives and to pages in the text, and are categorized by level of difficulty.

Instructor's Manual

The *Instructor's Manual*, prepared by Paul Rosenfeld and Horace Marchant at Westfield State College, includes student learning objectives, a detailed outline of each chapter, lecture topics and classroom discussion ideas, five essay questions and answers, references, and media sources for each chapter of the text. Also included are an appendix on how to organize and run a PSI (Personalized System of Instruction) course and reproduction masters for each chapter.

Other Teaching Aids

Also available with *Understanding Psychology*, Fifth Edition, are the following teaching aids:

- One hundred full-color transparencies

- One hundred full-color slides
- Films (available on a scheduling basis)
- *Computerized Activities in Psychology* (CAPSI), an experiential learning program for Apple II or IBM microcomputers, revised and expanded for this edition

- Test generator program for Apple and IBM microcomputers
- A customized testing service, for which you may telephone in your test orders (toll-free)

Note to the Student

Two unique study aids accompany this textbook: the *Student Self-Tutor* and the *Exercise and Practice Exam Book*. Each aid is valuable in its own right, and together they form a powerful learning and studying system that will markedly increase your mastery and enjoyment of this text.

Student Self-Tutor

What Is the *Student Self-Tutor?*
Have you noticed the booklet that's been wrapped along with this textbook? Unless your instructor assigns it, you don't *have* to read it—it's optional. But if you choose to use the *Student Self-Tutor* (*SST*), you may improve your grade in this course—and enjoy the course more, too.

The *SST* is a study tool that you can use side by side with the text as you read it. It is a highly effective learning aid, based on sound psychological principles.

The *SST* is easy and enjoyable to use. If you use it faithfully, you will need to read each chapter in the text only *once!*

Finally, the *SST* will help you develop good study habits that will serve you well throughout your college career—and beyond.

How Does the *Student Self-Tutor* Work?
The basis of the *Student Self-Tutor* is a study technique commonly known as SQ3R. SQ3R stands for *Survey, Question, Read, Recite,* and *Review.* In the *Student Self-Tutor,* SQ3R has been custom-tailored to *Understanding Psychology,* Fifth Edition. But once you learn the technique, you can apply it to *any* written material you want to master.

The introduction to the *SST* presents specific instructions that tell you, step by step, how to use this booklet. In brief, it works this way.

The *SST* has sixteen chapters to correspond to the chapters in the textbook. Before you read a text chapter you will read the *survey,* which gives you an overview of the important topics in the chapter and their organization.

The *SST* then proceeds one section of a text chapter at a time, and you will be led through the remaining steps of the study process for each chapter section. First, the *SST* suggests *questions* for you to keep in mind as you read, and then it directs you to the text pages to *read.* The next step—*recite*—is very important in this learning system. You will be asked to look up from your book and talk to yourself (or to a friend) about what you have just read. The *SST* provides cues and reminders to help you cover everything important in that chapter section. Finally, you will answer *review* questions that will test your mastery of the material.

Why Should You Use the *Student Self-Tutor?*
The *SST* is based on the fundamental psychological principle that *active learning is more effective* than passive learning. You probably know this from your own life. How many times have you just watched someone, say, play a guitar or cook a special meal? Did you learn very much? Now recall performing those activities yourself, and we're sure you'll agree that *doing* something is a more effective and enjoyable way of learning than *watching* something being done.

Because the *SST* is based on an active method of learning, using it along with the textbook will increase your mastery of introductory psychology—and make the learning process easier and more fun.

Exercise and Practice Exam Book

Whereas the *SST* is designed to be used along with the textbook as you read it, the *Exercise and Practice Exam Book* (*EPEB*) will help you to rehearse and prepare for exams. For each chapter, it includes:

- Learning objectives, which tell you the material to be mastered in the chapter

- An outline, which helps you refresh your memory of the broad concepts covered in the chapter

- Crossword puzzles, matching terms, and other activities, which help you remember terms and definitions—and are fun to do!

- Two multiple-choice exams, which are keyed to the learning objectives and to specific pages in the text. These will enable you to check your mastery of the material in the book and give you good practice in test taking.

- Self-assessment charts enable you to score your exercises and exams. In this way you can pinpoint your strengths and weaknesses and prepare better for exams.

We have written *Understanding Psychology*, Fifth Edition, and designed the *SST* and *EPEB* with *you* in mind. We hope you find this package effective and informative, and we hope you get the most knowledge and enjoyment possible from these materials.

Contents

PART 3
SOCIAL BEHAVIOR   287

Chapter 9
Human Interaction   289

Chapter 10
Attitudes and Group Processes   317

PART 4
HUMAN DEVELOPMENT   351

Chapter 11
Infancy and Childhood   353

Chapter 12
Adolescence and Adulthood   387

Boxed Inserts

Untitled drawing by Ed Butler.

1

What Is Psychology?

How do you manage to navigate crowded campus sidewalks and intersections so that you do not collide with your fellow students? Very likely you have never given the matter much thought. You simply take it for granted that somehow you get from here to there on campus. Yet if you and your classmates were to move like two sets of robots, each set maintaining its line of march, few if any of you would reach your destinations without being knocked down. Students at Ohio State University have looked into this matter and have identified a number of crash-avoidance devices:

- Most of us walk on the right side of walkways and follow the "first come, first through" principle at crowded intersections.

- At about fifteen to twenty feet we ordinarily "size up" the situation. We glance at pedestrians whom we are likely to encounter at an intersection and occasionally establish fleeting eye contact with them. We then shut down eye contact until we are about five feet apart.

- We communicate with other pedestrians on a nonverbal level. At about three to five feet we establish brief eye contact, signaling to them that we recognize their presence. We typically do not hold the visual contact unless we wish to take an assertive or aggressive stance.

- We often "negotiate" with other pedestrians on which of us will cross the intersection first. We slow our pace to signal to them that we would like them to increase their pace, or we quicken our pace to ask them to slow their pace. We incline our heads, shoulders, or bodies and dart our eyes in the direction we are headed. All the while we monitor their behavior, mentally note their responses to our body language, and infer what they are likely to do.

On a busy street people rarely touch or make lengthy eye contact. Rather, we make fleeting glances and negotiate ways to pass by, despite the close physical presence of others. *(Steve Hansen/Stock, Boston)*

- If we are alone we are likely to give way or detour around a group of people. Those of us in a group usually ignore the lone individual and assertively continue on course.

- We cooperate with other pedestrians to effect a "clean pass." We slightly angle our bodies, turn our shoulders, and take a slight step to the side; we pull our hands inward or away to avoid hand-to-hand contact; and we twist our bodies sideways to maximize face-to-face distance.

As this illustration suggests, the psychological perspective invites you to look more carefully at often-neglected or taken-for-granted aspects of the human experience and to examine them in fresh and creative ways. You will find that there are many layers of meaning in life and that things are not always what they seem. Just as you often overlook the ways you go about navigating campus walkways, so you also take for granted much of what is involved in navigating seventy or so years of the human life span.

Psychology is the study of behavior and mental processes. It equips you with a special kind of consciousness. From psychology you can gain a better understanding of what people say and do and new insights into yourself. As you look behind the outer edifice of human behavior and scrutinize its hidden fabric, you encounter new levels of reality. This approach to reality—a special form of consciousness and insight—is what psychology is all about. Psychology, then, offers you an invitation to take a new look at the human experience. We can make two promises about this book: first, it will answer some of the questions you have about yourself and other people, and second, it will show that everyday behavior is far more complex—and interesting—than most people imagine.

psychology: The study of behavior and mental processes.

WHY STUDY PSYCHOLOGY?

As the opening example suggests, one advantage of learning about psychology is that it offers new frameworks for viewing daily events: many things that you take for granted will be seen in a new way. There are other advantages as well.

Insight

Understanding psychology can provide useful insights into your own and other people's behavior. Suppose, for example, that a student is convinced he is hopelessly shy and doomed forever to feel uncomfortable in groups. Then he learns from social psychology that different kinds of groups tend to have different effects on their members. He thinks about this for a while and notes that although he is miserable at parties, he feels fine at meetings of the school newspaper staff and with the group he works with in the biology laboratory. (In technical terms, he is much more uncomfortable in unstructured social groups than in structured, task-oriented groups.) Realizing that he is uncomfortable in only some groups brings a flood of relief. He is not paralyzingly shy. He just does not like unstructured groups. Some people resemble him in this respect and thus he is not alone in his feelings. There is something about everyone in this book. You, too, may find that after studying one chapter or another, you see yourself in a new way. In sum, psychology offers you the potential for acquiring a greater measure of self-insight and thus, perhaps, the prospect for leading a fuller, richer, and more fruitful life.

Of course, you must be careful in applying your new insights. There are few people who are more obnoxious than the student who has taken an introductory psychology course and proceeds to terrorize family, friends, and strangers with an analysis of every action (not to mention all the neurotic puppies and goldfish that have been created by psychology students trying out new training methods on their pets). There is much truth to the old maxim, "A little knowledge is a dangerous thing." Nonetheless, the more psychology you study, the more respect you will gain for the complexity and the diversity of human behavior. An introductory psychology course is just one investment in a lifelong process of learning about yourself and others.

Practical Information

Some of the chapters in this book include material that has practical application to everyday life. You will read, in concrete and detailed form, how to employ a number of useful procedures that psychologists have developed. So you can gain much practical information and knowledge from psychology.

For example, Chapter 7 includes a description of several *mnemonic devices*, or memory aids, that will help you to learn information by rote. The rhyme beginning "Thirty days hath September," which helps many people to remember the number of days in each month, is an example. When using mnemonic devices you usually associate each item on a list with some sort of mental picture. Although this procedure may require time and effort (especially the first time), memory experts have shown that it is worth the trouble. The techniques described may help you to memorize almost any list of words or numbers—the names of the presidents of the United States and their dates in office (for a history course), the authors and titles of books (for an English course), phone numbers, shopping lists, and so on.

Chapter 6 describes the systematic way of dispensing rewards and punishments that psychologists call *shaping*. You will definitely find this method useful if you ever have to train a puppy. You may also find yourself wondering how to shape the behavior of people around you. Perhaps you have a friend who is always happy to join you for coffee or a movie but who never brings any money along. You have loaned him money many times, and just as many times he has failed to pay you back. You know he can afford to pay his share, and you have told him so repeatedly. But he is a good friend, so you end up paying his way again and again. In doing so, you are rewarding or reinforcing an undesirable behavior pattern. Is that what you really want to do?

In Chapter 11, on child development, you will recognize some of the experiences you had in your own childhood. Chapter 15, on disturbance and breakdown, may help you understand the more difficult periods in your own life and in the lives of those around you. And Chapter 16 will tell you about the different kinds of therapy available to people who are experiencing severe or chronic difficulties. But of course, you should not jump to conclusions on the basis of this introduction to psychology. It takes a trained professional to diagnose and treat psychological problems.

Animals can be taught surprisingly difficult tricks by a method called shaping, whereby the trainer rewards closer and closer approximations of the desired behavior. Humans, too, can be taught skills through shaping, as you will see in Chapter 6. *(Melissa Shook/The Picture Cube)*

Testing Your Intuitions

After reading this book, you will be able to check some of your assumptions about human behavior. Psychologists have put common sense to the test to find out whether the things that many people take for granted are in fact true. The statements about behavior printed in Figure 1.1 represent a small fraction of the beliefs psychologists have examined. Which of these statements do you think are true?

Before telling you the answers, we ask you to consider the implications of these opinions. Employers who believe that retarded people are mentally ill (item 13) and that many mentally ill people are dangerous (item 14) will undoubtedly refuse to hire a retarded person even though he or she may be perfectly suited for the job. Parents who believe that noisy, overly active children can be changed by

punishment (item 4) inflict a great many spankings and scoldings. Both reactions would be unfortunate, for psychologists have found that all the statements in this list are false.

HOW PSYCHOLOGISTS FIND THE ANSWERS

We have said that psychologists seek answers to questions having to do with behavior and mental processes. They approach their task with a scientific perspective. This focus involves the rigorous, disciplined pursuit of objectivity. Psychologists cultivate a disciplined approach to their subject matter so that they may determine facts as they are and not as they might wish them to be. As scientists, they are expected to avoid becoming so emotionally involved with their work that they cannot adopt a new approach or reject an old answer when their findings require that they do so. Let us consider, then, how psychologists go about finding answers to various questions.

Asking the Right Questions

You are sitting in the cafeteria with a group of people, waiting for your next class. Someone across the table says that she thinks psychotherapy is a waste of time and money. You think of a friend who has been seeing a therapist for some time. In your opinion, he is as mixed up now as he was when he started. But before you can say anything, a third person breaks in. He says that his brother has really changed since he entered therapy—he has stopped fighting with their parents, gotten a job, and assumed responsibility for himself. The person next to you comments, "It probably wasn't the therapy. The kid just needed time to grow up." Someone else chimes in, "I don't believe in the stuff. It's causing all kinds of trouble between my girlfriend and me. She wouldn't need a therapist if she would move away from her crazy family." Another person begins talking about how much he thinks therapy has helped him. The time for class rolls around, and you leave feeling more confused about this topic than you were before. Does therapy work or doesn't it?

How would a psychologist go about answering this question? The answer is that a researcher would

1. The behavior of most lower animals—insects, reptiles and amphibians, most rodents, and birds—is instinctive and unaffected by learning.
2. For the first week of life, a baby sees nothing but a gray blur regardless of what he or she "looks at."
3. A child learns to talk more quickly if the adults around the child habitually repeat the word he or she is trying to say, using proper pronunciation.
4. The best way to get a chronically noisy child to settle down and pay attention is to punish the child.
5. Slow learners remember more of what they learn than fast learners.
6. Highly intelligent people—"geniuses"—tend to be physically frail and prone to mental illness.
7. People who blame themselves, at least in part, for becoming the victim of a crime, accident, or illness have greater difficulty coping with the event than do individuals who do not blame themselves.
8. If you are mugged, you are more likely to receive help from a passerby in a crowded area of a park than in an area with only one or two other people.
9. The reason obese people are larger than slender people is that they eat more food than slender people do.
10. People who threaten suicide rarely follow through and take their own lives.
11. The largest drug problem in the United States, in terms of the number of people affected, is marijuana.
12. A good many people engage in bizarre and unusual activities when the moon is full.
13. Most mentally retarded people are also mentally ill.
14. A third or more of the people suffering from severe mental disorder are potentially dangerous.
15. The more severe the disorder, the more intensive the therapy required to cure it; for example, schizophrenics usually respond best to psychoanalysis.

FIGURE 1.1 Some of the beliefs about human behavior that psychologists have investigated and have found to be false.

not tackle such a broad and ill-defined question. As discussed in Chapter 16, the term "psychotherapy" covers everything from psychoanalysis to token economies. To answer this question you would have to investigate *all* the different kinds of therapy—an enormous task. You might concentrate on one form, leaving the investigation of other methods to other researchers. But even then you would have problems.

Some people see a therapist once a week for a few months, some five days a week for six or eight years. Some begin therapy because they want to grow; some because losing their job, getting divorced, or some other crisis has left them confused and unhappy; some because they are hospitalized and cannot function. Some start therapy as children, some in middle age. Some see a therapist of the same sex, some a therapist of the opposite sex. All these factors could make a difference. Whom would you study?

Then there is the question of what you mean by therapy "working." Do you accept a person's statement that she feels better about herself and her life,

or do you measure success in terms of observable changes in behavior? Suppose the people change during therapy. How do you know the change is due to therapy and not to other events in their lives? Wouldn't they have changed in some ways without therapy? Would some other form of therapy have been more or less effective? The more you think about this topic, the more questions you ask.

To do research on the effectiveness of psychotherapy, a psychologist has to take all these factors into account. And for this reason, researchers focus on a limited, well-defined set of questions. A psychologist might conduct research on whether people with similar problems and in similar life situations benefit from a specific kind of therapy. But he or she would not attempt to answer the whole question "Does therapy work?" The answers to big questions are usually arrived at by many psychologists researching limited questions in different ways and examining one another's work with respectful skepticism.

The first step, then, in all psychological research is to ask a precise question about a limited topic. In most cases, researchers also formulate a **hypothesis**—an educated guess about the relationship between two factors or variables. In a hypothesis, researchers state what they expect to find, and the statement is expressed in such a way that it can be proved or disproved. An example would be: hospitalized schizophrenics (individuals with a severe form of mental illness) who participate in a token economy program begin to make intelligible statements to other people sooner than hospitalized schizophrenics who do not participate in such a program (see Chapters 6 and 16). The research project is designed to test this hypothesis. The hypothesis may prove to be wrong—the researcher may find no difference between the two groups.

Thus psychology is an *empirical science*—one in which precise statements are tested to see whether they are true or false. There are many kinds of tests—surveys, experiments, naturalistic observations, and so on—and they are described in detail later in the chapter. But answers to general questions are arrived at only by general agreement on the part of experts after years of research on many different aspects of a problem.

Psychologists Disagree

Agreement takes time, and the experts in a given area often disagree. Sometimes this disagreement is very specific and concrete. For example, the psychologist Lee Salk (1962) suspected that unborn babies associate their mother's heartbeat with the security and comfort of the womb. If this is true, Salk reasoned, newborn infants should find the sound of a heartbeat soothing. He tested this idea by placing infants in two separate nurseries and playing the sound of an amplified heartbeat in one. It turned out that the babies in this nursery slept more, cried less, and gained weight faster than babies in the quiet nursery. Salk concluded that his original idea was correct.

Yvonne Brackbill and several of her colleagues (1966) were not entirely convinced, however. In a preliminary study, they found that two different

rhythmic sounds—a metronome (an instrument that makes regular clicking sounds) and a lullably—were just as effective in quieting babies as the heartbeat. Thus it appeared that infants were responding to the constant, monotonous rhythm, not to the heartbeat itself. Brackbill (1971) went on to test whether newborn infants responded favorably to other monotonous sensations—constant light, increased heat, and snug swaddling. She found that *all* of these seemed to comfort babies. Thus Salk's conclusions were not entirely wrong, but neither were they entirely correct. He had simply been too specific. Newborn babies seem to find a wide variety of monotonous, constant sensations reassuring. More recent research has further clarified these matters. Vocal music is more effective in soothing infants than monotonous noise is (Butterfield and Siperstein, 1972). And babies prefer the voice of their mother to that of other women or their father (DeCasper and Fifer, 1980; Prescott and DeCasper, 1981).

Similar challenges occur all the time. One researcher reports an interesting finding, and another comes along to examine the study critically and question some aspect of it. With variations on the same theme, the second researcher clarifies, corrects, and extends the results obtained by the first researcher. Indeed, Salk's work is recognized as a valuable contribution, particularly because it directed the attention of psychologists to the prenatal sensory experience of humans (DeCasper and Sigafoos, 1983).

But sometimes there are more fundamental disagreements among psychologists. B. F. Skinner investigated minute units of behavior (discrete actions), whereas Sigmund Freud focused on how unconscious motives and underlying personality patterns find expression in behavior. Thus, as will be seen in the section on the history of psychology, the followers of Skinner and of Freud have very different views of the nature of human beings, and they start out by examining different behaviors and by studying behavior at different levels of analysis. In turn, each set of psychologists has undertaken to formulate global theoretical statements about behavior based on their perspective and, not surprisingly, the

---

hypothesis (hi-PA-tha-sis): An educated guess about the relationship between two variables.

two sets have found themselves in fundamental disagreement.

The matter is somewhat like the old story of the three blind men and the elephant. Each man groped his way toward the elephant and encountered a different part of the animal's anatomy. "It's like a rope," announced the man who touched the elephant's tail. "No, it's like a wall," said the second man, who walked into the animal's side. "You're both wrong," said the third man, who had discovered the trunk. "This is obviously a snake."

As a psychology student, you will not be asked to resolve these differences of opinion, but you should be aware that they exist. Disagreement is the sign of a healthy, growing science. Indeed, a clash of ideas, rather than being a disaster, presents new opportunities for clarifying issues and initiating new studies.

Basic and Applied Psychology

Not uncommonly, various fields of study are categorized as being either "basic" or "applied" sciences. **Basic science** is the pursuit of knowledge for its own sake in order to satisfy curiosity about the nature of things. The immediate "usefulness" of the knowledge is not an issue. **Applied science,** on the other hand, involves using a basic science to accomplish practical goals. Hence physicists do not build bridges although engineers do, biologists do not treat people afflicted with cancer although physicians do, and chemists do not fill prescriptions at the drugstore although pharmacists do. Physics, biology, and chemistry are basic sciences, whereas engineering, medicine, and pharmacy are applied sciences.

In its early years, psychology was generally considered to be a basic science. However, in the intervening hundred or so years, psychology has increasingly evolved as a science having both basic and applied components. Most psychologists no longer see a hard-and-fast boundary separating basic from applied aspects of their discipline. Individual psychologists may concentrate their energies in the one realm or the other. Consequently, psychology encompasses both basic and applied dimensions, and one does not find within psychology the sharp division that separates physics from engineering, biology from medicine, or chemistry from pharmacy.

Today you can encounter the application of psychological findings in many areas of life. Take developmental psychology. Not too many years ago, newborns were isolated immediately after birth in special hospital nurseries. In many cases, parents could view their babies only through a glass window. Often parents did not get to hold their newborn until the mother and infant were discharged from the hospital. Premature infants were kept in incubators, deprived of normal skin contact and other kinds of stimulation.

These patterns have largely changed over the past twenty years. Research by developmental psychologists has established the importance for both newborns and their parents of close physical and interactive contact. And researchers have demonstrated the value of providing premature infants with extra human stimulation in the form of handling, cuddling, talking, singing, and rocking (Scarr and Williams, 1973; Gottfried et al., 1981). In the light of these findings, hospitals throughout the world have rather rapidly altered their practices to allow for newborn-parent contact and for the special stimulation of premature babies.

Psychology also affects public policy. A good illustration of this is the Head Start program. Psychological research on children's nursery-school experiences was influential in leading government officials to establish the Head Start program in 1965 as an offshoot of the War on Poverty. The program was designed to provide children from low-income families with early intervention education in nursery-school settings. It was believed that appropriate services from outside the family could compensate for the disadvantages these youngsters experienced during their early years. Over the years an accumulating body of research has shown that children in good preschool programs do indeed get a head start (Lazar and Darlington, 1982; Schweinhart and Weikart, 1985). Children who participated in Head Start programs in the 1960s have performed as well as or better than their peers in regular school and have had fewer grade retentions and special class

---

basic science: The pursuit of knowledge about natural phenomena for its own sake.
applied science: Discovering ways to use scientific findings to accomplish practical goals.

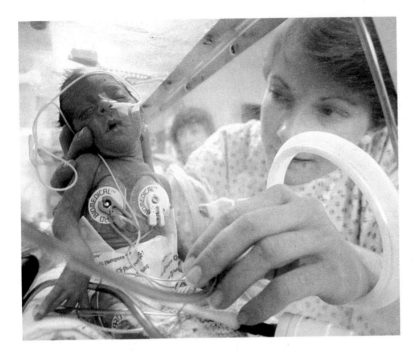

Prematurely born babies are kept in specially heated and humidified cribs, called isolettes, until they can maintain body temperature and breathe normally in the atmosphere of the nursery. But they benefit from the stimulation of handling, voices, music, and rocking even before they can join the world of normal newborns. These practices are an example of psychological findings being applied for human benefit. *(Tim Jewett/EKM-Nepenthe)*

placements. Likewise, youths who were in a Head Start program engage in less antisocial and delinquent behavior and are more likely to finish high school and get jobs or go to college than are their peers who were not in a program. The project has also provided hundreds of thousands of young children with essential health care services. In sum, psychology is a discipline with strong basic and applied components.

HOW PSYCHOLOGISTS DO RESEARCH

Both basic and applied psychology require reliable and valid information about behavior and mental processes. In this section we go behind the scenes to see how psychologists learn about these matters. We poke into laboratories where they are conducting experiments, follow them on surveys, and discuss some of the research problems psychologists have.

The surprise is that psychologists do what most people do in everyday life—only more carefully and more systematically. When you turn on the television and the picture is out of focus, you *experiment* with different knobs and dials until you find the one that works. When you ask a number of friends about a movie you are thinking of seeing, you are conducting an informal *survey*. Of course, there is more to doing scientific research than turning dials at random or asking friends what they think. Over the years psychologists, like other scientists, have transformed these everyday techniques for gathering and analyzing information into more precise tools.

Psychological research is also directed and guided by explicit hypotheses, whereas everyday research is typically governed by rather ill-defined, implicit ideas about the nature of the world. Of equal significance, should the theoretically guided hypotheses developed by psychologists be false, their research is designed to reveal this fact to them. But the same cannot be said for everyday research. Facts can usually be made to fit more than one explanation or theory. Consequently, the pursuit of scientific knowledge dictates that researchers seek evidence that will disconfirm a hypothesis if indeed it is false, rather than selectively looking for confirming evidence. In contrast, everyday research tends to be governed by a search for supporting, not disconfirming, evidence.

Whether of the everyday or psychological variety, all research is guided by some sort of underlying assumptions. Neither the layperson nor the psychologist simply goes out and "observes" behavior—any and all behavior—without prejudging what will be seen. Both kinds of activity involve initial expectations concerning what is likely to be found. As pointed out earlier in the chapter, it is simply not possible to observe or study everything about a phenomenon. One would be simply overwhelmed by an endless, unmanageable panorama of data. Instead, researchers must limit the scope of their observations by asking some questions and ignoring others. Thus they must begin by asking a specific question about a limited topic. The next step is to look for evidence.

How do psychologists collect information about the topic they have chosen to study? The method that researchers select depends partly on the research topic. For example, a social psychologist who is studying the effects of group pressure on conformity is likely to conduct an experiment. A psychologist who is interested in personality theories might begin with intensive case studies of individuals. But whatever approach to gathering data psychologists select, they must carefully plan how they will proceed.

Samples

Suppose a psychologist wants to know how the motivation to attend college affects the academic attitudes of high-school juniors and seniors. It would be impossible to study every junior and senior in the country. There are just too many. Instead, the researcher would select a **sample,** a relatively small group out of the total **population** under study (in this case, all high-school juniors and seniors).

Choosing a sample can be tricky. A sample must be *representative* of the population a researcher is studying. For example, if you wanted to know how tall American men are, you would want to make certain that your sample did not include a disproportionately large number of professional basketball players. This sample would be *biased;* it would not represent American men in general.

The editors of *Literary Digest* learned about sample bias the hard way. Before the 1936 presidential election, the magazine conducted a massive telephone survey to find out whether voters favored Franklin Roosevelt or Alf Landon. On the basis of the poll's results, the *Digest* predicted that Landon would win by a landslide. However, when the votes were counted on election night, it was Roosevelt who won by a landslide. What went wrong? The magazine had questioned only people who appeared on their subscription rolls or who were listed in the telephone book. In those Depression days, conservatives usually subscribed to this magazine, and only the affluent could afford the luxury of a telephone. And these were people who tended to be Republicans. The *Digest's* sample did not represent the views of American voters; it was biased toward Landon, the Republican candidate. Today, political polling is quite sophisticated. Even so, by virtue of their different sampling techniques, poll organizations arrive at somewhat different predictions (see Table 1.1). Some political scientists contend that the Harris sample seems consistently to include more Democratic-leaning respondents while the NBC sample seems weighted toward the Republicans (Farney, 1984).

There are two ways to avoid a biased sample. One is to take a purely **random sample,** so that each individual within the scope of the research has an *equal chance* of being represented. For example, a psychologist might choose every twentieth name on school enrollment lists for a study of schoolchildren in a particular town. Random sampling is like drawing names or numbers out of a hat while blindfolded.

The second way to avoid bias is deliberately to pick individuals who represent the various subgroups in the population being studied. For example, the psychologist doing research on schoolchildren might select students of both sexes, of varying ages, of all social classes, and from all neighborhoods. This procedure produces a **stratified sample.**

---

sample: A relatively small group out of the total population under study.

population: The total group of subjects from which a sample is drawn.

random sample: A sample that gives an equal chance of being represented to every individual within the scope of the research being conducted.

stratified sample: A sample that includes representatives of subgroups or variations of the population being studied.

TABLE 1.1   The Polls Versus the Results

Source	Reagan	Mondale	Margin of Victory
Actual results	59%	41%	18%
USA Today	60	35	25
NBC	58	34	24
New York Times/CBS	58	36	22
Gallup	59	41	18
Washington Post/ABC	54	40	14
Harris	56	44	12
Roper	55	45	10

Note: Figures reflect pollsters' allocation of undecided or leaning voters, where available. Where full allocation was unavailable, figures total less than 100 percent.

Source: Dennis Farney. 1984. Pollsters' predictions of election results varied as much as the methods they used. *Wall Street Journal* (November 8):7. Reprinted by permission.

A stratified sample can also include a random sample of each stratum, which yields a **stratified random sample.**

The size of the sample may also be important. If the sample is too small, the results will be meaningless. For example, a pollster who wants to know what Democrats think about a particular candidate will have to question a relatively large number of people. Why? Because Democrats vary considerably in their political attitudes. Northern and southern, rural and urban, blue-collar and white-collar, male and female Democrats often disagree. If the pollster interviews only six of the millions of Democrats in the country, the results will not reflect these differences. In most general surveys aimed at large populations (including national public-opinion polls), the researcher questions about a thousand people. However, a sample of one hundred may be sufficient *if* those one hundred individuals represent the population as a whole. Indeed, if Democrats were all of one mind, it would be necessary to interview only one! (The boxed insert on pages 14–15 tells how psychologists might go about determining the relationship between one set of observations, such as rural-urban background, and another set of observations, such as political attitudes, by computing a correlation coefficient.)

In practice, survey researchers have been far more careful about sampling than have experimenters. Psychologists undertaking experimental studies often use college students in introductory classes as their subjects, assuming that the students are representative of adults in the population. For some behaviors (including sensory reactions and physiological responses) college students may be representative of young adults but are hardly representative for intelligence, attitudes, and social background.

Sampling techniques apply to the collection of the data as well as to the choice of subjects for study. Psychologists who want to learn how children react to their first years in school might observe them every tenth day (a random sample). Alternatively, they might select typical experiences and spend several weeks observing children playing alone and in groups, with and without supervision, and engaged in different activities indoors and outside. Following this procedure would produce a stratified sample of observations.

---

stratified random sample: A stratified sample that includes a random sample of each stratum.

Surveys are valuable tools for understanding consumer reactions to new products, political views, and many other issues. Surveys are often conducted in places where ordinary people can easily be found, such as supermarkets, public libraries, and bus stations. *(Ellis Herwig/The Picture Cube)*

Surveys

Much of what we have had to say about sampling finds application within survey research. **Surveys** are impersonal data-collection tools that afford the most practical way to gather data on the attitudes, beliefs, and experiences of large numbers of people. A survey can take the form of interviews, questionnaires, or a combination of the two.

An interview allows a researcher to observe the subject and modify questions if the subject seems confused by them. On the other hand, a questionnaire takes less time to administer and the results are

more uniform. A questionnaire also eliminates the possibility that the researcher will influence the subject—for example, by unconsciously frowning at an answer he or she does not like. Of course, there is always a danger that subjects will give misleading answers in order to make themselves "look good." One way to detect this problem is to phrase the same question in several different ways. A person who says yes, she believes in racial integration of the schools but no, she would not want her child to marry someone of another race is probably not as free of prejudice as the first answer implied.

Survey research is not simply a matter of asking people a few questions. The questions must be carefully phrased, pretested on a sample, and then refined. By way of illustration, consider how one might go about determining the political orientation of Americans. At first sight this task does not seem to be particularly difficult. A good many people might observe, "All one has to do is go out and ask a representative sample of Americans a question or two." In fact, four polling organizations did just this. But as Table 1.2 shows, the findings of the organizations differed appreciably from one another. By asking the same questions in somewhat different ways, the pollsters secured somewhat different outcomes. Hence if a survey is to be worth its salt, it requires careful and skilled formulation and pretesting.

Experiments

The most rigorous investigative method available to psychologists is the **experiment**. The experiment enables the psychologist to *control* the situation so as to decrease the possibility that unnoticed, outside factors will influence the results. For example, the social psychologists Kenneth Gergen, Mary Gergen, and William Barton (1973) put groups of six or seven student volunteers who did not know each other in a dark room for an hour, told them they could do

---

survey: A relatively large sampling of data, obtained through interviews, questionnaires, or a combination of the two.

experiment: A rigorous investigative method in which the researcher controls the situation so as to decrease the possibility that unnoticed, outside factors will influence the results.

TABLE 1.2 The Political Orientation of Americans

Louis Harris and Associates

Question: How would you describe your own political philosophy, as conservative, middle-of-the-road, liberal, or radical?

Results: Conservative, 30 percent; middle-of-the-road, 43 percent; liberal, 15 percent; radical, 3 percent; undecided, 9 percent.

Gallup Organization

Question: If an arrangement of this kind, that is, two new political parties, were carried out, and you had to make a choice, which party would you personally prefer—the conservative party or the liberal party?

Results: Conservative, 40 percent; liberal, 30 percent; undecided, 30 percent.

National Opinion Center (NORC) of the University of Chicago

Question: We hear a lot of talk these days about liberals and conservatives. I'm going to show you a seven-point scale on which the political views that people might hold are arranged from extremely liberal to extremely conservative. Where would you place yourself on this scale?

Results: Conservative alternatives, 28 percent; liberal alternatives, 28 percent; the midpoint position, 37 percent; don't know, 6 percent.

Survey Research Center (SRC) of the University of Michigan

Question: We hear a lot of talk these days about liberals and conservatives. I'm going to show you a seven-point scale on which the political views that people might hold are arranged from extremely liberal to extremely conservative. Where would you place yourself on this scale or haven't you thought much about it? (Identical to the NORC question but for the last option.)

Results: Conservative alternatives, 25 percent; liberal alternatives, 21 percent; the midpoint position, 26 percent; haven't thought much about it, 21 percent.

Note: Polls were conducted between November 1974 and March 1975.

Source: Adapted from S. M. Lipset. 1976. The waving polls. *Public Interest,* 43 (Spring):70–89. Reprinted with permission of the publisher.

---

whatever they liked, then (unknown to the students) photographed their activities with infrared cameras and recorded their conversations. What was the purpose of this experiment? To test the hypothesis that a group of strangers left alone in a dark room will do and say things they would not do and say in a lighted room. Darkness provides a cloak of anonymity. The researchers thought that if people cannot see one another, they will not worry about being recognized after the experiment and so will feel uninhibited. The experiment was designed to test this hypothesis.

In designing and reporting experiments, psychologists think in terms of **variables**—conditions and behaviors that change in some manner. In the experiment we are describing, the two significant variables were the amount of light in the room and the amount of interaction (conversation, movement, and touch-

---

variable: In an experimental situation, any factor that is capable of change.

ing) in each of the groups. There are two types of variables: independent and dependent. The **independent variable** is the one experimenters deliberately change under controlled conditions so they can observe its effects. Here, the independent variable is the amount of light in the room. The **dependent variable** is the one that researchers believe will be affected by the independent variable. Here, interaction (conversation, movement, and touching) was the dependent variable. The researchers thought darkness would influence these behaviors.

Of course, there is always a chance that the very fact of participating in an experiment will change the way people act. For this reason, the researchers put similar groups of students in a lighted room, told them they could do whatever they liked, and photographed and recorded their behavior. Subjects such as these form the **control group.** Subjects who undergo the **experimental treatment**—here, functioning in a darkened room—are called the **experimental group.**

A control group is necessary in all experiments. Without it, researchers cannot be sure the experimental group is reacting to what they think it is reacting to—a change in the independent variable. By comparing the way control and experimental groups behaved in this experiment, the researchers could determine whether darkness did in fact influence behavior and how.

What were the results of this experiment? In the lighted room students remained seated (about three feet apart) for most of the hour and kept up a continuous conversation. No one touched anyone else. In the darkened room, the students moved around. Although conversation tended to slack off after half an hour or so, there was a great deal of touching—by accident and on purpose. In fact, half of the subjects in the experimenteal group found themselves hugging another person. Thus the researchers' hypothesis was supported. Anonymity does lessen inhibitions against letting conversation die out and against touching, even hugging, a stranger.

However, one experiment does not constitute the final word on a subject. Psychologists do not fully accept the results of their own or other people's studies until they have been *replicated*—duplicated by at least one other psychologist with different subjects. Why? Because there is always a chance that some unnoticed factor in the original experiment was not typical. For example, perhaps the subjects in the experimental group merely happened to be very outgoing people.

One example will illustrate why replication is so important. Some years ago, Neal Miller and Leo DiCara (1967) stunned the psychological and medical world by reporting that they had trained rats to control their heart rates. (Before the experiment, researchers believed that animals had no control over the autonomic nervous system.) But all attempts to replicate Miller and DiCara's study failed—including their own. What went wrong? To date, no one has found the answer.

Sometimes, a second group of researchers purposely changes one or more variables of the original study. For example, they may use elderly people instead of college students as subjects. The goal is to find out whether the conclusions drawn from the original study apply to people in general, or to just one segment of the population. For example, it is conceivable that older adults may have responded with fear and anxiety to the experiment in the darkened room. Consequently, rather than showing greater spontaneity as the college students did, elderly subjects may have exhibited greater inhibition.

---

independent variable: In an experiment, the factor that is deliberately manipulated by the experimenters to test its effect on another factor.

dependent variable: In an experiment, the factor that is not controlled by the experimenters but changes as a result of changes in the independent variable.

control group: In an experiment, a group of subjects that is treated in the same way as the experimental group, except that the experimental treatment is not applied.

experimental treatment: The manipulation of an independent variable in an experiment designed to observe its effects.

experimental group: The group of subjects to which an experimental treatment is applied.

Correlations and Explanations

Researchers often want to examine the *relationship* between two sets of observations—say, between students' grades and the number of hours the students sleep. Scientists use the word **correlation** to describe the degree of relatedness between two sets of data. Sometimes the relationship is quite close. For example, there is a **positive correlation** between IQ scores and academic success. High IQ scores tend to go with high grades; low IQ scores tend to go with low grades. But there is a **negative correlation** between smoking cigarettes and living a long, healthy life. The more a person smokes, the fewer years he or she may live. In this case, a high rank on one measure tends to go with a low rank on the other.

A **correlation coefficient** is a numerical measure of the degree of relationship between two variables or conditions. A correlation coefficient can range from -1.00 to $+1.00$. If it is $+1.00$, there is a perfect positive relationship between two variables (factors)—meaning that as one of the variables increases, the other also increases. If it is -1.00, there is a perfect negative relationship between two variables—meaning that as one of the variables increases, the other decreas-

es. If the correlation coefficient is $.00$, there is no relationship between the variables—meaning that a high value on one variable is just as likely to go with a lower as with a higher value on the other variable.

Establishing a correlation is useful because it enables scientists to make relatively accurate *predictions*. Knowing that there is a positive correlation between IQ and academic success, you can predict that a person with a high IQ will do well in school. You will not be right all the time: some people with high IQs do poorly in school. But you will be right most of the time. Similarly, you might predict that a person with high grades has a high IQ. Here, again, you will be right more often than you will be wrong.

But people often confuse correlations with explanations. Instead of looking at a correlation as a comparison of two things, they think of it as a cause-and-effect relationship. Some years ago, for example, medical researchers discovered a high correlation between cancer and drinking milk. It seemed that the number of cancer cases was increasing in areas where people drink a lot of milk (such as New England) but that cancer was rare in areas where they do not (some

Experimentation is sometimes impossible for practical or ethical reasons. Suppose a psychologist suspects that normal visual development in humans depends on visual experience as well as on physical maturation. An ideal way to test this hypothesis would be to raise an experimental group of infants in total darkness, thus depriving them of visual experience, and a control group of infants under similar conditions but with normal lighting. Such an experiment would be unthinkable, of course. But most ethical problems are not this clear-cut. In the last decade, the American Psychological Association and

correlation (cor-uh-LAY-shun): The degree of relatedness between two sets of data.

positive correlation: A correlation indicating that a high value for one variable corresponds to a high value for the other variable.

negative correlation: A correlation indicating that a high value for one variable corresponds to a low value for the other variable, and vice versa.

correlation coefficient (co-eh-FI-shent): A numerical measure of the degree of relationship between two variables or conditions.

regions of India). These data suggested to many people that milk causes cancer.

However, when researchers analyzed the data further, they found a third factor was involved. Cancer usually strikes people in middle age or later. As a result, cancer is more common in places where people enjoy a high standard of living and live longer than in places where people tend to die at an earlier age. Thus drinking milk is related to cancer, but only because they are both related to a high standard of living. Milk does not cause cancer, but the two factors may be correlated.

As this example illustrates, a correlation between two things may or may not indicate a cause-and-effect relationship. Consider, for instance, that when the winner of the Super Bowl is an original National Football League team, the stock market is very likely to end higher at the end of the year. When the opposite occurs, the stock market is likely to drop. The "indicator" has worked eighteen out of nineteen years, affording a high correlation (+.85). (See Table 1.3.) Would you conclude that the Super Bowl winner causes the performance of the stock market? Thus correlation studies may suggest cause-and-effect relationships that other studies can then test, using additional research procedures.

TABLE 1.3 The Football Connection

	Superbowl Winner	Original League	Stocks
1967	Green Bay	National	Up
1968	Green Bay	National	Up
1969	N.Y. Jets	American	Down
1970	Kansas City	American	Down
1971	Baltimore	National	Up
1972	Dallas	National	Down
1973	Miami	American	Down
1974	Miami	American	Down
1975	Pittsburgh	National	Up
1976	Pittsburgh	National	Up
1977	Oakland	American	Down
1978	Dallas	National	Up
1979	Pittsburgh	National	Up
1980	Pittsburgh	National	Up
1981	Oakland	American	Down
1982	San Francisco	National	Up
1983	Washington	National	Up
1984	L.A. Raiders	American	Down
1985	San Francisco	National	Up

Source: Columbus (Ohio) Dispatch. 1986. (January):G1. Reprinted by permission.

the United States government have developed a number of guidelines and regulations to ensure that the rights and health of people who take part in experiments are protected.

Naturalistic Observation

Researchers also need to understand the way people and animals behave naturally, when they are not conscious of being the subjects of an experiment. To obtain such information, psychologists use **naturalistic observation.** This is one of the most direct ways to learn about psychology. In this method, researchers listen and watch, without interfering, to see how humans and animals behave. For example, a social psychologist might join a commune or participate in a therapy group to study how leadership develops in these settings. A developmental psychologist might position himself or herself behind a two-way mirror to watch youngsters at play. *Ethologists* (scientists

naturalistic observation: Studying phenomena as they occur in natural surroundings, without interference by the researcher.

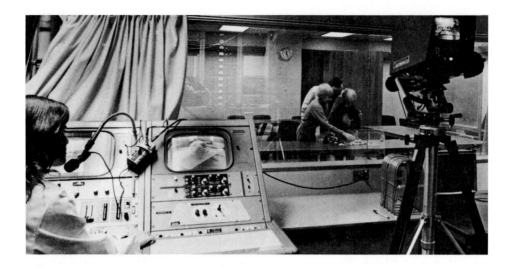

Naturalistic observation. This small-group laboratory at Ohio State University consists of two rooms that are separated by a one-way mirror. Researchers in the control room can observe subjects in the experimental room without themselves being observed (and thus interfering with the spontaneous behavior of the subjects). In the photograph above, an observer is watching from the control room. Viewed from the experimental room shown in the photograph below, the observer's window is a mirror. The Ohio State small-group laboratory also contains televisionlike equipment, so that in neighboring rooms individual subjects can view on a television screen the behavior that takes place in the experimental room. This allows subjects to observe and interpret behavior without influencing one another's perceptions and interpretations of it. Moreover, the equipment at Ohio State permits researchers to videotape behavior, so that they can replay the tapes later and study the behavior more closely. *(Patrick Reddy)*

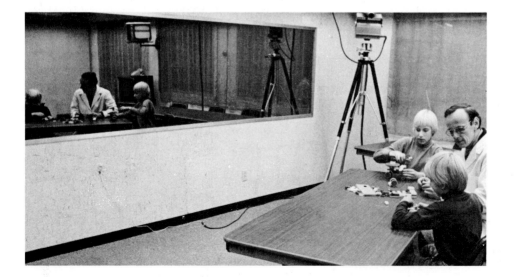

who specialize in studying animal behavior) often spend years observing members of a species before even considering an experiment. The cardinal rule of naturalistic observation is to avoid disturbing the people or animals you are studying, by concealing yourself or by acting as unobtrusively as possible. Otherwise, you may observe a performance produced for the researcher's benefit rather than natural behavior.

Naturalistic observation enjoys the advantage of allowing researchers to study behaviors that individuals may be unable or unwilling to tell about (for instance, illegal, taboo, or deviant behavior or behavior about which people lack self-insight). It also provides a rich source of ideas for future study. However, it is not a particularly strong method for testing hypotheses. The procedure does not allow researchers to "manipulate" variables as they can in experimental settings. Thus psychologists often employ naturalistic observation to identify critical variables that they can then manipulate in an experiment.

Case Studies

A **case study** is an intensive investigation of an individual or group. Many case studies focus on a particular mental disorder, such as schizophrenia, or a particular experience, such as being confined to prison. And most combine long-term observation (by one or more researchers), self-reports (such as diaries, tapes of therapy sessions, or perhaps artwork), and the results of psychological tests.

In the hands of an imaginative psychologist, case studies can be a powerful research tool. Sigmund Freud's theory of personality development, discussed in Chapter 13, was based on case studies of his patients. Jean Piaget's theory of intellectual development, described in Chapter 11, was based in part on case studies of his own children.

However, by itself, a case study does not typically allow researchers to reach firm conclusions regarding a subject. The primary problem is that the sample is too small and probably not representative of any larger population. Consequently, there is no way to know if the investigator's conclusions generalize to any other group.

By way of illustration, a researcher might conduct intensive case studies of families that include an individual diagnosed as schizophrenic. On the basis of these studies, she might conclude that a maladaptive kind of interaction within the family produces schizophrenia. However, unless she studies families that do *not* include schizophrenic individuals and finds that they interact differently, she has no way of reaching a firm conclusion. In other words, what is missing from case studies is a control group. The researcher might study a million families that include a schizophrenic person and find similar patterns. But unless she compares these families to others, she cannot be certain that normal families are different.

What, then, is the value of case studies? They provide a wealth of descriptive material that may generate new hypotheses which researchers can then test under controlled conditions with comparison groups.

Longitudinal Studies

Longitudinal studies cover long stretches of time. The psychologist studies and restudies the same group of subjects at regular intervals over a period of years to determine whether their behavior and feelings have changed, and if so, how (see Figure 1.2). For example, Lewis Terman followed 1,528 gifted children—who later became known as "Termites" —and a control group of children of average intelligence from an early age to adulthood. He found that

---

case study: An intense investigation of an individual or group, usually focusing on a single psychological phenomenon.

longitudinal (lon-jih-TOO-dih-null) study: A research method in which data on the same group of subjects are repeatedly gathered over a period of time for the purpose of studying consistencies and change.

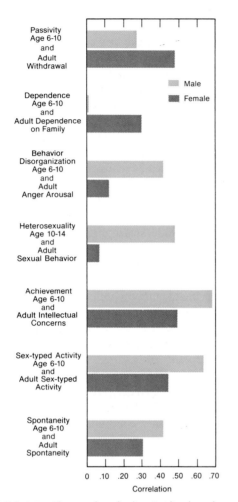

FIGURE 1.2 The results of a longitudinal study. Jerome Kagan and Howard A. Moss wanted to find out how much continuity there is between individuals' behavior in childhood and their behavior as adults. They found the correlations shown here. Traditional sex roles had a strong influence on whether a childhood behavior pattern died out or survived into adulthood. *(Data from Jerome Kagan and Howard A. Moss. 1962. Birth to Maturity: A Study in Psychosocial Development. New York: Wiley. Reprinted with permission of the authors.)*

the gifted ones were generally taller, heavier, and stronger than youngsters with average IQs. In addition, they tended to be more active socially and to mature faster than average children (Terman and Merrill, 1937). (So much for the stereotype of the skinny, unpopular bookworm.) After Terman's death, other psychologists continued the project (Sears, 1977; Sears and Barbee, 1977; Rafferty, 1984).

When Terman began his study in 1921, it was widely believed that if you were bright as a child, your later life would be marred by physical or mental illness, eccentricity, or social maladjustment. The Terman research dispelled these notions. Now in its seventh decade, the research has revealed that in later life the exceptionally bright youngsters had become better educated, more successful, better satisfied, and more effective and productive members of society than the average American. The Termites included a highly successful motion picture director, an atomic scientist, two dozen top-level research scientists, eight appellate court judges, and a nationally known science fiction writer. However, two members of the study had at some time in their lives received welfare payments and none had won a Nobel prize. There were also as many divorces, suicides, and alcohol problems among the Termites as among average Americans.

Longitudinal studies are time-consuming and precarious (subjects may disappear in midstudy). And then there is the additional problem that people retested many times may become "test-wise" and thus no longer be representative of people who have not been previously tested. But longitudinal studies are an ideal way to examine many consistencies and inconsistencies in behavior over time.

Cross-Cultural Studies

Cross-cultural studies are just what the term suggests: comparisons of the ways people in different cultures behave, feel, and think. The primary purpose of such research is to determine whether a behavior pattern is universal or whether it reflects the experiences that people have in a particular culture. For example, Lawrence Kohlberg (1981, 1984) studied the development of moral reasoning by

cross-cultural study: A research method in which comparable data are acquired from two or more cultures for the purpose of studying cultural similarities and differences.

presenting children and adolescents in eight societies with a series of dilemmas. He found that some children in all the societies progressed through six stages of moral awareness, from fear of punishment to an inner sense of justice (see Chapter 11). For instance, when Taiwanese village boys were asked whether a man should steal food for his starving wife, a typical answer from a preadolescent was: "Yes, because otherwise he will have to pay for her funeral, and that costs a lot." A Malaysian of the same age was likely to say: "Yes, because he needs her to cook his food." Although the cultural content of the replies differed (funerals are less important in Malaysia than in Taiwan), the same level of moral reasoning was found: the behavior was evaluated in terms of each youngster's own selfish needs. Kohlberg also finds that the percentage of those in each society who reach the most advanced stage varies. Thus, although certain values appear to be universal —including basic moral concepts relating to justice, equality, love, respect, and authority—cultural differences do affect the nature and course of moral reasoning (Harkness, Edwards, and Super, 1981).

Cross-cultural methods also present difficulties. For instance, there is the problem of deriving conclusions from test items that frequently mean different things to people in different cultures. This problem emerges with intelligence tests. For example, a number of years ago one portion of the National Intelligence Test asked individuals to underline the two words that best represented what the first word in the line must necessarily have. One line read: "Crowd: closeness, danger, dust, excitement, number." The "correct" answers (developed among middle-class whites in the United States) were "closeness" and "number." But on this item, Indian children in South Dakota commonly made the "error" of underlining the words "danger" and "dust," and frequently also "excitement." For these children, a crowd usually meant danger, dust, and excitement. Hence, materials suitable for testing people in one culture may be unsuitable for testing people in another culture. In sum, it is difficult to establish the extent to which test results can be generalized from one culture to another.

Conclusions

All the methods for gathering information we have described have advantages and disadvantages. No one technique is better than the others for all purposes. The method a psychologist chooses depends on what he or she wants to learn. It also depends on practical matters such as the amount of money available for research and the kind of training the researcher has had.

Although you may not undertake psychological research yourself, it is important that you have some idea of what these methods are. You would not vote for a political candidate simply because the individual promised to do something you agreed with. You would want to know whether the candidate had delivered on past campaign promises and whether he or she is indebted to special-interest groups. You would not purchase a new brand of soap merely because the company claimed that "tests prove" it is good for your skin. You would want to know what the tests were, who conducted them, and why other companies make the same claim.

By the same token, you should not accept what you read about psychology in magazines, newspapers, or for that matter this text just because a psychologist says so. (The "experts" can, and often do, disagree.) To evaluate psychological studies for yourself and weigh the evidence for conflicting views, you need to understand research methods. The goal of this section has been to make you a more informed "consumer" of psychology.

Finally, what distinguishes psychologists and other scientists from nonscientists is nagging skepticism. Scientists do not believe that they have any final answers, or that they ever will have. But they do believe they can learn more about feelings and behavior if they persist in studying them and asking questions systematically. Do people in fact behave in these ways? Does this method work? Does that way of thinking help? When the answer is yes, scientists do not stop asking questions. It is always possible that the next answer will be no, or that it is yes for some people and no for others. Hence it is essential for researchers to *invite* criticism by publishing detailed accounts of their methods as well as their results. (See the boxed insert on pages 20–21 for a discussion of some of the traps in psychological research and how psychologists attempt to avoid them.)

It is this approach that leads psychologists to question the common, cultural wisdom about behavior and its causes. And it leads psychologists to investigate in an objective manner behavior that

Traps in Doing Psychological Research and How to Avoid Them

In describing the methods and statistical techniques psychologists use, we have made research appear simpler and much more straightforward than it actually is. Science is a painstaking, exacting business. Every researcher must be wary of numerous pitfalls that can trap him or her into mistakes. Let us look at some of the most common problems psychological researchers confront and how they cope with them.

The Self-Fulfilling Prophecy

Psychologists are only human, and like most people they prefer to be right. No matter how objective they try to be in their research, there is always a chance that they will find what they want to find, unwittingly overlooking contrary evidence. This outcome is what we mean by the **self-fulfilling prophecy** (see Figure 1.3).

Researchers have shown how the self-fulfilling prophecy works in a study undertaken with experimenters (Rosenthal and Rosnow, 1969). The task involved administering the Wechsler Intelligence Scale for Children to twelve youngsters. Each child was tested by two experimenters, one of whom administered the odd-numbered questions, the other the even-numbered questions. With each child, one of the experimenters was told beforehand that the sub-

ject was above average in intelligence. The other was told that the subject was below average. The

FIGURE 1.3 The White Queen's fatalistic attitude is likely to be confirmed if she behaves in this way. This common phenomenon is called a self-fulfilling prophecy.

laypeople often take for granted. For instance, not too many decades ago, people believed that newborn infants were unresponsive vegetables who did nothing except eat, sleep, breathe, and cry. They thought that babies could not see or understand anything about their world. Nonetheless, psychologists investigated these matters and found that infants arrive with all sensory systems functioning. Through systematic responses to stimulating events, babies tell

us that they hear, see, and feel and that they know much about the sounds, sights, and other happenings in their environment.

A BRIEF HISTORY OF PSYCHOLOGY

Psychology has emerged and flourished as a scientific discipline because people desire information on why

self-fulfilling prophecy: A belief, prediction, or expectation that operates to bring about its own fulfillment.

results? The youngsters scored an average of seven and a half points higher on the half of the test administered by the experimenter who had been told that they were bright. Thus the experimenters found what they had expected; the prophecy that a given child would get a relatively high score was self-fulfilling.

The Double-Blind Procedure

One way to avoid the self-fulfilling prophecy is to use the double-blind technique. Suppose a psychologist wants to study the effects of a particular tranquilizer. She might give the drug to an experimental group and a placebo (a harmless substitute for the drug) to a control group. The next step would be to compare their performances on a series of tests. This procedure is known as a **single-blind experiment.** The subjects are "blind" in the sense that they do not know whether they have received the tranquilizer or the placebo.

A further guarantee of objectivity is for the researcher herself not to know who takes the drug or the placebo. She may ask the pharmacist to number rather than label the pills.) *After* she has scored the tests, she goes back to the pharmacist to learn which subjects took the tranquilizer and which took the placebo. This procedure is known as a **double-blind experiment.** Neither the subjects nor the experimenter knows which subjects received the tranquilizer. This technique

eliminates the possibility that the researcher will unconsciously find what she expects to find about the effects of the drug.

Observer Effects

Psychologists, like everyone else, are complex people, with attitudes, feelings, and ideas of their own, and their reactions to different subjects may distort the results of a study. Researchers may unknowingly react differently to male and female subjects, short and tall subjects, subjects who speak with an accent or who remind them of someone they particularly dislike. These attitudes, however subtly expressed, may influence the way subjects behave.

In addition, subjects may behave differently than they would otherwise just because they know they are being studied. The presence of an observer may cause them to change their behavior, just as the presence of a photographer can transform an assemblage of unruly children into a peaceful, smiling group. Under observation, people are apt to try to please or impress the observer—to act as they think they are expected to act. The use of a control group helps to correct for this problem. Since both the experimental group and the control group are being observed, differences between them are more likely to be due to the experimental situation than to being observed.

they think and behave as they do and because they seek to improve on the human condition. These motivations have prompted psychologists to develop and refine the research tools that were discussed in the preceding section. Interest in studying human behavior can be traced back to the Greeks. If from Greek sources psychologists have named their Oedi-

pus complex, their narcissism, their phobias, and their manias, it is because Greek 'mythology is an amazingly rich treasury of observations on human behavior. However, most historians agree that modern psychology began when the German scholar Wilhelm Wundt (1832–1920) established the first psychology laboratory in 1879. Wundt also edited

single-blind experiment: A research technique in which the experimenter but not the subjects knows which subjects have been exposed to the experimental treatment.

double-blind experiment: A research technique in which neither the subjects nor the experimenter knows which subjects have been exposed to the experimental treatment.

the first journal devoted to psychology and began experimental psychology as a science. His primary concerns were perception and sensation, areas of investigation that have again awakened psychological interest in recent decades (Chapter 5).

Over the past century, some of the most important historical trends in psychology have involved the study of unconscious processes, individual differences, observable behavior, and cognitive functioning. Different theoretical perspectives have arisen in psychology because, like knowledge of all kinds, scientific knowledge is a creation of the human mind (Gergen, 1985; Scarr, 1985b). As you will see in the chapters that follow, we fashion our notions of reality by taking sensory data and transforming them into images and thoughts. Viewed in this manner, facts do not have an independent existence. Rather, we mentally fashion facts by sorting out certain observations and finding meaningful links among them. Consequently, knowledge of the world is always constructed by the human mind. As evidence, consider the vast differences in the concepts that human beings had of the world before Galileo, Darwin, Einstein, and Freud.

Psychology as the Study of Unconscious Processes

For Sigmund Freud (1856–1939), a physician who practiced in Vienna until 1938, conscious experiences were only the tip of the iceberg. Beneath the surface, he believed, are primitive biological urges that are in conflict with the requirements of society and morality. According to Freud, these unconscious motivations and conflicts are responsible for much human behavior, including many of the medically unexplainable physical symptoms that troubled his patients (see Chapter 13).

Freud used a new method for indirectly studying unconscious processes. In this technique, known as *free association*, a patient gave a running account of everything that came to mind—no matter how absurd or irrelevant it sounded—without attempting to produce logical, meaningful statements. The person would do no editing or censoring, no thinking about the thoughts. Freud's role, that of psychoanalyst, was meant to be objective; he merely sat and listened, then interpreted the associations. Free association, Freud believed, reveals the operation of unconscious processes. Freud also believed that dreams

are an expression of the most primitive unconscious urges. To learn more about these urges, he developed dream analysis—basically an extension of free association whereby the patient free-associated to his or her dreams (Freud, 1940).

While working out his ideas, Freud took careful, extensive notes on all his patients and treatment sessions. He used these records, or case studies, to develop and illustrate a comprehensive theory of personality—the total, functioning person (Hall and Lindzey, 1978). Freud's theory of personality is discussed in Chapter 13, and his approach to therapy in Chapter 16.

In many areas of psychology today, Freud's view of unconscious motivation remains a powerful and controversial influence. Modern psychologists may support, alter, or attempt to disprove it, but most have a strong opinion about it. The technique of free association is still used by psychoanalysts.

Psychology as the Study of Individual Differences

Charles Darwin's (1809–1882) theory of evolution has had a continuing impact on psychological theory and research. Two major ideas are embodied in the notion of evolution: genetic variation and natural selection. As you may recall from courses in biology, within a population there is always genetic variation in the structure and functioning of individual organisms. Selection acts through the differential reproduction and mortality of people with different genes, creating new generations that are not exactly like those that preceded them. Hence, the variation that one observes in the behavior of people arises both from genetic variation and from environmental differences among individuals in the population (see Chapter 2).

Sir Francis Galton (1822–1911), like many of Darwin's followers, was interested in individual differences among human beings and sought to measure them. A nineteenth-century English mathematician and scientist, Galton sought to understand the way in which biology decides how one person's abilities, character, and behavior differ from those of other people. Galton (1869) traced the ancestry of various eminent people and found that greatness runs in families. (This interest was appropriate, since Galton himself was considered a genius and his family included at least one towering intellectual

Sigmund Freud in his Vienna office, 1938. (Edmund Engleman)

figure—his cousin Charles Darwin.) He therefore concluded that genius or eminence is a hereditary trait. Of course, this conclusion was premature. Galton did not consider the obvious possibility that the tendency of genius to run in eminent families might be a result of the exceptional environment and numerous socioeconomic advantages that also tend to "run" in such families.

The data Galton used were based on his study of biographies. However, not content to limit his inquiry to indirect accounts, he went on to invent procedures for directly testing the abilities and characteristics of a wide range of people. These tests were the primitive ancestors of the modern personality and intelligence tests that virtually everyone who reads this book has taken at some time. Galton also devised statistical techniques, notably the correlation coefficient, that are still in use today.

Although Galton began his work shortly before psychology emerged as an independent discipline, his theories and techniques quickly became central aspects of the new science. In 1883 he published a book, *Inquiries into Human Faculty and Its Development*, that is regarded as having defined the beginnings of individual psychology. Galton's writings raised the issue of whether behavior is determined by heredity or environment—a subject that has become the focus of controversy, especially in recent years. Galton's influence can also be seen in the current widespread use of psychological tests, in the continuing argument over their use, and in the statistical methods employed to evaluate their findings (matters that are discussed in Chapter 8).

Psychology as the Study of Observable Behavior

The pioneering work of Russian physiologist Ivan Pavlov (1849–1936), who won the Nobel prize in 1904, charted another new course for psychological investigation. In a now-famous experiment, Pavlov struck a tuning fork each time he gave a dog some meat powder. The dog, of course, would salivate the moment it saw the meat powder. After Pavlov had repeated the procedure many times, the dog would salivate when it heard the tuning fork, even if no food appeared.

The concept of the *conditioned reflex*—a response (salivation) elicited by a stimulus (the tuning fork) other than the one that first produced it (food)—was used by psychologists as a new tool, a means of exploring the development of behavior. Using this tool, they could begin to account for behavior as the product of prior experience. This insight enabled them to explain that certain acts and certain differences among individuals were the result of learning. These matters are discussed at length in Chapter 6.

Psychologists who stressed investigating observable behavior became known as *behaviorists*. Their position, as formulated by American psychologist John B. Watson (1879–1958), was that psychology should concern itself *only* with the observable facts of behavior. Watson (1924) further maintained that all behavior, even in its apparently instinctive aspects, is the result of conditioning and occurs because the appropriate stimulus is present in the environment. Hence the behaviorists denied the value of introspective insight for psychology and the notion that innate instincts underlie behavior.

Though it was Watson who defined and solidified the behaviorist position, it is B. F. Skinner (born 1904), the contemporary American psychologist, who has refined and popularized it. Skinner has attempted to show how, in principle, his laboratory techniques might be applied to a society as a whole. In his novel *Walden Two* (1948), he portrays his idea of Utopia—a small town in which conditioning, through rewarding those who display behavior that is considered desirable, governs every conceivable facet of life.

Skinner has exerted great influence on both the general public and the science of psychology. His face is familiar to television audiences, and his book *Beyond Freedom and Dignity* (1971) became a runaway best seller. A number of Walden Two communities have been formed in various parts of the country, and many people toilet train their children, lose weight, quit smoking, and overcome phobias by using Skinner-inspired methods.

But Skinner has also been widely criticized, because many people are convinced that he seeks to limit personal freedom with his "manipulative" conditioning techniques. Others have wholeheartedly applauded him as a social visionary. In any event, his theories and methods have permeated psychology. Behaviorist-inspired techniques compete with more traditional psychotherapy for primacy in the treatment of various psychological disorders. The techniques of *reinforcement,* or controlled reward and punishment, have become increasingly popular in education, and Skinner's teaching machine was the forerunner of modern programed instruction. Moreover, a vast number of today's psychologists use

Skinner's research methodology to obtain precise findings in their laboratory experiments.

Psychology as the Study of Cognitive Processes

In founding psychology, Wundt had viewed it as a field of study concerned with sensation and perception—indeed, the vast array of conscious elements that comprise human life. But under the onslaught of behaviorism, these concerns were largely shunted aside. Behaviorists such as Watson insisted that psychologists study only those things that can be observed. For Watson, the concept of "mind" was merely a modern synonym for the ancient notion of the "soul."

Much of this changed in 1967 with the publication of Ulric Neisser's *Cognitive Psychology*. Almost overnight, psychologists who had been doing research on human perception, sensation, language, learning, memory, information processing, and reasoning began viewing themselves as cognitive psychologists (Crowder, 1981; Gardner, 1985). Hence mental processes have once again become a lively focus of interest. Whereas in the preceding fifty-year period psychologists had come to view their field as the study of behavior, over the past two decades they have increasingly come to redefine it as the study of behavior *and* mental processes.

Neisser (1976:1) views cognition as the "activity of knowing: the acquisition, organization, and use of knowledge." Thus cognition has to do with those processes by which people perceive, represent, remember, and employ knowledge. Knowledge allows individuals to survive and adapt to their environment, to satisfy their social and biological needs, and to plan for the future (Bower, 1975).

Mental processes intrude themselves into most human psychological processes and activities. People are self-conscious beings; they are aware of their behavior and therefore are capable of intentionally choosing among alternative courses of action. They devise their behavior and reflect on their mental activities. Indeed, mental processes make it possible for individuals to fit their actions together to achieve meaningful *inter*action—to link themselves together within such enduring institutional arrangements as families, schools, churches, businesses, and organizations. Thus cognitive psychologists attribute primary significance to the fact that people *think*.

PSYCHOLOGY TODAY

Psychology today covers an enormous range. There are psychologists working in advertising, education, and criminology; there are psychologists studying death, art, and robots. Psychological themes and terminology have become part of everyday life, and of novels, films, and television programs.

In the process of growing, psychology has become divided into a number of subfields (Stapp, Tucker, and VandenBos, 1985). Nearly 60 percent of psychologists are found in *clinical* and *counseling psychology*. These specialists undertake to help people with adjustmental and psychological problems. Clinical psychologists are commonly psychotherapists. They work in mental hospitals, prisons, schools, clinics,

Psychologists fill many jobs in different settings: *(a)* one-to-one clinical psychology; *(b)* an experimental psychologist measuring the electronic functions of the brain; *(c)* retarded children learning with a computer program of the sort designed by educational psychologists, with a technician recording their responses; *(d)* a manual dexterity employment test, used in industrial psychology; and *(e)* a school psychologist doing play therapy with a student. *(a, Erich Hartmann/ Magnum; b, Van Bucher/Science Source-Photo Researchers; c, Dan McCoy/ Rainbow; d, Billy E. Barnes/Jeroboam; e, Alan Carey/The Image Works)*

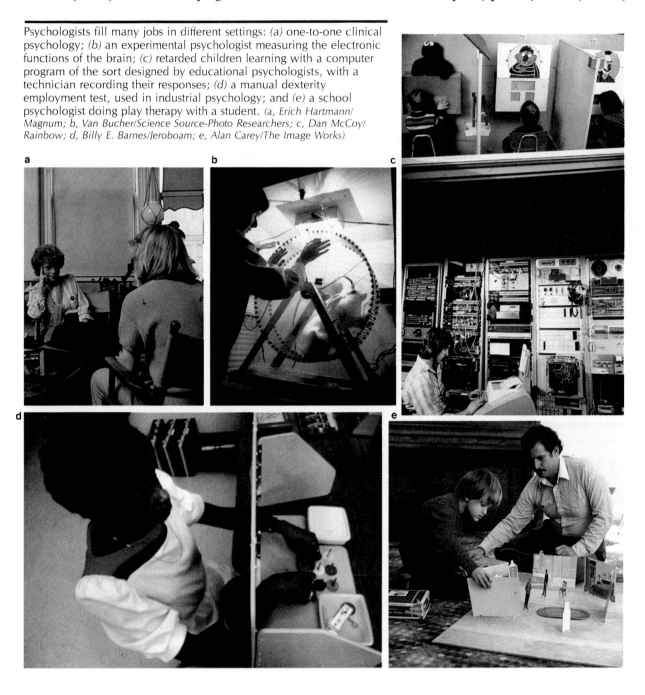

and private offices. Some specialize in giving and interpreting various diagnostic tests that are designed to determine whether or not a person needs treatment, and if so, of what type. Counseling psychologists work in schools, industrial firms, and similar settings, advising and assisting people who would be classified as normal rather than disturbed.

A large number of specialists are also attracted to *personality*, *social*, and *developmental psychology*. Personality psychologists study personality development and traits and devise personality tests. Social psychologists study groups and the way groups influence individual behavior. Some are particularly interested in public opinion and devote much of their time to conducting polls and surveys. Traditionally, developmental psychologists have focused on children from birth to age eighteen or thereabouts. However, in recent years they have moved toward a "life cycle" or "cradle to grave" approach —studying development as something that extends from birth to old age.

Educational psychology deals with topics related to teaching children and young adults, such as intelligence, memory, problem solving, and motivation. Educational psychologists are concerned with evaluating teaching methods, devising tests, and developing new instructional devices such as films and television. One of their contributions to education is computer programs that allow students to use computers to proceed through a subject at their own rate. *School psychologists* work with children who are experiencing difficulty in school, consult with parents and classroom teachers, and devise programs and materials for children with special needs. Their services have come to the forefront in recent years, as handicapped children and children with learning difficulties have been "mainstreamed" within regular classrooms.

Industrial psychology is another area of specializa-

tion. Psychological methods have been used to boost production, improve working conditions, place applicants in the jobs for which they are best suited, devise methods for training people, and reduce accidents. Psychologists have also been involved in improving machines—for example, by making control panels more readable. Industrial psychologists generally work as consultants to private firms or governmental agencies.

In recent years, new opportunities for *health care psychologists* have opened. As emotional stress has come to be identified as contributing to various disorders, including ulcers and heart disease, psychologists have been drawn into health care and disease prevention programs. Many medical problems, such as lung, heart, and liver disorders, have behavioral roots in patients who smoke, eat, and drink alcohol excessively. The treatments for these disorders often involve changing the behaviors of patients. Psychologists also use various behavioral techniques in working with patients who find their lives impaired by phobic fears.

Finally, about a fourth of all psychologists are engaged in *experimental psychology*. These psychologists do everything from testing how electrical stimulation of a rat's brain affects its behavior to studying how disturbed people think and observing how different socioeconomic groups vote in elections. They are basic scientists. Many of them work in colleges and universities, teaching and writing as well as conducting experiments.

All psychologists have an area of special interest, but most participate in diverse activities. A busy psychologist might divide his or her time between doing research, teaching, administering psychological tests, providing therapy or counseling, writing books and research papers, serving on college committees, figuring departmental budgets, and attending professional conventions.

SUMMARY

1. Psychology undertakes to answer the question, "Why do people think, feel, and act the way they do?" Psychology, therefore, is the study of behavior and mental processes.

2. From this text, you will be able to gain insights into your own and other people's behavior; practical information for everyday life; and an objective test of many of your beliefs.

3. When doing research, psychologists must be sure to ask precise questions about limited topics. They usually also formulate hypotheses: statements about what a researcher expects to find put in such a way that they can be proved or disproved.

4. Science thrives on debate. The results of a single study should not be mistaken for "the final answer" or for authoritative advice on how to handle everyday situations.

5. Basic science is the pursuit of knowledge for its own sake. Applied science, on the other hand, is the search for ways to put basic science to use in accomplishing practical goals.

6. The first step in psychological research is generating testable ideas. The next step is to select a sample of the population relevant to a study. A random sample (the equivalent of picking subjects while blindfolded) or stratified sample (one that mirrors variations in the population as a whole) helps a researcher avoid bias.

7. Psychologists often use experiments to test hypotheses about cause-and-effect relationships. The researchers observe the effects of the independent variable (the condition they manipulate) on the dependent variable (the condition they think will change) in an experimental group. They then compare the reactions of the experimental group to those of a control group that has not been exposed to the experimental treatment. Psychologists do not accept the results of an experiment until it has been replicated by another researcher using different subjects.

8. Other methods for gathering data on behavior and feelings include:

   A. surveys—gathering data from a large number of people through face-to-face interviews or questionnaires

   B. naturalistic observation—watching and recording behavior without intruding on the actors

   C. case studies—intensive investigations of individuals or groups that convey the quality of behavior and experiences

   D. longitudinal studies—studying and restudying the same group of subjects over a period of years

   E. cross-cultural studies—comparing the way people from different cultures behave and feel

9. Most historians agree that modern psychology began with the work of Wilhelm Wundt. He established the first psychological laboratory and the first journal devoted to psychology.

10. Sigmund Freud believed that people act the way they do as a result of primitive unconscious urges.

11. Charles Darwin and Sir Francis Galton saw psychology as the study of individual differences. Darwin's theory of evolution has had a continuing impact on psychological theory and research. Two major ideas are embodied in the notion of evolution: genetic variation and natural selection. Galton was one of the first to study systematically how one individual differs from the next, and today's psychological tests can be traced back to his work.

12. Ivan Pavlov, John Watson, and B. F. Skinner are three key figures in behaviorism, which studies the way learning shapes observable behavior.

13. Cognition entails those processes by which people perceive, represent, remember, and use knowledge. Over the past two decades the study of mental processes has once again become a lively area of concern for psychologists.

14. Psychology today covers an enormous range, including clinical, counseling, personality, social, developmental, educational, school, industrial, health care, and experimental psychology.

KEY TERMS

applied science (p. 7)
basic science (p. 7)
case study (p. 17)
control group (p. 13)

correlation (p. 14)
correlation coefficient (p. 14)
cross-cultural study (p. 18)
dependent variable (p. 13)

double-blind experiment (p. 21)
experiment (p. 11)
experimental group (p. 13)

experimental treatment (p. 13)
hypothesis (p. 6)
independent variable (p. 13)
longitudinal study (p. 17)
naturalistic observation (p. 15)
negative correlation (p. 14)
population (p. 9)

positive correlation (p. 14)
psychology (p. 2)
random sample (p. 9)
sample (p. 9)
self-fulfilling prophecy (p. 20)
single-blind experiment (p. 21)

stratified random sample (p. 10)
stratified sample (p. 9)
survey (p. 11)
variable (p. 12)

SUGGESTED READINGS

A number of magazines include articles on recent developments in the social sciences. Among them are *Psychology Today* and *Scientific American*.

AMERICAN PSYCHOLOGICAL ASSOCIATION. 1986. *Careers in Psychology*. Washington, D.C.: American Psychological Association. A useful booklet that provides information on the kinds of careers open to students interested in pursuing their study of psychology and describes the type of education required for each career.

BOAKES, ROBERT. 1984. *From Darwin to Behaviourism: Psychology and the Minds of Animals*. Cambridge: Cambridge University Press. An informative and anecdotal history of psychology from Darwin to Watson, focusing on the study of the minds of animals and addressing the nature/nurture controversy.

EYSENCK, HANS J. 1983. *Fact and Fiction in Psychology*. Baltimore: Penguin. Eysenck delves into popular notions of psychology and applies the scientific method to come up with some witty and entertaining conclusions. Topics range from criminal personality and the four temperaments to accident proneness. Also of interest are two other books by Eysenck that, together with this one, make up a trilogy: *Uses and Abuses of Psychology* (1983) and *Sense and Nonsense in Psychology* (1982).

FREUD, SIGMUND. 1949 (originally published 1940). *An Outline of Psychoanalysis*. Ed. and trans. by James Strachey. New York: Norton. A synopsis of thoughts on the nature of human feelings and behavior by the most influential psychological theorist of the early twentieth century.

JAMES, WILLIAM. 1962. *Psychology (Briefer Course)*. New York: Macmillan. Published originally in two volumes in 1890, this is the abridgment of James's *Principles of Psychology*, the first major classic in the field of psychology. This book, which remains highly readable and thought-provoking today, attracted many eminent psychologists to the field and has influenced innumerable others in their thinking and research.

MACKAY, CHARLES. 1932 (originally published 1841). *Extraordinary Popular Delusions and the Madness of Crowds*. New York: Farrar, Straus & Giroux. A remarkable book describing in vivid detail cases of human folly throughout the ages. Special emphasis is given to mass movements and the psychology of crowds.

SKINNER, B. F. 1953. *Science and Human Behavior*. New York: Macmillan. A classic presentation of the best-known behaviorist's ideas about reinforcement and human behavior. Skinner will surprise you.

part 1

BIOLOGY AND BEHAVIOR

Loren Maciver, *Skylight Moon*, 1958.

2
Brain and Behavior

Shakespeare called the brain "the soul's frail dwelling house." Since the brain is enclosed within a bony skull and three separate membranes, scientific observation of what is inside the "house" has been exceedingly difficult. Fortunately, recent technological advances are now allowing scientists to explore the "house" while only minimally disturbing the occupant. Some of the most imaginative and insightful research on the brain has been undertaken by Lars Olson and Ake Seiger at Stockholm's renowned Karolinska Institute. Over the past decade they have directed their attention to Parkinson's disease, a disabling disorder that afflicts more than a million older Americans. The disease is marked by a progressive rigidity of the arms and legs, shaking, and a shuffling gait. Patients with Parkinson's disease often benefit from treatment with L-dopa, a drug that boosts the brain's store of dopamine. Dopamine is a neurotransmitter, a chemical that brain cells use to communicate with one another.

Olson and Seiger began treating Parkinson-like symptoms in rats by transplanting cells from their adrenal glands (dopamine is made in small amounts in these walnut-sized glands perched atop the kidneys) to the symptom-producing region of their brains. Normally researchers perfect a new technique in rats, step up to larger mammals such as cats, and then try the method on nonhuman primates. However, in 1982, Erik-Olof Backlund, the neurosurgeon who works with Parkinson's patients at Karolinska Institute, approached Olson and Seiger. He asked them to try their method on patients whose symptoms could no longer be relieved by drugs. The ethics committee of the hospital gave its approval so long as three conditions were met: the patients had to be relatively young; they had to be in sufficient command of their faculties to render informed consent to the experimental procedure; and all conventional therapy must have failed.

"The first patient was truly burned out," Olson recalls. "He was almost totally disabled and under heavy doses of medication. He was rapidly going downhill" (Kiester, 1986:37). A portion of tissue from one of the man's adrenal glands was removed by a surgeon. Olson and Seiger then injected small units of the tissue into a very small location, the substantia nigra, on one side of the brain. The loss of cells in this region is thought to produce the Parkinsonian symptoms. The tissue grafted and the patient's condition stabilized. He regained some mobility in his arms, and researchers found increased amounts of dopamine by-products in his spinal fluid. Three and a half years later, the landmark patient was about the same as he had been at the time of the operation, but his downhill slide had been arrested.

The next patient was a forty-six-year-old woman who was so severely afflicted by Parkinson's disease that she was bedridden and could scarcely swallow food or medicine. The medical team decided to double the amount of tissue, inserting two implants on each side of her brain. Again the grafts took. The woman could move her hands and arms freely for the first time in years and could perform a number of simple functions for herself. The improvement lasted for four months. Similar operations have since been performed on two men. Initially the patients showed considerable improvement, but the positive effects gradually disappeared (Kiester, 1986).

Transplanting brain tissue is hardly a new idea. University of Chicago researcher Elizabeth Dunn successfully grafted tissue into rat brains in 1903. Nonetheless, conventional scientific wisdom long held that it could not be done. Now scientists are finding that when an area of the brain is damaged, nearby nerve cells sprout fibers that grow into the area and assume some of the functions of the old nerve cells. The work of the Scandinavian researchers and an American team headed by Richard Jed Wyatt at the National Institute of Mental Health now suggests that brain-tissue transplants are also possible (Young, 1983). Even in an age when diseased hearts, kidneys, and lungs are being replaced by transplanted healthy ones, the grafting of healthy cells into the human brain seems to be at the outer edge of science. Still, growing numbers of scientists are concluding that brain grafts are an idea whose time has come. In this chapter we explore the relationship between the brain and behavior, focusing our attention on the biological and chemical aspects of the nervous system. We begin our discussion with a consideration of the knowledge psychologists have derived from research with animals.

THE RELATIONSHIP BETWEEN HUMANS AND ANIMALS

Much of the understanding gained lately about the human brain has involved research seemingly unrelated to human beings or brains. For instance, one of the most exciting findings about learning has come from studies of what happens in the nervous system of a sea slug when its tail is poked or otherwise disturbed (Kandel and Schwartz, 1982; Hall, 1985). It responds by retracting a part of its feeding apparatus, the siphon. In a primitive way the slug "remembers" the poke and next time retracts its siphon more rapidly. Disturbing the slug's tail unleashes electrical processes that result in the rising and falling of cellular activities. *Ions* (electrically charged atoms) rush in and out through the membrane of a nerve cell, activating biochemicals that carry messages between nerve cells on a route from the tail to the siphon. The membrane of a tail nerve cell is studded with tiny pores, or channels, that open and close in response to electrical or chemical stimulation. Stimulation alters the pores of a nerve cell, and in effect, serves as a reminder that the tail was disturbed. This "memory" informs the nerve cell that it must quickly send out chemical instructions to withdraw the siphon when the tail is poked again. Thus, the slug's "memory" is contained in a series of interlinked chemical processes.

Researchers study nonhuman organisms because they cannot perform risky procedures on a human being with no better reason than scientific inquiry. For the most part the research that has been done on humans either has occurred as a part of some necessary medical procedure or has involved observing people who have suffered an injury by accident. It is now generally accepted that the study of animals can help in the study of human beings, even though direct experiments on humans would be even more useful if they could be done. Animal studies are particularly valuable for understanding vision and the effects that the stimulation of certain brain cells has on behavior. Additionally, drugs, vaccines, and new forms of surgery are regularly tested on animal subjects.

The reason such research is considered useful is that human beings have evolved from more primitive animal origins, and their bodies and brains are therefore similar in some respects to the bodies and brains of other animals. These similarities are most pronounced among the primates, with whom humans share recent evolutionary ancestors. Other animals, such as rodents and birds, are much more remotely related to humans. Nonetheless, they still provide some useful similarities and thus supply psychologists with insightful and ethically conscionable research opportunities (Burghardt, 1985).

Ethology

In 1859, the biologist Charles Darwin published his theory of evolution. This work contributed much to the understanding of how organisms are linked in time and space to their habitats and to other organisms with which they have contact. Central to evolutionary theory is the notion of *natural selection,* a remarkably simple idea. Organisms differ from one another. They may produce more offspring than the available resources can support. Those organisms that are best adapted survive, passing on their genetic characteristics to their offspring, whereas the others perish with few or no offspring. Consequently, later generations resemble their better-adapted ancestors. The result is evolutionary change (Ghiselin, 1969; Snowdon, 1983).

One of the major outgrowths of Darwin's theory of evolution is ethology. **Ethology** is the study of the natural behavior patterns of all species of animals. Ethologists attempt to understand how these patterns have evolved and changed, and how they are expressed in human beings.

Many people do not realize that evolution applies not only to anatomy and physiology but also to predispositions toward certain types of behavior. Consider the ordinary garden toad. When a toad sees a long, slender object—be it a snake or a garden hose—it reacts by filling its lungs to capacity with air and tilting its body in an awkward manner. By puffing itself up and positioning itself at an angle,

the toad complicates the task of a snake intent on capturing and swallowing it as a meal. Presumably the toad does not realize all this. Rather, the disposition to suck in air and tilt the body in the presence of a long, slender stimulus is a response "built into" the toad. The toad is said to be "prewired" or "primed" for these types of behaviors. And of course the behaviors have clear adaptive significance in promoting the survival of toads in a world replete with snakes. Such behavior patterns are subject to natural selection by processes not too different from those operating in the selection of various anatomical and physiological traits.

Species-Typical Behaviors

By observing animals in their natural environment, ethologists hope to discover the links between a species' surroundings and its behavior. They have been especially intrigued by **species-typical behaviors,** patterns of behaving that are characteristic of a particular animal species in particular environmental settings (Passingham, 1982).

Ethologists have found that the behavior and experience of more primitive creatures (such as insects or fish) are less flexible, or more stereotyped, than the behavior of higher animals (such as apes or humans). Stereotyped behaviors consist of patterns of responses that cannot change readily in response to changes in the environment. They work well only if the environment stays as it was when the behavior pattern evolved. Thus rigidity in behavior can be a disadvantage. But at the same time it affords an important advantage. The species-typical behavior is elicited by the appropriate environment even when a creature has been raised with little or no contact with other members of its species. In this sense the potential for a behavior has been "built into" its genes and hence need not be acquired over again with each new generation.

Ethologists have found that animals are born with special sensitivities to certain cues in the environment (as well as with special ways of behaving) (Walker, 1983). These cues are called *sign stimuli* or

---

ethology: The study of animal behavior in its natural environment.
species-typical behavior: Behavior that is characteristic of a particular animal species in particular environmental settings.

releasers. For example, for sexually receptive female stickleback fish, male sticklebacks with red bellies are an important sexual stimulus. The sign stimulus that triggers the attraction is the color red. In contrast, male sticklebacks interpret a red belly as a threat signal, and will either attack it or flee from it (Rowland, 1982a, 1982b).

Ethologists say that some forms of parenting behavior are released by the appropriate sign stimulus. For instance, occurring among cats are certain nesting behaviors in which a mother responds to a kitten's cries (the sign stimulus) by searching for and retrieving the kitten. But, as is very often the case, learning is also involved in the behavior. The mothers get better at the task with each successive litter. Psychologists refer to this link or mixture between innate and learned behavior as "easy learning." The animal is neurally prewired or hormonally primed for certain activities that are then released and gradually refined in interaction with particular environmental settings.

The noted ethologist Konrad Lorenz claims that human beings are also genetically programed for parenting behavior. Presumably caretaking tendencies are aroused by the "cuteness" of human babies. When Lorenz compared human infants with other young animals, he noticed that they all appear to display a similar set of sign stimuli that seem to stir up parental feelings. Apparently, short faces, prominent foreheads, round eyes, and plump cheeks all arouse the parental response. Infants come "equipped" with other types of "elicitors" as well (Bowlby, 1969; Eibl-Eibesfeldt, 1970). The abrasive, disconcerting sounds of a baby's cry typically "incite" such soothing activities as holding, caressing, and rocking. And a human face "triggers" an infant's smile, which in turn invites cuddling behaviors. As viewed by an ethologist, a baby is thus genetically prepared for a "people" environment and "in this sense is social from the beginning" (Ainsworth, Bell, and Stayton, 1974; MacDonald, 1984).

Yet here too some learning is involved. For instance, mothers and fathers soon "learn" that they can terminate the baby's piercing cries and thus allay

their own discomfort by holding, caressing, and rocking the child. And the baby "rewards" the caretaker with smiles and coos, thus reinforcing these behaviors. At the same time, caretakers assume rewarding properties for the infant as they feed, warm, dry, and snuggle it and reduce its pain and discomfort. Consequently, the attachment process is a two-way street that involves learning by all the parties (Gewirtz and Boyd, 1977).

Imprinting

The interaction among innate tendencies, maturational processes, and environmental experience is highlighted by imprinting. **Imprinting** is a set of responses by which an animal establishes social attachments during an early stage in its life. These attachments play a crucial part in patterning the animal's subsequent interactions with other members of its species.

Ethologists find that there is a short interval of time early in the life of chickens, goslings, and ducklings in which they begin slavishly to follow the first moving object that they encounter—their mother, a decoy, a human being, a beach ball, or whatever (Lorenz, 1935a; Hess, 1959). The object becomes "mother" to the birds, so thereafter they prefer it to all others and indeed will follow no other. The crucial time interval for "stamping in" a response is termed a **sensitive,** or **critical, period.** For instance, the peak interval for the imprinting effect among mallard ducklings is thirteen to sixteen hours after hatching.

A point of interest is that difficulty in following the object strengthens and intensifies the imprinting process. For example, administering shocks to the young followers increases rather than decreases the behavior. And ethologists claim that imprinted behaviors are irreversible, although some aspects of a response may not be evident until much later, when the appropriate stage of maturity has been reached. Hence adult geese who formed early attachments to human beings make courtship gestures and mating overtures to people rather than to other geese. But

---

imprinting: A process of rapid learning by which an animal establishes social attachments during an early stage in its life.

sensitive (critical) period: A short interval of time during which an organism is particularly susceptible to rapid learning.

Baby geese imprinted on Konrad Lorenz instead of on a mother goose. *(Thomas McAvoy, Time-Life Picture Agency,* © Time, Inc.)

ing of infants to their parents (called *attachment*) occurs some seven to nine months after birth, when infants come to recognize familiar caretakers and to form emotional attachments with them (Scarr, 1984). Whereas infants' attachment depends on their cognitive maturation, parental attachment to their infants does not. Pediatricians Marshall H. Klaus and John H. Kennell (1976) say that a bonding effect is indeed found to operate among human parents and their infants—what they term *maternal-infant bonding*. They claim that a sensitive period exists in the first several hours following birth, when close physical contact with the baby enhances the mother's attachment to the baby for months to come. Klaus and Kennell worry that the bonding process may be impaired in the absence of this contact, contributing to later child abuse and neglect. However, other psychologists, such as Michael Lamb (1982), have been unable to document any long-lasting effects of early physical contact for either the child or its mother. Bonding may well be less crucial for human parenting than for other mammals because human parents can *think* about the meaning of parenthood (Scarr, 1984).

Sociobiology

Closely related to ethology is a discipline that studies the evolutionary basis of social behavior in animals and human beings. This science, known as **sociobiology,** draws on the findings of biology, anthropology, and psychology. It has attracted a great deal of attention, and an even greater amount of controversy. In 1975, Harvard zoologist Edward O. Wilson published *Sociobiology: A New Synthesis*, in which he defined the discipline as "the systematic study of the biological basis of all social behavior" (1975:595). Wilson surveyed the social behavior of all known primates and suggested that certain traits humans share with most other primates—including prolonged maternal care of offspring and male dominance over females—are patterns that are easily learned because of a common evolutionary past.

One of the most startling assertions of sociobiology has to do with **altruism**—self-sacrificing behav-

some psychologists dispute these conclusions and fail to confirm the finding that imprinting is either immediate or irreversible (Hoffman and DePaulo, 1977). These psychologists prefer more traditional explanations for "imprinting," based on the learning processes detailed in Chapter 6.

Moreover, whether imprinting occurs among human beings is a highly controversial issue. Bond-

---

sociobiology: The study of the biological basis of social behavior.

altruism (AL-troo-ism): Self-sacrificing behavior that helps to ensure the survival of other members of one's own species.

People will sometimes endanger their own lives to spare others who are relatives or close companions. Some people choose dangerous jobs in which their efforts save others in their communities, at some risk to themselves. *(John E. Fogle/The Picture Cube)*

ior that helps to ensure the survival of other members of one's own species. Wilson notes, for instance, that a honeybee will attack an intruder about the hive with its fishhook-shaped sting. The sting remains embedded in the flesh of the enemy, together with the bee's entire venom gland and much of its viscera, causing the bee to die quickly. But the venom gland continues to leak poison into the wound of the predator. Viewed from the perspective of the colony as a whole, the suicide of the individual ensures the survival of the hive.

Similarly, termites will explode themselves to protect their colony from intruders. Robins, thrushes, and titmice sound warning calls to others of their kind should a hawk appear, thereby drawing the predator's attention to themselves. Baboons will charge a prowling leopard, allowing others in the troop to escape. And, of course, among human beings, parents die rescuing their children from fires, and soldiers throw themselves suicidally on grenades to save their buddies (individuals who, like relatives, are socially and emotionally close to them).

Altruistic behavior has long proven a puzzle for evolutionary theory. Why should altruistic tendencies be selected in the course of evolution if they entail surrendering one's own life? It seems more likely that individuals displaying self-sacrificing behavior would die out while selfish ones would survive and prosper. Sociobiologists provide a new twist to classical Darwinian theory by providing this answer:

in the course of evolution, natural selection has come to encompass kin selection (Blurton-Jones, 1984; Segal, 1984). **Kin selection** refers to evolutionary processes that favor behaviors that contribute to the survival of one's relatives. Evolution favors altruistic tendencies because, although some members of a society are sacrificed, the kin group as a whole survives (and has the capacity to reproduce the lost members' genes many times over). Hence Wilson (1975:3) asserts:

> In a Darwinian sense the organism does not live for itself. Its primary function is not even to reproduce other organisms; it reproduces genes and serves as their temporary carrier.

Wilson says that the emotions people experience as altruism ultimately derive from hereditary factors. What evolves through genes is the underlying altruistic sentiment, not the specific form that altruism takes in a particular society. Indeed, altruism finds different expressions among peoples of different cultures.

In appraising Wilson's formulations, it is important to keep in mind the fact that genes do not cause altruism. Indeed, for the most part we do not come equipped with genes for specific behaviors. Genes do not act at the behavioral level. They are components of cells. Cells themselves are involved at a higher level of organization as components of organs and physiological processes, including the functioning of the nervous and endocrine systems. In turn, these constituents are integrated with the environment at the behavioral level. Genes, therefore, do not mandate a particular type of behavior. They merely provide the capacity to develop certain behaviors —even more, the tendency to develop them in particular kinds of environments.

Some critics of Wilson believe that he moves too far toward a hereditarian interpretation of human behavior. And they worry lest sociobiology provide genetic rationalizations for the status quo and for the privileges that certain groups hold according to class, race, or gender. As such, Wilson's work has served to revive that old bugaboo of the behavioral sciences: the nature-nurture controversy (Pines, 1978).

Some anthropologists argue that the human brain is no longer rigidly tied to the calculus of "the selfish gene" (Barkow, 1978). Rather, genes have prescribed the construction of a liberated brain that permits a broad, flexible repertoire of behavioral responses. The evolution of the brain has gone hand in hand with the evolution of culture—a human-fashioned and socially transmitted adaptation to the environment (Scarr and Kidd, 1983). Consequently, the more culture that human beings developed, the more biological capacity for culture was evolved in their nervous systems, leading to more culture, and so on. And over time, cultural evolution, rather than biological evolution, came to be the greater source of behavioral change for human beings (Cavalli-Sforza and Feldman, 1981).

Sociobiology has provided psychology with both a hope and a challenge. The field permits psychologists to look beyond the nature-nurture controversy. By now science has established that both nature and nurture play crucial roles in behavior. Human behavior does not flow in some mystical fashion from genes, nor does environment imprint a human personality on a blank and infinitely plastic brain. Hence, psychology can now tackle the task of exploring the ways nature and nurture interact, a matter to which we now turn our attention.

HEREDITY AND ENVIRONMENT

Observant farmers have long been aware that they can improve certain qualities and traits in their animals by exercising care in their breeding. They may have cows that produce abundant milk, chickens that lay a good many eggs, horses that are swift, or sheep that grow prime-grade wool. Experience has demonstrated that by mating males and females from family lines possessing the desired characteristics, they can increase the likelihood that the resulting offspring will also possess these same characteristics. Laboratory experiments have confirmed that almost any characteristic can be promoted by selective breeding. The same principles apply to behav-

kin selection: Evolutionary processes that favor behaviors that contribute to the survival of one's relatives.

iors as to physical traits. Hence, mice have been bred to be more aggressive, more intelligent, or more sociable; dogs to be bold or timid (Plomin, DeFries, and McClearn, 1980). Through selection any breed of animals can be changed.

If selective breeding works to change animal behavior, why can it not be used to alter human behavior? Although there is no theoretical reason that artificial selection could not be used to change behaviors in the human population, ethical considerations have operated to bar experimentation (the Nobel laureate sperm bank notwithstanding). Human beings have been reluctant to admit that their behaviors are subject to the same evolutionary laws that apply to other organisms. All this has fueled the nature-nurture controversy.

The debate over the relative contributions that heredity and environment make to behavior has been going on for centuries. Indeed, even philosophers of the classical Greek era argued over whether ideas are innate to the human mind or are acquired through experience. As discussed in Chapter 1, Sir Francis Galton, a cousin of Charles Darwin, was one of the first in the modern era to preach the importance of nature. In 1869 he published *Hereditary Genius*, a book in which he analyzed the families of over one thousand eminent politicians, religious leaders, artists and scholars. He found that success ran in the families and concluded that hereditary differences caused differences in success.

But most psychologists have emphasized the importance of the environment. The tone was set by John Watson, the father of behaviorism, who wrote (1924:104):

> I should like to go one step further now and say, give me a dozen infants, well-formed, and my own specified world to bring them up in and I'll guarantee to take any one at random and train him to be any type of specialist I might select—doctor, lawyer, artist, merchant-chief, and yes, even beggar-man and thief, regardless of his talents, penchants, tendencies,

abilities, vocations, and the race of his ancestors. I am going beyond my facts and I admit it, but so have the advocates of the contrary and they have been doing it for many thousands of years.

Watson recognized that his statement went well beyond his data. He meant his statement to provoke a revolution in psychology, and he succeeded in his purpose.

How Genes and Environment Work Together

The question posed by Galton and Watson was essentially this: Which factor, heredity or environment, is more responsible for *differences* in people's intelligence, mental well-being, or worldly success? But the question has been misinterpreted by many to mean: Which factor, heredity *or* environment, is more responsible for behavior? And this erroneous formulation has caused the scientific community, and society at large, a great many difficulties. It has done so by creating a hopeless either/or type dichotomy. It is comparable to asking, Which is more important to water (H_2O), the hydrogen or the oxygen? Carried to its logical conclusion, the formulation defines biologically programed behavior as that which occurs in the absence of environment and learned behavior as that which does not require an organism. Obviously, we would have neither human beings nor behavior without having both heredity and environment. Considered in its broadest sense, **heredity** entails the biological transmission of traits from parents to their offspring through genes. **Environment** involves all those surrounding influences and factors that affect the organism.

In the course of our lives, our **genotype** (the set of genes we inherit) comes to be expressed as a **phenotype** (our observable characteristics). Although some genotypes, such as eye color and blood type, are expressed directly in the phenotype, this is not usually the case. Most phenotypes are the products

---

heredity: The biological transmission of traits from parents to their offspring through genes.

environment: Those surrounding influences and factors that affect the organism.

genotype (JEAN-oh-type): The set of genes organisms inherit from their parents.

phenotype (FEEN-oh-type): The observable characteristics of individuals (as distinct from their genotype).

of transactions between different genes and between genes and the environment. For instance, some people are genetically susceptible to clinical diabetes yet they never develop the disorder because they exercise care in their diets or because the action of other genes minimizes or counteracts the biochemical processes programed by the diabetes-disposing gene.

It is easy to simplify these matters and overlook their complexities. Consider the environment. You experience the environment in quite different ways. The developmental psychologist Joachim Wohlwill (1973) captures a number of these differences in four models:

1. *The hospital bed.* You often experience the environment passively, in that things "happen to you." You are the recipient of stimulation over which you have little control. Analogously, should you be immobilized on a hospital ward, medical personnel take your temperature, feed you, and wheel you from one procedure to another with little regard for your wishes.

2. *The amusement park.* In some settings you encounter a good many options as to what you might do. You typically ignore some things while attending to others. However, once you make a choice—decide on a particular ride such as a roller coaster or activity such as bumper cars—you exercise little control over what transpires. At this point the environment takes control.

3. *The swim meet.* Still other settings optimize your opportunities for acting in ways that you choose. In a swim meet, once the gun sounds, you dive into the water and swim as fast as you can. The water—the environment—simply provides the medium in which you carry out activities that you largely control and continually monitor.

4. *The tennis match.* There are some settings in which you must continually improvise behavior within an ever-changing environment. When you play a game of tennis, a tight "feedback loop" ties your responses to those of your opponent. If your opponent lobs a high return, you must retreat and extend your arm

and body to return the shot. Should the opponent slash a low return, you must dash forward to hit the ball. Your behavior and that of your opponent are bound together in a dynamic, complex interchange.

In your daily activities you are involved in all four types of environmental contexts. When you attend psychology class beginning at 1:00 P.M. on Mondays, Wednesdays, and Fridays, you encounter a hospital-bed experience. For the most part, you have little say in what you will see or hear. When you relax after class by watching a soap opera, you are involved in the amusement-park world of television. What transpires as you view the program has been determined by writers and a director. Should you then take your bike for a leisurely outing to rest your strained eyes, you find yourself in a swim-meet setting. When you return and talk to your friend on the telephone, your experiences resemble a tennis match. What each of you says is contingent on what transpired before and in turn influences the direction of the ensuing conversation.

As we will see in the chapters that follow, we are engaged in a continual interaction with our environment. In the course of our daily activities, we act upon, transform, and modify the world in which we live. In turn we are shaped and altered by the consequences of our own actions. For instance, our memory is not a tape recorder that transcribes an exact replica of whatever sounds we experience. In order to encode and store them in memory we must first interpret them and give them meaning. For instance, you may hear a foghorn and remember a terrifying Alfred Hitchcock movie, while your friend may hear one and remember a romantic walk along a Lake Michigan beach. As a result of the mental and biochemical processes that ensue—what we term "learning"—a change takes place in our capability for future behavior. When we again experience similar sound waves, we interpret or reinterpret them in ways that are influenced by our earlier memories. In brief, our brain molds and gives meaning to the experiences we have in our environment. Consequently, learning is not simply a process of maturation or unfolding. A microscopic examination of the tulip bulb reveals a blossom in miniature that, under proper environmental conditions, is merely elevated, enlarged, and colored until it assumes the familiar form of the spring flower. Much of human behavior is quite different because in the process of learning, we modify and transform ourselves as we respond. In sum, as we interact with others and the world about us, we literally "create" ourselves. Of course we do not do so indiscriminately, but in terms of the possibilities afforded by our genetic beings, a matter to which we now turn our attention.

Behavior Genetics

We hear a good deal nowadays about genes, much of this interest generated by exciting new developments in the war against various hereditary diseases. **Genes** are the building blocks of heredity. As such they have given their name to an academic discipline, **genetics**—the scientific study of the transmission of hereditary factors and the way these factors are expressed in the development and life of an individual. Genes are made up of numerous molecules called **deoxyribonucleic acid,** or **DNA.** DNA stores inherited information that serves as a "recipe" or "blueprint" that tells a cell how to manufacture such vital protein substances as enzymes, hormones, antibodies, and structural proteins.

Think of genes as regions or locations in chromosomes. (There are more than a thousand genes in each chromosome.) **Chromosomes** are long, threadlike bodies that contain the hereditary materials found in the nuclei of all cells. Most human cells contain forty-six chromosomes. At conception, the human being receives twenty-three chromosomes from the father's sperm and twenty-three chromosomes from the mother's ovum. When fertilization takes place, these chromosomes join together in twenty-three pairs.

Since genes are found in chromosomes, they too come in pairs (one gene from the sperm chromosome and one gene from the ovum chromosome). Some genes "average out" their instructions, whereas others are either *dominant* or *recessive* for a trait. Take the case of eye color. The gene for brown eyes is dominant and that for blue eyes is recessive. If you have two genes for brown eyes (dominant) or one gene for brown eyes (dominant) and one gene for blue eyes (recessive), you will have brown eyes. Only if you have two recessive genes for blue eyes will you have blue eyes (see Figure 2.1).

Some disorders that have behavioral implications are transmitted in the same manner as eye color. *Phenylketonuria,* or *PKU*—a disorder that occurs in about one out of every twelve thousand live births —is a case in point. PKU is caused by a defect in the gene involved with the body's use of phenylalanine, a protein present in milk and many other foods. The defective gene results in the lack of a body chemical needed to convert phenylalanine into other proteins. Unconverted phenylalanine builds up in toxic quantities and attacks the cells of the nervous system, causing progressive mental retardation. Like blue eye color, PKU derives from two recessive genes.

Fortunately, scientists have been able to break the tragic chain of events that would otherwise begin with defective PKU genes. Since the mid-1960s, physicians have pricked the heels of millions of American babies shortly after birth and have taken a few drops of blood for analysis of the phenylalanine level. An abnormally high level indicates the presence of the defective gene, and the baby is immediately started on a diet low in phenylalanine. Simply by adjusting one aspect of the infant's internal environment—the level of phenylalanine in the body— doctors can prevent the devastating effects of the faulty gene. Thus although PKU is inherited, PKU effects can be minimized by controlling the environment (Holtzman et al., 1986). This example shows

---

genes (jeans): The building blocks of heredity.

genetics (juh-NEH-tics): The scientific study of the transmission of hereditary factors and the way these factors are expressed in the development and life of an individual.

deoxyribonucleic (dee-OX-ee-rye-bow-new-CLAY-ic) acid (DNA): A molecule in which genetic information is stored; it tells a cell how to manufacture such vital protein substances as enzymes, hormones, antibodies, and structural proteins.

chromosome (CROW-ma-sewm): A long, threadlike body that contains the hereditary materials found in the nuclei of all cells.

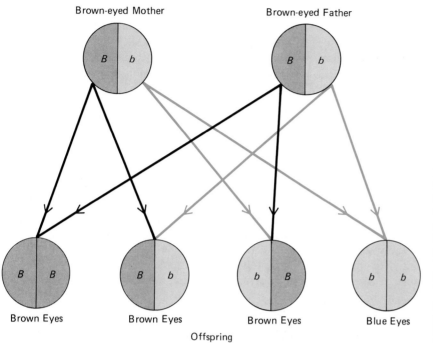

Brown-eyed Mother   Brown-eyed Father

B   b   B   b

B   B   B   b   b   B   b   b

Brown Eyes   Brown Eyes   Brown Eyes   Blue Eyes

Offspring

FIGURE 2.1 The transmission of eye color by dominant (B) and recessive (b) genes. Both parents are brown-eyed, but each carries a recessive gene for blue eyes. Four combinations of eye color are possible in their offspring. Three out of the four mixtures lead to brown-eyed offspring. Thus the chance that any child will have brown eyes is 75 percent, while the chance for blue eyes is only 25 percent.

that genetic screening and appropriate genetic counseling afford hope for environmental interventions to prevent undesirable consequences. Many other single-gene disorders of humans will one day be treated environmentally.

PKU children highlight a central theme of this chapter: heredity and environment interact in a relationship of varying dependence; both are essential for human behavior. Clearly, genes cannot be said to "cause" behavior. In the case of PKU, a gene fails to instruct cells to manufacture a crucial substance. In turn, because of the environmental intake of certain foods, other substances build up to toxic levels and destroy nerve cells. Progressive damage to the nervous system results in a deterioration of intellectual functioning. Simultaneously, language and motor performance are impaired.

PKU involves one gene. However, most human traits derive from **polygenic inheritance,** which involves the interaction of several genes. And the reverse also holds true. One gene often has multiple effects. Given the complexity of the processes gov-

erning genetic transmission, it is not surprising that at times something goes wrong. It is the *quality* of the genetic material that is associated with single-gene disorders. An error in metabolism interferes with the sequential chain whereby specific proteins are manufactured, distributed, and used.

Developmental or functional disorders can also be caused by the *quantity* of genetic material and the way it is *arranged*. For instance, there are some chromosomal defects in which the individual has too much chromosomal material. An illustration is *Down's syndrome*, which occurs in one out of six hundred live births and is associated with an extra chromosome. Children with Down's syndrome suffer from physical abnormalities and mental retardation. There are also some chromosomal defects in which the individual has too little chromosomal material. An example is *Turner's syndrome*, which is found among some women and is associated with one less chromosome than normal. Women with Turner's syndrome are short in stature, lack ovaries, and are deficient in female hormones.

polygenic (pol-ee-JEAN-ic) inheritance: Traits that derive from the interaction of several genes.

Studies of Family Resemblance

One way to find out what makes individuals differ is to conduct studies among family members. For instance, on occasion nature provides scientists with the makings of a natural experiment. By some accident, a fertilized egg sometimes gets split into two parts early in development. The two parts grow into separate and complete individuals, termed **identical**, or **monozygotic, twins.** Thus identical twins share the same genes. In contrast with identical twins, **fraternal**, or **dizygotic, twins** develop from two different eggs fertilized by two different sperm. Their genes are no more similar than those of ordinary brothers or sisters.

Obviously, twins growing up in the same house share the same general environment. But identical twins who grow up together also share the same genes. So if identical twins prove to be more alike on a specific trait than do fraternal twins, it probably means that genes are important for differences in that characteristic.

For example, many twin studies have been undertaken on the inheritance of mental disease. Schizophrenia is a serious mental illness that affects about 1 percent of the world population (see Chapter 15). Studies reveal that if one twin becomes schizophrenic, the other twin has about a 40 percent chance of also becoming schizophrenic if he or she is an identical twin, and a 4 to 10 percent chance if he or she is a fraternal twin (Gottesman and Shields, 1982). These statistics suggest that there is a genetic contribution to the development of schizophrenia. However, since in many cases only one identical twin develops the illness, environmental factors must also play a role.

Of particular scientific interest are pairs of identical twins who have been reared apart from each other. Such twins provide a means for studying the effects of the environment when heredity is the same. The psychologist Thomas J. Bouchard, Jr., and his associates at the University of Minnesota have collected a vast amount of psychological data on some thirty pairs of identical twins who were reared apart (Holden, 1980). The researchers find that on many psychological and ability tests the scores of the twins are closer than would be expected for the same person taking the same test a second time. And the brain-wave tracings of twins differ no more than do tracings taken from the same person at different times, suggesting that identical twins are almost identically "wired" (see the boxed insert on page 43). On the other hand, identical twins also differ to some degree—one twin, for instance, is likely to be more aggressive, more confident, and more outgoing than the other.

It is easy to come away from the Minnesota research with the impression that the effects of genes are carved in granite, somehow fixed for all time at the moment of conception. But this is hardly the case. Even when reared in different households, identical twins are filtering their environmental experiences through similar perceptual and interpretative screens. Consequently, as they go about their daily activities (even though living in quite different settings), they select roughly similar things from their environments to attend to and roughly similar things to ignore. And as they encounter a world of people, identical twins, since they look a great deal alike, evoke similar responses from others. Thus it is little wonder that they end up quite similar individuals. Not only do they have similar heredities, but they also tend to experience their environments, whatever they may be, in somewhat similar ways.

Another means that researchers use for assessing family resemblances is the study of children who were adopted at birth and reared by foster parents. Some characteristic of the adopted children, such as IQ score or the presence of a mental disorder, is compared with that of their biological parents and that of their foster parents. In this manner, researchers undertake to weigh the relative influences of the

---

identical (monozygotic) twins: Siblings that result when a fertilized egg accidentally gets split into two parts early in development; each part grows into a separate and complete individual who is genetically identical to the other.

fraternal (dizygotic [dye-zye-GAH-tic]) twins: Siblings that result when two different eggs supplied by the same female are fertilized by two different sperm; they are no more genetically related than ordinary sisters and brothers.

A Living Lab: Identical Twins Reared Apart

One of the most intriguing pair of identical twins who were reared apart and later reunited are two forty-seven-year-old brothers, Oskar Stöhr and Jack Yufe, studied by the University of Minnesota twin researchers (Holden, 1980).

These brothers reveal the most dramatically different backgrounds of all the twins in the study. Stöhr, who works as an engineer in West Germany, and Yufe, who owns a clothing store in California, were separated at six months of age, when their parents divorced. Stöhr went to live with his mother in Eastern Europe, while Yufe was reared in the Caribbean by his father. Hence, one was reared by a female and the other by a male.

Stöhr was brought up as a Catholic and later became involved in the Hitler Youth Movement. Yufe was raised as a Jew, joined an Israeli kibbutz in his youth, and served in the Israeli navy. Stöhr is married, a devoted union man, and a skier. Yufe is separated from his wife, describes himself as a workaholic, and sails as a hobby.

Despite the differences, striking similarities are found in the behavior of the two men:

- When they first met at the airport, both sported mustaches and two-pocket shirts with epaulets, and each carried a pair of wire-rimmed glasses with him.

- Both men like spicy foods and sweet liqueurs.

- Both are absent-minded, and both fall asleep in front of the television.

- Both flush the toilet before using it.

- Both find it quite humorous to sneeze in a crowd of strangers.

- Both store rubber bands on their wrists.

- Both read magazines from back to front.

- Both have similar personality profiles as measured by the Minnesota Multiphasic Personality Inventory.

- Both exhibit similar mannerisms, ask similar kinds of questions, and reveal a similar tempo in the way they do tasks.

- Both excel at sports and have difficulty with math.

Jack Yufe

Oskar Stöhr

(Photographs courtesy Thomas J. Bouchard Jr., Department of Psychology, University of Minnesota)

genetic factor and the home environment as they come to bear in behavior. The nervous system plays a critical part in mapping and channeling our behavior, a matter to which we now turn our psychological eye.

HOW THE NERVOUS SYSTEM AFFECTS BEHAVIOR

Consider the *Nimitz*, the ninety-thousand-ton, nuclear-powered aircraft carrier that can project

U.S. naval presence throughout the world. From its superstructure, complex electronic-radar gear twists and turns, ever hunting the seas and skies for potential adversaries. Linked to the radar equipment —the eyes and ears of a naval task force—are powerful computers that digest and interpret the data. In turn, communication networks channel this information to officers, crew, and pilots, who can promptly launch the carrier's ninety-five aircraft from a deck the size of three football fields. A protective ring of destroyers and other escort ships extends three hundred miles around the flagship, while hunter-killer submarines prowl below. All these activities are integrated and coordinated by a centralized high-tech nerve center aboard the vessel.

Striking parallels exist between the *Nimitz* and the human organism. Like the radar aboard an aircraft carrier, the mobile extremities and the eyes and ears allow humans to hunt stimuli. Like a computer, the human brain processes and interprets information. And like a communication network, the nervous system carries messages back and forth throughout the body.

Consider the marvelous way you go about recognizing a friend's face at different distances and in different positions (Hubel and Wiesel, 1979; N. Miller, 1982). You make such recognitions despite the fact that each change in position stimulates a different array of rods and cones on the retinas of your eyes. Even the most powerful computers on board the *Nimitz* are incapable of handling such an extraordinary series of detailed operations. Nonetheless, human beings manage the task in an orderly and effortless manner.

As your eyes, brain, and nervous system work with one another, you recognize the object as a person—indeed, as a friend. Even more important, you act. Your brain and spinal cord not only issue commands to muscles but also receive feedback signals that help you to orchestrate the commands (Evarts, 1979). Thus you may happily greet or embrace your friend.

Of course the *Nimitz* does not exist in isolation. It is a constituent part of an even more complex system—a naval task force. And it operates within a vast environmental arena. Similarly, the human organism is part of a more complex system—the human group or society. And like the *Nimitz*, human beings have the capacity to examine, engage, and alter their environment. The human organism is inherently active. Humans are the source of their own acts and are not simply activated by external forces. They influence the things and the people in their environment. In turn, physical objects and other people influence them. Thus human beings forge their personalities as they actively and relentlessly confront, master, and cope with the requirements of life. And in the process, they produce what psychologists term *behavior*.

The Nervous System

The human organism and its environment are linked within an encompassing behavioral system. What are the means by which this linkage is achieved? What are the mechanisms by which people adapt to the world about them and take their places within group life? Part of the answer lies with the nervous system and the brain. They provide the coordinating and control operations by which the perceptual, muscular, skeletal, digestive, and other systems achieve integration, allowing people to function as effective beings in a complex physical and social environment.

Consider how you respond to your environment. Your brain monitors what is happening inside and outside your body by receiving messages from **receptors**—cells whose function is to gather information and send messages to your brain. Your brain sifts through these messages, combines them, and sends out orders to the **effectors**—cells that work your muscles and your internal glands and organs. For example, receptors in your eye may send a message to your brain such as "Round object. Size increasing. Distance decreasing rapidly." Your brain instantly connects this image with information from memory to identify this object as a baseball. Almost simultaneously your brain orders the effectors in

---

receptors (ree-SEP-tors): Cells whose function it is to gather information and send messages to the brain.

effector (ih-FECK-ter): A cell that works the muscles, internal glands, and organs.

your arms to position themselves so you do not get beaned on the head when playing right field.

In some ways, the nervous system is like the telephone system in a city. Messages are constantly traveling back and forth. As in a telephone system, the messages are basically electrical. They travel along prelaid cables, linked with one another by relays and switchboards. In the body, the cables are nerve fibers. The relays are **synapses,** the gaps that occur between individual nerve cells. The switchboards are special cells that are found along the lines of communication (called *interneurons*) and the networks of nerve cells found in the brain and the spinal cord. One major difference is that a telephone system simply conveys messages, whereas the nervous system actively helps to run the body. The control system of the brain allows for at least two functions. The organism is *aroused* so that it becomes responsive to environmental inputs and *activated* so that it directs and concentrates its efforts on specific tasks (Plum and Posner, 1980; Tucker and Williamson, 1984). Nerve cells, termed *neurons,* make up the nervous system and the brain and assume a critical role in the performance of these functions.

Neurons

You can probably remember a time when you were just drifting off to sleep, enjoying the vague images and dreamy thoughts floating through your mind, when suddenly your whole body went into a spasm. You woke up startled, panicked, and confused. Although you were still in bed, you had a strong sense of having fallen. This feeling is a sign of miscoordination among the trillions of cells in your body. Most often, however, your body coordinates this mass of cells through a special type of cell, the neuron. **Neurons** are nerve cells that make up the nervous system and brain. Researchers are finding that a typical neuron is as complex as a small computer. Most neurons, consist of one major cell

A *photomicrograph* (microscopic photograph) of two human neurons with their connecting branches, called axons and dendrites. *(Dan McCoy/Rainbow)*

body. This cell body contains the nucleus of the neuron and the biochemical machinery for synthesizing enzymes and various life-support substances. A long, slender structure, the **axon,** emanates from the cell body. It is made up of tiny tubes, or filaments, along which biochemical signals are conveyed. Also radiating from the central cell body are a number of fibers, called **dendrites.** Dendrites resemble a bushy tree and differ in both structure and properties from an axon. In general, the dendrites and the cell body receive the incoming signals. The cell body combines and integrates the signals (roughly speaking, it

synapses (SIN-aps-es): The gaps that occur between individual nerve cells.

neurons (NEW-rons): The long, thin cells that constitute the structural and functional unit of nerve tissue, along which messages travel to and from the brain.

axon: A fiber of a nerve cell that conducts impulses away from the cell body.

dendrite: A relatively short, bushy fiber of a nerve cell that receives most incoming signals.

averages them) and emits outgoing impulses. The axon transports the outgoing signals to the axon terminals (knoblike tips called *synaptic knobs* or *terminal buttons*), which in turn distribute the information to other neurons (see Figure 2.2). Recent research reveals that transport in the axon also allows for a retrograde, or reverse, flow, by which substances needed by the cell body are brought back up the axon, at times even from beyond the synapses. Likewise, dendrites also transmit substances in the the opposite direction (Schmeck, 1984).

In some cases the axon is several feet in length; in other cases, less than an inch. Typically, the dendrites of one neuron form a "tree" about the axon and cell body of another neuron. A neuron commonly has from one thousand to ten thousand synapses and receives information from some one thousand other neurons. Most often the synapses form a narrow gap between the axon of one neuron and the dendrite of another, although in some instances the synaptic junctions occur between axon and axon, between dendrite and dendrite, and between axon and cell body. Since the brain contains between 10 billion and 100 billion neurons (estimates vary), each forming bridges to many others, the brain is abuzz with some one quadrillion connections.

A dense fatty coating termed **myelin** wraps around most axons and gives them electrical insulation (Morell and Norton, 1980). The myelin sheath apparently conserves the neuron's energy. Usually nerve fibers that are encased in myelin transmit signals faster than do those lacking myelin. Multiple sclerosis is a disease that destroys myelin and produces a variety of symptoms, including difficulty in seeing, muscle weakness, and lack of coordination. Apparently, the symptoms are caused by the failure of axons to conduct impulses properly once they have lost their myelin insulation.

Now consider how a message is transmitted (Hubel, 1979). On the input side there are receptors, some of which respond to light (vision), others to chemicals (taste and smell), and still others to mechanical pressure (touch and hearing). The receptors make contact with one set of neurons, which in turn establish contact with others, and so on. Each cell

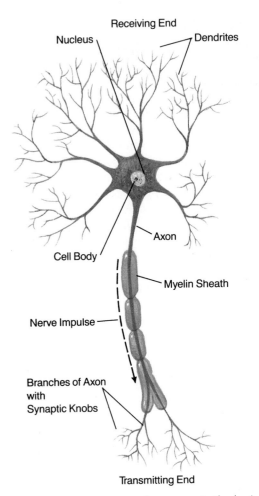

FIGURE 2.2 The structure of a neuron in the brain. From the cell body come the axon, or major branch, and many dendrites that receive incoming signals from other neurons.

combines and integrates the exciting or inhibiting impulses that converge on it from neurons farther down the line. As noted earlier in the chapter, *afferent*, or *receptor*, *neurons* carry impulses to the brain or spinal cord from receptors, while *efferent*, or *effector*, *neurons* convey signals away from the brain or spinal cord to muscles or glands, the output side of the nervous system.

myelin (MY-eh-lin): A dense fatty coating that wraps around an axon and gives it electrical insulation.

Neurotransmitters

Although the signal generated by a neuron and transmitted along its axon is an electrical impulse, information is conveyed across the synaptic gap from a neuron to a muscle cell, gland cell, or another neuron by chemical **neurotransmitters.** Scientists have identified more than fifty different neurotransmitters, including acetylcholine, norepinephrine, epinephrine, dopamine, and serotonin (S. H. Snyder, 1980, 1985). When an impulse reaches the end of an axon, the chemical-transmitted substance is released from small vesicles in the axon terminal button (see Figure 2.3). The substance diffuses across the synaptic gap and contributes to chemical changes in the other cell. The neurotransmitter typically affects another cell in one of two ways. It may excite the cell, leading it to generate impulses at a faster rate. Or it may inhibit the cell, reducing its rate of firing or canceling it altogether. Nerve cells frequently use two or even three substances to communicate with one another. Apparently a number of neurotransmitters, by working together, can convey subtler information than would be possible with a single substance (McGuiness and Pribram, 1980; S. H. Snyder, 1985). Neurotransmitters are critical substances for carrying messages that order muscles to contract or relax, turn "on" and "off" countless mental processes, and signal pain, fear, heat, hunger, and joy.

The neurotransmitters released from one neuron into the synaptic gap attach themselves to receptor sites (usually protein molecules) on the adjacent cell. The chemicals bind to their receptors like keys in their appropriate locks. Without the appropriate chemical key, nothing happens. Hence, by binding to the receptor, the neurotransmitter switches on or shuts down activities in the adjacent neuron. Acetylcholine is a case in point. It is a neurotransmitter found among neurons that terminate at muscle cells; it contributes to motor control. Some disorders, such as myasthenia gravis (a disease characterized by progressive muscular weakness, especially of the face, tongue, and neck), result from the failure of acetylcholine to move from a synapse to its appropriate receptors on the adjoining cell. Apparently a

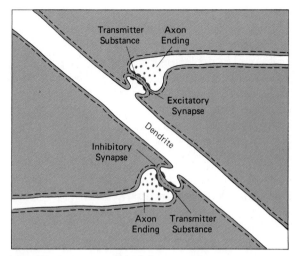

FIGURE 2.3 A simplified drawing of a synapse showing how neural transmission is controlled by axons that excite and inhibit the activity of the dendrite.

malfunctioning of the body's immune system leads to the blocking or destroying of the acetylcholine and its receptors.

Some substances facilitate the transfer of signals. For instance, scientists find that an individual who eats a large omelet or other foods that contain choline, such as meat or fish, will within a few hours have an extra supply of acetylcholine in the brain (Cohen and Wurtman, 1976; Wurtman, 1982). This increase amplifies the signals sent from one neuron to another by those cells that use acetylcholine for the signaling. Currently, a number of scientists are exploring the possibility that memory may be improved by increasing the activity of brain cells through the consumption of foods high in choline (Sitaram, Weingartner, and Gillin, 1978; Blustajn and Wurtman, 1983).

Neurotransmitters appear to be implicated in many mental disorders (see Chapter 15). Depression seems to be associated with a deficit of serotonin and norepinephrine in the synapse, while in mania, a surplus occurs. Some cases of schizophrenia may be due to disturbances in dopamine, as suggested by the action of antischizophrenic drugs that act selectively

neurotransmitters (new-roh-TRANS-mitt-ers): The chemicals released by neurons that determine the rate at which other neurons fire.

on dopamine receptors. Valium and other mood-influencing drugs appear to achieve their effect by altering the transmission of signals at synapses. Most drugs used in psychiatry exert their effects by acting on one or another neurotransmitter. In laboratories throughout the world, scientists are currently attempting to produce synthetic drugs that mimic the brain's natural neurotransmitters and correct the biochemical mix-ups that produce disorders (S. H. Snyder, 1980, 1985).

Divisions of the Nervous System

Psychologists find it helpful to organize information about the nervous system by describing its structural divisions (see Figure 2.4). The **central nervous system (CNS)** is composed of the brain and spinal cord. You might think of the **spinal cord** as the main cable. It is a bundle of nerves, about as thick as a pencil, running down the length of the back. The spinal cord transmits most of the messages back and forth between the body and the brain.

The spinal cord is well protected by the vertebrae, just as the brain is protected by the skull. This protection prevents interference with the line of communication between the brain and the rest of the body. Without the spinal cord, messages from the brain would never reach any of your muscles except those in the face. You would be paralyzed from the neck down, as is the case with quadriplegics.

Branching out from the spinal cord and, to a lesser extent, from the brain is a network of nerves called the **peripheral nervous system (PNS)** (see Figure 2.5). These nerves conduct information from the bodily organs to the central nervous system and take information back to the organs. The peripheral nervous system is divided into two parts: somatic and autonomic. The **somatic nervous system** controls voluntary movement of skeletal muscles (such as lifting your hand to turn a page, which involves a number of coordinated movements). The **autonomic nervous system** controls the glands, internal organs, and involuntary muscles (such as the heart). The autonomic nervous system itself has two parts: sympathetic and parasympathetic.

The **sympathetic nervous system** prepares your body for dealing with emergencies or strenuous activities. It speeds up the heart to hasten the supply of oxygen and nutrients to body tissues. It constricts some arteries and relaxes others so that blood flows to the muscles, where it is most needed in emergencies and strenuous activities. It increases the breathing rate and suspends some activities such as digestion. In contrast, the **parasympathetic nervous system** works to conserve energy and to enhance your body's ability to recover from strenuous activity. It reduces the heart rate, slows breathing, and the like.

Consider the following illustration. Suppose you have just eaten. You are now relaxing on the steps of the dining hall watching the sun set. Messages flow out along your parasympathetic nerves that stimulate your digestive processes. All the while, the sympathetic nerves to your digestive system are relatively inactive. The blood vessels that supply your digestive tract are fully open while those supplying your

---

central nervous system (CNS): The brain and spinal cord.

spinal cord: The bundle of nerves that runs down the length of the back and transmits most messages back and forth between the body and the brain.

peripheral nervous system (PNS): A network of nerves branching out from the spinal cord that conducts information from the bodily organs to the central nervous system and takes information back to the organs.

somatic (sew-MAA-tic) nervous system: The half of the peripheral nervous system that controls voluntary movement of skeletal muscles.

autonomic (aw-tuh-NOM-ic) nervous system: Part of the peripheral nervous system that controls internal biological functions, such as heart rate and digestion.

sympathetic nervous system: The system that prepares the body for dealing with emergencies or strenuous activities.

parasympathetic nervous system: The system that works to conserve energy and enhance the body's ability to recuperate after strenuous activity.

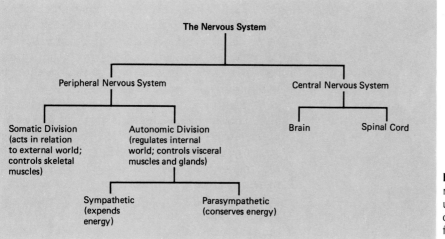

The Nervous System

Peripheral Nervous System — Central Nervous System

Somatic Division (acts in relation to external world; controls skeletal muscles) — Autonomic Division (regulates internal world; controls visceral muscles and glands)

Brain — Spinal Cord

Sympathetic (expends energy) — Parasympathetic (conserves energy)

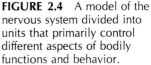

FIGURE 2.4 A model of the nervous system divided into units that primarily control different aspects of bodily functions and behavior.

FIGURE 2.5 The central nervous system (CNS) and the peripheral nervous system (PNS) in the human body.

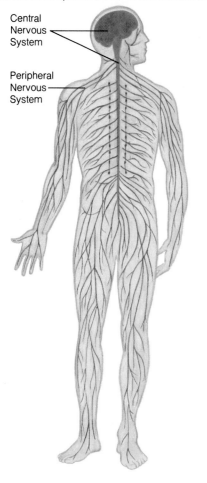

Central Nervous System

Peripheral Nervous System

limb muscles and kidneys are constricted. Suddenly the fire alarm goes off in the dining hall and students come charging down the steps. You become frightened. The chemical messages that rush through your body inhibit the parasympathetic nervous system and excite the sympathetic nervous system. Your digestive processes cease, your eyes open wide, and your heart starts pounding. When you learn it is a false alarm and the students file back into the dining hall, your nervous system again shifts its priorities, and your digestion resumes. In sum, the sympathetic nervous system arouses your body, whereas the parasympathetic nervous system quiets it.

It is the balance of the parasympathetic and sympathetic nervous systems that determines whether the organism is in an energy-conserving or energy-expending state. Not surprisingly, imbalances between the two systems may contribute to difficulties. For instance, the sympathetic nervous system may overreact to a situation that is not particularly menacing. A good example of this is stage fright: some individuals experience disabling feelings of anxiety —palpitating heart, tremors, sweating, and even a temporary loss of memory—when they have to speak or perform before an audience.

The Old Brain and the New Brain

Signals from the receptors in the peripheral nervous system travel up the spinal cord and enter the brain. The first part of the brain that the messages reach is

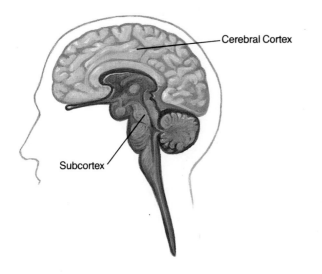

FIGURE 2.6 A cross section of the human brain, showing the subcortex, or "old brain," and the cerebral cortex, or "new brain."

the **subcortex** (see Figure 2.6). Together with the spinal cord, the subcortex controls and coordinates such vital functions as sleeping, heart rate, hunger, and digestion. It also controls many reflex actions, including blinking, coughing, and tearing.

The **cerebral cortex** partially surrounds the subcortex like a halved peach surrounds the pit (see Figure 2.7). The subcortex guides basic biological functioning. In contrast, the cerebral cortex enables you, among other things, to think, to read, and to solve problems.

The subcortex is sometimes called the "old brain" and the cortex the "new brain." Whereas the "old brain" is thought to have evolved millions of years ago in our prehuman ancestors, the "new brain" is more recent in origin. In fact, vague resemblances exist between the brain of a three-week-old human embryo and that of lower forms of life such as fish

and frogs. These organisms, like human beings, need to sleep, eat, and digest food. Thus it is not surprising that some areas of the brain such as the subcortex are somewhat similar across many species. The evolutionary ties are even closer among mammals, as are the brain resemblances.

It is said that ontogeny recapitulates phylogeny: an organism passes through stages of embryonic development that in some respects correspond to stages in the evolution of that organism. Thus the cerebral cortex, which evolved rather late among higher forms of life, is relatively slow to develop in the fetal period (Kalat, 1981). Indeed, the old brain or subcortex remains very important in newborn human functioning. Most reflexes—such as sucking, rooting, and grasping—are organized at the subcortical level (see Chapter 11). However, the range of functioning permitted an organism at the subcortical level is considerably less than that afforded at the cortical level. It is primarily at the cortical level that learning—acquired behavior—becomes possible. Consequently, the behavior available to a child increases with the maturation and myelination of the brain. And with this cortical development, the behavior of the child becomes less stereotyped and more flexible.

The Subcortex

The subcortex contains a number of structures (see Figure 2.7). A portion of the subcortex called the *reticular formation* controls an activating network of nerves that runs through the whole brain. This network, the **reticular activating system,** may be the brain's waking and attention system. It screens incoming messages, blocking out some signals and letting others pass. During sleep it blocks most inputs; but in response to a loud or unusual sound, it sends messages to the rest of the brain, alerting it and raising its activity level to a state of wakefulness.

---

subcortex: The part of the brain where all messages are first received and that, together with the spinal cord, controls and coordinates vital functions and reflex actions; sometimes called the "old brain."

cerebral (sair-REE-bral) cortex: The gray mass surrounding the subcortex that controls most of the higher brain functions, such as reading and problem solving.

reticular (reh-TIH-cue-lar) activating system: The system in the brain that screens incoming messages, blocking out some signals and letting others pass.

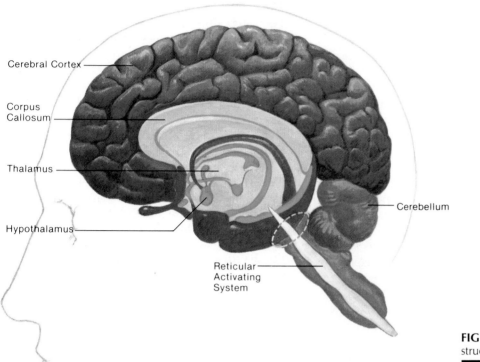

Cerebral Cortex

Corpus Callosum

Thalamus

Hypothalamus

Cerebellum

Reticular Activating System

FIGURE 2.7 The structures of the subcortex.

In the center of the brain is the **thalamus,** the brain's great relaying center. Like a switchboard, it sorts incoming impulses and directs them to various parts of the brain, and it relays messages from one part of the brain to another. The thalamus also has an important role in language. When the thalamus is impaired, we have difficulty associating sounds with their meanings (Crosson, 1984).

At the base of the brain, below and to the front of the thalamus, is the **hypothalamus,** a small, closely packed cluster of neurons that is one of the most important parts of the brain. This structure functions in two broad areas: it maintains a relatively constant internal body environment (such as the regulation of body temperature), and it activates,

regulates, and controls various expressions of behavior (such as the feelings associated with hunger, thirst, sexual arousal, fear, and rage) (Noback and Demarest, 1981).

The hypothalamus regulates body temperature by monitoring the temperature of the blood. If your body is too cold, the hypothalamus causes tiny vibrations in your muscles (shivering) that bring the temperature up to normal. If your body is too hot, the hypothalamus signals your sweat glands to perspire. As perspiration evaporates, your body is cooled. Thus your body possesses a variety of adaptive mechanisms that permit it to maintain a more or less stable existence in an unstable environment—a process termed **homeostasis.**

thalamus (THAL-uh-muss): The portion of the brain that sorts incoming impulses and then directs them to various parts of the brain. It also relays messages from one part of the brain to another part.

hypothalamus (hi-po-THAL-uh-muss): A small area deep inside the brain that regulates the autonomic nervous system and other body functions.

homeostasis (ho-me-oh-STAY-sis): The process that permits an organism to maintain a more or less stable existence in an unstable environment through a variety of adaptive mechanisms.

The hypothalamus also influences behavior in a number of ways. It regulates the autonomic nervous system, the system of peripheral nerves that controls bodily functioning. The structure thus regulates such biological functions as digestion, heart rate, and hormone secretion. By sensing the levels of water and sugar in your body, your hypothalamus can tell when you need food or water and can then cause you to feel hungry or thirsty. And by regulating the sugar level in your body, it influences your sense of well-being.

The hypothalamus likewise plays a critical part in determining your emotional responses of rage, fear, and pleasure, as well as your sexual responses. It does so in conjunction with the pituitary gland through the regulation of the endocrine system, matters that are discussed later in this chapter. In sum, the hypothalamus is so important because it is the place where many signals from the central nervous system, the endocrine system, and the autonomic nervous system converge, are integrated, and are responded to.

At the very back and bottom of the old brain is the **cerebellum,** the brain's "executive secretary." One of the cerebellum's main functions is to control posture and balance as you move about so that you do not fall over or bump into things. It also helps to regulate the details of commands from the cerebral cortex. Without your cerebellum, you might hit a friend in the stomach when you reach out to shake hands.

The Cerebral Cortex

The cerebral cortex, in which most of the higher brain functions take place, is a great gray mass of ripples and valleys, folded so that its huge surface area can fit inside the skull. These convolutions increase the surface area and thus the covering body of cells. With an increase in the number of cerebral cortex cells, the links among cells also increase, greatly augmenting the brain's capacity to process information (Kalat, 1981).

We still have much to learn regarding the functions of the various parts of the cortex. Nonetheless, it is amply clear that specific regions of the cortex —termed **lobes**—are associated with specific senses and types of activity (see Figure 2.8). In this localization of function, most visual information goes to the **occipital lobes** at the back of the brain. Auditory sensations, or sounds, go primarily to the **temporal lobes** on each side of the brain. The **parietal lobes** integrate visual, auditory, and other sensory input. The **somatosensory cortex,** located at the border of the parietal lobes, at the middle of the brain, receives information from the skin senses (such as touch) and from muscles. As you can see in Figure 2.9, the amount of brain tissue connected to a body part is proportional to that area's sensitivity rather than to its size. For example, the highly developed sense of touch in your hands involves a much larger brain area than your relatively insensitive calves, uppers arms, and thighs. For this reason, physicians administer skin tests and injections in these latter regions.

---

cerebellum (sair-un-BELL-um): A lower portion of the brain that controls posture and balance and regulates the details of motor commands from the cerebral cortex.

lobes: The different regions into which the cerebral cortex is divided.

occipital (ahk-SIH-pih-tull) lobes: The lobes located at the back of the brain that receive visual information.

temporal lobes: The lobes on each side of the brain that receive auditory information.

parietal (pa-RYE-eh-tull) lobes: The lobes located in the middle of the brain that contain the somatosensory cortex and integrate visual, auditory, and other sensory input.

somatosensory (sew-maa-tuh-SEN-so-ree) cortex: An area of the brain, within the cerebral cortex, that receives information from the skin and muscles.

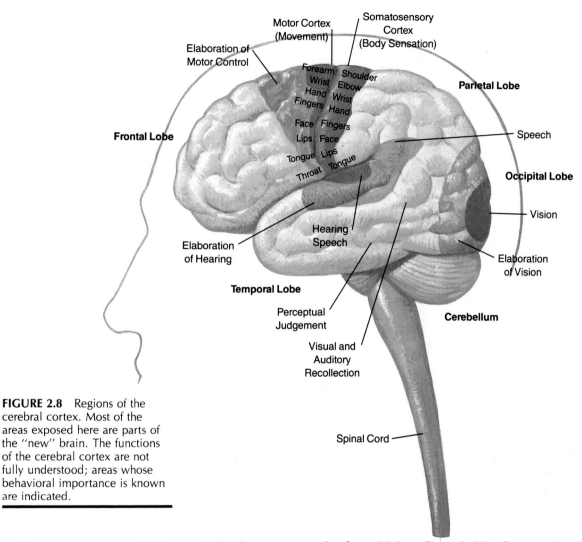

FIGURE 2.8 Regions of the cerebral cortex. Most of the areas exposed here are parts of the "new" brain. The functions of the cerebral cortex are not fully understood; areas whose behavioral importance is known are indicated.

The **motor cortex,** which controls body movement, is just in front of the somatosensory cortex, across a deep fold. The motor cortex is part of the **frontal lobes.** Some studies suggest that this area controls creativity and personality: it enables people to be witty, sensitive, or easygoing. For example, in the mid-1800s, a quarryman named Phineas Gage was injured in an explosion. The force of the blast drove an iron stake through Gage's head, damaging the frontal lobes. Remarkably, Gage survived and was back at work in a few months. The accident did not impair his bodily functions or his memory or skills. However, Gage's personality changed dramatically. This once trustworthy and dependable man became childish, fitful, impatient, and capricious. Later studies of large numbers of people with similar brain damage suggest that planning future action, monitoring personal behavior, handling sequential

motor cortex: The portion of the brain, located in the front of the somatosensory cortex, that controls body movement.

frontal lobes: The lobes, located in the front of the brain, that control intellect and personality.

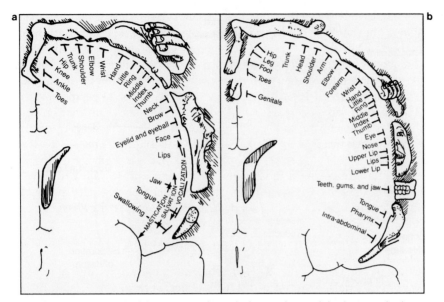

FIGURE 2.9 Both *a* and *b* represent the right hemisphere of the brain, which controls the voluntary muscles on the left side of the body. (a) The location and amount of cortical space devoted to the motor capacities of various body parts. Areas of the body capable of the most complex and precise movements take up the largest quantities of space in the motor cortex. (b) The location and amount of cortical space devoted to the sensory capacities of various body parts. In the sensory realm, those organs capable of the highest sensitivity have the largest representations in the somatosensory cortex. *(After W. Penfield and T. Rasmussen. 1950. The Cerebral Cortex of Man. New York: Macmillan. Reprinted by permission.)*

activities, persevering in carrying out tasks, translating knowledge into actual behavior, and integrating one's activities with other people's depend on the frontal lobes (Stuss and Benson, 1984). The frontal lobes reach their highest development in human beings. They take up only 3.5 percent of the cerebral cortex in cats, 7 percent in dogs, 17 percent in chimps, and 29 percent in humans.

Although various regions of the brain specialize in particular functions, other regions are frequently also involved. While neurons controlling our movements, senses, and information processing can be pinpointed in certain regions of the brain, axons from these regions can be traced back to other areas that serve as distant way stations along the path from receptor cells. We can gain an appreciation for some of these complexities by considering the hemispheres of the brain.

The Hemispheres of the Brain

The cortex is divided by a deep fissure into two halves, a left and a right hemisphere. (Each of the four lobes is present in both hemispheres.) The two hemispheres are connected by a thick band or cable of nerves called the **corpus callosum,** which carries messages back and forth between the two.

Lateralization of Functions

Although at first sight the two hemispheres seem to be rough mirror images of each other, they differ in

---

corpus callosum (kuh-LOW-sum): A band of nerves that connect the two hemispheres of the cortex and carries messages back and forth between them.

some functions. Each hemisphere is connected to half of the body in a crisscrossed fashion. The motor cortex of the left hemisphere of the brain controls most of the right side of the body; the motor cortex of the right hemisphere controls most of the left side of the body. Thus a stroke that causes damage to the right hemisphere will result in numbness or paralysis on the left side of the body. (A stroke occurs when an artery in the brain becomes blocked, resulting in the death of the tissues that the artery supplies.)

Each hemisphere also specializes in some functions. Typically the left hemisphere is more adept in some types of reasoning operations that involve the step-by-step processing of information. And in the vast majority of individuals, the left hemisphere also controls speech—the joining together of sounds to form words, and words to form sentences, for the communication of meaning. However, the right hemisphere adds emotional and humorous overtones important for understanding the full meaning of oral and written communication. The right hemisphere typically specializes in processing visual information, allowing you to recognize complex patterns and drawings. The two hemispheres differ in their perceptual roles in music. Discrimination and memory for single musical chords are superior in the right hemisphere. But the left hemisphere is critically important in discriminating and in producing temporally ordered sequences or melodies. Thus, as with most matters, both hemispheres are involved in the creation and appreciation of music (Levy, 1983, 1985).

Although language functions are partitioned primarily within the left hemisphere, damage to tissue in this area does not inevitably lead to permanent linguistic impairment. Some patients exhibit a remarkable capacity for recovery. For instance, if children, especially those under eight years of age, suffer damage to the left hemisphere, the right hemisphere typically takes over the function. These children may learn more slowly than other children, but they will learn to speak. However, many adults who suffer damage to the left hemisphere have extreme difficulty speaking—if they can speak at all. Apparently, because a child's central nervous system is still developing, a young brain is able to reorganize itself better than an older brain to compensate for the damage.

In everyday life, the lateralization of function between the hemispheres is in practice minimized because information is readily passed between them, especially through the corpus callosum. Both hemispheres are involved in thinking, logic, and reasoning, each from its own perspective and from its specialized domain of activity. Each hemisphere seems to have a limited and biased perspective that may allow adequate (but not excellent) performance in a highly restricted domain, but a deep grasp of or insight into language, music, mathematics, or some other area of endeavor derives from the fully integrated actions of the whole brain. Consequently, in most tasks the two hemispheres act in concert (Geschwind, 1979; Sergent, 1984; Levy, 1985).

"Split-Brain" Research

Psychologists became interested in differences between the cerebral hemispheres when "split-brain" operations were tried on epileptics such as Harriet Lees. For most of her life, Lees's seizures were mild and could be controlled with drugs. However, at age twenty-five they began to get worse, and by thirty Lees was having as many as a dozen violent seizures a day. (An epileptic seizure involves massive electrical activity—a violent storm of neural impulses—that begins in one hemisphere and spreads to the other.) To enable this woman to live a normal life, doctors decided to sever the corpus callosum so that seizures could not spread.

The operation was a success—Lees has not had a seizure since. But psychologists were even more interested in the potential side effects of this dramatic operation. Despite the fact that patients who had this operation now had "two separate, independent brains," they seemed remarkably normal. No fundamental changes in personality or intelligence appeared to result from the operation (Sperry, 1969, 1982; Gazzaniga, 1970, 1972, 1983). Researchers went on to develop a number of ingenious techniques to try to detect subtle effects of the operation. To understand the procedures, you need to know a little about brain anatomy. For example, the left field of vision is reversed by the lens to strike the right retina of each eye and is relayed by the optic nerve to the right hemisphere of the brain. To get a message to only one hemisphere at a time, the researchers asked each split-brain patient to stare at a dot while they briefly flashed a word or a picture on one side of the dot. If the word "nut" was flashed to the right of the dot, it went to the left hemisphere. The patient could usually read it quite easily under these circumstances, because the left hemisphere controls language for most right-handed people.

But when the same word was flashed to the right hemisphere (left side of each eye), the patient was not able to repeat it. For an ordinary person, the word "nut" would quickly go from one side of the brain to the other via the corpus callosum. Since this patient's corpus callosum had been cut, however, the message could not get from the nonverbal right hemisphere to the verbal left. Even more amazing was the fact that the patient really did recognize the word: with her left hand (which is also connected to the right hemisphere), she could feel and pick out a nut from a group of objects hidden behind a screen. But even after she had correctly picked out the nut and held it in her hand, she still could not remember the word!

In another experiment, a picture of a nude woman was flashed to the right hemisphere (left side of each eye) of another split-brain patient (see Figure 2.10). This woman laughed but said she saw nothing. Only her left hemisphere could speak, and it did not see the nude; but the right hemisphere, which did see the nude, produced the laugh. When the woman was asked why she had laughed, she acted confused and could not explain it.

Each hemisphere of the "split-brain" person processes information independently of the other. Consequently, the person may appear to be acting as if two people shared the same body. For instance, one patient reported that at times he found himself putting on his trousers with one hand while taking them off with the other. And on one occasion he violently shook his wife with his left hand while the right hand attempted to protect her from the left (Gazzaniga, 1970).

Left and Right Bias in Behavior

Most people show evidence of left or right bias in their everyday behavior. Left-handedness and right-handedness are good examples of this. About nine out of ten people prefer to use the right hand, and this seems to be a distinctly human characteristic with a long history. Even the people pictured in

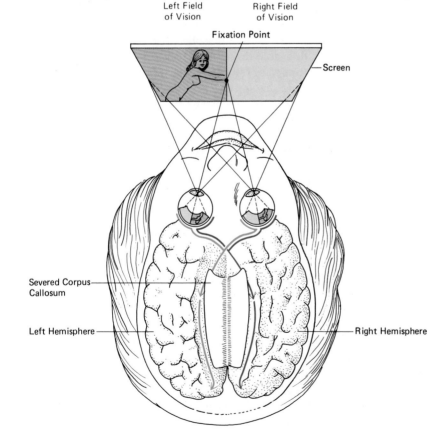

Left Field of Vision
Right Field of Vision

Fixation Point

Screen

Severed Corpus Callosum

Left Hemisphere

Right Hemisphere

FIGURE 2.10 The presentation of a visual stimulus to a single hemisphere of a person who has undergone split-brain surgery. The patient reacts with amusement to the picture of the nude woman flashed on the left side of the screen but is unable to say why.

An Egyptian tomb painting showing people at work, using their right hands. *(Brian Brake/Rapho-Photo Researchers)*

Egyptian tomb paintings usually use the right hand. Handedness is often mistakenly viewed as a specific trait comparable to eye color. However, it is actually relative: people prefer their right or left hands to a greater or lesser degree (Corballis, 1983). In fact, some people are hand-specific, preferring the right hand for some activities, such as playing tennis, and the left hand for others, such as pitching a baseball.

Left-handedness may be associated with some learning disabilities, autoimmune disease, and math giftedness (Marx, 1982; Kolata, 1983). About 10 percent of left-handers report some form of developmental problem such as dyslexia (a reading disorder) or stuttering, compared with only 1 percent of right-handers. Additionally, about 11 percent of left-handers have immunity diseases like allergies and asthma, compared with 4 percent of right-handers. Finally, 20 percent of the very best eleventh- and twelfth-grade math students (those

who are the top one in ten thousand) are left-handed; this incidence is twice that of left-handers in the population at large.

The neurologist Norman Geschwind suggests that left-handedness may be a product of an excess production of, or sensitivity to, the male hormone testosterone in the fetus. It would be expected that boys (who are exposed to more testosterone than girls in prenatal development) would be more likely than girls to be affected. Thus, not surprisingly, almost twice as many males as females are left-handed. Boys are also more susceptible to learning disorders. And among students in the top category of math performance, boys outscore girls by thirteen to one.

Testosterone is known to affect the development of brain structures. Geschwind believes that high levels of testosterone slow growth on the left side of the brain during the prenatal period and lead to a change in the usual dominance patterns of the brain. He conjectures that an increase in testosterone in some pregnancies is nature's way of providing for a greater diversity of brains in the human population. The brain organization that promotes left-handedness may lead to superior skills that are centered in the left hemisphere (including mathematical reasoning). However, if nature "overdoes" it, the result can be serious learning disorders, particularly language problems. Geschwind says that having children with learning problems may be the price a population pays for having some of its members gifted in mathematical thought and logic. Left-handers are overrepresented among architects, engineers, athletes, and artists. Examples of successful left-handed individuals include Michelangelo, Leonardo da Vinci, Benjamin Franklin, and Pablo Picasso.

Left or right bias also finds expression in other ways. One group of studies, for example, has looked at the brain waves (or EEG—see page 62) of right-handed people as they perform verbal and spatial tasks. The EEG showed greater activity in the right hemisphere for spatial tasks such as memorizing geometrical designs, remembering faces, or imagining an elephant in a swing. But when the same people were asked to perform verbal tasks—writing a letter in their heads, thinking of words that begin with "t," and listening to boring passages from the *Congressional Record*—their EEG showed relatively greater activity in the left hemisphere (Hassett,

Which Way Do the Eyes Move?

Did you know that the direction your eyes move when you think about a question may indicate which side of the brain you are using for the answer?

Ask some friends the following four questions, and secretly watch whether they first look to the right or the left as they consider each:

1. Make up a sentence using the words "code" and "mathematics."

2. Picture the last automobile accident you saw. In which direction were the cars going?

3. What does "Easy come, easy go" mean?

4. Picture and describe the last time you cried.

Questions 1 and 3 are verbal, nonemotional questions; a right-handed person should use the left hemisphere to answer and, as a result, tend to look to the right. Questions 2 and 4 are spatial-emotional questions that require the right hemisphere and should, on the average, yield more eye movements to the left than the right (Schwartz, Davidson, and Maer, 1975).

1978a). Likewise, right-handers move their eyes leftward when solving spatial problems, rightward when solving verbal problems (see the boxed insert above). In contrast, left-handers' eye movements turn out to be haphazard, again pointing to their greater bilaterality (Gur, Gur, and Harris, 1975).

THE ENDOCRINE SYSTEM

The nervous system is one of two communication systems for sending information to the brain and returning messages to the body's billions of cells. The second is the endocrine, or hormone, system.

The **endocrine system** is a group of glands that produce chemical substances called hormones. **Hormones** are chemicals that are manufactured in one part of the body and influence activities elsewhere in the body. They are distributed throughout the body by the blood and other body fluids. (The names and locations of major glands are shown in Figure 2.11.) In many ways the endocrine system resembles a postal system. Hormones, or chemical messages, circulate throughout the bloodstream but are deliv-

ered only to a specific address—the particular organs of the body that they influence (each target cell is equipped with receptors that recognize only the hormone molecules designed to act on that cell; the receptors—protein molecules—pull the hormone molecules out of the bloodstream and carry them into the cell).

The endocrine system is as essential as the nervous system in learning and memory, for integrating the body's activities, and for maintaining its internal homeostasis (McGaugh, 1983). However, the two systems differ in a number of respects. First, hormonal action (the postal system) is typically slower than neural action (the telephone system)—neuronal communication can take place in a few milliseconds, whereas in some cases hormonal communication can take several hours. Second, hormonal effects tend to be less specific and more general than the effects produced by neural activity. And third, the overall chemical impact of hormonal release on the body tends to be longer-acting than that associated with the firing of a series of neurons.

Although the two systems differ, on the molecular level they are not as dissimilar as they initially appear (S. H. Snyder, 1985). Both operate by bringing special messenger molecules in contact with specific

---

endocrine (EN-doh-crin) system: A group of glands that produces hormones, by which messages are sent through the bloodstream to particular organs of the body.

hormones: Control chemicals manufactured in one part of the body that influence activities elsewhere in the body; distributed by blood and other body fluid.

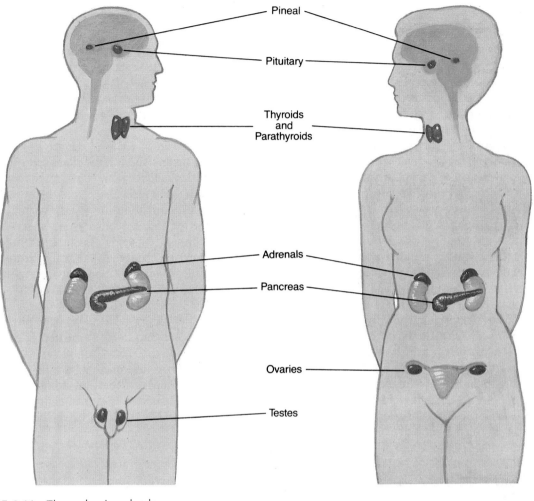

FIGURE 2.11 The endocrine glands.

receptors on a target cell. Moreover, neurotransmitters and hormones carry out quite specific tasks. Recently, researchers have found that there is an even closer relation between the two major systems of communication. Many of the messenger molecules employed by one system are also employed by the other. For example, the vasopressin molecule carries messages in both systems. As a hormone, vasopressin is released by cells in the pituitary gland. It raises blood pressure by constricting blood vessels, and it decreases the quantity of water in various parts of the body by increasing the kidneys' ability to reabsorb water. As a neurotransmitter, vasopressin is found in the brain, where it is believed to have a role in memory.

Although all the glands of the endocrine system have vital functions, the **pituitary gland** is particularly important (Fuhrmann et al., 1985). Together with the brain, the pituitary gland is the center of control for much of the system's activity. The pituitary secretes a large number of hormones, many of which control the output of hormones by other endocrine glands (and thus it is often called "the master gland"). Pituitary hormones play a critical part in regulating children's growth. Too little growth hormone can create a dwarf, while too much can

---

pituitary (pih-TOO-ih-tare-ee) **gland:** The center of control of the endocrine system, which secretes a large number of hormones.

produce a giant. Another pituitary hormone stimulates the production of milk in female mammals. Still other pituitary hormones affect the release of ova in women and the production of sperm in men.

The **thyroid gland,** located in the neck, produces the hormone thyroxin. Thyroxin stimulates certain chemical reactions that are important for all tissues of the body. Too little thyroxin makes people feel lazy and lethargic; too much makes them overactive. But the activity of the thyroid gland is itself controlled by a hormone released by the pituitary gland. In turn, in a feedback arrangement, thyroxin influences pituitary action: high levels of thyroxin in the blood reduce the output of the thyroxin-stimulating hormone by the pituitary gland; low levels of thyroxin cause the pituitary gland to produce greater levels of this hormone. The pituitary and thyroid glands thus mutually regulate each other, and the combination regulates general bodily activity. Additionally, when calcium levels in the blood rise, the thyroid gland secretes calcitonin, which inhibits the release of calcium from bone storage areas. Embedded in the back tissues of the thyroid are four **parathyroid glands.** They secrete parathyroid hormone, which counterbalances the effects of calcitonin by allowing the release of calcium into the bloodstream. The interaction of the thyroid and parathyroid glands keeps tight control over blood calcium levels (another example of homeostasis).

Few hormones produce more spectacular effects than **epinephrine** (also called **adrenaline**). It is manufactured by the **adrenal glands,** located just above the kidneys. Epinephrine plays a particularly critical role in arousing you and making you responsive to environmental stimuli. When your perceptual system encounters increasingly novel and complex stimuli, epinephrine is released that reaches widespread brain areas, making you alert and your brain receptive to additional perceptual input (Pribram and McGuinness, 1975; McGuinness and Pribram, 1980). Because these changes all serve to increase your body's ability to respond to external threat, whether in aggression or defense, the effect of epinephrine is to prepare you for "fight or flight." (See Chapter 14.)

We noted that in times of danger or excitement —times of stress—the adrenal glands pour epinephrine into the bloodstream. This response quickly prepares the body for action. Apparently what happens is this. Information concerning stress is picked up by the central nervous system from external sources, through the sense organs, or from internal sources, through changes in the body's temperature or in the blood's composition. The central nervous system integrates this information and relays a message to the hypothalamus. The hypothalamus then releases a substance that causes the pituitary to secrete the pituitary tropic hormone. In turn, the pituitary tropic hormone stimulates the adrenal glands to step up the manufacture of epinephrine and various other hormones, including steroids.

The entire operation is exquisitely regulated by a *feedback system.* For instance, when the level of the steroids circulating in the blood is elevated, the central nervous system picks up this information. It then shuts down the process that leads to secretion of the pituitary tropic hormone. Thus the control of the endocrine system is complex and delicately balanced. It maintains homeostasis through an integrated system of feedback loops (Levine, 1971; Snyder, 1985) (see Figure 2.12).

Through the combined action of the nervous and endocrine systems, the brain monitors and controls most human behavior. In Chapter 4 we will describe how the endocrine system influences emotion and motivation.

---

thyroid (THIGH-roid) gland: The gland in the endocrine system that produces several hormones, including thyroxin.

parathyroid (pair-uh-THIGH-roid) glands: Four glands situated in the back tissues of the thyroid glands that monitor calcium levels in the bloodstream.

epinephrine (eh-pih-NEH-frin) (adrenaline [ah-DREN-ah-lin]): A hormone secreted by the adrenal glands that among other things regulates the flow of blood to the various organs.

adrenal (uh-DREE-null) gland: An endocrine gland of vertebrates that is located near each of the kidneys and that produces epinephrine.

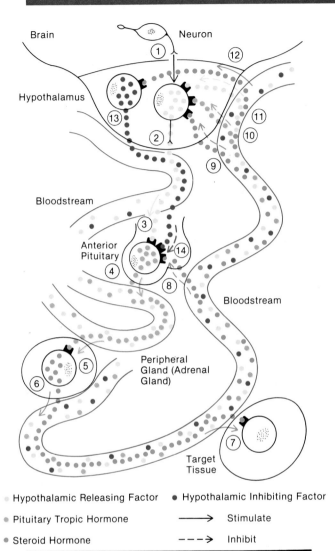

Brain

Neuron

①

⑫

Hypothalamus

⑬

⑪

②

⑩

⑨

Bloodstream

③

Anterior
Pituitary

⑭

④

⑧

Bloodstream

⑤

Peripheral
Gland (Adrenal
Gland)

⑥

⑦

Target
Tissue

○ Hypothalamic Releasing Factor   ● Hypothalamic Inhibiting Factor

● Pituitary Tropic Hormone   ⟶ Stimulate

● Steroid Hormone   - - -> Inhibit

FIGURE 2.12 The feedback system initiates the release of epinephrine into the bloodstream. When the hypothalamus is stimulated by neurons in the brain (1), it secretes a hypothalamic releasing factor (2) into the bloodstream. Some molecules of the releasing factor are pulled out of the blood by specialized receptors on the surface of cells in the pituitary (3) and induce the cells to produce and secrete the pituitary tropic hormone (4). The pituitary tropic hormone travels through the blood to the adrenal glands (5) and causes the glands to start producing a steroid hormone (6). The steroid hormone goes on to affect a target tissue (7). A number of feedback loops maintain the correct concentrations of steroid hormone in the bloodstream. For instance, the steroid hormone acts back on the pituitary (8) to inhibit the production of the pituitary tropic hormone; it also acts on the hypothalamus to limit the production of the hypothalamic releasing factor (9). The pituitary tropic hormone and the hypothalamic releasing factor also inhibit the hypothalamus from producing the releasing factor (10, 11). In addition the steroid hormone (12)

HOW PSYCHOLOGISTS STUDY THE BRAIN

The pace of brain research has quickened since World War II, contributing to a virtual explosion of new discoveries and insights (Hubel, 1979). This research has helped to clarify issues that have been the source of considerable debate among psychologists.

In the late 1860s, the French investigator Paul Broca advanced the view that specialized regions of the brain perform specific functions. While conducting an autopsy on a man who had been unable to speak for many years, Broca discovered evidence of brain damage in a portion of the man's left hemisphere. He labeled this section of the brain "the speech center" (since called, appropriately enough, *Broca's area*). During the 1870s, Gustav T. Fritsch and Eduard Hitzig explored the cerebral cortex by applying weak electrical currents at specific points of the brain. Depending on where they applied the current, they could stimulate different motor functions, such as the twitching of a toe or the darting of an eye. Findings such as these reinforced the notion that brain functions are localized in specific regions of the cortex.

However, in the 1920s, Karl Lashley (1929) advanced an alternative view—the principle that in producing behavior, the brain acts as a total mass with few localized centers (termed *equipotentiality*). Lashley and his associates tested the ability of rats to learn various tasks in a maze after one or another part of the cortex had been surgically destroyed. Although the destruction of large cortical areas resulted in slower learning, the animals seemed to learn just as well with one part of the cortex as with another. Apparently, the amount of cortical tissue remaining after the surgery was more important to behavior than was the specific region involved. All this led Lashley to conclude that one part of the cortex is essentially equal to another in its contribution to learned behavior. The generalized effects of

induces particular cells in the hypothalamus to produce a hypothalamic inhibiting factor (13) that acts to inhibit the release of the pituitary tropic hormone (14). *(After Solomon H. Snyder. 1985. The molecular basis of communication between cells. Scientific American, 253 (October):137. Copyright © 1985 by Scientific American, Inc. All rights reserved.)*

brain injuries have made it very difficult to discriminate local functions for one area of the brain or another (Stuss and Benson, 1984). In addition, some functions such as memory may be distributed throughout the cortex, while other skills such as speech production may be more localized.

New techniques for studying the brain have shed light on these controversies. Mappings of the brain's mountains, canyons, and inner recesses have revealed specific areas of the brain that are indeed associated with certain behaviors—a matter we have already considered in this chapter. Thus not all regions of the brain are interchangeable. But by the same token, much duplication of function does occur, particularly in those activities associated with the higher mental processes such as thinking, logical reasoning, and problem solving. Further, as discussed in our treatment of the left and right hemispheres, various parts of the brain operate in concert with one another, interacting to amplify and intensify mental effectiveness.

Psychologists have continually sought to develop better and more refined techniques for studying the brain. They cannot simply depend on naturally occurring accidents such as the one experienced by Phineas Gage to provide them with new findings. Let us turn, then, to consideration of a number of techniques that psychologists use to study the brain.

Generalized Brain Activity

Psychologists are concerned not only with how the brain is structured but also with how it functions. In other words, they wish to determine how the brain "works" as we go about our everyday lives. Such knowledge is crucial if we are to identify what goes wrong in the brain and leads to various motor, emotional, cognitive, and other problems. The earliest procedure for "listening" to the brain was invented in 1929 and is known as the electroencephalograph.

Electroencephalograph

The **electroencephalograph**, or **EEG**, relies on the recording of the brain's electrical activity. A psychologist or physician attaches electrodes to different areas of the scalp. The voltage emitted by the brain beneath each electrode is then graphed by a pen on a moving sheet of paper. Psychologists have observed that the overall electrical activity of the brain rises and falls rhythmically, and that the pattern of the rhythm depends on whether a person is awake, drowsy, or asleep (as is illustrated in Chapter 3). These rhythms, or brain waves, occur because the neurons in the brain tend to increase or decrease their amount of activity in unison.

EEGs can be used to monitor the brain disorder that causes epilepsy. When an epileptic seizure occurs, abnormal electrical activity begins in a small piece of damaged brain tissue. It then spreads to neighboring areas of the brain until much of the brain is showing abnormally large brain waves on the EEG. By monitoring these brain waves, psychologists can locate the site at which the seizure begins and can follow its spread through the brain. This helps doctors to determine what kind of surgical procedure (if any) would reduce violent seizures.

PET Scan

Another tool for diagnosing brain disorders is the **positron-emission-tomography**, or **PET**, scan. By injecting patients with a radioactive form of glucose, physicians can track the fuel consumption of brain cells. Areas that deviate from normal activity show where neurological disorders such as stroke damage, brain tumors, or epilepsy occur. For instance, live, healthy cells, which are using glucose at a normal rate, show up on a PET scan as a bright glow. Cells that are damaged but still partially functioning are less luminous, and dead cells register as dark patches. PET scanners are also providing information on

---

electroencephalograph (ih-LECK-troh-en-SEF-uh-la-graf) (EEG): A machine used to record the electrical activity of large portions of the brain.

positron (POS-ih-tron)-emission-tomography (PET) scan: A technique that permits the scanning of brain tissue. Individuals are injected with a radioactive form of glucose and the fuel consumption of the cells is tracked, yielding an image of brain activity.

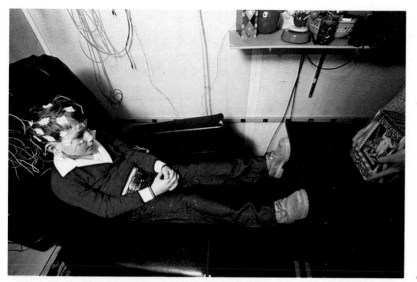

The many electrical leads from this boy's scalp are recording generalized activity in various parts of his brain. This recording is called an electroencephalograph, or EEG. *(Alexander Tsiaras/Science Source-Photo Researchers)*

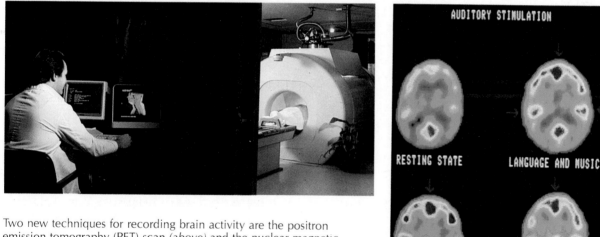

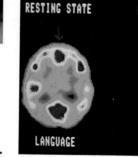

AUDITORY STIMULATION

RESTING STATE

LANGUAGE AND MUSIC

LANGUAGE

MUSIC

Two new techniques for recording brain activity are the positron emission tomography (PET) scan *(above)* and the nuclear magnetic resonance (NMR) imaging *(right)*, which use, respectively, radioactive injections and nuclear scanning techniques to illuminate active parts of the brain. In the PET scan shown, the dark red parts of the brain are most active. *(Above, Dan McCoy/Rainbow; right, Peter Menzel)*

the brain's internal chemistry. Scientists can ask an individual to think about moving a toe without actually moving it, and reveal through the scan the specific area of the brain that is in control of the behavior.

CAT Scan

Still another tool employing diagnostic radiology is the **computerized axial tomography, CT** or **CAT, scan.** Brain tissue absorbs the radiation directed at it

computerized axial (AX-ee-ull) tomography (tow-MAH-grah-fee) (**CT** or **CAT**) scan: A technique that uses radiation and high-speed computer analysis to yield constructed, cross-sectional pictures of body tissue.

Boxing: For Whom the Bell Tolls

"Duk Koo Kim. You may not have heard of him before—you will remember him today. Win or lose." This prediction, uttered on national television by a ringside announcer, was to be fulfilled in a tragic manner. It was November 13, 1982, the beginning of the fourteenth round, and Kim was making a valiant effort to take Ray Mancini's World Boxing Association lightweight championship. The fight promised to lift Kim out of obscurity and put him in line for big money in a boxing career. But it was not to be. Four days later Kim died of cerebral edema—swelling of the brain—resulting from a blow that sent him sliding to the canvas in the fourteenth round. Between 1945 and 1982, boxing took the lives of 349 boxers (Noonan, 1983; Cooke, 1984).

Most boxing fatalities result from acute brain trauma, caused by blows to the head or by a heavy fall to the canvas. A shot to the temple or the point of the chin is especially dangerous. These blows twist the head or tilt it sideways in a quick and violent movement. The brain is like jelly suspended in a bucket. When the bucket is struck sharply, the brain inside twists, whirls, and slams against the sides of the hard skeletal casing. If the jarred brain ruptures blood vessels, a massive build-up of blood (a hematoma) can occur. Because the skull is rigid, pressure quickly builds up, cutting off the brain's blood supply, reducing oxygen, and shutting down critical operations. Knockouts, which are technically concussions, are a different type of injury, in which the force of a punch is transmitted to the brain stem, causing a fighter to lose consciousness.

A good many professional boxers suffer chronic brain damage. The condition is termed *chronic encephalopathy*, better known as "the punch-drunk syndrome." Its symptoms include forgetfulness, speech impairment, unsteady gait, tremors, sudden mood shifts, and episodes of confusion. Muhammad Ali, three-time heavyweight champion of the world, may have incurred brain injury in the course of his many bouts. In 1980 and 1981 he underwent several tests, including a CAT scan, at New York University Medical Center to determine the cause of his sometimes-slurred speech and hand tremors. His physicians indicate he suffers from a collection of symptoms loosely called Parkinson's syndrome, similar to Parkinson's disease but not as severe. Dr. Ira R. Casson, a neurologist who examined Ali's NYU CAT scan at the behest of *Sports Illustrated*, says that Ali has enlarged ventricles and a cavum spetum pellucidum, neurological characteristics of long-time boxers (Boyle and

by the scanner in varying amounts depending on its density. A high-speed computer calculates the difference between the total radiation and the absorption of the X-rays as they enter different areas of the brain, and yields constructed, cross-sectional pictures with considerable detail and clarity. Before scanners were invented, scientists and physicians worked blind much of the time because their tools could not give them clear pictures of the brain's soft organs. Now surgeons can perform operations on the brain that once would have been too dangerous to attempt. CAT scanners also have shown the damage incurred by the brains of professional boxers (see the box above).

MRI

One of the latest advances in scanners is **magnetic resonance imaging,** or **MRI.** Using magnetic fields three thousand to twenty-eight thousand times

---

magnetic resonance (REZ-uh-nunce) imaging (MRI): A technique that uses magnetic fields and computer analysis to provide three-dimensional images of body tissue.

Ames, 1983). The ventricles are hollow spaces in which spinal fluid is stored. Punches jar the brain, enlarging the ventricles and causing a canal to open up between them (a condition termed *cavum spetum pellucidum*). This area of the brain apparently controls many motor activities, and when impaired, can contribute to tremors and unsteady gait.

There is probably no area of a professional boxer's brain that escapes injury. The outermost layer suffers an erosion of neurons and a gradual loss of tissue from being repeatedly bounced against the skull. Slurred speech tends to be associated with damage to portions of the left temporal lobe. Injury to the frontal lobes can result in sharp mood swings and related emotional difficulties. Damage to the cerebellum and the brain stem may contribute to an unsteady gait. Brain damage is related to the number of bouts a boxer fights.

The American Medical Association has called for a ban on boxing. But some critics contend that a ban may simply drive the sport to a less visible—and more dangerous—underground existence. The American Psychological Association, although stopping short of calling for a ban on boxing, seeks its eventual elimination by making the public aware of its hazards. It has also called for health measures to protect boxers through annual neuropsychological examinations.

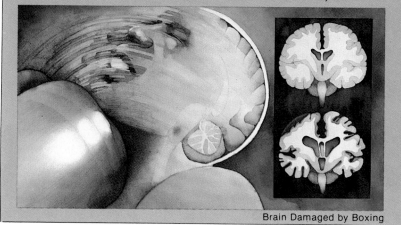

Healthy Brain

Brain Damaged by Boxing

When a boxer suffers a blow to the chin *(left)* the head moves rapidly, throwing the brain against the inside of the skull. Extensive bleeding, shown as the red patch in the cross section of a boxer's brain *(inset)*, can result in death. After years in boxing, a fighter's brain often looks different from a normal one, with enlarged ventricles in the interior (purple), and a canal or opening at the center (green). These injuries are associated with neurological problems. *(Greg Harlin/Stansbury, Ronsaville & Wood, Inc.)*

stronger than the Earth's, MRI makes the nuclei of atoms within the brain twirl like tops in the direction of the magnetic field. When the MRI device is turned off, the atoms shift in the manner peculiar to each element. A computer analyzes the currents induced by the nuclear flip-flops and from this information creates a three-dimensional picture. Tumors can be readily detected because cancerous tissue responds to the magnetic pull differently than normal tissue. The device is also valuable in detecting the plaques associated with multiple sclerosis. Additionally, it permits the intricate mapping of convoluted areas of the brain, allowing scientists to determine areas in the brain where epileptic seizures originate or where a person's response to touch is located. Unlike PET or CAT scans, the MRI scan does not require injecting substances into the body or exposing patients to radiation (Cherry and Cherry, 1985).

Specific Brain Activity

Psychologists find the techniques we have discussed valuable tools for learning about the generalized activity of the brain. For instance, the electroencephalograph measures the *cumulative* effects of massed electrical discharges. They use other procedures for measuring *specific* types of brain activity. Among these methods are single-unit recording, stimulation, and lesions in laboratory animals and in humans undergoing brain surgery.

Single-Unit Recording

By inserting wires called **electrodes** into the brain, it is possible to detect the minute electrical changes that occur when neurons fire. The wires are connected to electronic equipment that amplifies the tiny voltages produced by the firing neurons. Even single neurons can be monitored. For example, two researchers placed tiny electrodes in the sections of cats' and monkeys' brains that receive visual information. They found that different neurons fired, depending on whether a line, an edge, or an angle was placed before the animal's eyes (Hubel and Wiesel, 1962). Other researchers have inserted extremely sensitive microelectrodes into the visual regions of a frog's brain (Lettvin, 1959). They have found that the neurons fire more rapidly when dark spots are moved through a frog's field of vision. This response is a particularly useful adaptation for a creature that secures its food by catching flying insects.

Stimulation

Electrodes may be used to set off the firing of neurons as well as to record it. Brain surgeon Wilder Penfield stimulated the brains of his patients during surgery to determine what functions the various parts of the brain perform. In this way, he could localize the malfunctioning part for which the surgery was required—for example, for epilepsy. When Penfield applied a tiny electric current to points on the temporal lobe of the brain, he could trigger whole memory sequences. During surgery, one woman heard a familiar song so clearly that she thought a record was being played in the operating room (Penfield and Rasmussen, 1950).

Using the stimulation technique, other researchers have shown that there are "pleasure" and "punishment" centers in the brain. One research team implanted electrodes in certain areas of the subcortex (or "old brain") of a rat, then placed the rat in a box equipped with a lever that the rat could press. Each time the rat pressed the lever, a mild electrical current was delivered to its brain. When the electrode was placed in the rat's "pleasure" center, it would push the lever several thousand times per hour (Olds and Olds, 1965).

Scientists have used chemicals as well as electricity to stimulate the brain. In this method, a small tube is implanted in an animal's brain so that the end touches the area to be stimulated. Chemicals can then be delivered through the tube to the area of the brain being studied. Such experiments have shown that different chemicals in the hypothalamus can affect hunger and thirst in an animal.

The interpretation of brain stimulation research poses some problems (Carlson, 1977). Artificial stimulation never entirely duplicates the subtle interplay that naturally takes place in the brain between patterns of excitement and inhibition. Under artificial stimulation, neurons in an area simply fire in a mass. The procedure has been likened to attaching ropes to the arms of orchestra members and then shaking all the ropes simultaneously to find out what musical piece, if any, they can play.

Lesions

Localized brain damage often results from accidents or from natural events such as strokes. The injured or damaged tissue is termed a **lesion.** Scientists sometimes create lesions by cutting or destroying part of an animal's brain. If the animal behaves differently after the operation, they assume that the destroyed brain area is involved with that type of behavior. For example, in one classic lesion study, two researchers removed a certain area of the subcortex from rhesus monkeys. Normally, these animals are aggressive and vicious. After the operation they became less fearful, as well as less violent (Kluver and Bucy, 1937). The implication was that this area of the brain controlled aggression.

Subsequent researchers have learned that the relationships revealed by lesion research are far more subtle and complex than was at first believed (Carlson, 1977; Stuss and Benson, 1984). Interpretations are complicated by the fact that the various parts of the brain are interconnected. Invariably, researchers unintentionally sever the axons of neurons that

---

electrode (ih-LECK-trode): A type of wire used by scientists to detect the minute electrical changes that occur when neurons fire.

lesion: Injured or damaged tissue in the brain.

happen to pass through the lesioned region from other areas of the brain. Further, a lesion temporarily "knocks out" the synapses of other neurons in the vicinity of the injury. Hence, when the organism regains partial recovery of a function, it is difficult to determine its source. The recovery may have resulted from other parts of the brain "taking over" for the damaged structure or from the recovery of the temporarily incapacitated synapses.

Our discussion has highlighted the critical role that the brain plays in behavior. The brain functions as the master control center for the body. It receives a continuous stream of information from nerve endings sensitive to light, pressure, temperature, and other environmental cues. It then sorts, analyzes, and records this information. Finally, the brain directs and orchestrates the organism's responses to environmental inputs. Hence, in a very real sense, the human brain is the best organized, most functional three pounds of matter to be found in the universe. It is responsible for *Macbeth*, the Sistine Chapel, space vehicles, computers, the Vietnam War, prisons, income taxes, and a good deal more.

SUMMARY

1. Much of the understanding psychologists have gained about the human brain has derived from studies of nonhuman organisms. They study these organisms because they cannot perform risky procedures on a human being with no better reason than scientific inquiry. Animal studies are particularly valuable because human beings have evolved from more primitive animal origins, and their bodies and brains are therefore similar in some respects to the bodies and brains of other animals.

2. Evolution applies not only to anatomy and physiology but also to predispositions toward certain types of behavior. One of the major outgrowths of Darwin's theory of evolution is ethology. Ethology is the study of the natural behavior patterns of all species of animals from a biological point of view.

A. Ethologists attempt to understand how various patterns have evolved and changed, and how they are expressed in human beings. They call these natural patterns species-typical behaviors, behaviors that are characteristic of a particular animal species in particular environmental settings.

B. The interaction among innate tendencies, maturational processes, and environmental experiences is highlighted by imprinting. Imprinting is a set of responses by which an animal establishes social attachments during an early stage in its life.

3. Closely related to ethology is sociobiology, a discipline that studies the evolutionary basis of social behavior in animals and human beings. One of the most startling assertions of sociobiology has to do with altruism. Sociobiologists say that in the course of evolution, natural selection has come to encompass kin selection. Evolution favors altruistic tendencies because, although some members of a society are sacrificed, the group as a whole survives.

4. Scientists no longer ask the question, Which is more important, heredity or environment? Carried to its logical conclusion the question defines biologically programed behavior as that which occurs in the absence of environment and learned behavior as that which does not require an organism. Clearly, there could be neither human beings nor behavior without both heredity and environment.

5. Genes are the building blocks of heredity. They are made up of numerous molecules called deoxyribonucleic acid (DNA). We may think of genes as regions or locations on chromosomes. Chromosomes are long, threadlike bodies that contain the heredity materials found in the nuclei of all cells. Some genes "average out" their instructions, whereas others are either dominant or recessive for a trait. Given the complexity of the processes governing genetic transmission, it is not surprising that at times something goes wrong. The difficulty may derive from the quality of the genetic material or from the quantity of the genetic material and the way this material is arranged.

6. One way to find out what makes individuals differ is to conduct studies among family members. Of

particular scientific interest are identical twins who have been reared apart. Such twins provide a means for studying the effects of the environment when heredity is the same. Another means that researchers use for assessing family resemblances is to study children who were adopted at birth and reared by foster parents.

7. Messages are constantly traveling back and forth in the body through the nervous system to the brain. The spinal cord, a part of the nervous system, transmits most of the messages back and forth between the body and the brain. The messages to and from the brain are communicated by chemical-electrical signals traveling down long, thin cells called neurons.

A. Neurons make up the nervous system and brain. A typical neuron consists of one major cell body, an axon, and numerous dendrites. A dense fatty coating termed myelin wraps around an axon and gives it electrical insulation.

B. Although the signal generated by a neuron and transmitted along its axon is an electrical impulse, information is conveyed across the synaptic gap from neuron to neuron by chemical neurotransmitters.

C. Psychologists find it helpful to organize information about the nervous system by describing its structural divisions. The two chief divisions are the central nervous system and the peripheral nervous system.

8. Signals from the receptors in the peripheral nervous system travel up the spinal cord and enter the brain. The first part of the brain that the messages reach is the subcortex, or old brain. The cerebral cortex, or new brain, surrounds the subcortex like a halved peach surrounds the pit.

A. Major units of the subcortex are the reticular activating system, the thalamus, the hypothalamus, and the cerebellum. The hypothalamus is particularly important because it is where many signals from the central nervous system, the endocrine system, and the autonomic nervous

system converge, are integrated, and are responded to.

B. The cerebral cortex, in which most of the higher brain functions occur, is a great gray mass of ripples and valleys, folded so that its surface area can fit inside the skull. The regions of the cortex, termed lobes, are associated with specific senses and activity.

9. The cortex is divided by a deep fissure into two halves, a left and a right hemisphere. The two hemispheres are connected by a thick band or cable of nerves called the corpus callosum, which carries messages back and forth between the two.

A. Each hemisphere is connected to half of the body in a crisscrossed fashion. The motor cortex of the left hemisphere of the brain controls most of the right side of the body; the motor cortex of the right hemisphere controls most of the left side of the body. Each hemisphere also specializes in some functions.

B. Psychologists have gained considerable information concerning the differences in cerebral-hemisphere functions from "split-brain" research.

C. Most people show evidence of left or right bias in their everyday behavior. Left-handedness and right-handedness are good examples of this.

10. The endocrine, or hormone, system is a chemical system of communication between the body and the brain. Through the combined action of the nervous and endocrine systems, the brain monitors and controls human behavior. The operation of the endocrine system is exquisitely regulated by feedback systems.

11. Psychologists study the brain in two principal ways. One way involves the measurement of generalized brain activity, often by an electroencephalograph (EEG), a PET scan, a CAT scan, or MRI. A second way involves the measurement of specific brain activity, often by single-unit recordings, electrical or chemical stimulations, and lesions.

KEY TERMS

adrenal gland (p. 60)
altruism (p. 35)

autonomic nervous system (p. 48)
axon (p. 45)

central nervous system (CNS) (p. 48)
cerebellum (p. 52)

cerebral cortex   (p. 50)
chromosome   (p. 40)
computerized axial tomography
   (CT or CAT) scan   (p. 63)
corpus callosum   (p. 54)
dendrite   (p. 45)
deoxyribonucleic acid
   (DNA)   (p. 40)
effector   (p. 44)
electrode   (p. 66)
electroencephalograph
   (EEG)   (p. 62)
endocrine system   (p. 58)
environment   (p. 38)
epinephrine (adrenaline)   (p. 60)
ethology   (p. 33)
fraternal (dizygotic) twins   (p. 42)
frontal lobes   (p. 53)
genes   (p. 40)
genetics   (p. 40)
genotype   (p. 38)
heredity   (p. 38)

homeostasis   (p. 51)
hormones   (p. 58)
hypothalamus   (p. 51)
identical (monozygotic)
   twins   (p. 42)
imprinting   (p. 34)
kin selection   (p. 37)
lesion   (p. 66)
lobes   (p. 52)
magnetic resonance imaging
   (MRI)   (p. 64)
motor cortex   (p. 53)
myelin   (p. 46)
neurons   (p. 45)
neurotransmitters   (p. 47)
occipital lobes   (p. 52)
parasympathetic nervous
   system   (p. 48)
parathyroid glands   (p. 60)
parietal lobes   (p. 52)
peripheral nervous system
   (PNS)   (p. 48)
phenotype   (p. 38)

pituitary gland   (p. 59)
polygenic inheritance   (p. 41)
positron-emission-tomography
   (PET) scan   (p. 62)
receptors   (p. 44)
reticular activating system   (p. 50)
sensitive (critical) period   (p. 34)
sociobiology   (p. 35)
somatic nervous system   (p. 48)
somatosensory cortex   (p. 52)
species-typical behavior   (p. 33)
spinal cord   (p. 48)
subcortex   (p. 50)
sympathetic nervous system   (p. 48)
synapses   (p. 45)
temporal lobes   (p. 52)
thalamus   (p. 51)
thyroid gland   (p. 60)

SUGGESTED READINGS

BINKLEY, SUE. 1979. A time-keeping enzyme in the pineal gland. *Scientific American*, 240 (April):66–71. Describes a series of animal experiments that suggest that enzymes in the pineal gland can communicate information about time. Such a natural timing mechanism may regulate circadian physiological and behavioral processes.

GAZZANIGA, M. S., and LEDOUX, J. E. 1978. *The Integrated Mind*. New York: Plenum. A brilliant study of the bisected brain that illuminates the questions of how mind, life, and the essence of being relate to brain mechanisms.

KOLATA, GINA. 1985. Birds, brains and the biology of song. *Science 85*, 6 (December):58–61. A discussion of neurobiologist Fernando Notte-bohm's discoveries about the birth and death of neurons and lateralization in avian brains—like humans, songbirds have specialized right and left brain hemispheres.

LEVY, JERRE. 1985. Right brain, left brain: Fact and fiction. *Psychology Today*, 19 (May):38–39. An argument for harmony between the hemispheres.

LORENZ, KONRAD A. 1952. *King Solomon's Ring*. New York: Crowell. A classic study of nature by one of the world's outstanding scientists. An absorbing and beautiful book of essays; light and easy to read.

SCHNEIDER, ALLEN M., and TARSHIS, BARRY. 1985. *Introduction to Physiological Psychology*. 3d ed. A highly readable, balanced overview of the latest developments in the field. The experimental orientation challenges the reader to examine conclusions critically.

THOMPSON, R. F. *The Brain*. 1985. San Francisco: Freeman. A straightforward, uncomplicated explanation of one of the most complex structures in the universe—the brain.

TROTTER, ROBERT J. 1985. Lefty means larger. *Psychology Today*, 19 (November):24–25. A brief discussion of Dr. Sandra Witelson's discoveries of hemispheric specialization.

VALENSTEIN, ELLIOT. 1973. *Brain Control: A Critical Examination of Brain Stimulation and Psychosurgery*. New York: Wiley. The best introduction to this controversial area.

Wayne Thiebaud, *Fall River*, 1969.

3
States of Consciousness

When Scratches-face, a Crow Indian, was about thirteen years old, he began preparing himself for a "great dream" in which a spirit would appear to him and reveal his destiny. Since early childhood, his parents and other villagers had dinned into his ears the importance of such a dream. To succeed in life—to aspire to greatness—he would need to gain the blessing of some supernatural power. So, like the other adolescent boys, when his people's council said it is time for the puberty fast, Scratches-face goes off to a lonely spot near the summit of a mountain. Here, naked except for a breechclout and a buffalo robe to cover him at night, Scratches-face abstains from food and water for four days in hopes of inducing a trance state. All the while he concentrates intently on his special wish, to become a great warrior.

The hours pass. He smells the fragrant pine trees, hears the soft steps of animals farther down the mountain, and feels the breezes stir the fringe on his breechclout. At night he is frightened, his belly aches, and he feels lightheaded—indeed, he seems to "float." He knows that he must suffer if a spirit is to appear. As other Crow boys have done before him, he chops off a finger joint of his left hand as an offering to the supernatural beings. As he does so, he utters this prayer (Lowie, 1924:6):

> Old-woman's grandson, I give you this [joint], give me something good in exchange. . . . I am poor, give me a good horse. I want to strike one of the enemies and . . . I want to marry a good-natured woman. I want a tent of my own to live in.

After his sacrifice, Scratches-face hears footsteps but he cannot see anyone. He falls asleep and hears a voice: "What are you doing? You wanted him to come. Now he has come." Then Scratches-face sees six men riding horses, one of them seated on a bobtail horse, and this one says, "You have been poor, so I'll give you what you want . . . I am going to run." The trees around Scratches-face suddenly turn into enemies and begin shooting at the horsemen, who ride away and then return unscathed. The rider of the bobtail horse says to Scratches-face, "If you want to fight all the people on the earth, do as I do, and you will be able to fight for three or four days and yet not be shot." Then the horsemen begin to ride east. The enemies attack them once more, but the rider of the bobtail horse knocks them down with a spear.

Upon returning to his people's encampment, Scratches-face spends a few days recovering. Then he goes off and kills an enemy of the Crow without getting wounded. As the years pass, Scratches-face's confidence in the aid of his supernatural patron leads him to snap his fingers at danger. He establishes a reputation among the Crow for reckless bravery. He also obtains horses and marries a good-tempered and industrious woman.

Scratches-face was one of the Crow Indians that the anthropologist Robert H. Lowie interviewed in his visits to Montana between 1907 and 1916. The vision that Scratches-face sought was an established puberty right for Crow young men. But not all young men had Scratches-face's success. Some tried repeatedly to get a vision but failed. Little-rump told Lowie (1924:9): "All who had visions became well-to-do; I was destined to be poor, that is why I had no visions."

Dreams, visions, and trances are types of experiences that most of us view as different from the ordinary sensations, perceptions, emotions, and thought patterns that typify everyday life. They raise the question of what constitutes consciousness and what forms consciousness takes. As a human being, you are aware of yourself and of your own existence. There is something very special to this quality. Presumably the molecules of water composing a river do not know that they are part of a river, and yet the river flows on. But you sense yourself as alive, awake, and alert—as a being capable of think-ing, feeling, and acting. The matter of human awareness has long fascinated laypeople and psychologists. In this chapter we examine it and explore various states of consciousness.

THE NATURE OF CONSCIOUSNESS

Consciousness is the subjective awareness that you have at a given time of your inner sensations, images, thoughts, and feelings and of the world about you. It is the stream of mental processes that tell you what is happening to you and how you feel about it. You cannot touch, see, hear, taste, or smell consciousness. Nor can you directly count, weigh, or measure it. And, except as you may inform others about it, this internal mental world is quite private, something closed to other people.

Consciousness occupies a central place in the conception of what it means to be a human being. In your own view, you are aware of your behavior and therefore capable of altering your behavior with deliberate intent. Moreover, you take it for granted that you can and do reflect on your own mental activities. For instance, you undertake various measures to ensure that you will remember something, often by mentally rehearsing a name or an address several times. And when seeking to generate ideas in problem solving, you actively think about "thinking." As you experience yourself and your involvement with life, you believe not only that you consciously reflect on and control your behavior, but that this process results in even more intelligent behavior. Concern with these matters has guided the emergence of a now popular area of study, **metacognition** (Flavell, 1977, 1978b; Brown, 1982). Metacognition refers to your awareness and understanding of your mental state, abilities, memory, and processes of behavioral regulation.

Over the past several decades, exciting—even revolutionary—findings have linked various states of consciousness—including such events as sleep and dreaming—with electrical and chemical events in

---

consciousness: The subjective awareness that individuals have at a given time of their inner sensations, images, thoughts, and feelings and of the world about them.

metacognition (MEH-tuh-cog-NIH-shun): People's awareness and understanding of their mental states, abilities, memory, and processes of behaviorial regulation.

One of the many yoga exercises to control breathing and to alter consciousness. *(Joel Gordon)*

the brain. Physiological psychologists such as Roger W. Sperry (1976, 1982) have come to view consciousness as an integral part of brain activity and as a high-level, integrating aspect of cerebral function. Sperry says that the interplay among neutral events generates new and qualitatively higher levels of brain functioning that you in turn experience as inner conscious awareness.

Despite the interest in studying consciousness, Sperry (1976:9) points out that "subjective consciousness experience continues to pose the number-one problem for brain research and one of the most truly mystifying unknowns remaining in the whole of science." Indeed, psychologists currently know more about altered states of consciousness than they do about the normal state of consciousness. **Altered states of consciousness** are those mental processes that you experience as different from "usual," "ordi-nary," or "normal" processes. They are sensations, perceptions, thought patterns, judgments, memories, and emotions that have distinctive subjective qualities and are not typical of an awake and alert mental state.

The most obvious and familiar example of an altered state of consciousness is sleep. Other examples include daydreams, hallucinations, delirium, hypnotic states, being drunk or "high" on drugs, and the heightened awareness experienced during various forms of meditation (Tart, 1972). Likewise, when you fast, have a high fever, undergo sleep deprivation, or suffer from certain disorders such as motion sickness, you sense a distortion or disturbance in your typical psychological functioning. Psychologists have learned a good deal about these phenomena. Let us begin our consideration of them with sleep.

altered states of consciousness: Those mental processes that individuals experience as different from "usual," "ordinary," or "normal" processes.

SLEEP AND DREAMING

Sleep has long puzzled humankind. The ancient Greeks attributed its properties to the god Morpheus. Thus to be "in the arms of Morpheus" is to be in a deep sleep. People have long regarded sleep as a condition of complete relaxation and inactivity. However, when psychologists monitor the electrical activity of our brains while we sleep, they find that sleep is a complex and by no means inactive state. Indeed, the electrical activity in our brains in the phase of sleep in which dreams occur resembles wakefulness more closely than it does other phases of sleep. In sum, though our sensory contact with the environment is greatly reduced during sleep, our brain has not shut down (Morrison, 1983).

Sleep

Since sleep consumes about a third of your average day, it functions as a powerful organizing factor in your life. The distinction between being awake and being asleep pervades your notions of what constitutes a proper daily routine. Even so, considerable variability exists among people in their sleeping patterns. Some adults function well on four to five hours of sleep, others require nine to ten hours, while the vast majority get by on about seven to eight hours per night. To say that we all need eight hours' sleep is to say that we all should wear a size fifteen collar or a size twelve dress. Some individuals, particularly young adults, seem capable of reducing the time they spend sleeping by one or two hours a night while showing few if any ill effects (Horne and Wilkinson, 1985; Webb, 1985). Similarly, there are those people who like to go to bed early and rise early—"morning larks"—and those who prefer to go to bed late and rise late—"night owls."

As people pass across the life span, their sleeping patterns also undergo change. Newborns spend sixteen or more hours sleeping, packaged into seven or eight naps. They alternate sleep and wakefulness on rough four-hour cycles—three hours of sleep and one hour awake. By about six weeks of age, many infants begin sleeping through most of the night and

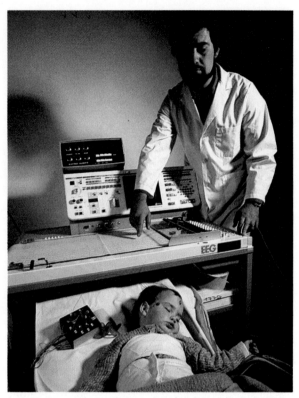

Even babies dream. In fact, they have more rapid-eye-movement (REM) sleep than is associated with dreaming that adults do. What do they dream? No one knows. *(Richard T. Nowitz/Phototake)*

reduce their naps to two to four during the day. Elderly people typically sleep less and wake up more often during the night than they did in middle life, although some may take a cat nap during the day.

Circadian Rhythm

Recent research has linked sleep to **circadian rhythm**—the 24-hour cycle of the body's biological clock. Many biological functions operate approximately on a 24-hour cycle. For instance, blood pressure is usually higher in the evening than in the morning, and body temperature fluctuates by 1½ to 2 degrees over the day around the accepted mean of 98.6 degrees. Scores of other body functions also regularly wax and wane, including vigor, alertness,

---

circadian (sir-KAY-dee-un) rhythm: The approximately twenty-four-hour cycle on which many bodily functions operate.

reaction time, distractibility, mood, memory, and chemicals in the blood and urine (Hilts, 1979; Moore-Ede, Sulzman, and Fuller, 1982). There are also shorter cycles (heartbeat and electrical activity in the brain) and longer cycles (menstruation).

In human beings, as in many other mammals, the circadian rhythm seems to be regulated by light (Binkley, 1979; Moore-Ede, Czeisler, and Richardson, 1983). The cues for setting the biological clock are provided by the daily cycle of alternating light and darkness that is associated with the earth's rotation on its axis. Apparently, the activity of the enzyme N-acetyltransferase in the pineal gland provides the basis for the mechanism. Constant darkness activates the release of the enzyme, while constant bright light suppresses its action.

For reasons that scientists do not as yet entirely understand, your body's sleep-wake schedule is linked to a 24.9-hour day—the period of the lunar day (Miles, Raynal, and Wilson, 1977). If you were isolated from clocks and other time cues and permitted to set your own sleep-wake schedule, you would typically go to sleep at 24.9-hour intervals. However —because of a job or class schedule—you are probably locked into a rigid routine based on the 24-hour clock. Consequently you are compelled to go to bed an hour earlier each night than your body clock would like. Not surprisingly, on weekends you probably tend to follow the body's natural clock and go to bed one hour later on Friday nights and two

hours later on Saturday nights. The net result is that you feel lethargic and somewhat out of sorts on Mondays when you return to the conventional schedule mandated by the cycle of a 24-hour day.

In modern life things often happen to throw off the circadian-timing system. Jet travel to a distant time zone puts our body time out of joint with clock time. Going to work on a night shift has a similar effect. For the night worker, critical time cues may be altered by eight hours—the equivalent of flying from Denver to Rome. The inner clock that governs body temperature resets itself by about an hour each day until it is again synchronized with external time cues, such as eating and going to bed. We naturally wake up when our temperature begins to rise, and we become sleepy when it begins to fall. If an alarm clock rouses us when our body temperature is still falling, we typically feel sluggish. So our performance is likely to be impaired for a number of days, sometimes with grave consequences. For instance, some have attributed the 1979 nuclear accident at Three Mile Island to these types of problems, since it occurred at four in the morning with a crew that had just started working the night shift.

Stages of Sleep

Psychologists measure the changes that come with sleep with a device known as an *electroencephalograph*, or *EEG*. As discussed in Chapter 2, the

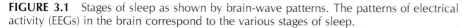

FIGURE 3.1 Stages of sleep as shown by brain-wave patterns. The patterns of electrical activity (EEGs) in the brain correspond to the various stages of sleep.

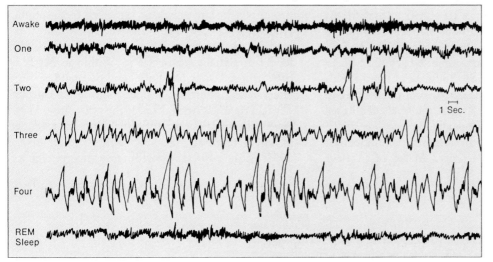

electroencephalograph records brain electrical activity, or brain waves. Researchers have found that sleep is not a single state. Instead, over the course of a night's sleep you pass in and out of several stages of sleep (see Figure 3.1).

In Stage I, sleep is marked by a growing irregularity in brain waves (as observed on an EEG), a slowing of the heart rate, and a developing unevenness in breathing. Your body may twitch, your eyes may roll, and brief visual images may flash across your mind (although your eyelids are shut). The stage typically lasts about five minutes.

In Stage II, your brain waves exhibit bursts of activity termed "spindles." Your eyes are generally still, and your heart and respiration rates fall slightly.

In Stage III, you move into even deeper sleep. The spindles disappear, and your brain waves become longer and slower. Your heart and breathing rates continue to decrease. It is now difficult to awaken you.

Stage IV is deep sleep. Large, regular waves indicate that you are in a state of oblivion. If you are awakened by a loud noise or sudden movement, you will not remember anything and may feel disoriented. Talking out loud, sleepwalking, and bed wetting —all of which may occur in this stage—leave no trace on memory. Deep sleep is important to physical and psychological well-being. Perhaps this is why people who, for one reason or another, are able to sleep only a few hours at a time descend rapidly into Stage IV and remain there for most of their nap.

However, on an average night, Stage IV sleep lasts only for an hour or an hour and a half. You then climb back through Stages III and II to Stage I. At this point, something curious happens. Although your muscles are even more relaxed than before, your eyes begin to dart rapidly back and forth behind your closed eyelids. You have entered **rapid-eye-movement, or REM, sleep.** Your pulse rate and breathing become irregular, and the levels of adrenal and sexual hormones in your blood rise—as if you were in the midst of an intensely emotional or physically demanding activity. Males often have erections, and females experience vaginal engorgement. Your brain sends out waves that closely resemble those of a person who is fully awake. It is during this stage that most dreaming takes place. However, sleepwalking and sleeptalking rarely occur during this phase, because motor output is inhibited during REM sleep, possibly as a protection against acting out dreams.

REM sleep lasts for about ten minutes, after which you retrace the descent to Stage IV. You go through this cycle every ninety minutes or so (see Figure 3.2). Each time, the period of Stage IV sleep decreases and the length of REM sleep increases —until you eventually wake up. But at no point does your brain become inactive. However, the quality of sleep changes with age. Apparently, the most "perfect" sleep is enjoyed by adolescents, many of whom could sleep through an earthquake; much of their night is spent in the deep sleep of Stages III and IV. In contrast, "normal" sleep in the elderly is typically light and fitful, mostly Stages I and II.

Sleep Disorders

From time to time most people have difficulty falling asleep or remaining asleep. However, in some instances the condition—termed **insomnia**—becomes chronic. Very often, persistent anxiety or depression underlies the disorder. But insomnia may also be produced by chronic pain, metabolic diseases (including diabetes and hyperthyroidism), and alcoholism. In some cases, insomnia becomes a consuming factor in people's lives, dominating their existence.

Barbiturates and other sedatives are frequently prescribed by physicians as remedies for insomnia. Nonetheless, most sleep experts agree that these medications simply mask the problem and in the long run actually aggravate it. Within a matter of days drugs such as Nembutal and Seconal lose their effectiveness. Further, people soon become dependent on them. When taken off the pills, they experience withdrawal symptoms, including an extended string of restless, miserable nights (Mitler et al., 1975; Mitler, 1983). Consequently, many sleep ex-

---

rapid-eye-movement (REM) sleep: The period of sleep during which the eyes dart
  back and forth and dreaming usually occurs.
insomnia: Difficulty falling asleep or remaining asleep.

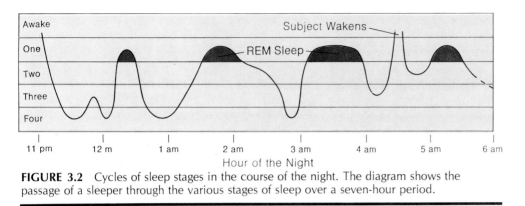

FIGURE 3.2 Cycles of sleep stages in the course of the night. The diagram shows the passage of a sleeper through the various stages of sleep over a seven-hour period.

perts prefer nonchemical remedies (see the boxed insert on page 78).

Another, but less common, sleep disorder is **narcolepsy** (Browman et al., 1982). Its victims suddenly fall asleep while working, driving an automobile, making love, engaging in sports, or virtually any activity, severely disrupting the quality of their lives. Many also experience *cataplexy*, a sudden weakening of body muscles and temporary paralysis. Victims begin sleep with a REM period (often associated with frightening hallucinations), leading some psychologists to believe that a neurological defect is implicated in the disorder. Unfortunately, narcoleptics are frequently stigmatized by their associates as lazy, shiftless people.

Apnea is still another sleep disorder, in which the sleeper periodically stops breathing during the night. The most common signs are loud, irregular snoring and excessive drowsiness during the day. During episodes in which breathing ceases, the oxygen level of the blood falls. The radical changes in brain chemistry alert the brain that the body needs air, activating the brain and causing the victim to awaken. This process is repeated hundreds of times during the night, contributing to the person's excessive sleepiness during the daytime. In some cases, apnea can contribute to high blood pressure, chronic

heart disease, and even lethal cardiac arrest. Serious cases often respond favorably to a *tracheotomy* (a hole is surgically produced in the throat, allowing air to move unimpaired in and out of the lungs at night). The typical apnea patient is a forty- to fifty-year-old man, overweight, with a thick, short, muscular neck, who has a long history of snoring and progressively worsening sleep (Mitler, 1983). Infants with apnea are in danger of sudden infant death syndrome (SIDS) and are often monitored through the night by an alarm that rings if they do not breathe every few seconds. Autopsies reveal that in about 60 percent of SIDS cases, there is evidence pointing to the underventilation of the lungs.

Dreaming

Dreams—the mini-dramas of sleep—have long captivated human interest. Indeed, people of many cultures believe that dreams arise from the nighttime travels of the soul outside the body. And they have viewed them as providing messages from the gods, divine prophecies of the future, and visitations from the dead. The Bible tells how Joseph interpreted the Pharaoh's dreams as predicting seven years of plenty followed by seven lean years and thus saved the people from starvation.

narcolepsy (NAR-coh-lep-see): A condition in which its victim suddenly falls asleep while performing some activity, such as working, driving an automobile, making love, or engaging in sports, among others.

apnea (AP-nee-uh): A sleep disorder in which the sleeper periodically stops breathing during the night.

Insomnia

Everyone has had a sleepless night at one time or another—a night when nothing you do brings the calm, soothing peace you want. Some people have sleep problems like this all the time, and they rarely get more than an hour or two of uninterrupted sleep a night. To help insomniacs, some psychologists recommend a number of ways to facilitate sleep (Bootzin, 1975; Mitler, 1983):

1. Stick to a regular schedule, going to bed and getting up at the same time each day.

2. Exercise regularly in the morning or afternoon, but do not engage in strenuous physical activity just before bedtime.

3. Stay away from caffeine-containing drinks—tea and coffee—after dinner.

4. Avoid alcohol before retiring. A nightcap disturbs sleep patterns and can contribute to early morning awakening.

5. Find a comfortable room temperature and maintain it throughout the night.

6. Try to relax before going to bed. Take a warm bath, engage in light reading, listen to music, and avoid stressful thoughts.

7. Do not use the bed for any activity other than sleep. This means no eating, reading, watching television, listening to the radio, or worrying in bed. The only exception is sexual activity.

8. If after you are in bed for about ten minutes you find that you cannot sleep, get up and go into another room. This will help you associate your bed with falling asleep quickly and dissociate it from tossing and turning. Return to your bed when you feel sleep coming on.

9. Repeat step 8 if you still cannot sleep. Get out of bed as many times as necessary during the night.

10. Be consistent about afternoon naps: Either take a nap every day or never nap at all.

Laboratory studies have shown the effectiveness of these techniques in helping insomniacs not only fall asleep but stay asleep. If you have a problem, they may work for you.

It seems that everybody dreams, although most people are able to recall few if any of their dreams. Sleep researchers sometimes make a point of waking subjects at regular intervals during the night to ask them about their dreams. The first few dreams are usually composed of vague thoughts left over from the day's activities. For example, a subject may report that she was watching television. As the night wears on, dreams become longer and more vivid, intense, and dramatic, especially dreams that take place during REM sleep. Whereas dreams that occur early in the night are usually rather simple, those that occur toward morning are often enriched in sagas with many scenes (Cartwright, 1978). These are the dreams that people are most likely to remember when they wake up.

When people are awakened randomly during REM sleep and asked what they had just been dreaming, the reports generally are commonplace, even dull (Hall and Van de Castle, 1966). The dreams people remember and talk about "are more coherent, sexier, and generally more interesting" than those collected in systematic research (Webb, 1975:140).

Researchers who have recorded the contents of thousands of dreams have found that most—even the late-night REM adventures—occur in such commonplace settings as living rooms, cars, and streets. Most dreams involve either strenuous recreational activities or passive events such as sitting and watching, not work or study. A large percentage of the emotions experienced in dreams are negative or unpleasant—anxiety, anger, sadness, and so on. Males—be they children, adolescents, college students, or adults—dream more often of men than women do (Hall, 1984). And contrary to popular

Dreams often contain vivid images of oneself in action, such as running up a hill or falling into a lake. Freud believed that dream images have meanings that are often hidden from the dreamer and that can be revealed through free associations to the images. *(Bohdan Hrynewych/Stock, Boston)*

belief, dreams do not occur in a "split second" but instead correspond to a realistic time scale (C. S. Hall, 1966).

The Freudian Interpretation of Dreams

Although dreams may contain elements of ordinary, waking reality, these elements are often jumbled in fantastic ways. The dreamer may see people in places they would never go, wander through strange houses with endless doors, find herself or himself transported backward in time. The dreamer may be unable to speak—or able to fly. What do these distortions mean?

Dream interpretations have been discovered dating back to 5000 B.C. Sigmund Freud (1900) was the first in the modern era to argue that dreams are an important part of people's emotional lives. Freud believed that no matter how simple or mundane, dreams typically contain clues to thoughts and desires that the dreamer is afraid to acknowledge or express in his or her waking hours. Indeed, he maintained that dreams are full of hidden meanings and disguises. Consequently, Freud concluded that dreams are really the "royal road to the unconscious."

Freud said that the symbolism of dreams is a private language that each individual invents for himself or herself. These symbols vary greatly from person to person. Suppose that a dreamer sees herself standing naked among fully clothed strangers. For one person, this dream may symbolize a desire to show her true self to people, without pretense. For another person, the dream may symbolize a fear of having her inadequacies exposed in public. In his work with patients, Freud attempted to break through the disguise of dream imagery. And he sought to use the emotions of a person displayed when recalling a dream to understand the deep-seated sexual wishes and aggressive drives of the dreamer. Freud believed dreams are useful in therapy because they harbor clues to the psychological issues and childhood conflicts that recur in a person's life.

The Activation-Synthesis Hypothesis

Some scientists are skeptical of Freud's view that dreams have some basic psychological function. Indeed, Nathaniel Kleitman (1960), one of the pioneers who discovered REM sleep, has asserted that dreaming may serve no function whatsoever. According to this interpretation, the experience of a dream is simply an unimportant by-product of having stimulated certain brain cells during sleep. This view finds expression in the *activation-synthesis hypothesis* of dreaming advanced by J. Allan Hobson and Robert W. McCarley (1977; McCarley, 1978).

The hypothesis derives from a variety of laboratory findings. When researchers monitor brain activity during REM sleep, they find that a surge of electrical activity is emanating from the "giant cells" in the pons area of the brainstem. These cells, as their name suggests, are rather large neurons. Their fibers extend into surrounding areas of the brain that control eye movement and motor activity. During non-REM sleep, the giant cells are relatively inactive. However, immediately before a REM episode, they become excited and retain a high pitch of activity throughout REM sleep. Apparently the giant cells "switch on" dreaming sleep. In contrast, other groups of nearby neurons "shut off" REM sleep and contribute to non-REM sleep or waking (Kiester, 1980).

According to the activation-synthesis hypothesis, the surge in the electrical activity of the giant cells of the brainstem flows toward the higher cells of the brain that control thought. In turn, those areas of the cortex that process and interpret information attempt to make sense out of this bombardment of electrical signals. Consequently, the thinking brain composes a dream that roughly fits the pattern of messages being received from the lower brain centers. The thinking brain, then, is simply making the best of a difficult situation.

Hobson and McCarley have also been intrigued by the rapid eye movements that occur during episodes of REM sleep. The conventional explanation is that the movements result from dreamers busily scanning the dream images as they pass before them. But Hobson and McCarley turn this explanation on its head. They say that the dream constitutes the efforts of the thinking brain to explain why the eyes are darting about. According to this view, the neural activity in the brainstem triggers rapid eye movement, which the cerebral cortex then struggles to interpret (perhaps as scene shifts in dreams).

Clearly, the views of Freud and those of Hobson and McCarley stand in sharp contrast with each other. For instance, Freud interprets the penile erections that men frequently experience while dreaming as an expression of their wish for sexual fulfillment. But Hobson and McCarley prefer the opposite view. They say that lower-brain-level activity causes penile erection, which the thinking brain then interprets through a dream about sex. Still another approach to these matters is the reverse learning, or unlearning, hypothesis.

The Reverse Learning, or Unlearning, Hypothesis

Two British scientists—Francis Crick and Graeme Mitchison—contend that dreaming is a way of cleansing the brain of information we have no need to remember (Melnechuk (1983). Crick may be more familiar to you as a Nobel laureate who shared the Nobel prize for the discovery of the gene's double-helix shape. Mitchison is a mathematician. They say that dreaming not only produces images in the mind but also erases the brain's redundant, bizarre, or otherwise useless memories, leaving behind only the ones that are useful. They term this mechanism *reverse learning*, or *unlearning*. Without such a mechanism, Crick and Mitchison believe, evolution could not have produced the highly refined cortex we have. As we store memories and associations, we encounter interference; information gets mixed up. Accordingly, some "garbage disposal" mechanism must be available to the mind to clear out all the useless information that interferes with rational thought and memory.

Crick and Mitchison theorize that the mechanism that culls false or nonsensical memories operates through the dreams that occur during REM sleep. In brief, we dream in order to forget. They believe that the random signals associated with REM sleep excite the vision system and produce the vivid images of dreams. The process somehow erases the brain's unneeded connections between neurons that formed during the day. With the slate wiped clean of extraneous information, the cortex is left uncluttered and ready for the next day's remembrances. Crick and Mitchison say that their hypothesis explains some facts about dreams that the Freudian view cannot. Newborn infants experience a great deal of REM sleep, yet presumably they suffer none of the repressed desires and psychological conflicts that Freudians contend arise in the course of childhood experience and that find expression in dreams. Large amounts of REM sleep make sense to Crick and Mitchison if the developing brains of newborns have to get rid of a good many undesired connections. Further, they argue that recalling dreams may be unhealthy because doing so may strengthen neural connections that should be discarded. However, the reverse learning, or unlearning, hypothesis has not been received enthusiastically by many leading sleep scientists. It is difficult to marshal compelling evidence to support it directly. Perhaps the safest conclusion we can reach on the various theories of dreams is that all the parties overstate their case. Traditional Freudian psychoanalysts neglect the physiological factors underlying dreaming, whereas activation-synthesis and reverse-learning theorists fail to take sufficient account of how daily experiences influence the content of dreams.

HYPNOSIS

Many people still associate hypnosis with magic shows, quackery, and hocus-pocus. Nonetheless, hypnosis has come to occupy a respected place in psychology, and it is an accepted supplement to some therapies. **Hypnosis** is a form of altered consciousness with a purpose—one in which individuals become more susceptible to suggestion and experience a heightened sense of selective attention. For example, by allowing the hypnotist to guide and direct them, people can "see" something that is not there. For instance, you can imagine a mouse running around on the top of your desk if you are not hypnotized. Under hypnosis, your imagination is augmented to the point that, if you are highly hypnotizable, you will perceive the mouse as real (Hilgard, 1986). Through hypnosis, people can be made conscious of things of which they are usually unaware and made unaware of things that they usually notice. People "tune in" those experiences that the hypnotist suggests and "tune out" those experiences that are sources of distraction. In so doing, they suspend their ordinary, everyday, critical approaches to reality (Hilgard, 1978).

Myths and Facts About Hypnosis

Many myths continue to plague popular understanding of hypnosis. For one thing, hypnosis is not sleep. The brain waves of a hypnotic trance and those of sleep are quite different. However, in order to encourage their subjects to relax, some hypnotists suggest to subjects that their eyelids feel heavy and that they are becoming sleepy.

Another myth derives from the old image of the hypnotist as a crafty, diabolical person who, with penetrating gaze and outstretched hands and arms, manipulates the will of his subjects and makes them slaves to his commands. Contemporary psychologists are pretty much in agreement that people cannot be hypnotized against their will. A good candidate for hypnosis must want to invest some control in another person. Indeed, people who are hypnotized for the first time often express amazement that they remained in touch with reality and even complain that they experienced no sensational or overwhelming feelings.

Moreover, not all people are likely candidates for hypnosis. Only about 10 percent of the population is highly hypnotizable; another 8 to 9 percent cannot be hypnotized at all (Williams, 1974). A leading researcher, Josephine R. Hilgard (1974), finds that

---

hypnosis: A form of altered consciousness in which individuals become more susceptible to suggestion and experience a heightened sense of selective attention.

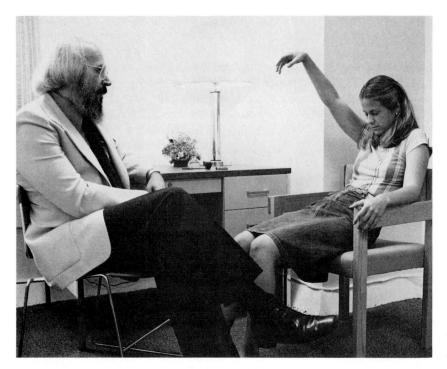

Under hypnosis people can behave in ways that are not typical of them, such as keeping an arm raised in the air for many minutes, but they cannot be made to commit acts that are against their will. *(Ken Robert Buck/The Picture Cube)*

the best potential subjects are those people who possess a vivid imagination and who as children used their imagination to escape from harsh realities. Most commonly, three characteristics are found among good hypnosis candidates: they are able to focus attention and concentrate; they are open to new experience; and they are willing to comply with suggestions (Goleman, 1977). Some psychologists use the Stanford Hypnotic Susceptibility Scale to evaluate an individual's potential for hypnosis (see Table 3.1).

Psychologists also find only limited truth in the notion that hypnosis can make people engage in dangerous or immoral acts that they would otherwise avoid. But they express caution in their discussions on the matter. Psychologists note that hypnotists can shape situations for subjects in such ways that an act that is not normally permissible can become permissible. For instance, under hypnosis a war veteran was informed he was walking down a jungle road and that an enemy was about to ambush him. He jumped at his attacker, in reality an assistant to the researcher, and began choking him. Ordinarily the man would not have attacked another person, since doing

so would have violated his moral code. But in a life-and-death situation, killing became self-defense (Williams, 1974).

Uses of Hypnosis

Hypnosis has many beneficial uses (Kihlstrom, 1985). In the hands of competent, well-trained therapists, it has proven itself a valuable tool. In particular, hypnotic suggestion has found clinical application as a weapon against pain (Hilgard and Hilgard, 1975; Knox et al., 1981). During World War II, it was used on some battlefields during surgery when analgesics and anesthetics were unavailable.

More recently, hypnosis has found use in dentistry and obstetrics—both health fields in which practitioners find their patients filled with considerable misinformation and intense fear. Since anxiety and tension are frequently implicated in the experience of pain, the relaxation afforded by hypnosis can serve a powerful therapeutic purpose. In some instances, hypnosis is used as an anesthetic during childbirth (for instance, the mother may imaginatively relive, step by step, a European vacation). Likewise, some

TABLE 3.1 Stanford Hypnotic Susceptibility Scale

Suggested Behavior	Criterion of Passing	Suggested Behavior	Criterion of Passing
Postural sway	Falls without forcing	Hallucination	Any movement, grimacing, or other acknowledgment of effect
Eye closure	Closes eyes without forcing		
Hand lowering	Lowers at least 6 inches by end of 10 seconds	Eye catalepsy	Eyes remain closed at end of 10 seconds
Immobilization	Arm rises less than 1 inch in 10 seconds	Posthypnotic	Any partial movement response at posthypnotic signal
Finger lock	Incomplete separation of fingers at end of 10 seconds	Amnesia test	Recall of 3 or fewer items
Arm rigidity	Less than 2 inches of arm bending in 10 seconds		
Hands moving apart	Hands at least 6 inches apart in 10 seconds		
Verbal inhibition	Name unspoken in 10 seconds		

Note: Items composing the scale have a high correlation with susceptibility to suggestions under hypnosis. Hence, the scale affords a technique for assessing a person's hypnotizability. The susceptibility of a subject primarily determines the degree of response to hypnotic suggestion.

Source: Adapted from Ernest Hilgard et al. 1961. *Psychological Monographs,* 75, No. 8. Reprinted/adapted by permission of the authors.

terminally ill cancer patients find relief from their intractable pain through hypnosis. And about one-third of amputees who experience phantom-limb pain in the stump respond favorably to hypnotic suggestion (Hilgard and Hilgard, 1975).

Some psychologists and psychiatrists use hypnosis as an adjunct to psychotherapy. One technique entails age regression. In **age regression,** people are told by a hypnotist that they are a certain age and are then instructed to tell about or act out their behavior during this earlier period of their lives. In so doing, the therapist attempts to assist a patient in unearthing the childhood roots of a subconscious problem

(see Chapter 16). However, in and of itself hypnosis is not a therapeutic tool. Rather, it is a technique by which people can reinstate memories that are otherwise unavailable to them and can thus ferret out subconscious problems (Williams, 1974).

Hypnosis may also be used to achieve selective forgetting, as in the case of **posthypnotic amnesia.** People are induced to "forget" particular events but can recall them again when the hypnotist provides the signal to do so. A hypnotist may likewise give people a command that they are to carry out at a later time—a procedure termed **posthypnotic suggestion.** For example, you might be told by the hypno-

age regression: A type of psychotherapy in which individuals are told by a hypnotist that they are a certain age and are then instructed to tell about or act out their behavior during this earlier period.
posthypnotic amnesia: A procedure in which an individual is induced to "forget" particular events for a while, but the events can be recalled again later when the hypnotist provides the signal to do so.
posthypnotic suggestion: A procedure in which the hypnotist gives a person a command that he or she is to carry out at a later time.

tist that you will no longer feel ravenously hungry or no longer care for the taste of cigarettes. This suggestion is often coupled with posthypnotic amnesia so that you would feel constrained to carry out the behavior without knowing why you are doing so. In some instances and with some people, such suggestions produce temporary abstinence from smoking or short-term dieting.

Theories About Hypnosis

Just how hypnosis achieves its effects is a matter of some controversy (Sarbin and Coe, 1979; Kihlstrom, 1985; Balthazard and Woody, 1985). Indeed, some psychologists, among them Theodore X. Barber (1965; Barber, Spanos, and Chaves, 1974), argue that hypnosis is not a "special" or "altered" state of consciousness. If people are simply given instructions and told to try their hardest, they can frequently do anything that hypnotized people can do. Barber has shown that unhypnotized people can hold a heavy weight at arm's length for several minutes; they can lie stiff as a board with only one chair under their shoulders and another under their feet to support them; they can even stick needles through their hands. According to some social psychologists, hypnotic behavior is merely a special case of compliance or obedience behavior (Wagstaff, 1981; Spanos and Gorassini, 1984). The hypnotic subject is seen as playing the "game" of hypnosis according to the rules laid down by the hypnotist, our cultural notion of "hypnosis," and an individual's personal attitudes and preconceptions. Thus, hypnotized people are said to behave as they do not because they have undergone a change in internal state, but because they are striving to enact the "role" of a "hypnotized subject." To the extent to which social factors are favorable, they provide performances that are convincing to both others and themselves.

Other psychologists, including Ernest R. Hilgard (1977, 1978, 1986), believe that there is something special about the hypnotic state. People who are hypnotized are very suggestible; they go along with the hypnotist and do not initiate activities themselves; and they can more easily imagine and remember things. Hilgard believes that consciousness is divided into multiple, simultaneous streams of mental activity. Consequently, some aspects of consciousness may become separated, or *dissociated*,

during hypnosis. He terms this view the *neodissociation theory*.

According to Hilgard, as you go about your daily life, you consciously take in only certain happenings. For instance, you may be engrossed in watching television, studying your notes for a test, or observing the cars as you cross a busy intersection. Other events are registering, but you are not consciously aware of them. Hypnosis assists people retrospectively to unlock these events and bring them into full, conscious awareness. Something of this sort is believed to occur when police hypnotize witnesses to assist them in recalling the specific details of a crime (see the boxed insert on pages 86–87). Hilgard says that hypnosis allows people to shut out competing mental inputs and to focus their attention only on those inputs suggested by the hypnotist. Hence, they mentally separate, or dissociate, various experiences that earlier they had consciously linked in a quite different manner.

In some of his experiments, Hilgard has demonstrated that consciousness can be broken down into a number of parts. For example, a person who is hypnotized may be told that her left hand is unable to feel pain even though it is immersed in ice water. She is further told that her right hand will act as a "hidden observer" and note how painful the water is but not consciously feel any pain itself. With appropriate hypnotic instructions, Hilgard later asks the "hidden observer" what the subject felt and is told that the right arm really did notice pain (even though the hypnotized person had earlier said that she did not feel anything at all). In this case the sensory component (the sensation of extreme cold) is separated from the emotional component (the experience of pain). Although a number of psychologists have insisted that the "hidden observer" effect is invalid and merely a "creation" of laboratory conditions (Spanos and Hewitt, 1980; Spanos, 1983), others have found solid support for its existence (Laurence, Perry, and Kihlstrom, 1983; Zamansky and Bartis, 1985).

Whether hypnosis is a special state of consciousness or not, it does reveal that people often have potential abilities that they do not use. Continued study may help us to understand where these abilities come from and how to use them better. Indeed, hypnosis may be a collection of phenomena, bound together in name only by the term "hypnosis," that demand a number of different explanations (Wagstaff, 1981).

Even when asleep or concentrating hard on getting a tan, one may be vaguely aware of other events and register them in memories that can be later recalled under hypnosis. *(Anestis Diakopoulous/Stock, Boston)*

THE SELF-REGULATION OF CONSCIOUSNESS

Clinical applications of hypnosis require that you relinquish some measure of control to another person: the hypnotist. But many people do not wish to take this road. Nonetheless, they find the prospect of deliberately gaining entry to their own inner states and consciously controlling these states quite appealing. Thus many people are attracted to such methods as meditation and biofeedback for increased self-awareness and achieving a measure of control over their own mental and bodily functions. These methods can be used to alleviate a good many conditions, including pain, some forms of heart disease, and emotional problems.

Meditation

Psychologists began studying meditation in the 1960s. In **meditation** an individual focuses attention on an image, a thought, a bodily process, or an external object with the goal of clearing his or her

---

meditation: Focusing of attention on an image, thought, bodily process, or external object with the goal of clearing one's mind and producing an "inner peace."

Hypnosis in Court Trials

On the evening of May 19, 1978, Nancy Simmons, a young Syracuse mother, put her four-year-old son to bed and then went to sleep herself. She left the apartment door unlocked for her husband, who worked the night shift. When Bart Simmons came home, he found his wife sprawled on the landing, bruised, and covered with dirt—the victim of a brutal rape. Unable to identify her assailant, Mrs. Simmons underwent hypnosis to "refresh" her memory. After a number of false starts, she declared, "I saw Kirk." Kirk Hughes was a next-door neighbor, friend, and occasional babysitter. Largely on the basis of Mrs. Simmons's identification, a jury convicted Hughes. However, on appeal, New York State's highest court held that hypnosis had not gained general acceptance in the scientific community and tends to produce "a mixture of accurate recall, fantasy or pure fabrication in unknown quantities." Accordingly, the court ordered a new trial for Hughes (Margolick, 1983).

Many experienced clinicians contend that hypnosis can improve a person's memory for events experienced outside hypnosis. This effect has been used to refresh the memories of witnesses, victims, and even suspects in criminal cases. Yet, alarmingly, there are striking incidents in which witnesses who were hypnotized have been wrong (Stark, 1984). For instance, in 1975, a sailor at the Philadelphia Naval Base was shot and wounded. The police apprehended a suspect, but the sailor was unable to identify him as the assailant. The sailor was then hypnotized and while under hypnosis said the suspect was definitely the person who had assaulted him. He remained adamant in his identification despite the fact that two people cleared the accused man by confirming his alibi. The suspect was not convicted.

An accumulating body of psychological research also suggests that some memories activated under hypnosis may be inaccurate. Although valid memory may be increased, it is often accompanied by corresponding increases in inaccurate recollection or confabulation. For example, Jane Dywan and Kenneth Bowers (1983) found in their study that hypnotized subjects correctly recalled twice as many pictorial items as did unhypnotized subjects. But the hypnotized subjects also made three times as many

mind and producing an "inner peace." In one of the first experiments, researchers simply asked people to concentrate on a blue vase. The participants soon reported that the color of the vase became very vivid and that time passed quickly. The people could not be distracted as easily as they normally might. Some individuals felt themselves merging with the vase. Others reported that their surroundings became unusually beautiful, filled with light and movement. All the meditators found the experience pleasant. After twelve sessions they all felt a strong attachment to the vase and missed it when it was not present during the next session (Deikman, 1963).

Other researchers went on to show that when people meditate, their physiological state changes. The most famous of these studies were those undertaken by Robert Keith Wallace at UCLA (1970). He measured the brain waves (EEG), heart rate, oxygen consumption, and sweat-gland activity of fifteen people as they practiced Transcendental Meditation. (*Transcendental Meditation* is a Westernized version of

yoga meditation techniques that was developed by the Indian guru Maharishi Mahesh Yogi.) For two twenty-minute periods each day, meditators sit in a comfortable position and repeat a special word —called a *mantra*—over and over again to themselves. Wallace found that when people did this, physiological measurements of their bodies proved that they were deeply relaxed.

Controversy exists over how meditation techniques differ and what their specific effects are. In the best-selling books *The Relaxation Response* (Benson, 1975) and *Beyond the Relaxation Response* (Benson and Proctor, 1984), Herbert Benson, a Harvard cardiologist, argues that most forms of meditation lead to a special state of reduced metabolism and deep relaxation, which he calls the "relaxation response." Benson believes that all through recorded history, people have been using various techniques to elicit the relaxation response. He cites many examples, including the contemplative practices indicated by Saint Augustine and the instructions for mistakes. Likewise, psychologists Jean-Roche Laurence and Campbell Perry (1983) have shown that hypnotized subjects are easily influenced by leading questions. They asked subjects under hypnosis to choose one night of the previous week and to relive the events of that night. Through this procedure the subjects were ascertained to have *no* specific memories of awakening during the specified night. While under hypnosis the subjects were asked if they had heard some loud noises that had awakened them. Thirteen of twenty-seven subjects accepted the suggestion and stated after hypnosis that they had been awakened on the night in question by loud noises. The results support the contention of psychologists who say that the memories of victims and witnesses of crime can be modified unsuspectingly through the use of hypnosis. Moreover, an initially unsure victim or witness can become highly credible in court after a hypnotic "refreshment" procedure (Orne et al., 1984).

Proponents of hypnosis in criminal cases commonly adhere to the *videotape theory of memory,* which says that every piece of information encountered by an individual is permanently stored somewhere in the brain and can be retrieved. Yet psychological research points to a *reconstructive theory of memory,* which holds that both new information and a person's own thoughts can alter a memory (Stark, 1984). In brief, individuals who are under hypnosis can unconsciously fill in gaps in their memories or fabricate facts in an effort to please their questioners. At times the contamination is so pervasive that it taints everything a subject had recalled before hypnosis. For this reason critics charge that testimony produced through hypnosis is inherently unreliable and should not be admitted in court. By 1984 at least twelve states had banned hypnotically induced testimony, and the number seems likely to grow. All this is not to say that hypnosis is of no value in criminal investigations. For example, in the 1976 Chowchilla, California, kidnaping of a busload of schoolchildren, the bus driver recalled, under hypnosis, all but one of the license-plate numbers of the kidnapers. On the basis of this clue, police found evidence enabling them to arrest and convict the abductors. And for their part, those who favor the use in court cases of evidence obtained through hypnosis contend that other pretrial techniques are also flawed and are just as likely to "lead" witnesses.

---

prayer provided by Martin Luther.

Benson contends that the relaxation response is directly opposite to the body's "fight or flight" response. Four basic elements seem to be required to elicit the relaxation response: a quiet environment, a comfortable position, a "mental device" (such as a word that is repeated over and over again, or a physical object that the meditator concentrates on), and a passive attitude. Many people have been helped by Benson's technique. (For a short form of the instructions Benson gives his own patients, see the boxed insert on page 89.)

Clinical applications of meditation techniques have proliferated. They have been employed in the treatment of anxiety, mild hypertension, insomnia, alcoholism, drug abuse, and stuttering. They are a mainstay of many stress-management programs and are often used in cardiac rehabilitation. Although few psychologists dispute that meditators experience benefits from the programs, some, like David S. Holmes (1984), contend that resting produces equivalent results. On the basis of his review of the literature on the physiology of meditation, Holmes says that a quiet time in an easy chair works just as well, and one does not have to bother with the mantras and the expense.

Biofeedback

Biofeedback involves learning conscious control of one's internal physiological processes with the help of information received from monitoring devices.

---

biofeedback: Learning conscious control of one's internal physiological processes with the help of information received from monitoring devices.

The *mandala* is a symbol of the universe that is used as an aid to meditation. This one is Tibetan. *(The Newark Museum Collection)*

For example, you can be hooked up to a biofeedback machine so that a light goes on every time your heart rate goes over 80. You could then learn to keep your heart rate below 80 by trying to keep the light off. How would you do it? When researcher David Shapiro (1973) asked a participant in one of his experiments how he changed his heart rate, the subject asked in return, "How do you move your arm?" In brief, it seems to be a process that people intuitively "know" and that they can improve on with training.

However it is done, biofeedback has been used to teach people to control a wide variety of physiological responses, including brain waves (EEG), heart rate, blood pressure, skin temperature, and sweat-gland activity (Hassett, 1978a). The basic principle of biofeedback is simple: feedback makes learning possible by providing people with information about their performance. Imagine trying to learn to play the saxophone if you were deaf. If you could not hear all the squeals and honks you mistakenly made, your version of "The Star-Spangled Banner" would probably cause the audience to leave. It is only through the feedback of hearing your errors that your playing improves.

But in many cases the body is not specifically designed to provide you with subtle feedback about your internal physiological states. It is very unlikely that you know whether your heart rate is now 60, 80, or 100 unless you take your pulse. Biofeedback involves using machines to tell you about very subtle, moment-to-moment changes in your body. You can then experiment with different thoughts and feelings while you watch how each affects your body. In time, most people can learn to change their physiological processes.

Neal Miller (1969, 1985) and his colleagues have demonstrated that a vast number of bodily functions can be voluntarily controlled if rewarding feedback follows the change in behavior. In a series of experiments, Miller taught rats to change either the rate of their intestinal contractions or the speed of their heart rate. He proceeded by temporarily paralyzing the animals with the drug curare and then maintaining them on artificial respiration. He designed this procedure so that the rodents could not "cheat" by exerting their muscles to speed up or slow down the processes. By administering electrical stimulation to their brains' "pleasure centers," Miller was able to monitor and control rewards that the rats received.

How to Meditate

Want to try meditation? Here are the instructions researcher Herbert Benson (1977; Benson and Proctor, 1984) gives his patients:

- Sit quietly in a comfortable position. Close your eyes. Deeply relax all your muscles, beginning at your feet and progressing up to your face. Keep them deeply relaxed.

- Breathe through your nose. Become aware of your breathing. As you breathe out, say the word "one" silently to yourself. Continue for twenty minutes. You may open your eyes to check the time, but do not use an alarm. When you have finished, sit quietly for several minutes, at first with closed eyes and later with opened eyes.

- Do not worry about whether you are successful in achieving a deep level of relaxation. Maintain a passive attitude and permit relaxation to occur at its own pace. Expect distracting thoughts. When these distracting thoughts occur, ignore them and continue repeating "one."

- Practice the technique once or twice daily, but not within two hours after a meal, since the digestive processes seem to interfere with elicitation of anticipated changes.

Some psychologists propose that meditation is relaxing and reduces stress. Other psychologists contend that resting in an easy chair is just as effective as meditation. *(Joel Gordon)*

Miller's research also revealed that the learning of the autonomic responses is specific and not general. That is, the subject is able to gain control over a specific response, not just the general autonomic response. Those rats rewarded for increases in intestinal contractions learned an increase, while the group rewarded for decreases learned a decrease. But neither of these groups displayed an appreciable change in heart rate. Conversely, the rodents rewarded for increases in heart rate learned an increase, while the group rewarded for decreases learned a decrease. But neither of these groups displayed an appreciable change in intestinal contractions. Miller's remarkable rats even learned to make one ear blush and not the other.

One of the most widely publicized uses of biofeedback is "alpha training." Alpha refers to a certain type of brain-wave activity, typically seen in the EEG when a person relaxes. Alpha has also been observed in the brain waves of some people when they meditate. As a result, a few years ago alpha biofeedback was widely advertised as a quick and easy way to achieve an altered state of consciousness —a sort of instant meditation. Most researchers are very skeptical of such claims. These days, most people feel that biofeedback has more potential for treating physical disease than for attaining spiritual well-being.

Over the past decade or so, biofeedback procedures have made considerable strides toward winning respectability within the medical community. Physicians and laypeople alike have gained new respect for the ability of individuals to increase their awareness and self-control of certain bodily processes and relate these processes to both their physical and mental well-being. As better instruments and techniques are devised, they hold promise of enhancing the remarkable capacity we have to control our bodies. For example, biofeedback has been found to be an effective tool for teaching violinists and violists to remove unwanted tension from their left hands (LeVine and Irvine, 1984). Excessive rigidity of the left hand decreases their finger speed and interferes with quick changes in the position of the hand. We will have more to say in Chapter 14 on the medical uses of biofeedback.

HALLUCINATIONS

Hallucinations are sensations or perceptions that have no actual external cause—seeing, hearing, smelling, tasting, or feeling things that do not exist. Hypnosis, meditation, certain drugs, withdrawal from addicting drugs, migraine headaches, high fever, and mental disorder may produce hallucinations. But they also occur under "normal" conditions. People hallucinate when they are dreaming and when they are deprived of the opportunity to sleep. Lonely explorers, isolated desert and polar wanderers, and prisoners in dark dungeons sometimes report experiencing them. Periods of high emotion, concentration, or fatigue may also produce false sensations and perceptions. For example, truck drivers on long hauls have been known to swerve suddenly to avoid stalled cars that did not exist. Even daydreams involve mild hallucinations.

Interestingly enough, it seems that some drug-induced hallucinations are very much alike from one person to the next. Soon after taking a drug that causes hallucinations, for example, people often see many geometric forms in a tunnellike perspective. These forms float through the field of vision, combining with one another and duplicating themselves. While normal imagery is often in black and white, hallucinations are more likely to involve color.

When Ronald K. Siegel (1977) traveled to Mexico's Sierra Madre to study the reactions of Huichol Indians who take peyote, he found that their hallucinations were much like those of American college students who took similar drugs. Siegel believes that these reactions are similar because of the way in which such drugs affect the brain. It seems that hallucinations are related to an arousal of the nervous system that is coupled with an underlying disorganization in brain functioning. Consequently, confusion occurs in the supervisory mechanisms that process information.

Louis Jolyon West (Siegel and West, 1975) suggests that hallucinations arise when the brain has difficulty separating newly arriving information from information that the memory system is supplying about past experience. Consider this analogy. You are looking out your living room window viewing the distant sunset. Behind you a fire burns in a fireplace. You are so engrossed by the scene outside the window that you are not consciously aware of the interior of the room. Darkness descends outside, but you continue to peer at the window. As the outside darkness deepens, the fire increasingly becomes the source of illumination in the room. You now see a vivid reflection of the room in the window, although it gives the appearance of being in the outdoors.

According to West's *perceptual-release hypothesis*, something similar to this process occurs with hallucination. The sensory input (the daylight) is reduced while the nervous system remains aroused (the interior illumination remains bright). Consequently, images within the brain (the interior room) may be perceived as though they have an external source (as though arising outside the window).

Interestingly, West's view parallels one interpretation of schizophrenia, a serious mental disorder in which hallucinations typically play a prominent role (see Chapter 15). One of the defining characteristics of the disorder is an impairment in perceptual functioning. Schizophrenics have difficulty focusing on relevant stimuli and ignoring irrelevant stimuli (Chapman and Chapman, 1973). It seems that schizophrenics are insufficiently alert and attentive to events in the external world. Instead, for reasons not as yet fully understood, they turn their focus inward on their own inner experiences.

Not untypical is Franz, a schizophrenic young man who says he is a riddle of bones (Rodgers, 1982b). He hears strange voices, buzzing noises, and penetrating squeals. He sees periodic flashes of light and shadows, which he claims are sent to him by

---

hallucination: A sensation or perception that has no actual external cause.

strangers. He tastes soap in his mouth and believes that he absorbs poison from the bedpost.

Much of Franz's attention is centered on experiences that derive from inner operations of the brain. He has difficulty processing information received from his sensory systems. Indeed, in some respects, Franz seems to suffer from a deprivation of sensory experience that resembles the experiences of some people isolated in sensory deprivation experiments, a matter to which we now turn our attention.

SENSORY DEPRIVATION

If consciousness plays a critical part in the monitoring and interpretation of environmental changes, then perhaps the absence of such changes may cause consciousness to alter. This possibility led psychologist Donald O. Hebb to begin a series of experiments to determine whether people who are deprived of normal stimulation over extended periods of time become more susceptible to hallucinations and related experiences. As one of the researchers (Heron, 1957:52) later described it: "The aim of this project was to obtain basic information on how human beings would react in situations where nothing at all was happening." This type of research assumes major importance at a time when the problem of on-the-job monotony is becoming more prevalent, as modern societies increasingly turn to the application of advanced technologies. Boredom is found among military personnel at radar installations, control-room operators at nuclear-power stations, and industrial workers in automated plants.

In Hebb's experiments, male college students were paid to lie all day on a comfortable bed—they would get up only for meals and to go to the bathroom. Plastic visors over their eyes kept them from seeing anything but diffuse light; U-shaped foam-rubber pillows around their heads and the hum of a small air conditioner and fan kept out any sounds; and cotton gloves and long cardboard cuffs restricted the sense of touch (see Figure 3.3). In short, the subjects could not see, hear, or touch anything—they were in a state of sensory deprivation.

FIGURE 3.3 Experimenting on the effects of boredom. Gloves and cotton cuffs prevented input to the hands and fingers; a plastic visor diffused the light coming into the eyes; a foam pillow and the continuous hum of the air conditioner and fan made input to the ears low and monotonous. Except for eating and using the bathroom, the subjects did nothing but lie on the bed. *(After Woodburn Heron. 1957. The pathology of boredom. Scientific American, 196 (January). Copyright © 1957 by Scientific American, Inc. All rights reserved.)*

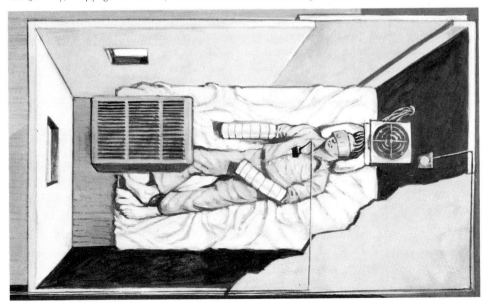

Most people had signed up for the experiment hoping to catch up on their work—planning term papers, lectures, and so on. But under these conditions they quickly became irritable and found they had trouble concentrating. After extended periods of isolation, many of the men reported seeing "images." One man said that he repeatedly saw a scene in which a rock was shaded by a tree. Another man was plagued by visions of babies, and still another by pictures of dogs. The experimenters did not appreciate the power and strangeness of these events until one of them himself underwent the isolation experience. It soon became clear to Hebb and his associates that the monotonous experimental setting was inducing the men to hallucinate.

The researchers concluded that prolonged exposure to monotonous events produces unhealthy outcomes. The men's thinking had become impaired. They displayed childish emotional responses. Their visual processes were disturbed. They experienced hallucinations. And their brain-wave patterns changed. All this led Hebb to theorize that there is an optimal level of sensory input that the organism needs in order to function well.

Many other studies of sensory deprivation have since been performed (Zubeck, 1969). They have used a variety of techniques for restricting sensory input, including lying in a tub of water for several days and submerging completely in a pool heated to body temperature while wearing only a diving helmet to supply oxygen. Not all techniques and conditions had the same effects. Hallucinations were generally not as common in later experiments, but sensory deprivation did consistently lead to irritability, restlessness, and emotional upset. Perhaps not surprisingly, some groups like the Shakers on St. Vincent, a Caribbean island, indulge in isolated conditions analogous to sensory deprivation experiments to induce trance states (Price-Williams, 1985).

Recognizing the powerful impact that sensory deprivation can have on people, a number of psychologists, among them Peter Suedfeld (Suedfeld and Ikard, 1977), have explored its use as a tool to facilitate long-term behavioral change. His hypothesis, supported by other research, is that a period of sensory deprivation typically leads to increased persuasibility and responsiveness to external cues (Suedfeld, 1969). Suedfeld has placed cigarette smokers in a socially isolated, monotonous environment for twenty-four hours. At ninety-minute intervals, the individuals heard two-minute messages telling about the hazards of smoking. A year later, the subjects had reduced their rate of smoking by an average of 48 percent. A comparable group of control subjects who heard the health-hazard messages but did not experience sensory deprivation reduced their cigarette consumption by only 16 percent.

PSYCHOACTIVE DRUGS

Human beings have long used drugs to alter their states of consciousness (Fort and Cory, 1975; Cox, 1984). More than ten thousand years ago Paleolithic people made an alcoholic beverage called mead. About 4000 B.C. a Sumerian tablet described opium as the "joy plant." And about 2737 B.C. the Chinese emperor Shen Nung recommended marijuana for "female weakness, gout, rheumatism, malaria, beriberi, constipation, and absent-mindedness." Chemical substances that individuals employ to change their moods, feelings, or perceptions are termed **psychoactive drugs.**

Although psychoactive drugs have a long history, various groups and societies have supplied different answers to the questions of which substances are legitimate, which effects are valuable, and which risks are tolerable (Orcutt, 1975; Zentner, 1977; Nicholi, 1983). Within the United States, the Federal Drug Administration, the Bureau of Narcotics, and other government agencies formally define whether particular drugs are "good" or "bad," and if "bad," how bad. Moreover, some drugs enjoy official approval. In adopting coffee as the approved beverage for breakfasts and "coffee breaks," Americans have institutionalized the use of caffeine, a mild stimulant. Most cola drinks, used around the world as a refreshment, include caffeine. And alcohol is a widely accepted—even mandatory—social "lubricant" in many recreational and business settings.

---

psychoactive (SIGH-koh-AK-tiv) drug: A chemical substance that an individual employs to change his or her mood, feelings, or perceptions.

Some drugs, such as alcohol, nicotine in cigarettes, and caffeine in colas and coffee, are legal for adults to use in most of the United States. Other drugs are outlawed or controlled by the Federal Drug Administration. *(Raoul Hackel/Stock, Boston)*

Psychoactive drugs produce their effects by temporarily altering aspects of brain activity. In Chapter 2 we discussed the chemical and electrical processes by which the brain and nervous system generate signals and transmit messages. Apparently, psychoactive drugs are capable of influencing these processes and intervening in their operation. As we will see later in this chapter, many of the drugs resemble in their chemical structure the brain's transmitter substances that excite or inhibit neuron firing.

Psychologists commonly make three broad divisions among psychoactive drugs: depressants, stimulants, and hallucinogens (see Table 3.2). Let us consider each of these categories in turn.

Depressants

Depressants are drugs that act on the brain and nervous system to reduce the responsiveness of the body and to slow its activities. They include alcohol, the barbiturates, the narcotics, and tranquilizers. Of these, alcohol is the most widely used. It is a comparatively safe drug when used in moderation and not in association with driving. But it can also be an exceedingly dangerous drug when abused. Indeed, alcohol abuse is so prevalent that, in spite of all we hear about the abuse of cocaine and marijuana, alcoholism is this nation's number-one drug problem (see the boxed insert on pages 96–98).

depressant: A drug that acts on the brain and nervous system to reduce the responsiveness of the body and to slow its activities.

TABLE 3.2 Major Substances Used for Mind Alteration

Drug	Slang Name	Source	Effects	Withdrawal Symptoms	Adverse/Overdose Reactions	Physical Dependence Potential	Psychological Dependence Potential
DEPRESSANTS Morphine	Drugstore dope, cube, first line, mud, white, stuff, M	Natural (from opium)	Apathy, difficulty in concentration, slowed speech, decreased physical activity, drooling, itching, euphoria, nausea	Anxiety, vomiting, sneezing, diarrhea, lower back pain, watery eyes, runny nose, yawning, irritability, tremors, panic, chills and sweating, cramps	Depressed levels of consciousness, low blood pressure, rapid heart rate, shallow breathing, convulsions, coma, possible death	Yes	Yes
Heroin	H, hombre, junk, smack, dope, horse, crap, scat	Semisynthetic (from morphine)				Yes	Yes
Codeine	Schoolboy	Natural (from opium), semisynthetic (from morphine)				Yes	Yes
Methadone	Meth, dolly	Synthetic (morphine-like)				Yes	Yes
Barbiturates	Barbs, red devils, yellow jackets, phennies, peanuts, blue heavens, candy	Synthetic	Impulsiveness, dramatic mood swings, bizarre thoughts, suicidal behavior, slurred speech, disorientation, slowed mental and physical functioning, limited attention span	Weakness, restlessness, nausea and vomiting, headache, nightmares, irritability, depression, acute anxiety, hallucinations, seizures, possible death	Confusion, decreased response to pain, shallow respiration, dilated pupils, weak and rapid pulse, coma, possible death	Yes	Yes
Alcohol	Booze, juice, sauce	Natural (from fruits, grains)	Drowsiness, decreased alertness and inhibitions	Delirium tremens (hallucinations, disorientation, convulsions, nausea, anxiety)	Toxic psychosis, addiction, neurologic damage, stupor, liver damage, obesity, violence, death	Yes	Yes
STIMULANTS Amphetamines	Bennies, dexies, hearts, pep pills, speed, lid proppers, wake-ups	Synthetic	Increased confidence, mood elevation, sense of energy and alertness, decreased appetite, anxiety, irritability, insomnia, transient drowsiness, delayed orgasm	Apathy, general fatigue, prolonged sleep, depression, disorientation, suicidal thoughts, agitated motor activity, irritability, bizarre dreams	Elevated blood pressure, increase in body temperature, face-picking, suspiciousness, bizarre and repetitious behavior, vivid hallucination, convulsions, possible death	Yes	Yes
Cocaine	Coke, blow, toot, snow, lady, gold dust, crack, rock	Natural (from coca leaves)				No	Yes
Caffeine (coffee, tea, colas)	Java, coke	Natural	Mood elevation, irritability, increased metabolism rate, in some cases irregular heartbeat, hallucinations, convulsions	Severe headache, drowsiness	Jitteriness, insomnia	Possible	Yes

Drug	Slang Name	Source	Effects	Withdrawal Symptoms	Adverse/Overdose Reactions	Physical Dependence Potential	Psychological Dependence Potential
Tobacco	Fag, coffin nail	Natural	Mood elevation, increased heart rate and blood pressure	Irritability	Heart disease, lung disease	Possible	Yes
HALLUCINOGENS							
LSD	Electricity, acid, quasey, blotter acid, microdot, white lightning, purple barrels, big D, sugar, trips, cubes, windowpane	Semisynthetic (from ergot alkaloids)	Fascination with ordinary objects; heightened esthetic responses; vision and depth distortion; hear colors, see music; slowing of time; heightened sensitivity to faces, gestures; heightened emotions; paranoia, panic, euphoria, bliss, impairment of short-term memory, projection of self into dreamlike images	Not reported	Nausea, chills; increased pulse, temperature, and blood pressure; trembling, slow, deep breathing, loss of appetite, insomnia, longer, more intense "trips"; bizarre, dangerous behavior possibly leading to injury or death	No	Possible
Mescaline	Peyote buttons, mesc	Natural (from peyote cactus)	Similar to LSD but more sensual and perceptual; fewer changes in thought, mood and sense of self; vomiting	Not reported	Resemble LSD, but more bodily sensations, vomiting	No	Possible
Psilocybin	Mushrooms, shrooms, rooms	Natural (from fungus on a type of mushroom)	Similar to LSD but more visual and less intense; more euphoria, fewer panic reactions	Not reported	Resemble LSD, but less severe	No	Possible
Marijuana/Hashish	Bhang, kif, ganja, dope, grass, pot, smoke, hemp, joint, weed, bone, Mary Jane, herb, tea, hash	Cannabis sativa	Euphoria, relaxed inhibitions, increased appetite, disoriented behavior	Hyperactivity, insomnia, decreased appetite, anxiety	Severe reactions are rare, but include panic, paranoia, fatigue, bizarre and dangerous behavior	No	Possible
Phencyclidine	PCP, angel dust, hog, rocket fuel, superweed, peace pill, elephant tranquilizer, dust, bad pizza	Synthetic	Increased blood pressure and heart rate; sweating, nausea, numbness, floating sensation, slowed reflexes, altered body image; altered perception of time and space; impaired short-term memory, decreased concentration, paranoid thoughts and delusions	Not reported	Highly variable and possibly dose-related; disorientation, loss of recent memory, lethargy/stupor; bizarre and violent behavior, rigidity and immobility; mutism, staring, hallucinations and delusions, coma	No	Possible

Source: Compiled from J. Kaufman, H. Schafter, and M. E. Burglass. 1983. The clinical assessment and diagnosis of addiction. II: The biological basics—drugs and their effects. In T. Bratter and G. Forrest, eds., Current Treatment of Substance Abuse and Alcoholism. New York: Macmillan; and Teaching About Drugs: A Curriculum Guide, K–12, by the American School Health Association and the Pharmaceutical Manufacturers Association.

The Abuse of Alcohol

Alcohol has always been part of American life (Peele, 1984a). Colonial Americans called it "the good creature of God." After the Revolutionary War, due to expanding frontiers and other social changes, the male-oriented saloon became the typical setting for drinking, and alcoholism rates rose dramatically. The temperance movement arose in response to the resulting explosion of alcohol problems. By the twentieth century, large numbers of Americans had come to view alcohol as "demon rum," leading to the enactment in 1920 of national prohibition. When prohibition was repealed in 1933, the goal of universal abstinence died with it. One reason Americans drink is that it is so easy to do. Alcoholic beverages are sold virtually everywhere. Moreover, they are comparatively cheap. And advertising, television, and movies routinely depict drinking as part of the smart life style.

Alcohol's effect on the mind and body depends on how much of it is consumed over what period of time. Five ounces of wine, twelve ounces of beer, and an ounce and a half of 80-proof spirits put the same amount of pure alcohol (about two-thirds of an ounce) into the bloodstream. How rapidly it passes into the bloodstream depends on a number of factors. Unlike most other substances, alcohol can be absorbed directly through the stomach, allowing it to reach the bloodstream more rapidly. Since the alcohol in beer and wine is less concentrated than that in spirits, beer and wine are absorbed more slowly than straight whiskey. On the other hand, the carbon dioxide in champagne and in drinks mixed with soda seems to speed the process of absorption. Eating before or while drinking, especially high-fat foods, slows down absorption.

According to the latest figures, alcohol causes or is associated with two hundred thousand deaths each year. These include deaths from alcohol-related diseases and automobile crashes (see Figure 3.4). When the body burns alcohol, acetaldehyde—a toxic substance—is produced. For this reason, chronic and excessive use of alcohol can seriously damage virtually every function and organ of the body. Alcohol is also an irritant to the stomach and adversely affects the way the small intestine transports and absorbs nutrients. It causes fatty deposits to accumulate in the liver, with cirrhosis—an incurable and often fatal illness—typically being the outcome. Alcohol contributes to chronic brain damage, making it second only to Alzheimer's disease as a cause of mental deterioration in adults. Moreover, excess drinking during pregnancy poses the risk of low birth weight, mental impairment, and birth defects to a fetus. It is estimated that alcohol-related diseases account for 30 to 50 percent of all hospital admissions (Franks, 1985).

Various explanations have been advanced to explain the biological effects of alcohol. One view looks to the fact that alcohol is soluble in fat and water. When individuals consume alcohol, the fatty membranes of neurons are thought to be affected. These membranes consist of protein "icebergs" afloat in seas of fats, or lipids. Because alcohol is a solvent, the fluidity of the fats increases. As a result, the protein "icebergs" begin drifting randomly, disrupting the channels that normally carry the messages controlling emotions and behavior. Withdrawal symptoms occur when alcohol is removed because the channels do not immediately recover their normal fluidity (contributing to hyperactivity in the central nervous system). Another view looks to the effects of alcohol on neurotransmitters. Animal studies show that when alcohol first enters the bloodstream, it stimulates the production of norepinephrine. Additionally, a number of alcohol-derived products, called TIQs (tetrahydroisoquiolines), are chemically related to opiates. Thus there may be a common mechanism for opiate and alcohol addiction (Blakeslee, 1984).

Individuals differ enormously in their responses to alcohol. Perhaps you have observed something of the following sort during a cocktail party: some guests remain talkative, friendly, charming, and witty; others become argumentative and pick fights; still others become ill and depressed; and some pass out. Researchers find

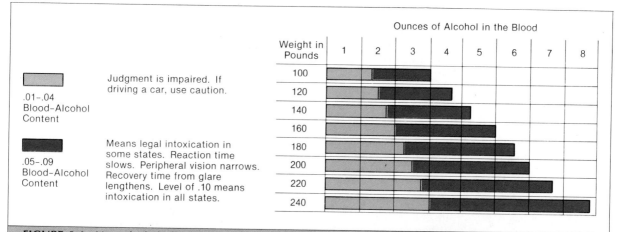

Ounces of Alcohol in the Blood

Weight in Pounds	1	2	3	4	5	6	7	8
100								
120								
140								
160								
180								
200								
220								
240								

.01–.04 Blood–Alcohol Content — Judgment is impaired. If driving a car, use caution.

.05–.09 Blood–Alcohol Content — Means legal intoxication in some states. Reaction time slows. Peripheral vision narrows. Recovery time from glare lengthens. Level of .10 means intoxication in all states.

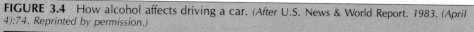

FIGURE 3.4 How alcohol affects driving a car. *(After U.S. News & World Report. 1983. (April 4):74. Reprinted by permission.)*

other differences as well. An estimated 50 percent of Orientals and 5 percent of Europeans do not produce the liver enzyme that metabolizes alcohol. The toxic effects of alcohol make these people feel dizzy, nauseated, and ill, and consequently they find the consumption of alcohol aversive. Some sons of alcoholics seem to have a higher tolerance for alcohol and are less intoxicated and less drowsy than others after drinking equal amounts of alcohol. And scientists at the University of Colorado have found that about 10 to 25 percent of individuals perform as well drunk as sober, particularly those who drink regularly. This evidence suggests that individuals metabolize alcohol differently, and that there are genes influencing how alcohol is handled by the body (Blakeslee, 1984; Franks, 1985).

Alcohol itself does not appear to be the cause of alcoholism. Paradoxically, most people can drink occasionally and sparingly throughout their lives and never succumb to alcohol abuse. One area currently under investigation is the part heredity plays in susceptibility to alcoholism. An *alcoholic* is commonly defined as someone who organizes his or her behavior around alcohol and continues to drink despite the serious problems it presents in everyday life. Researchers find that a significant number of children of alcoholic parents, when raised in a nonalcoholic household, become alcoholics. And a number of electroencephalogram (EEG) studies reveal differences between the brain waves of alcoholics and nonalcoholics as well as between those of children of alcoholics and children of nonalcoholics (Begleiter et al., 1984; Holden, 1985b). It seems that just as some people are born at risk for diabetes or hay fever, some people have a genetic vulnerability that can lead them to become alcoholics in specific environmental contexts. Yet everyone with the hereditary tendency need not become an alcoholic. Many genes are involved and there are many different roads to alcoholism. For instance, some individuals with depressive and anxiety disorders turn to alcohol as a means to deaden their unpleasant feelings (Wanberg and Horn, 1983).

Alcohol abuse is a treatable disorder (Moos and Finney, 1983). Therapists have devised many approaches to alcoholism. However, the key ingredient in successful programs seems to be the drinker's desire to stop drinking (Miller, 1985). Alcoholics Anonymous (AA) has made this principle a cornerstone of its approach. The organization was founded some fifty years ago in Akron, Ohio. Today AA claims it has nearly 631,000 members in the United States and another 400,000 in other nations. Although some therapists reject the self-help emphasis of Alcoholics Anonymous, preferring instead to focus on

(continued)

behavior modification or psychotherapy, they often urge patients to join AA as a companion program. Alcoholics Anonymous offers its members a social support system that encourages abstinence, self-validation as a person, and the sharing of experiences. It stresses that sobriety depends on alcoholics admitting that they no longer have control over alcohol and surrendering to a spiritual or personal power that is greater than themselves.

In recent years there has been a significant decline in average consumption of alcohol by Americans. The major shift has been away from distilled spirits, or liquor. In 1984, consumption of liquor was down by 14.4 percent from a decade earlier, although there was a rise of 32.6 percent in the consumption of wine and a rise of 6.1 percent in beer consumption (Shipp, 1985). A combination of greater concern for health and movements aimed at curtailing alcohol abuse has played a major role in the decrease in liquor sales. Mothers Against Drunk Driving (MADD) and the National Council on Alcoholism have conducted major educational campaigns against alcoholism, and these groups were instrumental in getting Congress to pass a bill requiring all states to raise the minimum drinking age to twenty-one or risk losing federal highway funds.

Alcohol acts by slowing down the activities of the higher brain centers. After the first few drinks, many individuals feel less tense and less inhibited than they previously did, and they experience an expansive sense of sociability and well-being. But as they ingest additional quantities, their complex mental processes are numbed, and their speech, vision, and motor coordination become impaired. In larger doses, alcohol induces sedation and sleep. For this reason it was often administered to patients about to undergo surgery before the advent of modern anesthetics. In large doses alcohol can kill by anesthetizing the lower brain, stopping breathing and heartbeat.

The barbiturates (Nembutal, Seconal, and phenobarbital) resemble alcohol in many of their effects and hence have been termed by some "solid alcohol." First synthesized at the turn of the century, barbiturates are used as an aid to relaxation and sleep. However, since they are highly addictive, physicians now prescribe them less frequently than in the past. The combination of alcohol and barbiturates has far more depressing effects than would be predicted from a summation of their individual doses. They interact. Taking barbiturates in combination with alcohol can prove fatal because the diaphragm muscles relax to such an extent that the person suffocates. Methaqualone (sold under the trade names Quaalude and Sopor) has effects similar to barbiturates and has emerged as a popular "street drug."

By virtue of the many problems that can arise from barbiturate use, some physicians prefer to prescribe tranquilizers such as Valium and Librium to alleviate their patients' anxiety and tension and to afford them relaxation. But these drugs also possess addictive properties and (like barbiturates) are made much more powerful when used with alcohol.

Narcotics such as morphine and heroin are derived from opium. They are painkilling and sleep-inducing drugs. Morphine was introduced on a large scale into American life during the Civil War. It was administered to wounded soldiers, and the men returned home addicted to the drug (they were said to be suffering from "the Army disease"). But the majority of addicts were women who had been given opiates for a myriad of complaints, including menstrual cramps, difficult childbirth, insomnia, "nervousness," and general aches and pains. In the 1890s, an even more potent narcotic—heroin—was extracted from opium and acclaimed as a "cure" for morphine addiction.

Users typically inject heroin into a vein. First-time users of heroin usually report that the drug makes them feel ill and nauseated. Only after "shooting" heroin on a number of occasions do individuals experience an ecstatic "thrill" or "rush" of pleasure that some say resembles a sexual orgasm. This sense of euphoria is followed within a few minutes by a warm, mellow, peaceful feeling—a pervasive sense of well-being. But as the euphoria wears off, the user experiences intense anxiety and a desperate preoccupation with obtaining new doses. The net result is addiction and physical dependency, matters we will consider later in the chapter.

Stimulants

Whereas depressants are "downers," stimulants are "uppers." **Stimulants** act on the brain and nervous system to increase the responsiveness of the body and to speed up its activities. Nicotine (found in tobacco) and caffeine (found in coffee, cola, and chocolate) are mild stimulants. Cocaine and amphetamines are much more powerful stimulants.

Cocaine produces a swift, surging high. It also raises the heart rate, blood pressure, and body temperature and produces sleeplessness, diminished appetite, sexual stimulation, and talkativeness. A cocaine high is short-lived, lasting only ten to thirty minutes. It is often followed by a crash marked by feelings of irritability, impatience, and depression. Traditionally, users have snorted white cocaine powder in small doses. However, more recently, an increasing number of users have taken to smoking cocaine paste, heating it and inhaling its vapers, or injecting it. Cocaine is expensive and considered by many to be the "aristocrat" or "Cadillac" of drugs—an elixir for those who live high, including entertainers, athletes, and aspiring young professionals. Considerable mystique surrounds cocaine, so that some users get high just believing that they are taking it although the substance is in fact fake cocaine (Van Dyke and Byck, 1982).

Cocaine is derived from the leaves of coca shrubs, which are native to the eastern slopes of the Andes. The Andean Indians of Ecuador, Peru, and Bolivia have chewed the leaves for at least five thousand years to combat fatigue, altitude sickness, and various ailments, and to help unhappy individuals forget their sorrows. Sigmund Freud and the fictional Sherlock Holmes used cocaine. In fact, for a time Freud, calling it a "magical substance," recommended it as a cure for digestive disorders and neuroses. And for a number of decades, cocaine was a primary ingredient of Coca-Cola. But a mounting antidrug movement led its producers to replace it with caffeine in 1903.

In the nineteenth century Coca-Cola contained cocaine, a stimulant used in small amounts to "soothe the Rattled Nerves." Today cocaine threatens to be the most widely abused drug in the United States. *(The Bettmann Archive)*

The National Institute on Drug Abuse, a federal agency, has repeatedly expressed alarm over the rapid growth in recent years in the use of cocaine. The agency disputes the widespread notion that cocaine is harmless. It and other health authorities (Lesko et al., 1982; Nicholi, 1983) find that chronic cocaine use is associated with such symptoms as weight loss, insomnia, anxiety, paranoia, and hallucination. Although users do not suffer the same agonizing withdrawal effects as do opiate users, they often experience a powerful compulsion to continue

---

stimulant: A drug that acts on the brain and nervous system to increase the responsiveness of the body and to speed up its activities.

taking it. And as highlighted by the 1982 death of the popular comedian John Belushi from an overdose of cocaine and heroin, the drug can destroy lives. Additionally, it has ruined countless marriages, destroyed careers, and wiped out fortunes.

Amphetamines are used medically in the treatment of depressive symptoms. But they have gained other uses as well (Fort and Cory, 1975). During World War II, the armed forces administered them on occasion to troops so that the men could perform their tasks for long periods without sleep. During the same period amphetamines found their way into illicit markets and were used by truck drivers on long hauls and by college students who wanted to remain awake all night to study for exams. Some physicians also have prescribed amphetamines to overweight patients to decrease their appetites (results that typically are short-lived once the patients go off the pills).

For years, amphetamines have been popular street drugs. Individuals who inject large doses are called "speed freaks." They claim that the procedure provides them with a powerful rush. When using amphetamines, speed freaks often go three to six days without sleep. Eventually, they "crash" into a long, deep sleep. They awake depressed and ready for another "run" on amphetamines to escape their "down" and get "up" once more.

Hallucinogens

Hallucinogens—so called because the main effect of these psychoactive drugs is to produce hallucinations—are found in plants that grow throughout the world (Schultes, 1976). The drugs are also called "psychedelic" ("mind-manifesting") because they demonstrate some of the ways in which the mind has the potential to function.

Among the more common hallucinogenic plants are belladonna, henbane, mandrake, datura (jimson weed), one species of morning-glory, peyote, many kinds of mushrooms, and also cannabis. While we still do not know the exact chemical effects of hallucinogens on the brain, some of them contain chemical compounds that seem to mimic the activity of certain neurotransmitters.

LSD (lysergic acid diethylamide) is one of the better known and more powerful hallucinogens. A synthetic substance, it is one hundred times stronger than psilocybin, which comes from certain mushrooms, and four thousand times stronger than mescaline, which comes from the peyote. A dose of a few millionths of a gram has a noticeable effect.

During an LSD "trip" a person can experience any number of mood states, often unusually intense and rapidly changing. The person's "set"— expectations, mood, and beliefs—and the circumstances under which he or she takes LSD can affect the experience, making it euphoric or terrifying. Perceptual hallucinations are very common with LSD. A typical hallucinatory progression begins with simple geometric forms, progresses to complex images, and then to dreamlike scenes (Siegel, 1977). The user may encounter such distortions in form that familiar objects become almost unrecognizable. A wall, for example, may seem to pulsate or breathe. The senses, too, seem to intermingle. Sounds may be "seen" and visual stimuli may be "heard." A person may experience a dissociation of the self into a being who observes and another who feels. Distortions of time, either an acceleration or a slowing down, are also common. A single stimulus may become the focus of attention for hours, being perceived as ever-changing or newly beautiful and fascinating.

Panic reactions ("bad trips") are the most common of LSD's unpleasant side effects, and they may be terrifying. Those who experience panic and later describe it often say that they felt trapped in the experience of panic and were afraid that they would never get out or that they would go mad. Panic usually arises when a person tries to ignore, change, or otherwise get rid of the effects of the drug (rather than yielding to the sensations it generates), then realizes he or she cannot. The best treatment, if the panic is not too severe, seems to be the comfort offered by friends and the security of pleasant, familiar settings. Medical attention is sometimes necessary for very intense reactions.

---

hallucinogen: A drug that often produces hallucinations.

LSD: An extremely potent psychedelic drug that produces hallucinations and distortions of perception and thought.

Another powerful hallucinogen is phencyclidine, also known as PCP, a cheap and easily produced chemical compound. On the street, PCP goes by many names, including "angel dust," "hog," "devil stick," "elephant juice," and "rocket fuel." It comes in a variety of forms, among them a white powder, pills, or colored liquids. PCP can be sniffed or swallowed, but it is commonly smoked with tobacco or marijuana. Once in the body, it accumulates in fat tissues, and thus it can remain active long after most other drugs dissipate. PCP alters users' perception of time and space, resulting in a disorienting quality in which surroundings may alternately appear crystal clear and spookily murky. In some individuals PCP produces euphoria, vivid thoughts, and hallucinations. But it may also create feelings of invincibility that alternate with paranoia, agitation, rage, and depression. Users often believe themselves impervious to pain and become heedless of consequences. Bizarre and violent behavior can ensue. The drug also has flashback effects in which psychedelic symptoms reappear weeks and months after it was taken. High doses can lead to convulsions, a suspension of sensation, muscle rigidity, and death.

Marijuana is still another hallucinogen. Its active ingredient is a complex molecule called tetrahydrocannabinol (THC), which occurs naturally in plants of the cannabis family. The plant has been grown for centuries as a psychoactive substance and as a source of hemp fiber. Marijuana is usually smoked, but it can also be cooked with food and eaten.

The effects of the drug vary somewhat from person to person and with the setting in which it is taken (Nicholi, 1983). But, in general, most sensory experiences seem greatly enhanced or augmented —music sounds fuller, colors are brighter, smells are richer, foods taste better, and sexual and other sensations are more intense. Users become elated, the world appears more meaningful, and even the most ordinary events may take on an extraordinary profundity. The sense of time is greatly distorted. A short sequence of events may seem to last for hours. Users may become so entranced with an object that they sit and stare at it for many minutes.

As many users of marijuana have discovered, however, the drug can heighten unpleasant as well as pleasant experiences. If a person is already in a frightened, unhappy, or depressed mood, the drug typically blows the negative feelings out of proportion. Consequently, the user's world becomes for a time very upsetting. In some cases, marijuana has activated psychological disturbances in people who were unstable before they used it.

In 1982, the National Academy of Sciences (1982) provided a detailed, critical review of the available scientific information about the health effects of marijuana. It found that there is no conclusive evidence that the drug produces long-term, permanent effects but that a variety of short-term reactions "justifies serious national concern." The study said that marijuana temporarily impairs motor coordination, memory, oral communication, and learning, and may trigger short-term confusion and delirium. It suggested the possibility that smoking marijuana ultimately may be linked to lung cancer and to heart and respiratory ailments, just as tobacco already has been. Chronic use decreases the number and movement of sperm, with unknown consequences for long-term male fertility. The Academy scientists said that in some cases marijuana may prove helpful in the treatment of glaucoma (and eye disorder) and in the control of the severe nausea and vomiting associated with cancer chemotherapy.

Physical and Psychological Dependence

People use psychoactive drugs for a great variety of reasons. Pleasure seeking or "fun" is certainly a compelling motive for many of them. The "thrill," "rush," or "high" associated with injecting narcotics and amphetamines or snorting cocaine provides an intrinsically rewarding experience. Drugs also offer an escape from boredom and reality. Moreover, they afford temporary relief from the physicial and mental aches and pains of life. And people may use drugs because other people expect them to do so. Peer pressures make many youths susceptible to drug use (see the box on pages 104–105). Likewise, in some American Indian societies, drugs play a socially approved and essential part in the quest for religious experiences.

The effects of a drug vary depending on the dose, the form in which the drug is taken, and the route by which it is administered (Van Dyke and Byck, 1982). The frequency of drug use is also important. The body accumulates some drugs or develops a tolerance to them. And the impact of psychoactive drugs is influenced by the expectations of the users, the social setting in which they use the drug, and the

For many young people, drug abuse begins with pressure from friends who use drugs. *(Dave Schaefer/Monkmeyer)*

history and personality of the individual user. Thus, as noted above, it is often difficult to determine just what portion of the cocaine experience is a function of the drug's biochemical properties and what portion derives from the user's expectations of a high.

Many people become physically dependent on drugs, a condition termed **addiction**. Physical dependence exists if the user of a drug develops severe withdrawal symptoms (Snyder, 1977). In the case of alcoholics, these symptoms include the shakes, convulsions, and hallucinations or *delirium tremens*. Narcotic addicts typically experience stomach cramps, diarrhea, restlessness, twitching, dilated pupils, and gooseflesh (thus the term "cold turkey"). Consequently, when the effects of a dose wear off, individuals undergo punishing withdrawal symptoms that lead them to seek relief in another dose (Dole, 1980). In this manner, they can become entrapped in drug-seeking behaviors. Addiction also commonly manifests itself in **tolerance**—increasingly higher

doses of a drug are required to produce effects that were previously produced by smaller doses.

Even in cases in which individuals are not physically hooked on a drug, they may experience a compulsive craving for it, termed **psychological dependence**. Hence, even after people have passed through the withdrawal phase and no longer experience severe physical discomfort, they still may have an overpowering desire to continue taking the drug. They come to yearn for the "high," or altered state of consciousness, as part of their daily routine. Further, the drug allows them to find temporary relief from feelings of low self-esteem, boredom, and depression. Much chronic drug use results not so much from the need for a "high" as the need to avoid the "lows." Since the drug experience is so central to the sense of well-being of these individuals, procurement and consumption of the drug become the focus of their thoughts and activities. Although long-term drug users periodically go off the drug, they continu-

---

addiction: A condition in which people are physically dependent on drugs.

tolerance: A condition in which increasingly higher doses of a drug are required to produce effects that were previously produced by smaller doses.

psychological dependence: A condition in which individuals, although not physically hooked on a drug, experience a compulsive craving for it.

Alcohol is the most widely used drug in the United States. Thanks to public campaigns, many people who abuse or are addicted to alcohol are seeking help. *(Kit Hedman/Jeroboam)*

ally return to it. A persistent disposition exists to relapse to drug use even when abstinence has been achieved and physical dependence reversed (Newman, 1983).

Many factors, operating at various levels of biochemical and psychological functioning, contribute to drug dependence. **Endorphins** (or **enkephalins**) are implicated at the physiological level. When first discovered in brain and certain other body tissues, these chemicals were called "the body's own morphine," because they have the capacity to dull pain and produce euphoric feelings. Endorphins are molecules that act as both neurotransmitters and hormones (S. H. Snyder, 1985). Apparently one of their functions is to regulate sensory information in those brain centers having to do with pain and emotional behavior. As we pointed out in Chapter 2, the nerve

cells of the brain have clusters of molecules called receptors. Opiate drugs such as morphine and heroin seek out certain of these receptors as targets, occupying the sites on neurons that normally are occupied by various types of endorphins. The drugs fit the receptors like keys fit their appropriate lock. This coupling of an opiate and a receptor changes the firing rate of neurons and contributes to the deadening of pain and to euphoric experiences. Researchers theorize that when all the receptors are occupied, the receptors send a message to the endorphin neurons that they are to stop releasing endorphins. Once the brain's natural endorphin production halts, the receptors use more and more of the opiate drug to compensate for the endorphin they are no longer receiving. When the addict stops taking the drug, the brain is suddenly left with neither morphine nor

endorphins (EN-door-fins) (enkephalins [en-KEH-fa-lins]): Chemical substances, called "the body's own morphine," that have the capacity to dull pain and produce euphoric feelings.

Drug Abuse

Over the past twenty-five years drug abuse has become a major national concern. The dimensions of the problem are enormous. Victims have included Keith Hernandez, a star first baseman, who testified in court that cocaine was "a demon in me" (Chass, 1985); John Belushi, the actor who died of a lethal combination of cocaine and heroin; Richard Pryor, the comedian who suffered nearly fatal burns when an ether and cocaine mixture exploded; and David A. Kennedy, a son of Robert F. Kennedy, who died at age twenty-eight of the combined effects of cocaine, Demerol, and Mellaril. Millions of Americans —from children in schoolyards to anesthesiologists in operating rooms, computer analysts in California's Silicon Valley and stockbrokers on Wall Street—are abusing all kinds of substances. Drug abuse is posing serious problems for the nation's businesses and schools. A Houston pharmaceutical company threw out a huge batch of contaminated products because its quality-control inspector was stoned. A high-tech West Coast company intentionally overproduced because it knew much of its output would be spoiled by spaced-out workers who snorted coke from microscope slides. And the San Onofre nuclear facility in California found it necessary to suspend twenty-one guards for suspected drug use (Brecher, 1983).

The United States had an earlier bout with drug abuse at the turn of the century (Cox, 1984). Drug use was so prevalent around 1900 that one contemporary historian called the nation "a dope fiend's paradise." Pure cocaine was freely available, found in many teas, cigarettes, chewing gum, and hundreds of patent medicines. Heroin was legal and lauded. Estimates of the number of opium and morphine addicts at the turn of the century run from 250,000 to 4 million out of a population of 80 million (roughly comparable to the share of narcotic addicts in the current population). The momentum for a crackdown on drugs began building about 1905 with an exposé of the patent-medicine industry's indiscriminate use of opium and cocaine. The first national antidrug law, the Harrison Act, was passed in 1914. It made the purchase of cocaine and narcotics illegal except through a physician's prescription. Overall, drug use was low in the general population in the intervening years and into the 1950s. The drug binge that began in the 1960s and that continues today occurred when a large population of "baby-boom" youth, a period of social turmoil, and new attitudes toward drug use coincided.

In 1962, only 4 percent of adults aged eighteen to twenty-five had ever smoked marijuana.

endorphin. This produces the symptoms of withdrawal. Under normal circumstances the body's natural endorphins do not addict, through a delicately adjusted internal feedback mechanism that regulates their rise and fall according to need, but always in natural balance (S. H. Snyder, 1977; Watkins and Mayer, 1982; Turkington, 1985).

Cocaine addiction apparently also has a chemical basis. Cocaine enhances the activity of dopamine, a neurotransmitter. Normally, when certain brain neurons are stimulated, they secrete dopamine, which crosses tiny gaps called synapses and stimulates other neurons (see Chapter 2). The neurons naturally reabsorb any excess dopamine that is released, a process termed *reuptake*. Each transmitting

neuron sends some dopamine back to the transmitting brain cell to keep its supply up for later use. But cocaine operates to block the reuptake. The dopamine remains in the synapse, where its presence brings more rapid transmission of neural signals, thus affording the user an emotional rush. With no mechanism for resupply, the nerve cells exhaust their supply of dopamine. The user experiences a sharp letdown and feels the need to take more of the drug to make up for the loss of the supply that the brain produces naturally (Milkman and Sunderwirth, 1983).

No single biochemical model seems to account for the effects of cocaine or the many other drugs that produce dependence. On the psychological level,

By 1982 the figure had risen to 64 percent; among all Americans aged twelve or older, one-third had tried marijuana. The picture is similar with respect to cocaine. Two decades earlier only a small fraction of the American population had encountered it. By 1982 some 22 million people had done so. However, except for cocaine, the last several years seem to have witnessed a decline in drug use among many segments of the population. Since 1975, University of Michigan social psychologists have conducted an annual survey of high school seniors for the National Institute on Drug Abuse (Zigli, 1985). The 1984 survey revealed that 5 percent of the nation's high-school seniors had used marijuana at least twenty times a month, down from a peak of 11 percent in 1978. Twenty-five percent reported they used marijuana occasionally, versus 37 percent in 1978. Six percent said they were users of cocaine, a relatively constant figure since 1979 (however, 16 percent reported they had tried the drug at least once). Sedative, tranquilizer, and stimulant use was also down from the peak rates of the early 1980s.

Despite a decrease in some types of drug abuse, cocaine dependence has been a growing problem in the 1980s. A surprising number of women are among the new users (Brozan, 1985b). The drug, by virtue of its image of glamour and status, has appealed mainly to middle- and upper-income women, mostly under the age of thirty-five, well educated, and involved in competitive, demanding jobs. It has also made inroads among financially comfortable homemakers who are dissatisfied with their lives. Besides having to juggle multiple roles, being a wife and mother and performing on the job, many women are rebelling against the double standard that once prohibited them from indulging in some types of behavior. Now they have access to cocaine and the income to afford it.

Drug problems have led more and more Americans to turn to a growing network of treatment programs for help (Seligman, 1984). The "getting straight" movement received a powerful impetus in 1978 when former First Lady Betty Ford announced she would enter a hospital for treatment to combat her dependency on alcohol and painkillers. Betty Ford made it acceptable, even respectable, to have a problem and deal with it. After she went public with her problems, many athletes and entertainers quickly joined the stream, including Elizabeth Taylor and Johnny Cash. The granddaddy of treatment programs is Alcholics Anonymous (AA). It has stimulated the formation of other self-help groups, such as Cocaine Anonymous. Additionally, a variety of agencies, churches, and hospitals throughout the nation now offer drug rehabilitation programs.

learning factors also come into play (see Chapter 6). People discover that alcohol, barbiturates, narcotics, tranquilizers, and various other drugs seem to reduce their tension, anxiety, and mental torment. In turn, the rewarding consequences of having taken the drug increase the probability that the behavior will be repeated. In like manner, the euphoric feelings·induced by many of the drugs reinforce their use. And individuals learn that they can avoid or escape punishing withdrawal symptoms by again resorting to the drug.

Programs for treating drug addiction and dependence typically begin with **detoxification,** in which patients are withdrawn from a drug under supervision. The aim of detoxification is to get the patients off the drug and over the hurdle associated with severe withdrawal symptoms. However, the problem of psychological dependence commonly presents the greatest difficulty. Organizations such as Alcoholics Anonymous seek to harness the powerful resources of group support to promote behaviors that are not drug dependent.

detoxification: A process in which individuals are withdrawn from a drug under professional supervision.

Some treatments use drug remedies. One of the most controversial treatments for heroin addiction is methadone maintenance. Methadone is a more benign narcotic than heroin and normally does not produce a "thrill" or "rush." Because it is dispensed inexpensively by clinics, the program presumably eliminates the need for addicts to engage in crime in order to support their habit. But critics charge that the program does not cure addiction and simply substitutes one addicting drug for another.

Treatment programs also frequently address their patients' drug-related health problems. For instance, alcoholics often suffer from *cirrhosis*, a condition in which liver cells are destroyed by alcohol and the tissue becomes scarred. And cocaine snorters commonly incur the ulceration and destruction of nasal membranes. Additionally, there is the need to identify and address the psychological and social factors that may contribute to drug use—for example, poor self-esteem, depression, monotonous work conditions, and peer pressures. Consequently, the treatment of drug addiction and dependence requires a comprehensive and rounded program.

SUMMARY

1. Consciousness is the subjective awareness that individuals have at a given time of their inner sensations, images, thoughts, and feelings and of the world about them. Over the past decade or so, psychologists have shown renewed interest in the study of consciousness. Nonetheless, they currently know more about altered states of consciousness than they know about consciousness.

2. Sleep is a state of altered consciousness characterized by its own distinctive patterns of brain activity.

   A. Recent research has linked sleep to the circadian rhythm of the body's biological clock. Many biological functions operate approximately on a 24-hour cycle. In human beings, as well as many other mammals, the circadian rhythm seems to be controlled by light.

   B. Researchers have found that sleep is not a single state. Instead, over the course of a night's sleep you pass in and out of several stages of sleep. The stage of sleep in which vivid dreams occur is called REM sleep.

   C. Some people suffer from sleep disorders. The most common is insomnia, in which the individual has difficulty falling asleep or remaining asleep.

3. Apparently everybody dreams, although most people are able to recall few if any of their dreams. Whereas dreams that occur early in the night are usually rather simple, those that occur toward morning are often enriched as sagas with many scenes.

   A. Sigmund Freud believed that no matter how simple or mundane, dreams contain clues to thoughts and desires that the dreamer is afraid to acknowledge or express in his or her waking hours. He viewed dreams as the "royal road to the unconscious."

   B. Psychologists who advance the activation-synthesis hypothesis of dreaming say that dreams result from electrical activity of the "giant cells" of the brainstem. In turn, the higher centers of the brain that control thought attempt to make sense out of this bombardment of electrical signals. Consequently, the thinking brain composes a dream that roughly fits the pattern of messages being received from the lower brain centers.

   C. Francis Crick and Graeme Mitchison set forth the reverse learning, or unlearning, hypothesis of dreaming. They contend that dreaming is a way of cleansing the brain of information we have no need to remember.

4. Hypnosis has come to occupy a respected place in psychology, and it constitutes an accepted adjunct of some therapies. It is a form of altered consciousness in which individuals become more susceptible to suggestion and experience a heightened sense of selective attention. Contemporary psychologists are pretty much in agreement that people cannot be hypnotized against their will. In the hands of competent, well-trained therapists, hypnosis has proven itself a valuable tool. In particular, hypnotic suggestion has found clinical application as a weapon against pain.

5. Meditation is a state of consciousness involving high levels of concentration—a drug-free "high" for many people. Experienced meditators are able to achieve a high state of relaxation with greatly reduced anxiety.

6. Biofeedback involves learning conscious control of one's physiological state with the help of monitoring devices that provide feedback about bodily processes.

7. Hallucinations—sensations or perceptions that have no actual external cause—may occur during drug states, after sleep deprivation, or under sensory deprivation, among various other conditions.

8. Psychologists find that individuals who are deprived of normal sensory stimulation over extended periods of time become more susceptible to hallucinations and related experiences. Prolonged exposure to monotony produces unhealthy outcomes.

9. Human beings have long used drugs to alter their states of consciousness. Psychologists commonly make three broad divisions among psychoactive drugs. Depressants are drugs that act on the brain and nervous system to reduce the responsiveness of the body and to slow its activities. Stimulants have the opposite impact. And hallucinogens have as their main effect the production of hallucinations.

10. Many people become physically dependent on drugs, a condition termed addiction. Physical dependence exists if the user of a drug develops severe withdrawal symptoms. Even in cases in which individuals are not physically hooked on a drug, they may experience a compulsive craving for it, which is called psychological dependence.

KEY TERMS

addiction (p. 102)
age regression (p. 83)
altered states of
  consciousness (p. 73)
apnea (p. 77)
biofeedback (p. 87)
circadian rhythm (p. 74)
consciousness (p. 72)
depressant (p. 93)
detoxification (p. 105)

endorphins (enkephalins) (p. 103)
hallucination (p. 90)
hallucinogen (p. 100)
hypnosis (p. 81)
insomnia (p. 76)
LSD (p. 100)
meditation (p. 85)
metacognition (p. 72)
narcolepsy (p. 77)

posthypnotic amnesia (p. 83)
posthypnotic suggestion (p. 83)
psychoactive drug (p. 92)
psychological dependence (p. 102)
rapid-eye-movement (REM) sleep (p. 76)
stimulant (p. 99)
tolerance (p. 102)

SUGGESTED READINGS

CASTENEDA, CARLOS. 1981. *The Eagle's Gift.* New York: Simon & Schuster. A description of the author's continuing efforts to learn to think in a new way, to move outside the old patterns of thought learned in his own culture.

DEMENT, WILLIAM. 1978. *Some Must Watch While Some Must Sleep.* New York: Norton. A brief, readable account of what is known about sleep and dreaming by one of the pioneers in modern dream research. Gives special attention to the relationship between sleep and psychological disorders.

FOULKES, DAVID. 1985. *Dreaming: A Cognitive-Psychological Analysis.* Hillsdale, N.J.: Erlbaum. A concise summary of the findings of empirical dream psychology that interprets those findings from a cognitive-psychological perspective.

HOLDEN, CONSTANCE. 1985. Genes, personality and alcoholism. *Psychology Today,* 19 (January):38–39. A discussion of familial alcoholism and alcoholics with antisocial personality; considers whether there is an inherited vulnerability to alcoholism.

ORNSTEIN, ROBERT. 1977. *The Psychology of Consciousness.* 2nd ed. New York: Harcourt Brace Jovanovich. An exploration of the idea that humans have two modes of consciousness, one in each brain hemisphere. Among the phenomena he discusses are meditation and biofeedback.

RAY, OAKLEY. 1978. *Drugs, Society, and Human Behavior.* St. Louis: Mosby. A lucid, lively, and thorough presentation of drug research and the impact of "recreational" drugs on society.

ROSE, STEVEN. 1976. *The Conscious Brain.* New York: Vintage. Very readable book that discusses a variety of topics, including the brain as a system, the evolution of consciousness, child and adult brains, and sleep.

Wayne Thiebaud, *Confections*, 1962.

4
Motivation and Emotion

Mark David McKee is a junior majoring in political science at the University of Kansas. He is also president of two companies that he founded. One is Pyramid Pizza, a franchise that supplies pizza to college students on three campuses. In 1985 the firm earned $700,000 in sales revenues. The other is Waddles Active Wear, a fashion-design company that specializes in Hawaiian clothing. "I never wanted to work for anyone else," he says, "and I don't think I could start now. I'd rather be in charge of my own destiny. My goal is to be a millionaire by the time I am twenty-five" (*New York Times*, 1985:21). Politics also excites McKee, who hopes to have a political career as well.

Bobby Kotick, a junior at the University of Michigan, has had difficulty settling on a major. But he has found a creative outlet in the Arktronics Corporation, a computer software company he founded with his friend Howard Marks. Kotick handles the firm's public relations and promotes its products. Marks designs the software. Kotick says, "This business is the most important thing to us" (*New York Times*, 1985:21). Over the past three years, they have sold their software to a variety of computer companies, including Apple and Commodore. Their 1985 gross revenues were about $2 million. Kotick has not been reluctant to ask more experienced business executives for advice, including those with Apple Computer. Steven Jobs, former president of the same company, has been Kotick's inspiration.

Maureen Lennon is a senior at UCLA and the founding director of the UCLA Entrepreneurs Association. She has found it difficult to convince men of her seriousness. "When people walk in and see a woman leading the meeting, they start gravitating to the men. They call the men and ask them the questions" (*New York Times*, 1985:21). Lennon indicates that she knows of other women who want to start their own companies but are finding campus business associations male-dominated. While men have found their entrepreneurial heroes in Steven Jobs, Andrew Carnegie, and other males, Lennon says it is her mother who inspires her: "She is incredible. She helped me start the organization. She stood behind me."

What sets McKee, Kotick, and Lennon apart from the other students on their campuses? Or are they indeed different? Is an achievement drive a major motivating force in their lives? Does a desire to accumulate money lead them to undertake new business ventures? Are they excited by new challenges? Do they have self-actualization needs? Are they propelled by a desire to acquire new skills? In sum, what leads people to enter into and sustain given lines of activity? And what feelings are associated with their decisions and activities?

Like most people, you like to know the causes of behavior. You are interested in what motivates people to act in the way they do. **Motivation** entails those inner states and processes that arouse, direct, and sustain activity. When you encounter active, moving, and energized organisms, you commonly assume that their behavior is focused. You infer that they are pursuing some goal—such as making money, securing food, alleviating thirst, finding a mate, or avoiding pain. Of course you never really know whether your inferences are correct. Like consciousness, motivation is something that you never directly observe. Rather, you observe people's behavior and the environment in which the behavior takes place. On the basis of these observations, you arrive at certain conclusions regarding their motivations (Mook, 1986).

THE ROOTS OF MOTIVATIONAL PSYCHOLOGY

Various notions and theories about motivation have constituted a central element of psychology. One of the earliest ideas was that of *instincts*. An instinct is an inherited disposition to think, feel, or act in a particular way. The psychologist William Mc-Dougall (1908) was an influential proponent of instinct theory. He began by listing twelve instincts, a number that he later increased to eighteen. Among the instincts outlined by McDougall were flight, repulsion, curiosity, pugnacity, self-abasement, self-assertion, reproduction, gregariousness, acquisition, and parental care. However, other psychologists also postulated additional instincts and by the 1920s several thousand instincts were listed in the psychological literature. The resulting confusion fueled considerable controversy, and soon the concept of instinct acquired an exceedingly poor scientific reputation. Moreover, instinct theory portrayed the organism as "hardwired" and biologically "programmed" for given behaviors, neglecting to analyze the interaction between nature and nurture in fashioning what we say and do (Whalen and Simon, 1984).

Drives and Incentives

As the instinct concept fell into disrepute, psychologists sought some alternative to it. One of these new proposals was the notion of drive, set forth by Robert S. Woodworth (1918). Like other mechanists, Woodworth viewed the human organism as modeled after a machine (Bolles, 1975). And in the manner of any other machine, it requires some fuel or motive force to get it to operate. Viewed from this perspective, a **drive** is a mechanism that goads an organism into action. It rests on the assumption that such "states" as hunger and thirst are unpleasant, and the organism will take steps to remove them.

Many psychologists distinguish between a drive and a need (Ferguson, 1976). **Needs** are those things that an organism requires if it is to survive or function in a reasonably healthy manner. For instance, a lack of food produces a physiological need for nutrients, and a lack of water produces a physiological need for liquids. Through evolutionary processes, physiological needs have become biochemically translated into psychological drives. Considered in

---

motivation: Those inner states and processes that arouse, direct, and sustain activity.

drive: A mechanism that goads an organism into action.

need: Something that an organism requires if it is to survive or function in a reasonably healthy manner.

An array of delectable food can overcome most people's resistance to eating, even if they are not very hungry. Environmental cues induce us to eat when we are not physiologically in need of food. *(Dan McCoy/Rainbow)*

this fashion, a drive is the psychological mechanism that incites the organism to meet a physiological need—such as the need to secure food or water. It is an internal tension that the organism experiences as discomfort and that induces the organism to pursue some goal (food or water).

The drive concept is closely associated with various drive-reduction theories. Basic to **drive-reduction theories** is the notion that when a drive is aroused, you are impelled to undertake those behaviors that in the past reduced the drive. For instance, you can reduce the hunger drive by eating and the thirst drive by consuming liquids (Hull, 1952).

Closely linked to drive-reduction processes is *homeostasis*, the process by which your body's adap-

tive mechanisms maintain a more or less stable existence in an unstable environment (see Chapter 2). These mechanisms operate to elevate or lower blood temperature, blood pressure, and other vital states in accordance with certain "ideal" levels. When internal or external events cause your body to deviate from these ideal levels, homeostatic reactions restore the steady state or balance. Consequently, drives play a critical part in motivating you to engage in those activities that contribute to the maintenance of homeostasis.

The drive concept was pretty much unquestioned until 1949, when Donald O. Hebb suggested that behavior is something more than activity prodded by internal forces (Bolles, 1975). Consider hunger. At

drive-reduction theory: The notion that when a drive is aroused, an organism is impelled to undertake those behaviors which in the past served to reduce the drive.

various times you have undoubtedly thought to yourself, "I'm starved." You then proceeded to prepare or purchase a snack. But at other times you are not "hungry." Indeed, you may feel somewhat "full" and even "bloated." But then a friend offers you a slice of pizza, some popcorn, or a scoop of ice cream. And you cannot resist. Why? Environmental cues entice you to eat. Perhaps you define the snack as a "treat," or perhaps you feel it necessary to be "a good sport" and join your friend in "just a little bite."

Psychologists term these types of external forces that instigate goal-related activity **incentives.** Whereas drives "push" organisms to act, incentives "pull" organisms into action. Hence, whereas drives originate from internal needs, incentives derive from external factors. Typically, behavior such as eating is a joint product of internal drives and external incentives. For instance, given equal need states, you will eat more steak than spinach if you consider steak to be a "good-tasting" food and spinach to be a "bad-tasting" food. In fact, you may even prefer to go hungry rather than cook and eat the protein-rich insects in your yard because you view them as inedible and repugnant. (The American belief that insects are not suitable for food is quite similar to the Islamic and Jewish belief that pork is unfit for consumption. Yet in many societies of the world, certain insects are considered to be delicacies.) People throughout the world reject some potential foods because they believe they taste bad (although they usually have never tasted them) and are offensive in odor and appearance (although the substance may be a nutritious food source). Likewise, food preferences and attitudes vary from one family to another (Pelchat and Rozin, 1982; Rozin, Fallow, and Mandell, 1984).

Drive-reduction theorists have typically assumed that organisms seek to reduce tension. Unquestionably the position has considerable merit, but there are exceptions to it. As pointed out in Chapter 3, Hebb has demonstrated through his sensory-deprivation experiments that there is an *optimal level of arousal* that an organism requires if it is to function well. When an organism's arousal level falls too low, it seeks stimulation. Conversely, should the organism's arousal level rise too high, it seeks to lower the stimulating aspects of its environment. Of course people differ in their susceptibility to stimulation (Wilson and Daly, 1985). At the one extreme are those who seem to need a good deal of excitement, including daredevils, mountain climbers, and many delinquents. At the other extreme are those who feel so overwhelmed by the usual stimulation of everyday life that they devote themselves to avoiding additional stress, risk, or adventure.

Traditional drive-reduction theories also have difficulty explaining risk taking as well as other tension-producing behaviors. Race-track drivers and skydivers yearn for the speedway or the parachuting experience. Whereas these people first feared the experience, they eventually come to crave the excitement. Richard L. Solomon and Robert Corbit (1974) explain these behaviors by their *opponent process theory,* in which thrill seeking builds its own acquired motivation. Over time, intense exhilaration comes to replace intense terror. Moreover, the euphoric effects are strengthened, thereby psychologically "hooking" the individual.

In recent years many old issues like the proper definitions of motivation and instinct have given way to new concerns. Increasingly, psychologists are turning their attention from motivation per se to "motivated behaviors." Accordingly, rather than studying hunger, thirst, the sex drive, or fear, they are investigating ingestion, mating, and flight. Likewise, twenty-five years ago psychologists usually limited their focus to the location in the brain of neural centers that govern motivated behaviors. Today they recognize that the brain is attached to the rest of the body. The activities and secretions of these organs play a vital part in the control and regulation of behavior. In sum, psychologists are seeing their task as one of understanding the integrated operation and functioning of the organism (Whalen and Simon, 1984). Abraham Maslow (1968, 1970) was a leading pioneer in this endeavor.

Maslow's Hierarchy of Needs

Any number of psychologists have attempted to identify and arrange human **motives** (drives and

---

incentive: An external force that instigates goal-related activity.
motives: Drives and incentives.

Physically terrifying experiences, such as skydiving, can become thrilling experiences when the initial terror of jumping into space is replaced by the exhilaration of safe landings on subsequent jumps. This transformation of emotional response is explained by opponent process theory. *(L. L. T. Rhodes/Taurus)*

incentives) in some systematic fashion. One of the most intriguing and popular approaches is that proposed by Abraham Maslow (1968, 1970), one of the founders of humanistic psychology (see Chapter 13). He has ordered human needs in a hierarchy, with basic survival needs ranked toward the bottom in a foundation position and self-actualizing needs ranked toward the top. Maslow maintains that satisfied needs do not motivate. Consequently, individuals proceed through the hierarchy in a sequential manner. As they satisfy one set of needs, the next higher set is activated and comes to occupy the focus of their attention.

As shown in Figure 4.1, Maslow classifies human needs in terms of three broad levels and five sets. The first level in the hierarchy is made up of **fundamental needs,** which include physiological and safety needs. The most basic and powerful needs are physiological and include all the primary drives that seem to be governed by homeostasis. These needs typically take priority over needs higher up in the hierarchy. For instance, if you are hungry, most of your activities will be motivated by the drive to acquire food, and you will not be able to function on a higher level. The next set of fundamental needs is for safety. When your physiological needs (the first order) are reasonably well satisfied, safety needs emerge as the preponderant motivating force.

The second level in Maslow's hierarchy consists of **psychological needs:** the need to belong and to give and receive love, and the need to acquire esteem through competence and achievement. Maslow suggests that these needs function in much the same way that biological needs do, and that they can be filled only by an outside source. A lack of love or esteem probably makes you anxious and tense. Your behavior then acquires a driven quality. You may engage in random, desperate, and sometimes neurotic or maladaptive activities to ease the tensions. Unless these needs are satisfied, you will be unable to move on. Most of your behavior will be motivated by unfulfilled psychological needs. Thus an unusually intelligent person, who does not feel loved may avoid success in the hope of being accepted as one of the crowd.

Self-actualizing needs are at the top of Maslow's hierarchy. These needs may include the pursuit of knowledge and beauty, or whatever else is required for the realization of your unique potential. Maslow believes that although relatively few people reach this level, everyone has self-actualizing needs. They provide a sense of self-worth and self-respect. In order to be self-actualized, you must be well adjusted

---

fundamental needs: In Maslow's hierarchy-of-needs theory, the needs to satisfy biological drives and to feel safe.

psychological needs: In Maslow's hierarchy-of-needs theory, an individual's need to belong and to give and receive love and to acquire esteem through his or her competence and achievement.

self-actualizing needs: The top of Maslow's hierarchy of needs. These include the pursuit of knowledge and beauty, or whatever else is required for the realization of one's unique potential.

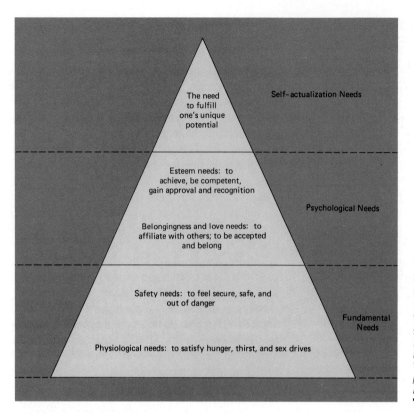

FIGURE 4.1 Maslow's hierarchy of needs. According to Maslow, it is only after satisfying the lower levels of needs that a person is free to progress to the ultimate need of self-actualization. *(After Abraham H. Maslow. 1970. Self-actualizing people. In Motivation and Personality. 2nd ed. New York: Harper & Row. Reprinted by permission of Harper & Row, Publishers, Inc.)*

and self-fulfilled. But as is true of other needs in the hierarchy, meeting your self-actualizing needs, and hence having potential for human growth, depends on your meeting prior lower-level needs. Maslow thus has added to motivation theory the idea that some needs take precedence over others and the suggestion that achieving one level of satisfaction releases new needs and motivations.

However, care must be exercised in the literal application of Maslow's scheme. Many people have risen from circumstances of deprivation in physiological, safety, and belongingness needs to realize great talent and self-actualization. And there are also those individuals—Henry Thoreau is an example—who have retreated to less hospitable settings and sacrificed lower-level needs in a search for self-fulfillment. (We discuss Maslow's theory in more detail in Chapter 13.)

MOTIVATION AND BIOLOGY

Thus far we have noted that there are several motivated behaviors, including those associated with

hunger and thirst, that depend in large part on biological processes. Although environmental factors play an important part in channeling these behaviors, biochemical processes seem to assume a critical role in their activation and regulation. Accordingly, let us take a closer look at the biological basis of motivation.

Hunger

Although eating is essentially an intermittent activity, hunger provides a powerful impetus to behavior. People who have gone without food for an extended period of time report that they become preoccupied with thoughts about food—its taste, aroma, texture, preparation, and consumption.

More than eighty years ago, Walter B. Cannon and A. L. Washburn (1912) sought a scientific explanation for hunger. They studied the rhythmic contractions of the stomach through an experimental procedure in which Washburn would swallow a balloon with a tube attached to it. Cannon then used the tube to fill the balloon with air and measured the contractions of Washburn's stomach with a record-

In Maslow's theory self-actualization can mean different things to different people. Some seek self-actualization in social service; other people find satisfaction in solitude and nature. *(Martin Rogers/Woodfin Camp & Associates)*

ing device. The researchers discovered that when Washburn's stomach contracted, he experienced "hunger pains." This finding led Cannon and Washburn to conclude that stomach contractions cause hunger.

However, there is much more to hunger than merely the feeling of discomfort in the stomach. If hunger were simply "in the stomach," then people who have had their stomachs removed surgically in ulcer or cancer operations would never feel hungry. But they continue to experience hunger sensations (Janowitz, 1967). This evidence suggests that cues from the stomach play only a secondary role in influencing hunger sensations and regulating eating behavior.

Research in the 1950s and 1960s focused on the regulatory role of the hypothalamus in hunger and

eating. Recall from Chapter 2 that the hypothalamus is a small, closely packed structure of neurons, located at the base of the brain, that regulates a great many bodily functions. Not surprisingly, researchers have also implicated the hypothalamus in those processes that tell people when they need to eat and when to stop eating.

If the portion of the hypothalamus called the **lateral hypothalamus (LH)** is stimulated with electrodes, a laboratory animal will begin eating, even if it has just finished a large meal. Conversely, if the LH is removed surgically, an animal will stop eating and eventually die of starvation if it is not fed artificially. Thus the LH provides the "go" signals: it tells you to eat (Hoebel and Teitelbaum, 1962).

If a different portion of the hypothalamus called the **ventromedial hypothalamus (VMH)** is stimulat-

---

lateral hypothalamus (hi-po-THAL-uh-muss) (LH): The part of the hypothalamus that is believed to produce hunger signals.

ventromedial hypothalamus (VMH): The part of the hypothalamus that is believed to produce feelings of fullness, as opposed to hunger, and to cause one to stop eating.

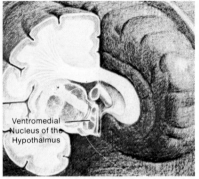

Ventromedial
Nucleus of the
Hypothalmus

FIGURE 4.2 (a) A rat that became obese after its ventromedial hypothalamus was removed. (b) A drawing showing the part of the human brain that corresponds to the part lesioned in the rat. The view is from the front of the brain, with one half shown in cross section *(Left: Courtesy, Neal Miller)*

ed, an animal will slow down or stop eating altogether, even if it has been kept from food for a long period (Hetherington and Ranson, 1940). However, if the VMH is removed, the animal will have an increased appetite and in time become obese (see Figure 4.2). This outcome indicates that the VMH provides a "stop" signal: it tells you when you have had enough food. The lateral hypothalamus and the ventromedial hypothalamus operate in balance: an increase in the firing rate of the neurons in the lateral hypothalamus is typically associated with a decrease in the firing rate of the neurons in the ventromedial hypothalamus, and vice versa (Oomura et al., 1967; Van Atta and Sutin, 1971).

Just how the hypothalamus goes about regulating eating patterns is not entirely clear. We do know that the hypothalamus seems to keep a close watch on the fat content of the body (Nisbett, 1972; Bennett and Gurin, 1982). One way the hypothalamus may learn about the state of the body's fat is through hormonal messages. By itself, the fat level cannot be interpreted. However, in conjunction with other input, such as the blood level of insulin, the hypothalamus may be able to glean information concerning the body's fat reserves. (*Insulin*, a hormone, promotes the storage of calories as fat.)

Another way the hypothalamus may learn about the fat content of the body is through its link to the liver via the vagus nerve (Novin, Gonzalez, and Sanderson, 1976). Should this be the case, the input to the hypothalamus is neural and not a bloodborne substance. However, whether the signal is hormonal

or neural is unclear at this point (Faust, Johnson, and Hirsch, 1977). Although the hypothalamus plays a major role in orchestrating feeding and satiety signals, it does not act alone. Other parts of the brain and outlying nervous system, as well as substances within the digestive tract and the characteristics of the food itself, combine to influence our appetite and eating behavior. The boxed insert on pages 118–120 provides additional information on many of these matters.

In search for the other factors that influence hunger, physiologists have investigated the changes people encounter in the taste and aroma of a food as they eat it. For instance, Michael Cabanac (1971) found that hungry individuals judge sweet-tasting and sweet-smelling food as "pleasant." But once they have consumed a sweet substance and feel "full," they judge the taste and aroma to be "unpleasant." You too have probably noticed that the first bite of food tastes better than the last. This mechanism initially encourages you to eat heartily but later discourages you from overeating. It assists your body in maintaining internal homeostasis by regulating your food intake. Very likely you have discovered that you can partially overcome the decline in your appetite as you increase the consumption of one food by switching to another food.

Taste and smell also contribute to the experience of hunger and to eating. They assist digestion by stimulating the flow of saliva, the secretion of various digestive enzymes, and the rhythmic contractions of the stomach and intestines. Indeed, the mere sight of a favorite food seems to activate the firing of neurons in those areas of the brain that control feeding (Rolls, Burton, and Mora, 1976). Thus when squirrel monkeys are shown peanuts, a favorite food, their neutronal responses quicken, whereas their responses remain unchanged when they are shown an egg, a disliked food.

Clearly it is an oversimplification to view food-seeking as merely "driven" behavior. It is behavior that is also "sought" because it is pleasure producing. Work by James Olds and others (Olds and Milner, 1954; Olds, 1958) has shown that there are several sites in the brain that, when electrically stimulated, seem to produce pleasurable sensations. Olds found that rats would press a lever over two thousand times an hour to receive electrical stimulation in certain areas of the hypothalamus. They preferred brain stimulation to eating, even when starving. Indeed, the rats would walk across an electrified grid floor that gave them shocks to reach the lever. Conceivably, neurotransmitters, particularly endorphins, act at these sites in the brain (Paul, Hulihan-Giblin, and Skolnick, 1982) (see Chapters 2 and 3). Drugs known to interfere with the functions of various neurotransmitters affect the rate at which a rat will press a lever when its brain is electrically stimulated; these same drugs affect mood in human beings and are administered to control anxiety and psychotic behavior (Routtenberg, 1978; Snyder, 1985). Rewards in everyday life, including food, drink, and sex, may be related to these brain centers. It is possible that electrical stimulation results in the release of neurotransmitters that customarily signal food (Olds and Fobes, 1981). However, psychologists are not as yet in full agreement on the mechanisms underlying brain-stimulation behaviors (Frank and Stutz, 1984).

Thirst

As with food intake, the body requires a continuous monitoring and regulation of its fluid levels in order to survive. But there is an important difference between the hunger and thirst systems. The mechanisms that control food intake operate within the context of substantial capacities for fat storage. But the absence of comparable storage reserves for fluids means that one can survive without water for only a few days.

The body has a variety of detectors for determining whether it needs fluid (Adolph, Barker, and Hoy, 1954; Epstein, 1960, 1982). Both the hypothalamus and the kidneys monitor fluid levels and contribute to thirst arousal (again demonstrating the link between the brain and the rest of the body in producing motivated behaviors). One indication that the body requires additional liquid is a falling of the ratio of water to salts in the bloodstream. Thus an organism experiences thirst either from decreased fluid or from increased concentrations of salt. For instance, the injection of salt solutions into the blood brings about drinking in amounts roughly proportional to the solution's concentration (Holmes and Gregersen, 1950). Bartenders understand this principle. In order to encourage their customers to buy drinks to quench their thirst, they commonly provide them with free salted pretzels, nuts, and potato chips.

Osmoreceptors in the hypothalamus are key mechanisms for monitoring low water and high sodium levels. When the receptor neurons begin dehydrating, they quicken their rate of firing (Ishikawa, Koizumi, and Brooks, 1966; Epstein, 1982). These messages reach the pituitary gland, which in turn secretes and releases *antidiuretic hormone (ADH)*. This hormone tells the kidneys to produce less urine and conserve water. Simultaneously, the osmoreceptors signal the fluid centers of the brain to activate thirst sensations. As the organism consumes water, the salinity of the blood decreases, the drinking stops, and water retention is lowered. All the while, receptors located elsewhere—particularly on some small blood vessels—monitor blood pressure as a means of detecting the flow of water. When they detect a decline in the volume of the blood, they send appropriate messages to the brain (Kalat, 1981).

In sum, there are at least two bodily changes that activate drinking: cellular dehydration and a drop in the volume of fluid in the vascular system. These processes operate as sensors that register the actual

---

osmoreceptors (OZ-moh-ree-SEP-ters): Receptors in the hypothalamus that monitor water and salt levels.

Obesity and Eating Disorders

An estimated 40 million Americans weigh at least 20 percent more than health experts say they should. In a society in which slimness is equated with beauty, health, and desirability and in which cultural stereotypes proclaim that "fat is ugly," obese people confront daily episodes of prejudice and discrimination. Moreover, obesity is associated with medical problems and lower life expectancy. Not surprisingly, many Americans are obsessed with their weight. A survey of UCLA students found that 27.3 percent of the women and 5.8 percent of the men said they were terrified of being fat (Lang, 1985).

Theories of obesity abound, in part reflecting the large number of factors that contribute to a person's weight. One fact nonetheless stands out above others. Adults who lose weight have difficulty maintaining the loss. And skinny people who seek to gain weight by overeating often find they are fighting a losing battle (Bennett and Gurin, 1982; Kolata, 1985).

A mounting body of data suggests that there may be a "normal" weight *range* for each individual. A particularly significant study was undertaken toward the close of World War II at the University of Minnesota by the epidemiologist Ancel Keys (1950). Keys hoped his research would provide useful information for rehabilitating the starved populations of war zones. The volunteers were thirty-six healthy young men who agreed to be placed on a diet consisting of half their usual caloric intake.

Although the men were always hungry, they were initially cheerful. Some even expressed euphoric highs, but these were invariably followed by the blues. Over time the men lost weight, most of it from their fat stores. By the end of six months, the subjects had become lethargic, irritable, and quarrelsome. They were then placed on a weight restoration program. Although the men proceeded to gain weight, they remained quite miserable. Their ravenous appetites could not be appeased even by large daily excesses of food. Only when the men returned to their "normal" weights and recovered their origi-

nal amounts of fat did their interest in food return to what it had been before the experiment began.

Ethan A. Sims and colleagues (1968) reversed Keys's procedures in an overeating experiment at Vermont State Prison. Here prisoner-volunteers agreed to commit themselves to a 25 percent weight gain. In order to reach their goal, the men had to double their food intake. Except for two men who had family histories of obesity and diabetes, the prisoners had difficulty putting on weight and then retaining it. To stay at the higher weight level, they had to overeat an average of two thousand extra calories a day, not simply the few hundred that would theoretically be required of them. Once the experiment was over, the men readily lost the excess weight. They also regained their usual activity levels, having become lethargic and apathetic at the peak of their obesity. This evidence suggests that each individual may have an optimal range for both weight and activity.

The psychologist Richard Nisbett (1972) believes that each person has a control system—a kind of fat thermostat—that dictates how much fat he or she should carry. Like a thermostat set to maintain a given temperature, the fat control system has its own baseline or "set-point." Whenever a person's weight goes below his or her ideal "set-point," the person tends to gain weight; whenever it goes above it, the person tends to lose weight. Some people seem to be biologically programed to be slender and others to be obese. For obese people, Nisbett says (1972:453), it is "as if their hunger switch were stuck in the 'on' position." According to this view, the body reacts to stringent dieting as though starvation were setting in. Dieters begin to experience the same unpleasant symptoms that were experienced by the subjects in Keys's study. Their bodies seem to rebel and cry out for food.

A person's "set-point" is influenced by a variety of factors, including genetic tendencies and early feeding patterns. People with overweight parents are much more likely to be overweight themselves than are other individuals. Further, the early overfeeding of children may lead them to develop a permanent excess of fat cells. Consequently, they go through life with an unusually large storehouse of fat cells waiting to be filled (Hirsch and Knittle, 1970). Unfortunately, it also seems that obese people may be primed so that the fatter they are, the fatter they become. This unhappy circumstance occurs because the larger a fat cell gets, the greater is its capacity to store fat and enlarge even more (Rodin, 1981; Kolata, 1985).

It has long been assumed that people are obese because they eat abnormally large amounts of food. Yet several decades of research have shown that a great many obese individuals eat no more than lean individuals do. Instead, it seems that obese people burn up calories less vigorously than their lean counterparts. In other words, obese persons may be more "fuel efficient" than are thin people. But rather than getting more miles per gallon, they end up with more pounds per calorie. Such a mechanism would provide a strong genetic advantage for people who lived in societies where famine was periodic and where a need existed for the body to be efficient in metabolizing food (DeLuise, Blackburn, and Flier, 1980).

New research also suggests that overweight people may eat too much because of an urge to change the way they feel, not because they are hungry. Many obese people crave carbohydrates —foods containing sugar or starch. Apparently they gobble snacks because these foods increase the level of serotonin in their brains. Serotonin is a neurotransmitter that relaxes us and raises our spirits. In contrast, foods high in protein lower the serotonin level. Another chemical messenger that affects eating is cholecystokinin. It was first found in the intestines and later discovered throughout the nervous system. When cholecystokinin is injected into the brain, animals stop eating, indicating that the substance affects satiety (Whalen and Simon, 1984). This appetite inhibitor may be what causes patients with anorexia nervosa and depression to lose their appetites.

Obese people may also differ from their lean counterparts in psychological ways. The psychologist Stanley Schachter (1971) finds that external cues have an especially strong effect on obese people even when they are not "hungry" (not experiencing hunger pangs). They are unusually sensitive to such things as the sight, aroma, taste, and attractiveness of food and the knowledge that it is mealtime. People of normal weight depend primarily on internal cues to tell them when they are hungry. For instance, in one study by Lee Ross (1974), overweight people ate twice as many cashews when the nuts were illuminated under bright light as they did when the light was dimmed. In contrast, people of normal weight ate about the same number of cashews regardless of how well the nuts were lighted. In brief, it seems that the obese respond to the prominence or availability of food rather than to internal, physical demands for it.

However, research over the past decade or so has shown that the distinction between an internal and an external orientation vastly oversimplifies the differences between overweight and normal-weight people (Rodin, 1978, 1981; Herman, Olmsted, and Polivy, 1983). Indeed, a number of psychologists have suggested that obese people may be unusually sensitized to food cues simply because they are more likely to be dieters and thus constantly compelled to exercise conscious restraint in relation to food (Herman and Polivy, 1975; Hibscher and Herman, 1977). Thus the continuous vigilance required of dieters may actually contribute to their ultimate doom.

In sum, psychologists are increasingly coming to the conclusion that there are different kinds of obesity with different causes. Even so, the fact remains that there are but two ways to lose weight: either by reducing food intake or by increasing the expenditure of calories through exercise. A good diet is characterized by a quantitatively reduced but qualitatively balanced daily intake and should be supplemented with daily exercise. Moreover, it is essential that these changes be integrated within the patterns of

(continued)

one's everyday life. Finally, it is worth remembering that much remains to be done in combating prejudice and discrimination directed toward obese individuals. The obese encounter a good many hardships, including job discrimination, social exclusion, inability to purchase health and life insurance, unsympathetic treatment by medical personnel, difficulty acquiring attractive clothes, and public ridicule and shaming (Archer, 1985).

The American preoccupation with slenderness has also contributed to two rapidly spreading eating disorders that may affect as many as 5 to 10 percent of American adolescent girls and young women (Herzog and Copeland, 1985). One is *anorexia nervosa*, a syndrome in which individuals have a severely distorted image of their own bodies as obese and willfully suppress their appetite, resulting in self-starvation. Particularly vulnerable are ballet dancers, gymnasts, and models. In some cases a woman begins dieting when she is overweight, then finds herself unable to stop (Polivy and Herman, 1985). The victims have a fierce desire to diet; have a morbid terror of having any fat on their bodies; and deny that they are thin or ill, although their self-induced starvation reduces them to the point where they resemble victims of Nazi concentration camps. Simultaneously, many anorexics long for food and even have secret binges of eating (often interrupted by self-induced vomiting). Approximately two-thirds of anorexic victims recover or improve, with one-third remaining chronically ill or dying of the disorder. The pop singer Karen Carpenter struggled against anorexia nervosa for years, and doctors said it contributed to her death in 1982 from cardiac arrest (starvation weakens the heart muscles). Most authorities now recognize that anorexia nervosa usually has multiple causes and that it requires a combination of treatment strategies.

Another disorder is *bulimia* (also termed the *binge-purge syndrome*). It is a syndrome characterized by repeated episodes of binging, particularly on high-calorie foods like candy bars and ice cream. The binge is followed by an attempt to get rid of the food through self-induced vomiting, taking laxatives or diuretics, chewing and spitting out food, or fasting (Schlesier-Stropp, 1983; Mitchell et al., 1985). Like anorexics, bulimics have an obsessive fear of becoming fat. However, bulimics are typically within normal weight range and have healthy, outgoing appearances, whereas anorexics are skeletally thin. Like anorexia nervosa, bulimia calls for treatment. Some researchers believe that hereditary depressive disorders may underlie some forms of both syndromes, and indeed some patients respond to antidepressant medication (Pope and Judson, 1984; Herzog and Copeland, 1985).

or impending depletion of body water. In turn, on the basis of the messages it receives, the brain acts to instruct the effector systems so that water-seeking occurs (see Chapter 2). When all these processes are functioning in concert, we are said to be thirsty.

Of course, social factors also play a part in the experience of thirst and the consumption of fluids. For instance, as noted in Chapter 3, cultural conventions mandate drinking coffee for breakfast, taking a "coffee break," and consuming alcoholic beverages or soft drinks with caffeine on social occasions.

Sex

When you experience hunger and thirst sensations, you are motivated to engage in behaviors that contribute to your own survival. A quite different outcome underlies your sexual urges. These wants ensure that reproduction occurs and that the species survives. Likewise, you do not typically view photographs or movies with the expectation that they will make you hungry or thirsty. Yet it would not be surprising if you periodically seek out enticing materials to stimulate your sexual interest. Whereas eating and drinking reduce drives by correcting body deficits and restoring energy, sexual motivation is often directed as much toward drive arousal as toward drive reduction.

Human sexuality differs from that of lower animals in that so much of human sexuality is learned and activated within a social context. The degree to which hormonal control governs sexual and gender

Thirst is a powerful physiological motivator. Long-distance runners require repeated administration of fluids over the course. *(Richard Pasley/Stock, Boston)*

behavior decreases from lower to higher species. At most it seems that hormones "flavor" a person for one kind of gender behavior or another. But even though hormones may predispose us toward given kinds of behavior, they do not dictate that the behavior be learned. Instead, hormones make it easier for us to learn certain gender-related behaviors. And these behaviors are constantly being shaped and modified by the environment (Reinisch, Gandelman, and Speigel, 1979; MacLusky and Naftolin, 1981; Hines, 1982).

The principal sex hormones are secreted by the reproductive glands, the testes in males and the ovaries in females. The chief male sex hormones are the **androgens** (primarily **testosterone**); those of females, the **estrogens**. These hormones play a particularly important role at puberty in bringing about the development of the secondary sex characteristics. Each sex has some male and some female hormones. Testosterone in women comes from the ovaries and from other tissues that convert steroids from the adrenal glands to testosterone. In men, small amounts of testosterone are converted to estrogen. The hormone-related sex differences in adults depend on the balance in levels of circulating hormones, rather than on absolute differences in hormonal make-up. Testosterone levels are roughly twenty times higher in men than in women, whereas estro-

androgens (AN-druh-jens): The principal male sex hormones.
testosterone (tes-TAHS-ter-own): A major male sex hormone.
estrogens (ESS-troh-jens): The principal female sex hormones.

gen levels are considerably higher in women than in men.

Among lower vertebrates, the sex hormones dominate sexual behavior (Bartke et al., 1973). When the animals are deprived of sex hormones by removal of their ovaries or testes, their sexual activity gradually decreases. Conversely, the administration of sex hormones restores their sexual behavior. Female animals are interested in mating only during the time that they are fertile, a period of receptivity termed **estrus** or "heat." Among human beings, female sexual interest is not limited to a fertile period, although some evidence suggests that women may experience a heightened interest in sexual behavior and be more likely to initiate sexual activity at the time of monthly ovulation (Adams, Gold, and Burt, 1978). However, not all researchers have been able to demonstrate a relationship between a woman's estrogen level and her sexual behavior (Persky et al., 1978).

In contrast to female animals, normal males are biologically capable of mating successfully at virtually any time. The arousal of their sex drive is closely tied to the behavior of a receptive female. Variety also plays a part. For instance, if a male rat is permitted to copulate with the same female until he becomes satiated, he will appear to lose interest in sex. But should the male be provided with a new partner, he experiences a spontaneous recovery. This phenomenon is termed the "Coolidge effect," after an anecdote told about a farm tour taken by President Calvin Coolidge and his wife (Walster and Walster, 1978). It seems that Mrs. Coolidge had reached the hen yard somewhat ahead of the President. Observing the vigor with which the rooster serviced one hen after the other, the First Lady asked the guide to make certain that her husband also took note of the rooster's performance. When President Coolidge arrived at the hen yard, the guide pointed to the rooster and recounted the bird's exploits. The guide mentioned that Mrs. Coolidge had instructed him to make the President aware of the rooster's prowess. The President reflected for a moment and replied, "Tell Mrs. Coolidge that there is more than one hen."

Animals' courtship rituals are often accompanied by flashy physical displays that attract females' attention. Here a male frigate bird, surrounded by females, shows off his red "bubble." *(John J. Bangma/Photo Researchers)*

Whatever the effect that variety may have on the sexual activities of human males, the level of testosterone circulating in their system is not significantly related to their willingness or readiness to copulate (Raboch and Starka, 1973; Brown, Monti, and Corriveau, 1978). Indeed, under favorable social conditions, even males with exceedingly low levels of testosterone are capable of engaging in normal sexual activity. Likewise, as a man sleeps his testosterone level tends to build up, reaching its highest peak early in the morning. The level decreases during the day and reaches its lowest level late in the evening. Yet late evening, when the testosterone level is lowest, is the time when sexual intercourse is most likely to occur (Schiavi et al., 1982). Testosterone levels are also influenced by psychological factors. The level increases in the presence of a sexually attractive and available partner, sexual stimulation, and sexual activity. It decreases with depression,

---

estrus (ESS-truss): The time of fertility in female animals; many nonhuman females are interested in mating only during this period of receptivity.

defeat, humiliation, and chronic stress (Kaplan, 1974). Although a number of medical researchers report that they have successfully used testosterone to increase the sexual appetite of some female patients, the treatment has not proven to be of much value in the treatment of male sexual impotence (Kupperman, 1963). Nor does the medical administration of testosterone alter the sexual preferences of homosexual men.

Human sexual behavior is so profoundly influenced by social factors that it is exceedingly difficult to sort out the effects of sex hormones on sexual motivation and behavior. Symbols and meanings pervade sexual arousal and orgasm. Consider that many of the same physical acts that occur in erotic encounters also occur in other situations: the palpation of the breast for cancer, the gynecological examination, the insertion of tampons, and mouth-to-mouth resuscitation. For people to define an activity as sexual, they typically must introduce a variety of words and gestures to the situation: they must say the "right things," wear "seductive" clothing, establish "sexy" eye contact, "deftly" remove clothing, and caress in the "proper" ritualistic sequence (Gagnon and Simon, 1973; Plummer, 1975).

Also, consider kissing. Most preadolescent boys regard kissing as "sissy stuff"; girls view it asexually. But as adolescents begin "hanging out" together, they begin to define the same physical activity as erotic. Consequently, they experience it as sexually arousing. No change has occurred in the act, only in the meaning that the individuals have attached to it (Gagnon, 1975).

Finally, it is worth pointing out that much "sexual" behavior has "nonsexual" motivations. The health faddist may have sex at prescribed and regular intervals, in the same way as he or she eats health foods and with the same goal in mind. A married couple may engage in sexual relations every Saturday night because each believes the other expects it, even

Reviving a nearly drowned person at the beach involves physical contact and mouth-to-mouth resuscitation, which do not have sexual connotations. Similar behaviors in a parked car or a bedroom are more likely to evoke sexual feelings. *(Owen Franken/Stock, Boston)*

though neither may want it. A prostitute or stripper engages in sexual activity to earn a living. A man may seek a regular flow of sexual partners in the hope of building a macho image. And a student may masturbate while studying for a test as a mechanism to relieve tension or boredom (Plummer, 1975).

Aggression

War, internal strife, violence, repression, terrorism, and rampant crime haunt people on all continents. Indeed, aggression seems everywhere about us. Psychologists view **aggression** as any act that is intentionally designed to harm another person. This definition excludes accidental injuries, such as those that result when we unintentionally knock someone down on a sidewalk or in a store. But it does include a wide variety of actions that are intended to hurt others, including verbal abuse. Psychologists have offered three primary explanations for aggression: (1) human beings possess an aggressive instinct, (2) aggression results from frustration, and (3) aggression, like other forms of social behavior, is learned.

The notion that we are by nature "brutish" creatures has been argued by Sigmund Freud and Konrad Lorenz. Influenced by the savagery of World War I, Freud surmised that aggression arises from a death instinct. He believed that destructive energy accumulates until it is discharged either inwardly against oneself or outwardly against others. Turned inward it results in self-destructive tendencies, including alcoholism, self-generated failure, and suicide. However, Freud thought that the death instinct is usually countered by a life instinct. So Freud concluded that human aggression derives from your channeling the energy associated with the death instinct away from yourself and toward others.

Konrad Lorenz (1966), a Nobel prize–winning ethologist, also contends that murderous and destructive impulses are instinctive. He believes that the human nervous system is "wired" for aggression by genes. Aggression, he says, has useful purposes in nature. For one thing, it spaces out organisms over

the available habitat, ensuring that adequate food is available to them. For another, aggression contributes to sexual selection—the best and strongest members of the species produce more offspring than do others. In sum, Lorenz contends that aggression is an adaptive mechanism evolved to promote the survival of a species. But whereas in lower animals instinctive aggression works to the advantage of the species, he believes it has gotten out of hand in human beings. Humans, he says, evolved as puny, harmless, omnivorous, but intelligent creatures. Paradoxically, it is our intelligence that has almost done us in. We have used our intelligence to develop lethal weaponry for which we lack inborn biological inhibitors.

As might be expected, the human-as-beast perspective has aroused considerable controversy. Critics contend that its assumptions are naive (Montagu, 1973; Freedman, 1975; McGuinness, 1984). They say that what is most striking about human beings is their remarkable diversity in behavior. For example, if we say that the murderous raids of the Brazilian Yanomamo Indians are prompted by an inborn aggressive instinct, how are we to account for the peacefulness of the Inuits (Eskimos) and the gentleness of the Philippine Tasaday tribe? Accordingly, psychologists are increasingly concluding that by nature, most of us are neither aggressive nor peaceful, but a product of complex interactions between our biology and our environment.

Although the human propensity to aggression may not qualify as an instinct, biological factors do influence aggression. Laboratory experiments show that when people are provoked, alcohol can enhance their aggressive responses (Steele, 1986). Significantly, about 54 percent of jail inmates convicted of violent crimes were drinking before they committed the offense. Low blood sugar can also boost aggressiveness (Bolton, 1973). And in males, aggressiveness can be heightened by the injection of male hormones (Reinisch, 1981).

Since its formulation nearly a half century ago, the **frustration-aggression hypothesis** has afforded another popular explanation for aggressive behavior

---

aggression: Any act that is intentionally designed to harm another person.
frustration-aggression hypothesis: A psychological theory that states that frustration activates angry and hostile impulses that find expression in aggressive behaviors.

(Dollard et al., 1939). **Frustration** refers to a state in which individuals are blocked in attaining some goal. According to frustration-aggression theorists, frustration activates angry and hostile impulses. Presumably, frustration remains a motivating force until it is discharged in aggressive behavior. At times the aggressive impulses become "free-floating"—detached from the frustrating source and discharged on another person or group. This process is termed **displacement**. Displacement—also called **scapegoating**—has been a popular explanation for racism, anti-Semitism, and prejudice. Hitler and Goebbels allegedly gave the German people—frustrated by defeat in World War I, plagued by poverty and uncontrolled inflation, and exasperated by life's problems—Jews, communists, and international bankers as targets on which to vent their rage.

Frustration-aggression theorists contend that we derive **catharsis**—a purging and lessening of pent-up energy—through discharging our angry impulses in aggressive behavior. The notion of catharsis has won wide popularity. Perhaps you have experienced a sense of relief after an emotional outburst: "I just had to get that out of my system," or "Gee, I'm glad I let off some steam." However, experimental evidence suggests that aggressive behavior does not necessarily lower subsequent aggression (Nelson, 1969; Geen, Stonner, and Shope, 1975). Indeed, watching someone behave aggressively appears to increase the likelihood of aggressive behavior (Bandura, 1973). And ventilative ("get it out") therapies, aimed at reducing aggressive drives, often inadvertently reinforce them (Berkowitz, 1970, 1973).

Although psychologists at first viewed aggression in simplistic terms as a product of instincts or frustration, they now see it as much more complicated. Many social factors operate to influence aggressive behavior. For instance, Leonard Berkowitz (1981) finds that the mere presence of guns can have an aggressive influence on behavior, what he terms the *weapons effect*. His research suggests that weapons themselves act as stimulants to violence. Social learning theorists (see Chapter 6) also cite an accumulating body of research that shows parents and other adults provide powerful models of aggression for children (Bandura, 1973). And a report prepared by the National Institute of Mental Health concludes that there is "overwhelming" scientific evidence that "excessive" violence on television leads directly to aggression and violent behavior among children and teenagers (Pearl, 1982). Accordingly, let us examine more carefully the part that learning plays in providing us with motivation to engage in various kinds of behavior.

MOTIVATION AND LEARNING

Hunger, thirst, and sex are motives that you share with all other mammalian species. Rats and cats are as driven by these biological motives as you are. But you also have other highly developed motives that the psychologist Keith J. Hayes (1962) calls *experience-producing drives*. You are curious about novel things, and you explore new environments simply because they are interesting. Other mammals, such as cats and rats, are also curious ("Curiosity killed the cat") but not as curious as primates. Monkeys and apes share the human interest in experiencing new events, and they will solve dull problems just to see a new picture or to watch an unfamiliar monkey. Most human beings like to travel to exotic places, see new films, and try novel foods.

The attraction to new experiences is crucial to learning. Without such a drive, you would stay in a rut and fail to learn much that is typically human. Imagine a well-fed, sexually satisfied person (perhaps yourself). Do you sit inert in your room simply because you are not hungry, thirsty, or sexually starved? At times, perhaps, but not often! More frequently, you are bored by monotonous events and tedious tasks (Berlyne, 1960). You find boredom an intensely unpleasant experience—you feel "itchy,"

---

frustration: A state in which individuals are blocked in attaining some goal.

displacement (scapegoating): Aggressive impulses become "free-floating"—detached from the frustrating source—and discharged on another person or group.

catharsis (kuh-THAR-sis): A purging and lessening of pent-up energy through discharging angry impulses in aggressive behavior.

you pace, and you search for some diversion. What you find distracting is likely to be some sort of change with a touch of novelty in it—perhaps a new shop down the street you can explore, a new record you can enjoy, or a party where you can hear new gossip. Through such activities, you reduce your boredom and gain new experiences. More serious examples are seeking knowledge from books, mastering electronics, or learning how to repair cars. Obviously, new experiences have a high adaptive value. Although not directly sought as physiological necessities, they have profound significance for human survival.

Closely related to Hayes's (1962) idea about experience-producing drives is Robert White's (1959) concept of *competence motivation*. White suggests that human beings are unique in their quest for mastery over their environment. He proposes an inner motive for competence that drives people to learn and to master new problems. White says that it is not the reduction of biological drives but the drive to be capable, fit, and skillful in manipulating the environment that motivates most human behavior. These views are consistent with those of Abraham Maslow, who placed motives in a hierarchical order. As discussed earlier in the chapter, Maslow stresses that when the biological drives are satisfied, attention turns to a variety of more human motives, many of which we subsume under the notion of happiness. Since happiness is profoundly influenced by our learning experiences, it merits our closer inspection.

Subjective Well-Being

Throughout history many philosophers and lay-people alike have considered happiness to be the highest good and ultimate motivation for behavior. In recent years psychologists have turned their attention to these matters by exploring **subjective well-being**—the mental assessments and feelings you have that your life is pleasant (Diener, 1984). People have had varying conceptions of what constitutes happiness. One view, traceable to Aristotle, holds that well-being derives from leading a virtuous life. Happiness is appraised not in terms of what people

themselves say and feel but in terms of a social or moral standard against which their lives can be judged. Another view, prevalent in the social sciences, defines well-being in terms of those things that lead people to evaluate their lives positively. The Roman philosopher-emperor Marcus Aurelius captured this sentiment when he wrote that "no man is happy who does not think himself so." Still another view of happiness comes closest to the way we use the term in everyday conversation. We typically conceive of happiness as circumstances in which we have more pleasant than negative feelings.

The domains that are closest and most immediate to people's personal lives are those that most influence their sense of well-being. Self-esteem is particularly important. People who think well of themselves tend to be happy people (Campbell, 1981). Good health also plays a critical part in life satisfaction (Sears, 1977; Flanagan, 1978; Quinn, 1983). Income is important, but it is often not the absolute level of goods and services that a person can afford that makes the difference. Education, status, and power commonly vary with income, and these ingredients in their own right contribute to many people's sense of well-being and allow them to feel they have choice or control in life. Marriage and family satisfaction are likewise important predictors of happiness (Emmons et al., 1983). Of all Americans, married couples in their twenties tend to be the happiest. In contrast, divorced women, especially those with children, appear to be the most dissatisfied Americans (Campbell, Converse, and Rogers, 1976; Campbell, 1981).

Many explanations have been advanced to account for happiness. But only recently have psychologists begun to subject them to scientific scrutiny (Diener, 1984). One question that philosophers have asked is whether happiness is gained by satisfying our desires or by suppressing them; hedonistic philosophers have recommended that we fulfill our needs, whereas ascetics have recommended we annihilate them. Likewise, philosophers have debated whether we derive greater satisfaction from already having fulfilled our desires or from the process of moving toward desired goals. The answers to these

---

subjective well-being: The mental assessments and feelings individuals have that their lives are pleasant.

Feeling good about yourself is an important part of feeling happy. *(Hap Stewart/Jeroboam)*

questions do not seem hard and fast. People differ greatly in how they experience happiness and in what produces it. Overall, it seems that people are happiest when they are in situations that match their personalities—in brief, where there is a comfortable person-environment fit (Diener, Larsen, and Emmons, 1984).

Philosophers have also differed on whether happiness is the sum of many small pleasures or the result of a global tendency to experience things in a positive way. According to the first view—termed the *bottom-up theory*—we judge whether or not our lives are happy by mentally calculating the balance between momentary pleasures and pains. A happy life, then, is one in which the happy moments outweigh the unhappy ones. According to the second view—termed the *top-down theory*—we enjoy pleasures because we are happy, not vice versa. The Greek philosopher Democritus captured this sentiment when he observed "that a happy life does not depend on good fortune or indeed on any external contingencies, but also, and even to a greater extent, on a person's cast of mind." For their part, psychologists are finding that neither theory is entirely accurate, and that both processes operate in everyday life. For

instance, many depressed people fail to feel pleasure when they engage in normally pleasant events (Sweeney, Schaeffer, and Golin, 1982). And lottery winners are no happier, and quadriplegics and spinal cord-injury victims no less happy, than the average person (Brickman, Coates, and Janoff-Bulman, 1978; Wortman and Silver, 1982). Even so, certain events are pleasurable to most people, and when carefully selected and accumulated, contribute to a sunny outlook. But much work is needed to develop more sophisticated theories of subjective well-being (Diener, 1984).

Since the central portion of the adult life span of both men and women is spent at work, job satisfaction plays a large part in people's personal happiness. Work has the potential for giving meaning to your life. By the same token, work that is not fulfilling can erode and undermine your sense of well-being and give rise to alienation. Research reveals that job satisfaction is associated with the opportunity to exercise discretion, accept challenges, and make decisions on the job (Kohn and Schooler, 1973; Kalleberg, 1977; Gruenberg, 1980). Hence, the most potent factors associated with satisfying work are those having to do with your self-respect, your chance to perform well, your opportunities for achievement and growth, and occasions to contribute something personal and quite unique. Overall, the problem confronting most of us in occupational life today is not so much that we are employees rather than employers, but that we cannot gain a sense of self-actualization in our work.

A 1980 Gallup survey revealed that 88 percent of all working Americans feel that it is personally important to them to work hard and to do their best on the job. And a 1982 Gallup survey found that 84 percent of Americans take a great deal of pride in their work (only 36 percent of Europeans and 37 percent of Japanese had this response). Although polls indicate that Americans *believe* that people now take less pride in their work than they did a decade ago, evidence suggests that the American work ethic remains strong (Wright and Hamilton, 1978; Yankelovich, 1982). But it may be in trouble. A 1983 survey of American workers found only 22 percent of them saying there is a direct relationship between how hard they work and how much they are paid (Serrin, 1983). Only 23 percent said they were performing to full capacity, and 44 percent admitted that they did not put any more effort into their work

Job satisfaction plays an important role in most adults' feelings of happiness. *(Freda Leinwand/Monkmeyer)*

amount of energy that Americans expend in the pursuit of success—good grades in school, high salaries at work, large profits in business, big congregations in religion, and winning games in sports. Part of the American dream is that "There is always another chance" and "If at first you don't succeed, try, try, again." This American exaltation of success is expressed in countless staple phrases such as "bettering yourself," "getting ahead," and "making it."

Achievement motivation entails behavior that seeks to develop or demonstrate high ability and competence (Nicholls, 1984). Over the past fifty years, it has been the focus of a variety of research programs. The initial impetus for these investigations derives from the work of the psychologist Henry A. Murray (1938), whose theory of personality identifies sixteen basic needs (see Table 4.1). Lists such as these are often quickly forgotten. But Murray's list has not been forgotten because other psychologists continued to study the needs. David C. McClelland and his associates (1953) took up one of them—the need for achievement—as an object of intensive study. The **need for achievement**, or **n-Ach**, entails the pursuit of success in competition that is determined by some standard of excellence.

than was required. Moreover, job satisfaction and job performance are only slightly related. Although the belief long has prevailed that a happy worker is a productive worker, research suggests otherwise. The findings indicate that each objective—job satisfaction and job performance—must be met by different interventions and programs because efforts to embellish both concurrently seldom succeed (Iaffaldano and Muchinsky, 1985). All this brings us to a consideration of achievement motivation.

Achievement Motivation

Foreign observers often remark about the hustle and bustle of American life. They are struck by the

Measuring and Teaching Achievement Motivation

McClelland's main tool for measuring achievement motivation was the *Thematic Apperception Test (TAT)*. This test consists of a series of pictures. Subjects are told to make up a story that explains each picture. Tests of this sort are called *projective tests*. (See also Chapter 13.) There are no right or wrong answers to the questions; the answers a person gives are believed to reflect his or her unconscious desires. Each story is "coded" by looking for certain kinds of themes and scoring these themes according to their relevance to achievement. Coding has by now been refined to the point where trained coders agree about 90 percent of the time.

---

achievement motivation: Behavior that seeks to develop or demonstrate high ability and competence.

need for achievement (n-Ach): The pursuit of success in competition that is determined by some standard of excellence.

TABLE 4.1 Henry Murray's List of Basic Needs

Acquisition
(to gain possessions and property)
n Conservance
(to collect, repair, clean, and preserve things)
n Order
(to arrange, organize, put away objects)
n Construction
(to organize and build)
n Achievement
(to overcome obstacles, to exercise power, to strive to do something difficult as well and as quickly as possible)
n Recognition
(to excite praise and commendation)
n Defendance
(to defend oneself against blame or belittlement)
n Dominance
(to influence or control others)
n Autonomy
(to resist influence or coercion)
n Aggression
(to assault or injure)
n Affiliation
(to form friendships and associations)
n Rejection
(to snub, ignore, or exclude)
n Nurturance
(to nourish, aid, or protect)
n Succorance
(to seek aid, protection, or sympathy)
n Play
(to relax, amuse oneself, seek diversion and entertainment)
n Cognizance
(to explore)

Note: Murray distinguishes between a class of primarily physical needs and a—much larger—class of psychological needs.
Source: H. A. Murray. 1938. *Explorations in Personality.* London: Oxford University Press.

People who succeed in business, such as Famous Amos, who invented and nationally merchandised his chocolate-chip cookies, are usually high in achievement motivation. *(Courtesy of Famous Amos Cookies)*

Over the past forty years, a large number of studies have explored the personality characteristics of individuals with high achievement motivation. McClelland finds a strong relationship between high need for achievement and entrepreneurial behavior. For instance, he followed up the careers of some students at Wesleyan University who had been tested with the TAT in 1947. He wanted to see which students had chosen entrepreneurial work—that is, work in which they had to initiate projects on their own. He found that eleven years after graduation, 83 percent of the entrepreneurs (business managers, insurance salespersons, real estate investors, consultants, and so on) had scored high in achievement, but only 21 percent of the nonentrepreneurs had scored that high (McClelland, 1965).

Encouraged by these and other findings, McClelland and others then set about devising a training course in achievement motivation. The trainees in this course learned to score their own TAT stories and to recognize achievement themes in them. They also rewrote their stories again and again, attempting to include more achievement themes in them. Then they discussed everyday life situations and case histories with other members of the group, focusing on achievement themes. Group members also played a business game that was designed to give them quick feedback for decision making and problem solving. Success with this program has been reported after applying it in such diverse places as Spain, Mexico, Italy, India, and poverty areas of Kentucky (McClelland and Winter, 1969). However, McClelland does not believe we should all train ourselves as high achievers. In fact, he has said that such persons are not always the most interesting, and they are usually not artistically sensitive (McClelland and Harris, 1971). They would also be less likely to value intimacy in a relationship.

Achievement Motivation and Gender

In the Western world, men have traditionally enjoyed greater power, privilege, and status than women have. Until relatively recently, men were assigned the economic-provider role and women the homemaking and child-rearing role. The prevalence of sexism in the United States led psychologists such as Matina S. Horner to speculate in the 1960s that women develop somewhat different achievement orientations than men do. Horner (1968, 1970, 1972) asked eighty-nine college men to write a story beginning with the line, "After first-term finals, John finds himself at the top of his medical school class." Substituting the name Anne for John in the opening line, she also asked ninety women to write a story. Ninety percent of the men wrote success stories. However, over 65 percent of the women predicted doom for Anne.

Some of the women feared for Anne's social life. They described her as undatable or unmarriageable, and suggested that she would be socially isolated if she excelled in her studies and career. Some wrote about the guilt and despair she would experience if she continued to succeed. On the basis of these findings Horner concluded that in pursuing achievement, women are hampered by a "fear of success." Females in our society are (or were) raised with the idea that being successful in any but a few careers is odd and unfeminine. Thus a woman who is a success in medicine, law, or other traditionally male occupations must be a failure as a woman.

Many changes have occurred in American life since the 1960s, when Horner undertook her research. It is questionable today whether vast numbers of women are still intimidated by achievement situations. Further, what Horner termed "fear of success" often reflected realistic appraisals by women of the negative consequences that would likely follow were they to deviate from gender-related stereotypes, and of the occupational opportunities then available to them in a sexist world (Condry and Dyer, 1976; Meeker and Weitzel-O'Neill, 1977). Rather than assuming that women have a deep-rooted disposition to avoid success, some psychologists suggest that both sexes will shun success when achievement conflicts with expectations relating to the gender role, and both will seek success when the norms permit success (Darley, 1976). Not surprisingly, as sexist barriers have been broken down, women have taken advantage of their new opportunities. For instance, between 1974 and 1984, the number of women in American medical schools nearly tripled from 7,731 (15.4 percent) to 20,685 (30.7 percent). And in the same period, the number of women holding bachelor's degrees in engineering increased from 744 to 10,761 (Teltsch, 1985).

EMOTION

It is difficult to draw a clear line between motives and emotions (Mook, 1986). When you need food, your stomach contracts, the level of sugar in your blood may drop, your neural and endocrine systems are altered, and your taste buds sense food to be more pleasant. When you are frightened, your heart and breathing rates quicken, your energy level rises, your senses mobilize, and your blood rushes away from the stomach into the brain, heart, and other muscles. Of course, a poet might diagnose a pounding heart, loss of appetite, and heightened awareness of the moonlight and scented breezes as love. Why, if all three involve identifiable physiological changes, is hunger called a biological drive, while fear and love are called emotions?

It depends on what is being described: the source of behavior or the feelings associated with behavior.

When we want to emphasize the determinants that lead to goal-directed behavior—various needs, desires, and mental calculations—we use the word "drive" or "motivation." When we want to stress the feelings associated with these decisions and activities, we use the word "emotion" or "affect."

Clearly, the two are intertwined. Motives are frequently explained in terms of emotions. Why did you walk out of the meeting? I was angry. Why do you go to so many parties? I enjoy meeting new people and love to dance. Why did you lend your notes to someone you do not particularly like? I felt guilty about talking behind her back. Why did you apply for a summer job overseas? The idea of flying to Saudi Arabia excites me—and so on. As these examples demonstrate, emotions push and pull people in different directions. All this brings us to the question: What is the source of our emotional experience? Psychologists have provided us with several answers to the question. Let us look at a number of these answers and then attempt an integration or synthesis of them.

Psychophysiological Approaches

Psychophysiological approaches to emotion can be traced back to 1884 when William James suggested that emotional experience consists of the arousal of our bodily responses and our perception of them (Katkin, 1985). In his classic work, *Principles of Psychology* (1884), James noted that nearly every description of emotions he read emphasized bodily changes. His observation of his own and other people's emotions seemed to confirm the point. People commonly associate feelings with sudden increases or decreases in energy ("Wild horses couldn't have dragged me away"), tension or relaxation ("My temples started pounding" and "I got hot under the collar"), and visceral sensations ("I felt butterflies in my stomach").

The James-Lange Theory

After much thought, James concluded that people use the word "emotion" to describe their visceral or "gut" reactions to the things that take place around them. In other words, James (1884:189–190) believed that emotions are the perception of certain internal bodily changes:

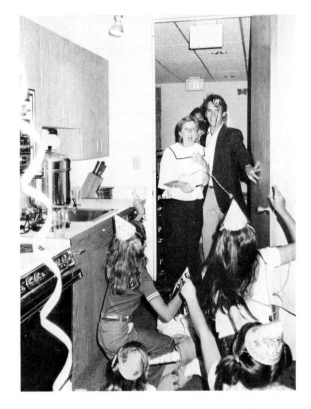

Surprises such as an unexpected party create bodily reactions that William James and Carl Lange said were the basis of emotion. First the body reacts and then we label the emotion. *(Midge Keator/Woodfin Camp & Associates)*

My theory . . . is that *the bodily changes follow directly the perception of the exciting fact, and that our feeling of the same changes as they occur IS the emotion.* Commonsense says, we lose our fortune, are sorry and weep; we meet a bear, are frightened and run; we are insulted by a rival, are angry and strike. . . . [T]he more rational statement is that we feel sorry because we cry, angry because we strike, afraid because we tremble. . . . Without the bodily states following on the perception, the latter would be . . . pale, colorless, destitute of emotional warmth.

In sum, we perceive a stimulus—a stock market crash, a surprise encounter with a bear in the forest, or the menacing words of a rival—that sets off some physiological reaction such as an increase in our heart rate. Our brain perceives this bodily change, the subjective experience of which is the emotion.

Before the publication of James's work, psychologists had assumed that emotions trigger bodily changes. James argued that the reverse is true. Because the Danish physiologist Carl Lange came to the same conclusion at about the same time, this position is known as the *James-Lange theory* (Lange and James, 1922).

The Cannon-Bard Theory

Techniques for studying bodily changes improved over the next three decades, and evidence that contradicted the James-Lange theory began to grow. In 1929, the physiologist Walter B. Cannon published a summary of this evidence. First, Cannon pointed out that people have considerable difficulty telling very different emotions from one another, since the bodily changes are so similar (for example, a pounding heart is commonly associated with both fear and love). Second, Cannon argued that physiological changes occur too slowly in the viscera and other internal organs to produce emotions (for instance, if bodily changes were the seat of emotion, everyone would be rather sluggish and dull in their emotional reactions). Contemporary research supports this argument (Chapman et al., 1980). And third, Cannon said that when researchers experimentally induce the bodily changes associated with an emotion (for example, by injecting subjects with epinephrine), people do not necessarily experience the same kind of emotional reaction.

Cannon advanced his own theory. He claimed that the thalamus (part of the lower brain) is the seat of emotion—an idea Philip Bard (1934) expanded and refined. According to the *Cannon-Bard theory,* certain experiences activate a nerve impulse in the thalamus. The nerve impulse then splits. One signal travels to the cortex (or higher brain) and the other to the body organs. (More sophisticated experiments showed that the thalamus is not involved in emotional experience, but the hypothalamus and reticular formation are.) Thus when people use the word "emotion," they are referring to the *simultaneous* burst of activity in the brain (associated with anger, fear, love, or other experiences of emotion) and in bodily functioning (contributing to such "gut" reactions as butterflies in the stomach).

Cannon also emphasized the importance of physiological arousal in many different emotions. He was the first to describe the "fight or flight" reaction of the sympathetic nervous system that prepares one for an emergency by increasing heart rate and blood pressure, releasing sugar into the bloodstream, and so on. Some of these signs of physiological arousal are measured in one of the most famous applications of psychological knowledge: lie detection (see the boxed insert on pages 134–135).

Biochemical Foundations of Emotion

Lovers commonly report that at the sight of one another they experience physiological arousal, including an increased heart rate and accelerated breathing. Cliché has it that "It's chemistry." The cliché may be correct (see the boxed insert on pages 136–137). Researchers are finding that neuropeptides may be the molecular bases of emotion (*peptides* are short chains of amino acids, the building blocks of proteins) (Cordes, 1985a). Many neurotransmitters and hormones, including endorphins, are neuropeptides (see Chapters 2 and 3). They often appear in clusters throughout the body—along the gastrointestinal tract, the testes, the ovaries, the spleen, and lymph nodes. In many cases neuropeptides meander through the glands, immune system, and brain in the manner of island-hopping cruise ships. Since the receptors for different neuropeptides are chemically distinct, they make their stops only at those cellular ports with the customized receiving docks. At these neural receptor sites—particularly those centers in the brain that are the processing stations for emotion—they sail in and unload their cargo of mood-influencing information. Consequently a receptor welcomes one neuropeptide that floats by while ignoring the others.

In Chapter 2 we noted that the traditional distinction between hormones and neurotransmitters is blurring, since neuropeptides function in some circumstances as hormones and in other circumstances as neurotransmitters. For instance, norepinephrine, as a hormone, is released by the adrenal gland to stimulate contractions of the heart, dilate the bronchial tract of the lungs, and increase the contracting capabilities of the arm and leg muscles (Snyder, 1985). As a neurotransmitter in the nervous system, it constricts blood vessels, thereby increasing blood pressure, and in certain areas of the brain, it influences a person's mood (a deficit of norepinephrine in the synapses is associated with depression). Although the molecular structure of norepinephrine remains the same regardless of its location in the body, its target receptors differ at various sites within the body. For example, stimulating one type of receptor (alpha$_1$) in the nervous system raises blood pressure (accordingly, many drugs for treating hypertension are designed to selectively block alpha$_1$ receptors). Stimulating other norepinephrine receptors (beta$_1$ or beta$_2$) dilates the bronchial tree of the lungs (accordingly, a beta stimulant can be used to treat asthma). Antidepressant drugs, by inhibiting the norepinephrine reuptake systems of brain neurons, make a greater quantity of neurotransmitter available to receptor sites and cause patients to feel more cheerful.

Knowledge of the biochemistry of emotion is still in its infancy. However, researchers have identified some sites in the brain that buzz with activity when a person feels excited, anxious, or sad. They have used PET scans to identify the parts of the neural orchestra that play when an individual feels particular emotions (see Chapter 2). Scans of depressed patients differ markedly from those of healthy individuals and from their own scans when they are no longer depressed (depressed people have a higher level of activation in the front portion of the right hemisphere than do people who are not depressed) (Davidson, 1984). Likewise, low levels of the neurotransmitter serotonin characterize the brains of many suicide victims. And low serotonin activity also seems common in highly aggressive and impulsive persons (Stanley, Virgilio, and Gershon, 1982; Brown et al., 1982; Ostroff et al., 1982).

Cognitive-Arousal Approaches

Our discussion of emotion has emphasized that we usually are aware something is going on within us when we are excited, anxious, angry, or afraid. At these times we may experience our heart pounding, our respiration rate increasing, sensations "in the pit of the stomach," and so on. But if we are asked to describe our emotions, we typically relate what excited, distressed, angered, or frightened us. Although we *define* our emotional states quite *differently,* in point of fact we *describe* our inner state of turbulence quite *similarly.* These observations form the base for what variously are termed *cognitive-arousal* and *cognitive-physiological* theories of emotion. Cognitive theorists say that physiological arousal accounts for only half the story of emotion. They

say that what you feel depends on how you *label* your symptoms. And this, in turn, depends on what is going on in your mind and in your environment (see the box on pages 136–137).

The theory of Stanley Schachter and Jerome Singer (1962) has served as a prototype for a large class of theories of emotion. In a classic experiment, they told all their subjects they were testing the effects of vitamin C on eyesight. In reality, most subjects received an epinephrine injection. One group was told that the "vitamin" injection would make their hearts race and their bodies tremble (which was true). Another group was deliberately misinformed: the injection would make them numb. A third group was not told anything about how their bodies would react to the shot. And a fourth group received a neutral injection that did not produce any symptoms. Like the third group, these subjects were not given any information about possible side effects.

After the injection, each subject was taken to a reception room to wait for the "vision test." There they found another person who was actually a "plant," a confederate of the researchers. The subjects thought the plant had had the same injection as theirs. With some subjects, the plant acted wild and crazy—dancing around, laughing, making paper airplanes with the questionnaire they had been asked to fill out. Other plants filled out a long and offensive questionnaire.

Subjects from the first group, who had been told how the injection would affect them, watched the plant with mild amusement. So did subjects who had received the neutral injection. However, those from the second and third groups, who either had no idea or an incorrect idea about the side effects, joined in with the plant. If the plant was euphoric, so were they; if he was angry, they became angry.

Schachter and Singer advance what they term a cognitive-physiological explanation for these findings. They suggest that (1) something in your environment typically serves to activate physiological arousal (an undifferentiated state of affect); (2) you in turn use information from past experience and your perception of the present situation to decide what you are experiencing (much like the subjects who took their cue from the behavior of the plant); and (3) you then attach a label to the reaction—love, anger, fear, or whatever. Viewed from this perspective, all your physiological reactions are relatively undifferentiated. What serves to distinguish one

Lie Detection

Most people associate lie detection with shifty-eyed criminals accused of murdering their grand-mothers. But in reality, American industry uses the lie detector far more often than the police do. No one knows exactly how many polygraph tests (**polygraph** is another name for a lie detector) are given each year, but current estimates place the figure at about a million. Companies use these tests for everything from finding out whether a job applicant has ever been in trouble to seeing who has his or her hand in the till at the local hamburger stand. Likewise, government is turning increasingly to the use of the polygraph. In 1983, the Reagan administration issued a set of rules under which any of the several hundred thousand federal workers with access to classified documents could be compelled to take lie-detector examinations—on pain of dismissal—if suspected of leaking sensitive information. The value of the lie detector is a matter of considerable controversy. However, it does serve one purpose probably expressed best by President Richard Nixon in a 1971 conversation recorded on the White House tapes: "Listen, I don't know anything about polygraphs, and I don't know how accurate they are, but I do know that they'll scare the hell out of people."

The first modern "lie detector" was invented by Leonarde Keeler, a member of the Berkeley, California, police force in the 1920s. Lie detectors work by measuring four body signals: blood pressure, thoracic respiration, galvanic skin response (the extent an individual sweats), and abdominal respiration. The theory is that if a person tells a lie, the fear, anxiety, or anger associated with the incorrect answer will cause measurable changes in signals picked up by the electronic probes. Lie detection is an art rather than a science, so the technique is only as good as the person who uses it (Hassett, 1978a). In fact, it is the form and mix of the questions that, according to polygraphers, are the key to the procedure (Meyer, 1982).

Since modern lie detection relies on nothing more than crude physiological indicators, subtle psychological insights, and skillful interviewing, many individuals attempt to fool the polygrapher. Outwitting a lie-detector test is not particularly easy, but it can be done (Barland and Raskin, 1973).

---

from the other is the situation in which it occurs and thus the label you ascribe to the state of arousal.

Schachter and Singer's theory has attracted considerable interest as well as criticism (Reisenzein, 1983). For one thing, not all people are affected by epinephrine in the same way. Indeed, some subjects in the study said that they did not experience any physiological reactions to the drug's administration. The researchers simply eliminated these subjects from their analysis, in effect providing much stronger support for their theory than the data warranted. But perhaps most devastating of all, other researchers have not been able to replicate Schachter and Singer's findings (Rogers and Deckner, 1975). In fact, some researchers find that subjects who receive epinephrine injections typically report unpleasant emotions, regardless of the situational context (Hogan and Schroeder, 1981). Additionally, some psychologists like Robert B. Zajonc (1980) contend that emotional reactions to stimuli can occur without any external cognitive labeling, can be made sooner than cognitive judgments, and can be made in the total absence of related memories. The part that facial expression plays in emotion is a case in point.

While understanding the origins of emotional experi-

---

polygraph: A machine used to measure physiological changes, particularly in lie detection.

Since the polygraph simply records the arousal of emotional responses, the trick is to respond emotionally at the wrong time. When you are asked for your name or address, before you respond simply picture yourself skydiving. You can also produce a physiological response by crossing your eyes or tensing the muscles in your leg. Pain also produces arousal. One old trick involves hiding a thumbtack in your shoe and pressing your toe on it whenever the examiner asks a question. Another countermeasure is to bite your tongue.

All these strategies work the same way—a polygraph test compares your relaxed physiological state to the response to an emotionally charged question. By confusing the issue when you're supposed to be relaxed, you may be able to make the test inconclusive. The key seems to be to use the countermeasures when you are first hooked up to get a baseline reading. Then later, should you lie, the test may not pick up your deception. Of course, if you get caught, it's not going to look good.

How effective are lie detectors? It is hard to say. Like all good businesspeople, polygraph experts advertise their successes and forget about their failures. The American Polygraph Association cites studies that it claims yield accuracy rates ranging from 87.2 to 96.2 percent. But their chief adversary, psychologist David Lykken, cites other studies that yield far lower rates, 64 to 71 percent (Meyer, 1982). Even if the incidence of error is low, that is not going to help you if you are one of the people the lie detector lies about.

A number of psychologists like Paul Ekman (1985) are also looking for behavioral clues to lying. Ekman's studies of people engaged in telling lies and the truth have shown that a lie frequently is betrayed by changes in voice, facial expressions, use of words, and body movements. Clues that can signal deception include hesitation in answering a question that should elicit an immediate response; tightening the lips; raising the tone of voice; an asymmetrical smile that yields a slightly lopsided expression; facial expressions that last longer than the usual five to ten seconds; and micro-expressions of fear such as a pulling of the eyebrows up and together. Ekman cautions that a lie catcher should not rely upon one clue to deceit; there must be many. The chances of detecting a lie vary considerably with the skill of both the liar and the person trying to detect the falsehood.

ence has been a longstanding concern of psychologists, an equally venerable tradition has examined the relationship between facial expression and emotion. Charles Darwin was one of the first investigators to study the matter scientifically. In *The Expression of Emotions in Man and Animals* (1872), Darwin argued that certain basic patterns of emotional expression are part of biological inheritance. These patterns evolved because of their survival value in providing human beings with standardized and mutually understood communicative symbols. For instance, like many other animals—including dogs and baboons—we grimace and bare our teeth when we are enraged.

A number of psychologists have recently followed up on Darwin's leads. One of these is Carroll E. Izard (1977). His approach, termed *differential emotions theory*, takes its name from its emphasis on ten distinct emotions: excitement, joy, startle, anguish, rage, revulsion, scorn, terror, humiliation, and remorse. Izard says that each of the specific emotions has its own distinctive facial pattern, thereby coloring the thinking brain's subjective awareness of affect. For instance, Izard suggests that when you experience rage, a specific pattern of muscle firings that is physiologically associated with anger "informs" your brain that you feel rage and not remorse or shame. Likewise, the muscular responses associated with smiling make you aware that you are joyful. In this manner facial patterning or facial muscle tension generates, sustains, and amplifies your experience of emotion. Hence, the facial-muscular movement that occurs with each emotion is part of an affect program wired into the organism.

Paul Ekman and his associates (Ekman, Friesen, and Ellsworth, 1972; Ekman, Friesen, and Ancoli,

Love

Love is an intense human emotion. Although we all have notions of what constitutes love, psychologists have difficulty defining it. If letters to "Dear Abby" and "Ann Landers" are any indication, it seems that a good many Americans—especially teen-agers—have similar concerns. Typical questions include: How can I be certain that I'm in love? How can I tell if my partner truly loves me? What can I do to make myself more lovable? Whatever the case may be, scientists and laypeople alike recognize that the intense emotion of love involves more than mild feelings of liking (Berscheid, 1983). Love, especially romantic or passionate love, typically entails a preoccupation (even obsession) with the loved one, a deeply felt desire to be with the person, a feeling of incompleteness without him or her, and a desire for physical intimacy with the partner. Friendship usually lacks the emotional intensity of love. However, the two types of relationships are commonly similar in such characteristics as enjoyment, acceptance, trust, respect, understanding, spontaneity, and confiding (Davis, 1985). Psychological interpretations of love tend to parallel the theoretical approaches to emotion discussed in the text.

Love as Brain Chemistry

Some scholars like Michael R. Liebowitz (1983) say that love has a unique chemical basis, associated with phenylethylamine (a compound related to the amphetamines). Amphetamine is believed to affect the nervous system indirectly by inducing the brain to release vast quantities of the neurotransmitters norepinephrine and dopamine. The action of the chemicals seems to operate on the threshold, or activation level, of the brain's pleasure centers. Love is often associated with a giddy response, much like an amphetamine high. The crash that follows the breakup of a romance resembles an amphetamine withdrawal. Endorphins may also be involved. Liebowitz finds that individuals with a history of roller-coaster love affairs frequently have a craving for chocolate after a breakup. Chocolate has a plentiful supply of the mood-altering chemical phenylethylamine. Liebowitz reasons that the brain pours out its own chemical correlate to amphetamine—phenylethylamine—when a person is in love and halts production of the substance when the romance ends. The person, suffering from the absence of phenylethylamine, binges on chocolate in an attempt at self-medication.

Love as Cognitive Arousal

Writing in *The Art of Love*, the first-century Roman poet Ovid said that an excellent time for a man to arouse romantic passion in a woman is while watching gladiators disembowel one another in the arena. Presumably the emotions of fear and repulsion that were excited by the grisly scene somehow become translated into romantic interest (Rubin, 1977). A number of "falling in love" studies suggest that there may be some truth in Ovid's observation. Social psychologists like Zick Rubin (1977) and Ellen Berscheid and Elaine Walster (Berscheid and Walster, 1974) say that passionate love, like other emotional states, requires arousal and then the assignment of a label to the arousal.

An experiment undertaken by Donald G. Dutton and Arthur R. Aron (1974) lends some support to this thesis. They conducted their study near two footbridges that cross the Capilano River in North Vancouver, Canada. One bridge was suspended 230 feet above a rushing rapids, had low cable handrails, and would tilt, sway,

1980) have also examined the part that facial expression plays in emotion. First, they selected a group of photographs of Americans that they thought depicted surprise, disgust, fear, anger, sadness, and happiness. Then they showed the photographs to people from five different cultures and asked them to say what the person in each photograph was feeling. The results of this experiment are shown in Figure 4.3. The overwhelming majority of the subjects identified the emotions as the researchers expected they would.

and wobble—a bridge with many arousal-inducing qualities. The other bridge was a solid wood structure farther upriver that was only ten feet above a babbling stream. An attractive female experimenter approached men who crossed each bridge and asked them to complete a questionnaire on "scenic attractions" and to write a short dramatic story based on a picture she showed them. When the men had completed the questionnaire, the woman gave each of them her name and telephone number in the event they wished more information on the study. The content of the men's stories revealed that those on the frightening suspension bridge were more sexually aroused by the woman than those on the solid bridge. Moreover, half of the men on the high-fear bridge called the woman (in contrast to only 13 percent of those who crossed the low-fear bridge). Presumably, the men on the frightening bridge had labeled their inner turbulence as the product of romantic attraction and sexual arousal. Such labeling is encouraged by popular stereotypes that portray falling in love as involving such symptoms as a pounding heart, shortness of breath, and trembling hands (also the physical symptoms of fear).

Whether the best place to look for answers to love is on high bridges in Vancouver or in the chemistry of people's heads remains a debatable issue. However, researchers like Robert J. Sternberg, who chart the course of love, find that people are initially drawn together for reasons that matter less as time goes on (Goleman, 1985c). Sternberg says that passion, intimacy, and commitment are the major components of love. Each of these elements blossoms at its own pace and follows a distinct course. Passion typically looms large in the early stages of a match, but it is the quickest to fade. Intimacy assumes greatest importance with the passage of time, although it too tends to fade (often remaining as a latent quality) as the partners become more familiar with one another. Commitment evolves over time, but it requires that the couple constantly work at rejuvenating the relationship. Sternberg's research suggests that the best predictor of how satisfied and happy a couple are is not how much or little the spouses love each other, but rather how equal their love is. The least satisfactory situation is one where a partner perceives the other partner as not reciprocating his or her love in like amounts (Sternberg and Grajek, 1984).

According to Robert J. Sternberg, passionate love is one of three components in an enduring relationship. The others are intimacy and commitment. (Joel Gordon)

Was this simply because they had met Americans, or at least seen American television shows and movies, and so learned how to "read" our facial expressions? Apparently not. A second study was conducted in a remote part of New Guinea among the Fore, a people who have had relatively little contact with outsiders and virtually no exposure to mass media. They too were able to identify the emotions being expressed (Ekman, Friesen, and Ellsworth, 1972; Ekman, 1980).

Photograph Judged						
Judgment	Happiness	Disgust	Surprise	Sadness	Anger	Fear
Culture	Percent Who Agreed with Judgment					
99 Americans	97	92	95	84	67	85
40 Brazilians	95	97	87	59	90	67
119 Chileans	95	92	93	88	94	68
168 Argentinians	98	92	95	78	90	54
29 Japanese	100	90	100	62	90	66

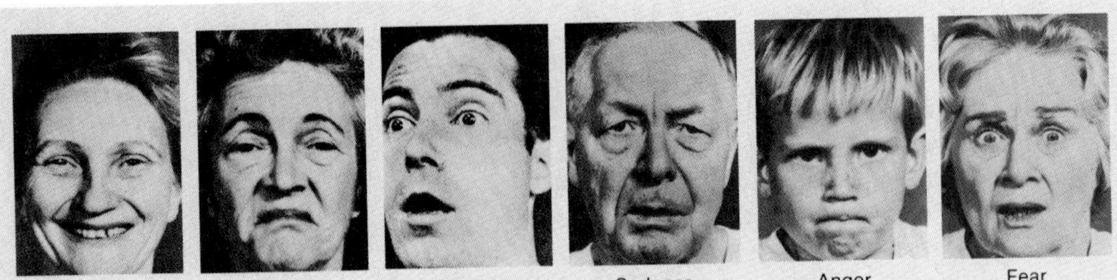

FIGURE 4.3 The data in this table show that there is substantial agreement among the members of different cultures about the meaning of various facial expressions. The muscular movements that produce these expressions are probably innate human responses. *(After P. Ekman, Ed. 1982. Emotion in the Human Face. 2nd ed. New York: Cambridge University Press. Reprinted with permission.*

Ekman claims that facial expressions of emotion (surprise, disgust, fear, anger, sadness, and happiness) are universal. However, each culture provides its own "display rules" that regulate how and when given emotions may be exhibited and with what consequences. In Ekman's view, your facial action accurately reflects your subjective experience of emotion. As such, it provides a window by which other people can gain access to your inner emotional life and by which you gain similar access to their inner life (Ekman, Friesen, and Ancoli, 1980).

More recently, Ekman and his associates (Ekman, Levenson, and Friesen, 1983) have taken the study of facial expression a step farther. They contend that the mechanics of facial muscle movement are closely tied to the autonomic nervous system, which controls heart rate, breathing, and other essential involuntary functions. Research has shown that we tend to mimic the facial expressions of those around us. But new findings suggest that such mimicry produces the same effects on the nervous system. By making a face, you can generate emotion. For example, Ekman and his colleagues asked subjects to combine the following actions: raise the eyebrows, pull the eyebrows together, raise the upper eyelids, tighten the lower lids, drop the jaw, and stretch the lower lip wide. Simultaneously, the volunteers' brain waves, heart rate, breathing rate, and skin temperature were monitored. Although the subjects were not told the emotion they were mimicking, they showed the physiological effects associated with anger. Similar findings apply to such emotions as disgust, fear, and sadness, and, possibly, surprise and contempt (strangely enough, the process does not seem to occur with smiles and happiness) (Rensberger, 1985). Ekman conjectures that the contraction or relaxation of certain facial muscles triggers a response in the nervous system that leads to a production of hormones capable of changing our mood (McDonald, 1985). The work of other researchers is buttressing Ekman's notion that there are unique brain pathways controlling each major emotion (Davidson, 1984).

A Synthesis

Our consideration of a number of leading theories of emotion suggests the incredible complexity of the mechanisms involved in our feelings. This proliferation and clash of ideas is not a disaster. Instead, it provides an opportunity for better understanding. Theories are simply tools that help us to explain what we observe. Any theory limits our vision by focusing on a few principal ideas. But a good theory also functions like a pair of binoculars and enlarges the horizon of what we see. It provides new perspectives through which we can uncover new relationships and extend the frontiers of knowledge.

It is probable that each theory is to some extent correct. But more particularly, psychophysiological, cognitive arousal, and facial expression interweave and collaborate in intricate and complicated ways. Consider what happens when a car unexpectedly looms as you cross an intersection. You very likely dart to safety and then experience emotional arousal and provide a cognitive interpretation for the situation. Similarly, there are other situations in which the cognitive interpretation anticipates the emotional arousal. You may be quietly thinking about an event earlier in the day when it suddenly occurs to you that you were victimized, and you then become enraged. And there are still other situations in which you smile in the presence of other people as part of a self-presentation strategy and then come to experience the true emotion of joy.

In sum, the three components—psychophysiological, cognitive arousal, and facial expression—can all be leaders in the determination of emotion, and each can also follow the other.

SUMMARY

1. Motivation entails those inner states and processes that arouse, direct, and sustain activity. One of the earliest theories about motivation concerned instincts, or the inherited disposition to think, feel, or act in a particular way.

2. As the instinct concept fell into disrepute, psychologists sought some alternative to it. One of these new proposals was the notion of drive, a concept associated with drive-reduction theories. According to this perspective, when a drive is aroused, an organism is impelled to undertake those behaviors that in the past served to reduce the drive. Closely linked to drive-reduction processes is homeostasis, those adaptive mechanisms by which the body maintains a more or less stable existence in an unstable environment.

3. Abraham Maslow believes that all people want to feel competent, to win approval and recognition, and to sense they have achieved something. According to his theory, there is a hierarchy of needs: fundamental needs, psychological needs, and self-actualizing needs. Some needs take precedence over others, and the achievement of one level of satisfaction releases new needs and motivations.

4. Hunger provides a powerful impetus to behavior. There is much more to hunger than merely the feeling of discomfort in the stomach. Research in the 1950s and 1960s focused on the regulatory role of the hypothalamus in hunger and eating, especially in keeping a close watch on the fat content of the body. But psychologists have increasingly come to recognize the importance of other factors as well, including the change that occurs in people's perception of the taste and aroma of a food as they eat it.

5. Both the hypothalamus and the kidneys monitor fluid levels and contribute to thirst arousal. Osmoreceptors in the hypothalamus are key mechanisms for monitoring low water and high sodium levels. Receptors located on some small blood vessels also monitor blood pressure as a means of detecting the flow of water.

6. Sexual urges ensure that reproduction occurs and that the species survives. Human sexuality differs from that of lower animals in that so much of human sexuality is learned and activated within a social context. The degree to which hormonal control governs sexual behavior decreases from lower to higher species.

7. Psychologists view aggression as any act intentionally designed to harm another. This definition excludes accidental injuries, such as those that result when we unintentionally knock someone down. But it does include a wide variety of actions that are intended to hurt others, including verbal abuse. Psychologists have offered three primary explanations for aggression: (1) human beings possess an aggressive instinct, (2) aggression results from frustration, and (3) aggression, like other forms of social behavior, is learned.

8. Social needs also motivate behavior. Human beings have experience-producing drives. We are curious about novel things and explore new environments simply because they are interesting. Our attraction to new experiences is crucial to learning. Without such a drive, we would stay in our ruts and fail to learn much that is typically human.

9. Throughout history many philosophers and laypeople have considered happiness to be the highest good and ultimate motivation for behavior. The domains that are closest and most immediate to people's personal lives are those that most influence their sense of well-being. Self-esteem and good health play particularly important roles in life satisfaction. Since the central portion of the adult life span of both men and women is spent at work, job satisfaction also plays a large part in people's personal happiness.

10. The need for achievement has been intensively studied by David McClelland. He and his associates devised a method for measuring achievement motivation. They also developed achievement training programs that have been successful cross-culturally. McClelland's work inspired a wide variety of research on other aspects of motivation. One researcher, Matina Horner, discovered another dimension of achievement motivation: the motive to avoid success. Although Horner believed that this was more of a problem for women than men, other researchers have questioned this.

11. It is difficult to draw a clear line between motives and emotions. Much depends on whether you are describing the source of your behavior or the feelings associated with that behavior. When people want to emphasize the determinants that lead to goal-directed behavior—various needs, desires, and mental calculations—they use the word "drive" or "motivation." When they want to stress the feelings associated with these decisions and activities, they use the word "emotion" or "affect."

12. Some psychologists consider the source of our emotional experiences to be psychophysical.

A. According to the James-Lange theory of emotion, bodily changes follow people's perception of an exciting event, and their feeling of these bodily changes is the source of the emotion.

B. In contrast, the Cannon-Bard theory suggests that certain experiences activate a nerve impulse in the thalamus. The nerve impulse then splits. One signal travels to the cortex (or higher brain) and the other to the body organs. Thus when one uses the word "emotion," one is referring to the simultaneous burst of activity in the brain and in the functioning of the body.

C. Recently, some research has shown there is a biochemical foundation of emotion.

13. Such cognitive theorists as Stanley Schachter and Jerome Singer believe that bodily changes and thinking work together to produce emotions. Physiological arousal accounts for only half the story of emotions. They say that what you feel depends on how you label your symptoms. Viewed from this perspective, all your physiological reactions are relatively undifferentiated.

14. A number of psychologists, among them Carroll E. Izard and Paul Ekman, add a third component (in addition to physiological and cognitive components) to the understanding of emotion—facial expression. The approach has been strongly influenced by Darwin's evolutionary theory. Darwin argued that certain basic patterns of emotional expression are part of biological inheritance. These patterns evolved because of their survival value in providing human beings with standardized and mutually understood communicative symbols.

15. Our consideration of the various theories of emotion suggests the incredible complexity of the mechanisms that operate in the experience of affect. In fact, it is probable that all the theories are to some extent right. The three components—psychophysiological, cognitive arousal, and facial expression—can all be leaders in the determination of emotion, and each can also follow the other.

KEY TERMS

achievement motivation (p. 128)
aggression (p. 124)
androgens (p. 121)
catharsis (p. 125)
displacement (scapegoating) (p. 125)
drive (p. 110)
drive-reduction theory (p. 111)
estrogens (p. 121)
estrus (p. 122)

frustration (p. 125)
frustration-aggression hypothesis (p. 124)
fundamental needs (p. 113)
incentive (p. 112)
lateral hypothalamus (LH) (p. 115)
motivation (p. 110)
motives (p. 112)
need (p. 110)

need for achievement (n-Ach) (p. 128)
osmoreceptors (p. 117)
polygraph (p. 134)
psychological needs (p. 113)
self-actualizing needs (p. 113)
subjective well-being (p. 126)
testosterone (p. 121)
ventromedial hypothalamus (VMH) (p. 115)

SUGGESTED READINGS

EKMAN, PAUL. 1975. Face muscles talk every language. *Psychology Today*, 8 (September):35–39. Does evolution or culture determine the way in which our faces express emotion? A discussion of research showing that at least some emotions produce the same facial expressions in fifteen different cultures.

GREENE, D., and LEPPER, M. R. 1974. Intrinsic motivation: How to turn play into work. *Psychology Today*, 7 (September):49–54. Suggests that rewarding children (or anyone) for something they like to do may turn enjoyment into drudgery. In the words of the authors, "a person's intrinsic interest in an activity may be decreased by inducing him to engage in that activity as a means to some . . . goal."

IZARD, CARROLL E. 1977. *Human Emotions*. New York: Plenum. Presents theoretical and research material valuable for a general understanding of the field of emotions.

MASLOW, ABRAHAM H. 1971. *The Farther Reaches of Human Nature*. New York: Viking. An elaboration of Maslow's concept of self-actualization and other aspects of human potential.

ROZIN, PAUL, and FALLON, APRIL. 1985. That's disgusting! *Psychology Today*, 19 (July):60–63. Discusses what makes something disgusting.

SALOVEY, PETER, and RODIN, JUDITH. 1985. The heart of jealousy. *Psychology Today*, 19 (September):22–25. A report on survey results that reveal how we deal with jealousy and envy —from looking through a lover's possessions to checking up with phone calls.

STRONGMAN, K. T. 1978. *The Psychology of Emotions*. New York: Wiley. A good introduction to contemporary views on and theories of emotion.

TAVRIS, CAROL. 1983. *Anger: The Misunderstood Emotion*. New York: Simon & Schuster. A controversial, readable review of the theory and research on anger; concludes that the unbridled expression of angry emotions is not as healthy as psychoanalysis would have us believe.

TAVRIS, CAROL, and OFFIR, CAROLE. 1984. *The Longest War*. 2nd ed. New York: Harcourt Brace Jovanovich. A delightful exploration of sex differences and relations between the sexes in history and in the social sciences; reviews the extensive literature on the battles of the sexes with wit and perspective.

part 2

FROM SENSING TO THINKING

Jane Freilicher, *In Broad Daylight*, 1979.

5
Sensation and Perception

Nels is a student majoring in computer science at the University of Illinois. Recently he was driving about Champaign-Urbana in a car with a female companion. He had taken a piece of candy from the glove compartment and placed it in his mouth. The young woman asked him what color the candy was and to let her see what it looked like. Nels tells what happened next: "I concealed the candy under my tongue, opened my mouth, and moved close to her with my mouth open. I then closed my mouth and moved back. I asked her whether or not she had seen the candy. She said, 'No.' Then I asked her if she had seen my tongue. She answered, 'Yes.' I next asked her, 'What color is my tongue?' She said, 'I don't know. I was looking for the candy.'" Nels observes that she was trying to perceive the color of the candy by looking at the candy and the candy only. But if she had not been so selective in her viewing and had taken notice of the color that the candy had stained his tongue, she would have known the color of the candy itself.

Jeff is a student at Ohio State University, where tickets to football games are exceedingly difficult to come by. It was mid-season and the Buckeyes were the number-four-ranked team in college football polls. Jeff's parents asked that he secure tickets so that they could come to Columbus and view a Big Ten game. There is a bulletin board in the lobby of his dorm with hundreds of items on it, mostly requesting or offering rides. Jeff explains that he placed a notice on the board offering to buy tickets together with his room and phone number. Nothing happened. Jeff concluded that no one was noticing his card among all the others. He tells what he did next: "I put up another card with a nude picture at the top. Replies galore! . . . The items on the bulletin board bombard a person's senses with a great many stimuli—even overwhelm the person. But putting a nude on my card, I made it stand out from

Mental Imagery

You are moving from one dorm room or apartment to another. You have a box in which you plan to pack some items. You stare at the objects stacked on your bed, mentally picture them arranged just so in the box, but then realize that your tennis shoes will not fit. So you mentally shift the items and "see" that you can make more room by rotating the position of three books. Such images, or "mental pictures," save you time and effort. They serve as a sort of "mental blackboard" on which you can experiment with various arrangements. What are these images, and what are their relationship to the images we see with our eyes in the real world?

Like laypeople, psychologists are struck by how closely mental imagery resembles actual perception (Kosslyn, 1980, 1981, 1983, 1985). Researchers find that images of both real and imagined objects are not photographic reproductions but internal representations that reflect the ways in which information is mentally processed and constructed. Moreover, we often use them in similar ways. For example, just as you would inspect a real object, subjects in laboratory experiments can inspect their mental images to find specific items or to make various perceptual judgments regarding them. Accordingly, an imaged object can "stand in" for an observed one, producing an effect indistinguishable from everyday perception. Indeed, it turns out that imagining yourself doing something can substitute, to some extent, for the actual activity. Researchers have asked subjects to practice in their minds shooting basketballs through a hoop for a number of minutes each day for a week; the subjects' actual shooting ability is better than that of other subjects in a control group who have no mental practice.

Mental imagery has a number of interesting properties. Although there is no actual screen in the brain, such as there is on a television set, your imagery seems to occur within the context of a mental screen. So if you "look" at objects in your images much as you look at actual objects, the

the other cards and people centered their attention upon it. If everyone else were to put a nude on each of their cards in the future, we would all be right back where we started."

Jennifer is also a student at Ohio State University. She is sitting next to Mirror Lake, a pond near the center of the campus, waiting for a friend. She is toying with a long, straight stick that she holds at one end and pokes in and out of the water. Jennifer notices that the stick appears to bend at an angle when she places it in the water. She is witnessing one of the oldest optical illusions experienced by human beings.

These matters are the subject of this chapter. Your knowledge of the external world—and of your internal state as well—comes entirely from chemical and electrical processes occurring in your nervous system, particularly in your brain. Physical change in the external or internal environment triggers chemical, electrical, and mechanical activity in your sense receptors. After complex processing in your nervous system, a pattern of activity is produced in certain areas of your brain. You experience this electrical activity as a **sensation**—an awareness of sights, sounds, smells, tastes, and touches. Usually you experience some meaningful whole—you see Clint Eastwood, hear your friend's voice, smell an old, dirty sock, or feel an ant crawling on your skin—rather than a collection of sensations. In brief, you order and interpret raw sense data to arrive at meaning. The process by which you give meaning to your sensations is termed **perception**.

This process can be seen in the act of eating. When someone puts a superhamburger in front of

sensation: Awareness of sights, sounds, smells, tastes, and touches.
perception: The process by which one gives meaning to one's sensations.

parts of small items are more difficult to see than those of large items. Likewise, the mental screen has a limited extent. Try the following mental experiment suggested by Stephen M. Kosslyn (1985:27):

> Image an elephant far off, facing to the left. Imagine you are walking toward it, fixing your gaze on the center of its flank. Does it seem to loom larger as you imagine getting closer? Most subjects say it does. Now, is there a point where you can't get any closer and still "see" the entire animal? Again, most subjects say there is. Now try it with a rabbit. Does the rabbit seem to be closer than the elephant was before it begins to overflow?

Kosslyn finds that the larger an object is, the further away it appears when it begins to overflow, much as if it is confronting the outer "edges" of a screen.

It seems that images resemble the representations formed during actual perception because the same parts of the brain are used for both. Consider what happens with stroke victims who suffer some types of brain damage. When cells in a particular area of the right hemisphere are affected, patients develop "visual neglect" on the left side. Although they are not blind, they ignore everything on the left side. For instance, male patients may forget to shave the left side of their face. Much the same thing happens with mental imagery. For example, when researchers asked a patient to imagine standing on one end of a plaza that he knew very well before suffering a stroke and report what he "saw," he mentioned only things to the right. He was then asked to imagine standing at the opposite end of the plaza. Once more he mentioned only things on the right, but they were the objects he had previously ignored because he had seen them on the left from the other perspective. In sum, brain damage seems to affect the mechanisms underlying both seeing and imagining in similar ways. Indeed, there is a mounting body of research suggesting that imagining an object leads to the activation of the very same perceptual mechanisms that are used in actually perceiving it (Finke, 1980, 1985, 1986).

you, receptors in your eyes send a message to your brain: the beef patties are stacked together in the sesame seed bun, along with some lettuce. Receptors in your nose may tell you there's ketchup and cheese inside. As you grasp this gourmet delight in your hands, receptors in your fingers tell you that the roll is soft and warm. When you take a bite, receptors in your mouth send messages about pickles and some mysterious sauce. And your brain combines all these inputs into one unified perception: the object is a Big Mac.

The senses function as intermediaries between you and your environment. Without sensation you would be devoid of experience. You would be imprisoned in your body without ties to the world about you. Your senses—seeing, hearing, smelling, tasting, and feeling—are your windows to the world. Moreover, they form the basis for your mental images, so you can conceive of objects and events in the absence of their actual display (see the boxed insert above).

BASIC ASPECTS OF SENSATION

Life is a bombardment of sights, sounds, smells, tastes, and touches, from which you select some information as the focus of your attention while ignoring all the rest (Wurtz, Goldberg, and Robinson, 1982). Consider that you are now chiefly aware of this page and, most of all, this sentence. But note. You are also seeing things below, above, and well to the sides of the book. What about the pressures on your skin, perhaps on your elbows or back? What sounds and odors do you detect? Clearly, at any given moment you are flooded with countless sensations that are capable of evoking a response; these are called **stimuli.** But you respond only to certain

stimulus: A sensation that is capable of evoking a response.

Whether a flower smells sweet or not depends both on the physical properties of the flower and the state of your olfactory system. A bad cold or a whiff of ammonia immediately before can prevent you from smelling or tasting many substances. *(Betsy Cole/The Picture Cube)*

stimuli, particularly—at this moment—to the items on this page.

A stimulus can be measured in some physical way—for instance, by its size, duration, intensity, or wavelength. A sensory experience can also be measured (at least, indirectly). But a sensory experience and a stimulus are not the same thing. For example, orange juice (stimulus) tastes (sensory experience) somewhat sweet if you drink it on an empty stomach; but the same orange juice tastes sour after you

have eaten ice cream. On the other hand, the same sensory experience (flashing lights, for example) may be produced by different stimuli (a blow to the head or a fireworks display).

Psychologists are interested in the relationship between physical stimuli and sensory experiences. In vision, for example, the sensation of color corresponds to the wavelength of the light, whereas brightness corresponds to the intensity of the light.

What is the relationship between color and wavelength? How does changing a light's intensity affect one's sensation of its brightness? The psychological study of such questions is called **psychophysics**. The goal of psychophysics is to develop a quantified relationship between stimuli from the world (such as frequency and intensity) and the sensory experiences (such as color and brightness) produced by them.

Thresholds

To establish laws about how people sense the external world, psychologists first try to determine how much of a stimulus is necessary for a person to sense it at all. For example, how much energy is required for you to hear a sound or to see a light? How much of a scent must be in the room before you can smell it? How much pressure must be applied to the skin before you will feel it?

Questions such as these take on practical significance in modern medicine. Consider the management of pain. One technique involves the use of *acupuncture*—a procedure in which specific areas of the skin are punctured with needles. Medical researchers have investigated the usefulness of acupuncture in the treatment of chronic back pain (Price et al., 1984). But in order to do so, they required a measure that distinguishes among various intensities of pain. As a first step, they determined an **absolute threshold**—the smallest amount of energy that will produce a sensation, in this case pain. Next, using the absolute threshold as a baseline, they developed a scale based on the ratings patients make of different levels of pain. One way to arrive at such a

psychophysics: The study of relationships between sensory experiences and the physical stimuli that cause them.

absolute threshold: The lowest level of physical energy that will produce a sensation in half the trials.

SIGHT
Candle flame seen from a
distance of 27 km (17 miles)

HEARING
Ticking of a watch in a room
6 meters (20 feet) away

TASTE
One teaspoon sugar dissolved
in 2 gallons of distilled water
(1 part in 2000)

SMELL
One drop of perfume in
a three-room house (1 part
in 500,000,000)

TOUCH
The wing of a bee falling on
your cheek from a distance of
1 centimeter (0.39 inch)

FIGURE 5.1 Absolute detection thresholds. *(Data from Eugene Galanter. 1962. Contemporary psychophysics. In R. Brown et al., Eds.,* New Directions in Psychology. *New York: Holt, Rinehart and Winston.)*

scale is to increase experimentally people's experience of pain through the application of successive increments of heat. Then, using the scale to determine a patient's level of pain before and after acupuncture, medical researchers have evaluated whether or not the procedure contributes to the reduction of pain. This research has revealed that acupuncture typically provides patients with pain relief. One explanation for the effectiveness of acupuncture is that it triggers the release of endorphins, chemical substances known to affect the pain and pleasure centers of the brain (see Chapter 3).

In everyday life, it is usually desirable that our senses have very low absolute thresholds (sensations will be experienced with very small amounts of stimulation). For example, the eardrum registers a sound if it moves as little as 1 percent of the diameter of a hydrogen molecule. If the ear were any more sensitive, you might hear the sound of air molecules bumping into one another. And if it were more sensitive to low frequencies, you might hear the vibrations of your body as you move about. And if your eyes were much more sensitive to the infrared range, you would be able to see the heat produced by your body in the dark (Békésy, 1957). Figure 5.1 provides some representative thresholds for the senses and illustrations of them.

Sensory Differences and Ratios

Another type of threshold is the **difference threshold**, or **just noticeable difference**. This term refers to the smallest change in a stimulus that will produce a change in sensation. So to return to our example of acupuncture, medical researchers would test for the difference threshold by asking patients to compare

difference threshold (just noticeable difference): The smallest change in a physical stimulus that produces a change in sensation in half the trials.

FIGURE 5.2 A change in sensory experience is proportional to the amount of physical change. In this case, each time the amount of sugar triples, the sweetness of the lemonade doubles.

the intensity of pain they experience in their backs and that produced by the experimental application of heat. They might gradually increase the heat until the person says, "Yes, this is now more painful than the pain I feel in my back." With this technique, it also is possible to identify the smallest increase in pain intensity that is noticeable to a patient.

Psychologists also have found that a particular sensory experience depends more on *changes* in the stimulus than on the absolute size or amount of the stimulus. For example, if you put a three-pound package of food into an empty backpack, the sensation of weight will be greatly increased. But if you add the same amount to a hundred-pound backpack, the sensation will hardly increase at all. This difference occurs because the sensation produced by the added weight reflects a proportional change—and three pounds does not provide much change in a one-hundred-pound load.

In psychophysics, this idea is knows as **Weber's law:** the larger or stronger a stimulus, the larger the change required for an observer to notice that any-

thing has happened to it (to experience a just noticeable difference) (Weber, 1834).

The amount of stimulus change necessary to produce some increase in sensory experience is different for different cases, but it is almost always proportional. Suppose, for example, that you have a glass of unsweetened lemonade. In order to make it sweet, you add two spoonfuls of sugar. Now to make the lemonade taste "twice as sweet," you must add six spoonfuls—three times the original amount of sugar. Then you discover that in order to make the lemonade "four times as sweet," you must add a total of eighteen spoonfuls (see Figure 5.2). Each time the sweetness doubles, the amount of sugar triples (Stevens, 1962).

By experimenting in this way with variations in sounds, temperatures, pressures, colors, tastes, and smells, psychologists are learning more about how each sense responds to stimulation. Some senses produce huge increases in sensation in response to small increases in energy. For example, the pain of an electric shock can be increased more than eight

---

Weber's law: The principle that the larger or stronger a stimulus, the larger the change required for an observer to notice a difference.

times by doubling the voltage. In contrast, the intensity of a light must be increased many times to double its brightness.

Sensory Adaptation

Psychologists have focused on people's responses to changes in stimuli because they find that the senses are tuned to change. The senses are more responsive to increases and decreases in the magnitude of stimulation than they are to a constant level of stimulation. They *adapt*, or adjust themselves, to ongoing, unchanging stimulation. They get used to a new level and respond only to changes that depart from this level. For example, receptors in your skin adapt to the cold water when you go for a swim. Disagreeable odors in a lab seem to disappear after a while. Street noises cease to bother you after you have lived in a city for a time. And you no longer feel the constant pressure of clothes on your body. These are all examples of *desensitization*, or negative adaptation. Another kind of adaptation, called *sensitization*, is positive. A good example is the increase in visual sensitivity that you experience after a short time in a darkened movie theater. At first you see only blackness, but after a while your eyes adapt to the new level, and you can see seats, faces, and wall fixtures. Indeed, the human eye is ten thousand times more sensitive to light after spending about forty minutes in the dark than it is directly after seeing a bright light (Kaufman, 1979).

Signal-Detection Theory

Thus far we have assumed that there is a threshold above which a stimulus will have an effect on a sense organ and below which it will have no effect. Consequently, all an experimenter need do is establish the point at which a given stimulus intensity shifts from being just perceptible to being imperceptible. However, a quite different view is advanced by the proponents of **signal-detection theory.** They consider the threshold concept to be superfluous.

Signal-detection theorists such as David Green and John Swets (1966) point out that a threshold level varies across situations depending on a person's motivation, experience, expectations, and other individual factors. These psychologists are not satisfied with asking subjects to report on their sensory experiences ("Yes, I hear it" or "No, I don't hear it"). Instead, they view subjects as making *decisions* as to whether or not a stimulus was presented. These decisions are not made in a vacuum but in settings having payoffs for individuals (rewards for correctness and costs for mistakes). Moreover, people differ in their sensitivity to various stimulus intensities.

The basic ideas of signal-detection theory can best be understood by an illustration. A radar operator must be able to detect an airplane on a radar screen—to decide yes if the "signal" is presented (blips indicating an airplane) or no if "noise" is presented (blips indicating a flock of birds or bad weather). Suppose that you are a radar operator watching a screen aboard an aircraft carrier in a war zone. How do you decide whether a blip on your screen is an enemy plane or a patch of noise? If you dispatch your own aircraft for every blip, you will create chaos. But if you mistakenly identify an enemy plane as noise, the results could be disastrous.

Signal-detection theorists are interested in the difficulties faced by people such as radar operators and how they go about making their decisions. Obviously, a radar operator's judgment will be influenced by many factors, and different operators appear to have different sensitivities to blips. Moreover, a specific person's sensitivity fluctuates depending on the situation. For example, being watched by a superior typically affects the operator's performance, as do fatigue and other distractions.

As a result of the information-processing and decision-making behavior that is involved in most real-life situations, signal-detection theory abandons the idea that there is a single true absolute threshold for a stimulus. Instead it adopts the notion that the stimulus, here called a *signal*, must be detected in the face of distractions that interfere with detection of the signal. Thus signal detection is similar to standing in a noisy bus terminal and listening for the announcement of your bus departure time over the loudspeaker. Although the volume of the loud-

---

signal-detection theory: The view that perception of an event varies across situations depending on a person's motivation, experience, and expectations.

Air traffic controllers must be able to detect an airplane on the radar screen even when the plane's blip is faint and difficult to distinguish from blips caused by natural phenomena such as flocks of birds or bad weather. *(Bohdan Hrynewych/Stock, Boston)*

speaker remains constant, the difficulty you have in detecting your "signal" depends on the amount of noise in the terminal building.

THE HUMAN SENSES

According to tradition, sight, hearing, smell, taste, and touch are the five human senses, each of which conforms to a basic organ (eye, ear, nose, tongue, and skin). Yet this list vastly oversimplifies your sensory experience. For instance, touch includes the sense of pressure and of temperature. It might more properly be viewed as two senses than as merely one. Similarly, in addition to hearing, your ear (through the vestibular apparatus) provides you with a sense

of balance and equilibrium. And although you typically think of vision as a single sense, in reality it comprises a set of systems, each one a sense in its own right (Wolfe, 1983). But an even greater shortcoming of the traditional list is that it leaves out your inner world. You experience hunger, thirst, pain, dizziness, anxiety, and countless other internal states.

In sum, your body possesses large numbers of external and internal receptors that take some sort of stimulus—light, chemical molecules, sound waves, pressure—and convert it into a chemical-electrical message that can be understood by your brain. The translation of the energy in environmental stimuli into neural impulses is termed **transduction**. Because most research has focused on vision and

---

transduction: The translation of the energy in environmental stimuli into neural impulses.

hearing, these senses receive a disproportionate amount of attention in the pages that follow.

Vision

In many ways, vision is your most remarkable and richest sense. The stimulus for visual experience is *light*—waves of radiant energy that, like waves in the ocean, flow in sequence. When they stimulate receptors in the eye, impulses are carried to the brain via the optic nerve and you experience visual events.

Characteristics of Light

Light consists of electromagnetic radiation that occurs within a very restricted range of wavelengths. The total electromagnetic spectrum ranges from gamma rays to the radiation given off by AC power lines (which your radio converts into static). The portion of this spectrum that affects your visual receptors—the "visible spectrum"—is but a narrow region (see Figure 5.3).

Two characteristics of light influence vision: wavelength and intensity. *Wavelength*—the distance between the crest of one wave and the crest of the next—determines color. *Intensity*—a measure of the height (amplitude) of the light waves—determines brightness. Both color and brightness influence whether you will see a light. For instance, if you project a dark purple light against a gray wall in a dark room, you must make it somewhat more intense than you would make a green light or you will not be able to see it.

The Structure of the Eye

Figure 5.4 depicts the human eye. Let us follow light inward and examine how visual perception occurs. Light energy enters the eye through the *cornea*, the protective window (the transparent outer layer) of the eye on which a contact lens rests. The amount of light entering the inner eye is controlled by the *iris*, a colored ring of muscle fiber that surrounds the pupil (brown-eyed individuals have pigmentation that blue-eyed individuals lack). The *pupil* is the opening in the center of the eye that has a black appearance. Light passes through the pupil to the *lens*, a transparent, elastic structure that can be expanded (becoming flatter) to focus on distant objects, or contracted (becoming rounder) to focus on near objects. Finally, light energy reaches the *retina*, the light-sensitive back surface of the eye that contains the receptor cells.

The Pathway from Eye to Brain

The retina contains two types of light-sensitive cells: rods and cones (see Figure 5.4). These cells are

FIGURE 5.3   The spectrum of electromagnetic energy. The small portion of this spectrum to which the human eye is sensitive is shown expanded. The scale on the large spectrum is a *logarithmic scale* of wavelength: each step on the scale corresponds to a tenfold increase in the wavelength of the electromagnetic radiation.

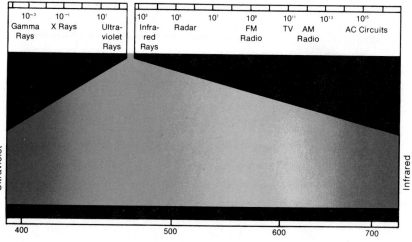

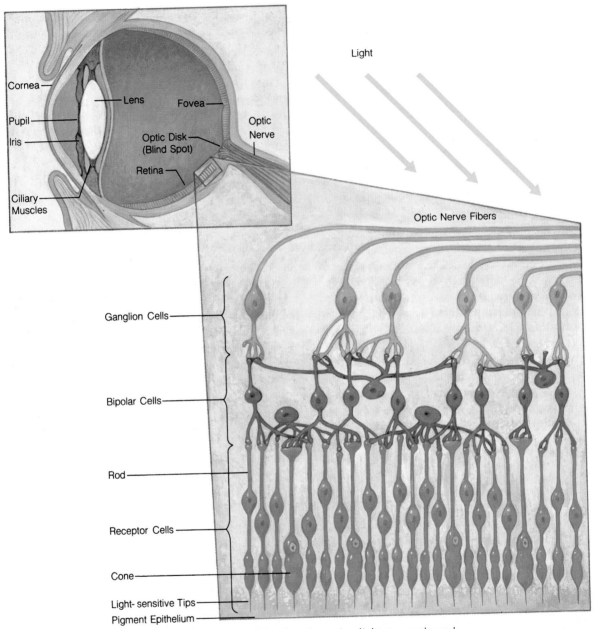

FIGURE 5.4 The structure of the human eye and retina. Incoming light passes through the cornea, pupil, and lens and hits the retina. As the inset shows, light filters through several layers of retinal cells before hitting the receptor cells (rods and cones), at the back of the eyeball and pointed away from the incoming light. The rods and cones register the presence of light and pass an electrical potential back to the adjacent bipolar cells. The bipolar cells relay the impulses to the ganglion cells, the axons of which form the fibers of the optic nerve, which transmits the impulses to the brain.

responsible for changing light energy into chemical and electrical impulses, which then travel over the *optic nerve* to the brain. (Note that light must penetrate several layers of cells before it encounters rods and cones, the actual receptors.) The retina surface, including the rods and cones, is covered by minute blood vessels (the eye is the only place in your body where these vessels can be directly seen, which is why physicians peer at them with an opthalmoscope when determining your state of health). You can see these blood vessels and the blood cells flowing through them by staring into a clear, bright sky. The blood vessels appear as pairs of parallel lines, while the blood cells are visible as small disks between the lines.

Rods and cones take their names from their shapes: rods are long, thin cells and cones are short, bulb-shaped ones. **Cones** are specialized for vision in bright light. They provide the clear, detailed, colored images that are associated with daytime vision. **Rods** are specialized for vision in dim light. They respond to extremely small amounts of light but do not transmit information about color or give sharp images with clear boundaries. Each eye has many more rods (75 to 150 million) than cones (6 to 7 million).

At the center of the retina is the *fovea*, a depressed area directly behind the lens. This region is where your vision is keenest and where you are picking up the words that you are now reading. The fovea contains mostly cones and few rods. You might try the following experiment. Stare at a word on this page. Notice that you cannot read very many other words without first moving your eyes. The reason for this is that the number of cones you have working for you trails off as your focus of attention moves away from the fovea.

Cones are found throughout the retina, while rods are most numerous in the areas surrounding the fovea and toward the sides of the retina. Since rods are very sensitive to light, you may improve your nighttime vision by looking to the side of an object rather than directly at it.

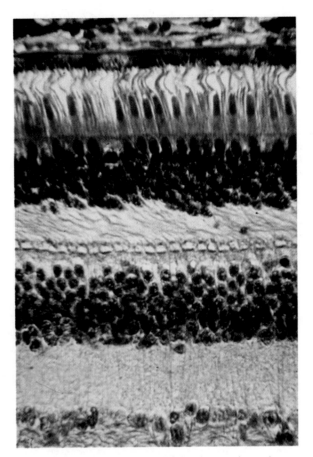

Rods and cones in the retina of the eye. Rods are long, thin cells that work well in dim light. Cones are short, round cells that operate in brighter light and give us color vision. (M. Cubberly/Phototake)

Once patterns of light and dark reach the retina, light impulses must be converted into nerve impulses by rods and cones. Rods contain a reddish-purple substance called *rhodopsin*, or "visual purple." When light strikes a rod, rhodopsin rapidly breaks down into its component parts. This chemical breakdown causes the rods to generate neural impulses. In bright light, rhodopsin disintegrates faster than it can be manufactured. However, in dim light, pro-

cones: Receptor cells in the retina sensitive to color. Because they require more light than rods to function, they are most useful in daytime vision.

rods: Receptor cells in the retina that are sensitive to light, but not to color. Rods are particularly useful in night vision.

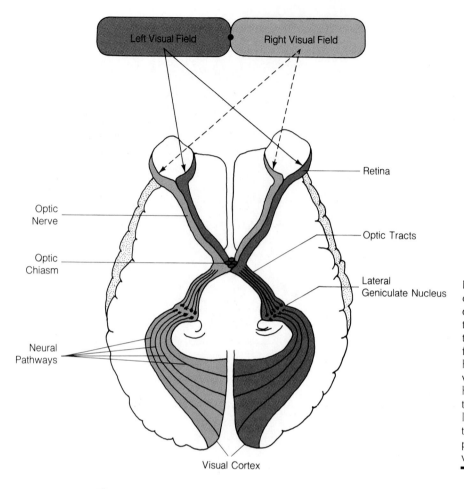

Optic Nerve

Optic Chiasm

Neural Pathways

Retina

Optic Tracts

Lateral Geniculate Nucleus

Left Visual Field

Right Visual Field

Visual Cortex

FIGURE 5.5 Pathway of the optic nerves, showing the division of the visual field by the brain. Light coming from the right side of the visual field is sent into the left hemisphere; light from the left visual field goes to the right hemisphere. The optic nerves terminate in synapses at the lateral geniculate nuclei. From there, geniculate cell axons project into the occipital lobe visual cortex areas.

duction keeps pace with the slower rate of break-down. Consequently, when you walk from the bright sunlight into a dimly lit room, you are temporarily "blinded" until your rods recharge the rhodopsin. In contrast, cones contain photosensitive chemicals that require bright light for their breakdown. Unlike rhodopsin, these chemicals reform rapidly (Tortora and Anagnostakos, 1978; O'Brien, 1982).

It is hardly surprising that a sense as complex as vision should require a complex organization of neurons (see Chapter 2). Once the rods and cones are stimulated, neural impulses are in turn transmitted to *bipolar nerve cells*. The bipolar cells then stimulate *ganglion cells* whose fibers (axons) form the optic nerve. Several rods or cones synapse with one bipolar cell, and several bipolar cells synapse with one ganglion cell (see Figure 5.4).

It is through the optic nerves (one from each eye) that information is channeled to the brain. The optic nerves meet at a crossover point termed the *optic*

chiasma, where each optic nerve splits. The fibers (axons) that arise from the left half of each retina go to the left side of the brain. Similarly, the fibers that arise from the right half of each retina go to the right side of the brain. However, objects seen on the left side of the body strike the right side of the retina and go into the right side of the brain. Thus the *left* half of each retina receives stimuli from the *right* half of the visual field and the *right* half of each retina receives stimuli from the *left* half of the visual field (see Figure 5.5). In other words, the left hemisphere of the brain "sees" objects on the right side of the body and the right hemisphere "sees" objects on the left side of the body (see Chapter 2).

From the optic chiasma, the optic nerve fibers proceed to the *lateral geniculate body* of the thalamus and then on to the visual cortex in the occipital lobes (see Figure 5.5). Here impulses bearing specific kinds of information diverge at specific sites. Nerve cells on the surface of the cortex are most receptive

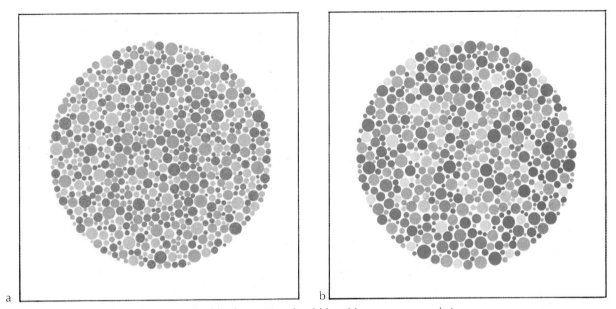

FIGURE 5.6 A test for red-green color blindness. You should be able to see numerals in the dot patterns that make up these two figures. In (a) normal subjects will see the number 8, and those with red-green deficiencies the number 3. In (b) normal subjects can read the number 16, but most people with red-green deficiencies cannot. Color-blind people use brightness differences to distinguish objects that most other people distinguish by color. In this test the dots are carefully equated for brightness, so the only way to see the numerals is to see the color differences. *(The Dvorine Pseudo-Isochromatic Plates)*

to positional information. Nerve cells in the next layer respond to information on orientation and movement. And finally, nerve cells still deeper in the cortex respond to even more complex visual elements.

Color Vision and Color Blindness

As noted, color vision is primarily mediated by the cones. One widely accepted view—the **trichromatic theory**—is that there are three types of cones and that each contains a different visual pigment. Each pigment absorbs light of a different color (or wavelength), so that each is maximally sensitive to light of a specific wavelength. (Review Figure 5.3.) Some cones respond best to red light, others to green light, and still others to blue light. Thus when red-

sensitive cones are stimulated, you see the color red. Further, colored lights can be mixed, so the color perceived by the brain depends on which class of cones is stimulated maximally, which minimally, and which not at all. Hence when red-sensitive and green-sensitive cones are equally stimulated, you "see" yellow. There is no wavelength of light that corresponds to white. You achieve the sensation of white when the three types of cones are about equally stimulated (Mollon, 1982). In sum, perceived color is the eye's measure and the brain's interpretation of electromagnetic wavelengths (Nassau, 1980).

When some or all of a person's cones do not function properly, the individual is said to have **color blindness.** There are several kinds of color blindness (see Figure 5.6); most color-blind people

---

trichromatic (TRI-crow-MAA-tic) theory: The view that there are three types of cones and that each contains a different visual pigment.

color blindness: Complete or partial inability to distinguish colors, resulting from malfunction in the cones.

FIGURE 5.7 The same scene as perceived by a person with normal vision and by people with three kinds of color blindness. (a) The scene as people with normal vision see it. (b) The experience of a person who is red-green blind; he or she sees everything in shades of blue and yellow. (c) Someone who is blue-yellow blind sees the world in shades of red and green. (d) The scene as experienced by individuals who are totally color blind. (Boulton-Wilson/Jeroboam)

do see *some* colors. For example, some people have trouble distinguishing between red and green. Other people are able to see red and green but cannot distinguish between yellow and blue. A very few people are totally color-blind. They depend on their rods, so to them the world looks something like black-and-white television programs—it consists of nothing but blacks and whites and shades of gray (see Figure 5.7).

Color blindness affects about 8 percent of American men and less than 1 percent of American women. It results from a hereditary defect in the cones. This defect is carried on one X-chromosome of women whose vision is normal. These women have a fifty-fifty chance of passing the X-chromosome with color-blindness genes on to their sons, who are born with color blindness.

Hearing

The auditory system, like the visual system, transduces energy into neural impulses. However, unlike

the visual system, it derives its energy from a mechanical rather than an electromagnetic source. Thus sound energy, unlike light, requires a medium such as air through which to travel. The denser the medium, the more effectively the sound energy travels.

Sound waves result from the alternate compression and decompression of molecules of air or water. Variations in the pressure of the atmosphere originate in vibrating strings (violin strings, human vocal cords), vibrating air columns (clarinet, organ), and vibrating membranes and plates (loudspeaker, drum, xylophone). The air transmits these disturbances outward from the source, much as the toss of a stone into a pool of water produces a series of ripples. Sonar, an underwater detection device, relies on the excellent sound conduction of water to "hear" heavy objects (such as ships) many miles away by bouncing sound waves off them.

The intensity of sound (associated with the psychological sensation of loudness) depends on the *amplitude* of sound waves (see Figure 5.8). The

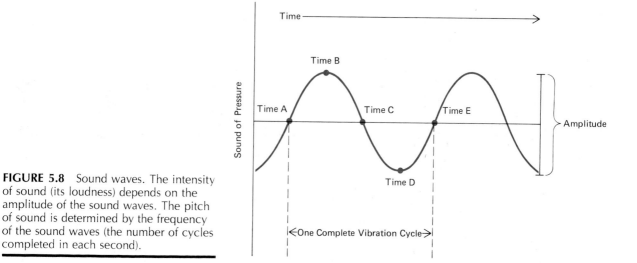

FIGURE 5.8 Sound waves. The intensity of sound (its loudness) depends on the amplitude of the sound waves. The pitch of sound is determined by the frequency of the sound waves (the number of cycles completed in each second).

greater the amplitude, the greater the intensity. Intensity of sound is expressed in *decibels (dB)*. The sounds one hears range upward from zero decibels, the softest sound the human ear can detect, to about 140 decibels, which is roughly as loud as a jet plane taking off. Any sound over 110 decibels can damage hearing, and any sound that is painful when you first hear it *will* damage your hearing if you hear it often enough. Some evidence suggests that today's nineteen-year-olds, particularly those who grew up with loud music from earphone-equipped portable stereos, do not hear as well as youths did two decades ago (Taylor, 1984). Figure 5.9 lists the decibel levels of some common sounds.

The pitch of sound is determined by the *frequency* of the sound waves and is expressed as cycles per second (see Figure 5.8). The greater the frequency, the higher the pitch. High frequencies produce shrill squeaks; low frequencies produce deep bass sounds. Human beings are restricted to a range of 20 to 20,000 cycles per second; cats respond to sounds up to 50,000 cycles per second; and bats and porpoises respond to frequencies as high as 100,000 cycles per second. If you hear a sound composed of a combination of different frequencies, you can hear the separate pitches even though they occur simultaneously. For example, if you strike two keys of a piano at the same time, your ear can detect two distinct pitches.

Vibrating objects alternately compress and expand neighboring molecules, producing mechanical waves of energy (sound waves) that strike the eardrum, or *tympanic membrane*, in the outer ear. These sound waves, or changes in air pressure, cause the

eardrum to vibrate with the same frequency. The middle ear consists of three bones: the *hammer*, the *anvil*, and the *stirrup*. These three bones transmit the vibrations of the eardrum to the *cochlea* in the inner ear (see Figure 5.10). The cochlea contains tiny hairlike cells that move back and forth (much like a field of wheat waving in the wind). These hair cells change sound vibrations into chemical-electrical signals that travel through the *auditory nerve* to the auditory area of the temporal lobe in the cerebral cortex (see Chapter 2).

Sounds are located through the interaction of the two ears. When a noise occurs on your right, for example, the sound comes to both ears, but it reaches your right ear a fraction of a second before it reaches the left. It is also slightly louder in the right ear. These differences typically tell you which direction the sound is coming from.

Smell and Taste

Smell and taste are known as the chemical senses because their receptors are sensitive to chemical molecules rather than to light energy or sound waves. Since the two senses are located close together and both have a chemical basis, people frequently confuse or blend their separate sensations. Indeed, smell and taste interact, especially in the appreciation of the subtleties of food flavor (Rozin, 1982). For instance, more than one person has remarked, "I really love the taste of Limburger cheese, but only if I can get it by my nose." The same odor, which constitutes the most distinctive aspect of its "taste,"

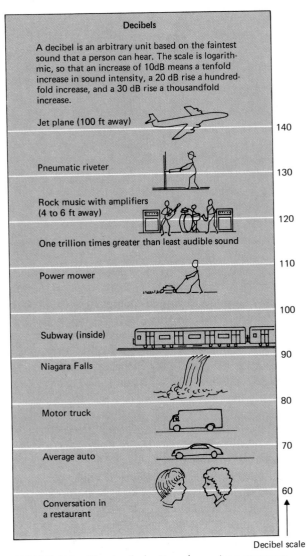

Decibels

A decibel is an arbitrary unit based on the faintest sound that a person can hear. The scale is logarithmic, so that an increase of 10dB means a tenfold increase in sound intensity, a 20 dB rise a hundredfold increase, and a 30 dB rise a thousandfold increase.

Jet plane (100 ft away) — 140

Pneumatic riveter — 130

Rock music with amplifiers (4 to 6 ft away) — 120

One trillion times greater than least audible sound

Power mower — 110

— 100

Subway (inside) — 90

Niagara Falls — 80

Motor truck — 70

Average auto

Conversation in a restaurant — 60

Decibel scale

FIGURE 5.9 The decibel ratings for various common sounds. Sound actually becomes painful at about 130 decibels. Decibels represent ratios: a 20-decibel difference between two sounds indicates that one sound is ten times more intense than the other. *(From George B. Dintiman and Jerrold S. Greenberg. 1986. Health Through Discovery. 3rd ed. New York: Newbery Award Records, p. 494. Reprinted by permission.)*

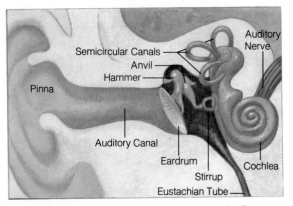

FIGURE 5.10 The hearing process. Sound vibrations in the air strike the eardrum (pinna) and set a chain of three tiny bones (hammer, anvil, and stirrup) into motion. Vibrations travel through the cochlea, a long coiled tube with a skinlike membrane running down the center of it. Stimulation of the hair cells on this membrane causes them to convert the vibrations into electrical impulses, which are relayed by the auditory nerve to the brain.

For you to smell something, the smell receptors in your nose must be stimulated by the appropriate molecules. The molecules enter your nose in vapors and reach the special membranes in the nasal passages on which the olfactory receptors are located (see Figure 5.11). When you sniff something, you create eddy currents that force air into the upper portions of your nose and increase your perception of odor. When you wish to savor something in your mouth, you exhale. This forces air from your mouth across the olfactory receptors (Murphy, Cain, and Bartoshuk, 1977; Murphy and Cain, 1980). In turn, the olfactory receptors send messages about smells over the *olfactory nerve* to the brain.

Laboratory tests show that most people can pick out one odor from another only about 70 percent of the time (Engen, 1980). In contrast, most people rarely make mistakes in distinguishing between visual objects or between sounds. Nonetheless, you can *recognize* a smell for a longer time and better than you can remember sights or sounds. For instance, the smell of turpentine may prompt you to recall the basement paint shelf in your grandfather's home, which you have not been in for forty years. The memory peg provided by odor allows animals to call on pertinent past experience in dealing with dangers or opportunities, and hence the ability provides survival value. Compared with many of the other

becomes pleasant when we sense it in our mouths. On the other hand, people who cannot smell can taste only sour, salty, bitter, and sweet, but none of the subtle flavors of chocolate, lemon, roast beef, or herbs. Not surprisingly, the majority of patients who complain of a loss of taste really have something wrong with their ability to smell.

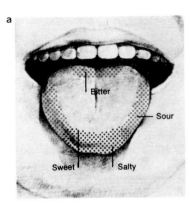

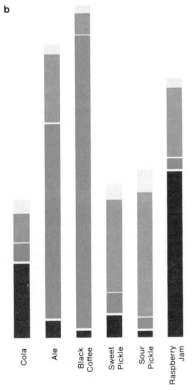

FIGURE 5.11 The sense of smell. The receptors for the sense of smell are located at the top of the nasal passages. The arrows show the path that the air we breathe takes to the receptors.

FIGURE 5.12 (a) A map of the human tongue showing the areas of maximum sensitivity to the four fundamental kinds of taste sensation. Interestingly, it is possible to be genetically taste blind as well as color blind: a chemical called PTC tastes extremely bitter to some people and is quite tasteless to others. (b) The tastes of a number of foods analyzed into the four components of taste shown in (a). The length of the colored bars indicates the amount of each component judged to be present in the taste of the food by a number of subjects in an experiment. (Data from J. G. Beebe-Center. 1949. Standards for the use of Gust Scale. Journal of Psychology, 28:411–419.)

senses, odor has a particularly powerful capacity to activate emotion (Engen, 1982). One of the most salient aspects of odor is hedonistic: we react to its pleasantness before we identify its quality or intensity. It is possible that the perception of odor evolved in part as a guide to the selection of food and to reinforce eating behaviors.

For you to taste something, appropriate chemicals must stimulate receptors in the taste buds on your tongue. Taste information is relayed to the brain along with data about the texture and temperature of the substance you have put in your mouth. Most scientists believe that there are four basic tastes: sour, salty, bitter, and sweet (Beebe-Center, 1949; Bartoshuk, 1974, 1980). As shown in Figure 5.12, different areas of the tongue are especially sensitive to one or more of these four basic qualities. You experience other taste sensations as mixtures of these four tastes or as various combinations of taste and smell.

Certain substances can suppress or distort one or more of the four tastes. You may have noticed that if you brush your teeth before breakfast, your orange juice acquires an unpleasant bitter-sour taste. One of the detergents found in some toothpastes (sodium laurel sulfate) produces this effect. However, even saliva contributes to taste modification. Not only does saliva have taste, but people differ in the taste produced by their saliva. For instance, a nonsmoker notices the difference immediately on kissing a smoker. The taste of saliva is also the source of the bitter or flat taste that many people attribute to distilled water (Bartoshuk, 1980).

The sense of taste illustrates the fact that people inhabit somewhat different sensory worlds. Culture and learning of course play an important part (Douglas, 1979). Very likely you shrink from the thought of eating grubs, grasshoppers, larks, blackbirds, and dogs, although they are served in various other parts of the world. And times also change. Nowadays beef, pheasant, and grouse are no longer kept and hung long enough to produce the rank, gamey flavor highly prized by earlier generations. Likewise, some children today seem to prefer the taste of orange juice made from frozen concentrate, complaining that the freshly squeezed kind "doesn't taste like the real stuff."

Differences in taste are also the product of complex chemical and genetic influences (Bartoshuk, 1974, 1980). For example, family studies reveal that the inability to taste the bitter substance phenylthiocarbamide (PTC) is a recessive trait (see Chapter 2). People with two recessive genes are relatively insensitive to PTC, whereas those with one or two dominant genes are quite sensitive to the substance. About two-thirds of the American population are PTC tasters. PTC tasters also commonly experience a bitter taste from such substances as the potassium chloride used as a salt substitute in low-sodium diets. Obviously, these taste differences have profound implications for firms marketing such products.

Another taste difference is the "artichoke effect." An estimated 60 percent of Americans find that water tastes sweet to them after eating artichokes. Thus if you are a wine fancier, you would be well advised to avoid artichokes when you expect to enjoy an unusual vintage of wine with dinner.

The chemical senses seem to play a less important role in human life than they do in lower animals. Insects, for example, often depend on smell to communicate with one another, especially in mating.

In human beings, smell and taste have become more a matter of aesthetics than of survival.

The Skin Senses

Receptors in the skin are responsible for providing the brain with at least four kinds of information about the environment: pressure, warmth, cold, and pain.

Sensitivity to pressure varies from place to place depending on the skin's location. Some spots, such as your fingertips, are densely populated with receptors and therefore are highly sensitive. Other spots, such as the middle of your back, contain relatively few receptors. Pressure sensations serve as a source of protection. For example, feeling the light pressure of an insect landing on your arm warns you of the impending danger of being stung.

Some skin receptors are particularly sensitive to hot or cold stimuli (Hensel, 1982). In order to create a hot or cold sensation, a stimulus must have a temperature that is greater or less than the temperature of the skin. If you plunge your arm into a sink of warm water on a hot day, you will experience little or no heat sensation. However, if you put your arm in the same water on a cold day, the water will feel quite warm.

Many kinds of stimuli—scratches, punctures, severe pressure, heat, and cold—can produce pain. Their common property is the real or potential injury that they pose to bodily tissues. Pain makes it possible for you to prevent damage to your body. It functions as an emergency system that demands immediate action.

Because pain acts as a warning system for your body, it does not easily adapt to stimulation—you rarely get "used to" pain. Pain tells you to avoid a stimulation that is harmful to you. Without this mechanism, you might "adapt" to a fire when you stand next to it. After a few minutes you would literally begin to cook, and your tissues would die.

In addition to the pain that derives from stimulation of the skin receptors, there is the pain that arises from stimulation of visceral receptors. Little is known about pain from the interior of the body except that it seems to be deep, dull, and much more unpleasant than the sharply localized pain from the skin. In some cases, internal pain receptors may send inaccurate messages. They may indicate, for example, that a pain is located in your shoulder when in reality the source of irritation is in your lower stomach. Such sensation of pain in an area that is away from the actual source is called **referred pain.**

Another type of bodily sensation comes from receptors that monitor internal body conditions. These receptors are sensitive to pressure, temperature, pain, and chemicals inside the body. For example, when your stomach is full, these internal receptors are stretched, informing your brain that you have eaten too much.

Balance and Kinesthesis

The body's sense of balance is regulated by the **vestibular system** inside the inner ear. Its prominent feature is the three semicircular canals (see Figure 5.13). When your head starts turning, the movement causes the liquid in the canals to move, bending the endings of receptor hair cells. The cells connect with the vestibular nerve, which then joins the auditory nerve and proceeds to the brain.

The stimuli for vestibular responses include movements such as spinning, falling, and tilting the body or head. Overstimulation of the vestibular sense by such movements can result in dizziness and "motion sickness"—the sorts of sensations you probably have experienced by going on amusement-park rides or by spinning around on a swivel stool. Although you are seldom directly aware of your sense of balance, without it you would be unable to stand without falling or walk without stumbling.

Kinesthesis allows you to recognize the location of one body part in relation to the others. It cooperates with the vestibular and visual senses to maintain posture and balance. The sensation of kinesthesis comes from receptors in and near your muscles, tendons, and joints. When any movement occurs, these receptors immediately send messages to your brain.

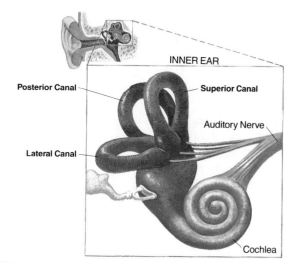

FIGURE 5.13 The vestibular system. The organs of balance consist of three semicircular canals at right angles to one another, filled with a freely moving fluid. Continuous motion in a straight line produces no response in this system, but starting, stopping, turning, speeding up, or slowing down makes the fluid in at least one of the canals move, stimulating the hair cells attached to the canal walls. These hair cells convert the movement into electrical impulses that are sent to the brain via the auditory nerve.

Without kinesthetic sensations, your movements would be jerky and uncoordinated. You would not know what your hand was doing if it was behind your back, and you would not be able to walk without looking at your feet. Furthermore, complex physical activities, such as surgery, piano playing, and acrobatics, would be impossible.

Interconnections Among the Senses

Our sensory systems hardly operate in isolation from one another. We expect to see things we hear, feel things we see, and smell things we taste. We fre-

referred pain: The sensation of pain in an area away from the actual source; most commonly experienced with internal pain.

vestibular (ves-TIH-bew-lar) system: Three semicircular canals located in the inner ear and connected to the brain by the vestibular nerve. They regulate the sense of balance.

kinesthesis (kin-es-THEE-sis): The sense of movement and body position, acquired through receptors located in and near the muscles, tendons, and joints.

Food not only smells good, but the sounds of frying fish and simmering rice increase their aesthetic appeal. (Katrina Thomas/Photo Researchers)

quently use information gained from one sensory system to "inform" our other systems (Acredolo and Hake, 1982). Earlier in the chapter we noted that our appreciation of the subtleties of food flavor is achieved through integrating knowledge from both smell and taste. Other senses are also involved. The appearance of food influences how appetizing we deem it to be. Even sound plays a part, such as the popping noises we associate with popcorn and the sizzling sounds we associate with a steak on an outdoor grill. Many of us also notice how the tastes "feel" as they are being washed over our tongue: salt and sweet often seem warm and pleasant; bitterness may curl the edges of the tongue; and sour may feel icy.

All the senses create a system that is a whole. Information gained from multiple senses is frequently more important than that gained from one sense precisely because it is interactive (Lamb and Sherrod, 1981). Interconnections between the senses are noted even in newborns. They will move their heads and their eyes in efforts to locate the source of

sounds, especially when the sounds are patterned and sustained. As infants mature, they become more adept at exploring their environment, selecting from fields of light, sound, odor, taste, and contact what is relevant. In brief, we are hardly passive beings. We actively use our organic receptors to search out information. We turn toward a sound, seeking to identify its location. We sniff an odor. We prod an object to determine what it is. Our perceptual system does not merely receive stimuli; it "hunts" additional stimuli until it achieves some sort of understanding.

In our everyday conversations we intermingle the five senses. We say, for example, that red is a "warm" color, but green is "cool"; her voice is "sweet," or sadness is "blue." These are termed *cross-modal associations*. In some people, cross-modal associations result in *synesthesia*, a condition in which perceptions typically confined to one sense overlap with two or more senses (Lemley, 1984). A person with synesthesia may report that roast beef "feels" like long marble archways, spearmint like cool glass columns, and lemonade like small spears against the face or that B-flat "sounds" purple.

PERCEPTUAL ORGANIZATION AND PROCESSES

Our discussion suggests that we do not usually experience a mass of colors, noises, temperatures, and pressures. Rather, we see cars and buildings, hear voices and music, feel pencils and desks, and touch close friends. We do not merely have sensory experiences; we perceive objects. Our brains receive information from the senses and then organize and interpret it into meaningful experiences. These processes are the core of perception.

Thus far in the chapter, we have directed most attention toward an understanding of the structure and functions of the human sense organs. For instance, in our discussion of vision we considered the mechanisms of the eye's operation, the part that light-sensitive rods and cones play in vision, the significance of electromagnetic wavelengths for the experience of color, and the neural pathways by which messages are transmitted to the brain. Ultimately, however, information from the sense organs must be processed and interpreted by the brain. The brain takes raw sensory data and gives them organi-

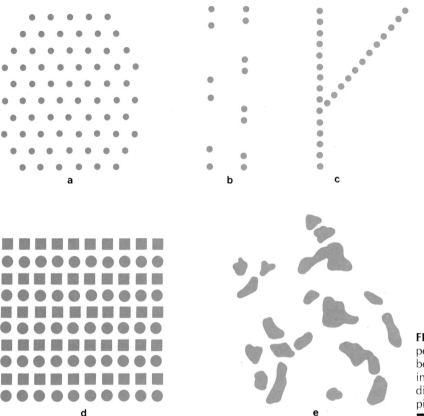

a   b   c

d   e

FIGURE 5.14 Principles of perceptual organization. Human beings see patterns and groupings in their environments rather than disorganized arrays of bits and pieces.

zation. In so doing, it enables you to grasp the *relatedness* of an object or event to all the other objects and events with which it is associated.

Grouping

Why do things look as they do? Why, for instance, when you look at an animal do you see a horse rather than simply fur, hoofs, legs, and a snout? Part of the answer lies in the fact that your brain constantly tries to build "wholes" out of the confusion of stimuli that bombard the senses. The "whole" experience that comes from organizing bits and pieces of information into meaningful objects and patterns is called a **Gestalt.** Here, the whole is greater than the sum of the parts. ("Gestalt" is a German word meaning pattern or configuration.)

The initial impetus to Gestalt psychology came in 1910, when the German psychologist Max Wertheimer (1880–1943) discovered the *phi phenomenon.* The phi phenomenon involves the illusion of motion. If two lights blink on and off at a certain rate, they give the impression that the light is moving back and forth. The apparent movement of neon-lighted arrows that point to a motel when lighted in succession is an example of the phi phenomenon. The experience of motion emerges as your brain organizes elements into wholes.

Gestalt psychologists have tried to identify the organizing principles that the brain uses in constructing perceptions. One kind of organization is called **grouping** (Koffka, 1963). Grouping depends on several principles, as demonstrated in Figure 5.14. In part *a,* dots of equal size are spaced equally

Gestalt (Geh-SHTAHLT) In perception, the experience that comes from organizing bits and pieces of information into meaningful wholes.

grouping: One of the organizing principles that the brain uses in constructing perceptions.

across a field, and you perceive no stable distinguishing pattern. In part *b*, the spacing of the dots has been changed so that elements that are close to one another seem to belong together—the principle of **proximity.** Consequently, stimuli that are found close to one another will be seen as a group.

In part *c*, the dots have been rearranged to illustrate the principle of **continuity.** Although the bottom dot in the inclined (slanted) series is closer to the vertical series than the dots in the vertical row are to each other, it is not seen as belonging to the vertical row. It is seen as a continuation of the inclined row and therefore as part of it. In this case, the principle of continuity overrules the influence of proximity.

Part *d* illustrates the principle of **similarity.** Similar events seem to belong together. Therefore, you see the array as a set of horizontal rows rather than as vertical columns, as you might do if all the elements were the same. Finally, part *e* demonstrates the principle of **closure.** You ignore the breaks and see the "whole" (a person riding a horse).

The knowledge most likely to become incorporated in our perceptual systems through evolutionary processes is knowledge that is relatively constant and simply represented (Shepard and Farrell, 1985). The Gestalt principles of organization are this sort of knowledge. They allow us to transform our inputs from the world about us in a relatively invariant and economical manner. And they permit us to fill in gaps in perceptual input in order to make sense of our experiences. For this latter reason computer scientists and engineers are having considerable difficulty replicating visual capabilities in machinery (see the boxed insert on page 169). Nor are Gestalt

principles limited to vision. For instance, by virtue of these principles, you tend to group musical notes on the basis of their closeness to one another in time—you hear melodies, not single notes. Similarity and continuity are also important. They allow you to follow the sound of a particular voice or instrument even when many other sounds are occurring. For example, you can follow the sound of a bass guitar through a song.

A number of psychologists have suggested that all the principles of grouping can be integrated under a single concept: **simplicity** (Attneave, 1954, 1982; Hochberg, 1978). (See Figure 5.15.) Perceptual tendencies toward simplicity—or economy—are termed the *minimum principle* (Hatfield and Epstein, 1985). One explanation for the minimum principle is that simplicity is adaptive because less complex representations require less mental activity than more complex representations do. Proximity, continuity, similarity, and closure all contribute to economy. Each of these grouping principles makes a mass of elements manageable by integrating the elements into a whole.

Figure and Ground

Another basic form of perceptual organization studied by Gestalt psychologists is **figure-ground**—the division of the visual field into two distinct parts, one being the objects (figure) and the other the background or spaces between the objects (ground). Look at Figure 5.16. What do you see? Sometimes the figure looks like a white vase against a black background. At other times it appears to be two black faces against a white background.

---

proximity: A principle in perceptual grouping in which stimuli that are found close to one another are seen as a group.

continuity: A principle in perceptual grouping in which stimuli are perceived as continuous.

similarity: A principle in perceptual grouping in which like elements are seen as belonging together.

closure: A principle in perceptual grouping in which breaks between elements are ignored and the whole is seen as a single image.

simplicity: A principle in perceptual grouping that states that people find it easier to perceive simple patterns than they do complex patterns.

figure-ground: The division of the visual field into two distinct parts, one being the objects (figure), the other the background or spaces between the objects (ground).

a   b

FIGURE 5.15   Two illustrations of the perceptual tendency toward simplicity. Despite conflicting cues, (a) is seen as two intersecting circles. The circle is among the simplest of perceived forms and provides the simplest means of interpreting this pattern. The figure in (b) is most often seen as a circle covering one large triangle, rather than a circle with three small points attached to it. The "one big triangle" interpretation fits and is simpler than the other. Note how the interpretation would change if the points were not aligned at the corners of a triangle.

When you look at three-dimensional objects against the sky or some other unstructured background, you have no trouble deciding which areas represent objects and which represent spaces between objects. It is when something is two-dimensional, as in Figure 5.16, that you may have trouble telling the figure from the ground. Nevertheless, such figure-ground problems give clues as to the active nature of perception. The fact that a single pattern can be perceived in more than one way demonstrates that you are not a passive receiver of stimuli. You *actively* explore the fields of light, selecting what is relevant and extracting information from them (Gibson, 1966).

Figure and ground are important in hearing as well as in vision. When you follow one person's voice at a noisy meeting, that voice is a figure and all other sounds become the ground. When you listen to a piece of music, a familiar theme may "leap out" at you: the melody becomes the figure, and the rest of the music merely background. Likewise, if you enter a kitchen filled with unfamiliar cooking odors and suddenly recognize the odor of a roast, the odor of the roast becomes the figure and the other odors become the ground.

Perceptual Constancies

When you have learned to perceive certain objects in your environment, you tend to see them in the same way, regardless of changing conditions. You probably judge the whiteness of the various portions of these pages to be fairly constant, even though you

FIGURE 5.16   What did you see the first time you looked at this famous illustration? Whatever you saw, you saw because of your past experiences and current expectations. People invariably organize their experience into figure and ground. Whatever appears as figure receives the attention, is likely to be remembered, and has a distinctness of form that is lacking in the vague, formless ground. But, as this figure shows, what is meaningless ground one minute may become the all-important figure the next.

may have read the book under a wide range of lighting conditions. The light, angle of vision, and distance—and, therefore, the image on the retina—all change, but your perception of the object does not. Thus despite changing physical conditions, you are able to perceive objects as relatively stable and

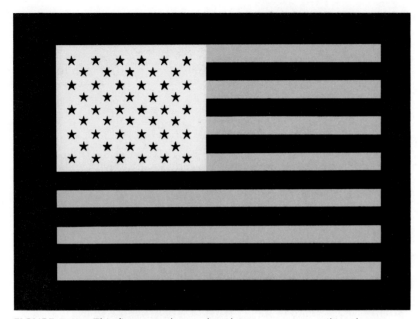

FIGURE 5.17 This figure can be used to demonstrate two striking features of vision, termed the *McCollough effect* after Celeste McCollough (1965), who was the first to describe it. Stare steadily at the lowest right-hand star for about forty-five seconds, or until the colors start to shimmer. Then stare at a blank piece of paper. After a second or two you should see a *negative afterimage* of this figure in which the flag shows the normal colors. This occurs because the receptors for green, black, and yellow become fatigued, allowing the complementary colors of each to predominate when you stare at the white paper. Since these complements are, respectively, red, white, and blue, you see a normal American flag. Now shift your glance to a blank wall some distance away. Suddenly the flag will appear huge. This happens because of the principle of *constancy*—the brain interprets the same image as large when it is far away (apparently on the wall) and small when it is close (apparently on a piece of paper in your hand). Typically, the more distant an object is from your eye, the smaller the image that is projected onto your retina. Your brain compensates for this effect by scaling up the apparent size of distant objects. When the image in the eye is field constant, as in the case of an afterimage, your brain compensates for changes in distance and you perceive a large flag. Studies suggest that the afterimage doubles in size for every doubling in the distance between the subject and the wall.

unchanging—a process that is termed **perceptual constancy.**

Figure 5.17 provides an experiment that allows you to explore the phenomenon of perceptual constancy. Your brain will automatically attempt to take into account the distance at which you perceive the object—with some interesting results. When you have completed the experiment in Figure 5.17, you may wish to try another one. Hold a coin at arm's length and look at it. Next bring the coin halfway toward your eyes. Does the coin seem to get larger? You will notice that it remains about the same size, illustrating perceptual constancy. This is a remarkable feat because at the halfway point the coin

perceptual constancy: The ability to perceive objects as relatively stable and unchanging.

The Quest to Match Human Vision

In pursuing one of humankind's most audacious dreams—creating machines that think—computer scientists have encountered a major roadblock. They are finding it difficult to replicate human vision (Ullman, 1979; Marr, 1982; Broad, 1984). After a quarter century of research, they have yet to design machines that are able to recognize a multitude of everyday objects and distinguish one from the other. Despite the problems, the goal has held considerable allure. Industry wants "vision machines" to robotize assembly lines, and the military wants them to guide land vehicles and planes.

Initially, the task did not seem particularly difficult. Psychologists like to tell the story of how twenty years ago Marvin Minsky, a pioneer in artificial intelligence, asked a graduate student to solve the problem of machine vision as a summer project. Moreover, early strides were impressive. In the 1960s engineers used tricks of lighting and contrast to heighten outlines in order to make objects visible to scanning equipment. A camera fed this information into a computer, which would analyze it for patterns and compare the image with ones stored in the computer's memory. Using techniques involving high-contrast images, engineers have designed machines that decide whether an object on an assembly line is the correct size and the right position. The major problem with current equipment is that conditions must be virtually perfect for the machine to make an identification.

As Gestalt psychologists have shown, much subtlety occurs in human vision. The brain "finds" a pattern—for instance, a circle in a series of random dots—even if only parts of a pattern are present. In brief, our brain "sees" things that are not there. We make inferences that allow us to identify objects whose parts are missing or indistinct. The challenge confronting engineers is how to design computers that go beyond the recognition of simple outlines. How do they get a computer to separate a bicycle from a child when their outlines merge? Or how can the computer identify a child when only an arm is viewed by the camera? Whereas the human eye sees a bus, dog, or carrot, a computer peering through the lens of a camera may see only disjointed jumbles of lines and circles. In sum, what the mind wants to see is frequently as important as what the eye actually sees.

Computer scientists are searching for solutions by developing computer programs that identify surfaces, textures, colors, and shadings. And they are attempting to build models that simplify the complexities of the real world by creating general patterns for making identifications (for example, using general surface contours rather than specific outlines of buses, dogs, and carrots). The task of enhancing the vision of computers is increasing the respect that scientists have for the human visual system. The biological system has considerable power and complexity. Moreover, the brain, with neurons that operate about a million times slower than silicon chips, is beating out computers. The difference is in the wiring. Neurons are doing millions and even billions of operations *simultaneously*. In contrast, most computers are still based on a serial, one-step-at-a-time architecture. Currently much research is centered on the development of "parallel" architectures that will allow computers to work on multiple problems at the same time. Even so, scientists have a considerable distance to go in designing machines that work as effectively as the human visual system in extracting the information necessary to construct a three-dimensional map of the environment.

---

projects an image on the retina that is double the size of that projected at arm's length. Even though the coin is moved nearer in vision, it does not balloon in size. Instead, your brain compensates for the changes in the retinal image and perceives the coin as more or less the same size.

From an evolutionary viewpoint, an animal that can see through the changeable aspects of its environment and pick up the stable aspects enjoys an advantage in meeting its survival needs. By recognizing familiar features in a new situation, the animal can bring prior experience and learning to bear in exploiting opportunities and minimizing perils. In so doing, it builds a world of enduring objects.

Brightness and Color Constancies

Although the amount of light available to your eyes varies a good deal, your perception of the brightness of familiar objects varies hardly at all. Thus, as noted above, you perceive portions of this page as being white whether you view it under light from the sun, a candle, a fluorescent lamp, or the moon. The reason for this is that the brightness (the whiteness or lightness) of an object depends on its surrounding field. Increasing the illumination of an object will not necessarily increase its brightness if the illumination received by its surrounding area is proportionally increased. It is the physical contrast between the lighting of an object and its field that gives you your sense that its brightness is increasing or decreasing.

You also perceive familiar objects as retaining their color, even though the information reaching your eyes varies. If you own a blue car, the car appears blue to you whether you see it in a parking lot under dim moonlight or under bright sunlight. Yet the information received by your eyes imparts a much blacker quality to the car under moonlight than under sunlight. However, should you be unfamiliar with an object, your experience of color will frequently vary. Hence, if you purchase a sweater in a store and later examine the sweater in daylight, you may infer that it has a somewhat different shade than it had previously.

Size and Shape Constancies

In order for your behavior to be adaptive, your perceived world must be predictable. Yet space relationships vary as a function of distance and orientation. Size and shape constancies allow you to perceive these aspects of your environment as constant despite the variations that occur in your retinal images.

The experiment you were asked to perform with a coin is an example of size constancy. It demonstrates that you have an automatic system for perceiving an object as being the same size whether it is far or near. In a similar fashion, a friend walking toward you does not seem to change into a giant even though the image inside your eyes becomes larger and larger as he or she approaches. To you, the friend's appearance stays the same size because at the same time that the size of your visual image is increasing, you are perceiving an additional piece of information: distance is decreasing. The enlarging eye image and the distance information combine to produce a perception of an approaching object that stays the same size.

Perceptual inference: even though you cannot see it, you assume that the road will continue beyond the slight rise—not stop abruptly at the limits of your vision from the car. *(Charles Harbutt/Magnum)*

Distance information compensates for the enlarging eye image to produce size constancy. If information about distance is eliminated, your perception of the size of the object begins to correspond to the actual size of the eye image. For example, it is difficult for most people to estimate the size of an airplane in the sky because they have little experience judging such huge sizes and distances. Pilots, however, can determine whether a flying plane is large and far away or small and close because they are experienced in estimating the sizes and distances of planes.

Shape constancy refers to the fact that the perceived shape of an object remains relatively invariant despite changes in spatial orientation. For instance, a rectangular book tilted away from you still looks like a rectangle even though its image on the retina becomes that of a trapezoid. Similarly, a desk top or a partially open door looks rectangular even though the retinal image is not.

Perceptual Inference

Often people have perceptions that are not based entirely on current sensory information (Hellstrom, 1985). When you hear barking as you approach your house, you assume it is your dog—not a cat or a rhinoceros or even another dog. When you take a seat in a dark theater, you assume it is solid and will hold your weight even though you cannot see what supports the seat. When you are driving in a car and see in the distance that the road climbs up a steep hill, then disappears over the top, you assume the road will continue over and down the hill, not come to an abrupt halt.

This phenomenon of filling in the gaps in what your senses tell you is known as **perceptual inference** (Gregory, 1978; Kawabata, 1984). Perceptual inference is largely automatic and unconscious. For instance, there are times when the things we hear do not correspond to the sounds at our ears. Consider that we live in a noisy environment. Loud sounds may drown out a portion of a message or melody. However, we possess mechanisms for reconstructing the masked segments, a process termed *auditory*

induction (Warren, 1984). In its simpler forms, the process allows us to restore sounds subject to intermittent interruption so that a message or melody seems continuous.

A variety of factors contribute to perceptual inference. For one thing you have typically encountered many of the stimuli and objects in the past, and you know what to expect from them in the present. So you need only a few cues to inform you that the noise you hear when approaching your home is your dog barking or that a theater seat is solid. Perceptual inference, then, may depend on experience. But it is also likely that people are born with some of their ability to make perceptual inferences. For example, experimenters have shown that infants just barely able to crawl will avoid falling over what appears to be a steep cliff—thus proving that they perceive depth (Gibson and Walk, 1960). (See Figure 5.18.) For this reason, many people walk around grates in sidewalks. Perceptual inference, whether an inherited or acquired property, plays a critical part in many skills, including hitting a baseball (see the boxed insert on page 174).

Illusions

Illusions are perceptions that are misrepresentations of reality. For example, look at the lines in Figure 5.19. Which lines are longer? Measure the lengths of the pairs of lines with a ruler, then look again. Do the "longer" lines *look* longer now that you *know* they are the same? For most people, the answer is no.

A possible explanation of this type of illusion is that even though the patterns are two-dimensional, your brain treats them as three-dimensional. These illusions have features that usually indicate distance in three-dimensional space. The left line in Figure 5.19a, for example, can be thought of as the inside corner of a building; the right line is like the near corner of the building. In Figure 5.19c and d the converging lines create the illusion of distance, so that the lower bar looks nearer and shorter than the upper bar. This "perceptual compensation" seems to be unconscious and automatic. Presumably for this reason your mind has difficulty making sense

perceptual inference: The process of assuming that certain objects remain the same and will function as they have in the past.
illusion: A perception that misrepresents physical stimuli.

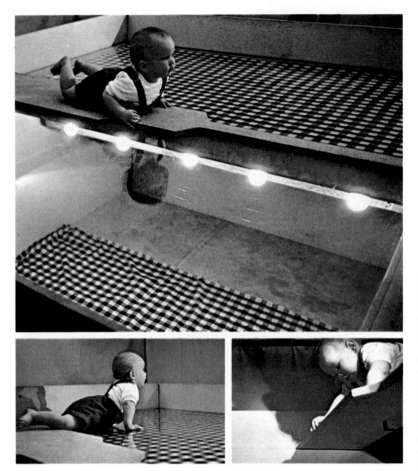

FIGURE 5.18 The visual cliff apparatus. A human infant of crawling age (about six months) will usually refuse to cross the glass surface of the "deep" side even if his or her mother is on the other side and is urging the child to join her. The infant is perfectly willing to cross the "shallow" side to reach his or her mother, however. Even though the child can feel the hard solid glass surface beneath him or her, he or she refuses to venture out over an edge that appears to be a sudden drop. *(Steve McCarroll)*

out of an image like the Necker Cube shown in Figure 5.20. The diagram does not contain a clue whether the shaded area is the front or the rear surface of the transparent cube. Accordingly, your brain first entertains one alternative—testing the input against it—and then proceeds to do the same with the other alternative. But it can never settle on an answer.

Figure 5.21 shows two people in a room. The sizes of the people look dramatically different because you perceive the room as rectangular. In fact, the ceiling and walls are slanted so that the back wall is both shorter and closer on the right than on the left. But even when you know how this illusion was achieved, you still accept the peculiar difference in the people's sizes because the windows, walls, and ceiling appear rectangular. Your experience with rectangular rooms overrides your knowledge of how this trick is done.

Illusions have long fascinated psychologists. Indeed, illusions have historically provided much of the impetus to the study of perception (McBurney and Collings, 1977). This fact derives in part from the belief that if one knows why illusions occur, one may gain new insights into how the brain and eyes work together to make sense out of the visual world. It seems that the phenomena that give rise to illusions, such as those encountered in certain drawings and photographs, are actually normal brain-eye mechanisms that seldom become noticeable in everyday life. These mechanisms work behind the scenes, so to speak, and provide interpretations of images that make sense to you.

Some illusions are related to perceptual constancies. In perceiving the illusions, your brain attempts to penetrate their structure to find underlying uniformities. In everyday life many possible configurations are consistent with a particular retinal image.

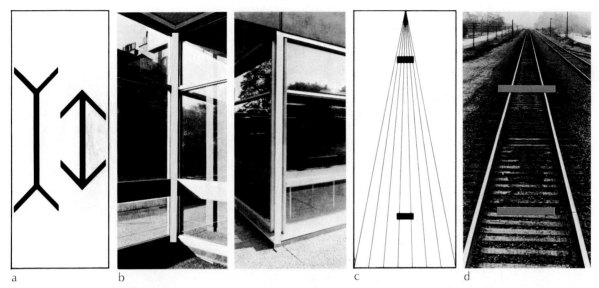

a   b   c   d

FIGURE 5.19 The *Muller-Lyer illusion* (a and b) and the *Ponzo illusion* (c and d) are two of the most famous illusions in psychology. The vertical lines of the figures in the Muller-Lyer illusion (a) are exactly the same length, although they appear to be different. One explanation for this illusion is suggested by the two scenes shown in (b). The arrow markings or fins on the lines in (a) lead us to perceive them as three-dimensional objects with corners. The corners activate the size-constancy effect. The center vertical line in the photograph on the left (b) seems to recede from us and hence appears to be further away. In contrast, the corresponding line in the photograph on the right seems to jut out toward us. Since the line on the left appears more distant, we perceive it as being larger. The horizontal lines in the Ponzo illusion (c) are also identical in length. As the photograph in (d) suggests, this figure can also be perceived as three-dimensional. The size-constancy principle leads us to scale up the size of the more "distant" object relative to the size of the "nearer" object. *(After R. L. Gregory. 1978. Eye and Brain. 3rd ed. New York: McGraw-Hill.)*

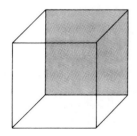

FIGURE 5.20 The Necker Cube. Study the figure intently. Observe that the shaded surface can appear as either the front or the rear surface of the cube.

Because they are ambiguous, retinal images require organization and interpretation. In part this ambiguity derives from the fact that the world is three-dimensional while each retinal image is basically two-dimensional (Hoffman, 1983; Prazdny, 1985). The specific devices—even "mental tricks"—that your brain uses serve this purpose remarkably well. Your visual system has developed so that under normal circumstances it provides you with the maximum amount of information. But there are situations in which the devices or "tricks" are turned against the system, as in the case of illusions (Parks, 1984).

In sum, vision is a process of inference. What you see depends not only on what is "out there" to be seen but also on how your visual system interprets and structures the images that fall on your retinas. Consequently, vision is an active process. Sensory data are filtered through the knowing apparatus of

Keep Your Eye Off the Ball!

From the sandlots to the big leagues, baseball batters have long been advised to "Keep your eye on the ball." Now researchers are calling this conventional wisdom into question (Lyons, 1984). When batting against a fastball pitcher, it may make more sense to take your eye off the ball. Data gained from complex tracking sensors and computers suggest that the big-league fastball moves more rapidly than the eye can follow. Even keen-eyed batters lose sight of the ball by the time it gets within five feet of the plate. The best advice seems to be to take your eye off the ball in the middle of its trajectory, then shift your vision closer to home plate and wait for the ball to arrive. You will not have to wait long, because a ninety- to one-hundred-mile-an-hour fastball will arrive at the plate in less than a second. Many good hitters seem to know this intuitively. Yogi Berra, longtime star with the New York Yankees, once confessed, "I can't think and hit at the same time."

Research suggests that at least three types of eye movements are implicated in hitting a baseball. First, there are *saccadic movements* —quick, jerky movements that our eye makes when we scan a page or a roomful of people. Second, there are *smooth-pursuit eye move-ments,* which we use to track an object in motion. Third, there are *vergence eye movements,* which we use to discriminate perspective and distance when we look between near and far objects. Finally, these eye movements operate in conjunction with the canals of the inner ear to help us orient our head to get a fix on the ball. Each of these operations is centered in a different area of the brain. Accordingly, hitting a baseball entails complex visual and mental operations. Not surprisingly, professional baseball players are much better at it than are rank-and-file college students.

When these research findings were presented to a number of the New York Yankees' better hitters, they disputed them. Steve Kemp said, "I try to watch the ball all the way to the plate, and if I'm hitting well, I do think I can follow it all the way." Don Mattingly observed, "There isn't time on a fastball to take your eye off it, then pick it up again, and the better you see the ball the better you hit it." And Don Baylor noted, "If every fastball came in the same way every time, the theory might hold, but different pitchers come at you different ways." Since most of you will not be batting against Nolan Ryan, the issue will probably remain an academic one.

the human senses and *made* into images and thoughts (Hoffman, 1983; Scarr, 1985b).

Depth Perception

You experience the world as three-dimensional. Yet the images cast on the retina are flat, occurring in only two dimensions. The eye by itself does not provide you with **depth perception**—the ability to tell the distances of various objects and to experience the world in three-dimensional terms. Consequently, depth perception depends in large measure upon the information-extracting and information-processing capabilities of the brain. In carrying out these operations, the brain relies on a variety of cues supplied to it by the eyes.

Binocular Vision and Stereopsis

Because you have two eyes, located about two and a half inches apart, the visual system receives two images. But instead of seeing double, you see a single image, probably a composite of the views of the two eyes. The combination of the two images into one is called **binocular vision.** Hence in effect the brain must act as a single, cyclopean eye (the Cyclops was

---

depth perception: The ability to tell the distances of various objects and to experience the world in three-dimensional terms.
binocular vision: The combination of the two images received by the visual system, so that despite the fact that one has two eyes, one sees a single image.

FIGURE 5.21 This boy appears to be a giant, whereas the woman looks tiny. In fact, both are normal-sized for their ages, but they are in a very peculiar room. This room, the true design of which is shown in the accompanying diagram, was constructed by psychologist Adelbert Ames. Again, the illusion is produced by tricking the brain into accepting an unusual situation as usual. *(Dan McCoy/Rainbow)*

the one-eyed creature encountered by Odysseus in *The Odyssey*).

Not only does the visual system receive two images, but there is a difference between the images on the retinas. This difference is called **retinal disparity.** You can easily observe retinal disparity by bringing an object such as an eraser close to your eyes. Without moving it, look at the eraser first with one eye, then with the other. You will see a difference in the two images because of the different viewpoint each eye has. When you open both eyes you will no longer see the difference, but will instead see the object as solid and three-dimensional (Mustillo, 1985). Your brain uses the cues received from retinal disparity to help it judge distances. The ability to see three-dimensional depth as a result of retinal disparity is termed **stereopsis** (see Figure 5.22). Other complex processes are also at work. Between our two eyes and our single perception of

the world about us lie processes that can "see" out of one eye, processes that can "see" out of either eye, and processes that can "see" only when both eyes are looking at the same thing (Wolfe, 1983). The brain combines these inputs to allow us to estimate the tilt of an object.

Monocular Depth Cues

You also use various *monocular cues* ("mono" —"one"; "ocular"—"eye") to provide you with a sense of depth. You rely on monocular cues when you use only one eye or when you look at a picture. One way the relative distance or depth of two objects is determined is by a comparison of their *relative size*. If two objects of similar structure are placed at the same distance on a landscape lacking other distance cues, the larger object appears to be closer.

---

stereopsis (stare-ee-OP-sis): The use by the visual system of retinal disparity to give depth information—providing a three-dimensional appearance to the world.
retinal (REH-tih-null) disparity (dis-PAIR-ih-tee): The difference between the images on the two retinas.

FIGURE 5.22 To experience stereoscopic depth perception, take a tall, thin piece of cardboard and place it perpendicular to the page on the line that marks the separation of the two pictures. Then, with the edge of the cardboard resting between your eyes (as shown in the drawing), look at the left photo with your left eye and the right photo with your right eye and try to let the two images come together as one. (It helps to concentrate on the white dot.) If you are successful in fusing the images, the scene will suddenly jump out in depth. This process of binocular vision contributes continuously to your ability to perceive depth. *(Tom Suzuki)*

Another monocular cue to depth is *linear perspective*. As shown in Figure 5.19*d*, the parallel lines representing a railroad track seem to draw together as they approach the horizon.

Still another cue is provided by *motion parallax* —the apparent movement of objects that occurs when you move your head from side to side or when you walk around. You can demonstrate motion parallax by looking toward two objects in the same line of vision, one near you and the other some distance away. If you move your head back and forth, the near object will seem to move more than the far object. In this way, motion parallax gives you clues as to which objects are closer than others.

You also judge distance by the *partial overlap* of objects. When a nearer object partially covers and hides another object, you perceive the object that is covered as being more distant.

Many surfaces present a *texture gradient*—some type of structural unit that is repeated over the entire surface. If you look across a landscape, the nearer units appear coarser in texture and the more distant ones appear finer.

Finally, an *aerial perspective* contributes to depth perception. As you look at objects in the distance, you notice that the more distant objects appear bluer or more violet in color. Hence, green vegetation on a distant mountain has a bluer cast than the vegetation on the mountain closer to you. Similarly, a blurring of detail occurs with distance, so that the image appears increasingly hazy. Fog, dust, and snow give a similar illusion.

Perceptual Development

Perception develops as infants mature and experience their environment. Although a full-term newborn is equipped at birth with a functional and intact visual apparatus, the eye contains a number of immaturities. For instance, the retina and optic nerve are as yet not fully developed (Abramov et al., 1982). And they lack the muscular ability to keep both eyes on the same object. Infants' eyes typically do not converge on the same point until babies are about three months old (Maurer and Maurer, 1976). With the passage of time, they also get better at discerning the human face. Infants under one month will smile at a nodding oval object the size of a human face, whether or not it has eyes, a nose, or other human features. At about twenty weeks, how-

An example of texture gradient as a cue to depth perception. *(Frank Siteman/Stock, Boston)*

they see a familiar face than when they see someone they do not know. But it takes seven or eight months for babies to distinguish among different people (Haaf, 1974; Maurer and Maurer, 1976; Barrera and Maurer, 1981a, 1981b).

Experiments show that people and animals must be actively involved in their environment to develop perception. An experiment with newborn kittens demonstrated this principle. A number of kittens were raised in the dark until they were ten weeks old. Then they were divided into two groups: actives and passives. For three hours a day an active kitten and a passive kitten were linked together, as shown in Figure 5.23. Notice that one kitten was able to move of its own accord while the other kitten was transported about in a carriage device as the first kitten moved. In this manner every action of the active kitten moved the passive kitten an equal distance, forward, backward, up, down, and from side to side. The visual stimulation for the two kittens was approximately the same, but the active animal produced its *own* changes in stimulation, primarily by walking. The other kitten was merely the passive receiver of the stimulation.

When the kittens were tested later, the passive one was not able to discriminate depth—to judge how close or far away various objects were. But the active kitten developed this ability. Not until the passive kitten had been allowed to live normally for

ever, a blank oval will not make most babies smile, but a drawing of a face or a mask will. The baby now distinguishes something that looks like a person from other objects. Babies twenty-eight weeks and older are more likely to smile at a female than a male face. By thirty weeks, most smile more readily when

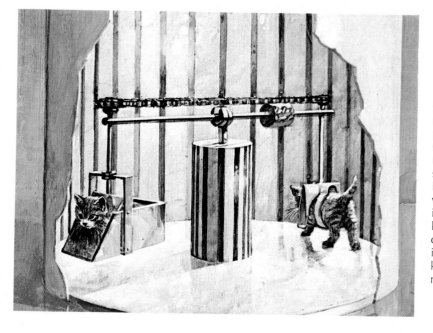

FIGURE 5.23 A cut-away view of the apparatus used to show that active involvement is necessary for perceptual learning. Both kittens are receiving roughly the same visual input as they move in relation to the vertical stripes painted on the walls of the cylinder, but one kitten is producing the changes in what it sees by its own muscular movements. The other kitten sees similar changes because of the way it is harnessed to the first kitten, but what it sees has nothing to do with its own movements. This second kitten was found not to have developed the ability to see depth in this situation, while the active kitten developed depth perception normally.

two days—to move around in a visual environment on its own—did it develop normal depth perception (Held and Hein, 1963). The experiment clearly demonstrates the importance of behavioral contact with the environment in the development of perceptual capabilities.

Experiments with human beings have also shown that active involvement in one's environment is important for accurate perception. People who have been blind from birth and who have had their sight restored by an operation (which is possible in only a few cases) have visual sensations. However, initially they cannot tell the difference between a square and a circle or determine that a red cube is like a blue cube (Valvo, 1971). In fact some have difficulty making such simple distinctions six months after their vision has been restored. Overall, their ability to make generalizations remains impaired. For instance, they fail to realize that what they have come to recognize as a triangle in one setting is also a triangle in a different setting.

Not all such cases end happily. For instance, researcher Richard L. Gregory (1978) describes the case of S.B., a man who had lost effective vision in both eyes by the time he was ten months of age and had his sight restored at the age of fifty-two. Before the operation, S.B. had lived an active and productive life. He liked making things in a shed in his garden. And he got about with little difficulty, even bicycling on occasion with a friend who guided him by holding his shoulder.

Immediately after his cornea transplant, S.B. could see only a blur, but his sight improved rapidly. He had some trouble judging distance—for example, he thought his hospital window was about six feet from the ground when it was really about sixty. But he recognized objects by sight that he had learned by touch. For years he had determined the time of day by feeling the position of the hands of his watch and this skill transferred to the visual sphere.

But S.B. never truly learned to trust his new sense. When he was blind, he would blithely cross the busiest intersections with only his cane to guide him. But after the operation, it would take two people on either side to force him across a street. He was terrified of traffic as never before in his life.

After the initial thrill of gaining his vision wore off, S.B. became progressively dispirited and bored. Little things like flaking paint and blemishes on objects disturbed and troubled him. His depressions gradually became deeper and more general. In the evening he would not turn on the lights but would sit alone in the darkness. It seemed that when his handicap was swept away, S.B. lost his sense of self-respect and well-being. Less than two years after the operation, S.B. died.

EXTRASENSORY PERCEPTION

In this chapter, we have discussed the perception of tangible and measurable aspects of the environment. But human beings are rarely content with understanding only what can be seen and directly measured. They are fascinated by things that cannot be seen, easily explained, or often even verified—such as extrasensory perception.

Extrasensory perception (ESP) involves the ability to receive information about the world through channels other than the normal senses. ESP is alleged to take a number of forms:

- **telepathy:** The ability to read another person's thoughts or to transfer thoughts from one person to another.

- **precognition:** The ability to see or predict future events. Precognition often takes the form of prophetic dreams.

- **clairvoyance:** The ability to gain knowledge of events that is not detectable by the usual senses.

---

extrasensory perception (ESP): The ability to receive information about the world through channels other than the normal senses.

telepathy (tel-LEH-puh-thee): The ability to read another person's thoughts or to transfer thoughts from one person to another.

precognition: The ability to see or predict future events.

clairvoyance: The ability to gain knowledge of events that is not detectable by the usual senses.

● **psychokinesis:** The ability to move objects through willpower without touching them.

Extrasensory perception is a hotly debated topic. Public-opinion polls show that 58 percent of American adults say that they have had an ESP experience (Hadden and Swann, 1981). Many people are convinced that ESP exists because of an intense personal experience that can never be scientifically validated. For instance, everyone has some fears before traveling, and people tend to imagine the worst: the plane will crash, the train will be derailed, they will have an automobile accident. These events almost never happen, and people easily forget their frightening premonitions. However, if the improbable should actually take place, their premonitions turn into compelling evidence for the existence of precognition.

One thing that contributes to people's willingness to accept ESP, even in the face of disproof, is the difficulty they have sorting out chance events from the nonrandom, patterned events of everyday life. One way we make sense of our sensory input is through the notion of *causality*—our attribution of a cause-and-effect relationship to two paired events that occur in succession. The ability to appreciate that a cause must always precede an effect has proved of enormous survival value for human beings in the course of evolution. But when the randomness of life produces natural coincidences, we are disposed to impute causation to them (Cornell, 1984; Hastie, 1984). Thus the acceptance of the paranormal may be a by-product of everyday strategies for processing information that typically serve us well. So coincidences sometimes become evidence supporting paranormal phenomena, and people quickly forget all the occasions when their premonitions were completely wrong. Thus, if one is truly interested in validating the existence of ESP, one must keep track of the frequency of its failures as well as its successes.

Scientists have been investigating ESP since the turn of the century. Probably the most famous **parapsychologist** (as these researchers into the su-

pernatural are called) is Joseph B. Rhine (1964). Around 1930, Rhine began a series of precise statistical tests of ESP. In tests of telepathy, for example, a "sender" focuses one at a time on each of twenty-five cards in a special deck. (The deck includes five cards for each of five different symbols.) A "receiver" locked in a distant room states which card he or she thinks the sender is focusing on. With luck alone, the receiver will guess about five cards correctly, sometimes a few more, sometimes a few less. Yet thousands of tests have shown that some people consistently respond above the average (Child, 1985). On the basis of this new information, the authors and other previously skeptical psychologists can no longer consider ESP a closed case.

While the results provided by these studies are statistically unlikely, in other ways they are not nearly as impressive. For example, in one study (described in Chance, 1976), Charles Tart screened 1,500 college students and found 25 who seemed to have ESP. The students were shown a machine that randomly turned on one of four lights. They had to guess which light would come on next. They guessed nearly 7,500 times, and were right 26.8 percent of the time. Since one would expect people without ESP to be right only 25 percent of the time (one out of four), and since they guessed so many times, the result was statistically significant: the odds were more than 2,500 to 1 against this performance occurring by chance. These outcomes provide impressive odds, but they are not particularly impressive results. This minimal performance would not be especially helpful for making "big" money by playing the stock market or betting in a football pool.

And there is one more problem with Tart's experiment. Unsupervised undergraduates collected the data. Many studies have shown that experimenters who believe in ESP tend to make errors supporting their belief, just as skeptics make errors showing that it does not exist. Another problem is the possibility of intentional fraud. It would not be the first time a student falsified data to please his professor or get a good grade. And there have been several rather

---

psychokinesis (sigh-coh-kin-EE-sis): The ability to move objects through willpower without touching them.

parapsychologist: A person who makes a systematic study of ESP and other unusual phenomena.

The Case of Uri Geller

Much interest and controversy have surrounded the supposedly paranormal abilities of Uri Geller, an Israeli "psychic." Geller claims that he bends keys, rings, and silverware simply by concentrating on them; reads the contents of hidden envelopes; fixes long-broken watches through psychic powers; and makes lost objects materialize. On the basis of their laboratory tests, two highly respected laser physicists, Russell Targ and Hal Puthoff (1974), concluded that Geller indeed possesses some telepathic abilities. They were unable to rule out the possibility that Geller receives unusual types of information through some unknown sensory channel.

However, professional magicians such as James (the Amazing) Randi (1978; Weil, 1974a, 1974b) insist that Geller is simply "a good magician, nothing more." Take the matter of the bent keys. Randi reveals how magicians employ a number of keys that are already bent and then substitute them for the unbent keys by sleight-of-hand. In other words, the human mind imposes its own interpretation on events. It registers what it expects the eyes to see. In so doing it "constructs" reality by selecting evidence and interpreting perceptions.

"Trickery" operates in other ways as well. Take the feat of reading the contents of hidden envelopes. Randi and other magicians take advantage of little opportunities to do the "dirty work" of sneaking a look inside an envelope to determine its contents. Randi claims that fully 80 percent of any good parapsychology demonstration entails the use of "psychology"—misdirection, showmanship, and just plain skullduggery.

More recently, Randi planted two accomplices in the McDonnell Laboratory for Psychical Research at Washington University in St. Louis. Skilled in sleight-of-hand, spoon-bending, mindreading, and "psychic photography," the two youths fooled the researchers into seeing "extraordinary things" and presenting their "findings" at a professional meeting. The ruse ended at a 1983 press conference, when Randi revealed the two "natural psychics" as nothing more than talented magicians (Broad, 1983). Critics have questioned the ethics of Randi's methods and have expressed concern lest psychologists now shun unorthodox but potentially enlightening paranormal research (Child, 1985).

spectacular cases of fraud in ESP research (Diaconis, 1978; Neher, 1980). (See the boxed insert above).

Another reason many scientists do not accept the results of experiments supporting ESP is that the findings are highly unstable. One of the basic principles of scientific research is that one scientist should be able to replicate another scientist's results. Not only do different ESP experiments yield contradictory findings, but the same individual seems to show ESP on one day but not on the next (Layton and Turnbull, 1975). Complicating matters even more, parapsychologists are in widespread disagreement, and they lack a coherent theoretical framework (Alcock, 1981).

Critics also point out that it is not unusual for some subjects to have temporary streaks in which they score well (Diaconis, 1978). Statisticians say that above-chance performance is a common phenomenon, one that laypeople often attribute to a "run of luck" in poker, horse racing, or dice games. But the run eventually ends. And when it does, it is unfair to claim that the individual has just temporarily lost ESP. Scientists must count *all* the attempts at psychic behavior, not just those that support its occurrence.

Proponents of ESP argue that this type of research cannot be consistently replicated because the special abilities are stifled in a laboratory situation. They say that ESP responses are best generated in highly emotional or relevant situations. Laboratory experiments that test people's ability to sense which symbols appear on cards are irrelevant to most people's lives, lack emotion, and are usually boring. According to this view, it is remarkable that ESP has been reported to appear in the laboratory setting at all.

Although ESP may indeed be a very fragile phenomenon, the inability to replicate results and the difficulty of verifying ESP events are crucial problems. Many people will remain skeptical about the existence of ESP until these problems are solved. However, such skepticism has often been overcome in the past. For example, just a century or so ago, the suggestion that many diseases were caused by invisible organisms was greeted with disbelief. Only after the work of Pasteur and other researchers proved that a clear relationship existed between these organisms and illness was the "germ theory" of disease accepted. Moreover, the scientific community did not accept the existence of meteorites before 1800.

Perhaps the development of appropriate techniques for testing ESP will similarly lead to establishing the existence of paranormal phenomena —and perhaps such techniques will not. For its part, the Pentagon has allegedly spent millions of dollars on secret projects to investigate ESP to determine if the human mind can perform acts of espionage, penetrate secret files, locate submarines, or blow up guided missiles in mid-flight (Targ and Harary, 1984). And the Soviet military has also shown interest in the possibilities for harnessing ESP for wartime use (Ebon, 1983). It is the intriguing possibility that ESP may exist that continues to interest a good many people. And should any of the claims of parapsychologists be proven, the way in which people conceive of the world will substantially change.

SUMMARY

1. Information about the outside world is received through the senses. The sense organs convert stimuli in the environment into chemical-electrical activity that travels to the brain. This process results in sensation.

2. Psychophysics is the study of the relationship between physical stimuli and the sensory experiences they produce. The smallest amount of energy that will produce a sensation is called an absolute threshold. The smallest change in a stimulus that produces a change in sensation is called the difference threshold.

3. Experiencing a sensation depends more on changes in the stimulus than on the absolute size or amount of the stimulus. The amount of stimulus change necessary to produce some increase in sensory experience is different for different cases, but it is almost always proportional.

4. The senses are more responsive to increases and decreases in the magnitude of stimulation than they are to a constant level of stimulation. They adapt, or adjust themselves, to ongoing, unchanging stimulation. They get used to a new level and respond only to changes that depart from this level.

5. Signal-detection theory considers the threshold concept to be superfluous. Signal-detection theorists point out that a threshold level varies across situations depending on a person's motivation, experience, expectations, and other individual factors. They view subjects as making decisions as to whether or not a stimulus was presented.

6. According to tradition, sight, hearing, smell, taste, and touch are the five human senses, each of which conforms to a basic organ (eye, ear, nose, tongue, and skin). Yet this list vastly oversimplifies your sensory experience. Moreover, it leaves out your inner experiences.

7. The stimulus for visual experience is light —waves of radiant energy that, like waves in the ocean, flow in sequence. When they stimulate receptors in the eye, impulses are carried to the brain via the optic nerve and you experience visual events.

A. Light consists of electromagnetic radiation that occurs within a very restricted range of wavelengths. Two characteristics of light influence vision: wavelength and intensity.

B. Light energy enters the eye through the cornea, the transparent outer layer of the eyeball. The amount of light entering the inner eye is controlled by the iris, a colored ring of muscle fiber that surrounds the pupil. Light passes through the pupil to the lens, a transparent, elastic structure. Finally, light energy reaches the retina, the light-sensitive back surface of the eye that contains the receptor cells.

C. The retina contains two types of light-sensitive cells: rods and cones. Cones are specialized for vision in bright light. Rods are specialized for vision in dim light. Once the rods and cones are stimulated, neural impulses are in turn transmitted to bipolar nerve cells. The bipolar cells then stimulate ganglion cells whose fibers form the optic nerve.

D. Color vision is primarily mediated by the cones. One widely accepted view—the trichromatic theory—is that there are three types of cones and that each contains a different visual pigment.

8. The auditory system, like the visual system, transduces energy into neural impulses. However, it derives its energy from a mechanical rather than an electromagnetic source. Sound waves result from the alternate compression and decompression of air molecules. The intensity of sound depends on the amplitude of sound waves. The pitch of sound is determined by the frequency of sound waves.

9. Smell and taste are known as the chemical senses because their receptors are sensitive to chemical molecules rather than to light energy or sound waves. Since the two senses are located close together and both have a chemical basis, people frequently confuse and blend their separate sensations.

10. Receptors in the skin are responsible for providing the brain with at least four kinds of information about the environment: pressure, warmth, cold, and pain. These sensations play an important role in warning the brain of possible external dangers.

11. The body's sense of balance is regulated by the vestibular system inside the inner ear. The stimuli for vestibular responses include movements such as spinning, falling, and tilting the body or head. Kinesthesis allows you to recognize the location of one body part in relation to the others. Without kinesthetic sensations, your movements would be jerky and uncoordinated.

12. Ultimately, information from the sense organs must be processed and interpreted by the brain. The brain takes raw sensory data and gives them organization.

13. Your brain constantly tries to build "wholes" out of the confusion of stimuli that bombards the senses. The "whole" experience that comes from organizing bits and pieces of information into meaningful objects and patterns is called a Gestalt. Gestalt psychologists have attempted to identify the organizing principles that the brain uses in constructing perceptions. One kind of organization is called grouping. Grouping depends on several principles: proximity, continuity, similarity, and closure. A number of psychologists have suggested that all the principles of grouping can be integrated under a single concept: simplicity.

14. Another basic form of perceptual organization studied by Gestalt psychologists is the division of experience into figure (the objects) and ground (the spaces between the objects).

15. When you have learned to perceive certain objects in your environment, you tend to see them in the same way, regardless of changing conditions. This fact is the basis for perceptual constancies.

A. Although the amount of light available to your eyes varies a good deal, your perception of the brightness of familiar objects varies hardly at all. Likewise, you perceive familiar objects as if they retained their color, even though the information reaching your eyes varies.

B. Size and shape constancies allow you to perceive size and shape as constant despite the variations that occur in your retinal images.

16. Often people have perceptions that are not based entirely on current sensory information. The phenomenon of filling in the gaps in what your senses tell you is known as perceptual inference.

17. Illusions are perceptions that are misrepresentations of reality. Apparently some illusions are related to perceptual constancies. In perceiving the illusions, the brain attempts to penetrate their structure to find the underlying uniformities.

18. You experience the world as three-dimensional. But the eye by itself does not provide you with depth perception. The images cast on the retina are flat, occurring in but two dimensions. Consequently, depth perception depends in large measure on the information-extracting and information-processing capabilities of the brain.

A. The brain uses the cues received from retinal disparity to assist it in judging distances. The ability to see depth as a result of retinal disparity is termed stereopsis.

B. You also use various monocular cues to provide you with a sense of depth. You rely on monocular cues when you use only one eye or when you look at a picture. Monocular depth cues include relative size, linear perspective, motion parallax, partial overlap, texture gradient, and aerial perspective.

19. Perception develops as infants mature and experience their environment. Experiments show that people and animals must be actively involved in their environment in order to develop perception.

20. Extrasensory perception is a hotly debated topic. For the most part, scientists have been skeptical about the claims of parapsychologists.

KEY TERMS

absolute threshold (p. 148)
binocular vision (p. 174)
clairvoyance (p. 178)
closure (p. 166)
color blindness (p. 157)
cones (p. 155)
continuity (p. 166)
depth perception (p. 174)
difference threshold (just noticeable difference) (p. 149)
extrasensory perception (ESP) (p. 178)
figure-ground (p. 166)

Gestalt (p. 165)
grouping (p. 165)
illusion (p. 171)
kinesthesis (p. 163)
parapsychologist (p. 179)
perception (p. 146)
perceptual constancy (p. 168)
perceptual inference (p. 171)
precognition (p. 178)
proximity (p. 166)
psychokinesis (p. 179)
psychophysics (p. 148)
referred pain (p. 163)
retinal disparity (p. 175)

rods (p. 155)
sensation (p. 146)
signal-detection theory (p. 151)
similarity (p. 166)
simplicity (p. 166)
stereopsis (p. 175)
stimulus (p. 147)
telepathy (p. 178)
transduction (p. 152)
trichromatic theory (p. 157)
vestibular system (p. 163)
Weber's law (p. 150)

SUGGESTED READINGS

ARNHEIM, RUDOLF. 1974. *Art and Visual Perception: A Psychology of the Creative Eye.* Berkeley: University of California Press. A revision of a classic book by a prolific writer on visual perception. Arnheim relates the Gestalt rules of organization to visual perception in general and to the perception and structure of works of art in particular.

GIBSON, JAMES J. 1979. *The Ecological Approach to Visual Perceptions.* Boston: Houghton Mifflin. Outlines the "Gibsonian" approach to the study of perception, which is characterized by a commitment to ecological validity and was the first to study perception by looking at actual perceptual phenomena rather than the physics of perception.

GOLDSTEIN, E. B. 1984. *Sensation and Perception.* Belmont, Calif.: Wadsworth. A general introduction to sensation and perception, whose main theme is that in order to understand perception, we need to understand how it relates to physiology.

GREGORY, RICHARD L. 1978. *Eye and Brain.* 3rd ed. New York: McGraw-Hill. One of the most popular and best-written introductions to the "psychology of seeing." Includes many illustrations.

HELD, RICHARD, and RICHARDS, WHITMAN, Eds. 1972. *Perception: Mechanisms and Models.* San Francisco: Freeman. A book of readings from *Scientific American* that provides accounts of some of the most famous research on perceptual processes in animals, including the visual cliff and the active and passive kittens.

KANIZSA, GAETANO. 1979. *Organization in Vision: Essays on Gestalt Perception.* New York: Praeger. An excellent example of the phenomenological approach to the study of perception.

ROCK, I. 1983. *The Logic of Perception.* Cambridge, Mass: MIT Press. Presents a most persuasive argument that visual perception is the result of problem solving; fully develops a hypothesis-testing view of perception.

SEKULER, R., and BLAKE, R. 1985. *Perception.* New York: Knopf. An up-to-date text presenting the study of visual, auditory, and olfactory perception as part of an ongoing intellectual process.

UTTAL, WILLIAM. 1981. *Taxonomy of Visual Processes.* Hillsdale, N.J.: L. Erlbaum Associates. Probably the most comprehensive book on visual perception available.

Henri Matisse, *Piano Lesson*, 1916.

6

Learning: Principles and Applications

The notion that animals have intelligence strikes a responsive chord in most of us. Perhaps for this reason, the fictional account of Dr. Doolittle, who talked with the animals, remains a perennial favorite. Psychologists have also been intrigued by these matters. For over thirteen years, the developmental psychologist Francine Patterson has worked with a female gorilla—Koko—and taught her some five hundred words by using the American Sign Language for the deaf. Patterson claims that Koko has spontaneously devised names for new objects, including "finger bracelet" for a ring, "white tiger" for a zebra, and "eye hat" for a mask. And in play, Koko will invent new signs. For example, for the English expression "you blew it," Koko jumps up, waves her arms, and blows as hard as she can (Patterson, 1985). Has Koko learned nothing more than an association between some action and a particular gesture, or does she "think" (Terrace, 1979b, 1985)?

Psychologists at the Language Research Center near Atlanta have documented a number of human-like capabilities in a four-year-old pygmy chimpanzee. The ape, Kanzi, shows an extensive understanding of spoken English words and identifies objects by name. He uses geometric symbols (made up of triangles, circles, squares, and lines) that visually represent words, since chimps lack the vocal apparatus of humans. As an infant, Kanzi had played in the laboratory while researchers taught the word symbols to his mother. When he was about two-and-a-half, Kanzi spontaneously began using several of the symbols correctly, apparently having mastered them by observing. He also understands somewhat complex spoken sentences. If asked, "Will you go get a diaper for your sister Mulika?" he will fetch one and

Kanzi, a pygmy chimpanzee, understands many English words, which he learned at first by observing his mother, who was taught to respond to words and to use geometric symbols to communicate with her trainers.
(Language Research Center, Yerkes Regional Primate Center, photo by Elizabeth Rubert)

take it to her (Eckholm, 1985a, 1985b). Are these responses simply "mechanical reproductions" of the behavior of humans, or is Kanzi "constructing" his behavior by using abstract mental representations (Premack, 1983)?

Other examples abound (Wyman, 1983). Pigeons in psychologist Richard Herrnstein's laboratory at Harvard have learned the ability to pick out fish in photographs, even though fish do not occur in their natural world. Is this an evolutionary adaptation, or have pigeons acquired the concept "fish"? Two female dolphins in Hawaii obey five-word commands like "bottom basket fetch surface hoop" that depend on word order for their meaning. Is this conditioned behavior, or do the dolphins understand syntax? And not only is the figure-eight waggle-dance of bees precise, but worker bees can store and translate the message overnight and even anticipate where a food source will be when it is moved a fixed distance. Is this behavior programed in bees, or do bees do math? The answers to these questions do not come easily (Fountain, Henne, and Hulse, 1984; Lubinski and MacCorquodale, 1984). Even so, there is a growing body of research that has appreciably advanced our understanding of learning and thinking. This chapter will focus on learning and the next chapter on thinking.

AN OVERVIEW OF LEARNING

Understanding the ways in which learning occurs is a first task in understanding behavior and experience (Mackintosh, 1983). We may view **learning** as a permanent change in behavior or capability that results from experience. Central to learning is the association (or link) between two elements (or events). Association is a critical process because it allows us to adapt to our environment. In this manner, for instance, we establish the relationship between a pizza and the relief of hunger sensations, between studying for a test and winning social recognition, and between shouting and upsetting a friend. Through our successes and failures in coping with events, we are able to modify and refine our actions. In sum, we achieve a better fit between ourselves and the realities of the world.

Although learning is responsible for a smaller portion of the behavior of lower species than of higher species, including human beings, it nonetheless often plays a critical role in their survival. For instance, young chickens learn essential pecking behaviors from the hen (Suboski and Bartashunas, 1984). And the ability to acquire aggressive biting and tailbeating behaviors by some species of fish

---

learning: A permanent change in behavior or capability that results from experience.

demonstrates the important evolutionary functions served by learning (Hollis, 1984). Even so, organisms are capable of learning only those things that the genes of its species permits (Seligman, 1970; Schwartz, 1978; Brush et al., 1985). Through its evolutionary history, each species has developed a kind of blueprint, or master plan, that facilitates, specifies, and constrains some aspects of behavior. Consequently, honeybees learn different things and in different ways than either pigeons or dolphins do. In turn each of these species learns different things and in different ways than human beings do.

Perhaps an analogy will help your understanding of this matter (Schwartz, 1978). A blueprint, or master plan (genetic factors), specifies in advance the rooms of a building. Within each room (category of behavior), experience comes into play. The room can be furnished with draperies or rugs, as well as with different varieties of draperies or rugs. But the structure of the room—its size, shape, and location in the building—imposes constraints on the interior designer. Further, some rooms—such as kitchens and bathrooms, with their special plumbing requirements—have their character rather rigidly specified by the blueprint. In a similar fashion, each organism's potential for learning certain kinds of things is influenced by the genetic blueprint of its species.

Learning is involved in nearly all the behavior of human beings. Thus if you wish to understand your behavior, a good place to begin is with the basic principles of learning. The careful application of these principles may be of assistance the next time you want to train a dog, help a child, improve your methods of study, or perhaps change an aspect of your behavior. Let us begin our consideration of these matters by examining classical conditioning.

CLASSICAL CONDITIONING

Like many great scientific discoveries, Ivan Pavlov's discovery of the principle of classical conditioning

was accidental. This Russian physiologist (1849–1936) had been studying the process of digestion around the turn of the century, work for which he won the Nobel prize in 1904. Initially, Pavlov wanted to understand how a dog's stomach prepares to digest food when something is placed in the dog's mouth. Then he noticed that the mere sight or smell of food was enough to start a dog salivating. (You may have had the same sensation when you read a menu describing a savory dish.) Pavlov became fascinated with these "psychic secretions" that occur before food is actually placed in the mouth, and he decided to investigate how they worked.

The Basic Elements of Classical Conditioning

Pavlov (1927) wondered whether what he had accidently stumbled on in the salivating behavior of dogs might be a product of learning. He began a series of experiments in which he would strike a tuning fork and then immediately place some meat powder on a dog's tongue. After following this procedure a number of times, Pavlov found that the dog salivated at the sound of the tuning fork even though food did not follow (see Figure 6.1).

Acquisition

By proceeding in this manner, Pavlov was dividing the *environment* into units called **stimuli** and segmenting *behavior* into units called **responses.** He was searching for the relationship or association between stimuli and responses that occurs in learning. In other words, he was attempting to identify the *conditions* that produce particular responses. Thus the process of learning new connections between stimuli and responses is termed **conditioning.**

Pavlov chose the tuning fork because it was a **neutral stimulus**—one that initially had nothing to do with the response (salivation). By pairing the sound of the tuning fork with meat powder, Pavlov established a *new* relationship, or connection, be-

---

stimuli: Environmental events or circumstances to which an organism responds.
responses: Units of behavior.
conditioning: Learning new connections between stimuli and responses.
neutral stimulus: A stimulus that does not initially elicit a response.

FIGURE 6.1 The apparatus Pavlov used to study conditioned salivation in dogs. The harness held the dog steady, while the tube leading from the dog's mouth deposited saliva on an arm connected to the recorder on the left. Drops of saliva moved the pen, making a permanent record of the salivation response to such stimuli as food and sights or sounds associated with food.

tween a stimulus (the sound of the tuning fork) and a response (salivation) that had not previously existed. This phenomenon is called **classical conditioning** —a process in which a new, previously neutral stimulus becomes able to evoke the response.

Classical conditioning involves responses that organisms naturally make. These responses include various reflex behaviors (such as salivation in dogs or sucking in infants), heart rate, and blood pressure. In classical conditioning, the experimenter or teacher merely arranges relations between events (for instance, between the sound of the tuning fork and the release of meat powder or between a sound and an electric shock) and hopes that the organism will catch on to the relationship.

Pavlov's work has led to a number of concepts that are used to describe classical conditioning (see Figure 6.2):

- The **unconditioned stimulus** (**UCS**) is the environmental factor (stimulus) that naturally brings about (elicits) a particular behavior (response). In Pavlov's experiment, the unconditioned stimulus was the presence of meat powder in the dog's mouth.

- The **unconditioned response** (**UCR**) is the unlearned, automatically occurring reaction brought about (evoked) by an unconditioned stimulus. The unconditioned response in Pavlov's experiment was salivation when meat powder was placed in the dog's mouth.

- The **conditioned stimulus** (**CS**) is a neutral stimulus that becomes capable of eliciting a particular response through being paired during training with an unconditioned stimulus. The animal uses the conditioned stimulus to

classical conditioning: A learning procedure in which a stimulus that normally elicits a given response is repeatedly preceded by a neutral stimulus (one that usually does not elicit the response). Eventually, the neutral stimulus will evoke a similar response when presented by itself.

unconditioned stimulus (UCS): A stimulus that elicits a certain response without previous training.

unconditioned response (UCR): In classical conditioning, an organism's automatic (or natural) reaction to an unconditioned stimulus.

conditioned stimulus (CS): In classical conditioning, a once-neutral stimulus that has become capable of eliciting a particular response through being paired during training with an unconditioned stimulus.

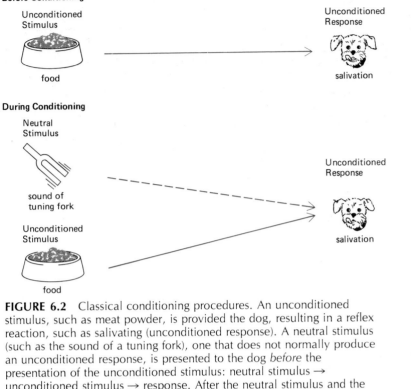

FIGURE 6.2 Classical conditioning procedures. An unconditioned stimulus, such as meat powder, is provided the dog, resulting in a reflex reaction, such as salivating (unconditioned response). A neutral stimulus (such as the sound of a tuning fork), one that does not normally produce an unconditioned response, is presented to the dog *before* the presentation of the unconditioned stimulus: neutral stimulus → unconditioned stimulus → response. After the neutral stimulus and the unconditioned stimulus have been paired a number of times, the neutral stimulus, now termed the conditioned stimulus, is capable of evoking the response in the absence of the unconditioned stimulus, and the dog salivates. The previously unconditioned response then becomes a conditioned response associated with the conditioned stimulus. *(After James W. Vander Zanden. 1981. Human Development. 2nd ed. New York: Alfred A. Knopf, p. 65. Reprinted by permission.)*

make predictions about events in the world (for instance, that food will follow). The conditioned stimulus in Pavlov's experiment was the sound of a tuning fork.

● The **conditioned response (CR)** is a response aroused by some stimulus other than the one that automatically produces it. After a number of pairings with the unconditioned stimulus, the conditioned stimulus elicits a response of the sort that is evoked by the unconditioned stimulus. The conditioned response in Pavlov's experiment was the salivation of the dog at the sound of the tuning fork.

In studying classical conditioning, it is important to remember that learning is an underlying process that cannot be directly observed. Consequently, psychologists must measure it indirectly through **performance**—what the organism does. Among the

---

conditioned response (CR): In classical conditioning, the response aroused by some
    stimulus other than the one that automatically produces it. In operant conditioning,
    an increase in the rate of responding.
performance: What an organism does.

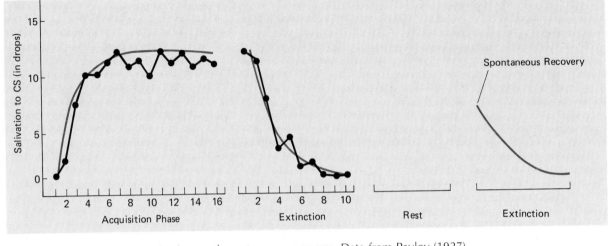

FIGURE 6.3 Acquisition, extinction, and spontaneous recovery. Data from Pavlov (1927) are shown in black, and idealized curves in color. During the acquisition phase, a dog begins to salivate rather quickly in response to the striking of a tuning fork (the conditioned stimulus). However, the conditioned response is extinguished in about ten trials if the conditioned stimulus is not followed by the unconditioned stimulus. Nonetheless, the conditioned response spontaneously recovers after a rest away from the experimental apparatus. Should a later series of trials not restore the link between the conditioned stimulus and the conditioned response, the response becomes inhibited. *(After Spencer Rathus. 1984. Psychology. 2nd ed. New York: CBS College Publishing, p. 176. Copyright © 1984 by CBS College Publishing. Reprinted by permission of CBS College Publishing.)*

major indexes of performance, and therefore of learning, are the frequency, speed, vigor, probability, and persistence of a response. At first, during the acquisition phase, the link between the conditioned stimulus and the conditioned response is weak. But the probability that the organisms will make the response in the presence of the stimulus (for instance, salivating at the sound of a tuning fork) typically increases over time (see Figure 6.3).

Extinction and Spontaneous Recovery

Pavlov discovered that if he stopped presenting food after sounding the tuning fork, the sound gradually lost its effect on a dog. After repeatedly striking the tuning fork without giving food, Pavlov found that a previously conditioned dog no longer associated the

sound with the arrival of food (the sound of the tuning fork was no longer able to evoke the salivation response). Pavlov called this effect **extinction** because the conditioned response had gradually died out (see Figure 6.3).

Pavlov found, however, that if he gave a dog a rest away from the experimental apparatus and later tried striking the tuning fork again, salivation once more occurred (see Figure 6.3). He termed this phenomenon **spontaneous recovery**. The existence of spontaneous recovery indicates that extinction is a kind of inhibition rather than simply forgetting. (In extinction, the organism has not forgotten that the conditioned stimulus formerly predicted the occurrence of the unconditioned stimulus. Rather, it has begun to use the conditioned stimulus to predict that the unconditioned stimulus will *not* occur.) Since it

extinction: The gradual disappearance of a response because the reinforcement is withheld.

spontaneous recovery: The reoccurrence of responses following an interval of time during which the responses had gradually died out.

typically takes a number of unrewarded sessions for spontaneous recovery itself to become inhibited, it takes time to reverse the conditioning process completely.

Stimulus Generalization and Stimulus Discrimination

In the same set of experiments, Pavlov also explored the phenomena of stimulus generalization and stimulus discrimination. **Stimulus generalization** occurs when an organism matches novel sensory inputs with previously established similar information. When Pavlov conditioned a dog to salivate at the sight of a circle (the conditioned stimulus), he found that the dog would salivate when it saw an oval shape as well. Psychologists find that the greater the resemblance between the original stimulus and the new stimulus, the greater the likelihood that the same response will occur and that it will be a strong response.

By virtue of stimulus generalization, the conditioning process does more than create a single conditioned stimulus. It creates, all at once, many conditioned stimuli that have closely related but varying characteristics. Were it not for stimulus generalization, organisms would not be able to profit from prior learning unless they encountered the *exact* same circumstances again. Stimulus generalization permits organisms to transfer learning from one situation to another. For instance, when you were a young child, you probably learned to stop at the red traffic sign near your home before you crossed the intersection. In turn, you came to recognize that you were to stop when you came across similar traffic signs at unfamiliar intersections.

In going about your daily life, it is not only essential that you recognize some stimuli as being similar. It is also essential that you distinguish among similar stimuli (for instance, between a cat and a skunk or among the letters of the alphabet). Only by differentiating among stimuli are you able to attune your behavior to the dictates of one situation or another (for example, keep away from a skunk but

Learning to discriminate between the real danger of a car careening out of control on the highway and a roller coaster ride where the car careens safely down a track at controlled speeds is an example of stimulus discrimination at a complex level. *(John Maher/ EKM-Nepenthe)*

not a cat or tell "u" from "v" and "b" from "d"). The ability of an organism to respond differently to two or more stimuli that are similar but distinct is **stimulus discrimination.**

Pavlov demonstrated the phenomenon of stimulus discrimination in his dog experiments. As noted, Pavlov would condition a dog to salivate at the sight of a circle. He found that on its own, the dog would generalize the conditioning to oval shapes. To teach the dog to respond only to the circle, Pavlov always

---

stimulus generalization: The ability of an organism to match novel sensory inputs with previously established similar information.

stimulus discrimination: The ability of an organism to respond differently to two or more stimuli that are similar but distinct.

paired meat powder with a circle but never with an oval. In due course, the dog would react to the circle by salivating but would not salivate in response to the oval. The dog had learned to react one way to one stimulus and another way to a different stimulus.

Higher-Order Conditioning

A form of classical conditioning that is quite relevant to real-world situations is **higher-order condition-ing.** In this process, after a second conditioned stimulus is paired with the first conditioned stimulus a number of times, the second conditioned stimulus takes on the functions of the first.

For example, we saw that when the sound of a tuning fork (the conditioned stimulus) was presented with the meat powder (the unconditioned stimulus) in Pavlov's experiments, the dog began to salivate when the tuning fork was sounded even in the absence of the meat powder. Now that we know that the sound of the tuning fork can elicit salivation, let us pair it with a second conditioned stimulus, say, a blinking light. We will first present the second conditioned stimulus (the blinking light) and then the first one (the sound of the tuning fork). Note that the meat powder is no longer used. After a number of these pairings, the blinking light alone will result in the dog salivating (Hergenhahn, 1976).

Russian experimenters have hypothesized that words, by being paired with conditioned stimuli, may serve as higher-order conditioned stimuli in bringing about conditioned responses (Hall, 1976). American researchers have also used words in higher-order conditioning experiments (Brackbill and Koltsova, 1967). For instance, the sound of a bell or the onset of a dim light have been used as conditioned stimuli in the development of a conditioned eyeblink response in young children. Following such conditioning, the word "bell" or "lamp" was spoken by the experimenter before presenting either the auditory or the visual stimulus. In short order, the verbal stimulus was sufficient to elicit the eyeblink. This type of link has profound adaptive value in human learning and communication. Words assume a central place in human signaling and in mental appraisal of different courses of action.

New Conceptions of Classical Conditioning

Understanding of classical conditioning has undergone major transformations over the past three decades (Rescorla and Holland, 1982; Mackintosh, 1983; Staddon, 1983). Psychologists no longer view conditioning as a simple, mechanical process involving the association of two events that occur rather closely in time. Conditioning is neither a simple nor a mechanical stamping together of a conditioned stimulus and an unconditioned stimulus, since organisms do not make pairings between events in a vacuum. The environmental context—the overshadowing of some stimuli, the blocking of others, and the highlighting of still others—assumes critical importance. According to a cognitive view of learning, organisms learn only when events violate their expectations (Kamin, 1969; Rescorla and Wagner, 1972). Over time they build an image of the external world and continually compare this image with reality. Thus by virtue of their previous experiences, they come to expect that certain events will follow the presentation of certain stimuli. When the expected environmental feedback is not forthcoming, their perception changes a bit; they must reevaluate the information that various stimuli provide them. Organisms then selectively associate the most informative or predictive stimuli with an unconditioned stimulus. Hence, for conditioning to occur, a potential conditioned stimulus must tell the organism something useful about the unconditioned stimulus that the organism does not already know.

In sum, classical conditioning flourishes only in conjunction with powerful environmental factors that foster the development of associative link (Staddon, 1983). Among human beings the contextual setting takes on particular importance because we possess conscious thought. Indeed, some evidence suggests that the critical relationship between the unconditioned and conditioned stimuli occurs only

---

higher-order conditioning: A process in which after a second conditioned stimulus has been paired with a first conditioned stimulus a number of times, it takes on the functions of the first conditioned stimulus.

when people understand the connection between them (Carpenter, 1985). Consider the following experiment. An instrument that measures sweat-gland activity is attached to the palm of a subject's hand as an indicator of stress. Each subject is told that five tones will be sounded and that a shock will be administered some time during the presentation of the tones. What the subjects are not told is that the shocks are applied according to a set plan, for example, after the highest tone. The subjects typically do not show high anxiety in anticipation of a shock because they have not figured out the pattern. When the experimenter tells them that the pattern may be predictable, most figure it out and begin exhibiting stress when they expect a shock. In brief, the subjects become conditioned *only* after they recognize the relationship between the shock and the tones. Let us explore these matters further by examining two examples of classical conditioning, taste aversions and systematic desensitization.

Taste Aversions

Considerable adaptive value resides in the development of strategies for determining the positive or negative nature of the foods we encounter. Suppose that you and a friend go out to a fancy restaurant. You may decide to try an expensive appetizer that you have never had before, such as snails. After dinner you attend a concert. As the evening wears on, you become progressively nauseated, even quite ill. As a result, you will very likely develop a *taste aversion*—you will never be able to look at another snail without feeling at least a little queasy in the stomach.

Your reaction to snails is a variety of classical conditioning. What makes this situation particularly interesting to learning theorists is that when human beings or other animals get ill, they seem to decide "It must have been something I ate," even if they ate several hours ago. In the foregoing situation, it is unlikely that the concert hall in which you got sick will be the conditioned stimulus. Nor will other stimuli from the restaurant—the wallpaper pattern or the type of china they use—make you sick in the future. What is more, psychologists can even predict which part of your meal will serve as the conditioned stimulus: you will probably blame a *novel* food, one that you have not had before. Thus if you get sick after a meal of salad, steak, and snails, you will

probably learn to hate snails, even if they are not really at fault.

John Garcia and R. A. Koelling (1966) first demonstrated the taste-aversion phenomenon with rats. These animals were placed in a cage with a tube containing flavored water. Whenever a rat took a drink, lights would flash and clicks would sound. Some rats were given an electric shock after they drank, and they showed traditional classical conditioning: the lights and the sounds became conditioned stimuli, and the rats tried to avoid them. But other rats were injected with a drug that made them sick, and they developed an aversion not to the lights or the sounds, but only to the taste of the flavored water. Researchers also find that rats will avoid consuming a novel food eaten by another rat before its becoming sick, a phenomenon called the *poisoned partner effect*. The poisoned partner effect—the product of associating a novel food with poisoning—is clearly adaptive. If members of a colony can learn about the toxic consequences of certain foods as a result of the acute poisoning of one of their number, they come to enjoy an evolutionary advantage (Bond, 1984).

Animals are more prepared by their evolutionary history to make associations between certain stimuli and responses than between others (Seligman and Hager, 1972; Kucharski and Spear, 1985). It seems that the animals are "wired" to discern certain stimuli and responses as naturally fitting together. Hence the associations between them are readily learned. Presumably such special cases of learning were developed and selected out because of their usefulness for survival. Thus taste-aversion behaviors are functional in discouraging animals from later consuming poisons that earlier made them sick. Birds such as quail that rely heavily on vision in their feeding behavior develop conditioned aversions to visual cues more easily than to taste cues (Wilcoxon, Dragoin, and Kral, 1971). However, the specific mechanisms by which taste aversions are conditioned remain a source of lively theoretical speculation among psychologists (Kalat and Rozin, 1971).

The special relationship between food and illness was exploited in a controversial study (Gustavson et al., 1974) that tried to make coyotes hate the taste of lamb. Researchers gave coyotes a drug that made them sick when they ate sheep. This induced aversion is an important application because sheep farmers in the western United States would like to

For many Westerners, the thought of eating raw fish is distasteful, but in Japan sushi (raw fish and rice) is a very desirable delicacy. If you eat a novel food such as sushi and later become ill, you are likely to develop a taste aversion for the novel food rather than a familiar food, even if the familiar food was the culprit that made you ill. *(Robert A. Isaacs/Photo Researchers)*

exposure to "scapegoat" tastes before chemotherapy may help prevent patients from developing aversions to normal diet items (Goodman, 1984).

Animals are also adept at learning to cope with deficiencies in their diet and to modify their preferences when presented with an adequate diet (Mehiel and Bolles, 1984). Thus many animals have a learning mechanism that allows them not only to avoid food that makes them ill but also to like food that provides calories and nutrients. Rats placed on restrictive diets will later offset the underrepresented nutrients when provided with adequate resources. They will regulate their diet by reducing those foods that they previously had in abundance while increasing those foods possessing the substances in which they are deficient. Another line of evidence in the area of learned taste preferences is based on the *medicine effect*. Researchers find that a rat will prefer a food that is paired with its recovery from an illness (Zahorik, Maier, and Pies, 1974; Zahorik and Bean, 1975). For some people, chicken soup has become a favorite food for this reason.

Systematic Desensitization

Psychologists have found still other applications for learning principles derived from classical conditioning research. **Systematic densensitization** is frequently used in the treatment of behavior disorders in which fear plays a prominent part (for instance, anxieties related to flying in airplanes, closed spaces, heights, death, sexual encounters, public speaking, or social contacts). The process entails gradually confronting patients with the fear-arousing stimulus after they have been trained to relax (Wolpe, 1958, 1969). (See Chapter 16, which deals with psychotherapy.)

In the first phase, the therapist constructs with the patient a list of fear-producing stimuli and then ranks them in terms of the amount of fear they produce (for example, viewing airplane-travel brochures, driving to an airport, entering the terminal building, approaching the check-in desk, walking to the departure gate, entering a plane, taxiing, taking short trips, and flying in turbulent weather). In the

eliminate the coyotes that threaten their flocks, while naturalists are opposed to killing the coyotes. The experimenters showed that coyotes could be trained to eat other kinds of meat and thus learn to coexist peacefully with sheep.

The scientific community is also looking for other applications of conditioned food aversions. For example, many cancer patients learn food aversions as an inadvertent side effect of chemotherapy that helps to retard tumors but also creates nausea and vomiting. Thus children given ice cream before chemotherapy frequently develop an aversion to it. Researchers are currently exploring whether deliberate

---

systematic desensitization: A process of gradually confronting patients with a fear-arousing stimulus after they have been trained to relax.

second phase, the patient is trained in techniques of deep muscle relaxation.

In the third phase, the therapist has the patient think about, dwell on, and imagine the *weakest* of the fear-producing stimuli (situations). The patient is instructed to relax and to visualize the fear-producing situation until it no longer produces any fear. Once the fear of the weakest stimulus has subsided, the patient progresses to the next step in the hierarchy. The therapy continues over a number of sessions until the patient feels comfortable with the most fear-inducing situation. Finally, if possible, the patient is put through a graded series of real-life situations arranged in the same fear hierarchy.

Interpretations of systematic desensitization vary. Some psychologists believe that counterconditioning is taking place: the fear response is being replaced by another response (relaxation) that is antagonistic to fear. Other psychologists think extinction is at work: patients are kept away from fear-evoking situations, and thus their expectation of negative outcomes following the stimulus (flying in airplanes) is not fulfilled. As yet, neither interpretation has been demonstrated in any definitive manner (Kalish, 1977; Schwartz, 1978).

Whatever interpretation may prove correct, the procedure has helped patients who have not responded to other therapies. For instance, many cancer patients undergoing chemotherapy experience anticipatory nausea and vomiting when they contemplate a forthcoming treatment session (during breakfast on the treatment day, while driving to the cancer center, or upon entering the center's waiting room). The syndrome is believed to be a learned response to the unpleasant effects of previous treatments. Anti-nausea medications do not help a good many of these patients. However, after only two hours of desensitization training, ten of twenty patients in a study conducted at the University of Rochester Cancer Center reported they no longer experienced anticipatory nausea and vomiting, and seven reported less severe problems than in the past (Morrow and Morrell, 1982).

The Molecular Bases of Classical Conditioning

While some psychologists explore learning at the level of observable behavior, others are looking at its chemical foundations. Significant advances have derived from the study of the foot-long sea slug *Aplysia* by Eric Kandel and his many collaborators (Kandel and Schwartz, 1982; Hawkins and Kandel, 1984). They have focused on the sea slug's brain because it contains only ten thousand neurons. Additionally, its neurons are large and identifiable, and the connections quite elementary. Though no genius, *Aplysia* learns in the same sense that Pavlov's dogs learned to salivate at the sound of a tuning fork. Classical conditioning occurs when a sea slug is touched lightly at two different sites; one of the stimuli is administered along with a mild electrical shock to the tail, and the other stimulus is not paired with a shock. Later, touching the animal at the site that was matched with the shock elicits a much greater withdrawal of its tubular feeding apparatus (siphon) than does touching the other site.

Kandel and his associates have studied the cellular changes that accompany behavioral modification in the sea slug. They contend that learning is not diffused throughout the brain but is localized in the activity of specific nerve cells. More particularly, learning results from changes that take place in the membranes of nerve cells and in the synaptic connections between them. When a neuron is stimulated, positive sodium ions flow in. Positive potassium ions rush out in an attempt to restore the original level of negative charge in the cell's interior. If the influx of sodium ions is sufficient to push the cell past a certain threshold, a dramatic spike of activity occurs (termed an *action potential*). This activity draws in calcium ions. A neuron fires only when the rapid exchange of ions provides its interior with a sufficient positive charge. In contrast, as a cell becomes increasingly negative, the firing process is inhibited. As we noted in Chapter 2, for a message from a firing neuron to travel to a target neuron, neurotransmitters must be released by the firing cell into the synapse between the two neurons.

Any mechanism that makes a neuron more or less likely to fire plays a role in the way information is processed and stored. Thus chemical alterations in the channels or pores of a cell's membrane contribute to learning. These changes affect the flow of each type of ion, altering the electrical charge. In turn, such changes have consequences for the firing of a neuron and for the release of neurotransmitters into the synapse. Viewed in this fashion, learning is a kind of symphony of rising and falling cellular activity in the neurological system, a confluence of electrical and biochemical notes (Hall, 1985).

Kandel believes there is a cellular alphabet of learning. He says that observing simple behavior in a simple animal provides the key to understanding even more complex forms of learning in higher animals. More complicated learning occurs when one neuron parlays changes in its chemistry and shape with changes in other neurons, or when additional chemicals prolong the changes (much in the manner that letters of the alphabet build into words, words into sentences, sentences into paragraphs, and so on). However, from a psychological perspective, *Aplysia* research does not account for many kinds of conditioning. One drawback is that the studies describe learning in terms of a "prewired" circuit that becomes experimentally strengthened or weakened. Although Kandel contends that the cellular mechanisms for learning are similar in all forms of life, some psychologists disagree. They say that any similarities found between *Aplysia*'s learning and human learning may be the product of *convergent evolution*—organisms that are not closely related become similar in a characteristic because of independent adaptation to similar environmental situations. Therefore the similarities may be merely accidental and not necessarily informative about the human condition.

OPERANT CONDITIONING

In his dog experiments, Pavlov was able to build on an inborn, automatic reflex (salivating at the taste of food). His procedures for classical conditioning involved the use of an already existing, involuntary response in the service of a new stimulus. But in many cases there is no preexisting unconditioned stimulus that can be linked to a new stimulus.

What alternative mechanisms are available for training a dog? Consider how you go about teaching a dog to "sit." With one hand you hold the dog so that it cannot jump about, while with the other hand

A rat pressing a bar in a Skinner box. The Skinner box is an artificial environment in which lights, sounds, rewards, and punishments can be delivered and controlled and in which some of the animal's behaviors, such as bar pressing, can be recorded by automatic switches. *(Steve McCarroll)*

you press the dog firmly down by its haunches. You then provide the dog with a morsel of food.

Note that in teaching the dog to "sit," you first get it to *enact* the behavior as best you can and then you reward the dog. The food *follows* the response. You are using **operant conditioning**—a type of learning in which the consequences of a behavior influence whether the organism will act (operate) in the same way in the future. Thus when a hungry dog engages in behavior that produces food, the tendency toward this behavior is strengthened by this consequence and therefore it is more likely to recur (Skinner, 1974). In contrast, in classical conditioning, it is the *food* that produces the behavior of salivation; the food comes *before* the response. In classical conditioning a stimulus is said to *elicit* the response, whereas in operant conditioning the response is *emitted* (see Table 6.1).

Reinforcement

Edward L. Thorndike (1874–1949), a pioneer American psychologist, is credited with developing many of the experimental procedures used in study-

---

operant (AH-per-ant) conditioning: A type of learning in which the consequences of a behavior influence whether the organism will act (operate) in the same way in the future.

TABLE 6.1 Comparison of Classical and Operant Conditioning

Characteristic	Classical Conditioning	Operant Conditioning
Stimulus-response sequence	The stimulus precedes the response.	The response occurs before the effect (reward).
Role of stimulus	Stimulus is elicited.	The response is emitted.
Specificity of stimulus	A specific stimulus results in a particular response.	No specific stimulus produces a particular response.
Process	One stimulus substitutes for another.	A substitution does not take place.
Content	Emotions such as fear are primarily involved.	Goal-seeking activity is primarily involved.

ing operant conditioning. He would place a hungry cat in a specially designed "puzzle box." When the cat accidentally hit a latch located in the cage, the door would spring open, allowing the animal to escape and secure a morsel of fish. During repeated exposures, a cat would progressively shorten the time needed to hit the latch, evidence that trial-and-error learning had occurred. From this research, Thorndike (1898) formulated the *Law of Effect:* the strength of a stimulus-response connection is increased when the response is followed by a satisfying state of affairs.

The psychologist B. F. Skinner (1953, 1974) built on Thorndike's work. For some four decades, students in college psychology courses have become familiar with Skinner's famous conditioning apparatus, the "Skinner box." The experimental chamber provides a soundproof enclosure that isolates the subject—pigeon, rat, or mouse—from stray stimuli.

Skinner's work with pigeons illustrates his procedure. He carefully watches a hungry pigeon strut about the box. When the bird makes a slight clockwise turn, Skinner instantly rewards it with a food pellet. Once more the bird struts about, and when it makes another clockwise turn, Skinner again rewards the pigeon. By repeating this procedure, Skinner is able in two to three minutes to teach a pigeon to make a full circle. He has also taught pigeons to "dance" with each other, to "play Ping-Pong," and to guide torpedoes.

Positive and Negative Reinforcement

In his experiments, Skinner modifies a pigeon's behavior by the consequence of that behavior. When the pigeon turns in a clockwise direction, it is rewarded with food. The food serves as a **reinforcer.** A reinforcer is any stimulus that follows a response and increases the probability that the response will occur again.

Skinner (1953) distinguishes between two types of reinforcers—positive reinforcers and negative reinforcers. A **positive reinforcer** is a pleasant stimulus that when *applied* following a behavior strengthens the probability of the behavior's future occurrence. Something pleasant (food, water, sex, sleep, warmth, comfort, or the like) is *added* to the situation. Skinner says that much of human life is given structure by arranging "payoffs" (reinforcing consequences). Business executives use wages to reward appropriate work behavior by employees. A man attracted to a woman attempts to ensure that she will go out with him on another occasion by "showing her a good time." A physician seeks to induce patients to return by making certain that they feel benefited by their first office visits.

---

reinforcer: Any stimulus that follows a response and increases the probability that the response will occur again.

positive reinforcer: A pleasant stimulus that when applied following a behavior strengthens the probability of the behavior's occurrence.

In contrast, a **negative reinforcer** is an aversive stimulus that when *removed* following a behavior strengthens the probability of the behavior's future occurrence. Something aversive (a loud noise, extreme heat or cold, a blinding light, or an electric shock) is removed from the situation. For example, when you get rid of a headache by taking two aspirin, taking aspirin is negatively reinforced. You are more likely to take aspirin for the next headache because the pain was removed. Psychologists classify reinforcers according to whether their presentation or removal strengthens a preceding behavior. Thus in negative reinforcement the organism must learn something to escape some consequence (Hilgard and Bower, 1975; Higgins and Morris, 1984). (Note that negative reinforcement differs from punishment in that the aversive consequence is *removed* following a behavior, rather than imposed.)

Often we cannot identify an already existing response in an organism's repertoire of behavior that represents the behavior we would like to reinforce. The behavior we desire may consist of several behaviors that are performed sequentially. For example, Skinner wished his experimental pigeons to move about in a perfect figure eight. So he instituted a procedure called **shaping**. In shaping, a desired behavior is broken down into successive steps that are taught one step at a time. Each step is reinforced until it is mastered, and then the subject is advanced to the next step. In this manner, the new behavior is gradually learned as the organism moves closer and closer to the final goal. Thus when Skinner wished to teach a pigeon to rotate through a figure eight, he would first teach the bird step-by-step to make a clockwise circle. Next he would reinforce the bird only when it would move in the opposite direction after making a full circle. Each time it made a counterclockwise turn, it received a food pellet. In due course, the pigeon would make a full counterclockwise circle, which, when combined with the clockwise circle, constituted the figure eight Skinner wanted.

We should exercise caution, however, in using findings regarding the behavior of pigeons (or other organisms) to arrive at conclusions about the behavior of human beings (Locurto, Terrace, and Gibbon, 1981). For example, pecking is peculiar to pigeons (and other birds) in feeding situations. As we pointed out earlier in the chapter, an organism's biology contributes to how and what it learns. A mounting body of evidence is causing psychologists to reevaluate studies that were presumed to have eliminated genetic predispositions as a significant factor in "learning" experiences (Schwartz, 1981). Psychologists call biological biases for learning certain kinds of behavior *autoshaping*, for automatic shaping.

Even so, despite these reservations, psychologists have found the concept of operant conditioning a useful tool. Consider the following example, in which positive reinforcers were used in a school setting (Hauserman, Walen, and Behling, 1973). In her first-grade class of twenty white students and five black students, a teacher noted that the students self-segregated themselves by race in their social activities. In order to promote integrated interaction, the teacher devised a "new friend" game. She produced a hat containing pairings of pupil names. Each black child was paired with a white child and consistent cliques of white children were mixed and paired with other white children. At lunchtime the teacher encouraged all the children "to sit in the cafeteria and to eat with your new friend."

When the children were eating their lunches, the teacher approached each table and observed, "Good! I'm glad you are sitting with your new friend." She then gave each child a pink, oak-leaf-shaped ticket and said, "This is for sitting with a new friend today. Later on, at recess, you give me your pink tag, and I will give you something good to eat." If the child and the "new friend" were still together at the end of the lunch period, each was provided with another tag entitling the pupil to an additional treat.

During the first four days of the experiment the teacher rearranged the pairings each day by means of

---

negative reinforcer: An aversive stimulus that when removed following a behavior strengthens the probability of the behavior's future occurrence.

shaping: A procedure in which a desired behavior is broken down into successive steps that are taught one step at a time.

A chimpanzee using a Chimp-O-Mat to "buy" peanuts and bananas with poker chips obtained by pulling down on a heavily weighted bar. Through operant conditioning, the animal has learned to value something that is neither edible nor fun to play with. *(Yerkes Regional Primate Center, Emory University)*

the names-in-the-hat technique. The experiment was then continued for an additional nine days. However, the teacher now dispensed with new daily pairings. She merely encouraged the children to "sit and eat with friends" and continued to reinforce the "new friend" behavior in the previous manner. By the end of the experimental period, the reinforcement program had tripled interracial free-time play.

Primary and Secondary Reinforcement

Psychologists distinguish between primary reinforcers and secondary reinforcers. A **primary reinforcer** is a stimulus that does not require an organism to learn its reinforcing property; it is an event that has natural, intrinsic value for the organism. For instance, food and water function as primary reinforcers for you when you are hungry and thirsty. Primary reinforcers are like unconditioned stimuli in classical conditioning.

A **secondary reinforcer** is a neutral stimulus that, through constant association with primary reinforcers, acquires its own reinforcing properties. In Skinner's view, money, honor rolls, and school grades are examples of secondary reinforcers. Take money. In and of themselves the small pieces of green paper are

primary reinforcer: A stimulus that does not require an organism to learn its reinforcing property; it is an event that has natural, intrinsic value for the organism.

secondary reinforcer: A neutral stimulus that, through constant association with primary reinforcers, acquires its own reinforcing properties.

of little value to you. Yet you work hard to obtain them (or you attend college in the anticipation that you will gain marketable skills that will allow you to earn them). The small pieces of green paper have acquired reinforcing properties by repeated association with primary reinforcers. Secondary reinforcers acquire their special value in much the manner that a second conditioned stimulus does in higher-order conditioning. Skinner's view of motivation is based on a deprivation model of simple animal drives in which hunger, thirst, and sex goad an organism into action. Other psychologists, including Abraham Maslow and Robert White, believe that human motives also encompass needs for approval and competence (see Chapter 4) and that these needs can assume the properties of primary reinforcers.

The psychologist John B. Wolfe (1936) has experimentally investigated secondary reinforcement with chimpanzees. Poker chips have no value for chimps —they are not edible and they are not very much fun to play with. However, Wolfe used operant conditioning to teach the chimps to value poker chips as much as human beings value money. He provided the animals with a "Chimp-O-Mat" that dispensed peanuts or bananas, which are primary reinforcers, or natural rewards. (Chimps like these foods.) However, to obtain food the chimps had first to pull down on a heavily weighted bar to obtain poker chips, then insert the chips in a slot in the machine. In time, the poker chips became secondary reinforcers. The value of the poker chips to the chimpanzees was evident from the fact that they would work for them, save them, and sometimes try to steal them from one another.

Schedules of Reinforcement

As noted earlier in the chapter, much of our understanding regarding the processes of operant conditioning has derived from the work of B. F. Skinner. Among other things, Skinner has demonstrated that the timing of reinforcement has a decided effect on the rate of learning. If the delay between a response

and its reinforcement is too great, learning is unlikely. The organism is simply unable to establish the association that exists between the response and its consequence.

Skinner also has shown that the frequency with which behaviors are reinforced has a considerable impact on learning. He accidentally stumbled on this fact one day while working in his laboratory. He had run low on food pellets. In order to conserve his limited supply, he started a pigeon off by rewarding it every time it engaged in the desired response. But once he had established the response, he would reward the bird only intermittently. In this manner he came to appreciate the important role that the patterning, or *scheduling*, of reinforcement plays in learning. In **continuous reinforcement** the organism is rewarded everytime it provides the desired or correct response. In **partial reinforcement** it is only occasionally rewarded for the proper response.

In later experiments, Skinner (1953) found that behavior that is partially reinforced is typically more stable and more ingrained than behavior that is continuously reinforced. Consider, for example, a man who has two cigarette lighters; one lights immediately every time (continuous reinforcement), whereas the other must be flicked four or five times before it lights (partial reinforcement). Next, suppose that both lighters stop lighting completely. Which lighter will he give up on first? Most likely, he will discard the first one immediately because it is now functioning differently from his expectations for it. But he will probably not consider it at all unusual for the second lighter to fail for the first four or five attempts. (See the boxed insert on page 203 for a discussion of how this process gives birth to superstitious practices.)

Although partial reinforcement may be arranged in a number of ways, four basic methods, or schedules, have been studied in the laboratory. Schedules of reinforcement may be based either on the number of correct responses that the organism makes between reinforcements (*ratio schedules*) or on the amount of time that elapses before reinforcement is

---

continuous reinforcement: A pattern in which an organism is rewarded every time it provides the desired or correct response.

partial reinforcement: A pattern in which an organism is only occasionally rewarded for providing the desired or correct response.

A child talks to the computer, which is programed to ask questions; all correct answers make the bear smile, and this gives the child continuous reinforcement.
(Hank Morgan/Rainbow)

made available *(interval schedules)*. In either case, reinforcement may appear on a regular, or fixed, schedule or an irregular, or variable, schedule. The four basic schedules result from the combination of these four possibilities (see Figures 6.4 and 6.5). People respond differently to each type.

On **fixed-ratio schedules,** reinforcement depends on a certain amount of behavior being emitted—for example, rewarding every fourth response. The student who receives a good grade after completing a specified amount of work and the typist who is paid every time he or she finishes a certain number of pages are on fixed-ratio schedules. People tend to work hard on fixed-ratio schedules, pausing briefly after each reward. However, if the amount of work or number of responses to be completed before the next reward is large, the student or piece-worker is likely to show low morale and few responses at the beginning of each new cycle because there is a long way to go before the next reinforcement.

On **variable-ratio schedules,** the number of required responses varies around some average, rather than being fixed. For example, a door-to-door salesperson may make a sale at the fourth house, the tenth house, and not again until the twentieth house. People on variable-ratio schedules tend to work or respond at a steady high rate. Why? Perhaps because the more the organism produces, the more reinforcement is obtained. Since the next reinforcement may follow the very next response, there is no pausing. The classic example of this schedule is a gambler at a slot machine. The faster he or she puts money into the machine, the sooner he or she will hit the jackpot.

On a **fixed-interval schedule,** reinforcement is available at a predetermined time no matter how many responses are emitted. Perhaps not surprisingly, a fixed-interval schedule produces a "scallop effect." If you record the responses of individuals on a graph, you find that at first they respond slowly

fixed-ratio schedule: A schedule of reinforcement in which a specific number of correct responses is required before reinforcement can be obtained.
variable-ratio schedule: A schedule of reinforcement in which a variable number of responses are required before reinforcement can be obtained.
fixed-interval schedule: A schedule of reinforcement in which a specific amount of time must elapse before a response will elicit reinforcement.

	RATIO (number)	INTERVAL (time)
FIXED	Fixed-Ratio	Fixed-Interval
VARIABLE	Variable-Ratio	Variable-Interval

FIGURE 6.4 Schedules of reinforcement. The fixed-ratio schedule reinforces the subject after a specific number of responses. The variable-ratio schedule provides the subject with a reinforcer after a different number of responses on different occasions (typically varying about an average). The fixed-interval schedule delivers a reinforcer only after a specific period of time has elapsed between responses. The variable-interval schedule affords reinforcement over a constantly changing period of time.

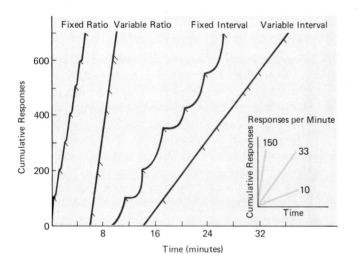

FIGURE 6.5 Typical cumulative recordings obtained by different schedules of reinforcement. The slash marks show when the reinforcements were introduced. Each curve represents the behavior of a pigeon pecking a key on the designated schedule. The vertical axis gives the number of responses emitted since the beginning of the time interval, so steeper curves indicate faster responding. *(Adapted from J. L. Williams. 1973. Operant Learning. Monterey, Calif.: Brooks/Cole. Copyright © 1973 by Wadsworth Publishing Company, Inc. Reprinted by permission of Brooks/Cole Publishing Company, Monterey, California 93940.)*

and in some cases not at all. But as the end of the time interval approaches, the subjects gradually increase their speed of responding in anticipation of the reinforcer. Good examples of common fixed-interval schedules are difficult to come by. However, the studying pattern of some students fits that of a fixed-interval schedule. They seldom study until just before an examination. A test reinforces more study-ing with a good grade—or lax studying with a poor grade. As the midterm approaches, the students increase their studying, reaching a feverish pitch immediately before the exam. After the test, their studying falls back to zero and begins to accelerate again only as the final approaches (Houston, 1976).

On a **variable-interval schedule,** the time at which a reinforcer will be available varies around

---

variable-interval schedule: A schedule of reinforcement in which varying amounts of time must elapse before a response will obtain reinforcement.

Sports Superstitions

Before the start of each inning, Mark Fidrych, a baseball pitcher with the Detroit Tigers, would get down on his hands and knees and smooth the dirt on the pitcher's mound; before he threw a pitch, he would talk to the baseball. Pitcher Mike Griffin always would wash his hair the day before he pitched. During the game, he would remove his cap after each pitch, and when the inning was over, he would sit in the same spot on the dugout bench (Gmelch, 1978). If you think these baseball players were using ritual and magic to help them win games, you are right. According to George Gmelch, once a pro baseball player and the author of several articles on baseball superstitions, pitchers have more magical rituals than fielders. It seems that pitchers have limited control over the results they achieve and use good-luck practices to help control the uncertainties (Zimmer, 1984). Thus superstition functions as a coping strategy, a way to handle the anxiety that comes with competition.

Experiments conducted by B. F. Skinner give us insight into how these rituals get started in the first place. Skinner rewarded pigeons with food pellets every fifteen seconds, no matter what they were doing. He soon found that the pigeons began to associate the onset of the feeding with a particular action—hopping from side to side, for example. Each time the pigeons were rewarded, their response was reinforced and they were more likely to repeat the response again. Even when they were fed irregularly, they did not give up. They still associated their action with the arrival of food, and the irregular feeding kept the connection going.

When a baseball player loads his mouth with a fresh pack of bubble gum before he bats and gets a home run, he may decide that the first event had something to do with the second. If he gets another hit, he is likely to chew bubble gum every time he is up. Since baseball statistics tell us that *on average* he will get a hit every fourth turn at bat; his ritualistic behavior will be intermittently reinforced on a variable-ratio schedule.

Of course, superstitious practices are not limited to baseball. They are found throughout sports. Even teams have superstitions. During the mid-1970s, the Philadelphia Flyers hockey team believed that Kate Smith's rendition of "God Bless America" brought them good luck. Accordingly, they had this song rather than the national anthem played before their home games. The result: fifty-four wins, nine losses, and two ties. However, the magic faded as the New York Islanders won a string of consecutive Stanley Cup titles. Perhaps not surprisingly, the Flyers returned to having the national anthem played (Zimmer, 1984).

---

some average, rather than being fixed. Dialing your friend's telephone number when her line is busy is a good example of a variable-interval schedule. When you finally get through, the sound of her voice will be a reinforcer. Meanwhile, no matter how many times you dial, you cannot increase the likelihood of getting through. Since you do not know when the line will be free, your best bet is to keep dialing at regular intervals. Similarly, a pigeon who is on a variable-interval schedule will tend to distribute its pecks at a key that releases a pellet much more evenly than does a pigeon who is on a fixed-interval schedule.

In general, responses are better learned and are more resistant to extinction when reinforced on a variable-interval or variable-ratio schedule. Likewise, the rate of responding is related to the reinforcement schedule. A fixed-ratio or a variable-ratio schedule tends to produce steady, rapid responses. A fixed-interval schedule results in a "scalloped" response curve. And a variable-interval schedule contributes to fairly steady, moderately paced responses (see Figure 6.5).

Punishment

Reinforcement differs from punishment. Reinforcement—be it of the positive or negative variety—*increases* the probability that an organism will act in

By paying off occasionally, slot machines put people on a variable-ratio schedule of reinforcement, which makes them keep feeding coins into the machine at a steady, high rate. *(Paul Fusco/Magnum)*

the same way in the future. In contrast, **punishment** serves to *decrease* the likelihood that a response will occur again. Whereas reinforcement *establishes* a behavior, punishment *suppresses* a behavior.

The Concept of Punishment

Students often have difficulty with the way learning psychologists use the concept of punishment. Admittedly, the psychological usage diverges from that of everyday life. You probably think of punishment as a penalty for some offense, most likely pain (a spanking) or physical coercion (imprisonment). Thus you view punishment as a kind of retribution or retaliation for misbehaving. But as learning psychologists use the term, punishment is defined by its *effect* on behavior: it *reduces* the frequency of a response (Azrin and Holz, 1966).

There are two types of punishment: *punishment by application* and *punishment by removal* (also called *extinction*). Punishment by application entails imposing a negative reinforcer (an aversive stimulus such as a spanking or jailing) after a response. Punish-

ment by removal involves taking away a positive reinforcer, for example, losing your television privileges, having your driver's license suspended, being fined money, or losing your job for misbehavior (Craighead, Kazdin, and Mahoney, 1976). A careful study of Figure 6.6 should assist you in grasping these distinctions.

The Effectiveness of Punishment

Although a controversial technique for suppressing unwanted behaviors, punishment is widely used. Even a scowl or a harsh word can take on punishing properties. Whether punishment works depends on a number of factors, of which timing and consistency seem to be the most important. The greater the time delay between a behavior and the punishing stimulus, the less effective it becomes (Aronfreed and Reber, 1965; Baron, 1965; Camp, Raymond, and Church, 1967). Likewise, the more consistently someone is punished, the more effective punishment is likely to be. Indeed, should people or animals find that they can occasionally get away with a behavior,

---

punishment: A consequence of behavior that decreases the likelihood that a response will occur again; punishment suppresses a behavior.

STIMULUS	APPLIED	WITHDRAWN
POSITIVE REINFORCER	**POSITIVE REINFORCEMENT** An increase occurs in the frequency of a response.	**PUNISHMENT BY REMOVAL (EXTINCTION)** A decrease occurs in the frequency of a response.
NEGATIVE REINFORCER	**PUNISHMENT BY APPLICATION** A decrease occurs in the frequency of a response.	**NEGATIVE REINFORCEMENT** An increase occurs in the frequency of a response.

FIGURE 6.6 Stimulus-response relationships. Positive reinforcement involves applying a positive reinforcer and results in a response's occurring more often. Negative reinforcement entails withdrawing a negative reinforcer and results in an increase in the incidence of a response. Punishment by removal (extinction) involves withdrawing a positive reinforcer and results in a response's occurring less often. Punishment by application entails adding a negative reinforcer and results in a decrease in the incidence of a response. *(Adapted from James W. Vander Zanden and Ann J. Pace. 1984. Educational Psychology. 2nd ed. New York: Random House, p. 139. Reprinted by permission.)*

they are likely to repeat it. Inconsistent punishment makes a behavior exceedingly resistant to change. Since inconsistency is unavoidable in most real-life situations, punishment often boomerangs (Azrin, Holz, and Hake, 1963).

Undesirable By-Products of Punishment

Most psychologists agree that punishment can have harmful side effects. First, although punishment may successfully suppress a particular behavior, it does not by itself provide an alternative "correct" response. Punishment simply says, "Stop what you're doing." It fails to say, "Do this instead." Reflect for a moment on how often you have heard a parent in a supermarket, a shopping mall, or some other public place tell a child, "Fred, stop that, you hear," "Jennie, quit fooling around," or "Mike, cut it out." Punishment is implied in such admonitions, but how effective are they? To be effective, the parent must also inform the child what the child is to do (Johnston, 1972).

A second problem with punishment is that the individual may attempt to avoid the punishing agent. Since the punishing agent is often a parent or a teacher, a child's avoidance behavior then poses a hindrance to learning. It deprives the child of the opportunity to acquire the desired attitudes and behaviors. Further, should escape be impossible, the child may simply "tune out" the stimulus through daydreaming and mental wanderings. Moreover, people who believe that they are unreasonably or unjustly punished often resort to alternative means for achieving the desired but forbidden end; for example, they cheat, lie, carry on the activity in secret, or invent excuses.

A third problem with punishment is that a parent or teacher who yells at or slaps a child is unwittingly providing a model for aggressive behavior. When a parent strikes a child for being aggressive toward peers, the parent provides a demonstration of how the child is "expected" to act when similarly confronted by frustration in later interactions. The command "Do as I say, not as I do" boomerangs. The individual is more influenced by the model's action—the "as I do" part of the command—than by the punishing stimulus associated with the "as I say" part (Bandura, 1967).

Learned Helplessness

Throughout the chapter we have emphasized that learning allows organisms to attune their behavior to the complexities of their environment. Thus, learning is an essential coping mechanism. However, the psychologist Martin Seligman (1975) has shown that under some circumstances organisms may learn behaviors that are maladaptive. When repeatedly exposed to uncontrollable events, they acquire a learned helplessness that then impairs their adjustment to later events that are controllable. **Learned helplessness** entails a generalized expectancy that unpleasant events are independent of one's own responses. Individuals experiencing learned helplessness consider their own actions to be causally unrelated to the events that follow. Hence they believe that their coping behaviors are futile.

Seligman performed a number of experiments to show how learned helplessness develops in animals. He strapped dogs into a harness from which they could not escape, and then gave them a series of shocks at irregular intervals. After days of shock treatment, the dogs were unharnessed. Now they could escape the shocks or avoid them entirely simply by jumping over a hurdle into a safe compartment. But more than half the dogs failed to learn to jump. When several dogs that had not been shocked were also tested, almost all of them quickly learned to jump to safety. Apparently, many of the dogs in the first group had learned to stand and endure the shocks, resigned to the fact that any effort to escape would be useless. (For obvious reasons, people concerned about unnecessary cruelty to animals have been highly critical of the research.)

Later experiments showed that people reacted in much the same way. In the first stage of one study (Hiroto, 1974), some college students were able to turn off an unpleasant loud noise, while others had no control over it. Later, all were placed in a situation in which they merely had to move a lever to stop a similar noise. Only the ones who had control over the noise in the first place learned to turn it off. The others did not even try.

It is easy to see how these results can apply to everyday situations. To be able to try hard and to be full of energy, people must learn that their actions *do* make a difference. If pain comes no matter how hard one tries, a person gives up (learned helplessness).

Seligman (1978; Abramson, Seligman and Teasdale, 1978) believes that learned helplessness contributes to some types of depression. He notes that many depressed people show a seeming paralysis of will. They interpret their responses to life situations as either failing or doomed to failure. It is as if the depressed person is locked within a mind-set that constantly exclaims, "I am a born loser."

Educational psychologists find that many school-children who give up when they confront failure in achievement settings are also victims of learned helplessness (Dweck, 1975; Diener and Dweck, 1978, 1980; Weisz, 1981; Friedlander, 1984). The children's belief that they do not control their learning outcomes leads them into apathetic responses. Nonetheless, they do think about their lack of success. Their passivity is not a function of simple indifference. They too would like to be successful; but since they attribute their poor performance to factors beyond their control, they do not search for ways to overcome failure. In contrast, mastery-oriented students approach their difficulties in a quite different fashion. These students look for new solutions to their problems.

"Helpless" students find their circumstances complicated by another factor. They attribute their poor performance to inadequate ability rather than to inadequate effort. But there is hope for these children. When they are taught to attribute their failure to lack of motivation rather than to lack of ability, they reveal striking improvements in their coping responses.

The notion of learned helplessness is important because it is a good example of several new trends in behavioral research. As learning theorists begin to study people rather than animals, they are finding that some of the old models are too simple. More important, they are finding that they cannot focus simply on what people *do*. What people *think* is also important.

Behavior Modification

The term "behavior modification" often appears in magazine articles describing research on changing people's behavior through drugs, "mind control," or even brain surgery. In fact, it is none of these things. **Behavior modification** refers to the systematic appli-

---

learned helplessness: A generalized expectancy that unpleasant events are independent of one's own responses.
behavior modification: The systematic application of learning principles to change people's actions and feelings.

When teachers control too much of children's learning, they can create bored, helpless-feeling students. *(Paul Fortin/Stock, Boston)*

cation of learning principles to change people's actions and feelings.

Behavior modification involves a careful series of well-defined steps to change behavior. And the success of each step is carefully evaluated to find the best solution for a given situation. The behavior modifier typically begins by defining a problem in quite specific terms. For example, a mother might complain that Pete, her son, is "messy." If she used behavior modification to reform the child, she would first have to define "messy" in objective terms. She would need to pinpoint exactly what behavior is to be modified: Pete does not make his bed in the morning, he drops his coat on the couch when he comes inside, and he leaves his dirty socks strewn about his bedroom. She would not worry about the underlying obscure or inner forces causing Pete's behavior. Rather, she would work out a system of

rewards and punishments aimed at getting Pete to make his bed, hang up his coat, and place his socks in the laundry basket.

One approach to behavior modification that has been used in classroom situations and with disturbed youngsters is a **token economy**. The approach usually operates as a miniature economy that in many ways parallels that of the larger society. Psychologists have used a token economy to motivate boys in the District of Columbia who had been labeled "uneducable" and placed in the National Training School. The youngsters received points for good grades on tests. They could "cash" these points in for such rewards as snacks, lounge privileges, or items in a mail-order catalog. In other words, the psychologists created a system that worked like the Chimp-O-Mat, discussed earlier. Within a few months, a majority of the students showed a signifi-

token economy: A form of conditioning in which desirable behavior is reinforced with tokens, which can be accumulated and exchanged for various rewards.

Breaking a Habit: Smoking

Medical authorities contend that cigarette smoking is the single most important source of preventable death (Fielding, 1985a). The annual death toll from diseases attributed to smoking, 350,000, is seven times the fatality rate of motor vehicle crashes and more than the total number of Americans killed in World War I, Korea, and Vietnam, combined. For its part, the Environmental Protection Agency lists tobacco smoke as the country's most dangerous airborne carcinogen.

There are about 33 million ex-smokers alive in the United States. Behavior modification techniques are one approach for breaking the smoking habit. Behavior therapists offer some tips on how to do it (Williams and Long, 1979; Brody, 1983):

● Start by keeping a diary for a week or so of the times and places you smoke every single cigarette. Identify the signals from the environment that are associated with smoking. The desire for a cigarette is activated by daily rituals or social situations: a cup of coffee, a cocktail, a meeting, or a waiting room may present special challenges.

● On the basis of your diary, rearrange your environment so that you avoid those circumstances or feelings that trigger the urge to smoke. For example, if every time you drink a cup of coffee you get a craving to smoke, switch to a different beverage or limit your coffee consumption to settings in which cigarettes are not available. Continue to keep records as you try to cut down or quit in order to find out which techniques work best for you.

● You can cut down impulsive smoking by switching the place you carry cigarettes and never carrying matches or a lighter. Searching for the pack each time and having to ask someone for a light will help make you more aware of your habit.

● Strike a bargain with yourself—for every day you go without a cigarette, for example, let yourself watch an extra hour of your favorite

cant increase in IQ scores (an average gain of twelve and a half points). The boys continued to improve in the months that followed, showing that they were, indeed, educable (Cohen and Filipczak, 1971).

In another experiment, teachers used a token economy to teach preschoolers in a Head Start program to write, and compared their scores on writing tests with those achieved by children who did not participate in a token economy. The youngsters who received tokens, which they could exchange for food, movies, and other rewards, improved dramatically. Equally important, they seemed to be developing a very positive attitude toward school. The youngsters who did not receive tokens made very little progress (Miller and Schneider, 1970).

In token economies, researchers set up an elaborate system of reinforcers to get people to act the way they want. One of the most important new trends in behavior modification is a growing emphasis on asking people to set up personal systems of rewards and punishments to shape their own thoughts and actions. Rather than depending on others to formulate their goals and to bring various reinforcers to bear, people assume these responsibilities for themselves.

As in other applications of behavior modification, the first step in self-control is to define the problem. Individuals who smoke too much would be encouraged to count how many cigarettes they smoke every hour of the day and note what kinds of situations lead them to smoke. (After a meal? When talking to friends? Driving to work?) (See the boxed insert above, which discusses a program for breaking the smoking habit.) Similarly, people who have a very poor opinion of themselves would have to define the problem more concretely. They might begin by counting the number of self-deprecating remarks they make and thoughts they have. Researchers have found that just keeping track of behavior in this way often leads people to start changing it.

The next step may be to set up a single behavioral

shows on television. Or you may allow yourself to buy a special book or an article of clothing.

● Practice self-restraint. When temptation presents itself, wait for ten minutes before deciding how to respond to it. This will give you time to regain your self-control. During the ten minutes try to distract yourself by substituting constructive daydreams or fantasies for the tempting thoughts.

● Institute replacement activities that can fill the void left by smoking. These may include physical exercise, Yoga, meditation, deep muscle relaxation, audiotapes, religious activity, creative activity, a new career, further education, or philanthropic work.

● Slips are common when seeking to break a long-standing habit like smoking. Avoid labeling yourself a loser and setting off a full relapse. Keep your eye on your long-term goal and focus on the successes you have had. Remind yourself after a slip that you made a mistake and that a slip merely means you have to be more careful in the future. Rather than harboring guilt or discouragement, get back on your program promptly.

Success in kicking the smoking habit varies from person to person. In most programs the initial rates at which people quit smoking are high, in the range of 70 to 90 percent. However, relapse rates are also high, with six-month and twelve-month abstinence rates in the range of 20 to 40 percent. The use of nicotine gum as an adjunct to behavioral approaches shows promise, with some studies suggesting that it can double the long-term abstinence rate. Most successful quitters who use nicotine gum gradually decrease their dependence on it and discontinue its use in several months. Another promising adjunct to traditional behaviorally oriented programs is the use of contests that pit teams of smokers against each other to win monetary prizes for team nonsmoking (Fielding, 1985b). Stop-smoking programs offered by employers at the work place also seem to be more successful than outside clinics in getting and keeping people off cigarettes. The work site affords an important social group. When the boss and coworkers say, "Good going, keep it up," people are more likely to stick with it (Elias, 1985b).

contract (see Figure 6.7). One soda lover who had trouble studying decided that she would allow herself a Pepsi only after she had studied for half an hour. Her cola addiction remained strong, but her study time increased dramatically under this system. A behavioral contract simply involves choosing a reinforcer (buying a new shirt, watching a favorite television program) and making it contingent on carrying out some unpleasant but necessary act (getting to work on time, washing the kitchen floor). These contracts are most likely to succeed if you also use successive approximations—starting with an easy task and gradually making it more difficult. For example, you might begin by studying ten minutes before rewarding yourself, and gradually increase it to an hour.

Behavior modifiers are now developing and testing many other techniques to help people learn to control their behavior. One program that may interest you has to do with the improvement of study habits (see the boxed insert on page 211).

COGNITIVE LEARNING

Cognitive psychology entails the study of the human mind (Sternberg, 1986). As such, it focuses on those processes by which you perceive, represent, remember, and employ knowledge. Operant-conditioning theorists such as Skinner view learning as a process by which particular responses are reinforced by environmental events. In contrast, cognitive psychologists credit learning to mental activity. They view symbols as the key to internal information processing (Bandura, 1977). Words and mental images—things that stand for something else—allow you to represent events, to analyze your experiences, and to plan your actions. Symbols permit you to solve problems without first having to try out various solutions on a trial-and-error basis. Indeed, some cognitive psychologists believe that stimuli and reinforcements have little impact on your behavior unless you first represent them in a mental fashion (that

FIGURE 6.7   Sample Behavior-Change Contract

I, _____, have decided to commit myself to the following behavioral change:

Behavior change: To lose weight.

More specifically, my goal is: To lose ten pounds.

Date I expect to reach my goal: July 10.

Subgoal(s):
- I will eat no more than 1,200 calories per day.
- I will lose two pounds each week.

Action steps and rules to follow that will help me accomplish my goal:
- I will write a three-day menu, which will contain no more than 1,200 calories for each day.
- I will stop eating before I feel full. I resign from the clean-plate club.
- I will eat carrot sticks and celery sticks for snacks.
- I will substitute water for soft drinks.
- When I go to someone's house for dinner, I will eat half the portion.
- Before going to a party, I will ask my roommate or a friend to remind me not to overindulge.
- At the end of each day, I will report my success to my roommate or friend.

I will get feedback by:
- Charting the number of calories I eat each day.
- Getting on the scale each Monday and charting the results. The chart will be posted on my bulletin board.
- Reporting my results to at least two friends.

If I reach my subgoals, I will reward myself by:
- Taking a bubble bath for each day that I stick to 1,200 calories.
- Buying a record for each week that I lose two pounds.

If I do not reach my subgoals, I will punish myself by:
- Confining myself to 1,000 calories for the day after I exceed 1,200 calories.
- Depriving myself of a party if I continue to exceed 1,200 calories day after day.

If I reach my goal by the date specified, I will reward myself by:
- Buying a new dress.

If I do not reach my goal by the date specified, I will punish myself by:
- Not watching TV for two weeks.

Signature _____   **Date** _____

(After Peggy Blake, Robert Frye, and Michael Pejsach. 1986. Discover Your Health Behaviors. New York: Random House, pp. 48–49. Reprinted by permission.)

Improving Your Study Habits

One psychologist (Fox, 1966) designed a program to help students improve their study habits and tried it on a group of volunteers. The students were told to set a time when they would go to a small room in the library they had not used before, taking only the materials they wanted to study. They were then to work for as long as they remained interested—and *only* for as long as they were interested. As soon as they found themselves fidgeting, daydreaming, becoming drowsy or bored, they were to make the decision to stop studying. There was only one condition. They had to read one more page, or solve one more simple problem, before they left. But even if this made them want to study longer, they were instructed to hold to their decision to leave the library, go for a cup of coffee, call a friend, or do whatever they wanted to do.

The next day they were asked to repeat the same procedure, adding a second page to the amount they read between the time they decided to leave and the time they actually left the library. The third day they added a third page, and soon. Students who followed this procedure found that in time they were able to study for longer periods than before, that they were studying more effectively, and that they did not mind studying so much.

Why did this procedure work? Many students force themselves to study. One common technique is to go to the library to avoid distractions. The result may be hours spent staring at a book without really learning anything. Repeated failures to get anything accomplished and sheer discomfort turn studying into a dreaded chore. The library becomes a conditioned aversive stimulus—you hate the place because you have spent so many uncomfortable hours there. The procedure was designed to change these negative feelings.

Requiring students to leave as soon as they felt distracted helped to reduce the negative, punishing emotions associated with studying. The students stopped when these feelings began. Studying in a new place removed the conditioned aversive stimulus. Thus aversive responses were not conditioned to the subject matter or the room, as they are when students force themselves to work.

Second, the procedure made use of successive approximations. The students began by reading just one page after they became bored, and only gradually increased the assignment. This also reduced the aversive response to studying. The task no longer seemed so difficult.

Finally, when they left their work, the students received two kinds of positive reinforcement. They had the satisfaction of knowing they had followed the procedure and had completed an assignment (namely, one more page). And they were free to do something they enjoyed. Thus they rewarded or reinforced themselves for however much studying they did. You might try this procedure.

is, symbolically portray and reflect on them in your mind) (Rosenthal and Zimmerman, 1978).

The work of cognitive psychologists affords a somewhat different view of human behavior than that of conditioning theorists. Conditioning theorists give a picture of humankind as made up of rather passive beings who are mechanically buffeted about by external influences (stimuli). Instead, cognitive theorists depict human beings as selecting, organizing, and transforming the stimuli that impinge on them. By virtue of mental (cognitive) processes, people come to exercise some degree of control over their own behavior. Cognitive theorists do not deny that direct experience makes a substantial contribution to human learning. But they emphasize that thought processes play an equally important role (Bandura, 1977; Rosenthal and Zimmerman, 1978).

Latent Learning

Learning provides you with the potential for engaging in a good many behaviors. Yet the fact that you have knowledge about certain matters or possess particular skills does not ensure that you will act in terms of your learning. For instance, accountants, bank officials, and computer programers often know a good deal about how to embezzle money by manipulating financial records, but they typically do not translate their knowledge into theft. Likewise, you undoubtedly know how to reach the nearest fast-food franchise, but you may not want to set out for it because you have just eaten. And since you are now reading this text, it is unlikely that you are currently using your automotive driving skills. Since organisms may know how to do something yet not do it, psychologists find it useful to distinguish between learning and performance.

The work of the psychologist Edward C. Tolman (1932, 1938, 1949) has highlighted the point that people know many things about their environment but that they act on this information only when they need to do so. In other words, knowledge remains dormant until a need arises. For example, let us suppose that you are currently reading this text in a library building. You feel thirsty. You reflect that you have passed by three drinking fountains in the building on numerous occasions but have never paused for a drink of water. Now, on experiencing thirst, you walk over to one of the fountains and take a drink (Hergenhahn, 1976). Tolman termed learning that is not translated into performance until the organism is motivated to show what it has learned **latent learning.**

Tolman demonstrated the existence of latent learning in a now famous experiment involving three groups of rats that were learning to solve a maze (Tolman and Honzik, 1930). One group was never rewarded for correctly navigating the maze. Another group was always rewarded. And still another group was not rewarded until the eleventh day of the experiment. Over the course of the experiment all the groups showed some improvement in their mastery of the maze. However, it was the group that had not been rewarded until the eleventh day that by the end of the experiment displayed the best performance. According to Tolman, the best-performing rats had not made use of their latent knowledge of the maze until they were given a reason to do so. In other words, the rats *learned* the layout of the maze,

but they did not *perform* in the maze until food motivated them to use the information.

Tolman stressed that there is often much more to learning than simply making connections between stimuli and responses. For instance, you do not simply go about life thinking to yourself, "If I do this, I will get that." You form ideas and conceptions about the way your environment is structured, about what things usually go together, and about what routes lead to what places. You then use these notions—*cognitions*—when you need them to achieve your goals.

In his rat experiments, Tolman demonstrated that organisms seem to learn "the lay of the land." They learn that if they turn to the left, they encounter one thing; if they turn to the right, they find something else. In this manner, organisms develop a "picture" of the environment that they use in dealing with reality and making their way about life. He termed this picture a *cognitive map*. Once organisms have developed a cognitive map, they can use alternative routes to reach a goal should one or more routes be blocked. Tolman believed that organisms, on the basis of their cognitive maps, typically choose the shortest route or the one requiring the least effort. He labeled this tendency the *principle of least effort*.

Over the past fifty years other psychologists have followed up on Tolman's leads. Like Tolman, they find that a cognitive map allows an animal to react to stimuli that are not immediately present. But in addition, psychologists have shown that a cognitive map allows animals to link conceptually parts of their environment that they have never experienced at the same time. Thus rats allowed to explore two runway mazes leading to food use their knowledge to navigate successfully a third maze that incorporates elements of the first two mazes (Ellen, Soteres, and Wages, 1984).

Modeling

Tolman's work drew the attention of psychologists to the part that inner, mental activity plays in some types of learning. He demonstrated that any number of factors may intervene in the process by which an

---

latent (LAY-tent) learning: Learning that is not translated into performance until the organism is motivated to show what it has learned.

Humans learn by watching others and imitating their behaviors. *(Frank Siteman/The Picture Cube)*

organism establishes a relationship or connection between a stimulus and a response. More recently psychologists such as Albert Bandura (1971, 1973, 1977) and Walter Mischel (1971, 1973) have built on Tolman's insights. They note that a person need not have direct experience with events to learn about the relationship between them. You may learn through **modeling** (also called **observational learning**). By watching other people, you can acquire new responses without first having to experience the response yourself.

Consider what occurs when you go to a concert for the first time. You may be very hesitant about where to go, when to enter (especially if you are late), when to clap, how to get a better seat after the first intermission, and so on. So you observe others, follow them, and soon you are an "old hand."

We would expect imitation to be responsible for more basic forms of behavior as well, when the proper response is essential to life. Trial-and-error learning is not useful if the punishment for failure to emit the response is to be eaten by a predator. Thus correct avoidance behavior often must be learned by imitating. Modeling influences an observer in at least three ways: learning new responses, inhibition and disinhibition, and facilitation.

Learning New Responses

We frequently acquire new behaviors by watching what other people say and do. When another person does something novel, we may try to imitate the behavior. For instance, a child may observe a parent standing on a kitchen chair to reach objects on a high shelf. In turn, the child may use the chair to reach otherwise inaccessible objects on the kitchen table. Your chemistry instructor employs this technique in using a blackboard to show you how to solve particular equations. It is not even necessary that you observe real-life models. Symbolic or pictorial

---

modeling (observational learning): The acquisition of new responses by watching other individuals, without first having to experience the response oneself.

Television Violence

Throughout history, most societies have provided their children with fictional materials that contain accounts of violent happenings. For example, fairy tales tell about fire-breathing dragons and dangerous giants. Thus children are not necessarily sheltered from knowledge of violence. However, today's children encounter an additional dimension of violence—television programs that depict human beings engaged in violent acts with which children can easily identify (Gentry, 1974).

Accordingly, a growing number of authorities have expressed concern over the effects that media violence has on the behavior of American youth (Eron et al., 1972). A report prepared by the National Institute of Mental Health concludes that there is "overwhelming" scientific evidence that "excessive" violence on television leads directly to aggression and violent behavior among children and teen-agers (Pearl, 1982). Labeling television a "beguiling" instrument that has become "a major socializing agent of American children," the report finds that "television violence is as strongly correlated with aggressive behavior as any other behavioral variable that has been measured." In 1985, the American Psychological Association, representing more than sixty thousand psychologists, voiced its concern. In a resolution passed by its council of representatives, the association said that "viewing televised violence may lead to increases in aggressive attitudes, values, and behavior, particularly in children" (Coughlin, 1985). The psychologists encouraged "parents to monitor and control television viewing by children" and asked the television industry to reduce "imitable violence in 'real-life' fictional children's programming."

According to the A. C. Nielsen Company, a firm that specializes in assessing the popularity of television programs, the average child between the ages of two and eleven watches twenty-seven hours and twenty-one minutes of television a week. By the time most young people leave high school, they have spent more time before a television screen than they have in the classroom. Many of the programs directed toward child audiences are saturated with mayhem, violence, and aggression. The A Team and the Bugs Bunny–Roadrunner cartoons are not atypical of the Saturday morning fare for children. On average, forty-six acts of violence occur per hour on The A-Team and fifty violent acts per hour in the Roadrunner cartoons (Tooth, 1985). At the same time, the number of educational programs for children (such as Captain Kangaroo) is declining, particularly on the three major commercial networks.

presentations—in newspapers, books, magazines, movies, and television—may do just as well. Researchers find that children are as likely to imitate aggressive behavior if they witness it in a movie or in an animated cartoon as they are if they witness it in person (Bandura, Ross, and Ross, 1963). (See the boxed insert above.)

Inhibition and Disinhibition

We may also exhibit *inhibition*, or avoidance, of a particular action as a result of observing what happens to others. When we see another person experiencing negative consequences for saying or doing something, we may become more reluctant to say or do this same thing. Teachers frequently punish one child in the presence of others to achieve a "spill-over" effect—other children are deterred by what they witness. Folklore, parables, and fables achieve somewhat similar outcomes through oral or written accounts. The expulsion of Adam and Eve from the Garden of Eden, for example, is meant to discourage people from engaging in religiously prohibited behavior (Zimmerman and Ghozeil, 1974).

Behavior may also undergo *disinhibition* by observing a model. Children who witness other children successfully violating school rules are encouraged to follow suit. If one child gets away with

Evidence suggests that all three of the modeling effects discussed in the text are associated with exposure to television violence (Liebert and Baron, 1972; Bandura, 1973; Andison, 1977; Withey and Abeles, 1980). First, people learn new ways of directing aggression against others from viewing violent scenes. Second, the inhibitions people have against committing antisocial acts are lowered and, in some instances, eradicated. And third, exposure to violent episodes facilitates similar behavior by increasing the probability that some viewers will imitate these actions.

Television violence also has other negative effects. Research shows that media violence increases children's tolerance for aggression in real life (Drabman and Thomas, 1974). Moreover, when television violence is watched by aggressive children, it provides opportunities for them to rationalize their own aggressive behavior as acceptable (Huesmann, Lagerspetz, and Eron, 1984). And televised violence may arouse some viewers, multiplying tendencies in angry and alienated youth to commit destructive acts (Tannenbaum, 1980; Zillmann, 1982).

Researchers at all the three major networks have challenged these findings. They contend that there is no direct evidence of a correlation between television violence and aggressive behavior in children. A number of psychologists tend to concur, believing that the link is not as significant as is commonly portrayed. But these psychologists are a minority (Milavsky et al., 1982; Walsh, 1983; Freedman, 1984; Coughlin, 1985). And there are some who say that there is a reverse causality between television violence and aggressive behavior. According to this view, aggressive individuals are socially ostracized, so they spend more time at home watching television. Another interpretation contends that aggressive personalities prefer violent shows (Fenigstein, 1979).

Psychologists are also investigating how television can be used to benefit children, or at least have fewer negative effects (Sprafkin, Swift, and Hess, 1983). Appropriate interventions can dramatically change children's reactions to television violence by altering their attitudes toward aggressive behavior (Huesmann et al., 1983). Researchers also find that the aggressive behavior of children can be reduced by their watching films depicting constructive solutions to conflicts that appear frequently in children's everyday lives (Pitkanen-Pulkkinen, 1979). And many children who watch episodes of *Mr. Rogers' Neighborhood* (a program that stresses such themes as kindness, cooperation, and sharing) display increases in sympathetic, friendly, and helping behaviors (Friedrich and Stein, 1975; Friedrich-Cofer and Huston, in press).

running down the hall, particularly if the floors are slippery enough to permit sliding, others quickly imitate. Should the child be rewarded by being the first to reach the playground and gaining access to the kickball, the effect is strengthened (Zimmerman, 1977). Conversely, many types of fear can be reduced by exposing children to a model who fearlessly approaches and deals with a feared stimulus, such as a dog or snake (Bandura and Menlove, 1968).

Facilitation

As Tolman's research documented, we have responses in our repertoire that we may not use. When we witness others engaging in these behaviors, we may recall the behavior later and be more inclined to apply it in a similar situation. Modeling, then, may facilitate our acting in ways that otherwise would be untypical of us. *Facilitation* is not the same thing as disinhibition. Disinhibition occurs only if some behavior is checked, as in the case of punishment. Facilitation takes place when a response that a person would be unlikely to make becomes more probable (Zimmerman and Ghozeil, 1974; Zimmerman and Koussa, 1979). For example, teen-agers may know how to smoke marijuana but never have done so. But when one teen-ager lights up, the others may join in the behavior.

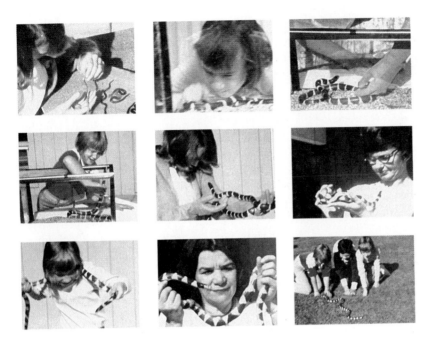

Bandura's modeling technique for eliminating snake phobia. In a procedure called live modeling with participation, subjects imitate a model's performance in handling the snake. *(Courtesy, A. Bandura)*

FACTORS THAT AFFECT LEARNING

The behavioral and cognitive approaches draw our attention to different but related processes in learning. Behaviorists emphasize how organisms adjust to their environments through the reinforcement of adaptive responses. Cognitive theorists examine the mental activities by which organisms process information that allows them to meet their needs and achieve their goals. Clearly, learning entails a good many processes. In complex forms of learning, several factors are involved that can help or hinder these processes. Among them are feedback, transfer, and practice.

Feedback

Information about the results of an action or performance is called **feedback.** Without feedback, you might repeat the same mistakes so many times that you would develop a skill incorrectly—you would never learn what you were doing wrong. If, for example, you always wore earplugs while you practiced the piano, you would never know just how bad your version of "Chopsticks" sounded. Even if you were performing correctly, without feedback you would not be receiving reinforcement for continuing to play.

Feedback has also been used as a means to encourage energy conservation (Seligman and Darley, 1977). Homeowners participating in a pilot study were informed four times a week how much electricity they were consuming to air-condition their homes. The information compared their "actual" consumption with their "expected" consumption in terms of the average outdoor temperature. The program contributed to an overall 10 percent saving in energy use.

Transfer

Learning is a cumulative process. The more knowledge and skill you acquire, the more likely it is that your new learning will be influenced and shaped by your past learning. Consequently, a skill that you have already learned can help you to learn a new

---

feedback: Information received after an action as to its effectiveness or correctness.

skill. **Transfer of learning** refers to the influence that prior learning has on performance in a new situation. From the earliest days of their discipline, psychologists have been concerned with the circumstances under which knowledge and principles learned in one context carry over to other contexts (James, 1984; Thorndike and Woodworth, 1901a, 1901b, 1901c; Judd, 1908). As you might expect, they have found that the extent to which knowledge and skills can be transferred from one realm to another varies with the knowledge and skills that are involved (Menzel and June, 1982, 1984; Schrier and Thompson, 1984).

Transfer effects may be positive, negative, or absent. In *positive transfer of learning*, the practice of one skill facilitates a second. For instance, if you have learned to play the saxophone, you can transfer many of the skills you already have to the clarinet, including reading notes and converting them to the proper lip, tongue, and finger movements. However, a previously learned task may also impede learning so that *negative transfer of learning* occurs. An American may find that learning to drive in England is more difficult than learning to drive in the United States. In England the steering wheel is on the right side of the car, and people are accustomed to traveling on the left side of the road. The experience of riding in cars American style thus makes it difficult to perform the necessary new mental and motor tasks. An American's responses are often the exact opposite of what is needed. Similarly, basketball training tends to interfere with a person's baseball skill. Throwing the ball may initially show negative transfer because of the differences in the size of the ball and in the distances the ball is usually thrown.

At one time psychologists debated whether or not transfer of learning occurs. Today the matter is no longer an issue. Instead they have come to see their task as one of identifying the *conditions* that influence transfer between tasks. The research of Harry F. Harlow (1949, 1959) has contributed a good deal to our understanding of these matters. Using both monkeys and children as his subjects, Harlow found that individuals improve their ability to learn new tasks because of their experiences with other similar or related tasks, termed a *learning set*. A learning set is an example of learning how to learn. He was able to show that monkeys and children display an ability to begin at successively higher levels when problems of a like kind are presented to them. Your schooling experiences very likely confirm Harlow's findings. For example, after you practice solving linear equations for a number of days, you improve your speed and accuracy in solving new and more difficult linear equations. You learn what you should attend to and what you should ignore in the problems. In brief, you discover *how to attack* similar tasks in an efficient manner; you learn to learn (Brown, 1982).

Practice

Practice, the repetition of a task, helps to bind responses together. It is the key element that makes for smooth and fluent movement from response to response.

Because practice takes time, psychologists have been interested in determining how to use that time most efficiently. They have found that whatever type of skill a person is learning, it is usually better to space out practice rather than do it all at once. Excessive repetition of a task without intervals of rest produces fatigue and boredom (Sage, 1971).

It is possible to practice by imagining oneself performing a skill. Athletes imagine themselves making golf swings over and over again or mentally shooting free throws in basketball to improve their performance. Psychologists call such effort *mental practice*. Although it is not as effective as the real thing, it is better than nothing at all.

SUMMARY

1. Learning is a permanent change in behavior or capability that results from experience. The association of or link between two events is central to learning. Learning is a critical process because it

---

transfer of learning: The effects of past learning on the ability to learn new tasks.
practice: The repetition of a task, which helps to bind responses together.

allows an organism to adapt to its environment. Although learning is responsible for but a small portion of the behavior of lower species, it is responsible for a substantial portion of the behavior of higher species, including human beings.

2. Classical conditioning was discovered by Ivan Pavlov. In this form of learning, a new, previously neutral stimulus becomes able to evoke a response because it is paired with a stimulus that has already evoked a response.

    A. Extinction of a classically conditioned response occurs when the conditioned response gradually dies out.

    B. Spontaneous recovery typically accompanies extinction. If the animal is given a rest away from the experimental equipment, the conditioned stimulus will again evoke the conditioned response.

    C. Stimulus generalization occurs when an organism matches novel sensory inputs with previously established but similar information.

    D. Stimulus discrimination involves the ability of an organism to respond differently to two or more stimuli that are similar but distinct.

    E. A form of classical conditioning that is quite relevant to real-world situations is higher-order conditioning. After a second conditioned stimulus has been paired with the first stimulus a number of times, the second stimulus may take on the functions of the first stimulus.

3. Psychologists no longer view conditioning as a simple, mechanical process involving the association of two events that occur rather closely in time. Organisms do not make pairings between events in a vacuum. Rather, they seem to evaluate the information that different stimuli provide them.

    A. Taste aversion is a type of classical conditioning in which there is a considerable delay in the association between the stimulus (feeling ill) and the response (avoiding the food). Other responses are also built on evolved biases in species' responses to particular stimuli.

    B. Systematic densensitization is frequently used in the treatment of behavior disorders in which fear plays a prominent part. The process entails gradually confronting patients with the fear-arousing stimulus after they have been trained to relax.

4. Significant advances in our knowledge of the molecular bases of classical conditioning have come from the study of *Aplysia*. Eric Kandel and his associates contend that learning is not diffused throughout the brain but is localized in the activity of specific nerve cells. More particularly, learning results from changes that take place in the membranes of nerve cells and in the synaptic connections between them. Kandel believes that a cellular alphabet underlies learning.

5. Operant conditioning is a type of learning in which the consequences of a behavior influence whether the organism will act (operate) in the same way in the future.

    A. Reinforcers play a prominent role in operant conditioning. A reinforcer is any stimulus that follows a response and increases the probability that the response will occur again. B. F. Skinner distinguishes between two types of reinforcers: positive reinforcers and negative reinforcers. Positive reinforcement entails adding something rewarding to the situation. Negative reinforcement entails removing something aversive from the situation.

    B. Psychologists also distinguish between primary reinforcers and secondary reinforcers. A primary reinforcer is an event that has natural, intrinsic value for an organism. A secondary reinforcer is a neutral stimulus that, through constant association with primary reinforcers, acquires its own reinforcing properties (for instance, money).

    C. In general, responses are better learned and are more resistant to extinction when reinforced on a variable-interval or variable-ratio schedule. Likewise, the rate of responding is related to the reinforcement schedule. A fixed-ratio or a variable-ratio schedule tends to produce steady, rapid responses. A fixed-interval schedule results in a "scalloped" response curve. Lastly, a variable-interval schedule contributes to fairly steady, moderately paced responses.

6. Reinforcement differs from punishment. Reinforcement increases the probability that an organism

will act in the same way in the future. In contrast, punishment serves to decrease the likelihood that a response will occur again. Whereas reinforcement establishes a behavior, punishment suppresses a behavior.

A. Punishment is of two types: punishment by application and punishment by removal. Punishment by application entails imposing a negative reinforcer after a response. Punishment by removal involves taking away a positive reinforcer.

B. Timing and consistency are variables that influence the effectiveness of punishment.

C. Punishment may produce a number of harmful side effects. First, although punishment may successfully suppress a particular behavior, it does not by itself provide an alternative "correct" response. Second, the individual may attempt to avoid the punishing agent. And third, a parent or teacher who yells at or slaps a child is unwittingly providing a model for aggressive behavior that the child may imitate.

7. Under some circumstances organisms may learn behaviors that are maladaptive. When repeatedly exposed to uncontrollable events, they acquire a learned helplessness that then impairs their adjustment to later events that are controllable.

8. Behavior modification refers to the systematic application of learning principles to change people's actions and feelings. One approach to behavior modification that has been used in classroom situations as well as with disturbed youngsters is a token economy.

9. Cognitive psychologists credit learning to mental activity. They depict human beings as selecting, organizing, and transforming the stimuli that impinge on them.

10. The work of the psychologist Edward C. Tolman has highlighted the point that individuals know many things about their environment but that they act on this information only when they need to do so. Latent learning and cognitive maps are good illustrations of this fact.

11. Building on Tolman's insights, contemporary psychologists note that a person need not have direct experience with events to learn about the relationships between them. Instead you may learn through modeling. Modeling influences an observer in at least three ways: learning new responses, inhibition and disinhibition, and facilitation.

12. Studies of more complex forms of learning have revealed that several factors help or hinder the process. Among them are feedback, transfer, and practice.

KEY TERMS

behavior modification (p. 206)
classical conditioning (p. 188)
conditioned response
   (CR) (p. 189)
conditioned stimulus
   (CS) (p. 188)
conditioning (p. 187)
continuous
   reinforcement (p. 200)
extinction (p. 190)
feedback (p. 216)
fixed-interval schedule (p. 201)
fixed-ratio schedule (p. 201)
higher-order
   conditioning (p. 192)
latent learning (p. 212)
learned helplessness (p. 206)

learning (p. 186)
modeling (observational
   learning) (p. 213)
negative reinforcer (p. 198)
neutral stimulus (p. 187)
operant conditioning (p. 196)
partial reinforcement (p. 200)
performance (p. 189)
positive reinforcer (p. 197)
practice (p. 217)
primary reinforcer (p. 199)
punishment (p. 204)
reinforcer (p. 197)
responses (p. 187)
secondary reinforcer (p. 199)
shaping (p. 198)
spontaneous recovery (p. 190)

stimuli (p. 187)
stimulus
   discrimination (p. 191)
stimulus generalization (p. 191)
systematic
   desensitization (p. 194)
token economy (p. 207)
transfer of learning (p. 217)
unconditioned response
   (UCR) (p. 188)
unconditioned stimulus
   (UCS) (p. 188)
variable-interval
   schedule (p. 202)
variable-ratio schedule (p. 201)

SUGGESTED READINGS

BOWER, GORDON, and HILGARD, ERNEST J. 1981. *Theories of Learning.* 5th ed. Englewood Cliffs, N.J.: Prentice-Hall. A comprehensive introduction to theories of learning. Covers all the major theories of learning since the time of Pavlov and Thorndike, including Freud's psychodynamics, information-processing accounts of learning, and recent work in artificial intelligence.

FLAHERTY, CHARLES F. 1985. *Animal Learning and Cognition.* New York: Random House. Discusses cognitive interpretations of animal behavior, the neural basis of conditioning, and recent work on the effects of drugs on conditioning. Includes fascinating material on how the study of animal learning illuminates human behavior.

GARBER, JUDY, and SELIGMAN, MARTIN, Eds. 1980. *Human Helplessness.* New York: Academic Press. Contains several excellent chapters on learned helplessness and the learned helplessness theory of depression. Of particular interest is the Abramson-Seligman-Teasdale reformulation of Seligman's learned helplessness theory.

GAZZANIGA, MICHAEL S. 1985. *The Social Brain.* New York: Basic Books. Describes the vital link between the way our brains are organized and the way we construct beliefs, and the modular organization of the human brain.

NEISSER, ARDEN. 1983. *The Other Side of Silence.* New York: Knopf. An extraordinary journey into the world of the deaf that illustrates one fascinating aspect of language learning.

SCHWARTZ, BARRY. 1978. *Psychology of Learning and Behavior.* New York: Norton. A quite readable account of the phenomena of Pavlovian and operant conditioning. Covers all of the major experimental findings on animal learning and their implications for contemporary theories of learning.

SHATTUCK, ROGER. 1980. *The Forbidden Experiment.* New York: Farrar, Straus, and Giroux. An account of the education of a boy who lived alone in the wild for at least six years between the ages of five and twelve that examines the influences of isolation and deprivation on learning.

SKINNER, B. F. 1968. *Walden Two.* New York: Macmillan. Originally published in 1949. Skinner's best-known work is a novel about an ideal, behaviorally engineered community. It is readable, interesting, and instructive.

Elizabeth Osborne, *Nava with Green Cup*, 1981.

7
Memory and Thought

In the 1920s a newspaper reporter came to the laboratory of the renowned Russian psychologist Alexander R. Luria (1968) to participate in a memory experiment. Luria was amazed to learn that S. (as he called the reporter) could easily repeat lists of thirty, fifty, or seventy numbers after he had heard them once. He could repeat the numbers backward and forward with equal ease. And when Luria asked him for some of the same lists more than fifteen years later, S. still remembered them.

Perhaps as a result of Luria's tests, S. began another career, this one as a professional mnemonist: he would repeat complicated lists that were supplied by people sitting in the audience. How did he manage to perform this feat? Every word or number would conjure up rich visual images, which S. easily remembered. For instance, in one performance the audience provided him with the following nonsensical formula:

$$N \cdot \sqrt{d^2 \, x \, \frac{85}{vx}} \cdot \sqrt[3]{\frac{276^2 \cdot 86x}{n^2v \cdot 264} \, n^2b}$$

$$= sv \, \frac{1,624}{32^2} \cdot r^2 \, s$$

S. was able to repeat the information perfectly after studying it for a few minutes. He later told Luria a story he had made up to help him remember the formula: "Neiman (N) came out and jabbed at the ground with his cane ($\cdot$). He looked up at a tall tree which resembled the square root sign ($\sqrt{}$), and thought to himself: 'No wonder the tree has withered and begun to expose its roots. After all, it was here when I built these two houses' (d^2)" (1968:49). And so on.

But being a professional mnemonist is not all roses. One of S.'s biggest problems was learning to forget. His brain was cluttered with old lists of

223

words, numbers, and letters. Even when he tried to relax, his mind would be flooded with vivid images from the past. S. also had trouble reading: every word brought a sea of images, and he had trouble focusing on the underlying meaning of a passage. Partly because of these problems, Luria wrote, "S. struck one as a disorganized and rather dull-witted person" (1968:65). S.'s amazing abilities to remember and his difficulties in thinking are the subject matter of this chapter. In it we turn our psychological eye upon the processes by which we remember and think about things.

MEMORY

Where in your brain is the sight of your favorite childhood friend, the smell of a chemistry lab, the taste of a roast beef sandwich, the texture of velvet, or the words to a hit song of three years ago? How is it that you can ride a bicycle, hit a baseball with a bat, or swim across a pool even if you have not done so for several years? As we saw in Chapter 6, learning involves the acquisition of skills and knowledge that allow you to adapt to your environment by building on previous experience. But adaptation requires more than simply learning new potentials for behavior. You must also retain them; you must be able to store these potentials over time and then activate them when you need them. Memory serves this function. **Memory** is the ability to recall, recognize, or relearn previously practiced behaviors more rapidly than new behaviors.

When memory fails, you do poorly on a test, cannot find your way home, or stare uncomprehendingly at friends and members of your family. Without memory, every experience would be isolated. Although what memory really is, how it works, and why it sometimes fails remain a difficult and complicated puzzle, many of the pieces are now falling into place. One way psychologists approach memory is by distinguishing among three stages in the memory process. When you remember something, three things happen: (1) **encoding** (also called **acquisition**), the process by which information is put into the memory system; (2) **storage** (also called **retention**), the process by which information is retained until it is needed; and (3) **retrieval**, the process by which information is regathered and brought back into awareness when needed.

Consider what takes place when you are asked the name of the person who is the current attorney general of the United States. If you cannot answer the question, a breakdown has occurred at some stage in the memory process. It may be that you never heard or read the name of the attorney general, in which case the difficulty resides in encoding. You simply never acquired the information. If you once knew the name of the attorney general but cannot recall it, the *memory trace* may have faded or decayed. A memory trace is a set of information; it is the residue of an event that remains in memory after the event (the visual image, the sound, the taste, or the smell) has vanished. When encoded, the trace is placed in storage. Finally, it is possible that you stored the name of the attorney general in your memory system but cannot recall it. You simply cannot activate the appropriate retrieval cues. At times the answer may be at the "tip of the tongue" —a word or name may lie tantalizingly outside your ability to recall it (Brown and McNeill, 1966). The condition has been likened to a state of mild torment (something on the order of the brink of a sneeze), and when you retrieve the word or name you feel considerable relief. Look at Figure 7.1. Should you be unable to identify an individual shown in a photograph, attempt to determine at which stage of memory a breakdown occurred.

Research on the encoding, storage, and retrieval of information has led many psychologists to con-

---

memory: The ability to recall, recognize, or relearn previously practiced behaviors more rapidly than new behaviors.

encoding (acquisition): The process by which information is put into the memory system.

storage (retention): The process by which information is retained until it is needed.

retrieval: The process by which information is regathered and brought back into awareness when needed.

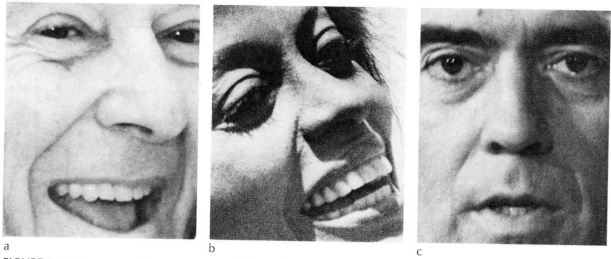

a   b   c

FIGURE 7.1 Fragments of faces. Try to identify these famous people. The answers are in Figure 7.2.

clude that there are three different types of memory stores: sensory storage, short-term memory, and long-term memory (Atkinson and Shiffrin, 1968, 1971; Gillund and Shiffrin, 1984). In **sensory storage** you hold an exact copy of what you have experienced for only an instant. To witness sensory storage at work, move a pencil back and forth before your eyes as you stare immediately ahead. Note that a shadowy image trails behind the moving pencil. Sensory storage allows you to hold on to information long enough to find meaning in it and transfer it to more durable memory. It bridges the receiving of information in perception and the storing of it in memory. In **short-term memory** you keep information in mind for about fifteen seconds. It is your working memory. It allows you to remember a phone number long enough to dial it, or to remember what a friend has said long enough to respond to it. In **long-term memory** you store information indefinitely. Here the information is related meaningfully to other information. By virtue of long-term memory, you can recognize a relative after an absence, find your way home, attend class on a regular basis, and drive an automobile. Let us explore these matters at greater length.

Sensory Storage

When you see or hear something, you are able to hold the input for a fraction of a second in sensory storage. *Iconic memory* is the sensory store associated with vision; *echoic memory*, the sensory store involved in hearing (Cowan, 1984). Unless the information goes into short-term memory, the image or sound of it is lost. For example, when you watch a movie, you do not notice the gaps between frames. The actions seem smooth because each frame is held momentarily in sensory storage until the next frame arrives. One frame, however, could strike your retina and disappear without your being aware of it or able to store it in memory.

---

sensory storage: The momentary storage of sensory information at the level of the sensory receptors.

short-term memory: Memory that is limited in capacity to about seven items and in duration to about fifteen seconds.

long-term memory: Information storage that has unlimited capacity and lasts indefinitely.

a   b   c

FIGURE 7.2 The famous people shown in Figure 7.1 are (a) Ronald Reagan, (b) Diana Ross, and (c) Dan Rather. If you were unable to identify a photograph correctly, at which stage of the memory process did the failure occur? (a, Bill Fitz-Patrick/The White House; b, UPI/Bettmann Newsphotos; c, CBS News)

The psychologist George Sperling (1960) demonstrated this phenomenon in an ingenious experiment. He used a tachistoscope (a device that presents a picture for a very brief time) to present a group of letters to people for one-twentieth of a second. Previous studies had shown that if you present a stimulus such as:

$$\begin{array}{ccc} T & D & R \\ S & R & N \\ F & Z & K \end{array}$$

people will usually be able to remember four or five of the letters after the array has disappeared. Sperling believed that people took a mental photograph of the letters, and were able to read back only a few before the picture faded. He told the people in his experiment that after he had flashed the letters on the tachistoscope screen, he would immediately present a tone. On hearing a high tone, the subjects were to tell him the top row, a medium tone the middle row, and a low tone the bottom row. Once people learned this system, they were indeed able to remember any row of letters. Thus he proved that subjects retain a brief image of the whole picture so that they can still read off the items in the correct row *just after* the picture has left the screen.

The information held by the senses is like a short-lived but highly detailed photograph or recording. You can demonstrate sensory storage for yourself.

- Close your eyes for about a minute. Then hold a quarter in front of your face and blink your eyes. Note that you will continue to see a fleeting image of the quarter for a split second after you close your eyes.

- Tap a pencil on your desk. Note how the distinctiveness of the sound in your mind has a very brief tapering-off period.

- Tap a pencil against your arm. At first you feel the immediate sensation. But then the feeling fades away and later you simply recall that you tapped yourself with a pencil.

Sensory storage maintains a rather complete reproduction of the world as it is received by your sensory system (Rock, 1985). It has a tremendous capacity. Indeed, there is virtually no limit to the amount of information that can be very temporarily recorded there. This fact could constitute a problem. Consider that at this very moment you are primarily aware of the page in front of you and, most of all, of this sentence. But reflect. Are you not also seeing

One illustration of selective attention is the cocktail party phenomenon. Sensory inputs, from background music to intimate conversations, are filtered through a perceptual system that can usually discriminate meaningful information from trivial noise. *(Elliot Erwitt/Magnum)*

things below, above, and well to the sides of this page? What about the pressures on your skin, perhaps on the soles of your feet or on your elbows? Do you notice any noises, detect any odors? Obviously, you are being bombarded by innumerable stimuli. Fortunately, you are capable of **selective attention**. You are able to "tune in" certain of the sensory messages reaching you while you "tune out" others. In brief, you seem able to control the selection of material from sensory memory (Logan and Cowan, 1984; Carlson and Dulany, 1985).

A good illustration of selective attention is the *cocktail party phenomenon*. In carrying on a conversation in a crowded setting, you encounter a confusing babble of sounds. You hear not only the person with whom you are chatting, but the din of other voices, the clink of glasses, and perhaps even music. But should someone in the room mention your name, you may become aware of it instantly. It seems that incoming sensory information is temporarily stored in sensory memory and that your higher mental

processes then inform you what you should and should not attend to. Initially you focus on the physical aspects of a message—the colors, shapes, tones, textures, odors, and other stimuli from your sense organs. You apparently switch your attention to the message's content when sufficient information is available to make sense out of it. The information then goes into short-term memory in a more meaningful form, including images, numbers, and words.

Short-Term Memory

The things you have in your conscious mind at any one moment are being held in short-term memory (Barnden, 1984; FitzGerald and Broadbent, 1985). The short-term store is your working memory. However, as you go about your daily activities you are not required to pay close attention to it. You have probably had the experience of listening to someone only partially and then having that person accuse you of not paying attention. You deny it, and in order to

selective attention: The ability to "tune in" certain sensory messages while "tuning out" others.

prove your innocence, you repeat to him or her, word for word, the last words said. You can do this because you are holding the words in short-term memory. Usually, however, the sense of what the person was saying does not register with you until you repeat the words out loud. Repeating the words makes you pay attention to them. This response is what psychologists mean by *rehearsal*.

Rehearsal

To keep information in short-term memory for more than a few seconds, you have to repeat it to yourself, in your mind or out loud. When you look up a telephone number, for instance, you can remember the seven digits long enough to dial them *if* you repeat them several times. If you are distracted or make a mistake in dialing, the chances are you will have to look up the number again. It has been lost from short-term memory. Hence each memory trace is "regenerated" or "reset" by rehearsal, at which point it begins decaying again.

Psychologists have measured short-term memory by seeing how long a subject can retain a piece of information without rehearsal. The experimenter shows the subject a card with three letters on it, such as CPQ. However, at the same time the experimenter makes the subject perform a task in order to prevent him or her from rehearsing the letters. For example, the researcher might ask the subject to start counting backward by threes from 798 as soon as the card is flashed. If the subject performs the task for only a short time, he or she will usually remember the letters. But if the subject is kept from rehearsing for more than eighteen seconds, the information will be forgotten (Brown, 1958; Peterson and Peterson, 1959). Thus short-term memory seems to last for less than twenty seconds without rehearsal.

Capacity

Short-term memory is quite limited in capacity. It can hold only about seven unrelated items. Consider, for example, what happens when someone quickly reels off a series of digits to you. You are able to keep only about seven or eight of them in your immediate memory. Beyond that number, you begin to confuse the digits. The same would be true if the unrelated items were a random set of words. You typically do not notice this limit to your capacity because you usu-

ally do not have to store so many unrelated items in your immediate memory. Either the items are linked (as when you listen to the words in a sentence) or they are rehearsed and put into long-term memory.

The most interesting aspect of this limit, discovered by George Miller (1956), is that it involves about seven items of *any* kind. Each item may consist of a collection of many other items, but if the items are all packaged into one "chunk," then there is still only one item. Thus you can remember about seven unrelated sets of initials, such as COMSAT, DDT, SST, or the initials of your favorite radio stations, even though you cannot remember all the letters separately. This capability occurs because you have connected, or "chunked," them together previously, so that DDT is one item, not three.

One of the tricks of memorizing a good deal of information quickly is to chunk together the items as you receive them. If you connect items in groups, you have fewer to remember. For example, you may find that you remember new phone numbers in two or three chunks (555-6794 or 555-67-94) rather than as a string of seven digits (5-5-5-6-7-9-4). As Figure 7.3 illustrates, you use chunking to remember visual as well as verbal input.

Displacement

The principle of *displacement* provides an explanation of how an item is lost from short-term memory (Waugh and Norman, 1965; Ellis and Hunt, 1977). As we have noted, there are approximately seven slots available in short-term memory for information. As items enter short-term memory, they are placed in the next available slot. When all the slots are in use, incoming information takes priority. It displaces or "bumps out" an old item from one of the slots. Hence the old item is "forgotten."

Long-Term Memory

Long-term memory is where you store information indefinitely for future use (see Figure 7.4). It can be thought of as a kind of filing cabinet or storage bin for names, dates, words, faces, and countless other items (see the boxed insert on page 230). When you say that someone has a good memory, you usually mean that the person can recall a good deal of this type of information. But long-term memory also contains representations of a great many experiences

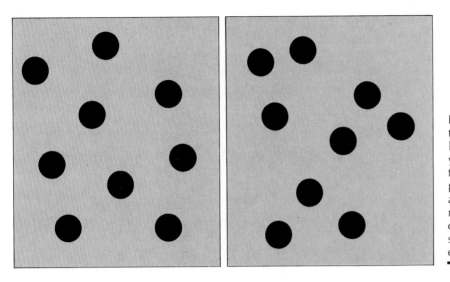

FIGURE 7.3 Glance quickly at the left figure in this pair, then look away. How many dots did you see? Now do the same with the right figure. You were probably more sure and more accurate in your answer for the right figure because the organization of the dots into a small number of chunks makes it easier to process the information.

and sensations. You may not have thought about your childhood home for years, but you can probably still visualize it.

Encoding Information

As we noted earlier in the chapter, *encoding* is the process by which information is put into the memory system. It involves perceiving information, abstracting from it one or more features, and creating corresponding memory traces for these features. Since the encoding process takes place during the presentation of to-be-remembered information, the distinction between learning and memory is becoming increasingly blurred by much current psychological research (Ellis and Hunt, 1977). Indeed, the

FIGURE 7.4 The flow of information processing. Input to the senses is stored temporarily, and some of it is passed on into short-term memory. Information may be kept in short-term memory by rehearsal or it may be passed on to long-term memory. Material stored in both short- and long-term memory is used in making decisions. The decision process results in outputs such as talking, writing, or moving. *(Adapted from James W. Vander Zanden and Ann J. Pace. 1984. Educational Psychology. 2nd ed. New York: Random House, p. 196. Reprinted by permission.)*

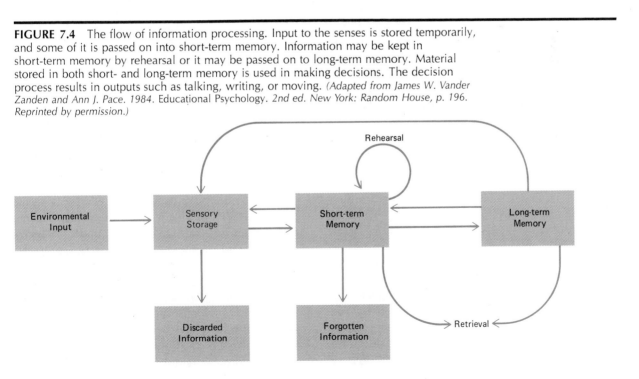

Remembering High-School Classmates

Few of you will ever forget your high-school days, with all their glory and pain. But how many of you will remember the names and faces of your high-school classmates ten, twenty, thirty, and even forty years after graduation? According to one study (Bahrick, Bahrick, and Wittinger, 1974), apparently more of you will than you might think.

To find out just how long long-term memory is, researchers showed nearly four hundred high-school graduates, ranging in age from seventeen to seventy-four, pictures from their high-school yearbooks. Here are some of the surprising results:

- Thirty-five years after graduation, people could identify the faces of nine out of ten classmates. The size of the high school made no difference in their response.

- Fifteen years after graduation, subjects could recall 90 percent of their classmates' names.

- Name recall began to fade to between 70 and 80 percent by the time people reached their late thirties.

- Women generally had better memories for names and faces than men did.

Researchers explain these amazing results by looking at the way this information is collected in the first place. The storehouse of names and faces is built over a four-year high-school career, and continual repetition helps cement this knowledge in the memory for decades.

A rare memory disorder, *prosopagnosia*, provides a clue as to how you remember faces (Tranel and Damasio, 1985). People with the disorder, which can result from a stroke or encephalitis, are normal except that they can no longer consciously recognize familiar faces, including their own face in a mirror or those of their spouse and children. Researchers find that victims can recognize faces on the unconscious level but fail to integrate the recognition into higher levels of memory. Consequently, they require some other cue—hearing the person's voice or seeing a familiar article of clothing—to activate their memory of a person.

It seems that you recognize familiar faces in the following manner. First, your eyes gather information on the shape of the face and the placement of its features. Next you create a *template*—a mental pattern or representation—for each face. The template is not an exact copy of a face, but a dynamic, developing record of it. Each facial template is connected to other memories of a person, including voice, conversations, and experiences. Accordingly, your memory of a person is embedded in a network that includes the facial template. When you see a familiar face, the template is activated and the associated memories stored in other areas of the brain are triggered. Victims of prosopagnosia must rely on other channels to the associated memories if they are to recognize a familiar person.

psychologist Endel Tulving (1968) says that learning is simply an improvement in retention. Thus, as viewed by Tulving, to investigate learning is to investigate memory.

Information processing is sometimes likened to an office filing system. Suppose that you work in the office of the college dean. One of your responsibilities is to file letters in the appropriate folders. You have a letter from the dean of another college suggesting that your school modify its form for transferring course credit from one institution to another. Under what category are you going to file the letter? Will you file it under the sender's name, under "Course Transfer Forms," under "Suggestions," or under some other category (perhaps creating a new category with a new folder)? The procedure you employ must be consistent. You cannot file this letter under the sender's name and the next similar letter under "Course Transfer Forms." How you file the item will have major implications for your ability to retrieve the letter at a later time. As with the filing system, how you encode information in memory has a profound impact on your subsequent ability to recognize or recall an item.

The order in which you receive and encode information also affects your retention of it. You tend to remember the information you first receive (a tendency called the *primary effect*) and material that you last receive before recall (a tendency called the *recency effect*). You typically forget the material in the middle. The first items in a list of to-be-remembered words get your attention; the last ones are still in short-term memory when you attempt to recall them. The words in the middle of the list enjoy neither advantage, and so you are more likely to forget them.

Retaining Information

A mounting body of evidence suggests that there are two distinct systems for the long-term storage of information: declarative and procedural (Squire and Cohen, 1979, 1982; Squire, 1982; Fisher, 1985a). **Declarative memory** centers on "facts," knowledge that can be brought consciously to mind and formulated in a statement, proposition, or image. By virtue of declarative memory, you can remember a vast array of cognitive information, including names, dates, faces, concepts, and formulas. **Procedural memory** entails "skills," knowledge associated with such learned habits as riding a bicycle, typing, expertly swinging a golf club, and solving puzzles. Often procedural memory cannot be consciously activated; much of what the brain does best it does unconsciously. In sum, the difference between declarative memory and procedural memory is the difference between "knowing that" and "knowing how." In practice, however, behavior is frequently an amalgam of both declarative and procedural processes.

The two forms of memory seem to reside in different structures of the brain (Mishkin, 1978, 1982). Apparently declarative memory is controlled through the hippocampus and amygdala, structures that are closely connected with the hypothalamus and the inner surface of the cerebral cortex (see Chapter 2). Procedural memory appears to be more diffused throughout many parts of the brain, although some of its activities are centered in the cerebellum. The notion that the brain contains two biologically and physically distinct memory systems derives from a variety of sources, including observations of amnesia victims—people who experience partial or complete memory loss because of trauma, disease, accident, or stroke. Like normal people, many amnesia victims can figure out how to solve difficult puzzles and how to read printed words upside down. But even though amnesiacs can remember how to do what they have learned, they cannot consciously remember doing it nor can they explain how they do it.

A number of psychologists such as Endel Tulving (1972, 1983, 1985) distinguish between two types of declarative knowledge: episodic memory and semantic memory. **Episodic memory** is the information we have about particular events that we experienced in the past. **Semantic memory** is the organized store of knowledge that we have about the world. Episodic memory is event knowledge. It is illustrated by the recollections you have regarding the gymnasium in your high school or college. Recall, for instance, the location of the doors, windows, and basketball hoops. Recall its pungent odor. And recall the drone of voices and the staccato of bouncing basketballs. Semantic memory is conceptual knowledge. It includes such things as the rules of grammar, chemical formulas, rules for addition and multiplication, and knowledge that summer follows spring. In brief, it

---

declarative memory: The storage of "facts," knowledge that can be brought consciously to mind and formulated in a statement, proposition, or image.

procedural (pro-SEE-dure-all) memory: The storage of "skills," knowledge associated with learned habits.

episodic (EP-ih-SAH-dic) memory: The information we have about particular events we experienced in the past.

semantic (suh-MAN-tick) memory: The organized store of knowledge we have about the world; conceptual knowledge.

involves facts that do not depend on a particular time or place but are simply facts.

"The grapefruit I had for breakfast yesterday was yellow" is an example of episodic memory. "Grapefruit is yellow" is an illustration of semantic memory. You typically have ready access to concepts in semantic memory and recall them without apparent search or effort. This is not the case with episodic memory. Further, semantic memory does not register the specific perceptual properties of stimuli but only their mental referents or symbolic representations. In contrast, episodic memory depends on the direct storage of specific perceptual inputs.

Retrieving Information

Memory is not simply a matter of encoding and storage. It also requires that you retrieve appropriate information when you need it. When you wish to recall information, you must use a cue that will allow you to narrow the domain in your memory in which you conduct the search.

Consider again the analogy of the office filing system. Let us say that you filed the letter to the dean in the folder labeled "Suggestions." Some four months later, the dean asks you to find the letter, since he or she is now ready to act on the matter. The dean's files contain thousands of folders. Whenever you are asked to retrieve a letter, you do not undertake your task by beginning with "A" and working your way alphabetically through all the folders until you locate the item. Instead, you use a cue to narrow the search. Thus you are likely to look under the letter-sender's name, under "Course Transfer Forms," and so on. And usually you will find the letter. However, if you filed it under "Suggestions" and you have neglected to search this folder, the letter will be technically available but inaccessible because of a retrieval breakdown. Likewise, an item may be contained in your memory store but be unavailable because you do not have the relevant cue. For practical purposes the item is forgotten.

In general, the better the cues that you use in memory search, the better will be your retrieval of information from long-term memory. For this reason, recognition is usually easier than recall. In **recognition,** your task is simply one of picking out certain information from a group of items as the remembered material. In contrast, **recall** requires that you supply for yourself all the information on a subject. For instance, in recognition questions you are asked: "Which of the following individuals was the fourth president of the United States? (a) John Adams; (b) Abraham Lincoln; (c) Thomas Jefferson; (d) James Madison" or "If you multiply 7 by 6 the answer is: (a) 12; (b) 34; (c) 42; (d) 63." Recall questions ask: "Name the fourth president of the United States" or "Recite the multiplication tables by seven."

In recognition tasks, you have both the cue and the item, and your job is to figure out which of the items is correct. In recall tasks, you must provide the cues for yourself. Hence recognition and recall share one process in common (decision on what item is correct) but differ in that recall requires an additional process (generation of the correct item) (Anderson and Bower, 1972). In the example, if you are asked to name the fourth president of the United States, you must search your long-term store for the names of presidents and *then* decide which person was the fourth president. But if you are provided with a recognition task (for instance, a multiple-choice question), you are not required to retrieve the names of the presidents. You need only decide which of the listed individuals is the president in question. Recognition permits you to by-pass the generation phase and move directly to the decision phase.

In sum, you typically can recognize a good deal more than you can recall. That is why you sometimes find yourself admitting to an acquaintance, "Your face looks familiar, but I just can't remember your name." Remembering a person's name is a recall task, while remembering the face is a recognition task because the face is there as a cue.

At times, of course, you cannot recall or recognize something. Yet it does not necessarily follow that you

---

recognition: The type of memory retrieval in which a person is required to pick out certain information from a group of items as the remembered material.

recall: The type of memory retrieval in which a person reconstructs previously learned material.

Recognizing the face of an old acquaintance is easier than recalling the person's name. In recognition, the cue is provided (in this case the face); in recall, one has to find one's own cues (for the person's name). *(Leonard Speier)*

have forgotten it. Often you can readily relearn information that you acquired earlier. You probably have discovered this fact for yourself when studying for a test. You may feel you have forgotten some material, yet with a small amount of reviewing it comes back rather quickly. In brief, through re-studying, a rather weak association regains its original strength in your memory. When **relearning** —learning the same material again on a later occasion—you need less time than would otherwise be required; you have saved the information from earlier learning.

Improving Memory

Many strategies for improving memory are based on efficient organization of the things you learn and on chunking information into easily handled packages (matters discussed earlier in the chapter). Hence techniques that assist you in organizing and

chunking otherwise unrelated items are likely to improve your memory. One of the advantages of note taking derives from this fact. Indeed, some research suggests that the probability of recalling an item that occurs in your notes is about seven times that of recalling items not in your notes (Howe, 1970). A number of strategies for improving your memory are discussed in the boxed inserts on page 234 and pages 236–237.

The Biochemistry of Memory

As we have noted in previous chapters, the brain is a collection of nerve cells, or neurons. Brain research-ers have long supposed that they are the repositories of memory. Now Gary Lynch (Lynch and Baudry, 1982, 1984; Lynch, 1984) has proposed a mechanism by which memory may result from a permanent change at neuron synapses. You will recall from

---

relearning: Learning the same material again on a later occasion. People need less time for relearning than for the initial learning; they have saved the information from earlier memory.

Preparing for Tests

One hears a good deal of talk nowadays about "memory pills." Researchers have found that some people given a chemical similar to vasopressin, a neuropeptide, show an improvement in memory (Weingartner et al., 1981). These findings have stirred debate about the value of so-called "memory pills" for healthy people. If science can correct impaired memories, the same breakthroughs conceivably could be used to improve normal memories. But much research is still required on these matters. There are, however, a number of strategies that are currently available to you for improving your memory for material you will be tested on. Let us look at some of these:

● If you are to study effectively, you must have at hand the appropriate information. This requires that you take adequate lecture notes. Lecture material seems to be encoded in memory in class as the information flows from ear to brain to hand to paper. Additionally, the external storage of the information (the notes) later provides you with a valuable aid to review. Having the notes may be of even greater significance than the act of note taking itself (Carter and Van Matre, 1975; Carrier and Titus, 1979; Barnett et al., 1981).

● After class, rewrite your notes and place them in an outline format. Organization is an important tool for learning new information (Reder and Ross, 1983; Myers et al., 1984). It involves dividing material into small units and placing these units within appropriate categories, so that each piece of information fits sensibly with the others. Improved recall is thought to result from organization, because you use category labels as retrieval cues and thus reduce memory overload in recall (Tulving and Pearlstone, 1966). Approach the material in your textbook in a similar way.

● In preparing your outline, try to provide a meaningful framework for the material. The more meaningful something is, the easier it will be to remember. You remember things more vividly if you associate them with things already stored in memory or with a strong emotional experience. For example, you would be more likely to remember the six letters "dfirne" if they were arranged to form the word "friend." Not surprisingly, teachers can increase their instructional effectiveness by relating new elements of information to students' existing knowledge (White and Gagné, 1976). As was mentioned earlier in the chapter, if information can be chunked or hooked into some meaningful category, you can retain it better.

● As noted in the text, rehearsal—the cycling of information through the memory store—plays an important part in the retention process (Bowles and Poon, 1985; Graf and Schacter, 1985). When preparing for a test, continually rehearse the material in your outline, reciting it to yourself. It often helps to recite the information aloud. Review the material in this same manner each day before the test.

● It helps in remembering something if you protect your memory from interference (Irwin and Pachella, 1985). For instance, when studying new material you would be well advised to avoid studying quite similar material with it. Instead of studying history right after political science, study biology in between. Another method is to space out your learning. Trying to absorb large amounts of information at one extended sitting results in a good deal of interference. It is more effective to study manageable units, each at its own time. Still another method to protect your memory from interference is overlearning material—rehearsing it even after you think you know it well.

By using these strategies, you should be able to improve your grades and the efficiency of your studying. You will accomplish a good deal more in the same time span. It would also help to take another look at the SQ3R approach discussed in the preface and the Student Self-Tutor for this book.

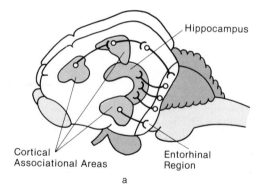

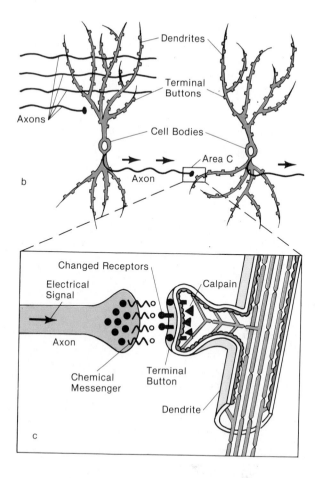

FIGURE 7.5 The formation of memories. According to the hypothesis advanced by Gary Lynch and his associates, memory storage takes place in the circuits of the mammalian brain that run from the associational areas of the cortex to the entorhinal region and from there to the hippocampus (a). Each neuron in the hippocampus (b) has thick dendrites covered with terminal buttons, and a thin axon that connects with other neurons. At the synapse (c), a neurotransmitter crosses the gap and causes calcium to enter the terminal button and activate calpain. This causes a physical change in the terminal button. The effect is believed to increase the strength of communication between the cells, resulting in memory formation. *(Adapted from PT conversation with Gary Lynch. 1984.* Psychology Today, *18 (April):30. Reprinted with permission.) Copyright © 1984 American Psychological Association.*

Chapter 2 that nerve signals are passed from cell to cell across synapses with the help of chemicals called neurotransmitters. Lynch finds that bursts of high-frequency electrical stimulation cause increased activity, which lasts for months, in some nerve cells in the cortex and neighboring hippocampus. He believes that this phenomenon—called *long-term potentiation (LTP)*—is involved in long-term memory.

Lynch theorizes that when a memory neuron fires repeatedly, calcium enters the cell and activates an enzyme called calpain at the excited synapse (see Figure 7.5). The calpain attacks the protein skeleton that shapes the neuron membrane. In the process of "chewing up" the protein meshwork, the calpain exposes hidden receptors at the synapse, reshapes the branches of the cell, and creates new synapses. Once the receptors are uncovered, they remain active. This allows the cell to process additional messages on a permanent basis while simultaneously strengthening the connections between memory neu-

rons. This type of link fits the needs of memory formation. Moreover, it is rarely found in parts of the brain that are not involved in memory. Lynch has tested this mechanism by chemically blocking the action of calpain in the brains of rats. As he predicted, this impairs the rodents' ability to learn cognitive tasks.

Lynch observes that memory differs from other biological systems in a critical way. Most systems in our bodies are homeostatic, or self-correcting (see Chapter 2). They are designed to keep us steady. But memory is a process that occurs in seconds and lasts for decades. In brief, the changes persist. Lynch says that this type of permanent change cannot involve protein synthesis because the process is too slow. Nor can it involve the cell's genetic machinery —chromosomes and genes—because their activity affects the entire cell.

An LTP mechanism of the type suggested by Lynch may explain the findings of the neuropsychol-

Mnemonic Techniques

Human beings have long been concerned with the practical art of memory. Various stage entertainers have capitalized on this interest and have advertised themselves as possessing unusual memory powers. Until recently, psychologists ignored the techniques used by memory performers, since they were thought to practice trickery and deception. Only in the past decade or so have psychologists come to appreciate the value of various memory procedures in simplifying certain memory tasks. Further, such techniques for remembering things—termed **mnemonic devices**—afford many insights into the organization and operation of memory (Norman, 1972). Two of the more useful techniques are the method of loci and the pegword system.

Method of Loci

The *method of loci,* or the method of places, was used by orators in classical Greece and Rome to perform what we today would consider prodigious feats of memory (Yates, 1966). It consists of two steps. First, learn in their naturally occurring sequential order some geographical locations with which you are intimately familiar, for instance, the layout of your living quarters, the paths you take between classes, or the floor plans of a building. Second, associate a visual image of the to-be-remembered item with a location in the series; place the items in the order you wish to remember them as you progress along your imaginary walk. In other words, deposit at each location a mental image constructed from the material you wish to memorize. Upon recall, revisit in your mind each place in the house (path or building) in their proper order, retrieving from each the image that you have left there.

By way of illustration, visualize a walk through your home or apartment. You enter the front door, move next through the entryway, then to the living room, to the dining room, to the kitchen, and so on. Use these loci for memorizing a shopping list, for instance, eggs, lettuce, coffee, soap, and milk. Imagine Humpty Dumpty blocking the doorway, heads of lettuce rolling down the hallway, a gigantic coffee pot hanging from the ceiling of the living room, soap suds overflowing in the dining room, and a cow sitting at your kitchen table (do not worry if the images are not logical; it may actually help if they are absurd). (See Figure 7.6.) Later, attempt to recall the items, in order, by taking an imaginary walk in which you again activate each visual image as you go from one room to the next. By using the method of loci, the ancients reeled off epic lengths of remembered literature.

Pegword System

The *pegword system* was introduced in England in 1879 by John Sambrook. It consists of memorizing a jingle that has the pegs on which you hang the to-be-remembered items by means of imagery. As with the method of loci, the pegword system can be used to remember shopping lists, errands, sets of facts in educational psychology, historical events, and the like.

First, learn the following jingle:

ONE is a BUN
TWO is a SHOE
THREE is a TREE
FOUR is a DOOR
FIVE is a HIVE
SIX is STICKS
SEVEN is HEAVEN
EIGHT is a GATE
NINE is a LINE
TEN is a HEN

Next, visually associate each item in your shopping list with one of the pegwords as in Table 7.1. To recall the items, you recite the

---

mnemonic (new-MON-ic) devices: Techniques that people use to help them remember things.

jingle and retrieve the item associated with each pegword.

The method of loci and the pegword system improve memory by a factor of two or three times over normal free recall. They allow you to place the information into storage in an organized and meaningful fashion and then to recall it with explicit retrieval cues. Further, the techniques employ visual imagery. Thus, both methods maximize memory by combining a number of potent mnemonic strategies. Likewise, using little associative crutches, like making up a rhyme

(Source: Box, table, and figure adapted from James W. Vander Zanden and Ann J. Pace. 1984. Educational Psychology. 2nd ed. New York: Random House, pp. 206–207. Reprinted by permission.)

for someone's name, helps you remember. It seems that the additional effort makes some sort of imprint on the brain.

TABLE 7.1 The Pegword System

Pegword	List Word	Mnemonic Image
one-bun	eggs	a bun eating Humpty Dumpty
two-shoe	lettuce	a head of lettuce growing out of a shoe
three-tree	coffee	coffee pots growing out of tree branches
four-door	soap	soap suds flowing through a doorway
five-hive	milk	milk running from a beehive

FIGURE 7.6 The method of loci. Mentally imagine items from a grocery list placed in sequential locations in your home. Then undertake an imaginary walk in which you retrieve each item in turn from its location as you pass from one room to the next.

ogist William Greenough (Greenough and Volkmar, 1973; Greenough, 1975). Greenough has shown that when rats learn, their nerve cells sprout more branches and form new synapses. He speculates that even though the number of neurons in the brain may be limited, the number of connections may be limitless, offering a chance for memory enhancement. Greenough has provided an "enriched" environment for certain rats—toys, the company of other rats, and a good many activities. Compared with rats kept in barren cages, the brains of the "advantaged" rats show greater branching of individual nerve cells into the structures that meet with other nerve cells. Apparently with greater mental stimulation, the "advantaged rats" need more elaborate interconnections between their fixed number of nerve cells to handle the extra traffic of learning. Other researchers confirm that giving rats either enriched experience in a complex environment or formal training leads to measurable changes in their brains (Rosenzweig, 1984). More recently, Greenough has found that when a nerve cell from the hippocampus is electrically stimulated—in an experimental dish and not in a living animal—new synapses form in seconds (Blakeslee, 1985).

Other evidence also points to the important part the hippocampus plays in memory. Memory impairment is an early, prominent expression of *Alzheimer's disease*—a disorder that results in progressive mental deterioration, memory loss, and confusion. It afflicts from 1.5 to 2 million elderly Americans and at least one hundred thousand of them die of it every year.

The hippocampus is one of the brain areas most consistently and heavily implicated in the disorder (Hyman et al., 1984; Rasool and Selkoe, 1985). Its nerve cells undergo drastic changes and come to resemble infinitesimal bits of braided yarn. It seems that the clumps of degenerating nerve cells disrupt the passage of electrochemical signals through the hippocampus to other parts of the brain and nervous system. Researchers also find that patients suffering from Alzheimer's disease have a huge deficit in the enzyme choline acetyltransferase and its neurotransmitter, acetylcholine (Francis et al., 1985). The result is that the neuronal lines of communication go dead, and people experience a loss of memory and intellect.

The cause of Alzheimer's disease is still unknown. However, some scientists suspect some infectious agent, perhaps a "slow-acting virus" (Prusiner, 1984). Others speculate that chromosomal factors may underlie the disorder, since Down's syndrome patients who survive to adulthood eventually succumb to Alzheimer's lesions (Sinex and Myers, 1982). And still others say that a variety of factors, including viruses and faulty genes, may interact to produce Alzheimer's disease (Wurtman, 1985).

Research dealing with the biochemistry of memory suggests that remembering is a complex and dynamic process. It cannot be understood simply in terms of one nerve cell triggering another. It is necessary to look at the bigger picture and see how the encoding, storage, and retrieval of information might be implemented by the firing of millions of

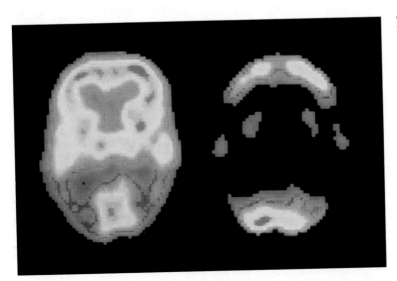

Scans of normal and abnormal brains. The left scan is normal. The darkened areas on the right image reveal abnormal brain tissue of a patient with Alzheimer's disease. *(N.I.H.—Science Source/Photo Researchers)*

neurons. Analogously, we would not attempt to discover the program that a computer is running by examining the states of its inner switches. We can understand a program only by examining the series of operations and functions it carries out. In brief, we have to look at much larger units. All this brings us to a consideration of constructive memory.

Constructive Memory

Although your memory for complex events is oftentimes startlingly accurate, it is also frequently incomplete and occasionally even highly distorted (Alba and Hasher, 1983). A good illustration of this is eyewitness accounts of crimes. As discussed in the boxed insert on pages 240–241, fleeting impressions of criminal behavior are elaborated by people into accounts that they believe to be "true." At times the wrong people are identified as criminals, and events are construed in ways that are consistent with an observer's emotions and prejudices. Findings such as these suggest to some psychologists that the knowledge contained in memory is the construction of your mind, what is termed *constructive memory*. You filter sensory data through the knowing apparatus of your senses where they are made into perceptions and cognitions. Consequently, your memories are in part created by the social and cultural context in which you come to know the world (Scarr, 1985c).

Scheme theories have appealed to some psychologists as an explanation for the constructed nature of various aspects of memory. A **scheme** is a knowledge framework or mental structure used in processing and organizing information. According to scheme theory, what you encode and store in memory is heavily determined by a guiding scheme. The scheme selects and actively modifies your experience in order to make the experience meaningful and consistent with your existing expectations and knowledge. Viewed in this manner, perception entails a search for those schemes in memory that permit us to make incoming sensory information intelligible.

Rand J. Spiro (1977) undertook an experimental study that shows the part that schemes having to do

with marriage and family life play in the fashioning of memory. He had subjects read one of two stories about an engaged couple, Margie and Bob. In both of the stories, Bob tells Margie that he is strongly opposed to having children. In one version, Margie feels the same way as does Bob. In the other version, she is shocked and dismayed by Bob's feelings because she strongly desires children.

After they had read the stories, Spiro had the subjects engage in an unrelated task (such as filling out consent forms for the experiment). While they were performing this task, he casually mentioned either that Bob and Margie eventually got married or that they broke up and never got married. Subjects returned anywhere from two days to six weeks later for a recall test. The results showed that subjects consistently reconciled their memories of the stories with the comments made by the experimenter. For example, in the condition where Margie is shocked and the experimenter says the couple got married, subjects "recalled" such things as "They underwent counseling" or "They decided to compromise and adopt children." But in the condition where Margie is shocked and the couple break up, the subjects did not introduce these "facts." Clearly, recall is often much more than the passive reproduction of stored memories.

Other researchers also find that we construct memories in accordance with schemes. For instance, after reading a brief story about a character who goes to a restaurant, subjects often recall statements about the person eating and paying for a meal even when these actions were not contained in the story (Bower, Black, and Turner, 1979). According to scheme theory, memory distortions occur when we attempt to fit our experiences into schemes. Much the same thing happens with stereotypes. As we will see in Chapter 9, we use stereotypes as "fuzzy" guides in sizing up people. Thus if we know that a person is a black, Hispanic, Jew, or Mormon, we use the information contained in our "black," "Hispanic," "Jewish," or "Mormon" scheme to "fill in" the gaps in our knowledge. These schemes often filter out incongruent information, or when incongruencies are noted, they are construed as special cases (you make

scheme (skeem): A knowledge framework or mental structure used in processing and organized information.

Eyewitness Testimony

In 1979, Father Bernard Pagano, a Roman Catholic priest from Wilmington, Delaware, went on trial for a series of armed robberies of small shops in the Wilmington area. The trial captured national attention. Newspapers had labeled the gunman the "gentleman bandit" because he was always well dressed and well groomed and displayed impeccable manners. Seven witnesses positively identified Father Pagano as the robber. Yet literally at the eleventh hour, another man, Ronald Clouser, confessed to the robberies. Clouser knew details of the crimes that only the real bandit could have known (details that had not come out in court or been carried by the press). The state then dropped the charges against the priest.

Father Pagano is not alone. Even more seriously, people are sometimes convicted of crimes that they never committed. Indeed, eyewitness testimony is not always the truth, the whole truth, and nothing but the truth. Memories change, and what people remember in the courtroom is not necessarily what they saw or heard at the scene (Thompson, 1985). The psychologist Elizabeth F. Loftus (1979, 1984) has shown that it is terribly easy to distort a person's memory. She has done a fascinating series of experiments showing that when people are asked to recall the details of auto accidents, they, too, are likely to distort the facts. After groups of college students had seen a filmed accident, she asked some of them, "About how fast were the cars going when they hit each other?" The average estimate was thirty-four miles per hour. When she substituted the word "smashed" for "hit" in the above question, another group of students remembered the cars as having gone significantly faster—an average estimate of forty-one miles per hour. Loftus has also shown subjects films of crimes and then introduced new information to them. She has made them believe a car sped through a red light that actually was green.

Other psychologists have also provided demonstrations of eyewitness fallibility. In one study at Brooklyn College, forensic psychologist Roger Buckhout (1974) staged a purse snatching in one of his classes. When fifty-two students who had seen the incident looked at two videotaped lineups, all but ten said they recognized the culprit. But thirty-five of these forty-two eyewitnesses picked the wrong man! Interestingly enough, the witnesses who were most sure of themselves were somewhat more likely to accuse an innocent man.

Lawyers have long been aware of the effects of leading questions, but the courts continue to act as if human memory were a videotape that enabled the witness to conjure up an instant replay of a crime. In reality, memory involves an active process of filling in the gaps on the basis of

---

the person an "exception to the rule") (Taylor and Crocker, 1981). In sum, stereotypes provide you with assumptions about people, and these assumptions may then affect your processing and recall of information.

Schemes also may come into play when you seek to reproduce a memory episode. If you try to remember something that happened in the past, you will find it hard to be entirely accurate. Probably you will recall a few facts and then use these facts to construct the "other facts." The process of bridging the gaps in memory with inferences about things that may have been true is termed **reconstruction**. For instance, the psychologist Donald Norman (Lindsay and Norman, 1977:372) has asked people such questions as, "What were you doing on Monday afternoon in the third week of September two years ago?" The types of responses he gets typically go something like this:

---

reconstruction: The process of bridging the gaps in memory with inferences about things that may have been true.

a person's attitudes and expectations. Buckhout, who has testified in over seventy trials, notes:

> Uncritical acceptance of eyewitness testimony seems to be based on the fallacious notion that the human observer is a perfect recording device—that everything that passes before his or her eyes is recorded and can be pulled out by sharp questioning or refreshing one's memory. . . . This is impossible—human perception and memory function effectively by being selective. A human being has no particular need for perfect recall; perception and memory are decision-making processes affected by the totality of a person's abilities, background, environment, attitudes, motives, and beliefs, and by the methods used in testing recollection of people and events. [Quoted by Rodgers, 1982a:33–34]

Complicating matters, the eyewitness to a crime or an accident frequently observes a confusing situation under heart-thumping stress levels. What is more, eyewitness testimony can be innocently flawed after an event when people make their own memories. Discussing the incident with friends, overhearing conversations, seeing news accounts of the incident, or answering leading questions from people can change memories. It is no surprise to psychologists, then, that eyewitnesses are so frequently wrong.

Father Bernard Pagano (*right*) was almost convicted of armed robbery when seven eyewitnesses mistook him for Ronald Clouser (*left*), the real culprit. (*UPI/Bettmann Archive*)

1. Come on. How should I know? (*Experimenter: Just try it, anyhow.*)

2. OK. Let's see. Two years ago . . .

3. I would be in high school in Pittsburgh . . .

4. That would be my senior year.

5. Third week in September—that's just after summer—that would be the fall term.

6. Let me see. I think I had chemistry lab on Mondays.

7. I don't know. I was probably in the chemistry lab.

8. Wait a minute—that would be the second week of school. I remember he started off with the atomic table—a big, fancy chart. I thought he was crazy, trying to make us memorize that thing.

9. You know, I think I can remember sitting . . .

This response protocol illustrates how your memory system operates with this type of retrieval problem. First you try to rephrase the question in the form of a specific date, then you attempt to determine what you were doing about that time. You organize your search around temporal "landmarks" (item 4: "my senior year"). The protocol reveals that the recall process is hardly easy. Note the fragmentary recall of what has in fact been experienced (item 8: "a big, fancy chart") with reconstructions of what "must" have been experienced (item 9: "I think I can remember sitting . . . "). The process appears as a looping, questioning activity, with the larger problem broken up into a series of subproblems. Hence the search is active and constructive.

Forgetting

You store vast amounts of information in memory, but you also forget a good deal. This fact undoubtedly troubles you. For instance, research reveals that about 66 percent of the concepts you "learned" in high-school and college courses are forgotten within two years (Pressey, Robinson, and Horrocks, 1959). And even though you seem to retain intellectual skills better than verbal information, two-thirds of the material you acquired in first-year algebra (composed primarily of rules or algorithms) was very likely lost within a year (Layton, 1932). Admittedly, forgetting results in the loss of many potential skills and valuable information. But if you did not forget, your mind would be cluttered with so many unrelated items that you would have great difficulty retrieving and selecting the information you need. Memory is best served by retaining only that information you find useful and relevant to your present interests.

Psychologists have identified a number of factors that contribute to forgetting. Among them are decay, interference, cue dependence, and motivation.

Decay

According to *decay theory*, the memory traces containing stored information deteriorate over time (Broadbent, 1963; Reitman, 1971, 1974; Loftus and Loftus, 1980). Unless the information is periodically used and hence rehearsed, it weakens and eventually is erased (Loftus, 1985). The process is like the gradual fading of a photograph or the progressive erosion of the inscription on a tombstone. Decay seems to account for losses from the fragile sensory and short-term memory stores. But the application of decay theory to long-term memory is open to question. For instance, not all long-term memories, particularly those associated with motor skills, dissipate with time.

The psychologist Larry R. Squire (1982) gives a somewhat different twist to decay theory. He says that remembering and forgetting are mirror images of each other. New memory requires time to become incorporated with other associations and preexisting knowledge. Consequently, axon terminals compete for space, and nerve cells constantly change their configuration over time. In sum, Squire contends that memory traces are constantly resculpted and

Some material, such as advanced mathematics, seems to be more easily forgotten than other material, such as vocabulary words, that we use frequently and have integrated into networks of meaning. *(Junebug Clark/Photo Researchers)*

reconfigured over time. Forgetting is simply a result of the inevitable changes that take place in the original configuration.

Interference

According to *interference theory*, a retrieval cue becomes less effective as more and new items come to be classed or categorized in terms of it. Whereas decay theory depicts forgetting as a storage failure, interference theory views it as a retrieval failure. One source of interference is termed *retroactive interference* —the learning of new material interferes with the recall of old material. Most commonly, interference of this sort is going on in the following type of situation. Someone asks you, "Who beat the Green Bay Packers three weeks ago?" If the Green Bay Packers have lost their last four games to four different teams, you may have difficulty recalling the information. Although you may have encoded the information three Sundays ago, you now have difficulty retrieving the material because you have since encoded information regarding the Packers' subsequent losses.

Another source of interference is termed *proactive interference*—material learned earlier interferes with the learning of new material. When children are trying to learn their multiplication tables, they commonly encounter this sort of interference problem. They do not find it difficult to remember a single multiplication item such as $5 \times 7 = 35$. But as soon as you begin teaching them $5 \times 9 = 45$ and $6 \times 7 = 42$, you are establishing for them competing associations to each of the elements in the original problem. The 5×7 and 35 that is already in storage interferes with their remembering something new: 5×9 and 45, and 6×7 and 42.

Interference leads to an interesting paradox. If facts about some topic (for instance, neurotransmitters) interfere with one another, then the more facts you know about the topic, the slower you should be at retrieving information about the topic. In other words, the more expert or knowledgeable you are on a matter, the worse you should be at answering questions about it. But this prediction contradicts your intuition that the more you know about something, the better you are at answering questions about the topic.

Cue-Dependent Forgetting

Endel Tulving (Tulving and Psotka, 1971; Tulving, 1974) advances a *cue-dependent theory* of forgetting. He suggests that memory is the product of information from two sources: first, the memory trace that you laid down in your memory store as a result of the original perception of an event; and second, the retrieval cue that is present at the time recall occurs. Accordingly, trace information may be available in the memory store. However, it may be inaccessible because the setting you are in lacks information that activates the memory. Hence, in the absence of an appropriate retrieval cue, the event is for all practical purposes forgotten.

Retrieval information plays the same role in remembering that illumination plays as you read a printed page. When the light is turned off in a dark room, you find it impossible to see the print. Likewise, remembering is impossible when the appropriate retrieval information is absent. In contrast, a good retrieval cue narrows the memory domain in which you have to search for an item.

Context need not be external, like a particular physical setting. What goes on inside of you at the time you encode information can likewise be a critical contextual ingredient. Your internal state —whether sober or drunk, happy or sad, calm or agitated—can serve as a retrieval cue (Weingartner et al., 1976; Bower, 1981; Ellis et al., 1985). In **state-dependent memory,** you can retrieve events from memory you acquired in one psychic state better when you are in this same state than when you are in other psychic states. A good illustration is the case of Sirhan Sirhan, the man who assassinated Bobby Kennedy in Los Angeles in 1968 (Bower, 1981). Afterward he had no recollection of the actual murder, which took place in the small kitchen of the Ambassador Hotel where he fired several bullets into

---

state-dependent memory: Memory you acquired in one psychic state, which is easier to retrieve when you are in this same state than when you are in other psychic states.

Kennedy. Sirhan carried out the deed in a highly agitated state. However, under hypnosis he could reconstruct the events of that fateful day. As he became more worked up and excited, the memories would come tumbling out. At the point of the shooting, Sirhan would scream out the death curses, "fire" the shots, and then choke as he reexperienced the Secret Service bodyguard pressing his hands against his throat.

Other contextual factors may also influence your ability to remember information. The failure to remember items may result from **cue overload,** a state in which you find yourself overwhelmed or engulfed by excessive stimuli (Watkins and Watkins, 1975). Consequently, you fail to process retrieval information effectively. You find that you cannot sharpen a retrieval cue to the point where you can adequately specify the event you wish to bring from memory (Craik, 1977; Riccio, Richardson, and Ebner, 1984).

Motivated Forgetting

At times you forget because you *want* to (Goleman, 1985e). According to the psychoanalytic theory of Sigmund Freud, you activate various ego defense mechanisms when you confront serious anxiety and emotional conflict. These mechanisms are mental devices by which you protect and insulate yourself from psychic pain. *Repression* is one of these devices. In repression, an unacceptable or threatening thought or impulse is driven from conscious awareness. For instance, when children have been taught that aggression and masturbation are "bad," they may repress knowledge of their own involvement in these practices. By repression they avoid conscious feelings of anxiety and guilt. However, the material has not disappeared from their memory store. Rather, they use retrieval mechanisms that by-pass routes leading to the repressed memory. We will have more to say on these matters in Chapter 14. Researchers also find that we tend to remember ourselves in ways

that enhance our self-esteem, for instance, as holding better-paying jobs or donating more to charity than is actually the case. In this respect, forgetting selected facts is a self-serving device (Loftus, 1980; Rubin, 1985). It helps us live a more pleasant life.

THOUGHT

If storage and retrieval were the only processes used to handle information, people would be little more than glorified cameras and projectors (Kanizsa, 1985). But in fact, human beings are capable of doing things with information that make the most complex computer seem simple by comparison. They are capable of thought. The study of thinking is an aspect of **cognitive science**—a domain in psychology concerned with the nature of various mental tasks and the operations that allow the mind to execute them. As we noted in Chapter 1, *cognition* entails those processes by which we perceive, represent, remember, and use knowledge.

Our ability to engage in complex thought—to ponder matters, to reason about them logically, to engage in complicated problem solving, and to have sudden bursts of creative insight—is a vital component of humanness. Moreover, it has been and continues to be a primary mechanism by which people adapt to their environment. Human beings have learned to adjust to geographical and climatic environments ranging from that experienced by Alaskan Eskimos to that of the nomads of the Sahara. Human civilization is a history of thought and problem solving, from the discovery of fire and the invention of the wheel to modern space travel.

Thinking

Thinking may be viewed as the process of changing and reorganizing the information stored in memory in order to create new information. For instance, by thinking, you are able to put together any combina-

---

cue overload: A state in which you find yourself overwhelmed or engulfed by excessive stimuli.

cognitive science: A domain in psychology concerned with the nature of various mental tasks and the operations that allow the mind to execute them.

thinking: The process of changing and reorganizing the information stored in memory in order to create new information.

tion of words from memory and create sentences never devised before (including this one). The processes of thought depend on several devices or units: images, symbols, concepts, and rules.

Units of Thought

As noted earlier in the chapter, human beings possess a remarkable capacity for mental visualization. It is one of the primary means for channeling information into memory (Paivio, 1971; Nelson, Reed, and McEvoy, 1977). Hence it is hardly surprising that imagery should play a central role in much of thinking activity. An **image**—a mental representation of a specific event or object—is the most primitive unit of thought. Evidence of mental operations using images abounds in everyday life. Consider this question. How do you get a card table through a narrow doorway without folding up the legs? Most people indicate that they first mentally envision the process of turning the table on its side, putting two legs through the opening, then rotating the table to get the other legs and top to pass through the doorway. Many scientists testify that their greatest achievements derived from imagined spatial relations and transformations. Albert Einstein's theory of relativity and James Watt's visualization of the mechanism for condensing steam in an engine were arrived at in this way (Cooper and Shepard, 1984).

A more abstract unit of thought is a **symbol**, a sound or design that stands for an object, event, or quality. The most common symbols in thinking are words: every word is a symbol that represents something other than itself. Symbols are arbitrary stand-ins for actual or imagined things. Although they stand for other things, symbols do not necessarily bear any relationship to them. For example, the word "small" is larger than the word "big," and on this page the symbol "yellow" appears just as black as the symbols "black" and "white." Whereas an image represents a specific sight or sound, a symbol may have a number of meanings. The fact that symbols differ from the things they represent enables you to think about things that are not present, to range over the past and future, to imagine things and situations that never were or will be. Numbers, letters, and punctuation marks are all familiar symbols of ideas that have no concrete existence.

When a symbol is used as a label for a class of objects or events with certain common attributes, or for the attributes themselves, it is called a **concept.** "Animals," "music," "liquid," and "beautiful people" are examples of concepts based on the common attributes of the objects and experiences belonging to each category. Thus the concept "animal" separates a group of organisms from such things as automobiles, carrots, and Roquefort cheese. Concepts enable you to chunk large amounts of information. You do not have to treat every new piece of information as unique, since you already know something about the class of objects or experiences to which the new item belongs. Thus by means of concepts you are able to sort large numbers of stimuli into manageable units and domains of related concepts. In this manner you reduce the complexity of your environment.

The fourth and most complex unit of thought is a **rule,** a statement of the relationship between two or more concepts. You do not live in a world characterized by just so many bits and pieces of information. Instead, some items are linked to other items in an orderly or recurrent manner. Examples of rules include "A person cannot be in two places at the same time" and "Mass remains constant despite changes in appearance."

Images, symbols, concepts, and rules are the building blocks of mental activity. They provide an economical and efficient way for people to represent reality, to manipulate and reorganize it, and to devise new ways of acting. A person can think about pursuing several different careers, weigh their pros and cons, and decide which to pursue without having to try them all. We will be examining a number of these matters more closely in the chapter that follows.

---

image: A rough mental representation of a specific event or object; the most primitive unit of thought.

symbol: An abstract unit of thought that represents an object, event, or quality.

concept: A label for a class of objects or events that share certain common attributes.

rule: A statement of the relationship between two or more concepts; the most complex unit of thought.

An old money-lender offered to cancel a merchant's debt and keep him from going to prison if the merchant would give the money-lender his lovely daughter. Horrified yet desperate, the merchant and his daughter agreed to let Providence decide. The money-lender said he would put a black pebble and a white pebble in a bag and the girl would draw one. The white pebble would cancel the debt and leave her free. The black one would make her the money-lender's, although the debt would be canceled. If she refused to pick, her father would go to prison. From the pebble-strewn path they were standing on, the money-lender picked two pebbles and quickly put them in the bag, but the girl saw he had picked up two black ones. What would you have done if you were the girl?

FIGURE 7.7 This problem was devised by psychologist Edward de Bono (1967), who believes that conventional directed thinking is insufficient for solving new and unusual problems. His approach to problem solving requires use of nondirected thinking in order to generate new ideas of looking at the problem situation. The answer to this problem is provided in Figure 7.11. *(After Edward de Bono. 1967. New Think: The Use of Lateral Thinking in the Generation of New Ideas. New York: Basic Books. © 1967, 1968 by Edward de Bono. Reprinted by permission of Basic Books, Inc., Publishers.)*

Kinds of Thinking

People think in two distinct ways. The first, called **directed thinking,** is a systematic and logical attempt to reach a specific goal. This kind of thinking depends heavily on symbols, concepts, and rules. Directed thinking is deliberate and purposeful. Through directed thinking people solve problems, formulate and follow rules, and set, work toward, and achieve goals.

The other type of thinking, called **nondirected thinking,** consists of a free flow of thoughts through the mind, with no particular goal or plan, and depends more on images (see Figure 7.7). Nondi-rected thinking is usually rich in imagery and feelings. Daydreams, fantasies, and reveries are typical examples. People often engage in nondirected thought when they are relaxing or trying to escape from boredom or worry. This kind of thinking may provide unexpected insights into one's goals and beliefs. Scientists and artists say that some of their best ideas emerge from drifting thoughts that occur when they have set aside a problem for the moment. A number of psychologists (Osborn, 1963; Parnes, 1971) have promoted **brainstorming** as a technique for fostering nondirected thinking. It is a process by which a great many solutions to a problem are encouraged by thinking out loud and deferring

---

directed thinking: Systematic, logical, goal-oriented thought.
nondirected thinking: The free flow of images and ideas, occurring with no particular goal.
brainstorming: A technique for fostering nondirected thinking. It is a freewheeling process for generating ideas.

judgment and evaluation. Freewheeling is welcomed, and individuals are urged to build on one another's ideas by improving on them or combining them in various ways with other ideas.

Problem Solving

One of the main functions of thinking is to solve problems—to bridge the gap, mentally, between a present situation and a desired goal. The gap may be between hunger and food, a column of figures and a total, a washed-out bridge and a destination, or cancer and a cure. In all these examples, getting from the problem to the solution requires thinking, which is sometimes nondirected and other times directed.

Strategies

Problem solving depends on the use of *strategies,* or specific methods for approaching problems. One strategy is to break down a complex problem into a number of smaller, more easily solved problems. This technique involves the use of *hierarchical measures,* in which complicated matters are decomposed into subproblems, until each subproblem becomes solvable. For example, it is the end of the semester and your life is falling apart. You find yourself drowning in a maze of tasks. You solve your problem by breaking it down into small pieces: studying for a science exam, finishing that overdue paper, canceling your dinner date, scheduling regular study breaks to maintain what is left of your sanity, and so on.

For some problems, you may use an *analogy* —using the solution to one problem to solve a similar problem. For instance, the automotive engineer Charles Duryea patterned the spray-injection carburetor after his wife's perfume atomizer. Success in using an analogy depends on recognizing the similarity between two problems. For other problems, you may work backward from the goal you have set. Mystery writers often use this method: they decide how to end the story ("who did it") and then devise a plot leading to the conclusion. These approaches entail the use of various *heuristic devices.*

Heuristic devices involve the use of shortcuts, rules of thumb, and other tried-and-true remedies to search for promising alternatives.

Heuristics, while often successful, do not guarantee success. In contrast, an *algorithm* is a procedure of steps that guarantees a solution if you apply it in the right circumstances and follow the steps correctly. The rules for division constitute an algorithm because a correct answer is guaranteed if you follow the steps in the prescribed manner.

To determine which strategy to use in a particular situation, most people analyze the problem to see if it resembles a situation they have experienced in the past. A strategy that worked in the past is likely to work again. The more unusual the problem, the more difficult it is to devise a strategy for dealing with it. Here nondirected thinking can be helpful.

Set

There are times when certain useful strategies become cemented into the problem-solving process. When a particular strategy becomes a habit, it is called a **set**—you are "set," or readied, to treat problems in a certain way. For example, a chess player may always attempt to control the four center squares of the chessboard. Whenever her opponent attacks, she responds by looking for ways to regain control of those four squares. She has a "set" for this strategy. If this set helps her to win, fine.

Sometimes, however, a set interferes with problem solving, resulting in *rigidity.* You probably know the old riddle, "What is black, white, and read all over? A newspaper." When you say the riddle, the word "read" sounds like "red," which is why some people cannot guess the answer. "Read" is heard as part of the black and white set—it is interpreted as being a color. If you asked, "What is read by people every day and is black and white?" the correct answer would be obvious. And boring.

One form of set that can interfere with problem solving is *functional fixedness*—the inability to imagine new functions for familiar objects. In experiments on functional fixedness, people are asked to solve a problem that requires them to use a familiar object in an unfamiliar way (Duncker, 1945). Be-

---

set: A habitual strategy or pattern of problem solving.

FIGURE 7.8 Given the materials pictured here, how would you go about mounting the candle vertically on a wooden wall in such a way that it can be lit? This problem was formulated by Carl Duncker to test how well people are able to overcome functional fixedness. The solution is presented in Figure 7.11. (Werner Kalber/PPS)

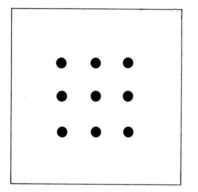

FIGURE 7.9 Connect these dots with four straight lines without lifting your pencil. The solution appears in Figure 7.11.

cause they are set to use the object in the usual way, people tend to pay attention only to the features of the object that relate to its everyday use (see Figure 7.8). They respond in a rigid way.

Another type of rigidity occurs when a person makes a wrong assumption about a problem. In Figure 7.9, for example, the problem is to connect the dots with four straight lines without lifting your pencil. Most people have trouble solving this puzzle because they falsely assume that they must stay within the area of the dots.

People trying to solve the kind of problem shown in Figure 7.10 experience a third kind of rigidity. Most people look for direct methods of solving problems and do not see solutions that require several intermediate steps.

Rigidity can be overcome if you realize that your strategy is not working and look for other ways to approach the problem. The more familiar the situation, the more difficult this will be. In contrast, rigidity is less likely to occur with unusual problems.

In sum, successful problem solvers first try to understand the problem situation. They consider alternative representations and relations among the variables. The process often requires that they break down a problem into small units. They then execute each task in turn, one after the other. These smaller goals and the methods to achieve them are the building blocks of expertise.

Artificial Intelligence

The rapid development of computer technology has stimulated interest in **artificial intelligence**—the design and construction of intelligent machines. When appropriately programed, computers can handle and process information in ways that bear close resemblances to human thinking and problem solv-

artificial intelligence: The design and construction of intelligent machines; the simulation of human thinking and problem solving by computer technology.

FIGURE 7.10 How would you go about solving this problem: eight soldiers need to cross a river, but the only way to cross is in a small boat in which two children are playing. The boat can carry at most two children or one soldier. How do the soldiers get across? You will find the answer in Figure 7.11.

ing (Waltz, 1982; Schank and Childer, 1985). This endeavor is teaching psychologists new ways to think about thinking (Gardner, 1985). It is also having a major impact on American industry and business. A New York market research firm estimates that the artificial intelligence market in the United States will rise from slightly over $155 million sales to $2 billion by 1989 (Eliot, 1985).

Programs that are currently available play games such as chess, checkers, and backgammon at the level of the human expert or master player (indeed, a program called Might Bee, written by Hans Berliner of Carnegie-Mellon University, defeated the world backgammon champion in 1979). And computers have been programed to diagnose medical problems, to navigate spaceships to the moon and distant planets, to solve complex mathematical problems, to give advice on stock market decisions, and to locate oil and mineral deposits. Although these operations initially seem incredible, there is a disconcerting fact. Such seemingly sophisticated tasks can often be relatively easy to program *because* they are specialized. In contrast, the ordinary, everyday things we do—walk, read a handwritten note, plan a trip to a shopping mall—turn out to be exceedingly difficult (Waldrop, 1985). A chess master seems to use the equivalent of roughly fifty thousand rules of expertise. Yet we know millions, and perhaps even bil-

lions, of commonsense things. We can only guess at how many "rules" that corresponds to.

Computer programs that are designed to mirror human thinking are termed *simulation models*. Researchers break down a problem to solvable dimensions by using organized sequences of elementary processes as the building blocks. Frequently, they identify the critical components by having human subjects "think aloud" as they solve actual problems. In turn, the researchers prepare a set of computer subprograms, each of which is designed to execute a specialized process that corresponds to one of the hypothesized human processes. For example, some subprograms transform or classify input information, others make comparisons and arrive at decisions, and still others compare calculations against various solution specifications (Newell and Simon, 1972; Davis, 1973).

The parallels between artificial and human problem solving do not rest on hardware (computer circuitry and semiconductor chips are not viewed as equivalent to brain nerve cells). Rather, the parallels derive from the processes used to reach given outcomes. Both computers and the human mind accept information, manipulate symbols, store items in memory, and retrieve them again (Conrad et al., 1984). Accordingly, researchers can formulate a theory about how human beings solve a problem.

They then program a computer to simulate these theoretical properties and test the theory by comparing the computer output with that produced by human beings (Dominowski, 1977; Dehn and Schank, 1982).

Allen Newell and Herbert A. Simon (1956, 1961) undertook the first successful attempt to simulate human thinking with computers. The accomplishment stands as a landmark in artificial intelligence. They used their program, termed the Logic Theorist, to prove the theorems in formal logic developed by Alfred North Whitehead and Bertrand Russell in their famous treatise *Principia Mathematica* (1925). Whenever the computer proved a theorem, it stored the information in memory. In this manner the computer could build on earlier theorems in deriving subsequent theorems (the same procedure employed by Whitehead and Russell). The Logic Theorist arrived at adequate proofs for thirty-eight of the fifty-two theorems. Moreover, some of the proofs were more ingenious and efficient than those originally advanced by Whitehead and Russell.

The Logic Theorist was programed to use many of the heuristics (shortcuts and informal rules of thumb) that you use in your everyday problem-solving activities. For example, one heuristic was "working backward" (it would begin with the answer and move backward step-by-step to the original problem, uncovering the procedure's underlying logic in the process). The computer did not blindly search through every possible sequence of logical operations until it eventually hit on the proof. Rather, by using heuristics, the computer evolved problem-solving strategies that allowed it to select the most promising acts for further examination while eliminating the less promising ones from full-scale consideration.

Another computer program called BACON has also been used to discover various scientific laws. For instance, if you provide BACON with the data that astronomer Johann Kepler worked with, it will discover Kepler's third law (the formula that relates the distance of a planet from the sun to the time it takes for the planet to go around the sun).

Artificial-intelligence research has considerably enriched the understanding of a complex human behavior. Yet computer models do not provide a perfect or even near-perfect analogy to human thinking processes. Present-day computers have a memory only if someone has put it there. And if one wishes to extract an item from memory, the computer must be told exactly where it is. In the human mind, things do not operate in this fashion. (Thus although Might Bee plays backgammon at the level of an expert player, it does not emulate the strategic decisions made by an actual human player.) Engineers, psychologists, and other specialists are currently attempting to design new generations of computers that will memorize and store images; read, write, and speak a language; and more important, "think" and figure out their own solutions to problems. The primary shortcoming of today's computers is that they must be given instructions at every step along the way.

Contemporary computers process information at a very rapid rate and serially (fetching pieces of information and acting on them one at a time in the manner of people passing through a doorway single file). In the human brain, in contrast, the rate of information processing is slower, but the information can be handled on millions of channels in parallel (West, 1985). Researchers in the United States and Japan are currently trying to copy the brain. They are attempting to design computer systems that will permit the parallel processing of information, allowing the computer to break a problem down into subproblems and work on several simultaneously.

However, even parallel processing will not provide computers with genuine "intelligence." Human beings can, in addition, infer meaning from sensory input and extract the underlying idea from words. The philosopher John Searle (1985) contends that a computer cannot truly think because it only manipulates symbols—and the symbols do not "mean" anything to the computer. In brief, it lacks an attribute that corresponds to consciousness or awareness. The concept of a conscious being is different from that of an unconscious being. Not only do conscious beings know something, they *know* that they know it.

Placing human-type intelligence within a computer remains a distant goal (and it is by no means certain that it is an achievable goal). As will be seen in the next chapter, the human capability for thinking and problem solving is so diverse and powerful that current computers are, in comparison, simply toddlers that can scarcely speak and stack blocks

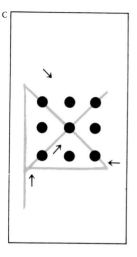

hen the girl put her hand into the bag to draw out the fateful pebble, she fumbled and dropped it, where it was immediately lost among the others. "Oh," she said, "well, you can tell which one I picked by looking at the one that's left." The girl's lateral thinking saved her father and herself.

FIGURE 7.11 Note that each solution to the problems in the chapter requires breaking certain habits of thought. (a) In the money-lender problem, it is difficult to imagine that control of the situation can be taken out of the hands of the powerful money-lender. *(After Edward de Bono. 1967.* New Think: The Use of Lateral Thinking in the Generation of Ideas. *New York: Basic Books. © 1967, 1968 by Edward de Bono. Reprinted by permission of Basic Books, Inc. Publishers.)* (b) Solving the candle problem requires looking at the matchbox as more than a container to be discarded. The presence of the useless piece of string usually confuses problem solvers. *(Werner Kalber/PPS)* (c) The solution to this problem is blocked if you avoid going beyond the boundaries of the dots. (d) The first steps in the solution of the river problem. Once you discover the first step, you may become further bogged down if you do not realize the lengthy cyclical nature of the process required.

(Stockton, 1980; Schank and Childers, 1985). The brain not only digests facts but also draws many inferences based on previous experiences (a matter addressed in Chapter 5 in the box "The Quest to Match Human Vision"). Moreover, the meaning of the bare facts differs for each person and changes for the same person over time. Finally, computers do not experience human emotions, nor do they learn from their mistakes.

SUMMARY

1. Learning involves the acquisition of skills and knowledge that allow individuals to adapt to their environment by building on previous experience. However, these new potentials for behavior must be retained. People must be able to store this potential over time and then activate it when they need it. Memory serves this function.

2. Sensory storage holds information for only an instant. This information is not as yet narrowed down or analyzed. It is like a short-lived but highly detailed photograph or tape recording.

3. The things you have in your conscious mind at any one moment are being held in short-term memory. The short-term store is your working memory.

A. To keep information in short-term memory for more than a few seconds, you have to repeat it to yourself. Each memory trace is "regenerated" or "reset" by rehearsal, at which point it begins decaying again.

B. Short-term memory is quite limited in capacity. You are able to keep only about seven unrelated items in your immediate memory.

C. The principle of displacement provides an explanation of how an item is lost from short-term memory. Since there are about seven slots available for information, items entering short-term memory are placed in the next available slot. When all the slots are in use, incoming information takes priority. It displaces or "bumps out" an old item from one of the slots.

4. Long-term memory is where you store information indefinitely for future use. It can be thought of as a kind of filing cabinet or storage bin for names, dates, words, faces, and countless other items.

A. Encoding is the process by which information is put into the memory system. It involves perceiving information, abstracting from it one or more features, and creating corresponding memory traces for these features.

B. There appear to be two distinct storage systems in long-term memory. Declarative memory centers on "facts," knowledge that can be brought consciously to mind and formulated in a statement, proposition, or image. Procedural memory entails "skills," knowledge associated with learned habits. The two forms of memory seem to reside in different structures of the brain.

C. Memory is not simply a matter of encoding and storage. It also requires that you retrieve appropriate information when you need it. In general, the better the cues that you use in memory search, the better will be your retrieval of information from long-term memory. For this reason, recognition is usually easier than recall.

5. Brain researchers believe that neurons are the repositories of memory. Gary Lynch finds that bursts of high-frequency electrical stimulation cause some nerve cells in the cortex and neighboring hippocampus to become far more active, and the increased activity lasts for months. He says that this phenomenon—called long-term potentiation (LTP)—is involved in long-term memory. William Greenough has shown that when rats learn, their nerve cells sprout more branches and form new synapses. He speculates that even though the number of neurons in the brain may be limited, the number of connections may be limitless, offering a chance for memory enhancement.

6. Although your memory for complex events is oftentimes startlingly accurate, it is also frequently incomplete and occasionally even highly distorted. Some psychologists contend that this is due to the fact that knowledge contained in memory is the construction of the mind. Scheme theory has appealed to many psychologists as an explanation for

the constructed nature of various aspects of memory. According to scheme theory, what you encode and store in memory is heavily determined by a guiding scheme.

7. You store vast amounts of information in memory, but you also forget a good deal. Psychologists have identified a number of factors that contribute to forgetting.

A. According to decay theory, the memory traces containing stored information deteriorate over time. Unless the information is periodically used and hence rehearsed, it weakens and eventually is erased.

B. According to interference theory, a retrieval cue becomes less effective as more and new items come to be classed or categorized in terms of it.

C. According to cue-dependent theory, memory is the product of information from two sources: the memory trace that you laid down in your memory store as a result of the original perception of an event, and the retrieval cue that is present at the time recall occurs. Thus, although trace information may be available in the memory store, it may be inaccessible because the setting you are in lacks information that activates the memory.

D. According to motivated forgetting theory, you forget because you want to.

8. Thinking may be viewed as the process of changing and reorganizing the information stored in memory in order to create new information.

A. The processes of thought depend on several devices or units: images, symbols, concepts, and rules.

B. People think in two distinct ways. The first, called directed thinking, is a systematic and logical attempt to reach a specific goal. The other type of thinking, called nondirected thinking, consists of a free flow of thoughts through the mind, with no particular goal or plan, and depends more on images.

9. One of the main functions of thinking is to solve problems—to bridge the gap mentally between a present situation and a desired goal.

A. Problem solving depends on the use of strategies, or specific methods for approaching problems. Hierarchical measures entail breaking down complicated matters into subproblems, until each subproblem becomes solvable. Analogies entail using the solution to one problem to solve a similar one. Heuristic devices involve the use of shortcuts, rules of thumb, and other tried-and-true remedies to search for promising alternatives.

B. There are times when certain useful strategies become cemented into the problem-solving process. When a particular strategy becomes a habit, it is called a set.

10. The rapid development of computer technology has stimulated interest in artificial intelligence. When appropriately programed, computers can handle and process information in ways that bear close resemblances to human thinking and problem solving. So far, however, computers are no match for the human mind.

KEY TERMS

artificial intelligence (p. 248)
brainstorming (p. 246)
cognitive science (p. 244)
concept (p. 245)
cue overload (p. 244)
declarative memory (p. 231)
directed thinking (p. 246)
encoding (acquisition) (p. 224)
episodic memory (p. 231)
image (p. 245)
long-term memory (p. 225)

memory (p. 224)
mnemonic devices (p. 236)
nondirected thinking (p. 246)
procedural memory (p. 231)
recall (p. 232)
recognition (p. 232)
reconstruction (p. 240)
relearning (p. 233)
retrieval (p. 224)
rule (p. 245)
scheme (p. 239)

selective attention (p. 227)
semantic memory (p. 231)
sensory storage (p. 225)
set (p. 247)
short-term memory (p. 225)
state-dependent memory (p. 243)
storage (retention) (p. 224)
symbol (p. 245)
thinking (p. 244)

SUGGESTED READINGS

ANDERSON, JOHN R. 1980. *Cognitive Psychology and Its Implications*. San Francisco: W. H. Freeman. A comprehensive introduction to the rapidly developing field of cognitive psychology. This book is especially good in its treatment of propositional memory and language.

CROWDER, R. G. 1982. *The Psychology of Reading*. New York: Oxford University Press. Examines theory and research on the processes of reading.

DE BONO, EDWARD. 1969. *The Mechanism of Mind*. New York: Simon & Schuster. A nonscientific book about how to use your mind effectively. It is particularly instructive about the nature of memory and models.

GLASS, A. L., and HOLYOAK, K. J. 1986. *Cognition*. New York: Random House. An introductory text that brings together the diverse areas and topics of cognitive psychology: attention, memory, perception, reasoning, problem solving, and language. At-tempts to integrate these rather diverse topics.

HUNT, MORTON. 1982. *The Universe Within: A New Science Explores the Human Mind*. New York: Simon & Schuster. A wonderfully readable, lucid, firsthand account of the latest discoveries and theories of cognitive science—the study of how our minds work. The author draws on two years of interviews with scientists at the cutting edge of this new discipline.

LOFTUS, G. R., and LOFTUS, E. F. 1976. *Human Memory: The Processing of Information*. Hillsdale, N.J.: Erlbaum. A thorough yet readable introduction to the study of human memory. Presents research and theory in an information-processing framework.

LURIA, A. R. 1968. *The Mind of a Mnemonist*. New York: Basic Books. A delightful discussion of the mnemonist S. and his amazing feats of memory.

NEISSER, ULRIC. 1982. *Memory Observed: Remembering in Natural Contexts*. San Francisco: W. H. Freeman. This edited collection of readings contains several excellent papers on remembering and forgetting in everyday situations. The book should serve as a "guidebook" to the phenomona of memory in "ordinary human experience." The topics covered are diverse and interesting, ranging from testifying in court to memory in the performing arts.

SMITH, E. E., and MEDIN, D. L. 1984. *Categories and Concepts*. Cambridge, Mass.: Harvard University Press. Provides a comprehensive, critical guide to the most recent developments in the psychology of human concepts; a tutorial review of this most hotly debated current topic in psychology.

Roger de La Fresnaye, *The Conquest of the Air*, 1913.

8

Intelligence, Creativity, and Their Assessment

On the weekend of July 4, 1942, psychologist Seymour Sarason, now a Yale professor, began work at Southbury Training School for the mentally retarded (McKean, 1985). The school occupied a picturesque, wooded site in a Connecticut valley. It was a hectic time because one of the students had escaped. In the 1940s it was not uncommon for the mentally retarded to be placed in institutions where they were held much like prisoners. Accordingly, it may not seem particularly surprising that the students would occasionally outwit their supervisors, slip into the woods, and head for home. School officials would then send out a search party to return the escapees to the institution.

Sarason set about his duties of providing psychological services to the students, including giving them the Porteus Mazes Test. It is an intelligence test that psychologists often use with the retarded because it does not require language skills but simply an ability to trace one's way out of printed mazes. Initially Sarason paid little attention to the escapees. But it soon dawned on him that something curious was occurring. Many of the escapees could not perform any of the puzzles correctly. "These kids couldn't get from point A to point B on paper, so how did they plan a successful runaway?" reasoned Sarason. "That was when I realized that what these kids could plan on their own was in no way reflected by how they did on tests" (quoted by McKean, 1985:25).

The insight that there is more to intelligence than how one performs on an intelligence test is hardly new or particularly startling. You probably have known people with below-average IQ scores who function exceedingly well in life and accomplish a good deal and others with high IQ scores who never

257

amount to much. Indeed, there are countless examples of seemingly intelligent people who never achieve their potential and come to untimely ends. Consider the sad case of Leonard Ross, a child prodigy who won $164,000 on a television show in the 1950s. He graduated from Yale Law School, where he was editor-in-chief of the law journal. His friends and associates assumed he was destined for a brilliant future. Instead, he drifted from one job to another, with happiness always eluding him. In May 1985, at the age of thirty-nine, Ross was found floating in a motel pool in Santa Clara, California, apparently a suicide.

There are also unusually gifted individuals who are mentally retarded. Consider Alonzo Clemons, who at twenty-five years of age is a resident in a private home for the mentally retarded in Boulder, Colorado (Schmidt, 1983). Although many of his verbal and social skills are those of a young child, Clemons has emerged as a sculptor of remarkable skill and talent. As a child he would sit silently for hours, kneading modeling clay into the shapes of tiny animals. Today professional artists recognize his hand-worked wax models of bulls, horses, and antelopes as outstanding. When a Denver gallery presented the first public exhibition of Clemons's work, a series of charging bulls cast in bronze realized $950 apiece.

In this chapter we will consider intelligence and creativity. We will examine a number of questions. What do we mean by intelligence? What are the sources of individual differences in intelligence? What factors underlie human creativity? What is the relationship between intelligence and creativity? What is the nature of intelligence tests? What do intelligence tests measure? What are the uses and abuses of intelligence tests?

HUMAN INTELLIGENCE

Intelligence is one of the most notable characteristics of the human species. In contrast with many other forms of life, human beings are not biologically prewired to adapt to specific environments. It is our intelligence that has allowed us to adapt to life in vastly differing environmental settings. Alaskan Eskimos and Siberian Chukchi, for instance, have adapted to arctic conditions, while various Arab nomads have adapted to the desert. Human beings

Human intelligence allows us to adapt to a variety of environments. We can survive in even the starkest and coldest of settings. *(Dave Johnston/The Picture Cube)*

have even fashioned vehicles that allow them to navigate and survive in outer space.

But simply being intelligent in the human sense does not necessarily mean that the human species is better adapted to the environment than other organisms. For example, the cockroach has displayed amazing versatility in surviving over a far longer span of history than have human beings. And it manages to propagate—indeed, even prosper —despite the best extermination programs.

Nonetheless, being intelligent has allowed human beings to occupy a unique environmental niche. This niche requires extensive use of learning and problem solving as coping mechanisms, in contrast with prewired adaptations that genetically program behavior. In this sense, human beings possess a more "open" program for development than cockroaches and other species. Learning allows us to transmit the social legacy afforded by culture from one generation to the next. Hence each new generation can build on the achievement of the preceding one and, by using the intelligence of its members, enrich this heritage.

Conceptions of Intelligence

In recent years, many people have become uncomfortable with the notion of intelligence and, more particularly, with intelligence testing. In a democratic society in which all people are in theory "born equal," the idea that people may differ in intelligence seems to smack of elitism, perhaps even of racism and sexism. The confusion of legal equality, guaranteed to all by the Constitution, and biological equality, an evolutionary impossibility, is at fault. The great achievement of the American Constitution is to guarantee equal rights to all in spite of individual differences (Dobzhansky, 1973). Intelligence of the human species is not a myth (Sternberg, 1976b, 1982). Nor are individual differences in intelligence (Scarr, 1981b). Intelligence is a primary adaptive mechanism for human beings, one that has evolved and shows typical patterns of individual variability.

Although laypeople and psychologists alike use the concept of intelligence, it remains a fuzzy concept (Sternberg et al., 1981; Sternberg, 1985). What psychologists typically mean by intelligence is captured in the definition proposed by David Wechsler (1975), a psychologist who has developed a number of widely used intelligence tests. He views **intelligence** as a global capacity to understand the world, think rationally, and cope resourcefully with the challenges of life. Considered in this manner, intelligence is a *capacity* to acquire knowledge and to function rationally and effectively, rather than the possession of a fund of knowledge. This capacity allows us to capitalize on our strengths, to compensate for our weaknesses, and to modify the environment so that it will better fit our adaptive skills (Sternberg, 1984a). Accordingly, intelligence finds a somewhat different expression in different environments and cultures (Kleinfeld, 1973; Ogbu, 1981; Gardner, 1983).

Popular Notions of Intelligence

The psychologist Robert J. Sternberg and his colleagues (1981) asked laypeople for their view regarding intelligence. They interviewed people in a New Haven supermarket, library, and commuter train station. For the most part, the people conceived of intelligence as having three components. First there was *problem-solving ability*, expressed in observations such as "reasons logically and well," "identifies connections among ideas," and "sees all aspects of a problem." Second, *verbal ability* emerged in statements such as "speaks clearly and articulately," "is verbally fluent," and "converses well." And third, *social competence* appeared in laypeople's comments such as "accepts others for what they are," "admits mistakes," and "displays interest in the world at large."

Sternberg and his colleagues also asked experts in psychology about their notions of intelligence. The laypeople and experts displayed considerable agreement (see Table 8.1). But there were two major differences in their answers. First, the psychologists believed motivation is an important ingredient in academic intelligence. They mentioned "dedication," "persistence," and "studying hard" as signs of an intelligent person. Second, the laypeople placed greater emphasis on social competence than the experts did. Experts did not consider sensitivity to others, honesty, and frankness as aspects of intelligence.

Likewise, people of different cultures often conceive of intelligence somewhat differently. Consider what happens when Kpelle tribespeople in Nigeria are asked to sort a series of objects in sensible order (Cole et al., 1971). If given the names of a number of fruits, animals, and tools, the Kpelle order the objects by the functions that they serve. For instance, they may place a potato with a hoe rather than with other foods. By Western standards this constitutes an inferior way of sorting. When shown the "right" way to go about the task, the Kpelle say that only stupid people sort things that way. What is of even greater interest is that when the Kpelle are asked to sort the way stupid people do, they are

---

intelligence: A global capacity to understand the world, think rationally, and cope resourcefully with the challenges of life.

TABLE 8.1 Comparison of Laypeople's and Experts' Ideas About Intelligence

LAYPEOPLE	EXPERTS
I. Practical problem-solving ability	***I. Verbal intelligence***
Reasons logically and well	Displays a good vocabulary
Identifies connections among ideas	Reads with high comprehension
Sees all aspects of a problem	Displays curiosity
Keeps an open mind	Is intellectually curious
Responds thoughtfully to others' ideas	Sees all aspects of a problem
Sizes up situations well	Learns rapidly
Gets to the heart of problems	Appreciates knowledge for its own sake
Interprets information accurately	Is verbally fluent
Makes good decisions	Listens to all sides of an argument before
Goes to original sources for basic	deciding
information	Displays alertness
Poses problems in an optimal way	Thinks deeply
Is a good source of ideas	Shows creativity
Perceives implied assumptions and	Converses easily on a variety of subjects
conclusions	Reads widely
Listens to all sides of an argument	Likes to read
Deals with problems resourcefully	Identifies connections among ideas
II. Verbal ability	***II. Problem-solving ability***
Speaks clearly and articulately	Is able to apply knowledge to problems at
Is verbally fluent	hand
Converses well	Makes good decisions
Is knowledgeable about a particular field	Poses problems in an optimal way
Studies hard	Displays common sense
Reads with high comprehension	Displays objectivity
Reads widely	Solves problems well
Deals effectively with people	Plans ahead
Writes without difficulty	Has good intuition
Sets aside time for reading	Gets to the heart of problems
Displays a good vocabulary	Appreciates truth
Accepts social norms	Considers the result of actions
Tries new things	Approaches problems thoughtfully
III. Social competence	***III. Practical intelligence***
Accepts others for what they are	Sizes up situations well
Admits mistakes	Determines how to achieve goals
Displays interest in the world at large	Displays awareness to world around him or
Is on time for appointments	her
Has social conscience	Displays interest in the world at large
Thinks before speaking and doing	
Displays curiosity	
Does not make snap judgments	
Makes fair judgments	
Assesses well the relevance of information to	
a problem at hand	
Is sensitive to other people's needs and	
desires	
Is frank and honest with self and others	
Displays interest in the immediate	
environment	

Source: Robert J. Sternberg. 1982. "Who's intelligent?" *Psychology Today,* 16 (April):32. Reprinted with permission. Copyright © 1982 American Psychological Association.

quite capable of employing the same categories used by Americans and Europeans. Clearly, the Kpelle and Westerners view intelligent behavior quite differently.

Intelligence: One or Many Skills?

When psychologists discuss the meaning of intelligence among themselves, they disagree about what "it" is. For the most part, psychologists can be assigned to one of two camps—the "lumpers" and the "splitters." The "lumpers" view intelligence as a *general capacity* for acquiring knowledge, reasoning, and solving problems. The "splitters" seek to identify *different types* of ability or intelligence.

Alfred Binet and Intelligence Testing

Modern psychological conceptions of intelligence and intelligence testing emerged about the turn of the century. At this time, the French psychologist Alfred Binet (1857–1911) undertook to help the schools of Paris identify pupils who would not be able to handle regular classroom work and who therefore could benefit from placement in special classes. He conceived of intelligence as a number of related abilities rather than as a specific trait.

Factor Approaches to Intelligence

About the same time that Binet was at work, Charles Spearman (1904, 1927) was achieving prominence in England by advancing a somewhat different view of intelligence. He concluded that there is a general mental ability that is used for abstract reasoning and problem solving. Spearman labeled this factor "g" for "general." He believed the "g" factor to be an underlying intellectual capacity—a property of the brain—that pervades all of a person's endeavors and functions as a wellspring of mental energy. However, Spearman recognized that each person performs better on some types of mental tasks than on others. Consequently, he sought to identify a number of "s" factors—"s" for "special"—that are peculiar to specific tasks (for example, arithmetic or spatial relations).

During the 1930s and 1940s, Louis Thurstone (1938, 1947) elaborated on Spearman's factor approach. He rejected the notion of a general intelligence and focused instead on seven specific spheres: verbal comprehension, word fluency, numerical ability, spatial visualization, associative memory, perceptual speed, and reasoning. More recently, J. P. Guilford (1967) has proposed that there are 120 separate types of mental ability. But not all psychologists are happy with such minute distinctions.

More recently the psychologist Howard Gardner has argued that human beings have evolved as a species to deal with at least seven separate kinds of information, what he terms "intelligences." As he views the matter, the seven basic competences cannot be collapsed into one intellectual heap (see the boxed insert on pages 262–263).

Levels of Intelligence: Arthur R. Jensen

A number of psychologists have distinguished between levels of intelligence, recognizing that simple learning differs in kind from complex learning (Thorndike, 1927, 1932). The educational psychologist Arthur R. Jensen (1973, 1980, 1982) has elaborated on this distinction in his identification of level I and level II skills. Level I skills revolve about simple learned associations and are reflected in tasks involving rote learning and memorization. One example would be digit span—the number of digits you can remember in a row (6–9–5–3–8–1). In contrast, level II skills entail conceptual reasoning—the sort of mental activity that most people mean by intelligence. Level II skills find expression in a capacity for abstract thinking and problem solving.

Levels of Intelligence: Sternberg's Model

Psychologist Robert J. Sternberg (1984a, b) has sought to advance our understanding by conceiving of intelligence not only in terms of the mind's work and what tests measure but also in terms of the context in which it occurs. His three-level (triarchic) theory of intelligence consists of contextual, experiential, and componential ingredients. Individual differences occur along all three dimensions. The first, or *contextual*, level deals with the environmental setting in which behavior occurs. Different life styles require and foster different abilities. Hence what is "intelligent" in one environment may be "stupid" in another (recall the differing Kpelle and Western approaches to ordering objects). For instance, until quite recently, the abilities to add, subtract, multiply, and divide were essential aspects of intelligent

Howard Gardner: Multiple Intelligences

Imagine two Martians who have just landed on Earth and are curious about the human mind. One wanders into a great American university and asks an educational psychologist about the mental powers of human beings. The educational psychologist responds that the key to the mind is intelligence and that it is measured by an IQ test. The Martian asks about the things one has to know and is told that an intelligent person should know what the word "belfry" means, who wrote *The Iliad,* how to multiply 8 X 3, and what a mountain and a lake have in common.

The second Martian also searches for the key to the human mind. This Martian orbits the globe and sees some amazing spectacles: sailors on the South Seas, dancers in Bali, yogis in India, computer programers, tennis players, concert pianists, productive peasants, and resourceful presidents. These observations lead the second Martian to decide that people on the planet Earth have a variety of mental processes—perhaps even different kinds of minds—and the Martian labels them *intelligences.*

The psychologist Howard Gardner (1983) uses this anecdote to introduce his theory of multiple intelligences. He observes that when we think of someone as smart, we usually refer to linguistic and logical-mathematical intelligences. But Gardner contends that there are five other kinds of intelligence that are equally important: spatial, musical, bodily-kinesthetic, and two forms of personal intelligence—interpersonal, knowing how to deal with others, and intrapersonal, knowledge of oneself.

The relative importance of the seven intelligences has shifted over time and varies from culture to culture. For instance, in a hunting society, it is more important to be quick, agile, and well coordinated than to be able to add and subtract rapidly. Among the Japanese, interpersonal intelligence—the ability to work well in groups and arrive at joint decisions—assumes critical importance. In the Caroline Islands of Micronesia, a Puluwat boy casts off in the dead of night, using his knowledge of waves, winds, and stars to reach any of hundreds of islands simply by fitting his observation to the spatial map in his head. And in Boston, an adolescent youngster struggling in a remedial reading course uses data from satellite photos in a newspaper to predict the week's weather.

Gardner not only carves up the mind into separate faculties, he also argues that the separate intelligences are located in different areas of

functioning in our society. But today calculators have made these skills less important. The ability to do mathematical computations on paper is typically of little value in getting you a good job. However, knowing how to use electronic equipment is of considerable value. Consequently, Sternberg contends that on the contextual level, intelligence consists of an ability to cope with one's environment.

The second level—the *experiential*—consists of capabilities that develop as we engage in various tasks. Here two general skills come into play: the ability to deal with novel situations (cleverness) and the ability to process information automatically with little conscious attention (expertise). As people become more accomplished in solving a problem, they can solve new but related problems rather quickly. By training themselves to solve familiar problems by rote, they free their minds for other problems.

The third level—*componential*—consists of three types of processes. The first type—*metacomponents* —are the higher order or executive processes that you use to plan what you are going to do, monitor what you are doing, and evaluate what you have done. Deciding on a strategy for solving a mathematical problem or organizing a term paper are illustrations of metacomponents at work. The second type of processes are *performance components.* Whereas metacomponents entail deciding what you will do, performance components center on what you actually do. Accordingly, the actual steps you use in the brain. Gardner observes that when a person suffers damage to the brain through a stroke or tumor, all abilities do not break down equally. Likewise, his work with gifted children shows that youngsters who are precocious in one area are often unremarkable in others. And idiots savants, otherwise retarded people, occasionally exhibit extraordinary ability in one area, usually mathematical calculation. All this leads Gardner to suggest that the much-maligned intelligence quotient (IQ) ought to be replaced with an "intellectual profile." Actually, Gardner is not saying anything new. Psychologists such as Arthur Jensen, Phillip Vernon, and Hans Eysenck have claimed for many years that intelligence consists of a *hierarchy* of skills, all of which are correlated but not perfectly so. Thus, humans have both a general intelligence and a set of related intelligences.

Gardner's seven intelligences include some talents that most psychologists would not want to call intelligence. Gardner's critics claim that what he is really talking about is talents, not intelligences. They have problems calling "intelligence" what people normally label as human virtues (Scarr, 1985a). His critics acknowledge that there are many human virtues that are not sufficiently rewarded in our society, including talent in music, dance, painting, and interper-

sonal relationships. But they question whether labeling them intelligence does justice to the research and theories dealing with intelligence or personality.

Dr. Howard Gardner and a young research participant in a study of artistic creativity. *(Rick Friedman/Black Star)*

solving an arithmetic or analogy problem, whether in everyday life or on an IQ test, are examples of performance components in action. The third type of processes are *knowledge-acquisition components*. You use these processes in learning new material; for instance, in learning how to solve a given type of arithmetic or analogy problem. Many componential processes consist of practical or tacit knowledge —those extremely important things that you "often don't know you know" and that you are not taught in school. Illustrations of these types of skills are contained in the Sternberg test found in Figure 8.1. They often become apparent in the processing of information, a matter to which we now turn our attention.

Intelligence as Cognitive Information Processing

Most of the approaches to intelligence that we have discussed so far focus on the search for "abilities" —whether general or specific—that distinguish among people in their performance on various tasks. These approaches assume that there is some property—intelligence—that *really* exists in human beings and that, if psychologists were good enough scientists, they could hope to identify and understand "it." Recently, a number of psychologists have taken a somewhat different tack (Sternberg, 1979b, 1981; Hunt, 1983; Pellegrino, 1985). In their opinion, the key to understanding our mental capabilities

a   b

c   d

FIGURE 8.1 Lovers and strangers. Robert J. Sternberg says that one form of intelligence is the ability to read body language and other nonverbal cues. Test your sensitivity to them by indicating which of the couples in the photographs are romantically involved and which are merely posing together. Answers are on page 266. *(Courtesy, Dr. Robert J. Sternberg)*

lies not in the answers we give on IQ tests but in how we arrive at them. Hence, rather than explaining mental behavior in terms of the outcomes of thinking, they seek to identify the processes involved in problem solving. They study how people mentally represent and process information. The step-by-step mental operations people use in tackling an intellectual task is termed **information processing.**

Consider the information-processing steps involved in the following analogy problem (Sternberg, 1979a): *Washington* is to *one* as *Lincoln* is to: (a) *five*, (b) *ten*, (c) *fifteen*, (d) *fifty*. Sternberg suggests that solving this sort of analogy requires several steps or *components*. First, you must *encode* the various items of the analogy, identifying each one and retrieving from long-term memory those attributes that may be relevant to the solution. For example, you may encode for *Washington* the following attributes: president, pictured on a piece of currency, and Revolutionary War hero. Possible encodings for *Lincoln* include: president, pictured on a piece of currency, and Civil War hero. Encoding is a critical first step.

information processing: The step-by-step mental operations people use in tackling an intellectual task.

In this illustration, failure to encode either man as having his portrait on a piece of currency will preclude solving the analogy.

Next, you must *infer* the relationship between the first two elements of the analogy: *Washington* and *one*. You may infer that the *one* has reference to Washington's being the first president or to his being portrayed on the $1 bill. Should you make the first link but not the second, you will be unable to solve the problem.

In the next step, you must turn to the second half of the analogy, the part having to do with *Lincoln*. You must *map* the higher-order relationship that links *Washington* to *Lincoln*. Here you may mentally note that both were presidents, both are pictured on currency, and both were war heroes. Should you fail to connect the two men as portraits on currency, you will fail to find the correct solution.

Next, you must *apply* the relation inferred between the first two items (*Washington* and *one*) and the third item (*Lincoln*) to each of the four possible answers. Washington is portrayed on the $1 bill and Lincoln on the $5 bill. However, you may not recognize the relationship because of a failure in application (you may mistakenly recall Lincoln as depicted on the $10 bill).

Finally, you *respond* with the answer that seems most appropriate. If earlier you had failed to encode *Washington* and *Lincoln* as portraits on currency but did encode them as presidents, you may seek the answer in the ordinal positions of the presidents. You may recall that Lincoln was the sixteenth president but, if not entirely certain, select *fifteen* as the response, assuming your memory to be slightly amiss.

The best performers on intelligence tests are not necessarily those who are fastest at executing each of the steps in problem solving (Sternberg, 1979a, 1984a). The higher scorers tend to be those people who spend more time "encoding" the problems. Because they are more likely to have at their disposal the relevant information that they later need to solve the problem, they can carry out the later operations more efficiently. Experts actually devote more time to encoding a physics problem than a beginner does, and they are repaid by an increased likelihood of finding the solution. Higher intelligence, then, seems to be associated with the faster execution of some components and the slower execution of others.

Intelligence as Brain Processes

Finally, other psychologists (Eysenck, 1985; Jensen, 1985) believe that intelligent behavior relies on neurological efficiency. Brains that process information reliably and quickly underlie what we call high intelligence. Low intelligence results from erratic or slow neural transmission.

By studying brain-wave responses to flashes of lights (evoked potentials), Hans Eysenck and his colleagues find a moderately high association between the reliability or regularity of brain waves and IQ test scores.

Arthur Jensen (1985) uses a choice-reaction time task to test intelligence. People must move quickly to push one button, or one of three, or one of eight to turn off a light that randomly appears. More time is required to respond to one of eight possible lights than to one of three or one of one. Jensen finds that people who respond more quickly to the choice-reaction time task have higher IQ test scores.

Neural efficiency and reliability must underlie intelligent behavior (see Chapter 2). But brain processes are not all there is to intelligent behavior.

Individual Differences in Intelligence

People differ in a great many respects—fortunately. A population that contains people with diverse talents adapts best to the environment. The distribution of skills benefits society by allowing people to work and live together in interdependent, socially organized ways. For instance, if you had to build your own home in its entirety, the result would undoubtedly be rather primitive. Instead, you can call on the services of a specialized architect, builder, carpenter, mason, and plumber. And so it is with the vast array of other human services that have come to characterize modern societies. Consequently, a well-adapted society is one that fosters diversity of intelligence (Scarr and Carter-Saltzman, 1983).

Both genetic and environmental factors are responsible for the intellectual variations observable among people (see Chapter 2). But to ask whether heredity or environment is more important to intellectual functioning is like asking whether fuel or oxygen is more necessary in making a fire. Indeed, if your hereditary potential were somehow annulled, you would immediately cease to exist. By the same token, if you were deprived of all environment, you would die (Woodworth, 1941).

Some people erroneously conclude that if genetic differences account for some portion of the intellectual differences among people, then genes have fixed each person's intelligence at a certain level and there is nothing that can be done about it. However, in point of fact, all behavioral characteristics have a considerable range of reaction in their development: the behavior that actually develops is only one of a number of possible forms that could have developed (Scarr and Kidd, 1983). In this sense, then, the development of competence is not precoded in the genes, only to emerge with maturation. Genes can only instruct cells to make a protein. It is a long chain of physiological events that leads to brain development and individual differences in intelligence. At each step, environmental differences can also play a role.

The process by which children come to differ in intellectual competence entails a variety of relationships between their heredity and their environment (Plomin, DeFries, and Loehlin, 1977; Scarr, 1981b; Scarr and McCartney, 1983). The first, the *passive relationship*, is one in which parents give their children both genes and an environment that are favorable (or unfavorable) to the development of a particular capability. For instance, parents who are gifted in verbal abilities are also likely to provide their children with an enriched verbal environment. They are more likely to carry on conversations with their children and to provide them with books and other reading matter. This combination of good genetic background and enriched environment produces a double dose of advantage—a "double whammy" effect.

The second, the *evocative relationship*, is one that derives from the fact that people respond differently to others with different genetic temperaments and dispositions. Socially engaging children typically evoke from other people more social interaction than do passive, sober children. Likewise, teachers frequently recognize the superior intellectual abilities of certain students and furnish them with additional and challenging materials to maximize their talents.

The third, the *active relationship*, is one in which people seek out the environment that they find compatible with their temperament and genetic propensities. For example, bright children often seek out people and settings that intellectually challenge them. And sociable children search for playmates and even create imaginary playmates if real ones are not at hand.

As pointed out in Chapter 2, one way to find out what makes people differ is to undertake family resemblance studies. One approach studies children who were adopted at birth and reared by foster parents. In turn, these children can be compared with those reared by their biological parents. In this way the effects of environment can be isolated. Children adopted in infancy share only a home environment with their genetically unrelated parents, whereas children reared by their biological parents share genes as well as home environment. The studies agree that children who are biological offspring are more similar to their parents in intelligence than adopted children are to their adoptive parents. Furthermore, the adopted children's IQ scores are similar to those of their natural parents, with whom they have never lived (Horn, 1983, 1986). These findings are evidence for the importance of genetic variability among people.

Another way to study the effects of genetic variability on intelligence is to compare identical and same-sex fraternal twins. Recall that identical twins are genetically the same person, whereas fraternal twins are no more alike than ordinary brothers and sisters—that is, they have about half of their genes in common. The finding from many twin studies is that identical twins' intellectual similarity far exceeds that of fraternal twins, even though the children in both cases are the same age and sex and are reared in the same household (Scarr and Carter-Saltzman, 1983).

Still another type of family resemblance study involves separated twins (McGue et al., 1984). Of particular interest to scientists are pairs of identical twins who have been reared apart. Chapter 2 discussed the twin research of Thomas J. Bouchard, Jr., and his associates at the University of Minnesota. You will recall that these researchers have found remarkable similarities between the twins in their scores on various ability tests. And their brain-wave tracings show no greater differences than do tracings taken from the same person at different times.

Answers to Figure 8.1: *(a)* real, *(b)* fake, *(c)* fake, *(d)* real. Sternberg finds that real couples, as compared with fake ones, tend to be more relaxed, to lean more toward one another, to stand closer together, to touch more, and to be similar in dress, age, and socioeconomic status.

From the studies of adopted and biological siblings and from the studies of identical and fraternal twins, it can be concluded that among white Americans and Europeans, about half of the variability in IQ test scores is due to genetic variability and about half to differences in environment. There have been too few studies of other populations to reach any conclusions about genetic differences in their IQ scores.

CREATIVITY

Like intelligence, creativity is a human quality that is commonly valued. And like intelligence, it serves an important adaptive function. Life demands that you continually fit yourself to your environmental surroundings. Creativity allows you to do so. But even more, it permits you to change your environment—indeed, to create new environments that better meet and express your needs. Underlying creativity is the notion that there is no particular virtue to doing things the way they have been done in the past. At times it may simply consist of turning up something that everyone else more or less sees but merely takes for granted. For example, consider that making right shoes different from left shoes was an idea first thought of only a little more than a hundred years ago.

Creativity is sometimes an elusive concept. Is an artist's wrapping of a public monument creative? *(Leonard Speier)*

Conceptions of Creativity

Most people have a pretty good idea of what they mean by the terms "intelligence" and "creativity." Intelligence seems to imply quick-wittedness in learning the predictable. In contrast, creativity is conceived of as entailing the production of unexpected ideas or materials, or their combination in some novel but comprehensible way. Thus **creativity** usually means the occurrence of original and useful responses.

Yet this definition leaves much to be desired. It does not specify what is original, since novelty is frequently more a matter of degree than of kind. For instance, glass was unquestionably an original invention, but how should its elaboration in costume jewelry and windowpanes be defined? And the question of what is useful is subjective. As Carl Rogers (1961) observes, one person may discover a new way to relieve pain while another may devise a more subtle form of torture for political prisoners. Although both these actions may be considered original, their social value is quite different. In fact, there are those who assert that creativity is not in itself an activity or even a process, but simply a "medal" that society pins on a public product. For instance, the social psychologist Teresa M. Amabile (1983) contends that creativity is a property of products, rather than of people. She says that a product is creative to

---

creativity: The occurrence of original and useful responses.

the extent that observers, familiar with the domain of activity, agree that it is so.

By virtue of the vague and subjective connotations associated with creativity, some psychologists, including J. P. Guilford (1959b, 1967), have proposed a somewhat different approach. Guilford distinguishes between convergent and divergent thinking processes. *Convergent thinking* requires integrative and focused responses; *divergent thinking*, fluent and flexible responses.

Much education promotes convergent thinking, by encouraging students to find the "right" answer to a problem. Such an approach assumes that there is but one correct answer. A task involving convergent thinking may ask you to provide an answer to a multiple-choice question or the solution to an arithmetic problem. In contrast, divergent thinking calls for speculation, imagination, and invention. Underlying divergent-oriented tasks is the assumption that there is more than one way in which to solve a problem. A task involving divergent thinking may ask you to list as many uses as possible for some item, such as a paper clip, a sock, or a book.

Guilford considers divergent thinking to be more characteristic of highly creative people than of less creative people. Research by other psychologists reveals that the observation has merit (Harrington, Block, and Block, 1983). However, still other psychologists point out that effective thinking requires both types of activity (Wallach, 1970, 1971; Kogan and Pankove, 1974). The first phase of problem solving calls for divergent thinking—the consideration of a variety of paths to a goal. The second phase demands convergent thinking—the process of reducing the array of possible solutions until one answer is produced. In sum, the creative process entails both responses: the first, to perceive the possibilities in a situation; the second, to settle on one possibility.

Intelligence and Creativity

It is often assumed that high intelligence and creativity go hand in hand, but firm conclusions have remained elusive. For one thing, psychologists have had difficulty agreeing on what intelligence is and what creativity is. For another, they have had difficulty finding suitable measures of each. Many tests of creativity have been so diffuse and global that they do not differentiate among various types of talents.

Finally, tests of intelligence and creativity have often been so much alike that they have ended up measuring the same attributes (Wallach and Kogan, 1965; Wallach, 1970).

Despite these difficulties, a mounting body of evidence suggests that high intelligence does *not* ensure creativity. Indeed, researchers find that differences between above-average and very high scores on intelligence tests have at best only a low association with creativity (Wallach and Kogan, 1965; Moran et al., 1983; Kershner and Ledger, 1985). But, while high intelligence does not guarantee creativity, low intelligence seems to work against it. For the most part, educational psychologists agree that an above-average, although not necessarily exceptional, level of intelligence is essential for creative achievement (MacKinnon, 1975). On the basis of his studies of history's renowned creators and leaders over the last century, the psychologist Dean Keith Simonton (1984) concludes that too much brainpower may even get in the way of creativity. His studies suggest that the optimal IQ for creativity is about nineteen points above the average of people in a given field. Moreover, many famous scientists, philosophers, writers, artists, and composers never complete college. The difficulty does not seem to be with knowledge itself. Rather, the danger in education comes from picking up rote methods for doing things that blind individuals to offbeat but creative solutions.

Characteristics of Creative Individuals

Few unusually creative people have bland personalities. Researchers at the Institute of Personality Assessment and Research (located on the Berkeley campus of the University of California) have studied the characteristics of creative people. They find, for instance, that the productive scientist is typically a person who has a strong and forceful personality, possesses considerable ego strength, is emotionally stable, resists conformity pressures, is self-sufficient and self-directing, has a strong need for independence, and enjoys abstract thinking (Taylor and Barron, 1963; Barron, 1969). These people tend to be distant and detached in their interpersonal relationships, preferring to deal with things and abstractions rather than with people.

The institute's researchers find that highly creative people describe themselves and are rated by others as inventive, independent, uninhibited, insightful, versatile, determined, enthusiastic, and industrious. In contrast, less creative people tend to emphasize their good character, their concern for other people, their reliability, and their conventionality (MacKinnon, 1962, 1975; Schaefer, 1969).

Psychologists have also examined the family backgrounds of creative people (Feldman, 1980). It seems that creative people do not spend their childhood years basking in parental love and warmth. Cool and even detached relationships frequently prevail between parents and their creative sons and daughters (Siegelman, 1973). One speculation is that this type of child rearing encourages independent thinking and action in children. Another interpretation is that creative children do not evoke warmth from others.

A team of University of Chicago researchers has investigated the backgrounds of one hundred exceptionally talented individuals between seventeen and thirty-five years of age: concert pianists, Olympic swimmers, tennis players, and research mathematicians (Pines, 1982b). These creative people immersed themselves in a world of music, sports, or intellectual activity at an early age. In many cases, the parents were involved in the activity, and the children thus learned its "language" easily. Moreover, the parents believed in and fostered a strong work ethic. Finally, the parents provided the child with special training and teachers. The Chicago researchers had anticipated finding that talented people showed early signs of special ability and were then provided with special attention and instruction. Instead, they found that the process seemed to work the other way around. The children blossomed because they had received special attention and instruction.

Creativity appears to be a mix of abilities and traits (Perkins, 1981). Five components stand out. First, as noted earlier, above-average intelligence is essential. Second, a problem-finding approach to tasks and a reluctance to accept quick and ready answers underlie creative thought. Third, creative people place a high value on originality and are imbued with a strong work ethic. Fourth, creative individuals believe both in their own capabilities and in the possibility of attaining new outcomes. And fifth, creative people attack problems in effective ways.

Assessed in terms of these components, unusually creative people differ from less creative people more in degree than in kind. A good analogy is afforded by extraordinary athletic achievement. Considerably more is involved in athletic excellence than just a person's innate abilities. Other factors—motivation, training, and tactics—are also important. Further, the abilities associated with athletic achievement do not substantially differ from the abilities that get the vast majority of people through everyday life. Strength, agility, and coordination are familiar aspects of a good many daily tasks.

Since the abilities associated with athletic achievement do not seem to differ in kind from the perceptual and motor abilities that most people possess, it does not seem necessary to advance a special explanation for them. You view the weight lifter's strength as similar to your own strength, but greater. The sprinter's speed resembles your own speed, but is much faster. Uncommon creative ability allows much the same explanation as does athletic excellence. Creativity, then, entails unusual versions of such familiar mental operations as remembering, reasoning, and problem solving (Perkins, 1981).

Social Factors in Creativity

Social and environmental factors also influence people's creativity (Amabile, 1983). Even seemingly insignificant factors can be detrimental or conducive to creativity in some people. For instance, in a letter to a friend the Russian composer Tchaikovsky (1906) described the devastating effect that simple interruptions had on his work. The poet Stephen Spender (1952) reports that in order for them to write well, Auden had to drink tea constantly, de la Mare had to smoke, and Schiller liked to have the scent of rotten apples about the room. The social environment may also have a critical impact. Albert Einstein (1949:17) described the stifling effects that the external constraints imposed by formal education had on his early scientific creativity: "The hitch in this was the fact that one had to cram all this stuff into one's mind for the examinations, whether one liked it or not. This coercion had such a deterring effect upon me that, after I had passed the final examination, I found the consideration of any scientific problem distasteful for an entire year."

L'art pour l'art—art for art's sake—was a rallying cry for artists during the Romantic era of art and literature in the late eighteenth and early nineteenth centuries. The phrase sums up the motivation that many people have for carrying out their creative activities. Research suggests that people are more creative when they are working to please themselves than when they are attempting to gain recognition and rewards from others (Amabile, 1983). When they are inspired by their own interests and enjoyment, people are more likely to explore unlikely paths, take risks, and in the end, produce something unique and useful. When their goals are imposed on them by others, or when they are goaded by lust for money or fear of firing, their creativity withers. The Nobel prize–winning physicist Arthur Schawlow confirms these findings. When asked about creativity, he responded, "The labor of love aspect is important. The successful scientists are often not the most talented, but the ones who are just impelled by curiosity—they've got to know what the answer is" (quoted by Bales, 1984:28).

Any number of psychologists suggest that it may be easier to stifle creativity through the social environment than it is to stimulate it (Amabile, 1983; Tyler, 1983; Bales, 1984). Many notable scientists arrive at much the same conclusion. Dr. Salvador E. Luria of the Massachusetts Institute of Technology, mentor to several famous scientists and himself a Nobel laureate, says, "The most important thing is to leave a good person alone." Adds Dr. Mahlon B. Hoagland, scientific director of the Worcester Foundation for Experimental Biology, "I've often said that running a scientific institution is a lot like running an artist colony. The best an administrator can do is leave people alone to do what they want to do" (quoted by Haney, 1985:C-1). In sum, creativity is most likely to emerge when we *allow* it, rather than when we attempt to prompt or produce it.

PSYCHOLOGICAL ASSESSMENT

To measure creativity and intelligence, psychologists need assessment tools they can trust. Measurement is a central ingredient in all scientific endeavors. In most cases, physical measurement proceeds in a fairly straightforward manner. Physical measures of light waves, volume, mass, and momentum are well established and accepted. They are indispensable tools for studying the length of ultraviolet light, the volume of a liquid, the mass of electrons, and the momentum of falling bodies. Measurement likewise finds applications in engineering.

Psychologists are concerned with measurement for many of the same reasons as physical scientists are. However, there is considerably more controversy in psychology about how concepts should be measured and about the precision of the measurements—and even about the concepts themselves. As we have observed, intelligence is a concept, or psychological construct, that has no universally agreed on definition among psychologists. As you might expect, lack of an agreed on definition of intelligence leads to all sorts of problems in measuring intelligence (Green, 1981).

Despite these limitations, psychological measurement—and especially testing—has constituted a central focus of much psychological work. Most research has depended on tools of assessment. But there have also been very practical reasons for testing. As long as it is impractical to give everyone a try at every school curriculum or every job, it is important that there be some shortcuts, some valid ways of selecting people for various environmental niches. Also required is information that will permit society to fashion environmental niches that better meet the needs of people. Psychological testing provides a mechanism for pursuing these goals.

By way of illustration, consider the testing of children by the schools (Scarr, 1981b; Sherman and Robinson, 1982). Ideally, educational institutions sort and select children into different programs in the interests of both the children and the larger society. Most people realize that any child cannot be made into any adult, and it is hopelessly silly to pretend otherwise. For whatever genetic and environmental reasons, children do have different talents. Hence the schools have the responsibility for matching a child to a curriculum *and* a curriculum to a child.

Admittedly, there are abuses and misuses of tests. Research has shown that children who were misclassified into vocational rather than academic programs do not gain intellectually as much as do children with similar abilities who were placed in academic programs (Härnquist, 1968; Husén, 1969). Findings such as these highlight that psychologists and educators must take care to use tests in the *interest* of children. They must ask the right questions about the right matters and then make the proper inferences from what they observe on the tests. Such appraisals are useful to school personnel in designing appropriate interventions for improving children's performance and school experience. Tests developed by psychologists have helped innumerable teachers to identify youngsters whose special skills and talents were concealed by shyness, cultural barriers, or "rebelliousness."

Basic Characteristics of Tests

All tests have one characteristic in common that makes them both fascinating and remarkably practical: they promise to make it possible to find out a great deal about a person in a very short time. The justification for using a test to make decisions about a person's future depends on whether a decision based on test scores would be fairer and more accurate than one based on other criteria. The fairness and usefulness of a test depend on several factors: its reliability, its validity, and the way its norms were established.

Test Reliability

The term **reliability** refers to a test's consistency —its ability to yield the same results under a variety of different circumstances. There are three basic ways of determining a test's reliability. First, if a person retakes the test, or takes a similar test, within a short time after the first testing, does the individual receive approximately the same score? To use an analogy, if you take your temperature five times in five minutes and the thermometer registers readings varying from 94 degrees to 106 degrees, you will have little confidence in the instrument. Nor would you feel easy with the measurements of a house taken by an elastic ruler. You want an instrument that yields a consistent measurement of the same thing —a criterion called *test-retest reliability* (see Figure 8.2).

The second measure of reliability is whether the test yields the same results when scored by different people. If both your teacher and a teaching assistant score an essay test that you have written, and one gives you a B while the other gives you a D, then you have reason to complain about the graders' reliability. The score you receive depends more on the grader than on your paper. On a reliable test, your

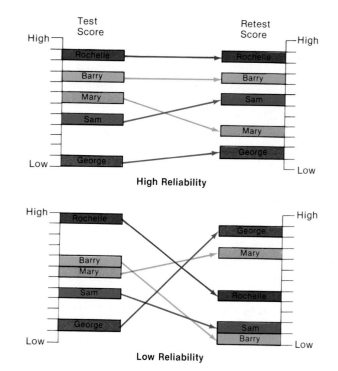

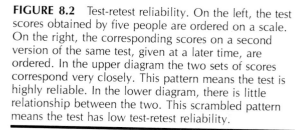

FIGURE 8.2 Test-retest reliability. On the left, the test scores obtained by five people are ordered on a scale. On the right, the corresponding scores on a second version of the same test, given at a later time, are ordered. In the upper diagram the two sets of scores correspond very closely. This pattern means the test is highly reliable. In the lower diagram, there is little relationship between the two. This scrambled pattern means the test has low test-retest reliability.

score would be similar no matter who graded your paper—a criterion called *interobserver reliability*.

One final way of determining a test's reliability is to find out whether, if you divide the test in half (for example, odd-numbered items versus even-numbered items) and score each half separately, the two scores are approximately the same. If a test is supposed to measure one quality in a person (for example, reading comprehension or administrative ability), then it should not result in the person's scoring high on one random part and low on the other. This kind of reliability is called *internal consistency*.

reliability: The ability of a test to give the same results under a variety of different circumstances.

In checking tests for reliability, psychologists are trying to prevent chance factors from influencing your score. All kinds of irrelevant matters can interfere with a test. If you are depressed because your pet goldfish is sick, or angry that you had to miss your favorite television program to take the exam, or if a broken radiator has raised the temperature in the testing room to 114 degrees, you will probably score lower than if you are reasonably relaxed, comfortable, and content.

Test Validity

A test cannot be valid without being reliable, but it may be reliable and still not be valid. **Validity** is the ability of a test to measure what it is supposed to measure (see Figure 8.3). For example, a test that consists primarily of vocabulary lists will not measure all aptitudes for engineering. Similarly, a test on American history will not measure general learning ability.

Determining the validity of a test is more complex than assessing its reliability. One of the chief methods for measuring validity is to find out how well a test *predicts* performance. For example, let us say that a group of psychologists designs a test to measure teaching ability. They ask questions about teaching methods, attitudes toward students, and so on. But do the people who score high on this test really make good teachers?

Suppose the test makers decide that a good way to check the validity of the test is to find out how much a teacher's students improve in reading in one year. If the students of those teachers who scored high on the test improve more in their reading skills than the students of those teachers who scored low on the test, the test may be considered valid. It identifies good teachers. School boards may then adopt it as one tool to use in deciding whom to hire to teach in their schools.

But what if teachers who are good at improving reading skills are poor at teaching other skills? It may be that this test measures talent for raising reading levels, not general teaching ability. This problem is the kind of difficulty psychologists encounter in trying to assess the validity of a test. As

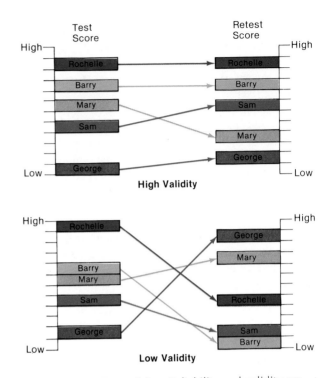

FIGURE 8.3 Test validity. Reliability and validity are assessed in exactly the same way, except that the assessment of validity requires that test scores be compared to some other measure of behavior. The lower diagram might represent the comparison of scores on the "head size" test of intelligence (on the left) with school grades (on the right). The upper diagram might represent the result of comparing Stanford-Binet scores with school grades. The Stanford-Binet is a valid test for predicting school grades; the head size measurement is not. The head size measurement is highly reliable but not a valid predictor of school grades.

the example shows, nothing can be said about a test's validity until the *purpose* of the test is absolutely clear.

Establishing Norms

When psychologists are designing a test to be used in a variety of schools, businesses, clinics, or other settings, they usually are interested in how a person compares with others in a group. The test is given to a large representative sample of the group to be

---

validity: The ability of a test to measure what it is intended to measure.

measured—for example, sixth graders, army privates, engineers, or perhaps the population as a whole. **Norms** are then established on the basis of the scores achieved by the group as a whole. They are standards of comparison. For instance, we may rank those who took a test on the basis of their scores from highest to lowest. If we give students a particular vocabulary test, we may find that Jerry can perform better than 85 percent of a national sample of sixth graders.

Test norms let us answer a number of questions:

- How does a person's test performance compare with that of other people with whom we wish to make a comparison?

- How does a person's performance on one test compare with the person's performance on another test?

- How does a person's performance on one form of the test compare with the person's performance on another form of the test that was administered at an earlier time?

Such comparisons make it possible to make certain predictions about a person's probable success in some area, to diagnose the person's strengths and weaknesses, and to measure growth in some capacity or skill.

In summary, when you take a test and obtain your score, you should consider the following questions in evaluating the results:

- Was the test a reliable one? If you took the same test or a similar test again, would you receive a similar score?

- Was the test a valid one? Does your performance on the test reflect your performance in the subject the test is designed to measure?

- How were the test's norms established? In other words, what group of people are you being compared to?

Intelligence Testing

Attempts to identify the gifted have a long history (*Psychology Today*, 1984). As early as 2200 B.C. the Chinese were using examinations to find talented and competent people to fill key government posts. They began the search at the local level, with the winner advancing to regional and national competition. Some 3 percent of the national finalists became mandarins, eligible for ruling positions. The examinations tested proficiency in music, archery, horsemanship, writing, arithmetic, and the rites and ceremonies of Chinese life.

In contemporary America, tests also play an important role in determining which people will be accorded various opportunities and positions. Among the most widely used—and widely disputed —tests are those that are designed to measure "intelligence" and yield an "IQ" score. Although there are over two hundred IQ measures available, only a few are widely used. This section describes some of the major intelligence tests and presents some of the issues that surround them.

Types of Intelligence Tests

As noted earlier in the chapter, the French psychologist Alfred Binet was the first to develop a useful intelligence test. In 1904, Binet was asked by the Paris school authorities to devise a means of picking out "slow learners" so that they could be placed in special classes from which they might better profit. Binet was unable to define intelligence, but he believed it was reflected in such things as the ability to make commonsense judgments, to tell the meanings of words, and to solve problems and puzzles. Binet assumed that whatever intelligence was, it increased with age. Consequently, older children had more intelligence than younger children. Therefore, in selecting items for his test he included only items on which older children did better than younger children. By asking the same questions of many children, Binet was able to determine the average age at which children could be expected to be able to answer a particular question. For example, he discovered that certain questions could be answered by

---

norms: Standards of comparison for test results developed by giving the test to large, well-defined groups of people.

most twelve-year-olds but not by most eleven-year-olds. If a child of eleven, or even nine, could answer these questions, the child was said to have a *mental age* of twelve. If a child of twelve could answer the nine-year-old-level questions but not the questions for ten-year-olds and eleven-year-olds, the child was said to have a mental age of nine. Thus a slow learner was one who had a *mental age* that was less than his or her *chronological age*. In sum, the original purpose of intelligence tests was to provide a more objective and reliable supplement to a teacher's subjective impression, in order to help students who were doing poorly.

The Stanford-Binet. Binet's intelligence test has been revised many times since he developed it. The Binet test currently in widespread use in the United States is a revision created at Stanford University: the Stanford-Binet Intelligence Test (Terman and Merrill, 1973). A new, thoroughly revised edition of the Stanford-Binet test was published in 1986. The new test consists of fifteen scales that are appropriate from the second birthday though adulthood. The scales are intended to assess a three-level, hierarchical model of intelligence. The first level is general reasoning ability. The second level includes three broad factors—crystallized abilities, fluid-analytic abilities, and short-term memory. The three abilities tested on the third level are verbal reasoning, quantitative reasoning, and abstract/visual reasoning. Nine of the scales are based on item types carried over from the preceding version of the test; the other six scales are based on new types of items.

The advantages of the new version over the old include broader coverage of cognitive skills, greater flexibility in administration, higher reliability and precision in scoring, and the opportunity for more detailed diagnostic assessments.

People are tested one at a time (see Figure 8.4).

The examiner must carry out standardized instructions—at the same time putting the person at ease, getting him or her to pay attention, and encouraging him or her to try as hard as possible.

In the final scoring, the mental age indicates how high a level the person has reached. If the test performance level is as high as the average twelve-year-old's, the person has a mental age of twelve. The **IQ,** or **intelligence quotient,** is called a quotient because it was originally computed by dividing mental age by actual (chronological) age and multiplying the result by 100 to eliminate decimals. (A nine-year-old with a mental age of twelve would have an IQ of 133.)

The Wechsler tests. Two other frequently used intelligence tests are the Wechsler Intelligence Scale for Children (Revised), or WISC-R, and the Wechsler Adult Intelligence Scale (Revised), or WAIS-R (Wechsler, 1958, 1975). The Wechsler tests differ from the Stanford-Binet in several important ways. For example, the Wechsler tests place more emphasis on performance tasks (such as doing puzzles) than the Stanford-Binet does, so that people who are not particularly skilled in the use of words will not be as likely to receive low IQ scores (see Figure 8.5).

Moreover, in addition to yielding one overall score, the Wechsler tests yield scores in several areas—vocabulary, information, arithmetic, picture arrangement, and so on. These ratings are used to compute separate IQ scores for verbal and performance abilities. This type of scoring provides a more detailed picture of the individual's strengths and weaknesses than does a single score.

Group tests. The Wechsler and Stanford-Binet tests, because they are given individually by a professional tester, are costly and time-consuming to administer. During World War I, when the United

---

intelligence quotient (QUO-shent) (IQ): Originally, a measure of a person's mental development obtained by dividing his or her mental age (the score achieved on a standardized intelligence test) by his or her chronological age and multiplying by 100; now, any standardized measure of intelligence based on a scale in which 100 is defined to be average.

FIGURE 8.4 Two tests of the Stanford-Binet Intelligence Scale being administered to a little boy. Both these tests are ones that would be easily passed by him unless he were severely retarded. *(left)* The examiner has built a tower of four blocks and has told the child, "You make one like this." The average two-year-old is able to build the tower. Three-year-olds are asked to copy a three-block bridge. *(right)* The examiner shows the child a card with six small objects attached to it and says, "See all these things? Show me the dog," and so on. The average two-year-old can point to the correct object as they are named. *(Photos by John Oldenkamp with permission of the Houghton Mifflin Company from Terman and Merrill Stanford-Binet Intelligence Scale)*

States Army found that it had to test nearly 2 million men, and quickly, individual testing was a luxury the army could not afford. Thus paper-and-pencil intelligence tests, which could be given to large groups of people at the same time, were developed. Current group IQ tests, such as the Armed Forces General Classification Test, have proved to be convenient and effective. They are used extensively in schools, employment offices, and many other settings.

The Uses and Meaning of IQ Scores

In general, the norms for intelligence tests are established in such a way that most people score near 100. Out of one hundred people, seventeen will score above 115 and seventeen will score below 85. About three in one hundred score above 130, and three score below 70.

What do these scores mean? What do the tests measure? Psychologists agree that IQ test results do not provide a measure of unlearned skills (Reschly, 1981). They agree that all skills sampled by tests are learned, if not explicitly taught (Scarr-Salapatek, 1977). IQ scores are useful when related to school achievement: they are quite accurate in predicting which people will do well in schools, colleges, and universities. Critics of IQ testing do not question this

predictive ability. They do wonder, however, whether such tests actually measure "intelligence." Most psychologists agree that intelligence is the ability to acquire new ideas and new behavior. Is success in school a real indication of such ability? Generally, IQ tests measure the ability to solve certain types of problems. But they do not directly measure the ability to pose those problems or to question the validity of problems set by others. The IQ test was developed to predict academic performance. If we want a measure that predicts life success, occupational success, marital success, or something else, we will have to invent a different test.

The Controversy over IQ

The history of IQ testing can be told as one of psychology's greatest achievements (Herrnstein, 1973) or as one of its most shameful (Kamin, 1974; Lewontin, Rose, and Kamin, 1984). Proponents of tests cite the tests' statistical and predictive virtues. Opponents criticize the tests' role in perpetuating social and economic injustice. Much of the controversy centers on one question: To what extent do either genetic differences or environmental inequalities explain the fact that two people receive different scores on intelligence tests? This debate becomes particularly heated when researchers consider differ-

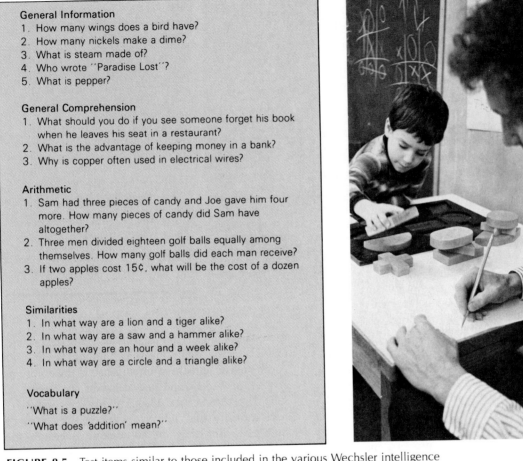

General Information
1. How many wings does a bird have?
2. How many nickels make a dime?
3. What is steam made of?
4. Who wrote ''Paradise Lost''?
5. What is pepper?

General Comprehension
1. What should you do if you see someone forget his book when he leaves his seat in a restaurant?
2. What is the advantage of keeping money in a bank?
3. Why is copper often used in electrical wires?

Arithmetic
1. Sam had three pieces of candy and Joe gave him four more. How many pieces of candy did Sam have altogether?
2. Three men divided eighteen golf balls equally among themselves. How many golf balls did each man receive?
3. If two apples cost 15¢, what will be the cost of a dozen apples?

Similarities
1. In what way are a lion and a tiger alike?
2. In what way are a saw and a hammer alike?
3. In what way are an hour and a week alike?
4. In what way are a circle and a triangle alike?

Vocabulary
''What is a puzzle?''
''What does 'addition' mean?''

FIGURE 8.5 Test items similar to those included in the various Wechsler intelligence scales. (*left*) A sampling of questions from five of the verbal subtests. (*right*) A problem in block design. Figuring out the relationship of shapes to a form board is an important skill for preschool children. (*Judith D. Sedwick/The Picture Cube*)

ences among segments of the population. On the average, people from middle-class backgrounds do better on IQ tests than people from poor backgrounds, and whites do better than blacks. For years many psychologists assumed that this difference in IQ scores was due primarily to cultural differences —the fact that middle-class white children have better schools, more books, more opportunities to travel, and more encouragement, both from their parents and from their teachers, to use their abilities and "get ahead." It was felt that if ghetto black children were given the same cultural advantages as middle-class white children, the black-white IQ gap would be closed. On the basis of this theory, the federal government instituted such programs as

Head Start, designed to enrich the environment of the culturally disadvantaged child. Some researchers find that the federally sponsored efforts have significantly improved the educational achievement of these youngsters (Lazar and Darlington, 1982; Miller and Bizzell, 1983; Stickney and Marcus, 1985).

However, since 1969, psychologist Arthur R. Jensen (1969, 1984a, 1984b, 1985) has questioned all these optimistic assumptions and findings. He has claimed that Head Start and other compensatory education programs have *not* succeeded in bringing about any permanent change in the IQ scores of the children in the programs. He goes on to contend that IQ differences are due primarily to genetic inheritance rather than to environment. Indeed, he argues

a

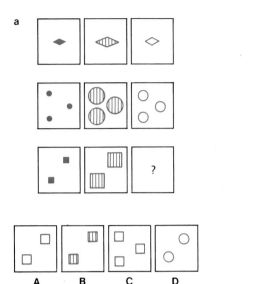

b

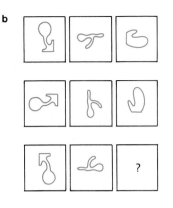

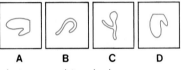

FIGURE 8.6 Typical matrix reasoning problems. The person being tested is asked to select one of the four answers at the bottom, labeled A, B, C, and D, that fits best the bottom right space. (a) The first row has one diamond in each space; the second row has three circles in each space; and the third row has two squares in the two completed spaces. Thus, the empty space will need an answer with two squares. Now notice the columns. The first column has solid figures; the second column, shaded figures; and the third column, open figures in the two completed spaces. The answer will need open figures. Thus, the information from the columns can be added to the information already observed from the rows. The correct answer is A, which has *two, open squares.* (b) Try this one yourself. *(After Paul Jacobs. 1977. Up the IQ. Ridgefield, Conn.: Wyden Books, pp. 41–42. Copyright © 1977 by Dr. Paul I. Jacobs. Reprinted by permission.)*

that between 50 and 80 percent of the difference in IQ scores between individuals is due to genetic difference. And if this is true of IQ differences, it may reasonably be true of IQ differences between races as well (Jensen, 1980, 1981, 1984a). Jensen says that the lower IQ average of blacks may be due to genetic disadvantage much more than to environmental disadvantage, and consequently that no amount of "cultural enrichment" programs will ever permit the average black child to keep pace with the average white child on an IQ test. At the other end of the intelligence distribution, Jensen credits the performance of Asian-Americans to genetic advantage. His studies of children from San Francisco's Chinatown suggest that Americans of Asian descent may be on average about fifteen IQ points brighter than children of European descent.

Needless to say, Jensen's position has raised a storm of protest. Sandra Scarr and Richard A. Weinberg (1976) studied black children raised by white

families to investigate racial differences in intelligence. Most studies reveal that black children in the United States, as a group, score lower than white children on intelligence tests. However, Scarr and Weinberg found that the IQ gap between blacks and whites is closed among black children who are adopted as infants by white middle-class foster parents. For instance, black children reared by middle-class white families are able to answer matrix reasoning problems at the same level as white children reared by white families (see Figure 8.6). These findings suggest that IQ tests and the schools share a common culture that differs to some extent from the culture experienced by black children reared by black parents. Hence being reared in the culture of the IQ tests and the school results in intellectual performance among black children that is comparable to that for white children adopted into similar families. On the basis of these findings, Scarr and Weinberg conclude that it is quite unlikely that

Children experience the culture of their families, so that black children adopted by white families develop the skills of the majority culture, just as white children adopted by similar families do. *(Steve Hanson/Stock, Boston)*

genetic differences between the races can account for the major portion of the usually observed differences in the performances of the two groups.

Other research supports this conclusion (Ginsburg and Russell, 1981; Mackenzie, 1984; Moore, in press). Data from the National Assessment of Educational Progress and from the College Entrance Examination Board show consistent reductions during recent years in the size of average achievement differences between white and black students (Jones, 1984). The difference in enrollment levels for high-school algebra and geometry courses between predominantly white schools and predominantly black schools accounts for part of the average white-black difference in mathematics achievement scores at age seventeen. It seems likely that white-black average differences might be reduced further were average enrollments in mathematics for black students to

become similar to average enrollments for white students.

Critics of IQ tests say they are unfair to minority-group children. For instance, black ghetto and Spanish-speaking children are often fearful of the testing process and expect to do poorly. Several researchers have coached disadvantaged youngsters in test taking—with good results. It seems that many do not fully understand the questions they are being asked or the tasks they are required to perform on the tests. In short, they have not learned the strategies to solve test problems. When they do, their scores improve (although they still do not match those of higher-income children). This finding suggests that a person's IQ score also reflects his or her skill and experience in taking tests. It is likewise worth noting that many black ghetto and Spanish-speaking children are typically competent problem solvers in their nonschool environment. They have mastered the skills, knowledge, and strategies essential for successful adjustment in their own culture. The children seem to learn and profit from their experiences in ways other than those revealed by their IQ scores and school-related achievements (Babad and Budoff, 1974).

In short, IQ test scores reflect cultural and social differences among people as well as individual differences in how much people have learned. This conclusion is not to say that the tests' use should be stopped altogether, however. Intelligence tests may be biased in some respects. But they may be less biased than many teachers, whose personal likes and dislikes can easily influence their evaluations of students. And although IQ tests may measure social class, motivation, and experience as well as intelligence, they do in fact test people on the kind of reasoning and problem-solving abilities required for success in school and careers in a complex society. Moreover, by studying the differences in average IQ among groups, ways may be found to correct inequalities in educational opportunity and experience. To condemn testing would be something like the ancient practice of killing the messenger who brought bad news. As the educational psychologist Lee J. Cronbach (1984:5) observes, "Sound policy is not *for* tests or *against* tests; what matters is how tests are used."

Measuring Abilities and Interests

Intelligence tests are designed to measure a person's overall ability to solve problems that involve symbols such as words, numbers, and pictures. Psychologists have developed other tests to assess special abilities and experiences. These include aptitude tests, achievement tests, and interest tests.

Aptitude Tests

Aptitude tests attempt to discover your talents and to predict how well you will be able to learn a new skill. The General Aptitude Test Battery (GATB) is the most widely used of these tests (see Figure 8.7).

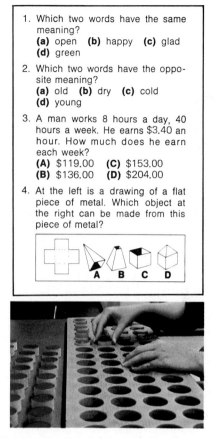

1. Which two words have the same meaning?
   (a) open **(b)** happy **(c)** glad **(d)** green

2. Which two words have the opposite meaning?
   (a) old **(b)** dry **(c)** cold **(d)** young

3. A man works 8 hours a day, 40 hours a week. He earns $3.40 an hour. How much does he earn each week?
   (A) $119.00 **(C)** $153.00
   (B) $136.00 **(D)** $204.00

4. At the left is a drawing of a flat piece of metal. Which object at the right can be made from this piece of metal?

FIGURE 8.7 The General Aptitude Test Battery (GATB) consists of a number of different kinds of tests. Shown here are items like those that test verbal and mathematical skills (*top*) and manual skills (*bottom*). Answers are given on page 286. (*Steve McCarroll*)

Actually, the GATB comprises nine different tests, ranging from vocabulary to manual dexterity. Test results are used to determine whether you meet minimum standards for each of a large number of occupations. In addition to the GATB, there are aptitude tests in music, language, art, mathematics, and other special fields. Another widely used aptitude test, taken by most prospective college students, is the Scholastic Aptitude Test, designed to predict success in college (see the boxed insert on pages 280–281).

---

aptitude test: An instrument used to discover a person's talents and to predict how well he or she will learn a specific new skill.

The College Boards

Every year, more than 1 million students take the College Board Scholastic Aptitude Test (SAT) as part of the process of applying to college. The College Board offered its first examinations in 1901. They consisted of essay tests in English, French, German, Latin, Greek, history, mathematics, chemistry, and physics. The tests had been devised by a group of educators who saw a need for a standard yardstick to help colleges compare applicants from different high schools. The tremendous success of mass testing to screen people for the armed services in World War I encouraged the College Board to move toward objective tests. In 1926, the SAT was offered for the first time. Today, the SAT aptitude tests include two separate seventy-five-minute examinations of verbal and mathematical ability. The tests have been carefully standardized, so that scores range from 200 to 800, with an average of 500. A combined score of 1,600 is a perfect score.

The SAT is most efficient as a testing device in making distinctions among above-average students. As such, it has served primarily the needs of Ivy League and other highly selective schools. However, to meet the needs of a larger spectrum of colleges and universities with a broader cross section of students, the American College Test (ACT) was developed, coming into existence in 1959. The ACT is modeled after the SAT and serves about 1 million students a year (primarily in the Midwest, South, and West).

College officials say that they want to admit students who will make satisfactory freshman grades and earn degrees, and reject those who will not finish their programs. Do college board examinations increase the number of "correct" admissions decisions? Critics respond with a resounding, "No!" For years consumer advocates, minority groups, and some educators have criticized the tests, contending that they are inadequate measures of academic skills (Nairn, 1980; Owen, 1985). Moreover, grades in college are correlated almost as powerfully with high-school grades alone as they are with an SAT score

taken singly or in combination with grades (Crouse, 1985). Critics also fault the monetary costs associated with the multi-million-dollar testing industry. And many students pay up to $1,000 for commercial coaching aimed at improving their test performance. Other costs include the anxiety of high-school students and their parents who nervously anticipate the test and the arrival of the scores. Finally, the tests are said to be biased against minority students.

Supporters of college board examinations say that because the tests are given nationally and cover subjects nearly all high-school students study, they place college applicants on a more equal footing than other admissions criteria such as grades. Also, defenders argue that college-bound students can use their test scores to help them select a college appropriate to their level of ability. For instance, students seldom apply to Ivy League schools unless they have good grades and high SAT scores. And some evidence suggests that test scores are especially valuable in predicting performance at the high and low extremes of the college-bound population. Proponents also deny charges that the tests are biased against black and Hispanic students. They point to evidence that the SAT and other aptitude tests overpredict academic performance for most groups targeted for affirmative action. The general rule is that when white students and minority students have identical test scores, the white students will do better as undergraduates (Klitgaard, 1985).

SAT scores fell sharply from a combined score peak of 980 in 1963 to an all-time low of 890 in 1980 and 1981, prompting national concern about declining educational standards and quality. The decline was reversed by 1982 high-school seniors, and the upward trend has continued. The 1985 scores were the highest since 1976 on the verbal section and since 1974 on the math section (see Figure 8.8). Minority-group students have also improved their test scores (see Figure 8.9). However, even though black students are continuing to improve their scores faster than whites, their average scores still lag behind the national average.

For all students, scores rise steadily in tandem with the income and associated intellectual levels of their families. But the scores of black students climb faster with increasing affluence and opportunity than do those of white students. Hence the score disparity shrinks significantly when the family income of a black student is about the same as that of a white student. Whereas the median score of whites is 239 points better than that of blacks when both come from families with incomes under $6,000, the gap narrows to 149 points when both come from families with incomes of $50,000 or over.

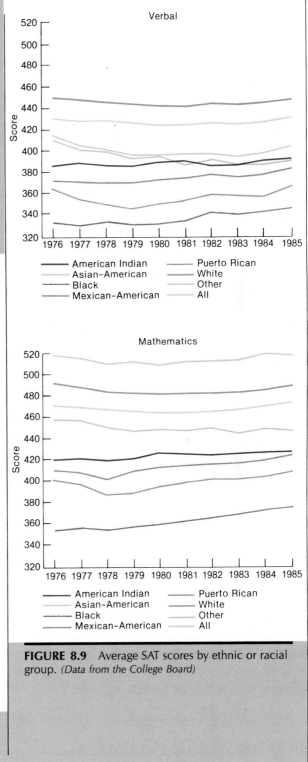

FIGURE 8.9 Average SAT scores by ethnic or racial group. (*Data from the College Board*)

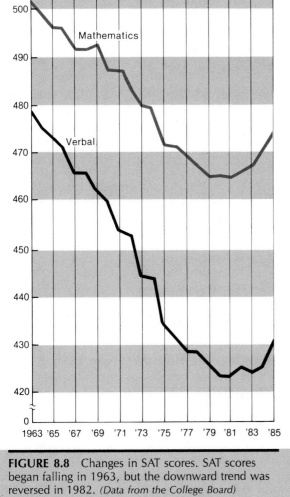

FIGURE 8.8 Changes in SAT scores. SAT scores began falling in 1963, but the downward trend was reversed in 1982. (*Data from the College Board*)

Achievement Tests

Whereas aptitude tests are designed to predict how well you will be able to learn a new skill, **achievement tests** are designed to measure how much you have already learned in a particular area. Such tests not only enable an instructor to assess your knowledge, they also help you to assess your progress for yourself.

The distinction between achievement and aptitude tests is not clear-cut (Sherman and Robinson, 1982). It rests more on purpose than on content. If a test is used to predict your future ability, it is considered an aptitude test; if it is used to assess what you already know, it is called an achievement test.

Nonetheless, scores on school achievement tests are so highly correlated with scores on school aptitude tests and IQ tests that, for practical purposes, they are not easily distinguished. As noted, in theory the tests attempt to tap different samples of learning: achievement tests are concerned with material *recently learned in school;* aptitude tests sample material *taught earlier in the school curriculum,* usually timing you on how rapidly you can solve familiar problems; and IQ tests tap material that is *not primarily taught in school* but acquired in the course of living in the culture. The primary problem is that people who find it easy to learn in school are typically people who learned school material well in years past and who learn a good deal outside of school. Thus, the samples of what people know and what they know how to do on achievement, aptitude, and IQ tests tend to rank them similarly on all three types of tests.

Interest Tests

The instruments for measuring interests are fundamentally different from the instruments for measuring abilities. Answers to questions on an intelligence test indicate whether you can, in fact, do certain kinds of thinking and solve certain kinds of problems. There are right and wrong answers. But the answers to questions on an interest or personality test cannot be right or wrong. The questions in this type of testing are not "How much can you do?" or "How much do you know?" but "What are you like?" and "What do you like?"

The essential purpose of an **interest test** is to determine your preferences, attitudes, and interests. Your responses are compared to the responses given by people in clearly defined groups, such as professions or occupations. The more your answers correspond to those of people in a particular occupation, the more likely that you are to enjoy and succeed in that profession.

In constructing the widely used Strong-Campbell Interest Inventory (Campbell, 1974), for example, psychologists compared the responses of people who are successfully employed in different occupations to the responses of "people in general." Suppose most engineers said they liked the idea of becoming astronomers but would not be interested in a coaching job, whereas "people in general" were evenly divided on these (and other) questions. If you responded as the engineers did you would rank high on the scale of interest in engineering—which really is a pattern of interests similar to those of already successful engineers. The Kuder Preference Record, part of which is shown in Figure 8.10, is based on the same principle. The purpose of these measures is to help people find the career that is right for them. The measures work because people who are happy in various occupations do have specific patterns of interests.

The Use and Misuse of Tests in Western Society

As suggested in the opening of this section, tests are widely used in Western societies. Indeed, testing is one of the major contributions that the science of psychology has made to Western culture. To some degree this has been an extremely beneficial contribution, for tests have a number of clear advantages over other evaluation techniques. In the first place,

---

achievement test: An instrument used to measure how much an individual has learned in a given subject or area.

interest test: An instrument designed to measure preferences for and attitudes toward certain activities.

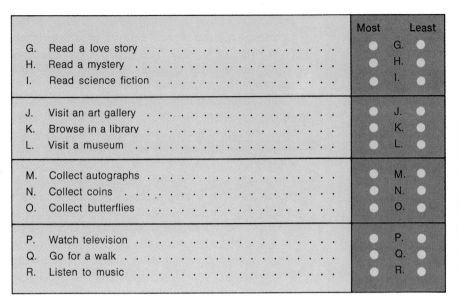

	Most		Least
G. Read a love story	●	G.	●
H. Read a mystery	●	H.	●
I. Read science fiction	●	I.	●
J. Visit an art gallery	●	J.	●
K. Browse in a library	●	K.	●
L. Visit a museum	●	L.	●
M. Collect autographs	●	M.	●
N. Collect coins	●	N.	●
O. Collect butterflies	●	O.	●
P. Watch television	●	P.	●
Q. Go for a walk	●	Q.	●
R. Listen to music	●	R.	●

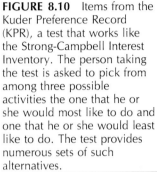

FIGURE 8.10 Items from the Kuder Preference Record (KPR), a test that works like the Strong-Campbell Interest Inventory. The person taking the test is asked to pick from among three possible activities the one that he or she would most like to do and one that he or she would least like to do. The test provides numerous sets of such alternatives.

they save time. They enable educators and others to measure large numbers of people in a matter of hours.

Second, tests can be extremely efficient measures for assisting decision makers in matching people to suitable positions. Tests have provided help in identifying people who will and will not do well in school, who will and will not make good mechanics, soldiers, typists, or salespeople. Schools use tests so that a brilliant child will not waste time on elementary mathematics, and a retarded child will not be forced to struggle with algebra. Tests are used by businesses to avoid putting clumsy people into jobs requiring great dexterity and precision, or highly intelligent people into jobs that are mechanical and repetitive. To replace cognitive ability tests with any instrument of lower validity would incur very high costs to the economy. Some estimates place the figure at between $3 billion and $16 billion a year (Hunter and Hunter, 1984).

A third important advantage is that tests are generally more objective than other forms of evaluation. A person cannot impress a test by wearing expensive and stylish clothing or by dropping names. A test cannot hear that a person has a foreign accent or see that he or she has a physical handicap —the sort of thing that might prejudice interviewers who rely solely on their own impressions.

Fourth, testing allows psychologists and others to identify problem areas in educational and training programs. On the basis of these assessments, appropriate adjustments can be made in existing programs or new programs can be designed. Tests can also be used for diagnostic purposes. For instance, when a student fails to master particular skills or knowledge, a more detailed search for the source of the learning difficulty is indicated. A remedy is possible only when a teacher understands the basis of the student's problem and then designs instruction to address the need. Hence testing provides the foundation for the development of appropriate interventions.

However, all these virtues depend on the validity of the tests involved. And, as discussed, psychological testing is far from infallible. Tests do make mistakes. Bright people do sometimes get low IQ scores. And tests usually turn out to measure much less than many people suspect. *The test results are probable*, within the limits of their reliability and validity.

Another limitation of psychological testing is that tests compare a person with others in his or her society according to prevailing social standards. Measures of intelligence are alway samples of culturally approved skills. Psychologists put together lists of questions that sample various skills thought to be important for school learning and job performance. The questions are those that people considered by the society to be "smart" answer more accurately than do those considered to be "dumb." Any new person's responses can then be compared with the

Some employment tests are samples of the tasks the candidate would actually be required to do on the job. This firefighter trainee is being tested in a simulated emergency. *(Walton Smith/EKM-Nepenthe)*

responses of those previously tested, to evaluate that person's standing. If social definitions of intelligence favor one group more than others, then tests will also. This is not a criticism of testing itself but a limitation in the meaning of test scores.

The widespread use of testing raises numerous ethical questions. Everyone would probably agree that it is appropriate for the law to require that people pass driving tests before taking the wheel alone. But is it appropriate for a business organization to pry into a person's fundamental beliefs and private fantasies before offering that person a job? Is it right for colleges to use attitude questionnaires in order to select their freshman classes? What does a student's attitude toward his or her mother or the opposite sex or freedom of the press have to do with whether he or she will be able to pass French 100 or Anthropology 101?

Such considerations lead to doubts about the use of tests in making major decisions about individual lives. Should people be denied a college education or be refused a particular job on the basis of test results? Should people be required to take tests at all, when many find it a traumatic, demanding experience of questionable value? The answers to these questions are not easy. Psychological tests, like other technological advances, have their uses and their limitations. Like automobiles, tranquilizers, and nuclear power, tests can be overused and badly used. But, as is the case with other technologies, they can be used well if people understand them and are determined to use them in the interests of the individual and of society. In sum, the making and taking of tests will surely persist in a great many forms. And so long as testing continues, we will need to guard against their misuse (Miller, 1984).

SUMMARY

1. Intelligence is one of the most notable characteristics of the human species. Being intelligent has allowed human beings to occupy a unique environmental niche. This niche requires extensive use of learning and problem solving as coping mechanisms, in contrast with prewired adaptations that genetically program behavior.

2. Although laypeople and psychologists alike use the concept of intelligence, it remains a fuzzy con-

cept. What psychologists typically mean by intelligence is a global capacity to understand the world, think rationally, and cope resourcefully with the challenges of life.

A. For the most part, laypeople conceive of intelligence as having three components: problem-solving ability, verbal ability, and social competence.

B. Some psychologists, among them Charles Spearman, Louis Thurstone, J. P. Guilford, and Howard Gardner, have proposed factor approaches to intelligence.

C. Arthur Jensen and Robert Sternberg distinguish between levels of intelligence. Jensen has identified level I skills (simple learned associations) and level II skills (capacity for abstract thinking and problem solving), while Sternberg proposes contextual, experiential, and componential ingredients.

D. Recently, a number of psychologists have taken a somewhat different approach to intelligence. They have directed their attention to information processing—the step-by-step mental operations people use in tackling an intellectual task.

E. Intelligence depends also on the reliability and efficiency of brain processes.

3. People differ in a great many respects, including intelligence. Both genetic and environmental factors are responsible for the intellectual variations observable among people. Some people erroneously conclude that if genetic differences account for some portion of the intellectual differences among people, then genes have fixed their intelligence at a certain level and there is nothing that can be done about it.

4. Like intelligence, creativity serves an important adaptive function. Creativity usually means the occurrence of original and useful responses. However, by virtue of the vague and subjective connotations associated with creativity, some psychologists prefer to distinguish between convergent thinking and divergent thinking.

5. Differences between above-average and very high scores on intelligence tests have at best only a low association with creativity. But while high intelligence does not guarantee creativity, low intelligence seems to work against it. For the most part, psychologists agree that an above-average, although not necessarily exceptional, level of intelligence is essential for creative achievement.

6. Unusually creative individuals often have strong, forceful personalities. It also seems that cool and even detached relationships frequently prevail between parents and their creative sons and daughters. Creativity appears to be a mix of abilities and traits. Uncommon creative ability entails unusual versions of such familiar mental operations as remembering, reasoning, and problem solving.

7. Social and environmental factors also influence people's creativity. Research suggests that people are more creative when they are working to please themselves than when they are attempting to gain recognition and rewards from others. When people are inspired by their own interests and enjoyment, they are more likely to explore unlikely paths, take risks, and in the end, produce something unique and useful.

8. All tests are designed to find out a great deal about a person in a relatively short time. Tests are useful to predict future performance in school or in a job, to assess what has been learned, or to diagnose problems. But test scores should not be regarded as ends in themselves.

9. The fairness and successfulness of a test depend on several factors: its reliability, its validity, and the way its norms were established.

A. Reliability is the ability of a test to yield the same results under a variety of circumstances.

B. Validity is the ability of a test to measure what it is supposed to measure.

C. Norms are established on the basis of the scores achieved by the group as a whole. They are standards of comparison. Standardization allows a test score to be interpreted in the light of the scores all people in a specified group achieved.

10. The first practical intelligence test was designed by Alfred Binet as a means of picking out slow learners. The test currently in widespread use is a revision of Binet's test known as the Stanford-Binet. The results of this test yield an IQ score that is a measure of "mental age." The Wechsler intelligence tests differ from the Stanford-Binet in that they place more emphasis on performance tasks and yield a number of separate scores for different abilities.

A. IQ tests are good at predicting school performance and success at certain jobs, regardless of why a person scores well or poorly on the test.

B. The debate over the causes of racial and socioeconomic differences in average IQ scores has called attention to the fact that IQ tests measure social class, motivation, and experience as well as the ability to reason and solve problems.

11. Psychologists have developed other tests to assess special abilities and experiences. These include aptitude tests, achievement tests, and interest tests.

A. Aptitude and achievement tests are virtually identical in content but serve different purposes. Aptitude tests are used to discover a person's talents and to predict how well he or she will be able to learn a new skill. Achievement tests measure how much a person has already learned.

B. Many other psychological tests have no right or wrong answers; they attempt to find out what a person is like. Interest tests measure preferences for and attitudes toward different activities.

12. As the most objective measure of intelligence, aptitude or achievement, and interests available, tests are extremely useful tools. But like any tool, they can be misused.

KEY TERMS

achievement test   (p. 282)
aptitude test   (p. 279)
creativity   (p. 267)
information processing   (p. 264)

intelligence   (p. 259)
intelligence quotient (IQ)   (p. 274)
interest test   (p. 282)
norms   (p. 273)

reliability   (p. 271)
validity   (p. 272)

SUGGESTED READINGS

AMERICAN PSYCHOLOGIST, 36, no. 11 (1981:whole issue). This issue of the *American Psychologist* contains review articles that illustrate the use, misuse, and history of the mental-measurement movement in the United States. The major public controversies over mental testing are summarized, and the use of mental tests with disadvantaged children is discussed.

BUROS, OSCAR K., ED. 1978. *The Eighth Mental Measurement Yearbook*. Highland Park, N.J.: Gryphon Press. A valuable reference work. Every major psychological test is reviewed by the experts.

GOULD, STEPHEN JAY. 1981. *The Mismeasure of Man*. New York: W. W. Norton. A well-written critique of the history of misguided attempts to measure intelligence, from counting bumps on the head to measuring immigrants' ignorance of American culture. Gould is a popular science writer with splendid academic credentials as a zoologist, and he attacks mental testing with vigor.

JENSEN, A. R. 1980. *Bias in Mental Testing*. New York: Free Press. The most thorough text on test construction, reliability, validity, and other issues of mental testing by one of the leading figures in the field. Jensen is a strong proponent of the usefulness of tests.

LOEHLIN, JOHN C., LINDZEY, GARDNER, and SPUHLER, J. N. 1975. *Race Differences in Intelligence*. San Francisco: W. H. Freeman. Sometimes rather technical, but an extremely thorough summary of racial differences in IQ.

MEAD, MARGARET. 1971. *Blackberry Winter*. New York: Simon & Schuster. The personal story behind the pioneering achievements of the world's most famous anthropologist. Mead vividly describes her early field trips to Samoa, New Guinea, and Bali, giving the reader insight into the life of a creative personality.

PERKINS, DAVID. 1981. *The Mind's Best Work*. Cambridge, Mass.: Harvard University Press. A popularly written book about creativity as a normal mental process rather than an extraordinary talent that only some people possess. Perkins maintains that everyone can think creatively.

RICE, BERKELEY. 1985. Why am I in this job? *Psychology Today*, 19 (January): 54–56. Contains practical advice on career counseling.

WELTY, EUDORA. 1984. *One Writer's Beginnings*. Cambridge, Mass.: Harvard University Press. A stunning book by one of America's best writers takes you to the core of writing as a creative enterprise.

Answers to Figure 8.7: (1) b and c, (2) a and d, (3) b, (4) c.

part 3

SOCIAL BEHAVIOR

Marc Klionsky, *On the Beach No. 1.*

9
Human Interaction

Have you had the experience of encountering someone in a distant city who knew one of your friends back home? And you exclaimed, "My, but it's a small world!" Very likely you also play the "small world game" in becoming acquainted with your fellow students. You usually inquire about their hometowns and academic majors and then ask, "Do you know . . . ?"

The "small world" phenomenon raises an interesting question. How many people do you think it would take to transmit a letter on an acquaintance-to-acquaintance basis to a stranger in a distant American city? Psychologist Stanley Milgram (1967) looked into this matter. He selected two arbitrary "target persons": the wife of a divinity-school student who lived in Cambridge, Massachusetts, and a stockbroker who worked in Boston but lived in Sharon, Massachusetts. His subjects or "starting persons" were people residing in Wichita, Kansas, and Omaha, Nebraska. Each starter was given a booklet telling the target person's name, address, occupation, and a few other facts. Milgram instructed each starter to begin moving the booklet on by mail toward the target. However, the booklet could be sent only to a first-name acquaintance. Each person in turn was to advance the booklet in like fashion until it reached its final destination. ·

Over a number of studies, from 12 to 33 percent of the booklets were delivered. The number of links in the completed chains ranged from two to ten, with averages between five and eight. Figure 9.1 shows a typical completed chain.

Milgram describes one case with two intermediate links (1967:64):

Our first target person was the wife of a student living in Cambridge. Four days after the folders were sent to a group of starting persons in Kansas, an instructor at the Episcopal Theological Seminary

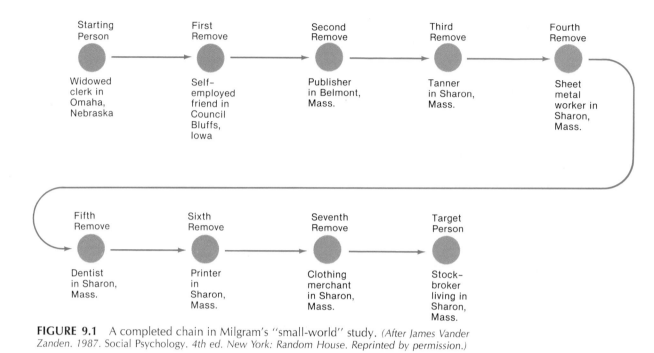

FIGURE 9.1 A completed chain in Milgram's "small-world" study. *(After James Vander Zanden. 1987. Social Psychology. 4th ed. New York: Random House. Reprinted by permission.)*

approached our target person on the street. "Alice," he said, thrusting a brown folder toward her, "this is for you." At first she thought he was simply returning a folder that had gone astray, but . . . we found to our pleased surprise that the document had started with a wheat farmer in Kansas. He had passed it onto an Episcopalian minister in his home town, who sent it to the minister who taught in Cambridge, who gave it to the target person.

You may find it surprising that only five to seven intermediaries will typically suffice to link any two randomly selected people, no matter where they happen to live in the United States. Even though we deal with only a small number of intermediaries, behind each of them stands a much larger group of 500 to 2,500 people. So each sender has an acquaintance pool of 500 to 2,500 people from which he or she selects the person believed best able to advance the chain. Geometric progression also works to your advantage. (Analogously, if you earn a penny a day and the sum is doubled each day, you will have a sum of more than $10 million at the end of thirty working days.) The net result is that with just a few removes, the search extends to an enormous number of people.

You can make the "small world" phenomenon work for you in getting a job. Employment experts find that only about 20 to 30 percent of all jobs are filled by want ads, employment agencies, or interview requests. The other 70 to 80 percent of jobs —especially the better ones—are never advertised. They are filled by word of mouth. You can gain access to a vast number of jobs by reaching out to friends, relatives, and acquaintances and letting them know you are job hunting. Many such jobs are "hidden"; they are made up of unannounced plans, emerging problems, impending retirements, and corporate expansions that are as yet only in people's minds. By working through your contacts, you gain access to the "hidden job market," you have someone who can "put in a good word for you," and you can get interviews directly with the people who have the power to hire you (Fader, 1984).

Clearly, you are the center of a good many social relationships that link you to a rather large number of people. For example, one network links you to your professor and classmates in your psychology course; other networks have strands that tie you to roommates, friends, parents, and perhaps coworkers. Central to these networks of relationships is human interaction, the process by which two or more people influence each other's feelings, attitudes, and actions. Human interaction is the essence of your social being. Whatever you want—be it food, clothing, shelter, sex, fame, sports, love—you must get by somehow involving yourself with other people. Indeed, the manner in which we have evolved has prepared and equipped us for living in groups, communicating with one another, perceiving and judging social situations, and establishing social ties and relationships.

Since you live your life in a social setting, you must continually make sense of your experiences with people. How you think about those experiences and how those experiences influence your thinking is termed **social cognition.** Of equal importance, on the basis of these mental processes you fashion your behavior—you say or do certain things.

SOCIAL PERCEPTION

As you will recall from reading Chapters 5 and 7, human beings perceive things in their own individual ways. Your thinking brain orders and interprets raw sensory data to arrive at meaning. Although there are over 4 billion people inhabiting planet Earth, we each experience a somewhat different world. Capitalists and communists, Christians and atheists, Israelis and Palestinians, bosses and employees, and parents and children typically perceive the same events in different ways. This is because different pasts, needs, and expectations—not to mention different genetic backgrounds—lead people to select, emphasize, and organize perceptual inputs in such a manner that they arrive at different meanings.

Cognitive Processes in Perception

Your senses enable you to extract information from the world about you, and your brain interprets this information. Receptor organs—your eyes, ears, nose, tongue, and skin—are aroused when the appropriate type of energy reaches them (see Chapter 5). But you do not merely await stimulation from external sources; you seek out information about the world. In crossing a busy intersection, you *actively* turn your head and scan the environment with your eyes and ears to pick up critical information that can guide your path in darting among the cars and pedestrians. You would soon become a traffic fatality if you passively relied on the hit-or-miss reception of perceptual cues regarding environmental happenings.

But not only do you "hunt" stimuli. Your brain transforms stimuli into organized systems of events to which you assign meaning. Through the processes described in Chapter 7, you form schemes that organize and preserve information about your environment. You will recall that a *scheme* is an abstract knowledge framework or mental structure used in processing and organizing information. A scheme allows you to give meaning to your perceptual inputs and make them consistent with your existing expectations and knowledge. Many schemes have two elements: *dimensions*, the attributes or characteristics you use for identifying something, and *categories*, the classes you use for sorting things into units based on certain similarities. For instance, you look at another person and appraise her height (a dimension). She is very short, so you place the person in the category "child."

Perhaps an additional illustration will help you to grasp the significance of schemes in your daily lives. Take the Big Dipper. When you look up into the northern sky on a cloudless night, you very likely identify a configuration of seven stars that you call the Big Dipper. Of course, a dipper is not literally to be found in the heavens. Instead, in viewing various celestial events, you undertake to organize your experience and make sense out of it. You use a cognitive structure—Big Dipper—as a mental model or working description of a particular group

---

human interaction: The process by which two or more people influence each other's feelings, attitudes, and actions.

social cognition: How you think about your social experiences and how your social experiences influence your thinking.

of stars. You use this structure as one tool for construing the world of celestial experience (Vander Zanden, 1987).

Some cloudless evening, try looking at this same combination of stars and discerning the image of a bear, a wagon, or a bushel. Americans typically find it impossible to "see" anything but a dipper. Other people have known this same group of stars by different names. To the ancient Greeks they were the Great Bear; to the Syrians, the Wild Boar; to the Hindus, the Seven Sages; to the Poles, the Heavenly Wagon; and to the Chinese, the Northern Bushel. The assignment of these names shaped each people's perception of this celestial configuration. For example, it is clear from their writings that the ancient Greeks, by calling these stars the Great Bear, actually *saw* the figure of a bear when they looked up into the northern sky.

Human beings use schemes to make sense of the countless stimuli that bombard the senses. We are concept-making creatures. The human brain operates so that we mentally group people, objects, and events into categories, give them labels, and thus think about the world in an efficient manner.

But there are also consequences associated with the use of schemes. As the illustration of the Big Dipper showed, we "construct" reality. We treat the Big Dipper *as if* it were real—as if there were a *naturally* occurring configuration of stars that form a dipper. The ancient Greeks carried the matter even further. They evolved an elaborate mythology based on "heavenly bodies" that supposedly influenced the destinies of earthly mortals. And believing in such mystical powers, they took the supernatural into account when fashioning their behavior, whether the pursuit of love, fame, or fortune. Thus if we define situations as real, our ideas or beliefs have real consequences for our actions (Thomas, 1931). (See the boxed insert on page 293 for a discussion of the importance of social definitions.)

The social philosopher Alfred Schutz (1971:5) makes the same point about schemes, which he terms "constructs":

> All our knowledge of the world, in common sense as well as in scientific thinking, involves constructs, i.e., a set of abstractions, generalizations, formalizations, and idealizations specific to the respective level of thought organization. Strictly speaking, there are no such things as facts, pure and simple. All facts are

People form rapid impressions of others whom they meet in social situations. Such stereotypes help to guide our behavior toward others, but may be very misleading. *(Peter Miller/Photo Researchers)*

from the outset facts selected from the universal context by the activities of our mind. They are, therefore, always interpreted facts.

In sum, we use schemes as abstract knowledge frameworks or mental structures to interpret the world of experience and to guide our behavior (Scarr, 1985b).

Forming Impressions of Others

We also use schemes to get about in a social environment. We construct images of others to make our social experiences manageable, stable, and predictable. Consider what happens when you attend a party. You typically attempt to "size up" the people. You look for cues that will tell you something about them—their age, occupation, marital status, person-

The Importance of Social Definitions: Who Is a Jew?

The following is a transcript of a classroom discussion:

INSTRUCTOR: Who is a Jew?

STUDENT 1: It's a religion. It means you are a member of a religious group.

INSTRUCTOR: You say it is a religion. I know a young woman by the name of Rebecca Cohen. Her parents are Jewish. Her brothers are Jewish. But she says she isn't Jewish. She's an atheist. She claims religion is a silly superstition. Is she a Jew?

STUDENT 1: No, she's not Jewish. If she says she isn't, she isn't.

INSTRUCTOR: You say she isn't Jewish. Last weekend she went to meet her boyfriend's parents, and his parents were horrified. They told their son they didn't want him going with a Jew. It would be even worse if he were to marry one. Rebecca insisted that she wasn't Jewish, but his parents were equally insistent that she was. Is she a Jew?

STUDENT 2: Yes, I think she is a Jew. She is a Jew because her ancestors were Jews. She was born a Jew.

INSTRUCTOR: Okay, let me give you another case. I know a young woman of Catholic background who married a Jewish fella and she converted to Orthodox Judaism. Her sons go to a Yeshiva [an Orthodox Jewish school]. Yet if you ask her about her religious ideas she indicates that she believes in Divine Science—sort of a spiritual healing, self-awareness, self-realization cult. If you ask her if she is a Jew, she'll respond affirmatively. Is she a Jew?

STUDENT 2: Yes, I'd say she is a Jew 'cause she says she is a Jew.

INSTRUCTOR: Okay, let's think about that for a moment. If I told you I was black [the instructor is a brown-haired, blue-eyed, white-skinned male], would you believe me?

STUDENT 2: [Hesitates] Yeah, I'd believe it. [Pause] Maybe deep down I wouldn't believe it, though. [Giggles]

INSTRUCTOR: Now I'm getting confused. On the one hand, you say you determine whether a person is a Jew by asking them. But then you tell me you don't always believe people.

STUDENT 3: A Jew is a person that is treated like a Jew.

INSTRUCTOR: Okay, let's look at this definition. As I understand it, Senator Barry Goldwater's father was Jewish and his mother was Episcopalian. If Barry Goldwater had beaten President Johnson in the 1964 presidential election, would Barry Goldwater have been America's first Jewish President?

STUDENT 3: No, I don't think so. I don't think Goldwater is Jewish.

INSTRUCTOR: Well, if Barry Goldwater had lived in Nazi Germany, would he have been identified as a Jew and gassed in a concentration camp?

STUDENT 3: I guess so.

INSTRUCTOR: What are we to make of all this? Who is a Jew? I think Jean-Paul Sartre put it best of all: "A Jew is a man whom other men call a Jew." It's a matter of social definition, what people believe to be the case and how they act. If people define situations as real [in this case, if they define one as a Jew], they are real in their consequences.

(Source: James W. Vander Zanden. 1987. Social Psychology. 4th ed. New York: Random House. Reprinted by permission.)

ality, and so on. By making inferences of this sort, you seek to identify the set of expectations that will guide your interaction with them. In so doing, you gain the information that you will need for fitting your actions to their actions.

It usually takes you very little time to make judgments regarding another person. From one brief conversation, or even by watching the person across a room, you form some sort of impression. In forming impressions of others, you typically scan their surface qualities and then look for less readily apparent qualities. This process has been compared to that of peeling an onion. The first and most superficial step entails the use of group stereotypes.

Stereotypes

Perhaps the most immediate attributes or characteristics that strike you about people are their sex, race, age, and social status. On the basis of these dimensions, you place them in various categories, for instance, male or female, black or white, child or adult, middle class or lower class (Bargh and Pietromonaco, 1982; Pryor et al., 1983). A variety of stereotypes are usually associated with the schemes that you use in identifying and placing people within a social context. A **stereotype** is a set of beliefs that you have about the people in a given category. When you encounter a member of some stereotyped group, you commonly infer that the person possesses a cluster of traits (Lord, Lepper, and Mackie, 1984).

Nowadays, a good many people—especially those who view themselves as "thinking" or "liberated" individuals—feel rather uncomfortable with the notion of stereotypes. They do not like to believe that they too may fall into "stylized modes of thought." Yet like it or not, we all must use stereotypes in making our way about life. The world is filled with so much subtlety and variety—so many differences and combinations—that we must simplify it in order to manage it. In the hustle and bustle of shopping, attending classes, and navigating hither and yon, it is virtually impossible to weigh every reaction of every person we encounter, minute by minute, in terms of the person's unique qualities. Instead, we type people in snap-judgment fashion: "assertive" male, "hardworking" father, "immature" youth, or "lazy" poor.

While stereotypes are convenient and have the virtue of efficiency, they frequently lack accuracy. When applied to an individual, they are often incorrect. They are thus the unscientific and unreliable generalizations that we use in evaluating other people.

Implicit Personality Theory and Prototypes

Undoubtedly you have had the following kind of experience. You are out with two close friends, perhaps shopping at a store. In the presence of your two companions, you purchase an item from a clerk. As you leave the store, you comment to your friends, "Gee, that person sure was timid!" But one of your friends immediately chimes in, asserting, "I think he was dull, real dull!" And your other friend takes issue with both of you, saying, "How can you say that? I think he was mysterious!" Thus you have three people, all having met the same stranger under similar circumstances, yet each having formed a quite different impression of the person.

One reason you form different impressions of the same stranger is that each of you is using a somewhat different scheme for processing and organizing information about the clerk. In recent years psychologists have used the concepts *prototype* and *implicit personality theory* to describe the influence that schemes have on our perception of people and our memories about them. A **prototype** is a category that you mentally use to represent a loose set of features that seem to belong together (Cantor and Mischel, 1979; Mischel, 1984). In like fashion, the term **implicit personality theory** implies that you typically assume a number of traits are associated with one another (Schneider, 1973; Schneider and Blankmeyer, 1983).

You use a prototype or an implicit personality theory as a "fuzzy" guide in sizing up a person. For instance, when you meet a person who seems unusually intelligent, you may assume she is also active, highly motivated, and conscientious. Another member of the group may have an altogether different "theory" about highly intelligent people—they are unrealistic, boastful, and insensitive. Whatever the person says or does provides "evidence" for both interpretations. You are impressed by how animated she becomes when talking about her work; the other group member is impressed by how little attention she pays to other people. Both of you are filling in gaps in what you know about the person, fitting her into your individual cognitive structure for typing "that kind of person."

---

stereotype: A set of unscientific beliefs about the people in a given category.

prototype: A category that you mentally use to represent a loose set of features that seem to belong together.

implicit personality theory: A set of assumptions about how people behave and what traits or characteristics go together.

Stereotypes. Note the importance of such attributes as sex, race, age, and appearance on the impressions that you form. What inferences do you make about each of these individuals? Which political party are they likely to support? Which one would be most likely to lend you a dollar? Which of these might own a sports car? *(top left: Tyrone Hall/Stock, Boston; top right: Steven Stone/The Picture Cube; bottom left: Pat Coffey/The Picture Cube; bottom right: J. D. Sloan/The Picture Cube)*

Experiments indicate that people's impressions are strongly influenced by a few traits (Asch, 1946; Zanna and Hamilton, 1972). (See Figures 9.2 and 9.3.) For example, the psychologist Harold Kelley (1950) invited a guest lecturer to a psychology class. Beforehand, all the students were given a brief description of the visitor. The descriptions were identical in all traits but one. Half the students were told that the speaker was cold, the other half that he was warm.

After the lecture, Kelley asked all the students to evaluate the lecturer. Reading their impressions, you would hardly know that the two groups of students were describing the same person. The students who

Intelligent
Warm
Confident
Practical

FIGURE 9.2 What is your impression of this person? Do you think you would like him? What do you think of the way he is dressed? What sort of expression does he have on his face? When you have formed an impression, turn to the drawing in Figure 9.3 and do the same.

had been told he was cold saw a humorless, ruthless, self-centered person. The other students saw a relaxed, friendly, concerned person. Changing one word—substituting "warm" for "cold"—had a dramatic impact on the audience's perception of the lecturer. It also affected their behavior. Students in the "warm group" were warm themselves, initiating more conversations with the speaker and asking him more questions than did the students in the other group. These differences occurred even though the lecturer gave the identical, memorized talk to both groups of students. In sum, when forming impressions of a person, you tend to round out the incomplete information and see him or her as a unit.

Some occupations highlight this process of impression formation. Take the case of customs inspectors. These inspectors look for particular traits that they believe will tip them off to other characteristics of a traveler. They are more likely to search a traveler if the person hesitates before answering questions, gives short answers, shifts his or her body about, avoids eye contact, or displays unusual items of clothing or hair style (Kraut and Poe, 1980).

Processing Inconsistent Information

For the most part we form and maintain impressions of people that are relatively consistent. We have a pretty good idea of which traits go together and

which do not. But what happens when the world presents us with inconsistent information (Erber and Fiske, 1984)? One way we react is to incorporate the inconsistent information within our overall impression. Consider what happens when subjects are presented with a pair of personality traits that do not seem to fit together, such as *shy* and *courageous* (Asch and Zukier, 1984). Taken in isolation, *shy* connotes reticence and withdrawal; *courageous*, outgoingness. When subjects bring the two traits together, *courageous* comes to imply unusual personal determination, and *shyness* ceases to suggest weakness. It is not too difficult to imagine a person who acts bravely despite being very reluctant to seem conspicuous. Thus subjects establish a coherent impression by looking for some sensible way to bring the two traits together in a meaningful and harmonious fashion.

Another way to handle inconsistent information is simply to ignore it (Hendrick, 1972; Erber and Fiske, 1984). We are usually better at examining and remembering information about people that is consistent with our expectations than information that is inconsistent (Berman, Read, and Kenny, 1983). We simply take the path of least resistance. But when we have a stake in some outcome (for instance, we may be working on a common task), we are more inclined to mull over the inconsistent information we receive about the person than if we have little motivation to modify our judgments. The conclusion we arrive at need be no more accurate than our initial impression, but it is nevertheless apt to be a more thoughtful one (Tetlock, 1983; Erber and Fiske, 1984).

Attribution

The previous section dealt with how you infer a person's characteristics on the basis of one central trait, such as age or "warmth." As you go about your daily activities, you must constantly size people up in a snap-judgment manner. Thus you like to know whether the strangers you encounter have honorable intentions and whether they are who they purport to be. In this way you attempt to make sense out of your experiences with people.

But usually you are not satisfied with simply describing a person's personality. You also like to understand an individual's behavior. You want to know what *causes* the person to act in a given manner. For instance, why did Brad flunk his chemistry test today? Why did Jean ignore me at work this morning? Why is the professor singling Mark out for special attention? These questions have do with **attribution**—the process by which ordinary people explain and interpret the events they encounter. Thus as you make your way about life, you act as an "intuitive psychologist," judging the causes and implications of your own and other people's behavior. You are most likely to search for explanations of people's behavior when they say or do things that you do not expect (Hastie, 1984).

Attribution of Responsibility

In analyzing a person's behavior, you typically attempt to determine whether it was caused by *personal* or *environmental* factors, or a combination of the two (Heider, 1958). For example, did Brad flunk his chemistry test because he forgot to study for the test (a personal, or *dispositional*, attribution), because his roommate got sick and Brad had to bring him to the doctor's office (an environmental, or *situational*, attribution), or because he initially thought the test was unimportant but later, changing his mind and deciding to study, discovered that someone had stolen his lecture notes (a combination of dispositional and situational attributions).

Social psychologists find that people tend to underestimate the impact of situational factors and overestimate the role of dispositional factors in controlling behavior—a tendency known as the **fundamental attribution error** (Ross, 1977). Thus if you are like most people, you typically exaggerate the part that "internal" factors (traits, abilities, or motives) play in a person's behavior as opposed to various "external" factors (the difficulty of the task, peer pressures, or incentives). For instance, if it seems to you that a friend indulges excessively in alcohol or marijuana, you are more likely to attribute the behavior to personality factors ("He's a very moody person" or "She's so darn self-critical") than to environmental circumstances ("He's in a tough field of study" or "She's under a lot of pressure at home"). Hence, as an "intuitive psychologist," you tend too often to be a "nativist" (a proponent of stable individual differences) and too seldom a "behaviorist" (a proponent of situational influences). (See the boxed insert on page 299 for a discussion of the effects of labeling people.)

The fundamental attribution error occurs in many settings. For instance, jurors in a criminal trial are often influenced by the personal characteristics of the defendant. They tend to be more lenient in their decision when the defendant possesses positive characteristics and more severe when the defendant possesses negative characteristics (Kalven and Zeisal, 1966). For instance, in one study subjects meted out an average jail term of ten years to an attractive rapist versus nearly fourteen years for a homely rapist (Jacobson, 1981). And in accounting for an event (a crime of negligent automobile homicide), subjects perceive a person's behavior as heavily weighted by internal factors.

However, it may make a difference if you are making attributions regarding your own or another person's behavior. You are more likely to view

---

attribution (AT-treh-BEW-shun): The process by which ordinary people explain and interpret the events they encounter.

fundamental attribution error: The tendency for people to underestimate the impact of situational factors and overestimate the role of dispositional factors in controlling behavior.

Intelligent
Cold
Confident
Practical

FIGURE 9.3 If your impressions of this person are different from your impressions of the person in Figure 9.2, the difference must be due to the change in a single word—the illustrations are otherwise identical.

Attractive trial defendants—like Sydney Biddle Barrows, known as "the Mayflower Madam" because she is descended from two old-line families and was accused of running a prostitution ring in New York City—are likely to receive more lenient treatment from juries than defendants with unappealing personal qualities. *(UPI/Bettmann Newsphotos)*

situational factors as underlying your own actions (Storms, 1973; Goldberg, 1978). People generally believe that they choose their own actions to fit the requirements of each situation, but that other people act the way that they do because of their inherent personal traits or qualities.

In part, these differences in attribution can be explained by differing informational bases. You know your own attitudes and motives. Consequently, you focus your attention on situational aspects in explaining why, in pursuing your goal, you took one course of action rather than another. But information on other people's inner states is normally lacking. When you examine other people's behavior, you know the situational context but not their motivations. So you direct your attention to the unknown element, their internal disposition.

If you are like most people, you are also more likely to attribute your successes to yourself while attributing your failures to the situation or to other people. The social psychologists Edward E. Jones and Richard E. Nisbett (1971:1) observe that when a student who is doing poorly in school discusses the matter with a faculty member, the two often see the matter quite differently:

The student, in attempting to understand and explain his inadequate performance, is usually able to point

The Effects of Labeling People

A major aspect of attribution involves identifying the causes and motivations that underlie people's behavior. In many instances, the final step in the attribution process is to assign to the person a *label*—a shorthand epithet or descriptive word that seems to summarize the various traits. For instance, you may label a person "dishonest," "stubborn," "stupid," "lazy," or "crazy." Once you have defined a person in this fashion, you then tend to act toward the individual as if he or she *were* dishonest, stubborn, stupid, lazy, or crazy.

David Rosenhan (1973) provides a dramatic demonstration of the consequences that can flow from attaching labels to people. He and seven others, including several graduate students in clinical psychology, feigned symptoms of mental illness to gain admission to twelve different psychiatric hospitals. They claimed to hear voices that said "hollow," "empty," and "thud." On this basis, they were diagnosed as schizophrenic and admitted as patients.

Once they had gained entry to a hospital, the researchers went back to their ordinary behavior. They dropped their claims of hearing voices, spoke to other patients and staff as they would to people outside the hospital, and told everyone that they were feeling fine.

The hospital staff was not at all suspicious of these changes. They never suspected that these "patients" were sane. For instance, while in the hospital, each researcher would take detailed notes concerning his or her experiences and the events of hospital life. Other patients soon noticed his behavior and concluded from it that the individual was not a real patient. But the staff placed a quite different interpretation on the behavior. They saw it as symptomatic of the "patient's" disturbance. Indeed, one nurse wrote on the "patient's" chart that the writing behavior was indicative of a disordered, abnormal compulsion. In sum, once the person had been assigned the label "mentally ill," the staff interpreted his or her actions in a manner consistent with the label. And when the pseudo-patients were finally released, they were described as "recovered schizophrenics" or "schizophrenics in remission," rather than as normal individuals.

to environmental obstacles such as a particularly onerous course load, to temporary emotional stress . . . , or to a transitory confusion about life goals that is now resolved. The faculty adviser may nod and may wish to believe, but in his heart of hearts he usually disagrees. The adviser is convinced that the poor performance is due neither to the student's environment nor to transient emotional states. He believes instead that the failure is due to enduring qualities of the student—to lack of ability, to irremediable laziness, to neurotic ineptitude.

In a similar fashion, teachers take credit for their students' successes but attribute their students' failures to low intelligence and poor motivation (Johnson, Feigenbaum, and Weiby, 1964; Schopler and Layton, 1972).

Self-Attributions

As the previous discussion has implied, people not only make attributions regarding the behavior of others but also seek to account for their own behavior. In coming to know and understand yourself you enjoy the advantage of introspection, an avenue not open to you when judging other people's inner attitudes and motivations. Indeed, from time to time you have probably asked yourself questions such as "How do I feel about this?" "What do I really want to do?" "Why do I act that way?" "What ever made me say such a thing?" or "Do I like this person?"

Yet in obtaining information about your own thoughts and feelings, you do not limit yourself to introspection. At times you cannot rely on internal cues because they are too weak, ambiguous, or inaccessible. On these occasions you find yourself in the same position as an outside observer. You must infer your inner state from external cues. Consequently, you observe your own actions and from them infer what your attitudes or motives must be. According to the psychologist Daryl Bem (1972), you use much the same kinds of evidence and logic in reaching conclusions about yourself as you do in perceiving other people. This approach to self-attribution is termed **self-perception theory.**

Consider the following illustration. If someone asks you whether or not your best friend likes milk, what do you do? You probably think to yourself, "Does she drink milk when I'm with her?" You then answer, "Yes, she drinks milk for breakfast and she often drinks milk with a snack, so she must like milk." Bem suggests that when someone asks you whether or not you like milk, you proceed in much the same fashion. You in effect observe or recollect your own behavior and then conclude: "If I can get milk with a meal, I always take it in preference to coffee or some other beverage. So I guess I must like it."

Evidence that external cues can shape your perceptions of your internal states is provided by social psychological research. For example, in one study (Valins, 1966), male college students were individually shown slides of *Playboy* nudes while their physiological reactions were supposedly being monitored. During the viewing session each man heard a rhythmic thumping. Some of the men were informed that the thumping sound was their heartbeat, whereas others were told it was irrelevant noise. With five of the ten slides, the thumping rate abruptly increased. Consequently, those men who believed they were monitoring their heartbeat concluded that the photos of these women had somehow affected their heart rate. Later the men were asked to rate the sexual attractiveness of each woman.

Apparently the external cues regarding their arousal level influenced the men's perceptions of how attractive they found each of the women. Of the men who thought they were listening to their heartbeat, 82 percent rated the women who had presumably increased their heart rate as more attractive than the other nudes. But for those men who believed that the sound was irrelevant noise, only 45 percent said the women associated with the sound change were the most attractive.

Follow-up interviews suggested that the men in the "heartbeat" group tried to understand the external cues afforded them by their "changing heart rate." They convinced themselves that their "sub-conscious" responses must have been right and that the nudes associated with the sound change indeed had nicer buttocks or breasts. Hence, having concluded from external cues that a woman had excited him, a man was more likely to find himself sexually attracted to the woman.

MONITORING AND MANAGING SOCIAL CUES

Your self-perceptions and your perceptions of other people set the stage for your behavior in a social environment. How you interact with people depends in large measure on the "readings" you take of yourself and of them. Does this stranger wish you well or harm or simply view you with indifference? Is your friend angry with you because you were not on time for your get-together? Is your professor likely to welcome your question if you interrupt her lecture now, or should you ask her the question after class? Will that salesclerk over there wait on you, or is he too busy chatting with the young woman? Does the driver of that car see you and intend to slow down so that you can safely cross the intersection?

You constantly confront questions such as these in your daily life. We have discussed how you go about forming impressions of others and how you explain and interpret events through attribution processes. Let us now consider some of the social cues that you use in monitoring the behavior of other people and in managing the impressions you in turn present to them.

Nonverbal Communication

In some respects you make your way about your social environment like an amateur detective. You attempt to piece together the bits and pieces of information you gain in your observations of people, in hopes of arriving at an interpretation of their behavior. You take into account what they say. But

---

self-perception theory: The use of much the same kinds of evidence and logic in reaching conclusions about oneself as are used in perceiving other people.

you also are influenced by their **nonverbal communication**—the gestures, postures, and facial expressions by which people transmit information, ideas, attitudes, and emotions to one another without the use of words.

All people are conscious of nonverbal communication from time to time. You have undoubtedly heard a friend tell you, "Oh, don't worry about it. It really doesn't matter." Nonetheless, you know that your friend, by speaking in a low voice and looking away, really means "You hurt my feelings and I feel bad." Very often you need not be told in so many words when a friend is elated or depressed, angry or pleased, nervous or contented. You sense such things. How do people communicate nonverbally? Let us consider this matter.

Body Language

The way you carry your body communicates information about you. If you stand tall and erect, you convey the impression of self-assurance. If you sit and talk with your arms folded and your legs crossed, you communicate that you are protecting yourself. But when you unfold your arms and stretch out (particularly when you fold your elbows away from your body, extend your hands and arms outward, hold your knees apart, and stretch out your legs), you communicate openness to other people.

One group of researchers (McGinley, LeFevre, and McGinley, 1975) found that women who adopt an open body position are better liked and are listened to more closely than women who assume a closed position. A number of students were given a questionnaire that measured their opinions on everything from the legalization of marijuana to the custom of tipping. A few weeks later they were invited back and asked to evaluate one student's responses. Some were shown a slide of the female student sitting in a closed position; others saw a slide of her sitting in a neutral or open position. A high percentage of those who saw the open-looking student indicated they liked her and changed many of their opinions in order to agree with hers when they filled out a second questionnaire.

Although people are not always directly aware of their use of body language, many of the postures they adopt and the gestures they make are governed by social rules. These rules are often very subtle. For instance, your boss is much more likely to touch you than you are to touch him or her—unilateral touching is a prerogative of higher status.

Body language also plays a critical role in courtship behavior (Scheflen, 1965; Schwarz, Foa, and Foa, 1983). People show a readiness to court by holding themselves more erect. Likewise, their eyes seem to brighten and their skin tends either to flush or to turn pale. And they commonly begin various "preening behaviors." A man may smooth his hair, readjust his clothes, tug at his tie, or pull up his socks. A woman may stroke her hair, check her make-up, rearrange her clothes, or push her hair off her face. Such signals say, "I'm interested in you. Notice me. I'm an attractive person."

Many nonverbal communications are understood in the same ways around the world (Ekman, 1980). Smiles show pleasant emotions, frowns unpleasant emotions. Crying means distress. Irenaus Eibl-Eibesfeldt (1970) photographed people greeting each other in settings ranging from the Amazon jungle to northern Europe. Humans typically raise and lower their eyebrows when saying "hello." Each species of animal also has its typical greeting behaviors (such as sniffing, circling, rubbing fur) that are universally understood within the species.

Perhaps not surprisingly, there are also cultural differences in body language (Ekman, Friesen, and Bear, 1984). For example, the thumbs-up gesture is favored by American and Western European airline pilots, truck drivers, and others to mean "all right." But in Sardinia and northern Greece, it is an insulting gesture comparable to the middle-finger gesture of American society. Likewise, Americans move their heads up and down to show agreement and shake them back and forth to show disagreement. In contrast, the Semang of Malaya thrust their heads sharply forward to agree and lower their eyes to disagree, while the Dayak of Borneo agree by raising their eyebrows and disagree by bringing them together.

---

nonverbal communication: The gestures, postures, and facial expressions by which people transmit information, ideas, attitudes, and emotions to one another without the use of words.

Personal space has different meanings in different cultures. *(top)* Leaders of the Druse religious sect of Lebanon and Syria confer in close physical proximity. *(Stephen H. Lewis/The Picture Cube)* *(bottom)* Two women keep a conversational distance comfortable for most middle-class Americans. *(Jerry Howard/Stock, Boston)*

But you do not have to go abroad to observe cultural variations in nonverbal communication. In a field study conducted in hospitals, airports, and fast-food restaurants, Marianne LaFrance and Clara Mayo (1976) found that American blacks and whites use eye contact in very different ways. Although blacks and whites look at each other for the same proportion of time during a conversation, the timing is different. Blacks tend to look at their partner while speaking and to look away while listening; whites do just the opposite. These differences may sometimes make blacks and whites uncomfortable when they talk to each other. There are also gender differences in communication processes, a matter discussed in the boxed insert on page 303.

The Language of Space

The anthropologist Edward T. Hall (1959, 1966) has drawn attention to the part that the **language of space** plays in human interaction. He uses this concept to refer to the methods that people use for communicating their sense of territorial privacy to others. Hall became acutely aware of the importance people attach to space when he found himself backing away from a colleague he particularly liked and

---

language of space: The methods that people employ for communicating to others their sense of territorial privacy.

Women and Men: Communication Processes

Popular belief has it that women are more adept than men in decoding nonverbal cues. In recent years researchers have looked into the matter and are finding truth to the belief (Hall, 1978; Blanck et al., 1981). Evidence shows that women are better judges than men of the meanings behind voice tones, facial expressions, and body movements, the sort of things that people have difficulty putting into words. Yet as women grow older, they seem to learn to be more nonverbally courteous or accommodating, and consequently they lose much of their advantage. Apparently there are social hazards in being "too good" at picking up messages that one is not intended to receive. "Knowing too much" about the inner states of one's associates often interferes with smooth interpersonal functioning (Rosenthal and DePaulo, 1979).

In talking with men, women also tend to carry the greater burden in keeping the conversation going. Pamela A. Fishman (1978) analyzed fifty-two hours of tapes made in the apartments of three middle-class couples between the ages of twenty-five and thirty-five. The women raised nearly twice as many topics for conversation as the men did. The men frequently would not respond to the women unless they regarded the topic the women presented as interesting. Consequently, the women would probe for topics in order to make the men full-fledged conversational participants. In contrast, the topics raised by men were seldom rejected by the women. Addi-tionally, the tapes revealed that the women would resort to attention-getting devices when they were confronted with the men's grunts or long silences. The women asked three times as many questions as the men did. A question does conversational "work" by eliciting a response. And the women would often preface their re-marks with such comments as "D'ya know what?" and "This is interesting." When a conver-sation lagged, they would often use the interjec-tion "you know." These phrases serve as go-ahead signals that the other person may speak up and that what is said will be heeded. Other research confirms that women do more of the routine maintenance work in conversations than men do (Roger and Schumacher, 1983).

Likewise, men are more likely to interrupt women than women are to interrupt men. In-deed, in cross-sex conversations in public plac-es, over 90 percent of the interruptions are made by men. Even in more relaxed settings men account for three in four interruptions (Zimmerman and West, 1975). Women also put more "color" in their speech than do men: they vary their pitch more, and they speak more tonefully. These techniques seem to be strategies for maintaining men's attention, because what women say is more likely to be ignored. Thus gender differences in social power affect the basic interaction of men and women (Kollock, Blumstein, and Schwartz, 1985; Pfeiffer, 1985).

respected. The associate was not an American, which led Hall to wonder if people from different cultures have different ideas about the proper dis-tance at which one should conduct an informal conversation. He decided to pursue the question.

After much observation, Hall concluded that Americans carry a two-foot "bubble" of privacy about them. If a strange person invades this space, an American feels imposed on, uncomfortable, and even threatened. In contrast, Hall found that the typical Arab does not have a private spatial barrier between himself and others. The Arab sees the person as existing somewhere down *inside* the body and not as extending in space beyond the body. Hence Arabs think nothing of touching one another on the street or on public conveyances.

Similarly, Arabs bathe the other person in their breath. To smell another is not only desirable, it is mandatory. To deny another person one's breath is to act ashamed. Whereas Arabs penetrate the olfac-tory bubble of others, Americans attempt to stay outside it. Thus Americans communicate shame to Arabs when in fact they are seeking to be polite. A "polite" American diplomat is an "ashamed" diplo-mat from the Arab's point of view. For Arabs, diplomacy is not only "eyeball to eyeball" but breath

"Public distance" at the beach. Strangers place themselves between twelve and twenty-five feet apart, a signal that no direct personal communication is desired. *(Barbara Alper/Stock, Boston)*

to breath, behavior that violates an American's privacy bubble and sense of propriety.

Germans have an even larger bubble of privacy than Americans. For Germans, an entire room of their home can represent personal privacy. They define space as an extension of themselves. During World War II, German prisoners of war, rather than pooling their resources to build a warm, shared shelter, would construct tiny individual units no larger than foxholes. In so doing, the men were protecting their sense of personal space.

Hall has observed Americans to see how they use space to communicate their feelings about other people and to define relationships. He found that Americans allow only intimates (lovers, close friends, and family members) closer than two feet, a point at which touching is almost inevitable. In contrast, when forced to stand very close to nonintimates, as in a crowded elevator, they try to hold their bodies immobile and avoid eye contact.

When people maintain a distance of four feet or so, they are essentially holding the other person "at arm's length." People who work together generally observe this boundary. Likewise, when you wish to transact impersonal business (for instance, the transactions between customers and clerks in a store), you typically create a four- to seven-foot bubble between yourself and the other person.

If you go to an uncrowded beach you will probably settle down between twelve and twenty-five feet from other people. At this distance—what Hall terms *public distance*—it is difficult to carry on a personal conversation. On the other hand, when you place your beach towel five feet from that of another person on a deserted beach, you are issuing either a threat or an invitation to that person.

People also use **markers** as signs of territorial defense, a "silent language" that includes such symbols as name plates, fences, hedges, and personal belongings. For example, they place books, handbags, and coats on a table or empty chair to reserve their place in the library, sunglasses and lotion on a towel to lay claim to a spot on the beach, and a drink on a bar to assert "ownership" of a bar stool (Becker, 1973; Schaffer and Sadowski, 1975).

Space is used to convey many other social meanings as well. Many of the terms we use in referring to status have spatial analogies: "head chair," "central figure," "dominant position," "upper echelon," and "high status" (Sommer, 1967; Schwartz, Tesser, and Powell, 1982). Figure 9.4 illustrates how status is subtly communicated in an office setting. Likewise,

marker: A sign of territorial defense; a "silent language" that includes symbols such as name plates, fences, and hedges.

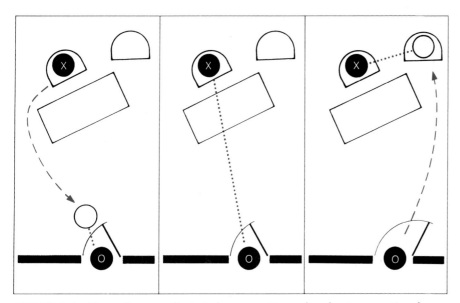

FIGURE 9.4 These diagrams illustrate how unwritten rules about occupational status are subtly communicated by physical position. O comes to visit X. The broken lines indicate movement; the dotted lines, conversation. See whether you can tell, before reading further, who has the superior status in each case. (*left*) X rises and moves to greet O. X's deference indicates that O is senior in rank. (*center*) O speaks from the doorway while X remains seated. O is deferring this time, suggesting that X is the superior. (*right*) O walks in and sits down beside X. This interaction indicates that X and O have roughly equal status.

firms usually reserve the highest floor for their top-ranking officials. On any given floor, the highest-ranking employees receive the corner offices, the next in rank have offices with windows, the lesser-ranked occupy partitioned cubicles, and so on. And studies of college classrooms reveal that dominant ethnic- and racial-group members occupy the spatial center of the seating area near the front of the room more often than do minority-group members, who more often occupy the spatial peripheries of a room (Haber, 1982).

Impression Management

Thus far in the chapter we have emphasized that people monitor the behavior of others so as to pick up cues regarding their attitudes, motives, and in-

tentions. In this manner they can fashion their own behavior in such a way that their actions are attuned to those of other people. They attempt to fit their actions to those of other people because they usually have a stake in such interaction. They often stand to gain or lose from it. Indeed, they are dependent on the behavior of other people to achieve many of their goals—be they employment, companionship, love, or whatever. Consequently, they find it in their interest to influence other people's behavior toward them.

But how can you influence other people's behavior? The sociologist Erving Goffman (1959) says that you can do so by influencing their conceptions of yourself. And you influence their conceptions by **impression management**—a process by which you attempt to shape people's definitions of yourself by

---

impression management: A process by which one attempts to shape people's definitions of oneself by generating words, gestures, and actions that will lead them to act in accordance with one's wishes.

generating words, gestures, and actions that will lead them to act in accordance with your wishes. Since human interaction is based on social cues and the meanings they convey, you possess the means for manipulating your behavioral performance in order to achieve favorable outcomes. You know that other people will take into account what you publicize about yourself. Thus you use the arts of concealment and strategic revelation to create various impressions. But impression management need not involve deception. At times you simply bring your actual attributes or accomplishments to the attention of others (Schlenker and Leary, 1982).

Central to the process of impression management is *front*—communications that assist you in defining the situation for other people (Goffman, 1959; Ball, 1966; Stone, 1970). One facet of front is the setting—the scenery and props you use in staging your performance. Consider, for example, the carefully tailored office of the typical physician. The waiting room is usually well carpeted and furnished with couches, chairs, large lamps, and tables with "appropriate" magazines—all communicating luxury and the special status of the doctor. Shelved medical books and framed diplomas adorn the physician's personal office, conveying a scientific mystique and competence. Family portraits are discreetly positioned to signal trustworthiness and to telegraph to others that the occupant is a pillar of "proper" community life.

Another aspect of impression management is *personal front*—the expressive equipment that you carry about. For instance, the physician's white lab coat, stethoscope, and black bag provide cues to the person's identity while the title "Doctor" (linked with the last name or simply employed by itself) establishes a rank that elicits social distance and deference.

Goffman's treatment of the presentation of self in everyday life highlights the subtle and manipulative features of human behavior in the presence of strangers, clients, patients, and others with whom one is not intimately associated. With them, you do not let your hair down, so to speak. But Goffman's treatment is insufficient. While it affords a discerning view of the chameleonlike behavior of people, it

Setting is an important aspect of impression management. In a doctor's office, the framed diplomas, white coat, stethoscope, and other elements of the setting help to define the doctor–patient situation. *(Rhoda Sidney/Monkmeyer)*

gives little consideration to "authentic" behavior. In many contexts, as with good friends, lovers, and family members, you experience genuine, honest, and sincere qualities in your relationships. You conceive of these people as meaningful in their own right and not merely as means to some ulterior end, a matter to which we now turn our attention.

SOCIAL RELATIONSHIPS

You form impressions of people and attempt to manage their impressions of yourself for a variety of reasons. But one reason that you attempt to understand others and want to impress them is because you wish to be with them. Indeed, as noted earlier, humans are social beings.

Barbra Streisand sang a song in which she said that "people need people." Social psychologists agree with this observation. It seems that most people do seek out other people and do want to *affiliate* with them (Deaux and Wrightsman, 1984). Prolonged absence from people, especially meaningful people, is typically experienced as utterly intolerable. Isolation—such as that experienced by prisoners in solitary confinement and scientists at South Pole research stations—disrupts a person's usual coping procedures (Suedfeld, 1974; Reinhold, 1982). In fact, the isolated person's behavior often becomes bizarre by ordinary standards. Clearly, our relationships with one another lie at the very core of our existence as human beings (Berscheid and Peplau, 1983).

Many interactions with people have a casual quality to them, for instance, occupying a seat next to a person on a bus, cashing a check at the teller's window, or sharing a table with someone at the library. Nonetheless, some interactions endure long enough so that a relatively stable set of expectations comes to link us with another person. This association is called a **social relationship.**

Two common types of relationship are *expressive ties* and *instrumental ties*. Sentiment is attached to relationships characterized by expressive ties—the kind of feelings associated with family, friends, and lovers. By contrast, the people in relationships characterized by instrumental ties are viewed as means to ends. On occasion people will even cooperate with their enemies, as in the old political saying, "Politics makes strange bedfellows." Let us consider, therefore, a number of factors that contribute to **social attraction**—the process by which people are drawn together.

Proximity

An important factor in determining whether two people will become friends is **proximity**—the distance from each other that the individuals live or work. In general, the closer two people are geographically to each other, the more likely they are to become attracted to each other. Not surprisingly, students typically develop closer friendships with those who share their classes, who sit near them, or who live in nearby rooms in the dormitory (Segal, 1974).

Psychologists have found that even in a small two-story apartment building, where each resident is in easy reach of everyone else, people are more likely to become close friends with the person next door than with anyone else (Festinger, Schachter, and Back, 1950). Even living two doors away makes a big difference. People are twice as likely to become friends with their next-door neighbor as with a person living two doors away. Moreover, people who live near the entrances, stairways, and mailboxes generally have more friends than other residents.

Proximity contributes to attraction by providing the *opportunity* for people to meet and interact with one another. People who are close by are simply more available than are those farther away. Hence proximity functions as a physical screen in determin-

---

social relationship: A tie that endures long enough to afford a relatively stable set of expectations.

social attraction: The process by which people are drawn together.

proximity (prok-SIM-ih-tee): The distance from one another that individuals live or work.

ing the probability of initial contact (Priest and Sawyer, 1967).

Physical Attractiveness

Proximity brings people together but it does not ensure that they will evolve a friendly relationship with one another. Indeed, proximity can also breed hatred, contempt, and emotional involvement. Police records reveal that aggravated assault and murder occur most often among acquaintances, neighbors, and family members. What then is likely to get you off to a good start with another person? A critical factor is physical attractiveness. Researchers find that we prefer the friendship and companionship of attractive people to that of unattractive people (Reis, Nezlek, and Wheeler, 1980; Marks, Miller, and Maruyama, 1981; Hatfield and Sprecher, 1986). And as discussed in the boxed insert on page 309, we often think that what is beautiful is good.

The power of physical attractiveness is also revealed by studies dealing with couples on blind dates. In one well-known experiment, social psychologists randomly paired male and female freshmen at a "computer dance" during "Welcome Week" at the University of Minnesota (Walster, Aronson, and Abrahams, 1966). While purchasing a ticket to the dance, each student was unknowingly judged for physical attractiveness by two observers. Later, after having attended the dance together, the students were interviewed and asked how much they liked their partners and whether they would like to date them in the future. To their surprise, the social psychologists found that only ratings of a man's or woman's attractiveness were useful predictors of liking; personality, intelligence, background, and social skills did not seem to matter.

Physical beauty is rewarding for both sexes, both as an individual experience and for the reflected prestige it provides (Sigall and Landy, 1973). Yet the supply of beautiful and handsome people is limited. Perhaps not surprisingly, observational studies of dating couples suggest that in real-life situations the partners tend to be similar to one another in their level of physical attractiveness (Walster and Walster, 1970; Berscheid et al., 1971; White, 1980). According to *the matching hypothesis of mate selection*, people fear rejection in the "mating and dating game" and select partners who are most likely to reciprocate their advances (Murstein, 1972). Thus they usually experience the greatest payoff and the least cost when they direct their efforts toward someone of approximately equal physical attractiveness.

Similarity

Few observations regarding human beings are older or more clearly established than the proposition that people tend to like others who are similar to them. Aristotle was one of the first to point out that "we like those who resemble us, and are engaged in the same pursuits." Countless studies have since documented that people prefer as friends others who share their beliefs and attitudes (Griffitt and Veitch, 1974; Vander Zanden, 1987). Indeed, the greater the proportion of similar attitudes held by two people, the greater the chances they will be attracted to each other (Gonzales et al., 1983). And the more likely they are to marry. Not uncommonly, husbands and wives have similar economic, religious, and educational backgrounds.

There are several explanations for the power of shared attitudes. First, agreement about what is stimulating, worthwhile, or fun provides the basis for sharing activities. We are likely to do more things with and to get to know people who have interests similar to our own.

Second, most of us feel uneasy around people who are constantly challenging our views, and we translate our uneasiness into hostility or avoidance. We are more comfortable around people who support us. According to the social psychologist Donn Byrne (1971), our attraction for another person is strongly influenced by the proportion of reinforcements and punishments associated with that person. He says that the perception of similarity is rewarding, whereas that of dissimilarity is punishing. According to Byrne, a friend's agreement bolsters our confidence and contributes to our self-esteem. (See the boxed insert on page 310 for a discussion of how these formulations about reinforcement can help you in relating to people.)

Third, we usually find it easier to communicate with people who agree with us. We have fewer arguments and misunderstandings with them; we are better able to predict each other's behavior and thus feel at ease with each other. In addition, most of us are self-centered enough to assume that people who share our values are basically decent and intelligent (unlike those who do not).

What Is Beautiful Is Good, or Is It?

The Greek philosopher Aristotle noted that "beauty is a greater recommendation than any letter of introduction." Studies reveal that Aristotle's observation is remarkably on target. And researchers are finding that the world is a more pleasant and satisfying place for attractive people because they are typically accorded many social advantages (Reis et al., 1982). These effects are embedded in the notion that "what is beautiful is good" (Dion, Berscheid, and Walster, 1972; Hatfield and Sprecher, 1986).

We commonly size up strangers on the basis of their physical attractiveness (Deaux and Lewis, 1984). Although it may seem unfair and unenlightened, we usually prefer attractive people over less attractive ones. And we assume that attractive people have more socially desirable traits than unattractive people. The beauty-is-good bias even operates in our appraisal of newborns. Physically attractive babies are deemed smarter, more likable, and less troublesome than unattractive infants (Stephan and Langlois, 1984). Later in life, teachers expect that attractive youngsters will earn higher school grades than their unattractive peers, and the attractive youngsters do (Clifford and Walster, 1973). Teachers also judge the misdemeanors of good-looking children as less serious than those of unattractive children (Dion, 1972); they discipline them less severely (Berkowitz and Frodi, 1979); and they expect they will have more successful careers (Dion, Berscheid, and Walster, 1972). Even in college, essays ostensibly written by attractive students are accorded higher grades than are the same essays when they are thought to be written by unattractive students (Landy and Sigall, 1974). And overall, most of us think that attractive adults have happier marriages, better sex lives, higher status, and better mental health than unattractive adults (Dion, Berscheid, and Walster, 1972; Dermer and Thiel, 1975; Cash et al., 1977).

However, it is not always to a person's advantage to be attractive, particularly if the person is a woman (Cash and Janda, 1984; Wilson et al., 1985). Attractive men and women seem to bring our gender stereotypes to mind. We perceive handsome men as being more masculine and beautiful women as more feminine than their less attractive peers. Such perceptions do not necessarily work a hardship on men (Reis et al., 1982). In fact, they are to a man's advantage. But the perceptions do pose problems for women who aspire to occupations in which "masculine" traits—being strong, independent, and decisive—are believed important to success. When it comes to jobs that clash with our society's traditional gender roles, we tend to rate beautiful women lower than less beautiful women. Accordingly, it seems that less attractive women enjoy an advantage over their more attractive counterparts when seeking management positions. It is hardly surprising that several "dress for success" books have made it to the best-seller list by advising women who wish to "get ahead" to wear their hair short, use cosmetics sparingly, and wear conservatively tailored suits. In sum, a sexist prescription holds: if a woman hopes to advance in a man's work, she should not appear too feminine.

Finally, Leon Festinger (1954) suggests a *social comparison theory* to account for the strong relationship between attitude similarity and attraction. He says that we have a need to evaluate our opinions and abilities. We like to know if our ideas are correct and if our appraisal of our abilities is accurate. We generally prefer some objective standard for checking these matters (for instance, we would prefer to measure how far we can throw a baseball than to have only a rough estimate). But when there is no objective basis for comparison, we seek to evaluate our opinions and abilities by comparison with others. Given a choice for comparison, we will choose someone close to our own opinion or ability (Wetzel and Insko, 1982; C. T. Miller, 1982). If only a divergent comparison is available, we will not be able to make a precise evaluation. For instance, if you are a graduating senior in accounting and wish to deter-

How to Relate to People

If you're like most people, you want others to like you, but knowing exactly how to make them like you is not always easy. Most psychologists believe that the principle of *reciprocal reinforcement* has a lot to do with how you get along with others. In simple terms, this principle states that people will like you if your behavior makes them feel good about themselves.

Here are some reinforcement techniques you can use to get a head start on winning and keeping friends (Williams and Long, 1979):

● When you are talking to another person, try to spend at least 50 percent of the time listening to what the other person says. That may mean cutting down on your chatter, but you will find the results to be well worthwhile.

● Be an active rather than a passive listener. By commenting directly on what the other person says, you will show that you are really interested in his or her conversation.

● Instead of focusing on your own accomplishments, ask questions about the person you are with. This tells the person in no uncertain terms that you care about what he or she has done. The best time to talk about yourself is when the other person asks.

● Approval is one of the best reinforcers if it is used correctly, but another person is easily turned off if it is not sincere. Be sure to praise only those things the other person considers important and do not use an overlavish or repetitive approach.

mine whether you should apply to the best firms for a job, you are unlikely to compare your achievements with those of a dance major or an electrical engineer. Rather, you compare yourself with others who will seek similar jobs. And in doing so, you are drawn to or attracted by other accounting majors.

Complementary Needs

Similarities undoubtedly play a considerable part in attraction. But there is also much truth to the old saying that "opposites attract." You probably have noticed that you feel comfortable with people who have certain personality traits but that other types of people "rub you the wrong way." Robert F. Winch (1958) has formulated a theory of attraction that is based on this everyday observation.

According to Winch, **complementary needs** are met between people who are different. He notes that some personality traits are the counterparts of others

and that people gain a sense of completeness when they are joined. Each person supplements the other and supplies the other's lack. For instance, if you are a dominant person, you would achieve a complementary relationship with submissive people. If you are talkative, you probably find yourself attracted to "good listeners." If you have a nurturance need (a need to sympathize with and help others), you may realize fulfillment with a person having a succorance need (a need to be helped and taken care of by others). And if you crave the limelight you probably find satisfaction with those who prefer to bask in the achievement of others.

Although the theory has been used to explain friendships, it has found its greatest application in the area of mate selection. According to Winch, people typically seek a partner who gives promise of providing them with the maximum gratification of their needs. Although the approach seems to find confirmation in everyday life (the domineering male

complementary needs: A condition in which each person in a social relationship supplies the other's lack. Individuals gain a sense of completeness when they enter into relationships with people with different traits.

According to the social exchange theory, the teacher–learner relationship, like all others, has rewards and costs that each member continually appraises as the relationship goes on. *(Hugh Rogers/Monkmeyer)*

and the mousy wife, or vice versa), actual studies have produced mixed findings (Kerckhoff and Davis, 1962; Levinger, Seen, and Jorgensen, 1970; Meyer and Pepper, 1977; Antill, 1983). One difficulty is that some needs are complemented by similarity rather than by contrast (Rosow, 1957; Levinger, 1964). Thus a quiet, thoughtful, introverted person usually prefers a similar person as a companion rather than a loud, active extrovert. Husbands and wives, in fact, are more similar in background, personality, talents, and interests than they are different.

Social Exchange

Over the past decade or so, a number of psychologists and sociologists have attempted to link various behavioral concepts with economic theory (Thibaut and Kelley, 1959; Homans, 1961; Blau, 1964). The result has been **social exchange theory.** Proponents of this view start with the notion that people like those who reward them and dislike those who punish them. Consequently, they enter into relationships with others much as they enter into economic transactions. They base their actions on the assumption that their actions will produce rewards, including love, recognition, a sense of security, or material benefit. So long as each provides the other with rewarding experiences, two people will maintain mutual attraction and continue associating with each other. Hence the reciprocal exchange of rewards contributes to mutual reinforcement.

Exchange theorists consider the relationship between rewards and costs to be critical. *Profit* is total reward minus costs. *Costs* include punishment as well as physical or mental effort (fatigue, anxiety, embarrassment). According to this view, people engage in mental bookkeeping, maintaining a ledger on rewards and costs. They keep track of their profits and losses and continue a relationship so long as they find it profitable.

As seen by social exchange theory, people go about life weighing the attractiveness of a relationship in terms of certain levels of expectation. They

social exchange theory: The view that people enter relationships with others much as they enter into economic transactions. They keep track of profits from a relationship and continue it so long as they find it beneficial.

ask themselves questions such as "Am I putting more into this relationship than I am getting out of it?" "What is the lowest level of reward I will take to continue in this relationship?" and "What rewards would I forgo if I were to try an alternative relationship?" On the basis of their answers to these questions, some people find a new roommate, break up with a lover, or secure a divorce. However, some research suggests that rewards play a more important part than costs in a good many relationships. Studies of heterosexual dating relationships and long-term college friendships reveal that benefit scores, and not cost or benefits-minus-costs scores, are the best predictor of the current and long-term status of relationships (Rusbult, 1983; Hays, 1985).

There are many values that people consider in evaluating a relationship. A friend has *stimulation value* if he or she is interesting or imaginative or can introduce you to new ideas or experiences. A friend who is cooperative and helpful, who seems willing to give time and resources to help you achieve your goals, has *utility value*. A third type of value in friendship is *ego-support value:* sympathy and encouragement when things go badly, appreciation and approval when things go well. These three kinds of rewards—stimulation, utility, and ego support—are evaluated consciously or unconsciously in every friendship. A man may like another man because the second man is a witty conversationalist (stimulation value) and knows a lot about gardening (utility value). A woman may like a man because he values her opinions (ego-support value) and because she has an exciting time with him (stimulation value).

A major advantage of social exchange theory is that it affords a unifying theme underlying many other factors of attraction. Consider the matter of physical beauty that was discussed earlier in the chapter. Suppose a physically unattractive man desires a beautiful woman (Murstein, 1972). Other things being equal, the woman would gain less profit from the relationship than the man would. Hence the man reasons that the woman will reject his advances. Further, he will suffer a cost, since rejection will cause him to lose in self-esteem. If he dates a less attractive woman, his cost is low since he stands little risk of rejection. But the reward from such a conquest is also low. Given this situation, he can obtain the greatest reward at the least cost by pursuing women of comparable attractiveness to himself. This interpretation underlies the matching hypothesis of mate selection.

Exchange theory is also useful in explaining other factors in attraction. People who live or work near one another (proximity) are more likely to interact because of the low cost of initiating interaction with each other. People who possess similar attitudes and values can provide one another with the reward of opinion validation and social support at low cost. And the partners in a complementary relationship offer each other high rewards by meeting needs at low cost to themselves.

SUMMARY

1. Human interaction is the foundation of group life. Since you live your life in a social setting, you must continually make sense of your experiences with people. How you think about those experiences and how those experiences influence your thinking is termed social cognition. Through the processes of social cognition you discriminate and organize various aspects of your social environment.

2. Human beings construct their perceptions of the world. Your brain orders and interprets raw sensory data to arrive at meaning. But you do not merely await stimulation from external sources. You seek out information. Your brain transforms stimuli into organized systems of events to which you assign meaning. You form schemes in memory that organize and preserve information.

3. People use schemes for getting about in a social environment. They construct images of others to make their social experiences manageable, stable, and predictable.

A. Perhaps the most immediate attributes or characteristics that strike you about people are their sex, race, age, and social status. On the basis of these dimensions, you place them in various categories to which you attach meaning—in this case, impressions of the average member of the group, called a stereotype.

B. One reason different people develop different impressions of the same stranger is that each person has his or her own implicit personality theory (a set of assumptions about how people behave and what traits or characteristics go together) and prototype (a category mentally used to represent a loose set of features that seem to belong together). Experiments indicate that people's impressions are strongly influenced by a few traits. When forming impressions of an individual, one tends to round out the incomplete information and see the person as a unit.

C. When presented with inconsistent information we usually either incorporate it within our overall impression or ignore it.

4. People usually want to understand another person's behavior. They want to know what causes the person to act in a given manner. The process by which they explain and interpret the events that they encounter is termed attribution.

A. In analyzing a person's behavior, one typically attempts to determine whether it was caused by personal (dispositional) or environmental (situational) factors. Social psychologists find that people tend to underestimate the impact of situational factors and to overestimate the role of dispositional factors in controlling behavior—the fundamental attribution error.

B. People also seek to account for their own behavior. But at times they cannot rely on internal cues because these are too weak, ambiguous, or inaccessible. They must then infer their inner state from external cues. They observe their own actions and from them determine what their attitudes or motives must be. This process of self-attribution is termed self-perception theory.

5. People use a variety of social cues in monitoring the behavior of others and in managing the impressions that they in turn present to others. In so doing they are influenced by nonverbal communication.

A. The way people carry their body communicates information about them. They can communicate either "openness" or "closeness" depending on the way they position their arms and legs.

B. People also use the language of space to communicate to others their sense of territorial privacy. People of different cultures have some-

what different ideas about privacy and the use of space.

6. Since human interaction is based on social cues and the meanings they convey, people possess the means for manipulating their behavioral performance in order to achieve favorable outcomes. They know that other people will take into account what they publicize about themselves. Thus they use the arts of concealment and strategic revelation to achieve impression management.

7. People form impressions of others and attempt to manage others' impressions of them because they wish to have companions. They establish social relationships—ties that endure long enough to afford a relatively stable set of expectations. Two common types of relationship are expressive ties and instrumental ties.

8. An important factor in determining whether two people will become friends is proximity. In general, the closer two people are geographically to each other, the more likely they are to become attracted to each other. Proximity contributes to attraction by providing the opportunity for people to meet and interact with one another.

9. A person's physical appearance greatly influences others' early impressions. Physically attractive people are typically viewed more positively than less attractive ones. We usually prefer the friendship and companionship of attractive people to that of unattractive people.

10. People tend to like others who are similar to them. There are several explanations for the power of shared attitudes. First, agreement about what is stimulating, worthwhile, or fun provides the basis for sharing activities. Second, people perceive similarity as rewarding and dissimilarity as punishing. Third, people who agree about things usually find it easier to communicate with each other. And finally, people use similarity in social comparison processes.

11. Similarities undoubtedly play a considerable part in attraction. But there is also much truth to the old saying that "opposites attract." Complementary needs are met between individuals who are different. In these cases, each person supplements the other and supplies the other's lack.

12. Social exchange theory attempts to link various behavioral concepts with economic theory. People

like those who reward them and dislike those who punish them. Consequently, they enter into relationships with others much as they enter into economic transactions. So long as each provides the other with rewarding experiences, two people will maintain their mutual attraction and continue to associate with each other.

KEY TERMS

attribution (p. 297)
complementary needs (p. 310)
fundamental attribution error (p. 297)
human interaction (p. 291)
implicit personality theory (p. 294)

impression management (p. 305)
language of space (p. 302)
marker (p. 304)
nonverbal communication (p. 301)
proximity (p. 307)

prototype (p. 294)
self-perception theory (p. 300)
social attraction (p. 307)
social cognition (p. 291)
social exchange theory (p. 311)
social relationship (p. 307)
stereotype (p. 294)

SUGGESTED READINGS

ARONSON, ELLIOT. 1980. *The Social Animal.* 3rd ed. San Francisco: Freeman. A conversationally written textbook in social psychology. Excellent reading for the person who wants to go deeper into the ideas in this and the next chapter.

CUSHMAN, DONALD P., and MCPHEE, ROBERT D., Eds., 1980. *Message-Attitude-Behavior Relationship: Theory, Methodology and Application.* New York: Academic Press. A challenging group of essays that define the relationship between messages, attitudes, and behaviors. Especially useful for anyone interested in behavioral research.

HALL, EDWARD T. 1966. *The Hidden Dimension.* Garden City, N.Y.: Doubleday. A thorough and well-written book that describes the bubbles of privacy people carry about them and the purpose of personal space.

MEER, JEFF. 1985. Loneliness. *Psychology Today*, 19 (July):28–33. Explains the many faces of ·loneliness from enjoyable solitude to miserable emptiness.

RUBIN, ZICK. 1973. *Liking and Loving: An Invitation to Social Psychology.* New York: Holt, Rinehart and Winston. A very readable presentation of topics in social psychology that help to develop principles of liking and loving.

SCHNEIDER, DAVID J., HASTORF, ALBERT H., AND ELLSWORTH, PHOEBE C. 1979. *Person Perception.* 2nd ed. Reading, Mass.: Addison-Wesley. Provides a brief but comprehensive overview of how people perceive one another. The authors pay special attention to attribution theory and implicit personality theory.

SHAW, MARVIN E. 1980. *Group Dynamics: The Psychology of Small Group Behavior.* 3rd ed. New York: McGraw-Hill. An excellent text in which the author reviews the field, summarizes what is known, and points to problems for future research.

VUCHINICH, SAMUEL. 1985. Arguments, family style. *Psychology Today*, 19 (October):40–43. Describes how video recordings of families reveal their patterns of bickering, an inevitable and often beneficial part of family life.

Anthony Toney, *New Yorkers*, 1979.

10

Attitudes and Group Processes

In 1977 the Federal Bureau of Investigation assigned agent Patrick Livingston to an undercover investigation of the pornography business in Florida. As "Pat Salamone," Livingston posed as a brash, loud-mouthed hustler of pornography. Within six months he succeeded in establishing himself with Mafia figures. For some three years Livingston enacted his role, eating in expensive restaurants, jetting coast-to-coast for sex-film conventions, and consorting with mobsters. In 1981 the Florida pornography investigation ended with the indictment of forty-five persons. But Livingston could not relinquish "Pat Salamone." He continued to visit his old bars, bookmakers, and underworld associates, even though most of them now knew he was an FBI agent. He maintained a bank account and a driver's license as Pat Salamone and sought to continue a high-living life style on funds borrowed from friends. The FBI returned him to its Louisville, Kentucky, office. Shortly thereafter, a store detective arrested Livingston for shoplifting. He gave his name as Pat Salamone and lied to the FBI about the incident. The FBI fired him in 1982.

Another agent, Dan A. Mitrione, had an impeccable record with the FBI. In 1982 the FBI selected him for an undercover assignment investigating narcotics dealing at the Fort Lauderdale, Florida, airport. Mitrione, posing as "Dan Micelli," and an informer set themselves up as electronic debugging experts and offered their services to drug-smuggling pilots worried about law-enforcement eavesdropping. According to a later indictment by federal authorities, Mitrione allowed the informer to close a cocaine deal worth $850,000 and took some of the proceeds for himself. He quit the FBI with the intention of going into the construction business.

Mitrione's wife says her husband did not revert to his former self until long after his clandestine assignment. However, in the interval, he was convicted of drug dealing and bribery.

Over the past decade, federal investigators and local police departments have employed undercover agents in operations against corrupt business executives and public officials, drug dealers, pornographers, and other racketeers (DeStefano, 1985). No one underestimated the physical dangers. But these dangers turned out to be more manageable than the psychological risks. A number of undercover agents have posed problems for their superiors, their associates, and their families. In a large number of cases they have ruined marriages and careers, botched prosecutions, and committed crimes.

The problems that many undercover operatives have in resuming their previous roles and identities highlight the crucial part that groups play in our lives. In the pages that follow we will address a number of questions. What are the sources of our attitudes? What part do attitudes assume in shaping our actual behavior? What are some mechanisms by which our attitudes and behavior are influenced? How do groups affect our daily lives and fortunes? What factors feed intergroup conflict and cooperation?

SOURCES OF ATTITUDES

Are you convinced that vitamin C is the best cure for the common cold? Do the oil companies periodically plunge the world into energy crises? How do you feel about Christianity? democracy? the national honor of the United States? What about the New York Yankees? daisies? termites? Each of you has a wide variety of attitudes on these and other topics. Some of them are deemed worth dying for; others are not considered worth the time it would take to explain them.

An **attitude** is a relatively enduring disposition or tendency to evaluate a person, object, or event in a particular way. When talking about attitudes—or attempting to measure them—one typically focuses on how people look at and feel about certain things. Do they judge them to be good or bad? Are they pleased or displeased by them?

Attitudes are states of mind. They are ways by which people organize and categorize their information and feelings on various matters (Deaux and Wrightsman, 1984; McGuire, 1985). As such, attitudes touch every phase of life. They influence the activities in which you engage and whom you engage in them with. And they guide you in such key decisions as your choice of a college, a profession, a spouse, a political candidate, and a life style.

Where Attitudes Come From

Each of you has very definite beliefs, ideas, and feelings about various matters, even matters about which you have no firsthand knowledge. Where do these attitudes come from? The culture in which you grew up, the people who raised you, those with whom you associate—your peers— and you yourself all shape your attitudes.

Culture

Out of the incredibly large number of ways of living successfully, we operate within the rather narrow domain provided by our *culture*—those customs, beliefs, values, and skills that guide our behavior along shared paths. Culture influences everything from taste in food to attitudes toward human relationships and political opinions. For example, most (if not all) Americans would consider it disgusting to eat snakes, curdled milk spiced with cattle blood, or monkey meat. Yet in some parts of the world these are considered delicacies. Most Americans believe eating meat is essential for good health. But many Hindus consider the relish for thick, juicy steaks and hamburgers barbaric and uncivilized.

Most Americans would also agree that parents who interfere in their children's choice of a marriage partner are behaving outrageously and that a person should be able to marry the person he or she loves. But in India, until relatively recently, parents chose husbands for their daughters, and many young

---

attitude: A relatively enduring disposition or tendency to evaluate a person, object, or event in a particular way.

Hindu women were relieved not to have to make such an important choice (Mace and Mace, 1960). Likewise, at one time the Manus of the Admiralty Islands (Melanesia) sought to prevent the development of adolescent love relationships by isolating their young people from potential mates. When a young woman experienced her first menstruation, the Manus removed her from her playmates and kept her at "home"—on stilts over a lagoon—under the close supervision of elders (Goode, 1959).

The list of culturally derived attitudes is endless. Indeed, it is only by traveling and reading about other ways of life that you can discover how many of the things taken for granted are *attitudes* and not common to all members of the human species.

Parents

For the first few years at least, parents represent to children a large portion of the social world (Himmelweit et al., 1981; Zern, 1983). They are the mirror in which children begin to view themselves. Parents control rewards and punishments and deliberately use them to shape their children's attitudes and behaviors. And parents often take considerable pains to filter the information that reaches their children. Hence parents are a powerful source for attitude formation.

Parental influences play an important role in the transmission of racial attitudes (Vander Zanden, 1983). However, it seems that racial attitudes are largely "caught rather than taught." Parents often have the impression that they are not the ones responsible for teaching their children prejudice. For the most part, they do not give their youngsters direct verbal instruction. But they allow their children to "overhear" adult conversations about other racial and ethnic groups. And by parental action and inaction, big and small—gestures, facial expressions, tone of voice, rapidity of speech, muscular movements, speed and rhythm of breathing, and other cues—sentiments are communicated.

Peers

It is not surprising that parental influence declines as children get older and are exposed to many other sources of influence (Caplow et al., 1982; Cherlin, 1983). In a now classic study, Theodore Newcomb (1943) investigated attitude change during the late 1930s among students at Bennington College (then a women's college) in Vermont. Most of the women came from wealthy, staunchly conservative families. In contrast, most Bennington faculty members were outspoken liberals. Rallies, money-raising drives, and discussion sessions fanned student enthusiasm for the causes of the day and demonstrated that the "good Bennington citizen" was properly concerned with current issues. The attitudes of the faculty were transmitted to the students, who then reinforced one another's views.

Newcomb found that many of the students were "converted" to the liberal point of view. In 1936, 54 percent of the juniors and seniors supported Franklin D. Roosevelt and the New Deal—although praising Roosevelt to their families would have produced about the same reactions as praising Karl Marx to Ronald Reagan. Indeed, nearly 30 percent of the students favored socialist or communist candidates. Newcomb contacted the subjects of his study twenty-five years after they had graduated, and found that most had maintained the attitudes they had acquired in college. One reason was that they had chosen friends, husbands, and careers that supported liberal values (Newcomb et al., 1967). People tend to adopt the likes and dislikes of groups whose approval and acceptance they seek.

Self

We, of course, evaluate evidence for ourselves. Our attitudes reflect our own conclusions about the world. Through our interaction with others and through the effects we produce on our material environment, we gain a sense of our adequacy, energy, skill, and industry. We come to know ourselves and evaluate ourselves on the basis of our actions and the outcomes of our actions. And we gain a sense of mastery from our accomplishments and the products of our efforts. Thus we are hardly placid beings at the mercy of our surroundings and the assessments of others. We fashion both ourselves and our attitudes as we make our way through life (Riegel, 1976).

Processes of Attitude Formation

Having considered where attitudes come from, let us now examine how they develop. Herbert Kelman (1961) suggests that three major processes are involved in forming or changing attitudes: compliance, identification, and internalization. He says that each of these processes constitutes a different type of social influence.

By way of illustration, consider your highway driving (Goldstein, 1980). You may conform to the posted speed limit because of external pressures. If you slow your car down to the speed limit when you spot a police patrol ahead, your response reveals *compliance*. Or you may drive at a speed that fits the behavior of someone you admire. If that person drives fast, you drive fast; if he or she drives slowly, you do so. This behavior reflects *identification*. Finally you may believe that fifty-five miles per hour is the safest and most efficient speed. Hence you drive at this highway speed whether or not a patrol car is ahead and whether or not someone who you know and admire observes the speed limit. In this case, you display *internalization*.

Compliance

At times you may yield to the pressures of others and act in conformity with their wishes even though you think you should act in some other way. Social psychologists term this response **compliance**. People often go along with others because they wish to be rewarded for conformity or to avoid being punished for nonconformity.

The case of Patricia Hearst provides a good example of compliance. As you may know, she was kidnaped in Berkeley, California, in 1974 by members of the Symbionese Liberation Army. Even though she loathed her captors, was forced to have sex with all three of the men, and was abused by the women, she did not escape even when they left her alone. She robbed banks with her captors and on occasion drove the getaway van. In her autobiography, Patricia Hearst says she never believed in what the group was doing and that she was not indoctrinated by the Maoist lectures. Rather, she had been made a member of the "team" and wanted to be a "team" player. She asserts, "I felt I owed them something, something like loyalty." In the process,

Many kidnaping victims and hostages show compliance with the attitudes of their captors, especially when they are held for long periods of time and are subjected to intense pressure to conform. Patricia Hearst is a well-known recent example of this phenomenon. *(UPI/Bettmann Newsphotos)*

she surrendered her autonomy and relinquished control over her body and destiny.

Group pressure to conform. The psychologist Solomon Asch (1952) launched a series of classic experiments to test conformity to pressure from peers. He found that groups can induce people to call true what they privately consider to be false. Hence individuals may conform to other people's ideas of the truth, even when they disagree. The following is what you would have experienced had you been a subject in one of Asch's experiments.

---

compliance: Yielding to the pressures of others and acting in conformity with their wishes even though one thinks one should act in some other way.

You and six other students meet in a classroom for an experiment on "visual judgment." Asch props up two large, white cards in the chalk tray of the blackboard (see Figure 10.1). He then explains to the seven of you that you are to match the length of the line on the first card with one of the three lines on the second card. There are to be eighteen comparisons and you are to give your answers aloud, each in turn.

You "happen" to be the sixth person, one other student following you. On the first comparison, everyone chooses the same matching line. The second set of cards is displayed, and once again the group is unanimous. The exercise seems easy, and you prepare for what you expect will be a rather boring experiment.

However, the third trial is a shock. You are certain that line 2 is the one that matches the standard. Yet the first person in the group announces confidently that line 1 is the correct match. Then the second person follows suit; she too declares that the answer is line 1. So do the third, fourth, and fifth subjects. Now it is your turn. You are confronted with two contradictory pieces of information: the evidence from your own senses tells you that one answer is clearly correct, but the unanimous and confident judgments of the preceding subjects tell you that you are wrong. Will you join the unanimous majority or be a minority of one?

You face the same dilemma on eleven of the remaining fifteen trials. After the trials are complete, Asch asks that you remain for a few minutes. He questions you about your experiences. Finally, he debriefs you, explaining to you the nature of the experiment. He tells you that the other students were really his assistants and that they had been instructed to provide the wrong answers.

How do subjects react to this experimental situation? Asch found that only one-fourth of the 123 subjects did not yield to group pressure and agree to an incorrect answer. Asch called those who did not conform "independents." Overall, one-third of all the subjects' estimates were in the direction of the majority. He termed the conformers "yielders." Most yielders explained to Asch afterward that they knew which line was correct but that they yielded to group pressure in order not to appear different from the others. Why so much conformity? According to one theory, most children are taught the overriding importance of being liked and accepted. Conformity

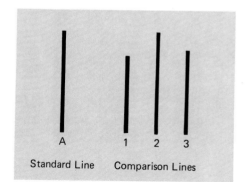

FIGURE 10.1 These two cards were shown to subjects in one trial of Asch's experiment on conformity. The actual discrimination is easy.

is the standard means of gaining this approval. Consequently, some people comply with the wishes of others in order to be liked by them (Insko et al., 1983; Insko et al., 1985).

However, Asch (1956) found that a single "deviant" can have a powerful effect on the conformity of other group members. As noted, over a third of the time subjects agreed with the unanimous majority on a line-judging task even when the response was clearly wrong. But the deviance of even one other group member—emboldened the subject to stick to his or her judgment. Under these circumstances, conformity dropped to about 8 or 9 percent. Indeed, one study found that the "deviant" need not give the correct answer (Allen and Levine, 1971). Even when the "deviant" provides an answer that is more incorrect than that of the majority, the compliance of the subjects drops off sharply. Hence, from the perspective of a totalitarian regime, permitting even one deviant can be exceedingly dangerous. It can result in others in the population also resisting the regime.

Dissenters not only show others that a variety of opinions and behavior is possible. People feel less vulnerable to group pressure when they have "company in deviance." Indeed, a minority that firmly and resolutely pursues its ends can exert considerable influence on the majority, even when the minority has no obvious advantages like wealth or recognized positions of power (Bray, Johnson, and Chilstrom, 1982). Such historical figures as Galileo, Abraham Lincoln, and Sigmund Freud steadfastly

Photographs taken during Asch's experiment on conformity. Subject 6 is the only real subject; the others are confederates of the experimenter (seen at the right in the upper-left photograph). The subject listens to the others express identical judgments that differ from his own. He is in a dilemma: does he express the judgment he knows to be correct and risk being different from the group, or does he conform to the group's judgment? *(William Vandivert)*

advanced a minority position and eventually induced the majority to adopt their beliefs. But for a minority to successfully challenge a majority, it must provide a consistent and stable alternative norm (for example, a program with respect to air pollution, women's rights, or abortion) (Moscovici, 1976). The consistency with which the minority promotes its program is also critical because the majority interprets consistency as an expression of certainty and confidence (Maass and Clark, 1984; Tanford and Penrod, 1984). But by the same token, the minority should not appear to be rigid lest the majority discount its opinions as dogmatic and narrow-minded (Ricateau, 1971).

Obedience to authority. The influence other people have on your attitudes and actions is consider-able. Sometimes this influence is indirect and subtle; at other times it is quite direct. People may simply tell you what to believe and what to do. Under what conditions do you *obey* them?

Everyone has had experience with various authorities—including parents, teachers, police officers, managers, judges, clergy, and military officers—who call for obedience. Under some circumstances, obeying the orders of another—for instance, a doctor or fire fighter in an emergency—can be constructive. But there are also circumstances in which obedience presents destructive possibilities. German crimes in Nazi Europe and atrocities during the Vietnam War reveal the cruel and dangerous outcomes that can follow from obedience to the commands of superiors (Cockerham and Cohen, 1980). And the 914 deaths at the People's Temple settlement in Guyana in 1978, following the suicide instructions of Reverend Jim Jones, provides stark testimony to the dangers of blind obedience in some cult settings. But perhaps most startling of all, research by the social psychologist Stanley Milgram (1974) reveals that there is a very good likelihood that you, or at least people like you, would carry out orders endangering another person's life. Critics have raised questions regarding the ethics of the research, since it exposed subjects to potential psychological trauma (Baumrind, 1964, 1985; Kelman, 1967). It is unlikely that such research could be undertaken now in light of various federal regulations governing the use of human subjects.

Milgram set up his controversial experiment as follows. Two subjects appeared for each session. They were told that they would be participating in an experiment to test the effects of punishment on memory. One of the subjects was to be the "teacher" and the other the "learner." (In reality, the learner was not a naive volunteer; he was Milgram's accomplice.) The teacher was to read a list of words into a microphone for the learner, who would be in a nearby room, to memorize. If the learner failed to recite the list correctly, the teacher was to administer an electric shock. The alleged purpose of the experiment was to test whether the shock would have any effect on learning. In actuality, however, Milgram wanted to discover how far the teacher would follow his instructions; how much shock would he be willing to give a fellow human being?

As the experiment began, the learner-accomplice continually gave wrong answers, and the teacher began to administer the prescribed shocks from an impressive-looking shock generator. The generator had a dial that ranged from 15 volts, which was labeled "Slight Shock," to 450 volts, which was labeled "Danger: Severe Shock." After each of the learner's mistakes, the teacher was told to increase the voltage by one level, thus increasing the severity of the shock. The teacher believed that the learner was receiving these shocks because he had seen the learner being strapped into a chair in the other room and had watched electrodes being attached to the learner's hands. In reality, however, the accomplice was receiving no shocks at all from the equipment.

Each increase in shock level was met by increasing shrieks of discomfort, cries of agony, and fervent pleas from the learner that the experiment be stopped. If the subject hesitated, the experimenter instructed him to continue. (You can see why a good many people have criticized the study as unethical.) Milgram found that 65 percent of the subjects gave the highest shock voltage—450 volts. No subject stopped before administering 300 volts, the point at which the learner began kicking the wall. Here are excerpts from the responses of one fifty-year-old subject. On administering the 180-volt shock, the subject turned to the experimenter and addressed him in agitated tones (Milgram, 1974:73–76):

SUBJECT I can't stand it. I'm not going to kill that man in there. You hear him hollering?
EXPERIMENTER As I told you before, the shocks may be painful, but—
SUBJECT But he's hollering. He can't stand it. What's going to happen to him?
EXPERIMENTER (*His voice is patient, matter-of-fact*) The experiment requires that you continue, Teacher.
SUBJECT Aaah, but, unh, I'm not going to get that man sick in there . . . know what I mean?
EXPERIMENTER Whether the learner likes it or not, we must go on, through all the word pairs.

At 195 volts the learner screamed, "My heart's bothering me, let me out!" By 450 volts the subject was no longer receiving any feedback from the learner:

SUBJECT That's that.
EXPERIMENTER Continue using the 450-volt switch for each wrong answer. Continue, please
SUBJECT But I don't get no anything!
EXPERIMENTER Please continue. The next word is "white."
SUBJECT Don't you think you should look in on him, please?
EXPERIMENTER Not once we've started the experiment.
SUBJECT But what if something has happened to the man?
EXPERIMENTER The experiment requires that you continue. Go on, please.
SUBJECT Don't the man's health mean anything?
EXPERIMENTER Whether the learner likes it or not . . .
SUBJECT What if he's dead in there? (*Gestures toward the room with the electric chair.*) I mean, he told me he can't stand the shock, sir. I don't mean to be rude, but I think you should look in on him. All you

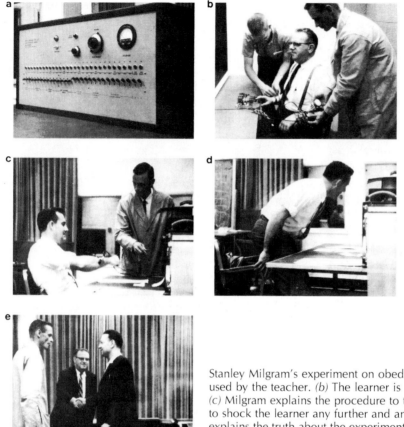

Stanley Milgram's experiment on obedience. (a) The fake shock generator used by the teacher. (b) The learner is connected to the shock apparatus. (c) Milgram explains the procedure to the teacher. (d) This subject refuses to shock the learner any further and angrily rises in protest. (e) Milgram explains the truth about the experiment. (By Stanley Milgram. From the film Obedience. Distributed by New York University Film Library.)

have to do is look in on him. All you have to do is look in the door. I don't get no answer, no noise. Something might have happened to the gentleman in there, sir.

EXPERIMENTER We must continue. Go on, please.

The teacher obeyed and administered additional shocks.

These subjects were not sadists. They were ordinary men—salespeople, engineers, postal workers —placed in an unusual situation. What accounts for the surprisingly high level of obedience? A large part of the answer is that the experimenter represents a legitimate authority. People assume that such an authority knows what he is doing, even when his instructions seem to run counter to their own standards of moral behavior.

Milgram's subjects could have walked out at any time—they had already been paid and had nothing to lose by leaving. Nevertheless, social conditioning

for obeying legitimate authorities is so strongly ingrained that people often lack the words or the ways to do otherwise. Simply getting up and leaving would have violated powerful unwritten rules of acceptable social behavior.

Subsequent experiments have revealed that there are a number of ways in which subjects can be helped to resist authority in this situation (Milgram, 1974). One is the removal of the physical presence of the experimenter (highest level of obedience dropped from 65 percent when the experimenter sat close by to 22 percent when he was simply a voice on the telephone). Also effective is putting the subject face to face with the victim (only 40 percent of the subjects conformed with full shock when the victim was in the room with them, and only 30 percent complied fully when they had to hold the learner's hand down on the electrical shock plate). The third and most effective variation of the experiment is to enhance an individual's sense of personal responsi-

Identification with a group such as a sorority or fraternity is one important way in which an individual's attitudes are formed or changed.
(Roy E. Roper/EKM-Nepenthe)

bility. For instance, when subjects must pass on the experimenter's orders to administer the shock to the victim, they are more obedient than when they must pull the shock switch themselves (Kilham and Mann, 1974). This finding helps explain why society generally assigns greater blame to the soldier who acts on an order than to the clerk who relays the order.

Identification

Another way in which attitudes may be formed or changed is through the process of **identification** —mentally associating yourself in thought, feeling, or action with another person or group. Suppose you have a favorite uncle who is everything you hope to be. He is a successful musician, has many famous friends, and seems to know a great deal about everything. In many ways you identify with him and copy his behavior. One night, during an intense conversation, your uncle announces he is an atheist.

At first you are confused by his statement. You have had a religious upbringing and have always considered religious beliefs as essential. However, as you listen to your uncle, you find yourself starting to agree with him. If a person as knowledgeable and respectable as your uncle holds such beliefs, perhaps you should, too. Later you find yourself feeling that atheism is acceptable. You have adopted a new attitude because of your identification with your uncle.

Identification occurs when you want to define yourself in terms of a person or group, and therefore adopt the person's or group's attitudes and ways of behaving. Identification is different from compliance because in identification you actually believe the newly adopted views. But because these attitudes are based on emotional attachment to another person or group rather than your own assessment of the issues, they are fragile. If your attachment to that person or group fades, the attitudes may also weaken. Thus in the Bennington College study discussed earlier in the

---

identification: Mentally associating oneself in thought, feeling, or action with another person or group.

chapter, one student ultimately rejected the liberal point of view (Newcomb, 1943:124):

> Family against faculty has been my struggle here. As soon as I felt really secure I decided not to let the college atmosphere affect me too much. Every time I've tried to rebel against my family I've found how terribly wrong I am, and I've very naturally kept to my parents' attitudes.

For this student, identification with the college community was only temporary.

As this quotation also illustrates, very often there is a group to which a person refers in order to evaluate and decide on attitudes and behaviors. A social unit with which people identify is called a **reference group.** Reference groups serve two functions (Kelley, 1952). First, they provide people with a framework for fashioning their attitudes and behavior. People view themselves as members in good standing within a particular group, or as wishing to become members in good standing. Consequently, they take on the group's political outlook, its clothing and hair styles, its sexual practices, or its drug-using behaviors. In this sense, their attitudes and behavior are group-anchored. Second, reference groups provide a comparison function. They serve as a standard against which people judge or evaluate themselves. Individuals continually make use of reference groups in assessing their physical attractiveness, intelligence, social ranking, standard of living, and health. But not all reference groups are positive. We also use *negative reference groups* in order to emphasize the dissimilarities between ourselves and others. For Cuban-Americans in Miami and Dade County, the Castro regime functions as a negative reference group (Carver and Humphries, 1981). Most of them fled their homeland after the revolution that brought Fidel Castro to power.

Internalization

Internalization entails the wholehearted acceptance of an attitude, so that it becomes an integral part of one's being. Internalization is most likely to occur when an attitude is consistent with your basic beliefs and values and supports your self-image. You adopt a new attitude because you believe it to be right —not because you want to please or be like someone else. Perhaps you have had an experience of this sort since attending college. Perhaps your attitude toward abortion has changed, for example.

Internalization is the most lasting of the three sources of attitude formation or change. Your internalized attitudes will be more resistant to pressure from other people because your reasons for holding these views have nothing to do with other people: they are based on your own evaluation of the merits of the issue. Internalization accounts for the fact that so many of the Bennington students still held their liberal attitudes a number of decades after leaving college (Newcomb et al., 1967). One coed put it this way (Newcomb, 1943:136):

> I became liberal at first because of its prestige value; I remain so because the problems around which my liberalism centers are important. What I want now is to be effective in solving the problems.

As this example suggests, compliance or identification may lead to the internalization of an attitude. Often the three overlap. You may support a political candidate in part because you know your friends will approve, in part because someone you admire speaks highly of the candidate, and in part because you believe his or her ideals are consistent with yours.

ATTITUDES AND BEHAVIOR

We have said that attitudes are states of mind. But what about behavior? What relationship is there between your attitudes and the way you act? Certainly how you evaluate people, objects, and events influences what you say and do. In this sense, attitudes ready you for certain kinds of action.

Yet your attitudes are not always in harmony. For instance, for more than a century many white Ameri-

---

reference group: A social unit with which people identify.

internalization: The wholehearted acceptance of an attitude, so that the attitude becomes an integral part of one's being.

cans accepted the American democratic creed that all people are equal under the law while simultaneously accepting racial discrimination in restaurants and theaters. Indeed, whites fought wars in the name of freedom, equality, and justice and yet tolerated slavery and later legalized segregation.

Nor do you necessarily act in accordance with your attitudes. In a classic study conducted a half-century ago, the sociologist Richard T. LaPiere (1934) traveled extensively across the United States with a Chinese couple. They stopped at 66 hotels, auto camps, and tourist homes (there were as yet no motels) and at 184 cafés and restaurants. Only once were they denied service. Several months later, LaPiere mailed questionnaires to the proprietors of the various establishments and asked if they would "accept members of the Chinese race as guests." Over 91 percent of the 128 replies were negative. This finding revealed a sharp contradiction between people's attitudes and their actual behavior. Let us then examine more carefully the relationships among attitudes and between attitudes and behavior.

Attitude Consistency

Much research in social psychology assumes that people strive for **attitude consistency**—they typically try to bring their attitudes into harmony with one another. Hence members of the Ku Klux Klan do not ordinarily make contributions to black civil-rights groups; Marxists do not usually enroll in graduate business schools; and environmentalists do not ordinarily vote for candidates who favor oil drilling along scenic coastlines. According to the principle of attitude consistency, people are impelled to reconcile their conflicting attitudes. They find that holding two opposing attitudes can create considerable internal conflict, throwing them off balance. Hence, they try to get their attitudes to fit together logically.

Few theories in social psychology have command-ed more interest than the formulation of Leon Festinger (1957) on attitude consistency—the theory of cognitive dissonance. **Cognitive dissonance** is the uncomfortable feeling that arises when you experience contradictory or conflicting attitudes. To reduce dissonance, it is necessary to change one or both of the attitudes. Consider, for example, the dilemma of a socialist who inherits $10 million. The newly rich socialist believes that wealth should be shared, but he may also be opposed to paying millions in taxes to the government or contributing to traditional charities. (Not to mention the temptation of high living and a Rolls Royce.) One solution is for him to give all the money to CARE and forget about his reservations regarding capitalist charities. Another is to decide that a mere $10 million cannot do much to stamp out poverty anyway, so he might as well hire an expensive tax lawyer and enjoy the money.

Some people attempt to evade dissonance by avoiding situations or exposure to information that would create conflict. For example, they may make a point of subscribing to newspapers and magazines that uphold their political attitudes, of surrounding themselves with people who share the same ideas, and of attending only those speeches and lectures that support their views. It is not surprising that such people get quite upset when a piece of conflicting information finally does get through.

People are not always explicitly aware of the process of dissonance reduction. Nonetheless, it is a frequent and powerful occurrence. In fact the social psychologist Milton Rokeach (1971) achieved remarkably long-lasting changes in attitudes by making white students aware that their emphasis on freedom was inconsistent with their indifference to equality and civil rights. In an initial forty-minute session, the students ranked a number of items by importance to themselves—including the key values of freedom and equality. They were also asked to express their attitudes toward civil rights.

The students then compared their answers with a table of typical answers, which the researchers inter-

---

attitude consistency: The tendency for people to try to bring their attitudes into harmony with one another.

cognitive dissonance: The uncomfortable feeling that arises when a person experiences contradictory or conflicting attitudes.

preted for them. The researchers told the students that a tendency to rank freedom high and equality low was evidence that such individuals are "much more interested in their own freedom than in other people's." Further, they were informed that such rankings are consistent with a lack of concern for civil rights. Finally, the students were asked whether their results left them satisfied or dissatisfied. (Another group of students, the control group, did not receive the researchers' explanation. They simply completed their rankings and went home, oblivious of any inconsistencies in attitude they might have expressed.)

In order to test whether students would act on the values they had expressed, three to five months later the researchers sent out a solicitation for donations or memberships on NAACP stationery. They received many more replies from students in the experimental group than in the control group. They concluded that the interpretation of students' conflicting attitudes had made the first group of students more receptive to civil-rights issues. Moreover, on tests fifteen to seventeen months later, changes in attitude were much more likely in subjects who had been dissatisfied with what they had been told about the results of their original test than in subjects who had not been dissatisfied. These findings suggest that cognitive dissonance spurred changes in attitudes toward civil rights.

The researchers had managed to produce a powerful and lasting impact from a forty-minute session and a few follow-up tests. In this case, the outcomes were consistent with the values esteemed by a democratic society. Nonetheless, Rokeach (1971:458) was disturbed by the implications of the study, for "If such socially important values as equality and freedom can be altered to become more important to human subjects, they can surely be altered to also become less important. Who shall decide . . .?"

Doing Is Believing

We have considered how people seek to reduce the dissonance they experience when holding conflicting attitudes. But what part do attitudes play in behavior? Obviously, your attitudes affect your actions. If

you like American cars, very likely you will buy an American car rather than a foreign car. Yet some of the relationships between attitudes and actions are not so obvious. For example, it turns out that if you like American cars but buy a foreign car for some reason (perhaps you can get a better deal on a foreign car), you will end up liking American cars less. In other words, actions affect attitudes.

In many instances, if you act and speak as though you have certain beliefs and feelings, you begin *really* to feel and believe this way. For example, people accused of a crime have, under pressure of police interrogation, confessed to crimes they did not commit. They have confessed in order to relieve the pressure; but having said that they did the deed, they begin to believe that they really *are* guilty.

Self-Justification Theory

One explanation for this phenomenon comes from the theory of cognitive dissonance. If you act one way but think another, you will experience dissonance. To reduce the dissonance, you will have to change either the behavior or the attitude. A closely related explanation is that you have a need for **self-justification**—a desire to view yourself as blameless and right.

In an experiment that demonstrated these principles, Leon Festinger and J. Merrill Carlsmith (1959) offered subjects a monetary incentive to say something opposed to their actual belief. They paid students either one dollar or twenty dollars to tell another person that a boring, tedious experiment in which both had to participate was really a lot of fun. Afterward, the experimenters asked the subjects how they felt about the experiment. They found that the subjects who had been paid twenty dollars to lie about the experiment continued to believe that it had been boring. They justified lying about the experiment's being fun by convincing themselves that the large reward warranted their behavior.

Those who had been paid one dollar, however, came to believe that the experiment had actually been fairly enjoyable. These people were given only a small payment to tell the lie. Consequently, they experienced more dissonance. To justify their lie,

---

self-justification theory: The view that people have a need to see themselves as blameless and right.

they had to believe that they had actually enjoyed the experiment.

The phenomenon of self-justification has serious implications. For example, David C. Glass (1964) led subjects in a psychological experiment to believe that they had injured or hurt other subjects in some way. The aggressors were then asked how they felt about the victims they had just harmed. It was found that the aggressors had convinced themselves that they did not like the victim of their cruelty. In other words, the aggressors talked themselves into believing that their defenseless victims had deserved their injury. The aggressors also considered their victims to be less attractive after the experiment than before —their self-justification for hurting another person was something like this: "Oh, well, this person doesn't amount to much, anyway." Soldiers frequently confront similar problems in wartime. They kill others and then must somehow justify their behavior. They commonly do this by dehumanizing their victims.

The self-justification phenomenon can also produce positive outcomes. It may help to explain why some patients realize benefits from psychotherapy. The effort involved in therapy, plus the decision to undergo the therapy, leads people to reduce cognitive dissonance by cultivating healthy modes of behavior (Axsom and Cooper, 1985). For example, obese people in weight-therapy programs seem to respond to the programs in part to justify their expenditure of effort. The fact that one has undergone highly taxing sessions is inconsistent with the notion that one does not usually engage in vigorous exercise. Justifying the effort enhances the attractiveness of the weight-loss behavior.

Self-Perception Theory

A somewhat different interpretation of the Festinger and Carlsmith findings is provided by Daryl Bem (1967, 1972). As we indicated in Chapter 9, Bem has formulated a self-perception theory. He says that people often come to know their attitudes and inner states by inferring them from the observations they make of their own behavior. Thus Bem claims that people's attitudes do not necessarily cause their behavior. Rather, their behavior frequently causes their attitudes.

Bem does not believe that cognitive dissonance theory offers the best explanation of why subjects in the small- and large-reward groups later reported different degrees of liking for the boring, tedious task. He says that the underlying mental process was not primarily an attempt to reconcile attitudes and behavior. Instead, the students were attempting to find out what their attitudes really were by observing their behavior. They looked at their own behavior and asked themselves, "What must my attitude be if I behave this way in this situation?" Those in the large-reward group reasoned, "Twenty dollars is enough money to induce me to lie; I really don't care for the task." In contrast, those in the small-reward group reasoned, "One dollar is not enough to induce me to lie; I must really have cared about doing the task." In sum, the subjects observed their own actions and from them inferred what their attitudes were.

Several experiments have been conducted to determine whether the self-justification or self-perception explanation is the more accurate (Snyder and Ebbesen, 1972; Green, 1974; Steele and Liu, 1983). The findings have been mixed. These inconclusive outcomes suggest that there may be some truth in each of the interpretations (McGuire, 1985; Ross and Fletcher, 1985).

Self-Fulfilling Prophecy Theory

Another relationship between attitudes and actions is rather subtle—but extremely widespread. It is possible, it seems, for people to act in such a way as to make their attitudes come true. This phenomenon is called a **self-fulfilling prophecy.** Suppose, for example, you are convinced that you are a bad cook. Every time you go into the kitchen, you think you will fail. Because you approach the task of baking a cake with a defeatist attitude, you fumble the measurements, pour in too much milk, leave out an ingredient, and so on. As a result, your cake is a flop. You thus confirm that you *are* a bad cook. One of the most difficult points to grasp in this connection is that there is no conspiracy to make the prophecy

---

self-fulfilling prophecy: The process by which individuals act in such a way as to make their attitudes come true.

come true. Rather you unintentionally cause the fulfillment to occur by virtue of your acting as if it were true—in keeping with your attitudes.

Self-fulfilling prophecies can influence all kinds of human activity (Stephan, 1985). Suppose you believe that people generally like you. Whenever you approach other people, you are friendly and open. Because of your smile and positive attitude toward yourself and the world, people like you. Thus your attitude that people like you produces your friendly behavior, which in turn causes people to respond favorably toward you. They confirm the belief "People like me."

But suppose you turn this example around. Imagine that you believe most people do not like you. Because of your negative attitude, you tend to avert your eyes from other people, to act gloomy, and to appear rather unfriendly. People think your actions are strange, and consequently, they act coldly toward you. Your attitude has produced the kind of behavior that confirms the belief "People don't like me."

The psychologist Robert Rosenthal (1966) has conducted a series of experiments that point to the role played in learning and education by self-fulfilling social expectations. He found that rats performed well in test situations if their handlers were told, falsely, that the rodents had been especially bred for intelligence. In contrast, rats consistently turned in poor performances when the handlers were falsely informed that the animals were dull. And when elementary school teachers were falsely told that certain children's IQ tests revealed that they were about to "spurt ahead" academically, these children sometimes surpassed their classmates on tests a year later (Rosenthal and Jacobson, 1968).

Prejudice and Discrimination

The dynamic interplay between attitudes and actions is highlighted by prejudice and discrimination. **Prejudice** refers to a predetermined attitude toward the members of a gender, race, family, or other group simply because the individuals belong to it and without regard to their personal traits or qualities (Allport, 1954). Prejudices may be in favor of a group's members, or against. You can be favorably prejudiced toward other members of your own social group and negatively prejudiced against members of another group.

Discrimination is behavior that arbitrarily gives or denies people privileges accorded to others by virtue of their group membership. Discrimination, like prejudice, can be pro or con. Note, though, that prejudice is an attitude; discrimination is behavior.

As in the case of other attitudes and actions, a one-to-one relationship does not necessarily hold between prejudice and discrimination (Vander Zanden, 1983). As revealed by LaPier's study of his trip with a Chinese couple, prejudiced people do not always translate their attitudes into discriminatory actions. Indeed, civil-rights legislation aims to deter discriminatory behaviors by penalizing people who otherwise might act in accordance with their prejudice. By the same token, nonprejudiced people may act in a discriminatory manner because segregation is mandated by law, as in South Africa and, until the 1960s, in the American South.

In determining how people will act in an intergroup situation, much depends on the social setting (Stephan, 1985). Observations made in Chicago during the 1950s by the sociologist Lewis Killian (1952, 1953) illustrate this proposition. He studied the behavior of southern rural and small-town white migrants to the North who harbored considerable hostility toward blacks. The men expressed strong preferences for segregated arrangements and in their daily talk constantly deplored that blacks were "taking over Chicago."

As patrons of a "redneck" tavern, the white migrants would have beaten up any black who entered the bar and asked to be served. Yet in the nonsegregated "greasy-spoon" restaurant next door, they ate their lunches as regular patrons side by side

---

prejudice: A predetermined attitude toward the members of a gender, race, family, or other group simply because the individuals belong to it and without regard to their personal traits or qualities.

discrimination: Behavior that arbitrarily gives or denies individuals privileges accorded to others by virtue of their group membership.

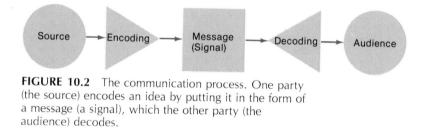

FIGURE 10.2 The communication process. One party (the source) encodes an idea by putting it in the form of a message (a signal), which the other party (the audience) decodes.

with blacks. Moreover, many of the men not only worked in plants with blacks but shared rest rooms with them. As the social psychologist Gordon W. Allport (1962:121) has pointed out, and research has consistently confirmed, "Segregationists act like integrationists where social prescription requires; integrationists behave like segregationists when it is socially appropriate to do so." Consequently, believing does not ensure doing.

PERSUASION

Persuasion is a deliberate attempt to influence attitudes and behavior through communication. At one time or another everyone engages in persuasion. When a smiling student who is working her way through college by selling magazine subscriptions comes to the door, she attempts to persuade you that reading *Newsweek* or *Sports Illustrated* or *Ms.* will make you better informed, giving you lots to talk about at parties. Parents often attempt to persuade a son or daughter to complete college or pursue a particular career. And some men try to persuade their dates that sex without love is perfectly natural. Even terrorism is used as a media event to shape public opinion (see the boxed insert on pages 332–333). In each case the persuader's main hope is that by changing the other person's attitudes, he or she can change that person's behavior as well.

Enormous amounts of time, money, and effort go into campaigns to persuade people to change their attitudes and behavior. Some succeed on a grand scale; others seem to have no effect. One of the most

difficult questions social psychologists have tried to answer is: What makes a persuasive communication effective?

Communication is the process by which people transmit attitudes, information, ideas, and feelings to one another. For persuasion to take place, three elements must mesh: the source, the message, and the audience (see Figure 10.2). The source sends a message to an audience, hoping to produce a desired outcome. However, not all messages succeed in bringing about the desired response. Let us consider each of these elements, examining in turn the part that the source, the message, and the audience play in persuasion.

The Source

How people see the source, or originator, of a message may be a critical factor in their acceptance or rejection of it. Individuals receiving the message ask themselves two basic questions: Is the person giving the message trustworthy and sincere? Does the source know anything about the subject? If the source seems reliable and knowledgeable, the message is likely to be accepted.

Suppose, for example, that you have written a paper criticizing a poem for your English class. A friend who reads the paper tells you about an article that praises the poem and asks you to reconsider your view. The article was written by Agnes Stearn, "a student at Mississippi State Teachers College." You might change your opinion—and you might not. But suppose your friend tells you that the same positive critique was written by T. S. Eliot. The

persuasion: A deliberate attempt to influence attitudes and behavior through communication.

communication: The process by which people transmit attitudes, information, ideas, and feelings to one another.

Terrorism

We are often reminded in one way or another of the frightening prevalence of terrorism in our contemporary world. According to one survey, ten years ago the world experienced an average of ten incidents of terrorist violence per week (bombings, assassinations, air hijackings, kidnapings, and maimings). By early 1985, there were nearly ten such incidents each day. Between 1970 and 1985, terrorists struck 22,171 times, killing an estimated 40,394 persons and wounding 24,588 others (*U.S. News & World Report,* 1985).

Terrorism entails the use of force or violence against persons or property to intimidate or coerce a government, an organization, or a civilian population in furtherance of political, religious, or social objectives. In practice, as with a great many other behaviors, what constitutes terrorism is a matter of social definition. Hence, it is frequently difficult to distinguish "our freedom fighter" from "your terrorist" or to differentiate aid to "terrorists" from "covert support of friendly forces" like the Nicaraguan contras, or counterrevolutionary fighters (in 1984 an eighty-nine-page booklet prepared under the auspices of the Central Intelligence Agency advocated blackmailing, kidnaping, and assassinating Nicaraguan government officials). Likewise, the Federal Bureau of Investigation labeled a "terrorist" the antinuclear activist who in 1982 drove up to the Washington Monument in a truck that he pretended was loaded with explosives, whereas the agency has failed to apply a similar label to those responsible for firebombing abortion clinics in various American cities.

For many years psychologists, sociologists, and historians viewed terrorism primarily as a "nuisance." However, as the historian Franklin L. Ford (1985) points out, terrorism has a long history. The attempts on the lives of President Reagan and Pope John Paul II and the successful murder of Anwar el-Sadat, all in 1981, may remind us that on March 15, 44 B.C., Julius Caesar was stabbed to death in the Roman Senate. We also encounter early prototypes of modern-day terrorists—the Israelite Zealots of the first century who murdered those who disagreed with their religious fundamentalism, and the radical Muslim schismatics who ten centuries later formed the sect of the Assassins and learned they could use the terror they inspired to extort funds that subsidized further terror. What distinguishes much contemporary terrorism is not so much its motivation or purpose as the extent to which nation-states have become involved in carrying out well-planned and highly destructive

chances are that you would begin to doubt your own judgment. Three psychologists tried this experiment. Not surprisingly, many more students changed their minds about the poem when they thought the criticism was written by T.S. Eliot (Aronson, Turner, and Carlsmith, 1963).

A person receiving the message also asks: Do I like the source? If the communicator is respected and admired, people will tend to agree with the message, either because they believe in the person's judgment or because they want to be like the person. The identification phenomenon explains the frequent use of athletes in advertisements. Football players and Olympic champions are not (in most cases) experts on deodorants, electric razors, or milk. Indeed, when an athlete endorses a particular brand of deodorant on television, everyone knows the individual is doing it for the money. Nevertheless, the process of identification makes these sales pitches highly effective (McGuire, 1985).

---

terrorism: The use of force or violence against persons or property to intimidate or coerce a government, an organization, or a civilian population in furtherance of political, religious, or social objectives.

acts against adversary nations. Terrorism has become a new mode of warfare. The 1983 attack on the U.S. Marine barracks in Beirut that resulted in the death of 240 Americans is a tragic example of this.

Another feature of recent terrorism has been the extent to which it has become a media event. Often the acts are aimed at a media audience, not the actual victims. Even though the terrorists write the script and perform the drama, the "theater of terror" becomes possible only when television and the press afford the stage and access to a worldwide audience. Measured in terms of the worldwide attention terrorist acts garner, and not in terms of the number of people who suffer or lose their lives, terrorism can attain a great deal of attention at relatively low cost to the perpetrators.

Media coverage frequently enhances the importance of "the problem" that ostensibly led to the terrorist acts. Television viewers and newspaper readers see "the problem" as of greater magnitude than previously and as justifying resolution by national or international action (Cunningham, 1984a). For example, the 1983 bombing of the Marine barracks led many Americans, including members of Congress, to conclude that the United States should not be involved in Lebanon. The grotesque scenes of young Marines being pulled out of the rubble sickened a good many people and led the American public to be wary of further entanglement in Lebanon's affairs.

Although the United States has often been seen as safe from terrorism, it too has had its share of terrorist acts. Over the past decade or so a variety of terrorist groups have surfaced, including the Symbionese Liberation Army, the Weather Underground, the Black Liberation Army, and the United Freedom Front. Some groups such as the anti-Turkish Armenians, nationalist Puerto Ricans, Croatian separatists, and anti-Castro Cubans have espoused nationalistic aims. And a number of groups, including such right-wing organizations as the Order, the Silent Brotherhood, the Covenant, and the Aryan Nations, have advanced programs of racial and religious hatred. (In 1985, the United States government indicted twenty-four members of the Order, charging them with the murder of Denver talk-show host Alan Berg, the attempted murder of FBI agents in gun battles in Washington and Oregon, armed robberies that included the paramilitary assault on a Brink's truck in Ukiah, California, and counterfeiting.) There also has been a trend in recent years toward issue-oriented terrorism, including the bombing of abortion clinics, damaging laboratories conducting animal experiments, and arson attacks on video shops selling pornography.

The Message

Suppose two people with opposing viewpoints are trying to persuade you to agree with them. Suppose further that you like and trust both of them. In this situation the message becomes more important than the source. The persuasiveness of a message depends on the way in which it is composed and organized as well as on the actual content.

Should the message arouse emotion? Are people more likely to change their attitudes if they are afraid or angry or pleased? The answer is yes, *but* the most effective messages combine emotional appeal with factual information and argument (McGuire, 1969; Leventhal, 1970; Leventhal and Nerenz, 1983). A communication that overemphasizes the emotional side of an issue may boomerang. If the message is too upsetting, it may force people to mobilize their defenses (Axelrod and Apsche, 1982).

For example, showing pictures of accident victims to people who have been arrested for drunken driving may convince them not to drive when they have been drinking. But if the pictures are so bloody that people are frightened or disgusted, they may also stop listening to the message. On the other hand, a communication that includes *only* logic and information may miss its mark because the audience does not relate the facts to personal lives.

The antismoking campaign provides a good illustration of a movement that has paid large dividends (Warner, 1981). Per capita cigarette consumption in the United States has declined annually since 1973.

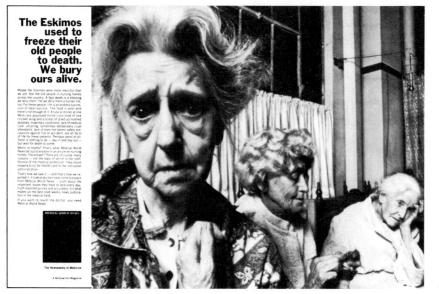

The Eskimos used to freeze their old people to death. We bury ours alive.

Maybe the Eskimos were more merciful than we are. Ask the old people in nursing homes across the country. A fast death is a blessing we deny them. Yet we deny them a human life, too. For these people, life is an endless succession of deprivations. The food is poor and there's not enough of it. A typical dinner at one Medicare approved home consisted of one chicken wing and a scoop of dried-up mashed potatoes. Insanitary conditions, lack of medical care, uncaring, sometimes deliberately cruel attendants, lack of even the barest safety precautions against fire or accident, are all facts of life for these patients. Perhaps worst of all, there is nothing to do — day in and day out — but wait for death to come.

Who's to blame? That's what Medical World News set out to explore in an article on nursing homes. The answer? There are of course many reasons — not the least of which is the indifference of the medical profession. They shunt responsibility for health care to the institution administration.

That's how we saw it — and that's how we reported it. It is what doctors have come to expect from Medical World News — truth about the important issues they have to face every day, truth reported quickly and accurately. It's what makes us the best-read weekly news publication in the medical field.

If you want to reach the doctor, you need Medical World News.

MEDICAL WORLD NEWS

The Newsweekly of Medicine

A McGraw-Hill Magazine

Successful advertising. This advertisement presents a powerfully emotional picture and headline to shock readers into attention and arouse their concern. It then gives some hard facts to further involve them in the subject matter. Readers might have ignored the ad if it had simply said, "Doctors need to know about current issues relevant to the medical profession. Subscribe to *Medical World News*." (Courtesy, Medical World News)

It is estimated, for instance, that the level of cigarette consumption would have been a third higher in 1978 had it not been for the campaign. Fear appeals try to get you to think about the dangers you confront when taking given courses of action. In the process you often gain a sense that you can effectively cope with or master a threatening situation. You may conclude, "Why should I take a chance?" and in turn follow a strategy of precaution. Or you may think, "I have nothing to lose by trying this approach, and much to gain," and then follow a strategy of defensiveness. In either case, you are made to feel safer (Maddux and Rogers, 1983).

When presenting an argument, is it more effective to present both sides of an issue or only one side? For the most part, a two-sided communication is more effective, because the audience tends to believe that the speaker is objective and fair-minded. Two-sided communication is especially effective when audiences are well informed and well educated or are initially opposed to the message. One-sided communications are the more effective approach when the audience already agrees with the message (McGinnies, 1966; McGuire, 1969, 1985).

The Audience

The audience includes all those people whose attitudes the communicator is trying to change. Being able to persuade people to alter their views depends on taking into account who the audience is and why it holds the attitudes it does. Individuals differ considerably in the extent to which they derive information from and elaborate on arguments provided by a message (Cacioppo, Petty, and Morris, 1983).

Suppose, for example, you are involved in a program to reduce the birth rate in a population that is outgrowing its food supply. The first step would be to inform people of various methods of birth control as well as how and where to obtain them. However, that people know how to limit their families does not mean that they will do so. Even the best technique will not be used unless people *want* to use it (Schnore, 1966; Davis, 1976). To persuade them to use available contraceptives, you need to know why they value large families. In some areas of the world, people have many children because they do not expect most babies to survive early childhood. In this case, you might want to tie the family-planning campaign to programs of infant care. In some areas, children begin working in the fields or at odd jobs at an early age and bring in needed income. In this case, you might want to promote an incentive system for families who limit themselves to two or three children.

If the people are not taking advantage of available means of birth control, you will want to know who is

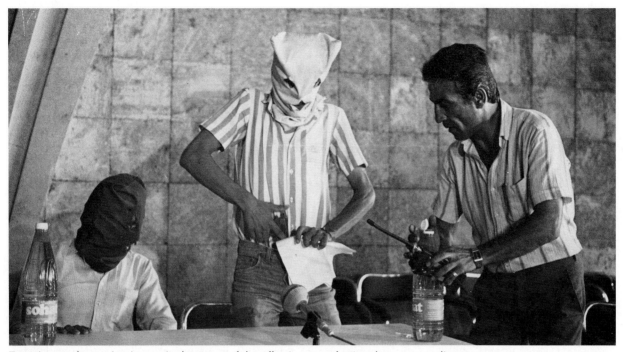

Terrorists are becoming increasingly aware of the effectiveness of using the news media to convey their messages to the public. Here a hooded hijacker prepares to make a statement to the press after the seizure of a TWA plane in Athens in 1985. *(Frederic Neema/Reuters-Bettmann Newsphotos)*

resisting and why. Perhaps men believe fathering a child is a sign of virility. Perhaps women consider motherhood an essential element of femininity. Or perhaps both sexes see parenthood as a symbol of maturity and adulthood (Coale, 1973). The more a person's attitude is "anchored" through linkage and integration with other supporting beliefs, the more resistant he or she is to changing the belief. Moreover, people draw on their existing beliefs and prior experiences to evaluate the validity of the arguments contained in a message (McFarland, Ross, and Conway, 1984; Schmidt and Sherman, 1984; Wood, Kallgren, and Preisler, 1985). To complicate matters, people selectively recall their past behaviors to make them consistent with their current attitudes (Ross et al., 1983). Accordingly, knowing who your audience is and what motivates it is crucial for mounting an effective campaign.

Some of the most effective techniques for changing people's attitudes and behavior use group processes (see the boxed insert on pages 336–337 for a description of the use of such processes in brainwashing), to which we now turn our attention.

BEHAVIOR IN GROUPS

In our discussion thus far in the chapter, we have noted the powerful role that groups play in shaping attitudes and behavior. Indeed, much of an individual's identity derives from group membership. People think of themselves and others as somehow clustered in social units: nations, races, families, organizations, teams, cliques, political parties, religions, and so on. And as has been pointed out, by identifying themselves with a group, people typically take on the attitudes prevalent in the group: it is *their* group, *their* attitudes. Moreover, a group exerts pressure on members to conform to its standards. Conformity is encouraged, approved, and rewarded; nonconformity is discouraged, disapproved, and punished. Let us begin this discussion of groups by considering their distinguishing characteristics.

The Nature of Groups

Social psychologists view groups as possessing three properties. First, the people composing a group

Brainwashing

The most extreme means of changing attitudes involves a combination of psychological gamesmanship and physical torture, aptly called **brainwashing.** The most extensive studies of brainwashing have been done with Americans who had been captured by the Chinese during the Korean War and subjected to "thought reform" (Schein, 1957; Lifton, 1963, 1973). The Chinese undertook to break down the Americans' convictions and to replace them with Marxist beliefs.

Perhaps the most significant feature of the Chinese POW program was the systematic destruction of the prisoners' formal and informal group structure. American officers were separated from their men and replaced by Chinese "leaders." "Noncooperative" prisoners and informal leaders were reassigned to other camps. The Chinese systematically fomented distrust by playing the prisoners off against one another in the allocation of necessities and privileges. The penetration of the American ranks by spies and informers led the men to believe that they could not trust anyone. These tactics reduced each man to a social isolate—exposed in a hostile environment—and thus prepared the way for indoctrination and collaboration with the enemy.

It is hard to say just where persuasion ends and brainwashing begins. (Some researchers believe that brainwashing is just a very intense form of persuasion.) Drawing this line has become particularly important to the courts in recent years —from the case of Patty Hearst to lawsuits over deprograming members of religious cults.

Although cult leaders deny that they use brainwashing, a number of people who have studied cults compare their techniques with the brainwashing methods practiced on American POWs in Korea (Lifton, 1979). Whatever the case may be, some groups use highly sophisticated techniques for inducing attitudinal and behavioral change. Adherents and ex-members describe constant exhortation, training in altered con-

conceive of themselves as having some degree of affiliation or connection with one another. The members feel a mutual affinity—an *awareness of belonging* that is not shared by those outside the group. This consciousness of oneness typically affords cohesiveness to a group, the sense that "I am one of them." These sentiments are fostered by shared attitudes and activities. Similarly, persecution, such as that experienced by Jews and other minorities, leads people to assume that their inner experiences and emotional reactions are closer to those of group members than to outsiders' (Shibutani and Kwan, 1965; Allen and Wilder, 1975). Because of this awareness of belonging, individuals are not merely *in* the group; they are *of* the group.

A second property of groups is that their members *interact* and *communicate* with one another. Group members reciprocally influence one another's atti-tudes, feelings, and actions (Davis, 1949; McGrath, 1984). Face-to-face contact facilitates group relationships. But people can also interact and communicate by writing or telephoning each other, a common practice among family members and business associates. Frequent contact deepens social ties as people gradually develop interlocking habits. And small group size allows people to see and talk with one another, making possible the subtle exchange of opinions, ideas, and feelings.

Third, the individuals making up a group share at least one *common goal*. As a result, the fates of group members are linked, making them interdependent. To achieve particular ends—food, shelter, love, security, or whatever—people find that they must somehow join their efforts with others. Members of a consumer group, for example, share the common goal of working for consumer protection. Members

---

brainwashing: A means of changing attitudes that involves a combination of psychological gamesmanship and physical torture.

sciousness, and automatic submission to directives. Some cults require long hours of prayer, chanting, meditation, marathon encounter groups, and psychodrama (Singer, 1979; Siegelman and Conway, 1979). Ex-cultists say that their critical faculties were held in abeyance while they were cult members: during this time they listened, believed, and obeyed. Even so, in most cases conversions are voluntary and occur in the absence of confinement or severe stress (Robbins and Anthony, 1980; Barker, 1984).

Many cult members join during periods of depression and confusion (Galanter et al., 1979; Singer, 1979; Paloutzian, 1981). The cults provide structure to daily activity and give life meaning: they give to members friends as well as ready-made decisions about marriage and careers, dating, and sex. Being cut off from the outside world typically increases a new member's sense of commitment.

Some ex-cultists have a good deal of difficulty reintegrating themselves into the larger society. At times former cult members experience depression, loneliness, indecisiveness, passivity, guilt, and blurring of mental activity. They may feel regret for the "lost years" during which they fell behind their peers in career and life pursuits (Singer, 1979). However, only a small minority remain in a cult for lengthy periods of time (Bird and Reimer, 1982). Consequently, for many people leaving is not an especially disturbing event. For a good many, the time they spend in the cult is a rather benign, even therapeutic, experience —a period when they are compelled to come to terms with themselves (Galanter, 1983; Levine, 1984). For this reason, coercive "deprograming" often fails. It operates against the possibility that cult members will resolve their conflicts, leave the group, and rejoin the larger community on their own. When young people are abducted from a cult, physically detained, and subjected to forcible "therapy," they may be driven back into the cult, or into a pattern of later "cult-hopping" (Levine, 1984).

of ethnic and religious groups desire to perpetuate a common heritage or set of beliefs. Thus groups commonly arise to perform tasks that no individual could handle alone. Since payoffs are frequently associated with group membership, people develop a stake in their group relationships, a factor strengthening social cohesiveness.

Leadership

Joint activity requires that the behavior of people be organized and channeled toward common ends. Accordingly, all groups, whether made up of monks, gangsters, soldiers, workers, or politicians, have leaders. Within a group, a leader initiates action, supplies direction, makes decisions, and settles disputes. **Leadership** entails a process of *influence* between a leader and followers to attain social goals. At times the term *power* is used with respect to leadership. However, power implies features of coercion and control, whereas leadership suggests influence, especially persuasion. Power does not require influence, nor does influence require power. Influence may persuade a friend but power coerces friend and foe alike (Bierstedt, 1950; Hollander, 1985).

Most people think of leadership as a quality or personality trait that some people have and that other people lack. To an extent this is true. Research reveals that leaders tend to be better adjusted, more self-confident, more energetic and outgoing, and slightly more intelligent than other group members (Gibb, 1969; Hare, 1976; Boyatzis, 1982). However, the nature of the group also determines who will lead. Indeed, groups draw some people into leadership roles even when they are not formally designated as leaders (Stein, 1975). Different circumstances and different functions also call for different kinds of leaders. A group that is threatened by internal

---

leadership: A process of influence between a leader and followers to attain social goals.

Through a combination of circumstances and personal characteristics, people such as Lee Iacocca emerge as leaders. *(Courtesy, Chrysler Corporation)*

conflict requires a leader who is good at handling people, settling disputes, and soothing tempers. A group that has a complex task to perform needs a leader with special experience to set goals and plan strategies for achieving them (Fiedler, 1967; Strube and Garcia, 1981). In sum, there may not be a "leader" for all people and all seasons (Mazlish, 1981).

In many groups, a single person has the most power and authority and is recognized as the group's leader. However, at times the leadership functions may be divided formally or informally among several group members (Cartwright and Zander, 1968; Hare, 1976). A common division of labor involves a *social-emotional leader* and *a task leader*. Their relationship with other members of the group emphasizes *expressive* and *instrumental* ties, respectively. The social-emotional leader tends to make encouraging remarks, to break any tension with a joke, and to solicit the reactions of others to whatever is going on. The task leader tends to take over when it is time to convey information, give opinions, or suggest how to do something. This leader is bossier and is not reluctant to disagree and press for a particular idea or course of action even if doing so creates tension in the group. A task leader usually has special knowledge or skills, and so different people may fill this role, depending on what the group is doing. The social-emotional leader is likely to be the same person across different settings because the need for promoting cohesion always exists. This person is usually quite popular and commands a good deal of loyalty within the group. (In some groups, of course, the same person may take on both functions.)

There are many ways in which a person can acquire enough influence to become the leader of a group. Three of the most common are expertise, charisma, and power. An expert directs the group's activity because such a person has the knowledge that the group needs to achieve its goals. For example, a ship's captain must know how to run a ship and how to meet an emergency at sea. Many leaders also possess a strong emotional appeal, or **charisma** (House, 1977). Presidents Franklin D. Roosevelt and John F. Kennedy are striking examples of political leaders with charisma who aroused strong feelings among both their followers and their enemies. Influence can also come from the power to

---

charisma (ka-RIZ-mah) The strong emotional appeal possessed by some leaders.

control rewards and punishments. Presidents of companies can give raises and promotions; they can also fire or demote people. They are leaders not because members necessarily like them but because they own the most shares in the company or because they have been appointed by those who own shares.

For whatever reason a member becomes a leader, the way a person leads will affect the structure of the group and the roles other members play (Hollander, 1985). An *authoritarian leader*—one who is domineering and unwilling to share power—may make all the important decisions for the group and assign relatively unimportant tasks to other members. A more *democratic leader* may try to involve as many members as possible in the decision-making process. In general, researchers find that authoritarian leadership is accompanied by high levels of frustration and some degree of aggression toward the leader. In part, these frustrations arise from the failure of authoritarian leaders to attend to the group members' social and emotional needs. In contrast, the members tend to be happier, more group minded, friendlier, and less aggressive under democratic leadership (Lewin, Lippitt, and White, 1939; White and Lippitt, 1960). Overall, subordinates who report high-quality relationships with their supervisors assume greater job responsibility, contribute more, and are rated better performers than subordinates who report low-quality relationships (Graen et al., 1970; Graen et al., 1977).

Group Structure

Leaders are not the only ones who play different parts in group life. Members also perform different tasks. **Group structure** consists of the parts various members play in a group and the interrelationships that exist among these parts. One technique psychologists use to analyze group structure is the **sociogram**. All members of a group are asked to name those people with whom they would like to interact on a given occasion or for a specific purpose, those they like best, and so on. For example, the members may be asked with whom they would like to go to a party, to discuss politics, to spend a vacation, or to

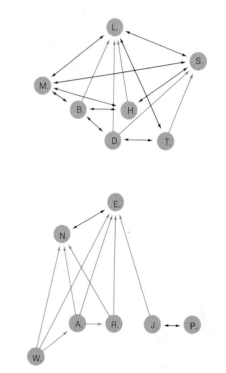

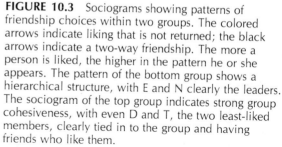

FIGURE 10.3 Sociograms showing patterns of friendship choices within two groups. The colored arrows indicate liking that is not returned; the black arrows indicate a two-way friendship. The more a person is liked, the higher in the pattern he or she appears. The pattern of the bottom group shows a hierarchical structure, with E and N clearly the leaders. The sociogram of the top group indicates strong group cohesiveness, with even D and T, the two least-liked members, clearly tied in to the group and having friends who like them.

complete an organizational task. Their choices can then be diagramed, as shown in Figure 10.3. Sociograms can help psychologists predict how that individual is likely to interact with other group members.

Another way to discover the structure of a group is to examine the communication patterns in the group—who says what to whom, and how often (Abelson and Levi, 1985). Harold Leavitt (1951) undertook an insightful experiment dealing with

---

group structure: The parts various members play in a group and the interrelationships that exist among these parts.

sociogram: (SO-see-oh-gram): A diagram representing relationships within a group.

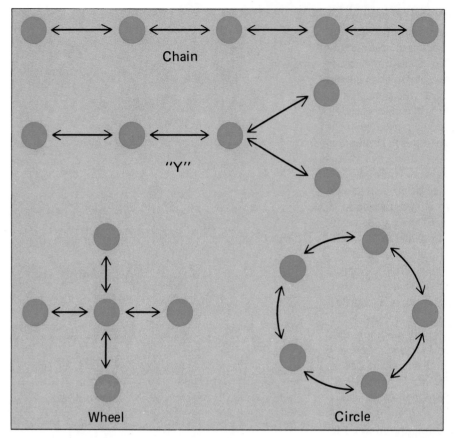

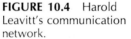

FIGURE 10.4 Harold Leavitt's communication network.

communication patterns. He gave a card with several symbols on it to each person in a group of five. (Leavitt put each person in a separate room or booth and allowed the members to communicate only by written message.) In this way he was able to create the networks shown in Figure 10.4. Each circle represents a person; the lines represent open channels. Subjects placed in each position could exchange messages only with the persons to whom they were connected by channels.

The most interesting result of this experiment was that the people who were organized into a "circle" were the slowest at solving the problem but the happiest at doing it. In this group everyone sent and received a large number of messages until someone solved the problem and passed the information on. In the "wheel," by contrast, everyone sent a few messages to one center person, who figured out the answer and told the rest what it was. These groups found the solution quickly, but the people on the outside of the wheel did not enjoy the job much.

Following the experiment, the members in each group were asked to identify the leader of their group. In the centralized groups (wheel, Y, and chain), the person in the center was usually chosen as the group leader. But in the circle network half the group members said they thought there was no real leader, and those who did say there was a leader disagreed on who that leader was. Thus a centralized organization seems more useful for task-oriented groups, whereas a decentralized network is more useful in socially oriented groups.

Groupthink

In 1961, the Kennedy administration set forth on the ill-fated Bay of Pigs invasion of Cuba. The United States dispatched fourteen hundred CIA-trained Cuban exiles to the Caribbean island with the intent of overthrowing the regime of Fidel Castro. Although the invaders were assisted by the CIA and the United States Air Force and Navy, everything went wrong. The Castro forces quickly crushed the attack and captured most of the invaders. The Bay of Pigs invasion was a colossal blunder. It deeply embarrassed the United States among Third World nations. It also solidified the Cuban-Russian alliance and encouraged the Russians in their attempt to place nuclear missiles in Cuba.

President John F. Kennedy later asked, "How could we have been so stupid?" Yet the President's advisers were hardly stupid. They comprised one of the most impressive arrays of intellectual talent in the history of American government. Nonetheless, the President and his advisers had overlooked such elementary facts as the size and strength of the Castro forces. Indeed, they failed to seek relevant intelligence information.

The psychologist Irving Janis (1982) has looked into what went wrong in the decision-making process that led to the Bay of Pigs invasion. He says the difficulty resided in "groupthink." **Groupthink** refers to the process of making decisions in a highly cohesive group in which the members are so intent on maintaining group consensus that their critical faculties become ineffective. Janis identifies eight symptoms of groupthink:

- *Invulnerability.* The members of the group share an illusion of invulnerability that leads to overconfidence and a willingness to take extraordinary risks. The Kennedy group had begun to think of themselves as immune to failure. Arthur Schlesinger, Jr. (1965:259), one of the inner circle, observed:

Everything had broken right for him [Kennedy] since 1956. He had won the nomination and the election against all the odds in the book. Everyone around him thought he had the Midas touch and could not lose.

- *Shared rationale.* The victims of groupthink collectively construct rationalizations in order to discount warnings. Thus the President and his advisers justified the invasion by saying it was the will of the Cuban people. Yet CIA surveys showed that the Castro government enjoyed mass support.

- *Morality.* Victims of groupthink believe unquestioningly in the inherent righteousness of their cause—in this case, the battle against communism.

- *Stereotypes.* Groupthink is characterized by stereotyped conceptions. The Kennedy group stereotyped the Cuban communists as weak, stupid, and ineffective.

- *Pressure.* Victims of groupthink demand conformity and apply pressure to any individual who even for a moment expresses doubts about the group's plans. For instance, at the most crucial meeting on the Cuban plan, the President asked each member to vote for or against the proposal. However, he did not call on Arthur Schlesinger, who he knew had serious misgivings.

- *Self-censorship.* Victims of groupthink withhold dissent. Thus members of the Kennedy inner circle kept silent about their misgivings and minimized to themselves their doubts.

- *Unanimity.* Victims of groupthink cultivate the illusion of unanimity. They want to believe that everyone is in agreement. Indeed, later evidence showed that the President, his secretary of state (Dean Rusk), and his secretary of defense (Robert McNamara) held widely differing assumptions about the invasion plan.

- *Mindguards.* One or more individuals commonly act as mindguards to protect the leader and group members from adverse information that might undermine consensus. Robert Kennedy performed this role in the Bay of Pigs deliberations.

Janis urges group members and their leaders to incorporate practices within their deliberations that lead to open consideration of alternative perspectives. Indeed, he recommends that they invite out-

---

groupthink: The process of making decisions in a highly cohesive group in which the members are so intent on maintaining group consensus that their critical faculties become ineffective.

side experts to important meetings and encourage the experts to challenge the views of the core members, or that they assign one of the group members to act as devil's advocate. And he suggests that when vital national concerns are at stake, leaders hold a "second-chance" meeting at which members can express their doubts and redefine the issues.

Prosocial Behavior and the Diffusion of Responsibility

Sometimes several people are faced with a common problem although they have no leader and may not even see themselves as a group. For instance, the mass media periodically carry reports of muggings, rapes, and murders that are committed in public while large numbers of people watch without intervening or calling for help.

One case in particular attracted national attention and spurred social psychologists to investigate **prosocial behavior**—helping responses that benefit other people. At 3:00 A.M. on March 13, 1964, a young woman named Kitty Genovese was attacked, beaten, and killed outside her apartment house in New York City. Her screams brought at least thirty-eight of her neighbors to their windows to watch. She was heard to yell, "He stabbed me! Please help me!" and later, "I'm dying! I'm dying!" The neighbors reported feelings of horror as they witnessed the attack. However, none attempted to come to the woman's aid or to call the police (despite the fact that the attack lasted for half an hour). More recently, in New Bedford, Massachusetts, a young mother of two entered a bar to buy cigarettes. A man grabbed her, stripped off her clothes, and raped her on the barroom floor. Other male patrons then lifted her onto a pool table and raped her again and again to the cheers and applause of a number of customers. Although the woman was assaulted and raped repeatedly for more than an hour before the eyes of at least fifteen other male patrons, no one came to her aid or called the police (*Newsweek*, 1983). Events such as these raise a frightening prospect for many of us. If we are in distress and need help, will other people help us?

By studying artificial crises, psychologists have tried to find out why people in such situations do not act. In one experiment, John M. Darley and Bibb Latané (1968) had college students participate in a "discussion of personal problems." They were asked to wait in separate rooms. Some were told they would be communicating with only one other person; others were given the impression that they would be talking with five other people. All communication, the psychologists told each student, was to take place over microphones so that everyone would remain anonymous and thus would speak more freely. Each person was to talk in turn.

In reality, there were no other people—all the voices the subjects heard were on tape. As the discussion progressed, the subject heard one of the participants go into what sounded like an epileptic fit. The victim began to call for help, making choking sounds. The experimenters found that most of the people who thought they were alone with the victim came out of their room to help him. But of those who believed there were four other people nearby, less than half did anything to help.

The experimenters suggested that this behavior was the result of **diffusion of responsibility.** In other words, because several people were present, each subject assumed someone else would help. The researchers found that in experiments where people could see the other participants, the same pattern emerged. In addition, bystanders reassured one another that it would not be a good idea to interfere. These findings on diffusion of responsibility suggest that the larger the crowd or group of bystanders, the more likely any given individual is to feel that he or she is not responsible for whatever is going on.

Another influence that inhibits action is the tendency to minimize the *need* for any response. To act, you must admit that an emergency exists. But you may not know exactly what is going on when you hear screams or loud thumps upstairs. You are likely to wait before risking the embarrassment of rushing to help where help is not needed or wanted. It is

---

prosocial behavior: Helping responses that benefit other people.
diffusion of responsibility: The tendency of the presence of others to lessen an individual's feelings of responsibility for his or her actions or failure to act.

Passersby may feel no need to help a stranger, either because they do not believe it is their responsibility to do so or because they are not sure the stranger requires assistance. *(Freda Leinwand/Monkmeyer)*

easier to persuade yourself that nothing needs to be done if you look around and see other people behaving calmly. Not only can you see that they think nothing is wrong, but you can see that not doing anything is entirely proper. You are able to minimize the need to act and to shift any responsibility to those around you (Clark and Word, 1972, 1974; Staub, 1978).

Much of the research undertaken on prosocial behavior has involved people who were strangers at the time of the emergency. In these situations, group cohesiveness is typically low. However, when bystanders know one another and have ties with one another, they are *more* likely to intervene in larger group settings than in smaller ones (Rutkowski, Gruder, and Romer, 1983). Apparently cohesiveness increases people's responsiveness to social norms. For instance, Americans are expected to help others who are in need. The awareness of a common group membership cancels the negative effect of diffusion of responsibility by activating the norm of social responsibility. Indeed, even informal social contact

arouses a latent sense of obligation. "Familiar strangers"—for example, the person one sees at the bus stop every day without ever exchanging a word —have been know to display heroic acts of assistance in a crisis (Cunningham, 1984b).

INTERGROUP DYNAMICS

Conflict between groups—whether between nations, social classes, races, religions, ethnic groups, or youth gangs—is a constant human occurrence. Social psychologists find the concepts "ingroup" and "outgroup" useful tools for examining and analyzing these matters. An **ingroup** is a social unit that individuals either belong to or identify with. An **outgroup** is a social unit that people either do not belong to or do not identify with. We often call ingroups *we-groups* and outgroups *they-groups*.

Ingroup identifications are fostered and strengthened by the existence of outgroups. Perhaps for this reason colleges and universities foster intercollegiate

---

ingroup (we-group): A social unit that people either belong to or identify with.
outgroup (they-group): A social unit that people either do not belong to or do not identify with.

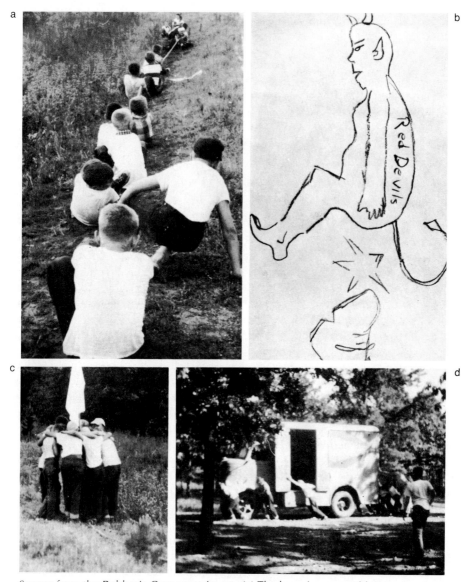

Scenes from the Robber's Cave experiment. *(a)* The boys in competition against one another in such activities as tug-of-war. *(b)* The considerable hostility that developed between the two groups was expressed in drawings like this one. *(c)* Hostility was also expressed in fights and in raids on "enemy" cabins. *(d)* The hostility was eliminated by having the boys perform tasks that needed cooperation, such as pushing a truck that supplied food to the camp. *(From Sherif and Sherif, 1969)*

athletic rivalries. The presence of an outgroup increases our consciousness of ingroup ties and promotes conformity to the ingroup's values and norms (Lauderdale et al., 1984; Wilder and Shapiro, 1984). By the same token, strong ingroup identities —particularly those associated with allegiance to a religious, racial, or ethnic group—provide powerful props to individual feelings of self-worth and self-esteem (Vander Zanden, 1983; Meindl and Lerner, 1984).

While ingroup–outgroup divisions promote a sentiment of oneness and social solidarity, they simultaneously generate the very opposite—social distance and conflict. Ingroup sentiments are a double-edged sword. They activate within the ingroup a feeling of "consciousness of kind" that overrides differences among members, such as those associated with economic conflicts or social gradations. Simultaneously, strong ingroup ties distance people from members of outgroups who are not of their kind (Ambedkar, 1955). In sum, those factors that promote ingroup allegiance are likely to be the very factors promoting distance from outgroups. Contemporary Lebanon provides a good illustration of this principle: religious and ethnic loyalties are so consuming that identity with the common nation-state of Lebanon is undermined.

One of the most interesting aspects of ingroup–outgroup divisions is the ease with which they are produced. The mere existence of social categories seems to result in ingroup–outgroup biases even when the basis for categorizing people into groups is arbitrary. Simply conceptualizing the world in terms of "us" and "them" is enough to arouse ingroup sympathies (Locksley, Ortiz, and Hepburn, 1980; Moreland, 1985). It leads us to discriminate against outgroup members and to favor ingroup members in the allocation of rewards, heightens ingroup attractiveness, and fosters the assumption that ingroup members have more in common with one another than is actually the case (Rabbie and Horowitz, 1969; Tajfel and Billig, 1974; Holtz and Miller, 1985). Few if any psychologists have made a greater contribution to our understanding of these processes than have Muzafer Sherif and his colleagues (Sherif et al., 1961).

For over a decade, Sherif studied conflict and cooperation between groups of boys. One of his more ingenious field studies was carried out in a boys' camp in the Robber's Cave area of the Southwest. From the beginning of the experiment, the boys (eleven and twelve years old) were divided into two separate groups. The boys hiked, swam, and played baseball only with members of their own group, and friendships and group spirit soon developed. After a while, the experimenters (working as counselors) brought the groups together for a tournament (baseball, touch football, a tug-of-war, a treasure hunt, and other games in which cumulative

group scores were kept). The psychologists had hypothesized that when these two groups of boys were placed in competitive situations, where one group could achieve its goals only at the expense of the other, hostility would develop. They were right.

Although the games began in a spirit of good sportsmanship, tension mounted as the tournament continued. Friendly competition gave way to name calling, fistfights, and raids on "enemy" cabins. The psychologists had demonstrated the ease with which they could produce unity *within* the two boys' groups and hatred *between* them. The experimenters then tried to see what they might do to end the conflict and create harmony between the two groups. They tried to bring the groups together for enjoyable activities, such as a movie and a good meal. This approach failed. Far from reducing conflict, the campers used these situations as opportunities to shove and push each other, throw food and insults, and continue their attacks.

Next, the psychologists deliberately invented a series of "emergencies" so that the boys would either have to help one another or lose the chance to do or get something they all wanted. For instance, one morning someone reported that the water line to the camp had broken. The boys were told that unless they worked together to find the break and fix it, they would all have to leave camp. By afternoon, they had jointly found and fixed the damage. Gradually, through such cooperative activities, intergroup hostility and tensions lessened. Friendships began to develop between individuals of the opposing groups, and eventually the groups began to seek out occasions to mingle. At the end of the camp period, members of both groups requested that they ride home together on the same bus.

The results of this experiment are striking. A group of boys from identical backgrounds had developed considerable hostility toward one another, simply because they were placed in competitive situations. The crucial factor in eliminating group hostility was bringing the boys together to achieve shared goals and to counter a mutual threat. The research convincingly demonstrated that the possibilities for achieving harmony are greatly enhanced when individuals are brought together to work toward common ends. It has implications for social dilemma situations, discussed in the boxed insert on pages 346–347.

Personal Interest Versus the Collective Welfare

Group living often confronts us with a dilemma. When the interests of the group conflict with those of the individual, whose interests should take precedence? Psychologists call this problem a **social dilemma**—a situation in which members of a group are faced with a conflict between maximizing their personal interest and maximizing the collective welfare (Komorita and Barth, 1985). Garrett J. Hardin's (1968) example of the "tragedy of the commons" is one type of social dilemma in which the long-run consequences of self-interested individual choice result in social disaster. Consider a situation in which a number of herders share a common pasture. Each person may reason that by putting another cow to graze he or she will realize a benefit from it. But if each individual follows this course, the commons will be destroyed and each will ultimately lose. Hardin was addressing the problem of population growth. However, the notion can be applied equally well to pollution, which is the reverse of the grazing problem; whereas grazing takes essential matter out of the commons, pollution puts harmful matter in.

In social dilemma situations, one member of a group may provide for the public good, making one's own contribution unnecessary (Kerr, 1983). This "let George do it" approach is called the **free-rider mechanism.** Consider the choice that a soldier faces at the outset of a battle. The safest thing the soldier could do is remain in a foxhole and not assault the enemy position. However, should every soldier take this course, the battle will be lost and everyone in the unit will be taken prisoner or captured. Something of this same sort happened in the Three Mile Island area in 1979 following the serious nuclear accident in which radiation was leaked from a nucle-

SUMMARY

1. Attitudes are ways by which people organize and categorize their information and feelings on various matters. As such, attitudes touch every phase of life.

2. All of us have beliefs, ideas, and feelings about various matters, even matters about which we have no firsthand knowledge. The culture in which you grew up, the people who raised you, those with whom you associate—your peers—and your own ability to perceive and think about social issues all help to shape your attitudes.

3. Three major processes are involved in forming or changing attitudes: compliance, identification, and internalization. Each constitutes a different type of social influence.

A. At times people yield to the pressure of others and act in conformity with others' wishes even though they think they should act in some other way. This response is compliance. People often go along with others because they wish to be rewarded for conformity or avoid being punished for nonconformity, or to obey authority.

B. Another way in which attitudes may be formed or changed is through the process of identification—mentally associating oneself in thought, feeling, or action with another person or group.

C. Finally, attitudes may be formed or changed through the process of internalization—the wholehearted acceptance of an attitude.

---

social dilemma: A situation in which members of a group are faced with a conflict between maximizing their personal interest and maximizing the collective welfare.

free-rider mechanism: The "let George do it" approach to dealing with social problems.

ar generator. Although most residents of the area were greatly disturbed and frightened by the event, only a relatively small proportion of them became politically active. While the vast majority agreed with the goals of the citizen protest groups, they contributed neither time nor money to the movement. Instead, they became free riders (Walsh and Warland, 1983).

The free-rider response has social consequences. In many group settings, there is the possibility not only that you can free ride on the efforts of others, but that other people may also free ride on your contributions. These circumstances lead to the **sucker effect.** Because you do not want to "play the sucker," you reduce your contributions to the group enterprise. The soldier in the foxhole may reason that if he alone were to charge the enemy, he would surely be killed and hence he may decide to desert his unit.

Given common social dilemmas, what social mechanisms does humankind possess to influence people to act for the common good rather than for selfish interest? Hardin sought an answer in social controls that restrict individual actions detrimental to the collective enterprise. Government often serves this role by regulating access to various scarce resources. Group norms may produce a similar effect through informal pressure (Messick et al., 1983). But there are also measures that induce people to act cooperatively and that elicit prosocial behaviors. Among these mechanisms are those that highlight group boundaries and foster a common identity (Kramer and Brewer, 1984). The research of Muzafer Sherif provides a good illustration of settings in which the pursuit of common goals lowers barriers to cooperation. Likewise, where people feel that they are being rewarded for their cooperative behavior (for instance, sharing in the profits or benefits equally), they are less likely to switch to self-centered, individualistic actions (Komorita and Barth, 1985).

4. Much research in social psychology relies on attitude consistency—people typically try to bring their attitudes into harmony with one another. Few theories on attitude consistency have commanded greater interest than Leon Festinger's theory of cognitive dissonance—the uncomfortable feeling that arises when you experience contradictory or conflicting attitudes. To reduce dissonance, it is necessary to change one or both of the attitudes.

5. Attitudes influence behavior, and behavior influences attitudes.

A. In many instances, if you act and speak as though you have certain beliefs and feelings, you begin really to feel and believe this way. One explanation for this phenomenon—the self-justification theory—derives from the theory of cognitive dissonance. People rationalize their behavior by finding supporting attitudes.

B. According to self-perception theory, attitudes do not necessarily cause behavior. Rather, behavior frequently causes attitudes. People observe their own actions and from them infer what their attitudes must be.

C. It is also possible for people to act in such a way as to make their attitudes come true. This phenomenon is called a self-fulfilling prophecy. There is no conspiracy to make the prophecy come true. Rather, people unintentionally cause the fulfillment to occur by acting in accordance with their attitudes.

6. Prejudice is an attitude; discrimination is behavior. As in the case of other attitudes and actions, a one-to-one relationship does not necessarily hold between prejudice and discrimination. In determining how people will act in an intergroup situation, much depends on the social setting.

---

sucker effect: Because individuals do not want others to free ride on their contributions, they reduce their contributions to the group enterprise.

7. Persuasion is a deliberate attempt to influence attitudes and behavior through communication. How people see the source, or originator, of a message may be a critical factor in their acceptance or rejection of it. If the source seems reliable and knowledgeable, the message is likely to be accepted. Also, if the communicator is respected and admired, people will tend to agree with the message.

8. The most effective messages combine emotional appeal with factual information and argument. A communication that overemphasizes the emotional side of an issue may boomerang. Also a two-sided communication is more effective than a one-sided communication because the audience tends to believe that the speaker is objective and fair-minded.

9. The audience includes all those people whose attitudes the communicator is trying to change. Being able to persuade people to alter their views depends on taking into account who the audience is and why it holds the attitudes it does.

10. Groups possess three properties. First, the individuals composing a group feel an awareness of belonging. Second, the members interact and communicate with one another. And third, the individuals making up a group share at least one common goal.

11. The nature of the group determines who will lead. Groups draw some people into leadership roles even when they are not formally designated as leaders. In many groups a single person has the most

power and authority and is recognized as the group's leader. However, at times the leadership functions may be divided formally or informally among several group members. A common division of labor involves a social-emotional leader and a task leader.

12. Group structure consists of the parts various members play in a group and the interrelationships that exist among these parts. One technique psychologists use to analyze group structure is the sociogram. Sociograms help psychologists predict the interaction and communication patterns among the members of a group.

13. Groupthink refers to the process of making decisions in a highly cohesive group in which the members are so intent on maintaining group consensus that their critical faculties become ineffective. Eight symptoms of groupthink are a sense of invulnerability, a shared rationale, a highly moral outlook, shared stereotypes, conformity pressures, self-censorship, the illusion of unanimity, and the use of mindguards.

14. In certain group situations, people undergo a diffusion of responsibility. They fail to engage in prosocial behavior because they assume that others will help.

15. Intergroup conflict is fostered by competition for scarce, divisible resources, such as prizes. Cooperation is promoted when people together work toward common ends.

KEY TERMS

attitude (p. 318)
attitude consistency   (p. 327)
brainwashing   (p. 336)
charisma   (p. 338)
cognitive dissonance (p. 327)
communication (p. 331)
compliance (p. 320)
diffusion of responsibility
    (p. 342)
discrimination (p. 330)

free-rider mechanism (p. 346)
group structure (p. 339)
groupthink (p. 341)
identification (p. 325)
ingroup (we-group) (p. 343)
internalization (p. 326)
leadership (p. 337)
outgroup (they-group) (p. 343)
persuasion (p. 331)
prejudice (p. 330)

prosocial behavior (p. 342)
reference group (p. 326)
self-fulfilling prophecy (p. 329)
self-justification theory (p. 328)
social dilemma (p. 346)
sociogram (p. 339)
sucker effect (p. 347)
terrorism (p. 332)

SUGGESTED READINGS

ALLPORT, GORDON. 1958. *The Nature of Prejudice*. New York: Doubleday-Anchor. A classic book on the topic of prejudice.

DELLA FEMINA, JERRY. 1970. *From Those Wonderful Folks Who Gave You Pearl Harbor*. New York: Simon & Schuster. A hilarious and insightful look at the world of advertising agencies through the eyes of a creative man with plenty of firsthand experience.

HOFFER, ERIC. 1951. *The True Believer*. New York: Harper & Row. Hoffer identifies and analyzes the characteristics of the "true believer"—the person who identifies so much with a group that he or she has no identity away from it.

JANIS, IRVING L. 1982. *Groupthink*. Boston: Houghton Mifflin. This revised and enlarged edition of *Victims of Groupthink* describes policy fiascoes and successes to elucidate further the groupthink syndrome. Chapters also discuss how to prevent groupthink.

MC GINNESS, JOE. 1970. *The Selling of the President, 1968*. New York: Pocket Books. Shows how advertising people manufacture, package, and market their most lucrative product: the President of the United States. Fascinating, frightening, and essential reading for anyone interested in the use of psychology in advertising and the way that advertising is used to shape public opinion.

RUBIN, THEODORE ISAAC. 1985. *Overcoming Indecisiveness*. New York: Harper & Row. The president of the American Institute for psychoanalysis and board member of the Karen Horney Clinic describes the eight stages of effective decision making.

SHAVER, KELLY G. 1985. *The Attribution of Blame: Causality, Responsibility and Blameworthiness*. New York: Springer-Verlag. Develops a comprehensive theory of how people assign blame as a social explanation of responsibility.

SINGER, MARGARET T. 1979. Coming out of the cults. *Psychology Today*, 12 (January):72–82. Describes Singer's research on why people join cults and what happens to them when they quit.

ZIMBARDO, PHILIP G., EBBESEN, E. B., AND MASLACH, CHRISTINA. 1977. *Influencing Attitudes and Changing Behavior*. 2nd ed. Reading, Mass.: Addison-Wesley. A short introduction to methodology, experimentation, and theory in the field of attitude change. Designed for readers without extensive background.

HUMAN DEVELOPMENT

Mary Cassatt, *The Family,* ca. 1892.

11
Infancy and Childhood

What is a human being? Is there such a thing as "human nature"? Are we born human or do we become human through our experiences in society? Ordinarily these questions do not come to mind. But when we encounter strange people—an individual from a quite different culture, a person hallucinating and suffering from severe mental illness, or a "wild" child—these issues confront us with terrifying force.

Such an event took place in a small village in southern France in the winter of 1800 (Shattuck, 1980). A boy of about nine or ten—"naked, speechless, and filthy"—came out of the forest and dug for vegetables in a tanner's garden. He was captured by villagers and quickly gained international notoriety as "the wild boy of Aveyron." The boy seemed to have lived in almost total isolation for a number of years. For several months the child was maintained as a "curiosity," kept on a leash, and paraded before crowds of jeering people. In the summer of 1800 he was taken to the Institute for Deaf-Mutes in Paris, where he came under the tutelage of a young physician, Jean Itard.

A product of the revolutionary time in which he lived, Itard held an optimistic view of humankind. He rejected the notion of genetically fixed behavior and believed that human beings were products of their social experiences. Accordingly, he set to work to transform the boy, now named Victor, into a functioning member of society. He hoped to give the boy the ability to relate to other people, to develop his senses, to extend his physical and social needs, to speak, and to think clearly. Although many of his colleagues thought that Victor was a "hopeless idiot," Itard persevered in his efforts for some five years. He was never able to teach Victor to speak, in part, very likely, because the child was deaf. Nonetheless, Victor achieved the ability to read, compose, and write three-word sentences. He could solve various sorts of problems and use tools in his tasks.

When Victor entered puberty, Itard concluded he could contribute little more to his intellectual development and withdrew from the case. Itard's housekeeper continued to care for Victor until he died in 1828. Never a normal adult, Victor nonetheless made considerable progress with education and loving care.

Through the years other cases of extremely isolated children have come to public attention (Davis, 1949). One such case was that of Genie, a girl who was found in 1970 at the age of thirteen after having experienced a childhood of severe deprivation and abuse (Curtiss, 1977; Pines, 1981). From the age of twenty months, she had been locked in a small room by her father and rarely saw anyone. Her vocalizations and noises were punished by beatings. Under these conditions, Genie was unable to speak and only whimpered. When a social worker discovered her, she was naked and restrained by a harness on a potty seat. Public authorities placed her in a special rehabilitation program. Over the course of eight years Genie made considerable progress in the comprehension and production of language. Yet her speech was still far from normal, resembling a somewhat garbled telegram. After living for a few years with a foster family, Genie was able to approach strangers and initiate physical contact, and she seemed to expect kindness, not hostility, from adults. Even so, some of her behavior remained strange. In 1978, Genie's mother became her legal guardian and removed her from the special program in which she had been participating. Consequently, all research on Genie's language and intellectual development halted.

Cases like those of Victor and Genie raise a variety of questions. What are human beings born with? How do we learn to walk and talk, to think, to love, to hate? What makes each of us a unique person? How do we change over the years? These are questions dealt with by **developmental psychology**—the study of the changes that occur across the life cycle. In this chapter the many different aspects of development experienced from infancy through childhood will be described. In the next chapter, adolescence and adulthood will be considered.

THE BEGINNINGS OF LIFE

Development begins long before an infant is born. In this section we will discuss the genetic and prenatal factors that affect the newborn, as well as the first experiences of the newborn.

Genetic and Prenatal Factors in Development

Life begins as a single fertilized cell. Blueprinted in the original cell, termed the *zygote,* are the more than 200 billion cells that characterize the newborn nine months later. At conception, the sperm penetrates the wall of the ovum, an event that determines biological inheritance. In this manner people acquire the hereditary material that links them to their parents and, through them, to previous generations. As we saw in Chapter 2, this hereditary material is found in *chromosomes*, the long, threadlike bodies located in the nuclei of all cells. You receive twenty-three chromosomes from your father and twenty-three chromosomes from your mother. Therefore each cell contains twenty-three pairs of chromosomes, a total of forty-six chromosomes.

Chromosomes contain a number of smaller units called *genes.* Whereas a chromosome is like a book in a library, a gene is like a page in the book. Genes are the mechanisms by which a physical bridge is achieved between generations. As such, they provide for the continuity of life and they structure the biological potential of the new organism. (Chapter 2 discussed the part that heredity and environment play in producing that organism.)

In typical pregnancies, approximately 266 days elapse between conception and birth. This developmental time span is known as the *prenatal period.* It is divided into three phases: the germinal phase, the embryonic phase, and the fetal phase. The germinal phase begins with fertilization. For the first four days, the zygote drifts down the Fallopian tube, which connects the ovary with the uterus. For another three days it floats freely within the uterus.

---

developmental psychology: The study of the changes that occur across the life cycle.

During this time the zygote undergoes rapid cell division, producing a cluster of several dozen, then hundreds of cells. In the interval, the uterus readies itself for the zygote, thickening the outer layers of tissue lining its cavity, termed the *endometrium*. About the sixth or seventh day, the zygote begins to burrow into this tissue and gradually becomes completely implanted in it. However, not all pregnancies are successful. One of every three or four pregnancies ends in spontaneous abortion (the majority caused by chromosomal or lethal genetic defects in the embryo).

About two weeks after fertilization the zygote is solidly implanted in the uterus, and it is now termed the *embryo*. The developing organism resembles a small object encased in liquid within a hollow ball. It rapidly takes on humanlike features. Eight weeks after conception the embryo is about an inch long. It has acquired a recognizable but miniature form with eyes, mouth, ears, and many internal organs. Indeed, as early as the third week, the embryo's blood is pumped by its own developing heart. The blood flows through the embryo's aorta and on into connective tissue at the middle of its abdomen. Here the embryo is linked with the mother's uterus through a connecting lifeline, the *umbilical cord*. The umbilical cord and its attaching membranes—the *placenta* —function as an exchange terminal that permits the entry of food materials and oxygen to the embryo and the exit of waste products.

The final phase in prenatal life begins at the conclusion of the second month and ends with birth. The developing organism is called a *fetus* during this period. During the fetal phase, the nervous system develops, reproductive organs are formed, the digestive organs start functioning, and the fetus begins periodic movement. By seven months, the typical fetus weighs a little more than two pounds and measures about fifteen inches in length. If born at this time, it is likely to live with the aid of modern hospital care. Over the remaining two months, it gains additional weight and its organs become more finely developed. The fetus is then prepared for independent life.

Throughout the prenatal period, developing embryos and fetuses are vulnerable to various harmful substances and diseases that can cross from the mother. Generally the risks are greater during early than later pregnancy because the internal organs and nervous system are just beginning and contain critical foundation cells. Mothers who are chronic smokers are twice as likely to give birth to premature babies as nonsmokers are. Further, major congenital abnormalities are more prevalent among the infants of women who smoke. A mother's use of alcohol can also contribute to fetal defects. Other potentially harmful agents are venereal disease, German measles, tranquilizers such as thalidomide, and addictive drugs such as heroin.

The Newborn

Birth puts staggering new demands on the capacity of babies to adapt and survive. They go from an environment in which they are totally protected from the world to one in which they are assaulted by lights, sounds, touches, and a far wider range of temperatures. Newborns are capable of certain coordinated movement patterns, called reflexes, that can be triggered by the right stimulus. A **reflex** is a relatively simple, involuntary, and unlearned response to a stimulus. One response that is triggered automatically through built-in circuits is the **grasping reflex.** If the palm of an infant's hand is touched, the baby will clasp the object with its fingers. Infants can grasp an object, such as a finger, so strongly that they can be lifted into the air.

Also vital are the **rooting reflex** and the **sucking reflex.** In the rooting reflex, if alert newborns are touched anywhere around the mouth, they will move

---

reflex: A relatively simple, involuntary, and unlearned response to a stimulus.
grasping reflex: An infant's clinging response to a touch on the palm of his or her hand.
rooting reflex: An infant's response toward the source of touching that occurs
    anywhere around his or her mouth.
sucking reflex: An infant's response to having the soft palate of the mouth touched;
    it takes the form of a rapid burst of five to twenty-five sucks.

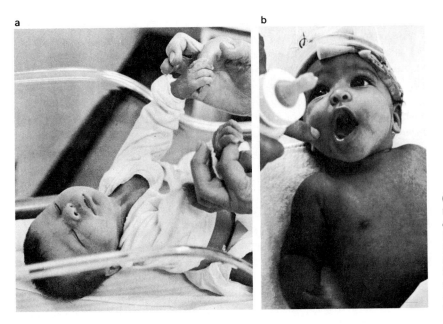

(a) The strength of the grasping reflex is demonstrated in a baby only a few days old. (Bill MacDonald) (b) This infant is responding to a touch on the cheek by opening his mouth and turning his head. The response is called the rooting reflex. (Jason Lauré)

their head and mouth toward the source of the touch. In this way, the touch of a mother's breast on a baby's cheek guides the baby's mouth toward her nipple. The sucking that follows contact with the nipple is one of the baby's most complex reflexes. The baby is able to suck, breathe air, and swallow milk twice a second without getting confused. This task is at least as difficult as learning to walk while balancing a book on one's head.

The grasping, rooting, and sucking reflexes have obvious adaptive significance. There are also other reflexes that do not seem to have significance for human infants but are leftovers from the evolutionary past (Cratty, 1970). For example, the *Babinski reflex*, triggered by gently stroking the sole of a newborn's foot, results in the fanning out of the toes and their curling downward in a fashion that sharply differs from their later use in walking. Infants also have reflexes for swimming movements and stepping motions that do not seem to be continuous with later development (Thelen and Fisher, 1982).

The behavior of newborns is organized by the subcortex of the brain. Many of the reflexes and organizing principles of early behavior, including grasping, rooting, and sucking, disappear by about three months of age. Maturation of the cortex brings with it myelination and the development of dendrites throughout the brain (see Chapter 2). In the process, cortical control increasingly replaces subcortical con-

trol, and infants become more uniquely human than they were in the first three months of life. Consequently, as behavior becomes unhinged from its initial reflexive foundation, human beings progressively part company with the primates of other species. And simultaneously they become much more susceptible to learning from their environment.

Besides grasping, sucking, and other reflex behavior, newborns spend a lot of time just looking. From birth, unless they are sleeping, feeding, or crying, babies are watching with curiosity, directing their gaze toward bright patterns and tracing the outlines of those patterns with their eyes. By measuring these eye movements while stimulating the baby in different ways, it is possible to infer how the infant perceives the world. For example, infants spend less time looking at out-of-focus movies than they do looking at the same movies in focus. Moreover, infants quickly learn to suck vigorously on a pacifier attached to the focusing mechanism of a movie projector in order to cause an out-of-focus picture to become more sharply defined. This suggests that babies are attuned to distinct edges; if the visual world were a blurry confusion for infants, they would not care that a movie was slightly blurry (Kalnins and Bruner, 1973).

Similarly, newborns younger than three days can tell the voice of their mother from that of other people. Indeed, they seek out their mother's voice from the voices of other women (DeCasper and Fifer, 1980). They also know the odor of their own mother and on this basis alone can distinguish their mother from other nursing mothers (Macfarlane, 1978; Cernoch and Porter, 1985). Evidence of this sort has refuted the notion that the world is essentially disorganized and chaotic to babies.

PROCESSES OF DEVELOPMENT

In the space of two years, grasping, rooting, searching infants will develop into children who can walk, talk, and feed themselves. This transformation is the result of both maturation and learning.

Maturation

To some extent babies are like plants that shoot up and unfold according to a built-in plan. Unless something is wrong with them, infants will begin to lift their heads at about three months, smile at four months, and grasp objects at five to six months. Crawling appears at eight to ten months. By this time babies may be able to pull themselves into a standing position, although they will fall if they let go. Three or four months later they will begin to walk, tentatively at first, but gradually acquiring a sense of balance.

Psychologists call internally programed growth **maturation.** It entails the more or less automatic unfolding of biological potential in a set, irreversible sequence. Maturation is as important as learning or experience, especially in the first year. Unless children are persistently underfed, severely restricted in their movements, or deprived of human contact and things to look at, they will develop more or less according to this schedule. Conversely, no amount of coaching will push children to walk or speak before they are physiologically ready.

Maturation is a feature of children's growing capacities throughout development. As the brain matures (particularly as the cortex becomes myelinized), new opportunities in the environment become available to children. For example, even though young infants are growing up in a linguistic environment, they do not speak. But by twelve to eighteen months of age they begin to use words. They have reached a point where the linguistic environment to which they have been exposed for many months becomes relevant to them. As children mature, their capacities for learning expand.

The process of maturation is easiest to understand when considering motor development. Psychologists identify and chart the development of various capabilities such as sitting, standing, creeping, reaching, and climbing (Figure 11.1). Maturation also provides the foundation for other behaviors, including the development of a fear of strangers at about eight months and the development of speaking (first words) at about twelve months. Schedules such as these help doctors and other professionals to spot problems and abnormalities. If a child has not begun to talk by the age of two and a half, a doctor will recommend tests to determine if something is wrong.

One recurrent theme emerging from psychological research is that the maturational plan inside each child is unique (Scarr and Weinberg, 1983; Wilson, 1983). On the average, babies start walking at twelve to thirteen months. However, some are ready at nine months, and others delay walking until eighteen months. And each baby has his or her own temperament. Some infants are extremely active from birth and some extremely quiet. Some are cuddly and some object to close physical contact. Some cry a great deal while others hardly ever whimper. No two babies are exactly alike, and no two mature according to the same timetable. Even identical twins (who genetically are essentially carbon copies of each other) differ slightly, since their experiences invariably differ in some respects. (The part that sex differences may play in these processes is discussed in the boxed insert on pages 360–361.)

Environmental conditions encourage or retard maturation. In order for children to express their capabilities, there must be some sort of environment —for example, there must be somewhere for them to crawl or walk and someone to listen to and talk to. The environment provides the arena in which children's potentialities are developed.

---

maturation: The internally programed growth of a child.

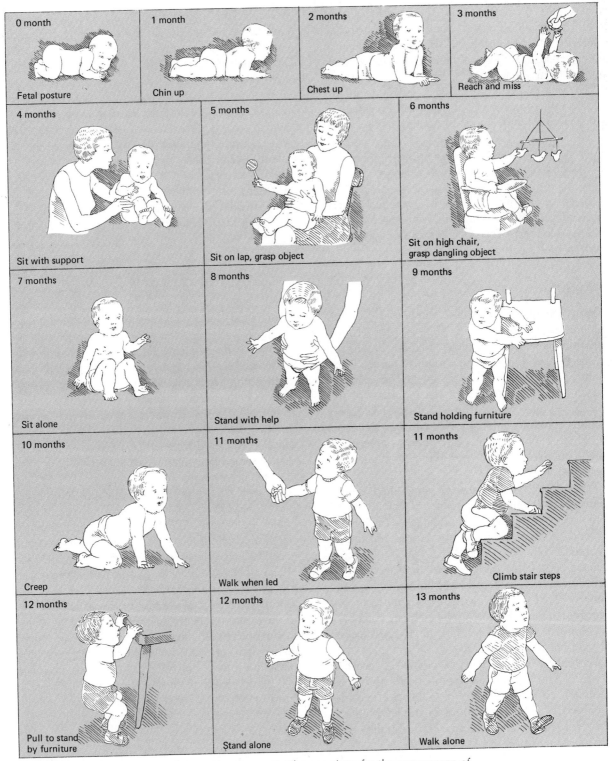

FIGURE 11.1 The sequence of motor development. The age given for the appearance of each skill is approximate; there is a wide range of individual differences. *(Adapted from M. M. Shirley. 1933. The First Two Years. Minneapolis: University of Minnesota Press. Reprinted with permission.)*

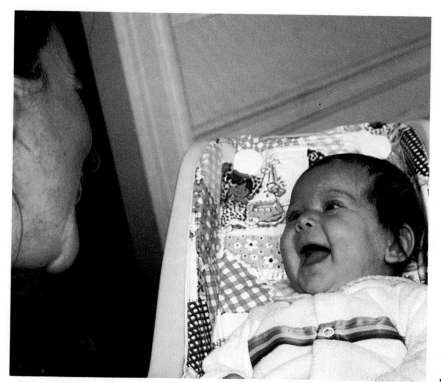

By two months of age, babies smile at human faces, especially when adults smile broadly, nod their heads, and speak in high-pitched tones. At this age infants do not smile more readily at familiar people than at unfamiliar ones, but parents respond warmly to their babies' smiles. *(Julie O'Neil/The Picture Cube)*

Learning

Although maturation is a critical factor in development, its importance lies primarily in making learning possible. Infants and small children are exceedingly responsive to social and psychological experience. Each experience changes children, teaches them something, pushes them in some direction. Children learn to make associations, to expect certain events—such as mother and food—to come together. They learn to do things that produce rewards and to avoid doing things that produce punishments. They also learn by imitating other people. And children learn for learning's sake, as discussed in Chapter 4 in the section entitled "Motivation and Learning."

But children do not merely respond to their environment (Bell, 1968, 1979). Newborns are hardly passive lumps of clay waiting to be molded by the environment. Human infants are marvelous creatures, active agents in their development. They explore their environment—prod an object, sniff an odor, and hunt people with their eyes. Indeed, normal babies compel their caretakers to notice and respond to them if the caretakers are to find relief from their piercing and unnerving cries. For years

psychologists have described how mothers shape their babies; but they are now beginning to appreciate how much babies shape their mothers—and fathers as well.

Experiments indicate how infants learn new behaviors. Even newborn babies change their behavior in response to the environment—which, as you will recall from Chapter 6, is the basic definition of "learning." One psychologist apparently taught two- and three-day-old infants to turn their heads at the sound of a buzzer by rewarding them with a bottle each time they did so (Marquis, 1931).

Research also reveals that infants learn through imitation (Restak, 1982). For instance, infants are especially attracted to human faces. In fact, soon after birth infants recognize the mother's face and begin to fasten a special kind of attention on it. Should the mother open her mouth, babies will imitate the behavior and open their mouth.

To be effective, the skills and knowledge that infants acquire in the course of learning must be retained. As was pointed out in our discussion of memory in Chapter 7, memory is the storage of experiences and their recollection. Insight into infants' early memory processes is gained through

The Psychology of Sex Differences

"A snail starts at the bottom of a well twelve feet deep and crawls up four feet each day. Each night, however, the poor thing slips back three feet. How long will it take the snail to reach the top of the well?" (The answer is at the conclusion of the box.) For over thirty-five years psychologists have tested men and women on these and other types of puzzles and have found that men are far better than women at solving them (Johnson, 1984). Given findings that, on average, women do better in certain verbal skills and men in spatial and mathematical skills, it is but a short step to the conclusion that male and female brains are organized differently (Kimura, 1985).

For centuries intense debate has surrounded questions about the nature of men and women. In order to find out which generalizations are justified and which are not, the psychologists Eleanor E. Maccoby and Carol N. Jacklin (1975) spent three years compiling, reviewing, and interpreting over two thousand books and articles on sex differences in intellectual ability, motivation, and social behavior. They concluded that the following notions are *myths*:

- Girls are more sociable, empathic, and socially oriented than boys are.

- Girls are more suggestible and susceptible to outside influences than boys are.

- Girls have less self-esteem and less self-confidence than boys do.

- Girls are better than boys at rote learning and simple repetitive tasks; boys are better at tasks requiring creative thinking.

- Boys are better than girls at tasks requiring analysis.

- Boys are more affected by environment and girls by heredity.

- Girls lack the achievement motivation of boys.

Maccoby and Jacklin did find four fairly "well-established" sex differences between boys and girls:

- Beginning at about age eleven, girls show greater verbal ability than boys do.

- Boys perform better than girls on visual-spatial tasks in adolescence and adulthood, although not in childhood.

- At about age twelve or thirteen, boys move ahead of girls in mathematical ability.

- Males are more aggressive than are females at all ages.

Not surprisingly, these summary findings have been the source of considerable controversy. Other psychologists have surveyed the literature and arrived at contrary conclusions (Caplan, MacPherson, and Tobin, 1985; Thomas and French, 1985). For instance, Julia Sherman (1978, 1980) and Janet Shibley Hyde (1981) reexamined the evidence for the three cognitive gender differences that Maccoby and Jacklin considered to be "well-established" (verbal ability, visual-spatial ability, and mathematical ability). They conclude that either the differences are nonexistent or their magnitude is inconsequential.

studies of **habituation** (Cohen, 1979; Cohen and Menten, 1981), a process by which infants pay less and less attention to the same stimulus presented over and over again. If the same stimulus—for instance, a sound, a color, or a geometric shape—is repeatedly presented to infants, they will soon become bored with it (habituated to it). Consequently, if infants pay less attention to a stimulus the tenth

---

habituation: The process by which infants pay less and less attention to the same stimulus presented over and over again.

However, the controversy persists (Johnson, 1984; Linn and Petersen, 1985). Two psychologists at Johns Hopkins University, Camella P. Benbow and Julian C. Stanley (1980), have compared the 1972 through 1979 Scholastic Aptitude Test (SAT) scores of 9,927 intellectually gifted junior-high-school students. Although the boys and girls performed equally well on the verbal sections, more than twice as many boys as girls had math scores greater than 500 (1,817 versus 675). The greatest differences were between the top-scoring boys and girls. On the basis of this evidence, Benbow and Stanley offer the hypothesis that sex differences in mathematics achievement derive from "superior male mathematical ability."

A number of other psychologists have challenged Benbow and Stanley's interpretation (Schafer and Gray, 1981; Tobias, 1982). They contend that until and unless girls experience the same world as boys do, one cannot assume that gender differences in math have a biological or genetic basis. Current stereotypes lead many women to believe that mathematics is a "male domain." A 1982 study by the National Science Foundation found that 40 percent of the boys who graduated from high school in 1980 had taken three or more years of math, compared to 25 percent of the girls. Moreover, 25 percent of the boys had taken three or more years of science, compared to 20 percent of the girls (Engelgau, 1984). Other researchers also dispute the notion that boys do better than girls in higher levels of reasoning (Beckman and Fraser, 1985). Analyses of SAT data suggest that a male-female difference occurs primarily on algebraic items; it is not evident on arithmetical or geometric problems (Becker, 1983).

The matter of biological differences between men and women in innate levels of aggressiveness is likewise an area of controversy. Researchers find that males of many species are hormonally primed for aggression. By the same token, hormones seem to prenatally "masculinize" or "feminize" the brain (Phoenix, Goy, and Resko, 1969; Reinisch, 1981; Kimura, 1985). But the evidence in support of gender differences in aggression is by no means firmly established. Some psychologists point to data suggesting that the magnitude of the differences is at best small (Elias, 1984; Hyde, 1984). Further, these and other patterns are quite variable from person to person, and on most cognitive and behavioral measures there is enormous overlap of men and women.

It is clear that the psychology of sex differences is full of controversy. This condition is likely to persist in the future because the findings of psychology and other sciences can be used to buttress or challenge various social arrangements. Even so, evidence suggests that while one's gender may be related to some capabilities, it is a very poor screening device for the assessment of human beings. A great many environmental events interact with our genetic heritage from prenatal development onward. Moreover, the human brain is extraordinarily malleable and variable. Consequently, we can predict very little about people's abilities—mental or otherwise—based on their sex. Any number of men and women can and do excel in activities that, on average, favor the other sex (Kimura, 1985).

(The answer to the snail problem is nine days.)

---

time they experience it than they did the first time, one has evidence that they have "remembered" it.

Clearly, then, the processes of maturation and learning occur hand in hand. In the pages that follow, we will explore how inner plans and outside influences—maturation and learning—work together in the development of intellect, language, love, and morality.

COGNITIVE DEVELOPMENT

During the preadolescent years, children's mental capabilities develop rapidly and gradually evolve into those attributes called adult intelligence. Children become progressively more adept at processing information, attending to salient features of their environment, encoding and retrieving information from memory, and monitoring their own thinking processes. All too often, preschool children fail to comprehend what it is that they know, and when and how to use information to best advantage. They proceed in life in a willy-nilly, hit-or-miss fashion, as if they already possess all the information that they need to know. Consequently, they encounter gaps in their knowledge that prevent them from completing a task or reaching their goal. In contrast, school-age children are more likely to ask themselves before tackling a problem, "What do I need to know?" and "Do I know how to proceed?" They mentally bring together the necessary information and formulate their strategies beforehand. In this manner, they can cope more effectively with their environment and deal with the problem at hand.

The work of the Swiss psychologist Jean Piaget (1895–1980) has had a considerable impact on our understanding of intellectual development. Common sense told Piaget that intelligence, or the ability to think, develops gradually, as the child grows. The sharpest, most inquisitive four-year-old simply cannot understand things a seven-year-old grasps easily. What accounts for the dramatic changes between the ages of four and seven?

Piaget spent years observing, questioning, and playing games with babies and young children —including his own. He concluded that younger children are not just ignorant, in the sense of lacking a given *amount of information*. Rather they think in a different *way* than older children and adults; they use a different kind of logic. A seven-year-old is completely capable of answering the question "Who was born first, you or your mother?" but a four-year-old is not (Chukovsky, 1963). Intellectual development involves quantitative changes (growth in the *amount* of information) as well as qualitative changes (differences in the *manner* of thinking).

In time, Piaget was able to detail the ways in which a child's thinking changes, month by month, year by year. Although the rate at which different children develop varies, he believed that every child passes through the same predictable stages. Each stage builds on the last, increasing the child's ability to solve more complex problems. Thus children develop by continually sharpening the way they view and think about themselves and the world.

Changes in Ways of Knowing

Understanding the world involves the construction of *schemes*, or mental plans for knowing. Each of us is an architect and engineer in this respect, constructing intellectual schemes, applying them, and changing them as necessary. When you put a scheme into action, you are trying to understand something. In this process, you **assimilate**—you try to fit the world into your scheme. Piaget said that people seek to stretch a scheme as far as possible to fit new observations. But at times they find that their scheme does not work. They are then compelled to reorganize their view of the world in accordance with the new experience. That is, they **accommodate** —they change the scheme to fit the characteristics of the world.

According to Piaget, babies begin with two schemes, grasping and sucking—two of the reflexes discussed earlier in the chapter. In other words, babies understand things by grasping or sucking them—whether they be breasts, bottles, fingers, rattles, wooden blocks, or bars of soap. Consider what happens when children attempt to pick up an object with their hand. They begin with an existing scheme. Normally the scheme that was used to pick up a previously experienced wooden block or bottle will work as well with a newly experienced rattle. Piaget said that children *assimilate* the rattle to their existing scheme for picking up objects. But if the newly encountered object is a wet bar of soap, the slippery quality of the object will not allow children to grasp it in the same manner as a wooden block, bottle, or rattle. Consequently, they must change their scheme in order to make allowance for the new

---

assimilation: In Piaget's theory of cognitive development, the process of fitting objects and experiences into one's scheme for understanding the environment.

accommodation: In Piaget's theory of cognitive development, the adjustment of one's scheme for understanding the world to fit newly observed events and experiences.

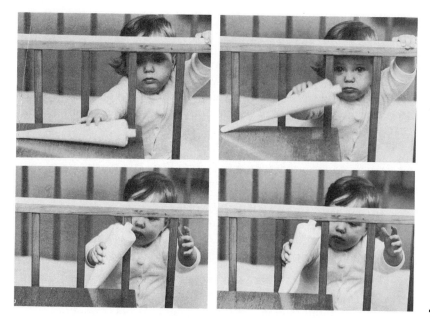

From left to right and top to bottom: This child possesses a scheme for grasping objects and pulling them to her that does not adequately match the features of the environment she is now trying to assimilate. Her scheme will not get the toy through the bars of the playpen. An accommodation—the addition of turning to grasping and pulling—achieves a state of equilibrium. *(George Zimbel/Monkmeyer)*

quality. In so doing, Piaget said, children *accommodate* their scheme to fit the new reality of their experience.

Assimilation and accommodation work together to produce intellectual growth. When events do not fit into existing schemes, new and grander schemes have to be created. Children begin to see and understand things in a new light. Piaget distinguished four stages in the development of intelligence. (Table 11.1 summarizes each stage.)

Sensorimotor Stage (Birth to Two Years)

Infants must discover the relationship between their sensations and their motor responses. For instance, they have to learn that their hands are a part of themselves, whereas a wooden block, bottle, rattle, or bar of soap is not. A major element in distinguishing between themselves and what is outside themselves involves the notion of **object permanence** —the knowledge that a thing has a reality of its own that extends beyond your immediate perception of it.

Consider what happens when a toy is hidden from an infant. She acts as if it had ceased to exist. She doesn't look for it. She grabs whatever else she can find and plays with that, or simply starts crying. However, at ten to twelve months, this pattern begins to change. If the toy rolls behind a chair, the child will watch closely as it rolls out of sight and then search for it behind the chair.

The mastery of object permanence is a giant step in intellectual development. The child has progressed from a stage where she apparently believed that her own actions created the world, to a stage where she realizes that people and objects are independent of her actions. This new scheme, object permanence, might be expressed as: "Things continue to exist even though I cannot see or touch them." The child now conceives of a world of which she is only a part.

Preoperational Stage (Two to Six Years)

The achievement of object permanence suggests that a child has begun to engage in what Piaget called

---

object permanence: A child's realization, developed between the ages of one and two, that an object exists even when he or she cannot see or touch it.

TABLE 11.1   Summary Highlights: Piaget's Stages of Cognitive Development

Stage	Age	Characteristics
Sensorimotor	Birth to two years	Thinking is displayed in action, such as the grasping, sucking, and looking schemes. Beginning at ten to twelve months, the child gradually learns to discover the location of hidden objects, until about eighteen months, when the concept of object permanence is fully understood.
Preoperational	Two to six years	Beginning of symbolic representation. Language first appears; the child begins to draw pictures that represent things. The child cannot represent a series of actions in his or her head in order to solve problems.
Concrete operational	Six to twelve years	Ability to understand conservation problems. Ability to think of several dimensions or features at the same time. The child can now do elementary arithmetic problems, such as judging the quantity of liquid containers and checking addition of numbers by subtraction.
Formal operational thought	Twelve years to adulthood	Thinking becomes more abstract and hypothetical. The individual can consider many alternative solutions to a problem, make deductions, contemplate the future, and formulate personal ideals and values.

representational thought, the hallmark of the preoperational stage. The child's intelligence is no longer one of action only. Now children can picture (or represent) things in their mind. At fourteen months of age, Piaget's daughter demonstrated this. When she was out visiting another family, she happened to witness a child throwing a temper tantrum. She had never had a tantrum herself, but the next day she did—screaming, shaking her playpen, and stamping her feet as the other child had. She had formed so clear an image of the tantrum in her mind that she was able to create an excellent imitation a day later (Ginsburg and Opper, 1969). To Piaget, this meant that his daughter was using symbols. Soon she would learn to use a much more complex system of symbols—spoken language. Whereas infants are limited to solving problems with their actions, older children can mentally represent problems and use language to think them through.

Thinking with actions, in other words, comes before thinking with language.

Stage of Concrete Operations (Six to Twelve Years)

More complex intellectual abilities emerge as the infant grows into childhood. Between the ages of five and seven, most children begin to understand what Piaget called **conservation,** the major milestone of the stage of concrete operations. Conservation is the principle that a given quantity does not change when its appearance is changed. If you have two identical short, wide jars filled with water and you pour the contents of one of them into a tall, thin jar, a child under five will say that the tall jar contains more water than the short one. If you pour the water back into the short jar to show the amount has not changed, the child will still maintain that there was

representational thought: The intellectual ability of a child to picture something in his or her mind.

conservation: The principle that a given quantity does not change when its appearance is changed. The discovery of this principle between the ages of five and seven is important to the intellectual development of the child.

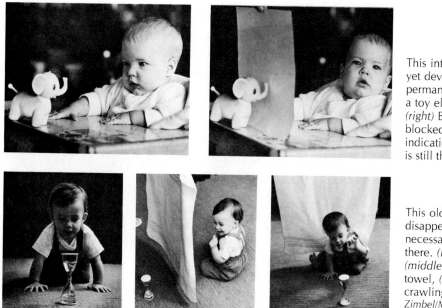

This infant of about six months has not yet developed a concept of object permanence. *(left)* She looks intently at a toy elephant that is in front of her. *(right)* But when the elephant is blocked from view, she gives no indication that she understands the toy is still there. *(George Zimbel/Monkmeyer)*

This older infant realizes that the disappearance of an object does not necessarily mean that it is no longer there. *(left)* When the object he sees *(middle)* is shielded from view by a towel, *(right)* the baby searches for it, crawling under the towel to it. *(George Zimbel/Monkmeyer)*

more water in the tall jar. Children under five do not seem to be able to think about two dimensions at the same time. That is, they do not understand that a change in width is made up for by a change in the height of the tall glass.

Within two years, the same child will tell you that the second jar contains the same amount of water as the first. If you ask why, the child may say because the short jar is fatter than the tall jar—indicating an ability to coordinate perceptions of height and width. Or the child may point out that if you poured the water back into the short jar, it would be the same—indicating an ability to think in reverse, to retrace the steps of the experiment. Younger children generally cannot do this.

This experiment dealt with the conservation of liquid. The same principle applies to the conservation of mass, which is demonstrated by another experiment. An experimenter shows a four-year-old child two identical balls of clay. Then the child watches the experimenter flatten one ball and roll it into the shape of a sausage. Again, the young child believes that the amount of clay has changed. The older child conserves. That is, he or she recognizes that the amount of clay is unaffected by the change in appearance.

Four-year-old children can tell you whether they are boys or girls, and many are fully informed about anatomical differences. Yet if you question children this age, you'll find that they believe people can change their sex by wearing clothes designed for the opposite sex, changing their haircut, playing games associated with the opposite sex, and the like. In other words, if you pour a boy into a female container, he will change. Only when children understand conservation do they realize that a person's sex is permanent.

Many such cognitive advances take place between the years of five and twelve. This is the stage when children develop a working knowledge of the world. They develop skills in the trial-and-error approach to problem solving. But in general, the thinking of children this age is extremely concrete. They need to try solutions out; they cannot work through problems in their heads; and they have a difficult time thinking about hypothetical situations or abstract concepts.

Stage of Formal Operational Thought (Twelve Years to Adulthood)

In the stage of concrete operations, a child's thought remains fixed on the immediate or concrete evidence provided by the senses. But as children enter their teens, they begin thinking in abstract terms. Adoles-

The girl taking part in this demonstration thinks there is more water in the tall beaker; she has not yet acquired conservation. Although she has seen the liquid poured from one beaker to another, she bases her decision on the height of the column of water and ignores its diameter. *(Steve Wells)*

cents learn to engage in **hypothesis testing,** the chief achievement of the stage of formal operations. Hypothesis testing is thinking of how things might be or could be under other circumstances and trying them out. This is the type of logical reasoning associated with scientific activity.

Piaget highlighted the unique quality of formal operational thought with his pendulum experiments. He supplied students with a graduated set of weights that they could suspend from a string (Ginsburg and Opper, 1969). Piaget would show each student how to vary the length of the string and how to replace one weight with another. Then he would ask the student to find out why a pendulum swings rapidly or slowly. The correct answer entails cause-and-effect reasoning. The student should discover that the length of the string is the critical factor: the shorter the string, the faster the movement.

Young children approach the pendulum problem without an overall plan. They do one thing and then another haphazardly, without any underlying logic or order. For instance, one child lengthened the string, attached a light weight to it, and then pushed the pendulum. Next he swung a short pendulum with a heavy weight. Finally, he removed the weight altogether.

Now consider how an adolescent capable of logical thought approached the task. She first tested an intermediate weight with a long string and then followed with tests of shorter strings. Then she reran the procedure, varying the length of the string with a light weight. She concluded her experiment by swinging a heavy weight with a long and then a short string. Reflecting on her results, she observed: "It's the length of the string that makes it go faster or slower; the weight doesn't play a role" (Ginsburg and Opper, 1969:184).

The young woman handled the problem quite differently from the child. She undertook to test *all* possible combinations in a systematic fashion. In contrast, the child proceeded aimlessly, hoping to stumble on the answer by chance.

Logical thought opens a vast new world to adolescents. They can now grasp the relationship between facts and events—a relationship that previously escaped them. But this new way of knowing also

---

hypothesis testing: Thinking of how things might be or could be under other circumstances and trying them out.

confronts adolescents with new realities and dilemmas (Kagan, 1971). How should they respond to peer pressure to experiment with drugs? How should they deal with the temptations of masturbation, petting, intercourse, and, perhaps, homosexuality? Is school worth the effort it requires? Should they look for a job? Is it moral to lie, shoplift, vandalize school property, or cheat on tests?

Logical thought often results in adolescents' questioning some of their basic values and convictions. A fourteen-year-old may brood about inconsistencies in her beliefs (Kagan, 1971): How can God be all-loving and just and still permit human suffering? How can my parents be wise and kind and yet fight so much? How can sex be so much fun but nonetheless get me into difficulty? It is little wonder that some teen-agers find adolescence an unsettling experience.

Not all teen-agers, or for that matter all adults, reach full operational thinking (Elkind, 1975; Roberge and Flexer, 1979). And it makes a difference where one lives. Thus many rural villagers in Turkey do not seem to reach the formal operational stage, although urbanized and educated Turks often do (Kohlberg and Gilligan, 1971). Some evidence suggests that secondary schools may provide students with experiences in mathematics and science that facilitate the development of formal operational thought. A number of psychologists speculate that these experiences may be necessary to its development (Sharp, Cole, and Lave, 1979; Hobbs and Robinson, 1982). There are also those who suggest that a higher or postformal operational stage may also exist. It is characterized by even more powerful and complex thought processes—a type of cognition found in high-level and abstract mathematical and scientific thinking (Commons, Richards, and Kuhn, 1982; Kramer, 1983).

LANGUAGE DEVELOPMENT

Language and thought are closely intertwined. Both abilities involve the use of symbols. You are able to think and talk about objects that are not present and about ideas that are not necessarily true. **Language** is a systematic arrangement of spoken and written symbols and rules for combining them in socially meaningful ways. As such, language allows people to enter one another's worlds. Clearly, the acquistion of language provides children with a formidable tool for learning, coping with the environment, and reaching new levels of intellectual development.

Animal Communication

Language is basic to the human condition. It allows people to communicate with one another and thus to fit their actions together to constitute group life. Various other organisms, such as bees, also aggregate in organized groups. But bees integrate their activities primarily on the basis of ritualistic communication that is biologically programed within them. In contrast, human language entails the manipulation of acquired symbols. And it is abstract and versatile, permitting the formation of innumerable word combinations.

By investigating the communicative patterns of nonhuman organisms, scientists seek to ascertain whether sophisticated language acquisition and use is indeed unique to the human species. They have been able to learn a good deal about language from studies of our nearest relative in the animal kingdom, the chimpanzee. Any number of psychologists have tried to teach chimpanzees to use language, but only recently have such efforts had any success (Savage-Rumbaugh et al., 1980; Premack and Premack, 1983; Eckholm, 1985a, 1985b). One husband-and-wife team, Allen and Beatrice Gardner (1971), raised a baby chimp named Washoe in their home and taught her to use the American Sign Language for deaf people. At three and a half years of age, Washoe knew eighty-seven signs for words such as "food," "dog," "toothbrush," "gimmee," "sweet," "more," and "hurry." She could also put words together, producing simple sentences: "Listen dog"; "More tickle"; and "Susan [a trainer] stupid."

Making signs at the appropriate times would not be enough to be called language, though (Terrace,

language: A systematic arrangement of spoken and written symbols and rules for combining them in socially meaningful ways.

Washoe at about five years of age. She is shown here using the American Sign Language sign for "hat." (R. A. and B. T. Gardner)

1979; Sebeok and Umiker-Sebeok, 1980). A dog or a parrot might make signs that its owner could interpret as demands for a walk or for food. Washoe's remarkable achievement was that some of her signs had abstract meanings and that she occasionally put signs together in new ways to produce new meanings. For example, she learned the sign for "more" (putting her fingertips together over her head) because she loved to be tickled and wanted more. But she was not simply doing something like a dog does when it rolls over to be tickled. She was able to use the same sign later in entirely new circumstances—asking for more food or more hair brushing. In brief, Washoe *generalized* the sign for "more" to related situations; she could apply a response learned with respect to one stimulus to other, similar stimuli. But of course, Washoe's "language" was no match for that of a normal human two-year-old.

The ability to arrange symbols in new combinations to produce new meanings is especially well developed in the human brain. The rules for such organization of symbols are called *grammar*. Grammatical rules are what make the sentence "The rhinoceros roared at the boy" mean the same thing as "The boy was roared at by the rhinoceros." On the surface, these sentences appear different because the word position is changed. But on a deeper level, one knows that the first is an active sentence and the second a passive transformation of it. In their ability to use such grammatical rules to produce meaningful sentences, human beings far surpass the chimpanzee. All this suggests that the degree of communicative ability varies with the level of evolutionary

sophistication. Although the skills displayed by chimps are related to human language skills, they are not truly equivalent to human skills (Limber, 1977; de Villiers and de Villiers, 1979).

Language Acquisition

The example of Washoe shows that becoming competent in a language is not necessarily an easy matter. And the methods by which Washoe and other chimps must be trained are quite different from the relatively spontaneous way in which children acquire a language. Chimps lack the unique capacity for language and thought that characterizes normal human beings. Even under difficult circumstances such as deafness, the human child reveals a natural inclination to develop languagelike systems of communication (Goldin-Meadow and Mylander, 1983).

Communication is central to social behavior, and consequently language is a critical aspect of much communication. Yet language is not the only means by which people transmit messages. Newborns cry —perhaps the most noticeable sound they make (Schaffer, 1971). Variations in the intensity and rhythm of their cries produce a "mad cry" (rhythmical and energetic) and a "pain cry" (beginning with a sudden shriek and then punctuated with gasping wailing). About four weeks or so after birth, infants begin social smiling; their mouths broaden and their eyes crinkle in the presence of another person (Gewirtz, 1965). By nine months, about one-quarter of infants communicate with others by pointing to interesting events, and two-thirds do this by four-

Language development starts early with parents' naming objects and giving babies the ideas that things have names and that speech communicates ideas to others. (Joel Gordon)

teen months of age (Murphy, 1978). All these behaviors set the stage for language acquisition.

In order to communicate effectively with others, children must have social intent. They must have some message to transmit, "encode" an idea and put it in signal form, learn to listen to what others say, "decode" the signals of others, and tailor their own responses to the preceding message from the other person. In addition, they must learn to initiate a conversation, take turns in speaking, and articulate meaning and intentions (Harding, 1982).

The Sequence of Language Development

Children pass through a sequence of stages in their acquisition of language: babbling, one-word speech, two-word speech, telegraphic speech, and complex sentences. Each child takes these steps at his or her own rate. During the first year of life, the "average child" makes many sounds. Crying lessens, and the child starts making mostly cooing sounds, which

develop into a babble. In *babbling*, infants utter soft gurgling or murmuring sounds, in which they alternate vowels and consonants in a recurrent pattern, for example, "ba-ba-ba" or "lo-lo-lo." By the time of their first birthday, babies can make every sound that adults can make—Chinese vowels, African clicks, the German rolled "r," and the English "o" (Osgood, 1953). However, they retain only those sounds that are contained in their own language community.

Late in the first year, the strings of babbles begin to sound more like the language that the child hears. Children imitate the speech of their parents and their older brothers and sisters, and are greeted with approval whenever they say something that sounds like a word. In this way children learn to speak their own language, even though they could just as easily learn any other.

Deaf babies also pass through a babbling phase, even though they never hear any spoken sounds. Seemingly, a hereditary mechanism underlies the babbling process. But unless they receive special training, children with moderate to severe hearing loss do not become competent users of language. Profoundly deaf children rarely learn to speak. While maturing processes activate vocal behavior, adequate environmental stimulation is also essential (Lenneberg, 1973).

Children do not acquire language by simply *hearing* others speak it. Take the case of a boy with normal hearing whose deaf parents communicated by American Sign Language (Moskowitz, 1978). The parents had the boy watch television every day so that he would learn English. By the time the child was three, he was fluent in sign language but he neither understood nor spoke English. The case suggests that in order to learn language, children must *interact* with people in that language.

The leap to using sounds as symbols occurs some time in the second year. The first attempts at saying words are primitive, and the sounds are not exactly like adult sounds. These early utterances are termed **holophrases.** Holophrases are single words that the child uses to convey different meanings, depending on the situation. Thus "mama" may mean "I want a

---

holophrases (HOLE-uh-frayz-es): Single words that a child uses to convey different meanings, depending on the situation.

cookie," "Let me out of my playpen," "Don't wash my face," "I hurt myself," "Daddy's home and at the door," and "I'm frightened of that dog." In time, the words become more intelligible and more precise in their discriminatory power. Typical two-year-olds have a vocabulary of at least fifty words.

Beginning about eighteen months of age, children start to express themselves by joining words into two-word phrases such as "Allgone milk," "No down," "Mama sock," and "Toy there." By the time children are about thirty months old, they use short but nonetheless intelligible sentences, what psychologists term **telegraphic speech**—for instance, "Where my apple?" "Daddy fall down," and "Jimmy want that." Children leave out letters and words but still get the message across—much as adults do when composing a telegram (Brown, 1973).

Around four years of age, children construct their sentences in much the same manner as adults. True, the ideas that they convey are hardly on the level of those of adults. Nevertheless, and this is crucial, they have mastered the basics of grammar. They can correctly use rules for structuring language. Language includes four ingredients: *phonology*—rules for putting sounds together to form words; *syntax* —rules for putting words together to form sentences; *semantics*—rules for interpreting the meaning of words and sentences; and *pragmatics*—rules for the use of speech to communicate with others (such as taking turns and following the topic of conversation).

Foundations of Language Acquisition

The psychologist Noam Chomsky (1965, 1968, 1975) has marveled at the ease with which children learn their native language and the young age at which they learn it. Indeed, as Chomsky suggests, speech is no small accomplishment. Reflect on how a conversation carried on in another language sounds to you. Think of the enormous number of grammatical forms that are poured over a youngster's head. All this brings Chomsky to ask whether human beings are endowed with a special biological capacity for language. He answers the question affirmatively.

Chomsky speculates that children are born with some sort of language-generating mechanism, which he terms the **language acquisition device (LAD)**. He finds that all languages of the world permit the individual to string together nouns and verbs, give commands, ask questions, deny statements, and much more. Consequently, children may already "know" certain universal aspects of language by the time they approach the task of language acquisition. In contrast, Washoe and other chimps seemingly lack the prewired mechanism that disposes human children to language use. And unlike the brain of chimps, that of human beings is lateralized, with language centered in the left hemisphere.

Although essential, an adequate biological foundation is not sufficient for language development. As pointed out before, suitable environmental input is also required. For their part, parents and other caretakers are anxious that children master language as soon as possible. Language "humanizes" children and assists them in learning other crucial self-care skills. By playing with children, talking to them, and reading to them, parents stimulate their language development (Clarke-Stewart, 1973; Cunningham et al., 1985). Caregivers reinforce the learning of words, phrases, and sentences in much the same fashion that they condition other behaviors (Catania, 1979; Salzinger, 1979; Julia, 1983).

Caretakers facilitate children's acquisition of language in a variety of ways. **Caretaker speech** is a good example of this. It differs from everyday speech in its simplified vocabulary, higher pitch, exaggerated intonation, and short sentences (Snow, 1972; Moskowitz, 1978). Mothers also use a high proportion of questions ("Baby hungry?"); fathers, a high

---

telegraphic speech: The kind of speech used by young children. Words are left out, but the meaning is still clear.

language acquisition device (LAD): The innate language-generating mechanism that Noam Chomsky speculates children are born with.

caretaker speech: A systematically modified version of language that adults use in addressing infants and young children. Caretaker speech differs from everyday speech in its simplified vocabulary, higher pitch, exaggerated intonation, short, simple sentences, and high proportion of questions and imperatives.

proportion of imperatives ("Baby walk!"). Baby talk is a type of caretaker speech—speech with high pitch, an exaggerated intonation, and the duplication of syllables (in the English language, "wa-wa" = "water," "choo-choo" = "train," "bebe" = "baby," and "tum-tum" = "stomach"). Baby talk is found in all languages, from Gilyak and Comanche (the languages of small, isolated, preliterate Old and New World communities) to Arabic and Marathi (languages of people with literary traditions) (Caporael, 1981).

When youngsters begin uttering meaningful, identifiable words (around twelve to fourteen months of age), their caretakers invariably speak **motherese**—a simplified, redundant, and highly grammatical sort of language. Many of the features of motherese result from the process of trying to carry on a conversation with immature conversational partners (Snow, 1977). Mothers and fathers typically restrict their utterances to the present tense, to concrete nouns, and to comments on what the child is doing or experiencing (for instance, statements as to what objects are called, what color they are, and where they are located). They seek to get and hold a child's attention by using the child's name ("Mary, what is that?") and prefacing statements with exclamations ("Hey! See that!").

Language and Thought

Scientists have long interested themselves in the relationship between language and thought. Some anthropologists, among them Edward Sapir (1949) and his student Benjamin L. Whorf (1956), say that language controls the way people experience and think about the world—the *linguistic relativity thesis*. According to Sapir and Whorf, people with different languages have different views of the world. For instance, the Hanunoo, a Philippine people, have a name for each of ninety-two varieties of rice, whereas English-speaking Americans have but one word. Linguistic relativity theorists claim that the Hanunoo, by virtue of their ninety-two words, attune themselves to differences in rice that Americans typically overlook. With respect to rice, the Hanunoo and Americans are said to inhabit different sensory worlds and hence to experience different realities.

Most psychologists agree with the notion that the words people use reflect their chief cultural concerns—for instance, if they have many words for rice they are likely to be much more concerned with rice than if they have only one word for it. But Americans' lack of a word for each variety of rice does not mean that they fail to notice differences in rice. Rather than determining thought, most psychologists would say that language merely helps or hinders some types of thinking. Thus it is easier to refer to *small brown grains of rice with dark brown spots* with one word rather than with nine English words.

The linguistic relativity thesis claims that language shapes thought. The contrary view (that thought shapes language) holds that language is not essential for thought but only for conveying it—the *container of thought thesis*. Piaget (1952, 1962) said that speech presupposes that young children have already formed mental images of objects (water, ball, and Mommy) and events (drinking, holding, and sucking). For instance, children first form visual representations associated with the actions having to do with a bottle—holding a bottle, sucking from a bottle, and pouring from a bottle. Only later do children come to represent these various activities with the word "bottle." "Bottle" then becomes a verbal marker for the prior mental images (Zachry, 1978). Other researchers confirm that children's first words are typically names for preexisting mental categories (Lenneberg, 1967; Nelson, 1972; Bornstein, Kessen, and Weiskopf, 1976).

The Soviet psychologist Lev Vygotsky (1962) suggests a way by which the conflicting positions on language and thought can be reconciled. His research indicates that thought and speech initially develop in a separate but parallel manner. At about two or so years of age, the two independent streams come together, whereupon "thought becomes verbal and speech rational" (p. 44). Speech and thought then *interact*, so that each reciprocally influences and shapes the other. What children think affects what they say. And what they and others say affects

---

motherese: A simplified, redundant, and highly grammatical form of language employed by parents in communicating with their young children.

children's thought. Indeed, in some situations speech and thought blend. In *inner speech*, children "talk" to themselves by carrying on an internal conversation. Later, in adolescence (in the stage of formal operations), they engage in *verbal thought* when involved, for instance, with political and ethical reasoning.

EMOTIONAL AND SOCIAL DEVELOPMENT

While children are developing their ability to use their bodies, to think, and to express themselves, they are also developing emotionally and socially. They begin to attach themselves to specific people and to care what these significant others think and feel. And they gradually learn those skills that will fit them for participation in group life. In the process they become social beings who look to their association with others for affection, acceptance, security, recognition, and a general sense of well-being.

Emotional Development

The idea that healthy children pass through a series of well-defined stages of motor and intellectual development is now well-established and a valuable concept for physicians and pediatricians. Recently Stanley I. Greenspan and his colleagues (Greenspan and Greenspan, 1985) at the National Institute of Mental Health have investigated children's emotional development. They believe that knowledge about the emotional side of growth is as critical as is knowledge about the growth of physical and intellectual capabilities. The researchers have identified six milestones in children's emotional development.

Stage One (Birth to About Two Months)

During this phase, infants learn how to calm themselves while simultaneously increasing their interest in the world about them. Already they show their personal preferences for certain kinds of sensory experiences and their dislike for others. On the basis of the foundations established during this stage, they

gradually expand their repertoire of feelings and behavior and their ability to integrate and organize them in purposeful ways. Special problems may result from immature central nervous systems or abnormal sensory patterns. Should a baby be unable to respond through any of the primary sensory channels, particularly seeing and hearing, parents should have the child professionally evaluated.

Stage Two (About Two Months to Four or Five Months)

This phase in emotional development is a time for "falling in love" in which infants display a joyful interest in the *human* world. At first they become responsive to human beings as a general class of stimuli. Later, at about seven months of age, they begin linking themselves with specific individuals (Schaffer and Emerson, 1964a). Psychologists term this bonding process **attachment**—the affectional tie that the infant forms with another person. Infants reveal attachment by engaging in behavior that promotes closeness and contact. These activities include crying, smiling, calling, clinging, and approaching. Usually the mother is the first object of attachment, but in some instances the first attachment is to the father or a grandparent (Weinraub, Brooks, and Lewis, 1977; Schaffer, 1977; Ainsworth, 1984). The ideal environment for an infant during the early months of attachment is one of wooing, in which caregivers draw out a baby's affection and bring him or her pleasure. A pattern of despondency, withdrawal, a shallow capacity for joy, or a greater interest in things than people may signal an underlying difficulty.

Stage Three (About Four to Eight Months)

Children build on the foundation of sensory interest in the world and learn about emotional "dialogues" with others. They lift their arms to caretakers, play give-and-take games with caregivers, and gurgle in response to another person's speech. They may display normal anger by throwing a toy away. Should caretakers consistently misread a child's cues for attention or affection, the infant may regress and

---

attachment: The affectional tie that the infant forms with another person.

shut itself off from meaningful relationships with other people.

Stage Four (About Nine or Ten Months to Eighteen Months)

During this period, children begin developing an organized sense of self, make a bid for independence, and exhibit more complex behavioral and emotional patterns. For instance, they will take a caretaker's hand and guide the person to the refrigerator when they are hungry, instead of simply crying for dinner. Children begin piecing small cause-and-effect units into meaningful chains. In fact, children appear to operate on an implicit theory of causality. The ability to appreciate that a cause must always precede an effect is of enormous survival value in the course of evolution (Pines, 1983a). Difficulties may also appear during this phase. Some parents, threatened by their child's emerging independence, may become overly strict. When strictness is carried to extremes, the result can be a withdrawn, compliant child.

Stage Five (Eighteen Months to About Two-and-a-Half Years)

Children begin developing an ability to create their own mental images of the world and to use ideas in expressing emotions. They can mentally conjure an image of their last interaction with a caregiver in the person's absence. Moreover, children gain the capacity to enact emotional dramas, and they can play organized games because they are now better able to internalize social rules. During this phase, children gain knowledge of particular physical attributes that distinguish them from other children and adults (Lewis and Brooks-Gunn, 1979). They also achieve a sense of "mine" with respect to toys and territory (Levine, 1983). However, some children may become stalled at a "more primitive" level, able to express emotions only in "behavioral discharges" like temper tantrums.

Stage Six (Two-and-a-Half to Four Years)

A flowering of emotional capacity occurs in this phase. Children develop an ability for emotional thinking; they learn to distinguish among different emotional feelings and to understand how these feelings are related. They now use such words as "because" and "but" that allow them greater precision in thought and speech. Their imagination is richer, and their pretend dramas often contain several subplots. Mood disorders, sleeping and eating problems, and an inability to concentrate may suggest problems in this stage.

Greenspan and his associates contend that attention to children's emotional state is as important as an assessment of their rate of growth, IQ, or physical health. They find that the more factors that interfere with a child's mastery of the emotional milestones, the greater the probability of compromised intellectual and emotional development later. When infants show difficulty at an early age, such as four months, it is easier to nudge them and the parents back onto a healthier path than it is at four years of age. The longer problems persist, the greater the likelihood that maladaptive emotional coping strategies build up. In an early phase the solution to a problem may be as simple as teaching a parent that an emotionally disorganized newborn is too easily overstimulated or finds stroking or cuddling discomforting.

At times the relationship between the parent and the infant may be troubled (Crittenden, 1983). Consider the following two episodes. In one case, a mother reaches out her arms to her six-month-old son and asks him to "come to Mommy." The infant, as yet too young to be mobile, stares at her intently. When the child fails to come, the mother turns away, saying, "OK, if you don't love me, I don't love you." In another case, an animated three-year-old girl sings and dances around a room, while her depressed mother slumps over a table, ignoring her. Finally, the child drops dejectedly to the floor. The mother turns to the child for the first time, and asks, "You're tired, too, huh?" Specialists at the Clinical Infant Research Unit at the National Institute of Mental Health are devising psychological intervention techniques to improve the chances of youngsters like these, whose parents have difficulty relating to them. For instance, a therapist may have to teach mothers who never received proper nurturing themselves how to hold, feed, and even talk to their infants. By monitoring children's emotional growth, researchers hope that emotional difficulties can be detected before they become serious psychological problems.

Over the past several decades, more and more mothers with young children have found employ-

Mother Care/Other Care

Since 1950, the proportion of mothers active in the American work force has tripled, with the working mother now being the norm. As of 1985, some 20 million women, or 62 percent of all women with children under eighteen, held jobs. In addition, 41 percent of all mothers with infants under age one were working. As increasing numbers of mothers with children have found employment outside the home, new arrangements for the care of infants and young children have emerged (see Figure 11.2).

Although some experts have reservations about the consequences of these trends for American youngsters, an accumulating body of research suggests that many of the concerns are unwarranted (Scarr, 1985). For the most part, psychologists and sociologists are no longer asking whether it is good or bad that mothers work. Instead, they are finding that a more important issue is whether the mother, regardless of employment, is satisfied with her situation (Hoffman and Nye, 1974; Stuckey, McGhee, and Bell, 1982; Easterbrooks and Goldberg, 1985). The working mother who obtains personal satisfaction from employment, who does not feel excessive guilt, and who enjoys satisfactory household arrangements is likely to perform as well as or better than the nonworking mother. Women who are not working and would like to, and working mothers whose lives are beset by harassment and strain, are the ones whose children are most likely to display maladjustment and behavior problems (Lerner and Galambos, 1985).

There is no evidence that children do better if a mother stays at home for the first three months of life, or for that matter for the child's first three years (Scarr, 1985). Babies respond naturally to caretakers other than their biological parents. However, infants may experience greater difficulty in day care between the ages of seven and fifteen months, when they become more sensitive to separation from a primary caretaker. Even so, children are quite adaptable and they seem to suffer few, if any, long-term harmful effects from day-care experiences. Most child psychologists agree that high-quality day care and nursery schools afford parents acceptable alternative care arrangements for their children (Kagan, Kearsley, and Zelazo, 1978; Ainslie, 1984). High-quality programs are characterized by small group size, high staff-child ratios, well-trained staffs, good equipment, and attractive and nurturing environments.

However, the quality of the day care currently available and affordable leaves many people dissatisfied. Ralph Nader, the consumer activist, describes some centers as "children's warehouses." Additionally, sex-abuse scandals at centers from California to New York have terrified a good many parents. And low-quality facilities function as networks for spreading a variety of diseases, especially colds, diarrhea, and dysentery (Ricks, 1984). The United States is one of the few industrialized nations that does not have a comprehensive day-care program. European nations like Sweden have established nationally subsidized support systems. More than eighteen hundred American companies offer help with day care, but such programs are still in their infancy (Collins, 1985; Meyers, 1985).

ment outside the home, and many are returning to work earlier after the birth of their babies. Consequently, the quality of out-of-home care for infants and young children is a major concern of parents, psychologists, educators, and policymakers. The boxed insert above addresses a number of these issues.

Personality Development

Humanness is a social product. People become human as they interact with other members of their society and acquire those ways of behavior typical of their culture. Psychologists call this process **socialization**. Socialization is the sum of the ways a society

---

socialization: The process of learning the rules of behavior of the culture within which an individual is born and will live.

Many incidents of day-care abuse or neglect can be avoided if parents spend time carefully choosing a center. Parents should ask themselves, "Would I like to be here?" They should look at how sensitive the caregivers are to each child and the sorts of interactions that take place among the children themselves. It is advisable that they drop in at unexpected times. If a caregiver says, "Do not come except at these times," there are grounds for concern. Parents should also appraise the physical facilities; for instance, does the center have adequate space for play, accessible toilets and wash basins, ample facilities for children when the weather is inclement, and inviting playthings? It is often helpful to ask neighbors and acquaintances about their experiences with various centers.

Parents can rest assured that most children show remarkable resilience. Throughout the world children are raised under a great variety of conditions, and the day-care arrangement is just one of them. The effects of day care depend to some extent on the amount of time a child spends at a center and on the quality of parent-child interaction during the time that the family is together (Stith and Davis, 1984). However, these findings should not lead to the conclusion that "it doesn't matter what happens during the early years." Nor should they be taken as an invitation to excuse or overlook child neglect and abuse.

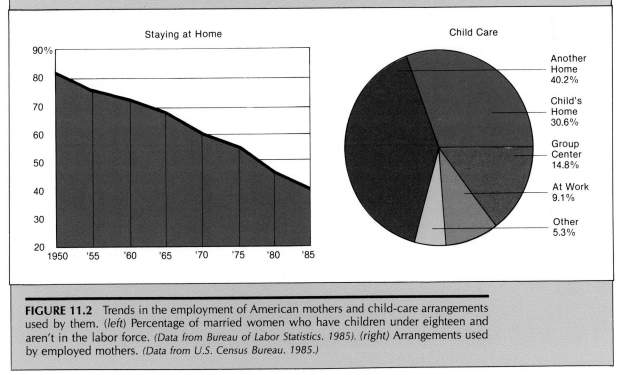

FIGURE 11.2 Trends in the employment of American mothers and child-care arrangements used by them. *(left)* Percentage of married women who have children under eighteen and aren't in the labor force. *(Data from Bureau of Labor Statistics. 1985.)* *(right)* Arrangements used by employed mothers. *(Data from U.S. Census Bureau. 1985.)*

shows its children how to be acceptable adults. By so doing, it recreates itself in the young. Simultaneously, socialization is the mechanism by which the young become capable of effective participation in group life. In sum, socialization is both a process by which society renews itself and a process by which a mere biological human is transformed into a human person.

In becoming functioning members of society, children learn many things. They typically gain an understanding of what constitutes acceptable and unacceptable behavior. They acquire ideas about what is meaningful, valuable, beautiful, and worth striving for. And they learn those skills and roles that enable them to interact and live with other people. Of equal importance, the child gains an answer to the question "Who am I?" and develops an identity. In the pages that follow, we examine several theories about how the child becomes socialized. We begin with Freud's theory of psychosexual development, which has been a major influence on the understanding of socialization.

Freud's Theory of Psychosexual Development

Sigmund Freud (1856–1939) believed that all children are born with powerful sexual and aggressive urges that must be tamed. In learning to control these impulses, children acquire a sense of right and wrong. They become "civilized." The process—and the results—are different for boys and girls.

In the first few years of life, boys and girls have similar experiences. Their erotic pleasures are obtained through the mouth, sucking at their mother's breast. Weaning is a period of frustration and conflict —it is children's first experience with not getting what they want. Freud called this the **oral stage** of development. Later the anus becomes the source of erotic pleasure, giving rise to what Freud called the **anal stage.** Children enjoy holding in or pushing out their feces—until they are required, through toilet training, to curb this freedom.

The major conflict comes between the ages of three and five, when children discover the pleasure they can obtain from their genitals. As a consequence, they become extremely aware of the differences between themselves and members of the opposite sex. In this **phallic stage,** according to Freud, the child becomes a rival for the affections of the parent of the opposite sex. The boy wants to win his mother for himself and finds himself in hostile conflict with his father. The girl wants her father for herself and tries to shut out her mother. These struggles take place on an unconscious level; generally the child and the parents do not have any clear awareness that it is going on. Freud called this crisis the **Oedipal conflict,** after Oedipus, the king in Greek tragedy who unknowingly killed his father and married his mother.

According to Freud, children successfully resolve the Oedipal conflict by identifying with the parent of the same sex. Boys come to terms with the fact that they cannot hope to vanquish their fathers, and girls make their peace with the fact that they cannot outdistance their mothers. Simultaneously, both boys and girls give up their incestuous desire for the parent of the opposite sex. In this manner, boys acquire a sense of masculinity and girls acquire a sense of femininity.

The oral, anal, and phallic stages occupy the center stage of Freud's theory. He believed that what happens to people in later life is simply a ripple on the surface of a core personality that is fashioned during the preschool years. Nonetheless, Freud also identified two additional periods, the latency stage and the genital stage.

The **latency stage** begins at about five years of age and ends with puberty. Sexual desires are pushed into the background, and children busy themselves with exploring the world and learning new skills. This process of redirecting sexual impulses into learning tasks is called **sublimation**. Although children this age often avoid members of the opposite sex, sexual interest reappears in adolescence and

oral stage: According to Freud, the stage at which infants associate erotic pleasure with the mouth.
anal stage: According to Freud, the stage at which children associate erotic pleasure with the elimination process.
phallic (FAL-ic) stage: According to Freud, the stage at which children associate sexual pleasure with their genitals.
Oedipal (EE-di-pull) conflict: According to Freud, a boy's wish to possess his mother sexually, coupled with hostility toward his father. Correspondingly, girls desire their fathers sexually and feel hostile toward their mothers. In order to reduce his or her fear of punishment from the same-sex parent, the child begins to identify with the parent of the same sex.
latency stage: According to Freud, the stage at which sexual desires are pushed into the background and the child becomes involved in exploring the world and learning new skills.
sublimation: The process of redirecting sexual impulses into learning tasks that begins at about the age of five.

launches the **genital stage**. The way in which children resolve the Oedipal conflict in childhood influences the kind of relationships they will form with members of the opposite sex throughout life. Ideally, when a person reaches the genital stage, he or she derives as much satisfaction from giving pleasure as from receiving it. Freud thought that most of the key processes that underlie personality development occur at the unconscious level and stem from impulses buried below the level of awareness.

Today, relatively few psychologists believe that sexual feelings disappear in childhood. Further, Oedipal conflict, to the extent it actually exists, may be limited to nuclear family arrangements characterized by two parents and their offspring. Children in non-Western societies in which extended family arrangements prevail seem untouched by conflicting Oedipal sentiments. Moreover, psychologists find it difficult to test Freud's formulations by established scientific procedures (Greenberg and Fisher, 1978). Since unconscious motivation is, by definition, beyond awareness, how does one go about observing, studying, and measuring it in an objective manner?

Freud was attempting to set off a revolution in society's thinking about childhood. Like many revolutionaries, he probably overstated the case. Yet the idea that children have to learn to control powerful sexual and aggressive desires, and the belief that such early childhood experiences can have a long-term effect on adult personality and behavior, would be difficult to deny. (We shall return to Freud in Chapter 13.)

Erikson's Theory of Psychosocial Development

Freud's work has had a major impact on twentieth-century thought. He directed the attention of scientists to the crucial part that social experience plays in human development. It is hardly surprising, therefore, that one of Freud's major contributions has been the impetus that his work has given other psychologists to delve more deeply into the human experience. One of the most insightful of these is the neo-Freudian psychoanalyst Erik Erikson.

To Erikson (1959, 1963), socialization is neither so sudden nor so emotionally violent an experience as that depicted by Freud. Moreover, Erikson takes a broader view of human development than Freud in terms of both time and scope. Although he recognizes the child's sexual and aggressive urges, he believes that the need for social approval is just as important (hence his term "psychosocial development"). And although he believes that childhood experiences have a lasting impact on a person, he sees development as a lifelong process.

All of us face a series of "crises" as we grow from infancy to old age, as we mature and people expect more from us. Each of these crises represents an issue. And as children—or adolescents or adults—we may develop more strongly in one way or another, depending on how other people respond to our efforts to cope with such issues.

For example, two-year-olds are delighted with their new-found ability to walk, to get into things, to use words, and to ask questions. The very fact that they have acquired these abilities adds to their self-esteem. They are eager to use them. If the adults around them applaud their efforts and acknowledge their achievements, they begin to develop a sense of autonomy, or independence. However, if the adults ignore them except to punish them for going too far or being a nuisance, children may begin to doubt the value of their achievements. They may also feel shame because the people around them act as if their new desire for independence is bad. The tug between the forces of autonomy and shame provides the foundation for the second of eight stages in Erikson's theory. (The other stages and a table showing all stages are presented in Chapter 12, where we continue our discussion of the life cycle.)

Each stage builds on the last. It is this feature that forms the basis for Erikson's *epigenetic principle:* at each stage of the life span there emerges a new characteristic that is dependent for its development on the successful resolution of the crisis posed by the previous stage; in turn, this new characteristic becomes an essential building block for the stage that follows it (Erikson, 1968). For instance, children who have learned to trust the world (the chief

---

genital stage: According to Freud, the stage during which a person's sexual satisfaction depends as much on giving sexual pleasure as on receiving it.

developmental gain of Erikson's first stage) are better equipped to seek autonomy than those who are mistrustful; children who have achieved autonomy take initiative more readily than those who doubt themselves; and so on. The basic question in each stage is whether the individual will find ways to direct his or her needs, desires, and talents into socially acceptable channels and learn to think well of himself or herself.

Learning Theories of Social Development

Both Freud and Erikson stress the emotional dynamics of social development. Their theories suggest that learning social rules is altogether different from learning to ride a bicycle or to speak a foreign language. Many psychologists disagree. They believe that children learn the ways of their social world because they are rewarded for conforming and because they copy older children and adults in anticipation of future rewards. In other words, social development is simply a matter of conditioning and imitation (see Chapter 6).

Conditioning. Adults—especially parents and teachers—have the power to reward and punish. Consciously and unconsciously they use praise, smiles, and hugs to reward children for behaving in ways they consider good and for expressing attitudes that support their own. They tend to ignore or to be hostile toward the expression of opinions that are contrary to their own and toward behavior of which they disapprove.

Gender-role training provides obvious examples of this (Eisenberg et al., 1985; Power, 1985). At home and in school, boys are encouraged to engage in athletics and to be assertive. Girls are discouraged from doing these things, but are rewarded for being helpful and nice, looking neat, and acting cute. Indeed, gender typing and gender-role socialization begin at birth (Rubin, Provenzano, and Luria, 1974). Although male and female newborns are indistinguishable except for their genitals, parents (especially fathers) typically describe their daughters as "weak," "soft," "fine-featured," "awkward," and "delicate." In contrast, they describe their sons as "strong," "firm," "large-featured," "well coordinated," and "hard."

Teachers perpetuate and reinforce gender-typed behaviors in their classrooms (Serbin et al., 1973; Fagot, 1985; Fagot et al., 1985). They are more willing to overlook aggression in girls than in boys, and they scold boys more sharply than girls. Moreover, teachers encourage dependence in girls by ignoring them except when the girls are directly beside them. In these and many other ways, adults use conditioning to shape children's development. Children gradually learn to behave in the way that leads to the greatest satisfaction, even when no one is watching. To avoid punishment and gain rewards from those around them, they learn to reward and punish themselves. For example, a child may criticize herself for making a mistake that has led to punishment in the past. The mistake may be a moral one—lying, for example. A boy may learn to be hard on himself for showing sensitivity, because in the past his tears and blushes were met with humiliating laughter.

All this is not to say that children always do as they are told. Adults also teach youngsters how to get away with misbehavior—for example, by apologizing or by giving a present to someone they have wronged. In this way, some children learn that they may receive praise instead of punishment for bad conduct (see Chapter 6).

Imitation. A second way in which children learn social rules is by observing other people. When youngsters see another child or an adult being congratulated for behaving in certain ways or expressing certain attitudes, they are likely to imitate that person in the hope of obtaining rewards themselves.

Albert Bandura's experiments indicate that children are very quick indeed to imitate other people's behavior (Bandura and Walters, 1963). Bandura's basic technique is to show children movies of a person reacting to a situation. He then puts the children in the same situation to see how they behave.

In a classic experiment Bandura showed a film of a frustrated adult taking out her anger on a "Bobo" doll. The woman assaulted the doll—yelling, kicking, and punching it with all her might. After the film, children who had been deliberately frustrated with broken promises and delays were led to a room that contained an identical doll. Taking their cue from the film, they launched furious attacks —imitating the actress's behavior down to the last kick.

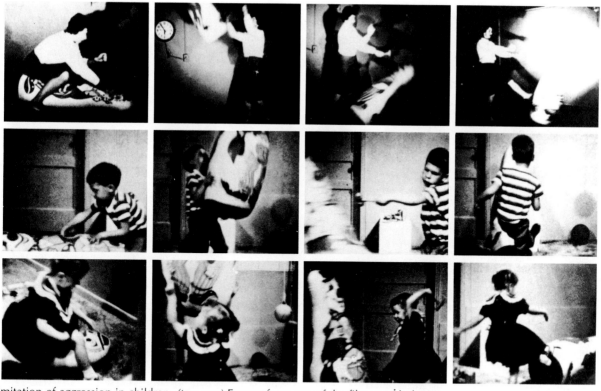

Imitation of aggression in children. *(top row)* Frames from one of the films psychologist Albert Bandura showed to children. *(bottom two rows)* Behavior of children who watched the film and were given a chance to play with similar objects. *(Courtesy, Albert Bandura)*

Later Bandura added two different endings to the film. In one the actress was praised and given candy and soft drinks after she had attacked the doll. In the other she was severely scolded for her behavior. Most of the children who saw the second version learned from the actress's experience and did not attack the doll so they would not be punished. What this suggests is that conditioning and modeling work together. Children do not imitate everything they see, only the behavior that seems to bring rewards.

The Cognitive-Developmental Approach to Understanding Social Development

Theorists who emphasize the role of cognition, or thinking, in development view growing children quite differently. Learning theory implies that children are essentially passive—pieces of clay to be shaped. The people who administer rewards and punishments and serve as models do the shaping. Cognitive theorists see the *children* as the shapers.

Taking their cue from Piaget, they argue that social development is the result of children's acting on the environment and trying to make sense out of their experiences. The games children play illustrate this process.

Play. People commonly think of play as activities that are voluntary, ephemeral, and not terribly serious. Yet whereas much of adult play is largely frivolous and frequently light-hearted, much of children's play is basic, useful, earnest, and often intense (Garvey, 1977; King, 1979; Rubin, Fein, and Vandenberg, 1983). And very often play fulfills different needs and produces different satisfactions for children than it does for adults (Piaget, 1962; Erikson, 1963; Smith and Vollstedt, 1985). During the sensorimotor stage described by Piaget, play provides opportunities for exploratory learning. Later, fantasy play allows children, like imaginative writers, to create a world of their own and in so doing to come to terms with new and often frighten-

"Dress-up" is a favorite role-taking game of preschool children. Role-taking is dress rehearsal for understanding the adult world and for becoming an adult. *(Joseph Schuyler/Stock, Boston)*

ing experiences. Still later, games become a vehicle by which children make up their own rules and structure group activities; the world of play then becomes a miniature society, with its own rules and codes.

Play makes other contributions to children's development. In play, children can trim the world down to manageable size and manipulate it to suit their whims (Caplan and Caplan, 1973). Further, games allow children to test various kinds of competition in an atmosphere that permits them to fail without grave frustrations or severe consequences. And play offers opportunities for children to explore equal and cooperative relationships with others, in contrast with their largely unequal and subordinate relationships with adults. In all these contexts, children shape and mold their self-conceptions and evolve their identities.

Much of children's play involves **role taking.** Youngsters try on such adult roles as mother, father, teacher, storekeeper, explorer, and rock star. Role taking allows them to learn about different points of view firsthand. Suppose a child plays a mother opposite another child who plays a whiny, disobedient baby. When she finds herself totally frustrated by the other child's nagging she begins to understand why her mother gets mad. You cannot cook even a pretend meal when the baby keeps knocking over the pots and pans.

Friendship. Children's friendships undergo changes as they grow older (Berndt, 1978; Berndt and Hoyle, 1985). Five-year-olds conceive of friends as people whom they know and like and with whom they play and spend time. Later, especially about ten to twelve years of age, children come to think of friends as people with whom they share intimacies, confidences, and problems. They view friends as people who stick up for them and who display other evidence of loyalty. And friends are people with whom they have common interests. In adolescence, friendships take on additional dimensions and allow even more intimate and personal kinds of experiences. Therefore, while virtually nonexistent in the

role taking: An important aspect of children's play that involves assuming adult roles, thus enabling the child to experience different points of view firsthand.

TABLE 11.2   Kohlberg's Stages in a Child's Moral Development

Level One	Preconventional	Reactions to Example of Theft of Drug
Stage 1	*Obedience and punishment orientation.* The child obeys rules to avoid punishment. "Conscience" is the fear of punishment.	Pro: Theft is justified because the drug did not cost much to produce. Con: Theft is condemned because the thief would get caught and go to jail.
Stage 2	*Naïve hedonistic and instrumental orientation.* The child's action is motivated by a desire for reward or benefit. Morality is judged in terms of whether or not a given action provides a "payoff."	Pro: Theft is justified because the wife needs the drug and Heinz needs his wife's companionship. Con: Theft is condemned because his wife will probably die before Heinz gets out of prison so it will not do him much good.

Level Two	Conventional	Reactions to Example of Theft of Drug
Stage 3	*"Good boy"–"nice girl" orientation.* The child is preoccupied with the approval of others. In judging the morality of behavior, consideration is given to the person's intentions. The child views a moral person as one who possesses a set of virtues, thus the emphasis on being "nice."	Pro: Theft is justified because Heinz is unselfish in looking after the needs of his wife. Con: Theft is condemned because Heinz will feel bad thinking of how he brought dishonor on his family; his family will be ashamed of his action.
Stage 4	*Law and authority orientation.* The child blindly accepts social rules. Emphasis falls on "doing one's duty," showing respect for authority, and maintaining social order.	Pro: Theft is justified because Heinz would be responsible for his wife's death. Con: Theft is condemned because Heinz is a lawbreaker.

Level Three	Postconventional	Reactions to Example of Theft of Drug
Stage 5	*Social-contract orientation.* The child is concerned with balancing the rights of the individual and the protection of society. Morality is viewed as a social contract among people that can be adjusted to promote basic human rights.	Pro: Theft is justified because the law is not fashioned for situations in which a person would forfeit a life in obeying the rules. Con: Theft is condemned because others may also have great need.
Stage 6	*Universal ethical-principle orientation.* The child condemns himself for violating his own principles. He follows self-selected ethical principles based on abstract values (e.g., the Golden Rule, the fundamental equality of all human beings). Unjust laws may be broken when they conflict with basic moral principles.	Pro: Theft is justified because Heinz could not have lived with his conscience if he had allowed his wife to die. Con: Theft is condemned because Heinz could not have lived up to the standards of his conscience if he had engaged in thievery.

Source: Based on Lawrence Hohlberg. 1963. The development of children's orientations toward a moral order. *Vita Humana,* 6:11–33.

preschool years, intimacy takes on a progressively important role in friendships as children move from the early school years through adolescence.

Moral development. Lawrence Kohlberg's studies show just how important being able to see other people's points of view is to social development in general and to moral development in particular. Kohlberg (1968, 1981, 1984) studied the development of moral reasoning—deciding what is right and what is wrong—by presenting children of different ages with a series of moral dilemmas. For example:

In Europe, a woman was near death from cancer. One drug might save her, a form of radium that a druggist in the same town had recently discovered. The druggist was charging $2,000, ten times what the drug cost him to make. The sick woman's husband, Heinz, went to everyone he knew to borrow the money, but he could only get together about half of what it cost. He told the druggist that his wife was dying and asked him to sell it cheaper or let him pay later. But the druggist said, "No." The husband got desperate and broke into the man's store to steal the drug for his wife. Should the husband have done that? Why?

At every age, some children said that the man should steal, some that he should not. What interested Kohlberg, however, was how the children arrived at a conclusion. He wanted to know what sort of reasoning they used. After questioning about a hundred children, Kohlberg identified six stages of moral development. He then replicated his findings in several different cultures.

Table 11.2 summarizes Kohlberg's levels and stages of moral development and provides the typical types of responses that individuals provide to the story of Heinz. Study the table carefully for a thorough understanding of Kohlberg's approach. Note that the stages are not based on whether the moral decision made about Heinz is pro or con. Rather, Kohlberg considers the style of reasoning that a person uses in reaching a decision.

To reach the highest levels of moral development, a child must first be able to see other people's points of view. But this understanding is no guarantee that a person will respect the rights of others. Thus cognitive abilities influence moral development, but there is far more to morality than simple understanding.

Likewise, some psychologists, such as Carol Gilligan (1982), contend that there are sex differences in moral reasoning. Men typically define moral problems in terms of rights and rules—the "justice approach." In contrast, women often perceive morality as an obligation to exercise care and to avoid hurt—the "responsibility approach." Whereas men deem autonomy and competition to be central to life, women tend to view life as a web of human relationships with obligations and privileges. However, not all researchers find support for the notion that men and women differ so often in their approaches to moral issues (Gibbs, Arnold, and Burkhart, 1984; Walker, 1984). It may be that moral judgments of men and women are more alike than different but that nuances are not captured by standard interviews.

It is important to remember that our discussion in this chapter has focused primarily on normal children and the changes that occur as they mature. However, development does not always proceed in a normal manner, a matter that is considered in the boxed insert on page 383.

SUMMARY

1. Developmental psychology is the study of the changes that occur across the life cycle.

2. Life begins as a single fertilized cell. In typical pregnancies approximately 266 days elapse between conception and birth. The prenatal period is divided into three phases: the germinal phase, the embryonic phase, and the fetal phase.

3. At birth an infant is capable of certain coordinated movement patterns that can be triggered by the right stimulus. One of these, the grasping reflex, is a response to a touch on the palm. Another, the rooting reflex, involves the movement of the infant's head toward the source of any touch near his or her mouth.

(continued on p. 384)

Atypical Development

About one in eight American schoolchildren has a problem that requires special instruction (see Table 11.3). Through the years, a variety of terms and labels have been applied to children afflicted with one or more difficulties: mentally retarded, emotionally disturbed, hyperactive, autistic, learning disabled, physically handicapped, language-disordered, perceptually impaired, and others. However, psychologists and educators are increasingly coming to recognize that terms and labels disguise the considerable differences that exist among children, even those in the same diagnostic category. Moreover, once labeled, it is frequently difficult for a child to regain the status of being "normal." The label becomes a stigma, a harmful badge, that can psychologically damage the child.

During their early years, children typically develop basic perceptual, motor, cognitive, language, emotional, and social behaviors. Difficulties in any of these areas can have major consequences for development in other areas (Gardner, 1974). For instance, if a child is visually handicapped, she will have difficulty acquiring basic eye-hand coordination skills—cutting with a scissors, stringing beads, or completing puzzles. Or if a child is hyperactive or has emotional difficulties, he will encounter problems in making friends. The absence or slow development of basic skills frequently has a cumulative effect. For this reason, it is important that children receive professional evaluation and assistance as early as possible.

As we saw in Chapter 2, both genetic and environmental factors affect development, and so either one of them separately or in combination can contribute to atypical development (Robinson and Robinson, 1976). For instance, at least 10 percent of mentally retarded children exhibit Down's syndrome, a condition that results from an extra chromosome. In other genetic disorders, such as phenylketonuria (or PKU), the central nervous system becomes gradually damaged due to the body's inability to metabolize an amino acid. In still other cases, genetic factors render the individual more vulnerable to certain kinds of environmental dangers. (In various convulsive disorders in which hereditary factors play a part, some individuals are especially likely to respond to stress with seizures.) Hunger and malnutrition also take a devastating toll on children throughout the world and, when sustained, can contribute to mental impairment. And, as noted earlier in the chapter, unhealthy social environments, such as those associated with foundling homes and orphanages, can interfere with children's development.

Psychologists and educators stress that even children with the most unusual and severe learning and behavioral difficulties can and do learn. Further, in most cases the child's condition is caused by factors beyond the scope of normal child-rearing practices. Consequently, parents need not experience guilt or shame because of their child's difficulties. Treatment programs for atypical children can help. Home-intervention programs, which have as their aim the enhancement of the parent-child relationship and the involvement of the parent as a central educator, have sometimes been effective (Levenstein, 1974). And over the past decade, mainstreaming programs have integrated students with special needs into regular classrooms. Some children benefit from mainstreaming; others do not. The search for effective treatment for all such children goes on (Madden and Slavin, 1983).

TABLE 11.3 Percentage of Handicapped Students in Regular Classes, by Type of Handicap

Learning disability	78%
Mentally retarded	29%
Deaf	38%
Deaf and blind	9%

Source: Data from National Center for Education Statistics, 1985.

4. As a result of maturation (internally programed growth) and learning, infants are able to walk, talk, and feed themselves in about two years' time. Learning and maturation work together in the development of intellect, language, love, and morality.

5. Swiss psychologist Jean Piaget formulated a comprehensive theory of intellectual development. Intellectual growth involves changes in the amount of information children have as well as in the way they think.

A. Children's grasp of object permanence at about eighteen months marks a giant step in their intellectual development. Understanding that objects still exist when out of sight means children can now engage in representational thinking. They can picture an object in their minds without seeing or touching the object.

B. More complex intellectual abilities develop as the infant grows into childhood. Somewhere between the ages of five and seven, most children begin to understand what Piaget calls conservation. However, in the stage of concrete operations (six to twelve years), a child's thought remains fixed on the immediate or concrete evidence provided by the senses. As children enter their teens, they begin thinking in abstract terms. Adolescents learn to engage in hypothesis testing, the hallmark of the stage of formal operational thought.

6. Language is basic to the human condition. It allows human beings to communicate with one another and thus to fit their actions together to constitute group life. Researchers have been able to learn a good deal about language from studies of our nearest relative in the animal kingdom, the chimpanzee. Although the skills displayed by chimps are related to human language skills, they are not truly equivalent to human skills.

7. In order to acquire language children spend the first year of life practicing sounds, then imitating the speech they hear around them. In the second year they use sounds as symbols, and their first real words usually refer to something they can see or touch. By four or five years of age, children have usually mastered the basics of their native language.

8. Scientists have long interested themselves in the relationship between language and thought. According to the linguistic relativity thesis, language controls the way people experience and think about the world. The contrary view, the container of thought thesis, claims that language is not essential for thought but only for conveying it. The Soviet psychologist Lev Vygotsky suggests a way by which the conflicting positions on language and thought can be reconciled. He says that thought and speech initially develop in a separate but parallel manner. At about two or so years of age, the two independent streams come together and merge.

9. Stanley I. Greenspan and his colleagues have identified six milestones in the emotional development of children. Each stage confronts the child with a somewhat different task. The more factors that interfere with a child's mastery of the emotional milestones, the greater the probability of compromised intellectual and emotional development later. The longer problems persist, the greater the likelihood that maladaptive emotional coping strategies will build up.

10. Socialization involves learning the rules of behavior of the culture in which a child is born and will grow up.

A. The theories of Sigmund Freud and Erik Erikson stress the emotional dynamics of social development. They both believe that children must learn to control the sexual and aggressive urges they are born with, but Erikson would add that the need of children for social approval is just as important to their social development.

B. Learning theorists give much less emphasis to the emotional dynamics of social development. They argue that children learn appropriate social behavior through conditioning and imitation.

C. Cognitive theorists argue that social development is more than just the result of the child being shaped by rewards and punishments. These psychologists see the *child* as the shaper. They argue that social development results from the child acting on the environment, trying to make sense out of his or her experience. Play and friendship with peers are part of the normal process of growing up, and change in nature with development.

D. Lawrence Kohlberg has observed that the moral development of a child progresses in six stages. Essentially, each stage represents an advance in the child's ability to take the roles of other people.

KEY TERMS

accommodation (p. 362)
anal stage (p. 376)
assimilation (p. 362)
attachment (p. 372)
caretaker speech (p. 370)
conservation (p. 364)
developmental psychology
 (p. 354)
genital stage (p. 377)
grasping reflex (p. 355)
habituation (p. 360)

holophrases (p. 369)
hypothesis testing (p. 366)
language (p. 367)
language acquisition device
 (LAD) (p. 370)
latency stage (p. 376)
maturation (p. 357)
motherese (p. 371)
object permanence (p. 363)
Oedipal conflict (p. 376)
oral stage (p. 376)

phallic stage (p. 376)
reflex (p. 355)
representational thought
 (p. 364)
role taking (p. 380)
rooting reflex (p. 355)
socialization (p. 374)
sublimation (p. 376)
sucking reflex (p. 355)
telegraphic speech (p. 370)

SUGGESTED READINGS

BODEN, MARGARET. 1979. *Jean Piaget.* Harmondsworth, Middlesex, England: Penguin Books. A useful summary of Piaget's theories of the development of human intelligence.

BOWER, THOMAS G.R. 1982. *Development in Infancy.* 2nd ed. San Francisco: W. H. Freeman. A brief and very readable survey of psychological development during infancy.

GARVEY, CATHERINE. 1977. *Play.* Cambridge, Mass.: Harvard University Press. Describes the emergence of play in infants' smiles and laughter, and follows the development of play to the more ritualized games of older children. The central focus is on the function of play in children's cognitive, social, and emotional development.

GINSBURG, HERBERT, and OPPER, SYLVIA. 1969. *Piaget's Theory of Intellectual Development: An Introduction.* Englewood Cliffs, N.J.: Prentice-Hall. The clearest, most popular introduction to Piaget's work available.

HALL, ELIZABETH, LAMB, MICHAEL, and PERLMUTTER, MARION. 1986. *Child Psychology Today.* 2nd ed. New York: Random House. A topically organized text on development in childhood and adolescence, with a strong emphasis on recent research.

KOHLBERG, LAWRENCE. 1969. Stage and sequence: The cognitive-developmental approach to socialization. In D. Goslin, Ed., *Handbook of Socialization.* Chicago: Rand McNally, 347–480. An inspired summary of Kohlberg's work on moral development that shows how he developed his six-stage theory.

LAMB, MICHAEL, and BORNSTEIN, MARC. 1987. *Development in Infancy: An Introduction.* 2nd ed. New York: Random House. An overview of development from the prenatal period to 36 months, this book is unique in its portrayal of the infant as an active shaper of his or her environment.

LEACH, PENELOPE. 1978. *Your Baby and Child: From Birth to Age Five.* New York: Knopf. An invaluable guide for parents that offers medical advice and clear descriptions of young children's development of social, intellectual, and physical skills.

LERNER, RICHARD. 1986. *Concepts and Theories of Human Development.* 2nd ed. New York: Random House. An analysis of historical and philosophical bases for developmental issues and theories and of their interrelationships. Includes excellent discussions of research methodology.

PINES, MAYA. 1966. *Revolution in Learning: The Years from Birth to Six.* New York: Harper & Row. An exciting, easy-to-read account of what children learn before they start elementary school.

SCARR, SANDRA. 1985. *Mother Care/Other Care.* New York: Warner Books. An examination of critical issues surrounding child care in contemporary America.

SCARR, SANDRA, WEINBERG, RICHARD A., and LEVINE, ANN. 1986. *Understanding Development.* San Diego: Harcourt Brace Jovanovich. A comprehensive text on human development from birth through adolescence.

SINGER, DOROTHY, and SINGER, JEROME. 1981. *Television, Imagination and Aggression: A Study of Preschoolers.* Hillsdale, N.J.: L. Erlbaum Associates. A review of all the research on the effects of television on children.

SPOCK, BENJAMIN. 1978 (originally published 1946). *Baby and Child Care.* New York: Pocket Books. For decades this book has served as a handy and practical guide for parents on almost every conceivable issue of child rearing. In recent editions, Dr. Spock has recommended a less rigid approach to child rearing than he used to advocate.

Fairfield Porter, *Katie and Anne*, 1955.

12
Adolescence and Adulthood

At age 113 Khfaf Lasuria joined a troupe of thirty performers, each of whom was 90 years of age or older (Benet, 1974). An excellent dancer, she still performed happily for her audiences at 131 years of age. Not too distant from her lived Akhutsa Kunach, age 114. The previous winter, while cutting timber in the woods, he suffered three broken ribs when a tree fell on him. Within two months he had recovered and resumed all his former duties. In the neighboring village of Gumista, E. J. Jachava was an outgoing, good-natured, and talkative man of 116 years. The only thing that annoyed him was that he had some difficulty hearing.

These three centenarians are not exceptional. They are Abkhasians, residents of a small, mountainous Soviet republic wedged between the Black Sea and the High Caucasus. In the 1979 Soviet census, 548 Abkhasians—out of a population of 520,000—were reported to be 100 years of age or older. When the cases were investigated, the number of centenarians was pared to 241, still five times the American average (Sullivan, 1982). The Abkhasians are a tall, slender, narrow-faced, and fair-skinned people. Old men develop bushy eyebrows, which, together with their luxuriant mustaches, give them a dignified, stern appearance. The women are typically a bit shorter than the men, graceful, with high foreheads and long, slender necks. Medical observers are uniformly impressed by the alertness, excellent muscle tone, and mental and physical capabilities of the Abkhasians of all ages.

Explanations abound for the long lives enjoyed by the people of Abkhasia. For one thing, they reside in a hard land, one that according to their legends was one of God's afterthoughts. But more important, they seem blessed with a good genetic endowment and their life style contributes to good health. The elderly never retire, and continue working at what they are capable of doing until they die. Consequently, at no stage of life do they become sedentary. Their diets coincide with precepts that contemporary nutritionists define as ideal. Overeating is seen as dangerous, and obese people are regarded as ill. Age is an honored and esteemed status, one that takes precedence over wealth and social position. Strong kinship ties pervade and regulate Abkhasian interpersonal relationships. These and other cultural mechanisms reduce stress and minimize intergenerational conflict. Their high degree of social integration and the continuity in their personal lives permit them to adapt to changing conditions at a comfortable pace.

All of this is not to say that the Abkhasians have discovered the fountain of youth. However, they may have developed the next best thing—youthful old age. Their use of time, attitudes toward people and life, social roles and behavior, work habits, patterns of relaxation, eating habits, and health practices apparently make it possible for an exceptionally large number of them to live to very advanced ages. And they do so without the ravages that once led General Charles de Gaulle to say that old age is a dreadful illness, as he, a vigorous and long-lived person, faced final decline.

In this chapter we continue our treatment of the life span by considering adolescence, adulthood, and old age. We will deal with a number of issues, all of which focus on the question of how people change and adapt over the life span. What is uniquely human is that we remain in an unending state of development. Life is always an unfinished business, which only death ends (Montagu, 1981).

ADOLESCENCE

In many preliterate societies, the village or tribe holds elaborate initiation ceremonies—*puberty rites*—that socially mark the transition from childhood to adulthood. Once a young person has been initiated, he or she is considered ready for courtship and marriage and is expected to assume adult responsibilities. Choices in life style are limited: the economic, social, and sexual roles of adulthood are clearly defined. As a result, there are few questions about

"how far to go" sexually or what to do with one's life—and hence few conflicts (Dragastin and Elder, 1975; Herdt, 1981, 1982). The transition between childhood and adulthood that we call "adolescence" simply does not exist.

In 1904, the psychologist G. Stanley Hall published a book entitled *Adolescence* that made "adolescence" a household word in America. Hall pointed out that through most of the nineteenth century, the family functioned as a basic economic unit in this country. All hands were needed. Youngsters worked alongside their parents in fields and shops and small factories, gradually assuming more and more responsibility. The line between children and adults was not as clearly drawn as it is today (Kett, 1977).

Industrialization changed this pattern. First, machines made it possible for one person to do the work of many. The economy no longer needed child and teen-age labor. Second, the demand for specialized skills increased, and parents could not teach children these new skills. Moreover, with the decline of family farms and businesses and the rise of wage labor, young people could not know for sure what they would be doing with their lives. The solution to all of these problems was school. School kept unemployed young people off the streets, gave them training, and provided some of them with career options not available to their parents.

This combination of events created what has come to be called **adolescence**—a developmental stage between childhood and adulthood. Young people who were physically mature began to remain in training, doing economically nonproductive work, depending on their families for support, and delaying decisions about their future for longer and longer periods. Consequently, adolescence has become a noteworthy life experience primarily due to societal demands (Brooks-Gunn and Petersen, 1984).

Hall believed adolescence to be a period of great "storm and stress"—perhaps the most difficult stage of human development. Being an adolescent is something like being a fully grown animal in a cage, an animal who sees freedom but does not know quite when he will experience it or how he will handle it. Society treats the adolescent as a child one minute, as an adult the next. Adolescents are expected to act

---

adolescence: The developmental stage between childhood and adulthood.

The last stage of a New Guinea puberty rite, when the boys gather in the hut from which they will emerge as adults of the tribe. *(Malcolm Kirk/Peter Arnold)*

maturely but also to do as they are told. They are denied the chance to earn a living (unemployment rates are higher among teen-agers than any other group) but often are reminded that their parents had to work at their age. They are envied for their youth but resented for their lack of responsibility.

Physical Changes

Although societies differ in the way they treat young people, one aspect of adolescence is found everywhere: males and females undergo dramatic physical changes. **Puberty,** or sexual maturation, is the biological event that marks the end of childhood. At about nine or ten, girls rather suddenly begin to grow—sometimes as much as two or three inches a year. During this growth spurt, a girl's breasts and hips begin to fill out, and she develops pubic hair. Between ten and fifteen, she has her first menstrual period, or **menarche.** Another year or so will pass before her periods become regular and she is capable of conceiving a child. In general, girls must achieve a critical level of body fat before they begin to men-

struate (Frisch, 1978). Those who restrict their weight for athletic reasons (for instance, gymnasts, dancers, and runners) reach menarche a year to several years later than nonathletic girls (Wyshak and Frisch, 1982; Bullen et al., 1985).

Menarche is a pivotal event in an adolescent girl's experience (Greif and Ulman, 1982; Brooks-Gunn and Petersen, 1983). Most young women are both happy and frightened by their first menstruation (Petersen, 1983). It is a symbol of a girl's developing sexual maturity and portends her full-fledged status as a woman. Consequently, menarche plays an important part in shaping a girl's image of her body and her sense of identity as a woman. Postmenarcheal girls report that they experience themselves as more womanly and that they give greater thought to their reproductive role.

At about twelve, boys begin to develop pubic hair and larger genitals. Within a year or two they become capable of ejaculation. They too begin to grow rapidly and to fill out, developing the broad shoulders and thicker trunk of an adult man. Their voices gradually deepen. Hair begins to grow on

---

puberty: Sexual maturation; the biological event that marks the end of childhood.
menarche (men-ARK): A woman's first menstrual period.

their faces and later on their chests. Overall, boys enter and conclude puberty about two years later than similarly aged girls.

The male experience of first ejaculation is not particularly traumatic, just as menarche is not an especially negative experience for girls (Gaddis and Brooks-Gunn, 1985). Earlier generations of men often described their first ejaculation in negative terms: "It scared the hell out of me"; "I thought I was ill"; and "I thought I had hurt myself" (Shipman, 1971). But contemporary adolescents seem better informed. Although many boys say they were a little scared, the majority report that their positive reactions to their first ejaculation outweighed their negative feelings.

The changes associated with puberty are regulated by the activities of the endocrine glands, which in turn are controlled by the hypothalamus (see Chapter 2). The hypothalamus signals the pituitary gland to step up the production of various hormones. Through elaborate feedback mechanisms, the pituitary and other endocrine glands constitute a complex system that secretes the necessary growth and sex hormones (the masculinizing androgens and the feminizing estrogens). It seems that before puberty the hormonal system operates to suppress the reproductive system (Klein, 1984; Kolata, 1984).

Early and Late Maturers

Young people display considerable variation in the age at which they reach puberty. In general, girls begin to develop earlier than boys and for a year or two may tower over male age-mates. Even within the same sex, some adolescents may have largely completed their growth and sexual maturation at an age when others are just beginning the process (Tanner, 1973). This fact causes many young people considerable anguish. In the United States, students move in chronological lockstep through elementary and secondary school. But since children mature at varying rates, some adolescents are advantaged while others are disadvantaged in the "ideals" associated with physical attractiveness, height, strength, and athletic prowess. Hence the feedback that young people receive regarding their overall worth and desirability varies, with consequences for their self-image and behavior.

Research reveals that boys who mature early have a decided advantage (Jones and Bayley, 1950;

Mussen and Jones, 1957; Weatherley, 1964; Tobin-Richards, Boxer, and Petersen, 1983). They become heroes in sports, leaders in formal and informal social activities. Other boys look up to them; girls have crushes on them; adults tend to treat them as more mature. As a result, they are generally more self-confident and independent than other boys. The late-maturing boys, whose high-pitched voices and less-than-ideal physiques may make them feel inadequate, tend to be withdrawn or rebellious. Follow-up studies of men in their thirties show early maturers to be more poised, relaxed, cooperative, sociable, and conforming, and late maturers to be more eager, talkative, self-assertive, rebellious, and touchy (Jones, 1957).

With girls, the pattern is somewhat different. Early-maturing girls are more independent and popular with boys, whereas late-maturing girls have more positive body images and fewer school problems. These differences often persist into ninth or tenth grade, possibly because the adult stature of early-maturing girls is, on average, shorter and plumper than that of late-maturing girls. Overall, being "on time" for girls is associated with a more positive set of self-perceptions than being "off time" —either earlier or later in maturing than their peers (Tobin-Richards, Boxer, and Petersen, 1983). Additionally, American standards for female attractiveness—the "lean, lithe look"—make girls extremely sensitive to the configuration of their bodies and generate negative feelings regarding even moderate amounts of fat. Consequently, being "off time" may produce personal crises because of social judgments about body image, attractiveness, and ideal weight (Brooks-Gunn and Petersen, 1983).

Sexual Attitudes and Behavior

Physical maturation typically occurs concurrently with a social process in which a person develops sexual interests and assumes sexual roles. And signs of physical maturation result in a person being perceived as a potential sexual partner (Smith, Udry, and Morris, 1985). Perhaps not surprisingly, first sexual intercourse is a developmental milestone of major personal and social significance (Jessor et al., 1983). Youths view sexual intercourse as a declaration of independence from their parents, an affirmation of their sexual identity, and a statement of their capacity for interpersonal intimacy (Jessor and Jes-

Having the "right" body build is important to the self-esteem of most adolescents, even though they can make fun of their own concerns. (Alan Carey/The Image Works)

sor, 1975). American teen-age boys also experience a good deal of peer pressure to prove themselves through sexual intercourse: sex is seen as a rite of passage; fear of homosexuality is widespread; and "virginity" is a negative word. Boys who admit they are virgins or do not pressure their dates into having sex are sometimes labeled "gay." One recent survey reveals that 60 percent of boys report that they felt "glad" about their first sexual experience; 61 percent of the girls were ambivalent (Coles and Stokes, 1985). Fifty percent of teens say they learn about reproduction from school, but hear about masturbation, homosexuality, and sexual techniques from friends.

Substantial changes have occurred over the past twenty-five years in teen-age sexual attitudes and activity. Earlier, between 1920 and 1965, American attitudes had become more permissive, but little overall change in actual sexual behavior had occurred (Reiss, 1976). However, beginning in the mid-1960s and continuing through the 1970s, not only did attitudes liberalize but the proportions of young people engaging in premarital sexual relations increased. Before this period, the premarital sexual experience of men exceeded that of women. But coital rates for unmarried women increased moderately in the latter 1960s, and accelerated in the 1970s. Male rates held steady in the latter 1960s, and increased in the 1970s, but not as rapidly as female rates. Accordingly, the rates have tended to converge (Reed and Weinberg, 1984). By age nineteen, two out of three females and four out of five males have had sexual intercourse (Lincoln, 1981).

Although the use of birth control has increased, nearly two-thirds of teen-age women either have never used contraceptives or use them only erratically. And while teen-agers in the United States constitute only 18 percent of sexually active women considered capable of bearing children, they account for 46 percent of out-of-wedlock births and 31 percent

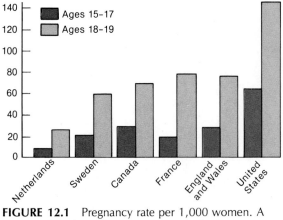

FIGURE 12.1 Pregnancy rate per 1,000 women. A comparative view of teen-age pregnancies in Western nations shows the United States with the highest rate. *(Data from Alan Guttmacher Institute. 1985.)*

of abortions. Indeed, American teen-agers become pregnant, have abortions, and give birth at significantly higher rates than adolescents in other industrialized nations (Brozen, 1985a). The pregnancy rate for American young women fifteen to nineteen years old is 96 per 1,000 compared with 14 per 1,000 in the Netherlands, 35 in Sweden, 43 in France, 44 in Canada, and 45 in England and Wales (see Figure 12.1). Nor do the lower pregnancy rates of other industrialized nations reflect more frequent recourse to abortion. By the time they are eighteen years old, 60 of every 1,000 American women have had an abortion. By contrast, in the Netherlands only 7 of every 1,000 women age eighteen had an abortion. For England and Wales, the figure is about 20 per 1,000, for France and Sweden about 30, and for Canada about 24. Moreover, the level of sexual activity does not account for differences in the pregnancy rates of Western nations. The primary difference is that teen-agers in the United States are less likely to use contraception. And those who do use contraception are less likely to use the most effective method: birth-control pills. In other nations birth control tends to be free or inexpensive for teen-agers and is readily available to them. Further,

American culture tends to be prudish—intolerant of premarital sexual activity and unwilling to deal with sexual topics openly (Morrison, 1985).

It is important to emphasize, however, that recent changes in patterns of sexual behavior have not been accompanied by a complete change in sexual values. Many young people judge the acceptability of sexual relations in terms of a couple's love and affection for each other (Reiss, 1976). One survey revealed that 41 percent of teen-agers in the United States say it is "okay" to have sex if you are "in love," and 60 percent say it is "okay " if marriage is planned (Coles and Stokes, 1985). Overall, most young people do not regard the "new morality" as license for promiscuous thrill seeking. But neither do they take the necessary precautions to prevent unwanted pregnancies.

Evolving a Stable Identity

A major developmental task confronting adolescents is building a stable identity. **Identity** consists of the answers you give to the questions "Who am I?" and "Who am I to be?" It is your sense of placement in the world. Just as you must find meaning in the events, objects, and people that make up your daily experience, so must you also attach meaning to yourself. As you make your way about your everyday life, you interact with others in terms of the conceptions you hold both of others and of yourself. Moreover, your identity is not fixed once and for all time. It is shaped and reshaped over the course of your entire life span (Adams and Fitch, 1982).

According to Erik Erikson (see Chapter 11), adolescence constitutes that psychosocial stage in life in which people struggle to develop and clarify their identities. As children, they were aware of what other people (adults and peers) thought of them. They knew the labels others applied to them (good, naughty, silly, talented, brave, pretty). They may also have dreamed of being this or that person and enacted various roles in their play. But they did not brood about who they were or where they were going in life. As children, they lived in the present; as adolescents, they begin to think about the future.

identity: The answers people give to the questions "Who am I?" and "Who am I to be?" A sense of placement within the world.

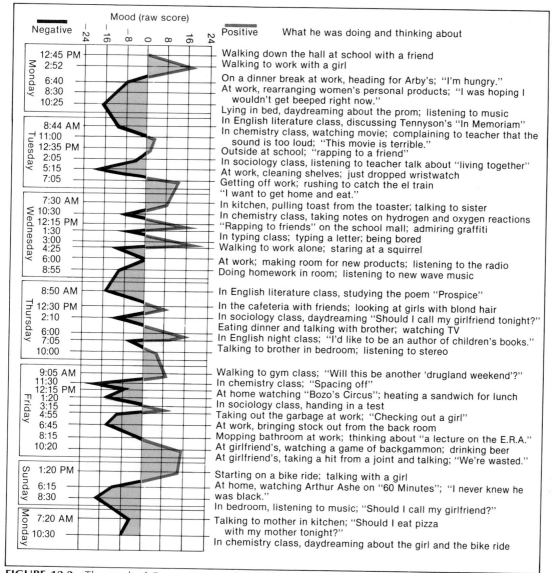

FIGURE 12.2 The week of Gregory Stone. Researchers at the University of Chicago studied seventy-five teen-agers in a Chicago suburb. The teen-agers were equipped with small electronic pagers. A transmitter was used to activate the pagers at random moments during the week, signaling the teen-agers to record their thoughts, feelings, and activities at the time. *(Adapted from Mihaly Cszikszentmihalyi and Reed Larson. 1984. Being Adolescent: Conflict and Growth in the Teen-Age Years. Copyright © 1984 by Basic Books, Inc., Publishers. Reprinted by permission of the publisher. Adapted by Sandra Scarr, Richard A. Weinberg, and Ann Levine. 1986. Understanding Development. San Diego: Harcourt Brace Jovanovich, p. 498. Reprinted by permission.)*

Such changes seem to contribute to the dramatic swings in mood that appear to be a normal feature of adolescent life (Cszikszentmihalyi and Larson, 1984). One boy's mood swings during a single week are shown in Figure 12.2. Adolescents whose moods change the most report being as happy and as much in control as do their peers with less drastic changes, and they are as well adjusted in other areas of their lives.

Erikson (1968) says that adolescents often suffer an *identity crisis*—worrying about who they are (see Table 12.1). Many factors contribute to this self-

TABLE 12.1   Erikson's Stages of Psychosocial Development

Approximate Age	Crisis
0–1	TRUST VS. MISTRUST: If infants are well cared for, they will develop faith in the future. But if they experience too much uncertainty about being taken care of, they will come to look at the world with fear and suspicion.
1–2	AUTONOMY VS. DOUBT: Here children learn self-control and self-assertion. But if they receive too much criticism, they will be ashamed of themselves and have doubts about their independence.
2–5	INITIATIVE VS. GUILT: When children begin to make their own decisions, constant discouragement or punishment could lead to guilt and a loss of initiative.
5–Puberty	INDUSTRY VS. INFERIORITY: Children master skills and take pride in their competence. Too much criticism of their work at this stage can lead to long-term feelings of inferiority.
Adolescence	IDENTITY VS. ROLE CONFUSION: Teen-agers try to develop their own separate identity while "fitting in" with their friends. Failure leads to confusion over who they are.
Early adulthood	INTIMACY VS. ISOLATION: People secure in their own identity can proceed to an intimate partnership in which they make compromises for another. Isolated people may have many affairs or even a long-term relationship, but always avoid true closeness.
Middle age	GENERATIVITY VS. STAGNATION: People who become stagnated are absorbed in themselves and try to hang on to the past. Generativity involves a productive life that will serve as an example to the next generation.
Later adulthood	INTEGRITY VS. DESPAIR: Some people look back over life with a sense of satisfaction, and accept both the bad and the good. Others face death with nothing but regrets.

confrontation: the physiological changes we have described; awakening sexual drives and the possibility for establishing a new kind of intimacy with the opposite sex; and cognitive developments associated with the attainment of logical thought (see Chapter 11 for a discussion of Piaget's stage of formal operational thought). Adolescents begin to see the future as a reality, not just a game. They know they have to confront the almost infinite and often conflicting possibilities and choices that lie ahead. In the process of reviewing their past and anticipating their future, they begin to think about themselves. Establishing a strong sense of identity in adolescence contributes to a person's capacity to develop and maintain intimate relationships in adulthood (Kahn et al., 1985).

Erikson suggests that the adolescent's identity crisis is compounded by the desire to feel unique and distinctive on the one hand and to "fit in" on the other. Some young people have great difficulty satisfying these contradictory desires. This may be one reason why so many American adolescents are drawn to radical political or religious movements, fraternities and sororities, or gangs. These groups provide a ready-made identity. Strict codes of dress and behavior relieve the individual of the burden of making choices. In what Erikson calls **totalism,** or complete

---

totalism: Complete immersion in a group.

Even older adolescents and adults find important parts of their identities in being members of peer groups. *(Roy E. Roper/EKM-Nepenthe)*

immersion in a group, the adolescent rebels against adult rules by rigidly conforming to peer-group standards. (Obviously, in other cultures, adolescent conflicts and concerns may be very different.)

Erikson's notions regarding adolescence have gained considerable popular acceptance and some support from social psychological research on groups (see Chapter 10). They underlie many of the prescriptions offered in advice columns and books to parents and teachers for "dealing" with teen-agers. Yet psychologists are not entirely convinced that Erikson's portrayal of adolescence is correct in all its details. Unquestionably, youths in Western societies undergo some changes in their self-concepts during adolescence (Montemayor and Eisen, 1977; Waterman, 1982). But while psychiatrists and clinical psychologists do encounter youths in their practices who are experiencing disturbances in their self-concepts, it is becoming increasingly clear that most adolescents do not experience anything approaching an identity "crisis" (Adelson, 1979; Offer, Ostrov, and Howard, 1981; Blyth and Traeger, 1983). Indeed, adolescent "disturbance" is often limited to bickering with parents (Offer, 1969). And the overall self-esteem of most individuals *increases* with age across the adolescent years (McCarthy and Hoge, 1982; O'Malley and Bachman, 1983).

A mounting body of psychological literature suggests that a high degree of stability and consistency characterizes the adolescent years (Nawas, 1971; Monge, 1973; Savin-Williams and Demo, 1984). Thus in one study, University of Michigan researchers followed up some two thousand young men over the course of a number of years (Bachman, O'Malley, and Johnston, 1978). For the most part, the men did not display abrupt changes in their self-concepts, aspirations, or political and racial attitudes. By the time they had reached tenth grade, these components were already well established. Similarly, other studies do not reveal a sharp discontinuity between childhood and adolescent self-concepts and attitudes. Rather, adolescents seem to evolve their self-concepts through processes of gradual and continual growth that are associated with their social circumstances and their emergent cognitive abilities and skills (Prawat, Jones, and Hampton, 1979; Dusek and Flaherty, 1981).

Social Development: Family and Friends

One of the principal developmental tasks for adolescents is to begin becoming independent of their families. Unfortunately, the means of achieving this status are not always clear, either to the adolescents or to their parents. First, mixed feelings often characterize both sides. Some parents build their life style around the family and are reluctant to let a child go. Also, parents whose children are old enough to leave home sometimes have to wrestle with their own fears of advancing age. And many parents worry about whether their children are really ready to cope with the harsh realities of life—and so do adolescents. At the same time that young people long to get out on their own and try themselves against the world, they typically worry a lot about failing. This internal struggle is often mirrored in the adolescent's unpredictable behavior, which parents may interpret as "adolescent rebellion."

Schools are important as places for adolescents to get together. And they do get together in fairly predictable ways. Most schools contain easily recognizable and well-defined sets, or crowds. And these sets are arranged in a fairly rigid hierarchy —everyone knows who belongs to which set and what people in that set do with their time. Early in adolescence the sets are usually divided by sex, but later the sexes mix. Sets usually form along class lines. Some school activities bring teen-agers of different social classes together, but it is the exception rather than the rule that middle-class and lower-class adolescents are close friends. Belonging to a **clique** (a group within a set) gives adolescents status and a means of defining themselves; it is a handle they can hold on to while shaping an identity (Dunphy, 1963).

A good deal is made of generational differences between young people and their parents. Indeed the term "generation gap" is commonly used to imply mutual antagonism, misunderstanding, and distance between the two groups. Yet the gap between generations is hardly as pervasive or as widespread as popular stereotypes imply. For instance, a recent poll sponsored by the National Association of Secondary School Principals (Cromer, 1984) found that three-fourths of the nation's young people (grades seven to twelve) reported having no serious family problems and feeling free to discuss their concerns with a parent. Ten years earlier, only half of the

youths had felt that way and more than 40 percent had said they would be happier living away from home. In 1983, 80 percent of the students agreed with their parents on the topics of drugs, education, and work, and 60 percent agreed on the topic of sex. Fifty-four percent of 1983's students planned to attend four-year colleges, compared with a third in 1974. Said Janis Cromer, an educational analyst who authored the report, "If there was a generation gap in the 60's, it narrowed to a crack in the 1970's and it's a hairline fracture in the 1980's."

Formulations depicting a generation gap vastly oversimplify the relationship between young people and their parents. They imply that attachment to the peer group bars attachment to the adult group. Nonetheless, research reveals that both the peer group and the family are anchors in the lives of most teen-agers (Biddle, Bank, and Marlin, 1980; Davies and Kandel, 1981; Krosnick and Judd, 1982; Pipp et al., 1985). For the most part, no behavior comes under the exclusive dominance of either generation. However, the relative influence of peers and parents differs with the issue involved. When the issues entail immediate gratification (such as smoking, marijuana use, drinking, and academic cheating) or peripheral matters (such as musical tastes, personal adornment, and entertainment idols), teen-agers are typically more responsive to the preferences of peers. But when the issues have to do with future goals, fundamental behavioral codes, and core values, teen-agers are usually more responsive to the parental generation (Kandel and Lesser, 1972; Kandel, 1974; Wright and Keple, 1981).

It is also easy to overlook the fact that teen-agers typically feel most comfortable within peer groups that adopt values similar to those found within the home environment (Offer and Offer, 1975; Cohen, 1983; Billy and Udry, 1985). Thus researchers find little support for the "hydraulic" view—that the greater the influence of one generation, the less the influence of the other. In fact, a substantial proportion of young people see no reason to differentiate between the value system of their parents and that of their friends (Larson, 1972; Troll and Bengtson, 1982).

---

clique (CLEEK): A group within a set.

ADULTHOOD

Until quite recently, psychologists knew little about adulthood. Like many laypeople, they often used the term "adulthood" as a kind of catchall category for all that happens to individuals after they "grow up." One reason for this neglect is that it is difficult to study the entire life cycle. A *cross-sectional study* (which compares individuals of different ages at the same point in time) may reflect changes in the way different generations were raised and the challenges they face, not changes that occur as a result of aging. A *longitudinal study* (which compares the way the same people think and act at different points in time) takes years to complete. However, by combining these techniques, psychologists have begun to shed new light on the process of growing older. The opportunities and problems people face and the nature of their interests do change significantly over the adult years.

Young Adulthood

Adulthood is not a steady state of being. Instead, it is a process of *becoming*. This fact is highlighted by young adulthood. It is during this period that people are exploring and negotiating new levels of intimacy, with many entering marriage and embarking on parenthood. And many of them are joining the labor force, with major implications for their life style and community placement.

In 1985 the typical American was in his or her early thirties. Marriage and remarriage had slowed somewhat, but nuptial bliss remained nearly everybody's dream. Young people were not rushing into marriage as rapidly as in the past (see Figure 12.3), opting to do other things—invest in education and careers or gain more life experience. Although people are now waiting longer to marry, they are much more willing to call it quits than they used to be (see Figure 12.3). If you married between 1975 and 1979, the chances of your marriage breaking up are twice as high as if you married between 1960 and 1964. Among the biggest changes in American life has been the sharp rise in the proportion of families headed by a single parent, especially in black households. Nearly half of all children born in the 1980s will live in a single-parent home for at least a part of their childhood. There has also been a sharp increase

in nonfamily households—people living alone or with nonrelatives. Nonfamily households constituted 26.7 percent of all households in 1980, compared with 19.7 in 1970. By 1990, fully 45 percent of all households are expected to be headed by a man or woman without a spouse.

It is easy to conclude from census figures that marriage and family life are going out of style. Yet this is hardly the case. Most Americans say that they prefer to be married—indeed, almost 95 percent get married at some point in their lives. Likewise, most divorced people remarry. People get married for a variety of reasons (Dacey, 1982). First there are *pull factors*, such as the desires for love, a regular sex partner, children, and companionship. Second, there are *push factors*, such as premarital pregnancy, conformity to group expectations, escape from an unpleasant home life, and the avoidance of loneliness.

Most American women still expect to have two children (but not three or more). Yet they have also become increasingly interested in pursuing careers and are more inclined to delay childbirth or avoid it altogether. Over the past twenty-five years, the fertility rate of American women has dropped sharply. In 1960, the United States had 36 million women of childbearing age, and they produced 4.3 million children. In 1984, 50.3 million women were in the childbearing years, and they produced only 3.3 million babies. Other factors have also contributed to the drop in fertility rates: later marriage, rising divorce rates, the availability of legal abortions, economic hard times, and stiff home mortgage rates.

Perhaps one of the most pronounced developments in recent years has been the movement of women into the work force. In 1940, only 27.9 percent of the female population sixteen years and older were in the labor force. By 1984, the figure had nearly doubled, standing at 53.7 percent. Further, as noted in Chapter 11, 62 percent of all women with children under eighteen held jobs.

Along with these developments, young adults are encountering greater difficulties than did the preceding generation in securing jobs and launching careers. In recent years, America's industrial base has undergone a steady erosion. The auto, steel, machinery, and other basic industries have been devastated by difficult economic times and by tough, more efficient, technologically up-to-date foreign competitors. Traditionally, these industries provided an

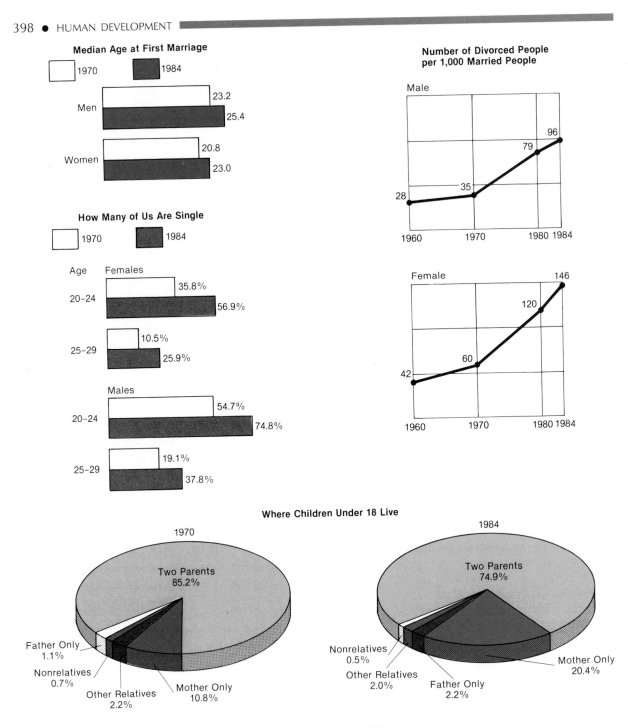

FIGURE 12.3 The way Americans live. *(Data from Census Bureau. 1985.)*

entry point into the labor force for many blue-collar youths. But by the same token, new computer-based technologies have afforded growing opportunities for young people possessing the necessary skills and training.

Physical Changes

In general, human beings are at their physical peak between the ages of eighteen and twenty-five. This is the period when they are strongest and healthiest

More than half of American women are employed outside of the home, and increasing numbers work at jobs that were closed to them a generation ago, such as newscasting. *(John Maher/EKM-Nepenthe)*

and have the quickest reflexes. One has only to think of the average age of professional athletes or dancers to verify this. Most Olympic athletes fall between these ages. However, in some events, such as women's gymnastics, women of eighteen are deemed "old." Usually professional football and baseball players are thought to be "over the hill" by thirty-five, if not earlier. The George Blandas and Pete Roses are the exception and not the rule.

For most adults, the process of physical decline is slow and gradual. Strength and stamina begin to decline in the late twenties. A twenty-year-old manages to carry four heavy bags of groceries; a forty-year-old finds it is easier to make two trips. In middle age, appearance changes. The hair starts to turn gray and perhaps to thin out. The skin becomes somewhat dry and inelastic; wrinkles appear. People may become overweight or develop hypertension or arthritis, which accelerate the aging process. In old age, muscles and fat built up over the years break down, so that people often lose weight, become shorter, and develop more wrinkles, creases, and loose skin.

With time, the senses require more and more stimulation. During their forties most people begin having difficulty seeing distant objects, adjusting to the dark, and focusing on a printed page, even if their eyesight has always been good. Many experience a gradual or sudden loss of hearing in their later years, especially in the higher frequencies. Long-term exposure to noise in urban and industrial environments appears to be a contributing factor. In addition, reaction time slows (Kimmel, 1974; Birren and Schaie, 1977).

Some of the changes associated with growing older are the result of the natural processes of aging. Others result from diseases and from simple disuse and abuse. A person who eats sensibly; exercises; avoids cigarettes, drugs, and alcohol; and is not subjected to severe emotional stress will look and feel younger than someone who neglects his or her health.

Menopause

Between the ages of forty-seven and fifty-two, most women experience a profound drop in the production of female hormones. This biological event is called **menopause.** The woman stops ovulating (producing eggs) and menstruating, and therefore cannot

---

menopause: The stage of life between the ages of forty-seven and fifty-two, when a woman stops ovulating and menstruating and her production of sex hormones is sharply reduced.

have any more children. However, menopause does not cause any reduction in a woman's sexual drive. The stoppage of menstruation typically takes two to four years to be completed, with an intermittent missing of periods and an extension of the intervals between periods.

During menopause, some women experience hot flashes (a feeling of being overly warm), hot flushes (the flushing of the skin), fatigue, dizziness, headaches, insomnia, nervousness, and depression. Women are more likely to encounter difficulties with menopause if they view it as signaling the end of their attractiveness, usefulness, and sexuality. These feelings may be intensified by America's youth-oriented culture, which devalues aging.

Research suggests that the negative effects of menopause are frequently exaggerated (Neugarten et al., 1963; Goodman, Grove, and Gilbert, 1978; Lennon, 1982). Often the most upsetting thing about menopause is the anticipation of it. Fortunately, at least two-thirds of postmenopausal women believe that they "feel better after menopause than they have for years" and that "after the change of life, a woman feels freer to do things for herself" (Neugarten et al., 1963). Many women are relieved that they no longer have to think about their periods or about getting pregnant. Their relations with their husbands often improve; they enjoy sex as much as or more than they did before. Clearly, in and of itself menopause should not be seen as some sort of "illness" (McCrea, 1983).

Men do not go though any biological change equivalent to menopause, because testosterone levels decrease slowly, if at all (Vermeulen, Rubens, and Verdonck, 1976; Tsitouras, Martin, and Horman, 1982). The number of sperm that a man's body produces declines gradually over the years, but men have fathered children at an advanced age.

Sexual Behavior

Is there sex after forty? According to one study (Pocs et al., 1977), most college students believe their parents have intercourse no more than once a month, never have oral sex, and never had intercourse before they were married. Many of the midwestern university students who answered this questionnaire were upset by the very idea of the survey. For example, one wrote: "Whoever thinks about their parents'

sexual relations, except perverts?" One-fourth of the students believed that their parents had had intercourse only once or not at all in the last year.

Of course, what people believe about their parents' sexual activity may be different from what they believe about that of other people their parents' age. Still, it is interesting to compare this belief with the following statistics and observations: in the studies by Alfred Kinsey (Kinsey et al., 1953), the average reported frequency of sexual intercourse for men sixty-five and older was about four times a month; 25 to 30 percent of the older married men and women in the studies also claimed to supplement intercourse with masturbation. Other, more recent studies (Masters and Johnson, 1970; Botwinick, 1978) have found essentially the same thing: that rather than suddenly reaching an age at which sexual interest disappears, most old people for whom a partner is available maintain relatively vigorous sex lives (Jasso, 1985). Those who are most sexually active tend to be those who also were most active in their youth (Newman and Nichols, 1960; Tsitouras, Martin, and Horman, 1982).

It is true that with aging, hormone production decreases in both sexes, and vaginal lubrication and erectile vigor diminish; but these changes are gradual. William H. Masters and Virginia E. Johnson (1970) emphatically point out that for most people who are in good health there is no physiological reason for stopping sexual activity with advancing age. The reasons people do so are usually related to other factors: lack of a partner; boredom with a partner of long standing; poor physical condition caused by a lack of exercise, obesity, or excessive use of alcohol; socially defined expectations that aging results in a loss of "sex drive"; and illness (such as advanced heart disease) not directly related to sexual physiology and functioning. Perhaps one significant contribution that modern sex research has made to society is to provide rational arguments against the expectation that sex stops or somehow becomes "improper" after a certain age. This understanding has enabled a large segment of the population to continue to enjoy a healthy sex life (Jasso, 1985).

Intellectual Changes

People are better at learning new skills and information, solving problems that require speed and coordi-

When they have an incentive and are given plenty of time, older people are efficient learners. This woman, who was never taught to read or write, is now on the road to literacy. *(Mark Mittelman)*

nation, and shifting from one problem-solving strategy to another in their mid-twenties than they were in adolescence (Baltes and Schaie, 1974; Schaie, 1983). These abilities are considered signs of intelligence; they are the skills intelligence tests measure.

At one time, many psychologists thought that intellectual development reached a peak in the mid-twenties and then declined. The reason is that people typically do not score as high on intelligence tests in middle age as they did when they were younger. Further investigation has revealed, however, that some parts of these tests measure speed, not other aspects of intelligence (Bischof, 1976; Cerella, 1985). A person's reaction time begins to slow in the early thirties. Therefore, intelligence tests "penalize" older adults for this fact.

Allowing for the decline in speed, one finds that people continue to acquire knowledge and skills and to expand their vocabularies throughout adulthood and until late in life (Bayley, 1968; Gilbert, 1973; Hayslip and Sterns, 1979). For the most part, the ability to comprehend new material improves with the years. This is particularly true if a person has had higher education, lives in a stimulating environment, and works in an intellectually demanding career (Blum and Jarvik, 1974; Jarvik, 1975; Kohn and Schooler, 1978). One researcher (Dennis, 1966) studied over seven hundred people who were engaged in scholarship, science, or the arts. Although the patterns varied from profession to profession, most people reached their peak of creativity and productivity in their forties. Overall, the most reasonable conclusion to be drawn from research data is that some decline in intellectual performance occurs among the elderly but that the decline is not great until very late in life (Botwinick, 1978; Schaie and Hertzog, 1983; Schaie, 1983). Moreover, individual differences are substantial at all ages, and they become greater with advancing age.

Memory is another area of cognitive functioning that in some cases is affected by aging (Burke and Light, 1981; Duchek, 1984; Lehman and Mellinger, 1984). However, memory loss is not inevitable. Rather, some memory loss is found in an increasing proportion of older people with each advance in chronological age. This means that some elderly people retain a sound memory regardless of age (Botwinick, 1967). Apparently environmental factors play an important part. Inactivity, alienation, hopelessness, and defensiveness all have an impact on memory (Jarvik, 1975; Langer et al., 1979; Scogin, Storandt, and Lott, 1985). Moreover, not all aspects of memory appear to be equally affected by aging; for example, age-related decreases are more severe for recall tasks than for recognition tasks (Craik, 1977; Inman and Parkinson, 1983). Memory loss may also result from hardening of the arteries, tumors, vitamin deficiencies, anemia, metabolic disorders, and Alzheimer's disease. However, it is important to stress that many elderly people continue to be alert, productive, and inventive throughout their lives. Leo Tolstoy, Pablo Picasso, Artur Rubinstein, Eleanor Roosevelt, Ronald Reagan, and Winston Churchill are some of the obvious examples.

Personality and Social Development

Increasingly, psychologists have come to portray the individual as undergoing change across the entire life span (Riegel, 1973, 1976; Baltes and Willis, 1977; Lerner and Busch-Rossnagel, 1981; Eichorn et al., 1982). They do not accept the notion of Sigmund Freud that adulthood is essentially a ripple occurring on the surface of a personality structure fixed in childhood. And they consider Jean Piaget's premise that no additional cognitive changes occur after adolescence a gross oversimplification. As seen by contemporary psychologists, adulthood is hardly a single, uniform stage—an undifferentiated phase of life between adolescence and old age.

Erikson's View

A major impetus to the study of life-span development has been provided by Erikson's theory of the eight crises of psychosocial adjustment (see Table 12.1). Erikson (1950, 1968) believes that the chief crisis confronting young adults revolves about questions of *intimacy versus isolation*. The ability to establish intimate relationships depends in large part on whether people have achieved a stable sense of identity. People who are insecure are likely to avoid closeness: they fear that other people will see through them, or they feel uncomfortably dependent on people with whom they are close. Erikson says that the failure to achieve intimacy leads to isolation. In some cases, isolating patterns are disguised by a series of intense but brief affairs or by stable but distant relationships. The ability of many contemporary youths to successfully resolve the crisis posed by this stage may be complicated by remaining or returning home (see the boxed insert on page 403).

Middle age may trigger either a new sense of generativity or a slide into stagnation. By *generativity*, Erikson means being a productive member of one's community and using one's accumulated wisdom to guide future generations—directly, as a parent, or indirectly, as a mentor. *Stagnation* occurs when a person wants to hang on to the past. The most graphic examples of this are women who try to recapture youth with face-lifts and men who attempt to recapture it by having affairs with young women. Stagnation may take the form of childish self-absorption, preoccupation with one's health, and bitterness about the direction one's life has taken.

Ideally, middle-aged people feel that the way they see themselves, what they would like to be, and the way others perceive them fit meaningfully together. They have developed their own strategies for dealing

Mentor and protégé. The desire to transmit one's knowledge and experience to the next generation is a sign of what Erikson calls the generativity resolution of the crisis of middle age. The opposite resolution—stagnation—results in self-absorption, bitterness, and looking backward. (Ken Heyman)

The Cluttered Nest

Over the past century norms have dictated that American youths leave home and make their own way in the world. It seemed as if "Americans had revised the commandment, 'Honor thy father and mother' to read 'Honor thy father and mother—but get away from them' " (Blumstein and Schwartz, 1983:26). But today's under-thirty generation is remaining home longer than any generation since the early 1940s. And adult children have been making their way back to the parental home in increasing numbers. In 1984, the Census Bureau reported that 15,543,000 people, or 54 percent of Americans between the ages of eighteen and twenty-four, were still living at home, up from 10,582,000, or 47.3 percent, in 1970. A total of 4,174,000 people, or 10.4 percent, of those between twenty-five and thirty-four were also still home, compared with 1,950,000, or 8 percent, in 1970.

A good many factors have contributed to these trends: postponed marriages, high divorce rates, high housing costs, high levels of unemployment, expectations for a high standard of living, more liberal sexual attitudes, high rates of illegitimate births, and damaged lives resulting from drug abuse. Anita Tarjan, a twenty-four-year-old teacher who lives with her parents, says (Lindsey, 1984:10):

I want to strike out on my own, be independent, take care of my own affairs and have privacy. But unfortunately I can't afford to. You get out of college believing you're going to have this terrific job, and then when you finally do get a job, your salary just doesn't meet your expectations. You can't survive and there you are, living at home again, just like a teenager.

Living with their parents has proven highly successful for some and disastrous for others, with many gradations in between (Langway, 1980; Brooks, 1981; Clemens and Axelson, 1985). Those who find themselves pleased with the arrangement say that it affords them the benefits historically available in extended family living. There is a sense of warmth, closeness, and emotional support at a time of widespread personal alienation. Young couples find built-in babysitting advantages, and grandparents have an opportunity to know and enjoy their grandchildren.

Young adults are remaining or returning home during periods of the family life cycle that traditionally served as launching- and empty-nest periods. Family therapists express concern about the hidden emotional and psychological costs that may be involved. Those who stay on do not have opportunities to fully develop their sense of individuality. Staying at home tends to aggravate tendencies toward excessive protectiveness in parents and a lack of self-confidence in youths, and thus can delay maturity, even in healthy family settings (Brooks, 1985; Clemens and Axelson, 1985).

Perhaps the most common complaint voiced by members of both generations concerns the loss of privacy. Couples report that they feel uncomfortable fighting in front of family members. Young adults, especially the unmarried, complain that parents cramp their sex lives or their stereo-playing, treat them like children, and impair their independence. Parents often grumble that additional strain is placed on their own marriage, their peace and quiet is disturbed, the phone rings at odd hours, they lie awake at night worrying and listening for the adult child to return home, meals are rarely eaten together because of conflicting schedules, and too much of the burden of babysitting falls on them. Then, too, higher expenses may compel parents to relinquish long-awaited vacations, and a need for space means they must postpone a move to a smaller, cheaper home. Usually the happiest refilled nests are those with ample space and open, trusting communication. Those that are most difficult are associated with grown children who lack resilience and maturity and who have drug problems. Under these circumstances parents may treat the twenty-five-year-old like a fifteen-year-old, and the twenty-five-year-old behaves accordingly. The tensions that result may be severe enough to lead some families to seek professional help.

effectively with stress and the complexities of life. They have a new self-assurance born of the feeling that they know they can handle things. And they want to share this experience with others.

In middle age, many people begin to devote more time and energy to the outside world. Although their interest in family and friends continues, they become more deeply involved in organizations—professional associations, unions, political campaigns, civic committees, and the like. This new outward orientation may be most obvious among mothers who now have the time to go back to school or to full-time work, to chair committees or run for political office. But it is also true of working people whose experience and heightened productivity command new respect. Involvement in outside affairs is an extension of generativity beyond the family.

Male Development

A number of psychologists, among them Daniel J. Levinson and his colleagues (1978) at Yale, have attempted to go beyond Erikson and to construct a descriptive framework defining the stages in adult male development. They have studied forty men in their mid-thirties to mid-forties, including blue- and white-collar workers in industry, business executives, academic biologists, and novelists. The Yale researchers conclude that the overriding task running throughout adulthood is the constant need to structure and restructure goals and goal-seeking behaviors. This process involves the man in a continual interaction with his environment and leads him through a series of stages or levels in life organization. These stages are depicted in Figure 12.4 and may be summarized as follows.

Entering the adult world. From about age twenty-two to age twenty-eight, the young man is considered, both by himself and by society, to be a novice in the adult world—not fully established as a man, but no longer an adolescent. During this time he must attempt to resolve the conflict between the need to explore the options of the adult world and the need to establish a stable life structure. He needs to sample different kinds of relationships, to keep choices about career and employment open, to explore the nature of the world now accessible to him as an adult. But he also needs to begin a career and to establish a home and family of his own. The first life

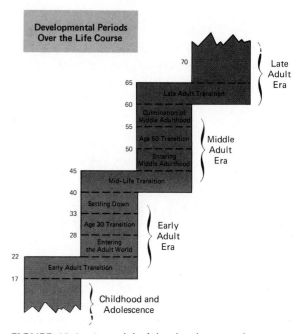

FIGURE 12.4 A model of the developmental sequence of a man's life proposed by Levinson and his colleagues (1978). The scheme emphasizes that development is a process that requires continual adjustment.

structure, then, may have a tentative quality. The young man may select a career or a job but not be committed to it. He may form romantic attachments and may even marry during this period; but the life structure of early adulthood often lacks a full sense of stability or permanence.

The age-thirty crisis. The motto of the rebellious, politically oriented young people who sought to change American society in the 1960s was "Never trust anyone over thirty." Levinson's data reveal that the years between twenty-eight and thirty-three are indeed often a major transition period. The thirtieth birthday can truly be a turning point; for most men in Levinson's sample, it could be called "the age-thirty crisis." During this transitional period, the tentative commitments that were made in the first life structure are reexamined, and many questions about the choices of marriage partner, career, and life goals are reopened, often in a painful way. The man feels that any parts of his life that are unsatisfying or incomplete must be attended to now, because it will soon be too late to make major changes.

Settling down. Having probably made some firm choices in the previous stage about his career, family, and relationships, the man begins actively carving out a niche in society. He now concentrates on what Levinson calls "making it" in the adult world. The man attempts to move up the ladder of prestige and achievement in his chosen career or profession.

Becoming one's own man. Levinson found that near the end of the settling-down period, approximately between the ages of thirty-six and forty, there is a distinctive phase that he has labeled "becoming one's own man." Whereas earlier the young man had looked to an older, more experienced man as a mentor, someone who would share his experience and wisdom, the relationship with the mentor is often fundamentally changed, or even broken off, in the process of becoming one's own man. Now it is time to become fully independent. During this period, the man strives to attain the seniority and position in the world that he identified as his ultimate goal at the beginning of the settling-down period.

The mid-life transition. At about age forty, the period of early adulthood comes to an end and the mid-life transition begins. From about age forty to age forty-five, the man begins again to ask questions, but now the questions concern the past as well as the future. He may ask: "What have I done with my life?" "What have I accomplished?" "What do I still wish to accomplish?" At age thirty, the man had primarily looked ahead toward goals. Now, at the mid-life transition, he is in a position to assess his accomplishments and to determine whether they have been satisfying. During this transition he begins to evolve yet another life structure that will predominate during the period of middle adulthood.

The Yale researchers plan to continue their study into the years beyond the mid-forties. Other researchers (Gould, 1972, 1978; Vaillant, 1977) have also investigated the phases of adult life. On the basis of a study involving patients, medical students, and hospital workers at a major western university hospital, the psychiatrist Roger L. Gould provides insight on later age periods.

From about forty-five to fifty, Gould finds that adults tend to conclude that the die has pretty well been cast as to what their life fortunes are to be. Consequently, they begin to resign themselves to many of life's negative aspects. This coming to terms with one's fate sets the stage for the period between fifty and sixty.

During the fifties, people typically mellow. They become more accepting of themselves and of their spouses, children, and friends. They no longer experience the intense combative impulses or the driving pressures that often characterized their lives when they were thirty. They recognize that life is time-bound and that they too will die. But these thoughts do not particularly trouble them. Instead, they find a new serenity as they reflect on the meaning of their lives and their accomplishments.

Female Development

The phases in adult female development remain largely unexplored. Studies of women such as those conducted by Levinson and Gould of men are currently being undertaken, but their findings are as yet unavailable. Nonetheless, it is clear that the same phases that apply to adult men do not necessarily apply to the development of adult women (Sassen, 1980; Gilligan, 1982). For instance, whereas Erik Erikson (1963) says the formation of identity in adolescence is followed by the capacity for intimacy in early adulthood, many women describe the opposite progression, with the sense of identity developing more strongly in mid-life (Baruch and Barnett, 1983).

Traditionally, women have experienced numerous combinations of career, marriage, and child rearing that have provided a different cast to their lives than that experienced by men. Until recent decades, a woman's life was defined primarily in terms of her reproductive role. But with 90 percent of all women now working outside the home at some point in their lives, jobs and careers are coming to occupy an increasingly important part in the identity and self-esteem of women. It seems that work outside the home acts as a stabilizing force for women during critical junctures of the life cycle. A national survey reveals that working women at mid-life are healthier, have higher self-esteem, and suffer less anxiety than homemakers do (Coleman and Antonucci, 1983).

The economist Lester C. Thurow (1981) points out that women encounter a substantial disadvantage should they have children. The years between ages twenty-five and thirty-five constitute the decade in the life span that is particularly critical in the development of a career. During this period lawyers and accountants become partners in the top firms, business managers make it onto the "fast track," college professors secure tenure at good universities, and blue-collar workers find positions that generate high earnings and seniority. But it is this period of life when women are most likely to leave the labor force to have children. When they do, the present system for achieving promotions and acquiring critical skills extracts a high lifetime price. Even when new mothers return to work within a few months, male managers often assume that the women are no longer free to take on time-consuming tasks and pass them over for promotion (Fraker, 1984).

The more successful a man is, the more likely it is that he will marry and have a family. But for women it is the other way around. Hence, whereas 51 percent of women executives at top corporations are single, only 4 percent of their male counterparts are single; in addition, whereas 61 percent of the women are childless, only 3 percent of the men have no children (Fraker, 1984). Also of significance are the growing numbers of women who rear their children first in two-parent, then in one-parent, and then again in two-parent homes (Neugarten, 1979). Differing combinations of career, marriage, and chil-

dren occur with respect to both timing and commitment, and each pattern has different ramifications.

In many cases, women who are now in their forties and fifties stopped their schooling or work on the birth of their first child and remained in the home during their children's early years. When they attempt to resume their careers, they find that jobs are now scarcer in the fields in which they were originally trained (traditional "women's jobs" such as teaching and social work). In other fields, such as nursing, their knowledge is likely to be dated (Mogul, 1979). Further, women who have functioned as homemakers often find that their decision to return to the paid labor force gives rise to friction even in the most supportive families. The husband may feel threatened by expectations that he assume additional household responsibilities, and so the major portion of housework continues to be performed by the woman (Crosby, 1982).

Women encounter other obstacles as well. Almost half of all employed women work in occupations that are at least 80 percent female, while slightly more than half of all men are in occupations at least 80 percent male (see Table 12.2). A 1985 report by the National Academy of Sciences says that, despite recent progress, most American women will contin-

Older women who want to return to the work force after their children are grown may not only doubt themselves but also encounter resistance from their husbands and their employers. (Hazel Hankin)

TABLE 12.2 Percentages of Women in Occupations That Employ the Most Men and That Employ the Most Women

	1970	1980
Men		
1. Managers	15.3%	26.9%
2. Heavy truck drivers	1.5	2.3
3. Janitors and cleaners	13.1	23.4
4. Production supervisors	9.9	15.0
5. Carpenters	1.1	1.6
6. Sales supervisors	17.0	28.2
7. Laborers	16.5	19.4
8. Sales representatives	7.0	14.9
9. Farmers	4.7	9.8
10. Auto mechanics	1.4	1.3
Women		
1. Secretaries	97.8	98.8
2. Elementary schoolteachers	83.9	75.4
3. Bookkeepers	80.9	89.7
4. Cashiers	84.2	83.5
5. Office clerks	75.3	82.1
6. Managers	15.3	26.9
7. Waitresses and waiters	90.8	88.0
8. Sales workers	70.4	72.7
9. Registered nurses	97.3	95.9
10. Nursing aides	87.0	87.8

Source: Data from National Research Council, 1985.

ue to work in largely low-paying occupations dominated by women for the foreseeable future (Ilchman, 1985). Women's average wages are about 60 percent of men's for full-time jobs, and the report finds that about 35 to 40 percent of the gap is caused by the segregation of women and men into different occupations. A number of factors have limited women's progress and continue to do so, including social stereotyping, referrals from predominantly male settings, veterans' preference policies, and departmental rather than plantwide seniority systems. In sum, the adult experience is likely to be different for women than for men.

LATER ADULTHOOD

Aging is not an event, like a birthday, that suddenly descends on a person. People carry much the same baggage with them into their later years that they carried earlier in life. If they lived active lives, they typically will be active when they are older; if they did not, they will not be particularly active when they enter later life. Aging does not destroy the continuity between what people were, what they are, and what they will be. Life's course is a seamless web.

According to Erikson (1950, 1959), as people approach the end of life, they take stock of the years that have gone before (see Table 12.1). Growing old and the prospect of dying lead some people to a heightened sense of ego integrity and others to despair. By *ego integrity*, Erikson means greater self-acceptance. Looking back, the elderly person concludes that if he or she had life to live over, the choice would be to relive it like it was—with all the bumps, false starts, and disappointments as well as the joys and triumphs. By *despair*, Erikson means the inability to accept oneself and one's life. Looking back, the old person may see little but lost chances, bad decisions, people who spoiled his or her plans.

The psychologist Robert N. Butler (1963, 1971) also finds that elderly people tend to look back on their lives and to reflect and reminisce about what has transpired, a process he terms the **life review.** Such a review most frequently occurs at the time of retirement, the death of a spouse, or one's own imminent death. When people are satisfied with their lives, the process helps them to adjust to their impending death and represents the continuation of development right to the very end.

The Elderly

What happens to people as they grow older? Seen from the perspective of younger Americans, people over the age of sixty-five have serious problems with poverty, health, fear of crime, and loneliness. Yet the

---

life review: The tendency of elderly people to look back on their lives and to reflect and reminisce about what has transpired.

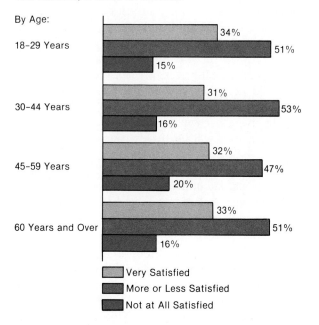

Question: How satisfied are you with the way things are going for you *personally*? Are you very satisfied, more or less satisfied, or not at all satisfied?

By Age:

18–29 Years
34%
51%
15%

30–44 Years
31%
53%
16%

45–59 Years
32%
47%
20%

60 Years and Over
33%
51%
16%

Very Satisfied
More or Less Satisfied
Not at All Satisfied

Question: People feel differently about what years are the best time of a person's life. Which of these do *you* think are the best time of life?

By Age:	Childhood	Teen-age Years	The Twenties	The Thirties	The Forties	The Fifties	Retirement Years
18–29 Years	22%	29%	42%	9%	4%	1%	3%
30–44 Years	22%	21%	28%	31%	13%	4%	5%
45–59 Years	17%	16%	24%	22%	20%	13%	8%
60 Years and Over	14%	14%	19%	20%	16%	11%	31%

FIGURE 12.5 Taken as a group, America's elderly are growing old gracefully and contentedly. (top: *Data from Roper Organization. 1984.* Roper Report 84-9. *September 15–22.* bottom: *Data from Roper Organization. 1984.* Roper Report 84-4. *March 17–24.)*

Note: Multiple responses per respondent. Don't know/no answer (not shown) ranged from 4–8 percent.

general public's view of older people's circumstances is far grimmer than the elderly's own perceptions (Weaver, 1981) (see Figure 12.5). Americans are being forced to revise their conceptions of aging because many stereotypes no longer hold (if in fact they ever did). Older Americans are themselves doing much to redefine the notion of old age. They are, on the whole, better educated, better off, healthier, and more active than were previous generations.

Growing Numbers

The elderly are becoming more visible within American society as their proportion grows. People sixty-five years of age and older currently make up 11 percent of the population and will make up 13 percent by the year 2000 and 21 percent by the year 2030. Today, a sixty-five-year-old woman can expect to survive to eighty-four. However, a sixty-five-year-old man has a statistical chance of living only to seventy-nine. The life expectancy gap between men and women has been widening over recent decades. By age sixty-five, only sixty-eight men are still alive for every one hundred women (by age seventy-five, the figure falls still further, to fifty-five men). One result of women's greater life expectancy is that only one-third of women over age sixty-five are married, in contrast to 75 percent of older men (Robey, 1982).

Retirement

Retirement has often been portrayed as having profoundly negative consequences for people. Partly in response to this view, Congress in 1978 prohibited most mandatory retirement before age seventy. Yet the trend toward early retirement has continued. Fewer than 12.5 percent of workers in the United States currently remain in the labor force once they reach the age of sixty-five. The proportion has dropped steadily since 1950, when 26.7 percent of the elderly stayed at work.

There is no good evidence that retirement poses a crisis for most people. Money is what is most missed in retirement; and when people are ensured an adequate income, most of them retire early (Atchley, 1971; Shanas, 1972; Beck, 1982; Fillenbaum,

George, and Palmore, 1985). Contrary to popular notions, only a small minority of workers are forced out of jobs by mandatory retirement plans (Parnes, 1981). Poor health forces out eight times as many men as mandatory retirement does. Most people who retire for reasons other than poor health are "very happy" in retirement and would, if they had to do it over again, retire at the same age. Only a minority —13 percent of whites and 17 percent of blacks— say they would retire later if they could choose again. However, some people do experience "retirement shock." Most commonly they are workers who failed to develop interests outside their jobs or who never worked out the details of their retirement with their spouses (Brody, 1981b).

Income

In 1959, one-third of the nation's elderly lived below the poverty line. Today, only 14 percent fit this category (and the percentage is smaller if food stamps and other benefits are included). Although public-opinion surveys show that 68 percent of those under age sixty-five think a lack of money is a "very serious problem" for the elderly, only 17 percent of those over sixty-five believe it to be a personal problem (Weaver, 1981). In fact, as shown in Figure

Retirement need not have negative consequences for people who have worked out the details and have interests outside their jobs. *(Harry Wilks/Stock, Boston)*

Question: We are interested in how people are getting along financially these days. So far as you and your family are concerned, would you say that you are pretty well satisfied with your present financial situation, more or less satisfied, or not satisfied at all?

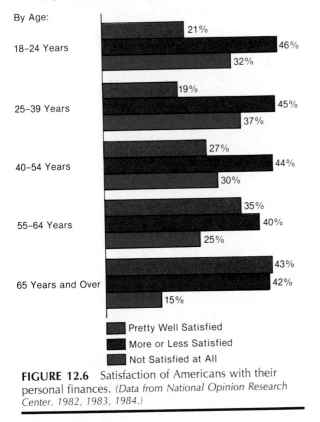

FIGURE 12.6 Satisfaction of Americans with their personal finances. *(Data from National Opinion Research Center. 1982, 1983, 1984.)*

12.6, Americans sixty-five and over are better satisfied with their personal financial situation than younger Americans. Currently, more than 92 percent of the elderly receive social security benefits, which constitutes 38 percent of the total income of older Americans (Gottschalk, 1983).

Crime and Victimization

It is popularly believed that fear of crime constitutes a serious problem for the elderly. But a 1981 survey revealed that only 25 percent of the elderly themselves view crime as a major concern (Harris Poll, 1981). Further, the elderly are less likely to be victims of crime than younger people. Crimes against the person (rape, robbery, and assault) occur to the elderly at a rate of 30 per 1,000. These same crimes occur in the population as a whole four times as often, at a rate of 130 per 1,000 (Russell, 1980).

Health

Perceived good health is the single strongest predictor of an elderly person's ability to maintain optimism and good morale (Hinds, 1980). Fortunately, fully 56 percent of people over age sixty-five who are not in nursing homes rate their health as good or excellent. In comparison, 74 percent of all Americans say their health is good or excellent (see Figure 12.7). Although the elderly have more health problems than younger people, they seem less prone to injury. Some 35 percent of Americans report at least one injury per year, but only 21 percent of older people do so (Turner, 1982). However, 43 percent of the elderly indicate that their activities are limited

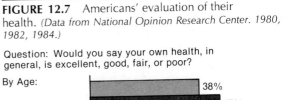

FIGURE 12.7 Americans' evaluation of their health. *(Data from National Opinion Research Center. 1980, 1982, 1984.)*

Question: Would you say your own health, in general, is excellent, good, fair, or poor?

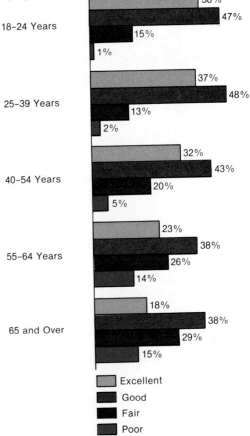

because of illness or disability. They visit physicians an average of seven times a year and report being sick in bed fifteen days a year. These figures are about twice those for the population as a whole (Russell, 1980).

Some 80 percent of long-term home care for the elderly is provided by family members, and a majority of the elderly live within a half-hour car trip of one of their children. Seventy-five percent of older Americans never see a nursing home. Only 5 percent of all persons aged sixty-five and over are institutionalized. For those over seventy-five, the figure is 9.4 percent, and for those over eighty-five, it is 19 percent (Brozan, 1980). The sense of social obligation among relatives is strong even when the emotional ties between parent and child were previously weak (Cicirelli, 1981; Neugarten, 1982). Many of the residents in nursing homes have had little education and less than the best medical care over their life span. Further, as the final insult, they find themselves planted in a desolate kind of institution (Rodin and Langer, 1977).

Loneliness

Thirty percent of noninstitutionalized individuals over sixty-five live alone: 16 percent of the men and 40 percent of the women (Russell, 1980). But whereas 65 percent of younger people regard loneliness as a serious problem for the elderly, only 13 percent of the elderly agree (Weaver, 1981). Further, the elderly watch no more television than do people in general; the majority watch three hours a day or less (Hinds, 1980).

Dying

Western cultures have long been extremely uncomfortable with death. In fact, some people have labeled the United States a "death-denying" society because Americans often take such great pains to keep death out of sight and out of mind. Even medical schools have done little to prepare physicians for dealing with death in their practices. Not surprisingly, many physicians do their best to ignore death when treating dying patients and working with

Friends are important social supports throughout life. Most older adults have close relationships with others that they find emotionally satisfying. *(Alan Carey/The Image Works)*

their families. Moreover, less than 25 percent of Americans have prepared wills, and insurance agents frequently try to circumvent the topic of death when selling life insurance policies.

Over the past decade or so, these patterns have altered and in some respects Western societies have begun to "rediscover" death. Television, newspapers, and magazines have featured programs or articles on the topic. And the relatively new field of **thanatology**—the study of dying and death—has

---

thanatology: The study of dying and death.

Hospices

Death is one of the few taboos that has lingered late into twentieth-century America. The breakdown of extended families and the rise of modern medicine have insulated most people in our society from seeing death. Many people have no direct experience with death, and partly as a result, they are afraid to talk about it. In 1900, two-thirds of those who died in the United States were under fifty, and most of them died at home in their own beds. Today, most Americans live until at least sixty-five, and many die in hospitals or nursing homes. Elaborate machines may prolong existence long after a person has stopped living a normal life.

A new movement to restore the dignity of dying revolves around the concept of the *hospice*—usually a special place where terminally ill people go to die. Doctors in hospices do not try to prolong life but rather to relieve pain and provide contact with loved ones during the last days of life. The first and most famous facility of this sort was St. Christopher's Hospice in London, England, which opened in 1967. Then, as now, the vast majority of patients have been cancer patients, since hospice care is particularly suited to this disease. Patients in a hospice lead the most normal life they are able to and are taken care of as much as possible by their family members. More recently, many hospice programs have focused on care of the dying person at home. Visiting physicians, nurses, and other support personnel provide both emotional and medical care. The number of hospice programs in the United States, including both home-care and inpatient services, jumped from only one in 1975 to 1,345 a decade later (Maloney, 1985).

Hospices are also being organized in hospitals and nursing homes. Proponents of hospice care say that hospitals and their staffs are geared to

Patients at St. Christopher's Hospice in England. In the United States, the hospice movement seeks to retain the person's dignity in the face of immanent death. Terminally ill patients are given emotional comfort and pain relief, rather than life-prolonging medical interventions. More and more older adults who are near death choose to live their final days outside of hospitals. *(Dr. Cicely Saunders/Hospice)*

curing illness and prolonging life; death represents embarrassing evidence of failure. Hospices seek to provide an alternative care arrangement that accepts the inevitability of death and provides for the needs of dying patients and their families. Many Americans see the hospice as a humane alternative to the hospital ward where gravely ill patients are kept alive by respirators and other "heroic" measures. The success of the movement may signal a change in American attitudes toward death.

gained in popularity. This new interest has been accompanied by a surge in controversies revolving about death, including such matters as abortion, the

death penalty, "clinical death," "the right to die," and the "quest for a healthy death." (The boxed insert above deals with the hospice movement, which aims to provide comfort and care for the terminally ill.)

Fear of Death

Death is a highly personal matter. Since it means different things to different individuals, people confront death in different ways (Jeffers and Verwoerdt, 1969). Some erect formidable denial mechanisms to shield themselves from the fact of death. However, in a study of 140 elderly persons, Duke University researchers found that only 5 percent denied that they ever thought about death. Nearly half reported that they were reminded of death in one fashion or another at least once a day, while 20 percent said it came to mind about once a week and 25 percent reported that they thought about death less than once a week. In any event, most researchers agree that less than 10 percent of elderly people are terrified of death (Swenson, 1961; Jeffers and Verwoerdt, 1969). Overall there seems to be no relationship between age and strong fears of death (Conte, Weiner, and Plutchik, 1982). High levels of death anxiety appear to be more related to personality maladjustment and depression at any age than to the decline of physical abilities.

The Dying Process

The work of Elisabeth Kübler-Ross (1969, 1981) has done much to restore dignity and humanity to death. She has helped people to appreciate that dying, like living, is a process. When physicians and the family know that a person is dying and seek to hide this fact, difficulties are created for the dying person. Kübler-Ross finds that death can be a growing experience for all parties if individuals are allowed to express their true feelings and if these emotions are respected.

On the basis of interviews with over two hundred patients, Kübler-Ross finds that there are a number of common elements to the death experience. People typically pass through five stages. Not everyone goes through all the stages and there may be movement back and forth between the stages. The first stage is *denial*. The most common response is "It can't happen to me: there must be a mistake." The second stage is *anger*: "Why me?" Dying people may resent the healthy and show hostility toward the people who will survive them. In the third stage, the dying attempt to *bargain* (perhaps with God) for more time. The next stage entails a growing sense of loss and the experience of *depression*. Dying people begin to mourn their own impending death, the loss of close friends and relatives, and the surrendering of meaningful things, experiences, and dreams. Finally, near the end, when they are tired and weak, they *accept* the inevitable. It is almost as if the dying have said their good-byes, made their peace with themselves, and are resting before the final journey. Of course, such factors as the nature of the disease, the degree of pain, the extent of mobility, and the length of the terminal period also play a part in people's adjustment to death (Kastenbaum, 1975).

Grief and Bereavement

Every year about 8 million Americans suffer the death of a close family member. The event has major consequences for those who survive (Joyce, 1984). It can disrupt their patterns of life for as long as three years and often for at least a year. In some cases, four to seven years after the death of a spouse or child, survivors still have not entirely "put the loss behind them." Grief and mourning vary widely among people. Phyliss Silverman (1983:63), an authority on bereavement, has this to say about the process:

> It isn't a problem or an illness that can be solved or cured. That's why it is really inappropriate for someone to say: "You can get over this. You can recover." In fact, people can't recover in the sense of going back to the way things were. You must make changes in your life in order to go on. The death and the bereavement wizen you, weather you and make you look at life differently.

Not uncommonly a person who has lost a family member or close friend experiences for a time periodic mood swings between sadness, anger, guilt, anxiety, and irritability. The survivor may also feel physically sick, experience a loss in appetite, sleep poorly, and fear he or she is going crazy, sometimes hallucinating or "seeing" the deceased person in the street. Sadness is most likely to flare up on anniversaries or other significant dates. Although most bereaved people do not become seriously ill following the loss of someone close, they often do experience adverse health reactions. On the whole, bereaved people show a more than average incidence of illness, accidents, mortality, unemployment, and other indices of a damaged life (Greenblatt, 1978; Fenwick and Barresi, 1981; Stroebe and Stroebe, 1983). Health problems in survivors are likely to be more severe among those who are already in poor physical or mental health, who are alcohol or drug abusers, and who lack integration in a social network.

Unfortunately, cultural expectations, social values, and community practices at times interfere with the bereavement process. Dying is left to medical technology and often takes place in a hospital or nursing home. Funerals are abbreviated and simplified, while mourning is frequently seen as a form of mental pathology (the cultural ideal is the self-contained widow who displays a "stiff upper lip"). In contrast, such traditions as the Irish wake and the Jewish *shivah* assist the bereaved in coming to terms with the loss and in reconstructing new life patterns through family and friends. These rituals signal that the feelings of grief have their rightful place in life.

SUMMARY

1. Puberty, or sexual maturation, is the biological event that marks the end of childhood. The changes associated with puberty are regulated by the activities of the endocrine glands, which in turn are controlled by the hypothalamus.

A. Young people display considerable variation in the age at which they reach puberty. In general, girls begin to develop earlier than boys and for a year or two may tower over male age-mates. Research reveals that boys who mature early have a decided advantage. They are typically more self-confident and independent than other boys. The differences between early maturers and late maturers do not seem to be as pronounced among girls as they are among boys.

B. First sexual intercourse is a major event in a young person's experience. Among the meanings that youths attach to sexual intercourse are a declaration of autonomy and of independence from parents, an affirmation of sexual identity, and a statement of capacity for interpersonal intimacy.

2. A major developmental task confronting adolescents is building a stable identity. Erik Erikson says that adolescents often suffer an identity crisis. His notions have gained considerable popular acceptance. However, research is increasingly indicating that most adolescents do not experience anything approaching an identity "crisis."

3. A good deal is made of generational differences between young people and their parents. Yet the gap between generations is hardly as pervasive or as widespread as popular stereotypes imply. The relative influence of peers and parents differs with the issue involved.

4. Adulthood is not a steady state of being but a process of becoming. This fact is highlighted by young adulthood. It is during this period that individuals are exploring and negotiating new levels of intimacy, with many entering marriage and embarking on parenthood. And many of them are joining the labor force, with major implications for their life style and community placement.

5. In general, human beings are at their physical peak between the ages of eighteen and twenty-five. For most adults, the process of physical decline is slow and gradual. Some of the changes associated with growing older are the result of the natural processes of aging. Others result from diseases and from simple disuse and abuse.

A. Between the ages of forty-five and fifty, a woman's production of sex hormones is sharply reduced. This biological event is called menopause. Research suggests that the negative effects of menopause are frequently exaggerated.

B. For most people who are in good health, there is no physiological reason for stopping sexual activity with advancing age.

6. Allowing for the decline in speed of functioning, people continue to acquire knowledge and skills and to expand their vocabularies throughout adulthood and until late in life. For the most part, the ability to comprehend new material improves with the years. Some decline in intellectual performance occurs

among the elderly, but the decline is not great until very late in life.

7. Increasingly psychologists have come to portray the individual as undergoing change across the entire life span. Adulthood is hardly a single, uniform stage.

A. Erik Erikson portrays people as confronting crises at various periods of the life span. These crises pose the opportunity for individuals to achieve a new dimension of personal and social growth.

B. Daniel J. Levinson and his colleagues at Yale have constructed a framework defining the stages in adult male development. They conclude that the overriding task running throughout adulthood is the constant need to structure and restructure goals and goal-seeking behaviors.

C. The same phases that apply to adult men do not necessarily apply to the development of adult women. Until recent decades, a woman's life was defined primarily in terms of her reproductive role. In the past two decades there has been a decrease in the importance of marital status and motherhood in determining the types of activities and roles a woman adopts.

8. Aging is not an event, like a birthday, that suddenly descends on a person. People carry much the same baggage with them into old age that they carried earlier in life. Aging does not destroy the continuity between what people were, what they are, and what they will be. Thus, many stereotypes no longer hold.

9. Dying, like living, is a process. Elisabeth Kübler-Ross identifies five stages through which dying people typically pass: denial, anger, bargaining, depression, and acceptance. Not everyone goes through all the stages and there may be movement back and forth between the stages.

KEY TERMS

adolescence (p. 388)
clique (p. 396)
identity (p. 392)

life review (p. 407)
menarche (p. 389)
menopause (p. 399)

puberty (p. 389)
thanatology (p. 411)
totalism (p. 394)

SUGGESTED READINGS

CONGER, JOHN J., AND PETERSON, ANNE C. 1983. *Adolescence and Youth.* 3rd ed. New York: Harper & Row. An excellent overview of physical, personality, and intellectual development that takes place during adolescence. Also includes such topics as alienation and commitment, dropping out and delinquency, sexual attitudes, and drug use.

ERIKSON, ERIK H. 1969. *Gandhi's Truth.* New York: W.W. Norton. The Pulitzer Prize winning account of Gandhi's creative search for truth. Erikson skillfully describes Gandhi's growth to adulthood and, eventually, one of the century's most important historical and spiritual figures.

EVANS, RICHARD I. 1967. *Dialogue with Erik Erikson.* New York: Dutton. A long interview with Erikson, in which he discusses his eight stages of psychosocial development and problems young people have in finding their identity, a satisfying life career, and an intimate relationship with another person.

FRIEDENBERG, EDGAR Z. 1959. *The Vanishing Adolescent.* Boston: Beacon. One of the best-known authorities on adolescence presents his views in an exciting and highly readable fashion. Friedenberg stresses the importance of adolescent conflict as a means of establishing a relationship between the individual and the society.

KÜBLER-ROSS, ELISABETH. 1969. *On Death and Dying.* New York: Macmillan. Through a number of very moving interviews with patients who are terminally ill, the author allows us to share their private pain and final dignity. We see the stages they pass through: from denial, anger, bargaining, and depression to eventual acceptance.

LEVINSON, DANIEL J., ET AL. 1978. *The Seasons of a Man's Life.* New York: Knopf. The long-awaited report of Levinson's research on stages of development in adult males. On the basis of intensive interviews with forty men from four different occupational groups, Levinson proposes a model of the stages, crises, and transitions experienced by most men.

SHEEHY, GAIL. 1976. *Passages*. New York: Dutton. A popular account of the predictable crises of adulthood. Sheehy is not the systematic theorist that Levinson (above) is, but she has a rich data base in the interviews she personally conducted, and she deals with the life crises of women as well as of men.

STEINBERG, LAURENCE. *Adolescence*. 1985. New York: Random House. A multidisciplinary survey of theories and research on individual development, which also examines the effects of the contexts in which adolescents grow up.

WINN, MARIE. 1983. *Children Without Childhood*. Hammondsworth, Middlesex, England: Penguin Books. A provocative examination of childhood and adolescence today that addresses the disintegration of family life; the emphasis on sex in books, films, and television; and society's casual acceptance of "recreational" drugs as factors contributing to the emergence of prematurely "adult" children.

part 5

PERSONALITY AND CHANGE

Paul Cézanne, *Boy in a Red Waistcoat*, 1893–95.

13
Personality Theory

A few years ago, New York City homicide detective Thomas Foley was having considerable difficulty cracking an unusually vicious murder. The nude body of a twenty-six-year-old special-education teacher had been found on the roof of her Bronx apartment building. The murderer had brutally beaten the woman about the face and strangled her with the strap of her purse. The killer then mutilated her body and scrawled obscenities in ink on her thigh.

When months of investigation turned up few solid leads, Foley's superior suggested that he contact the Behavioral Science Unit at the FBI Academy in Quantico, Virginia. The FBI unit provides profiles of criminals to local police departments in cases involving multiple rape, "motiveless" murders, and brutal crimes that suggest major psychological abnormality in the perpetrator. A few days after providing the FBI with photographs of the murder scene and a copy of the autopsy report, Foley received a "profile" of the probable murderer. The killer would be a white man, most likely between twenty-five and thirty-five years of age. In all probability he knew the victim and either worked or lived nearby, perhaps in her apartment building. He would be a high-school dropout, live by himself or with a single parent, and maintain an extensive collection of pornography. And very likely he would be a person the police had already interviewed.

Over the next ten months Foley and other detectives followed up leads suggested by the FBI sketch and eventually identified the murderer. He was a thirty-two-year-old high-school dropout who knew the victim and lived on the fourth floor of her building. The police had questioned the man's father, with whom he maintained a pornography collection. Initially Foley had not thought the man was a likely suspect because Foley was told that he had been in a mental hospital at the time of the killing.

419

However, because the man fit the FBI's profile so closely, Foley checked the hospital and learned that patients were permitted to come and go more or less at will. Accordingly, Foley thoroughly investigated the man and accumulated enough evidence to allow the district attorney to obtain a murder conviction. "What the FBI description did," says Foley, "was to keep me on course" (Porter, 1983:45).

In working up its profiles, the FBI unit gives microscopic attention to photographs of the crime scene and autopsy reports. For instance, in the case of the Bronx murder there was a good deal of beating about the victim's face. As a general rule, FBI researchers find that a brutal facial attack means that the killer knew the victim, and that the more vicious the attack, the closer the relationship. Killers in their teens or early twenties usually kill a person immediately, in a kind of blitz assault. In contrast, if a murderer has shown mastery of the situation, if he has killed his victim slowly and methodically, a more sadistic personality is probably involved—very likely a man in his late twenties or early thirties. The murderer is unlikely to be a man in his late thirties or forties, because the urge to commit brutal sex murders typically surfaces at an earlier age, so the chances are that by the time such a person reached that age, he would already be in jail.

In most murders, the perpetrator and the victim are of the same race. Consequently, the FBI presumed that since the murder victim was white, the murderer was also white. The FBI also knows from statistics that killers of this nature commonly come from single-parent homes and have difficulty sustaining a lasting relationship with a woman. From this the researchers concluded that the Bronx murderer lived by himself or with only one parent. Finally, evidence at the murder scene suggested that the killer had conducted himself in a leisurely fashion (for instance, he had removed the woman's earrings and placed them neatly by her head, and had carefully arranged the body in a spread-eagle position). This lack of haste indicated a confidence that suggested that the man must have been fairly familiar with the surroundings by virtue of his working or living in the area.

The uncanny accuracy of the FBI sketch of the murderer persuaded Foley and his colleagues to join a growing number of police officers across the United States who believe that profiling can provide crucial help in solving some kinds of crimes. Underlying the use of profiles is the assumption that certain regularities characterize human behavior and that personality traits or predispositions account for many of these regularities. However, profiling lends itself more readily to highly deviant crimes than to more everyday varieties. "The more bizarre the crime scene," said agent John Douglas, who helped prepare the Bronx murderer's profile, "the easier it is to tell what kind of person did it" (Porter, 1983:45–46).

All this brings us to a consideration of personality, the subject matter of this chapter. Among the issues we will consider are the extent to which behavior is the product of a person's unique and enduring set of psychological tendencies and the extent to which it is the product of the characteristics of the situation in which the person finds himself or herself.

Everyone has a unique and enduring set of psychological tendencies that he or she reveals in the course of daily living (Pervin, 1985; Snyder and Ickes, 1985). The concept of **personality** allows you to account both for the differences among people and for the consistencies in an individual's behavior over time and in different situations.

WHAT PERSONALITY THEORIES TRY TO DO

A *personality theory* is an attempt to explain the observable continuities in a person's behavior despite great complexity and even contradictions in the behavior. While some psychologists confine their studies to more limited problems (such as how the eye works, or why people remember some events better than others), personality theorists deal with a broader problem: Why do people do the things they do? The psychologists and psychiatrists whose insights we will be describing have based their theories on what they have learned from patients whose

---

personality: The relatively unique and enduring set of psychological tendencies that a person reveals in the course of interacting with his or her environment.

Even when people are dressed alike, individual differences among them are obvious—differences not only of appearance but also of personality. *(Dan McCoy, Rainbow)*

psychological difficulties they have helped to ease, from their reading of literature and philosophy, from their research activities, and from their own lives. Directly and indirectly, these theorists have changed the ways people think about themselves.

Psychologists develop personality theories for a number of reasons. First, people differ from one another in many ways. In fact, they differ in so many ways that you can quickly find yourself overwhelmed by their sheer number and detail. So as to order this mass of information—to render it manageable and intelligible—psychologists look for specific *dimensions* along which people vary (Buss and Plomin, 1975). For instance, psychologists find that people differ in their *temperament*—those "raw material" aspects of personality that revolve about a person's pattern of activity, sociability, impulsiveness, and susceptibility to emotional stimulation. Temperament involves behavioral style, or the "how" of behavior, rather than the content or the "what" of behavior (Rothbart, 1981; Hubert et al., 1982). Moreover, many psychologists suggest that

people also differ in their *personality traits*—those relatively enduring ways that people have for dealing with other people in a wide variety of situations (for example, friendliness, generosity, and aggressiveness).

A second purpose of any personality theory is to explain how the observable differences among people come about. In so doing, theorists probe beneath the surface. Suppose a man you know is humble to the point of being self-effacing. When the conversation turns to him, he seems embarrassed. He is much happier bustling about, making people comfortable, and asking about their lives than he is talking about himself. A woman you know is just the opposite. She enjoys nothing better than talking about the work she is doing, the people she has met, her plans for the future. When she asks about your life you suspect it is either because she is being polite or because you might be useful to her.

You explain the different behaviors in terms of motives: the man's primary goal in life is to please other people; the woman is extremely ambitious. But these explanations are little more than descriptions. How did these two people come to have different motives in the first place? What factors are at work in their lives? Different personality theorists stress different factors. Some, such as psychoanalysts, might attempt to gather information on early child-rearing practices associated with breast-feeding and toilet-training that they feel underlie the man's fear of aggressive behavior and the woman's achieving behavior. Others, such as behaviorists, might look to the rewarding and punishing aspects of the environment that reinforce the respective behaviors. And still others, such as cognitive theorists, might focus on how each person comes to perceive, interpret, and think about aggression and achievement. Each theory provides a different level of analysis and insight.

A third goal of personality theory is to explore how people conduct their lives. It serves as a tool by which psychologists can assess the match between a specific individual and his or her environment. Hence a personality theory helps to explain how well people are adapted and how successfully they manage their lives. Personality theorists try to explain why problems arise, and why such problems are more difficult for some people to manage than for others.

Finally, personality theorists are concerned with how life can be improved. It seems obvious that many people are dissatisfied with themselves, their parents, their husbands or wives, their children, their work lives. People resign themselves to unrewarding jobs, and there is a widespread feeling that much is wrong with society and the world. Almost everyone recognizes that people need to grow and change, individually and collectively. But what are the proper goals of growth and change? How can people cope with the inevitable conflicts of life? Hence personality theory is concerned with advancing the frontiers of knowledge so that all people, not simply those who are psychologically troubled, can lead richer and more satisfying lives.

Personality psychologists attempt to pursue these goals with systematic theories about human behavior. These theories are used to guide research; and research, in turn, can test the parts of a theory to see whether the theory is a useful way to think about human behavior. Thus while everyone has pet theories about why people act in certain ways, formal personality theories try to make such ideas more scientific by stating them very precisely and then testing them.

INTERNAL THEORIES

We pointed out earlier in the chapter that personality is a unique and enduring set of psychological tendencies that each person reveals in daily living. Hence personality is not a fixed entity that locks a person for all time within a preprogramed destiny regardless of environment. Instead, it must be understood as a product of the dynamic interplay between internal and external factors (see Chapter 2). Put another way, personality is a learned set of adaptations based on genetic differences in personal tendencies (internal factors) and on experience (external factors).

While most personality theorists recognize the importance of both internal and external factors, some assign greater weight to one set of factors than to the other. Those who stress internal factors look to the part that personal characteristics play in shaping behavior. They see these characteristics as rendering a person's behavior fairly consistent across time and situations. Those who emphasize external factors focus on the particular situation in which behavior is carried out. These psychologists see behavior as varying from setting to setting depending on the specific dictates of the situation. Thus they say that personality has only limited consistency. Let us proceed by examining a number of leading personality theories, organizing our discussion in terms of the distinction between internal and external approaches.

Genetic-Influence Theory

According to much popular wisdom, the reason that people have different personalities is that they are "just born that way." Although a vast oversimplification, the statement contains an element of truth (Scarr et al., 1981; Scarr, 1985c; Buss, 1984). As parents of large families know and developmental psychologists confirm, babies are individualists from the moment they draw breath (Goldsmith and Gottesman, 1981; Hubert et al., 1982). One particularly striking difference is in their reaction to cuddling (Schaffer and Emerson, 1964b). Some babies are "cuddlers," whereas others are "noncuddlers." Parents of a cuddler describe their baby in these

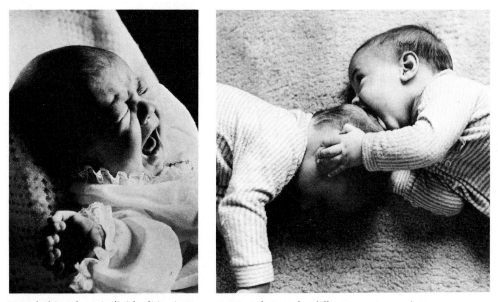

Even babies show individualities in temperament that evoke different responses from others. *(left: Steve McCarroll; right: Elizabeth Crews)*

terms: "He snuggles into you"; "She cuddles you back"; and "He'd let me cuddle him for hours." In contrast, parents of a noncuddler say that they run into difficulty when they hold the baby on their laps or press him or her against their shoulders. They report: "He won't allow it—he fights to get away"; "Try and snuggle him against you and he'll kick and thrash, and if you persist he'll begin to cry"; and "She struggles, squirms, and whimpers when you try to hold her close." However, the noncuddlers enjoy being swung, bounced, and romped with so long as they are not restrained, and they generally like kissing, tickling, and other games that do not restrain them.

In a series of studies of more than two hundred infants, Alexander Thomas and Stella Chess (1977) found that during the first weeks of life babies show a distinct individuality in temperament that is independent of their parents' handling or personalities. About 10 percent of all infants are "difficult babies" —they wail and cry a good deal, spit out new foods, eat and sleep irregularly, and are difficult to pacify. Another 15 percent are "slow-to-warm-up babies" —they have low activity levels, adapt slowly, are wary in new situations, and tend to be somewhat withdrawn. Still another 40 percent are "easy babies"—they have sunny, cheerful dispositions and readily adapt to new foods and people. Finally, the remaining 35 percent display a mixture of traits that do not suggest simple categories.

The characteristics of the infant—cuddliness, intensity of responses, and temperament—elicit different kinds of responses from adults (Yarrow, Waxler, and Scott, 1971; Dion, 1974; Marcus, 1975). Indeed, you do not have to be around babies very long to realize that you experience different feelings toward babies who wail no matter what you do to calm them and babies who promptly and cheerfully respond to your soothing efforts. Tragically, but not surprisingly, difficult and unsoothable babies are overrepresented among abused children (Korner, 1979). In turn, in an interacting spiral, the child's experiences with caretakers shape his or her developing personality (see Chapter 11).

The kind of environment that children experience is related to their temperament in another way. For instance, a very sociable child is likely to get considerably more social interaction than a child who prefers to play alone with toys. The more sociable child searches out opportunities to relate to others, while the less sociable child is overlooked and ignored by others. Consequently, the environment of the sociable child is quite different from the environment of the less sociable child. In brief, the environment does not simply impose itself on the child from outside. The child's own responsiveness evokes in others an environment that encourages or discourages social interaction (Scarr and McCartney, 1983). The same principle holds for adults. Our choice of the settings in which we live our lives reflects features of our personality. For example, we may seek out situations in which it is appropriate to be serious, reserved, and intellectual because we are serious, reserved, and thoughtful people (M. Snyder, 1981; Snyder and Ickes, 1985). And as discussed in the boxed insert on page 425, there are relatively situational individuals (high self-monitors) and relatively dispositional individuals (low self-monitors).

Finally, children do not react in the same ways to the same environmental influences. Whereas domineering, highly authoritarian parental behavior makes one child anxious and submissive, it leads another to engage in rebellious and aggressive behavior (Tower, 1980). In sum, children come into the world with temperamental differences that over time and in interaction with the environment often devel-

op into personality differences (Scarr et al., 1981; Scarr, 1985c).

Psychodynamic Theory

The following classified advertisement appeared in the *New York Times:*

> Charming, spacious, homelike 1 rm apts. Modern kitchenette. Hotel service. Weekly rats available.

The person who set the ad at the *Times* probably did not leave the "e" out of "rates" deliberately. But was it simply an innocent mistake?

Slips like these are common. One usually laughs at them. But sometimes they can be disturbing. You have probably had the experience of making some personal remark that hurt a friend and have later asked yourself, "Why did I say that? I didn't mean it." Yet when you think about it, you may realize that you were angry at your friend and wanted to "get back" at him.

The frequency of physical aggression declines from the preschool to the adolescent years, as most children learn to express anger in socially more acceptable ways. A few older children—both boys and girls—continue to get into trouble with peers and adults by attacking others. *(Frank Siteman/The Picture Cube)*

Self-Monitoring: The Quality of Intimate Relationships

People often choose to enter situations that allow them to express their personalities and choose to avoid situations that interfere with this expression (Snyder and Ickes, 1985). Yet people differ. They vary in the level of self-awareness that they bring to new situations and in the strategies they use to get others to act in accordance with their plans. According to the psychologist Mark Snyder (1979, 1980), some people—those he terms *high self-monitors*—are actors on a social stage. They are more concerned with playing a role than with presenting a true picture of themselves. At parties, job interviews, professional meetings, and chance encounters they are especially sensitive to the ways they express and present themselves. In chameleonlike fashion they swing with ease from bubbly sociability to reserved withdrawal as the situation dictates. In contrast, *low self-monitors* seem to have much less concern for how others view their behavior. They pay less attention to the behavioral cues generated by others, and they monitor and consciously control their behavior to a lesser extent than high self-monitors do. Low self-monitors subscribe to the credo, "To thine own self be true." Their behavior more closely approximates their underlying attitudes, values, and personality traits.

In keeping with their situationally guided focus, high self-monitors seek to maximize the fit between their friends and the kinds of situations in which they interact with them. On the other hand, low self-monitors seek to maximize the fit between their friends and their own personal attributes. These differing social worlds find expression in the choices of friends that high and low self-monitors make for leisure activities (Snyder, Gangestad, and Simpson, 1983). High self-monitors like to have a wide range of friends and to have different friends for different activities. They bowl with Mike and ski with Pete. Moreover, they pick friends who are highly skilled in some area. Hence Mike is likely to be particularly good at bowling and Pete at skiing. In searching the world for friends, they typically ask themselves, "How well-suited is this person for this activity?" and "Does this person have what it takes to do this activity well?" Low self-monitors take a different approach. They like to bowl and ski with the same person. They typically ask themselves, "How much do I like this person?" and "All other things being equal, how much do I want to spend time with this person?"

High self-monitors are also less willing to commit themselves to a romantic relationship, are more willing to end one romance in favor of another, and are slow to become emotional intimates of dating partners. They tend to be particularly concerned with the physical attractiveness of potential partners, perhaps because they are preoccupied with managing the images they project to others. In contrast, low self-monitors are more willing to commit themselves to a romantic relationship, are more faithful lovers, and are more willing to invest themselves emotionally with those they date (Snyder and Simpson, 1984). They tend to be particularly concerned with the personality characteristics of potential dating partners. In fact, when forced to sacrifice one dimension for the other, over 80 percent of low self-monitors prefer to date a partner who has a desirable personality even though the partner may be physically unattractive; almost 70 percent of high self-monitors choose a partner who is physically attractive even though the person possesses an undesirable personality (Snyder, Berscheid, and Glick, 1985).

These patterns reflect the unique orientation of each type of self-monitoring. High self-monitors, in keeping with their situational orientation, look for dating relationships on the basis of the competencies of their prospective partners. Low self-monitors are governed by their relatively stable personality traits, which contribute to longer and stronger commitments. For high self-monitors the satisfaction of a relationship derives primarily from the pleasure of *doing* things with others. For low self-monitors, the satisfaction springs chiefly from the pleasure of simply *being* with their partners.

Sigmund Freud: Psychosexuality and the Unconscious

It was Sigmund Freud (1856–1939) who first suggested that the little slips that people make, the things they mishear, and the odd misunderstandings they have are not really mistakes at all. Freud believed there was something behind these mistakes, even though people claimed they were just accidental and quickly corrected themselves. Similarly, when he listened to people describe their dreams, he believed the dreams had some meaning, even though the people who dreamed them did not know what they meant. (But see the discussion of dreams in Chapter 3.)

Freud was a physician who practiced in Vienna in the early 1900s. Since he specialized in nervous diseases, a great many people talked to him about their private lives, their conflicts, fears, and desires. In the course of working with his patients, he concluded that some of the most powerful influences on human personality are things people are *not* conscious of.

Freud was the first to suggest that every personality has a large **unconscious** component. Life includes both pleasurable and painful experiences. Freud maintained that experiences include feelings and thoughts as well as actual events. He believed that many experiences, particularly the painful episodes of childhood, are forgotten or buried in the unconscious. But although a person may not consciously recall these experiences, they continue to influence behavior. For example, children who never fully please a demanding parent may feel unhappy much of the time and will doubt their abilities to succeed and to be loved. As adults, they may suffer from feelings of unworthiness and low self-esteem, despite their very real abilities. Freud believed that unconscious motives and the feelings people experience as children have an enormous impact on adult personality and behavior (see the discussions of human development in Chapters 11 and 12).

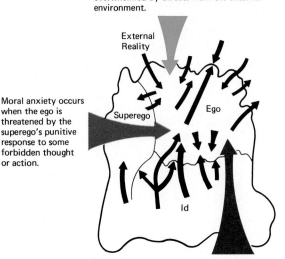

Reality anxiety occurs when the ego feels overwhelmed by threats from the external environment.

Moral anxiety occurs when the ego is threatened by the superego's punitive response to some forbidden thought or action.

Neurotic anxiety occurs when the id threatens to overwhelm ego constraints, leading to unacceptable or impulsive behavior.

FIGURE 13.1 A visual interpretation of the Freudian theory of personality structure. The ego tries to balance the id's desires against the superego's demands and the realities of the world. In doing this it sometimes suppresses the irrational tendencies of the id, but it may also be able to deflect the id's energy into channels acceptable to both the superego and the outside world.

The Id, Ego, and Superego

By 1923, Freud had formulated his view of the structural components of the mind: id, ego, and superego (see Figure 13.1). Although Freud often spoke of them as if they were actual parts of the personality, he introduced and regarded them simply as a *model* of how the mind works. In other words, the id, ego, and superego do not refer to actual portions of the brain. Instead, they explain how the mind functions and how the instinctual energies are regulated.

In Freud's theory, the **id** is the reservoir or container of the instinctual urges. It is the lustful or

---

unconscious: According to Sigmund Freud, the part of the mind that contains material that a person is unaware of but that strongly influences his or her conscious processes and behaviors.

id: According to Sigmund Freud, that part of the unconscious personality that contains needs, drives, and instincts as well as repressed material. The id strives for immediate gratification of desires.

drive-ridden part of the unconscious. The id seeks immediate gratification of desires, regardless of the consequences of the actions that are undertaken.

The personality process that is mostly conscious is called the **ego.** The ego is the rational, thoughtful, realistic personality process. For example, if people are hungry, the id might drive them to seek immediate satisfaction by dreaming of food or by eating all the available food at once instead of keeping some of it for a later time. The ego would recognize that the body needs real food and that it will continue to need food in the future. It would use the id's energy to preserve some of the food available now and to look for ways of finding more.

Suppose you thought of stealing the desired food from someone else. The part of the personality that would suggest you should not steal is called the **superego.** The id is concerned with what people *want* to do and the ego is concerned with planning what they *can* do; the superego is concerned with what they *should* do. It is the moral part of the personality, the source of conscience and of high ideals. But the superego can also create conflicts and problems. It is sometimes overly harsh, like a very strict parent. The superego, then, is also the source of guilt feelings that come from serious as well as mild deviations from what it defines as "right."

The id and the superego frequently come into conflict with each other. Because neither is concerned with reality, they may both come into conflict with the outside world as well. Freud saw the ego as part of the person that must resolve these conflicts. Somehow, the ego must find a realistic way to satisfy the demands of the id without offending the superego. If the id is not satisfied, the person feels an intolerable tension of longing or anger or desire. If the superego is not obeyed, the person feels guilty and inferior. And if outside reality is ignored, the person suffers such outcomes as starvation or dislike by other people (Freud, 1943).

Defense Mechanisms

According to Freud, the ego's job is so difficult that unconsciously all people resort to psychological defenses. Rather than face intense frustration, conflict, or feelings of unworthiness, people deceive themselves into believing nothing is wrong. If the demands of the id and the ego cannot be resolved, it may be necessary to distort reality. Freud called these techniques **defense mechanisms** because they defend the ego from experiencing anxiety about failing in its tasks. Freud felt that these defense mechanisms stem mainly from the unconscious part of the ego, and ordinarily become conscious to a person only during psychotherapy.

To some degree, defense mechanisms are necessary to psychological well-being. They relieve intolerable confusion, help us weather intense emotional crises, and give us additional time to work out our problems. However, if we resort to defense mechanisms all or most of the time, continually deceiving ourselves and others about our true feelings and aspirations, we will avoid facing and solving our problems realistically. A few of the defense mechanisms identified by Freud and elaborated by his daughter, Anna (Freud, 1946), are discussed next.

Repression. When people have some thought or urge that causes the ego too much anxiety, they may push that thought or urge out of consciousness down into the unconscious. This process is called **repression.** Individuals seemingly "forget" the thing that disturbs them, forcing it out of awareness without even realizing it. For example, an adult woman whose father is meddling in her life may have the

---

ego: According to Sigmund Freud, the part of the personality that is in touch with reality. The ego strives to meet the often conflicting demands of the id and the superego in socially acceptable ways.

superego: According to Sigmund Freud, the part of the personality that inhibits the socially undesirable impulses of the id. The superego may cause excessive guilt if it is overly harsh.

defense mechanism: According to Sigmund Freud, a certain specific means by which the ego unconsciously protects itself against unpleasant impulses or circumstances.

repression: The exclusion from conscious awareness of a painful, unpleasant, or undesirable memory.

impulse to say, "I hate you, Dad." But the woman may feel so anxious and afraid about having such an impulse that she will come to believe—without realizing what she is doing—that what she feels is not hatred. She replaces the feeling with apathy, a feeling of not caring at all. Essentially she says to herself, "I don't hate you at all, Dad. I have no special feelings about you." Nevertheless, her anger and hostility remain on an unconscious level. She may reveal these negative feelings by making cutting remarks or sarcastic jokes about her father, through slips of the tongue, or by hostile dreams involving her father.

Projection. Another way the ego avoids anxiety is by believing that impulses coming from within are really coming from other people. For example, angry children who have learned that rage is socially unacceptable may attribute their own aggressive tendencies to their playmates: "They're always picking on me and starting fights." Or the extremely jealous husband who does not wish to admit to himself that he is threatened by his wife's independence may claim, "I'm not jealous—she's the one who is always keeping track of where I've been and what I'm doing." This mechanism is called **projection** because inner feelings are thrown, or projected, outside oneself. Hence in projection, people attribute to others motives or traits that they sense within themselves but that would be too painful to acknowledge.

Displacement. **Displacement** occurs when the object of an unconscious wish provokes anxiety. This anxiety is reduced when the ego unconsciously shifts the wish to another object. The energy of the id is displaced from one object to another, more accessible, object. For example, your professor may make you exceedingly angry and you would like to "tell him off." But it is too threatening or dangerous to do so (he might retaliate by giving you a low grade). When you return home a relative or roommate makes some trivial remark about your hair and you explode with an angry diatribe. More than one relative or roommate has complained to a frustrated person after receiving an unwarranted attack, "Don't take it out on me!"

Reaction formation. **Reaction formation** involves replacing an unacceptable feeling or urge with its opposite. For example, a divorced father may resent having his child for the weekend. Unconsciously, he feels it is terribly wrong for a father to react that way, so he showers the child with expressions of love, toys, and exciting trips. Or a fifth-grade boy may have a "crush" on one of his classmates. But as yet he feels uncomfortable about liking girls. So instead he unconsciously finds opportunities to tease and squabble with the girl, thus covering his true feelings.

Regression. **Regression** means going back to an earlier and less mature pattern of behavior. When people are under severe pressure and their other defenses are not working, they may start acting in ways that helped them in the past. An illustration is the severely stressed adult who regresses to eating three hot fudge sundaes at a sitting, just as she did in early adolescence.

Rationalization. People often find a convincing reason for doing something that they would otherwise deem to be unacceptable. This process is termed **rationalization**. Indeed, people are quite ingenious in coming up with excuses for their behavior. Take a college student who would like to break off with his girlfriend but feels guilty about it because they have gone together now four years. He

---

projection: The attribution to others of motives or traits that one senses within oneself but that would be too painful to acknowledge.

displacement: The redirection of desires, feelings, or impulses from their proper object to a substitute.

reaction formation: The replacement of an unacceptable feeling or urge with its opposite.

regression: A return to an earlier stage of development or pattern of behavior in a threatening or stressful situation.

rationalization: The process by which individuals find a convincing reason for doing something that would otherwise be viewed as unacceptable.

can go ahead and make the break, however, if he can justify his behavior: "She'd be better off if she got a little more experience dating other guys."

Evaluating Freud's Contributions

Freud offered the first major theory of personality. But his ideas were controversial when they were proposed at the turn of the century, and they are controversial today. Some psychologists treat Freud's writings as a sacred text—if Freud said it, it must be so. At the other extreme, many have accused Freud of being unscientific. He made few predictions that can be tested by accepted scientific methods. Unconscious motivation is, by definition, not in the conscious mind. Hence scientists have few ways to study the process objectively. (Hypnotism is one; see Chapter 3.)

In recent years, interest in the many child-rearing factors that Freud deemed critical has gradually waned (Kagan, 1979) because most psychologists see personality as developing *across* the life span (see Chapter 12). The historic significance of Freud's work is his recognition that human behavior is the outcome of psychological conflicts, many of which are not conscious. Revealing the difficulty of controlling and handling conflicting forces was Freud's great contribution to understanding life.

Freud also highlighted the part that childhood experience plays in shaping a person's personality (see Chapter 11). And we are indebted to Freud for identifying and defining the various psychological defense mechanisms that have just been discussed. Finally, he opened up the scientific study of sexuality—a highly taboo topic at the turn of the century.

Freud's psychoanalytic theory continues to intrigue many psychologists and to stimulate psychological research (Silverman, 1982; Masling, 1983; Erdelyi, 1985). Seymour Fisher and Roger Greenberg (1977:396) put it well in their assessment of more than fifty years of research on Freud's ideas: "But like all theorists, he has proved in the long run to have far from a perfect score. He seems to have been right about a respectable number of issues, but he was also wrong about some important things."

Carl G. Jung. One of the most mystical and metaphysical of the pioneer theorists, Jung has had, until recently, a wider acceptance in Europe than in America. *(The Granger Collection)*

In Freud's Footsteps: Jung and Adler

Freud's revolutionary ideas attracted many followers, and a number of these psychoanalysts came to develop important theories of their own. One of these was Carl Jung (1875–1961), who for a time was Freud's closest associate. But when Freud and Jung started to argue about psychoanalytic theory, their personal relationship became strained. Finally, they stopped speaking to each other entirely, a mere seven years after they met.

Jung (1963) disagreed with Freud on two major points. First, he took a more positive view of human nature, believing that people try to develop their potential as well as to handle their instinctual urges. Second, he distinguished between the personal unconscious (which was similar to Freud's idea of the unconscious) and the **collective unconscious,** which is a storehouse of memory traces inherited through the course of human evolutionary development. He

---

collective unconscious: According to Carl Jung, that part of the mind that contains the inherited instincts, urges, and memories common to all people.

called these deep-rooted, universal ideas **archetypes.** Jung said that the same archetypes are present in every person. They reflect the common experiences of humanity over many generations in coping with nature, war, parenthood, love, and evil.

Jung undertook to identify the archetypes by studying dreams, paintings, poetry, folk stories, myths, and religions. He found that the same themes appear again and again. For example, the story of Jack and the Beanstalk is essentially the same as the story of David and Goliath. Both tell how a small, weak, good person triumphs over a big, strong, bad person. Jung believed such stories are common and easy to understand because the situations they describe have occurred over and over again in human history. As such, they have been built into the unconscious of every human being and are embodied in the tales of every culture.

Like Jung, Alfred Adler (1870–1937) was an associate of Freud's who left his teacher in the early part of this century to develop his own approach to personality. Adler (1959) developed his psychology along social lines, emphasizing the influence on personality of an individual's interpersonal relationships. Whereas Freud viewed behavior as driven by instinctual forces residing in the id, Adler looked to the role of social forces in the fashioning of behavior. And whereas Freud stressed the unconscious determinants of behavior, Adler insisted that humans are first and foremost conscious beings who can identify their motivations and strive toward future goals. This latter notion of the creative self led Adler to the view that human beings enjoy the capacity to choose among alternatives and to shape their own destinies.

Adler believed that people strive toward one overriding goal—self-acceptance. Self-acceptance finds expression in the pursuit of personal development, accomplishment, and self-realization. Phrased somewhat differently, Adler thought that the desire to overcome inferiority is the prime determining force in behavior. Classic examples include Demos-

Alfred Adler. Adler's writings on psychotherapy offer more optimism and practicality than those of Freud or Jung. His intuitive and commonsense approach to human life has greatly affected the thinking of psychologists throughout this century. *(The Granger Collection)*

thenes, who overcame a speech impediment by practicing speaking with pebbles in his mouth and became the greatest orator of ancient Greece; Napoleon, a short man who conquered Europe in the early 1800s; and Glenn Cunningham, an Olympic runner who had lost his toes in a fire as a child and had to plead with doctors who wanted to amputate his legs because they thought he would never be able to use them again.

Everyone struggles with inferiority, said Adler. He described a person who continually tries to cover up and avoid feelings of inadequacy as having an **inferiority complex** (a term he introduced). Children first feel inferior because they are so little and so dependent on adults. But gradually they learn to do the things that older people can do.

---

archetype (ARK-uh-type): According to Carl Jung, an inherited idea, based on the experiences of one's ancestors, that shapes one's perception of the world.
inferiority complex: According to Alfred Adler, a pattern of avoiding feelings of inadequacy and insignificance, rather than trying to overcome their source.

Adler believed that the way parents treat their children has a great influence on the styles of life the children choose. Overpampering, in which the parents attempt to satisfy the child's every whim, tends to produce a self-centered person who has little regard for others and who expects everyone else to do what he or she wants. On the other hand, the child who is neglected by his or her parents may seek revenge by becoming an angry, hostile person. Both the pampered and the neglected child tend to grow up into adults who lack confidence in their ability to meet the demands of life. Ideally, said Adler, a child should learn self-reliance and courage from the father and generosity and a feeling for others from the mother (Adler, 1959)—a sexist view that now should be taken to mean that children should learn these virtues from their parents!

Although Jung and Adler were the first major figures to break with Freud, many others followed. Erich Fromm's (1947) theory centered on the need to belong and the loneliness freedom brings. Karen Horney (1945) stressed the importance of basic anxiety, which children feel because they are helpless, and basic hostility, a resentment of their parents that generally accompanies this anxiety. She also attacked several basic beliefs of Freud's, including his emphasis on the importance of penis envy in the development of women. Erik Erikson accepted Freud's basic theory, but he expanded it to emphasize adaptation and change across eight psychosocial stages that constitute the life span (described in Chapters 11 and 12). Harry Stack Sullivan (1953) insisted that personality develops out of interpersonal experience. These and other neo-Freudians have helped to keep psychoanalytic theory alive and growing.

Humanistic Theory

One might look at **humanistic psychology** as a rebellion against the rather negative, pessimistic view of human nature that dominated psychoanalytic theory in the first part of this century. As we have

indicated, Freudians emphasized the struggle to control primitive, instinctual urges on the one hand, and to come to terms with the authoritarian demands of the superego or conscience on the other. Similarly, the behaviorists (to be discussed later in the chapter) saw human behavior as shaped entirely by rewards and punishments. Humanistic psychologists object to both approaches, on grounds that they demean human beings. They criticize psychoanalytic theorists for depicting people as locked by irrational and destructive instincts within a lifetime programed by childhood events. And they fault behavioral theorists for portraying people as little more than "robots" who are mechanically programed by the conditioning force of external stimuli. In contrast, the humanists stress people's ability to fashion their own lives, to choose among alternatives, and to develop positive values for group living. Thus humanistic psychology provides an optimistic vision of human potential.

Humanistic psychology is founded on the belief that all human beings strive for **self-actualization** —the realization of one's potential as a unique human being. Self-actualization involves an openness to a wide range of experiences; an awareness of and respect for one's own and other people's intrinsic worth; an acceptance of one's responsibility for freedom and commitment; a desire to become more and more authentic and true to oneself; and an ability to grow. It requires the courage, in Kipling's words, "to trust yourself when all men doubt you." Humanists view this striving as a basic human force and the essence of human dignity.

Abraham Maslow: Growth and Self-Actualization

Abraham Maslow (1908–1970) was one of the guiding spirits of the humanistic movement in psychology. He deliberately set out to create what he called "a third force in psychology" as an alternative to psychoanalysis and behaviorism. Maslow (1968, 1970) tried to base his theory of personality on studies of

---

humanistic psychology: An approach to psychology that stresses the uniqueness of the individual; focuses on the value, dignity, and worth of each person; and holds that healthy living is the result of realizing one's full potential.

self-actualization: The humanistic term for realizing one's unique potential.

(left) Abraham Maslow. Maslow's work, as well as that of Carl Rogers and Alfred Adler, helped create a humanistic orientation toward the study of behavior by emphasizing growth and the realization of an individual's potential. (The Granger Collection) (right) Carl Rogers. Rogers's theories have had a considerable impact on modern psychology and on society in general. He has emphasized personal experience rather than drives and instincts. (John Oldenkamp)

healthy, creative, self-actualizing people who fully utilize their talents and potential, rather than on studies of disturbed individuals. He criticized other psychologists for their pessimistic, negative, and limited conceptions of human beings. Where is the psychology, he asked, that deals with gaiety, exuberance, love, and expressive art to the same extent that it deals with misery, conflict, shame, and hostility?

When Maslow decided to study the most productive people he could find—in history as well as in his social and professional circles—he was breaking new ground. The psychodynamic theories of personality we discussed earlier in this chapter were developed by therapists after years of working with people who could not cope with everyday frustrations and conflicts. In contrast, Maslow was curious about people who not only coped with everyday problems effectively but also created exceptional lives for themselves—such people as Abraham Lincoln, Albert Einstein, and Eleanor Roosevelt.

Maslow found that although these people sometimes had great emotional difficulties, they adjusted to their problems in ways that allowed them to become highly productive. Maslow also found that such self-actualized people share a number of traits. First, they *perceive reality accurately*—unlike most people, who, because of prejudices and defenses, perceive it inaccurately. Self-actualized people also *accept themselves*, other people, and their environments more readily than "average" people do. Without realizing it, most people project their hopes and fears onto the world around them. Often they become upset with people whose attitudes differ radically from their own. They also spend a good deal of time denying their own shortcomings and trying to rationalize things they do not like about themselves.

On the other hand, self-actualizing people come to terms with themselves and accept themselves as they are.

Secure in themselves, healthy people are more *problem-centered* than self-centered. They are able to focus on tasks in a way that people concerned about maintaining and protecting their self-image cannot. They are more likely to base decisions on ethical principles than on calculations of the possible costs or benefits to themselves. They have a strong sense of *identity with other human beings*—not just members of their family, ethnic group, or country, but all humankind. They have a strong *sense of humor*, but they laugh with people, not at them.

Maslow also found that self-actualizing people are exceptionally *spontaneous*. They are not trying to be anything other than themselves. And they know themselves well enough to maintain their integrity in the face of opposition, unpopularity, and rejection. In a word, they are *autonomous*. They *value privacy* and frequently seek out solitude. That is not to say that they are detached or aloof. But rather than trying to be popular, they focus on deep, *loving relationships with the few people* to whom they are truly close.

Finally, the people Maslow studied had a rare ability to appreciate even the simplest things. They approached their lives with a *sense of discovery* that made each day a new day. They rarely felt bored or uninterested. Given to moments of intense joy and satisfaction, or "peak experiences," they got high on life itself. Maslow believed this to be both a cause and an effect of their creativity and originality (Maslow, 1970).

As indicated in Chapter 4, Maslow believed that to become self-actualizing a person must first satisfy

Feeling good about oneself is an essential characteristic of the self-actualized person. *(Owen Franken/Stock, Boston)*

admiration for certain people and because he assumed before even undertaking his research that they were in fact self-actualized people. He showed, however, how successfully some people can live out their lives, which was a valuable counterweight to the pessimism of psychoanalysis and behaviorism.

Maslow's influence has been great. He has inspired many researchers to pay more attention to healthy, productive people and has led many group leaders and clinicians to seek ways to promote the growth and self-actualization of workers, students, and clients in therapy.

Carl Rogers: Your Organism and Yourself

The people Carl Rogers (born 1902) counsels are "clients," not "patients." The word "patient" implies illness, a negative label that Rogers rejects. As a therapist, Rogers is primarily concerned with the roadblocks and detours on the path to self-actualization (or "full functioning," as he calls it). He believes that many people suffer from a conflict between what they value in themselves and what they learn other people value in them.

Rogers explains how this conflict develops as follows: there are two sides or aspects to every person. One is the **organism,** which is the whole person, including his or her body. Rogers believes that the organism is constantly struggling to become more and more complete and perfect. Anything that furthers this end is good: the organism wants to become everything it can possibly be. For example, children want to learn to walk and run because their bodies are built for these activities. People want to shout and dance and sing because their organisms contain the potential for these behaviors. Different people have different potentialities, but every person wants to realize them, to make them real, whatever they are. It is of no value to be able to paint and not to do it. It is of no value to be able to make witty jokes and not to do so. Whatever you can do, you want to do—and to do as well as possible. (This optimism about human nature is the essence of humanistic psychology.)

his or her basic, primary needs—for food and shelter, physical safety, love and belonging, and self-esteem. Of course, to some extent the ability to satisfy these needs depends on factors beyond the person's control. Still, no amount of wealth, talent, beauty, or any other asset can totally shield someone from frustration and disappointment. The affluent as well as the poor, the brilliant as well as the slow, have to adjust to maintain themselves and to grow.

Maslow's work has not gone without criticism. His claim that human nature is "good" has been called an intrusion of subjective values into what should be a neutral science. Of course, scientists' assumptions are always present in their theories and in their research, so that in this respect Maslow is no different from other scientists. His study of self-actualizing people has been criticized because the sample was chosen on the basis of his personal

---

organism: Carl Rogers's term for the whole person, including all of his or her feelings, thoughts, and urges as well as body.

The other aspect of each individual is what Rogers calls the **self.** The self is essentially your image of who you are and what you value—in yourself, in other people, in life in general. The self is something you acquire gradually over the years by observing how other people react to you. At first, the most significant other person in your life is your mother (or whoever raises you). You want her approval, or **positive regard.** You ask yourself, "How does she see me?" If the answer is, "She loves me. She likes what I am and what I do," you begin to develop positive regard for yourself.

But often this does not happen. The image you see reflected in your mother's eyes and actions is mixed. Whether or not she approves of you often depends on whether or not you spit up your baby food or do your homework on time. In other words, she places conditions on her love: *if* you do what she wants, she likes you. Young and impressionable, you accept these verdicts and incorporate **conditions of worth** into yourself. "When I use obscene language at the dinner table, I am bad." You begin to see yourself as good and worthy only if you act in certain ways. You have learned from your parents and from other people who are significant to you that unless you meet certain conditions you will not be loved.

Rogers's work as a therapist convinced him that people cope with conditions of worth by rejecting or denying parts of themselves that do not fit their self-concept. For example, if your mother grew cold and distant whenever you became angry, you learned to deny yourself the right to express or perhaps even feel anger. Being angry "isn't you." In effect, you are cutting off a part of yourself; you are allowing yourself to experience and express only part of your being.

In Rogers's theory, the greater the gap between the self and the organism, the more limited and defensive a person becomes. Rogers believes the cure for this situation is **unconditional positive regard.** If significant others (parents, friends, a mate, perhaps a therapist) convey the feeling that they value you for what you are, in your entirety, you will gradually learn to grant yourself the same unconditional positive regard. The need to limit yourself declines. You will be able to accept your organism and become open to *all* your feelings, thoughts, and experiences—and hence to other people. This is what Rogers means by **fully functioning.** The organism and the self are one: the individual is free to develop all his or her potentialities. Like Maslow and other humanistic psychologists, Rogers (1951, 1961) believes that self-regard and regard for others go together and that the human potentials for good and for self-fulfillment outweigh the potentials for evil and despair.

Rogers's theory has been criticized for not recognizing the importance of *contingencies*—rewards that depend on how the person acts. For instance, behaviorists say it is unrealistic and even harmful for people to be loved unconditionally and without regard for how they act toward other people.

Trait Theory

Everyday experience seems to tell us that people have fairly stable personalities. Betsy spends many hours talking to other people, circulates freely at parties, and strikes up conversations while she waits in the dentist's office. Dan, though, spends more time with books than with other people and seldom goes to parties. In commonsense terms, one says that Betsy is friendly and Dan is not. Friendliness is a

---

self: Carl Rogers's term for one's experience or image of oneself, developed through interaction with others.

positive regard: Carl Rogers's term for viewing others or oneself in a positive light; in the case of oneself, the result of positive feedback.

conditions of worth: Carl Rogers's term for the conditions a person must meet in order to regard himself or herself positively.

unconditional positive regard: Carl Rogers's term for complete emotional support and complete acceptance of one person by another.

fully functioning person: Carl Rogers's term for an individual whose organism and self coincide, allowing him or her to be open to experience, to possess unconditional positive regard, and to have harmonious relations with others.

personality trait, and some theorists have argued that studying such traits in detail is the best approach to solving the puzzle of human behavior.

Psychologist J. P. Guilford (1959a) has defined a trait as "any relatively enduring way in which one individual differs fron another." A **trait,** then, is a predisposition to respond in a certain way in many different kinds of situations—in a dentist's office, at a party, or in a classroom. More than other personality theorists, trait theorists emphasize and attempt to explain the consistency of an individual's behavior across different situations. And they search for predictability or coherence in what appear to be different behaviors (Loevinger and Knoll, 1983).

Assumptions of Trait Theorists

Trait theorists generally make two basic assumptions about these underlying sources of consistency: every trait applies to all people (for example, everyone can be classified as more or less independent), and these descriptions can be quantified (for example, we might establish a scale on which an extremely dependent person scores 1 while a very independent person scores 10).

Thus every person can be classified in terms of each trait. Aggressiveness, for example, may be viewed as a continuum: a few people are extremely aggressive or extremely unaggressive and most people fall somewhere in the middle. You can understand people by specifying their traits, and you can use traits to predict people's future behavior. If you were hiring someone to sell vacuum cleaners, you would probably choose Betsy over Dan. This choice would be based on two assumptions: friendliness is a useful trait for salespeople, and a person who is friendly in the dentist's office and at parties will be friendly in another situation—namely, in the salesroom.

Trait theorists go beyond this kind of common-sense analysis and try to discover the underlying sources of the consistency of human behavior. What is the best way to describe the common features of Betsy's behavior—as friendly, extroverted, socially aggressive, interested in people, self-confident, or

something else? What are the underlying *traits* that best explain her behavior?

Most (but not all) trait theorists believe that each person is characterized by a few basic, or core, traits. For example, an underlying trait of high self-confidence might be used to explain more superficial characteristics such as social aggressiveness, or low self-confidence might be used to explain dependence. If this were true, it would mean that people are aggressive because they possess self-confidence or dependent because they lack self-confidence. Psychologists who accept this approach set out on their theoretical search for basic traits with very few hard-and-fast assumptions regarding the nature of personality.

This approach is very different from the starting point of other personality theorists we have considered. Freud, for example, began with a well-defined theory of instincts. When he observed that some people were stingy, he set out to explain this behavior in terms of his theory of psychosexual development. Trait theorists do not start by trying to understand the childhood origins of stinginess. Rather, they try to determine whether or not stinginess is a trait. In brief, they try to find out whether people who are stingy in one type of situation are also stingy in others. Then they may ask whether stinginess is a sign of a more basic trait such as possessiveness: Is the stingy person also very possessive in relationships? Thus the first and foremost question for the trait theorist is: What behaviors go together?

Instead of theories telling them *where* to look, trait theorists have complex and sophisticated methods that tell them *how* to look. These methods begin with the statistical technique of correlation (discussed in Chapter 1), in which researchers use one set of scores to predict another. For example, if I know that someone talks to strangers in line at the supermarket, can I predict that the person will be likely to strike up conversations in a singles bar? Such predictions are never perfect. Perhaps the reason Betsy is so talkative in the dentist's office is that she is terrified, and she jabbers to keep her mind off the impending drill.

When traits are used to explain behavior, care must be taken to avoid circular reasoning. Why does

---

trait: A predisposition to respond in a certain way to different kinds of situations.

Marie get so little done? Because she is lazy. How do you know she is lazy? Because she gets so little done. This kind of circularity can be avoided, at least in part, by investigating whether the trait also predicts other kinds of behavior that form a consistent pattern.

Individual Differences in Consistency

For the most part, trait theorists have assumed that people differ from one another only in the *amount* of a trait that they possess (for instance, how much aggressiveness, independence, or friendliness they typically exhibit). However, over the course of the past decade, a number of researchers have challenged this assumption (Mischel, 1973; Underwood and Moore, 1981). They say that although people are consistent on some traits, they are not necessarily consistent on other traits. Psychologists Daryl Bem and Andrea Allen (1974) tested this idea. They asked college students if they were consistently or only occasionally friendly. Bem and Allen then observed how often the students spoke in small groups and how quickly they started up a conversation with strangers. They found that students who deemed themselves consistently friendly were more likely to be friendly in both situations than were those students who said they were only intermittently friendly. Moreover, when the students' parents and friends were asked to rate their friendliness, the evaluations were quite similar to the students' self-ratings and predicted accurately how they would act in the two situations. This evidence suggests that we can judge ourselves with considerable accuracy and that others tend to confirm our self-assessments.

Most of us implicitly recognize that people vary in their consistency on different traits. When you are asked to characterize a friend, you do not list an inventory of fixed dimensions that you use for all people. Rather, you select a small set of traits that strike you as particularly pertinent and discard as irrelevant the other ten thousand or so potential properties. Moreover, you typically pick those characteristics of the person that impress you as being salient because they are consistent across situations as well as because they are distinctive for this person—which usually means that the person is especially high or low on those traits compared to other people. It seems that when you develop a close relationship with a person, you evolve a stable idea of what he or she is like in general. Consequently, you can predict rather accurately how the person is likely to react in particular situations. In sum, although we hesitate to characterize people along every personality dimension, we usually can identify those traits that serve as their trademarks (Peele, 1984b).

People very often give the appearance of being inconsistent when they are observed by others across situations. But if their behavior is examined from their own perspective, consistency rather than inconsistency is at work. For instance, researchers find that most children will "lie," "cheat," and "steal" in some situations and not in others (Hartshorne and May, 1928). Traditionally, trait theorists would place a child along the honesty-dishonesty scale depending on the frequency with which he or she engaged in these behaviors.

Yet it is questionable whether children can be assessed as being honest or dishonest if they have different frames of reference for their behavior. For instance, one child may "lie" to avoid hurting the feelings of a teacher, while another may "steal" money in order to purchase social acceptance from classmates. The first child may also be the most likely to compliment the teacher on a new dress, use good manners with friends' parents, and be considered the "perfect little lady" by adults. The second may be far more concerned with the opinions of peers at school, in clubs, and in the neighborhood. Hence, if the behavior of the first child is assessed in terms of "concern for adults" and the other in terms of "concern for peers," considerable consistency may be observed in each child's behavior across many situations. However, when appraised in terms of "honesty," each child may be judged "inconsistent." In brief, people will be consistent to the extent that situations are similar to their most important frames of reference (Bem, 1983; Funder, 1983).

Gordon W. Allport: Identifying Traits

The psychologist Gordon W. Allport (1937, 1961) contributed a good deal to the understanding of traits. He pointed out that your ability to discern "traits" in other people and in yourself helps in finding your way about daily life. Traits allow you to assume that there is some measure of patterning and stability to behavior. As a result, you can undertake joint action with others on the assumption that there will be continuity in your relationships across time.

Belonging to some groups, like the Boy Scouts, encourages socially desirable behaviors. *(Gabor Demjen/Stock, Boston)*

Thus Allport asserted that a trait makes a wide variety of situations "functionally equivalent." In sum, it enables a person to realize that many different situations call for a similar response.

Allport provided a number of classification schemes for distinguishing among kinds of traits. For example, he was concerned with emphasizing the differences between two major ways of studying personality. In the *nomothetic* approach, researchers study large groups of people in the search for general laws of personality. This focus can be contrasted with the *idiographic* approach, in which the researcher studies a particular person in detail, emphasizing his or her uniqueness. On the basis of this distinction, Allport defined *common traits* as those characteristics that apply to everyone, and *individual traits* as those characteristics that apply more to a specific person.

An example of the latter is found in Allport's book *Letters from Jenny* (1965), which consists of 172 letters a woman whom Allport calls Jenny Masterson wrote to a friend. Jenny reveals herself in these letters (which she wrote between the ages of fifty-eight and seventy) as a complex and fiercely independent woman. In his preface to the book, Allport writes:

> To me the principal fascination of the Letters lies in their challenge to the reader (whether psychologist or layman) to "explain" Jenny—if he can. Why does an intelligent lady behave so persistently in a self-defeating manner?

Allport's own attempt to understand Jenny Masterson began with a search for the underlying traits that would explain the consistency of her behavior. He asked thirty-nine psychologists to read Jenny's letters and list her most important traits. They came up with a total of 198 words, which Allport broke down into eight basic categories, including "independent-autonomous," "self-centered," and "sentimental." Allport then compared these labels with the results of a more quantitative technique (in which a computer analyzed how often Jenny used certain words in her letters) and found that the two procedures led to similar conclusions. Jenny's outstanding traits made her a unique personality on the basis of the enduring consistencies in her approach to life.

Raymond B. Cattell: Factor Analysis

More recent theorists have concentrated on what Allport called common traits, and they have further tried to quantify them in a precise, scientific manner. Their primary tool in this task has been an extremely sophisticated mathematical technique called **factor analysis** (Sells and Murphy, 1984). Basically, factor analysis is a high-powered way of looking for underlying sources of consistency. Researchers might note, for example, that people's test scores in math predict their chemistry grades (although not perfectly, of course), that chemistry grades predict history

---

factor analysis: A complex statistical technique used to identify the underlying reasons that variables are correlated.

grades less well, and that scores in English predict scores in French. If they used factor analysis to study all these scores, they might find two underlying factors to explain their results: mathematical skills and verbal skills. These factors explain why chemistry grades predict performance in physics better than they predict performance in political science.

Raymond B. Cattell (1965, 1983) has used factor analysis extensively to study personality traits. Cattell defines a trait as a tendency to react to related situations in a way that remains more or less stable over time. He distinguishes between two kinds of tendencies: surface traits and source traits. *Surface traits* are clusters of behavior that tend to go together. An example of a surface trait is altruism, which involves a variety of related behaviors such as helping a neighbor who has a problem or contributing to an annual blood drive. Other examples of surface traits are integrity, curiosity, realism, and foolishness. *Source traits* are the underlying roots or causes of these behavioral clusters—for example, ego strength, dominance, and submissiveness. Cattell believes that discovering and learning to measure surface and source traits will enable us to identify those characteristics that all humans share and those that distinguish one person from another and make him or her an individual.

EXTERNAL THEORIES

The personality theories that we have considered thus far have focused on factors that are primarily "within" people. They are concerned with what people bring with them, as functioning organisms, to environmental settings. In other words, they take as their starting point the tendencies or predispositions that people already have to respond in certain ways.

We now turn our attention to another group of theories—those that emphasize the part that external factors play in calling forth or drawing out given behaviors. They explain how people's behavior is shaped and fashioned in the context of different environmental settings. Thus these personality the-

B. F. Skinner. Skinner's pioneering work in behavioral psychology has resulted in a number of new therapeutic techniques that have been markedly successful in treating certain kinds of problems. *(Ted Polumbaum)*

ories view people as thinking, feeling, and acting in ways that are fundamentally influenced by their experiences in the world. For example, when viewed in this manner, heroism is primarily the product of the situation in which a person is momentarily immersed (see the boxed insert on page 439).

Classic Behaviorism

Although his classic **behaviorism** was not proposed as a theory of personality, B. F. Skinner (born 1904) has had a major impact on personality theory. Skinner sees no need for a general concept of personality structure. He focuses instead on precisely what is causing a person to act in a specific way. More particularly, Skinner contends that the causes of behavior reside outside the organism. It is a very pragmatic approach, one that is less concerned with

---

behaviorism: The school of psychology that holds that the proper subject matter of psychology is objectively observable behavior—and nothing else.

Heroism: Extraordinary Individuals or Hero-Producing Situations?

Are heroes extraordinarily brave people, or does the situation make heroes of ordinary individuals? Reuven Gal (1985), at one time chief psychologist for the Israeli Defense Forces, looked into this matter. Israeli soldiers and officers often receive personality evaluations when they are inducted into their nation's armed forces. Accordingly, Gal was able to compare the average scores of 77 soldiers who received decorations for bravery in the 1973 Yom Kippur War with 273 others who had not won medals. He found that the decorated men had received substantially higher ratings on four personality traits: decisiveness, leadership, perserverance under stress, and devotion to duty.

Four types of situations accounted for 70 percent of the heroic acts. Twenty-eight percent had taken place when a unit had its "back to the wall." In this setting, a group of soldiers had been outnumbered and surrounded by a superior enemy unit and was fighting defensively. Another 18 percent of the courageous acts occurred in a "last remnant" setting. The unit had taken many casualties and its commander was dead or incapacitated. In the course of face-to-face fighting, one of the men assumed leadership of the group and conducted himself valiantly. Still another 14 percent took place when "fighting to the last bullet." Either a single soldier or a few survivors had fought to the death in order to accomplish their mission. Finally, 10 percent of the heroic acts had been of a "self-sacrificing" nature. The group was encircled and one soldier laid down his life in order to save the unit.

Gal found that many of the decorated heroes doubted whether they had been more worthy of the medals than some of the other men in their units. On the question of whether heroism results from an extraordinary person or a hero-producing situation, Gal concludes that it is primarily the specific constellation of situational factors that evokes heroic behavior. He says that whether one or another person performs the heroic act is almost a matter of chance. Thus, heroism is a combination of situational factors and personal characteristics.

understanding the underlying sources of behavior than with predicting it and controlling it.

Consider the case of Tom, a college sophomore who has been rather depressed lately. Freud might have sought the roots of Tom's unhappiness in events in his childhood. But Skinner's approach is more direct. First of all, Skinner would reject the vague label "depressed." Instead he would ask, Exactly how does Tom behave? The answer may be that Tom spends most of the day in his room, cuts all his classes, and rarely smiles or laughs.

Next, Skinner would try to understand the **contingencies of reinforcement** that are operating in Tom's life. What conditions are maintaining these behaviors? What reinforces Tom for never leaving his room? One hypothesis is that Tom's girlfriend, Ethel, has unintentionally reinforced this behavior by spending a lot of time with Tom, "babying" him and trying to cheer him up. Perhaps she did not pay much attention to him before he was depressed. Note that Skinner's approach immediately suggests a hypothesis that can be proved true or false. If indulging Tom encourages his moroseness, then ignoring him should decrease the likelihood of this behavior. So Ethel might try ignoring Tom for a few days. If he then starts leaving his room, she has discovered the contingencies of reinforcement that govern Tom's behavior. If not, she will know that the hypothesis is wrong and can try something else. Perhaps Tom is glued to the TV in his room all day

---

contingency of reinforcement: B. F. Skinner's term for the occurrence of a reward or punishment following a particular behavior.

Through training, retarded adults are able to learn many self-help skills, such as cooking, and to live in group homes with some supervision. *(Alan Carey/The Image Works)*

and has become a game-show addict. Take away the TV and you will find out whether that is the reinforcer.

Skinner's approach has been popular among many psychologists, partly because it is so practical. It is a very action-oriented, very American approach: "Don't get all agitated about what's wrong—jump in and fix it." And it is true that behaviorism often works. Skinnerians have applied the techniques to a wide range of behaviors, from teaching pigeons to play Ping-Pong to teaching severely retarded people to dress themselves, feed themselves, and take part in simple activities once believed beyond their abilities.

The idea of controlling people with systematic rewards is a frightening concept to many people, more reminiscent of Aldous Huxley's *Brave New World* than of Plato's *Republic*. But Skinner's novel *Walden Two* (1948) describes how these principles might be applied to form a utopian society. In another of his popular books, *Beyond Freedom and Dignity* (1971), Skinner argues the philosophical position that freedom is an illusion. You may think you are free to read this book or put it down, but in fact your behavior has been shaped by your history of reinforcements. You are reading this book right now because you have been reinforced in the past for

studying—by getting a good grade and by winning the approval of your parents. Or perhaps you are now thinking of putting it down because you have been rewarded in the past for independence, and you want to demonstrate that your behavior is not shaped by rewards.

Skinner argues that since the way reinforcers shape behavior cannot be changed, people might as well make the most of it. Today's society, for example, often rewards immoral behavior—slumlords get more profits if they let their property run down than if they spend money to maintain it. Skinner suggests that to change this situation, appeals should not be made to the inherent goodness of the slumlords—unless approval is a reinforcer for them. The more likely course would be to change society (perhaps by providing tax breaks) so that they will be rewarded for taking care of their buildings.

Social Learning Theory

Skinner's behaviorism seeks to answer the question "Why do people behave as they do?" He answers that people's actions are shaped and controlled by environmental rewards and punishments. Yet as discussed in Chapter 6, people do not require direct experience with events to learn the connection or association between them. They also learn through *modeling:* they watch other people and learn new responses that are based on their observations of others' behavior. Nor are people simply organisms buffeted about by external influences. They select, organize, and transform the stimuli that they receive from the environment. They symbolically represent their world of experience, mentally process information, and devise their own actions. This view of behavior is variously termed *observational learning, cognitive learning,* or *social learning theory.*

Social learning theorists such as Albert Bandura (1977) and Walter Mischel (1971, 1973) consider learning to be the core of psychology. Learning revolves about the changes that occur in a person's behavior as a result of experience (see Chapter 6). It is the primary process by which people adapt to their environment. For social learning theorists, personality exists largely in the beliefs that people hold about themselves (Bandura, 1978; Mischel, 1979; Mischel and Peake, 1983a, 1983b). People's behavior varies so much from one situation to another that the notion of personality traits that exist apart from self-beliefs is rendered meaningless (see the boxed insert on page 442).

Mischel's position runs counter to commonsense assumptions that your friends, relatives, and co-workers have certain basic consistencies that run through their behavior. It seems "self-evident" that the people you know do indeed have distinctive sets of personal qualities or characteristics that allow you to predict their behavior in new situations with reassuring accuracy. We all know "live wire" people, easygoing people, friendly people, overbearing people.

Social learning theorists present a number of arguments for believing that intuitions about "personality" are in error (Mischel, 1968, 1983, 1984; Bem and Allen, 1974). First, they point out, people encounter many acquaintances only within a restricted range of situations—perhaps in the role of neighbor, coworker, or fellow student. Hence, people are excluded from a host of situations in which their acquaintances are likely to show a greater diversity of behavior than in commonly observed situations. Second, as was pointed out in our discussion of attribution processes in Chapter 9, people tend to overestimate the degree to which behavior is controlled by dispositional factors and to underestimate the impact of situational factors. We find it reassur-

ing to attribute behavior to something unchanging within us rather than acknowledge how much we change with each situation. Third, as was also noted in Chapter 9, people hold "implicit personality theories"—preconceived ideas as to which traits and behaviors go with which other traits and behaviors. Consequently, they generalize beyond their observations and fill in the "missing" information with "consistent" information of their own manufacture (Shweder and D'Andrale, 1980).

The argument that personality traits do not exist strikes at the very heart of personality theory. Hence it is hardly surprising that many psychologists have taken issue with Mischel's view that behavioral consistency is largely in the eye of the beholder (Alker, 1972; Bowers, 1973; Epstein, 1983, 1984). For one thing, Mischel's critics argue, the research on which he based his conclusion used too few observations of a person's behavior to extract from them meaningful themes or traits. They contend that traits provide a reasonably accurate prediction of behavior when behavior is averaged over a sample of situations and occasions (Epstein and O'Brien, 1985). For another, people in self-reports of their own behavior view themselves as having considerable consistency in what they say and do across some kinds of situations (Bem and Allen, 1974; Kenrick and Stringfield, 1980). For still another, people rate their friends and relatives as having discernible clusters of traits. Finally, situations vary in the constraints they impose on behavior and in the range of behavior that is deemed appropriate to them (Price and Bouffard, 1974; Monson, Hesley, and Chernick, 1982). When in church or at a job interview, you typically enjoy fewer behavioral options than when you are in the park or in your own home. Thus in some situations your behavior may be highly consistent while in others much less consistent.

Developmental psychologists add another element to our understanding of these matters. A sample of Berkeley and Oakland youths—first studied in the 1930s when they were in their teens and assessed again when they were in their mid-thirties and mid-forties—reveals that their basic personalities remained much the same through the years (Block, 1971, 1977, 1980). The picture gained from the research undertaken by psychologists at the Gerontology Research Center in Baltimore is quite similar (Costa and McCrae, 1980). On such personality dimensions as warmth, impulsiveness, gregari-

Personality in a Severe Environment

The psychologist Philip G. Zimbardo and his colleagues (1973) undertook a study that high-lights the part situational factors play in shaping the behavior of people judged to have "normal personalities." To investigate the consequences of being a prisoner or a prison guard, the re-searchers converted the basement of the Stanford University psychology building into a mock pris-on.

Some seventy-five male student volunteers were given intensive clinical interviews and per-sonality tests. Of these, twenty-one were se-lected on the basis of their emotional stability, adjustment and maturity, physical health, and absence of a jail record or a record for violence or drug abuse. Half of the men were assigned at random to serve as "guards" and the other half to serve as "prisoners." To enhance the realism of the experiment, the men were unexpectedly picked up at their homes by Palo Alto police in a squad car. Each subject was charged with a felony, told of his constitutional rights, spread-eagled against the car, searched, handcuffed, and then delivered to the station for finger-printing.

At the mock prison, the prisoners were stripped naked; skin-searched; sprayed for lice; issued a uniform, bedding, soap, and a towel; and placed in a six-by-nine-foot barred cell with two other "convicts." The men were imprisoned around the clock and permitted out only for meals, exercise, toilet privileges, head-count lineups, and work details.

"Guards" worked on three eight-hour shifts and returned home when they were not on duty. The researchers instructed them to "maintain law and order" and not to take any nonsense from the prisoners. They wore khaki uniforms and carried billy clubs, whistles, and handcuffs.

Over the remarkably short period of six days, a "perverted" symbiotic relationship developed. As the guards became more aggressive, the pris-oners became more passive. The guards' asser-tion led to the prisoners' dependence, the guards' self-aggrandizing tendencies to the prisoners' self-deprecation, and the guards' authority to the prisoners' helplessness.

Each day, the guards escalated their aggressive behavior, insulting the prisoners, inventing petty rules for prisoner conduct, and improvising de-grading and meaningless punishments. They made the prisoners sing songs, laugh or smile on command, and curse and vilify one another. Although scheduled to run for two weeks, the study had to be discontinued after six days so as to prevent any lasting negative effects on the subjects.

The study starkly reveals that healthy, normal, and well-educated college men can be profound-ly transformed under the institutional pressures of a prison environment. Zimbardo observes (Zimbardo and Ruch, 1975:561):

No personality test scores or other variables related to the subjects' past history were found to be related to the extreme differences in reaction observed between the prisoners and the guards. Thus the pathology witnessed here cannot be reasonably attributed to preexisting personality traits—such as those of "psychopathic" or "sadistic" guards, or of "criminal, weak impulse-controlled" prisoners. Rather, the abnormal personal and social behavior in both groups is best viewed as a product of transactions with an environment that supports such behavior.

In sum, the bizarre social and personal reac-tions of the subjects arose out of the situational factors in a severe institutional environment.

---

ousness, assertiveness, anxiety, and proneness to depression, high correlations are found in the order-ing of persons from one decade to another. An assertive nineteen-year-old is typically an assertive thirty-five-year-old and later an assertive eighty-

year-old. Likewise, "complainers" remain "com-plainers" (they may complain about their love life in early adulthood while bemoaning their poor health in late adulthood). In sum, for many facets of our personality there is strong evidence of continuity across the adult years (Costa, McCrae, and Arenberg, 1980; Conley, 1985; Stevens and Truss, 1985).

Some measure of stability in behavior is adaptive; we know what we are like and hence can make more intelligent choices regarding our living arrangements, careers, spouses, and friends. If our personality continually changed in an erratic manner, our ability to map our future and make wise decisions would be severely impaired. By the same token, however, rigid, generalized types of responses are often not appropriate for competent functioning (Mischel, 1984). Adaptation also requires that we vary our behavior depending on the dictates of the situation. Accordingly, most personality psychologists would agree that our concept of personality should reflect patterns of change and variation as well as consistency and stability (Pervin, 1985).

In sum, there is both variation and consistency in behavior. On this matter psychologists agree. They disagree about the amount of consistency and variability, and about the usefulness of the trait concept in accounting for the regularities that do exist (Epstein, 1983; Mischel and Peake, 1983a).

Cognitive Theory

Cognitive theorists, especially those with an interactionist orientation, contend that the question of which is more important, personality traits or the situation, is a meaningless one. Behavior is always a joint product of the person and the situation. In some respects, the interactionist position may be viewed as a compromise between the trait position and the situationist position. While it acknowledges the existence of behavioral consistency and stability, it also insists that situations exert a strong influence on behavior (Bowers, 1973; Ekehammar, 1974; Magnusson and Endler, 1977; Buss and Craik, 1983a, 1983b).

According to interactionist theorists, people do not show strong behavioral tendencies independent of the setting. Thus people and situations are interdependent. A person's cognitions and perceptual processes, as much as the objective characteristics of the stimuli, influence what he or she says and does. Consequently, people with different cognitive frameworks, or schemes, interpret and respond to the same stimuli in different ways (Markus, 1977; Markus and Smith, 1981). In this sense, behavior

constitutes a transaction between the individual and the situation, each component influencing the other. Since behavior does not occur in a vacuum but always in a situational context, it is senseless to talk about the traits of a person without specifying the situation in which the behavior takes place (Epstein, 1979); Aries, Gold, and Weigel, 1983).

Jean Piaget's theory of cognitive development (discussed in Chapter 11) is a good example of an interactionist approach. You will recall that Piaget suggested that children pass through four major stages in the growth and maturing of their thinking capabilities. He depicts children as engaged in a continuous interaction with their environment. As acting individuals, they transform and modify the world in which they live. In turn, they are shaped and altered by the consequences of their own actions.

According to Piaget, new experiences interact with the child's existing structure or mode of thought, thereby changing the structure and rendering it better equipped to deal with reality. This modified structure then influences the child's new perceptions, and in turn, these new perceptions become incorporated within a more complex structure. In this manner, experience modifies structure, and structure modifies experience. Through this interchange between the child and the environment, new mental capabilities arise, and the child gains an expanded repertoire of behaviors for meeting environmental demands. In sum, the human organism modifies itself through responding to its environment.

PERSONALITY ASSESSMENT

Thus far in the chapter we have had much to say about personality but little to say about how psychologists go about the task of assessing a person's characteristics, emotional adjustment, interpersonal relations, interests, attitudes, and motivation. Underlying the process of psychological assessment is the premise that individuals differ in certain identifiable and measurable dimensions. Tests are one means that psychologists use to quantify and describe these differences. However, personality psychologists do not typically view assessment as simply a matter of administering tests and interpreting the scores. They see their task as one of using all the information available to them—test data, biographical information, oral reports, and observation—to characterize a person (Korchin and Schuldberg, 1981). Let us turn, then, to a consideration of some of the techniques that psychologists employ in personality assessment.

Objective Personality Assessment

The objective approach to personality assessment commonly involves the use of standardized self-report questionnaires and inventories. It aims to measure a person's personality by obtaining a sample of answers to predetermined questions. The psychologist proceeds in much the manner of a chemist who tests a city's water supply by analyzing a few samples of the water, or a physician who examines a patient's blood by analyzing a few samples of blood. Just as it is impractical to test all the water or all the blood drop by drop, so is it impractical to test all aspects of a person's adaptation to life—personality.

The *Minnesota Multiphasic Personality Inventory* *(MMPI)* is the most widely used and researched objective test of personality. It was developed by a team of psychologists at the University of Minnesota in the late 1930s and early 1940s. Their purpose was to provide an objective assessment of some of the major personality characteristics that affect personal and social adjustment (Hathaway and McKinley, 1967). Like other personality tests, the MMPI has no right or wrong answers. The test consists of 550 statements to which a person can respond "true," "false," or "cannot say." Examples of items are "I like tall women"; "I am an agent of God"; "I wake up tired most mornings"; "I am envied by most people"; "I often feel a tingling in my fingers."

The items on the MMPI reveal habits, fears, delusions, sexual attitudes, and symptoms of mental problems. Although the statements that relate to a given characteristic (such as depression) are scattered throughout the test, the answers to them can be pulled out and organized into a single depression scale. There are ten such clinical scales to the MMPI.

In scoring the MMPI, a psychologist looks for patterns of responses, not a high or a low score on all the scales. This is because the items on the test do not, by themselves, identify personality types. In creating the MMPI, the test makers did not try to decide which statements would identify depression,

anxiety, and serious forms of mental disorder such as schizophrenia. Rather, they invented a wide range of statements about all sorts of topics; gave the test to groups of people already known to be well adjusted, depressed, schizophrenic, and so on; and retained for the test those questions that discriminated among these groups—questions, for example, that people suffering from depression or from anxiety disorders answered differently from normal groups (Hathaway and McKinley, 1940). Many of the items on the MMPI may sound like sheer nonsense. But they work. One unique aspect of the MMPI is that it has a built-in "lie detector." If people give false responses to statements, they are likely to be detected by answering differently rephrasings of the same questions later in the test and by answering questions in ways that are too socially desirable. (No one is *that* good.)

The MMPI has proved useful in helping to diagnose various forms of mental disturbance and in providing data for personality research (Dahlstrom and Welsh, 1960; Gynther and Gynther, 1983). It has also been used—and misused—in employment offices to screen job applicants. A person who is trying to get a job is likely to give answers he or she thinks the employer would like to see—thereby falling into some of the traps built into the test. Administering the MMPI under such circumstances can produce misleading, even damaging results. Innocently trying to make a good impression, the job applicant ends up looking like a liar instead. As an aid to counseling and therapy, however, it is a valuable tool.

Other objective tests, such as the California Psychological Inventory (Gough, 1964) and several interest inventories (Strong-Campbell, Edwards Personal Preference Schedule), have been developed to help counsel people about their future plans (Gynther and Gynther, 1983). As such, normal personality tests can help people learn what kinds of activities and careers they are most likely to enjoy and what traits in themselves they might like to change.

Phenomenological Techniques

Earlier in the chapter, we discussed the humanistic perspectives of Abraham Maslow and Carl Rogers. At the core of these approaches is the notion that

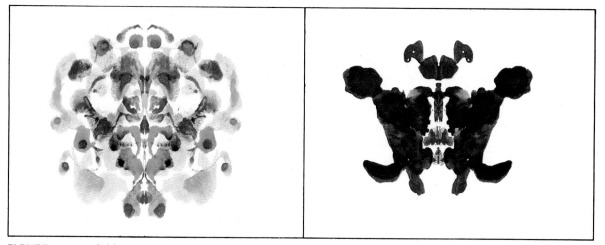

FIGURE 13.2 Ink blots similar to those used on the Rorschach test. In interpretations of a person's responses to the ink blots, as much attention may be paid to the style of the responses as to their content.

individuals possess the ability to strive for self-actualization and hence to achieve their full potential as human beings. Each person is seen as a unique individual with worth and dignity. Humanistic theorists stress **phenomenology**—the view that each person's personality can best be understood by seeing the world through his or her own eyes. Thus the phenomenological approach focuses on people's subjective experience. Humanistic psychologists attempt to understand how each person experiences various events, without imposing preconceptions or preexisting theoretical notions on the person's perceptions or interpretations.

In keeping with this focus, humanists have searched for self-report techniques that allow people more range for self-expression than that accorded them when they respond to standardized items on objective tests. They use biographical data and people's free-form reports of their internal experiences. In this way, they attempt to capture each person's own construction of reality. They are especially interested in what people say about themselves and the concepts they use to describe themselves, rather than in how these people compare to other individuals.

Projective Measures

Projective measures are usually open-ended tests that invite people to tell stories about pictures, diagrams, or objects. The idea is that because the test material has no established meaning, the story a person tells must say something about his or her needs, wishes, fears, and personality traits. In other words, subjects will project their feelings onto the test items. The interpretation of the responses rests with the examiner, however, which raises many questions of reliability and validity (see Chapter 8).

Perhaps the best-known and most widely discussed projective measure is the *Rorschach ink-blot test*, developed by the Swiss psychiatrist Hermann Rorschach. Rorschach created ten ink-blot designs and a system for scoring responses to them. To administer the test, a psychologist hands the ink blots, one by one, to the subject, asking the person to say what he or she sees. The person might say that a certain area represents an airplane or an animal's head. This phase is the free-association period of the test. The psychologist then asks certain general questions in an attempt to discover what aspects of the ink blot determined the person's response (see Figure 13.2).

phenomenology: The view that each person's personality can best be understood by seeing the world through the person's own eyes.

There are a number of systems for scoring Rorschach responses. Some are very specific and concrete. For example, according to one system, a person who mentions human movement more often than color in the ink blots is probably introverted while an extrovert will mention color more than movement. Other systems are far more intuitive —for example, simply noting whether the person taking the test is open or hostile. Many researchers have criticized the Rorschach, charging that scoring systems are neither reliable nor valid. But it continues to be widely used by therapists.

The second most widely used projective measure was developed by Henry Murray. The *Thematic Apperception Test (TAT)* consists of a series of twenty cards containing pictures of vague but suggestive situations. The person is asked to tell a story about the picture, indicating how the situation shown on the card developed, what the characters are thinking and feeling, and how the story will end (see Figure 13.3).

Situational Tests

The use of psychological tests for such things as job placement has become extremely controversial in recent years. Is there any direct relation between people's responses to statements on the MMPI and their everyday behavior? Do people's perceptions of an ink blot really tell whether they will be able to remain calm under pressure or to give and take orders efficiently? Many psychologists think not. They believe that the closer a test is to the actual situation the examiner wants to know about, the more useful the results will be. A test that measures a person's performance in terms of emotional, attitudinal, and behavioral responses to real-life situations is called a *situational test*. An example is a test for a driver's license, requiring that the person actually drive. The photograph below shows an airplane simulation, used to assess the performance of pilots. Samples of job performance are used widely in business and have proved very successful in selecting

Using this airplane flight simulator, pilots are trained and tested before they are given the responsibility of flying a real airliner. None of the standard objective tests described in this chapter could predict accurately whether a pilot would panic in such a situation. (*Courtesy, United Airlines*)

FIGURE 13.3 A picture of the sort that might be used in the measurement of the need for achievement. Examples of stories that would be scored from fairly high to low are also shown. The portions of the stories printed in italics are the kinds of themes considered to reflect need for achievement. (*Harry Crosby*)

This guy is just getting off work. These are all working guys and they don't like their work too much either. The younger guy over on the right knows the guy with the jacket.

Something bad happened today at work—*a nasty accident that shouldn't have happened.* These two guys don't trust each other *but they are going to talk* about it. *They mean to put things to rights. No one else much cares,* it seems.

The guy with the jacket is *worried.* He feels that *something has to be done. He wouldn't ordinarily talk* to the younger man *but now he feels he must.* The young guy is ready. He's *concerned* too but doesn't know what to expect.

They'll both realize after talking that you never know where your friends are. *They'll both feel better* afterward because they'll feel

they have someone they can rely on next time there's trouble.

Harry O'Silverfish has been working on the Ford assembly line for thirteen years. Every morning he gets up, eats a doughnut and cup of coffee, takes his lunch pail, gets in the car, and drives to the plant. It is during this morning drive that his mind gets filled with *fantasies of what he'd like to be doing* with his life. Then, about the same time that he parks his car and turns off his ignition, he also *turns off his mind*—and it remains turned off during the whole working day. In the evenings, he is *too tired and discouraged to do much* more than drink a few beers and watch TV.

But this morning Harry's mind didn't turn off with the car. He had witnessed a car accident on the road—in which two people were

killed—soon after leaving home. Just as he reaches the plant gate, Harry suddenly turns. Surprised, he discovers that he has made *a firm decision* never to enter that plant again. He knows that *he must try another way* to live before he dies.

These are hard-hats. It's the end of the shift. There is a demonstration outside the plant and the men coming out are looking at it. Everyone is just walking by. They are not much interested. One person is *angry* and *wants to go on strike,* but this does not make sense to anyone else. He is out of place. Actually he is not really angry, he is just bored. He looks as though he might do a little dance to amuse himself, which is more than the rest of them do. *Nothing will happen* at this time *till more people join* this one man in his needs.

qualified managers and evaluating candidates for promotion.

In sum, psychologists find that personality assessment is a valuable tool for identifying the consistencies in people's behaviors, attitudes, and feelings across time and situations. Some of your behavior is specific to a situation. For instance, if you are walking alone down an unlighted street about midnight, you may warily pass a stranger without speaking to him. But you may initiate a conversation with this same stranger if he takes the seat next to you in Psychology 101. Even so, whether you are judged by yourself and by others to be a friendly person depends on the patterns that recur in your behavior when it is compared with that of other people. Given a large number of settings, are you more likely to be a retiring person or more likely to initiate interaction with others? It is this type of question that psychologists undertake to answer by personality assessment.

Because personality theorists attempt to describe how people function as whole human beings in their environments, their task is more complex than that confronting psychologists in other areas of study. Since personalities have so many dimensions, it is easy to appreciate the diversity of approaches that psychologists use to study human personalities.

SUMMARY

1. Underlying most psychological definitions of personality is the notion that everyone has a unique and enduring set of psychological tendencies that he or she reveals in the course of interacting with the environment. The concept of personality accounts both for the differences among people and for the consistencies in an individual's behavior over time and in different situations.

2. Psychologists develop theories of personality for a number of reasons. First, people differ from one another in so many ways that psychologists look for specific dimensions along which people vary, to make the information manageable. Second, personality theories attempt to explain how the observable differences among people come about. Third, they serve as tools by which psychologists can assess the match between a specific individual and his or her environment. And finally, personality theories are concerned with how life can be improved.

3. Personality theories may be divided into those that stress internal factors and those that stress external factors in the development of personality. The genetic-influence view holds that children are born with intellectual and temperamental differences that over time and in interaction with the environment often develop into personality differences.

4. Freudian theory centers on the unconscious and the important role it plays in personality.

    A. According to Freud, the ego tries to balance the id's desires against the demands of the superego and the realities of the world.

    B. Defense mechanisms are unconscious solutions to conflict situations. They protect the ego from experiencing anxiety about failing in its tasks. Some common defense mechanisms are repression, projection, displacement, reaction formation, regression, and rationalization.

    C. Later psychoanalysts proposed changes in Freud's theory. Carl Jung believed that the collective unconscious is a universally shared inheritance of instincts, urges, and memories called archetypes. Alfred Adler developed his psychology along social lines, emphasizing the influence on personality of interpersonal relationships.

5. Humanistic theories of personality emphasize human dignity and potential.

    A. After studying highly productive people who fulfilled their capabilities, Abraham Maslow concluded that self-actualized people were not free of emotional problems. Rather, they adjusted to their problems in ways that allowed them to become highly productive.

    B. Carl Rogers suggests that full functioning depends on a person's opening the self to include all of the organism, shedding others' evaluations of one's worth.

6. Trait theorists, such as Gordon Allport and Raymond Cattell, emphasize and attempt to explain the consistency of an individual's behavior across different situations. They generally make two basic assumptions about these underlying sources of consistency: every trait applies to all people to a greater

or lesser degree, and descriptions, or trait classifications, can be quantified.

7. Taking an external perspective, behaviorists such as B. F. Skinner contend that psychologists should focus on the way rewards and punishments shape behavior. Situations and their contingencies, not internal predispositions, determine how people act.

8. Social learning theorists consider learning—the changes that occur in a person's behavior as a result of experience—to be the core of psychology. Thus, by implication, personality theory is superfluous. Indeed, Walter Mischel says that people's behavior varies so much from one situation to another that the notion of personality traits is largely useless.

9. Cognitive theorists, especially those with an interactionist orientation, say that the question of which is more important, personality traits or the situation, is a meaningless one. Behavior is always a joint product of the influence of the person and the situation on each other.

10. Underlying the process of psychological assessment is the premise that individuals differ in certain identifiable and measurable dimensions. Tests are one means that psychologists use to quantify and describe these differences. They have a variety of techniques at their disposal.

   A. Objective measures include standardized self-report questionnaires and inventories.

   B. Phenomenological techniques emphasize people's free-form reports of internal experiences.

   C. Projective measures employ open-ended tests that invite people to tell stories about pictures, diagrams, or objects.

   D. Situational tests seek to measure people's performance within "real-life" settings.

KEY TERMS

archetype (p. 430)
behaviorism (p. 438)
collective unconscious (p. 429)
conditions of worth (p. 434)
contingency of
   reinforcement (p. 439)
defense mechanism (p. 427)
displacement (p. 428)
ego (p. 427)
factor analysis (p. 437)

fully functioning person (p. 434)
humanistic psychology (p. 431)
id (p. 426)
inferiority complex (p. 430)
organism (p. 433)
personality (p. 420)
phenomenology (p. 445)
positive regard (p. 434)
projection (p. 428)
rationalization (p. 428)

reaction formation (p. 428)
regression (p. 428)
repression (p. 427)
self (p. 434)
self-actualization (p. 431)
superego (p. 427)
trait (p. 435)
unconditional positive
   regard (p. 434)
unconscious (p. 426)

SUGGESTED READINGS

HALL, CALVIN S. 1954. *A Primer of Freudian Psychology.* Cleveland: World. A good, clearly written introduction to Freudian theory that emphasizes Freud's contributions to the psychology of "normal" people.

HORNEY, KAREN. 1967. *Feminine Psychology.* New York: Norton. This gem seems as current today as when it was originally published over fifty years ago. Horney addresses issues that affect women's personality development.

JUNG, CARL. 1963. *Memories, Dreams, Reflections.* New York: Pantheon. A beautifully written autobiography.

MASLOW, ABRAHAM. 1968. *Toward a Psychology of Being.* New York: Van Nostrand. Maslow directs current thinking away from its obsession with the "normal" person and focuses on the "healthy" person.

RABIN, ALBERT I. (ED.). 1981. *Assessment with Projective Techniques.* New York: Springer. A careful, comprehensive presentation of projective test approaches to personality assessment.

ROGERS, CARL. 1961. *On Becoming a Person.* Boston: Houghton Mifflin. An important work on the humanistic theory of personality, Freudian theory's first major rival.

SKINNER, B. F. 1962; originally published 1948. *Walden Two.* New York: Macmillan. A novel describing a behaviorist's utopia.

Richard Diebenkorn, *Woman in a Window,* 1957.

14
Health and Stress

As described by political scientist Doris Kearns (1976), Lyndon Johnson's last years were filled with frustration and despair. The retired President was deprived of power and influence and subjected to harsh criticism for his Vietnam policies. In discussing the efforts of his successor, Richard Nixon, to cut off funds for his domestic programs, Johnson compared his Great Society to a starving woman. "And when she dies," remarked Johnson, who had survived a severe heart attack in 1955, "I too will die." On January 21, 1973, the day following Nixon's inauguration to his second term, the Republican administration announced plans for the dismantling of the Great Society. The following day, Johnson died of a heart attack.

The timing of Johnson's death could have been coincidental. Nevertheless, the notion that sudden death can accompany emotional flooding has long been an element popular in folklore. One of the earliest reported cases dates back to A.D. 50. According to Saint Luke, when Ananias was charged by Peter, "You have not lied to man but to God," Ananias fell dead (Acts 5:1–2).

Mohammad Reza Pahlavi, the shah of Iran, was another world leader who incurred serious health problems after suffering a severe political reversal. The shah came down with a virulent, progressive form of cancer three to four months after being forced from the throne. The son of the founder of Iran's Pahlavi dynasty, he had assumed leadership of his nation in 1941. However, in the late 1970s, mounting opposition from Muslim leaders, the political left, students, and some merchants compelled the shah to flee into exile on January 16, 1979. His doctors at the Cornell Medical Center in New York City said the shah had suffered secretly for years with a slow leukemia. But in April 1979, while he was in the Bahamas, the new cancer—lymphoma—was detected. He died from the disease in Cairo on July 27,

1980. While it is not possible to blame a particular cancer on an especially stressful loss or event, cancer experts said the shah's case was not unusual. Dr. Burton Lee of Memorial Sloan-Kettering Cancer Center, an expert on lymphoma, observed, "You take a chairman of the board who's run a huge conglomerate for fifteen years, take that away and make him retire to the beach in Florida and he can go to pieces like a one-horse shay" (*Columbus Dispatch*, October 28, 1979:A–8).

Medical workers have often noted that people who suffer a great personal loss, such as the death of a spouse, a bitter divorce, or a forced retirement, frequently lose their health as well. Is there any scientific support for the inference that stress plays a role in the onset of illness? What are the links between behavioral influences and our health? What are the mechanisms by which stress may trigger disease processes? Is stress always harmful, or may it be beneficial? What are the major sources of stress in our lives? Do people differ in how they experience and handle stress? What are some particularly useful strategies for coping with stress? In this chapter we will look for answers to these questions.

HEALTH IN A PSYCHOSOCIAL ENVIRONMENT

In the course of your daily life, you are asked countless times, "How are you?" And you very likely automatically respond, "Fine. How about you?" Clearly, health plays a pivotal role in our sense of well-being. Many of us believe that life is not merely being alive, but being well. In health we find freedom. Some have termed it "a liberty," others the "first wealth," and still others "the vital principle of bliss." Yet whereas we "feel" sickness, we usually do not "feel" health. Rather, we tend to take health for granted.

Most of us would agree that health is much more than the absence of illness. The World Health Organization recognizes this fact, defining health as "a state of complete physical, mental, and social well-being and not merely the absence of disease or infirmity." The biologist René Dubos (1968:67) provides a complementary view of health as a way of life that enables imperfect human beings "to achieve a rewarding and not too painful existence while they cope with an imperfect world." We can measure people's health by how well they are able to function and adapt to a continually changing environment. Health, then, will take on somewhat different properties in the lives of a professional football player, a reclusive monk, a homemaker, a movie idol, a park ranger, a political revolutionary, a computer programmer, and an unemployed worker.

We commonly think of disease as a serious, prolonged, and deep-rooted condition. It may be an organic illness like cancer or a serious mental dysfunction like schizophrenia. The word "disease" literally means "dis-eased"—not feeling at ease. The traditional medical model has seen disease as a purely biological phenomenon, a product of bacteria and viruses and bodily dysfunction. However, in recent years the medical establishment has increasingly come to recognize that behavioral factors also are crucial ingredients in causing disease and in its effective treatment and management (Engel, 1977b; Miller, 1983; Taylor, 1986). This has given rise to a new interdisciplinary field, **behavioral medicine,** that integrates behavioral and biomedical knowledge regarding health and disease processes. Viewed from the perspective of behavioral medicine, we are sick when we are not in harmony with our inner and outer environments. Let us begin our discussion of these matters by looking at the links between behavior and illness.

Links Between Behavior and Physical Disease

Behavior influences health and disease in a variety of ways (Krantz, Grunberg, and Baum, 1985). For one thing, our habits and styles of life affect our health. As we pointed out in Chapter 6, cigarette smoking is the single most important source of preventable death in the United States today. Diets high in cholesterol, lack of exercise, excessive consumption of alcohol, and poor hygienic practices also have

---

behavioral medicine: An interdisciplinary field that integrates behavioral and biomedical knowledge regarding health and disease processes.

Not all appetizing foods and drinks are good for you. Foods high in animal fats, such as steaks, fried potatoes, onion rings, and whipped cream, are thought by many nutrition experts to be a cause of high blood pressure and obesity. *(Raoul Hackel/Stock, Boston)*

been linked to illness, including coronary heart disease (Pell and Fayerweather, 1985). Many of these practices, such as eating what we think is a "hearty meal" and using alcohol as a "social lubricant," are deeply rooted in cultural patterns. In many cases, they are initiated by social influences, as when a teen-ager starts smoking to obtain peer-group approval. A good deal of research has documented the part that cultural and social influences play in a person's susceptibility to cancer. Consider skin cancer, by far the most common form of cancer. An estimated 400,000 new cases are detected each year in the United States, and almost all of them are attributable to overexposure to the sun. In many Western societies, a luxuriant tan bespeaks health and glamour. But with each hour of exposure, the sun's ultraviolet radiation produces irreversible damage (Tucker et al., 1985).

Another process through which behavior influences health occurs when people minimize the significance of their symptoms, delay obtaining medical care, or fail to comply with treatment regimens.

Many people put off seeking help for early signs of cancer or heart disease, thereby diminishing their chances for survival. Thus how people react to being ill and to the experience of being in the role of "sick person" has important consequences for their health. When we assume the "sick person" role, we incur a set of expectations and privileges that are defined for us by society. The social group obligates us to behave in a way that will lead to recovery. Indeed, with some illnesses, we are entitled to stay in bed, free from responsibilities that might sap our strength. But with others we are expected to continue our daily activities (Jaco, 1979). A pulled muscle, a broken finger, or poison ivy may make us just as uncomfortable as symptoms of influenza, but within American culture only the flu is labeled a sickness.

People with some illnesses may face a variety of nonmedical problems, from social isolation to job discrimination. Patients with AIDS—acquired immune deficiency syndrome—often are shunned by a frightened public. And cancer patients suffer from a host of day-to-day psychological and social problems

Sunbathing may give you a fashionable bronzed look, but it may also give you skin cancer. Experts today advise against extended exposure to strong sunlight, especially if you have a fair complexion. *(Alan Carey/The Image Works)*

resulting from their illness. One survey found that 85 percent of cancer patients encountered problems interacting with their friends and relatives because their friends and relatives felt uncomfortable with their illness; 70 percent said they experienced tension in talking with their spouses about their illness; 91 percent reported that their sex lives were adversely affected; and 72 percent admitted having difficulties communicating their feelings, symptoms, and questions to the physicians and nurses treating them. The majority also reported disruption in their daily activities, including problems eating, sleeping, carrying out household chores, and participating in recreational activities (Bridgwater, 1985).

Emotional factors also have implications for the functioning of our bodies. That emotions are implicated in physical illness has long been a basic tenet of folk wisdom and psychotherapy. Almost 2,000 years ago the Greek physician Galen observed that 60 percent of his patients had symptoms of emotional rather than physical origin—a figure close to contemporary estimates (Shapiro, 1978). More recently, Norman Cousins (1979) wrote a best-selling book, *Anatomy of an Illness*, contending that emotions play

a profound part in bringing on disease and in helping to combat it. And researchers are finding that traumatic life events are often correlated with the onset of disease. For instance, studies of rape victims have shown significant elevations in reported health problems in the years following the rape (Kilpatrick, Resick, and Vernonen, 1981; King and Webb, 1981). Likewise, two large surveys indicate that people who report having been raped or molested before the age of seventeen are more likely to report having ulcers, stomach problems, kidney and bladder infections, headaches, cardiovascular symptoms, and related problems than those who had more normal childhoods (Pennebaker and O'Heeron, 1984). This same research shows that people who are able to confide in others about their troubled feelings, rather than bear the turmoil in silence, are less vulnerable to illnesses. All this brings us to a consideration of the part that stress plays in health and disease processes.

The Nature of Stress

Stress is a central process in the relationship between behavior and health. It helps to explain how psycho-

FIGURE 14.1   This figure illustrates the three phases of Selye's general adaptation syndrome (1974). Phase A is the alarm response, in which the body first reacts to a stressor. At this time, resistance is diminished. Phase B, the stage of resistance, occurs with continued exposure to a stressor. The bodily signs associated with an alarm reaction disappear and resistance rises above normal. Phase C is the stage of exhaustion that results from long-term exposure to the same stressor. At this point resistance may again fall to below normal. *(After Shelley E. Taylor. 1986.* Health Psychology. *New York: Random House, p. 148. Reprinted with permission.)*

logical events translate into health-impairing physiological changes and illness (Krantz, Grunberg, and Baum, 1985). "Stress" is one of those words that we think we all understand, at least until we have to become precise about its meanings and consequences. Stress may be viewed as external events that make demands on an organism, but most scientists now suggest that stress is the organism's *response* to the events that challenge it (Selye, 1976). Still others emphasize that both external and internal events are implicated in stress and focus on the interaction between the environment and a person's reaction to it (Lazarus and Launier, 1978; Lazarus et al., 1985). Common to all these notions is the idea that **stress** is a process involving the recognition of and response to threat or danger (Fleming, Baum, and Singer, 1984).

Initially, stress was defined in physiological terms, as a collection of bodily responses, including a more rapid heart rate, elevated blood pressure, rapid breathing, sweating palms, and increased muscle tension. Physiologist Walter B. Cannon (1932) suggested that these components were part of the "fight or flight" response, a series of physical reactions that prepare an organism to face danger or flee from it. Later the endocrinologist and biologist Hans Selye

(1956) popularized the word "stress" in describing the **general adaptation syndrome.** He viewed stress as the common denominator of all the body's adaptive reactions, a nonspecific response of the body to any demand made of it. Selye said that our body responds to stress in several stages (see Figure 14.1). The first stage is the *alarm reaction.* The nervous system is activated; digestion slows; heartbeat, blood pressure, and breathing rate increase; and the level of blood sugar rises. In brief, the body pulsates with energy. Then the stage of *resistance* sets in. The body mobilizes its resources to overcome stress. During this phase the heart and breathing rates may return to normal. But the appearance of normality is superficial, since the pituitary hormone ACTH remains at high levels (see the discussion of ACTH in Chapter 2). Finally, if some measure of equilibrium is not restored, a stage of *exhaustion* is reached. The body's capacity to handle stress is progressively undermined, the organism seemingly gives up, and eventually it dies. In some cases, however, death may occur immediately (see the boxed insert on pages 456–457). Selye believed the damage produced by stress accumulates over time and finds expression in cardiovascular disease, mental disorders, ulcers, and possibly cancer. However, Selye's critics contend that in many cases stress is not a nonspecific but a specific response and that he overlooks psychological factors in his laboratory experiments (Mason, 1971, 1975).

Another tradition has viewed stress from a cognitive perspective (Taylor, 1983). Seen in this fashion, stress is an interaction between a situation that requires readjustment and a person's ability to cope. What is crucial is the person's definition of a situation as stressful. The philosopher Epictetus made a similar observation centuries ago when he noted that

---

stress: A process involving the recognition of and response to threat or danger.
general adaptation syndrome: A series of stages described by Hans Selye by which an organism responds to stress: the alarm reaction stage, the resistance stage, and the exhaustion stage.

Sudden Death and Emotional Stress

On November 19, 1983, Pearl Pizzamiglio, sixty, was working at the desk of a motel in Chevy Chase, Maryland. Late that evening the door burst open and a deranged-looking young man demanded that she fill a paper bag with money. Terrified, she complied and gave the robber $176. When the man ran out the door, she phoned the police. The police took her to the station house, where she began gasping for breath and clutching at her chest. Although rushed to a nearby hospital, Pizzamiglio died within two hours of the robbery from a series of wildly erratic heart rhythms. She had had no previous history of heart disease or hypertension. One year later a Montgomery County jury found twenty-year-old Michael Steward guilty of felony murder. It was one of the few cases in American history in which a defendant was convicted of scaring a person to death. Expert witnesses testified that bands of heart tissue ruptured by a sudden flood of adrenalinelike substances, sometimes released by people in the grip of terror, had short-circuited the beating of her heart (Monagan, 1986).

Psychiatrist George Engel (G. Engel, 1977) has collected histories of some 275 sudden deaths. **Sudden death** is the term applied to many forms of death, but in most situations it encompasses a death that is totally unexpected as well as sudden. The deaths studied by Engel occurred within minutes or hours of a major event in the person's life, usually centered on losses, situations of personal danger, and occasionally some para-doxical situations of great relief, pleasure, or triumph. In one case, a thirty-eight-year-old man collapsed and died when he failed to revive his two-year-old daughter after she had fallen into a wading pool while her father's attention had wandered. In another case, a fifty-six-year-old woman who saw the wreckage of her husband's truck and ran 150 yards to the accident scene collapsed and died upon reaching the truck.

Numerous accounts are found in the anthropological literature of otherwise healthy people dying inexplicably after being hexed or violating some taboo (Cannon, 1942). Canon Roscoe, long a missionary in British East Africa, recounts one voodoo death. Three men came to him to have their wounds dressed after having been attacked by a leopard. Two of them had been badly clawed, whereas the third bore only a scratch on the neck (quoted by Webster, 1948:488):

> I attended to him last and after dressing his wound I said, "There is not much the matter with you; you will soon be well." To my surprise he said, "I am dying." Thinking he had got an exaggerated idea of his wound, I talked to him for a few moments and then dismissed them all, telling them to come again in the morning. Next morning two of the men came, but the third with the scratch on his neck was missing, and when I asked for him I was told that he was dead. He had gone home and, saying that he had been killed by magic, died in a short time. So far as it was possible to discover, no complications had

we are not disturbed by things, but by our opinions about things. This notion is captured by the humorous definition of an optimist as a person who sees a glass as half full, while a pessimist sees it as half empty. Within psychology the cognitive approach to stress has been popularized by Richard S. Lazarus and his colleagues (1985). They emphasize that stress resides neither in the individual nor in the situation alone, but in how a person evaluates an event.

When most people talk about stress, they mention its negative consequences—tension headache,

---

sudden death: A term applied to many forms of death. In most situations it encompasses a death that is totally unexpected as well as sudden.

arisen, but he was convinced that the animal had been caused by magic to attack him and the power of his imagination had done the rest.

Sudden death in situations of severe stress is not confined to human beings. Curt Richter (1957) has demonstrated experimentally that healthy rats placed in a hopeless situation will give up struggling and die. Normally, a rat can stay afloat for hours before becoming exhausted and drowning. But in Richter's experiments each rat was traumatized by being immobilized in a bag while its whiskers and facial hair were shaved off. Then each rat was released and dropped into a tank of water. Richter (1957:194) reports, "The first rat swam around excitedly on the surface for a very short time, then dove to the bottom where it began to swim around nosing its way along the glass wall. Without coming to the surface a single time, it died two minutes after entering the tank." At first Richter thought that shaving the whiskers destroyed a rat's adaptive mechanism for achieving contact with the outside world. But additional research revealed that some of the wild rats died while merely being held in his hand. He related his findings to voodoo death, in that the human victim, like the rat, is not set for fight or flight, but rather, is resigned to his or her fate—a hopeless situation.

The psychological and physiological mechanisms that contribute to sudden death in situations of severe stress are largely a matter of conjecture (Griffiths, 1960; Hughes and Lynch, 1978). One hypothesis suggests that emotional stress contributes to changes in the cardiovascular system, resulting in a surge in blood pressure and a disruption of heart rhythm. According to this view, many cases of sudden death result from a temporary malfunction—a kind of electrical accident—in which a torrent of electrochemical impulses wildly overaccelerate the heart (Monagan, 1986). But as psychiatrist Joel E. Dimsdale notes, the central question is why so few people die a sudden death from emotional causes. He concludes (1977:1364): "We must assume that sudden death occurs only when a number of factors are present simultaneously and that, fortunately, the odds of this occurring must be small." Existing heart disease is an important precipitating factor in many cases. Even so, some 15 to 20 percent of sudden death victims have no detectable coronary atherosclerosis; 50 percent have no history of smoking, hypertension, high cholesterol, or obesity; and as many as 75 percent show no evidence of previous myocardial infarctions (Monagan, 1986).

Rapid death unpreceded by obvious illness also occurs in concentration and prisoner-of-war camps, where some people seemingly "turn their faces to the wall and die." Likewise, hospital personnel recount cases in which patients who, although not critically ill, die soon after some disappointment or loss has led them to "lose their will to live." And sociologists find dips in the death rate immediately before holidays and days of special significance (such as presidential elections), followed by a "catching up" soon after the important event has passed (Philips and Feldman, 1973).

churning stomach, tight throat, aching back, crying jags, short temper, sleepless nights, dizzy spells, ulcers, asthma attacks, and countless other unpleasant symptoms. It is little wonder that most of us think that stress is bad. Yet without some stress, we would find life quite drab, boring, and purposeless. Significant gains in personal growth can be made under stressful circumstances that increase our confidence and skills for dealing with future events (Goodhart, 1985). This is reflected in the Chinese word for stress, which is composed of two characters —one meaning danger and the other opportunity. Danger and opportunity are not so much opposites as two sides of a single coin. A stressful situation for one person may be a splendid opportunity for another. Indeed, many people thrive on stress. They find that working under pressure or against deadlines provides them with the motivation to do their best. Nor do these people necessarily succumb to adverse stress reactions. Indeed, slowing a "racehorse" down to the pace of a "turtle" would be as stressful as attempting to make a turtle keep up with a race-

Working under pressure is invigorating for some people, and they thrive on it. Other people experience health-threatening stress from the same pressures. *(Mark Antman/The Image Works)*

horse. Although a certain amount of pressure may encourage productivity, efficiency, and well-being, people differ considerably in the amount of stress that they find optimal and in their ability to cope with it (Kobasa, 1982; Taylor, 1986). We will have more to say on this matter later in the chapter.

PSYCHOSOCIAL STRESSORS

Students often complain that college life is a "rat race." Textbook assignments, term papers, and exams abound. Moreover, many students have to balance a job with their schooling. All the while young people are compelled to restructure their lives. They find themselves in a transition period between adolescent life, which was centered in family and peer relationships, and their entry into the adult world. They must become less financially dependent, formulate new goals, enter new roles and living arrangements, modify long-held assumptions, and achieve greater autonomy and self-responsibility (see Chapter 12).

In brief, life requires continual adjustment. Stress is often associated with changing life circumstances. What are some of the sources of stress that we experience in the course of our lives? Psychologists have provided a number of answers to this question.

Life Change

The concept of *life change* as formulated by Thomas H. Holmes, Richard H. Rahe, and their colleagues (Holmes and Masuda, 1974; Rahe, 1974) refers to any event that requires a modification in your accustomed way of living. Life events that create change and require adaptation may occur in any aspect of your life. You may evaluate these events either positively or negatively. Holmes and Rahe (1967) developed a forty-three-item Social Readjustment Rating Scale to measure the amount of change required by life events (see Table 14.1). Each of these life events is given a numerical rating in "life-change units" on a scale from 1 to 100. The highest score is 100 points, which is assigned to the death of a

Major life transitions, even rewarding ones like graduating from college, are stressful. *(Ken Robert Buck/The Picture Cube)*

TABLE 14.1 Stress Ratings of Various Life Events

Events	Scale of Impact	Events	Scale of Impact
Death of spouse	100	Son or daughter leaving home	29
Divorce	73	Trouble with in-laws	29
Marital separation	65	Outstanding personal achievement	28
Jail term	63	Wife begins or stops work	26
Death of close family member	63	Begin or end school	26
Personal injury or illness	53	Change in living conditions	25
Marriage	50	Revision of personal habits	24
Fired at work	47	Trouble with boss	23
Marital reconciliation	45	Change in work hours or	
Retirement	45	conditions	20
Change in health of family member	44	Change in residence	20
Pregnancy	40	Change in schools	20
Sex difficulties	39	Change in recreation	19
Gain of new family member	39	Change in church activities	19
Business readjustment	39	Change in social activities	18
Change in financial state	38	Mortgage or loan less than $10,000	17
Death of close friend	37	Change in sleeping habits	16
Change to different line of work	36	Change in number of family get-	
Change in number of arguments		togethers	15
with spouse	35	Change in eating habits	15
Mortgage over $10,000	31	Vacation	13
Foreclosure of mortgage or loan	30	Christmas	12
Change in responsibilities at work	29	Minor violations of the law	11

Source: Adapted from T. S. Holmes and T. H. Holmes. 1970. Short-term intrusions into life-style routine. *Journal of Psychosomatic Research, 14:121–132.* Reprinted with permission of Pergamon Press, Ltd. Copyright © 1970 by Pergamon Press, Ltd.

spouse. Divorce is weighted at 73 points, being fired from one's job at 47 points, pregnancy at 40 points, change in schools at 20 points, and minor violations of the law at 11 points (the lowest score). A risk score is them computed by adding your life-change units for a given time period. (A version of this rating scale has been developed for people of college age. You may want to take the self-test on pages 460–462 to estimate the level of stress you have experienced in the past year.)

In one study, Holmes and a colleague (Holmes and Masuda, 1972) followed the health of eighty-four young physicians at the University of Washington over an eight-month period. In this time, 49 percent of those in the high-risk category (those with 300 or more life-change units), 25 percent in the medium-risk category (those with 200 to 299 units), and 9 percent in the low-risk category (those with 150 to

199 units) reported illness. In another study, Holmes evaluated the injury rates of college football players. At the end of the athletic season, he found that 50 percent of the high-risk group, 25 percent of the medium-risk group, and 9 percent of the low-risk group had been injured (Holmes and Masuda, 1974). In still another study, Rahe (1968) asked some twenty-five hundred officers and enlisted men aboard three United States Navy cruisers to report their life changes and histories for the previous six months. He then followed the men's health over the next six months through their shipboard medical records. In the first month at sea, those men who were judged to be in a high-risk category by virtue of the stressful events they had experienced in the preceding six months had nearly 90 percent more first illnesses than did those men who were in a low-risk category. One explanation given for the

Self-Test: Social Readjustment Rating Scale

Directions

Below is a list of 100 adjustment events that college students have identified as causing stress in their lives. Read each event and determine the number of times it has occurred in the past twelve months. (Do not enter a number larger than 5.) Enter this number in the Frequency column.

Event	Value	Frequency	Total
1. Death of a spouse, lover, or child	94		
2. Death of parent or sibling	88		
3. Beginning formal higher education	84		
4. Death of a close friend	83		
5. Miscarriage or stillbirth of pregnancy of self, spouse, or lover	83		
6. Jail sentence	83		
7. Divorce or marital separation	82		
8. Unwanted pregnancy of self, spouse, or lover	82		
9. Abortion of unwanted pregnancy of self, spouse, or lover	80		
10. Detention in jail or other institution	79		
11. Change in dating activity	79		
12. Death of a close relative	79		
13. Change in marital situation other than divorce or separation	78		
14. Separation from significant other whom you like very much	77		
15. Change in health status or behavior of spouse or lover	77		
16. Academic failure	77		
17. Major violation of the law and subsequent arrest	76		
18. Marrying or living with lover against parents' wishes	75		
19. Change in love relationship or important friendship	74		
20. Change in health status or behavior of a parent or sibling	73		
21. Change in feelings of loneliness, insecurity, anxiety, boredom	73		
22. Change in marital status of parents	73		
23. Acquiring a visible deformity	72		
24. Change in ability to communicate with a significant other whom you like very much	71		
25. Hospitalization of a parent or sibling	70		
26. Reconciliation of marital or love relationship	68		
27. Release from jail or other institution	68		
28. Graduation from college	68		
29. Major personal injury or illness	68		
30. Wanted pregnancy of self, spouse, or lover	67		
31. Change in number or type of arguments with spouse or lover	67		
32. Marrying or living with lover with parents' approval	66		
33. Gaining a new family member through birth or adoption	65		
34. Preparing for an important exam or writing a major paper	65		
35. Major financial difficulties	65		
36. Change in the health status or behavior of a close relative or close friend	65		
37. Change in academic status	64		
38. Change in amount and nature of interpersonal conflicts	63		

Event	Value	Frequency	Total
39. Change in relationship with members of your immediate family	62	_____	_____
40. Change in own personality	62	_____	_____
41. Hospitalization of yourself or a close relative	61	_____	_____
42. Change in course of study, major field, vocational goals, or work status	60	_____	_____
43. Change in own financial status	59	_____	_____
44. Change in status of divorced or widowed parent	59	_____	_____
45. Change in number or type of arguments between parents	59	_____	_____
46. Change in acceptance by peers, identification with peers, or social pressure by peers	58	_____	_____
47. Change in general outlook on life	57	_____	_____
48. Beginning or ceasing service in the armed forces	57	_____	_____
49. Change in attitudes toward friends	56	_____	_____
50. Change in living arrangements, conditions, or environment	55	_____	_____
51. Change in frequency or nature of sexual experiences	55	_____	_____
52. Change in parents' financial status	55	_____	_____
53. Change in amount or nature of pressure from parents	55	_____	_____
54. Change in degree of interest in college or attitudes toward education	55	_____	_____
55. Change in the number of personal or social relationships you've formed or dissolved	55	_____	_____
56. Change in relationship with siblings	54	_____	_____
57. Change in mobility or reliability of transportation	54	_____	_____
58. Academic success	54	_____	_____
59. Change to a new college or university	54	_____	_____
60. Change in feelings of self-reliance, independence, or amount of self-discipline	53	_____	_____
61. Change in number or type of arguments with roommate	52	_____	_____
62. Spouse or lover beginning or ceasing work outside of the home	52	_____	_____
63. Change in frequency of use of amounts of drugs other than alcohol, tobacco, or marijuana	51	_____	_____
64. Change in sexual morality, beliefs, or attitudes	50	_____	_____
65. Change in responsibility at work	50	_____	_____
66. Change in amount or nature of social activities	50	_____	_____
67. Change in dependencies on parents	50	_____	_____
68. Change from academic work to practical fieldwork experience or internship	50	_____	_____
69. Change in amount of material possessions and concomitant responsibilities	50	_____	_____
70. Change in routine at college or work	49	_____	_____
71. Change in amount of leisure time	49	_____	_____
72. Change in amount of in-law trouble	49	_____	_____
73. Outstanding personal achievement	49	_____	_____
74. Change in family structure other than parental divorce or separation	48	_____	_____
75. Change in attitude toward drugs	48	_____	_____
76. Change in amount and nature of competition with same sex	48	_____	_____
77. Improvement of own health	47	_____	_____
78. Change in responsibilities at home	47	_____	_____
79. Change in study habits	46	_____	_____

(continued on next page)

Event	Value	Frequency	Total
80. Change in number or type of arguments or conflicts with close relatives	46	_____	_____
81. Change in sleeping habits	46	_____	_____
82. Change in frequency of use or amounts of alcohol	45	_____	_____
83. Change in social status	45	_____	_____
84. Change in frequency of use or amounts of tobacco	45	_____	_____
85. Change in awareness of activities in external world	45	_____	_____
86. Change in religious affiliation	44	_____	_____
87. Change in type of gratifying activities	43	_____	_____
88. Change in amount or nature of physical activities	43	_____	_____
89. Change in address or residence	43	_____	_____
90. Change in amount or nature of recreational activities	43	_____	_____
91. Change in frequency of use or amounts of marijuana	43	_____	_____
92. Change in social demands or responsibilities due to your age	43	_____	_____
93. Court appearance for legal violation	40	_____	_____
94. Change in weight or eating habits	39	_____	_____
95. Change in religious activities	37	_____	_____
96. Change in political views or affiliations	34	_____	_____
97. Change in driving pattern or conditions	33	_____	_____
98. Minor violation of the law	31	_____	_____
99. Vacation or travel	30	_____	_____
100. Change in number of family get-togethers	30	_____	_____
TOTAL			_____

Scoring

For each event, multiply the frequency times the value and write the product in the Total column. To determine your final score, add up all the numbers in the Total column.

Interpretation

- Up to 1500   = Minor stress

- 1501–3500   = Mild stress

- 3501–5500   = Moderate stress

- More than 5501   = Major stress

Your total score is a measure of the amount of stress you have experienced in the past year. It can be used to predict your chances of suffering illness within the next year. For example, if you have experienced only minor stress, your chance of becoming ill is 28 percent. Mild stress carries a 45 percent chance, moderate stress a 70 percent chance, and major stress an 82 percent chance of suffering illness. Furthermore, as your score increases, so do the odds that the illness will be serious.

Remember, however, that a low score does not protect you from illness, just as a high score does not guarantee illness. Your score is simply an indication of your chance of becoming ill based on the stress you have experienced.

(Source: Peggy Blake, Robert Fry, and Michael Pesjack. 1984. Self-Assessment and Behavior Change Manual. New York: Random House, pp. 43–47. Reprinted by permission of Random House, Inc.)

association between life change and health change is that changing life situations require adaptive behavior and evoke significant alteration in the body's metabolism, which lowers resistance to illness.

Since the publication of the Social Readjustment Rating Scale, some psychologists have questioned whether all the events should be treated the same way. They argue it is not change per se that is crucial, but the meaning that an event has to the person involved (Mueller, Edwards, and Yarvis, 1977; Ross and Mirowsky, 1979). Others fault the scale because the risk score is contaminated by items closely related to physical health, including such items as "major personal injury or illness," "major changes in sleeping habits," and "sexual difficulties." Consequently, these critics say that the scale exaggerates the link between environmental stress and illness (Schroeder and Costa, 1984). And critics observe that not all people develop chronic diseases or psychiatric disorders after exposure to stressful conditions. Indeed, they say that most people do not become sick even when terrible things happen to them, and those who do usually "bounce back" in a reasonably short time (Hudgens, 1974; Rabkin and Struening, 1976).

Chronic Stress

Psychologists have also examined the effects that a single, chronic life stressor has on people. Whereas single episodes of acute exposure to stressors usually have only a temporary effect, repeated exposure to stressful circumstances may produce more serious problems (DeLongis et al., 1982; Lazarus and DeLongis, 1983). Chronic stressors include long-term unemployment and wartime combat.

Economic Hard Times

A number of psychologists and sociologists contend that changes in the economy affect the incidence of

health problems (Kasl and Cobb, 1982; Catalano and Dooley, 1983; Horwitz, 1985). They point out that bad economic times have adverse consequences for diet and life style. But hard times also create additional stress that has been implicated in disease processes. The sociologist Harvey Brenner (1973, 1975, 1976) calculates that for each rise of 1 percent in the unemployment rate, 4 percent more people wind up in state prisons, 5.7 percent more are murdered, 4.1 percent more commit suicide, 4.3 percent more men and 2.3 percent more women are admitted to state mental institutions for the first time, and 1.9 percent more people die of heart disease, cirrhosis of the liver, and other ailments.

Undergoing an undesirable job or financial event nearly doubles the odds that you will become ill or be injured (Catalano and Dooley, 1983). It seems that economic hardship creates a stressful state. Unemployed people are far more likely than those who are employed to experience demoralization, low self-esteem, feelings of unhappiness, dissatisfaction with life, and a good deal of personal strain (Campbell, 1981; Veroff, Douvan, and Kulka, 1981). When workers are reemployed, their distress levels typically decline dramatically (Banks and Jackson, 1982; Liem, Atkinson, and Liem, 1983). Moreover, the impact of unemployment is not limited to the family member who is out of work. It frequently engulfs the family unit. Psychiatric symptoms among the wives

For most people, being unemployed is a major stressor. (Péter Tartsányi/EKM-Nepenthe)

of unemployed men increase, as do arguments and tensions in the household (Scholzman and Verba, 1978).

Combat Stress and Trauma

Studies of veterans from World War II and the Vietnam War reveal that the psychological effects of combat and traumatic war experiences often linger for a long time (Stouffer et al., 1949; Archibald et al., 1962; Laufer, Gallops, and Frey-Wouters, 1984). Exposure to combat involves many sources of stress, including being far away from home and loved ones, the threat to life and limb, physical discomfort from exposure to the elements, disease, the dying of friends, the requirement to kill and harm others, and the feeling of helplessness in the face of forces beyond one's control. What veterans of earlier wars called "battle fatigue" or "shell shock" is now categorized by psychiatrists as *post-traumatic stress disorder* (PTSD), along with rape, catastrophic natural disaster, concentration camp confinement, and kidnaping. Its symptoms include guilt feelings about surviving when others have not, sleep disturbances, exaggerated startle responses, impaired memory, identity confusion, cynicism, and loss of intimacy (Frye and Stockton, 1982; Wilmer, 1982). In some cases, veterans relive over and over in flashbacks and nightmares the fires of battle and the screams of comrades. Some psychologists believe that PTSD afflicts about 50 percent of all combat veterans. In recent years public attention has focused on a small number of "tripwire vets" who have abandoned life in the larger community and reportedly survive in the wild using skills they learned in Vietnam (Davidson and Lang, 1984; Turkington; 1984b).

The social context of the Vietnam War was new to the American experience in a number of ways. For one thing, veterans had to return from the combat theater to a civilian society in which the war was not popular and in which veterans received little moral support. For another, Vietnam was not primarily a war of confrontation along front lines, but a guerrilla war in which the enemy was mobile and elusive. Finally, the scope and intensity of guerrilla activity made it unclear who the enemy was and placed the noncombatant status of civilians in question. The net result was that American soldiers participated in many types of violence, including attacks on civilian villages, the mistreatment of civilians, and the physical harassment of prisoners. Reseachers have found direct links between these experiences and the incidence of stress symptoms and disorders among veterans in the postwar period (Laufer, Gallops, and Frey-Wouters, 1984).

Daily Hassles

We have seen that big events—the death of a loved one, a divorce, the loss of a job, or combat experience—affect our well-being and health. This is most apparent when stressful events accumulate, straining our problem-solving capacities. But small, frustrating events are also important. These smaller occurrences, or microstressors, are called **hassles** —the irritating demands and troubled relationships that plague us day in and day out (Lazarus and DeLongis, 1983; Lazarus et al., 1985). Hassles come in many forms, including annoying household chores, concern about one's weight, too many things to do, misplacing or losing things, a noisy neighborhood, money worries, uncooperative coworkers, and taxes.

People differ in the hassles that they report (Kanner et al., 1981). Middle-aged people most frequently cite economic concerns (rising prices, money worries, or taxes), whereas college students more often mention academic and youthful problems (wasting time, meeting high standards, or being lonely). The counterpart of hassles are positive psychological experiences, or **uplifts**: pleasant, happy, or satisfying events like hearing good news, getting a good night's sleep, or solving a difficult problem. Here too age differences come into play. For middle-aged adults, the most frequent uplifts are health- or family-related. For the college population, the most frequent uplifts have a hedonic quality—having fun, partying, and laughing.

Richard S. Lazarus and his colleagues (Lazarus and DeLongis, 1983; Lazarus et al., 1985) find a relationship between the incidence of daily hassles and illness. Indeed, they contend that life's daily

---

hassles: The irritating demands and troubled relationships that plague us day in and day out. Compare **uplifts**.

uplifts: Pleasant, happy, or satisfying psychological experiences. Compare **hassles**.

Everyday life is full of minor hassles—so many for some people that they become depressed and unable to cope. *(Ray Solomon/Monkmeyer)*

hassles are more closely linked to and may have a greater effect on our moods and our health than life's major misfortunes. However, the degree to which people feel stress seems to depend less on the number or intensity of the hassles they experience than whether a particular stressful event is central to their sense of self-esteem. Other hassles are usually transitory. We may be irritated by a traffic jam, but it has little long-lasting significance. The hassles that affect us most severely typically impinge on our personal values, commitments, goals, and spheres of vulnerability. However, people also thrive on some kinds of hassles. For instance, an executive who has just changed to a better job with more responsibility may report an exuberant mood. As yet, the psychological study of hassles is a relatively new area of investigation and much controversy rages among

psychologists on how best to go about measuring them (Dohrenwend et al., 1984; Dohrenwend and Shrout, 1985).

Crowding

We commonly think that crowding is bad for us because it produces stress. According to popular belief, crowding contributes to violence, crime, chronic physical and mental illness, family breakdown, alcoholism, and suicide. The notion that crowding breeds pathology derives in part from studies of animal populations. Researchers find that after population build-ups, interaction among the members of a community intensifies and leads to progressively greater levels of stress (Evans, 1978). For instance, a study of the Sika deer population on James Island in Chesapeake Bay revealed that as overcrowding increased, so did stress (Christian, 1963). Prolonged stress contributed to severe metabolic disturbance and to the enlargement and overactivity of the animals' adrenal glands. Later, when a winter cold spell set in, the deer were unable to withstand the shock and a massive die-off resulted. In a related study of the Norway rat, John Calhoun (1962) found that overcrowding led to the disintegration of family life, high infant mortality rates, small litters, inadequate nesting, abandonment of the young, cannibalism, and sadism—a condition Calhoun termed a "behavioral sink." However, there is some question whether these outcomes resulted from the limited space available for each animal or from the large size of the group (Freedman, 1979).

Although population build-up apparently has a negative effect on deer, rats, and many other creatures, it does not seem to have a similar impact on human beings. Consider crime. Although it may sound implausible, over the past thirty-five years American urban population *and* household crowding have sharply *declined*, while crime rates have soared. Nor have researchers been able to show a significant statistical link between crowding and aggression (Loo, 1972; Freedman, 1975; Sundstrom, 1978).

All this does not mean that crowding has no impact upon human behavior. It does. However, density and crowding are not the same things (Desor, 1972; Stokols, 1972). **Density** is a physical

density: A physical condition that entails spatial limitations.

Some work environments are so crowded and noisy that they are highly stressful for many employees. *(Scott Thode/International Stock)*

condition that entails spatial limitations. **Crowding** is the perception people have that they are receiving excessive stimulation from social sources. What matters most is not density per se but the definition we have of a situation as being crowded or uncrowded. For example, architectural designs of doors, windows, partitions, and dividers that reduce our perception of one another—providing us with a sense of privacy—lead us to feel "less crowded" even though the actual density of a space remains constant (Desor, 1972). Likewise, the sense of crowding and stress experienced by students living on long-corridor dormitories can be alleviated by modifying the hallways so as to cluster residents in small groups of fewer than twenty members (Baum and Davis, 1980).

Many factors influence whether people will define a setting as crowded (Sundstrom, 1978; Worchel and Brown, 1984). Duration of exposure is one consideration. We usually find it easier to tolerate a brief exposure to conditions of high density, such as a ride on a crowded elevator, than prolonged exposure, such as a ride on a crowded cross-country bus. Another factor is predictability. We find situations more stressful when they are unpredictable than when they are predictable. Still another consideration revolves about our need for stimulation. There are times when we prefer intensive interaction, as at a football game, and times when we prefer solitude, as when we are studying for a test. And finally, we find it easier to tolerate many people in an impersonal, public place (a shopping mall or an airline terminal) than we do in a personal, private place (our home or dorm room).

In sum, density is most likely to produce stress when it involves conditions that disturb our sense of

---

crowding: The perception people have that they are receiving excessive stimulation from social sources.

control over our relationships with other people (Edney, 1975; Sundstrom, 1975; Darley and Gilbert, 1985). This finds expression in the colloquialism "Don't crowd me!" By the same token, complicated or disorderly settings tax our capacity to pay attention and our ability to assimilate information. In crowds we pick up too many thermal, olfactory, and visual cues and feel ourselves "overloaded" with excessive stimulation (Cohen, 1978; Schaeffer and Patterson, 1980). Complicating matters further, excessive interpersonal proximity makes us think that our personal space is being invaded (Karlin, Epstein, and Aiello, 1978). Even so, we differ considerably in our experience of crowding and our ability to cope with it (Baum et al., 1982).

The Workplace

Occupational stress is related to physical illness, psychological impairment, and lowered job performance and satisfaction (Caplan et al., 1975; Cooper and Payne, 1978; House et al., 1979; Knight, 1984). Many facets of the workplace can produce stress, including deadlines, unmanageable work loads, inadequate salaries, poor relationships with bosses and coworkers, few opportunities to participate in decision making, role conflicts, and lack of appreciation. The greatest stress is found in jobs in which heavy demands are made on workers but workers exercise little control over how the work is done. People in machine-paced jobs, such as assembly-line workers, freight handlers, punch-press operators, and garment stitchers, fall into this category. So do workers in certain service jobs in which employees have little say in how they relate to the client. Examples include cashiers, telephone operators, and nurses' aides. In contrast, jobs that allow workers a good deal of control over the work process are typically low in stress. Many laboratory scientists, forest rangers, skilled machinists, and appliance repairers can set their own work pace, define their style of working, and determine their methods for handling job-related demands.

Some positions make high demands on their occupants, but afford them a high measure of control over their work. Executives are a case in point. They set their own pace and have a voice in the procedures that they will employ in carrying out their tasks. Moreover, executives can often determine their work associates. And they have opportunities to grow and develop new skills and capabilities in their work. Although they commonly label their jobs as "stressful," for them a "stressful job" translates into a "responsible job," a "decision-pressured job," an "important job," or a "powerful job." Even though reports of stress are associated with high position, job success, influence, and power, the crippling health effects of stress are not. In sum, while executives may find their work environments demanding, they generally perceive their jobs positively and derive a good deal of satisfaction from them.

Some research suggests that women typically encounter more work-related stress than male workers (Stewart and Salt, 1981; Haw, 1982; Reskin and Coverman, 1985). In part this seems due to the fact that women are more likely to hold jobs in which they have little influence on decisions, engage in redundant operations, exercise little control over the pace of their work, and lack authority. Despite recent increases in the occupational mobility of women, there has been little substantial change in the gender segregation of occupations since 1900 (Scott, 1982). Additionally, working women not only may experience role overload, they also must integrate the often conflicting role demands of worker, spouse, and mother. Even so, a mounting body of research suggests that work is not necessarily inimical to the health of women, and indeed is often beneficial to them (Haynes and Feinleib, 1980; Kandel, Davies, and Raveis, 1985; Zappert and Weinstein, 1985).

One approach to job stress is *person-environment fit theory* (French, 1973; Harrison, 1978; Chemers et al., 1985). According to this view, people whose abilities, needs, and work styles are "in match" with the demands, resources, and opportunities of their jobs show less stress, fewer health problems, and fewer days missed from work than do individuals who are "out of match." For example, workers whose job complexity is either greater or less than they desire report more depression than do employees whose degree of job complexity matches their preferences (Caplan et al., 1975). Likewise, what one person finds a challenge another may view as an unendurable pressure. Even assessments of monotony vary widely. Indeed, almost any job will seem boring to some people (Stagner, 1975).

Work that once was fulfilling and satisfying may over time become unfulfilling and unsatisfying, a condition called **job burnout.** Its symptoms include a sense of boredom, apathy, reduced efficiency, fatigue, frustration, and sometimes even despair (Perlman and Hartman, 1982). Psychologist Christina Maslach (1976) says that job burnout typically evolves through three phases. First, people experience emotional exhaustion, a feeling of being drained, used up, and having nothing more to give. Second, they become increasingly cynical, callous, and insensitive toward the people they encounter in their work. Finally, they conclude that their careers have been unsuccessful and their efforts are in vain. Victims of burnout are commonly highly efficient, competent, and energetic people. They often enter their occupations with idealistic fervor and dedication, hoping to make the world a better place (Farber, 1983; Shinn et al., 1984). But the reality eventually crushes their humanism and disillusions them. Moreover, being available to others in need can be emotionally draining. Nurses, police officers, teachers, social workers, divorce and criminal lawyers, and staffers in mental hospitals and hospices are especially prone to job burnout. Other victims of burnout are ambitious people who are blocked in climbing the corporate ladder and people motivated by strong creative impulses. The boxed insert on page 469 presents a number of techniques for handling job-related stress.

COPING WITH STRESS

Coping behaviors are a key aspect of stress. When we face trying circumstances, we typically seek some way of dealing with them. **Coping** entails the responses we make in order to master, tolerate, or reduce stress (Lazarus and DeLongis, 1983; Fleming, Baum, and Singer, 1984). Coping is a complex combination of emotions, thoughts, and behaviors. This is hardly surprising, for life itself is anything but simple. Consider illness. In dealing with a serious illness, a patient must frequently confront many sources of stress, including pain and incapacitation, hospital environments, and the demands

imposed by medical personnel and special treatment procedures (Moos and Tsu, 1977). No one coping strategy is likely to fit all these situations. Accordingly, in dealing with stress, an array of shifting strategies is called for. Depending on the situation, patients may actively attack a problem, seek to downplay the threat, or attempt to protect themselves from unpleasant reality by simply denying it.

Coping Behaviors

Coping involves a number of types of behavior. At the most basic level, we can distinguish between *emotion-focused coping* and *problem-focused coping* (Folkman and Lazarus, 1985). Problem-focused coping changes the troubling situation, whereas emotion-focused coping changes your appraisal of the situation. If you resolve the trouble through problem-focused efforts, you no longer have reason to feel threatened. If you engage in emotion-focused efforts, the objective situation remains the same but you experience it as less distressful or menacing. Under the latter circumstances, you may attempt to shift your thoughts to other matters, intellectually detach yourself from the problem, engage in magical or wishful thinking, deny that the problem exists, laugh the difficulty off, or have recourse to religious faith. Psychologists find that you are more likely to use problem-focused coping at work and emotion-focused coping to deal with many health stresses. You can also combine problem-focused coping with emotion-focused coping in a great many different ways. Consider how you cope with a coming midterm examination (Krantz, 1983; Folkman and Lazarus, 1985). You tackle the task at hand and study for the test. But simultaneously, you may attempt to regulate your emotional stress by visiting friends, engaging in some recreational activity, daydreaming that you will do exceedingly well, or praying for divine assistance.

We undertake coping behaviors in response to our appraisals of a stressful situation. We evaluate an event with respect to what is at stake (*primary appraisal*) and what coping resources and options we

---

job burnout: A job-related stress syndrome marked by boredom, apathy, reduced efficiency, fatigue, frustration, and sometimes even despair.
coping: The responses individuals make in order to master, tolerate, or reduce stress.

Dealing with Stress on the Job

Stress is an inescapable aspect of any job. Many of us find that we do our best and most satisfying work when we perform it under some degree of stress. Indeed, it can be argued that eliminating stress entirely would mean never getting up in the morning. But job stress can also take its toll. At times it is associated with emotional problems and medical ailments. It causes resignations and absenteeism by employees who are too bored, upset, or angry to come to work. And it plays a role in industrial accidents as well. Given that stress is inescapable, what might we do to minimize its harmful effects? Psychological studies suggest a number of answers (Lazarus, 1966; Antonovsky, 1979; Pines and Aronson, 1981):

● Listen to your body. It lets you know when you are pushing too hard: your muscles may tense, your stomach may seem queasy, your head may ache, you may clench your teeth, or you may experience dizziness. Identify and monitor the situations that trigger tension so that you can evolve strategies for dealing with them.

● Exercise is one of the best ways to relieve the pressures caused by job stress. In fact, physical fitness may serve as a sort of inoculation against stress. But if heavy exercise is not enjoyable, do not do it. Otherwise you may only create new tensions.

● Find a project at work that means a good deal to you and that is consistent with your employer's goals. You generally do not burn out in a job because of overwork and stress, but because the work you are doing is no longer rewarding. Accordingly, select some project that you can "sink your teeth into" and that will reconnect you with your work. Greater variety may also lend spice to the workplace.

● Organize your time. Figure out what are your most essential and important tasks. Pace yourself by scheduling these tasks when you are most productive and least likely to be interrupted. Learn to set priorities. Get a handle on time so that you use it rationally and wisely.

● Communicate with your superior. Let your boss know how things are going, where the problems are, and what your achievements have been. A good relationship with a superior is a two-way street. Avoiding your boss tends to be a poor coping technique.

● Leave your work at the shop or office and thus minimize conflicts with your family and home responsibilities.

● Develop outside interests and hobbies. Allow yourself time to recharge your batteries. You cannot expect your job to give your life all its meaning.

● Virtually all job settings require that you work closely with someone who constantly annoys you. Minimize the impact that your nemesis has for you. See if you can find a way to deal with the person in an easier, friendlier way. Be generous. The good will you extend may come back to benefit you. Also find ways to team up with coworkers whom you enjoy working with.

● Acquire new skills and build your self-confidence. Attend workshops and conferences. Take courses to gain additional competence.

● If you see little hope for improvement in your present job situation, consider looking for another job. Procrastination is almost guaranteed to prolong your distress. But do not quit your current job until you have a job to replace it.

● Do not be afraid to seek outside help. Job counseling may be helpful should you find yourself unhappy with your job and confused as to what you should do about it. In some cases, training in assertiveness may assist you in gaining self-confidence.

Do not sit around waiting for the day when you can relax and when your problems will be over. The struggles associated with daily living never end. If you follow some of the above suggestions, you can make your work a more satisfying experience.

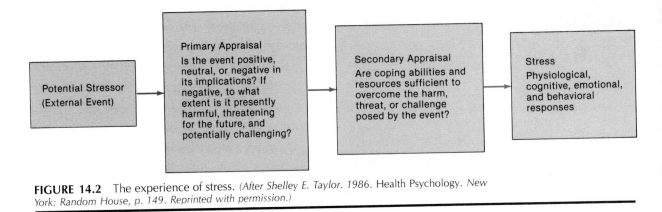

FIGURE 14.2 The experience of stress. *(After Shelley E. Taylor. 1986. Health Psychology. New York: Random House, p. 149. Reprinted with permission.)*

have available to us (*secondary appraisal*) (see Figure 14.2). We may arrive at any number of different appraisals. Some appraisals involve an assessment that harm or loss has already occurred. Others entail the belief that harm or loss has not yet occurred but will in the future. And still others involve an assessment that an opportunity presents itself for mastery or gain. As we noted earlier in the chapter, people differ greatly in how they evaluate a situation and whether they see it negatively, as a threat, or positively, as a challenge. And they may even see the situation in both ways. Hence, if you are like a good many students, you experience feelings of both threat and challenge at the prospect of a midterm examination.

Stress-Hardiness

We have seen that much depends on how we appraise a situation. Not surprisingly, some of us seem to be more stress-resistant than others by virtue of the attitudes we bring to our day-to-day lives. Psychologist Suzanne C. Kobasa and her colleagues (Kobasa, Maddi, and Kahn, 1982) find that hardiness is associated with an openness to change, a feeling of involvement in what one is doing, and a sense of control over events. Take the matter of a person's attitude toward change. Stress-hardy people see a potentially difficult event as something challenging rather than something to be feared. Rather than viewing loss of a job as a catastrophe, they define the situation as an opportunity to begin a new career that is more to their liking. Likewise, psychologically hardy people get involved in life rather than hanging back on its fringes; they immerse themselves in

meaningful activity. And stress-hardy people believe that they can actively influence many of the events in their lives and that they have an impact on their surroundings.

A study of Vietnam combat veterans found that those who did not develop post-traumatic stress disorder handled stress in somewhat similar ways (Hendin and Haas, 1984). During combat the men had exhibited calmness under pressure, intellectual control, acceptance of fear, and a lack of excessively violent or guilt-arousing behavior. Other researchers also find that those who adapt to stress with little physical or psychological strain are more easygoing and less inclined to use avoidance coping than are persons who become ill under stress (Holahan and Moos, 1985). Additionally, men who are self-confident and women who have family support seem better able to handle stress than other people. In sum, people differ in their orientations or dispositions to stress and in their strategies for handling it (Fleishman, 1984; Ganellen and Blaney, 1984; Taylor, 1986).

A Sense of Control

A recurring theme in the psychological literature is that people who feel in control of a situation experience a sense of empowerment (Lefcourt et al., 1981; Frankenhaeuser, 1983; Fiske and Taylor, 1984; Fleishman, 1984). People with a high sense of mastery believe that they can control most aspects of their lives. In contrast, those unable to gain mastery —to exert influence over their circumstances—feel helpless (see the discussion in Chapter 6 on learned helplessness). People with a low sense of mastery

Older adults who have some responsibilities and control over their lives tend to be healthier and more content. *(Ellis Herwig/Stock, Boston)*

believe that their attempts at control are futile. It seems that a general sense of mastery moderates the negative effects of stress and encourages problem-focused as opposed to emotion-focused coping (Folkman, 1984).

The important part that feelings of personal choice and control play in our lives is highlighted by the experiences of the elderly residents of a Connecticut nursing home. Psychologists Ellen J. Langer and Judith Rodin (1976) assessed the effects of an intervention designed to encourage elderly residents to make a greater number of choices and to feel they had more control over their day-to-day lives. They sought to determine whether the decline in health, alertness, positive attitude, and activity that frequently occurs in residents of institutions could be slowed, reversed, or even prevented by giving residents more responsibility for making daily decisions. The results showed that the elderly given more responsibility became more active and reported feeling less unhappy than did a comparison group on another floor, who were encouraged to feel that the staff would care for them and try to satisfy their needs. In an eighteen-month follow-up, Rodin and Langer (1977) found that during the period following the intervention the responsible patients exhibited significantly greater improvement in health than patients in the comparison group. Even the death

rates of the two groups were marginally different, suggesting that enhanced feelings of control may have life-promoting effects. Animal studies also show that if animals have control over an unpleasant stimulus, they are less likely to develop ulcers, depressed appetite, sleep disturbances, or brain-chemistry changes characteristic of stress responses (Abbott, Schoen, and Badia, 1984; Maier and Laudenslager, 1985).

Biofeedback

Biofeedback is a useful tool in training people to exert more control over their physical reactions to situational stresses.

Before biofeedback, scientists believed that such responses as heart rate and sweat-gland activity were involuntary, that people could not consciously control them. When researchers in the 1960s began to find that people could, there was a great deal of excitement about these newly discovered potentials of the nervous system. Many began experimenting with biofeedback to cure such medical and stress-related conditions as high blood pressure, migraine headaches, and tension headaches. (For a discussion of lowering blood pressure with biofeedback, see the boxed insert on page 472.) At first, many biofeedback cures were reported in the press. But psycholo-

Lowering Blood Pressure

One out of every three American adults has high blood pressure. More than 90 percent of these cases are diagnosed as *essential hypertension*—a euphemism that means nobody really knows what is causing it. Traditionally, physicians have treated this problem with pills. But now doctors are shifting their emphasis from pills to people. Patients with high blood pressure are being taught to relax, often with the help of medication and biofeedback (Hassett, 1978b).

Blood pressure is the force of the blood moving away from the heart, pushing against the artery walls. It changes from instant to instant, peaking as the heart beats and blood spurts through the arteries, and gradually decreasing to a minimum just before the next beat. Blood pressure is expressed as two numbers: systolic pressure (the maximum value when the heart beats) over diastolic pressure (the minimum pressure between beats). Normal blood pressure is somewhere around 120/80.

Blood pressure varies constantly and increases under stress. Visiting the dentist, taking an examination, thinking about trying out skydiving with the new friend you are trying to impress, even drinking a cup of coffee (a mild stimulant) will increase your blood pressure temporarily. Strong emotions, particularly suppressed anger, will also raise blood pressure.

When blood pressure goes up and stays up, the medical condition is called **hypertension.** Definite hypertension refers to a blood pressure greater than 160/95. Hypertension is called "the silent killer" because it usually produces no pain and no other symptoms or warnings before causing severe damage to the cardiovascular system or other organs. But a killer it is. It is a primary cause of *stroke* (which is blood-vessel damage in the brain).

After researchers discovered that normal people could raise and lower blood pressure with the help of biofeedback, it was but a small step to using the idea to help hypertensives. But biofeedback's effects do not always last after the subject leaves the laboratory. For instance, a researcher noticed that one man had a puzzling pattern of successes and failures. Five days a week, this hypertensive man faithfully attended training sessions, collecting thirty-five dollars every Friday for his success in lowering his systolic pressure. When he returned each Monday morning, however, he again had high blood pressure. After several weeks of this, the researcher took the patient aside and asked for an explanation of the problem. It seemed that Saturday nights the man took his biofeedback earnings to the race track, gambled, and lost both his money and his controlled level of blood pressure.

So it was clear from the start that biofeedback was not a magical cure, only part of the answer. Since blood-pressure biofeedback requires complex and expensive equipment, it is not practical to use with large numbers of patients.

Herbert Benson (1975; Benson and Proctor, 1984) has experimented with meditation as a partial treatment for high blood pressure and has found it to be successful. Other researchers (Surwit, Shapiro, and Good, 1978) have directly compared the effects of blood-pressure biofeedback, muscle-tension biofeedback, and meditation. All three reduced blood pressure; there were no significant differences among the groups. Since biofeedback requires elaborate instruments and meditation does not, it seems likely that the latter will be more widely used (Hassett, 1978b).

---

hypertension: A medical condition characterized by chronically high blood pressure.

gists were suspicious that these miraculous cases had more to do with the power of suggestion than with biofeedback itself. (Doctors are very familiar with what they term the *placebo effect*, the fact that patients often improve when they believe in a treatment, even if it is only a sugar pill.)

Therefore, more careful studies were started to see what medical conditions could be helped by biofeedback (Tarler-Benlolo, 1978; Victor, Weipert, and Shapiro, 1984). Some of the best-documented biofeedback cures involve special training in muscular control. Tension headaches often seem to result from constriction of the frontalis, or forehead muscle. Thomas Budzynski and others (1973) used biofeedback to teach people to relax this specific muscle. The practice went on for several weeks while other people were given similar treatments without biofeedback. Only the biofeedback group improved significantly. Likewise, patients suffering from a number of neuromuscular disorders, ranging from simple nerve and muscle damage to cerebral palsy and paralysis caused by strokes, have been able to recover some portion of their lost abilities through biofeedback treatment (Miller, 1985).

Some patients who suffer from migraine headaches have also been helped by biofeedback (Tarler-Benlolo, 1978). Biofeedback therapists teach migraine sufferers how to raise the temperature in their hands at the onset of an attack (Dalessio et al., 1979). It seems that when the flow of blood to the head and brain becomes excessive, the blood vessels greatly expand and cause piercing pain. Redirecting the blood flow to the hands instead of the head apparently diminishes the pressure and aborts the headache. However, other researchers say that the technique works simply because it relaxes the patient. And a third group wonders whether the power of suggestion is not the most important element underlying the remedy.

Social Support

Interpersonal relationships are central to the quality of our lives. As social beings, we require other people to meet many of our needs. In few areas of life is this more evident than in our patterns of health and illness (Shumaker and Brownell, 1984). One strength of the human species is the tendency of people to give and receive support. We may view **social support** as the exchange of resources among people that derives from their interpersonal ties in networks, groups, and the larger community. Social support plays a crucial role in our physical and mental health through its health-sustaining and stress-buffering functions.

Health-Sustaining Functions

People who have social ties live longer and have better physical and mental health than those without such ties (Berkman and Breslow, 1983). Studies over a vast range of illnesses, from depression to arthritis to heart disease, show that the presence of social support helps people fend off illness, and the absence of such support makes poor health more likely (Cohen and McKay, 1984; Wallston et al., 1984; Reis et al., 1985). Moreover, the death rate from all causes is greater among people with relatively low levels of social support (Blazer, 1982; House, Robbins, and Metzner, 1982). Studies of college students also reveal that social environments low in cohesion, student participation, and social activities are associated with a higher incidence of health problems (Moos and VanDort, 1976). In sum, it seems that social resources have a beneficial effect on people whether or not they are under stress.

Large social networks provide us with regular positive experiences and a set of stable, socially rewarded roles in the community. This kind of support contributes to our well-being because it affords a positive frame of mind, lends a sense of predictability and stability to our lives, and accords us a sense of self-worth. A support network may also help us to avoid negative experiences—unwise decisions or legal problems—that would increase the probability of psychological or physical difficulties. And it may encourage us to exercise and take care of ourselves, avoiding excessive use of alcohol and poor diets.

---

social support: The exchange of resources among individuals that derives from their interpersonal ties in networks, groups, and the larger community.

Stress-Buffering Functions

Social support buffers people from the potentially harmful influence of stressful events. People who have a strong social support system are better able to cope with major life changes; those with little or no social support are more vulnerable to life changes, especially undesirable ones. Social support operates to cushion stress in a number of ways (Cohen and Wills, 1985; Seeman, Seeman, and Sayles, 1985). For one thing, friends and relatives may tell us that they care about and value us. Our self-esteem is strengthened when we know that we are accepted by others despite our difficulties or faults. For another, we often receive informational support from others. They help us to define and understand our problems and cope with them. For still another, we derive companionship from people. Spending time with others in leisure and recreational activities fulfills our social needs, distracts us from our worries, and encourages positive mental attitudes. Finally, interpersonal ties can afford us *instrumental support*—the financial aid, material resources, and needed services provided by others. Such help may reduce stress by resolving our problems or giving us increased time for relaxation or entertainment.

Although the preponderance of evidence supports the view that social networks are positive factors in our lives, they may have negative or harmful effects in certain circumstances (Shinn, Lehmann, and Wong, 1984; Rook and Dooley, 1985). For instance, bereaved people often receive well-meaning but inappropriate remarks from friends and relatives that try to stem and control grief prematurely—"It's probably for the best," "Don't take it so hard," "She's better off now," or "You can have another child." Others can also be sources of conflict, strew obstacles in our path, violate our privacy, or provide us with well-intentioned help that may backfire. At times, lay support prevents us from seeking the help we need from professionals like physicians or mental health workers. And support extended to some medical patients inadvertently reinforces sick-role behavior and undermines independent coping (Taylor, 1979).

BEHAVIORAL FACTORS IN DISEASE

Today the purely biological model of disease based on the notion "one germ, one disease, and one therapy" is recognized as being much too simple (Miller, 1983; Krantz, Grunberg, and Baum, 1985). A more complex and holistic model is winning acceptance; it directs attention to the interactions among biological, social, and psychological factors that produce illness (see Figure 14.3). It seems that conditions are optimal for illness when there is (1) a preexisting biological susceptibility to a given disorder, such as diabetes, asthma, or heart disease; (2) the presence of a disease agent; (3) a condition that a person perceives to be stressful; and (4) an inability to cope with or adapt to the stressful condition (Hinkle, 1974; Rabkin and Struening, 1976; Jemmott and Locke, 1984).

Most of us recognize that such temporary symptoms as an "upset stomach" or a "tension headache" may be related to stressful circumstances. But what about more serious and chronic diseases? Here the waters become murky, or at least less clear. In real life, people and animals sometimes get sick under stressful conditions and sometimes do not. Let us take a closer look at this matter.

The Immune System

The **immune system** is a surveillance mechanism that protects an organism from disease-causing viruses, bacteria, fungi, and tumors. Until relatively recently scientists thought that the immune system operated in a biological vacuum, independent and isolated from other systems. Now evidence is accumulating that links the immune system with the nervous system. This research suggests that anatomical and physiological ties between the two systems help to explain how psychological events may affect our susceptibility to disease. A new field of study, awkwardly christened **psychoneuroimmunology,** has arisen to investigate how psychological events affect physical health. The picture that is emerging

---

immune system: A surveillance mechanism that protects an organism from disease-causing viruses, bacteria, fungi, and tumors.

psychoneuroimmunology: An interdisciplinary field of study concerned with the ties between psychological events and disease, and more particularly the links between emotions and the immune system.

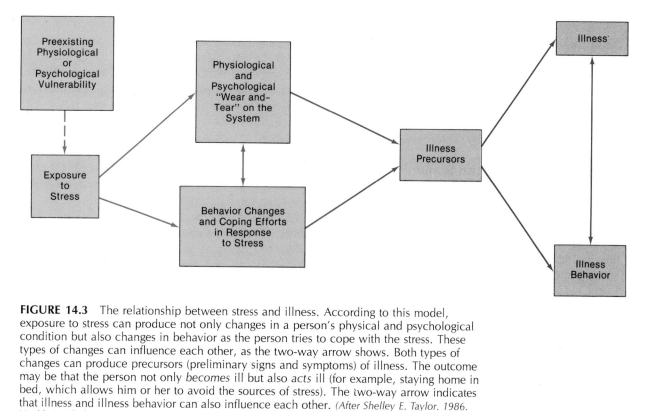

FIGURE 14.3 The relationship between stress and illness. According to this model, exposure to stress can produce not only changes in a person's physical and psychological condition but also changes in behavior as the person tries to cope with the stress. These types of changes can influence each other, as the two-way arrow shows. Both types of changes can produce precursors (preliminary signs and symptoms) of illness. The outcome may be that the person not only *becomes* ill but also *acts* ill (for example, staying home in bed, which allows him or her to avoid the sources of stress). The two-way arrow indicates that illness and illness behavior can also influence each other. *(After Shelley E. Taylor. 1986. Health Psychology. New York: Random House, p. 161. Reprinted with permission.)*

from psychoneuroimmunology is one in which the immune and nervous systems are highly integrated, able to communicate back and forth to coordinate their activities.

The functioning of the immune system is highly complex and as yet not fully understood. Apparently the immune system has two principal reactions. One

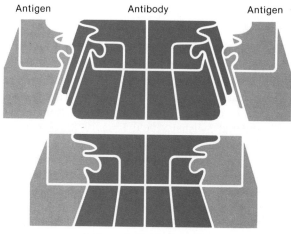

Antigen-Antibody Complex

is the *humoral immune response*, which is primarily responsible for our body's defense against bacterial infections. It involves the production of specific, soluble proteins, called *antibodies*, that are released into the blood and other body fluids in response to an invasion by harmful bacteria. The antibodies coat the bacteria or neutralize their toxins, making it easier for scavenger cells called *macrophages* to engulf and destroy them (see Figure 14.4). The second type of reaction, known as the *cellular immune response*,

FIGURE 14.4 Antigen–antibody reaction. An *antigen* is a foreign substance that stimulates an organism's immune system to produce antibodies against it. Research suggests that in many cases an antibody molecule has two identical halves, each with one large and one small component. Each antibody has only one antigen that it fits, because the configuration of its combining site interlocks with that of the antigen. When the antigen and antibody make contact at the proper angle, so that the two patterns fit together, a union between antigen and antibody occurs, thus inactivating the antigen. *(After Marvin R. Levy, Mark Dignan, and Jan Shirreffs. 1984. Life and Health. 4th ed. New York: Random House. Reprinted with permission.)*

constitutes the body's primary defense against cancer cells and many viruses and is responsible for the rejection of surgically transplanted organs. It consists of specifically armed cells in the blood that directly attack foreign cells. In general, humoral responses take place rapidly, whereas cellular responses evolve more slowly.

Links Between Mind and Immunity

Animal and human studies show that emotional reactions can suppress or stimulate the disease-fighting cells—*lymphocytes*—described above, and can trigger the release of hormones, neurotransmitters, and neuropeptides that in turn affect dozens of body processes (Anderson, 1982; Jemmott and Locke, 1984). One mechanism is the hypothalamic-pituitary axis discussed in Chapter 2. As a consequence of brain-immunity links, researchers find that mice exposed to loud noises, chickens introduced to new pecking orders, rodents that fight with one another, and bighorn sheep exposed to the stress of capture all experience reduced resistance to disease.

Among human beings, virtually every ill that befalls the body—from the common cold to diabetes to heart disease and cancer—can be influenced, positively or negatively, by our mental state. Consider the stressful effects of bereavement. Researchers find that otherwise healthy men show a significant decline in lymphocyte function within a month or two of the death of their wives from breast cancer (Schleifer et al., 1980). Likewise, herpes patients who are depressed suffer significantly more recurrences of the disease, and these depressed people also have much lower immune-cell function than optimistic people (Elias, 1985a). And West Point cadets who have high motivation and overachieving fathers but do poor academic work are more likely than other cadets to develop clinical symptoms of infectious mononucleosis (Kasl, Evans, and Niederman, 1979). Apparently even small contributions from psychosocial factors can make a difference. The immune system is balanced delicately like a seesaw, with half a dozen children on each side of the fulcrum; should another child jump onto one side, the balance is tipped.

Conditioning the Immune System

Additional evidence that the brain can influence immune responses comes from the work of psychologist Robert Ader and immunologist Nicholas Cohen (1981, 1984). Several years ago, Ader made an unexpected observation while studying conditioned taste aversion in mice (see Chapter 6). He provided the experimental mice with water sweetened with saccharin, which mice love. Then he conditioned an aversion to saccharin by following the drinking period with an injection of cyclophosphamide, a nausea-inducing drug. As Ader expected, the mice learned to avoid the saccharin-sweetened water.

Then came a surprise. After about forty days, the conditioned mice began dying at an unusually high rate, although the unconditioned mice showed no ill effects. Ader took a closer look at this puzzling development and learned that cyclophosphamide suppresses the immune system. It dawned on him that at the same time he was conditioning an aversion to saccharin, he was inadvertently conditioning a suppression of the organism's immune response. And when the immune response is suppressed, animals become more susceptible to disease-causing organisms (see Figure 14.5).

In the intervening years, Ader and Cohen have checked and rechecked their techniques. They have examined different kinds of immune response, varied the interval between conditioning and testing, tried a different conditioning drink, and tested other animals as well as mice. This work has convinced them that both humoral and cellular immune responses can be conditioned. They are now investigating whether this finding can be used to treat *autoimmune diseases*, in which the immune system goes awry and begins attacking the body's own tissues. However, some scientists remain skeptical of this research (Fisher, 1985b).

Cancer

Stress may play a role in the onset and course of cancers in animals and humans (Sklar and Anisman, 1981). Several studies reveal that many cancer patients had experienced some personal tragedy about a year before the onset of disease (Greene, 1966; Greene and Swisher, 1969; Fox, 1978). The notion that psychological factors can contribute to cancer is hardly a new one. As early as the second century, the Greek physician Galen said that women who are depressed are more likely to develop cancer than those who are more confident and vital. And in recent years a good many books by lay writers have advocated positive thinking techniques for forestall-

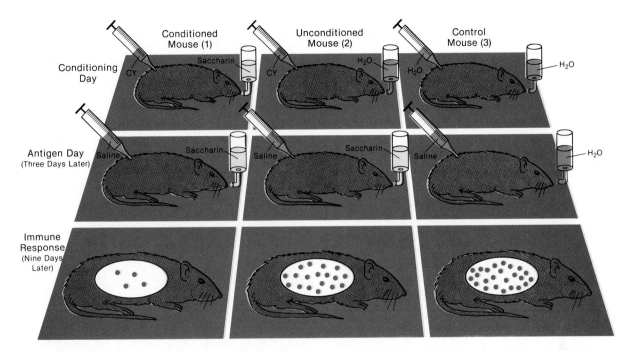

FIGURE 14.5 In an experiment demonstrating the link between the brain and the immune system, Robert Ader and Nicholas Cohen employed three test groups: (1) conditioned, (2) unconditioned, and (3) control. On conditioning day, the conditioned group got saccharin plus cyclophosphamide (CY), a substance that makes mice feel nauseated and weakens their immune response. The unconditioned group got water plus CY. The control group received plain water. On antigen day, both the conditioned and unconditioned groups got saccharin and saline. The control group received water and saline. All three got an antigen that normally causes the immune system to form antibodies as a defense. The unconditioned and control groups formed the normal number of antibodies (shown as dots in the diagram). However, the conditioned group formed very few antibodies. By virtue of conditioning, the mice reacted to the saccharin as if it had been CY. In brief, the saccharin became associated with CY, and the response was a weakened immune reaction. *(After Alan Anderson. 1982. How the mind heals.* Psychology Today, *16 (December):54. Reprinted with permission. Copyright © 1982 American Psychological Association. Courtesy Genigraphics ® Corporation.)*

ing and fighting the disease (Sontag, 1977; Simonton, Matthews-Simonton, and Creighton, 1978; Cousins, 1979). However, much of this work has been open to compelling criticism (Krantz, Grunberg, and Baum, 1985). In most of the studies people with cancer were questioned about their psychological symptoms and recent stressful happenings. It is usually impossible to tell by this method whether the emotions caused the disease or the disease caused the emotional reactions. Another frustrating factor is that most cancers take years to develop, making it difficult to isolate the stresses that may have predisposed a person to malignancy. And finally, people's reports of long-ago events are not necessarily accurate (see Chapter 7).

Animal Research

One difficulty in studying links between emotions and human cancers is that scientists cannot inoculate human beings with tumor cells or feed them substances that may produce cancer. Nor is it ethical to subject human beings to the types of stress that may result in immune impairment or illness. Accordingly, many researchers have undertaken cancer research with animals, a practice that has outraged animal rights advocates (Gallup and Suarez, 1985).

Psychologist Mark L. Laudenslager and his associates (1983) have conducted experiments with rats that demonstrate that animals unable to escape stress or cope with it may be more susceptible to cancer and other diseases. When the researchers subjected one group of rats to mild electrical shocks that the animals were unable to control, the rodents developed weakened immune systems. Another group of rats who were able to shut off the shocks by turning a wheel in their chamber remained normal. Laudenslager tested the rats' immune systems by counting the number of disease-fighting lymphocytes in their bloodstream. When the rats suffering inescapable shocks were given drugs that cause cells to multiply as they do in tumors, they failed to muster enough lymphocytes to fight the foreign substances. In contrast, the lymphocytes in the rats that could control the shocks multiplied as readily as did those from unstressed rats.

Microbiologist Vernon Riley (1975, 1981) also found that stress appears to weaken the immune system of animals, lessening their capacity to combat cancer. He studied a cancer-causing virus in mice that passes from mother to offspring in milk. The virus typically produces breast tumors in 80 percent of female mice by the time they are about four hundred days of age. Riley placed one group of mice in a high-stress environment filled with noxious noises and odors. He placed another group in a low-stress environment. After four hundred days, 92 percent of the mice in the high-stress condition had developed tumors compared with only 7 percent of those in the low-stress group. The stressed mice showed a dramatic increase in a hormone that impairs the immune response and a decline in disease-fighting lymphocytes. However, the low-stress environment only delayed the onset of the disease. After six hundred days, the incidence of tumors in the two groups were similar. Riley concluded that his studies indicate that if an underlying disease agent or genetic proclivity is lacking, stress will have no effect on cancer.

Human Studies

A number of psychological studies suggest that patients who respond to cancer by apathy, depression, and helplessness have poor survival rates. In contrast, patients who are openly angry and display a fighting spirit—"I'm going to lick this thing!" —show more favorable outcomes (Sklar and Anisman, 1981). Psychologist Sandra M. Levy (1982) has assessed women recovering from surgery for breast cancer and monitored their levels of

Some studies have found that "fighting back" against cancer, instead of passively accepting the disease, improves chances of recovery. New York City policewoman Vivian Picciarelli has fought a winning battle against both lymph cancer and a police department hierarchy that tried to force her out of her job because of her illness. *(Paul DeMana/N.Y. Daily News Photo)*

lymphocytes. Women who accepted the disease and adjusted to their condition displayed lower lymphocyte activity than those women who complained and were open about their emotional distress and hostility. The passive patients were also more likely to show signs of the spread of cancerous cells to the lymph nodes, a clinical indicator that the cancer was spreading. Levy suggests that passivity in the face of a life-threatening disease may reflect feelings of helplessness that in turn affect hormonal and immune responses. But as yet the issue remains an unsettled one. An alternative explanation is that lowered immunity levels and the progress of the disease may have caused the women to feel more sickly and hence apathetic.

Other research has also raised questions about the ability of a healthy mental attitude and fighting spirit to affect cancer. Researchers at the University of Pennsylvania Cancer Center assessed cancer patients on social background and personality measures that other studies had found to be predictive of survival (Cassileth et al., 1985). The patients were asked about their satisfaction with their jobs and life in general, the feelings they had about their health, and their sense of hopelessness. The researchers then followed the patients to determine the length of their survival and the time it took for symptoms of cancer to recur. In general, the more cheerful patients showed no greater capacity than the apathetic ones for fighting their cancers, and the pessimists were at no greater risk of death or recurrence than the optimists.

Although the University of Pennsylvania researchers do not deny that psychological attitudes play a role in illness, they contend that there is not a cause-and-effect relationship between them. They think that mental state and emotional factors have but limited roles and that other factors are more critical to malignant disease, with respect both to who gets it and to what happens after the disease is established. But with scientific caution, the Pennsylvania researchers emphasize that their conclusions apply only to patients with advanced cancer. They concede that their study "did not address the possibility that psychosocial factors or events may influence the cause of disease or the outcome for patients with more favorable cancer diagnoses" (p. 1555).

The Pennsylvania researchers express concern that media interest in the links between psychosocial factors and cancer will lead some patients to reject conventional cancer treatment. They caution cancer patients and their families that positive attitudes are no substitute for competent medical attention. They say that there are increasing numbers of practitioners around the country who offer mind tricks as cures for cancer. Other medical professionals say that when patients are already suffering from disease "they should not be further burdened by having to accept responsibility for the outcome" (Angell, 1985:1572). People may blame themselves for falling ill and feel even more guilty should they get worse.

Clearly the links between emotions and illness are incredibly complex (Levy et al., 1985). Psychologists do not argue that we get cancer just because we undergo stress or become depressed. However, they do insist that there is a substantial body of research findings linking psychological factors to health. Genetic susceptibility, disease agents, personality, environmental conditions, and stress factors interact in the disease process. Accordingly, medical treatment can often be enhanced by psychological interventions (Taylor, Lichtman, and Wood, 1984).

Cardiovascular Diseases

Medical researchers have sought to identify people who are at risk for developing *cardiovascular diseases* —disorders affecting the heart and blood vessels. They also have been concerned with determining those behavioral influences that may activate genetic predispositions to *hypertension* (high blood pressure), *atheroscleosis* ("hardening" of the arteries), and *cerebrovascular events* (strokes). Despite a decline in cardiovascular mortality in recent years, disorders of the cardiovascular system still account for one in two deaths in the United States.

Researchers have found that some people are more likely to develop cardiovascular diseases than others. They are usually older males who have high levels of cholesterol or other fats in their blood, high blood pressure, diabetes, and parents who had heart disease, and who are overweight, exercise little, and smoke. The search for the mechanisms and influences that contribute to coronary risk has also included the study of stress factors. Certain conditions, such as chronic environmental stresses and excessive work load, job responsibility, and dissatisfaction, may enhance risk, but much depends on how people perceive these situations (Krantz, Grunberg, and Baum, 1985).

The **Type A behavior pattern** is thought to be another risk factor in coronary disease (Friedman and Rosenman, 1974; Haynes, Feinleib, and Kannel, 1980; Matthews, 1982). Strictly speaking, the Type A pattern is not a trait but a set of behaviors that characterizes people having a high incidence of

Type A behavior pattern: Behaviors that characterize individuals having a high incidence of cardiovascular problems. Type A's are hard-driving, competitive, ambitious, impatient, time-urgent, and easily angered when things go wrong.

Self-Test: Are You Type A or Type B?

Directions

Each scale below is composed of a pair of adjectives or phrases separated by a series of dashes. Each pair has been chosen to represent two kinds of contrasting behavior. Each of us belongs somewhere along the line between the two extremes. For each item on the test, place a check mark at the point where you think you belong.

Assessment

1 2 3 4 5 6 7

1. Doesn't mind leaving things temporarily unfinished   _ _ _ _ _ _ _   Must get things finished once started

2. Calm and unhurried about appointments   _ _ _ _ _ _ _   Never late for appointments

3. Not competitive   _ _ _ _ _ _ _   Highly competitive

4. Listens well, lets others finish speaking   _ _ _ _ _ _ _   Anticipates others in conversation (nods, interrupts, finishes sentences for the other)

5. Never in a hurry, even when pressured   _ _ _ _ _ _ _   Always in a hurry

6. Able to wait calmly   _ _ _ _ _ _ _   Uneasy when waiting

7. Easygoing   _ _ _ _ _ _ _   Always going full speed ahead

8. Takes one thing at a time   _ _ _ _ _ _ _   Tries to do more than one thing at a time, thinks about what to do next

9. Slow and deliberate in speech   _ _ _ _ _ _ _   Vigorous and forceful in speech (uses a lot of gestures)

10. Concerned with satisfying himself or herself, not others   _ _ _ _ _ _ _   Wants recognition by others for a job well done

11. Slow doing things   _ _ _ _ _ _ _   Fast doing things (eating, walking, etc.)

12. Easygoing   _ _ _ _ _ _ _   Hard driving

13. Expresses feelings openly   _ _ _ _ _ _ _   Holds feelings in

14. Has a large number of interests   _ _ _ _ _ _ _   Few interests outside work

15. Satisfied with job   _ _ _ _ _ _ _   Ambitious, wants quick advancement on job

16. Never sets own deadlines   _ _ _ _ _ _ _   Often sets own deadlines

17. Feels limited responsibility   _ _ _ _ _ _ _   Always feels responsible

cardiovascular problems. Type A's are hard-driving, competitive, ambitious, impatient, time-urgent, and easily angered when things go wrong. They walk and eat quickly, interrupt others, gesture with their hands, and drive themselves relentlessly. A noncoronary-prone pattern—the **Type B behavior pattern**—is defined by a more relaxed, easygoing life style. (The self-test above will give you an idea of whether your personality tends more toward Type A or Type B.)

Type B behavior pattern: Behaviors that characterize individuals having a low incidence of cardiovascular problems. Type B's follow a more relaxed, easygoing life style.

18. Never judges things in terms of numbers   —————— Often judges performance in terms of numbers (how many, how much)

19. Casual about work   —————— Takes work very seriously (works weekends, brings work home)

20. Not very precise   —————— Very precise (careful about detail)

Scoring

Assign a value from 1 to 7 for each score. Total them.

Interpretation

- 110–140 = Type A1: If you are in this category, and especially if you are over forty and smoke, you are likely to have a high risk of developing cardiac illness.

- 80–109 = Type A2: You are in the direction of being cardiac-prone, but your risk is not as high as the A1. You should, nevertheless, pay careful attention to the advice given to all Type A's.

- 60–79 = Type AB: You are a mixture of A and B patterns. This is a healthier pattern than either A1 or A2, but you have the potential for slipping into A behavior and you should recognize this.

- 30–59 = Type B2: Your behavior is on the less-cardiac-prone end of the spectrum. You are generally relaxed and cope adequately with stress.

- 20–29 = Type B1: You tend to the extreme of noncardiac traits. Your behavior expresses few of the reactions associated with cardiac disease.

This test will give you some idea of where you stand in regard to your susceptibility to cardiac illness. The higher you score, the more cardiac-prone you tend to be. Remember, though, even B persons occasionally slip into A behavior, and any of these patterns can change over time.

Source: "The Glazer-Stress Control Life-Style Questionnaire," reprinted with permission from Journal of Chronic Diseases, 22; Rayman W. Bootner, "A Short Rating Scale as a Potential Measure of Pattern of Behavior," 1969, Pergamon Press, Ltd.

Although most Type A's do not develop cardiovascular disorders, one study found that Type A men had more than twice the rate of heart disease during eight-and-a-half years of follow-up than men originally judged to be Type B (Rosenman et al., 1975). The American Heart Association includes Type A behavior as one of the factors that increases the risk of cardiac disease. However, it ranks it as a secondary factor, and questions have recently been raised about whether it actually plays any role at all in coronary problems (*Newsweek*, May 19, 1986). Indeed, some aspects of Type A behavior may be beneficial, indicative of a hardy, vigorous, coherent, and competent person. Other components may be harmful. A person's level of hostility and cynicism seems to be a better predictor of heart disease than his or her overall level of Type A behavior. In sum, impatience and ambition may be less damaging than a constant state of annoyance (Dembroski and Mac-Dougall, 1985).

SUMMARY

1. Health is more than the absence of illness. We can measure people's health by how well they are able to function and adapt to a continually changing environment. Health, then, takes on somewhat different properties for people in different walks of life. The traditional medical model has seen disease as a purely biological phenomenon, a product of bacteria and viruses and bodily dysfunction. However, in recent years the medical establishment has increasingly come to recognize that behavioral factors also are crucial in both causing and managing disease.

2. Behavior influences health and disease in a variety of ways. For one thing, our habits and styles of life affect our health. Another process through which behavior influences health occurs when people minimize the significance of their symptoms, delay securing medical care, or fail to comply with treatment regimens. And finally, emotional factors also have implications for the functioning of our bodies.

3. Stress is a central process in the relationship between behavior and health. It helps to explain how psychological events translate into health-impairing physiological changes and illness. Hans Selye popularized the word stress in describing the general adaptation syndrome. He said that our body responds to stress in several stages. The first stage is the alarm reaction. Then the stage of resistance sets in. Finally, if some measure of equilibrium is not restored, a stage of exhaustion is reached. Another tradition, the cognitive perspective, holds that the person's definition of a situation as stressful is crucial.

4. The concept of life change refers to any events that require a modification in a person's accustomed way of living. Life events that create change and require adaptation may occur in any aspect of an individual's life. Thomas H. Holmes, Richard H. Rahe, and their associates have developed a Social Readjustment Rating Scale to measure the amount of change required by life events. Holmes and Rahe contend that a person's risk score—the sum of his or her life-change units over a given period—tends to be related to his or her incidence of illness.

5. Whereas single episodes of acute exposure to stressors usually have only a temporary effect, repeated exposure to stressful circumstances may produce more serious problems. Chronic stressors include long-term unemployment and wartime combat. A number of psychologists and sociologists say that changes in the economy affect the incidence of health problems. And studies of combat veterans reveal that the psychological effects of traumatic war experiences often remain long afterward.

6. Richard S. Lazarus and his colleagues find a relationship between the incidence of daily hassles and illness. Indeed, they contend that life's daily hassles may have a greater effect on our moods and our health than life's major misfortunes. However, the degree to which people feel stress seems to depend less on the number or intensity of the hassles they experience than on whether a particular stressful event is central to their sense of self-esteem.

7. Although population build-up apparently has a negative effect on deer, rats, and many other creatures, it does not seem to have a similar impact on human beings. It is important to distinguish between density and crowding. Whereas density has to do with spatial or physical limitations, crowding is the perception people have that they are receiving excessive stimulation from social sources. What matters most is not density per se but the definition people have of a situation as being crowded or uncrowded.

8. Occupational stress is related to physical illness, psychological impairment, and lowered job performance and satisfaction. Many facets of the workplace can produce stress, including deadlines, unmanageable work loads, inadequate salaries, poor relationships with bosses and coworkers, few opportunities for decision making, role conflicts, and lack of appreciation. The greatest stress is found in jobs in which workers experience heavy demands but exercise little control over how the work is done.

9. Coping behaviors are a key aspect of stress. When we face trying circumstances, we typically seek some way of dealing with them. Coping involves a number of types of behavior. At the most basic level, we can distinguish between emotion-focused and problem-focused coping. Problem-focused coping changes the troubling situation, whereas emotion-focused coping changes your appraisal of the situation. Further, some people seem more stress-hardy than others.

10. Interpersonal relationships are central to the quality of our lives. As social beings, we require others to meet many of our needs. One strength of the human species is the tendency of people to render one another social support, which plays a crucial role in our physical and mental health through its health-sustaining and stress-buffering functions.

11. Until relatively recently, scientists thought that the immune system operated in a biological vacuum, independent and isolated from other systems. Now evidence is accumulating that links the immune system with the nervous system. This research suggests that anatomical and physiological ties between the two systems help to explain how psychological events may affect our susceptibility to disease.

12. Stress may play a role in the onset and course of cancers in animals and humans. Researchers find that stress weakens the immune system of animals, lessening their capacity to combat cancer. A number of psychological studies suggest that patients who respond to cancer by apathy, depression, and hope-lessness have poor survival rates. However, people do not get cancer just because they undergo stress or become depressed. Genetic susceptibility, disease agents, personality, environmental conditions, and stress factors interact in the disease process.

13. The search for the mechanisms and influences that contribute to coronary risk has included the study of stress factors. Certain conditions, such as chronic environmental stresses and excessive work load, job responsibility, and dissatisfaction, may enhance risk, but much depends on how people perceive these situations. The Type A behavior pattern is thought by some psychologists to be another risk factor in coronary disease. Compared to Type B individuals, Type A persons have higher levels of psychological arousal and may spend a greater portion of their daily lives reacting with "fight or flight" responses. As a result, they may sustain an intense state of hormonal and cardiovascular readiness for long periods, cumulatively producing high blood pressure, high blood cholesterol levels, and permanent damage to coronary arteries.

KEY TERMS

behavioral medicine (p. 452)
coping (p. 468)
crowding (p. 466)
density (p. 465)
general adaptation
   syndrome (p. 455)
hassles (p. 464)

hypertension (p. 472)
immune system (p. 474)
job burnout (p. 468)
psychoneuroimmunology
   (p. 474)
social support (p. 473)
stress (p. 455)

sudden death (p. 456)
Type A behavior pattern (p. 479)
Type B behavior pattern (p. 480)
uplifts (p. 464)

SUGGESTED READINGS

ARENDT, RUTH P. *Stress and Your Child*. 1984. Englewood Cliffs, N.J.: Prentice-Hall. Stress can affect children and their relationships with others, including parents, siblings, and friends. This guide offers adults suggestions for helping their children cope with stress.

LAZARUS, RICHARD S. *Psychological Stress and the Coping Process*. 1966. New York: McGraw-Hill. A compendium of information on the field of stress and its relationship to personality. Includes a discussion of the measurement of psychological stress.

MAIER, STEVEN F., and LAUDENSLAGER, MARK. 1985. "Stress and Health: Exploring the Links," *Psychology Today* 19, No. 8: 48–49.

MOOS, R. H. (ED.). *Coping with Life Crises: An Integrated Approach*. 1985. New York: Plenum. An anthology of articles on effective coping behavior, long-term effects of life crises, and ways in which life stressors can promote personal growth and maturity.

TAYLOR, SHELLEY E. 1986. *Health Behavior*. New York: Random House. Explores the influence of psychological factors on health-related behaviors, with extensive coverage of the relationship between stress and physical illness.

Rod MacKillop, *Blue Shoes for My Father*, 1984.

15
Disturbance and Breakdown

As a youngster, Paul spent a good deal of time designing and building model airplanes out of balsa wood. He carried this interest into adulthood, fashioning ever more sophisticated planes that he flew by remote control in a field near his San Francisco home. Over time he accumulated a number of trophies for his gracefully executed circles and loops in local aviation-club competitions. He also welcomed the opportunity that his job as a hospital-equipment technician gave him to crisscross the nation by plane to make repairs in distant cities.

About the time Paul had logged his 150,000th air mile, a 747 jet on which he was traveling began to bounce about in turbulence associated with a thunderstorm. He broke out in a cold-sweat panic—his heart raced, he felt dizzy, and he experienced tingling in his hands and feet. Later he brushed the incident aside, relieved that it was over. But the matter did not end so simply. His anxiety recurred when he flew again, and, after a terror-filled flight from Atlanta to San Francisco, he vowed never to fly again. "I felt flying wasn't good for me or my body," says Paul (Salholz, 1984:72).

Andrea was viewed by those who knew her throughout the first thirty-one years of her life as "hopelessly, incurably crazy." Strange things seemed to go on within her head. Sometimes she was Super Andrea, who held down a high-level, high-pressure job and performed her duties superlatively; then she was Bridget, who enjoyed casual sex; Sheba and Anton, who killed cats; Dara, who would burn her arms with oven cleaner to punish herself for her sinfulness; Philippe, who would try to make certain that her sinfulness would never occur again with suicide attempts that landed her in the hospital —indeed, some twenty-eight different "beings" who governed her often bizarre and incomprehensible behavior. Until five years ago, when she met Eugene Bliss, a University of Utah psychiatrist, it had never occurred to Andrea that she might be a victim of "multiple personalities," or what mental health professionals term a "dissociative disorder." As a toddler and young child she had experienced unremitting physical and sexual abuse at the hands of her deranged father. All the while, her mother had blamed the little girl for her "strange" behavior, telling her it was "God's will." In response, Andrea had "created" protective or numbing personalities that later turned against her, producing the self-mutilating behavior. In the course of her therapy with Dr. Bliss, Andrea has undertaken to consciously relive her lifetime of horrors, episode by episode, and to evolve an integrated personality. Although she now seems to have developed a fused personality, when in highly stressful situations she still experiences an urge to fall back on one or another of the earlier personalities (Bliss and Bliss, 1985).

As these two cases indicate, disturbance and breakdown in behavior result from both a vulnerability of the person and environmental stresses. Some people are genetically so vulnerable that it is very difficult to provide them with an environment that is sufficiently low in stress to prevent psychological disorder. In some cases, the hereditary predisposition takes the form of a defect in the metabolism of one or more neurotransmitters (see Chapter 2). There are also people who are so resistant to stress that few, if any, environments would produce breakdown. For instance, some political prisoners, despite being placed in solitary confinement for years and enduring periodic torture, manage to retain their sanity. Most people fall somewhere between these extremes in vulnerability. Thus people differ in their risk for developing psychological disorders (Zubin and Spring, 1977).

Cases like those of Paul and Andrea raise a number of questions. What is a normal human quirk, and what is distorted, abnormal behavior? What constitutes psychological health? Is it possible to classify various kinds of abnormal behavior? What are some of the major forms of psychological disturbance that people may experience? These issues are the subject matter of this chapter.

NORMAL AND ABNORMAL BEHAVIOR

A man living in the Ozark Mountains has a vision in which God speaks to him. He begins preaching to his

The line between normal and abnormal is a fine one and depends very much on the observer and the standard being used. What some people consider deviant, others may see as just a little odd. (© *Diane Tong*)

relatives and neighbors, and soon he has the whole town in a state of religious fervor. People say he has a "calling." His reputation as a prophet and healer spreads, and in time he is drawing large audiences everywhere he goes. However, when he ventures into St. Louis and attempts to hold a prayer meeting, blocking traffic on a main street at rush hour, he is arrested. He tells the police officers about his conversations with God, and they hurry him off to the nearest mental hospital.

A homemaker is tired all the time, yet she has trouble sleeping. The chores keep piling up because she has no energy. Applications for evening courses and "help wanted" clippings from the classified ads lie untouched in a drawer. She consults the family doctor, but he says she is in perfect health. One night she tells her husband that she thinks she is depressed and would like to see a psychotherapist. He thinks this is ridiculous. According to him, she is just lazy. He says that all she needs to do is get out of her chair and get busy.

Who is right? The "prophet" or the police officers? The homemaker or her husband? It is often difficult to draw a line between "sanity" and "madness," normal and abnormal behavior. Behavior that some people consider normal seems crazy to others. Many non-Western peoples, along with religious fundamentalists in our own country, feel that having visions and hearing voices are an important part of a religious experience. Other people believe these are symptoms of mental disturbance. The man in the previous example was interviewed by psychiatrists, diagnosed as "paranoid schizophrenic," and hospitalized for mental illness. Had he stayed home, he could have been considered perfectly okay. Indeed, more than okay—special (Slotkin, 1955).

What Is Abnormality?

In our first example, the man was classified as mentally troubled because his behavior was so different from what other people felt was "normal." Yet the fact that people are different does not necessarily mean that they are insane. Indeed, going along with the crowd may at times be self-destructive. Most readers—and most psychologists—would agree that teen-agers who use cocaine because nearly everyone in their social circle does have problems.

In the case of the homemaker, she was the one who decided she was psychologically troubled, simply because she was so unhappy. Yet unhappiness and even depression are certainly not foolproof signs of psychological disturbance or of impending breakdown. Everyone feels low from time to time.

How, then, do psychologists distinguish the normal from the abnormal? It is this matter to which we now turn our attention.

Deviation from the Average

One approach to defining abnormality is to say that whatever most people do is normal. Abnormality, then, is any deviation from the average or from the majority. It is normal to bathe periodically, to be attracted to the opposite sex, and to laugh when tickled, because most people do so. And because very few people take ten showers a day, find horses sexually attractive, or laugh when a loved one dies, those who do may be considered abnormal.

However, the deviance approach has serious limitations. If most people cheat on their income-tax returns, are honest taxpayers abnormal? If most people are noncreative, was Shakespeare abnormal? If from time to time most people drink alcoholic beverages, are teetotalers abnormal? Because the majority is not always right or best, the deviance approach to defining abnormality is not a generally useful standard.

Deviation from Social Norms

Deviance may be defined in terms other than departures from the average. All societies have **social norms**—rules that specify appropriate and inappropriate behavior. Behavior that departs significantly from social norms may be viewed as abnormal. Yet this criterion also represents numerous difficulties. As the example of the "Ozark prophet" demonstrated, a person deemed "insane" in one cultural context may be highly valued in another. Similarly, the person who has the courage to be "maladjusted" in an unjust society—who refuses to submit to racial segregation or tyranny—can hardly be considered psychologically disordered.

Critics of normative conceptions of abnormality point out that deviance is not a property inherent in certain forms of behavior (Becker, 1963; Lemert, 1972, 1976; Kaplan, 1983). It is simply a property that people confer on these behaviors by social definitions. Indeed, the psychiatrist Thomas Szasz (1961) views mental illness as a "myth." He says some people are merely "labeled" by others as mentally ill and "stigmatized" because their behavior differs from societal standards. Although Szasz acknowledges that mental disorders exist, he claims they are simply "a problem in living." Szasz's view is not shared by the majority of psychologists, who consider most psychological disorders to be something more than simply defective strategies for handling life.

---

social norm: A rule that specifies appropriate and inappropriate behavior.

In recent years gay and lesbian rights groups have mobilized to fight many forms of discrimination against them. Among their victories is the fact that homosexuality is no longer classified as a psychiatric disorder. *(EKM-Nepenthe)*

Normative definitions of abnormality confront another difficulty. Social norms alter over time. Consider the changes that have taken place over the past decade or so in American attitudes toward homosexuality. The American public has relaxed its view on what constitutes "permissible"—or, perhaps more accurately, "tolerable"—sexual behavior, particularly when performed in private by consenting adults. Until 1974, the American Psychiatric Association considered homosexuality a "sickness," listing it as a mental disorder.

Inability to Function Effectively

Another way to distinguish normal from abnormal people is to say that normal people are able to get along in the world. They can feed and clothe themselves, work, find friends, and live by the rules of society. By this definition, abnormal people are the ones who are unable to function effectively.

Abnormal people have difficulty coping with their environment. Although they appear physically capable, they lack the internal resources to be contributing members of the community. They cannot find a place for themselves in the broad social fabric, and thus they fail to become knitted within meaningful and productive relationships. Examples include people who refuse to leave their homes because they become overwhelmed by intense anxieties in public settings, individuals who are so unhappy and lethargic that they cannot carry out routine work responsibilities, and drug addicts who cannot hold a job or maintain family ties.

Lack of a Sense of Well-Being

A final criterion for abnormality considers how people themselves feel, rather than how others view them. Normal people have a subjective sense that "things are mostly right with them." They say that on the whole they feel "good" about their lives and their experiences. In contrast, abnormal people indicate that they are basically "unhappy," "troubled," or internally "turbulent." They may also complain about a loss of appetite, insomnia, listlessness, headaches, or other physical symptoms. However, psychologists do not always rely on people's self-reports. In some cases of mental illness, such as mania, people say they feel "great"—even ebullient. However, their behavior, when judged by most social standards, is inappropriate and detrimental to themselves.

None of these four approaches provides an infallible standard for defining abnormal behavior. (There is also the matter of legal definitions of insanity, which are examined in the boxed insert on pages 490–491.) In the course of daily life you are influenced by multiple criteria in sizing up people and their behavior. Perhaps the best approach to the matter is to recognize that normality and abnormality are extremes on a continuum and that actual behavior typically falls somewhere in between. All of us vary in certain ways from the average, violate some social norms, function better in some environments than in others, and periodically have our share of fears, anxieties, confusions, conflicts, and lows.

That it is difficult to define abnormality should of course not lead you to conclude that no such thing exists. What it does mean is that you should be very cautious in labeling people "mentally ill" just because they act in ways that you do not understand. Further, in this and the following chapter you will find that many popular notions about mental illness simply do not hold. These myths include the following:

- Abnormal behavior is always bizarre.

- Mental illness is not treatable.

- All mental patients are dangerous.

- Mental illness results from a defect in will.

- Mental illness is punishment for sin.

- Mental illness is entirely genetically inherited.

In sum, it is important to keep an open mind when exploring the matter of "abnormality."

The Madwoman, painted by Chaim Soutine in 1920. Many people stereotype the mentally ill in quite unfavorable terms. *(National Museum of Western Art, Tokyo)*

Psychological Health

It is not particularly difficult to extract a conception of mental health from our discussion of abnormality. Two features stand out, one social and the other psychological (Strupp and Hadley, 1977). From a social perspective, mental health entails your ability to function effectively in your social roles and to meet the requirements associated with group life. From a psychological perspective, mental health involves your subjective feelings of well-being —your happiness, contentment, and satisfaction.

Some psychologists believe that the normal or healthy person is one who is functioning ideally or who at least is striving toward ideal functioning.

Psychology in the Courtroom

Considerable controversy has been generated in recent years by the use of "insanity" pleas in cases in which people are charged with serious crime. One of the most notable trials was that of John W. Hinckley, Jr., who was accused of shooting President Reagan. Hinckley's attorneys argued that he was "not guilty by reason of insanity" and secured his acquittal. The defense claimed that Hinckley was enacting the film *Taxi Driver* and attempting to impress the actress Jodie Foster, who had portrayed a teen-age prostitute in the film. Although he was acquitted, Hinkley did not go free, since he was committed to a mental institution for treatment of his condition (Perr, 1983). Successful invocation of the insanity defense is rare, involving a fraction of 1 percent of all felony cases (Pasewark, 1981).

The insanity plea derives from the notion prevalent in Western societies that criminal law is based on morality. Since morality requires that people have free will, guilt or innocence resides in their ability to choose between good and evil. Hence a jury must typically decide whether a person lacked free will at the time a crime was committed. More specifically, in order to convict a person in a federal court, it must be established that he or she had "substantial capacity to conform his or her conduct to the requirements of the law" and "to appreciate the wrongfulness of his or her conduct." In sum, a longstanding premise of the criminal law is that unless defendants intentionally choose to commit a crime, they are not morally blameworthy and should not be punished.

In a legal sense "insanity" is quite different from mental illness. For instance, the jury could have convicted Hinckley if it had believed that he was mentally ill but that mental illness did not cause his crimes. By the same token, the vast majority of mentally ill people do not engage in criminal or violent acts. Thus "sanity" is a legal matter. To ask whether an accused person is sane is akin to asking, "Is this person responsible for the actions that led to this crime?"

In well-publicized trials such as that of Hinckley, it is quite common to find psychiatrists and psychologists delivering diametrically opposite opinions on a defendant's mental state. Such happenings have led some people to question whether mental health experts belong in the courtroom.

Personality theorists such as Carl Jung and Abraham Maslow (see Chapter 13) have tried to describe this striving process, which is often referred to as *self-actualization*. According to this line of thinking, to be normal or healthy involves full acceptance and expression of your own individuality and humanness. One problem with this approach to defining mental health is that it is difficult to determine whether you are doing a good job of actualizing yourself. How can you tell when you are doing your best? What are the signs that you are losing the struggle? Answers to such questions must often be arbitrary.

Common to most psychological conceptions of mental health is the notion that social and psychological well-being is not so much a state of being as a process. Mental health is not some sort of plateau or static existence. Rather, it necessitates your continuous change and adaptation in order to cope effectively with life. It is that process by which you undertake to find a meaningful and comfortable fit between yourself and the world—the continuing endeavor to "get it all together."

Classification of Abnormal Behavior

For years mental health professionals have been trying to devise a logical and useful method for classifying psychological disorders. This task is difficult because psychological problems do not lend themselves to the same sort of categorizing that many physical illnesses do. The causes, symptoms, and cures for psychological disturbances and breakdowns are rarely obvious or clear-cut.

It should be stressed that such concepts as "insanity," "competence," and "dangerousness" are neither scientific nor clinical. They are arbitrary standards evolved by society to meet certain regulatory needs. Hence when asked questions about these subjects, psychiatrists and psychologists are involved with matters of opinion—even morality—and not science. However, mental health experts are equipped to help judicial authorities in deciding whether defendants are capable of cooperating with their attorneys and understanding court procedures. They can also explain to juries what part mental illness typically plays in given behaviors and what motivations frequently underlie given acts.

Mental health professionals are often called on to evaluate people to determine their potential for violent behavior. The situations include decisions about involuntary commitment and the treatment of hospitalized patients (Tanke and Yesavage, 1985). However, psychiatrists and psychologists tend to agree that they should not be asked to testify on the likelihood that a defendant will commit an act of violence or be a danger to society in the future. Henry J. Steadman, a sociologist for the New York State Office of Mental Health, followed up 257 mental patients who had committed felonies in 1971 and 1972 and had been examined by psychologists for dangerousness. Over a three-year period, only 14 percent of those judged dangerous were later rearrested for a violent crime. But 16 percent of those labeled *not* dangerous, a slightly higher figure, were rearrested (Pines, 1982a). Indeed, in a Texas case, the American Psychiatric Association asked that psychiatrists' long-term predictions about criminal behavior be barred from the court because such testimony "gives the appearance of being based on expert medical judgment, when in fact no such expertise exists" (Tierney, 1982:28).

More recently, the American Psychiatric Association (1983:686) has decided that the "dangerousness" of insanity acquittees who have perpetrated violence has already been demonstrated. Their future dangerousness need not be inferred; it may be assumed, at least for a reasonable period of time. The American Psychiatric Association is therefore quite skeptical about procedures in many states requiring mental health professionals (or others) to decide periodically whether patients who have committed previous violent offenses are still "dangerous." There is little objective basis for such judgments.

In 1952, the American Psychiatric Association (APA) agreed on a standard system for classifying abnormal symptoms—the *Diagnostic and Statistical Manual of Mental Disorders*, or DSM. A revised version, accepted in 1968, became known as DSM-II. In 1980, the APA published a still newer system, DSM-III. (A fourth edition is being prepared for publication in the late 1980s.)

Each new system has constituted an attempt to solve some of the problems of the earlier approaches (Spitzer, Williams, and Skodol, 1980; Spitzer, 1985). For example, DSM-II had been criticized as being vague: two professionals often gave different diagnoses for the same patient. DSM-III is much more concrete and specific, and it seeks to produce more reliable diagnoses (Spitzer, Forman, and Nee, 1979). Whereas DSM-I listed 60 disorders and DSM-II 145, DSM-III has established more than 230.

DSM-III

DSM-III offers extensive and highly detailed descriptions for different diagnostic categories. These descriptions include:

- The *essential features* that "define" a disorder
- The *associated features* that usually accompany a disorder
- The *diagnostic criteria* (a list of symptoms taken from the lists of essential and associated features) that *must* be present for the patient to be given a particular diagnostic label

Mental health may be defined as feelings of well-being and the ability to function effectively in everyday life. *(Alan Carey/The Image Works)*

- Information on *differential diagnosis* that allows professionals to distinguish a particular disorder from other disorders with which it might be confused.

DSM-III requires that a good deal of information be provided about a patient in the process of diagnosis. It instructs the diagnostician to evaluate the patient on five different "axes," or areas of functioning:

- *Axis I—Clinical Psychiatric Syndrome:* the diagnostic label that is applied to the patient's most serious psychological problem (the problem usually consists of a cluster of core symptoms)

- *Axis II—Personality Disorders (adults) or Specific Development Disorders (children and adolescents):* any accompanying adjustment disorders not covered by the Axis-I label

- *Axis III—Physical Disorders:* any medical problems that may be relevant to the psychological problem

- *Axis IV—Psychosocial Stressors:* any current sources of stress (for example, divorce, retirement, miscarriage) that may have contributed to the patient's psychological problem

- *Axis V—Highest Level of Adaptive Functioning during the Past Year:* a rating of the patient's adjustment—social relationships, occupational functioning, use of leisure time—within the past year

Whereas the earlier diagnostic system might have diagnosed a patient under the label "alcohol addiction," under DSM-III the person might be diagnosed as follows:

- Axis I: alcohol dependence

- Axis II: avoidant personality disorder

- Axis III: diabetes

- Axis IV: loss of job, one child moved out of house, marital conflict

- Axis V: fair

This procedure provides a good deal of information that may be useful in devising a treatment program. Furthermore, the five-part diagnosis offers researchers invaluable data for uncovering connections among psychological disorders and other factors such as stress and physical illness.

DSM-III avoids any suggestion about the cause of a disorder unless the cause has been definitely established. This policy has contributed to some substantial changes in the classification system. For example, the term "neurosis" has been dropped altogether, since it is a Freudian concept and implies a psychoanalytic interpretation (namely, that the disorder derives from anxiety over repressed wishes or conflicts). Similarly, research has not demonstrated that some severe depressions are environmental in origin while others are biological, so this distinction has been dropped. DSM-III aims simply at naming the disorders and describing them as clearly and specifically as possible; their causes, if not established, are not speculated on.

As might be expected, DSM-III—like its predecessors—has its critics (Smith and Kraft, 1983; Klerman et al., 1984; Schacht, 1985). Some of the most vocal have been practicing psychotherapists who are not medical doctors. They charge that the American Psychiatric Association—a professional organization of medical doctors—has attempted to turn every human problem into an organic disease. They believe that most of the emotional problems of living, including marital conflict, delinquency, and dehumanization, do not belong in the category of disease. Hence these therapists see DSM-III as a power ploy by psychiatrists to preempt their territory. Similarly, psychoanalysts are quite critical of DSM-III because it abandons such categories as "neurosis" and in their view constitutes a repudiation of Freud's work. And some psychologists contend that DSM-III is biased against women and codifies "masculine-biased assumptions about what behaviors are healthy and what behaviors are crazy" (Kaplan, 1983:786; Caplan, 1984; Holden, 1986).

Advantages and Disadvantages of Classification

Classifications of this sort inevitably produce considerable controversy. But even apart from these differences of opinion, there is the question whether the benefits of classification outweigh the disadvantages. Among the arguments in support of categorization are the following:

- Classification facilitates communication among professionals. Grouping abnormal behavior within manageable classes based on certain similarities allows mental health workers to unscramble and order symptoms that otherwise would overwhelm them by virtue of their sheer complexity.

- The systematic and reliable classification of people with certain patterns of behavior expedites research and the accumulation of knowledge about psychological disorders. Obviously, any research on diagnostic groups—for instance, schizophrenia or manic-depressive disorder—is no better than the validity of the diagnoses that are secured and used (Garfield, 1978; Klerman et al., 1984).

- By classifying patients, psychiatrists and psychologists can better understand the causes of their disordered behavior. More important, good classification permits professionals to generate reasonable approaches to treatment and to predict patients' future behavior and recovery.

- Classification makes it possible to identify specific behavior problems and to marshal resources of money, facilities, and talent to combat these problems. For instance, categorizing is necessary to write legislation, to appropriate funds, and to design programs.

Disadvantages may also flow from categorization:

- Once given diagnoses such as "a person with schizophrenia" or "a person with manic-depressive disorder," people have difficulty regaining the status of being "normal." The label often becomes a stigma, a harmful badge, that is psychologically damaging and that functions to isolate them from meaningful social experiences and relationships (Rosenhan, 1973; Langer and Abelson, 1974).

- The "mentally ill" label enables family members and professionals to "explain" a person's lack of progress in terms of the label ("What can you expect? Henry is schizophrenic"). The label diminishes a person's sense of responsibility and portrays the patient simply as a victim of his or her own neurological malfunctioning.

- Labeling a person "mentally ill" results in behavior that otherwise might be considered of little consequence being perceived as deviant (Langer and Abelson, 1974; Kaplan, 1983). People not so labeled can blame their own impatience, anger, and antisocial behavior on external causes. But "mentally ill" people are not permitted this luxury.

- Categories may bias professionals in their treatment of patients. For instance, categorizing a person as "an individual with alcohol dependence" may lead mental health workers to overlook the fact that the patient is depressed. Further, placing a patient in a category makes it easy to ignore the person's individuality and unique experience of the disorder.

Implicit in systems for classifying abnormal behavior is the assumption that the benefits of classification do outweigh the disadvantages. In the following pages we will discuss a number of the disorders covered in DSM-III. As you read this material, you will probably feel that at times some of the descriptions could be applied to your own behavior. They probably could. But remember, a psychologically disturbed person is one who turns normal human quirks into extreme and distorted *patterns* of thought and behavior. When we speak of the psychologically disturbed, we are not talking about people who have their normal share of difficulties, but rather about people who are exceedingly unhappy, whose minds are confused and chaotic, who have a difficult time doing the simple things in life, or who act in ways that are truly harmful to themselves or to others.

Prevalence of Mental and Addictive Disorders

A survey undertaken by the National Institute of Mental Health (NIMH) suggests that about one in five adult Americans, or about 29 million people, suffers from mental problems in any given six-month period (Fox, 1984). Moreover, between 29 and 38 percent of the population had experienced at least one psychiatric problem in their lifetime. The survey involved household interviews with about ten thousand people in three localities: New Haven, Baltimore, and St. Louis. The study is still in progress and will cover twenty thousand people in five regions when complete. Based on DSM-III criteria, the researchers concluded that women tend to suffer from phobias and depression more often than men, while men score significantly higher than women in the abuse of alcohol or dependence on drugs and in long-term antisocial behavior. When all disorders are taken into account, men and women are about equally troubled. The study showed no "major differential" between blacks and whites in the general incidence of mental disorders. College graduates reported a lower incidence of psychiatric disorders than individuals who had not attended or did not graduate from college.

As shown in Table 15.1, anxiety disorders (including phobias, compulsive behavior, and attacks of panic) are most common, affecting about 8.3 percent of adults. Substance abuse disorders, including alcohol abuse, are next at 6.4 percent. Another 6 percent of the population suffers from depression and 1 percent from schizophrenia. The study found that only a fraction of the population identified as having mental disorders sought or received treatment for them. Only half of those who received treatment went to specialists. The finding that one of five Americans is troubled at any given time roughly coincides with the Midtown Manhattan study, done in the 1950s, that reported 23 percent of the population had severe disorders, and up to 80 percent had some mild level of impairment (Srole, 1962).

ANXIETY DISORDERS

Anxiety is a vague, generalized apprehension or feeling that one is in danger. For people who experience anxiety disorders, the world is fraught with apprehension and fear. Until recently, mental health professionals termed them "neurotic." But since little consensus exists on the meaning of "neurosis," DSM-III eliminated the term as a category (APA, 1980). Under DSM-III, people with anxiety are classified by their major behavioral symptoms and stresses before they were diagnosed.

People with anxiety disorders do not typically lose touch with reality. Nor does their behavior grossly depart from socially permissible standards. Nonetheless, the lives of such people are impaired and crippled, since their anxieties interfere with normal social and psychological functioning.

Generalized Anxiety and Panic Disorders

Once in a while everyone feels nervous, especially in stressful circumstances such as taking an important exam, interviewing for a job, anticipating a key

---

anxiety: A vague, generalized apprehension or feeling that one is in danger.

TABLE 15.1 Mental Health of Adult Americans

Disorder	Number Affected	Percentage of Population Affected	Percentage Treated*
Anxiety	13.1 million	8.3%	23%
Alcohol and drug abuse	10.0 million	6.4	18
Depression	9.4 million	6.0	32
Schizophrenia	1.5 million	1.0	53

*Highest rate of treatment

Source: News release, National Institute of Mental Health, October 2, 1984.

athletic event, or presenting a public speech. For the most part, we know why we are "uptight." Moreover, we "settle down" once we have immersed ourselves in the task or soon after we have completed the activity.

But matters are otherwise for people who suffer from **generalized anxiety disorder.** These individuals experience frequent high levels of tension for months on end. However, they do not know why they are apprehensive or fearful. Since their anxiety is not limited to a particular stimulus or situation, it is termed "free-floating." At times the anxiety blossoms into a full-fledged attack, which may include choking sensations, racing heart, chest pains, dizziness, trembling, hot flashes, and numbness and tingling in the hands or feet. Moreover, sufferers frequently have a nagging worry that disaster will befall them or their loved ones.

In other cases of anxiety, people experience what is termed **panic disorder.** They have sudden, intense attacks of fear, apprehension, or terror (APA, 1980; Sheehan, 1982; Barlow et al., 1985). Usually, the bouts of anxiety begin in late adolescence or early adulthood. The attacks are more acute than in generalized anxiety disorder, and they differ from normal responses to danger in that there seems to be a sudden activation of the body's alarm system for no explainable reason. During an attack, sufferers complain of rubbery legs, a pounding heart, dizziness, hot flashes, nausea, or choking feelings. Others say their surroundings become strange, unreal, or foggy. The attacks may last from a few minutes to hours.

Why do some people become so anxious? According to Freudian psychoanalytic theorists, anxiety is caused by desires and conflicts that people find exceedingly disturbing. These unresolved conflicts operate on an unconscious level. The individuals live in constant fear of bringing the desires to the surface and unleashing their pent-up emotions. When something happens to bring the feelings closer to the surface, they become terrified, that is, have an anxiety attack. For example, people who are unable to face or express feelings of anger may become tense and fearful when they encounter others arguing or when hostile images flash into mind because these things remind them of feelings they are trying to deny. Their anxiety appears to be unfounded and irrational, but only because they are hiding their true emotions from both themselves and others.

Some mental health professionals reject the psychoanalytic view of anxiety and instead advance a genetic-susceptibility model (Crowe et al., 1980; Klein and Rabkin, 1981; Sheehan, 1982). They suggest that anxiety disorders are associated with biochemical abnormalities in the nervous system, to which there is a genetic vulnerability. For instance,

generalized anxiety disorder: A disturbance in which individuals experience frequent high levels of tension for months on end but do not know why they are apprehensive or fearful.

panic disorder: A condition in which individuals experience sudden, intense attacks of fear, apprehension, or terror.

Anxiety attacks produce physical distress, including nausea, heart palpitations, and weakness in the limbs. The primary psychological symptom is an overwhelming feeling of panic about some unknown danger. *(Dave Schaefer/The Picture Cube)*

the expression of emotion (Fishman and Sheehan, 1985). Other researchers find a common underlying vulnerability for panic disorder and major depressive illness in many patients. A significant proportion of patients with panic disorder experience major depressive episodes in the course of their lives (Breier, Charney, and Heninger, 1985).

Learning theorists advance still another explanation for the development of anxiety disorders. They claim that environmental experiences are critical. For instance, if teen-agers feel extremely anxious and uncomfortable on a first date, even the thought of another date may make them nervous. Consequently, they may seek to avoid similar kinds of unsettling experiences in the future. Should they no longer go out on dates, they never have a chance to confront their anxiety and come to terms with it. Indeed, in some cases, individuals may generalize their discomfort from one type of social setting to other social situations. Hence they suffer anxiety attacks whenever they confront the prospect of dealing with new people.

Phobias

Severe anxiety focused on a particular object or situation is called a **phobia.** A person with a phobia has an intense, persistent, irrational fear of something. A phobia can develop toward almost anything. Common phobias include:

- *Acrophobia*—fear of high places
- *Agoraphobia*—fear of open places
- *Claustrophobia*—fear of closed, cramped spaces
- *Nyctophobia*—fear of darkness
- *Pathophobia*—fear of disease
- *Thanatophobia*—fear of death
- *Xenophobia*—fear of strangers

Phobic individuals develop elaborate plans to avoid the situations they fear. For example, people with agorophobia may stop riding on buses or shop-

should one of a pair of identical twins have the problem, the other has a 40 percent chance of also developing it; among fraternal twins, in contrast, the risk of the second twin developing it is only 5 percent. One indication of the chemical nature of the problem is that injections of sodium lactate can precipitate a panic attack in people who suffer from anxiety disorder, but not in others. Moreover, the blood flow in areas of the brain that are thought to control panic and anxiety reactions is much higher in lactate-sensitive people than in others. This finding suggests an exaggeration of the normal hemispheric specialization in the part of the brain that regulates

phobia: A form of severe anxiety in which a person focuses on a particular object or situation.

ping in large, busy stores. The first attack may occur with no warning, perhaps when the person is on a bus or in a supermarket. Should the attacks become more frequent, the victim comes to associate them with these places. Very shortly a sense of "anticipatory panic" wells up every time the victim finds himself or herself in such a setting. The home is seen as a refuge, the only place the person feels safe. In time the victim may become totally "housebound." But of course some phobias are more troublesome than others. For instance, if you are an acrophobic but do not have to frequent high places, the phobia may not be a problem to you in everyday life.

There are a number of theories about how people develop phobias. In some cases, phobias result from frightening experiences in the past (Faravelli et al., 1985). For example, if a person who is genetically vulnerable to anxiety was attacked and bitten by a dog as a child, he or she may develop an intense fear of dogs, having linked or associated the two events (biting and dogs). But people also acquire phobias without having had contact with the feared object, as when they develop a phobic fear of airplanes without ever having flown. Modeling theorists (Bandura and Rosenthal, 1966) suggest that phobias can be learned from other people who have such fears, from television accounts of airplane crashes, or through other communications that arouse anxiety about flying. Some people are susceptible to such information, while others are not.

Some psychologists, among them Martin Seligman (1971), note that phobias are readily learned (often after only one encounter) and are exceedingly resistant to change. These facts lead them to speculate that common phobias—especially the fear of heights, darkness, and open spaces—are *prepared responses*. The phobias are "easily learned" because human beings have been biologically equipped by their evolutionary history to be especially sensitive to certain environmental cues (heights, darkness, and open spaces).

Psychoanalytic theorists say that phobic fears have a less straightforward explanation. They interpret phobias as projection mechanisms. What the people really fear is some deep-seated impulse within themselves. To avoid conscious confrontation with the "unacceptable" impulse, they unconsciously project it onto something outside themselves. For instance, Sigmund Freud (1959) had a patient called "Little Hans," a five-year-old boy, who had a phobia regarding horses. Freud concluded that the boy was sexually attracted to his mother and wished his father dead—both intolerable ideas to the boy. One day, the boy went to a park with his father and saw a horse fall over. From that day on, the boy was terrified of horses. Freud contended that the boy projected his fear onto horses because he found it safer than dealing with the fear engendered by his forbidden wishes regarding his parents. (Many other theorists dispute such interpretations of phobias.)

Obsessions and Compulsions

Some people experience an uncontrollable and unwelcome pattern of thoughts, called an **obsession.** For instance, a young mother may periodically be flooded with thoughts of knifing her child, a business executive may feel persistent anxiety lest he lose control and run through the office shouting obscenities, or a student may be plagued with the recurrent thought, "I wonder if I locked the door before leaving home?" The images, words, or presumed desires intrude into awareness, against people's will and beyond their conscious ability to stop them.

People may also feel constrained to perform repeatedly certain irrational and ritualized actions. This behavior is called a **compulsion.** For example, a person may feel compelled to avoid walking on the cracks of sidewalks or to touch every third windowpane along the walkway of shopping centers. Frequently, obsessive thoughts are tied to compulsive acts. Thus persistent thoughts about being germ-ridden may cause people to wash their hands countless times during the day. DSM-III groups these difficulties with anxiety disorders because people experience anxiety if they resist the obsessions or compulsions (APA, 1980).

In contrast to anxieties produced by obsessive-compulsive fears, some psychologists speak of an *obsessive-compulsive personality*. Such individuals do

---

obsession: An uncontrollable and unwelcome pattern of thoughts.
compulsion: The impulsive and uncontrollable repetition of an irrational action.

In his play *Macbeth,* Shakespeare portrayed Lady Macbeth as compulsively involved in a hand-washing ritual in an attempt to erase her guilt for having taken part in the murder of the king. *(The Museum of Modern Art/Film Stills Archive)*

not have specific obsessions or compulsions. Rather, they display a style of behavior—inflexibility, perfectionism, stubbornness, frugality, and punctuality —that runs throughout their daily activities (Salzman and Thaler, 1981). They are typically dependable and reliable workers, have high standards and ethical values, and appreciate order and discipline. They live highly ritualized lives and allow themselves little expression of spontaneity.

Why do some people develop obsessions and compulsions? Possibly because the disorders serve as diversions from their real fears. Moreover, obsessions and compulsions allow people to "control" their anxiety through the performance of "magical" acts (for instance, misfortune can be avoided by not walking on sidewalk cracks). Obsessions and com-

pulsions also provide people with evidence that there is structure and order in a confusing and turbulent world. And in some cases they function as a ritual to erase guilt for misdeeds (for example, Shakespeare portrays Lady Macbeth as continually washing her hands in guilt for the murder of Duncan). But understanding of the underlying causes of obsessive-compulsive behavior is not complete (Turner, Beidel, and Nathan, 1985).

SOMATOFORM DISORDERS

In **somatoform disorders** ("body-form" disorders), people experience physical symptoms for which there is no apparent organic cause. Sufferers do not

---

somatoform disorder: A type of disturbance in which individuals exhibit physical symptoms for which there is no apparent organic cause.

intentionally seek to mislead either themselves or others about their physical condition. Their difficulties are quite real. Often they complain of backache, stomach pains, or chest pains (a condition categorized as *psychogenic pain disorder*). Others report blindness, deafness, the loss of sensation in body limbs, false pregnancy, or partial paralysis (a condition categorized as *conversion disorder*). Evidence suggests that both categories of symptoms are linked to psychological factors or conflicts (Theodor and Mandelcorn, 1973; APA, 1980). Here we will limit our discussion to conversion disorders.

Conversion disorders get their name from the belief among some psychologists that patients experiencing the disorders "convert" anxiety into physical symptoms. From time to time most people experience mild conversion disorders; for instance, you may become so frightened or terrified that you cannot move. Later you may comment that you were "frozen stiff." But people suffering a conversion disorder do not momentarily lose functioning due to fright. Their difficulty persists.

Victims of a conversion disorder experience a real and prolonged handicap—they may not be able to hear or speak, to feel anything in a hand, to move their legs, or to exercise some other normal function (see Figure 15.1). In some cases, they may wake up one morning and find themselves paralyzed from the waist down. Most people would respond to this state of affairs by becoming deeply distressed. But often in cases of conversion disorder, the person accepts his or her loss of function with relative calm. Psychologists take this response as one sign that the person is suffering from a psychological rather than a physiological problem. Symptoms also typically disappear when the person is asleep, anesthetized, or hypnotized.

Some psychologists believe that sufferers unconsciously invent physical symptoms to gain freedom from unbearable anxiety. For instance, people who live in terror of blurting out something that they do not want to say may lose the power of speech. This

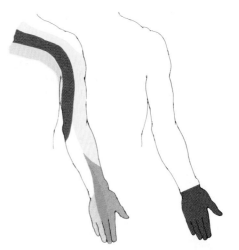

FIGURE 15.1 A patient who complained to a doctor that his right hand had become numb might be diagnosed as suffering from hysteria, depending on the exact pattern of the numbness. (a) The skin areas served by different nerves in the hand. (b) The "glove" numbness shown here could not result from damage to the nerves shown in (a). *(John Dawson)*

approach "solves" the problem. Likewise, during both world wars, a large number of men developed conversionlike symptoms either before or during combat. They were unable to move, fire their weapons, or storm the next hill.

Conversion disorders should be distinguished from **hypochondriasis,** in which a person who is in good health becomes preoccupied with imaginary ailments and blames his or her problems on them. They should also be distinguished from **psychosomatic illnesses,** in which emotional problems produce real physical damage such as ulcers or high blood pressure. In conversion disorders, something real has happened to the victim, but not physically. Once the psychological problem has been solved, the person's normal functioning is restored.

conversion disorder: A psychological disorder in which the individual loses some body function without an apparent organic cause.
hypochondriasis: A preoccupation with imaginary ailments, on which the person blames his or her other problems.
psychosomatic illness: A condition in which emotional problems produce real physical damage such as ulcers and high blood pressure.

DISSOCIATIVE DISORDERS

In **dissociative disorders,** it is psychological rather than physical functioning that is affected. People experience a disturbance in memory or identity. The disorders get their name from the psychoanalytic view that one part of the mind or consciousness splits off, or "dissociates," from another part. These psychological phenomena fascinate many people, and so a good deal is heard about amnesia and "split personalities." Actually, dramatic cases are quite rare. On the other hand, temporary dissociative states, in which people cannot remember what happened to them, are common.

Amnesia, or loss of memory, may be an attempt to escape from problems by blotting them out completely. During wartime, for example, some hospitalized soldiers block out their names, when they were born, where they lived, and their war experiences. However, the amnesiac remembers how to speak and usually retains a fund of general knowledge. Another explanation of amnesia rests on the distinction between automatic and effortful encoding of information (Hirst, 1982). Information that normal people encode automatically may require effort in amnesiacs, leading to memory impairment.

In **fugue,** another type of dissociative disorder, amnesia is coupled with active flight to a different environment. The person may suddenly disappear and "wake up" three days later in a restaurant two hundred miles from home. Or on discovering himself or herself in a new location, the person may establish a new identity—assume a new name, take a job, and even marry—repressing all knowledge of a previous life. A fugue state may last for days or for decades. However long it lasts, the person comes out of it with no memory of what he or she has done in the interim. Fugue, then, is a sort of traveling amnesia, and it probably serves the same psychological function as amnesia: escape from unbearable conflict or anxiety.

In **multiple personality,** a third type of dissociative disorder, the individual seems to have two or more distinct identities. Robert Louis Stevenson's story *Dr. Jekyll and Mr. Hyde* provides a fictional illustration of this disorder. Eve White, a young woman who sought psychiatric treatment for severe headaches and blackouts, has become a well-known real-life example. She was a conscientious, self-controlled, rather shy person. However, during one of her therapy sessions, her expression—and her personality—suddenly changed. Eve Black, as she now called herself, was childlike, fun-loving, and irresponsible—the opposite of the woman who originally walked into the psychiatrist's office. Eve Black was conscious of Eve White's existence but considered her a separate person. Eve White did not know about Eve Black, however, and neither was she conscious of Jane, a third personality that emerged during the course of therapy. (This case served as the basis for the book and film *The Three Faces of Eve.*)

In cases of multiple personality, psychologists find that the various personalities are relatively independent and distinct, with only a small degree of personality linkage among them (Ludwig et al., 1972). Brain-wave measurements reveal that each personality has a distinctive pattern (Putnam, 1982). In fact, allergies, vision problems, and diabetic symptoms associated with some personalities may be absent with others. Typically, certain of the personalities operate in a particular realm or emotional domain. The primary personality—for instance, that of Eve White—carries out most activities and handles most situations. But the experience of strong sexual, aggressive, or interpersonal conflict within the primary personality serves as a "switch-over mechanism" for the appearance of the appropriate

---

dissociative disorder: A psychological disorder characterized by a disturbance in memory or identity.

amnesia: A dissociative disorder characterized by memory loss.

fugue: A rare dissociative disorder in which complete or partial amnesia is combined with a move to a new environment.

multiple personality: A rare dissociative disorder in which one person shows two or more separate consciousnesses with distinct personalities.

A still from the film *The Three Faces of Eve.* Eve White, shown here, was self-controlled and shy, unaware of the irresponsible Eve Black or of her third personality, Jane. *(The Museum of Modern Art/Film Stills Archive)*

"specialist" personality. Hence when the individual feels threatened or inadequate, the more expert personality emerges and assumes control.

Two predisposing factors seem to be implicated in the disorder. The first is an underlying capacity to go into a spontaneous hypnotic trance. The second is an early childhood of harsh abuse. According to one view, the child uses the hypnotic state as a kind of psychological protection, a temporary defense against an unbearable situation. The temporary defense becomes stabilized when the child is repeatedly confronted with the same kinds of circumstances. Each personality allows the child to cope with certain kinds of difficult realities without other aspects of his or her personality having to know about or confront them (Bliss and Bliss, 1985).

AFFECTIVE DISORDERS

Mood disturbances underlie **affective disorders.** (**Affect** is the term psychologists use to refer to a person's emotional state or mood.) From time to time everyone undergoes changes in mood, ranging from elation to sadness. Typically, these changes are associated with events in one's life. Feeling joyous after receiving an A in a difficult course and dejected after quarreling with a friend or a lover are normal experiences of life. However, moods of elation or depression can be abnormal when they persist for long periods, interfere with a person's daily functioning, and distort an individual's outlook on life. At times the disorders can be life-threatening, culminating in suicide.

---

affective disorder: A mood disturbance disorder associated with extreme elation and sadness.

affect: A person's emotional state or mood.

Depression

By depression, psychologists do not mean the blues —those feelings of gloom and despair that pervade everyday life at one time or another. They do not mean the short-term bout of sadness and anxiety that accompanies a stressful experience. Rather, **depression** is an affective disorder characterized by a mood drop that lasts for months (severe depressions average about eight months), even years. As depression deepens, people commonly experience insomnia, disinterest in work, loss of appetite, reduced sexual desire, low energy, hopeless feelings, persistent sadness, and profound emotional despair. Often even routine tasks become difficult for depressed people to perform. They have difficulty concentrating, remembering things, and getting their thoughts together. Some people also suffer deep anxiety as part of their depression (Nelson and Charney, 1981).

Depression is frequently termed "the common cold of mental ailments." It is much more widespread and pervasive than is sometimes thought (see the boxed insert on page 503). The National Institute of Mental Health estimates that seven out of every one hundred Americans are affected by depression at any given time. And the U.S. Office of Education blames depression as a major cause of dropping out of college.

According to Freudian theory, depression reflects anger directed inward on the self. Depressed people are viewed as guilt-ridden individuals who unconsciously seek self-punishment. For instance, they may feel that they have neglected someone who just died and unconsciously hold themselves responsible for that person's death. In this case, depression acts as a self-imposed jail term: the victims will not permit themselves to be happy.

In recent years, the cognitive theories of Aaron Beck and Martin Seligman have provided an impetus to much psychological research on depression. Beck (1967, 1976) believes that depressed people draw illogical conclusions about themselves. They blame themselves for normal problems, read disapproval into innocuous statements by others, and constantly devalue their accomplishments. In short, they are overwhelmed with negative thoughts about themselves, the world, and the future. For instance, depressed individuals may fail a driver's test and conclude that they are worthless and hopeless people who do not deserve to own or drive a car. As described in Chapter 6, Seligman (1975) suggests that some types of depression are caused by a feeling of learned helplessness. Depressed people learn to believe that they have no control over events in their lives, that nothing they do makes any difference, and that it is useless even to try. In sum, maladaptive cognitive schemes are responsible for the self-derogating thought patterns of the depressed (Pietromonaco and Markus, 1985).

Peter M. Lewinsohn (1974, 1976) provides a different interpretation of depression, which is based on behaviorism. He looks to the part that a person's social relations play in producing and maintaining affective disorders. On the basis of his research, he concludes that depressed persons are on the whole less socially skillful than nondepressed persons. Since they have difficulty interacting with others, they live more passive and inactive lives. They are more likely to isolate themselves by staying home and avoiding social activities. And when they do interact with others, their social deficits interfere with their ability to enjoy themselves. Consequently, they receive little positive reinforcement from their social experiences and find life devoid of pleasure.

Another theory explains depression as a chemical imbalance in the brain. A growing body of research suggests that victims of depression have a shortage of certain neurotransmitters (Wender and Klein, 1981; Siever and Davis, 1985). Among the most important of these delicate compounds are serotonin and norepinephrine. As discussed in Chapter 2, as a "message" is passed along by the nervous system, a few drops of the neurotransmitters are squirted out of the various root branches of the nerve cell into the synapse, the gap between two neurons. The balance between these compounds at the nerve-cell synapses is thought to be decisive in the maintenance of normal mood states. (It seems that low levels of

---

depression: An affective disorder characterized by a pattern of sadness, anxiety, fatigue, insomnia, underactivity, and reduced ability to function and to work with others.

Lincoln's Depressive Episodes

Throughout his life, Abraham Lincoln suffered recurrent periods of mental depression. His depressions are documented in his letters, in newspaper accounts of the period, and in the journals of those who knew him well. When he was twenty-nine, he was plunged into a deep depression by the death of his first love, Ann Rutledge. He was frequently observed wandering along the river banks, distracted and filled with deep grief. His landlady observed, "The community said he was crazy, but he was not crazy, but simply very despondent for a long time." Believing that he might be suicidal, friends deprived him of knives and razors. Lincoln consulted his physician, Dr. Anson Henry, who told him he had a nervous condition.

Lincoln experienced another severe depression in 1841. He wrote gloomily at the time, "If what I feel were equally distributed to the whole human family, there would not be one cheerful face on earth." During this time he was to be married to Mary Todd. But Lincoln did not show up for the wedding. Friends later found him agitated, desperate, and deeply despondent. Again, fearing that he might take his own life, knives and razors were kept from him. Eventually, upon recovering, he was able to go through with the marriage.

Lincoln apparently suffered another depressive episode during the great Lincoln-Douglas debates. Portraits show him as a man with the look of melancholy. After his crowning speech in Quincy, he broke down, agitated and exhausted. While President, Lincoln experienced another serious bout with depression that was triggered by the death of his son, Willie.

It is very likely that Lincoln's depressive history would today rule him out as a presidential candidate. In 1972, for instance, Senator Thomas Eagleton was the vice-presidental nominee of the Democratic party. When in the course of the campaign his history of severe mental depression and electroshock treatment became known, public opinion compelled him to resign from the ticket.

(For more details, see Ronald R. Fieve, *Moodswing* [New York: William Morrow, 1975].)

Lincoln about the time of the Lincoln-Douglas debates. His profoundly sad look is characteristic of depression. *(The Bettmann Archive)*

norepinephrine are associated with depression, high levels with mania.) Proponents of the biochemical view point out that depressive disorders run in families and that a person having a close relative who suffers from depression is at greater than average risk (Winokur, Tsuang, and Crowe, 1982; Coryell et al., 1985; Klein, Depue, and Slater, 1985). All of the theories of depression are compatible with the view that biochemically vulnerable people are more likely to have isolated social lives full of anxiety.

Mania and Bipolar Disorders

Another mood disorder is **mania,** in which people experience an extended "high"—they feel revved up and on top of the world. More often, they alternate between elated, excited "highs" and dejected, depressed "lows" (NIMH/NIH Consensus Development Panel, 1985). This latter disturbance is termed **bipolar disorder** and also, by some mental health professionals, **manic-depressive disorder.**

When in the manic phase, these people vibrate with energy and have a decreased need for sleep. Their thoughts and feelings race at machine-gun speed. Frequently, the "high" spirals out of control and sufferers become confused and disorganized, as illustrated by the following case of acute mania (Karnash, 1945):

> On admission she slapped the nurse, addressed the house physician as God, made the sign of the cross, and laughed loudly when she was asked to don the hospital garb. This she promptly tore to shreds. . . . She sang at the top of her voice, screamed through the window, and leered at the patients promenading in the recreation yard.

Bipolar swings between highs and lows may occur over the course of several days to several months. Some people experience interim periods of normality. Others may have only brief highs and long lows or, more rarely, brief lows and long highs. And then there are people who are normal most of the time except for relatively minor dips and elevations.

Some people who are quite successful in life have a mild form of bipolar disorder. They function exceedingly well when they are in a mild high. In fact, psychiatrist Ronald R. Fieve (1975) claims that some of the most gifted people in our society, including some playwrights, scientists, politicians, and business executives, suffer from this condition. Their tremendous drive, energy, and imagination during their manic upswings allow them to achieve the heights of success. In severe cases, however, what usually happens is that the manic phase escalates out of control and then there is a crash. After the manic episode, the person is often in financial ruin because of reckless spending or unwise investment strategies.

Suicide

Not all people who commit suicide are depressed, and not all depressed people attempt suicide (Leonard, 1974). But many depressives do think about suicide, and some of them translate these thoughts into action.

People may take their own lives for any number of reasons: to escape from insufferable physical or emotional anguish (perhaps a terminal illness or the loneliness of old age), to end the torment of unacceptable feelings (such as desire for a friend's wife), to punish themselves for wrongs they feel they have committed, or to punish others who have not perceived their needs (Mintz, 1968). In many cases the reason for the suicide simply is not known. The very person who takes his or her life may be the least aware at the decisive moment of the reasons and emotions underlying the behavior (Schneidman, 1976). Indeed, a mounting body of evidence suggests that low levels of the neurotransmitter serotonin characterize the brains of many suicide victims (Brown et al., 1982; Ostroff et al., 1982). Although a low serotonin level does not determine suicidal behavior, it seems to make people more vulnerable to distressing aspects of their environment (Pines, 1983b).

But every year between twenty thousand and thirty thousand Americans do end their lives—about one every thirty minutes. However, official figures underestimate suicide—because of insurance considerations, religious reasons, and social worries, and most often because of uncertainty, particularly in the case of automobile accidents. The actual suicide figure very likely exceeds one hundred thousand deaths a year.

---

mania: A mood disorder in which people experience an extended "high."
bipolar (manic-depressive) disorder: An affective disorder characterized by mood
    swing from depression to mania.

Suicide attempts are often dangerous cries for help. Through miscalculation of the risks of the pills they swallow, many people who attempt suicide die when they did not really intend to. (© T.C. Fitzgerald/The Picture Cube)

Suicide rates vary from culture to culture. In the United States the suicide rate is 11.5 per one hundred thousand population; in Hungary it is 45.6 per one hundred thousand population—the highest in the world (see Figure 15.2). Other countries of Central Europe also have high rates. This is true also of nations like Japan, where suicide under certain circumstances is for many people part of a distinct moral code. Predominantly Roman Catholic countries such as Ireland and Spain, where suicide is considered a mortal sin, have suicide rates among the lowest in the world.

Within the United States, more women than men attempt suicide, but more men than women succeed. Men are more likely to shoot themselves, whereas women are more likely to take sleeping pills—a culturally determined difference in approach with differences in likelihood of success. Suicide is most common among the elderly, with separated, divorced, and widowed elderly males living alone being particularly susceptible. It also ranks as the third most common cause of death among college students. Contrary to popular belief, people who threaten suicide or make an unsuccessful attempt usually *are* serious. Studies show that about 70 percent of people who kill themselves have threatened to do so within the three months preceding the suicide, and an unsuccessful attempt is often a trial run (Alvarez, 1970).

For every actual suicide there are about eight attempts, and some estimates place the ratio much higher (Schneidman, 1976). However, many people who attempt suicide do not really wish to die. They may slash their wrists or swallow a handful of pills and then telephone someone with a tearful farewell. In effect they are saying, "Get me help! Save me from myself!" The goal of "attempted suicide" is often to change one's life (or that of significant others), rather than to end it. Nonetheless, an attempted suicide may unintentionally become an actual suicide through miscalculation of the margin of safety.

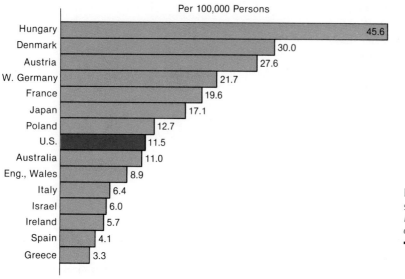

Per 100,000 Persons

Hungary	45.6
Denmark	30.0
Austria	27.6
W. Germany	21.7
France	19.6
Japan	17.1
Poland	12.7
U.S.	11.5
Australia	11.0
Eng., Wales	8.9
Italy	6.4
Israel	6.0
Ireland	5.7
Spain	4.1
Greece	3.3

FIGURE 15.2 Suicide rates in selected countries. *(Data from World Health Organization and U.S. Department of Health and Human Services, 1984.)*

SCHIZOPHRENIC DISORDERS

Schizophrenic disorders are a group of severe, baffling psychological disturbances that account for half the patients in U.S. mental hospitals. Many more schizophrenics live in society but must on occasion return to hospitals. According to the National Institute of Mental Health (1980), about 2 million Americans—some 1 percent of the population—can be classified as schizophrenics. The illness usually appears in late adolescence or early adulthood. On the average, about one-fourth of sufferers fully recover from a first attack, the majority remain chronically ill and require long-term medication, and another one-fifth do poorly, regardless of treatment (Strauss and Carpenter, 1979; Neale and Oltmanns, 1980).

The Nature of Schizophrenic Disorders

Although "madness" has existed throughout human history, in 1911 Eugen Bleuler, a Swiss psychiatrist, named the illness "schizophrenia." The term literally means "split mind," reflecting Bleuler's belief that

the fundamental property of the disorder is the split between thought and emotions. However, the label is widely misunderstood as applying to cases of multiple personality, such as that of Eve White, in which the mind is divided into several selves. But in dissociative disorders, people at least have identifiable personalities. In contrast, in chronic cases of schizophrenia, the personality appears to wear away. Indeed, the disintegration of the mind as an operating whole makes it seem that *no* personality—*no* unity of self—is discernible. Hence, Bleuler used the term to describe the disjointed perceptions, emotions, and thoughts—the disorganized bits and pieces of behavior—that characterize its victims.

Schizophrenia is an umbrella term used to cover a variety of disorders with a broad spectrum of symptoms. Some schizophrenics gradually lose interest in what is happening around them, becoming increasingly apathetic, listless, and noncommunicative. They may be able to hold menial jobs or survive as "drifters," but their interpersonal contacts are few and of limited quality. Other people commonly view them as "eccentric," "odd," or "shiftless." "Bag ladies" who haunt city streets are often suffering from this disorder. So are many recluses.

---

schizophrenic disorders: A group of serious disorders characterized by confused and disconnected thoughts, emotions, and perceptions.

Other schizophrenics experience **delusions** (false beliefs maintained in the face of contrary evidence) and **hallucinations** (sensations in the absence of appropriate stimulation). Sufferers commonly believe that others are plotting against them —contriving ways to confuse them, to make them appear ridiculous, and even to injure or murder them. In psychoanalytic terms, they are using the defense mechanism of projection. Alien forces constantly watch them and monitor their thoughts. When they view television, read the newspaper, or go to the movies, they find—to their horror—that somehow the content deals with them. They must remain eternally vigilant, always on guard lest they be victimized. Their delusions are usually supported by hallucinations, in which their senses detect the evidence of plots. They may taste poison in their food, smell gas in their bedroom, or hear voices telling them why they have been singled out for some special mission.

Still other schizophrenics alternate between periods of paralytic stupor and periods of excited agitation. They may remain totally immobile, rigid, and unresponsive for hours. Periodic frenzied flare-ups, when they display enormous energy and flail about, may be the only sign of emotional life displayed.

In schizophrenia, it is as if the gears of a person's mental machinery have slipped and the connections have gone haywire. One patient described the experience as losing the ability to focus his thoughts (McGhie and Chapman, 1961):

> I can't concentrate. It's diversion of attention that troubles me. I am picking up different conversations. It's like being a transmitter. The sounds are coming through to me but I feel my mind cannot cope with everything. It's difficult to concentrate on any one sound.

Another told of being unable to organize his perceptions:

> Everything is in bits. You put the picture up bit by bit into your head. It's like a photograph that's been torn to bits and put together again. You have to absorb it again. If you move it's frightening. The picture you had in your head is still there but it's broken up.

Factors in Schizophrenic Disorders

Multiple factors are implicated in schizophrenic disorders. Stress appears to play a role in the onset of the illness and in relapses, but apparently only in people who are predisposed to schizophrenia. Hence genetic vulnerability and environmental stress interact in producing the disorder (Zubin and Spring, 1977; Lykken, 1982).

Genetic Factors

Today most psychologists agree that at least some types of schizophrenia have genetic roots. This genetic component seems to derive from genes that code for proteins regulating brain function, particularly the neurotransmitters. The hereditary factor has been implicated in schizophrenia by family, adoption, and twin studies.

The logic underlying family studies is that biological relatives have a greater proportion of their genes in common than unrelated persons do. Hence, to the extent that a disorder is genetically influenced, relatives of affected people are more likely to have inherited the predisposing genes than people in the general population. Family studies reveal that relatives of schizophrenics are more likely to be at risk for schizophrenia than other people (Gottesman and Shields, 1982; Kendler, 1983; Kendler and Robinette, 1983; Baron et al., 1985). Among the brothers and sisters of schizophrenics, the average risk for the disorder is roughly between 8 and 10 percent.

Some of the most compelling evidence that genetic factors are involved with schizophrenia comes from adoption studies. Seymour Kety and his colleagues (1975; Kety, 1983) have investigated the psychiatric status of American and Danish adults born of schizophrenic parents but adopted in infancy. The research shows that adopted children born of schizophrenic parents have a higher incidence of schizophrenia (21 percent) than adopted children born of normal parents (5 percent). Regardless of

---

delusion: A false belief maintained in the face of contrary evidence.
hallucination: A sensation in the absence of appropriate stimulation.

Paintings by schizophrenic patients that suggest the disturbances of feelings and sense of self that are characteristic of the disorder. *(National Library of Medicine)*

rearing environment, children of schizophrenic parents have high rates of breakdown. Children born of schizophrenic parents and reared by them do not show a higher rate of psychological disorder than children born of schizophrenics and reared by normal parents. Finally, children born to normal parents but adopted by schizophrenic parents do not show increased rates of schizophrenia. Thus genetic vulnerability to schizophrenia is the major source of breakdown.

However, as revealed by twin studies, genetic factors are not the only influence. Although the tendency for both twins to have schizophrenia is far greater among identical than among fraternal twins, in approximately half the cases in which an identical twin has been diagnosed as schizophrenic, the other twin is not schizophrenic. (Among fraternal twins the rate of concordance is only 4 to 10 percent.) These findings suggest that hereditary factors alone are not responsible for the development of schizophrenia. Environmental factors must also be at work.

Biochemical Factors

Some of the most promising research of recent years has dealt with the part that brain chemistry plays in schizophrenia. A prominent hypothesis is that dopamine, a neurotransmitter, is excessively active in the brains of schizophrenics (Carlsson, 1978; Haracz, 1982). Dopamine's specific functions still remain a riddle. However, it is localized in those parts of the brain that regulate emotion and that are believed to mediate the interpretation of sensory perceptions. Virtually all the drugs that are effective in reducing the symptoms of schizophrenia work by blocking the receptor sites where dopamine is normally received (Pickar et al., 1984; Zemlan et al., 1985).

Another brain chemical under investigation is monoamine oxidase, or MAO (Wyatt, Potkin, and Murphy, 1979). A number of studies have shown that schizophrenics in general and paranoid schizophrenics in particular are deficient in the enzyme (Potkin et al., 1978; Baron et al., 1984). MAO plays a critical part in breaking down chemicals known as monoamines after they have completed their work in the brain. However, low MAO activity is also found in some patients with other disorders and even among some normal individuals (Sullivan et al., 1978). Hence the role of MAO remains an inconclusive factor in the causation of schizophrenia.

Scientists have produced schizophrenialike effects in rats by injecting into their brains small amounts of beta-endorphin (Bloom et al., 1976; Jacquet and Marks, 1976). The substance is found naturally in animal brains and seems to have morphinelike characteristics. In rats, the beta-endorphins produce a prolonged muscular rigidity and immobility reminiscent of catatonic schizophrenia. The rodents become so rigid that if they are placed across two bookends supported only at the neck and base of the tail, they will remain fixed in the horizontal position. The effect lasts for hours but can be erased within seconds by injections of naloxone, an antidote used for morphine overdose.

Another avenue of research has been opened up by two kinds of computer-generated brain scans —the CAT scan, which shows the brain's anatomy, and the PET scan, which shows brain metabolism and functioning (see Chapter 2). For instance, researchers report that about two-thirds of chronic schizophrenics show at least some structural differences from normal individuals, including atrophy of the cortex and enlarged brain ventricles (fluid-filled portions of the brain) (Weinberger et al., 1979; Wender and Klein, 1981; Seidman, 1983).

Still another area of investigation has been opened by chemical tests of the spinal fluid of schizophrenics. These tests suggest that in some cases a slow virus may be at work. Perhaps certain nerve cells become the targets of viral attacks, somewhat like the progressive mental deterioration associated with senility (also termed Alzheimer's disease). This interpretation is supported by the fact that individuals who later in life become schizophrenic tend to be born more often in the late-winter and spring months than at other times of the year. Studies of South Africa, Australia, and other southern hemisphere nations with reversed seasons confirm that schizophrenic patients are born in the cooler months, when viral infections are more common (Torrey, 1979; Bradbury and Miller, 1985).

Environmental Factors

Concern for the contribution of the social environment in schizophrenia has led to the study of family patterns. Some psychologists suggest that the parents of individuals who later become schizophrenic use communication patterns that contain contradictory words and actions (Bateson et al., 1956; Wynne et al., 1977). According to the **double-bind** theory of schizophrenia, a childhood full of such contradictory messages produces people who perceive the world as a confusing, disconnected place and who believe that their words and actions have little significance. Consequently, some researchers believe such children may develop the kinds of disordered perceptions, thoughts, and emotions characteristic of schizophrenia. More likely, however, schizophrenia in a family member is a cause rather than a result of disordered communications (Hirsch and Leff, 1975).

PERSONALITY DISORDERS

Personality disorders are different from the problems we have been discussing. People with personality disorders generally do not suffer from acute anxiety; nor do they behave in bizarre, incomprehensible ways. Psychologists consider these people "abnormal" because they seem unable to establish meaningful relationships with other people, to assume social responsibilities, or to adapt to their social environment. This diagnostic category includes a wide range of self-defeating personality patterns, from painfully shy, lonely types to vain, pushy show-offs. Although there are many types of personality disorders, in this section we focus on the **antisocial personality**, sometimes called the **sociopath** or **psychopath**.

Antisocial individuals are irresponsible, immature, emotionally shallow people who seem to court trouble. Extremely selfish, they treat other people as

double bind: A situation in which a person receives conflicting demands, so that no matter what he or she does, it is wrong.
personality disorder: A psychological disturbance characterized by lifelong maladaptive patterns that are relatively free of anxiety and other emotional symptoms.
antisocial personality (psychopath, sociopath): A personality disorder characterized by irresponsibility, immaturity, shallow emotions, and lack of conscience.

objects—as things to be used for gratification and to be cast coldly aside when no longer wanted. Intolerant of everyday frustrations and unable to save or plan or wait, they live for the moment. Seeking thrills is their major occupation. If they should injure other people along the way or break social rules, they do not seem to feel any shame or guilt. It is the other person's tough luck. Nor does getting caught seem to rattle them. No matter how many times they are reprimanded, punished, or jailed, they never learn how to stay out of trouble. They simply do not profit from experience (Schmauk, 1970; Hare, Frazelle, and Cox, 1978).

Many antisocial people can get away with destructive behavior because they are intelligent, entertaining, and able to mimic emotions they do not feel. They win affection and confidence from others whom they then take advantage of. This ability to charm while exploiting helped Charles Manson to dominate the gang of runaways whom he eventually led into the gruesome Tate-LaBianca murders in 1969.

If caught, antisocial people will either spin a fantastic lie or simply insist, with wide-eyed sincerity, that their intentions were utterly pure. Guilt and anxiety have no place in the antisocial personality. A fine example is that of Hugh Johnson, a con man caught after having defrauded people of thousands of dollars in sixty-four separate swindles. When asked why he had victimized so many people, "he replied with some heat that he never took more from a person than the person could afford to lose, and further, that he was only reducing the likelihood that other more dangerous criminals would use force to achieve the same ends" (Nathan and Harris, 1975:406–407). More recently, a man with more than fifty aliases was convicted of bigamy and fraud in the case of one woman. But he confessed to having married 105 women over thirty years for their money, without benefit of divorce!

How do psychologists explain such a lack of ordinary human decency and shame? According to one theory, the psychopath has simply imitated his or her own antisocial parents. Other theories point to lack of discipline or inconsistent discipline during childhood. Finally, some researchers believe that psychopaths have a "faulty nervous system." While most people get very aroused when they do something that they have been punished for in the past, psychopaths never seem to learn to anticipate punishment.

A scratched cross on his forehead still visible, Charles Manson is brought into court in 1969. An antisocial personality helped him to charm a group of runaways, leading them to commit the notorious Tate–LaBianca mass murders. *(Wide World Photos)*

PSYCHOSEXUAL DISORDERS

All societies have sexual standards that tell their members what is "normal" and what is "deviant" behavior. It is hardly surprising, therefore, that sexual behavior one society defines as conventional may be defined by another society as abnormal. Indeed, mental health professionals have changed their minds in recent years on the dividing line between the normal and the abnormal. DSM-II, published in 1968, defined as sexually deviant "individuals whose sexual interests are directed primarily toward objects other than people of the opposite sex, toward sexual acts not usually associated with coitus [sexual intercourse], or toward coitus performed under bizarre circumstances" (American Psychiatric Association, 1968:44). Twelve years later DSM-III classified as psychosexual disorders "those deviations from standard sexual behavior that involve gross impairments in the capacity for affectionate sexual activity between adult human partners" (American Psychiatric Association, 1980). Perhaps the most practical and least harmful approach is to consider **psychosexual disorders** to be those sexual acts that people feel compelled to perform, that make them unhappy, or that cause physical or psychological harm to another person (Rosen and Hall, 1984).

When people are attracted to unacceptable sources of sexual gratification, we call their disorders **paraphilias.** These are conditions that are associated with a preference for the use of a nonhuman object for sexual arousal, repetitive sexual activity with humans involving real or simulated suffering or humiliation, or repetitive sexual activity with nonconsenting or inappropriate partners. Examples of paraphilias include:

- *Exhibitionism:* Obtaining sexual gratification by exhibiting one's genitals to an involuntary observer

- *Fetishism:* Using some object or nongenital part of the body as a stimulus in achieving sexual gratification, such as a lock of hair, an undergarment, or a shoe

- *Incest:* Having sexual relations with close blood relatives

- *Masochism:* Achieving sexual gratification through having pain inflicted on oneself

- *Pedophilia:* Using physical or sexual contact with children to secure sexual gratification

- *Rape:* Engaging in sexual intercourse by threatening or using force on another person

- *Sadism:* Achieving sexual gratification by inflicting pain on another individual

- *Transvestism:* Impersonating and dressing in the clothing of the opposite sex to attain sexual gratification

- *Voyeurism:* Securing sexual gratification through secret observations of another person's sexual activities or genitals

- *Zoophilia:* Obtaining sexual gratification with animals, usually through masturbation or intercourse

Gender identity disorders constitute another category of psychosexual disorders; people with these disorders form gender identities contrary to their sexual anatomy. **Transsexuals,** people who have normal sexual organs but who psychologically feel like members of the opposite sex, are a case in point. Their sexual identities have developed in opposition to their anatomy—it is "as if their mind is in the wrong body." James/Jan Morris (1974) explained the matter in these terms: "I was born with the wrong body, being feminine by gender but male by sex, and I could achieve completeness only when the one was adjusted to the other." Some transsexuals, like Morris and Renée Richards, seek sex-reassignment surgery and hormone therapy to resolve their dilemma.

Disturbance and breakdown, then, are the products of a complex set of factors associated with genetic vulnerability and environmental stress. Every person is more or less vulnerable to psychological disorder, depending on the mix of such factors. The course of a disorder also varies from one person to another. Even in cases of schizophrenia, about

---

psychosexual disorders: Those sexual acts that people feel compelled to perform, that make them unhappy, or that cause physical or psychological harm to another person.
paraphilias: Psychosexual disorders that are associated with a preference for the use of a nonhuman object for sexual arousal, repetitive sexual activity with humans involving real or simulated suffering or humiliation, or repetitive sexual activity with nonconsenting or inappropriate partners.
gender identity disorders: Psychosexual disorders in which individuals form gender identities that are contrary to their sexual anatomy.
transsexuals: People who have normal sexual organs but who psychologically feel like members of the opposite sex.

one-fourth to one-third of its victims make a full recovery. Although the outcome for schizophrenia is somewhat poorer than that for other disorders, pessimism or defeatism is hardly warranted (Strauss et al., 1978; Mosher and Keith, 1980). In the next chapter we consider a number of therapies for intervention and change.

SUMMARY

1. There is no absolute standard for determining whether behavior is normal or abnormal. Common approaches for defining abnormality include deviation from the average, deviation from social norms, an inability to function effectively, and lack of a sense of well-being. In the course of daily life one is influenced by multiple criteria in sizing up people and their behavior.

2. Disturbance and breakdown in behavior result from both a vulnerability of the person and environmental stresses. Some people are genetically so vulnerable that it is difficult to provide them with an environment that is sufficiently low in stress to prevent psychological disorder. There are also those people who are so resistant to stress that few, if any, environments would produce breakdown.

3. From a social perspective, mental health entails the ability to function effectively in one's social roles and to meet the requirements associated with group life. From a psychological perspective, mental health involves people's subjective feelings of well-being —their happiness, contentment, and satisfaction.

4. In 1980, the American Psychiatric Association published a revised system for classifying psychological disorders: DSM-III. Classifications of this sort inevitably produce considerable controversy. Apart from differences of opinion, there is also the question of whether the benefits of classification outweigh the disadvantages.

5. For people who experience anxiety disorders, the world is fraught with apprehension and fear. Among the anxiety disorders are generalized anxiety, panic disorders, phobias, and obsessions and compulsions.

6. In somatoform disorders, individuals experience physical symptoms for which there is no apparent organic cause. Often they complain of backache, stomach pains, or chest pains (psychogenic pain disorder). Others report blindness, deafness, the loss of sensation in body limbs, false pregnancy, or partial paralysis (conversion disorder).

7. In dissociative disorders—amnesia, fugue, and multiple personality—it is psychological rather than physical functioning that is affected. Individuals experience a disturbance in memory or identity.

8. Mood disturbances underlie affective disorders. Moods of elation or depression can be abnormal when they persist for long periods, interfere with a person's daily functioning, and distort an individual's outlook on life. Depression, mania, and bipolar disorders fall into this category.

9. Depression is an affective disorder characterized by a mood drop that lasts for several months, even years. As depression deepens, individuals commonly experience insomnia, a lack of interest in work, loss of appetite, reduced sexual desire, low energy, and profound emotional despair. According to Freudian theory, depression reflects anger directed inward on the self. Cognitive theorists believe that depressed people draw illogical conclusions about themselves. Another interpretation, based on behavior, stresses the role of social relations in depression. Still another approach explains depression as a chemical imbalance in the brain.

10. Another mood disorder is mania, in which people experience an extended "high." More often, they alternate between elated, excited "highs" and dejected, depressed "lows"; this disturbance is termed bipolar disorder (also manic-depressive disorder).

11. Not all people who commit suicide are depressed, and not all depressed people attempt suicide. But many depressives do think about suicide and some of them translate these thoughts into action. Suicide rates vary from culture to culture.

12. In schizophrenia the personality appears to wear away. The disintegration of the mind as an operating whole makes it seem that no personality is discernible. Schizophrenia is an umbrella term used to cover a variety of disorders with a broad spectrum of symptoms, which may include delusions, hallucinations, and alternating periods of stupor and frenzied activity.

13. Multiple factors are implicated in schizophrenic disorders. Stress appears to play a role in the onset of the illness and in relapses, but apparently only in people who are predisposed to schizophrenia. Hence, genetic vulnerability and environmental stress interact in producing the disorder.

14. Personality disorders are different from other types of psychological disorders in that the victims typically do not suffer from acute anxiety or behave in bizarre, incomprehensible ways. Rather, people with personality disorders are unable to establish meaningful relationships with others, to assume social responsibility, or to adapt to their social environment.

15. All societies have sexual standards that tell their members what is "normal" and what is "deviant" behavior. From a psychological perspective, the most practical and least harmful approach seems to be to consider as psychosexual disorders those acts that individuals feel compelled to perform, that make them unhappy, or that cause physical or psychological harm to another person. Disorders that emphasize the deviation to which the individual is attracted are termed paraphilias. Another category of psychosocial disorders is gender identity disorders, in which individuals form gender identities contrary to their sexual anatomy.

KEY TERMS

affect (p. 501)

affective disorder (p. 501)

amnesia (p. 500)

antisocial personality
   (psychopath, sociopath)
   (p. 509)

anxiety (p. 494)

bipolar (manic-depressive)
   disorder (p. 504)

compulsion (p. 497)

conversion disorder (p. 499)

delusion (p. 507)

depression (p. 502)

dissociative disorder (p. 500)

double bind (p. 509)

fugue (p. 500)

generalized anxiety disorder
   (p. 495)

gender identity disorders
   (p. 511)

hallucination (p. 507)

hypochondriasis (p. 499)

mania (p. 504)

multiple personality (p. 500)

obsession (p. 497)

panic disorder (p. 495)

paraphilias (p. 511)

personality disorder (p. 509)

phobia (p. 496)

psychosexual disorders (p. 511)

psychosomatic illness (p. 499)

schizophrenic disorders
   (p. 506)

social norm (p. 487)

somatoform disorder (p. 498)

transsexuals (p. 511)

SUGGESTED READINGS

FISHMAN, SCOTT M., and SHEEHAN, DAVID V. 1985. Anxiety and panic: Their cause and treatment. *Psychology Today*, 19 (April):26–30. A new approach to a very common problem.

GREEN, HANNAH. 1964. *I Never Promised You a Rose Garden*. New York: New American Library. A moving and compelling story about the terrifying world and successful treatment of an adolescent girl who had been diagnosed as schizophrenic.

KAPLAN, BERT, ED. 1964. *The Inner World of Mental Illness*. New York: Harper & Row. A fascinating collection of first-person accounts of what it is like to experience severe mental disturbance.

NEALE, JOHN M., and OLTMANNS, THOMAS F. 1980. *Schizophrenia*. New York: Wiley. Consolidates research on schizophrenia: diagnosis, language and information processing, genetics, biochemistry, psychophysiology, the role of the environment, high-risk research, and treatment.

PAYKEL, EUGENE S., ED. 1982. *Handbook of Affective Disorders*. New York: Guilford Press. Offers everything one wants to know about affective disorders—description, theories of causation, and treatments.

PLATH, SYLVIA. 1971. *The Bell Jar*. New York: Bantam. An autobiographical novel about a young woman's mental breakdown. Plath was an excellent writer, and the book is especially powerful because she was able to articulate her feelings so well.

ROSENFELD, ANNE. 1985. Depression: Dispelling despair. *Psychology Today*, 19 (June): 28–32. An overview of drug and talk therapies for depression, describing the benefits and drawbacks of each.

Alex Katz, *Good Afternoon II*, 1974.

16
Intervention and Change

Renée Bigler's son suffers from schizophrenia. She had hoped that he might be cured. But as he grew into adulthood, still unable to function independently, her problems increased. She was unable to find a place where he could live. In her anguished and relentless search for help, Renée came across other families with members who also suffered from long-term mental illness. She says, "I found out I was not alone in this terrible kind of hell" (Turkington, 1984a:20). Renée Bigler concluded that what her son, and thousands of others like him, needed was a supportive residence that would allow him to combine independent living with caring support.

Unfortunately for Renée Bigler and many other families, few programs for the chronically mentally ill are available in the United States. As a result, most of the three hundred thousand to 3 million mentally ill Americans who cannot find shelter seek it in doorways, in bus stations, and under bridges in crowded cities. Because there was no home for the mentally ill in Greenwich, Connecticut, where Renée Bigler and her son lived, she decided to establish one. In 1982 she organized Pathways, Inc., raised funds in the community, and bought a three-story stone house near the center of town.

But her difficulties had just begun. Pathways discovered that Greenwich regulatory agencies had no classification for halfway homes. Accordingly, the city's zoning appeals board decided to consider Pathways a convalescent home. However, the building department ruled that as a convalescent home, Pathways had to undertake extensive and impractical renovations. To sidestep this requirement, the building department deemed Pathways to be a three-family dwelling. The fire department disagreed, saying the house did not qualify as a three-family dwelling because the residents were not related. So Pathways became a rooming house. In turn, the zoning board held that as a rooming house it violated the zoning code.

Eventually Greenwich's three departments agreed to consider Pathways a multifamily dwelling and issued it a certificate of occupancy. But the neighbors were outraged. Although Greenwich citizens thought the idea of a residential program for the mentally ill a good one, none of them wanted it located next door. The neighbors banded together as the Central Greenwich Association and sued the zoning board and Pathways for failing to observe the city's zoning laws.

Volunteers had raised $340,000 for Pathways in the first two years. The house cost $164,000, and more than $54,000 was consumed in legal fees. Although the privately raised funds were ample to get the program going, money for the home's day-to-day operation was another matter. Pathways assumed it would be eligible for assistance from the state's mental health department. But the state informed Pathways that it would have to join Connecticut's mental health consortium, a nonprofit organization that oversees the state's mental health programs, before it could receive funds. However, a Catch-22 stood in the way. Pathways was barred from the consortium unless it was already a provider of services. Yet it could not provide housing services until it joined the consortium. To meet the state's requirement, Pathways set up a social club in a local Presbyterian church where it provided services for the mentally ill. Although it now qualifies for state assistance, as a new program it receives only 13 percent of its operating budget from state sources (Turkington, 1984a).

The story of Renée Bigler and Pathways illustrates the struggle that many of the mentally ill and their families experience in securing help. This chapter addresses a number of questions. What kinds of helping relationships are available to the mentally ill? What settings offer help? What types of help are available? And does intervention work?

To live is to change. Indeed, life dictates constant coping and adaptation. Even the assumption of welcomed roles—adulthood, a career, marriage, parenthood—requires adjustment. Thus to live an abundant, full, and fruitful life, you must continually fit your behaviors to those of other people and to the world.

At times the processes associated with living are more difficult than at other times. Everyone confronts a share of difficulties and problems. In periods of unusual flux or crisis, one may feel a need to find some trustworthy person with whom to share doubts and dilemmas. A parent, relative, or close friend may prove helpful in such times of need. Or one may seek out a self-help group, such as Parents Without Partners, Weight Watchers, or Alcoholics Anonymous. Should psychological problems become too complex or bewildering, one may look for assistance to people with special experience or training.

A growing number of psychologists also contend that traditional conceptions of the role of clinical psychology need to be expanded (Levy, 1984). They broaden their perspective to encompass a *human services psychology*—a sector of professional psychology that promotes human well-being through the acquisition and application of psychological knowledge related not only to the treatment of psychological and physical disorders but also to their prevention. This approach seeks to promote better parenting and social change to restore or increase social justice, to reduce powerlessness, and to lessen the stresses of contemporary society. The emphasis is on preventing problems from appearing in the first place (Albee, 1982, 1985).

LOOKING FOR HELP

People do not have to "break down" before seeking professional help. Nor are people who seek help a small minority of the population. Indeed, the probabilities are quite high that people you know and feel close to will want professional help for their personal and psychological difficulties at some point in their lives. It is also possible that you have already received help or that you will do so at some time for some problem. Clearly, seeking professional assistance is becoming much more commonplace in American life. Yet as noted in Chapter 15, although a recent National Institute of Mental Health survey reveals that one in five American adults suffers from mental illness, only 19 percent of people with psychological problems seek help.

Public attitudes have changed considerably from earlier times, when psychological disturbances were thought to represent moral or religious problems. People with emotional or mental disorders were often viewed as being inhabited by devils or demons. Treatment consisted of driving out the evil spirits by religious ceremonies or subjecting such people to punishment for their wayward ways.

Today people seek professional psychological help for a good many reasons. Much depends on what is happening in their lives. Some people need help to cope with a crisis—an immediate and acute problem (for instance, a person may "break down" or be the victim of rape or violent assault). Others finally become fed up with chronic problems (for example, they may experience persistent loneliness or recurrent depressive episodes). Still others seek help for another person whom they believe is causing them continuing distress (for instance, a person may seek professional help for an alcoholic spouse or for a delinquent teen-age family member).

In Chapter 15, we pointed out that two features typically characterize psychological health. First, people are able to function effectively in their social roles and meet the requirements associated with group life. Second, people have a subjective feeling of well-being; they are fundamentally happy, contented, and satisfied with their lives—as Freud said,

they are able to love and to work. Noticeable departures from these standards provide signals of trouble that may warrant professional attention.

People typically seek professional help when they conclude that the approaches they are using for dealing with their problems are not working. They find that their own efforts and the help of their friends and relatives are inadequate to the task. Frequently, they feel that their difficulties are worsening. And they expect that professionals will be able to help them in solving their problems.

In looking to outsiders for help, people commonly lack personal acquaintance with specific professionals and often distrust those whom they do not personally know. Under these circumstances, they may turn to someone who worked with or treated a friend or relative in time of difficulty (McKinlay, 1973; Griffith, 1985). Or they may be referred to a professional by a physician, teacher, employer, lawyer, or member of the clergy. There are many therapies, and those who offer them differ in theory, technique, and training. Table 16.1 distinguishes

---

TABLE 16.1 Kinds of Mental Health Therapists

Psychiatrists	Physicians who specialize in the treatment of mental illness. They generally take a post-M.D. residency in a mental institution. Because of their medical background, pyschiatrists are the only group licensed to prescribe drugs.
Psychoanalysts	Psychiatrists who have taken special training in the theory of personality and techniques of psychotherapy of Sigmund Freud and his followers, usually at a psychoanalytic institute. They must themselves be psychoanalyzed before they can practice.
Lay analysts	Psychoanalysts who do not have degrees in medicine but who have studied with established psychoanalysts.
Clinical psychologists	Therapists with a Ph.D. or Psy.D. degree. They are the product of a four- to five-year research-oriented program in psychology, which also includes a one-year predoctoral or postdoctoral internship in psychotherapy and psychological assessment.
Counselors	People who generally have a master's or doctor's degree in counseling psychology. They usually work in educational institutions or personnel-related settings, where they are available for consultation about personal problems. They customarily refer clients with serious problems to psychiatrists or clinical psychologists.
Psychiatric social workers	People with a graduate degree in psychiatric social work. They generally receive supervised practical training coupled with two years of courses in social work.
Nonprofessionals	Include clergy, physicians, teachers, and others who dispense a great deal of advice despite the fact that they have little, if any, formal training in therapy or counseling. Nevertheless, troubled people turn more to nonprofessionals than to professionals.

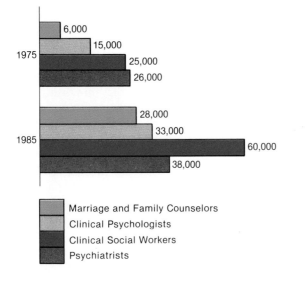

6,000
15,000
25,000
26,000

1975

28,000
33,000
60,000
38,000

1985

Marriage and Family Counselors
Clinical Psychologists
Clinical Social Workers
Psychiatrists

FIGURE 16.1 Estimated rate of growth among the chief professional categories of mental-health therapists. *(After Daniel Goleman. 1985. Social workers vault into a leading role in psychotherapy. New York Times (April 30):17. Copyright © 1985 by the New York Times Company. Reprinted by permission.)*

among various types of practitioners. As Figure 16.1 shows, clinical social workers now constitute the largest group of mental health professionals, followed by psychiatrists, clinical psychologists, and marriage and family counselors. Psychiatry, which at one time was the largest single group of therapists, has seen a sharp decrease in members in the past decade. Over the same period, the number of clinical psychologists has doubled (Goleman, 1985d).

HELPING SETTINGS

During the nineteenth century, and well into the twentieth century, many forms of psychological disorder were viewed as illnesses to be treated in a hospital setting. Large mental hospitals were built in rural areas, where space could be obtained cheaply and patients could be concealed from the public, who thought them unsightly and dangerous. But the social isolation of patients, their removal from familiar surroundings and family life, often made later

readjustment to society even more difficult. Released patients found themselves too far from the hospital for any supplementary care and too fragile to cope independently with the pressures of the outside world. Hence over the past sixty years, and especially since the 1950s, many new settings have evolved for dealing with psychological disorders.

Private Office Settings

Many mental health professionals treat patients on a one-to-one basis in a private office. For the most part, the patients continue to function in the workaday world and see their practitioner at regularly scheduled appointments. Psychoanalysts usually see patients over two or more years for three to five sessions a week. In contrast, behaviorally oriented and medically oriented practitioners typically see patients once or twice a week over three months to a year. Most patients treated in private offices either can afford to pay the fees or have insurance that covers them.

Group Settings

Since human beings live in groups and since many of their problems derive from group living, it is not surprising that troubled people should turn to groups for assistance. In **group therapy**, patients work together with the aid of a group leader to resolve interpersonal problems. As noted in Chapter 10, groups play a powerful role in shaping attitudes and behavior. Hence much of the therapeutic effectiveness of groups comes from people's identification with them, their feelings of group support, and their sense of gaining new levels of self-control in a group whose goals are compatible with their own. Therapeutic groups take a great many forms. Some are organized by mental health professionals, others by nonprofessionals, and still others by troubled people themselves.

Traditional Group Therapy

Traditional group-therapy sessions are typically provided by trained therapists. An advantage of this

---

group therapy: A form of therapy in which patients work together with the aid of a group leader to resolve interpersonal problems.

The traditional custodial mental hospital setting: a bare room, barred windows, a hospital gown. Such a setting contributes to the person's isolation and feeling of separation from the everyday world and can actually decrease the chances of recovery. *(Mary Ellen Mark/Magnum)*

arrangement is that one therapist can help a large number of people, and people in the groups can help one another. The therapist leads the sessions, makes suggestions, clarifies points, and keeps matters from getting out of hand. In this manner, therapists can use their training and experience to help from six to ten (in some cases up to twenty) patients at once.

Group therapy gives troubled people practical experience with one of their major problems—getting along with others. They also have a chance to see how other people are struggling with problems similar to their own. Moreover, they can discover what others think of them, gain feedback on how they appear to others, and in turn, express what they think of the other members of the group. In this exchange, group members discover where they are mistaken in their conceptions of themselves and of others, and where they are correct.

Encounter and Sensitivity Groups

Over the past quarter century, group therapy took a number of new directions. Among these developments was the emergence in the late 1960s and early 1970s of encounter and sensitivity groups. The groups were primarily for people who functioned adequately in everyday life but who, for some rea-

son, felt unhappy, dissatisfied, or stagnant. Their purpose was to provide people with experiences that would help them to live more open and meaningful lives. Many of their techniques were directed toward overcoming various self-imposed constraints to personal liberation and growth.

Some *encounter groups* met only once or twice, in "marathon" sessions that lasted eighteen or more hours. The emphasis fell on emotional release and the tearing down of encrusted defenses and façades. People were encouraged to focus only on here-and-now feelings. Sometimes exercises entailed touching, weeping, and yelling. Many encounter groups also employed discussions in which group members were encouraged to "tell it as it is." Such confrontations could be exceedingly frank, even brutal.

Sensitivity groups were typically less confrontational than encounter groups. In them, the emphasis fell on developing "trusting" relationships with others. Thus the atmosphere tended to be relaxed and the members were usually warm, sympathetic, and supportive of one another. Often sensitivity sessions were used to broaden the interpersonal awareness of coworkers in office relationships.

Today many of the practices pioneered by encounter and sensitivity groups have become commonplace and have been absorbed into the mainstream.

An encounter group session. The purpose of these groups was to provide experiences that would help people to live more intense lives; the methods used were intended to increase sensitivity, openness, and honesty. *(Dan O'Neill/EPA, Inc.)*

Other practices have fallen by the wayside and even into disrepute (Goleman, 1985b). In some cases techniques for rapidly breaking down defense mechanisms resulted in casualties. Indeed, about a third of those who engaged in the more confrontational encounter groups responded negatively to their experiences (Lieberman, Yalom, and Miles, 1975; Hartley, Roback, and Abramowitz, 1976). Impulsive dissolutions of marriages, acute panic states, depressive reactions, and even breakdowns were among the consequences of group participation. Although such groups often posed no problems for psychologically healthy individuals, and even provided benefits for them, people who were less secure or stable discovered they were better off elsewhere.

Self-Help Groups

Some of the most successful group-therapy programs are provided by nonprofessional self-help organizations such as Alcoholics Anonymous (AA) (Silverman, 1980). The purpose of Alcoholics Anonymous is "to carry the AA message to the sick alcoholic who wants it." According to AA, the only way for alcoholics to change is to admit that they are powerless over alcohol and that their lives have become unmanageable. They must come to believe that only some power greater than themselves can help them. Drinkers who think they can battle their problem alone will not be successful.

Members of AA usually meet at least once a week to discuss the meaning of this message, to talk about the horrors of their experiences with alcohol, and to describe the new hope they have found with AA. Mutual encouragement, friendship, and an emphasis on personal responsibility are the main techniques used to keep people "on the wagon." Every member must be willing to come to the aid of another member who is tempted to take a drink.

Alcoholics Anonymous has served as a model for a variety of other groups. The Public Health Service estimates that 15 million citizens have banded together in five hundred thousand groups, including those formed by displaced homemakers, single parents, parents of handicapped children, unmarried pregnant teen-agers, former drug addicts, smokers, overeaters, child-abusing parents, and former mental patients (Mann, 1983). Psychologists find that people who have the support of such groups are much better off emotionally than those who face their problems alone (Albee, 1985).

Carl Rogers is shown here (on the left, top photograph) leading a sensitivity group. Many group leaders, including Rogers, felt that their role in the group was the same as that of any other member. Only if the group as a whole or any one of its members got into trouble would the leader intervene to rescue the situation. Typically, other group members would exhibit leadership or therapeutic skills and the designated leader would remain in the background. (H. Lee Pratt)

Hospital Settings

When the demands of everyday life cannot be met, psychologically troubled people may require hospitalization. Approximately 25 percent of the total hospital days in the United States are for mental disorders (Kiesler, 1982). But whether a person ends up in a mental hospital also depends on a number of factors beyond the person's mental state. People with family and friends who are willing to care for them are less likely to be hospitalized than those without family or friends. Moreover, recent budget cutbacks in funds for state mental health agencies mean that people in need of help are finding it increasingly difficult to gain admission to state hospitals. Many private institutions and for-profit psychiatric hospitals scattered across the United States offer care, but they are usually expensive.

Ideally, a mental hospital should be a place where patients are temporarily freed from social pressures that they cannot bear. Limited and carefully planned demands should be made by an understanding and concerned staff. Unfortunately, the reality of many public and private hospitals generally does not fit this ideal. Conditions in some state institutions have improved in recent decades. Nonetheless, the quali-

ty and quantity of care vary from state to state, from hospital to hospital, and from ward to ward within a single hospital. One still finds in many facilities inappropriate prescribing and careless monitoring of medication, excessive use of electroshock therapies, and inadequate therapeutic programs.

Most psychiatric hospitals serve three sets of patients. The first group consists of chronically ill people whose condition has deteriorated beyond the point where existing therapies seem to afford benefit. For these patients, the hospitals provide custodial care. The second group of patients consists of seriously ill people who live outside a hospital environment when their condition is in remission but who are readmitted during periods of acute illness. The third group is in acute crisis. They may be suicidal or unable to cope with everyday life. Some people in the acute crisis group will never have another breakdown, while others will become members of the first and second groups.

Over the past two decades, many general hospitals have added psychiatric units. (State and private mental hospitals now account for only 25 percent of the total incidence of mental hospitalization.) The advent of health insurance coverage for short-term hospitalization associated with psychological disorder has contributed to the trend. Further, a wide array of psychoactive drugs has made intensive medical treatment of mental problems possible. The average length of stay in most psychiatric units is now from three to four weeks, although many people stay for several months.

A statistical profile of the nation's mental health by the National Institute of Mental Health (1985) describes a trend toward a two-tiered mental health care system. One tier consists of mental health care for more affluent (mostly white) Americans and a second, inferior tier for poorer (predominantly minority) Americans. According to 1980 figures, non-

whites are admitted to state and county mental hospitals at a rate more than double that of whites: 328 versus 137 per 100,000 (see Figure 16.2). Yet there is very little difference in the incidence of various disorders between white and minority populations. People who need and can afford care are able to find it. But people who cannot afford to pay for care themselves, or who do not have medical insurance, have a harder time finding the kind of treatment they require. Much the same pattern holds for white youngsters and minority youngsters showing behavioral disorders. White children are more likely to be channeled into the mental health system and

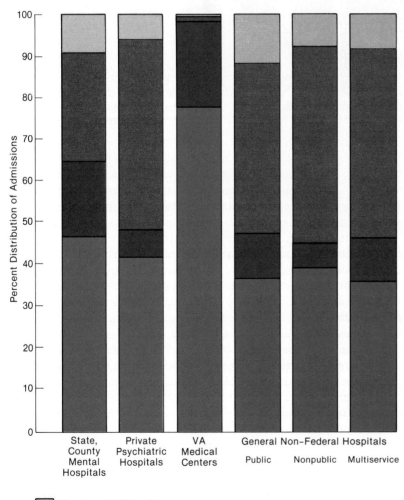

FIGURE 16.2 Percent distribution of mental-health hospital admissions, by race, sex, and type of inpatient psychiatric service, United States, 1980. *(After National Institute of Mental Health, 1985, Mental Health, United States, 1985. Washington, D.C.: U.S. Government Printing Office.)*

Halfway houses, day treatment centers, and community mental health centers try to return as many people as possible to the community. This group of ex-hospital patients meets to discuss problems and help one another make the adjustment from inmate to functioning member of a community. *(Michael Weisbrot & Family)*

minority children into the penal system or a training school.

Community Settings

Mental health professionals have long held that it is better if people do not stay too long in mental hospitals. It seems that mental hospitalization becomes self-perpetuating—the bulk of admissions are readmissions, ranging from 86 percent at Veterans Administration (VA) medical centers to 70 percent at general hospitals (Kiesler, 1982; National Institute of Mental Health, 1985). After a while, patients become dependent on a sheltered environment, lose social skills, and avoid self-responsibility. Many become apathetic and resign themselves to the routine of institutional life. Hence experts have championed community programs that allow people to retain some measure of community involvement and rootedness. Further, community programs allow people to receive help before their difficulties become so acute as to require hospitalization.

Researchers find that community care for the mentally ill does make a difference. Matched groups of schizophrenic patients in Portland, Oregon, and Vancouver, British Columbia, were compared one year following their discharge from psychiatric facilities (Beiser et al., 1985). Whereas Vancouver boasts a rich network of accessible private services and a model public mental health system, Portland's aftercare facilities at the time of the study were limited. One year after discharge the Vancouver patients experienced fewer readmissions, were more apt to be employed, and reported a higher level of well-being than the Portland patients. These findings suggest that community aftercare positively affects the symptoms of schizophrenia.

Community Mental Health Centers

The Community Mental Health Centers Act of 1963 was designed to solve some of the problems faced by patients trying to reenter society. One mental health center was required for every fifty thousand members of the U.S. population, to supply needed psychological services for the ex-patient attempting to function within the community. These centers were also supposed to educate community workers such as police, teachers, and clergy in the principles of preventive mental health, to train paraprofessionals, and to carry out research (Dowell and Ciarlo, 1983).

Outpatients can walk into a clinic and receive therapy once, twice, or several times a week, without separating themselves from school, job, or family, and without feeling as stigmatized as institutionalized mental patients. Thus the centers serve as a bridge between hospitalization and complete independence by giving care to patients after they are released from hospitals.

Many community mental health centers also maintain storefront clinics that are open around the clock to deal with such emergencies as acute anxiety attacks, suicide attempts, and bad drug trips. The centers may have teams of psychologically trained personnel on call to go to city hospital emergency rooms to deal with psychological traumas.

In some respects, the movement for community mental health centers has not lived up to the high expectations held for it by its proponents. For one thing, a countrywide system of centers has not yet been achieved. For another, the programs have been underfunded and understaffed (see the boxed insert on pages 526–527). They have also had difficulty providing adequate services for minority-group clients.

Still another difficulty has been that in community settings, mental health workers often lose contact with former patients. Once discharged from a hospital, patients in theory become the community's responsibility. But in practice many released patients do not voluntarily come to the centers. They lack the resources, social skills, and self-direction necessary for seeking assistance. Consequently, large numbers of released patients live in isolation and squalor on the streets or in unlicensed group homes, boarding houses, and single-occupancy hotels in the central cities. Many are victims of crime, medical neglect, and fires. These problems have led some mental health professionals to argue that the time has come to reconsider the notion of humane institutionalization for chronically disabled individuals—not necessarily in hospitals but in special community residential facilities.

Halfway Houses

There are thousands of people who spend time in mental hospitals, prisons, and homes for delinquents and who, when finally released, are psychologically unprepared to return to life in society. They may be able to behave well under structured conditions, but they find the freedom and immensity of society confusing and overwhelming. Such people can ease back into society through halfway houses.

Halfway houses give their inhabitants the support they need in order to build enough confidence to reenter society. Unwritten rules and informal social

Many mental patients are discharged from hospitals without adequate provision for follow-up care and end up living on the street. The plight of the mentally ill and homeless has become a major social issue. (Alan Carey/The Image Works)

pressures guide the members in their efforts to readjust to the larger world (Raush and Raush, 1968).

Psychiatric Day Treatment Centers

Psychiatric day treatment centers care for people during the day, permitting them to return home in the evening and remain in a family environment. Such centers serve as alternatives to full-time hospitalization. They also function as transitional facilities from hospital to community, as rehabilitation centers for chronic patients, and as intensive treatment centers for adolescents and drug abusers. The arrangement minimizes the disruption of ties with significant others and the processes of regression, infantilization, and social stigmatization associated with hospitalization. More particularly, day treatment centers allow patients to maintain and enhance their social roots and skills (Greene and De La Cruz, 1981).

Crisis hot lines allow people in distress to call at any time and find a sympathetic, helpful person to talk to. Most areas of the country now have such hot lines, and some mental health agencies have even installed special telephones on bridges and in other locations where depressed people are likely to attempt suicide. *(Mark Antman/The Image Works)*

Crisis Intervention: The Hot Line

Community services of the type already outlined are costly and complicated to set up, but the crisis hot line provides an instant, economical, and effective way to deal with emergency situations. People who are in trouble can telephone at any time and receive immediate counseling, sympathy, and comfort. The best known of these systems is the Los Angeles Suicide Prevention Center, established in 1958. Sim-

ilar hot lines have been set up for alcoholics, rape victims, battered women, runaway children, gamblers, and people who just need a shoulder to cry on. In addition to providing sympathy, hot-line volunteers give information on the community services available to deal with each kind of problem.

TYPES OF HELP

Numerous types of help are available to people suffering from psychological disorders. Most therapies fall into one of two major categories. The first is made up of **psychotherapies,** which use psychological means for the treatment of mental disorders; the second is composed of various **biological therapies,** which use drugs and electroshock procedures. But psychotherapies and biological therapies are not mutually exclusive; they are often used together (Karasu, 1982; Cooper, 1985).

The Nature of Psychotherapy

A major function of psychotherapy is to help people realize that they are responsible for their own problems and, even more important, that they are the only ones who can really solve these problems. This approach does not imply that people become disturbed on purpose or that no one should need outside help. People often adopt certain techniques for getting along in life that seem appropriate at the time but that lead to trouble in the long run. Such patterns can be difficult for a person to see or change. The major task of the therapist, therefore, is to help people examine their way of living, understand how their present way of living causes problems, and start living in new, more beneficial ways. The therapist can be thought of as a guide who is hired to help people find the source of their problems and some possible solutions.

Psychotherapeutic interventions are based on psychological theories of personality and behavior (see Chapters 13 and 15). For the most part, the interven-

---

psychotherapies: The use of psychological means for the treatment of mental disorders.

biological therapies: The use of drugs and electroshock procedures for the treatment of mental disorders.

The Plight of the Homeless Mentally Ill

A massive program to discharge the mentally ill from large state mental hospitals—termed *deinstitutionalization*—began in the mid-1950s. As a result, state-hospital populations declined 75 percent from 1955 to 1980. The process was assisted by the advent of tranquilizers and other antipsychotic drugs, concern for the civil rights of institutionalized patients, and a political ideology supporting a less restrictive setting for the treatment of the mentally ill. Deinstitutionalization had two primary goals: to reduce the inpatient populations of publicly supported state mental hospitals and to provide community-based programs for the care and treatment of the chronically mentally ill (Shadish, 1984; Gronfein, 1985).

The magnitude and complexity of the change have precipitated a large and growing social problem. Community acceptance of former patients, adequate housing, vocational and social rehabilitation, medical care, and aftercare services are often lacking or substandard. Deinstitutionalization has meant that many patients have been released unsupervised into the community, where they find themselves helpless, sleeping on sidewalk grates, panhandling, and traveling aimlessly around the country (termed by some "Greyhound therapy"). Food is found in garbage cans or at a mission. The pattern may be interrupted by random encounters with the police and

periodic short-term visits to the psychiatric ward of a local hospital.

At any given time there are about 2 to 3 million homeless Americans; of these, an estimated 25 to 50 percent are mentally ill (Boffey, 1984). Some studies show even higher proportions. A 1983 study of 193 people in a Philadelphia shelter found that 84 percent were mentally ill, including 37 percent who were schizophrenic and 25 percent who were long-term alcohol and drug abusers. And a New York City study showed that almost all the homeless were mentally ill, with 72 percent of those studied being diagnosed as schizophrenic (Nelson, 1983). Longtime advocates of mental health reform, like Dr. Leona Bachrach of the University of Maryland, concede that deinstitutionalization has been a "failure in implementation" because very little of the hoped-for community psychological and psychiatric support was ever provided. That shortfall, says Bachrach, has created "a big mess" for the mentally ill (Morganthau, 1986:14). The American Psychiatric Association has echoed this view, terming the release of the mentally ill into communities "a major societal tragedy" (Boffey, 1984).

Should the homeless mentally ill be hospitalized (or, more often, rehospitalized)? If so, what therapy should they receive? Who should make the decisions? Will treatment be of value if they

---

tions are primarily either insight or action (behavior) therapies. **Insight therapies** typically involve "a conversation with a therapeutic purpose" (Korchin, 1976). The assumption underlying the approach is that many people carry on their lives in ways that block them from finding fulfillment, happiness, and satisfaction. If they can uncover and identify these unhealthy patterns and discern their true reasons for

acting as they do, then they may be able to change their behavior.

Insight therapies share the premise that people must understand the causes of their behavior before they can alter it. In contrast, **behavior therapies** are not too concerned with the inner sources of behavior. Instead, they focus on people's actions in the here and now—what they say and do. Behavior

---

insight therapy: A form of psychotherapy whose basic premise is that people must understand the causes of their behavior before they can alter it.

behavior therapy: A form of therapy aimed at changing undesirable behavior through conditioning techniques.

are then merely released into the community without outpatient services? Mental health professionals and lawyers have debated these questions since the early 1970s. At that time, in response to activism by civil libertarians, reform of involuntary civil commitment laws swept the nation. Due-process procedures, including right to counsel, right to treatment, and limited duration of hospitalization, were put in place. The reforms sought to eliminate gross abuses, such as arbitrary commitment, "warehousing" with no treatment, and indeterminate hospital stays (Holden, 1985a).

However, the reforms of the 1970s have also resulted in situations in which it is exceedingly difficult to get a person who is obviously mentally incompetent and in need of help—occasionally even overtly suicidal—admitted to a hospital for care. The common legal standard is that a person must be "a danger to himself or others" in order to secure even a short-term commitment. In practice, however, the phrase has often meant that a person must commit some overt act of violence before a court will intervene. The result has too often been an arrangement in which the mentally ill are abandoned on the streets of American cities. Considerable controversy surrounds the issue of how to respect the civil rights of the mentally ill while assuring them of the care they need.

Getting people out of the hospitals was relatively easy to accomplish. But it has proven exceedingly difficult to secure alternative care for them. Although 63 percent of the chronically mentally ill are at large in the community, two-thirds of all state and local mental health funding goes to mental institutions (the National Institute of Mental Health estimates that 2.4 million Americans should be classified as chronically mentally ill and that some 1.5 million of them now reside in the community). This lack of funds has contributed to the mounting numbers of homeless people. Most mental health professionals still believe that humane and cost-effective community-based care represents the best hope for the majority of chronically mentally ill individuals. There is clearly a shortage of long-term care facilities and a shortage of community residences, adult homes, halfway houses, and treatment programs to ensure that patients secure the help they require. And it is not at all certain that taxpayers are prepared to foot the bill.

The verdict of the nation's experience with deinstitutionalization is that if it is to succeed, considerably more financial and human resources will have to be spent on the programs. Simultaneously, political and social pressures are mounting to move some of the homeless off the streets and back to the custody of state institutions. In any event, there seems to be a developing consensus that something must be done to help the nation's homeless (Cordes, 1985b; Morganthau, 1986; Shipp, 1986).

therapies deal with the specific and observable symptoms of a problem. Whereas insight therapies have grown up outside the mainstream of academic and experimental psychology, behavior therapies rely heavily on discoveries made by experimental psychologists. In particular, they draw from learning research. Today the majority of therapies combine methods of behavioral change and insight because the most effective ways of treating personal problems consist of both showing people that they can cope more effectively with the world and helping them to understand how to avoid crises in the future.

Whatever the emphasis, most psychotherapies have certain features in common. Clients work with a therapist whose goal is to assist them in establishing harmony with themselves, with other people, and with the requirements of social life. Much of the success of the enterprise depends on the patient-therapist relationship. Patients are encouraged to develop trust in the therapist and to share with the therapist their most intimate thoughts, feelings, and experiences. In turn, the therapist typically maintains a nonjudgmental attitude, attempting to help patients devise more effective measures for dealing with problems. Some therapists use *directive approaches*, in which they actively provide guidance, interpretations, and solutions. Others use *nondirective approaches*, in which they make the clients responsible for discovering their own insights and remedies, although the therapist may help in clarifying feelings and values.

Psychoanalytic Therapies

Psychoanalysis is the most famous insight therapy. It is both a theory of mental disorder and a form of psychotherapy. Classical psychoanalysis traces its origins to the formulations and work of Sigmund Freud. According to Freud's views, psychological disturbances arise from anxieties rooted in unconscious conflicts. (Freud's theory of personality is described in Chapters 11 and 13.) One task of the psychoanalyst, therefore, is to help make patients aware of the unconscious impulses, desires, and fears that are causing the anxiety. Psychoanalysts believe that if patients can understand their unconscious motives, they have taken the first step toward gaining control over their behavior and freeing themselves of their problems.

Psychoanalysis is a slow procedure. It usually takes years of fifty-minute sessions several times a week before a patient is able to show appreciable progress. Throughout this time, the analyst assists the patient in a thorough examination of the unconscious motives underlying his or her thoughts, feelings, and actions. In classical psychoanalysis, the patient reclines on a couch. The therapist asks the patient to give full rein to all thoughts and feelings that come to mind and to verbalize them. This method is called **free association.** Patients may consider their passing thoughts too trivial, too embarrassing, or too distressing to mention. But the analyst encourages the patient to express everything.

Patients describe their dreams, talk about their private lives, or recall long-forgotten experiences.

The psychoanalyst typically sits out of sight behind the patient and often says nothing for long periods during the session. Occasionally the analyst asks a question or makes a remark that guides the patient. Or the therapist may suggest an unconscious motive or factor that "explains" something the patient has been talking about. However, most of the talking is done by the patients themselves. Thus psychoanalysis is nondirective; the therapist is distant and seemingly uninvolved, and the primary agent of analysis and change is the patient's experience with his or her own thoughts.

Patients are understandably reluctant to reveal painful feelings and to examine lifelong patterns that need to be changed. Not surprisingly, as the analysis proceeds, they consciously—more often, unconsciously—try to hold back the flow of information. This phenomenon—in fact, any behavior that impedes the course of therapy—is called **resistance.** At times, in spite of a wish to cooperate, patients find that their mind goes blank. They may report to the analyst that they no longer can think of anything to say. At these times, the analyst merely points out that the patient is trying to censor disturbing material that is threatening to break out of the unconscious into the conscious mind. The therapist may wait for the patient to continue or may suggest another line of approach for overcoming the area of resistance. By analyzing the patient's resistances, both the therapist and the patient can understand how the patient deals with anxiety-provoking matters.

Sooner or later, the analyst begins to appear in the patients' associations and dreams. According to psychoanalytic theory, patients come to feel toward the analyst the way they felt toward some important figure in their childhood. This process is called **transference.** (The therapist may in turn become

---

psychoanalysis: A form of therapy aimed at making patients aware of their unconscious motives so that they can gain control over their behavior and free themselves of self-defeating patterns.

free association: A method used by psychoanalysts to examine the unconscious. The patient is instructed to say whatever comes into his or her mind.

resistance: The reluctance of a patient to reveal painful feelings and to examine longstanding behavior patterns.

transference: The process, which is experienced by the patient, of feeling toward an analyst or therapist in the way that he or she felt toward some other important figure in his or her life.

The famous couch on which Freud's patients reclined while he analyzed them. Freud sat at the head of the couch, out of the patient's view, and urged the patient to talk freely about the past. The couch technique was designed to make the patient comfortable (note the pillows and coverlets) and free of the inhibition that might have accompanied confronting the analyst face to face. *(Edmund Engleman)*

overly preoccupied with the long-term patient. This is called **countertransference.**)

If patients can recognize what is occurring, transference may help them identify their true feelings toward this key individual. But often, instead of grasping and understanding their true feelings, patients begin acting toward the therapist in the same way they used to act toward the significant person, usually one of their parents. Often these patterns are also being repeated in other relationships, causing the patients many problems and deep distress.

Therapists do not allow their patients to "get away" with these tactics. They remain impersonal and professional. They attempt to direct patients back to themselves. For instance, therapists may ask, "What do you see when you imagine my face?" Patients may reply that they see the therapist with an angry, frowning, unpleasant face. But therapists do not take this sort of response personally. Instead, they may calmly say, "Who does this make you think of?" Gradually, it becomes clear to patients that they are reacting to the neutral figure of the therapist as though the therapist were a threatening father or some other childhood figure of authority.

Through this kind of process, patients become aware of their genuine feelings and motivations. For example, a man may begin to understand why he has trouble with other authority figures, such as his boss. He may be seeing his boss, his therapist, and indeed any man in a position of authority, in the same way that as a child he saw his father.

In addition to classical psychoanalysis, there are any number of *psychodynamic therapies.* Although influenced by Freud's theory of unconscious conflicts, they depart in some respects from his views and techniques. Some of these approaches are derived from the theories of neo-Freudian psychiatrists such as Karen Horney (1945) and Harry Stack Sullivan (1947, 1953), who have stressed the role played by interpersonal factors and relationships in the shaping of people's personalities. Other approaches derive from the work of analysts such as

countertransference: The process by which a therapist becomes overly preoccupied with a patient.

Carl Jung (1912), who emphasized the importance for mental health of various ego functions (especially a person's self-conceptions).

Psychodynamic therapies seek to draw on the adaptive and creative abilities that reside in people. The therapies typically involve more direct dialogue between patient and therapist than is used in classical analysis. For the most part, they are face-to-face, active, and supportive endeavors that aim to assist patients in the strengthening of their coping capacities.

Recently Lloyd H. Silverman (1983; Silverman and Weinberger, 1985) has provided still another new direction in psychoanalytic therapy. He contends that most adults have powerful wishes, typically unconscious, for a state of oneness with "the good mother of early childhood." These wishes originate in the infant's experience with the mother as a comforting, protective, and nurturing figure. Silverman finds that gratification of these wishes can enhance a person's adaptation. In laboratory settings he exposes patients for four milliseconds to the words MOMMY AND I ARE ONE in order to activate "unconscious symbiotic-like fantasies." The message is called *subliminal* because it operates below the threshold of consciousness. Many schizophrenics and other patients experience a reduction in their pathology when exposed to the MOMMY AND I ARE ONE stimulus. Other subliminally presented stimuli such as MOMMY AND I ARE THE SAME and DADDY AND I ARE ONE do not seem to reduce pathology. Silverman conjectures that psychotherapy benefits many people because the qualities of the "good therapist" parallel the qualities of the "good mother."

Humanistic Therapies

Humanistic psychology has given rise to several new approaches to psychotherapy, known collectively as the **human potential movement.** We discussed these schools of psychology in Chapter 13. To review,

humanistic psychologists stress the actualization of each person's unique potential through personal responsibility, freedom of choice, and authentic relationships.

Like psychoanalytic approaches, humanistic therapies are insight-oriented. However, they are based on a much more optimistic view of humankind than that provided by Freud. They do not take as a basic premise the notion that people tend to be locked by unconscious instincts and irrational forces into a lifetime programed by childhood events.

As viewed by humanists, the major goal of therapy is the development of the total person. They stress that the uniqueness of the human condition resides in the fact that human beings can actively intervene in the course of events to control their destinies and to shape the world around them. Humanistic therapists assign particular emphasis to the emotional realm—people's ability to experience empathy for one another and to come to terms with their own and others' emotional feelings. Thus the therapies have as their focus the experiencing individual.

Client-Centered Therapy

Client-centered therapy is based on the theories of Carl Rogers (1951). (See Chapter 13.) The use of the term "client" instead of "patient" gives one an insight into the reasoning behind Rogers's method. "Patient" may suggest inferiority, whereas "client" implies an equal relationship between the therapist and the person seeking help. Further, a therapist is viewed primarily as a "facilitator."

Client-centered therapists assume that people are basically good and that they are capable of handling their own lives. Psychological problems arise when the true self becomes lost and people come to view themselves according to the standards of others. One of the goals of therapy, therefore, is to help clients recognize their own strengths so that they can learn

---

human potential movement: An approach to psychotherapy that stresses the actualization of each person's unique potential through personal responsibility, freedom of choice, and authentic relationships.

client-centered therapy: A form of therapy aimed at helping clients recognize their own strengths and gain confidence so that they can learn to be true to their own standards and ideas about how to live effectively.

to be true to their own standards about how to live effectively.

In the course of a session, clients are encouraged to speak freely about intimate matters that may be bothering them. They are told that what they talk about is up to them. The therapist listens and encourages the client's conversation but tries to avoid giving opinions. Instead, the therapist tries to "echo back" or "mirror" as clearly as possible the feelings the client has expressed. The therapist may try to extract the main points from the client's hesitant or rambling explanations. For example, a client may tell a long story about an incident with her father, and the therapist may respond by saying, "This kind of thing makes you feel very stupid." The client may in turn say, "No, not stupid, angry. It's really he who is being stupid." And the therapist will say, "Oh, I see, you really feel angry at him when he acts this way." Between them, they form a clearer and clearer picture of how the client really feels about herself, her life, and the people around her.

Client-centered therapy is conducted in an atmosphere of emotional support that Rogers calls **unconditional positive regard.** As in psychoanalysis, the therapist never rejects or passes judgment on the client. Instead, the therapist attempts to foster a climate of trust and confidence. Thus a primary task for the therapist is the creation of a warm, understanding, and accepting relationship.

This acceptance, coupled with concern, makes it easier for clients to explore thoughts about themselves and their experiences. They are able to abandon old values without fear of disapproval, and they can test new patterns of behavior without fear of embarrassment. They can try out new or hidden aspects of their personality. And they can begin to see themselves, their situation, and their relationships with others in a more favorable light.

As they reduce their tensions, let go of encrusted constraints, and express their emotions, clients begin to experience themselves as more complete people. They gain the courage to accept parts of their personality that they previously considered weak or bad. As they come to recognize their self-worth, they can establish realistic goals and consider the steps needed to reach them. The achievement of independence signals the end of formal therapy. Clients can then continue the lifetime process of growth and mastery on their own.

Existential Therapy

Like Rogers, other therapists in the human potential movement see their role as helping people achieve self-determination. Existential therapists believe that for most people, freedom and autonomy are threatening and discomforting experiences. To acknowledge that you are a unique and independent person is to acknowledge that you are alone. Unconsciously many people avoid this realization, burying their feelings and desires. Existential therapists, such as Rollo May (1969), attempt to help people overcome the fear of freedom, get in touch with their true feelings, and accept responsibility for their lives.

Viktor Frankl (1970) is also an existentialist, but he approaches therapy somewhat differently. After listening to a person express despair, he might ask, "Why don't you commit suicide?" Frankl is not being cruel or sarcastic. He is trying to help the person find meaning in life. The answer (whether it is "my husband and children," "my religion," or "my work") provides clues about what the person values.

In Frankl's view, feelings of emptiness and boredom are the primary source of emotional problems (1970:165–166):

> Mental health is based on a certain degree of tension between what one has already achieved and what one still ought to accomplish, or the gap between what one is and what one should become. Such a tension is inherent in the human being and is therefore indispensable to mental well being. . . . What people actually need is not a tensionless state but rather the striving and struggling for some worthy goal.

---

unconditional positive regard: In client-centered therapy, the atmosphere of emotional support provided by the therapist. The therapist shows the client that he or she accepts anything the client may say and does not become embarrassed or angry.

Frankl believes a therapist should help to open the patient's eyes to the possibilities in life and guide the patient toward new challenges.

Gestalt Therapy

Developed by Fritz Perls in the 1950s and 1960s, **Gestalt therapy** aims to make the person "whole" or "complete" by developing self-awareness, overcoming incapacitating defenses, releasing pent-up feelings, and giving full range to the potential for growth (Perls, Hefferline, and Goodman, 1965; Perls, 1970). Although taking its name "Gestalt" (meaning "pattern" or "configuration" in German) from a distinct school of psychological thought (see Chapter 5), the approach does not strictly follow traditional Gestalt theory. However, it resembles other humanistic approaches in its emphasis on the expressive and dynamic aspects of people, rather than on the unhealthy and distorted features stressed by psychoanalytic theorists.

Clients of Gestalt therapy are encouraged to immerse themselves in the here and now. More particularly, they are asked to experience things rather than imagine them and to feel rather than think. Therapeutic techniques teach people to pick up cues associated with bodily sensations, perceptions, and feelings. More particularly, therapeutic work is directed toward the identification of a person's needs and of legitimate ways by which these needs can be met. People are helped to come to terms with themselves—to accept themselves for what they *are* and to give expression to their true feelings and desires in a responsible manner. In brief, each person is encouraged to do his or her own thing.

The relationship between the patient and the therapist reflects the "living in the now" emphasis. It attempts to drive home the need to get in touch with one's feelings and to express them without fear or embarrassment. Suppose that toward the middle of a session a patient runs out of material to discuss and sits mute, staring blankly out the window. Instead of waiting for the patient to speak up, a Gestalt therapist would say what she feels: "I can't

stand the way you just sit there and say nothing. Sometimes I regret ever becoming a therapist. You are impossible. . . . There, now I feel better" (Kempler, 1973:272). The therapist is not blowing off steam in an unprofessional way. She does this to encourage (by example) the patient to express his feelings, even if it means risking a relationship.

Behavior Therapies

Psychoanalysis and the human potential movement have sometimes been criticized for being "all talk and no action." In behavior therapy there is much more emphasis on action. Rather than spending large amounts of time going into the patient's past history or the details of his or her dreams, the behavior therapist concentrates on finding out what is specifically wrong with the patient's current life and takes steps to change it. Thus the aim of behavior therapies is not to alter a person's personality (which is the aim of psychoanalysis) but to change only certain problem behaviors (Woolfolk and Richardson, 1984). The approach has proven of particular value in the treatment of anxiety disorders (Barlow and Beck, 1983).

The idea behind behavior therapy is that a disturbed person is one who has learned to behave in the wrong way. The therapist's job, therefore, is to "reeducate" the patient. The reasons for the patient's undesirable behavior are not important. What is important is to change the behavior. To bring about such changes, the therapist uses techniques based on the principles of learning detailed in Chapter 6. The strategy rests on the assumption that learning depends on the connections or links that people make between two events.

Systematic Desensitization

One technique used by behavior therapists is *systematic desensitization*. You will recall from Chapter 6 that therapists use this method to help patients overcome various fears. These anxieties may be associated with closed spaces, heights, death, sexual

---

Gestalt (ga-SHTALT) therapy: A form of therapy that emphasizes the relationship between the patient and therapist in the here and now; it aims to make the patient "whole."

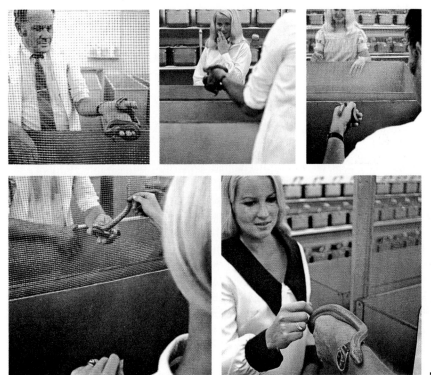

These photographs illustrate the desensitization of a snake phobia. First, the woman simply observes the snake in the hands of the attendant, who is on the other side of a screen. Just seeing another person handling the snake helps decrease her fear. Next she gradually gets closer to the snake until she is able to touch it without fear. *(Steve McCarroll)*

encounters, public speaking, flying in airplanes, or social contacts. Systematic desensitization involves gradually confronting patients with various levels of a fear-rousing stimulus after they have first been trained to relax.

In systematic desensitization, the therapist takes the patient through the feared situation step by step. In contrast, in "implosive" or "flooding" therapy, the therapist guides the patient through the entire feared situation all at once, either by imagining it (*implosion*) or actually experiencing it (*flooding*). For instance, a patient may fear her father's anger should she assert herself. In implosion, the therapist would have the patient imagine telling her father something of which he would certainly disapprove, and then hold the scene in mind until her anxiety peaks and decreases. As an example of flooding, if a patient fears heights, the therapist may accompany him to a high building and have him look out a window. The patient remains in the anxiety-provoking situation until it no longer elicits anxiety. Flooding resembles the end stages of desensitization but without the gradual build-up to the feared situation (Goisman, 1985).

Aversive Conditioning

Another form of behavior therapy is **aversive conditioning**. People learn to associate a strong negative response with an undesirable behavior such as drinking, using drugs, gambling, or smoking. The aversive stimulus may be an electric shock, a loud noise, or nausea.

Aversive conditioning has been used in the treatment of alcoholism (Craighead, Kazdin, and Mahoney, 1976). Clients take the drug Antabuse each day in pill form. If they drink alcohol while Antabuse is in their system, they experience intense

---

aversive conditioning: A type of behavior therapy in which individuals learn to associate a strong negative response with an undesirable behavior.

nausea, dizziness, and vomiting. After sufficient pairings between alcohol and the noxious symptoms, the mere thought of the severe reaction inhibits drinking. However, the main problem with this strategy is that alcoholics stop taking Antabuse when they have a strong urge to drink. In brief, they learn that they can circumvent the negative consequences and still use alcohol.

Joseph Cautela (1966, 1967, 1973) has developed a modified form of aversive conditioning known as *covert sensitization*. Clients first imagine some maladaptive behavior and then imagine distressing consequences. For instance, Cautela (1967:462) uses the following imagery with obese patients:

> I want you to imagine you've just had your main meal and you are about to eat your dessert, which is apple pie. As you reach for the fork, you get a funny feeling in the pit of your stomach. You start to feel queasy, nauseous, and sick all over. . . . As you're about to open your mouth, you puke; you vomit all over your hands, the fork, over the other people's food. Your eyes are watering. Snot mucus is all over your mouth and nose. Your hands feel sticky. There is an awful smell. As you look at this mess you just can't help but vomit again and again until just watery stuff is coming out.

Although the findings on the effectiveness of covert sensitization are still tentative, the approach seems to produce only marginal results (Mahoney and Arnkoff, 1978).

Contingency Management

Still another form of behavior therapy is called **contingency management.** In this method, the therapist and patient decide what old, undesirable behavior needs to be eliminated and what new, desirable behavior needs to appear. Arrangements are then made for the old behavior to go unrewarded and for the desired behavior to be reinforced. In its simplest form, contingency management consists of the therapist agreeing with the patient, "If you do X, I will give you Y." This form of agreement is similar to systems of reward that people often use on

themselves. For instance, a college student may say to himself, "If I get a good grade on the exam, I'll treat myself to a great dinner." The reward is *contingent* (dependent) on getting a good grade.

Contingency management is used in prisons, mental hospitals, schools, and army bases, as well as with individual patients. In these situations, it is possible to set up whole miniature systems of rewards, called *token economies* (see Chapter 6). For example, psychologists in some mental hospitals select behaviors they judge desirable. Patients are then rewarded for these behaviors with "hospital," or token, money. Thus if patients clean their rooms or work in the hospital garden, they are rewarded with token money. The patients are able to cash in their token money for things they want, such as candy or cigarettes, or for certain privileges, such as time away from the ward. These methods are successful in inducing depressed mental patients, who often sit around doing nothing day after day, to begin leading active lives. They learn to take care of themselves and to take on responsibility instead of having to be cared for constantly.

Modeling

Finally, as we pointed out in Chapter 6, much human behavior is socially transmitted, either deliberately or inadvertently, through the behavioral examples provided by other people. Thus, not surprisingly, *modeling* principles have been successfully used in treating phobias. The therapies have been used to rid people of snake phobias (Rosenthal and Bandura, 1978) and children of their fear of dogs (Bandura, Grusec, and Menlove, 1967). *Diversified modeling*, in which clients observe the feared activity being repeatedly and safely performed by a variety of models, is more effective than the same performances by a single model (Bandura and Menlove, 1968).

Treatments combining modeling with guided participation have proven themselves effective in eliminating disabling fears and inhibitions (Bandura, 1978). Therapists structure the environment so that clients can perform successfully despite their phobias. The therapists first model the threatening activi-

---

contingency management: A form of behavior therapy in which undesirable behavior is not rewarded, while desirable behavior is reinforced.

The behavior therapy approach to the treatment of some childhood disorders involves the use of contingency management, also known as operant conditioning (see Chapter 6). The therapist is rewarding the child with (*left*) affection and (*top right*) food for performing such desirable behaviors as coming toward the therapist and eating and drinking at the table. (*bottom right*) The therapists are introducing two children to the experience of holding hands. (*Costas Manos/Magnum*)

ties in easily mastered steps. Then the clients enact the modeled behavior with appropriate guidance until they can perform it skillfully and fearlessly. At times, the therapists may physically assist fearful clients to engage in the threatening activities. When clients participate in a daring or frightening task, they seem to acquire a sense of "self-efficacy," or mastery over the situation.

Cognitive-Behavioral Therapies

As noted in Chapter 15, psychologists such as Martin Seligman and Aaron T. Beck stress the part that negative thinking plays in depressive disorders. Depressed people look at life through dark-colored glasses. They dwell on bad experiences, minimize their accomplishments, and forget happy times. These elements constitute the *cognitive* components of depression. Depression is also characterized by

behavioral components, including withdrawal, lack of energy, insomnia, and loss of appetite.

Cognitive-behavioral therapists attack their patients' problems on both the cognitive and the behavioral levels (Kovacs, 1980; Freeman, 1983). They insist that depressed patients confront their negative view of themselves and the world and question the evidence that they use. And they assist their patients in tackling the behavioral aspects of their problems by scheduling positive self-reinforcements.

Beck's Cognitive Therapy

In recent years, the **cognitive therapy** of Beck (1976) has gained considerable popularity and acceptance. He assigns primary importance to the fact that people *think*. In turn, how they think and the conclusions they reach determine what they feel and

cognitive therapy: A form of therapy aimed at assisting people to overcome negative styles of thought.

do. Thus Beck reasons that if depressed people come to see themselves as winners instead of losers, they will feel better. His approach is designed to correct these major distortions characteristic of depressed people: seeing themselves as deficient and unworthy; seeing the world as frustrating and unfulfilling; and seeing the future as hopeless.

In early sessions, Beck has his patients record their daily activities in a notebook, plan productive activities, and schedule enjoyable events. He also assigns tasks at which the patient is likely to succeed (it can be as simple as getting out of bed, preparing a snack, or writing a letter). These measures "break into" the self-defeating and circular components of depressive thought. They focus the patient's attention on his or her behavior and away from melancholy preoccupations. Simultaneously, they provide the patient with a sense of accomplishment (Beck, 1976, 1977; Kovacs and Beck, 1978).

Later, the patient and the therapist work together to pinpoint the patient's distorted, negative, and unrealistic thoughts. Patients are made to confront their pessimistic ideas and see that they do not make sense. For example, they come to recognize the danger of such either-or premises as "Either I'm popular with everybody or I'm a total flop." They learn to realize that such unreasonable and inflexible expectations lock them within cycles of inevitable failure, that their pursuit of unattainable goals feeds their feelings of guilt and worthlessness.

Finally, the patient and therapist set about to modify the maladaptive beliefs. They seek to increase the patient's problem-solving repertoire through the acquisition of effective verbal and behavioral strategies. Research suggests that cognitive therapy is a particularly effective type of directive therapy in combating depressed feelings associated with hopelessness and in strengthening a person's sense of worth and self-esteem (Rush et al., 1982).

Ellis's Rational-Emotive Therapy

Rational-emotive therapy (RET) is a form of therapy developed by Albert Ellis in the late 1950s (Ellis,

1973). Ellis believes that people behave in deliberate and rational ways, given their assumptions about life. Emotional problems arise when a person's assumptions are unrealistic.

Suppose a man seeks therapy when a woman leaves him. He cannot stand the fact that she has rejected him. Without her his life is empty and miserable. She has made him feel utterly worthless. He must get her back. An RET therapist would not look for incidents in the past that are making the present unbearable for this man, as a psychoanalyst would. RET therapists do not probe; they reason. Like a spoiled child, the man is demanding that the woman love him. He expects—indeed, insists—that things will always go his way. Given this assumption, the only possible explanation for her behavior is that something is dreadfully wrong, either with him or with her.

What is wrong, in the therapist's view, is the man's thinking. By defining his feelings for the woman as need rather than desire, he—not she—is causing his depression. When you convince yourself that you need someone, you will in fact be unable to carry on without that person. When you believe that you cannot stand rejection, you will in fact fall apart when you encounter rejection.

The goal of rational-emotive therapy is to correct these false and self-defeating beliefs. Rejection is unpleasant, but it is not unbearable. The woman may be very desirable, but she is not irreplaceable. To teach the man to think in realistic terms, the RET therapist may use a number of techniques: role playing (so that the person can see how his beliefs affect his relationships); modeling (to demonstrate other ways of thinking and acting); humor (to underline the absurdity of his beliefs); and simple persuasion. The therapist may also assign homework to give the man practice in acting more reasonably. For example, the therapist may instruct him to ask out women who are likely to reject him. Why? So that he will learn that he can cope with things that do not go his way.

Ellis believes that people must take three steps to cure or correct themselves. First, they must realize

---

rational-emotive therapy (RET): A form of therapy aimed at changing unrealistic assumptions about oneself and other people. It is believed that once a person understands that he or she has been acting on false beliefs, self-defeating thoughts and behaviors will be avoided.

that some of their assumptions are false. Second, they must see that they are making *themselves* disturbed by acting on false beliefs. Finally, they must work to break old habits of thought and behavior. They have to practice, to learn self-discipline, to take risks.

Other cognitive therapies, such as those of Donald Merchenbaum (1977), Arnold Lazarus (1971), and Jerome L. Singer (1969), offer similar approaches. Self-defeating thoughts and feelings that people have can be changed, and they will learn to both feel and behave in more adaptive ways.

Family Therapies

Psychological interventions have traditionally had as their focus the individual. Conventional therapists have viewed the individual as the site of pathology and have arrived at a diagnostic label for the person's disorder (for example, obsession, schizophrenia, amnesia, or bipolar depression). However, in recent years **family therapy** has become an increasingly important type of treatment (Olson, Russell, and Sprenkle, 1980; Epstein and Vlok, 1981). Its roots go back to Alfred Adler (see Chapter 13). The individual is seen as functioning in a disturbed environment, in which family members interact with one another in maladaptive ways. Very often, these patterns are passed on from one generation to the next. For example, in such families there may be recurring patterns of women victimized by husbands who have mistresses, or generation after generation in which incest or physical abuse prevails (Goleman, 1986). Consequently, therapeutic progress depends on remedying the home situation. Treatment consists of helping family members understand their difficulties, identify their unhealthy patterns of dealing with one another, and work out more effective methods for living together.

Family therapists look at the family as a structure. Within this arrangement, people's behavior is channeled and organized through recurrent patterns that shape their experience of reality (Minuchin, 1974). For instance, consider a family in which the parents are troubled by the behavior of their adolescent son. The son stays out late, fails to do his schoolwork, experiments with drugs, and does not obey family rules. His father responds by imposing a curfew. The son complains that his father is a "dictator," and the wife criticizes her husband's disciplinary measures as being too harsh. The father withdraws into his work, attempting to avoid further friction. The mother implores the son to behave himself and to get his life on track. The son tells the mother to mind her own business and to stay out of his affairs. The mother, confused and guilt-ridden, backs off. The son continues to misbehave. And the cycle continues.

In this situation, talking to the son about the problem may not be nearly as effective as helping the parents to get better control over the son and perhaps over themselves. The difficulty is not simply a matter for individual therapy. It is one that calls for the straightening out of family patterns of interaction, the formulation of a division of authority, and the definition of the rights and responsibilities of each family member.

Most commonly, family members do not grasp how they fit within a maladaptive family web and how their behavior is a necessary link in the perpetuation of the disordered functioning. Family patterns put blinders on people. Consequently, the individuals find themselves entrapped by rigid and recurrent modes of interaction.

In the previous illustration, the family therapist would typically see all of the family members together and individually. She would help the parents to see that they both are threatened by friction and conflict. They prefer to withdraw and retreat from confrontation with their son, rather than following through and exercising parental constraint. Further, the mother is undercutting the authority of the father. The net effect is that the parents have abandoned control of their son, who simply is taking advantage of his situation. It may be discovered that the son's behavior is only one of the family's problems. His misbehavior is being maintained by a malfunctioning family system.

---

family therapy: A form of therapy aimed at understanding and improving relationships that have led one or more members in a family to experience emotional suffering.

Family therapy is also used in cases of severe mental illness. The therapist operates on the principle that if one can change the patterns of interaction among people, one can change the people. Researchers have found that schizophrenic patients living in households characterized by high levels of stress have poorer outcomes than do those living in low-stress households (Brown, Birley, and Wing, 1972; Vaughn and Leff, 1976; Breier and Strauss, 1984; Spiegel and Wissler, 1986). Thus, not surprisingly, family therapy has been shown to be beneficial in the home management of persons suffering from schizophrenia and in the prevention of their rehospitalization (Goldstein, 1981; Leff, Kuipers, and Berkowitz, 1982). Among the goals of family therapy are accepting a person's vulnerability to the disorder, identifying precipitating stresses, looking at future events that may contain similar elements of stress, and developing strategies for avoiding, minimizing, and coping with these stresses (Mosher and Keith, 1979; Falloon et al., 1982).

Biological Therapies

Major advances have taken place over the past thirty years in the biological treatment of many psychological disorders. Perhaps the most notable advances have occurred in drug therapies. Drugs have been developed to treat schizophrenia, depression, mania, anxiety, and other psychological difficulties. As discussed in Chapter 15, researchers have implicated biological malfunctioning in some of these disorders. Hence drugs are used to relieve symptoms by normalizing the biochemical imbalance. The approach parallels the treatment of diabetes by administering insulin to patients even though the underlying pancreatic malfunctioning remains uncorrected. However, there is some measure of trial and error in drug prescription. It is not unusual for patients to respond to the second or third medication that is prescribed rather than to the first.

Just as not all patients respond to "talking" and "learning" therapies, not all patients respond to drug therapy. Clearly, correct diagnosis is essential if patients are to receive the most appropriate type of help for their particular difficulty. In many cases, drugs are used in conjunction with psychotherapy. A growing body of research suggests that patients who suffer from schizophrenia or depression and receive both psychotherapy and drugs do better than those receiving only psychotherapy or drugs (Schooler,

In the last twenty years antipsychotic drugs have reduced the antisocial and bizarre symptoms of the seriously disturbed patients in mental hospitals. Tens of thousands of drug-treated patients have been released from hospitals, but such drugs do not ensure their adjustment to the outside world of relationships and work. *(Richard Wood/The Picture Cube)*

1978; White and Sloane, 1979; Falloon and Liberman, 1983). In many cases, then, the integration of treatments affords the greatest potential. Patients receiving drug therapy often benefit from the support provided by psychotherapy, especially in coping with the demoralizing aspects of their illness. Further, psychological interventions assist the patients in identifying sources of stress in their lives, gaining insight on crucial matters, confronting reality, and coping with problems.

Antipsychotic drugs (also known as major tranquilizers) are used in the treatment of schizophrenia. The most popular of these drugs are the phenothiazines, which include Thorazine (chlorpromazine) and Stelazine (trifluoperazine). The drugs are believed to block dopamine and thus decrease neurotransmission in dopamine neurons. Schizophrenic patients who take these drugs typically improve in a number of ways: they become less withdrawn, become less confused and agitated, have fewer auditory hallucinations, and are less irritable and hostile (Wender and Klein, 1981). Studies directly comparing phenothiazines with other forms of therapy suggest that these drugs are the most effective form of treatment now available for schizophrenia (Davis et al., 1980; Donaldson, Gelenberg, and Baldessarini, 1983).

Although the patients who take antipsychotic drugs often improve enough to leave the hospital, they may have trouble adjusting to the outside world. Many patients now face the "revolving door" syndrome of going to a mental hospital, being released, returning to the hospital, being released again, and so on. Phenothiazines also have a number of unpleasant side effects, including a dry mouth, blurred vision, grogginess, constipation, and muscle disorders. Some 40 percent or more of schizophrenics placed on antipsychotic drugs for many years develop *tardive dyskinesia*, a neurological disorder. Symptoms include twitching of the arms and legs and grotesque, involuntary movements of the mouth and facial muscles (for example, protrusions of the tongue, lip smacking, and grimaces).

Another class of drugs, called *antidepressants*, alleviates the symptoms of severely depressed patients (NIMH/NIH Consensus Development Panel, 1985). Interestingly, they do not affect the mood of normal people. As noted in Chapter 15, victims of depression seem to suffer from an imbalance in brain chemicals. By acting on these chemicals, the drugs relieve the symptoms of depression in up to 80 percent of all cases. The tricyclic compounds (Elavil, Tofranil, Aventyl, Sinequan, and Vicactil) affect the levels of norepinephrine and serotonin. The MAO (monoamine oxidase) inhibitors (Marplan, Nardil, and Parnate) block an enzyme that breaks down various neurotransmitters, including norepinephrine. The side effects of the tricyclics include dryness of the mouth, constipation, and dizziness, but these symptoms generally subside in a number of weeks. Patients taking MAO inhibitors may develop high blood pressure if they eat foods containing the amino acid tryamine (found in chocolate, aged cheese, and chicken livers).

Lithium, a naturally occurring chemical, is now widely used in the treatment of bipolar (manic-depressive) disorders (NIMH/NIH Consensus Development Panel, 1985). Regular doses of lithium given under careful medical supervision can prevent attacks in many patients, especially the manic component. However, when used for periods of up to twenty years, lithium may contribute to kidney disorders (Jefferson and Greist, 1981; Ramsey and Cox, 1982). The probability of kidney disorders in the use of lithium over long periods of time must be weighed against the risk of suicide in patients who experience frequent depressive episodes. There is also a growing consensus that lithium may play a useful role in the treatment of some patients who suffer from schizophrenia (Donaldson, Gelenberg, and Baldessarini, 1983).

Commonly known as sedatives or mild tranquilizers, *anti-anxiety drugs* are used to reduce excitability and cause drowsiness. Since anxiety and insomnia are conditions that most people have experienced at one time or another, these drugs are in wide use. The most popular of these drugs are Miltown (meprobamate), Librium (chlordiazepoxide), and Valium (diazepam).

While these drugs are effective for helping normal people cope with difficult periods in their lives, they are also prescribed for the alleviation of agitation, psychosomatic problems, and symptoms of alcohol withdrawal. The major effect of Valium, Librium, and Miltown is to depress the activity of the central nervous system. If the drugs are taken properly, the side effects are few and consist mainly of drowsiness. However, prolonged use may lead to dependency, and heavy doses taken along with alcohol can result in death (see the boxed insert on page 540).

"Shock treatment," as *electroconvulsive therapy (ECT)* is commonly called, has proved effective in the treatment of depression, although no one is certain exactly how it works. However, animal research demonstrates that electroconvulsive therapy causes numerous changes in the brain's chemistry (Sackeim, 1985). The procedure involves administering, generally about three times a week for two to four weeks, a series of brief electrical shocks via electrodes fixed to the scalp. The shock induces a convulsion similar to an epileptic seizure. As it is now applied, electroconvulsive therapy entails very little discomfort. Before treatment, the patient is given a sedative and injected with a muscle relaxant to alleviate involuntary muscular contractions and prevent physical injury.

The procedure is usually reserved for cases of severe depression in which patients fail to respond to drug therapy (Crowe, 1984). It is also used for cases in which patients exhibit strong suicidal tendencies

---

Valium

Valium is one of the most frequently prescribed drugs in the United States today. It is also the most abused prescription drug. Each year, tens of millions of Americans spend over a half billion dollars to have Valium in their medicine chests.

Valium (generic name diazepam) is not a life-saving drug or a remedy for some dreaded disease. Rather, it is a soother of anxiety; for many it is the only thing that makes today's fast-paced society livable. Tranquilizers such as Valium act by binding to the entire constellation of benzodiazepine receptors in the brain (Kolata, 1982; Greenblatt, Shader, and Abernethy, 1983). Consequently, the drug has several effects, of which the dampening of anxiety is one. But it also acts as a sedative, muscle relaxant, and anticonvulsant. Most doctors believe that

Valium serves these functions in a way that no other minor tranquilizer can.

However, many mental health professionals believe that Valium is too freely prescribed by physicians. When taken in combination with alcohol or other central nervous system depressants, the drug can be deadly. Extended use also produces dependence. Withdrawal symptoms are similar in character to those noted with barbiturates and alcohol. Abrupt discontinuance of Valium is associated with convulsions, tremors, abdominal and muscle cramps, vomiting, difficulty in sleeping, and sweating.

It must be remembered that Valium is a drug and a potentially dangerous one at that. Consequently, Valium use should never be taken for granted, and it requires careful monitoring.

---

that require prompt therapeutic intervention. Electroconvulsive therapy can cause some temporary memory loss, but whether it results in permanent memory deficits or brain damage is a matter of considerable controversy (Palmer, 1981; Sackeim, 1985). Indeed, it remains the most controversial treatment in psychiatry. Recently a panel of experts assembled by the National Institutes of Health gave cautious endorsement to the procedure as a treatment of last resort in severe depression. In 1980 the National Institute of Mental Health (NIMH) reported 33,384 cases, but treatment has increased in the past several years, with estimates of the annual number of patients treated ranging up to 100,000 (Holden, 1985c).

DOES INTERVENTION WORK?

In 1952, Hans Eysenck published a review of five studies of the effectiveness of psychoanalytic treatment and nineteen studies of the effectiveness of *eclectic psychotherapy*, treatment in which several different therapeutic approaches are combined. Eysenck concluded that psychotherapy was no more

effective than no treatment at all. According to his interpretation of these twenty-four studies, only 44 percent of the psychoanalytic patients improved with treatment, while 64 percent of those given eclectic psychotherapy were "cured" or had improved. Most startling, Eysenck argued that even this 64 percent improvement rate did not demonstrate the effectiveness of psychotherapy, since it had been reported that 72 percent of a group of hospitalized neurotics improved *without* treatment. If no treatment at all leads to as much improvement as psychotherapy, the obvious conclusion is that psychotherapy is not effective. Eysenck (1966) vigorously defended his controversial position, which generated a large number of additional reviews and a great many studies of the effectiveness of psychotherapy.

One of the most thoughtful and carefully reasoned reviews was written by Allen Bergin (1971). Bergin made the following points in reply to Eysenck. First, he demonstrated that when some different but equally reasonable assumptions about the classification of patients were made, the effectiveness of psychoanalytic treatment was much greater than Eysenck had reported; perhaps as many as 83 percent of the patients improved or recovered. Second, he reviewed a number of studies that showed that the rate of improvement without treatment was only about 30 percent (Bergin and Lambert, 1978).

Bergin's review leads one to question the validity of Eysenck's sweeping generalization that psychotherapy is no more effective than no treatment at all. But much of Bergin's argument is based on differences of opinion about how patients should be classified. Precise criteria for "improvement" are difficult to define and to apply. The nature of "spontaneous remission" (sudden disappearance) of symptoms in persons who have not received formal psychotherapy is difficult to assess, for these people may have received help from unacknowledged sources—friends, relatives, religious advisers, family physicians. And if, as some researchers believe, the prime ingredient in therapy is the establishment of a close relationship, then "spontaneous remission" in people who have received continuing help from such sources is not spontaneous at all.

There is also the matter of the **placebo effect.** This name comes from giving medical patients *placebos*—harmless sugar pills—when they complain of ailments that do not seem to have any physiological basis. The patients take the tablets and their symptoms disappear. The placebo effect does not imply that problems can be solved simply by fooling the patient. It does demonstrate, however, the tremendous importance of the patient's attitude in finding a way to change. Patients who do not believe they can be helped probably cannot be. Patients who believe they can change and believe they have the power to change will often find a way. However, therapy goes beyond the placebo effect. It combines patients' beliefs that they can change with hard work and professional guidance.

An analysis of nearly four hundred studies of the effectiveness of psychotherapy, conducted by Mary Lee Smith and Gene V. Glass (1977), used elaborate statistical procedures to estimate the effects of psychotherapy. They found that therapy is generally more effective than no treatment and that on the average most forms of therapy have similar effects.

Considerable controversy also revolves about the issue of whether training makes a therapist more effective. Indeed, some researchers have concluded that patients treated by *paraprofessionals* (individuals who have not received formal or clinical training in a post-baccalaureate program) improve more than those treated by professionals (Hattie, Sharpley, and Rogers, 1984). Other researchers find that professionals may be better for brief treatments and older patients, but they do not enjoy any substantial superiority in effectiveness over paraprofessionals (Berman and Norton, 1985). Overall, it seems that empathy, warmth, and genuineness are the core conditions underlying successful counseling and psychotherapeutic relationships (Patterson, 1984).

All this raises the question, Will any therapy do for any client? Probably not (Marshall, 1980; VandenBos and Pino, 1980; Epstein and Vlok, 1981). Smith and Glass (1977) were able to show that for some specific clients and situations, some forms of therapy would be expected to have a greater effect than others (see Figure 16.3). For example, if the client is of average intelligence, has generalized interpersonal difficulties, and is seen in individual sessions by a therapist with five years of experience, psychodynamic therapy would be expected to have a greater effect than systematic desensitization. But in the case of a highly intelligent person with a phobia, systematic desensitization would be expected to have greater impact. However, these are educated guesses based on the interpretation of some complex statistical analyses. Studies that are designed to answer more specific questions are currently needed (Miller and Berman, 1983; Berman, Miller, and Massman, 1985).

Perhaps, in the final analysis, the question is not which technique of intervention is better than others, but rather, "*What* treatment, by *whom*, is most effective for *this* individual with *that* specific problem, and under *which* set of circumstances?" (Paul, 1967:111). Thus, should you have difficulties of one sort or another and decide to seek therapy, you might consider the material contained in this and the previous chapter.

The kind of therapy you consider using must be suitable for the kind of problem it is meant to resolve (Smith, Glass, and Miller, 1980). Thus behavior therapies seem better suited for dealing with phobi-

---

placebo (pluh SEE bo) effect: The influence that a patient's hopes and expectations have on his or her improvement.

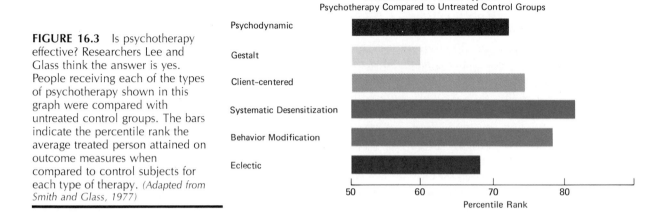

FIGURE 16.3 Is psychotherapy effective? Researchers Lee and Glass think the answer is yes. People receiving each of the types of psychotherapy shown in this graph were compared with untreated control groups. The bars indicate the percentile rank the average treated person attained on outcome measures when compared to control subjects for each type of therapy. *(Adapted from Smith and Glass, 1977)*

as, smoking, and overeating. Family therapy or counseling may be more advisable for marriage problems. If you experience considerable loneliness or have difficulties in interpersonal relationships, group therapy or cognitive-behavioral therapy may be the preferable approach. Mild depression may best respond to cognitive therapy. Severe depression or schizophrenia may require drugs, and perhaps

hospitalization. The time and financial resources available to you are also important considerations. In sum, as in other matters, it is necessary that you undertake to become an informed consumer and that you use good sense in arriving at some course of action (Frances, Clarkin, and Perry, 1984). (See the boxed insert on page 543.)

SUMMARY

1. People seek professional psychological help for a good many reasons. Much depends on what is happening in their lives. Some people need help to cope with a crisis. Others become fed up with chronic problems. Still others seek help for another person whom they believe is causing them continuing distress. Noticeable departures from standards of good mental health provide signals of trouble that may warrant professional attention.

2. People typically seek professional help when they conclude that the approaches they are using for dealing with their problems are not working. They find that their own efforts and the help of their friends and relatives are inadequate to the task. There are many therapies and those who offer them differ in theory, technique, and training.

3. Many mental health professionals maintain private offices and treat patients in these settings. For the most part, the patients function in the workaday world and see their practitioner at regularly scheduled appointments.

4. Since human beings live their lives in groups, and since many of their problems derive from group living, it is not surprising that troubled individuals should turn to groups for assistance.

A. Traditional group-therapy sessions are typically provided by trained therapists. An advantage of this arrangement is that one therapist can help a large number of people.

B. Over the past two decades, group therapy took a number of new directions. Among these developments was the emergence of encounter and sensitivity groups. These groups sought to provide people with experiences that would overcome self-imposed constraints and lead to personal liberation and growth.

C. Some of the most successful group-therapy programs are provided by nonprofessional self-help organizations such as Alcoholics Anonymous.

5. When the demands of everyday life cannot be met, psychologically troubled people may require

What to Look for in Psychotherapy

If you are to get the most out of psychotherapy, you should select a therapist carefully and with realistic expectations. The most frequent way to find a therapist is to ask your friends or consult your physician. You may wish to do additional reading on the different types of therapy that are available to you. Popular books describing them can be secured from your campus or local library or purchased at a bookstore. Brochures are also available from the American Psychological Association, 1200 17th St., Washington, DC 20036.

Once you find a therapist and enter therapy, do not expect to solve your problems or feel better immediately. On the basis of studies of three thousand patients, psychologist Kenneth I. Howard finds that 53 percent of depressed patients show significant improvement within eight sessions, 54 percent of those with anxiety symptoms respond within thirteen sessions, and 50 percent of those with more severe disorders improve within twenty-six sessions. In fact, the simple act of making an appointment with a therapist brings noticeable relief to 20 percent of all patients (Sperling, 1984).

It is advisable that you and your therapist set goals for your therapy. You should agree on what you can expect to achieve. And you should have some idea on how long the therapy can be expected to last. Do not hesitate to ask the therapist any questions you have. You should also determine whether your medical insurance covers psychotherapy. Most employer-supplied policies cover from 50 to 80 percent of the cost of psychotherapy undertaken with a psychiatrist or clinical psychologist. However, many companies limit their financial coverage for psychotherapy to a set number of sessions or limit the dollar amounts payable in a given time period.

You may feel that you are not getting what you had hoped for out of therapy or that you do not work well with your therapist. Accordingly, you may consider changing therapists. However, dissatisfaction with therapy is common and does not necessarily signal that your therapy is failing. Patients' reactions to their therapists may simply result from what psychoanalysts term "negative transference." Moreover, patients who have already switched therapists several times would be well advised to examine why they have done so instead of switching yet again. If you are dissatisfied with your therapist, you might consider seeking an outside consultation with another therapist. Such a consultation may help you correct any mistaken notions you have about therapy or suggest that a change in therapists is indicated (Goleman, 1985a).

Overall, you should trust your own sense of how well you are doing. Researchers find a strong relationship between whether you think you are being helped and objective ratings of your progress. Psychoanalyst Lester Luborsky (1984) finds that if the working alliance between you and your therapist does not become strong early in therapy, the prospect for success is less favorable. He concludes that three aspects of a working alliance are critical. First, you need to believe that your therapist is competent and your treatment is proving beneficial. Second, you need to trust the therapist and the therapist's ability to understand and empathize with your difficulties. And third, you and your therapist need to have common ideas about your problems and hold similar expectations for your treatment. One sign of a good fit between you and your therapist is the ease with which you can communicate your negative feelings to him or her.

hospitalization. Many institutions tend to be under-funded and understaffed and designed to care for chronically ill patients. Over the past two decades, many general hospitals have added psychiatric units for short-term care.

6. Mental health professionals have long held that it is better if people do not stay too long in mental hospitals. After a while, patients become dependent on a sheltered environment, lose social skills, and avoid responsibility for themselves. Hence experts

have championed community programs that allow individuals to retain some measure of community involvement and rootedness. The Community Mental Health Centers Act of 1963 was designed to solve some of the problems faced by patients trying to reenter society.

7. Most therapies fall into one of two major categories. The first is made up of psychotherapies, which use psychological means for the treatment of mental disorders. The second is composed of various biological therapies, which use drugs and electroshock procedures. A major function of psychotherapy is to help people realize that they are responsible for their own problems and, even more important, that they are the only ones who can really solve these problems.

8. Psychoanalysis is a form of psychotherapy, based on the theories of Sigmund Freud, aimed at making patients aware of the unconscious impulses, desires, and fears that are causing anxiety. Psychoanalysts believe that if patients can achieve insight—that is, understand their unconscious motives—they may be able to gain control over their behavior and thus free themselves of recurring problems.

9. Humanistic psychology has given rise to several forms of therapy known collectively as the human potential movement. They stress the actualization of an individual's potential through personal responsibility, freedom of choice, and authentic relationships.

   A. Client-centered therapy, based on the theories of Carl Rogers, provides an atmosphere of unconditional positive regard, in which clients are encouraged to speak freely.

   B. Existential therapy helps patients to overcome their fear of freedom and get in touch with their true feelings.

   C. Gestalt therapy aims to make a person "whole" by giving full range to the potential for growth.

10. Unlike psychoanalysis and the human potential movement, which emphasize the resolution of conflicts through understanding, behavior therapy focuses on changing specific behaviors through conditioning techniques.

11. Cognitive-behavioral therapies stress the part that negative thinking plays in psychological disorders, especially depressive disorders. Therapists attack their patients' problems on both the cognitive and the behavioral levels.

   A. Aaron T. Beck's cognitive therapy aims to change the way people think about themselves.

   B. Rational-emotive therapy, developed by Albert Ellis, attempts to correct a person's self-defeating beliefs. Ellis believes that emotional problems arise when a person's assumptions about life are unrealistic.

12. Family therapists look at the family as a structure. The individual is seen as functioning in a disturbed environment, in which family members interact with one another in maladaptive ways. Consequently, therapeutic progress depends on remedying the home situation.

13. Major advances have taken place over the past thirty years in the biological treatment of many psychological disorders. Since researchers have implicated biological malfunctioning in some disorders, drugs are used to relieve symptoms by normalizing the biochemical imbalance. In many cases drugs are used in conjunction with psychotherapy.

14. In the final analysis, the question is not which technique of intervention is better than others, but rather, "*What* treatment, by *whom*, is most effective for *this* individual with *that* specific problem, and under *which* set of circumstances?" (Paul, 1967:111). The kind of therapy a person considers using should be suited for the kind of problem it is meant to resolve. As in other matters, it is necessary that individuals undertake to become informed consumers and use good sense in arriving at some course of action.

KEY TERMS

aversive conditioning (p. 533)
behavior therapy (p. 526)
biological therapies (p. 525)

client-centered therapy (p. 530)
cognitive therapy (p. 535)
contingency management (p. 534)

countertransference (p. 529)
family therapy (p. 537)
free association (p. 528)

Gestalt therapy (p. 532)
group therapy (p. 518)
human potential movement
  (p. 530)
insight therapy (p. 526)

placebo effect (p. 541)
psychoanalysis (p. 528)
psychotherapies (p. 525)
rational-emotive therapy
  (RET) (p. 536)

resistance (p. 528)
transference (p. 528)
unconditional positive
  regard (p. 531)

SUGGESTED READINGS

BRY, ADELAIDE, ED. 1972. *Inside Psychotherapy*. New York: Basic Books. Conversations with nine clinicians, including Erwin Singer, Joseph Wolpe, Ian Alger, and Frederick Stoller, about how they work and what they are trying to accomplish.

CORSINI, RAYMOND J., ED. 1979. *Current Psychotherapies*. 2nd ed. Itasca, Ill.: Peacock. Most of the chapters were written by distinguished leaders of the various approaches, and major current therapies are covered. Each author follows the same format and outline, which makes comparison of therapies easier.

FRANKS, CYRIL M., and WILSON, G. TERENCE. Published annually. *Annual Review of Behavior Therapy: Theory and Practice*. New York: Brunner/Mazel. Presents up-to-date information on behavioral approaches to intervention. Includes a broad range of topics by experts in specific fields.

GURMAN, ALAN S., and KNISKERN, DAVID P., EDS. 1981. *Handbook of Family Therapy*. New York: Brunner/Mazel. A collection that addresses the history and models of family therapy and then reviews research on its effectiveness. Includes a special section on enriching family life and dealing with divorce.

SARASON, SEYMOUR. 1974. *The Psychological Sense of Community: Prospects for a Community Psychology*. San Francisco: Jossey-Bass. Presents a strong plea for a person's integration into effective communities as the source of psychological health. Reviews failures of communities and proposes new models for community-based intervention.

TORREY, E. FULLER. *Surviving Schizophrenia*. 1983. New York: Harper & Row. Comprehensive, realistic, and compassionate approach to schizophrenia by a former special assistant to the director of NIMH. Recommended by *Psychology Today*, Public Citizen Health Research Group, and the *American Journal of Psychiatry*.

TURNER, SAMUEL M., CALHOUN, KAREN S., and ADAMS, HENRY E., EDS. 1981. *Handbook of Clinical Behavior Therapy*. New York: Wiley. An excellent collection that presents reviews of behavioral approaches to a broad range of disorders.

APPENDIX
Statistics in Psychology

When psychologists set out to study any particular question, they may design an experiment, carry out a survey, or use some other research method that in some way involves measuring people. These techniques and other methods of investigation were described in Chapter 1. Whatever method psychologists use, however, at some point they are likely to accumulate a quantity of data about their subjects. If they are studying the relationship of IQ scores to school performance, for example, they will accumulate many subjects' IQ scores and school grades —perhaps over several years. If they are studying the prevalence of phobias in women, they will gather survey information from many women—whether they've ever had a phobia, when, of what, and so on. Eventually, the psychologist has on hand a mass of raw data—hundreds of thousands of numbers, survey responses, or the like.

By themselves, the raw data cannot be easily understood. To put them into a form in which they have more meaning, psychologists use statistics. **Statistics** summarize and make more understandable a mass of information. Although psychologists must be familiar with a good many statistical formulas and calculations, as a student you need be familiar with only a few basics. If the term "statistics" nevertheless brings to mind a lot of complex mathematics and obscure computations, it might be comforting to consider some statistics you are familiar with. If your favorite baseball player has a .335 batting average, you know that he is having an excellent season. Likewise, if your grade-point average in June is a 3.8 (on a 4.0 basis), you know you've had an excellent year. As these averages show, many

---

statistics: Methods of summarizing a mass of information and making it more understandable.

useful statistics are not complex—and they have the advantage of reducing a lot of information into a form that is concise and easy to use.

WHAT ARE STATISTICS?

Statistics come in two basic kinds: those that *describe* a collection of data—such as measurements of height, heart rate, or income—and those that tell us how *reliable* our research data are. **Descriptive statistics** summarize and characterize a set of measurements by telling us the average (mean) and other information about variations among the individual measurements in a distribution. In a few numbers, they summarize a lot of individual observations. The second kind of statistics, **inferential statistics,** tells us how reliable the results of a study are—how much faith we should put in them. Inferential statistics tells us how likely it is that our results could have occurred by chance.

DESCRIPTIVE STATISTICS

The Normal Distribution

Individual differences show up in everything that can be measured. There are no measurements —whether they be of heart rate, vocabulary size, or political opinion—that do not show individual variation. Most often, if we measure a representative sample of the population, the individual differences that we can identify will show up in a certain characteristic pattern. If we measure height, we will find a few very short people, a few very tall people, and a great many medium-sized people. If we mea-

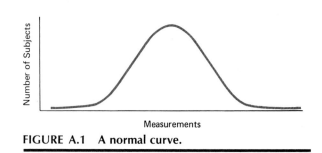

FIGURE A.1   A normal curve.

sure years of education completed, we will find a few grade-school dropouts, a few people with several advanced degrees, and a great many people who have graduated from high school or have had a year or two of additional training. If we measure opinions of the President's performance in office, we will find a handful of people who think he's been brilliant, a few people who think he's done a miserable job and deserves to be impeached, and a lot of people who think he's done a more or less competent job. What we find, then, is that more of our measurements typically fall in the middle of a distribution than at the extremes. If we express this discovery graphically, we get what is known as a **normal curve.** It has a characteristic bell shape because the greatest number of measurements fall at the center (see Figure A.1).

Skewed Distributions

In the general population, as we have seen, many distributions are "normal"—that is, they conform to the normal curve. But other distributions are **skewed.** This means that instead of being normal and bell-shaped, they have a "tail" on one side. If the tail is on the right, we call this **positive skew** (see

descriptive statistics: Analyses that summarize and characterize a set of measurements by giving the average (mean) and other information about variations among the individual measurements in a distribution.

inferential statistics: Analyses that indicate how reliable the results of a study are—how likely it is that the results could have occurred by chance.

normal curve: A graphic description of data that has a characteristic bell shape because more measurements fall in the middle than at the extremes.

skewed distribution: A graphic description of data on which measurements create a "tail" on one side.

positive skew: A graphic description of data that has a "tail" on the right side.

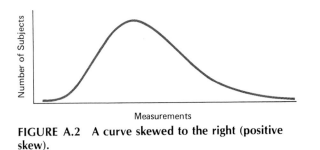

FIGURE A.2 A curve skewed to the right (positive skew).

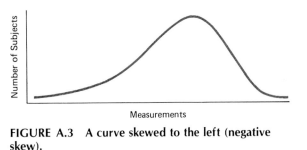

FIGURE A.3 A curve skewed to the left (negative skew).

Figure A.2). If the tail is on the left, we call this **negative skew** (see Figure A.3). Many samples can have skewed distributions, especially those that are not representative of the general population. Suppose we went to a remedial math class at the local junior high and tested the students' knowledge of elementary mathematics. Although a few would show that they had learned math skills by scoring in the upper portion of the distribution, most would pile up at the bottom of the distribution. This is positive skew, and the distribution of scores would look something like the curve in Figure A.2. Now suppose we went to a Wall Street brokerage and gave the same math tests to a group of stockbrokers. Although there might be a few who were such habitual users of electronic calculators that they had forgotten how to do simple math, most would probably do well on the test and pile up on the right of the distribution. This is negative skew, and our distribution would look something like the curve in Figure A.3.

Measures of Central Tendency

If we wanted to summarize the performance of the two groups just discussed—or of any two groups —with a single descriptive statistic, we would want what is known as a **measure of central tendency,** which locates the center of the distribution. There are three measures of central tendency: the mean, the median, and the mode. Each of these gives us a particular characterization of a distribution.

The **mean** is the arithmetic average of all the individual measurements in the distribution. For example, suppose ten advanced students in a seminar take an exam. Their scores are 98, 96, 92, 88, 88, 86, 82, 80, 78, and 72. We find the mean score by adding all the scores and dividing by the number of scores. In this case, the sum of the scores is 860; 860 ÷ 10 = 86, the mean. The **median** is the measurement above which and below which half of the individual measurements fall. In our group of scores, the median is 87, the score between the fifth and sixth scores. The **mode** is the most frequent measurement. In this group of scores, the mode is 88.

In our example, the mean, median, and mode are quite close together. This is not always the case, however. In some distributions, particularly those that are strongly skewed, the three figures may be significantly different, and all three may be needed to describe the distribution adequately. Let us consider an example.

The graph in Figure A.4 represents the distribution of salaries at a plastics company. The mean

---

negative skew: A graphic description of data that has a "tail" on the left side.

measure of central tendency: A statistic that locates the center of a distribution and thus summarizes the measurements in the distribution. The mean, the median, and the mode are measures of central tendency.

mean: The arithmetic average of all individual measurements in a distribution.

median: The measurement above which and below which half the individual measurements fall in a distribution.

mode: The measurement that appears most frequently in a distribution.

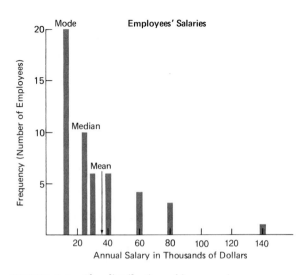

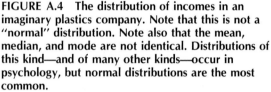

FIGURE A.4 The distribution of incomes in an imaginary plastics company. Note that this is not a "normal" distribution. Note also that the mean, median, and mode are not identical. Distributions of this kind—and of many other kinds—occur in psychology, but normal distributions are the most common.

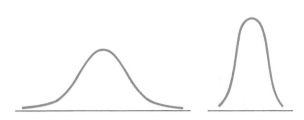

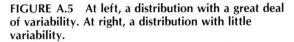

FIGURE A.5 At left, a distribution with a great deal of variability. At right, a distribution with little variability.

Variability and Standard Deviation

A measure of central tendency, such as the mean, tells us what, on the average, a group is like. Often we want to know the extent to which measurements spread out away from the average, that is, how much variability there is within a distribution. The measures that show how closely clustered or how widely spread any distribution of scores is are called **measure of variability.** Even though the curve representing a distribution is not skewed, it may be wider or narrower, depending on whether the measurements cluster together or spread out widely. If there is a great deal of variability in the distribution, the curve will be short and broad; if there is little variability, it will be tall and narrow (see Figure A.5).

The most commonly used measure of variability is the **standard deviation.** It shows how widely the measurements in a distribution are scattered above and below the mean.

If the measurements cluster closely around the mean, the standard deviation is small and the distribution is said to have little variability. If the measurements are dispersed widely from the mean, the standard deviation is large, and the distribution is said to have considerable variability. Thus, the standard deviation tells us how representative the mean is. If the variation is small, we know that the individual measurements are close to it; if large, we have less assurance as to the use of the mean as a representative value.

income of its fifty employees is about $31,000 a year, but look at the distribution. The president of the company earns $140,000 a year; he pays three executives $80,000 and four executives $60,000. There are six managers at $40,000 and six salespeople who earn $30,000. The majority of the employees, the thirty people who run the machines, all earn $25,332 or less. Although the mean of all fifty salaries is $36,000, this measure of central tendency is not a fair representation of the actual distribution of salaries.

In the case of the plastics company, the median is a better measure of central tendency, because it tells us the point at which the same number of salaries fall above and below it. The median income is $25,332. However, the mode, or the most frequent salary, is only $12,666 a year; more people make this salary than make any other.

measure of variability: A measurement that shows how closely clustered or how widely spread a distribution of scores is.

standard deviation: A measure of how widely the measurements in a distribution are scattered above and below the mean.

How to Find the Standard Deviation

Ascertaining the standard deviation is not difficult, although it is tedious to compute without the aid of a calculator. To calculate the standard deviation:

1. Determine the mean of the measurements.

2. From each measurement, subtract the mean and square the difference. (Measurements are squared to eliminate the negative signs that result when dealing with numbers that fall below the mean.)

3. Add the squares together.

4. Divide the sum by the number of measurements.

5. Take the square root of the value you have obtained. This figure is the standard deviation.

The standard deviation divides the normal curve into regular portions, each of which has a certain percentage of the distribution (see Figure A.6).

The standard deviation can be computed by means of a simple formula (see the boxed insert above). Knowing the standard deviation, we can relate a measurement to the mean by comparing it with the standard deviation. Suppose that a large group of students takes a quiz with 100 questions, in which the mean score is 60 and the standard deviation is 10. Since the typical score will fall within 10 units of the mean, a student with a score of 90 (3 standard deviations above the mean) obviously is doing outstanding work, and a student with a score of 30 (3 standard deviations below the mean) is unlikely to pass the course. But students with scores varying from 50 to 70 are within the expected range for the typical student in this course.

Establishing Norms

When psychologists are designing a test to be used in a variety of schools, businesses, clinics, or other settings, they usually are interested in how a person compares with others in a group. The test is given to a large representative sample of the group to be measured—for example, sixth graders, army privates, engineers, or perhaps the population as a whole. Then those who took the test are ranked on

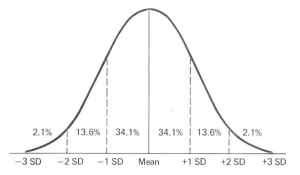

FIGURE A.6   A normal distribution, showing the percentage of measurements that will fall within 1, 2, or 3 standard deviations from the mean.

the basis of how well they did on it. For instance, on a particular vocabulary test, we may find that Jerry can perform better than 85 percent of a national sample of sixth graders. Scores on psychological tests are most commonly interpreted by reference to **norms**, standards of comparison developed for assessing the test performance of those who took the test. Most of the intelligence, aptitude, and personality tests you will encounter have been provided with norms in this way. Your percentile on the College Boards, for example, reflects your standing among people of your age and grade who have taken these exams.

---

norms: Standards of comparison for test results developed by giving the test to a large representative sample.

It should be remembered, however, that norms are not really standards—even though a norm group is sometimes misleadingly referred to as a "standardization group." Norms refer only to what has been found normal or average for some group of people at one point in time. Thus American IQ scores have been rising for the past half century—nearly 15 IQ points. Consequently, someone who scores 100 today would have scored 115 on the 1932 version of the same test (Flynn, 1984). All this is to say that if Johnny can read at the fiftieth percentile level, this does not mean that he has met some absolute standard for ability to read. It only means that he reads better than half the population his age (50 percent) and worse than the other half.

INFERENTIAL STATISTICS

In addition to the descriptive statistics we have just discussed, psychologists make use of inferential statistics. As the name suggests, these statistics involve mathematical inferences: if our data pass certain statistical tests, we may infer that our research is reliable.

Reliability

Why, you may ask, don't we just "know" if our data are reliable? Why do we need mathematical procedures to test our research results? Of course, some observations and experiments yield such clear-cut results that there is no argument about how to interpret them. Suppose we want to know if Great Danes are larger dogs than miniature poodles. We could sample 100 Great Danes and 100 miniature poodles and weigh them. Each dog's weight can be shown on a chart called a **frequency distribution.** It is an arrangement of data that shows the number of instances of each measure of a variable, in this case, weight. If we drew a graph of the frequencies of the dogs' weights per five-pound interval, we would discover that none of the poodles is as large as the smallest Great Dane (see Figure A.7). The distribu-

tions do not overlap. In this case we do not need statistics to tell us that Great Danes are a larger breed than miniature poodles (as if this were not obvious from the start).

But suppose that we wanted to know if Labrador retrievers weigh more or less, on the average, than German shepherds. The answer to this question is not immediately obvious. At least we can anticipate that if there is an average difference between the two breeds, it will be much smaller than that between Great Danes and miniature poodles. Again, we can take a sample of each breed and arrange their weights in a frequency distribution. Suppose we have 100 retrievers and 100 shepherds, as shown in Figure A.8. The weights of the retrievers vary from 50 to 80 pounds, as do those of the shepherds. The retrievers' average weight is 65 pounds, the shepherds', 67 pounds. Although the shepherds *in this sample* weigh 2 pounds more than the retrievers *in this sample*, would we find the same result with another sample of the two breeds? Perhaps we would get a slightly heavier sample of retrievers and a slightly lighter sample of shepherds the next time we sampled, and therefore we would not find an average difference in weight between the breeds. The fact that we must take samples (we can never weigh *all* retrievers and shepherds) means that the inferences we make are *probabilistic* statements about the whole populations of shepherds and retrievers.

To estimate how reliable our samples of dogs are in representing their breeds, we need to be assured that the samples were random (see Chapter 1) and that the variation between the breeds *reliably* exceeds the variation of individuals within each breed. The test of how reliable the difference in weight is depends on the sizes of the two samples of dogs and on the size of the average difference between the two breeds compared with how much individual variation there is within each breed.

The *t*-Test

The test of the breed difference is called a **t-test,** which compares the size of the average difference

---

frequency distribution: An arrangement of data that shows the number of instances
    of each measure of a variable.
t-test: An estimation of the reliability of the difference between two means.

How to Calculate the *t*-Test

The *t*-test is an estimation of the reliability of the difference between two means (averages). To find out whether the difference could have occurred by chance, we need to know how large the average difference is (mean 1 minus mean 2). We also need to know how variable the individual dogs' weights are within each breed. This is the *variance* of each breed. The *t*-test compares the variance within each breed to the size of the mean difference between the breeds. Finally, we need to know how many dogs we sampled—in this case 100 of each breed. How reliable the average difference is depends on how large it is (remember the miniature poodles and Great Danes), how much individual dogs within each breed vary in weight, and how many dogs we studied in each sample.

To calculate the *t*-test, just follow these steps:

1. Determine the mean of the scores for each breed and subtract one from the other.

2. Go back to the box on the standard deviation. Stop at Step 4. That gives you the variance of each distribution.

3. Add the two variances.

4. Add the numbers of dogs minus 2 (200 − 2 = 198).

5. Divide the summed variances by 198, and take the square root.

6. Divide the mean difference in weights by the square root from Step 5.

If the samples add up to more than 50 individuals, any value of *t* over 2 is statistically reliable more than 95 percent of the time.

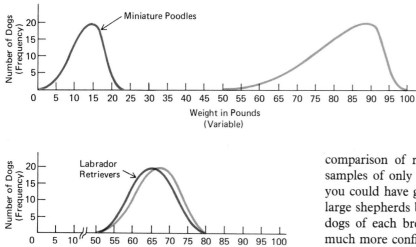

FIGURE A.7 A graph of the frequencies of miniature poodles' and Great Danes' weights. Note that the frequencies do not overlap.

FIGURE A.8 A graph of the frequencies of German shepherds' and Labrador retrievers' weights. Note that the frequencies do overlap.

comparison of retrievers and shepherds based on samples of only two dogs of each breed. After all, you could have gotten two small retrievers and two large shepherds by chance. Random samples of 100 dogs of each breed, on the other hand, give us a much more confident basis on which to make judgments about the average difference in weight between the two breeds. It is highly unlikely that our large random samples of each breed would have been biased toward heavy or light dogs. (For a description of how the *t*-test is performed, see the boxed insert above.)

Analysis of Variance

To execute more complicated comparisons among the averages of three or more groups, and among

between the breeds with the variation within each breed. The formula weights the probability of the breed difference by how many dogs there are in the two samples. You would not put much faith in a

TABLE A.1 Voter Preference in a 2 × 2 Table

Sex	Omnivores	Vegetarians	Row total
Females			100
Males			100
Column total			200 Grand total)

TABLE A.2 No Sex Difference in Voting Pattern

Sex	Omnivores	Vegetarians	Row total
Females	60	40	100
Males	60	40	100
Column total	120	80	200 (Grand total)

TABLE A.3 Sex Difference in Voting Pattern

Sex	Omnivores	Vegetarians	Row total
Females	40	60	100
Males	60	40	100
Column total	100	100	200 Grand total)

groups classified in more than one way (for example, males and females in two or more breeds), psychologists perform an **analysis of variance (ANOVA)**, which is rather like a more complex *t*-test.

Chi-Square

Some information psychologists collect does not consist of individual scores or measures, but of counts of who does what or is of what kind. For example, if we want to know how many male and female voters prefer the Vegetarian Party and how many the Omnivores, we do not want average voter preferences by sex but actual counts of voters by sex. The most efficient way to look at voter preference by sex is in a 2 × 2 table (see Table A.1).

Suppose that we want to know if men are more likely to prefer the Omnivores than women are and that we have a sample of 100 people of each sex. To decide if the sex difference between these samples is likely to be a reliable representation of the population of men and women from whom the samples are drawn, we can use the chi-square statistic. The **chi-square** estimates the reliability of differences between two distributions (in this case, men and women voters). It calculates the expected distribution if voters were randomly distributed between the two political parties and the deviation of the observed distributions from the expected values.

Suppose that 40 percent of both the men and the women voted for the Vegetarians and that 60 percent voted for the Omnivores (see Table A.2). There would be no sex difference in voting pattern. But

---

analysis of variance (ANOVA): A more complex form of the *t*-test, which allows comparisons among means in three or more groups.

chi-square: An estimation of the reliability of the difference between two distributions.

How to Calculate Chi-Square

Chi-square (χ^2) is an estimate of how sure we can be that a distribution of events or people, such as voters, did not happen by chance. Chi-square calculates the *expected* numbers of people who would by chance fall into each cell of the table. Then it compares the *observed* number of people to fall into each cell with the expected number. If the difference between the expected and observed numbers is large, then the distribution is not likely to have happened by chance.

To calculate a chi-square statistic on the distribution of men and women voters for the Vegetarian and Omnivore parties, follow these steps:

1. Figure how many people would by chance fall into the upper-left cell by multiplying the first row total by the first column total (100 × 100) and divide by the grand total (200). The expected number is 50.

2. Subtract the expected number (50) from the observed number in the upper-left cell (60).

The difference is 10 (60 − 50 = 10). Square the difference to eliminate negative signs (10 × 10 = 100) and divide it by the expected number: 100 ÷ 50 = 2.

3. Repeat Steps 1 and 2 for each of the four cells. In this example the expected values are the same for each cell, but that will not always be true.

4. Sum the four values you get from calculating the difference between the expected and observed numbers for each cell. This is the chi-square.

The reliability of the chi-square value must be looked up in a table. In this example, men preferred the Omnivores and women the Vegetarians by such a margin that this distribution could occur only two times in a hundred by chance.

---

suppose that 40 percent of the men and 60 percent of the women voted for the Vegetarians (leaving 60 percent of the men and 40 percent of the women to vote for the Omnivores) (see Table A.3). Would there be a reliable basis for concluding that women are more likely than men to prefer the Vegetarians?

Given samples of 100 of each sex, we can be sure that men are more likely to prefer the Omnivores and women the Vegetarians. To learn how to perform the chi-square calculation, see the boxed insert above.

SUMMARY

1. Statistics is the science concerned with summarizing a mass of information and making it more understandable. When psychologists accumulate a quantity of data about their subjects, they use statistics to put the data into a concise and easy-to-use form in which they have more meaning.

2. There are two basic kinds of statistics.

A. Descriptive statistics summarize numerous individual observations, giving information about the average (mean) measurement and about variations among the measurements in the distribution.

B. Inferential statistics indicate the reliability of a study. They show how likely it is that the results could have occurred equally well by chance.

3. Many measurements fall into what is known as a normal curve, with more measurements in the middle of the distribution than at the extremes.

4. Other distributions are skewed, with a "tail" on one side. A positive skew has a tail on the right; a negative skew, on the left.

5. Measures of central tendency—mean, median, and mode—summarize information with a single descriptive statistic.

A. The mean is the arithmetic average of all individual measurements in a distribution.

B. The median is the measurement above which and below which half the individual measurements fall in a distribution.

C. The mode is the measurement that appears most frequently in a distribution.

6. Another descriptive statistic is the standard deviation, which shows how much variability exists within a distribution, that is, how representative the mean is.

7. A norm is yet another descriptive statistic. It is a standard of comparison, based on the performance of a large representative sample, against which an individual's performance on an intelligence, aptitude, or personality test can be measured.

8. The *t*-test is an inferential statistic that estimates the reliability of the difference between two means. It compares the size of the average difference between two population samples with the variation within each sample.

9. The analysis of variance (ANOVA) is a more complex *t*-test used with three or more groups.

10. The chi-square is an inferential statistic that estimates the reliability of the difference between two distributions. It compares the expected distribution of a population sample with the observed distribution.

KEY TERMS

analysis of variance (ANOVA) (p. 554)
chi-square (p. 554)
descriptive statistics (p. 548)
frequency distribution (p. 552)
inferential statistics (p. 548)
mean (p. 549)

measure of central tendency (p. 549)
measure of variability (p. 550)
median (p. 549)
mode (p. 549)
negative skew (p. 549)
norms (p. 551)

normal curve (p. 548)
positive skew (p. 548)
skewed distribution (p. 548)
standard deviation (p. 550)
statistics (p. 547)
t-test (p. 552)

SUGGESTED READINGS

FREEMAN, DAVID, PISANI, R., and PURVES, R. 1978. *Statistics*. New York: Norton. Presents basic statistics in nonmathematical terms.

MARKEN, RICHARD. 1981. *Methods in Experimental Psychology*. Monterey, Calif.: Brooks/Cole. A fine discussion of methods of conducting and writing up research.

RAY, WILLIAM J., and RAVIZZA, RICHARD. 1981. *Methods Toward a Science of Behavior and Experience*. Belmont, Calif.: Wadsworth. An introductory text on methods in psychology. Nicely written, with good examples.

ROBINSON, P. W. 1981. *Fundamentals of Experimental Psychology*. 2nd ed. Englewood Cliffs, N.J.: Prentice-Hall. Emphasizes procedures; shows how to analyze different types of data step by step.

SIEGEL, MICHAEL H., and ZEIGLER, H. PHILLIP, EDS. 1976. *Psychological Research: The Inside Story*. New York: Harper & Row. Contains chapters by psychologists in which they describe how they got into doing the particular research that they do. They talk about their mistakes and their triumphs.

Glossary

absolute threshold: The lowest level of physical energy that will produce a sensation in half the trials.

accommodation: In Piaget's theory of cognitive development, the adjustment of one's scheme for understanding the world to fit newly observed events and experiences.

achievement motivation: Behavior that seeks to develop or demonstrate high ability and competence.

achievement test: An instrument used to measure how much an individual has learned in a given subject or area.

activation-synthesis hypothesis: The suggestion that, rather than serving a psychological function, dreams may simply represent an unimportant by-product of having stimulated certain brain cells during sleep.

acupuncture: Technique in which specific areas of the skin are punctured by needles; used for the management of pain.

addiction: A condition in which people are physically dependent on drugs.

adolescence: The developmental stage between childhood and adulthood.

adrenal (uh-DREE-null) **gland:** An endocrine gland of vertebrates that is located near each of the kidneys and that produces epinephrine.

affect: A person's emotional state or mood.

affective disorder: A mood disturbance disorder associated with extreme elation and sadness.

afferent (receptor) neuron: A nerve cell that carries impulses to the brain or spinal cord from a receptor.

age regression: A type of psychotherapy in which individuals are told by a hypnotist that they are a certain age and are then instructed to tell about or act out their behavior during this earlier period.

aggression: Any act that is intentionally designed to harm another person.

alcoholic: Someone who organizes his or her behavior around alcohol and continues to drink despite the serious problems it presents in everyday life.

altered states of consciousness: Those mental processes that individuals experience as different from "usual," "ordinary," or "normal" processes.

altruism (AL-troo-ism): Self-sacrificing behavior that helps to ensure the survival of other members of one's own species.

amnesia: A dissociative disorder characterized by memory loss.

anal stage: According to Freud, the stage at which children associate erotic pleasure with the elimination process.

analysis of variance (ANOVA): A more complex form of the *t*-test, which allows comparisons among means in three or more groups.

androgens (AN-druh-jens): The principal male sex hormones.

anorexia nervosa: A disorder in which individuals willfully suppress their appetite, resulting in self-starvation.

anti-anxiety drug: A sedative or mild tranquilizer used to reduce excitability and cause drowsiness.

antidepressant: A drug used in the treatment of psychological depression.

antipsychotic drug: A major tranquilizer, chiefly phenothiazine, used in the treatment of schizophrenia to make patients less withdrawn, less confused or agitated, less prone to auditory hallucinations, and less irritated or hostile.

antisocial personality (psychopath, sociopath): A personality disorder characterized by irresponsibility, immaturity, shallow emotions, and lack of conscience.

anvil: One of the three bones of the middle ear, shaped like an anvil.

anxiety: A vague, generalized apprehension or feeling that one is in danger.

apnea (AP-nee-uh): A sleep disorder in which the sleeper periodically stops breathing during the night.

applied science: Discovering ways to use scientific findings to accomplish practical goals.

aptitude test: An instrument used to discover a person's talents and to predict how well he or she will learn a specific new skill.

archetype (ARK-uh-type): According to Carl Jung, an inherited idea, based on the experiences of one's ancestors, that shapes one's perception of the world.

artificial intelligence: The design and construction of intelligent machines; the simulation of human thinking and problem solving by computer technology.

assimilation: In Piaget's theory of cognitive development, the process of fitting objects and experiences into one's scheme for understanding the environment.

attachment: The affectional tie that the infant forms with another person.

attitude: A relatively enduring disposition or tendency to evaluate a person, object, or event in a particular way.

attitude consistency: The tendency for people to try to bring their attitudes into harmony with one another.

attribution (AT-treh-BEW-shun): The process by which ordinary people explain and interpret the events they encounter.

auditory induction: Mechanism for reconstructing masked segments of heard messages.

auditory nerve: The nerve that carries information from the ear to the auditory area of the temporal lobe in the cerebral cortex.

authoritarian leader: A leader who is domineering and unwilling to share power.

autoimmune disease: Disease in which the immune system goes awry and begins attacking the body's own tissues.

autonomic (aw-tuh-NOM-ic) **nervous system:** Part of the peripheral nervous system that controls internal biological functions, such as heart rate and digestion.

autoshaping: Biological bases for learning certain kinds of behavior; automatic shaping.

aversive conditioning: A type of behavior therapy in which individuals learn to associate a strong negative response with an undesirable behavior.

axon: A fiber of a nerve cell that conducts impulses away from the cell body.

babbling: The soft gurgling or murmuring sounds in which infants alternate vowels and consonants in a recurrent pattern.

Babinski reflex: A reflex exhibited in newborns that is triggered by gently stroking the sole of the infant's foot, resulting in the fanning out of the toes and their curling downward.

basic science: The pursuit of knowledge about natural phenomena for its own sake.

behavior modification: The systematic application of learning principles to change people's actions and feelings.

behavioral medicine: An interdisciplinary field that integrates behavioral and biomedical knowledge regarding health and disease processes.

behavior therapy: A form of therapy aimed at changing undesirable behavior through conditioning techniques.

behaviorism: The school of psychology that holds that the proper subject matter of psychology is objectively observable behavior—and nothing else.

binocular vision: The combination of the two images received by the visual system, so that despite the fact that one has two eyes, one sees a single image.

biofeedback: Learning conscious control of one's internal physiological processes with the help of information received from monitoring devices.

biological therapies: The use of drugs and electroshock procedures for the treatment of mental disorders.

bipolar (manic-depressive) disorder: An affective disorder characterized by mood swing from depression to mania.

bipolar nerve cells: Cells that receive impulses when the rods and cones of the eye are stimulated.

bottom-up theory: We judge whether or not our lives are happy by mentally calculating the balance between momentary pleasures and pains.

brainstorming: A technique for fostering nondirected thinking. It is a freewheeling process for generating ideas.

brainwashing: A means of changing attitudes that involves a combination of psychological gamesmanship and physical torture.

bulimia: A disorder in which individuals engage in a punishing cycle of binge eating and self-induced vomiting purges.

Cannon-Bard theory: The belief that emotion involves a simultaneous burst of activity in the brain and in bodily functioning.

cardiovascular diseases: Disorders affecting the heart and blood vessels.

caretaker speech: A systematically modified version of language that adults use in addressing infants and young children. Caretaker speech differs from everyday speech in its simplified vocabulary, higher pitch, exaggerated intonation, short, simple sentences, and high proportion of questions and imperatives.

case study: An intense investigation of an individual or group, usually focusing on a single psychological phenomenon.

catharsis (kuh-THAR-sis): A purging and lessening of pent-up energy through discharging angry impulses in aggressive behavior.

cellular immune response: One of two major immune system reactions in which specifically armed cells in the blood directly attack foreign cells.

central nervous system (CNS): The brain and spinal cord.

cerebellum (sair-uh-BELL-um): A lower portion of the brain that controls posture and balance and regulates the details of motor commands from the cerebral cortex.

cerebral (sair-REE-bral) **cortex:** The gray mass surrounding the subcortex that controls most of the higher brain functions, such as reading and problem solving.

charisma (ka-RIZ-mah): The strong emotional appeal possessed by some leaders.

chi-square: An estimation of the reliability of the difference between two distributions.

chromosome (CROW-ma-sewm): A long, threadlike body that contains the hereditary materials found in the nuclei of all cells.

circadian (sir-KAY-dee-un) **rhythm:** The approximately twenty-four-hour cycle on which many bodily functions operate.

clairvoyance: The ability to gain knowledge of events that is not detectable by the usual senses.

classical conditioning: A learning procedure in which a stimulus that normally elicits a given response is repeatedly preceded by a neutral stimulus (one that usually does not elicit the response). Eventually, the neutral stimulus will evoke a similar response when presented by itself.

client-centered therapy: A form of therapy aimed at helping clients recognize their own strengths and gain confidence so that they can learn to be true to their own standards and ideas about how to live effectively.

clique (CLEEK): A group within a set.

closure: A principle in perceptual grouping in which breaks between elements are ignored and the whole is seen as a single image.

cochlea: A part of the inner ear containing tiny hairlike cells that move back and forth in the presence of sound.

cocktail party phenomenon: A type of selective attention.

cognitive dissonance: The uncomfortable feeling that arises when a person experiences contradictory or conflicting attitudes.

cognitive map: The picture of their environment organisms develop to use in dealing with reality and making their way about life.

cognitive science: A domain in psychology concerned with the nature of various mental tasks and the operations that allow the mind to execute them.

cognitive therapy: A form of therapy aimed at assisting people to overcome negative styles of thought.

collective unconscious: According to Carl Jung, that part of the mind that contains the inherited instincts, urges, and memories common to all people.

color blindness: Complete or partial inability to distinguish colors, resulting from malfunction in the cones.

communication: The process by which people transmit attitudes, information, ideas, and feelings to one another.

competence motivation: The causation of behavior by capability, fitness, and skillfulness.

complementary needs: A condition in which each person in a social relationship supplies the other's lack. Individuals gain a sense of completeness when they enter into relationships with people with different traits.

compliance: Yielding to the pressures of others and acting in conformity with their wishes even though one thinks one should act in some other way.

compulsion: The impulsive and uncontrollable repetition of an irrational action.

computerized axial (AX-ee-ull) **tomography** (tow-MAH-grah-fee) (**CT** or **CAT**) **scan:** A technique that uses radiation and high-speed computer analysis to yield constructed, cross-sectional pictures of body tissue.

concept: A label for a class of objects or events that share certain common attributes.

conditioned response (CR): In classical conditioning, the response aroused by some stimulus other than the one that automatically produces it. In operant conditioning, an increase in the rate of responding.

conditioned stimulus (CS): In classical conditioning, a once-neutral stimulus that has become capable of eliciting a particular response through being paired during training with an unconditioned stimulus.

conditions of worth: Carl Rogers's term for the conditions a person must meet in order to regard himself or herself positively.

cones: Receptor cells in the retina sensitive to color. Because they require more light than rods to function, they are most useful in daytime vision.

consciousness: The subjective awareness that individuals have at a given time of their inner sensations, images, thoughts, and feelings and of the world about them.

conservation: The principle that a given quantity does not change when its appearance is changed. The discovery of this principle between the ages of five and seven is important to the intellectual development of the child.

contingency management: A form of behavior therapy in which undesirable behavior is not rewarded, while desirable behavior is reinforced.

contingency of reinforcement: B. F. Skinner's term for the occurrence of a reward or punishment following a particular behiavor.

continuity: A principle in perceptual grouping in which stimuli are perceived as continuous.

continuous reinforcement: A pattern in which an organism is rewarded every time it provides the desired or correct response.

control group: In an experiment, a group of subjects that is treated in the same way as the experimental group, except that the experimental treatment is not applied.

convergent thinking: Thinking that results in integrative and focused responses.

conversion disorder: A psychological disorder in which the individual loses some body function without an apparent organic cause.

coping: The responses individuals make in order to master, tolerate, or reduce stress.

corpus callosum (kuh-LOW-sum): A band of nerves that connects the two hemispheres of the cortex and carries messages back and forth between them.

correlation (cor-uh-LAY-shun): The degree of relatedness between two sets of data.

correlation coefficient (co-eh-FI-shent): A numerical measure of the degree of relationship between two variables or conditions.

countertransference: The process by which a therapist becomes overly preoccupied with a patient.

creativity: The occurrence of original and useful responses.

cross-cultural study: A research method in which comparable data are acquired from two or more cultures for the purpose of studying cultural similarities and differences.

crowding: The perception people have that they are receiving excessive stimulation from social sources.

cue dependence: The need for a relevant cue in order to retrieve an item from memory; without such a cue, an item is forgotten for all practical purposes.

cue overload: A state in which you find yourself overwhelmed or engulfed by excessive stimuli.

decay theory: The idea that memory traces containing stored information deteriorate unless the information is periodically used and hence rehearsed.

decibels: A measurement of the intensity of sound.

declarative memory: The storage of "facts," knowledge that can be brought consciously to mind and formulated in a statement, proposition, or image.

defense mechanism: According to Sigmund Freud, a certain specific means by which the ego unconsciously protects itself against unpleasant impulses or circumstances.

delusion: A false belief maintained in the face of contrary evidence.

democratic leader: A leader who tries to involve as many group members as possible in the decision-making process.

dendrite: A relatively short, bushy fiber of a nerve cell that receives most incoming signals.

densensitization: The negative adaptation to a stimulus in which the senses get used to a level of stimulation, such as traffic noise, and respond only to departures from it.

density: A physical condition that entails spatial limitations.

deoxyribonucleic (dee-OX-ee-rye-bow-new-CLAY-ic) **acid (DNA):** A molecule in which genetic information is stored; it tells a cell how to manufacture such vital protein substances as enzymes, hormones, antibodies, and structural proteins.

dependent variable: In an experiment, the factor that is not controlled by the experimenters but changes as a result of changes in the independent variable.

depressant: A drug that acts on the brain and nervous system to reduce the responsiveness of the body and to slow its activities.

depression: An affective disorder characterized by a pattern of sadness, anxiety, fatigue, insomnia, underactivity, and reduced ability to function and to work with others.

depth perception: The ability to tell the distances of various objects and to experience the world in three-dimensional terms.

descriptive statistics: Analyses that summarize and characterize a set of measurements by giving the average (mean) and other information about variations among the individual measurements in a distribution.

detoxification: A process in which individuals are withdrawn from a drug under professional supervision.

developmental psychology: The study of the changes that occur across the life cycle.

difference threshold (just noticeable difference): The smallest change in a physical stimulus that produces a change in sensation in half the trials.

differential emotions theory: The belief that facial patterning or facial muscle tension generates, sustains, and amplifies the experience of emotion.

diffusion of responsibility: The tendency of the presence of others to lessen an individual's feelings of responsibility for his or her actions or failure to act.

directed thinking: Systematic, logical, goal-oriented thought.

discrimination: Behavior that arbitrarily gives or denies individuals privileges accorded to others by virtue of their group membership.

displacement: The redirection of desires, feelings, or impulses from their proper object to a substitute.

dissociative disorder: A psychological disorder characterized by a disturbance in memory or identity.

divergent thinking: Thinking that results in fluent and flexible responses.

double bind: A situation in which a person receives conflicting demands, so that no matter what he or she does, it is wrong.

double-blind experiment: A research technique in which neither the subjects nor the experimenter knows which subjects have been exposed to the experimental treatment.

Down's syndrome: A disorder associated with the presence of an extra chromosome that results in physical abnormalities and mental retardation.

drive: A mechanism that goads an organism into action.

drive-reduction theory: The notion that when a drive is aroused, an organism is impelled to undertake those behaviors which in the past served to reduce the drive.

echoic memory: The sensory store involved in hearing.

educational psychology: A subfield of psychology that deals with topics related to teaching children and young adults, such as intelligence, memory, problem solving, and motivation.

effector (ih-FECK-ter): A cell that works the muscles, internal glands, and organs.

efferent (effector) neuron: A nerve cell that carries impulses away from the brain or spinal cord to muscles or glands.

ego: According to Sigmund Freud, the part of the personality that is in touch with reality. The ego strives to meet the often conflicting demands of the id and the superego in socially acceptable ways.

electrode (ih-LECK-trode): A type of wire used by scientists to detect the minute electrical changes that occur when neurons fire.

electroconvulsive therapy: A controversial form of treatment for psychological disorders in which electrical shocks are administered to a patient to induce a convulsion.

electroencephalograph (ih-LECK-troh-en-SEF-uh-la-graf) (**EEG**): A machine used to record the electrical activity of large portions of the brain.

embryo: The developing organism during the prenatal period from the second week to the end of the second month.

empirical science: An approach to knowledge in which precise statements are tested to see whether they are true or false.

encoding (**acquisition**): The process by which information is put into the memory system.

endocrine (EN-doh-crin) **system:** A group of glands that produces hormones, by which messages are sent through the bloodstream to particular organs of the body.

endorphins (EN-door-fins) (**enkephalins** [en-KEH-fa-lins]): Chemical substances, called "the body's own morphine," that have the capacity to dull pain and produce euphoric feelings.

environment: Those surrounding influences and factors that affect the organism.

epinephrine (eh-pih-NEH-frin) (**adrenaline** [ah-DREN-ah-lin]): A hormone secreted by the adrenal glands that among other things regulates the flow of blood to the various organs.

episodic (EP-ih-SAH-dic) **memory:** The information we have about particular events we experienced in the past.

estrogens (ESS-troh-jens): The principal female sex hormones.

estrus (ESS-truss): The time of fertility in female animals; many nonhuman females are interested in mating only during this period of receptivity.

ethology: The study of animal behavior in its natural environment.

experience-producing drive: The human need to explore new environments and experiences simply because they are interesting.

experiment: A rigorous investigative method in which the researcher controls the situation so as to decrease the possibility that unnoticed, outside factors will influence the results.

experimental group: The group of subjects to which an experimental treatment is applied.

experimental psychology: A type of psychology devoted to producing new knowledge through the use of experimental methodologies.

experimental treatment: The manipulation of an independent variable in an experiment designed to observe its effects.

extinction: The gradual disappearance of a response because the reinforcement is withheld.

extrasensory perception (**ESP**): The ability to receive information about the world through channels other than the normal senses.

facilitation: The process by which a response that a person would be unlikely to make becomes more probable.

factor analysis: A complex statistical technique used to identify the underlying reasons that variables are correlated.

family therapy: A form of therapy aimed at understanding and improving relationships that have led one or more members in a family to experience emotional suffering.

feedback: Information received after an action as to its effectiveness or correctness.

fetus: The final phase in prenatal life, beginning with the conclusion of the second month and ending with birth.

figure-ground: The division of the visual field into two distinct parts, one being the objects (figure), the other the background or spaces between the objects (ground).

fixed-interval schedule: A schedule of reinforcement in which a specific amount of time must elapse before a response will elicit reinforcement.

fixed-ratio schedule: A schedule of reinforcement in which a specific number of correct responses is required before reinforcement can be obtained.

fovea: A depressed area directly behind the lens at the center of the retina where vision is keenest.

fraternal (**dizygotic** [dye-zye-GAH-tic]) **twins:** Siblings that result when two different eggs supplied by the same female are fertilized by two different sperm; they are no more genetically related than ordinary sisters and brothers.

free association: A method used by psychoanalysts to examine the unconscious. The patient is instructed to say whatever comes into his or her mind.

free-rider mechanism: The "let George do it" approach to dealing with social problems.

frequency distribution: An arrangement of data that shows the number of instances of each measure of a variable.

frustration: A state in which individuals are blocked in attaining some goal.

frustration-aggression hypothesis: A psychological theory that states that frustration activates angry and hostile impulses that find expression in aggressive behaviors.

fugue: A rare dissociative disorder in which complete or partial amnesia is combined with a move to a new environment.

fully functioning person: Carl Rogers's term for an individual whose organism and self coincide, allowing him or her to be open to experience, to possess unconditional positive regard, and to have harmonious relations with others.

functional fixedness: The inability to imagine new functions for familiar objects.

fundamental attribution error: The tendency for people to underestimate the impact of situational factors and overestimate the role of dispositional factors in controlling behavior.

fundamental needs: In Maslow's hierarchy-of-needs theory, the needs to satisfy biological drives and to feel safe.

ganglion cell: A cell whose fibers (axons) form the optic nerve; ganglion cells are stimulated by the bipolar cells.

gender identity disorders: Psychosexual disorders in which individuals form gender identities that are contrary to their sexual anatomy.

general adaptation syndrome: A series of stages described by Hans Selye by which an organism responds to stress: the alarm reaction stage, the resistance stage, and the exhaustion stage.

generalized anxiety disorder: A disturbance in which individuals experience frequent high levels of tension for months on end but do not know why they are apprehensive or fearful.

genes (jeans): The building blocks of heredity.

genetics (juh-NEH-tics): The scientific study of the transmission of hereditary factors and the way these factors are expressed in the development and life of an individual.

genital stage: According to Freud, the stage during which a person's sexual satisfaction depends as much on giving sexual pleasure as on receiving it.

genotype (JEAN-oh-type): The set of genes organisms inherit from their parents.

Gestalt (ga-SHTALT): In perception, the experience that comes from organizing bits and pieces of information into meaningful wholes.

Gestalt (ga-SHTALT) **therapy:** A form of therapy that emphasizes the relationship between the patient and therapist in the here and now; it aims to make the patient "whole."

grammar: The rules for the organization of language symbols.

grasping relfex: An infant's clinging response to a touch on the palm of his or her hand.

group structure: The parts various members play in a group and the interrelationships that exist among these parts.

group therapy: A form of therapy in which patients work together with the aid of a group leader to resolve interpersonal problems.

grouping: One of the organizing principles that the brain uses in constructing perceptions.

groupthink: The process of making decisions in a highly cohesive group in which the members are so intent on maintaining group consensus that their critical faculties become ineffective.

habituation: The process by which infants pay less and less attention to the same stimulus presented over and over again.

hallucination: A sensation or perception that has no actual external cause.

hallucinogen: A drug that often produces hallucinations.

hammer: One of the three bones of the middle ear, shaped like a hammer.

hassles: The irritating demands and troubled relationships that plague us day in and day out. Compare **uplifts.**

health care psychology: The use of psychological techniques in the treatment of medical problems with behavioral roots.

heredity: The biological transmission of traits from parents to their offspring through genes.

heuristic device: A shortcut, rule of thumb, or other tried-and-tested remedies used to search for promising alternatives.

hierarchical strategy: A problem-solving technique in which complex problems are divided into solvable subproblems.

higher-order conditioning: A process in which after a second conditioned stimulus has been paired with a first conditioned stimulus a number of times, it takes on the functions of the first conditioned stimulus.

holophrases (HOLE-uh-frayz-es): Single words that a child uses to convey different meanings, depending on the situation.

homeostasis (ho-me-oh-STAY-sis): The

process that permits an organism to maintain a more or less stable existence in an unstable environment through a variety of adaptive mechanisms.

hormones: Control chemicals manufactured in one part of the body that influence activities elsewhere in the body; distributed by blood and other body fluid.

human interaction: The process by which two or more people influence each other's feelings, attitudes, and actions.

human potential movement: An approach to psychotherapy that stresses the actualization of each person's unique potential through personal responsibility, freedom of choice, and authentic relationships.

human services psychology: A sector of professional psychology that promotes human well-being through the acquisition and application of psychological knowledge to both treatment and prevention of disorders.

humanistic psychology: An approach to psychology that stresses the uniqueness of the individual; focuses on the value, dignity, and worth of each person; and holds that healthy living is the result of realizing one's full potential.

humoral immune response: One of two major immune system reactions which involves the production of antibodies in response to an invasion by harmful bacteria.

hypertension: A medical condition characterized by chronically high blood pressure.

hypnosis: A form of altered consciousness in which individuals become more susceptible to suggestion and experience a heightened sense of selective attention.

hypochondriasis: A preoccupation with imaginary ailments, on which the person blames his or her other problems.

hypothalamus (hi-po-THAL-uh-muss): A small area deep inside the brain that regulates the autonomic nervous system and other body functions.

hypothesis (hi-PA-tha-sis): An educated guess about the relationship between two variables.

hypothesis testing: Thinking of how things might be or could be under other circumstances and trying them out.

iconic memory: The sensory store associated with vision.

id: According to Sigmund Freud, that part of the unconscious personality that contains needs, drives, and instincts as well as repressed material.

The id strives for immediate gratification of desires.

identical (monozygotic) twins: Siblings that result when a fertilized egg accidentally gets split into two parts early in development; each part grows into a separate and complete individual who is genetically identical to the other.

identification: Mentally associating oneself in thought, feeling, or action with another person or group.

identity: The answers people give to the questions "Who am I?" and "Who am I to be?" A sense of placement within the world.

illusion: A perception that misrepresents physical stimuli.

image: A rough mental representation of a specific event or object; the most primitive unit of thought.

immune system: A surveillance mechanism that protects an organism from disease-causing viruses, bacteria, fungi, and tumors.

implicit personality theory: A set of assumptions about how people behave and what traits or characteristics go together.

impression management: A process by which one attempts to shape people's definitions of oneself by generating words, gestures, and actions that will lead them to act in accordance with one's wishes.

imprinting: A process of rapid learning by which an animal establishes social attachments during an early stage in its life.

incentive: An external force that instigates goal-related activity.

independent variable: In an experiment, the factor that is deliberately manipulated by the experimenters to test its effect on another factor.

industrial psychology: A subfield of psychology concerned with human behavior in the work place.

inferential statistics: Analyses that indicate how reliable the results of a study are—how likely it is that the results could have occurred by chance.

inferiority complex: According to Alfred Adler, a pattern of avoiding feelings of inadequacy and insignificance, rather than trying to overcome their source.

information processing: The step-by-step mental operations people use in tackling an intellectual task.

ingroup (we-group): A social unit that people either belong to or identify with.

inhibition: Avoidance of a particular action as a result of observing what happened to others.

insight therapy: A form of psychotherapy whose basic premise is that people must understand the causes of their behavior before they can alter it.

insomnia: Difficulty falling asleep or remaining asleep.

instrumental support: The financial aid, material resources, and needed services provided by others.

intelligence: A global capacity to understand the world, think rationally, and cope resourcefully with the challenges of life.

intelligence quotient (QUO-shent) (**IQ**): Originally, a measure of a person's mental development obtained by dividing his or her mental age (the score achieved on a standardized intelligence test) by his or her chronological age and multiplying by 100; now, any standardized measure of intelligence based on a scale in which 100 is defined to be average.

intensity: A measure of the height (amplitude) of light waves; the higher the intensity, the brighter the light.

interest test: An instrument designed to measure preferences for and attitudes toward certain activities.

interference: The recall of irrelevant items when searching for an item in long-term memory.

internal consistency: A characteristic of tests that exists if one divides the items on a test in half, scores each half separately, and finds the two scores to be approximately the same.

internalization: The wholehearted acceptance of an attitude, so that the attitude becomes an integral part of one's being.

interobserver reliability: A test criterion in which a score is the same no matter who grades the paper.

interval schedule: A schedule of reinforcement in which time must elapse before reinforcement is made available.

James-Lange theory: The belief that bodily changes trigger emotions, not vice versa.

job burnout: A job-related stress syndrome marked by boredom, apathy, reduced efficiency, fatigue, frustration, and sometimes even despair.

kin selection: Evolutionary processes that favor behaviors that contribute to the survival of one's relatives.

kinesthesis (kin-es-THEE-sis): The sense of movement and body position, acquired through receptors located in and near the muscles, tendons, and joints.

label: A shorthand epithet or descriptive word that seems to summarize the various traits.

language: A systematic arrangement of spoken and written symbols and rules for combining them in socially meaningful ways.

language acquisition device (**LAD**): The innate language-generating mechanism that Noam Chomsky speculates children are born with.

language of space: The methods that people employ for communicating to others their sense of territorial privacy.

latency stage: According to Freud, the stage at which sexual desires are pushed into the background and the child becomes involved in exploring the world and learning new skills.

latent (LAY-tent) **learning:** Learning that is not translated into performance until the organism is motivated to show what it has learned.

lateral geniculate body: An area of the thalamus that receives impulses from the optic nerve fibers.

lateral hypothalamus (hi-po-THAL-uh-muss) (**LH**): The part of the hypothalamus that is believed to produce hunger signals.

Law of Effect: Thorndike's formulation that the strength of a stimulus-response connection is increased when the response is followed by a satisfying state of affairs.

leadership: A process of influence between a leader and followers to attain social goals.

learned helplessness: A generalized expectancy that unpleasant events are independent of one's own responses.

lesion: Injured or damaged tissue in the brain.

life change: Any event that requires a modification in a person's accustomed way of living.

life review: The tendency of elderly people to look back on their lives and to reflect and reminisce about what has transpired.

linear perspective: A monocular cue to depth; for example, the parallel lines representing a railroad track seem to draw together as they approach the horizon.

lobes: The different regions into which the cerebral cortex is divided.

longitudinal (lon-jih-TOO-dih-null) **study:** A research method in which data on the same group of subjects are repeatedly gathered over a period of time for the purpose of studying consistencies and change.

long-term memory: Information storage that has unlimited capacity and lasts indefinitely.

LSD: An extremely potent psychedelic drug that produces hallucinations and distortions of perception and thought.

magnetic resonance (REZ-uh-nunce) **imaging** (**MRI**): A technique that uses magnetic fields and computer analysis to provide three-dimensional images of body tissue.

mania: A mood disorder in which people experience an extended "high."

marker: A sign of territorial defense; a "silent language" that includes symbols such as name plates, fences, and hedges.

maternal-infant bonding: The special attachment between human mothers and their children that forms in the first several hours after birth.

maturation: The internally programed growth of a child.

mean: The arithmetic average of all individual measurements in a distribution.

measure of central tendency: A statistic that locates the center of a distribution and thus summarizes the measurements in the distribution. The mean, the median, and the mode are measures of central tendency.

measure of variability: A measurement that shows how closely clustered or how widely spread a distribution of scores is.

median: The measurement above which and below which half the individual measurements fall in a distribution.

meditation: Focusing of attention on an image, thought, bodily process, or external object with the goal of clearing one's mind and producing an "inner peace."

memory: The ability to recall, recognize, or relearn previously practiced behaviors more rapidly than new behaviors.

memory trace: A set of information; the residue of an event that remains in memory after the event has vanished.

menarche (men-ARK): A woman's first menstrual period.

menopause: The stage of life between the ages of forty-seven and fifty-two, when a woman stops ovulating and menstruating and her production of sex hormones is sharply reduced.

metacognition (MEH-tuh-cog-NIH-shun): People's awareness and understanding of their mental states, abilities, memory, and processes of behavioral regulation.

minimum principle: Perceptual tendencies toward simplicity or economy.

Minnesota Multiphasic Personality Inventory (**MMPI**): Five hundred and fifty true-false-cannot say statements that constitute the most widely used and researched objective test of personality.

mnemonic (new-MON-ic) **devices:** Techniques that people use to help them remember things.

mode: The measurement that appears most frequently in a distribution.

modeling (observational learning, cognitive learning): The acquisition of new responses by watching other individuals, without first having to experience the response oneself.

motherese: A simplified, redundant, and highly grammatical form of language employed by parents in communicating with their young children.

motion parallax: The apparent movement of objects that occurs when you move your head from side to side or when you walk around.

motivation: Those inner states and processes that arouse, direct, and sustain activity.

motives: Drives and incentives.

motor cortex: The portion of the brain, located in the front of the somatosensory cortex, that controls body movement.

multiple personality: A rare dissociative disorder in which one person shows two or more separate consciousnesses with distinct personalities.

myelin (MY-eh-lin): A dense fatty coating that wraps around an axon and gives it electrical insulation.

narcolepsy (NAR-coh-lep-see): A condition in which its victim suddenly falls asleep while performing some activity, such as working, driving an automobile, making love, or engaging in sports, among others.

naturalistic observation: Studying phenomena as they occur in natural surroundings, without interference by the researcher.

need: Something that an organism requires if it is to survive or function in a reasonably healthy manner.

need for achievement (n-Ach): The pursuit of success in competition that is determined by some standard of excellence.

negative correlation: A correlation indicating that a high value for one variable corresponds to a low value for the other variable, and vice versa.

negative reinforcer: An aversive stimulus that when removed following a behavior strengthens the probability of the behavior's future occurrence.

negative skew: A graphic description of data that has a "tail" on the left side.

neurons (NEW-rons): The long, thin

cells that constitute the structural and functional unit of nerve tissue, along which messages travel to and from the brain.

neurotransmitters (new-roh-TRANS-mitt-ers): The chemicals released by neurons that determine the rate at which other neurons fire.

nondirected thinking: The free flow of images and ideas, occurring with no particular goal.

nonverbal communication: The gestures, postures, and facial expressions by which people transmit information, ideas, attitudes, and emotions to one another without the use of words.

normal curve: A graphic description of data that has a characteristic bell shape because more measurements fall in the middle than at the extremes.

norms: Standards of comparison for test results developed by giving the test to large, well-defined groups of people.

object permanence: A child's realization, developed between the ages of one and two, that an object exists even when he or she cannot see or touch it.

obsession: An uncontrollable and unwelcome pattern of thoughts.

obsessive-compulsive personality: A disorder characterized by the pervasiveness of inflexibility, perfectionism, stubbornness, frugality, and punctuality in daily activities.

occipital (ahk-SIH-pih-tull) **lobes:** The lobes located at the back of the brain that receive visual information.

Oedipal (EE-di-pull) **conflict:** According to Freud, a boy's wish to possess his mother sexually, coupled with hostility toward his father. Correspondingly, girls desire their fathers sexually and feel hostile toward their mothers. In order to reduce his or her fear of punishment from the same-sex parent, the child begins to identify with the parent of the same sex.

olfactory nerve: The nerve that carries information from the nose to the brain.

operant (AH-per-ant) **conditioning:** A type of learning in which the consequences of a behavior influence whether the organism will act (operate) in the same way in the future.

opponent process theory: The theory that motivation develops as a result of two opposing processes. For example, thrill seeking develops as terror is gradually replaced by its opponent process, exhilaration.

optic nerve: The nerve that carries information from the eye to the brain.

oral stage: According to Freud, the stage

at which infants associate erotic pleasure with the mouth.

organism: Carl Rogers's term for the whole person, including all of his or her feelings, thoughts, and urges as well as body.

osmoreceptors (OZ-moh-ree-SEP-ters): Receptors in the hypothalamus that monitor water and salt levels.

outgroup (they-group): A social unit that people either do not belong to or do not identify with.

panic disorder: A condition in which individuals experience sudden, intense attacks of fear, apprehension, or terror.

paraphilias: Psychosexual disorders that are associated with a preference for the use of a nonhuman object for sexual arousal, repetitive sexual activity with humans involving real or simulated suffering or humiliation, or repetitive sexual activity with nonconsenting or inappropriate partners.

paraprofessionals: Individuals who have not yet received formal or clinical training in a post-baccalaureate program.

parapsychologist: A person who makes a systematic study of ESP and other unusual phenomena.

parasympathetic nervous system: The system that works to conserve energy and enhance the body's ability to recuperate after strenuous activity.

parathyroid (pair-uh-THIGH-roid) **glands:** Four glands situated in the back tissues of the thyroid glands that monitor calcium levels in the bloodstream.

parietal (pa-RYE-eh-tull) **lobes:** The lobes located in the middle of the brain that contain the somatosensory cortex and integrate visual, auditory, and other sensory input.

partial reinforcement: A pattern in which an organism is only occasionally rewarded for providing the desired or correct response.

perception: The process by which one gives meaning to one's sensations.

perceptual constancy: The ability to perceive objects as relatively stable and unchanging.

perceptual inference: The process of assuming that certain objects remain the same and will function as they have in the past.

performance: What an organism does.

peripheral nervous system (PNS): A network of nerves branching out from the spinal cord that conducts information from the bodily organs to the central nervous system and takes information back to the organs.

personal front: One aspect of impression management that consists of the expressive equipment that one carries about to provide cues about one's identity and rank.

personality: The relatively unique and enduring set of psychological tendencies that a person reveals in the course of interacting with his or her environment.

personality disorder: A psychological disturbance characterized by lifelong maladaptive patterns that are relatively free of anxiety and other emotional symptoms.

personality psychology: A subfield of psychology that studies personality development and traits.

personality theory: An attempt to explain the observable continuities in a person's behavior despite the complexity and contradictions in the behavior.

persuasion: A deliberate attempt to influence attitudes and behavior through communication.

phallic (FAL-ic) stage: According to Freud, the stage at which children associate sexual pleasure with their genitals.

phenomenology: The view that each person's personality can best be understood by seeing the world through the person's own eyes.

phenotype (FEEN-oh-type): The observable characteristics of individuals (as distinct from their genotype).

phenylketonuria (PKU): A disorder caused by a defect in the gene involved with the body's use of a common protein. As a result the protein (phenylalanine) builds up in toxic quantities and contributes to mental retardation.

phobia: A form of severe anxiety in which a person focuses on a particular object or situation.

phonology: Rules for putting sounds together to form words.

pituitary (pih-TOO-ih-tare-ee) **gland:** The center of control of the endocrine system, which secretes a large number of hormones.

placebo (pluh-SEE-bo): Harmless sugar pill.

placebo (pluh-SEE-bo) **effect:** The influence that a patient's hopes and expectations have on his or her improvement.

poisoned partner effect: The product of associating a novel food with poisoning; seen in rats.

polygenic (pol-ee-JEAN-ic) **inheritance:** Traits that derive from the interaction of several genes.

polygraph: A machine used to measure physiological changes, particularly in lie detection.

population: The total group of subjects from which a sample is drawn.

positive correlation: A correlation indicating that a high value for one variable corresponds to a high value for the other variable.

positive reinforcer: A pleasant stimulus that when applied following a behavior strengthens the probability of the behavior's occurrence.

positive skew: A graphic description of data that has a "tail" on the right side.

positron (POS-ih-tron)**-emission-tomography (PET) scan:** A technique that permits the scanning of brain tissue. Individuals are injected with a radioactive form of glucose and the fuel consumption of the cells is tracked, yielding an image of brain activity.

posthypnotic amnesia: A procedure in which an individual is induced to "forget" particular events for a while, but the events can be recalled again later when the hypnotist provides the signal to do so.

posthypnotic suggestion: A procedure in which the hypnotist gives a person a command that he or she is to carry out at a later time.

practice: The repetition of a task, which helps to bind responses together.

pragmatics: Rules for the use of speech to communicate with others (such as taking turns and following the topic of conversation).

precognition: The ability to see or predict future events.

prejudice: A predetermined attitude toward the members of a gender, race, family, or other group simply because the individuals belong to it and without regard to their personal traits or qualities.

prenatal period: The time span between conception and birth.

primacy effect: The tendency to remember the information we first receive prior to recall.

primary reinforcer: A stimulus that does not require an organism to learn its reinforcing property; it is an event that has natural, intrinsic value for the organism.

principle of least effort: The tendency identified by Edward C. Tolman for organisms to choose the shortest route to a goal or the one requiring the least effort.

proactive interference: The tendency for material learned earlier to interfere with the learning of new material.

procedural (pro-SEE-dure-all) **memory:** The storage of "skills," knowledge associated with learned habits.

projection: The attribution to others of motives or traits that one senses within oneself but that would be too painful to acknowledge.

projective test: A test with no right or wrong answers—instead, answers are thought to reflect the subject's unconscious desires.

prosocial behavior: Helping responses that benefit other people.

prototype: A category that you mentally use to represent a loose set of features that seem to belong together.

proximity (prok-SIM-ih-tee): The distance from one another that individuals live or work.

psychoactive (SIGH-koh-AK-tiv) **drug:** A chemical substance that an individual employs to change his or her mood, feelings, or perceptions.

psychoanalysis: A form of therapy aimed at making patients aware of their unconscious motives so that they can gain control over their behavior and free themselves of self-defeating patterns.

psychodynamic therapy: A therapeutic approach that seeks to draw on patients' adaptive and creative abilities; predominantly face-to-face, active, supportive efforts to assist patients to strengthen their coping capacities.

psychoneuroimmunology: An interdisciplinary field of study concerned with the ties between psychological events and disease, and more particularly the links between emotions and the immune system.

psychokinesis (sigh-coh-kin-EE-sis): The ability to move objects through willpower without touching them.

psychological dependence: A condition in which individuals, although not physically hooked on a drug, experience a compulsive craving for it.

psychological needs: In Maslow's hierarchy-of-needs theory, an individual's need to belong and to give and receive love and to acquire esteem through his or her competence and achievement.

psychology: The study of behavior and mental processes.

psychophysics: The study of relationships between sensory experiences and the physical stimuli that cause them.

psychosexual disorders: Those sexual acts that people feel compelled to perform, that make them unhappy, or that cause physical or psychological harm to another person.

psychosomatic illness: A condition in which emotional problems produce real physical damage such as ulcers and high blood pressure.

psychotherapies: The use of

psychological means for the treatment of mental disorders.

puberty: Sexual maturation; the biological event that marks the end of childhood.

public distance: A distance (between twelve and twenty-five feet) from others from which it is difficult to carry on a personal conversation.

punishment: A consequence of behavior that decreases the likelihood that a response will occur again; punishment suppresses a behavior.

random sample: A sample that gives an equal chance of being represented to every individual within the scope of the research being conducted.

rapid-eye-movement (REM) sleep: The period of sleep during which the eyes dart back and forth and dreaming usually occurs.

ratio schedule: A schedule of reinforcement in which an organism must make a number of correct responses between reinforcements.

rational-emotive therapy (RET): A form of therapy aimed at changing unrealistic assumptions about oneself and other people. It is believed that once a person understands that he or she has been acting on false beliefs, self-defeating thoughts and behaviors will be avoided.

rationalization: The process by which individuals find a convincing reason for doing something that would otherwise be viewed as unacceptable.

reaction formation: The replacement of an unacceptable feeling or urge with its opposite.

recall: The type of memory retrieval in which a person reconstructs previously learned material.

recency effect: The tendency to remember the information we last received prior to recall.

receptors (ree-SEP-tors): Cells whose function it is to gather information and send messages to the brain.

recognition: The type of memory retrieval in which a person is required to pick out certain information from a group of items as the remembered material.

reconstruction: The process of bridging the gaps in memory with inferences about things that may have been true.

reference group: A social unit with which people identify.

referred pain: The sensation of pain in an area away from the actual source; most commonly experienced with internal pain.

reflex: A relatively simple, involuntary, and unlearned response to a stimulus.

regression: A return to an earlier stage of development or pattern of behavior in a threatening or stressful situation.

rehearsal: The process of mentally repeating something so as to remember it.

reinforcer: Any stimulus that follows a response and increases the probability that the response will occur again.

relearning: Learning the same material again on a later occasion. People need less time for relearning than for the initial learning; they have saved the information from earlier memory.

reliability: The ability of a test to give the same results under a variety of different circumstances.

replication: The duplication of research by another scientist with different subjects.

representational thought: The intellectual ability of a child to picture something in his or her mind.

repression: The exclusion from conscious awareness of a painful, unpleasant, or undesirable memory.

resistance: The reluctance of a patient to reveal painful feelings and to examine longstanding behavior patterns.

reticular (reh-TIH-cue-lar) **activating system:** The system in the brain that screens incoming messages, blocking out some signals and letting others pass.

reticular formation: A portion of the subcortex that controls an activating network of nerves that runs through the whole brain.

retinal (REH-tih-null) **disparity** (dis-PAIR-ih-tee): The difference between the images on the two retinas.

retrieval: The process by which information is regathered and brought back into awareness when needed.

reverse learning (unlearning): A function of dreaming in which the brain is cleansed of information the person has no need to remember.

rhodopsin: A reddish-purple substance in the rods of the eye that breaks down in the presence of light.

rods: Receptor cells in the retina that are sensitive to light, but not to color. Rods are particularly useful in night vision.

role taking: An important aspect of children's play that involves assuming adult roles, thus enabling the child to experience different points of view firsthand.

rooting reflex: An infant's response toward the source of touching that occurs anywhere around his or her mouth.

rule: A statement of the relationship between two or more concepts; the most complex unit of thought.

sample: A relatively small group out of the total population under study.

scheme (skeem): A knowledge framework or mental structure used in processing and organized information.

schizophrenic disorders: A group of serious disorders characterized by confused and disconnected thoughts, emotions, and perceptions.

school psychology: Working with children experiencing difficulty in school; consulting with parents and teachers; devising programs and materials for children with special needs.

secondary reinforcer: A neutral stimulus that, through constant association with primary reinforcers, acquires its own reinforcing properties.

selective attention: The ability to "tune in" certain sensory messages while "tuning out" others.

self: Carl Rogers's term for one's experience or image of oneself, developed through interaction with others.

self-actualization: The humanistic term for realizing one's unique potential.

self-actualizing needs: The top of Maslow's hierarchy of needs. These include the pursuit of knowledge and beauty, or whatever else is required for the realization of one's unique potential.

self-fulfilling prophecy: The process by which individuals act in such a way as to make their attitudes come true.

self-justification theory: The view that people have a need to see themselves as blameless and right.

self-perception theory: The use of much the same kinds of evidence and logic in reaching conclusions about oneself as are used in perceiving other people.

semantic (suh-MAN-tick) **memory:** The organized store of knowledge we have about the world; conceptual knowledge.

sensation: Awareness of sights, sounds, smells, tastes, and touches.

sensitive (critical) period: A short interval of time during which an organism is particularly susceptible to rapid learning.

sensitization: The positive adaptation to a stimulus in which acuity increases after exposure; for example, visual sensitivity becomes more acute in low light.

sensory storage: The momentary storage of sensory information at the level of the sensory receptors.

set: A habitual strategy or pattern of problem solving.

shaping: A procedure in which a desired behavior is broken down into successive steps that are taught one step at a time.

short-term memory: Memory that is limited in capacity to about seven items and in duration to about fifteen seconds.

signal-detection theory: The view that perception of an event varies across situations depending on a person's motivation, experience, and expectations.

similarity: A principle in perceptual grouping in which like elements are seen as belonging together.

simplicity: A principle in perceptual grouping that states that people find it easier to perceive simple patterns than they do complex patterns.

simulation model: A computer program that is designed to mirror human thinking.

single-blind experiment: A research technique in which the experimenter but not the subjects knows which subjects have been exposed to the experimental treatment.

situational test: A test that measures an individual's performance in terms of emotional, attitudinal, and behavioral responses to real-life situations.

skewed distribution: A graphic description of data on which measurements create a "tail" on one side.

social attraction: The process by which people are drawn together.

social cognition: How you think about your social experiences and how your social experiences influence your thinking.

social comparison theory: The idea that people seek to evaluate their opinions and abilities by comparison with others—preferably others close to their own opinion or ability.

social dilemma: A situation in which members of a group are faced with a conflict between maximizing their personal interest and maximizing the collective welfare.

social-emotional leader: A leader who tends to make encouraging remarks, to break tension with jokes, and to solicit the reactions of others.

social exchange theory: The view that people enter relationships with others much as they enter into economic transactions. They keep track of profits from a relationship and continue it so long as they find it beneficial.

social norm: A rule that specifies appropriate and inappropriate behavior.

social psychology: A subfield of psychology that studies groups and the way they influence individual behavior.

social relationship: A tie that endures long enough to afford a relatively stable set of expectations.

social support: The exchange of resources among individuals that derives from their interpersonal ties in networks, groups, and the larger community.

socialization: The process of learning the rules of behavior of the culture within which an individual is born and will live.

sociobiology: The study of the biological basis of social behavior.

sociogram (SO-see-oh-gram)**:** A diagram representing relationships within a group.

somatic (sew-MA-tic) **nervous system:** The half of the peripheral nervous system that controls voluntary movement of skeletal muscles.

somatoform disorder: A type of disturbance in which individuals exhibit physical symptoms for which there is no apparent organic cause.

somatosensory (sew-maa-tuh-SEN-so-ree) **cortex:** An area of the brain, within the cerebral cortex, that receives information from the skin and muscles.

source trait: An underlying root or cause of a surface trait.

species-typical behavior: Behavior that is characteristic of a particular animal species in particular environmental settings.

spinal cord: The bundle of nerves that runs down the length of the back and transmits most messages back and forth between the body and the brain.

spontaneous recovery: The reoccurrence of responses following an interval of time during which the responses had gradually died out.

standard deviation: A measure of how widely the measurements in a distribution are scattered above and below the mean.

state-dependent memory: Memory you acquired in one psychic state, which is easier to retrieve when you are in this same state than when you are in other psychic states.

statistics: Methods of summarizing a mass of information and making it more understandable.

stereopsis (stare-ee-OP-sis)**:** The use by the visual system of retinal disparity to give depth information—providing a three-dimensional appearance to the world.

stereotype: A set of unscientific beliefs about the people in a given category.

stimulant: A drug that acts on the brain and nervous system to increase the responsiveness of the body and to speed up its activities.

stimulus: A sensation that is capable of evoking a response.

stimulus discrimination: The ability of an organism to respond differently to two or more stimuli that are similar but distinct.

stimulus generalization: The ability of an organism to match novel sensory inputs with previously established similar information.

stirrup: One of the three bones of the middle ear, shaped like a stirrup.

storage (retention): The process by which information is retained until it is needed.

strategy: A specific method for approaching a problem.

stratified random sample: A stratified sample that includes a random sample of each stratum.

stratified sample: A sample that includes representatives of subgroups or variations of the population being studied.

stress: A process involving the recognition of and response to threat or danger.

subcortex: The part of the brain where all messages are first received and that, together with the spinal cord, controls and coordinates vital functions and reflex actions; sometimes called the "old brain."

subjective well-being: The mental assessments and feelings individuals have that their lives are pleasant.

sublimation: The process of redirecting sexual impulses into learning tasks that begins at about the age of five.

sucker effect: Because individuals do not want others to free ride on their contributions, they reduce their contributions to the group enterprise.

sucking reflex: An infant's response to having the soft palate of the mouth touched; it takes the form of a rapid burst of five to twenty-five sucks.

sudden death: A term applied to many forms of death. In most situations it encompasses a death that is totally unexpected as well as sudden.

superego: According to Sigmund Freud, the part of the personality that inhibits the socially undesirable impulses of the id. The superego may cause excessive guilt if it is overly harsh.

surface trait: A cluster of behaviors that tend to go together.

survey: A relatively large sampling of data, obtained through interviews, questionnaires, or a combination of the two.

symbol: An abstract unit of thought that represents an object, event, or quality.

sympathetic nervous system: The system that prepares the body for dealing with emergencies or strenuous activities.

synapses (SIN-aps-es): The gaps that occur between individual nerve cells.

syntax: Rules for putting words together to form sentences.

systematic desensitization: A process of gradually confronting patients with a fear-arousing stimulus after they have been trained to relax.

t-test: An estimation of the reliability of the difference between two means.

tardive dyskinesia: A neurological disorder associated with the use of antipsychotic drugs, manifested by grimaces and smacking together of lips.

task leader: A leader who tends to take over when it is time to convey information, give opinions, or suggest how things should be done.

telegraphic speech: The kind of speech used by young children. Words are left out, but the meaning is still clear.

telepathy (tel-LEH-puh-thee): The ability to read another person's thoughts or to transfer thoughts from one person to another.

temperament: Behavioral style; the aspects of personality that revolve around a person's pattern of activity, sociability, impulsiveness, and susceptibility to emotional stimulation.

temporal lobes: The lobes on each side of the brain that receive auditory information.

terrorism: The use of force or violence against persons or property to intimidate or coerce a government, an organization, or a civilian population in furtherance of political, religious, or social objectives.

testosterone (tes-TAHS-ter-own): A major male sex hormone.

test-retest reliability: A measure of whether an instrument consistently tests the same thing.

texture gradient: Any type of structural unit that is repeated over an entire surface.

thalamus (THAL-uh-muss): The portion of the brain that sorts incoming impulses and then directs them to various parts of the brain. It also relays messages from one part of the brain to another part.

thanatology: The study of dying and death.

Thematic Apperception Test (TAT): A projective test in which subjects are asked to make up stories to explain each picture in a series.

thinking: The process of changing and reorganizing the information stored in memory in order to create new information.

thyroid (THIGH-roid) **gland:** The gland in the endocrine system that produces several hormones, including thyroxin.

token economy: A form of conditioning in which desirable behavior is reinforced with tokens, which can be accumulated and exchanged for various rewards.

tolerance: A condition in which increasingly higher doses of a drug are required to produce effects that were previously produced by smaller doses.

top-down theory: We enjoy pleasures because we are happy, not vice versa.

totalism: Complete immersion in a group.

trait: A predisposition to respond in a certain way to different kinds of situations.

transduction: The translation of the energy in environmental stimuli into neural impulses.

transfer of learning: The effects of past learning on the ability to learn new tasks.

transference: The process, which is experienced by the patient, of feeling toward an analyst or therapist in the way that he or she felt toward some other important figure in his or her life.

transsexuals: People who have normal sexual organs but who psychologically feel like members of the opposite sex.

trichromatic (TRI-crow-MAA-tic) **theory:** The view that there are three types of cones and that each contains a different visual pigment.

Turner's syndrome: A chromosomal abnormality in some women caused by one less chromosome than normal and associated with short stature, lack of ovaries, and deficiency in female hormones.

tympanic membrane: The eardrum; the membrane separating the outer ear and the inner ear.

Type A behavior pattern: Behaviors that characterize individuals having a high incidence of cardiovascular problems. Type A's are hard-driving, competitive, ambitious, impatient, time-urgent, and easily angered when things go wrong.

Type B behavior pattern: Behaviors that characterize individuals having a low incidence of cardiovascular problems. Type B's follow a more relaxed,

easygoing life style.

unconditional positive regard: Carl Rogers's term for complete emotional support and complete acceptance of one person by another.

unconditioned response (UCR): In classical conditioning, an organism's automatic or natural reaction to an unconditioned stimulus.

unconditioned stimulus (UCS): A stimulus that elicits a certain response without previous training.

unconscious: According to Sigmund Freud, the part of the mind that contains material that a person is unaware of but that strongly influences his or her conscious processes and behaviors.

uplifts: Pleasant, happy, or satisfying psychological experiences. Compare **hassles.**

validity: The ability of a test to measure what it is intended to measure.

Valium: An anxiety-damper, sedative, muscle relaxant, and anticonvulsant minor tranquilizer that is one of the most frequently prescribed drugs in the United States today.

variable: In an experimental situation, any factor that is capable of change.

variable-interval schedule: A schedule of reinforcement in which varying amounts of time must elapse before a response will obtain reinforcement.

variable-ratio schedule: A schedule of reinforcement in which a variable number of responses are required before reinforcement can be obtained.

ventromedial hypothalamus (VMH): The part of the hypothalamus that is believed to produce feelings of fullness, as opposed to hunger, and to cause one to stop eating.

vestibular (ves-TIH-bew-lar) **system:** Three semicircular canals located in the inner ear and connected to the brain by the vestibular nerve. They regulate the sense of balance.

wavelength: The distance between the crest of one wave of light and the crest of the next, which determines color.

weapons effect: The idea that weapons themselves act as stimulants to violence; one of the factors influencing aggressive behavior, according to Berkowitz.

Weber's law: The principle that the larger or stronger a stimulus, the larger the change required for an observer to notice a difference.

References

Abbott, B. B., Scheen, L. S., and Badia, P. 1984. Predictable and unpredictable shock: Behavioral measures of aversion and physiological measures of stress. *Psychological Bulletin*, 96:45–71.

Abelson, R. P., and Levi, A. 1985. Decision making and decision theory. In Lindzey, G., and Aronson, E., Eds., *Handbook of Social Psychology*. Vol. 1. 3rd ed. New York: Random House.

Abramov, I., Gordon, J., Hendrickson, A., Hainline, I., Dobson, V., and LaBossiere, E. 1982. The retina of the newborn infant child. *Science*, 217:265–267.

Abramson, L. Y., Seligman, M. E. P., and Teasdale, J. D. 1978. Learned helplessness in humans: Critique and reformulation. *Journal of Abnormal Psychology*, 87:49–74.

Acredolo, L. P., and Hake, J. K. 1982. Infant perception. In Wolman, B. B., Ed., *Handbook of Developmental Psychology*. Englewood Cliffs, N.J.: Prentice-Hall.

Adams, D. B., Gold, A. R., and Burt, A. D. 1978. Rise in female-initiated sexual activity at ovulation and its suppression by oral contraceptives. *New England Journal of Medicine*, 299:1145–1150.

Adams, G. R., and Fitch, S. A. 1982. Ego stage and identity status development: A cross-sequential analysis. *Journal of Personality and Social Psychology*, 43:574–583.

Ader, R., and Cohen, N. 1981. Conditioned immunopharmacologic responses. In Ader, R., Ed., *Psychoneuroimmunology*. New York: Academic Press.

——— and ———. 1984. Behavior and the immune system. In Gentry, W. D., Ed., *Handbook of Behavioral Medicine*. New York: Guilford.

Adler, A. 1959. *What Life Should Mean to You*. New York: Putnam.

Adolph, E. F., Barker, J. P., and Hoy, P. A. 1954. Multiple factors in thirst. *American Journal of Physiology*, 178:538–562.

Ainslie, R. C., Ed. 1984. *The Child and the Day Care Setting: Qualitative Variations and Development*. New York: Praeger.

Ainsworth, M. D. S. 1984. Attachment. In Erdler, N. F., and McVhunt, J., Eds., *Personality and Behavior Disorders*. Vol. 1. 2nd ed. New York:

Wiley. Pp. 559–602.

———, Bell, S. M., and Stayton, D. J. 1974. Infant–mother attachment and social development. In Richards, M. P. M., Ed., *The Integration of a Child into a Social World*. Cambridge: Cambridge University Press.

Alba, J. W., and Hasher, L. 1983. Is memory schematic? *Psychological Bulletin*, 93:203–231.

Albee, G. W. 1982. Preventing psychopathology and promoting human potential. *American Psychologist*, 37:1043–1050.

———. 1985. The answer is prevention. *Psychology Today*, 19 (February): 60–62.

Alcock, J. E. 1981. *Parapsychology: Science or Magic? A Psychological Perspective*. Elmsford, N.Y.: Pergamon Press.

Alker, H. A. 1972. Is personality situationally specific or intrapsychically consistent? *Journal of Personality*, 40:1–16.

Allen, V. L., and Levine, J. M. 1971. Social support and conformity: The role of independent assessment of reality. *Journal of Experimental Social Psychology*. 7:48–58.

——— and Wilder, D. A. 1975. Categorization, belief similarity, and intergroup discrimination. *Journal of Personality and Social Psychology*, 32:971–977.

Allport, G. W. 1937. *Personality: A Psychological Interpretation*. New York: Holt.

———. 1954. *The Nature of Prejudice*. Reading, Mass.: Addison-Wesley.

———. 1961. *Pattern and Growth in Personality*. New York: Holt, Rinehart and Winston.

———. 1962. Prejudice: Is it societal or personal? *Journal of Social Issues*, 18:120–134.

———, Ed. 1965. *Letters from Jenny*. New York: Harcourt, Brace & World.

Alvarez, A. 1970. *The Savage God: A Study of Suicide*. New York: Random House.

Amabile, T. M. 1983. *The Social Psychology of Creativity*. New York: Springer.

Ambedkar, B. R. 1955. *Thoughts on Linguistic States*. Delhi, India: B. R. Ambedkar.

American Psychiatric Association. 1968. *Diagnostic and Statistical Manual of Mental Disorders (DSM-II)*. Washington, D.C.: American

Psychiatric Association.

———. 1980. *Diagnostic and Statistical Manual of Mental Disorders (DSM-III)*. Washington, D.C.: American Psychiatric Association.

———. 1983. APA statement on the insanity defense. *American Journal of Psychiatry*, 140:681–688.

Anderson, A. 1982. How the mind heals. *Psychology Today*, 16 (December): 51–56.

Anderson, J. R., and Bower, G. H. 1972. Recognition and retrieval processes in free recall. *Psychological Review*, 79:97–123.

Andison, F. S. 1977. TV violence and viewer aggression: A cumulation of study results 1956–1976. *Public Opinion Quarterly*, 41:314–331.

Angell, M. 1985. Disease as a reflection of the psyche. *New England Journal of Medicine*, 312:1570–1572.

Antill, J. K. 1983. Sex role complementarity versus similarity in married couples. *Journal of Personality and Social Psychology*, 45:145–155.

Antonovsky, A. 1979. *Health, Stress, and Coping*. San Francisco: Jossey-Bass.

Archer, D. 1985. Social deviance. In Lindzey, G., and Aronson, E., Eds., *Handbook of Social Psychology*. Vol. 2. 3rd ed. New York: Random House.

Archibald, H. C., Long, D. M., Miller, C., and Tuddenham, R. D. 1962. Gross stress reaction in combat: A 15-year follow-up. *American Journal of Psychiatry*, 119:317–322.

Arien, E. J., Gold, C., and Weigel, R. H. 1983. Dispositional and situational influences on dominance behavior in small groups. *Journal of Personality and Social Psychology*, 44:779–786.

Aronfreed, J., and Reber, A. 1965. Internalized behavior suppression and the timing of social punishment. *Journal of Personality and Social Psychology*, 1:3–16.

Aronson, E., Turner, J., and Carlsmith, M. 1963. Communicator credibility and communicator discrepancy as determinants of opinion change. *Journal of Abnormal and Social Psychology*, 67:31–36.

Asch, S. E. 1946. Forming impressions of personality. *Journal of Abnormal and Social Psychology*, 41:258–290.

———. 1952. *Social Psychology*. Englewood Cliffs, N.J.: Prentice-Hall.

———. 1956. Studies of independence and conformity: I. A minority of one against a unanimous majority. *Psychological Monographs*, 70:No. 416.

———, and Zukier, H. 1984. Thinking about persons. *Journal of Personality and Social Psychology*, 46:1230–1240.

Atchley, R. C. 1971. Retirement and work orientation. *Gerontologist*, 2:29–32.

Atkinson, R. C., and Shiffrin, R. M. 1968. Human memory: A proposed system and its control process. In Spence, K. W., and Spence, J. T., Eds., *The Psychology of Learning and Motivation*. Vol 2. New York: Academic Press.

——— and ———. 1971. The control of short-term memory. *Scientific American*, 224:82–90.

Attneave, F. 1954. Some information aspects of visual perception. *Psychological Review*, 61:182–193.

———. 1982. Pragnanz and sopa-bubble systems: A theoretical exploration. In Beck, J., Ed., *Organization and Representation in Perception*. Hillsdale, N.J.: Erlbaum.

Axelrod, S., and Apsche, J. 1982. *The Effects of Punishment on Human Behavior*. New York: Academic Press.

Axsom, D., and Cooper, J. 1985. Cognitive dissonance and psychotherapy: The role of effort justification in inducing weight loss. *Journal of Experimental Social Psychology*, 21:149–160.

Azrin, N. H., and Holz, W. C. 1966. Punishment. In Honig, W. K., Ed., *Operant Behavior: Areas of Research and Application*. New York: Appleton-Century-Crofts.

———, ———, and Hake, D. F. 1963. Fixed-ratio punishment. *Journal of the Experimental Analysis of Behavior*, 6:141–148.

Babad, E. Y., and Budoff, M. 1974. Sensitivity and validity of learning-potential measurement in three levels of ability. *Journal of Educational Psychology*, 66:439–447.

Bachman, J. G., O'Malley, P., and Johnston, J. 1978. *Youth in Transition*. Vol. 6: *Adolescence to Adulthood—Change and Stability in the Lives of Young Men*. Ann Arbor: Institute for Social Research, University of Michigan.

Bahrick, H. P., Bahrick, P. O., and Wittinger, R. P. 1974. Those unforgettable high school days. *Psychology Today*, 8 (December): 50–56.

Bales, J. 1984. Freedom, support boost creativity. *APA Monitor* (November):28.

Ball, D. W. 1966. An abortion clinic ethnography. *Social Problems*, 14:293–301.

Baltes, P. B., and Schaie, K. W. 1974. Aging and IQ: The myth of the twilight years. *Psychology Today*, 7 (March):35–40.

——— and Willis, S. L. 1977. Toward psychological theories of aging and development. In Birren, J. E., and Schaie, K. W., Eds., *Handbook on the Psychology of Aging*. New York: Van Nostrand.

Balthazard, C. G., and Woody, E. Z. 1985. The "stuff" of hypnotic performance: A review of psychometric approaches. *Psychological Bulletin*, 98:283–296.

Bandura, A. 1967. The role of modeling processes in personality development. In Hartup, W. W., and Smothergill, N. L., Eds., *The Young Child: A Review of Research*. Washington, D.C.: National Association for the Education of Young Children.

———. 1971. *Social Learning Theory*. Morristown, N.J.: General Learning Corporation.

———. 1973. *Aggression: A Social Learning Analysis*. Englewood Cliffs, N.J.: Prentice-Hall.

———. 1977. *Social Learning Theory*. Englewood Cliffs, N.J.: Prentice-Hall.

———. 1978. The self system in reciprocal determinism. *American Psychologist*, 33:344–358.

———, Grusec, J. E., and Menlove, F. L. 1967. Vicarious extinction of avoidance behavior. *Journal of Personality and Social Psychology*, 5:16–23.

——— and Menlove, F. L. 1968. Factors determining vicarious extinction of avoidance behavior through symbolic modeling. *Journal of Personality and Social Psychology*, 8:99–108.

——— and Rosenthal, T. L. 1966. Vicarious classical conditioning as a function of arousal level. *Journal of Personality and Social Psychology*, 3:54–62.

———, Ross, D., and Ross, S. 1963. Imitation of film-mediated aggressive models. *Journal of Abnormal and Social Psychology*, 63:575–582.

——— and Walters, R. M. 1963. *Social Learning and Personality Development*. New York: Holt, Rinehart and Winston.

Banks, M. H., and Jackson, P. R. 1982. Unemployment and risk of minor psychiatric disorder in young people: Cross-sectional and longitudinal evidence. *Psychological Medicine*, 12:789–798.

Barber, T. X. 1965. Measuring "hypnotic-like" suggestibility with and without "hypnotic induction": Psychometric properties, norms, and variables influencing response to the Barber Suggestibility Scale (BSS). *Psychological Reports*, 16:809–844.

———, Spanos, N. P., and Chaves, J. F. 1974. *Hypnosis, Imagination, and Human Potentialities*. New York: Pergamon.

Bard, P. 1934. On emotional expression after decortication with some remarks of certain theoretical views. *Psychological Review*, Part I, 41:309–329; Part II, 41:424–449.

Bardwick, J. 1971. *Psychology of Women: A Study of Bio-Cultural Conflicts*. New York: Harper & Row.

Bargh, J. A., and Pietromonaco, P. 1982. Automatic information processing and social perception: The influence of trait information presented outside of conscious awareness on impression formation. *Journal of Personality and Social Psychology*, 43:437–449.

Barkow, J. H. 1978. Culture and sociobiology. *American Anthropologist*, 80:5–20.

Barland, G. H., and Raskin, D. C. 1973. The detection of deception. In Prokasy, W. F., and Raskin, D. C., Eds., *Electrodermal Activity in Psychological Research*. New York: Academic Press.

Barlow, D. H., and Beck, J. G. 1983. The psychosocial treatment of anxiety disorders: Current status, future directions. In Williams, J. B. W., and Spitzer, R. L., Eds., *Psychotherapy Research: Where Are We and Where Should We Go?* New York: Guilford.

———, Vermilyea, J., Blanchard, E. B., Vermilyea, B. B., DiNardo, P. A., and Cerny, J. A. 1985. The phenomena of panic. *Journal of Abnormal Psychology*, 94:320–328.

Barnden, J. A. 1984. Diagrammatic short-term information-processing by neural mechanisms. *Cognition and Brain Theory*, 7:285–328.

Barnett, J. E., DiVesta, F. J., and Rogozinski, J. T. 1981. What is learned in note-taking? *Journal of Educational Psychology*, 73:181–192.

Baron, A. 1965. Delayed punishment of a runaway response. *Journal of Comparative Physiological Psychology*, 58:112–134.

Baron, M., Gruen, R., Kane, J., and Asnis, L. 1985. Modern research criteria and the genetics of schizophrenia. *American Journal of Psychiatry*, 142:697–701.

———, Levitt, M., Gruen, R., Kane, J., and Asnis, L. 1984. Platelet monoamine oxidase activity and genetic vulnerability to schizophrenia. *American Journal of Psychiatry*, 141:836–842.

Barrera, M. E., and Maurer, D. 1981a. Discrimination of strangers by the three-month-old. *Child Development*, 52:558–563.

——— and ———. 1981b. Recognition of mother's photographed face by the three-month-old infant. *Child Development*, 52:714–716.

Barron, F. 1969. *Creative Person and Creative Process*. New York: Holt, Rinehart and Winston.

Bartke, H., Steele, R. E., Musto, N., and Caldwell, B. V. 1973. Fluctuations in plasma testosterone levels in adult male rats and mice. *Endocrinology*, 92:1223–1228.

Bartoshuk, L. M. 1974. After-dinner talk: Taste illusions. *Annals of the New York Academy of Sciences*, 237:279–283.

———. 1980. Separate worlds of taste. *Psychology Today*, 14 (September): 48–56+.

Baruch, G., and Barnett, R. C. 1983. Adult daughters' relationships with their mothers. *Journal of Marriage and the Family*, 45:601–606.

Bateson, G., Jackson, D., Haley, J., and Weakland, J. 1956. Toward a theory of schizophrenia. *Behavioral Science*, 1:241–264.

Baum, A., Calesnick, I. E., Davis, G. E., and Gatchel, R. J. 1982. Individual differences in coping with crowding: Stimulus screening and social overload. *Journal of Personality and Social Psychology*, 43:821–830.

——— and Davis, G. E. 1980. Reducing the stress of high-density living: An architectural intervention. *Journal of Personality and Social Psychology*, 38:471–481.

Baumrind, D. 1964. Some thoughts on ethics of research: After Milgram's "Behavioral study of obedience." *American Psychologist*, 19:421–423.

———. 1985. Research using intentional deception: Ethical issues revisited. *American Psychologist*, 40:165–174.

Bayley, N. 1968. Behavioral correlates of mental growth: Birth to thirty-six years. *American Psychologist*, 23:1–17.

Beck, A. T. 1967. *Depression: Clinical, Experimental, and Theoretical Aspects*. New York: Harper & Row.

———. 1976. *Cognitive Therapy and the Emotional Disorders*. New York: International Universities Press.

———. 1977. A new, fast therapy for depression. *Psychology Today*, 10 (January):94–102.

Beck, S. H. 1982. Adjustment to and satisfaction with retirement. *Journal of Gerontology*, 37:616–624.

Becker, B. J. 1983. Item characteristics and sex differences on the SAT-M for mathematically able youth. Paper presented at Annual Meetings, American Educational Research Association, Montreal.

Becker, F. D. 1973. Study of spatial markers. *Journal of Personality and Social Psychology*, 26:439–445.

Becker, H. S. 1963. *Outsiders: Studies in the Sociology of Deviance*. New York: Free Press.

Beckman, R. A., and Fraser, L. 1985. Investigating gender differences. *Science 85*, 6 (June):14.

Beebe-Center, J. G. 1949. Standards for the use of Gust Scale. *Journal of Psychology*, 28:411–419.

Begleiter, H., Porjesz, B., Bihari, B., and Kissin, B. 1984. Event-related brain potentials in boys at risk for alcoholism. *Science*, 225:1493–1496.

Beiser, M., Shore, J. H., Peters, R., and Tatum, E. 1985. Does community care for the mentally ill make a difference? A tale of two cities. *American Journal of Psychiatry*, 142:1047–1052.

Békésy, G. von. 1957. The ear. *Scientific American*, 197 (February):66–78.

Bell, R. Q. 1968. A reinterpretation of effects in studies of socialization. *Psychological Review*, 75:81–95.

———. 1979. Parent, child, and reciprocal influences. *American Psychologist*, 34:821–826.

Bem, D. J. 1967. Self-perception: An alternative interpretation of cognitive dissonance phenomena. *Psychological Review*, 74:183–200.

———. 1972. Self-perception theory. In Berkowitz, L., Ed., *Advances in Experimental Social Psychology*. Vol. 6. New York: Academic Press.

———. 1983. Further *déjà vu* in the search for cross-situational consistency: A response to Mischel and Peake. *Psychological Review*, 90:390–393.

——— and Allen, A. 1974. On predicting some of the people some of the time: The search for cross-situational consistencies in behavior. *Psychological Review*, 81:506–520.

Benbow, C. P., and Stanley, J. C. 1980. Sex differences in mathematical ability: Fact or artifact? *Science*, 210:1262–1264.

Benet, S. 1974. *Abkhasians: The Long-Living People of the Caucasus*. New York: Holt, Rinehart and Winston.

Bennett, W., and Gurin, J. 1982. *The Dieter's Dilemma*. New York: Basic Books.

Benson, H. 1975. *The Relaxation Response*. New York: Avon.

———. 1977. Systemic hypertension and the relaxation response. *New England Journal of Medicine*, 296:1152–1156.

——— and Proctor, W. 1984. *Beyond the Relaxation Response*. New York: Times Books.

Bergin, A. E. 1971. The evaluation of therapeutic outcomes. In Bergin, A. E., and Garfield, S. L., Eds., *Handbook of Psychotherapy and Behavior Change: An Empirical Analysis*. New York: Wiley.

——— and Lambert, E. 1978. The evaluation of therapeutic outcome. In Garfield, S. L., and Bergin, A. E., Eds., *Handbook of Psychotherapy and Behavior Change*. 2nd ed. New York: Wiley.

Berkman, L. F., and Breslow, L. 1983. *Health and Ways of Living: The Alameda County Study*. New York: Oxford University Press.

Berkowitz, L. 1973. Words and symbols as stimuli to aggressive responses. In Knutson, J. F., Ed., *The Control of Aggression*. Chicago: Aldine.

———. 1981. How guns control us. *Psychology Today*, 15:11–12.

——— and Frodi, A. 1979. Reactions to a child's mistakes as affected by her/his looks and speech. *Social Psychology Quarterly*, 42:420–425.

Berlyne, D. E. 1960. *Conflict, Arousal, and Curiosity*. New York: McGraw-Hill.

Berman, J. S., Miller, R. C., and Massman, P. J. 1985. Cognitive therapy versus systematic desensitization: Is one treatment superior? *Psychological Bulletin*, 97:451–461.

——— and Norton, N. C. 1985. Does professional training make a therapist more effective? *Psychological Bulletin*, 98:401–407.

———, Read, S. J., and Kenny, D. A. 1983. Processing inconsistent social information. *Journal of Personality and Social Psychology*, 45:1211–1224.

Berndt, T. J. 1978. Children's conceptions of friendship and the behavior expected of friends. Paper presented at the annual meeting of the American Psychological Association, Toronto, August.

——— and Hoyle, S. G. 1985. Stability and change in childhood and adolescent friendships. *Developmental Psychology*, 21:1007–1015.

Berscheid, E. 1983. Emotion. In Kelley, H. H., Ed., *Close Relationships*. New York: W. F. Freeman.

———, Dion, K., Walster, E., and Walster, G. 1971. Physical attractiveness and dating choice: A test of the matching hypothesis. *Journal of Experimental Social Psychology*, 35:577–586.

—— and Peplau, L. A. 1983. The emerging science of relationships. In Kelley, H. H., Ed., *Close Relationships*. New York: W. H. Freeman.

—— and Walster, E. 1974. A little bit about love. In Huston, E. L., Ed., *Foundations of Interpersonal Attraction*. New York: Academic Press.

Biddle, B. J., Bank, B. J., and Marlin, M. M. 1980. Parental and peer influences on adolescents. *Social Forces*, 58:1057–1079.

Bierstedt, R. 1950. An analysis of social power. *American Sociological Review*, 15:730–738.

Billy, J. O. G., and Udry, J. R. 1985. Patterns of adolescent friendship and effects on sexual behavior. *Social Psychology Quarterly*, 48:27–41.

Binkley, S. 1979. A timekeeping enzyme in the pineal gland. *Scientific American*, 204 (April):66–71.

Bird, F., and Reimer, B. 1982. Participation rates in new religious movements and para-religious movements. *Journal for the Scientific Study of Religion*, 21:1–14.

Birren, J. E., and Schaie, K. W., Eds. 1977. *Handbook of the Psychology of Aging*. New York: Van Nostrand.

Bischof, L. J. 1976. *Adult Psychology*. 2nd ed. New York: Harper & Row.

Blakeslee, S. 1984. Scientists find key biological causes of alcoholism. *New York Times* (August 14):19, 22.

——. 1985. Clues hint at brain's two memory maps. *New York Times* (February 19):17, 20.

Blanck, P. D., Rosenthal, R., Snodgrass, S. E., DePaulo, B. M., and Zuckerman, M. 1981. Sex differences in eavesdropping on nonverbal cues: Developmental changes. *Journal of Personality and Social Psychology*, 41:391–396.

Blau, P. M. 1964. *Exchange and Power in Social Life*. New York: Wiley.

Blazer, D. G. 1982. Social support and mortality in an elderly community population. *American Journal of Epidemiology*, 115:684–694.

Bliss, J., and Bliss, E. 1985. *Prism: Andrea's World*. New York: Stein and Day.

Block, J. 1971. *Lives Through Time*. Berkeley, Calif.: Bancroft Books.

——. 1977. Advancing the psychology of personality: Paradigmatic shift or improving the quality of research. In Magnusson, D., and Endler, N. S., Eds., *Personality at the Crossroads: Current Issues in Interactional Psychology*. Hillsdale, N.J.: Erlbaum.

——. 1980. From infancy to adulthood: A clarification. *Child Development*, 51:622–623.

Bloom, F., Segal, D., Ling, N., and Guillemin, R. 1976. Endorphins: Profound behavioral effects in rats suggest new etiological factors in mental illness. *Science*, 194:630–632.

Blum, J. E., and Jarvik, L. F. 1974. Intellectual performance of octogenarians as a function of educational and initial ability. *Human Development*, 17:364–375.

Blumstein, P., and Schwartz, P. 1983. *American Couples*. New York: Morrow.

Blurton-Jones, N. G. 1984. A selfish origin for human food sharing: Tolerated theft. *Ethology and Sociobiology*, 5:1–3.

Blusztajn, J. K., and Wurtmow, R. J. 1983. Choline and cholinergic neurons. *Science*, 221:614–620.

Blyth, D. A., and Traeger, C. M. 1983. The self-concept and self-esteem of early adolescents. *Theory into Practice*, 22:91–97.

Boffey, P. M. 1984. Failure is found in the discharge of mentally ill. *New York Times* (September 13):1, 13.

Bolles, R. C. 1975. *Theory of Motivation*. 2nd ed. New York: Harper & Row.

Bolton, R. 1973. Aggression and hypoglycemia among the Qolla: A study in psychobiological anthropology. *Ethnology*, 12:227–257.

Bond, N. W. 1984. The poisoned partner effect in rats: Some parametric considerations. *Animal Learning and Behavior*, 12:89–96.

Bootzin, R. R. 1975. *Behavior Modification and Therapy: An Introduction*. Cambridge, Mass.: Winthrop.

Bornstein, M. A., Kessen, W., and Weiskopf, S. 1976. Color vision and hue categorization in young human infants. *Journal of Experimental Psychology: Human Perception and Performance*, 2:115–129.

Botwinick, J. 1967. *Cognitive Processes in Maturity and Old Age*. New York: Springer.

——. 1978. *Aging and Behavior*. New York: Springer.

Bower, G. H. 1975. Cognitive psychology: An introduction. In Estes, W. K., Ed., *Handbook of Learning and Cognitive Processes*. Vol. 1. New York: Wiley.

——. 1981. Mood and memory. *American Psychologist*, 36:129–148.

——, Black, J. B., and Turner, T. R. 1979. Scripts in memory for text. *Cognitive Psychology*, 11:177–221.

Bowers, K. S. 1973. Situationism in psychology: An analysis and critique.

Psychological Review, 81:506–520.

Bowlby, J. 1969. *Attachment*. New York: Basic Books.

Bowles, N. L., and Poon, L. W. 1985. Effects of priming in word retrieval. *Journal of Experimental Psychology: Learning, Memory, and Cognition*, 11:272–283.

Boyatzis, R. E. 1982. *The Competent Manager*. New York: Wiley.

Boyle, R. H., and Ames, W. 1983. Too many punches, too little concern. *Sports Illustrated* (April 11):44–67.

Brackbill, Y. 1971. Cumulative effects of continuous stimulation on arousal level in infants. *Child Development*, 42 (1971):17–26.

——, Adams, G., Crowell, D., and Gray, L. 1966. Arousal level in neonates and preschool children under continuous auditory stimulation. *Journal of Experimental Child Psychology*, 4:177–188.

—— and Koltsova, M. M. 1967. Conditioning and learning. In Brackbill, Y., Ed., *Infancy and Early Childhood*. New York: Free Press.

Bradbury, T. N., and Miller, G. A. 1985. Season of birth in schizophrenia: A review of evidence, methodology, and etiology. *Psychological Bulletin*, 98:569–594.

Bray, R. M., Johnson, D., and Chilstrom, J. T., Jr. 1982. Social influence by group members with minority opinions: A comparison of Hollander and Moscovici. *Journal of Personality and Social Psychology*, 43:78–88.

Brecher, J. 1983. Taking drugs on the job. *Newsweek* (August 22):52–60.

Breier, A., Charney, D. S., and Heninger, G. R. 1985. The diagnostic validity of anxiety disorders and their relationship to depressive illness. *American Journal of Psychiatry*, 142:787–797.

—— and Strauss, J. S. 1984. The role of social relationships in the recovery from psychotic disorders. *American Journal of Psychiatry*, 141:949–955.

Brenner, M. H. 1973. *Mental Illness and the Economy*. Cambridge, Mass.: Harvard University Press.

——. 1975. Trends in alcohol consumption and associated illnesses: Some effects of economic changes. *American Journal of Public Health*, 65:1279–1292.

——. 1976. Estimating the social costs of national economic policy: Implications for mental and physical health and criminal aggression. Paper No. 5., Report to the Congressional Research Service of the Library of Congress and Joint Committee of Congress. Washington, D.C.: U.S.

Government Printing Office.

Brickman, P., Coates, D., and Janoff-Bulman, R. 1978. Lottery winners and accident victims: Is happiness relative? *Journal of Personality and Social Psychology*, 36:917–927.

Bridgwater, C. A. 1985. Cancer: The psychosocial effects. *Psychology Today*, 19 (April):13.

Broad, W. J. 1983. Magician's effort to foil scientists raises questions. *New York Times* (February 15):19, 21.

———. 1984. Computer scientists stymied in their quest to match human vision. *New York Times* (September 25):19, 20.

Broadbent, D. E. 1963. Flow of information within the organism. *Journal of Verbal Learning and Verbal Behavior*, 2:34–39.

Brody, J. E. 1981a. Guide through maze of psychotherapies. *New York Times* (October 26):17, 20.

———. 1981b. Planning to prevent retirement "shock." *New York Times* (May 27):13.

———. 1983. Breaking a habit: Road to success is rocky. *New York Times* (February 23):17.

Brooks, A. 1981. When married children come home to live. *New York Times* (January 19):28.

———. 1985. Staying on at home of parents. *New York Times* (November 4):19.

Brooks-Gunn, J., and Petersen, A. C., Eds. 1983. *Girls at Puberty: Biological and Psychosocial Perspectives*. New York: Plenum.

——— and ———. 1984. Problems in studying and defining pubertal events. *Journal of Youth and Adolescence*, 13:181–196.

Browman, C. P., Sampson, M. G., Gujavarty, K. S., and Mitler, M. M. 1982. The drowsy crowd. *Psychology Today*, 16 (August):35–38.

Brown, A. L. 1982. Learning and development: The problems of compatibility, access and induction. *Human Development*, 25:89–115.

Brown, G. L., Ebert, M. H., Goyer, P. F., Jimerson, D. C., Klein, W. J., Bunney, W. E., and Goodwin, F. K. 1982. Aggression, suicide, and serotonin: Relationships to CSF amine metabolites. *American Journal of Psychiatry*, 139:741–746.

Brown, G. W., Birley, J. L. T., and Wing, J. K. 1972. Influence of family life on the course of schizophrenic disorders: A replication. *British Journal of Psychiatry*, 121:241–258.

Brown, J. 1958. Some tests of the decay theory of immediate memory. *Quarterly Journal of Experimental Psychology*, 10:12–21.

Brown, R. A. 1973. *A First Language: The Early Stages*. Cambridge, Mass.: Harvard University Press.

Brown, R. W., and McNeill, D. 1966. The "tip-of-the-tongue" phenomenon. *Journal of Verbal Learning and Verbal Behavior*, 5:325–337.

Brown, W. A., Monti, P. M., and Corriveau, D. P. 1978. Serum testosterone and sexual activity and interest in men. *Archives of Sexual Behavior*, 7:97–102.

Brozan, N. 1985a. U.S. leads industrialized nations in teen-age births and abortions. *New York Times* (March 13):1, 22.

———. 1985b. Women and cocaine: A growing problem. *New York Times* (February 18):18.

Brunjes, P. C. 1985. A stereological study of neocortical maturation in the precocial mouse, *Acomys cahirinus*. *Developmental Brain Research*, 19:279–287.

Brush, F. R., Baron, S., Froehlich, J. C., Ison, J. R., Pellegrino, L. J., Phillips, D. S., Sakellaris, P. C., and Williams, V. N. 1985. Genetic differences in avoidance learning by *Rattus norvegicus*: Escape/avoidance responding, sensitivity to electric shock, discrimination learning, and open-field behavior. *Journal of Comparative Psychology*, 99:60–73.

Buckhout, R. 1974. Eyewitness testimony. *Scientific American*, 231 (December):23–31.

Budzynski, T. H., et al. 1973. EMG biofeedback and tension headache: A controlled outcome study. *Psychosomatic Medicine*, 35:481–496.

Bullen, B. A., Skrinar, G. S., Beitins, I. Z., von Mering, G., Turnbull, B. A., and McArthur, J. W. 1985. Induction of menstrual disorders by strenuous exercise in untrained women. *New England Journal of Medicine*, 312:1349–1353.

Burghardt, G. M. 1985. Animal awareness: Current perceptions and historical perspective. *American Psychologist*, 40:905–919.

Burke, D. M., and Light, L. L. 1981. Memory and aging: The role of the retrieval process. *Psychological Bulletin*, 90:513–546.

Buss, D. M. 1984. Evolutionary biology and personality psychology. *American Psychologist*, 39:1135–1147.

——— and Craik, K. H. 1983a. The act frequency approach to personality. *Psychological Review*, 90:105–126.

——— and ———. 1983b. The dispositional analysis of everyday conduct. *Journal of Personality*, 51:393–412.

Buss, H. A., and Plomin, R. 1975. *A Temperament Theory of Personality Development*. New York: Wiley.

Butler, R. N. 1963. The life review: An interpretation of reminiscence in the aged. *Psychiatry*, 26:65–76.

———. 1971. The life review. *Psychology Today*, 5 (December):49–51+.

Butterfield, E. C., and Siperstein, G. N. 1972. Influences of contingent auditory stimulation upon nonnutritional sucking. In Bosma, J., Ed., *Oral Sensation and Perception: The Mouth of the Infant*. Springfield, Ill.: Thomas.

Byrne, D. 1971. *The Attraction Paradigm*. New York: Academic Press.

Cabanac, M. 1971. Physiological role of pleasure. *Science*, 173:1103–1107.

Cacioppo, J. T., Petty, R. E., and Morris, K. J. 1983. Effects of need for cognition on message evaluation, recall, and persuasion. *Journal of Personality and Social Psychology*, 45:805–818.

Calhoun, J. B. 1962. Population density and social pathology. *Scientific American*, 206:139–146.

Camp, D. S., Raymond, G. A., and Church, R. A. 1967. Temporal relationship between response and punishment. *Journal of Experimental Psychology*, 74:114–123.

Campbell, A. 1981. *The Sense of Well-Being in America: Recent Patterns and Trends*. New York: McGraw-Hill.

———, Converse, P. E., and Rodgers, W. L. 1976. *The Quality of American Life: Perceptions, Evaluations, and Satisfactions*. New York: Russell Sage.

Campbell, D. P. 1974. *Manual for the Strong-Campbell Interest Inventory T 325 (Merged Form)*. Stanford, Calif.: Stanford University Press.

Cannon, W. B. 1929. *Bodily Changes in Pain, Hunger, Fear and Rage*. New York: Appleton-Century-Crofts.

———. 1932. *The Wisdom of the Body*. New York: Norton.

———. 1942. Voodoo death. *American Anthropologist*, 44:169–181.

——— and Washburn, A. L. 1912. An explanation of hunger. *American Journal of Physiology*, 29:441–454.

Cantor, N., and Mischel, W. 1979. Prototypes in person perception. In Berkowitz, L., Ed., *Advances in Experimental Social Psychology*, 12:3–52.

Caplan, F., and Caplan, T. 1973. *The Power of Play*. Garden City, N.Y.: Anchor Books.

Caplan, P. J. 1984. The myth of women's masochism. *American Psychologist*, 39:130–139.

————, MacPherson, G. M., and Tobin, P. 1985. Do sex-related differences in spatial abilities exist? *American Psychologist*, 40:786–799.

Caplan, R. D., Cobb, S., French, J. R. P., Jr., Harrison, R. V., and Pinneau, S. R., Jr. 1975. Job demands and worker health. HEW Publication No. NIOSH-75-160. Washington, D.C.: U.S. Government Printing Office.

Caplow, T., Bahr, H. M., Chadwick, B. A., Hill, R., and Williamson, M. H. 1982. *Middletown Families: Fifty Years of Change and Continuity*. Minneapolis: University of Minnesota Press.

Caporael, L. R. 1981. The paralanguage of caregiving. *Journal of Personality and Social Psychology*, 40:876–884.

Carlson, N. R. 1977. *Physiology and Behavior*. Boston: Allyn and Bacon.

Carlson, R. A., and Dulany, D. E. 1985. Conscious attention and abstraction in concept learning. *Journal of Experimental Psychology: Learning, Memory, and Cognition*, 11:45–58.

Carlsson, A. 1978. Antipsychotic drugs, neurotransmitters, and schizophrenia. *American Journal of Psychiatry*, 135:164–173.

Carpenter, E. 1985. Conditioning: It's the thought that counts. *Psychology Today*, 19 (May):8–10.

Carrier, C. A., and Titus, A. 1979. The effects of notetaking: A review of studies. *Contemporary Educational Psychology*, 4:299–314.

Carter, J. F., and Van Matre, N. H. 1975. Note-taking versus note having. *Journal of Educational Psychology*, 67:900–904.

Cartwright, D., and Zander, A. 1968. *Group Dynamics: Research and Theory*. 3rd ed. New York: Harper & Row.

Cartwright, R. D. 1978. Happy endings for our dreams. *Psychology Today*, 12 (December):66–76.

Carver, C. S., and Humphries, C. 1981. Havana day-dreaming: A study of self-consciousness and the negative reference group among Cuban Americans. *Journal of Personality and Social Psychology*, 40:545–552.

Cash, T. F., and Janda, L. H. 1984. The eye of the beholder. *Psychology Today*, 18:46–52.

————, Kehr, J., Polyson, J., and Freeman, V. 1977. Role of physical attractiveness in peer attribution of psychological disturbance. *Journal of Counseling Psychology*, 45:987–993.

Cassileth, B. R., Lusk, E. J., Miller, D. S., Brown, L. L., and Miller, C. 1985. Psychosocial correlates of survival in advanced malignant disease. *New England Journal of Medicine*, 312:1551–1555.

Catalano, R., and Dooley, D. 1983. Health effects of economic instability: A test of economic stress hypothesis. *Journal of Health and Social Behavior*, 24:46–60.

Catania, A. C. 1979. *Learning*. Englewood Cliffs, N.J.: Prentice-Hall.

Cattell, R. B. 1965. *The Scientific Analysis of Personality*. Baltimore: Penguin.

————. 1983. *Structural Personality-Learning Theory*. New York: Praeger.

Cautela, J. R. 1966. Treatment of compulsive behavior by covert sensitization. *Psychological Record*, 16:33–41.

————. 1967. Covert sensitization. *Psychological Reports*, 20:459–468.

————. 1973. Covert processes and behavior modification. *Journal of Nervous and Mental Disease*, 157:27–36.

Cavalli-Sforza, L. L., and Feldman, M. W. 1981. *Cultural Transmission and Evolution: A Quantitative Approach*. Princeton, N.J.: Princeton University Press.

Cerella, J. 1985. Information processing rates in the elderly. *Psychological Bulletin*, 98:67–83.

Cernoch, J. M., and Porter, R. H. 1985. Recognition of maternal axillary odors by infants. *Child Development*, 56:1593–1598.

Chance, P. 1976. Telepathy could be real. *Psychology Today*, 9 (February):40–44, 65.

Chapman, L., and Chapman, J. 1973. *Disordered Thought in Schizophrenia*. Englewood Cliffs, N.J.: Prentice-Hall.

Chapman, R. M., McCrary, J. W., Chapman, J. A., and Martin, J. K. 1980. Behavioral and neural analyses of connotative meaning: Word classes and rating scales. *Brain and Language*, 11:319–339.

Chass, M. 1985. Hernandez of the Mets tells jury of his experiences with cocaine. *New York Times* (September 7):1, 17.

Chemers, M. M., Hays, R. B., Rhodewalt, F., and Wysocki, J. 1985. A person-environment analysis of job stress: A contingency model explanation. *Journal of Personality and Social Psychology*, 49:628–635.

Cherlin, A. 1983. Changing family and household: Contemporary lessons from historical research. *Annual Review of Sociology*, 9:51–66.

Cherry, L., and Cherry, R. 1985. Another way of looking at the brain. *New York Times Magazine* (June 9):56+.

Child, I. L. 1985. Psychology and anomalous observations: The question of ESP in dreams. *American Psychologist*, 40:1219–1230.

Chomsky, N. 1965. *Aspects of a Theory of Syntax*. Cambridge, Mass.: MIT Press.

————. 1968. *Language and Mind*. New York: Harcourt Brace Jovanovich.

————. 1975. *Reflections on Language*. New York: Pantheon.

Christian, J. J. 1963. The pathology of overpopulation. *Military Medicine*, 128:571–603.

Chukovsky, K. 1963. *From Two to Five*. Berkeley: University of California Press.

Cicirelli, V. G. 1981. *Helping Elderly Parents: The Role of Adult Children*. Boston: Auburn House.

Clark, R. D., III, and Word, L. E. 1972. Why don't bystanders help? Because of ambiguity? *Journal of Personality and Social Psychology*, 24:392–400.

Clarke-Stewart, K. A. 1973. Interactions between mothers and their young children: Characteristics and consequences. *Monographs of the Society for Research in Child Development*, 38:6–7, Serial No. 153.

Clemens, A. W., and Axelson, L. J. 1985. The not-so-empty nest: The return of the fledgling adult. *Family Relations*, 34:259–264.

Clifford, M. M., and Walster, E. 1973. The effect of physical attractiveness on teacher expectation. *Sociology of Education*, 46:248–258.

Coale, A. J. 1973. The demographic transition reconsidered. In *International Population Conference*, Liége.

Cockerham, W. C., and Cohen, L. E. 1980. Obedience to orders: Issues of morality and legality in combat among U.S. army paratroopers. *Social Forces*, 58:1272–1288.

Cohen, E. L., and Wurtman, R. J. 1976. Brain acetylcholine: Control by dietary choline. *Science*, 191:561–562.

Cohen, H., and Filipczak, J. 1971. *A New Learning Environment*. San Francisco: Jossey-Bass.

Cohen, J. 1983. Peer influence on college aspirations with initial aspirations controlled. *American Sociological Review*, 48:728–734.

Cohen, L. B. 1979. Our developing knowledge of infant perception and cognition. *American Psychologist*, 34:894–899.

———— and Menten, T. G. 1981. The rise and fall of infant habituation. *Infant Behavior and Development*, 4:269–280.

Cohen, S. 1978. Environmental load and

the allocation of attention. In Baum, A., Singer, J., and Valines, S., Eds., *Advances in Environmental Psychology.* Vol. 1. Hillsdale, N.J.: Erlbaum.

———— and McKay, G. 1984. Social support, stress and the buffering hypothesis: A review of naturalistic studies. In Baum, A., Singer, J. E., and Taylor, S. E., Eds., *Handbook of Psychology and Health.* Vol. 4. Hillsdale, N.J.: Erlbaum.

———— and Wills, T. A. 1985. Stress, social support, and the buffering hypothesis. *Psychological Bulletin,* 98:310–357.

Cole, M., Gay, J., Glick, J., and Sharp, D. 1971. *The Cultural Context of Learning and Thinking.* New York: Basic Books.

Coleman, L. M., and Antonucci, T. C. 1983. Impact of work on women at midlife. *Developmental Psychology,* 19:290–294.

Coles, R., and Stokes, G. 1985. *Sex and the American Teenager.* New York: Harper & Row/Rolling Stone Press.

Collins, G. 1985. More corporations are offering child care. *New York Times* (June 21):25.

Columbus (Ohio) Dispatch. 1979. Shah's cancer seems to underscore possible link between stress, disease. *Columbus (Ohio) Dispatch* (October 28):A-8.

Commons, M. L., Richards, F. A., and Kuhn, D. 1982. Systematic and metasystematic reasoning: A case for levels of reasoning beyond Piaget's stage of formal operations. *Child Development,* 53:1058–1069.

Condry, J., and Dyer, S. 1976. Fear of success: Attribution of cause to the victim. *Journal of Social Issues,* 32:63–83.

Conley, J. J. 1985. Longitudinal stability of personality traits: A multitrait-multimethod-multioccasion analysis. *Journal of Personality and Social Psychology,* 49:1266–1282.

Conrad, M., Harth, E., Holland, J., Martinez, H., Pattee, H., Rada, R., Waltz, D., and Zeigler, B. 1984. Natural and artificial intelligence. *Cognition and Brain Theory,* 7:89–104.

Conte, H. R., Weiner, M. B., and Plutchik, R. 1982. Measuring death anxiety: Conceptual, psychometric, and factor-analytic aspects. *Journal of Personality and Social Psychology,* 43:775–785.

Cooke, P. 1984. For whom the bell tolls. *Science 84,* 5 (December):88–89.

Cooper, A. M. 1985. Will neurobiology influence psychoanalysis? *American Journal of Psychiatry,* 142:1395–1402.

Cooper, C. L., and Payne, R., Eds. 1978. *Stress at Work.* New York: Wiley.

Cooper, L. A., and Shepard, R. N. 1984. Turning something over in mind. *Scientific American,* 251 (December):106–114.

Corballis, M. C. 1983. *Human Laterality.* New York: Academic Press.

Cordes, C. 1985a. Chemical cruise steers emotions. *APA Monitor,* 16 (September):18.

————. 1985b. A step back. *APA Monitor* (April):12–14.

Cornell, J. 1984. Science vs. the paranormal. *Psychology Today,* 18 (March):28–31+.

Coryell, W., Endicott, J., Andreasen, N., Keller, M. 1985. Bipolar I, bipolar II, and nonbipolar major depression among the relatives of affectively ill probands. *American Journal of Psychiatry,* 142:817–821.

Costa, P. T., Jr., and McCrae, R. R. 1980. Still stable after all these years: Personality as a key to some issues in adulthood and old age. In Baltes, P. B., and Brim, O. G., Jr., Eds., *Life-Span Development and Behavior.* Vol. 3. New York: Academic Press.

————, ————, and Arenberg, D. 1980. Enduring dispositions in adult males. *Journal of Personality and Social Psychology,* 38:793–800.

Coughlin, E. K. 1985. Is violence on TV harmful to our health? Some scholars, a vocal minority, say no. *The Chronicle of Higher Education* (March 13):5, 8.

Cousins, N. 1979. *Anatomy of an Illness.* New York: Norton.

Cowan, N. 1984. On short and long auditory stores. *Psychological Bulletin,* 96:341–370.

Cox, M. 1984. Abuse of narcotics in U.S. is by no means a recent phenomenon. *Wall Street Journal* (December 3): 1, 24.

Craighead, W. E., Kazdin, A. E., and Mahoney, M. J. 1976. *Behavior Modification: Principles, Issues, Applications.* Boston: Houghton Mifflin.

Craik, F. I. M. 1977. Age differences in human memory. In Birren, J. E., and Schaie, K. W., Eds., *Handbook of the Psychology of Aging.* New York: Van Nostrand.

Cratty, B. J. 1970. *Perceptual and Motor Development in Infants and Children.* New York: Macmillan.

Crittenden, A. 1983. New insights into infancy. *New York Times Magazine* (November 20):84+.

Cromer, J. 1984. *The Mood of American Youth.* Washington, D.C.: National Association of Secondary School Principals.

Cronbach, L. J. 1984. *Essentials of Psychological Testing.* 4th ed. New York: Harper & Row.

Crosby, F. 1982. *Relative Deprivation and Working Women.* New York: Oxford University Press.

Crossom, B. 1984. Role of the dominant thalamus in language: A review. *Psychological Bulletin,* 96:491–517.

Crouse, J. 1985. Does the SAT help colleges make better selection decisions? *Harvard Educational Review,* 55:195–219.

Crowder, R. G. 1981. Contributions of experimental and cognitive psychology to clinical psychology. Paper presented at American Psychological Association symposium, Los Angeles, August 26.

Crowe, R. R. 1984. Electroconvulsive therapy—A current perspective. *New England Journal of Medicine,* 311: 163–167.

————, Pauls, D. L., Slymen, D. J., and Noyes, R. 1980. A genetic study of anxiety neurosis. *Archives of General Psychiatry,* 37:77–79.

Cszikszentmihalyi, M., and Larson, R. 1984. *Being Adolescent; Conflict and Growth in the Teen-Age Years.* New York: Basic Books.

Cunningham, C. E., Siegel, L. S., van der Spay, H. I. J., Clark, N. L., and Bow, S. J. 1985. The behavioral and linguistic interactions of specifically language-delayed and normal boys with their mothers. *Child Development,* 56:1389–1403.

Cunningham, S. 1984a. The new terrorism: Devotion or deviancy? *APA Monitor* (March):1, 14.

————. 1984b. Genovese: 20 years later, few heed a stranger's cries. *APA Monitor* (May):30.

Curtiss, S. 1977. *Genie: A Psycholinguistic Study of a Modern Day "Wild Child."* New York: Academic Press.

Dacey, J. S. 1982. *Adult Development.* Glenview, Ill.: Scott, Foresman.

Dahlstrom, W. G., and Welsh, G. S. 1960. *An MMPI Handbook: A Guide to Use in Clinical Practice and Research.* Minneapolis: University of Minnesota Press.

Dalessio, D. J., Kunzel, M., Sternbach, R., and Sovak, M. 1979. Conditioned adaptation-relaxation reflex in migraine therapy. *Journal of the American Medical Association,* 242:2102–2104.

Darley, J. M., and Gilbert, D. T. 1985. Social psychological aspects of environmental psychology. In Lindzey, G., and Aronson, E., Eds., *Handbook of Social Psychology.* Vol. 2. 3rd ed. New York: Random House.

———— and Latané, B. 1968. Bystander intervention in emergencies:

Diffusion of responsibility. *Journal of Personality and Social Psychology*, 8:377–383.

Darley, S. A. 1976. Big-time careers for the little woman: A dual-role dilemma. *Journal of Social Issues*, 32:85–98.

Darwin, C. 1872. *The Expression of Emotions in Man and Animals*. Chicago: University of Chicago Press. Republished 1967.

Davidson, J., and Lang, J. S. 1984. Vietnam's sad legacy: Vets living in the wild. *U.S. News & World Report*, (March 12):38–39.

Davidson, R. 1984. *Emotion, Cognition, and Behavior*. New York: Cambridge University Press.

Davies, M., and Kandel, D. B. 1981. Parental and peer influences on adolescents' educational plans: Some further evidence. *American Journal of Sociology*, 87:363–387.

Davis, G. A. 1973. *Psychology of Problem Solving*. New York: Basic Books.

Davis, J. M., Schaffer, C. B., Killian, G. A., Kinard, C., and Chan, C. 1980. Important issues in the drug treatment of schizophrenia. In *Special Report: Schizophrenia 1980*. Washington, D.C.: U.S. Government Printing Office.

Davis, K. 1949. *Human Society*. New York: Macmillan.

———. 1976. The world's population crisis. In Merton, R. K., and Nisbett, R., Eds., *Contemporary Social Problems*. New York: Harcourt Brace Jovanovich.

Davis, K. E. 1985. Near and dear: Friendship and love compared. *Psychology Today*, 19 (February): 22–30.

Deaux, K., and Lewis, L. L. 1984. Structure of gender stereotypes: Interrelationships among components and gender labels. *Journal of Personality and Social Psychology*, 46:991–1004.

——— and Wrightsman, L. S. 1984. *Social Psychology in the 80s*. 4th ed. Monterey, Calif.: Brooks/Cole.

deBono, E. 1967. *New Think: The Use of Lateral Thinking in the Generation of New Ideas*. New York: Basic Books.

DeCasper, A. J., and Fifer, W. P. 1980. Of human bonding: Newborns prefer their mother's voice. *Science*, 208:1174–1176.

——— and Sigafoos, A. D. 1983. The intrauterine heartbeat: A potent reinforcer for newborns. *Infant Behavior and Development*, 6:19–25.

Deikman, A. J. 1963. Experimental meditation. *Journal of Nervous and Mental Disease*, 136:329–373.

DeLongis, A., Coyne, J. C., Dakof, G.,

Folkman, S., and Lazarus, R. S. 1982. Relationship of daily hassles, uplifts, and major life events to health status. *Health Psychology*, 1:119–136.

DeLuise, M., Blackburn, G. L., and Flier, J. S. 1980. Reduced activity of the red-cell sodium-potassium pump in human obesity. *New England Journal of Medicine*, 303:1017–1022.

Dembroski, M., and MacDougall, J. M. 1985. Beyond gloabal Type A: Relation of paralinguistic attributes, hostility, and anger-in in coronary heart disease. In Field, T., McCabe, P., and Schneiderman, N., Eds., *Stress and Coping*. Hillsdale, N.J.: Erlbaum.

Dennis, W. 1966. Creative productivity between the ages of twenty and eighty years. *Journal of Gerontology*, 21:1–8.

———. 1973. *Children of the Crèche*. New York: Appleton-Century-Crofts.

——— and Dennis, M. G. 1951. Development under controlled conditions. In Dennis, W., Ed., *Readings in Child Psychology*. Englewood Cliffs, N.J.: Prentice-Hall.

Dermer, M., and Thiel, D. L. 1975. When beauty may fail. *Journal of Personality and Social Psychology*, 31:1168–1176.

Desor, J. A. 1972. Toward a psychological theory of crowding. *Journal of Personality and Social Psychology*, 21:79–83.

DeStefano, A. M. 1985. Undercover jobs carry big psychological risk after the assignments. *Wall Street Journal* (November 4):1, 12

de Villiers, P. A., and de Villiers, J. G. 1979. *Early Language*. Cambridge, Mass.: Harvard University Press.

Diaconis, P. 1978. Statistical problems in ESP research. *Science*, 201:131–136.

Diener, C. I., and Dweck, C. S. 1978. An analysis of learned helplessness: Continuous changes in performance, strategy, and achievement cognitions following failure. *Journal of Personality and Social Psychology*, 36:451–462.

——— and ———. 1980. An analysis of learned helplessness: II. The processing of success. *Journal of Personality and Social Psychology*, 39:940–952.

Diener, E. 1984. Subjective well-being. *Psychological Bulletin*, 95:542–575.

———, Larsen, R. J., and Emmons, R. A. 1984. Person X situation interactions: Choice of situations and congruence response models. *Journal of Personality and Social Psychology*, 47:580–592.

Dimsdale, J. E. 1977. Emotional causes of sudden death. *American Journal of*

Psychiatry, 134:1361–1366.

Dintiman, G., and Greenberg, J. 1986. *Health Through Discovery*. New York: Random House.

Dion, K. 1972. Physical attractiveness and evaluations of children's transgressions. *Journal of Personality and Social Psychology*, 24:207–213.

———. 1974. Children's physical attractiveness and sex as determinants of adult punitiveness. *Developmental Psychology*, 10:772–778.

———, Berscheid, E., and Walster, E. 1972. What is beautiful is good. *Journal of Personality and Social Psychology*, 24:285–290.

Dobzhansky, T. 1973. *Genetic Diversity and Human Equality*. New York: Basic Books.

Dohrenwend, B. P., and Shrout, P. E. 1985. "Hassles" in the conceptualization and measurement of life stress variables. *American Psychologist*, 40:780–785.

Dohrenwend, B. S., Dohrenwend, B. P., Dodson, M., and Shrout, P. E. 1984. Symptoms, hassles, social supports, and life events: Problem of confounded measures. *Journal of Abnormal Psychology*, 93:222–230.

Dole, V. P. 1980. Addictive behavior. *Scientific American*, 243 (December):138–154.

Dominowski, R. L. 1977. Problem solving. In Marx, M. H., and Bunch, M. E., Eds., *Fundamentals and Applications of Learning*. New York: Macmillan.

Donaldson, S. R., Gelenberg, A. J., and Baldessarini, R. J. 1983. The pharmacologic treatment of schizophrenia: A progress report. In Carpenter, W. T., Jr., and Schooler, N. R., Eds., *New Directions in Drug Treatment for Schizophrenia*. Rockville, Md.: National Institute of Mental Health.

Douglas, M. 1979. Accounting for taste. *Psychology Today*, 13 (July):44–51.

Dowell, D. A., and Ciarlo, J. A. 1983. Overview of the community mental health centers program from an evaluation perspective. *Community Mental Health Journal*, 19:95–125.

Drabman, R. S., and Thomas, M. H. 1974. Does media violence increase children's toleration of real-life aggression? *Developmental Psychology*, 10:418–421.

Dragastin, S. E., and Elder, G. H., Jr. 1975. *Adolescence in the Life Cycle*. New York: Wiley.

Dubos, R. 1968. *Man, Medicine, and Environment*. New York: Praeger.

Duchek, J. M. 1984. Encoding and retrieval differences between young and old: The impact of attentional capacity usage. *Developmental Psychology*, 20:1173–1180.

Duncker, K. 1945. On problem solving. Trans. by L. S. Lees. *Psychological Monographs*, 58:No. 270.

Dusek, J. B., and Flaherty, J. F. 1981. The development of the self-concept during the adolescent years. *Monographs of the Society for Research in Child Development*, 46:No.4.

Dutton, D. G., and Aron, A. P. 1974. Some evidence for heightened sexual attraction under conditions of high anxiety. *Journal of Personality and Social Psychology*, 30:510–517.

Dweck, C. S. 1975. The role of expectations and attributions in the alleviation of learned helplessness. *Journal of Personality and Social Psychology*, 31:674–685.

Dywan, J., and Bowers, K. 1983. The use of hypnosis to enhance recall. *Science*, 222:184–185.

Easterbrooks, M. A., and Goldberg, W. A. 1985. Effects of early maternal employment on toddlers, mothers, and fathers. *Developmental Psychology*, 21:774–783.

Ebon, M. 1983. *Psychic Warfare*. New York: McGraw-Hill.

Eckholm, E. 1985a. Pygmy chimp readily learns language skills. *New York Times* (June 24):1, 14.

———. 1985b. Kanzi the chimp: A life in science. *New York Times* (June 25):19, 20.

Edney, J. J. 1975. Territoriality and control: A field experiment. *Journal of Personality and Social Psychology*, 31:1108–1115.

Eibl-Eibesfeldt, I. 1970. *Etiology: The Biology of Behavior*. Trans. by E. Klinghammer. New York: Holt, Rinehart and Winston.

Eichorn, D. H., Clausen, J. A., Haan, N., Honzik, M. P., and Mussen, P. H., Eds. 1982. *Present and Past in Middle Life*. New York: Academic Press.

Einstein, A. 1949. Autobiography. In Schilpp, P., Ed., *Albert Einstein: Philosopher-Scientist*. Evanston, Ill.: Library of Living Philosophers.

Eisenberg, N., Wolchik, S. A., Hernandez, R., and Pasternack, J. F. 1985. Parental socialization of young children's play: A short-term longitudinal study. *Child Development*, 56:1506–1513.

Ekehammar, B. 1974. Interactionism in personality from a historical perspective. *Psychological Bulletin*, 81:1026–1048.

Ekman, P. 1980. *The Face of Man: Expressions of Universal Emotions in a New Guinea Village*. New York: Garland STPM Press.

———. 1985. *Telling Lies: Clues to Deceit in Marketplace, Politics and Marriage*. New York: W. W. Norton.

———, Friesen, W. V., and Ancoli, S. 1980. Facial signs of emotional experience. *Journal of Personality and Social Psychology*, 39:1125–1134.

———, ———, and Bear, J. 1984. The international language of gestures. *Psychology Today*, 18 (May):64–69.

———, ———, and Ellsworth, P. 1972. *Emotion in the Human Face: Guidelines for Research and an Integration of Findings*. New York: Pergamon Press.

———, Levenson, R. W., and Friesen, W. V. 1983. Autonomic nervous system activity distinguishes among emotions. *Science*, 221:1208–1210.

Elias, M. 1984. Kid's gender doesn't rule behavior. *USA Today* (April 23):D1.

———. 1985a. Be upbeat and beat illness, stress. *USA Today* (August 26):D1.

———. 1985b. Office no-smoke programs work best. *USA Today* (October 1):D1.

Eliot, L. B. 1985. Book reviews. *Artificial Intelligence*, 26:361–366.

Elkind, D. 1975. Recent research on cognitive development in adolescence. In Dragastin, S. E., and Elder, G. H., Jr., Eds., *Adolescence in the Life Cycle*. New York: Wiley.

Ellen, P., Soteres, B. J., and Wages, C. 1984. Problem solving in the rat: Piecemeal acquisition of cognitive maps. *Animal Learning & Behavior*, 12:232–237.

Ellis, A. 1973. Rational-emotive therapy. In Corsini, R., Ed., *Current Psychotherapies*. Itasca, Ill.: Peacock.

Ellis, H. C., and Hunt, R. R. 1977. Memory: The processing of information. In Marx, M. H., and Bunch, M. E., Eds., *Fundamentals and Applications of Learning*. New York: Macmillan.

———, Thomas, R. L., McFarland, A. D., and Lane, J. W. 1985. Emotional mood states and retrieval in episodic memory. *Journal of Experimental Psychology: Learning, Memory, and Cognition*, 11:363–370.

Emmons, R. A., Larsen, R. J., Levine, S., and Diener, E. 1983. Factors predicting satisfaction judgments. Paper presented at the meeting of the Midwestern Psychological Association, Chicago, May.

Engel, G. 1977. Emotional stress and sudden death. *Psychology Today*, 11 (November):114+.

Engelgau, D. 1984. NSF supports role models. *The Chronicle of Higher Education* (July 5):5–6.

Engen, T. 1980. Why the aroma lingers on. *Psychology Today*, 13 (May):138.

———. 1982. *The Perception of Odors*. New York: Academic Press.

Epstein, A. N. 1960. Water intake without the act of drinking. *Science*, 131:497–498.

———. 1982. The physiology of thirst. In Pfaff, D. W., Ed., *The Physiological Mechanisms of Motivation*. New York: Springer.

Epstein, N. B., and Vlok, L. A. 1981. Research on the results of psychotherapy: A summary of evidence. *American Journal of Psychiatry*, 138:1027–1035.

Epstein, S. 1979. The stability of behavior: I. On predicting most of the people much of the time. *Journal of Personality and Social Psychology*, 37:1097–1126.

———. 1983. The stability of confusion: A reply to Mischel and Peake. *Psychological Review*, 90:179–184.

———. 1984. The stability of behavior across time and situation. In Zucker, R., Aronoff, J., and Rabin, A. I., Eds., *Personality and the Prediction of Behavior*. San Diego, Calif.: Academic Press.

——— and O'Brien, E. J. 1985. The person-situation debate in historical and current perspective. *Psychological Bulletin*, 98:513–537.

Erber, R., and Fiske, S. T. 1984. Outcome dependency and attention to inconsistent information. *Journal of Personality and Social Psychology*, 47:709–726.

Erdelyi, M. 1985. *Psychoanalysis: Freud's Cognitive Psychology*. San Francisco: W. H. Freeman.

Erikson, E. H. 1950. *Childhood and Society*. New York: Norton.

———. 1959. Identity and the life cycle. *Monograph, Psychological Issues*. Vol. 1. New York: International Universities Press.

———. 1963. *Childhood and Society*. Rev. ed. New York: Norton.

———. 1968. *Identity: Youth and Crisis*. New York: Norton.

Eron, L. D., Huesmann, L. R., Lefkowitz, M. M., and Walder, L. O. 1972. Does television violence cause aggression? *American Psychologist*, 27:253–263.

Evans, G. W. 1978. Crowding and the developmental process. In Baum, A., and Epstein, Y. M., Eds., *Human Responses to Crowding*. Hillsdale, N.J.: Erlbaum.

Evarts, E. V. 1979. Brain mechanisms of movement. *Scientific American*, 241 (September):164–179.

Eysenck, H. J. 1957. *The Dynamics of Anxiety and Hysteria*. London: Routledge & Kegan Paul.

———. 1966. *The Effects of Psychotherapy*. New York: International Science Press.

Fader, S. S. 1984. Start here: Finding "hidden" jobs. *Working Woman* (June):42–45.

Fagot, B. I. 1985. Beyond the reinforcement principle: Another step toward understanding sex role development. *Developmental Psychology*, 21:1097–1104.

———, Hagan, R., Leinbach, M. D., and Kronsberg, S. 1985. Differential reactions to assertive and communicative acts of toddler boys and girls. *Child Development*, 56:1499–1505.

Falloon, I. R. H., Boyd, J. L., McGill, C. W., Razani, J., Moss, H. B., and Gilderman, A. M. 1982. Family management in the prevention of exacerbations of schizophrenia. *New England Journal of Medicine*, 306:1437–1440.

——— and Liberman, R. P. 1983. Interactions between drug and psychosocial therapy in schizophrenia. In Carpenter, W. T., Jr., and Schooler, N. R., Eds., *New Directions in Drug Treatment for Schizophrenia*. Rockville, Md.: National Institute of Mental Health.

Farber, B. A., Ed. 1983. *Stress and Burnout in the Human Service Professions*. Elmsford, N.Y.: Pergamon.

Farney, D. 1984. Pollsters' predictions of election results varied as much as the methods they used. *Wall Street Journal* (November 8):7.

Faust, I. M., Johnson, P. R., and Hirsch, J. 1977. Surgical removal of adipose tissue alters feeding behavior and the development of obesity in rats. *Science*, 197:393–96.

Feldman, D. 1980. *Beyond Universals in Cognitive Development*. Norwood, N.J.: Ablex.

Fenigstein, A. 1979. Does aggression cause a preference for viewing media violence? *Journal of Personality and Social Psychology*, 37:2307–2317.

———. 1984. Self-consciousness and the overperception of self as a target. *Journal of Personality and Social Psychology*, 47:860–870.

Fenwick, R., and Barresi, C. M. 1981. Health consequence of marital-status change among the elderly: A comparison of cross-sectional and longitudinal analyses. *Journal of Health and Social Behavior*, 22:106–116.

Ferguson, E. D. 1976. *Motivation: An Experimental Approach*. New York: Holt, Rinehart and Winston.

Festinger, L. A. 1954. A theory of social comparison processes. *Human Relations*, 7:117–140.

———. 1957. *A Theory of Cognitive Dissonance*. Stanford, Calif.: Stanford University Press.

——— and Carlsmith, J. M. 1959. Cognitive consequences of forced compliance. *Journal of Abnormal and Social Psychology*, 58:203–210.

———, Schachter, S., and Back, K. 1950. *Social Pressures in Informal Groups*. New York: Harper & Row.

Fiedler, F. E. 1967. *A Theory of Leadership Effectiveness*. New York: McGraw-Hill.

Fielding, J. E. 1985a. Smoking: Health effects and control: I. *New England Journal of Medicine*, 313:491–498.

———. 1985b. Smoking: Health effects and control: II. *New England Journal of Medicine*, 313:555–561.

Fieve, R. R. 1975. *Moodswing*. New York: William Morrow.

Fillenbaum, G. G., George, L. K., and Palmore, E. B. 1985. Determinants and consequences of retirement among men of different races and economic levels. *Journal of Gerontology*, 40:85–94.

Finke, R. A. 1980. Levels of equivalence in imagery and perception. *Psychological Review*, 87:113–132.

———. 1985. Theories relating mental imagery to perception. *Psychological Bulletin*, 98:236–259.

———. 1986. Mental imagery and the visual system. *Scientific American*, 254 (March):88–94.

Fisher, K. 1985a. Brain structure affects what, how we know. *APA Monitor*, 16 (September):3+.

———. 1985b. Psychoneuroimmunology. *APA Monitor* (August):8+.

Fisher, S., and Greenberg, R. P. 1977. *The Scientific Credibility of Freud's Theories and Therapy*. New York: Basic Books.

Fishman, P. M. 1978. Interaction: The work women do. *Social Problems*, 25:397–406.

Fishman, S. M., and Sheehan, D. V. 1985. Anxiety and panic: Their cause and treatment. *Psychology Today*, 19 (April):26–32.

Fiske, S. T., and Taylor, S. E. 1984. *Social Cognition*. Reading, Mass.: Addison-Wesley.

FitzGerald, P., and Broadbent, D. E. 1985. Order of report and the structure of temporary memory. *Journal of Experimental Psychology: Learning, Memory, and Cognition*, 11:217–228.

Flanagan, J. C. 1978. A research approach to improving quality of life. *American Psychologist*, 33:138–147.

Flavell, J. H. 1977. *Cognitive Development*. Englewood Cliffs, N.J.: Prentice-Hall.

———. 1978. Metacognitive development. In Scandura, J. M., and Brainerd, C. J., Eds., *Structural/Process Theories of Complex Human Behavior*. The Netherlands: Sijthoff and Noordoff.

Fleishman, J. A. 1984. Personality characteristics and coping patterns. *Journal of Health and Social Behavior*, 25:229–244.

Fleming, P., Baum, A., and Singer, J. E. 1984. Toward an integrative approach to the study of stress. *Journal of Personality and Social Psychology*, 46:939–949.

Flynn, J. R. 1984. The mean IQ of Americans: Massive gains 1932 to 1978. *Psychological Bulletin*, 95:29–51.

Folkman, S. 1984. Personal control and stress and coping processes: A theoretical analysis. *Journal of Personality and Social Psychology*, 46:839–852.

——— and Lazarus, R. S. 1985. If it changes it must be a process: Study of emotion and coping during three stages of a college examination. *Journal of Personality and Social Psychology*, 48:150–170.

Ford, F. L. 1985. *Political Murder: From Tyrannicide to Terrorism*. Cambridge, Mass.: Harvard University Press.

Fort, J., and Cory, C. T. 1975. *American Drugstore: A (Alcohol) to V (Valium)*. Boston: Educational Associates/Little, Brown.

Fountain, S. B., Henne, D. R., and Hulse, S. H. 1984. Phrasing cues and hierarchical organization in serial pattern learning by rats. *Journal of Experimental Psychology*, 10:30–45.

Fox, B. H. 1978. Premorbid psychological factors as related to cancer incidence. *Journal of Behavioral Medicine*, 1:45–133.

Fox, J. L. 1984. NIMH study finds one in five have disorders. *Science*, 226:324.

Fox, L. J. 1966. Effecting the use of efficient study habits. In Ulrich, R., Stachnik, T., and Mabry, J., Eds., *Control of Human Behavior*. Glenview, Ill.: Scott, Foresman.

Fraker, S. 1984. Why women aren't getting to the top. *Fortune* (April 16):40–45.

Frances, A., Clarkin, J., and Perry, S. 1984. *Differential Therapeutic in Psychiatry: The Art and Science of Treatment Selection*. New York: Brunner/Mazel.

Francis, P. T., Palmer, A. M., Sims, N. R., Bowen, D. M., Davison,

A. N., Esiri, M. M., Neary, D., Snowden, J. S., and Wilcock, G. K. 1985. Neurochemical studies of early-onset Alzheimer's disease. *New England Journal of Medicine*, 313:7–10.

Frank, R. A., and Stutz, R. M. 1984. Self-deprivation: A review. *Psychological Bulletin*, 96:384–393.

Frankenhaeuser, M. 1983. The sympathetic-adrenal and pituitary-adrenal response to challenge: Comparison between the sexes. In Dembroski, T. M., Schmidt, T. H., and Blumchen, G., Eds., *Biobehavioral Bases of Coronary Heart Disease*. Basel: Karger.

Frankl, V. 1970. *Man's Search for Meaning: An Introduction to Logotherapy*. New York: Clarion.

Franks, L. 1985. A new attack on alcoholism. *New York Times Magazine* (October 20):47–49+.

Freedman, J. L. 1975. *Crowding and Behavior: The Psychology of High-Density Living*. New York: Viking.

———. 1979. Reconciling apparent differences between the responses of humans and other animals to crowding. *Psychological Review*, 86:80–85.

———. 1984. Effect of television violence on aggressiveness. *Psychological Bulletin*, 96:227–246.

Freeman, A., Ed. 1983. *Cognitive Therapy with Couples and Groups*. New York: Plenum Press.

French, J. R. P., Jr. 1973. Person-role fit. *Occupational Mental Health*, 3:15–20.

Freud, A. 1946. *The Ego and the Mechanisms of Defense*. New York: International Universities Press.

Freud, S. 1900. The interpretation of dreams. In *The Complete Psychological Works*. Trans. by J. Strachey. London: Hogarth Press. Republished in 1966.

———. 1940. *An Outline of Psychoanalysis*. Ed. and trans. by J. Strachey. New York: Norton. Republished in 1949.

———. 1943. *A General Introduction to Psychoanalysis*. Trans. by J. Riviere. Garden City, N.Y.: Garden City Publishing.

———. 1959. *Collected Papers*. Jones, E., Ed. New York: Basic Books.

Friedlander, S. 1984. Learned helplessness in children: Perception of control and causal attributions. *Imagination, Cognition, and Personality*, 4:99–116.

Friedman, M., and Rosenman, R. 1974. *Type A Behavior and Your Heart*. New York: Knopf.

Friedrich, L. K., and Stein, A. H. 1975. Prosocial television and young children: The effects of verbal labeling and role playing on learning and behavior. *Child Development*, 46:27–38.

Friedrich-Cofer, L., and Huston, A. In press. Television violence and aggression: The debate continues. *Psychological Bulletin*.

Frisch, R. E. 1978. Menarche and fatness. *Science*, 200:1509–1513.

Fromm, E. 1947. *Man for Himself: An Inquiry into the Psychology of Ethics*. New York: Holt, Rinehart and Winston.

Frye, J. S., and Stockton, R. A. 1982. Discriminant analysis of posttraumatic stress disorder among a group of Viet Nam veterans. *American Journal of Psychiatry*, 139:52–56.

Fuhrmann, G., Durkin, T., Thiriet, G., Kempf, E., and Ebel, A. 1985. Cholinergic neurotransmission in the central nervous system of the Snell Dwarf Mouse. *Journal of Neuroscience Research*, 13:417–430.

Funder, D. 1983. Three issues in predicting more of the people: A reply to Mischel and Peake. *Psychological Review*, 90:283–289.

Gaddis, A., and Brooks-Gunn, J. 1985. The male experience of pubertal change. *Journal of Youth and Adolescence*, 14:61–70.

Gagnon, J. 1975. *Human Sexuality*. Boston: Little, Brown.

——— and Simon, W. 1973. *Sexual Conduct*. Chicago: Aldine.

Gal, R. 1985. Heroism. Paper presented at the Northeast Regional Conference of the Inter-University Seminar on Armed Forces and Society, Albany, New York.

Galanter, E. 1962. Contemporary psychophysics. In Brown, R., et al., Eds., *New Directions in Psychology*. New York: Holt.

Galanter, M. 1983. Unification Church ("Moonie") dropouts: Psychological readjustment after leaving a charismatic religious group. *American Journal of Psychiatry*, 140:984–989.

———, Rabkin, R., Rabkin, J., and Deutsch, A. 1979. The "Moonies": A psychological study of conversion and membership in a contemporary religious sect. *American Journal of Psychiatry*, 136:165–170.

Gallup, G. G., Jr., and Suarez, S. D. 1985. Alternatives to the use of animals in psychological research. *American Psychologist*, 40:1104–1111.

Galton, F. 1869. *Hereditary Genius: An Inquiry into Its Laws and Consequences*.

London: Macmillan.

———. 1883. *Inquiries into Human Faculty and Its Development*. London: Macmillan.

Ganellen, R. J., and Blaney, P. H. 1984. Hardiness and social support as moderators of the effects of life stress. *Journal of Personality and Social Psychology*, 47:156–163.

Garcia, J., and Koelling, R. A. 1966. The relation of cue to consequence in avoidance learning. *Psychonomic Science*, 4:123–124.

Gardner, B. T., and Gardner, R. A. 1971. Two-way communication and an infant chimpanzee. In Schrier, A., and Stollnitz, F., Eds., *Behavior of Non-Human Primates*. Vol. 4. New York: Academic Press.

Gardner, H. 1983. *Frames of Mind: The Theory of Multiple Intelligences*. New York: Basic Books.

———. 1985. *The Mind's New Science: A History of the Cognitive Revolution*. New York: Basic Books.

Gardner, W. I. 1974. *Children with Learning and Behavior Problems*. Boston: Allyn and Bacon.

Garfield, S. L. 1978. Research problems in clinical diagnosis. *Journal of Consulting and Clinical Psychology*, 46:596–607.

Garvey, C. 1977. *Play*. Cambridge, Mass.: Harvard University Press.

Gazzaniga, M. S. 1970. *The Bisected Brain*. New York: Appleton-Century-Crofts.

———. 1972. One brain—Two minds? *American Scientist*, 60:311–317.

———. 1983. Right hemisphere language following brain bisection: A 20-year perspective. *American Psychologist*, 38:525–537.

Geen, R. G., Stonner, D., and Shope, G. L. 1975. The facilitation of aggression by aggression: Evidence against the catharsis hypothesis. *Journal of Personality and Social Psychology*, 31:721–726.

Gentry, W.D. 1974. Aggression in fairy tales: A study of three cultures. Paper presented to the meetings of the Southeastern Psychological Association, April.

Gergen, K. J. 1985. The social constructionist movement in modern psychology. *American Psychologist*, 40:266–275.

———, Gergen, M. M., and Barton, W. H. 1973. Deviance in the dark. *Psychology Today*, 7 (October):129+.

Geschwind, N. 1979. Specializations of the human brain. *Scientific American*, 241 (September):180–199.

Gewirtz, J. L. 1965. The course of infant smiling in four child-rearing environments in Israel. In Foss,

B. M., Ed., *Determinants of Infant Behavior.* Vol. 3. New York: Wiley.

———— and Boyd, E. F. 1977. Experiments on mother-infant interaction underlying mutual attachment acquisition: The infant also conditions the mother. In Alloway, T., Pliner, P., and Krames, L., Eds., *Attachment Behavior.* New York: Plenum.

Ghiselin, M. 1969. *The Triumph of the Darwinian Method.* Berkeley: University of California Press.

Gibb, C. A. 1969. *Leadership: Selected Readings.* Baltimore: Penguin.

Gibbs, J. C., Arnold, K. D., and Burkhart, J. E. 1984. Sex differences in the expression of moral judgment. *Child Development,* 55:1040–1043.

Gibson, E. J., and Walk, R. D. 1960. The visual cliff. *Scientific American,* 202:64–71.

Gibson, J. J. 1966. *The Senses Considered as Perceptual Systems.* Boston: Houghton Mifflin.

Gilbert, J. G. 1973. Thirty-five-year follow-up study of intellectual functioning. *Journal of Gerontology,* 28:68–72.

Gilligan, C. 1982. *In a Different Voice: Psychological Theory and Women's Development.* Cambridge, Mass.: Harvard University Press.

Gillund, G., and Shiffrin, R. M. 1984. A retrieval model for both recognition and recall. *Psychological Review,* 91:1–67.

Ginsburg, H., and Opper, S. 1969. *Piaget's Theory of Intellectual Development: An Introduction.* Englewood Cliffs, N.J.: Prentice-Hall.

Ginsburg, H. P., and Russell, R. L. 1981. Social class and racial influences on early mathematical thinking. *Monographs of the Society for Research in Child Development,* 46 (6).

Glass, D. C. 1964. Changes in liking as a means of reducing cognitive discrepancies between self-esteem and aggression. *Journal of Personality,* 32:531–549.

Gmelch, G. 1978. Baseball magic. *Human Nature* (August):32–39.

Goffman, E. 1959. *The Presentation of Self in Everyday Life.* Garden City, N.Y.: Doubleday.

Goisman, R. M. 1985. The psychodynamics of prescribing in behavior therapy. *American Journal of Psychiatry,* 142:675–679.

Goldberg, L. R. 1978. Differential attribution of trait-descriptive terms to oneself as compared to well-liked, neutral, and disliked others: A psychometric analysis. *Journal of Personality and Social Psychology,*

36:1012–1028.

Goldin-Meadow, S., and Mylander, C. 1983. Gestural communication in deaf children: Noneffect of parental input on language development. *Science,* 221:372–373.

Goldsmith, H. H., and Gottesman, I. I. 1981. Origins of variation in behavioral style: A longitudinal study of temperament in young twins. *Child Development,* 52:91–103.

Goldstein, J. H. 1980. *Social Psychology.* New York: Academic Press.

Goldstein, M. J. 1981. *New Developments in Interventions with Families of Schizophrenics.* San Francisco: Jossey-Bass.

Goleman, D. 1977. Hypnosis comes of age. *Psychology Today,* 11 (July):54–56+.

————. 1985a. Dissatisfied patients urged to consider therapist switch. *New York Times* (July 23):17, 18.

————. 1985b. Esalen wrestles with a staid present. *New York Times* (December 10):15, 16.

————. 1985c. Patterns of love charted in studies. *New York Times* (September 10):13, 18.

————. 1985d. Social workers vault into a leading role in psychotherapy. *New York Times* (April 30):17.

————. 1985e. *Vital Lies, Simple Truths: The Psychology of Self-Deception.* New York: Simon & Schuster.

————. 1986. Clues to behavior sought in history of families. *New York Times* (January 21):17, 20.

Goode, W. J. 1959. The theoretical importance of love. *American Sociological Review,* 24:38–47.

Goodhart, D. E. 1985. Some psychological effects associated with positive and negative thinking about stressful event outcomes: Was Pollyanna right? *Journal of Personality and Social Psychology,* 48:216–232.

Goodman, H. 1984. Eat, drink and be wary. *Psychology Today,* 18 (August):17.

Goodman, M. J., Grove, J. S., and Gilbert, F., Jr. 1978. Age at menopause in relation to reproductive history in Japanese, Caucasian, Chinese, and Hawaiian women living in Hawaii. *Journal of Gerontology,* 33:688–694.

Gottesman, I. I., and Shields, J. 1982. *Schizophrenia: The Epigenetic Puzzle.* Cambridge, England: Cambridge University Press.

Gottfried, A. W., Wallace-Lande, P., Sherman-Brown, S., King, J., and Coen, C. 1981. Physical and social environment of newborn infants in special care units. *Science,* 214:673–675.

Gottschalk, E. C., Jr. 1983. The aging made gains in the 1970s, outpacing rest of the population. *Wall Street Journal* (February 17):1, 16.

Gough, H. 1964. *California Psychological Inventory.* Palo Alto, Calif: Consulting Psychologists Press.

Gould, R. L. 1972. The phases of adult life: A study in developmental psychology. *American Journal of Psychiatry,* 129:33–43.

————. 1978. *Transformations.* New York: Simon & Schuster.

Graen, G., Alvares, K. M., Orris, J. B., and Martella, J. A. 1970. Contingency model of leadership effectiveness: Antecedent and evidential results. *Psychological Bulletin,* 74:285–296.

————, Cashman, J. F., Ginsburg, S., and Schiemann, W. 1977. Effects of linking-pin quality on the quality of working life of lower participants. *Administrative Science Quarterly,* 22:491–504.

Graf, P., and Schacter, D. L. 1985. Implicit and explicit memory for new associations in normal and amnesic subjects. *Journal of Experimental Psychology: Learning, Memory, and Cognition,* 11:501–518.

Green, B. F. 1981. A primer of testing. *American Psychologist,* 36:1001–1011.

Green, D. 1974. Dissonance and self-perception analysis of "forced compliance": When two theories make competing predictions. *Journal of Personality and Social Psychology,* 29:819–828.

Green, D. M., and Swets, J. A. 1966. *Signal Detection Theory and Psychophysics.* New York: Wiley.

Greenberg, R. P., and Fisher, S. 1978. Testing Dr. Freud. *Human Behavior,* 1 (September):28–33.

Greenblatt, D. J., Shader, R. I., and Abernethy, D. R. 1983. Drug therapy: Current status of benzodiazepines. *New England Journal of Medicine,* 309:354–358.

Greenblatt, M. 1978. The grieving spouse. *American Journal of Psychiatry,* 135:43–47.

Greene, L. R., and De La Cruz, A. 1981. Psychiatric day treatment as alternative to and transition from full-time hospitalization. *Community Mental Health Journal,* 17:191–202.

Greene, W. A. 1966. The psychosocial setting of the development of leukemia and lymphoma. *Annals of the New York Academy of Sciences,* 125:794–801.

———— and Swisher, S. N. 1969. Psychological and somatic variables associated with the development and course of monozygotic twins discordant for leukemia. *Annals of the New York Academy of Sciences*, 164:394–408.

Greenough, W. T. 1975. Experimental modification of the developing brain. *American Scientist*, 63:37–46.

——— and Volkmar, F. R. 1973. Pattern of dendritic branching in occipital cortex of rats reared in complex environments. *Experimental Neurology*, 40:491–504.

Greenspan, S. I., and Greenspan, N. T. 1985. *First Feelings: The Emotional Care of the Infant and Young Child*. New York: Viking Press.

Greenwald, A. G., and Pratkanis, A. R. 1984. The self. In Wyer, R. S., and Srull, T. K., Eds., *Handbook of Social Cognition*. Hillsdale, N.J.: Erlbaum.

Gregory, R. L. 1978. *Eye and Brain: The Psychology of Seeing*. 3rd ed. New York: McGraw-Hill.

Greif, E. B., and Ulman, K. J. 1982. The psychological impact of menarche on early adolescent females: A review of the literature. *Child Development*, 53:1413–1430.

Griffith, J. 1985. Social support providers: Who are they? Where are they met? and the relationship of network characteristics to psychological distress. *Basic and Applied Social Psychology*, 6:41–60.

Griffiths, W. J. 1960. Responses of wild and domestic rats to forced swimming. *Psychological Reports*, 6:39–49.

Griffitt, W., and Veitch, R. 1974. Preacquaintance attitude similarity and attraction revisited: Ten days in a fall-out shelter. *Sociometry*, 37:163–173.

Gronfein, W. 1985. Incentives and intentions in mental health policy: A comparison of the Medicaid and community mental health programs. *Journal of Health and Social Behavior*, 26:192–206.

Gruenberg, B. 1980. The happy worker: An analysis of educational and occupational differences in determinants of job satisfaction. *American Journal of Sociology*, 86:247–271.

Guilford, J. P. 1959a. *Personality*. New York: McGraw-Hill.

———. 1959b. Three faces of intellect. *American Psychologist*, 14:469–479.

———. 1967. *The Nature of Human Intelligence*. New York: McGraw-Hill.

Gur, R. E., Gur, R. C., and Harris, L. J. 1975. Cerebral activation, as measured by subjects' lateral eye movements, is influenced by experimenter location. *Neuropsychologia*, 13:35–44.

Gustavson, C. R., et al. 1974. Coyote predation control by aversive conditioning. *Science*, 184:581–583.

Gynther, M. D., and Gynther, R. A. 1983. Personality inventories. In Weiner, I. B., Ed., *Clinical Methods in Psychology*. New York: Wiley.

Haaf, R. 1974. Complexity and facial resemblance as determinants of response to facelike stimuli by 5- and 10-week-old infants. *Journal of Experimental Child Psychology*, 18:480–487.

Haber, G. M. 1982. Spatial relations between dominants and marginals. *Social Psychology Quarterly*, 45:219–228.

Hadden, J. K., and Swann, C. E. 1981. *Prime Time Preachers: The Rising Power of Televangelism*. Reading, Mass.: Addison-Wesley.

Hall, C. S. 1966. *The Meaning of Dreams*. New York: McGraw-Hill.

———. 1984. "A ubiquitous sex difference in dreams" revisited. *Journal of Personality and Social Psychology*, 46:1109–1117.

——— and Lindzey, G. 1978. *Theories of Personality*. 3rd ed. New York: Wiley.

——— and Van de Castle, R. L. 1966. *The Content Analysis of Dreams*. New York: Appleton-Century-Crofts.

Hall, E. T. 1959. *The Silent Language*. Garden City, N.Y.: Doubleday.

———. 1966. *The Hidden Dimension*. Garden City, N.Y.: Doubleday.

Hall, G. S. 1904. *Adolescence*. Vols. 1 and 2. New York: Appleton-Century-Crofts.

Hall, J. A. 1978. Gender effects in decoding nonverbal cues. *Psychological Bulletin*, 85:845–857.

Hall, J. F. 1976. *Classical Conditioning and Instrumental Learning: A Contemporary Approach*. Philadelphia: Lippincott.

Hall, S. S. 1985. Aplysia & Hermissenda. *Science 85*, 6 (May):30–39.

Haney, D. Q. 1985. Creativity is fragile and easily stifled. *Columbus (Ohio) Dispatch* (February 3):C-1.

Haracz, J. L. 1982. The dopamine hypothesis: An overview of studies with schizophrenic patients. *Schizophrenia Bulletin*, 8:438–469.

Hardin, G. J. 1968. The tragedy of the commons. *Science*, 162:1243–1248.

Harding, C. G. 1982. Development of the intention to communicate. *Human Development*, 25:140–151.

Hare, A. P. 1976. *Handbook of Small Group Research*. 2nd ed. New York: Free Press.

Hare, R. D., Frazelle, J., and Cox, D. N. 1978. Psychopathy and

physiological responses to threat of an aversive stimulus. *Psychophysiology*, 15:165–172.

Harkness, S., Edwards, C. P., and Super, C. M. 1981. Social roles and moral reasoning: A case study in a rural African community. *Developmental Psychology*, 17:595–603.

Harlow, H. F. 1949. The formation of learning sets. *Psychological Review*, 56:51–65.

———. 1959. Learning set and error factor theory. In Koch, S., Ed., *Psychology: A Study of a Science*. Vol. 2. New York: McGraw-Hill.

Härnquist, K. 1968. Relative changes in intelligence from 13 to 18: I. Background and methodology. *Scandinavian Journal of Psychology*, 9:50–82.

Harrington, D. M., Block, J., and Block, J. H. 1983. *Journal of Personality and Social Psychology*, 45:609–623.

Harrison, R. V. 1978. Person–environment fit and job stress. In Cooper, C. L., and Payne, R., Eds., *Stress at Work*. New York: Wiley.

Harris Poll: National Council on the Aging, 1981. *The Myth and Reality of Aging in America*. Washington, D.C.: National Council on the Aging.

Hartley, D., Roback, H. B., and Abramowitz, S. I. 1976. Deterioration effects in encounter groups. *American Psychologist*, 31:247–255.

Hartshorne, H., and May, M. A. 1928. *Studies in the Nature of Character*. New York: Macmillan.

Hassett, J. 1978a. *A Primer of Psychophysiology*. San Francisco: Freeman.

———. 1978b. Teaching yourself to relax. *Psychology Today*, 12 (August):28–40.

Hastie, R. 1984. Causes and effects of causal attribution. *Journal of Personality and Social Psychology*, 46:44–56.

Hatfield, E., and Sprecher, S. 1986. *Mirror, Mirror: The Importance of Looks in American Life*. Albany: State University of New York Press.

Hatfield, G., and Epstein, W. 1985. The status of the minimum principle in the theoretical analysis of visual perception. *Psychological Bulletin*, 97:155–186.

Hathaway, S. R., and McKinley, J. C. 1940. A multiphasic personality schedule (Minnesota): I. Construction of the schedule. *Journal of Psychology*, 10:249–254.

——— and ———. 1967. *The Minnesota Multiphasic Personality Inventory*

Manual. New York: Psychological Corporation. Originally published 1951.

Hattie, J. A., Sharpley, C. F., and Rogers, H. J. 1984. Comparative effectiveness of professional and paraprofessional helpers. *Psychological Bulletin,* 95:534–541.

Hauserman, N., Walen, S. R., and Behling, M. 1973. Reinforced racial integration in the first grade: A study in generalization. *Journal of Applied Behavior Analysis,* 6:193–200.

Haw, M. A. 1982. Women, work and stress: A review and agenda for the future. *Journal of Health and Social Behavior,* 23:132–144.

Hawkins, R. D., and Kandel, E. R. 1984. Is there a cell-biological alphabet for simple forms of learning? *Psychological Review,* 91:375–391.

Hayes, K. J. 1962. Genes, drives, and intellect. *Psychological Reports,* 10:299–342.

Haynes, S. G., and Feinleib, M. 1980. Women, work and coronary heart disease: Prospective findings from the Framingham heart study. *American Journal of Public Health,* 70:133–141.

———, ———, and Kannel, W. B. 1980. The relationship of psychosocial factors to coronary heart disease in the Framingham study. *American Journal of Epidemiology,* 111:37–58.

Hays, R. B. 1985. A longitudinal study of friendship development. *Journal of Personality and Social Psychology,* 48:909–924.

Hayslip, B., and Sterns, H. L. 1979. Age differences in relationships between crystallized and fluid intelligences and problem solving. *Journal of Gerontology,* 34:404–414.

Heider, F. 1958. *The Psychology of Interpersonal Relations.* New York: Wiley.

Held, R., and Hein, A. 1963. A movement-produced stimulation in the development of visually guided behavior. *Journal of Comparative Physiology and Psychology,* 56:606–613.

Hellstrom, A. 1985. The time-order error and its relatives: Mirrors of cognitive processes in comparing. *Psychological Bulletin,* 97:35–61.

Hendin, H., and Haas, J. 1984. The reliving experience in Vietnam veterans with post-traumatic stress disorder. *Comprehensive Psychiatry,* 25:165–173.

Hendrick, C. 1972. Effects of salience of inconsistency on impression formation. *Journal of Personality and Social Psychology,* 22:219–222.

Hensel, H. 1982. *Thermal Sensations and Thermoreceptors in Man.* Springfield,

Ill.: Charles C. Thomas.

Herdt, G. H. 1981. *Guardian of the Flutes: Idioms of Masculinity.* New York: McGraw-Hill.

———, Ed. 1982. *Rituals of Manhood.* Berkeley: University of California Press.

Hergenhahn, B. R. 1976. *An Introduction to Theories of Learning.* Englewood Cliffs, N.J.: Prentice-Hall.

Herman, C. P., and Polivy, J. 1975. Anxiety, restraint, and eating behavior. *Journal of Abnormal Psychology,* 84:666–672.

Heron, W. 1957. The pathology of boredom. *Scientific American,* 196 (January):52–56.

Herrnstein, R. J. 1973. *IQ in the Meritocracy.* Boston: Atlantic–Little, Brown.

Hess, E. H. 1959. Imprinting. *Science,* 130:133–141.

Hetherington, A. W., and Ranson, S. W. 1940. Hypothalamic lesions and adiposity in the rat. *Anatomical Record,* 78:149–172.

Hibscher, J. A., and Herman, C. P. 1977. Obesity, dieting, and the expression of "obese" characteristics. *Journal of Comparative and Physiological Psychology,* 91:374–380.

Higgins, S. T., and Morris, E. K. 1984. Generality of free-operant avoidance conditioning in human behavior. *Psychological Bulletin,* 96:247–272.

Hilgard, E. R. 1977. *Divided Consciousness.* New York: Wiley.

———. 1978. Hypnosis and consciousness. *Human Nature,* 1:42–49.

———. 1986. Conversation: A study in hypnosis. *Psychology Today,* 20 (January):23–27.

——— and Bower, G. H. 1975. *Theories of Learning.* 4th ed. Englewood Cliffs, N.J.: Prentice-Hall.

——— and Hilgard, J. R. 1975. *Hypnosis in the Relief of Pain.* Los Altos, Calif.: Kaufman.

———, Weitzenhoffer, A. M., Landes, J., and Moore, R. K. 1961. *Psychological Monographs,* 75:No. 8.

Hilgard, J. R. 1974. Imaginative involvement: Some characteristics of the highly hypnotizable and the non-hypnotizable. *International Journal of Clinical and Experimental Hypnosis,* 22:138–156.

Hilts, P. 1979. The clock within. *Science 80,* 1:61–67.

Himmelweit, H. T., Humphreys, P., Haegers, M., and Katz, M. 1981. *How Voters Decide: A Longitudinal Study of Political Attitudes and Voting Extending Over Fifteen Years.* London: Academic Press.

Hinds, M. D. 1980. Happy old age tied

to spouses' health. *New York Times* (June 12):C3.

Hines, M. 1982. Prenatal gonadal hormones and sex differences in human behavior. *Psychological Bulletin,* 92:56–80.

Hinkle, L. E., Jr. 1974. The effect of exposure to culture change, social change, and changes in interpersonal relationships on health. In Dohrenwend, B. S., and Dohrenwend, B. P., Eds., *Stressful Life Events: Their Nature and Effects.* New York: Wiley.

Hiroto, D. S. 1974. Locus of control and learned helplessness. *Journal of Experimental Psychology,* 102:187–193.

Hirsch, J., and Knittle, J. L. 1970. Cellularity of obese and nonobese human adipose tissue. *Federation Proceedings,* 29:1516–1521.

Hirsch, S. R., and Leff, J. P. 1975. *Abnormalities in Parents of Schizophrenics.* London: Oxford University Press.

Hirst, W. 1982. The amnesic syndrome: Descriptions and explanations. *Psychological Bulletin,* 91:435–460.

Hobbs, N., and Robinson, S. 1982. Adolescent development and public policy. *American Psychologist,* 37:212–223.

Hobson, J. A., and McCarley, R. W. 1977. The brain as a dream state generator: An activation-synthesis hypothesis of the dream process. *American Journal of Psychiatry,* 134:1335–1348.

Hochberg, J. E. 1978. *Perception.* Englewood Cliffs, N.J.: Prentice-Hall.

Hoebel, B. G., and Teitelbaum, P. 1962. Hypothalamic control of feeding and self-stimulation. *Science,* 135:375–376.

Hoffman, D. D. 1983. The interpretation of visual illusions. *Scientific American,* 249 (December):154–162.

Hoffman, H. S., and DePaulo, P. 1977. Behavioral control by an imprinting stimulus. *American Scientist,* 65:58–66.

Hoffman, L. W., and Nye, F. I. 1974. *Working Mothers.* San Francisco: Jossey-Bass.

Hogan, R., and Schroeder, D. 1981. Seven biases in psychology. *Psychology Today,* 15 (July):8–14.

Holahan, C. J., and Moos, R. H. 1985. Life stress and health: Personality, coping, and family support in stress resistance. *Journal of Personality and Social Psychology,* 49:739–747.

Holden, C. 1980. Identical twins reared apart. *Science,* 207:1323–1328.

———. 1985a. Broader commitment laws sought. *Science,* 230:1253–1255.

———. 1985b. Genes, personality and alcoholism. *Psychology Today*, 19 (January):38–44.

———. 1985c. A guarded endorsement for shock therapy. *Science*, 228:1510–1511.

———. 1986. Proposed new psychiatric diagnoses raise charges of gender bias. *Science*, 231:327–328.

Hollander, E. P. 1985. Leadership and power. In Lindzey, G., and Aronson, E., Eds., *Handbook of Social Psychology*. Vol. 2. 3rd ed. New York: Random House.

Hollis, K. L. 1984. The biological function of Pavlovian conditioning: The best defense is a good offense. *Journal of Experimental Psychology: Animal Behavior Processes*, 10:413–425.

Holmes, D. S. 1984. Meditation and somatic arousal reduction: A review of the experimental evidence. *American Psychologist*, 39:1–10.

Holmes, J. H., and Gregersen, M. I. 1950. Observations on drinking induced by hypertonic solutions. *American Journal of Physiology*, 162:326–337.

——— and ———. 1972. Psychosomatic syndrome. *Psychology Today*, 5 (April):71+.

——— and ———. 1974. Life change and illness susceptibility. In Dohrenwend, B. S., and Dohrenwend, B. P., Eds., *Stressful Life Events: Their Nature and Effects*. New York: Wiley.

——— and Rahe, R. H. 1967. The Social Readjustment Rating Scale: A comparative study of Negro, Mexican and white Americans. *Journal of Psychosomatic Research*, 11:213–218.

Holtz, R., and Miller, N. 1985. Assumed similarity and opinion certainty. *Journal of Personality and Social Psychology*, 48:890–898.

Holtzman, N. A., Kronmal, R. A., Van Doorninck, W., Azen, C., and Koch, R. 1986. Effect of age at loss of dietary control on intellectual performance and behavior of children with phenylketonuria. *New England Journal of Medicine*, 314:593–598.

Homans, G. C. 1961. *Social Behavior: Its Elementary Forms*. Rev. ed. New York: Harcourt. Republished 1963, 1974.

Horn, J. 1983. The Texas Adoption Project: Adopted children and their intellectual resemblance to biological and adoptive parents. *Child Development*, 54:268–275.

———. 1986. Models of intelligence. In *Intelligence: Measurement, Theory and Public Policy*. A Symposium marking the occasion of the retirement of Lloyd G. Humphreys from the Department of Psychology, University of Illinois. Champaign, Ill.: University of Illinois Press.

Horne, J. A., and Wilkinson, S. 1985. Chronic sleep reduction: Daytime vigilance performance and EEG measures of sleepiness, with particular reference to "practice" effects. *Psychophysiology*, 22:69–78.

Horner, M. S. 1968. Sex differences in achievement motivation and performance in competitive and noncompetitive situations. Unpublished doctoral dissertation. University of Michigan.

———. 1970. Femininity and successful achievement: A basic inconsistency. In Bardwick, J., Douvan, E. M., Horner, M. S., and Gutman, D., Eds., *Feminine Personality and Conflict*. Belmont, Calif.: Brooks/Cole.

———. 1972. Toward an understanding of achievement-related conflicts in women. *Journal of Social Issues*, 28:157–175.

Horney, K. 1945. *Our Inner Conflicts*. New York: Norton.

Horwitz, A. V. 1985. The economy and social pathology. *Annual Review of Sociology*, 10:95–119.

House, J. S., McMichael, A. J., Wells, J. A., Kaplan, B. H., and Landerman, L. R. 1979. Occupational stress and health among factory workers. *Journal of Health and Social Behavior*, 20:139–160.

———, Robbins, C., and Metzner, H. L. 1982. The association of social relationships and activities with mortality: Prospective evidence from the Tecumseh Community Health Study. *American Journal of Epidemiology*, 116:123–140.

House, R. J. 1977. A 1976 theory of charismatic leadership. In Hunt, J. G., and Larson, L. L., Eds., *Leadership: The Cutting Edge*. Carbondale: Southern Illinois Press.

Houston, J. P. 1976. *Fundamentals of Learning*. New York: Academic Press.

Howe, M. J. 1970. Using students' notes to examine the role of the individual learner in acquiring meaningful subject matter. *Journal of Educational Research*, 64:61–63.

Hubel, D. H. 1979. The brain. *Scientific American*, 241 (September):45–65.

——— and Wiesel, T. N. 1962. Receptive fields, binocular interaction, and functional architecture in the cat's visual cortex. *Journal of Physiology*, 106:106–154.

——— and ———. 1979. Brain mechanisms of vision. *Scientific American*, 241 (September):150–63.

Hubert, N. C., Wachs, T. D., Peters-Martin, P., and Gandour, M. J. 1982. The study of early temperament: Measurement and conceptual issues. *Child Development*, 53:571–600.

Hudgens, R. W. 1974. Personal catastrophe and depression. In Dohrenwend, B. S., and Dohrenwend, B. P., Eds., *Stressful Life Events: Their Nature and Effects*. New York: Wiley.

Huesmann, L. R., Eron, L. D., Klein, R., Brice, P., and Fischer, P. 1983. Mitigating the imitation of aggressive behaviors by changing children's attitudes about media violence. *Journal of Personality and Social Psychology*, 44:899–910.

———, Lagerspetz, K., and Eron, L. D. 1984. Intervening variables in the TV violence-aggression relation: Evidence from two countries. *Developmental Psychology*, 20:746–775.

Hughes, C. W., and Lynch, J. J. 1978. A reconsideration of psychological precursors of sudden death in infrahuman animals. *American Psychologist*, 33:419–429.

Hull, C. L. 1952. *A Behavior System*. New Haven: Yale University Press.

Hunt, E. 1983. On the nature of intelligence. *Science*, 219:141–146.

Hunter, J. E., and Hunter, R. F. 1984. Validity and utility of alternative predictors of job performance. *Psychological Bulletin*, 96:72–98.

Husén, T. 1969. *Talent, Opportunity and Career*. Stockholm: Almquest & Wiksell.

Hyde, J. S. 1981. How large are cognitive gender differences? *American Psychologist*, 36:892–901.

———. 1984. How large are gender differences in aggression? A developmental meta-analysis. *Developmental Psychology*, 20:722–736.

Hyman, B. T., Van Hoesen, G. W., Damasio, A. R., and Barnes, C. L. 1984. Alzheimer's disease: Cell-specific pathology isolates the hippocampal formation. *Science*, 225:1168–1170.

Iaffaldano, M. T., and Muchinsky, P. M. 1985. Job satisfaction and job performance: A meta-analysis. *Psychological Bulletin*, 97:251–273.

Ilchman, A. S. 1985. *Women's Work, Men's Work: Sex Segregation on the Job*. Washington, D.C.: National Academy Press.

Inman, V. W., and Parkinson, S. R. 1983. Differences in Brown-Peterson recall as a function of age and retention interval. *Journal of*

Gerontology, 38:58–64.

Insko, C. A., Drenan, S., Smith, R., and Wage, T. J. 1983. Conformity as a function of the consistency of positive self-evaluation with being liked and being right. *Journal of Experimental Social Psychology*, 19:341–358.

———, Smith, R. H., Alicke, M. D., Wade, J., and Taylor, S. 1985. Conformity and group size: The concern with being right and the concern with being liked. *Personality and Social Psychology Bulletin*, 11:41–50.

Irwin, D. E., and Pachella, R. G. 1985. Effects of stimulus probability and visual similarity on stimulus encoding. *American Journal of Psychology*, 98:85–100.

Ishikawa, T., Koizumi, K., and Brooks, C. 1966. Activity of the supraoptic nucleus of the hypothalamus. *Neurology*, 16:101–106.

Izard, C. E. 1977. *Human Emotions*. New York: Plenum.

Jaco, E. G., Ed. 1979. *Patients, Physicians, and Illness*. 3rd ed. New York: Free Press.

Jacobs, P. I. 1977. *Up the IQ!* New York: Wyden Books.

Jacobson, M. B. 1981. Jurors go easy on handsome rapists with homely victims. *Psychology Today*, 15 (October):27.

Jacquet, Y. F., and Marks, N. 1976. The C-fragment of B-lipotropin: An endogenous neuroleptic or antipsychotogen? *Science*, 194:632–635.

James, W. 1884. *Principles of Psychology*. New York: Holt.

Janis, I. L. 1972. *Victims of Groupthink*. Boston: Houghton Mifflin.

———. 1982. *Groupthink*. Boston: Houghton Mifflin.

Janowitz, H. D. 1967. Role of the gastrointestinal tract in regulation of food intake. In Code, C. F., Ed., *Handbook of Physiology: Alimentary Canal I*. Washington, D.C.: American Physiological Society.

Jarvik, L. F. 1975. Thoughts on the psychobiology of aging. *American Psychologist*, 30:576–583.

Jasso, G. 1985. Marital coital frequency and the passage of time: Estimating the separate effects of spouses' ages and marital duration, birth and marriage cohorts, and period influences. *American Sociological Review*, 50:224–241.

Jeffers, F. C., and Verwoerdt, A. 1969. How the old face death. In Busse, E. W., and Pfeiffer, E., Eds., *Behavior and Adaptation in Late Life*.

Boston: Little, Brown.

Jefferson, J. W., and Greist, J. H. 1981. Some hazards of lithium use. *American Journal of Psychiatry*, 138:93–94.

Jemmott, J. B., III, and Locke, S. E. 1984. Psychosocial factors, immunologic mediation and human susceptibility to infectious diseases: How much do we know? *Psychological Bulletin*, 95:78–108.

Jensen, A. R. 1969. How much can we boost IQ and scholastic achievement? *Harvard Educational Review*, 39:1–123.

———. 1973. *Educability and Group Differences*. New York: Harper & Row.

———. 1980. *Bias in Mental Testing*. New York: Free Press.

———. 1981. *Straight Talk About Mental Tests*. New York: Free Press.

———. 1982. Level I/Level II: Factors or categories? *Journal of Educational Psychology*, 74:868–873.

———. 1984a. Political ideologies and educational research. *Phi Delta Kappan*, 65 (March):460–462.

———. 1984b. Objectivity and the genetics of IQ: A reply to Steven Selden. *Phi Delta Kappan*, 66 (December): 284–286.

———. 1985. Compensatory education and the theory of intelligence. *Phi Delta Kappan*, 66 (April):554–558.

Jessor, R., Costa, F., Jessor, R., and Donovan, J. E. 1983. Time of first intercourse: A prospective study. *Journal of Personality and Social Psychology*, 44:608–626.

Jessor, S., and Jessor, R. 1975. Transition from virginity to nonvirginity among youth: A social-psychological study over time. *Developmental Psychology*, 11:473–484.

Johnson, E. S. 1984. Sex differences in problem solving. *Journal of Educational Psychology*, 76:1359–1371.

Johnson, T. J., Feigenbaum, R., and Weiby, M. 1964. Some determinants and consequences of the teacher's perception of causation. *Journal of Educational Psychology*, 55:237–246.

Johnston, J. M. 1972. Punishment of human behavior. *American Psychologist*, 27:1033–1054.

Jones, E. E., and Nisbett, R. E. 1971. *The Actor and the Observer: Divergent Perceptions of the Causes of Behavior*. Morristown, N.J.: General Learning Corporation.

Jones, L. V. 1984. White-black achievement differences: The narrowing gap. *American Psychologist*, 39:1207–1213.

Jones, M. C. 1957. The later careers of

boys who were early- or late-maturing. *Child Development*, 28:113–128.

——— and Bayley, N. 1950. Physical maturing among boys as related to behavior. *Journal of Educational Psychology*, 41:129–148.

Joyce, C. 1984. A time for grieving. *Psychology Today*, 18 (November):42–44.

Judd, C. H. 1908. The relation of special training to general intelligence. *Educational Review*, 36:28–42.

Julia, P. 1983. *Explanatory Models in Linguistics: A Behavioral Perspective*. Princeton, N.J.: Princeton University Press.

Jung, C. G. 1912. *The Psychology of the Unconscious*. Leipzig: Franz Deuticke.

———. 1963. *Memories, Dreams, Reflections*. Ed. by A. Jaffe, trans. by R. Winston and C. Winston. New York: Pantheon.

Kagan, J. 1971. A conception of early adolescence. *Daedalus*, 100:997–1012.

———. 1979. Overview: Perspectives on human infancy. In Osofsky, J. D., Ed., *Handbook of Infant Development*. New York: Wiley.

———, Kearsley, R. B., and Zelazo, P. R. 1978. *Infancy: Its Place in Human Development*. New York: Wiley.

——— and Moss, H. A. 1962. *Birth to Maturity: A Study in Psychological Development*. New York: Wiley.

Kahn, S., Zimmerman, G., Csikszentmihalyi, M., and Getzels, J. W. 1985. Relations between identity in young adulthood and intimacy at midlife. *Journal of Personality and Social Psychology*, 49:1316–1322.

Kalat, J. W. 1981. *Biological Psychology*. Belmont, Calif.: Wadsworth.

——— and Rozin, P. 1971. Role of interference in taste-aversion learning. *Journal of Comparative and Physiological Psychology*, 77:53–58.

Kalish, H. I. 1977. Conditioning and learning in behavior modification. In Marx, M. H., and Bunch, M. E., Eds., *Fundamentals and Applications of Learning*. New York: Macmillan.

Kalleberg, A. L. 1977. Work values and job rewards: A theory of job satisfaction. *American Sociological Review*, 42:124–143.

Kalnins, I. V., and Bruner, J. S. 1973. The coordination of visual observation and instrumental behavior in early infancy. *Perception*, 2:304–314.

Kalven, H., Jr., and Zeisal, H. 1966. *The American Jury*. Boston: Little, Brown.

Kamin, L. J. 1969. Predictability,

surprise, attention and conditioning. In Campbell, B. A., and Church, R. M., Eds., *Punishment and Aversive Behavior*. New York: Appleton-Century-Crofts.

———. 1974. *The Science and Politics of IQ*. Hillsdale, N. J.: Erlbaum.

Kandel, D. B. 1974. Inter- and intragenerational influences on adolescent marijuana use. *Journal of Social Issues*, 30:107–135.

Kandel, D. B., Davies, M., and Raveis, V. H. 1985. The stressfulness of daily social roles for women: Marital, occupational and household roles. *Journal of Health and Social Behavior*, 26:64–78.

——— and Lesser, G. S. 1972. *Youth in Two Worlds*. San Francisco: Jossey-Bass.

Kandel, E. R., and Schwartz, J. H. 1982. Molecular biology of learning: Modulation of transmitter release. *Science*, 218 (October 29):433–443.

Kanizsa, G. 1985. Seeing and thinking. *Acta Psychologica*, 59:23–33.

Kanner, A. D., Coyne, J. C., Schaefer, C., and Lazarus, R. S. 1981. Comparison of two modes of stress measurement: Daily hassles and uplifts versus major life events. *Journal of Behavioral Medicine*, 4:1–39.

Kaplan, H. S. 1974. *The New Sex Therapy*. New York: Brunner/Mazel.

Kaplan, M. 1983. A woman's view of DSM-III. *American Psychologist*, 38:786–798.

Karasu, T. B. 1982. Psychotherapy and pharmacotherapy: Toward an integrative model. *American Journal of Psychiatry*, 139:1102–1113.

Karlin, R. A., Epstein, Y. M., and Aiello, J. R. 1978. A setting-specific analysis of crowding. In Baum, A., and Epstein, Y. M., Eds., *Human Responses to Crowding*. Hillsdale, N.J.: Erlbaum.

Karnash, L. J. 1945. *Handbook of Psychiatry*. St. Louis: Mosby.

Kasl, S. V., and Cobb, S. 1982. Variability of stress effects among men experiencing job loss. In Goldberger, L., and Breznitz, S., Eds., *Handbook of Stress*. New York: Free Press.

———, Evans, A. S., and Neiderman, J. C. 1979. Psychosocial risk factors in the development of infectious mononucleosis. *Psychosomatic Medicine*, 41:445–467.

Kastenbaum, R. 1975. Is death a life crisis? On the confrontation with death in theory and practice. In Datan, N., and Ginsberg, L. H., Eds., *Life-Span Developmental Psychology: Normative Life Crisis*.

New York: Academic Press.

Katkin, E. S. 1985. Blood, sweat and tears: Individual differences in autonomic self-perception. *Psychophysiology*, 22:125–137.

Kaufman, L. 1979. *Perception: The World Transformed*. New York: Oxford University Press.

Kawabata, N. 1984. Perception at the blind spot and similarity grouping. *Perception & Psychophysics*, 36:151–158.

Kazdin, A. E. 1977. *The Token Economy: A Review and An Evaluation*. New York: Plenum Press.

Kearns, D. 1976. *Lyndon Johnson and the American Dream*. New York: Harper & Row.

Kelley, H. H. 1950. The warm-cold variable in first impressions of persons. *Journal of Personality*, 18:431–439.

Kelley, H. H. 1952. Two functions of reference groups. In Swanson, G. E., Newcomb, T. M., and Hartley, E. L., Eds., *Readings in Social Psychology*. New York: Holt, Rinehart and Winston.

Kelman, H. C. 1961. Processes of opinion change. *Public Opinion Quarterly*, 21:57–78.

———. 1967. Humane use of human subjects: The problem of deception in social psychological experiments. *Psychological Bulletin*, 67:1–11.

Kempler, W. 1973. Gestalt therapy. In Corsini, R., Ed., *Current Psychotherapies*. Itasca, Ill.: Peacock.

Kendler, K. S. 1983. Overview: A current perspective on twin studies of schizophrenia. *American Journal of Psychiatry*, 140:1413–1425.

——— and Robinette, C. D. 1983. Schizophrenia in the National Academy of Sciences National Research Council Twin Registry: A 16-year update. *American Journal of Psychiatry*, 140:1551–1563.

Kenrick, D. T., and Stringfield, D. O. 1980. Personality traits and the eye of the beholder: Crossing some traditional philosophical boundaries in the search for consistency in all of the people. *Psychological Review*, 87:88–104.

Kerckhoff, A. C., and Davis, K. E. 1962. Value consensus and need complementarity in mate selection. *American Sociological Review*, 27:295–303.

Kerr, N. L. 1983. Motivation losses in small groups: A social dilemma analysis. *Journal of Personality and Social Psychology*, 45:819–828.

Kershner, J. R., and Ledger, G. 1985. Effect of sex, intelligence, and style of thinking on creativity: A

comparison of gifted and average IQ children. *Journal of Personality and Social Psychology*, 48:1033–1040.

Kett, J. F. 1977. *Rites of Passage: Adolescence in America 1790 to the Present*. New York: Basic Books.

———. 1983. Mental illness in the biological and adoptive relatives of schizophrenic adoptees: Findings relevant to genetic and environmental factors in etiology. *American Journal of Psychiatry*, 140:720–727.

Kety, S. S., Rosenthal, D., Wender, P. H., Schulsinger, F., and Jacobsen, B. 1975. Mental illness in the biological and adoptive familes of adopted individuals who have become schizophrenic: A preliminary report based on psychiatric interviews. In Fieve, R. R., Rosenthal, D., and Brill, H., Eds., *Genetic Research in Psychiatry*. Baltimore: Johns Hopkins Press.

Keys, A. 1950. *The Biology of Human Starvation*. Minneapolis: University of Minnesota Press.

Kiesler, C. A. 1982. Public and professional myths about mental hospitalization. *American Psychologist*, 37:1323–1339.

Kiester, E., Jr. 1980. Images of the night. *Science 80*, 1 (May/June): 36–43.

———. 1986. Spare parts for damaged brains. *Science 86* (March):33–38.

Kihlstrom, J. F. 1985. Hypnosis. *Annual Review of Psychology*, 36:385–418.

Kilham, W., and Mann, L. 1974. Level of destructive obedience as a function of transmitter and executant roles in the Milgram obedience paradigm. *Journal of Personality and Social Psychology*, 29:696–702.

Killian, L. M. 1952. The effects of southern white workers on race relations in northern plants. *American Sociological Review*, 17:327–331.

———. 1953. The adjustment of southern white migrants to northern urban norms. *Social Forces*, 33:66–69.

Kimmel, D. C. 1974. *Adulthood and Aging*. New York: Wiley.

Kimura, D. 1985. Male brain, female brain: The hidden difference. *Psychology Today*, 19 (November):50–58.

King, H. E., and Webb, C. 1981. Rape crisis centers: Progress and problems. *Journal of Social Issues*, 37:93–104.

King, N. R. 1979. Play: The kindergartners' perspective. *Elementary School Journal*, 80:81–87.

Kinsey, A. C., Pomeroy, W. B., Martin, C. E., and Gebhard, P. H. 1953. *Sexual Behavior in the Human Female*. Philadelphia: Saunders.

Klaus, M., and Kennell, J. 1976.

Maternal–Infant Bonding. St. Louis: Mosby.

Klein, D. F., and Rabkin, J. G. 1981. *Anxiety: New Research and Concepts*. New York: Raven Press.

Klein, D. N., Depue, R. A., and Slater, J. F. 1985. Cyclothymia in the adolescent offspring of parents with bipolar affective disorder. *Journal of Abnormal Psychology*, 94:115–127.

Kleinfeld, J. S. 1973. Intellectual strengths in culturally different groups: An Eskimo illustration. *Review of Educational Research*, 43:341–359.

Kleitman, N. 1960. Patterns of dreaming. *Scientific American*, 203 (November):82–88.

Klerman, G. L., Vaillant, G. E., Spitzer, R. L., and Michels, R. 1984. A debate on DSM-III. *American Journal of Psychiatry*, 141:539–553.

Klitgaard, R. 1985. *Choosing Elites*. New York: Basic Books.

Kluver, H., and Bucy, P. C. 1937. Psychic blindness and other symptoms following bilateral temporal lobectomy in rhesus monkeys. *American Journal of Physiology*, 119:532–535.

Knight, R. C. 1984. Can stress make you sick? *Working Women* (April):142–150.

Knox, V. J., Gekoski, W. L., Shum, K., and McLaughlin, D. M. 1981. Analgesia for experimentally induced pain: Multiple sessions of acupuncture compared to hypnosis in high- and low-susceptible subjects. *Journal of Abnormal Psychology*, 90:28–34.

Kobasa, S. C. 1982. The hardy personality: Toward a social psychology of stress and illness. In Sanders, G., and Suls, J., Eds., *Social Psychology of Health and Illness*. Hillsdale, N.J.: Erlbaum.

———, Maddi, S. R., and Kahn, S. 1982. Hardiness and health: A prospective study. *Journal of Personality and Social Psychology*, 42:168–177.

Koffka, K. 1963. *Principles of Gestalt Psychology*. New York: Harcourt Brace Jovanovich.

Kogan, N., and Pankove, E. 1974. Long-term predictive validity of divergent-thinking tests: Some negative evidence. *Journal of Educational Psychology*, 68:802–810.

Kohlberg, L. 1968. The child as moral philosopher. *Psychology Today*, 2 (September):25–30.

———. 1976. Moral stages and moralization. In Lickona, T., Ed., *Moral Development and Behavior Theory, Research, and Social Issues*.

New York: Holt, Rinehart and Winston.

———. 1981. *Essays on Moral Development*. Vol. 1: *The Philosophy of Moral Development*. San Francisco: Harper & Row.

———. 1984. *Essays on Moral Development*. Vol. 2: *The Psychology of Moral Development*. San Francisco: Harper & Row.

——— and Gilligan, C. F. 1971. The adolescent as philosopher: The discovery of the self in a postconventional world. *Daedalus*, 100:1051–1086.

——— and Kramer, R. 1969. Continuities and discontinuities in child and adult moral development. *Human Development*, 12:93–120.

Kohn, M., and Schooler, C. 1973. Occupational experience and psychological functioning: An assessment of reciprocal effects. *American Sociological Review*, 38:97–118.

Kohn, M. L., and Schooler, C. 1978. The reciprocal effects of the substantive complexity of work and intellectual flexibility: A longitudinal assessment. *American Journal of Sociology*, 84:24–52.

Kolata, G. 1982. New Valiums and anti-Valiums on the horizon. *Science*, 216:604–605.

———. 1983. Math genius may have hormonal basis. *Science*, 222:1312.

———. 1985. Why do people get fat? *Science*, 227:1327–1328.

Kollock, P., Blumstein, P., and Schwartz, P. 1985. Sex and power in interaction: Conversational privileges and duties. *American Sociological Review*, 50:34–46.

Komorita, S. S., and Barth, J. M. 1985. Components of reward in social dilemmas. *Journal of Personality and Social Psychology*, 48:364–373.

Korchin, S. J. 1976. *Modern Clinical Psychology: Principles of Intervention in the Clinic and Community*. New York: Basic Books.

———, and Schuldberg, D. 1981. The future of clinical assessment. *American Psychologist*, 36:1147–1158.

Korner, A. F. 1979. Conceptual issues in infancy research. In Osofsky, J. D., Ed., *Handbook of Infant Development*, New York: Wiley.

Kosslyn, S. M. 1980. *Image and Mind*. Cambridge, Mass.: Harvard University Press.

———. 1981. The medium and the message in mental imagery: A theory. *Psychological Review*, 88:46–66.

———. 1983. *Ghosts in the Mind's Machine: Creating and Using Images in

the Brain*. New York: W. W. Norton.

———. 1985. Stalking the mental image. *Psychology Today*, 19 (May):24–28.

Kovacs, M. 1980. The efficacy of cognitive and behavior therapies for depression. *American Journal of Psychiatry*, 137:1495–1501.

——— and Beck, A. T. 1978. Maladaptive cognitive structures in depression. *American Journal of Psychiatry*, 135:525–533.

Kramer, D. A. 1983. Post-formal operations? A need for further conceptualization. *Human Development*, 26:91–105.

Kramer, R. M., and Brewer, M. B. 1984. Effects of group identity on resource use in a simulated commons dilemma. *Journal of Personality and Social Psychology*, 46:1044–1057.

Krantz, D. S., Grunberg, N. E., and Baum, A. 1985. Health psychology. *Annual Review of Psychology*, 36:349–383.

Krantz, S. E. 1983. Cognitive appraisals and problem-directed coping: A prospective study of stress. *Journal of Personality and Social Psychology*, 44:638–643.

Kraut, R. E., and Poe, D. 1980. Behavioral roots of person perception: The deception judgments of customs inspectors and laymen. *Journal of Personality and Social Psychology*, 39:784–798.

Krosnick, J. A., and Judd, C. M. 1982. Transitions in social influence at adolescence: Who induces cigarette smoking? *Developmental Psychology*, 18:359–368.

Kübler-Ross, E. 1969. *On Death and Dying*. New York: Macmillan.

———. 1981. *Living with Death and Dying*. New York: Macmillan.

Kucharski, D., and Spear, N. E. 1985. Potentiation and overshadowing in preweanling and adult rats. *Journal of Experimental Psychology: Animal Behavior Processes*, 11:15–34.

Kupperman, H. S. 1963. *Human Endocrinology*. San Francisco: Davis Publishing Co.

LaFrance, M., and Mayo, C. 1976. Racial differences in gaze behavior during conversations: Two systematic observational studies. *Journal of Personality and Social Psychology*, 33:547–552.

Lamb, M. 1982. Second thoughts on first touch. *Psychology Today*, 16 (April):9–11.

——— and Sherrod, L. R. 1981. *Infant Social Cognition: Empirical and Theoretical Considerations*. Hillsdale, N.J.: Erlbaum.

Landy, D., and Aronson, E. 1969. The influence of the character of the criminal and his victim on the decisions of simulated jurors. *Journal of Experimental Social Psychology*, 5:141–152.

Landy, D., and Sigall, H. 1974. Beauty is talent: Task evaluation as a function of the performer's physical attractiveness. *Journal of Personality and Social Psychology*, 29:299–304.

Lang, S. 1985. Fear of fat: Women, yes; men, no. *USA Today* (May 30):1A.

Lange, C. G., and James, W. 1922. *The Emotions*. Ed. by Knight Dunlap, trans. by I. A. Haupt. Baltimore: Wilkins & Wilkins.

Langer, E. J., and Abelson, R. P. 1974. A patient by any other name . . . : Clinician group differences in labeling bias. *Journal of Consulting and Clinical Psychology*, 42:4–9.

———, Beck, P., Weinman, C., Rodin, J., and Spitzer, L. 1979. Environmental determinants of memory improvement in late adulthood. *Journal of Personality and Social Psychology*, 37:2003–2013.

——— and Rodin, J. 1976. The effects of choice and enhanced personal responsibility for the aged: A field experiment in an institutional setting. *Journal of Personality and Social Psychology*, 34:191–198.

Langway, L. 1980. Flying back to the nest. *Newsweek* (April 7):86.

LaPiere, R. T. 1934. Attitudes versus actions. *Social Forces*, 13:230–237.

Larson, L. E. 1972. The influence of parents and peers during adolescence. The situation hypothesis revisited. *Journal of Marriage and the Family*, 34:67–74.

Lashley, K. 1929. *Brain Mechanisms and Intelligence*. Chicago: University of Chicago Press.

Laudenslager, M. L., Ryan, S. M., Drugan, R. C., Hyson, R. L., and Maier, S. F. 1983. Coping and immunosuppression: Inescapable but not escapable shock suppresses lymphocyte proliferation. *Science*, 221:568–570.

Lauderdale, P., Parker, J., Smith-Cunnien, P., and Inverarity, J. 1984. External threat and the definition of deviance. *Journal of Personality and Social Psychology*, 46:1058–1068.

Laufer, R. S., Gallops, M. S., and Frey-Wouters, E. 1984. War stress and trauma: The Vietnam veteran experience. *Journal of Health and Social Behavior*, 25:65–85.

Laurence, J. R., and Perry, C. 1983. Hypnotically created memory among highly hypnotizable subjects. *Science*, 222 (November):523–524.

———, ———, and Kihlstrom, J. 1983. "Hidden observer" phenomena in hypnosis: An experimental creation? *Journal of Personality and Social Psychology*, 44:163–169.

Layton, B. D., and Turnbull, B. 1975. Belief, evaluation, and performance in an ESP task. *Journal of Experimental Social Psychology*, 11:166–179.

Layton, E. T. 1932. The persistence of learning in elementary algebra. *Journal of Educational Psychology*, 23:46–55.

Lazar, I., and Darlington, R. 1982. Lasting effects of early education: A report from the Consortium for Longitudinal Studies. *Monographs of the Society for Research in Child Development*, Vol. 47, Nos. 2–3.

Lazarus, A. A. 1971. *Behavior Therapy and Beyond*. New York: McGraw-Hill.

Lazarus, R. S. 1966. *Psychological Stress and the Coping Process*. New York: McGraw-Hill.

——— and DeLongis, A. 1983. Psychological stress and coping in aging. *American Psychologist*, 38:245–254.

———, ———, Folkman, S., and Gruen, R. 1985. Stress and adaptational outcomes. *American Psychologist*, 40:770–779.

——— and Launier, R. 1978. Stress-related transactions between person and environment. In Pervin, L. A., and Lewis, M., Eds., *Perspectives in Interactional Psychology*. New York: Plenum.

Leavitt, H. J. 1951. Some effects of certain communication patterns on group performance. *Journal of Abnormal Social Psychology*, 46:38–50.

Lefcourt, H. M., Miller, R. S., Ware, E. E., and Sherk, D. 1981. Locus of control as a modifier of the relationship between stressors and moods. *Journal of Personality and Social Psychology*, 41:357–369.

Leff, J., Kuipers, L., and Berkowitz, R. 1982. A controlled trial of social intervention in the families of schizophrenic patients. *British Journal of Psychiatry*, 141:121–134.

Lehman, E. B., and Mellinger, J. C. 1984. Effects of aging on memory for presentation modality. *Developmental Psychology*, 20:1210–1217.

Lemert, E. M. 1972. *Human Deviance, Social Problems and Social Control*. Englewood Cliffs, N.J.: Prentice-Hall.

———. 1976. Response to critics: Feedback and choice. In Coser, L. A., and Larsen, O. N., Eds., *The Uses of Controversy in Sociology*. New York: Free Press.

Lemley, B. 1984. Synesthesia: Seeing is feeling. *Psychology Today*, 18 (June):65.

Lenneberg, E. H. 1967. *The Biological Foundations of Language*. New York: Wiley.

———. 1973. *Biological Foundations of Language*. 2nd ed. New York: Wiley.

Lennon, M. C. 1982. The psychological consequences of menopause: The importance of timing of a life stage event. *Journal of Health and Social Behavior*, 23:353–366.

Leonard, C. V. 1974. Depression and suicidality. *Journal of Consulting and Clinical Psychology*, 42:98–104.

Lerner, J. V., and Galambos, N. L. 1985. Maternal role satisfaction, mother-child interaction, and child temperament: A process model. *Developmental Psychology*, 21:1157–1164.

Lerner, R. M., and Busch-Rossnagel, N. A. 1981. *Individuals as Producers of Their Development*. New York: Academic Press.

Lesko, L. M., Fischman, M. W., Javaid, J. I., and Davis, J. M. 1982. Iatrogenous cocaine psychosis. *New England Journal of Medicine*, 307:1153.

Lettvin, J. Y. 1959. What the frog's eye tells the frog's brain. *Proceedings of the Institute of Radio Engineers*, 47:1940–1951.

Levenstein, P. 1974. A message from home: A home-based intervention method for low-income preschoolers. Paper presented at conference on "The Mentally Retarded and Society: A Social Science Perspective." Niles, Michigan, April 18.

Leventhal, H. 1970. Findings and theory in the study of fear communications. In Berkowitz, L., Ed., *Advances in Experimental Social Psychology*. Vol. 6. New York: Academic Press.

——— and Nerenz, D. 1983. Representations of threat and the control of stress. In Meichenbaum, D., and Jaremko, M., Eds., *Stress Reduction and Prevention: A Cognitive Behavioral Approach*. New York: Plenum.

Levine, L. E. 1983. Mine: Self-definition in 2-year-old boys. *Developmental Psychology*, 19:544–549.

Levine, S. V. 1984. Radical departure. *Psychology Today*, 18 (August):21–27.

LeVine, W. R., and Irvine, J. K. 1984. In vivo EMG biofeedback in violin and viola pedagogy. *Biofeedback and Self-Regulation*, 9:161–168.

Levinger, G. 1964. Note on need complementarity in marriage. *Psychological Bulletin*, 61:153–157.

———, Seen, D. J., and Jorgensen, B. W. 1970. Progress toward permanence in courtship: A test of the Kerckhoff-Davis hypothesis. *Sociometry*, 33:427–443.

———, Darrow, C. N., Klein, E. B., Levinson, M. H., and McKee, B. 1978. *The Seasons of a Man's Life*. New York: Knopf.

Levy, J. 1983. Research synthesis on right and left hemispheres. *Educational Leadership*, 40:66–72.

———. 1985. Right brain, left brain: Fact and fiction. *Psychology Today*, 19 (May):38–44.

Levy, L. 1984. The metamorphosis of clinical psychology. *American Psychologist*, 39:486–494.

Levy, S. M., Ed. 1982. *Biological Mediators of Behavior and Disease: Neoplasia*. New York: Elsevier Biomedical.

———, Winkelstein, A., Rabin, B. S., Lippman, M., and Cohen, S. 1985. Psychosocial variables and the course of cancer. *The New England Journal of Medicine*, 313:1355–1356

Lewin, K., Lippitt, R., and White, R. K. 1939. Patterns of aggressive behavior in experimentally created "social climates." *Journal of Social Psychology*, 10:271–299.

Lewinsohn, P. M. 1974. A behavioral approach to depression. In Friedman, R. J., and Katz, M. M., Eds., *The Psychology of Depression: Contemporary Theory and Research*. Washington, D. C.: V. H. Winston.

———. 1976. Manual of instructions for behavior ratings for the observation of interpersonal behavior. In Mash, E. J., and Terdal, L. G., Eds., *Behavior Therapy Assessment: Diagnosis, Design, and Evaluation*. New York: Springer.

Lewis, M., and Brooks-Gunn, J. 1979. *Social Cognition and the Acquisition of Self*. New York: Plenum.

Lewontin, R. C., Rose, S., and Kamin, L. J. 1984. *Not in Our Genes*. New York: Pantheon Books.

Lieberman, M. A., Yalom, I. D., and Miles, M. B. 1975. *Encounter Groups*. New York: Basic Books.

Liebert, R. M., and Baron, R. A. 1972. Some immediate effects of televised violence on children's behavior. *Developmental Psychology*, 6:469–475.

Liebowitz, M. R. 1983. *The Chemistry of Love*. Boston: Little, Brown.

Liem, R., Atkinson, T., and Liem, J. 1983. The work and unemployment project. Personal and family effects of job loss. Paper presented at 1st National Conference on Social Stress. Concord, N.H.

Lifton, R. J. 1963. *Thought Reform and the Psychology of Totalism: A Study of "Brainwashing" in China*. New York: Norton.

———. 1973. *Home from the War*. New York; Simon & Schuster.

———. 1979. The appeal of the death trap. *New York Times Magazine* (January 7):26–31.

Limber, J. 1977. Language in child and chimp. *American Psychologist*, 32:280–295.

Lincoln, R. 1981. *Teenage Pregnancy: The Problem That Hasn't Gone Away*. New York: Alan Guttmacher Institute.

Lindsay, P. H., and Norman, D. A. 1977. *Human Information Processing*. 2nd ed. New York: Academic Press.

Lindsey, R. 1984. A new generation finds it hard to leave the nest. *New York Times* (January 25):10.

Linn, M. C., and Petersen, A. C. 1985. Emergence and characterization of sex differences in spatial ability: A meta-analysis. *Child Development*, 56:1479–1498.

Lipset, S. M. 1976. The waving polls. *Public Interest*, 43 (Spring):70–89.

Lipsitt, L. P. 1971. Babies: They're a lot smarter than they look. *Psychology Today*, 5 (December):70–72+.

Locksley, A., Ortiz, V., and Hepburn, C. 1980. Social categorization and discriminatory behavior: Extinguishing the minimal intergroup discrimination effect. *Journal of Personality and Social Psychology*, 39:773–783.

Locurto, C. M., Terrace, H. S., and Gibbon, J. 1981. *Autoshaping and Conditioning Theory*. New York: Academic Press.

Loevinger, J., and Knoll, E. 1983. Personality: Stages, traits, and the self. *Annual Review of Psychology*, 34:195–222.

Loftus, E. F. 1979. *Eyewitness Testimony*. Cambridge, Mass.: Harvard University Press.

———. 1980. *Memory*. Reading, Mass.: Addison-Wesley.

———. 1984. Eyewitnesses: Essential but unreliable. *Psychology Today*, 18 (February):22–26.

——— and Loftus, G. R. 1980. On the permanence of stored information in the human brain. *American Psychologist*, 35:409–420.

Loftus, G. R. 1985. Evaluating forgetting curves. *Journal of Experimental Psychology: Learning, Memory, and Cognition*, 11:397–406.

Logan, G. D., and Cowan, W. B. 1984. On the ability to inhibit thought and action: A theory of an act of control. *Psychological Bulletin*, 91:295–327.

Loo, C. 1972. The effects of spatial density on the social behavior of children. *Journal of Applied Social Psychology*, 2:372–381.

Lord, C. G., Lepper, M. R., and Mackie, D. 1984. Attitude prototypes as determinants of attitude-behavior consistency. *Journal of Personality and Social Psychology*, 46:1254–1266.

Lorenz, K. 1935. Der kumpan in der umwelt des vogels. *Journal of Ornithology*, 83:137–213, 289–413.

———. 1966. *On Aggression*. New York: Harcourt, Brace and World.

Lowie, R. H. 1924. *Primitive Religion*. New York: Liveright.

Lubinski, D., and MacCorquodale, K. 1984. "Symbolic communication" between two pigeons (*Columba livia*) without unconditioned reinforcement. *Journal of Comparative Psychology*, 98:372–380.

Luborsky, L. 1984. *Principles of Psychoanalytic Psychotherapy: A Manual for Supportive-Expressive Treatment*. New York: Basic Books.

Ludwig, A. M., Brandsma, J. M., Wilbur, C. B., Bendfeldt, F., and Jameson, D. H. 1972. The objective study of a multiple personality. *Archives of General Psychiatry*, 26:298–310.

Luria, A. R. 1968. *The Mind of a Mnemonist*. New York: Basic Books.

Lykken, D. T. 1982. Research with twins: The concept of emergenesis. *Psychophysiology*, 19:361–373.

Lynch, G. 1984. A magical memory tour. *Psychology Today*, 18 (April):28–39.

——— and Baudry, M. 1982. Rapid structural modification in rat hippocampus: Evidence for its occurrence and an hypothesis concerning how it is produced. In Morrison, A., and Strick, P., Eds., *Changing Concepts of the Nervous System*. New York: Academic Press.

——— and ———. 1984. The biochemistry of memory: A new and specific hypothesis. *Science*, 224:1057–1063.

Lyons, R. D. 1984. Take your eye off the ball, scientist coaches sluggers. *New York Times* (June 12):19, 20.

Maass, A., and Clark, R. D., III. 1984. Hidden impact of minorities: Fifteen years of minority influence research. *Psychological Bulletin*, 95:428–450.

McBurney, D. H., and Collings, V. B. 1977. *Introduction to Sensation/ Perception*. Englewood Cliffs, N.J.: Prentice-Hall.

McCarley, R. W. 1978. Where dreams come from: A new theory. *Psychology*

Today, 12 (December):54–65+.

McCarthy, J. D., and Hoge, D. R. 1982. Analysis of age effects in longitudinal studies of adolescent self-esteem. *Developmental Psychology*, 18:372–379.

McClelland, D. C. 1965. Need achievement and entrepreneurship: A longitudinal study. *Journal of Personality and Social Psychology*, 1:389–392.

———, Atkinson, J. W., Clark, R. A., and Lowell, E. L. 1953. *The Achievement Motive*. New York: Appleton-Century-Crofts.

——— and Harris, T. G. 1971. To know why men do what they do: A conversation with David C. McClelland. *Psychology Today*, 4 (January):35–39.

——— and Winter, D. G. 1969. *Motivating Economic Achievement*. New York: Free Press.

Maccoby, E. E., and Jacklin, C. N. 1975. *The Psychology of Sex Differences*. Stanford, Calif.: Stanford University Press.

McCollough, C. 1965. Color adaptation of edge detectors in the human visual system. *Science*, 149:1115–1116.

McCrea, F. B. 1983. The politics of menopause: The "discovery" of a deficiency disease. *Social Problems*, 31:111–123.

MacDonald, K. 1984. An ethological-social learning theory of the development of altruism: Implication for human sociobiology. *Ethology and Sociobiology*, 5:97–109.

McDonald, K. 1985. Changes in facial expression can alter a person's moods. *Chronicle of Higher Education* (June 5):15.

McDougall, W. 1908. *An Introduction to Social Psychology*. London: Methuen.

Mace, D., and Mace, V. 1960. *Marriage: East and West*. New York: Doubleday.

McFarland, C., Ross, M., and Conway, M. 1984. Self-persuasion and self-presentation as mediators of anticipated attitude change. *Journal of Personality and Social Psychology*, 46:529–540.

Macfarlane, J. A. 1978. What a baby knows. *Human Nature*, 1 (February):74–81.

McGaugh, J. L. 1983. Hormonal influences on memory. *Annual Review of Psychology*, 34:297–323.

McGhie, A., and Chapman, J. 1961. Disorders of attention and perception in early schizophrenia. *British Journal of Medical Psychiatry*, 34:103–116.

McGinley, H., LeFevre, R., and McGinley, P. 1975. The influence of a communicator's body position on opinion change in others. *Journal of Personality and Social Psychology*, 31:686–690.

McGinnies, E. 1966. Introducing resistance to persuasion. In Berkowitz, L., Ed., *Advances in Experimental Social Psychology*. Vol. 1. New York: Academic Press.

McGrath, J. E. 1984. *Groups: Interaction and Performance*. Englewood Cliffs, N.J.: Prentice-Hall.

McGue, M., Bouchard, T. J., Jr., Lykken, D. T., and Feuer, D. 1984. Information processing abilities in twins reared apart. *Intelligence*, 8:239–258.

McGuinness, D. 1984. Aggression and war. *ICF Report*, 2 (December): 10–11.

——— and Pribram, K. 1980. The neuro-psychology of attention: Emotional and motivational controls. In Wittrock, M. C., Ed., *The Brain and Psychology*. New York: Academic Press.

McGuire, W. J. 1969. The nature of attitudes and attitude change. In Lindzey, G., and Aronson, E., Eds., *The Handbook of Social Psychology*. Reading, Mass.: Addison-Wesley.

———. 1985. Attitudes and attitude change. In Lindzey, G., and Aronson, E., Eds., *Handbook of Social Psychology*. Vol. 2. 3rd ed. New York: Random House.

McKean, K. 1985. Intelligence: New ways to measure the wisdom of man. *Discover* (October):25–41.

Mackenzie, B. 1984. Explaining race differences in IQ. *American Psychologist*, 39:1214–1233.

McKinlay, J. B. 1973. Social networks, lay consultation, and help-seeking behavior. *Social Forces*, 51:275–292.

MacKinnon, D. W. 1962. The nature and nurture of creative talent. *American Psychologist*, 17:484–495.

———. 1975. IPAR's contribution to the conceptualization and study of creativity. In Taylor, I. A., and Getzels, J. W., Eds., *Perspectives in Creativity*. Chicago: Aldine.

Mackintosh, N. J. 1983. *Conditioning and Associative Learning: Oxford Psychology Series, No. 3*. Oxford, England: Clarendon Press.

MacLusky, N. J., and Naftolin, F. 1981. Sexual differentiation of the central nervous system. *Science*, 211: 1294–1303.

Madden, N. A., and Slavin, R. F. 1983. Mainstreaming students with mild handicaps: Academic and social outcomes. *Review of Educational Research*, 53:519–569.

Maddux, J. E., and Rogers, R. W. 1983. Protection motivation and self-efficacy: A revised theory of fear appeals and attitude change. *Journal of Experimental Social Psychology*, 19:469–479.

Magnusson, D., and Endler, S. 1977. Interactional psychology: Present status and future prospects. In Magnusson, D., and Endler, S., Eds., *Personality at the Crossroads: Current Issues in Interactional Psychology*. Hillsdale, N.J.: Erlbaum.

Mahoney, M. J., and Arnkoff, D. B. 1978. Cognitive and self-control therapies. In Garfield, S. L., and Bergin, A. E., Eds., *Handbook of Psychotherapy and Behavior Change: An Empirical Analysis*. New York: Wiley.

Maier, S. F., and Laudenslager, M. 1985. Stress and health: Exploring the links. *Psychology Today*, 19 (August):44–49.

Maloney, L. D. 1985. Now hospices ease last days of the dying. *U.S. News & World Report* (February 11):70.

Mann, J. 1983. Behind the explosion in self-help groups. *U.S. News & World Report* (May 2):33–34.

Marcus, R. F. 1975. The child as elicitor of parental sanctions for independent and dependent behavior: A simulation of parent-child interaction. *Developmental Psychology*, 11:443–452.

Margolick, D. 1983. Courts, citing dangers, take a dimmer view of hypnosis. *New York Times* (July 10):8E.

Marks, G., Miller, N., and Maruyama, G. 1981. Effect of targets' physical attractiveness on assumptions of similarity. *Journal of Personality and Social Psychology*, 41:198–206.

Markus, H. 1977. Self-schemata and processing of information about the self. *Journal of Personality and Social Psychology*, 35:63–78.

——— and Smith, J. 1981. The influence of self-schemas on the perception of others. In Cantor, N., and Kilstrom, J. F., Eds., *Personality, Cognition, and Social Interaction*. Hillsdale, N.J.: Erlbaum.

Marquis, D. P. 1931. Can conditioned responses be established in the newborn infant? *Journal of Genetic Psychology*, 39:479–492.

Marr, D. 1982. *Vision: A Computational Investigation into the Human Representation and Processing of Visual Information*. San Francisco: Freeman.

Marshall, E. 1980. Psychotherapy works, but for whom? *Science*, 207:505–507.

Marx, J. L. 1982. Autoimmunity in left-handers. *Science*, 217:141–144.

Maslach, C. 1976. Burned-out. *Human Behavior*, 5 (September):16–22.

Masling, J. M., Ed. 1983. *Empirical Studies of Psychoanalytical Theories*.

Hillsdale, N.J.: Erlbaum.

Maslow, A. H. 1968. *Toward a Psychology of Being*. 2nd ed. New York: Van Nostrand.

———. 1970. *Motivation and Personality*. Rev. ed. New York: Harper & Row.

Mason, J. W. 1971. A re-evaluation of the concept of "non-specificity" in stress theory. *Journal of Psychiatric Research*, 8:323–333.

———. 1975. A historical view of the stress field: Part II. *Journal of Human Stress*, 1:22–36.

Masters, J. C. 1984. Psychology, research, and social policy. *American Psychologist*, 39:851–862.

Masters, W. H., and Johnson, V. E. 1970. *Human Sexual Inadequacy*. Boston: Little, Brown.

Matthews, K. A. 1982. Psychological perspectives on the Type A behavior pattern. *Psychological Bulletin*, 91:293–323.

Maurer, D. M., and Maurer, C. E. 1976. Newborn babies see better than you think. *Psychology Today*, 10 (October):85–88.

May, R. 1969. *Existential Psychology*. 2nd ed. New York: Random House.

Mazlish, B. 1981. Leader and led, individuals and group. *Psychohistory Review*, 9:214–237.

Meeker, B. F., and Weitzel-O'Neill, P. A. 1977. Sex roles and interpersonal behavior in task-oriented groups. *American Sociological Review*, 42:91–105.

Mehiel, R., and Bolles, R. C. 1984. Learned flavor preferences based on caloric outcome. *Animal Learning and Behavior*, 12:421–427.

Meichenbaum, D. H., 1977. *Cognitive Behavior Modification: An Integrative Approach*. New York: Plenum.

Meindl, J. R., and Lerner, M. J. 1984. Exacerbation of extreme responses to an out-group. *Journal of Personality and Social Psychology*, 47:71–84.

Melnechuk, T. 1983. The dream machine. *Psychology Today*, 17 (November):22–34.

Menzel, E. W., Jr., and Juno, C. 1982. Marmosets (*Saguinus fuscicollis*): Are learning sets learned? *Science*, 217:750–752.

——— and ———. 1984. Are learning sets learned? Or: Perhaps no nature-nurture issue has any simple answer. *Animal Learning and Behavior*, 12:113–115.

Messick, D. M., Wilke, H., Brewer, M. B., Kramer, R. M., Zemke, P. E., and Lui, L. 1983. Individual adaptations and structural change as solutions to social dilemmas. *Journal of Personality and Social Psychology*, 44:294–309.

Meyer, A. 1982. Do lie detectors lie? *Science 82*, 3:24–27.

Meyer, J. P., and Pepper, S. 1977. Need compatibility and marital adjustment in young married couples. *Journal of Personality and Social Psychology*, 35:331–342.

Meyers, W. 1985. Child care finds a champion in the corporation. *New York Times* (August 4):1F, 6F.

Milavsky, J. R., Kessler, R. C., Stripp, H. H., and Rubens, W. S. 1982. Television and aggression: Results of a panel study. In Pearl, D., Bouthilet, L., and Lazar, J., Eds., *Television and Behavior*. Vol. 2: *Technical Reviews*. Washington, D.C.: U.S. Government Printing Office.

Miles, L. E. M., Raynal, D. M., and Wilson, M. A. 1977. Blind man living in normal society has circadian rhythms of 24.9 hours. *Science*, 198:421–423.

Milgram, S. 1967. The small-world problem. *Psychology Today*, 1:61–67.

———. 1974. *Obedience to Authority*. New York: Harper & Row.

Milkman, H., and Sunderwirth, S. 1983. The chemistry of craving. *Psychology Today*, 17 (October):36–44.

Miller, C. T. 1982. The role of performance-related similarity in social comparison of abilities: A test of the related attributes hypothesis. *Journal of Experimental Social Psychology*, 18:513–523.

Miller, G. A. 1956. The magical number seven plus or minus two: Some limits on our capacity for processing information. *Psychological Review*, 63:81–97.

———. 1984. The test. *Science 84*, 5 (November):55–57.

Miller, L. B., and Bizzell, R. P. 1983. Long-term effects of four preschool programs: Sixth, seventh, and eighth grades. *Child Development*, 54:727–741.

Miller, L. K., and Schneider, R. 1970. The use of a token system in Project Headstart. *Journal of Applied Behavior Analysis*, 3:213–220.

Miller, N. 1982. Psychology today: The state of the science. *Psychology Today*, 16(May):51–52.

Miller, N. E. 1969. Learning of visceral and glandular responses. *Science*, 163:434–445.

———. 1983. Behavioral medicine: Symbiosis between laboratory and clinic. *Annual Review of Psychology*, 34:1–31.

———. 1985. Rx: Biofeedback. *Psychology Today*, 19 (February):54–59.

——— and Di Cara, L. 1967. Instrumental learning of heart rate

changes in curarized rats: Shaping and specificity to discriminative stimulus. *Journal of Comparative and Physiological Psychology*, 63:12–19.

Miller, R. C., and Berman, J. S. 1983. The efficacy of cognitive behavior therapies: A quantitative review of the research evidence. *Psychological Bulletin*, 94:39–53.

Mintz, R. S. 1968. Psychotherapy of the suicidal patient. In Resnik, H. L. P., Ed., *Suicidal Behaviors*. Boston: Little, Brown.

Minuchin, S. 1974. *Families and Family Therapy*. Cambridge, Mass.: Harvard University Press.

Mischel, W. 1968. *Personality and Assessment*. New York: Wiley.

———. 1971. *Introduction to Personality*. New York: Holt, Rinehart and Winston.

———. 1973. Toward a cognitive social learning reconceptualization of personality. *Psychological Review*, 80:252–283.

———. 1979. On the interface of cognition and personality: Beyond the person-situation debate. *American Psychologist*, 34:740–754.

———. 1983. Alternatives in the pursuit of predictability and consistency of persons: Stable data that yield unstable interpretations. *Journal of Personality*, 51:578–604.

———. 1984. Convergences and challenges in the search for consistency. *American Psychologist*, 39:351–364.

——— and Peake, P. K. 1983a. Analyzing the construction of consistency in personality. In Page, M. M., Ed., *Personality: Current Theory and Research*. Lincoln: University of Nebraska Press.

——— and ———. 1983b. Some facets of consistency: Replies to Epstein, Funder, and Bem. *Psychological Review*, 90:394–402.

Mishkin, M. 1978. Memory in monkeys severely impaired by combined but not separate removal of amygdala and hippocampus. *Nature*, 273:297–298.

———. 1982. A memory system in the monkey. In *Philosophical Transactions of the Royal Society of London*. London: The Royal Society.

Mitchell, J. E., Hatsukami, D., Eckert, E. D., and Pyle, R. L. 1985. Characteristics of 275 patients with bulimia. *American Journal of Psychiatry*, 142:482–485.

Mitler, M. M. 1983. How to get a good night's sleep—expert's advice. *U.S. News & World Report* (January 20):65–67.

———, Guilleminault, C., Orem, J., Zarcone, V. P., and Dement, W. C.

1975. Sleeplessness, sleep attacks, and things that go wrong in the night. *Psychology Today*, 9 (December): 45–50.

Mogul, K. M. 1979. Women in midlife: Decisions, rewards, and conflicts related to work and careers. *American Journal of Psychiatry*, 136:1139–1143.

Mollon, J. D. 1982. Color vision. *Annual Review of Psychology*, 33:41–85.

Monagan, D. 1986. Sudden death. *Discover* (January):64–71.

Monge, R. H. 1973. Developmental trends in factors of adolescent self-concept. *Developmental Psychology*, 8:382–393.

Monson, T. C., Hesley, J. W., and Chernick, L. 1982. Specifying when personality traits can and cannot predict behavior: An alternative to abandoning the attempt to predict single-act criteria. *Journal of Personality and Social Psychology*, 43:385–399.

Montagu, A., Ed. 1973. *Man and Aggression*. 2nd ed. New York: Oxford University Press.

———. 1981. *Growing Young*. New York: McGraw-Hill.

Montemayor, R., and Eisen, M. 1977. The development of self-conceptions from childhood to adolescence. *Developmental Psychology*. 13:314–319.

Mook, D. G. 1986. *Motivation*. New York: Norton.

Moore, E. G. Q. In press. Family socialization and the IQ test performance of traditionally and transracially adopted black children. *Developmental Psychology*.

Moore-Ede, M. C., Czeisler, C. A., and Richardson, G. S. 1983. Circadian timekeeping in health and disease. *New England Journal of Medicine*, 309:469–476.

———, Sulzman, F. M., and Fuller, C. A. 1982. *The Clocks That Time Us: Physiology of the Circadian Timing System*. Cambridge, Mass.: Harvard University Press.

Moos, R., and Tsu, V. D. 1977. The crisis of physical illness: An overview. In Moss, R., Ed., *Coping with Physical Illness*. New York: Plenum.

——— and VanDort, B. 1976. Student physical symptoms and the social climate of college living groups. Unpublished manuscript. Social Ecology Laboratory, Department of Psychiatry and Behavioral Sciences, Stanford University.

Moos, R. H., and Finney, J. W. 1983. The expanding scope of alcoholism treatment evaluation. *American Psychologist*, 38:1036–1044.

Moran, J. D., III, Milgram, R. M.,

Sawyers, J. K., and Fu, V. R. 1983. Original thinking in pre-school children. *Child Development*, 54:921–926.

Moreland, R. L. 1985. Social categorization and the assimilation of "new" group members. *Journal of Personality and Social Psychology*, 48:1173–1190.

Morell, P., and Norton, W. T. 1980. Myelin. *Scientific American*, 242 (May):88–119.

Morganthau, T. 1986. Abandoned. *Newsweek* (January 6):14–19.

Morris, J. 1974. *Conundrum*. New York: Harcourt Brace Jovanovich.

Morrison, A. R. 1983. A window on the sleeping brain. *Scientific American*, 248 (April):94–102.

Morrison, D. M. 1985. Adolescent contraceptive behavior: A review. *Psychological Bulletin*, 98:538–568.

Morrow, G. R., and Morrell, C. 1982. Behavioral treatment for the anticipatory nausea and vomiting induced by cancer chemotherapy. *New England Journal of Medicine*, 307:1476–1480.

Moscovici, S. 1976. *Social Influence and Social Change*. London: Academic Press.

Mosher, L. R., and Keith, S. J. 1979. Research of the psychosocial treatment of schizophrenia: A summary report. *American Journal of Psychiatry*, 136:623–651.

——— and Keith, S. J. 1980. Psychosocial treatment: Individual, group, family, and community support approaches. In *Special Report: Schizophrenia 1980*. Washington, D.C.: U.S. Government Printing Office.

Moskowitz, B. A. 1978. The acquisition of language. *Scientific American*, 239 (November):92–109.

Mueller, D. P., Edwards, D. W., and Yarvis, R. M. 1977. Stressful life events and psychiatric symptomatology: Change or undesirability? *Journal of Health and Social Behavior*, 18:307–317.

Murphy, C., and Cain, W. S. 1980. Taste and olfaction: Independence vs. interaction. *Physiology & Behavior*, 24:601–605.

Murphy, C. M. 1978. Pointing in the context of a shared activity. *Child Development*, 49:371–380.

Murray, H. A. 1938. *Explorations in Personality*. London: Oxford University Press.

Murstein, B. I. 1972. Physical attractiveness and marital choice. *Journal of Personality and Social Psychology*, 22:8–12.

Mussen, P. H., and Jones, M. C. 1957.

Self-conceptions, motivations, and interpersonal attitudes of late- and early-maturing boys. *Child Development*. 28:243–256.

Mustillo, P. 1985. Binocular mechanisms mediating crossed and uncrossed stereopsis. *Psychological Bulletin*, 97:187–201.

Myers, J. L., O'Brien, E. J., Balota, D. A., and Toyofuku, M. L. 1984. Memory search without interference: The role of integration. *Cognitive Psychology*, 16:217–242.

Nairn, A. 1980. *The Reign of ETS: The Corporation That Makes Up Minds*. Washington, D.C.: Ralph Nader.

Nassau, K. 1980. The cause of color. *Scientific American*, 243 (October):124–154.

Nathan, E., and Harris, S. L. 1975. *Psychopathology and Society*. New York: McGraw-Hill.

National Academy of Sciences. 1982. *Marijuana and Health*. Washington, D.C.: National Academy Press.

National Institute of Mental Health. 1980. *Special Report: Schizophrenia: 1980*. Washington, D.C.: U.S. Government Printing Office.

———. 1985. *Mental Health, United States, 1985*. Washington, D.C.: U.S. Government Printing Office.

Nawas, M. M. 1971. Change in efficiency of ego functioning and complexity from adolescence to young adulthood. *Developmental Psychology*, 4:412–415.

Neale, J. M., and Oltmanns, T. F. 1980. *Schizophrenia*. New York: Wiley.

Neher, A. 1980. *The Psychology of Transcendence*. Jamaica, N.Y.: Spectrum.

Neisser, U. 1967. *Cognitive Psychology*. New York: Appleton-Century-Crofts.

———. 1976. *Cognition and Reality*. San Francisco: Freeman.

Nelson, B. 1983. Studies report mental illness in most homeless in 2 cities. *New York Times* (October 2):17.

Nelson, D. L., Reed, V. S., and McEvoy, C. L. 1977. Learning to order pictures and words: A model of sensory and semantic encoding. *Journal of Experimental Psychology: Human Learning and Memory*, 3:485–497.

Nelson, E. A. 1969. Social reinforcement for expression versus suppression of aggression. *Merrill-Palmer Quarterly*, 15:259–278.

Nelson, J. C., and Charney, D. S. 1981. The symptoms of major depressive illness. *American Journal of Psychiatry*, 138:1–13.

Nelson, K. 1972. The relation of form recognition to concept development.

Child Development, 43:67–74.

Neugarten, B. L. 1979. Time, age, and the life cycle. *American Journal of Psychiatry*, 136:887–894.

———. 1982. Age or need? *National Forum*, 42:25–27.

———, Wood, V., Kraines, R. J., and Loomis, B. 1963. Women's attitudes towards the menopause. *Vita Humana*, 6:140–151.

Newcomb, T. 1943. *Personality and Social Change*. New York: Dryden.

———, Koenig, K. E., Flacks, R., and Warwick, D. P. 1967. *Persistence and Change: Bennington College and Its Students After 25 Years*. New York: Wiley.

Newell, A., and Simon, H. A. 1956. The logic theory machine: A complex information-processing system. *IRE Transactions on Information Theory*, IT-2:61–69.

——— and ———. 1961. Computer simulation of human thinking. *Science*, 134:2011–2017.

——— and ———. 1972. *Human Problem Solving*. Englewood Cliffs, N.J.: Prentice-Hall.

Newman, G., and Nichols, C. R. 1960. Sexual activities and attitudes in older persons. *Journal of the American Medical Association*, 173:33–35.

Newman, R. G. 1983. The need to redefine "addiction." *New England Journal of Medicine*, 308:1096–1098.

Newsweek. 1983. The tavern rape: Cheers and no help. *Newsweek* (March 21):25.

New York Times. 1985. Entrepreneurs: New heroes. *New York Times* (December 11):21.

Nicholi, A. M., Jr. 1983. The nontherapeutic use of psychoactive drugs. *New England Journal of Medicine*, 308:925–933.

Nicholls, J. G. 1984. Achievement motivation: Conceptions of ability, subjective experience, task choice, and performance. *Psychological Review*, 91:328–346.

NIMH/NIH Consensus Development Panel. 1985. Mood disorders: Pharmacologic prevention of recurrence. *American Journal of Psychiatry*, 142:469–476.

Nisbett, R. E. 1972. Hunger, obesity, and the ventromedial hypothalamus. *Psychological Review*, 79:433–453.

Noback, C. R., and Demarest, R. J. 1981. *The Human Nervous System*. New York: McGraw-Hill.

Noonan, D. 1983. Boxing and the brain. *New York Times Magazine* (June 12):40+.

Norman, D. A., Ed. 1972. *Memory and Attention*. 2nd ed. New York: Wiley.

Novin, D., Gonzalez, M. F., and

Sanderson, J. D. 1976. Paradoxical increased feeding following glucose infusions in recovered lateral rats. *American Journal of Physiology*, 230:1084–1089.

O'Brien, D. F. 1982. The chemistry of vision. *Science*, 218:961–966.

Offer, D. 1969. *The Psychological World of the Teen-ager: A Study of Normal Adolescent Boys*. New York: Basic Books.

——— and Offer, J. B. 1975. *From Teenage to Young Manhood*. New York: Basic Books.

———, Ostrov, E., and Howard, K. I. 1981. *The Adolescent: A Psychological Self-Portrait*. New York: Basic Books.

Ogbu, J. U. 1981. Origins of human competence: A cultural-ecological perspective. *Child Development*, 52:413–429.

Olds, J. 1958. Self-stimulation of the brain. *Science*, 127:315–324.

——— and Milner, P. 1954. Positive reinforcement produced by electrical stimulation of septal area and other regions of rat brain. *Journal of Comparative and Physiological Psychology*, 47:419–427.

——— and Olds, M. E. 1965. Drives, rewards and the brain. In Barron, F., Ed., *New Directions in Psychology II*. New York: Holt, Rinehart and Winston.

Olds, M. E., and Fobes, J. L. 1981. The central basis of motivation: Intracranial self-stimulation studies. *Annual Review of Psychology*, 32:523–574.

Olson, D. H., Russell, C. S., and Sprenkle, D. H. 1980. Marital and family therapy: A decade review. *Journal of Marriage and the Family*, 42:973–993.

O'Malley, P. M., and Bachman, J. G. 1983. Self-esteem: Change and stability between ages 13 and 23. *Developmental Psychology*, 19:257–268.

Oomura, Y., Ooyama, H., Yamamoto, T., and Naka, F. 1967. *Physiology and Behavior*, 2:97–115.

Orcutt, J. D. 1975. Deviance as a situated phenomenon: Variations in the social interpretation of marijuana and alcohol use. *Social Problems*, 22:346–356.

Osborn, A. F. 1963. *Applied Imagination*. 3rd ed. New York: Scribner.

Osgood, C. 1953. *Method and Theory in Experimental Psychology*. New York: Oxford University Press.

Ostroff, R., Giller, E., Bonese, K., Ebersole, E., Harkness, L., and Mason, J. 1982. Neuroendocrine risk factors of suicidal behavior. *American*

Journal of Psychiatry, 139:1323–1325.

Owen, D. 1985. *None of the Above*. Boston: Houghton Mifflin.

Paivio, A. 1971. *Imagery and Verbal Processes*. New York: Holt, Rinehart and Winston.

Palmer, R. L. 1981. *Electroconvulsive Therapy: An Appraisal*. New York: Oxford University Press.

Paloutzian, R. F. 1981. Purpose in life and value changes following conversion. *Journal of Personality and Social Psychology*, 41:1153–1160.

Parks, T. E. 1984. Illusory figures: A (mostly) atheoretical review. *Psychological Bulletin*, 95:282–300.

Parnes, H. S. 1981. *Work and Retirement—A Longitudinal Study of Men*. Cambridge, Mass.: MIT Press.

Parnes, S. J. 1971. Can creativity be increased? In Davis, G. A., and Scott, J. A., Eds., *Training Creative Thinking*. New York: Holt, Rinehart and Winston.

Pasewark, R. A. 1981. Insanity plea: A review of the research literature. *Journal of Psychiatry and Law*, 9:357–401.

Passingham, R. E. 1982. *The Human Primate*. New York: Oxford University Press.

Patterson, C. H. 1984. Empathy, warmth, and genuineness in psychotherapy: A review of reviews. *Psychotherapy*, 21:431–438.

Patterson, F. 1985. Talking with apes. *USA Today* (March 1):11A.

Paul, G. L. 1967. Strategy of outcome research in psychotherapy. *Journal of Consulting Psychology*, 31:109–119.

Paul, S. M., Hulihan-Giblin, B., and Skolnick, P. 1982. (+) – Amphetamine binding to rat hypothalamus: Relation to anorexic potency of phenylethylamines. *Science*, 218:487–490.

Pavlov, I. P. 1927. *Conditioned Reflexes*. Trans. by G. V. Anrep. London: Oxford University Press.

Pearl, P. 1982. *Television and Behavior: 10 Years of Scientific Research*. Washington, D.C.: U.S. Government Printing Office.

Peele, S. 1984a. The cultural context of psychological approaches to alcoholism. *American Psychologist*, 39:1337–1351.

———. 1984b. The question of personality. *Psychology Today*, 18 (December):54–56.

Pelchat, M. L., and Rozin, P. 1982. The special role of nausea in the acquisition of food dislikes by humans. *Appetite: Journal of Intake Research*, 3:341–351.

Pell, S., and Fayerweather, W. E. 1985.

Trends in the incidence of myocardial infarction and in associated mortality and morbidity in large employed population, 1957–1983. *New England Journal of Medicine*, 312:1005–1011.

Pellegrino, J. W. 1985. Anatomy of analogy. *Psychology Today*, 19 (October):49–54.

Penfield, W., and Rasmussen, T. 1950. *The Cerebral Cortex of Man*. New York: Macmillan.

Pennebaker, J. W., and O'Heeron, R. C. 1984. Confiding in others and illness rate among spouses of suicide and accidental-death victims. *Journal of Abnormal Psychology*, 93:473–476.

Perkins, D. N. 1981. *The Mind's Best Work*. Cambridge, Mass.: Harvard University Press.

Perlman, B., and Hartman, A. 1982. Burnout: Summary and future research. *Human Relations*, 35:283–305.

Perls, F. S. 1970. Four lectures. In Fagan, J., and Shepard, I. L., Eds., *Gestalt Therapy Now: Therapy, Techniques, Applications*. Palo Alto, Calif.: Science and Behavior Books.

———, Hefferline, R. F., and Goodman, P. 1965. *Gestalt Therapy*. New York: Dell.

Perr, I. N. 1983. The insanity defense: A tale of two cities. *American Journal of Psychiatry*, 140:873–874.

Persky, H., Charney, N., Lief, H. I., O'Brien, C. P., Miller, W. R., and Strauss, D. 1978. The relationship of plasma estradiol level to sexual behavior in young women. *Psychosomatic Medicine*, 40:523–535.

Pervin, L. A. 1985. Personality: Current controversies, issues, and directions. *Annual Review of Psychology*, 36:83–114.

Petersen, A. C. 1983. Menarche: Meaning of measures and measures of meaning. In Golub, S., Ed., *Menarche: The Transition from Girl to Woman*. Lexington, Mass.: Heath.

Pfeiffer, J. 1985. Girl talk, boy talk. *Science 85*, 6 (February):58–63.

Philips, D. P., and Feldman, K. A. 1973. A dip in deaths before ceremonial occasions: Some new relationships between social integration and mortality. *American Sociological Review*, 38:678–696.

Phoenix, C. H., Goy, R. W., and Resko, J. A. 1969. Psychosexual differentiation as a function of androgenic stimulation. In Diamond, M., Ed., *Reproduction and Sexual Behavior*. Bloomington: Indiana University Press.

Piaget, J. 1952. *The Origins of Intelligence in Children*. Trans. by M. Cook. New York: International Universities Press.

———. 1962. *Play, Dreams, and Imitation in Childhood*. New York: Norton.

Pickar, D., Labarca, R., Linnoila, M., Roy, A., Hommer, D., Everett, D., and Paul, S. M. 1984. Neuroleptic-induced decrease in plasma homovanillic acid and antipsychotic activity in schizophrenic patients. *Science*, 225:954–956.

Pietromonaco, P. R., and Markus, H. 1985. The nature of negative thoughts in depression. *Journal of Personality and Social Psychology*, 48:799–807.

Pines, A. M., and Aronson, E. 1981. *Burnout: From Tedium to Personal Growth*. New York: Free Press.

Pines, M. 1978. Is sociobiology all wet? *Psychology Today*, 11 (May):23–24.

———. 1981. The civilizing of Genie. *Psychology Today*, 15 (September): 28–34.

———. 1982a. Violence termed hard to foretell. *New York Times* (June 27):20.

———. 1982b. What produces great skills? Specific pattern is discerned. *New York Times* (March 30):21–22.

———. 1983a. Can a rock walk? *Psychology Today*, 17 (November): 46–54.

———. 1983b. Suicide signals. *Science 83*, 4 (October):55–58.

Pipp, S., Shaver, P., Jennings, S., Lamborn, S., and Fischer, K. W. 1985. Adolescents' theories about the development of their relationships with parents. *Journal of Personality and Social Psychology*, 48:991–1001.

Pitkanen-Pulkkinen, L. 1979. Self control as a prerequisite for constructive behavior. In Feshbach, S., and Fraczek, A., Eds., *Aggression and Behavior Change*. New York: Praeger.

Plomin, R., DeFries, J. C., and Loehlin, J. C. 1977. Genotype-environment interaction and correlation in analysis of human behavior. *Psychological Bulletin*, 84:309–322.

———, and McClearn, G. E. 1980. *Behavioral Genetics: A Primer*. San Francisco: Freeman.

Plum, E., and Posner, J. B. 1980. *The Diagnosis of Stupor and Coma*. 3rd ed. Philadelphia: Davis.

Plummer, K. 1975. *Sexual Stigma: An Interactionist Account*. London: Routledge.

Pocs, O., et al. 1977. Is there sex after 40? *Psychology Today*, 10 (June):54–57.

Polivy, J., and Herman, C. P. 1985. Dieting and bingeing: A causal analysis. *American Psychologist*, 40:193–201.

Porter, B. 1983. Mind hunters. *Psychology Today*, 17 (April):44–52.

Potkin, S. G., Cannon, H. E., Murphy, D. L., and Wyatt, R. J. 1978. Are paranoid schizophrenics biologically different from other schizophrenics? *New England Journal of Medicine*, 298:61–66.

Power, T. G. 1985. Mother– and father–infant play: A developmental analysis. *Child Development*, 56:1514–1524.

Prawat, R. S., Jones, H., and Hampton, J. 1979. Longitudinal study of attitude development in pre-, early, and later adolescent samples. *Journal of Educational Psychology*, 71:363–369.

Prazdny, K. 1985. On the nature of inducing forms generating perceptions of illusory contours. *Perception & Psychophysics*, 37:237–242.

Premack, D. 1983. Animal cognition. *Annual Review of Psychology*, 34:351–362.

——— and Premack, A. J. 1983. *The Mind of an Ape*. New York: Norton.

Prescott, P., and DeCasper, A. J. 1981. Do newborns prefer their father's voice? Apparently not. Paper presented at the biennial meeting of the Society for Research in Child Development, Boston.

Pressey, S. L., Robinson, F. P., and Horrocks, J. E. 1959. *Psychology in Education*. New York: Harper & Row.

Pribram, K. H., and McGuinness, D. 1975. Arousal, activation, and effort in the control of attention. *Psychological Review*, 82:116–149.

Price, D. D., Rafii, A., Watkins, L. R., and Buckingham, B. 1984. A psychophysical analysis of acupuncture analgesia. *Pain*, 19:27–42.

Price, R. H., and Bouffard, D. L. 1974. Behavioral appropriateness and situational constraint as dimensions of social behavior. *Journal of Personality and Social Psychology*, 30:579–586.

Price-Williams, D. R. 1985. Cultural psychology. In Lindzey, G., and Aronson, E., Eds., *Handbook of Social Psychology*. Vol. 2. 3rd ed. New York: Random House.

Priest, R. R., and Sawyer, J. 1967. Proximity and peership: Bases of balance in interpersonal attraction. *American Journal of Sociology*, 72:633–649.

Prusiner, S. B. 1984. Some speculations about prions, amyloid, and Alzheimer's disease. *New England Journal of Medicine*, 310:661–663.

Pryor, J. B., Ostrom, T. M., Dukerich, J. M., Mitchell, M. L., and Herstein, J. A. 1983. Preintegrative categorization of social information:

The role of persons as organizing categories. *Journal of Personality and Social Psychology*, 44:923–932.

Psychology Today. 1984. Gifted and talented. *Psychology Today*, 18 (June):19.

Putnam, F. W. 1982. The brain: Trace of Eve's faces. *Psychology Today*, 16 (October):88.

Quinn, W. H. 1983. Personal and family adjustment in later life. *Journal of Marriage and the Family*, 45:57–73.

Rabbie, J. M., and Horowitz, M. 1969. Arousal of ingroup–outgroup bias by a chance win or loss. *Journal of Personality and Social Psychology*, 13:269–277.

Rabkin, J. G., and Struening, E. L. 1976. Life events, stress, and illness. *Science*, 194 (December):1013–1020.

Raboch, J., and Starka, L. 1973. Reported coital activity of men and levels of plasma testosterone. *Archives of Sexual Behavior*, 2:309–15.

Rafferty, C. 1984. Study of gifted from childhood to old age. *New York Times* (April 23):18.

Rahe, R. H. 1968. Life-change measurements as a predictor of illness. *Proceedings of the Royal Society of Medicine*, 61:1124–1126.

———. 1974. Life change and subsequent illness reports. In Gunderson, E. K. E., and Rahe, R. H., Eds., *Life Stress and Illness.* Springfield, Ill.: Charles C. Thomas.

Ramsey, T. A., and Cox, M. 1982. Lithium and the kidney: A review. *American Journal of Psychiatry*, 139:443–449.

Randi, J. 1978. The psychology of conjuring. *Technology Review*, 80 (January):56–63.

Rasool, C. G., and Selkoe, D. J. 1985. Sharing of specific antigens by degenerating neurons in Pick's disease and Alzheimer's disease. *New England Journal of Medicine*, 312:700–705.

Rathus, S. A. 1984. *Psychology.* 2nd ed. New York: Holt, Rinehart and Winston.

Raush, H. L., and Raush, C. 1968. *The Halfway House Movement: A Search for Sanity.* New York: Appleton-Century-Crofts.

Reder, L. M., and Ross, B. H. 1983. Integrated knowledge in different tasks: The role of retrieval strategy on fan effects. *Journal of Experimental Psychology: Learning, Memory, and Cognition*, 9:55–72.

Reed, D., and Weinberg, M. S. 1984. Premarital coitus: Developing and established sexual scripts. *Social Psychology Quarterly*, 47:129–138.

Reinhold, R. 1982. Strife and despair at South Pole illuminate psychology of isolation. *New York Times* (January 12):17, 19.

Reinisch, J. M. 1981. Prenatal exposure to synthetic progestins increases potential for aggression in humans. *Science*, 211:1171–1173.

———, Gandelman, R., and Speigel, F. S. 1979. Prenatal influences on cognitive abilities: Human genetic and endocrine syndromes. In Wittig, M. A., and Peterson, A. C., Eds., *Sex-Related Differences in Cognitive Functioning.* New York: Academic Press.

Reis, H. T., Nezlek, J., and Wheeler, L. 1980. Physical attractiveness in social interaction. *Journal of Personality and Social Psychology*, 38:604–617.

———, Wheeler, L., Kernis, M. H., Spiegel, N., and Nezlek, J. 1985. On specificity in the impact of social participation on physical and psychological health. *Journal of Personality and Social Psychology*, 48:456–471.

———, ———, Spiegel, N., Kernis, M. H., Nezlek, J., and Perri, M. 1982. Physical attractiveness in social interaction: II. Why does appearance affect social experience? *Journal of Personality and Social Psychology*, 43:979–996.

Reisenzein, R. 1983. The Schachter theory of emotion: Two decades later. *Psychological Bulletin*, 94:239–264.

Reiss, I. L. 1976. *Family Systems in America.* 2nd ed. Hinsdale, Ill.: Dryden Press.

Reitman, J. S. 1971. Mechanisms of forgetting in short-term memory. *Cognitive Psychology*, 2:185–195.

———. 1974. Without surreptitious rehearsal, information in short-term memory decays. *Journal of Verbal Learning and Verbal Behavior*, 13:365–377.

Rensberger, B. 1985. Feigned emotion often becomes real. *Washington Post* (May 30):A7.

Reschly, D. J. 1981. Psychological testing in educational classification and placement. *American Psychologist*, 36:1094–1102.

Rescorla, R. A., and Holland, P. C. 1982. Behavioral studies of associative learning in animals. *Annual Review of Psychology*, 33:265–308.

——— and Wagner, A. R. 1972. A theory of Pavlovian conditioning: Variations in the effectiveness of reinforcement and nonreinforcement. In Black, A. H., and Prokasy, W. F., Eds., *Classical Conditioning II: Current Research and Theory.* New York: Appleton-Century-Crofts.

Reskin, B. F., and Coverman, S. 1985. Sex and race in the determinants of psychophysical distress: A reappraisal of the sex-role hypothesis. *Social Forces*, 63:1038–1059.

Restak, R. M. 1982. Newborn knowledge. *Science 82*, 3 (January): 58–65.

Rhine, J. B. 1964. *Extra-Sensory Perception.* Boston: Branden.

Ricateau, P. 1971. Processus de categorisation d'autrui et les mecanismes d'influence. *Bulletin de Psychologie*, 24:909–919.

Riccio, D. C., Richardson, R., and Ebner, D. L. 1984. Memory retrieval deficits based upon altered contextual cues: A paradox. *Psychological Bulletin*, 96:152–165.

Richter, C. 1957. On the phenomenon of sudden death in animals and man. *Psychosomatic Medicine*, 19:190–198.

Ricks, T. E. 1984. Researchers say day-care centers are implicated in spread of disease. *Wall Street Journal* (September 5):15.

Riegel, K. F. 1973. Dialectic operations: The final period of cognitive development. *Human Development*, 16:346–370.

———. 1976. The dialectics of human development. *American Psychologist*, 31:689–700.

Riley, V. 1975. Mouse mammary tumors: Alteration of incidence as an apparent function of stress. *Science*, 189:465–468.

———. 1981. Psychoneuroendocrine influences on immunocompetence and neoplasia. *Science*, 212:1100–1109.

Robbins, T., and Anthony, D. 1980. The limits of "coercive persuasion" as an explanation for conversion to authoritarian sects. *Political Psychology*, 2:22–37.

Roberge, J. J., and Flexer, B. K. 1979. Further examinations of formal operational reasoning abilities. *Child Development*, 50:478–484.

Robey, B. 1982. Older Americans. *American Demographics*, 4 (June):40–41.

Robinson, N. M., and Robinson, M. B. 1976. *The Mentally Retarded Child.* New York: McGraw-Hill.

Rock, I. 1985. Perception and knowledge. *Acta Psychologica*, 59:3–22.

Rodgers, J. E. 1982a. The malleable memory of the eyewitness. *Science 82*, 3 (June):32–35.

———. 1982b. Roots of madness. *Science 82* (July/August):85–91.

Rodin, J. 1978. Has the distinction between internal versus external control of feeding outlived its usefulness? In Poray, G. A., Ed., *Recent Advances in Obesity Research*, London: Newman.

———. 1981. Current status of the internal-external hypothesis for obesity. *American Psychologist*, 36:361–372.

——— and Langer, E. J. 1977. Long-term effects of a control-relevant intervention with the institutionalized aged. *Journal of Personality and Social Psychology*, 35:897–902.

Roger, D. B., and Schumacher, A. 1983. Effects of individual differences on dyadic conversational strategies. *Journal of Personality and Social Psychology*, 45:700–705.

Rogers, C. 1951. *Client-centered Therapy*. Boston: Houghton Mifflin.

———. 1961. *On Becoming a Person*. Boston: Houghton Mifflin.

Rogers, R. W., and Deckner, C. W. 1975. Effects of fear appeals and physiological arousal upon emotion, attitudes, and cigarette smoking. *Journal of Personality and Social Psychology*, 32:222–330.

Rokeach, M. 1971. Long-range experimental modification of values, attitudes, and behavior. *American Psychologist*, 26:453–459.

Rolls, E. T., Burton, M. J. and Mora, F. 1976. Hypothalamic neuronal responses associated with the sight of food. *Brain Research*, 111:53–66.

Rook, K. S., and Dooley, D. 1985. Applying social support research: Theoretical problems and future directions. *Journal of Social Issues*, 41:5–28.

Rosen, R., and Hall, E. 1984. *Sexuality*. New York: Random House.

Rosenhan, D. L. 1973. On being sane in insane places. *Science*, 179:250–258.

Rosenman, R. H., Brand, R. J., Jenkins, C. D., Friedman, M., Straus, R., and Wurm, M. 1975. Coronary heart disease in the Western Collaborative Group Study: Final follow-up experience of 8½ years. *Journal of the American Medical Association*, 233:872–877.

Rosenthal, R. 1966. *Experimenter Effects in Behavioral Research*. New York: Appleton-Century-Crofts.

——— and DePaulo, B. M. 1979. Sex differences in accommodation in nonverbal communication. In Rosenthal, R., Ed., *Skill in Nonverbal Communication*. Cambridge, Mass.: Oelgeschlager, Grinn, and Hain.

——— and Jacobson, L. 1968. *Pygmalion in the Classroom*. New York: Holt, Rinehart and Winston.

——— and Rosnow, R. L., Eds. 1969. *Artifact in Behavioral Research*. New York: Academic Press.

Rosenthal, T. L., and Bandura, A. 1978. Psychological modeling: Theory and practice. In Garfield, S. L., and Bergin, A. E., Eds., *Handbook of Psychotherapy and Behavior Change: An Empirical Analysis*. New York: Wiley.

——— and Zimmerman, B. J. 1978. *Social Learning and Cognition*. New York: Academic Press.

Rosenzweig, M. R. 1984. Experience, memory, and the brain. *American Psychologist*, 39:365–376.

Rosow, I. 1957. Issues in the concept of need-complementarity. *Sociometry*, 20:216–233.

Ross, C. E., and Mirowsky, J., II. 1979. A comparison of life-event-weighting schemes: Change, undesirability, and effect-propositional indices. *Journal of Health and Social Behavior*, 20:166–177.

Ross, L. 1974. Effects of manipulating the salience of food upon consumption by obese and normal eaters. In Schachter, S., and Rodin, J., Eds., *Obese Humans and Rats*. Washington, D.C.: Erlbaum/Halsted.

———. 1977. The intuitive psychologist and his shortcomings: Distortions in the attribution process. In Barkowitz, L., Ed., *Advances in Experimental Social Psychology*. Vol. 10. New York: Academic Press.

———, Greene, D., and House, P. 1977. The "false consensus" effect: An egocentric bias in social perception and attribution processes. *Journal of Experimental Social Psychology*, 13:279–301.

Ross, M., and Fletcher, G. J. O. 1985. Attribution and social perception. In Lindzey, G., and Aronson, E., Eds., *Handbook of Social Psychology*. Vol. 2. 3rd ed. New York: Random House.

———, McFarland, C., Conway, M., and Zanna, M. P. 1983. Reciprocal relation between attitudes and behavior recall: Committing people to newly formed attitudes. *Journal of Personality and Social Psychology*, 45:257–267.

Rothbart, M. K. 1981. Measurement of temperament in infancy. *Child Development*, 52:569–578.

Routtenberg, A. 1978. The reward system of the brain. *Scientific American*, 239 (November):154–164.

Rowland, W. J. 1982a. Mate choice by male sticklebacks, *Gasterosteus Aculeatus*. *Animal Behavior*, 30:1093–1098.

———. 1982b. The effects of male nuptial coloration on stickleback aggression. *Behaviour*, 80:118–126.

Rozin, P. 1982. "Taste–smell confusions" and the duality of the olfactory sense. *Perception & Psychophysics*, 31:397–401.

———, Fallon, A., and Mandell, R. 1984. Family resemblance in attitudes to foods. *Developmental Psychology*, 20:309–314.

Rubin, D. C. 1985. The subtle deceiver: Recalling our past. *Psychology Today*, 19 (September):39–46.

Rubin, J. Z., Provenzano, F. J., and Luria, Z. 1974. The eye of the beholder: Parents' views on sex of newborns. *American Journal of Orthopsychiatry*, 44:512–519.

Rubin, K. H., Fein, G. G., and Vandenberg, B. 1983. Play. In Hetherington, E. M., Ed., *Handbook of Child Psychology*. Vol. 4: *Socialization, Personality, and Social Development*. New York: Wiley.

Rubin, Z. 1977. The love research. *Human Behavior*, 6 (February):56–59.

Rusbult, C. E. 1983. A longitudinal test of the investment model: The development (and deterioration) of satisfaction and commitment in heterosexual involvements. *Journal of Personality and Social Psychology*, 45:101–117.

Rush, A. J., Beck, A. T., Kovacs, M., Weissenburger, M., and Hollon, S. D. 1982. Comparison of the effects of cognitive therapy and pharmaco-therapy on hopelessness and self-concept. *American Journal of Psychiatry*, 139:862–866.

Russell, C. 1980. The elderly: Myths and facts. *American Demographics*, 2 (March):30–31.

Rutkowski, G. K., Gruder, C. L., and Romer, D. 1983. Group cohesiveness, social norms, and bystander intervention. *Journal of Personality and Social Psychology*, 44:545–552.

Sager, G. H. 1971. *Introduction to Motor Behavior*. Reading, Mass.: Addison-Wesley.

Salholz, E. 1984. Unfriendly skies. *Newsweek* (April 23): 72.

Salk, L. 1962. Mother's heartbeat as an imprinting stimulus. *Transactions of the New York Academy of Sciences*, 24:753–763.

Salzinger, K. 1979. Language behavior. In Catania, A. C., and Brigham, T. A., Eds., *Handbook of Applied Behavior Analysis*. New York: Irvington.

Salzman, L., and Thaler, F. H. 1981. Obsessive-compulsive disorders: A review of the literature. *American Journal of Psychiatry*, 138:286–296.

Sapir, E. 1949. *Selected Writings in Language, Cultural Personality*.

Berkeley: University of California Press.

Sarbin, T. R., and Coe, W. C. 1979. Hypnosis and psychopathology: Replacing old myths with fresh metaphors. *Journal of Abnormal Psychology*, 88:506–526.

Sassen, G. 1980. Success anxiety in women: A constructivist interpretation of its source and significance. *Harvard Educational Review*, 50:13–24.

Savage-Rumbaugh, E. S., Rumbaugh, D. M., Smith, S. T., and Lawson, J. 1980. Reference: The linguistic essential. *Science*, 210:922–924.

Savin-Williams, R. C., and Demo, D. H. 1984. Developmental change and stability in adolescent self-concept. *Developmental Psychology*, 20:1100–1110.

Scarr, S. 1981. Testing for children: Assessment and the many determinants of intellectual competence. *American Psychologist*, 36:1159–1166.

———. 1984. *Mother Care/Other Care*. New York: Basic Books.

———. 1985a. An author's frame of mind (Review of *Frames of Mind* by H. Gardner). *New Ideas in Psychology*, 3:95–100.

———. 1985b. Constructing psychology: Making facts and fables of our times. *American Psychologist*, 40:499–512.

———. 1985c. Personality and experience: Individual encounters with the world. Paper delivered at the Henry A. Murray Lectures in Personality, Michigan State University, April 12–13.

——— and Carter-Saltzman, L. 1983. Genetic differences in intelligence. In Sternberg, R. A., Ed., *Handbook of Intelligence*. Cambridge, Mass.: Harvard University Press.

——— and Kidd, K. K. 1983. Developmental and behavior genetics. In Haith, M., and Campos, J., Eds., *Manual of Child Psychology: Infancy and the Biology of Development*. Vol. 2. New York: Wiley, pp. 343–433.

——— and McCartney, K. 1983. How people make their own environments: A theory of genotype → environment effects. *Child Development*, 54:424–435.

———, Webber, P. L., Weinberg, R. A., and Wittig, M. A. 1981. Personality resemblance among adolescents and their parents in biologically related and adoptive families. *Journal of Personality and Social Psychology*, 40:885–898.

——— and ———. 1983. The Minnesota Adoption Study: Genetic differences and malleability. *Child Development*, 54:260–267.

——— and Weinberg, R. A. 1976. IQ test performance of black children adopted by white families. *American Psychologist*, 31:726–739.

——— and Williams, M. L. 1973. The effects of early stimulation on low-birth-weight infants. *Child Development*, 44:94–101.

Scarr-Salapatek, S. 1977. Learning, intelligence, and intelligence testing. In Marx, M. H., and Bunch, M. E., Eds., *Fundamentals and Applications of Learning*. New York: Macmillan.

Schacht, T. E. 1985. DSM-III and the politics of truth. *American Psychologist*, 40:513–521.

Schachter, S. 1971. *Emotion, Obesity, and Crime*. New York: Academic Press.

——— and Singer J. 1962. Cognitive, social, and physiological determinants of emotional state. *Psychological Review*, 69:379–399.

Schaefer, C. E. 1969. The self-concept of creative adolescents. *Journal of Psychology*, 72:233–242.

Schaeffer, G. H., and Patterson, M. L. 1980. Intimacy, arousal, and small group crowding. *Journal of Personality and Social Psychology*, 38:283–290.

Schafer, A. T., and Gray, M. W. 1981. Sex and mathematics. *Science*, 211:231.

Schaffer, D. R., and Sadowski, C. 1975. This table is mine: Respect for marked barroom tables as a function of gender of spatial marker and desirability of locale. *Sociometry*, 38:408–419.

Schaffer, H. R. 1971. *The Growth of Sociability*. Baltimore: Penguin.

———. 1977. *Mothering*. Cambridge, Mass.: Harvard University Press.

——— and Emerson, P. E. 1964a. The development of social attachments in infancy. *Monographs of the Society for Research in Child Development*, 29 (3).

——— and ———. 1964b. Patterns of response to physical contact in early human development. *Journal of Child Psychology and Psychiatry*, 5:1–13.

Schaie, K. W., Ed. 1983. *Longitudinal Studies of Adult Psychological Development*. New York: Guilford.

——— and Hertzog, C. 1983. Fourteen-year cohort-sequential analyses of adult intellectual development. *Developmental Psychology*, 19:531–543.

Schank, R. C., and Childers, P. G. 1985. *The Cognitive Computer: On Language, Learning, and Artificial Intelligence*. Reading, Mass.: Addison-Wesley.

Scheflen, A. E. 1965. Quasi-courtship behavior in psychotherapy. *Psychiatry*, 28:245–257.

Schein, E. H. 1957. Reaction patterns to severe, chronic stress in American army prisoners of war of the Chinese. *Journal of Social Issues*, 13:21–30.

Schiavi, R. C., Fisher, C., White, D., Beers, P., Fogel, M., and Szechter, R. 1982. Hormonal variations during sleep in men with erectile dysfunction and normal controls. *Archives of Sexual Behavior*, 11:189–200.

Schleifer, S. J., Keller, S. E., McKegney, F. P., and Stein, M. 1980. Bereavement and lymphocyte function. In *New Research*. San Francisco: American Psychiatric Association.

Schlenker, B. R., and Leary, M. R. 1982. Social anxiety and self-presentation: A conceptualization and model. *Psychological Bulletin*, 92:641–669.

Schlesier-Stropp, B. 1983. Bulimia: A review of the literature. *Psychological Bulletin*, 95:247–257.

Schlesinger, A., Jr. 1965. *A Thousand Days*. Boston: Houghton Mifflin.

Schmauk, F. J. 1970. Punishment, arousal, and avoidance learning in sociopaths. *Journal of Abnormal Psychology*, 76:325–335.

Schmeck, H. M., Jr. 1984. Explosion of data on brain cell reveals its great complexity. *New York Times* (March 6):17, 21.

Schmidt, D. F., and Sherman, R. C. 1984. Memory for persuasive messages: A test of a schema-copy-plus-tag model. *Journal of Personality and Social Psychology*, 47:17–25.

Schmidt, W. E. 1983. Mysteries lie locked away in some minds. *New York Times* (July 12):17, 20.

Schneider, D. J., and Blankmeyer, B. L. 1983. Prototype salience and implicit personality theories. *Journal of Personality and Social Psychology*, 44:712–722.

Schneidman, E. S. 1976. Introduction. In Schneidman, E. S., Ed., *Suicidology: Contemporary Developments*. New York: Grune and Stratton.

Schnore, L. F. 1966. Population problems in perspective. In Becker, H. S., Ed., *Social Problems: A Modern Approach*. New York: Wiley.

Schooler, N. R. 1978. Antipsychotic drugs and psychological treatment in schizophrenia. In Lipton, M. A., DiMascio, A., and Killam, K. F., Eds., *Psychopharmacology: A Generation of Progress*. New York: Raven Press.

Schopler, J., and Layton, B. 1972. Determinants of the self-attribution of having influenced another person. *Journal of Personality and Social Psychology*, 22:326–332.

Schrier, A. M., and Thompson, C. R. 1984. Are learning sets learned? A reply. *Animal Learning and Behavior*, 12:109–112.

Schroeder, D. H., and Costa, P. T., Jr. 1984. Influence of life event stress on physical illness: Substantive effects or methodological flaws? *Journal of Personality and Social Psychology*, 46:853–863.

Schultes, R. E. 1976. *Hallucinogenic Plants*. New York: Golden Press.

Schutz, A. 1971. *Collected Papers*. The Hague: Martin Nijhoff.

Schwartz, B. 1978. *Psychology of Learning and Behavior*. New York: Norton.

———. 1981. Autoshaping: Driving toward a psychology of learning. *Contemporary Psychology*, 26:823–825.

———, Tesser, A., and Powell, E. 1982. Dominance cues in nonverbal behavior. *Social Psychology Quarterly*, 45:114–120.

Schwartz, G. E., Davidson, R., and Maer, F. 1975. Right hemisphere lateralization for emotion in the human brain: Interactions with cognition. *Science*, 190:286–288.

Schwarz, L. M., Foa, U. G., and Foa, E. B. 1983. Multichannel nonverbal communication: Evidence for combinatory rules. *Journal of Personality and Social Psychology*, 45:274–281.

Schweinhart, L. J., and Weikart, D. P. 1985. Evidence that good early childhood programs work. *Phi Delta Kappan*, 66 (April):545–551.

Scogin, F., Storandt, M., and Lott, L. 1985. Memory-skills training, memory complaints, and depression in older adults. *Journal of Gerontology*, 40:562–568.

Scott, J. W. 1982. The mechanization of women's work. *Scientific American*, 247:167–187.

Searle, J. 1985. *Minds, Brains and Science*. Cambridge, Mass.: Harvard University Press.

Sears, P. S., and Barbee, A. H. 1977. Career and life satisfaction among Terman's gifted women. In Stanley, J. C., George, W. C., and Solano, C. H., Eds., *The Gifted and the Creative: Fifty-Year Perspective*. Baltimore: Johns Hopkins University Press.

Sears, R. R. 1977. Sources of life satisfactions of the Terman gifted men. *American Psychologist*, 32:119–128.

Sebeok, T. A., and Umiker-Sebeok, J. 1980. *Speaking of Apes: A Critical Anthology of Two-Way Communication with Man*. New York: Plenum Press.

Seeman, M., Seeman, T., and Sayles, M.

1985. Social networks and health status: A longitudinal analysis. *Social Psychology Quarterly*, 48:237–248.

Segal, M. W. 1974. Alphabet and attraction: An unobtrusive measure of the effect of propinquity in a field setting. *Journal of Personality and Social Psychology*, 30:654–657.

Segal, N. L. 1984. Cooperation, competition, and altruism within twin sets: A reappraisal. *Ethology and Sociobiology*, 5:163–177.

Seidman, L. J. 1983. Schizophrenia and brain dysfunction: An integration of recent neurodiagnostic findings. *Psychological Bulletin*, 94:195–238.

Seligman, C., and Darley, J. M. 1977. Feedback as a means of decreasing residential energy consumption. *Journal of Applied Psychology*, 62:363–368.

Seligman, M. E. P. 1970. On the generality of the laws of learning. *Psychological Review*, 77:406–418.

———. 1971. Phobias and preparedness. *Behavior Therapy*, 2:307–320.

———. 1975. *Helplessness*. San Francisco: Freeman.

———. 1978. Comment and integration. *Journal of Abnormal Psychology*, 87:165–179.

——— and Hager, J. L. 1972. *Biological Boundaries of Learning*. New York: Appleton-Century-Crofts.

Sells, S. B., and Murphy, D. 1984. Factor theories of personality. In Eroller, N. S., and Hunt, J. M., Eds., *Personality and the Behavioral Disorders*. New York: Wiley.

Selye, H. 1956. *The Stress of Life*. New York: McGraw-Hill.

———. 1974. *Stress Without Distress*. Philadelphia: Lippincott.

———. 1976. *Stress in Health and Disease*. Woburn, Mass.: Butterworth.

Serbin, L. A., O'Leary, K. D., Kent, R. N., and Tonick, I. J. 1973. A comparison of teacher response to the preacademic and problem behavior of boys and girls. *Child Development*, 44:796–804.

Sergent, J. 1984. Inferences from unilateral brain damage about normal hemispheric functions in visual pattern recognition. *Psychological Bulletin*, 96:99–115.

Serrin, W. 1983. Study says work ethic is alive but neglected. *New York Times* (August 14):1, 14.

Shadish, W. R., Jr. 1984. Lessons from the implementation of deinstitutionalization. *American Psychologist*, 39:725–738.

Shanas, E. 1972. Adjustment of retirement: Substitution or accommodation? In Carp, F., Ed.,

Retirement. New York: Behavioral Publications.

Shapiro, A. K. 1978. Placebo effects in medical and psychological therapies. In Garfield, S. L., and Bergen, A. E., Eds., *Handbook of Psychotherapy and Behavior Change: An Empirical Analysis*. New York: Wiley.

Shapiro, D. 1973. Preface. In Shapiro, D., et al., Eds., *Biofeedback and Self-Control 1972*. Chicago: Aldine.

Sharp, D., Cole, M., and Lave, C. 1979. Education and cognitive development: The evidence from experimental research. *Monographs of the Society for Research in Child Development*, 44 (178).

Shattuck, R. 1980. *The Forbidden Experiment: The Story of the Wild Boy of Aveyron*. New York: Farrar, Straus and Giroux.

Sheehan, D. V. 1982. Panic attacks and phobias. *New England Journal of Medicine*, 307:156–58.

Shepard, R. N., and Farrell, J. E. 1985. Representation of the orientation of shapes. *Acta Psychologica*, 59:103–121.

Sherif, M., Harvey, O. J., White, B. J., Hood, W. R., and Sherif, C. W. 1961. *Intergroup Conflict and Cooperation*. Norman: Institute of Group Relations, University of Oklahoma.

Sherman, J. 1978. *Sex-Related Cognitive Differences*. Springfield, Ill.: Charles C. Thomas.

———. 1980. Mathematics, spatial visualization, and related factors: Changes in girls and boys, grades 8–11. *Journal of Educational Psychology*, 72:476–482.

Sherman, S. W., and Robinson, N. M., Eds. 1982. *Ability Testing: Uses, Consequences, and Controversies, Parts I and II*. Washington, D.C.: National Academy Press.

Shibutani, T., and Kwan, K. M. 1965. *Ethnic Stratification*. New York: Macmillan.

Shinn, M., Lehmann, S., and Wong, N. W. 1984. Social interaction and social support. *Journal of Social Issues*, 40:55–76.

———, Rosario, M., Morch, H., and Chestnut, D. E. 1984. Coping with job stress and burnout in the human services. *Journal of Personality and Social Psychology*, 46:864–876.

Shipman, G. 1971. The psychodynamics of sex education. In Muuss, R. E., Ed., *Adolescent Behavior and Society: A Book of Readings*. New York: Random House.

Shipp, E. R. 1985. Alcohol abuse becomes a public policy issue. *New York Times* (October 1):1, 14.

————. 1986. Half in poll say more should be done for homeless. *New York Times* (February 3):14.

Shirley, M. M. 1933. *The First Two Years*. Minneapolis: University of Minnesota Press.

Shumaker, S. A., and Brownell, A. 1984. Toward a theory of social support: Closing conceptual gaps. *Journal of Social Issues*, 40:11–36.

Shweder, R. A., and D'Andrade, R. G. 1980. The systematic distortion hypothesis. In Shweder, R., Ed., *New Directions for Methodology of Social and Behavior Science*. San Francisco: Jossey-Bass.

Siegel, R. K. 1977. Hallucinations. *Scientific American*, 237 (October): 132–140.

———— and West, L. J. 1975. *Hallucinations: Behavior, Experience, and Theory*. New York: Wiley.

Siegelman, J., and Conway, F. 1979. Snapping: Welcome to the eighties. *Playboy*, 26 (March):59+.

Siegelman, M. 1973. Parent behavior correlates of personality traits related to creativity in sons and daughters. *Journal of Consulting and Clinical Psychology*, 40:139–147.

Siever, L. J., and Davis, K. L. 1985. Overview: Toward a dysregulation hypothesis of depression. *American Journal of Psychiatry*, 142:1017–1031.

Sigall, H., and Landy, D. 1973. Radiating beauty: Effects of having a physically attractive partner on person perception. *Journal of Personality and Social Psychology*, 28:218–224.

Silverman, L. H. 1982. A comment on two subliminal psychodynamic activation studies. *Journal of Abnormal Psychology*, 91:126–130.

————. 1983. The subliminal psychodynamic activation method: Overview and comprehensive listing of studies. In Masling, J., Ed., *Empirical Studies of Psychoanalytic Theories*. Hillsdale, N.J.: Erlbaum.

———— and Weinberger, J. 1985. Mommy and I are one: Implications for psychotherapy. *American Psychologist*, 40:1296–1308.

Silverman, P. R. 1980. *Mutual help groups: Sage Human Services Guide*. Beverly Hills, Calif.: Sage.

————. 1983. Coping with grief—It can't be rushed. *U.S. News & World Report* (November 14):65–68.

Simonton, D. K. 1984. *Genius, Creativity, and Leadership*. Cambridge, Mass.: Harvard University Press.

Simonton, O. C. Matthews-Simonton, S., and Creighton, J. 1978. *Getting Well Again: A Step-by-Step, Self-Help Guide to Overcoming Cancer for Patients and Their Families*. Los Angeles: J. P. Tarcher.

Sims, E. A., Goldman, R. F., Gluck, C. M., Horton, E. S., Kelleher, P. C., and Rowe, D. W. 1968. Experimental obesity in man. *Transcripts of the Association of American Psychiatrists*, 81:153–170.

Sinex, F. M., and Myers, R. H. 1982. Alzheimer's disease, Down's syndrome, and aging: The genetic approach. *Annuals of the New York Academy of Science*, 396:3–13.

Singer, J. L. 1969. Drives, affects, and daydreams: The adaptive role of spontaneous imagery of stimulus-independent meditation. In Antrobus, J., Ed., *Cognition and Affect: The City University of New York Symposium*. Boston: Little, Brown.

Singer, M. T. 1979. Coming out of the cults. *Psychology Today*, 12 (January):72–82.

Sitaram, N., Weingartner, H., and Gillin, J. C. 1978. Human serial learning: Enhancement with arecholine and choline and impairment with scopolamine. *Science*, 201:274–276.

Skinner, B. F. 1948. *Walden Two*. New York: Macmillan. Republished in 1964.

————. 1953. *Science and Human Behavior*. New York: Free Press.

————. 1971. *Beyond Freedom and Dignity*. New York: Knopf.

————. 1974. *About Behaviorism*. New York: Knopf.

Sklar, L. S., and Anisman, H. 1981. Stress and cancer. *Psychological Bulletin*, 89:369–406.

Slotkin, J. J. 1955. Culture and psychopathology. *Journal of Abnormal and Social Psychology*, 51:269–275.

Smith, D., and Kraft, W. A. 1983. DSM-III: Do psychologists really want an alternative? *American Psychologist*, 38:777–785.

Smith, E. A., Udry, J. R., and Morris, N. M. 1985. Pubertal development and friends: A biosocial explanation of adolescent sexual behavior. *Journal of Health and Social Behavior*, 26:183–192.

Smith, M. L., and Glass, G. V. 1977. Meta-analysis of psychotherapy outcome studies. *American Psychologist*, 32:752–760.

————, ————, and Miller, F. I. 1980. *The Benefits of Psychotherapy*. Baltimore: Johns Hopkins University Press.

Smith, P. K., and Vollstedt, R. 1985. On defining play: An empirical study of the relationship between play and various play criteria. *Child Development*, 56:1042–1050.

Snow, C. E. 1972. Mothers' speech to children learning language. *Child Development*, 43:549–65.

————. 1977. The development of conversation between mothers and babies. *Journal of Child Language*, 4:1–22.

Snowdon, C. T. 1983. Ethology, comparative psychology, and animal behavior. *Annual Review of Psychology*, 34:63–94.

Snyder, M. 1979. Self-monitoring processes. In Berkowitz, L., Ed., *Advances in Experimental Social Psychology*. New York: Academic.

————. 1980. The many me's of the self-monitor. *Psychology Today*, 13 (March):33–40+.

————. 1981. On the influence of individuals on situations. In Cantor, N., and Kihlstrom, J., Eds., *Personality, Cognition, and Social Interaction*. Hillsdale, N.J.: Erlbaum.

————, Berscheid, E., and Glick, P. 1985. Focusing on the exterior and the interior: Two investigations of the initiation of personal relationships. *Journal of Personality and Social Psychology*, 48:1427–1439.

———— and Ebbesen, E. B. 1972. Dissonance awareness: A test of dissonance theory versus self-perception theory. *Journal of Experimental Social Psychology*, 31:64–67.

————, Gangestad, S., and Simpson, J. A. 1983. Choosing friends as activity partners: The role of self-monitoring. *Journal of Personality and Social Psychology*, 45:1061–1072.

———— and Ickes, W. 1985. Personality and social behavior. In Lindzey, G., and Aronson E., Eds., *Handbook of Social Psychology*. Vol. 2. 3rd ed. New York: Random House.

———— and Simpson, J. A. 1984. Self-monitoring and dating relationships. *Journal of Personality and Social Psychology*, 47:1281–1291.

Snyder, S. H. 1977. Opiate receptors and internal opiates. *Scientific American*, 236 (March):44–56.

————. 1980. Matter over mind. *Psychology Today*, 14 (June):66–76.

————. 1985. The molecular basis of communication between cells. *Scientific American*, 253 (October): 132–141.

Solomon, R. L., and Corbit, J. D. 1974. An opponent-process theory of motivation. *Psychological Review*, 81:119–145.

Sommer, R. 1967. Small group ecology. *Psychological Bulletin*, 67:145–152.

————. 1985. Local studies offer large-scale rewards. *APA Monitor* (December):6.

Sontag, S. 1977. *Illness as Metaphor*. New York: Farrar, Straus and Giroux.

Spanos, N. P. 1983. The hidden observer as an experimental creation. *Journal of Personality and Social Psychology*, 44:170–176.

———, and Gorassini, D. R. 1984. Structure of hypnotic test suggestions and attributions of responding involuntarily. *Journal of Personality and Social Psychology*, 46:688–696.

———, and Hewitt, E. C. 1980. The hidden observer in hypnotic analgesia: Discovery or experimental creation? *Journal of Personality and Social Psychology*, 39:1201–1214.

Spearman, C. 1904. General intelligence objectively determined and measured. *American Journal of Psychology*, 15:201–293.

———. 1927. *The Abilities of Man*. New York: Macmillan.

Spender, S. 1952. The making of a poem. In Ghiselin, B., Ed., *The Creative Process: A Symposium*. Berkeley: University of California Press.

Sperling, D. 1984. Psychotherapy: When to expect some results. *USA Today* (September 28):D-1.

Sperling, G. 1960. The information available in brief visual presentations. *Psychological Monographs*, 74:No. 11.

Sperry, R. W. 1969. A modified concept of consciousness. *Psychological Review*, 76:532–536.

———. 1976. Changing concepts of consciousness and free will. *Perspectives in Biology and Medicine*, 20 (Autumn):9–19.

———. 1982. Some effects of disconnecting the cerebral hemispheres. *Science*, 217:1223–1226.

Spiegel, D., and Wissler, T. 1986. Family environment as a predictor of psychiatric rehospitalization. *American Journal of Psychiatry*, 143:56–60.

Spiro, R. J. 1977. Remembering information from text: The "state of schema" approach. In Anderson, R. C., Spiro, R. J., and Montague, W. E., Eds., *Schooling and the Acquisition of Knowledge*. Hillsdale, N.J.: Erlbaum.

Spitzer, R. L. 1985. DSM-III and the politics-science dichotomy syndrome: A response to Thomas E. Schacht's "DSM-III and the politics of truth." *American Psychologist*, 40:522–526.

———, Forman, J. B. W., and Nee, J. 1979. DSM-III field trials: I. Initial interrater diagnostic reliability. *American Journal of Psychiatry*, 136:815–817.

———, Williams, J. B. W., and Skodol, A. E. 1980. DSM-III: The major

achievements and an overview. *American Journal of Psychiatry*, 137:151–164.

Sprafkin, J., Swift, C., and Hess, R., Eds. 1983. *Rx Television: Enhancing the Prevention Impact of TV*. Prevention in Human Services. Vol. 2, Nos. 1–2. New York: Haworth Press.

Squire, L. R. 1982. The neuropsychology of human memory. *Annual Review of Neuroscience*, 5:241–273.

——— and Cohen, N. 1979. Memory and amnesia: Resistance to disruption develops for years after learning. *Behavioral and Neural Biology*, 25:115–125.

———and———. 1982. Remote memory, retrograde amnesia, and the neuropsychology of memory. In Cermak, L., Ed., *Human Memory and Amnesia*. Hillsdale, N.J.: Erlbaum.

Srole, L., et al. 1962. *Mental Health in the Metropolis: The Midtown Manhattan Study*. Vol. 1. New York: McGraw-Hill.

Staddon, J. E. R. 1983. *Adaptive Behavior and Learning*. Cambridge, England: Cambridge University Press.

Stagner, R. 1975. Boredom on the assembly line: Age and personality variables. *Industrial Gerontology*, 2:23–44.

Stanley, M., Virgilio, J., and Gershon, S. 1982. Tritiated imipramine binding sites are decreased in the frontal cortex of suicides. *Science*, 216:1337–1339.

Stapp, J., Tucker, A. M., and VandenBos, G. R. 1985. Census of psychological personnel: 1983. *American Psychologist*, 40:1317–1351.

Stark, E. 1984. Hypnosis on trial. *Psychology Today*, 18 (February): 34–36.

Staub, E. 1978. *Positive Social Behavior and Morality: Social and Personal Influences*. Vol. 1. New York: Academic Press.

Steele, C. M., and Liu, T. J. 1983. Dissonance processes as self-affirmation. *Journal of Personality and Social Psychology*, 45:5–19.

Stein, R. T. 1975. Identifying emergent leaders from verbal and nonverbal communications. *Journal of Personality and Social Psychology*, 32:125–135.

Stephan, C. W., and Langlois, J. H. 1984. Baby beautiful: Adult attributions of infant competence as a function of infant attractiveness. *Child Development*, 55:576–585.

Stephan, W. G. 1985. Intergroup relations. In Lindzey, G., and Aronson, E., Eds., *Handbook of*

Social Psychology. Vol. 2. 3rd ed. New York: Random House.

Sternberg, R. J. 1979a. Stalking the IQ quark. *Psychology Today*, 13 (September):42–54.

———. 1979b. The nature of mental abilities. *American Psychologist*, 34:214–230.

———. 1981. Testing and cognitive psychology. *American Psychologist*, 36:1181–1187.

———. 1982. Who's intelligent? *Psychology Today*, 16 (April):30–39.

———. 1984a. *Beyond IQ: A Triarchic Theory of Human Intelligence*. New York: Cambridge University Press.

———. 1984b. Testing intelligence without I.Q. tests. *Phi Delta Kappan*, 65:694–698.

———. 1985. Implicit theories of intelligence, creativity, and wisdom. *Journal of Personality and Social Psychology*, 49:607–627.

———. 1986. Inside intelligence. *American Scientist*, 74:137–143.

———, Conway, B. E., Ketron, J. L., and Bernstein, M. 1981. People's conceptions of intelligence. *Journal of Personality and Social Psychology*, 41:37–55.

——— and Grajek, S. 1984. The nature of love. *Journal of Personality and Social Psychology*, 47:312–319.

Stevens, D. P., and Truss, C. V. 1985. Stability and change in adult personality over 12 and 20 years. *Developmental Psychology*, 21:568–584.

Stevens, S. S. 1962. The surprising simplicity of sensory metrics. *American Psychologist*, 17:29–39.

Stewart, A. J., and Salt, P. 1981. Life stress, life-styles, depression, and illness in adult women. *Journal of Personality and Social Psychology*, 40:1063–1069.

Stickeny, B. D., and Marcus, L. R. 1985. Education and the disadvantaged 20 years later. *Phi Delta Kappan*, 66 (April):559–564.

Stith, S. M., and Davis, A. J. 1984. Employed mothers and family day-care substitute caregivers: A comparative analysis of infant care. *Child Development*, 55:1340–1348.

Stockton, W. 1980. Creating computers that think. *New York Times Magazine* (December 7):40–42+.

Stokols, D. 1972. On the distinction between density and crowding: Some implications for future research. *Psychological Review*, 79:275–277.

Stone, B. P. 1970. Appearance and the self. In Stone, G. P., and Farberman, H. A., Eds., *Social Psychology Through Social Interaction*. Waltham, Mass.: Xerox College Publishing.

Storms, M. D. 1973. Videotape and the attribution process: Reversing actors' and observers' points of view. *Journal of Personality and Social Psychology,* 27:165–175.

Stouffer, S. A., Lumsdaine, A. A., Lumsdaine, M. H., Williams, R. M., Jr., Smith, M. B., Janis, I. D., Star, S. A., and Cottrell, L. S., Jr. 1949. *The American Soldier.* Vol. 2: *Combat and Its Aftermath.* Princeton, N.J.: Princeton University Press.

Strauss, J. S., and Carpenter, W. T., Jr. 1979. The prognosis of schizophrenia. In Bellak, L., Ed., *Disorders of the Schizophrenic Syndrome.* New York: Basic Books.

———, Kokes, R. F., Carpenter, W. T., Jr., and Ritzler, B. A. 1978. The course of schizophrenia as a developmental process. In Wynne, L. C., Cromwell, R. L., and Matthysee, S., Eds., *The Nature of Schizophrenia: New Approaches to Research and Treatment.* New York: Wiley.

Stroebe, M. S., and Stroebe, W. 1983. Who suffers more? Sex differences in health risks of the widowed. *Psychological Bulletin,* 93:279–301.

Strube, M. J., and Garcia, J. E. 1981. A meta-analytic investigation of Fiedler's contingency model of leadership effectiveness. *Psychological Bulletin,* 90:307–321.

Strupp, H. H., and Hadley, S. W. 1977. A tripartite model of mental health and therapeutic outcomes. *American Psychologist,* 32:187–204.

Stuckey, M. F., McGhee, P. E., and Bell, N. J. 1982. Parent–child interaction: The influence of maternal employment. *Developmental Psychology,* 18:635–644.

Stuss, D. T., and Benson, D. F. 1984. Neuropsychological studies of the frontal lobes. *Psychological Bulletin,* 95:3–28.

Suboski, M. D., and Bartashunas, C. 1984. Mechanisms for social transmission of pecking preferences to neonatal chicks. *Journal of Experimental Psychology: Animal Behavior Processes,* 10:182–194.

Suedfeld, P. 1969. Changes in intellectual performance and susceptibility to influence. In Zubek, J. P., Ed., *Sensory Deprivation: Fifteen Years of Research.* New York: Appleton-Century-Crofts.

———. 1974. Social isolation: A case for interdisciplinary research. *Canadian Psychologist,* 15:1–15.

——— and Ikard, F. F. 1977. Use of sensory deprivation in facilitating the reduction of cigarette smoking. In Kammerman, M., Ed., *Sensory*

Isolation and Personality Change. Springfield, Ill.: Thomas.

Sullivan, H. S. 1947. *Conceptions of Modern Psychiatry.* Washington, D.C.: William A. White Psychiatric Foundation.

———. 1953. *The Interpersonal Theory of Psychiatry.* New York: Norton.

Sullivan, J. L., Stanfield, C. N., Schanberg, S., and Cavenar, J. 1978. Platelet MAO and serum DBH activity in chronic alcoholics. *Archives of General Psychiatry,* 35:1209–1212.

Sullivan, W. 1982. Clues to longevity in Soviet. *New York Times* (November 30):17.

Sundstrom, E. 1975. An experimental study of crowding: Effects of room size, intrusion, and goal blocking on nonverbal behavior, self-disclosure, and self-reported stress. *Journal of Personality and Social Psychology,* 32:645–654.

———. 1978. Crowding as a sequential process. Review of research on the effects of population density on humans. In Baum, A., and Epstein, Y. M., Eds., *Human Responses to Crowding.* Hillsdale, N.J.: Erlbaum.

Surwit, R. S., Shapiro, D., and Good, M.I. 1978. Comparison of cardiovascular feedback, neuromuscular feedback, and meditation in the treatment of borderline essential hypertension. *Journal of Consulting and Clinical Psychology,* 46:252–263.

Sweeney, P. D., Schaeffer, D. E., and Golin, S. 1982. Pleasant events, unpleasant events, and depression. *Journal of Personality and Social Psychology,* 43:136–144.

Swenson, W. M. 1961. Attitudes toward death in an aged population. *Journal of Gerontology,* 16:49–52.

Szasz, T. S. 1961. *The Myth of Mental Illness.* New York: Harper & Row.

Tajfel, H., and Billig, M. 1974. Familiarity and categorization in intergroup behavior. *Journal of Experimental Social Psychology,* 10:159–170.

Tanford, S., and Penrod, S. 1984. Social influence model: A formal integration of research on majority and minority influence processes. *Psychological Bulletin,* 95:189–225.

Tanke, E. D., and Yesavage, J. A. 1985. Characteristics of assaultive patients who do and do not provide visible cues of potential violence. *American Journal of Psychiatry,* 142:1409–1413.

Tannenbaum, P. H. 1980. Entertainment as vicarious emotional experience. In Tannenbaum, P. H., Ed., *The*

Entertainment Functions of Television. Hillsdale, N.J.: Erlbaum.

Tanner, J. M. 1973. Growing up. *Scientific American,* 229 (September):34–43.

Targ, R., and Harary, K. 1984. *The Mind Race.* New York: Villard Books.

——— and Puthoff, H. 1974. Information transmission under conditions of sensory shielding. *Nature,* 251 (October 18):602–607.

Tarler-Benlolo, L. 1978. The role of relaxation in biofeedback training: A critical review of the literature. *Psychological Bulletin,* 85:725–755.

Tart, C. T. 1972. *Altered States of Consciousness.* 2nd ed. New York: Wiley.

Taylor, C. W., and Barron, F. 1963. *Scientific Creativity: Its Recognition and Development.* New York: Wiley.

Taylor, R. A. 1984. What all that noise pollution is doing to our lives. *U.S. News & World Report* (July 16):50.

Taylor, S. E. 1979. Hospital patient behavior: Reactance, helplessness, or control? *Journal of Social Issues,* 35:156–184.

———. 1983. Adjustment to threatening events: A theory of cognitive adaptation. *American Psychologist,* 38:1161–1173.

———. 1986. *Health Psychology.* New York: Random House.

——— and Crocker, J. 1981. Schematic bases of social information processing. In Higgins, E. T., Herman, C. A., and Zanna, M. P., Eds., *Social Cognition: The Ontario Symposium on Personality and Social Psychology.* Hillsdale, N.J.: Erlbaum.

———, Lichtman, R. R., and Wood, J. V. 1984. Attributions, beliefs about control, and adjustment to breast cancer. *Journal of Personality and Social Psychology,* 46:489–502.

Tchaikovsky, P. 1906. Letter, 1879. In Newmarch, R., Ed. *Life and Letters of Peter Tchaikovsky.* London: John Lane.

Teltsch, K. 1985. "One of the guys": The engineer of today is often a woman. *New York Times* (September 19):19, 21.

Terman, L. M., and Merrill, M. A. 1937. *Measuring Intelligence.* Boston: Houghton Mifflin.

——— and ———. 1973. *Stanford-Binet Intelligence Scale: Manual for the Third Revision. Form L-M.* Boston: Houghton Mifflin.

Terrace, H. S. 1979a. How Nim Chimpsky changed my mind. *Psychology Today,* 13 (November): 65–76.

———. 1979b. *Nim.* New York: Knopf.

Tetlock, P. E. 1983. Accountability and the perseverance of first impressions. *Social Psychology Quarterly*, 46:285–292.

Thelen, E., and Fisher, D. M. 1982. Newborn stepping: An explanation for a "disappearing" reflex. *Developmental Psychology*, 18:760–775.

Theodor, L. H., and Mandelcorn, M. S. 1973. Hysterical blindness: A case report and study using a modern psychophysical technique. *Journal of Abnormal Psychology*, 82:552–553.

Thibaut, J. W., and Kelley, H. H. 1959. *The Social Psychology of Groups*. New York: Wiley.

Thomas, A., and Chess, S. 1977. *Temperament and Development*. New York: Brunner/Mazel.

Thomas, J. R., and French, K. E. 1985. Gender differences across age in motor performance: A meta-analysis. *Psychological Bulletin*, 98:260–282.

Thomas, W. I. 1931. The relation of research to the social process. In *Essays on Research in the Social Sciences*. Washington, D.C.: The Brookings Institution.

Thompson, C. P. 1985. Voice identification: Speaker identifiability and a correction of the record regarding sex effects. *Human Learning*, 4:19–27.

Thorndike, E. L. 1898. Animal intelligence. An experimental study of the associative processes in animals. *Psychological Monographs*, 2:No. 8.

———. 1927. The law of effect. *American Journal of Psychology*, 39:212–222.

———. 1932. *The Fundamentals of Learning*. New York: Teachers College Press.

——— and Woodworth, R. S. 1901a. The influence of improvement in one mental function upon the efficiency of other functions. I. *Psychological Review*, 8:247–261.

——— and ———. 1901b. The influence of improvement in one mental function upon the efficiency of other functions. II. The stimulation of magnitudes. *Psychological Review*, 8:384–395.

——— and ———. 1901c. The influence of improvement in one mental function upon the efficiency of other functions. III. Functions involving attention, observation, and discrimination. *Psychological Review*, 8:553–564.

Thurow, L. C. 1981. Why women are paid less than men. *New York Times* (March 8):E-5.

Thurstone, L. L. 1938. *Primary Mental Abilities*. Chicago: University of Chicago Press.

———. 1947. *Multiple Factor Analysis: A Development and Expansion of "The Vectors of the Mind."* Chicago: University of Chicago Press.

Tierney, J. 1982. Doctor, is this man dangerous? *Science 82*, 3: (June):28–31.

Tinbergen, N. 1951. *The Study of Instinct*. New York: Oxford University Press.

———. 1965. *Animal Behavior*. New York: Time-Life Books.

Tobias, S. 1982. Sexist equations. *Psychology Today*, 16 (January):14–17.

Tobin-Richards, M., Boxer, A. M., and Petersen, A. C. 1983. The psychological significance of pubertal change: Sex differences in perceptions of self during early adolescence. In Brooks-Gunn, J., and Petersen, A. C., Eds., *Girls at Puberty*. New York: Plenum.

Tolman, E. C. 1932. *Purposive Behavior in Animals and Men*. New York: Nailburg.

———. 1938. The determiners of behavior at a choice point. *Psychological Review*, 45:1–41.

———. 1949. There is more than one kind of learning. *Psychological Review*, 56:144–155.

——— and Honzik, C. H. 1930. Introduction and removal or reward, and maze performance in rats. *University of California Publications in Psychology*, 4:257–275.

Tooth, G. 1985. Why children's TV turns off so many parents. *U.S. News & World Report* (February 18):65.

Torrey, E. F. 1979. Tracking the causes of madness. *Psychology Today*, 12 (March):79–80+.

Tortora, G. J., and Anagnostakos, N. P. 1978. *Principles of Anatomy and Physiology*. 2nd ed. San Francisco: Canfield Press.

Tower, R. 1980. The influence of parents' values on preschool children's behavior. Doctoral dissertation, Yale University.

Tranel, D., and Damasio, A. R. 1985. Knowledge without awareness: An utonomic index of facial recognition by prosopagnosics. *Science*, 228:1453–1454.

Troll, L. E., and Bengtson, V. L. 1982. Intergenerational relations throughout the life span. In Wolman, B. B., Ed., *Handbook of Developmental Psychology*. Englewood Cliffs, N.J.: Prentice-Hall.

Tsitouras, P. D., Martin, C. E., and Horman, S. M. 1982. Relationship of serum testosterone to sexual activity in healthy elderly men. *Journal of Gerontology*, 37:288–293.

Tucker, D. M., and Williamson, P. A. 1984. Asymmetric neural control systems in human self-regulation. *Psychological Bulletin*, 91:185–215.

Tucker, M. A., Shields, J. A. Hartge, P., Augsburger, J., Hoover, R. N., and Fraumeni, J. F., Jr. 1985. Sunlight exposure as risk factor for intraocular malignant melanoma. *New England Journal of Medicine*, 313:789–792.

Tulving, E. 1968. Theoretical issues in free recall. In Dixon, T. R., and Horton, D. L., Eds., *Verbal Behavior and General Behavior Theory*, Englewood Cliffs, N.J.: Prentice-Hall.

———. 1972. Episodic and semantic memory. In Tulving, E., and Donaldson, W., Eds., *Organization of Memory*. New York: Academic Press.

———. 1974. Cue-dependent forgetting. *American Scientist*, 62:74–82.

———. 1983. *Elements of Episodic Memory: Oxford Psychology Series, No. 2*. New York: Oxford University Press.

———. 1985. How many memory systems are there? *American Psychologist*, 40:385–398.

——— and Pearlstone, Z. 1966. Availability versus accessibility of information in memory for words. *Journal of Verbal Learning and Verbal Behavior*, 5:381–391.

——— and Psotka, J. 1971. Retroactive inhibition in free recall: Inaccessibility of information available in the memory store. *Journal of Experimental Psychology*, 87:1–8.

Turkington, C. 1984a. Supportive homes few, barriers many. *APA Monitor* (August):20, 22.

———. 1984b. Trip-wire vets find niche in the wild. *APA Monitor* (April):7–8.

Turner, B. F. 1982. Sex-related differences in aging. In Wolman, B. B., Ed., *Handbook of Developmental Psychology*. Englewood Cliffs, N.J.: Prentice-Hall.

Turner, S. M., Beidel, D. C., and Nathan, R. S. 1985. Biological factors in obsessive-compulsive disorders. *Psychological Bulletin*, 97:430–450.

Tyler, L. E. 1983. *Thinking Creatively*. San Francisco: Jossey-Bass.

Ullman, S. 1979. *The Interpretation of Visual Motion*. Cambridge, Mass.: MIT Press.

Underwood, B., and Moore, B. S. 1981. Sources of behavioral consistency. *Journal of Personality and Social Psychology*, 40:780–785.

U.S. News & World Report. 1985. The rise of world terrorism. *U.S. News & World Report* (July 8):27.

Vaillant, G. E. 1977. *Adaptation to Life.* Boston: Little, Brown.

Valins, S. 1966. Cognitive effects of false heart-rate feedback. *Journal of Personality and Social Psychology,* 4:400–408.

Valvo, A. 1971. *Sight Restoration After Long-Term Blindness: The Problems and Behavior Patterns of Visual Rehabilitation.* New York: American Foundation for the Blind.

Van Atta, L., and Sutin, J. 1971. The response of single lateral hypothalamic neurons to ventromedial nucleus and limbic stimulation. *Physiology and Behavior,* 6:523–536.

VandenBos, G. R., and Pino, C. D. 1980. Research on the outcome of psychotherapy. In VandenBos, G. R., Ed., *Psychotherapy: Practice, Research, Policy.* Beverly Hills, Calif.: Sage.

Vander Zanden, J. W. 1981. *Human Development.* 2nd ed. New York: Random House.

———. 1983. *American Minority Relations.* New York: Knopf.

———. 1984. *Social Psychology.* 3rd ed. New York: Random House.

———. 1987. *Social Psychology.* 4th ed. New York: Random House.

——— and Pace, A. 1984. *Educational Psychology: In Theory and Practice.* 2nd ed. New York: Random House.

Van Dyke, C., and Byck, R. 1982. Cocaine. *Scientific American,* 246 (March):128–141.

Vaughn, C. E., and Leff, J. P. 1976. The influence of family and social factors on the course of psychiatric illness: A comparison of schizophrenic and depressed neurotic patients. *British Journal of Psychiatry,* 129:125–137.

Vermeulen, A., Rubens, R., and Verdonck, L. 1976. Testosterone secretion and metabolism in male senescence. *Journal of Clinical Endocrinology and Metabolism,* 34:730–735.

Veroff, J., Douvan, E., and Kulka, R. 1981. *The Inner American: A Self-Portrait from 1957 to 1976.* New York: Basic Books.

Victor, R., Weipert, D., and Shapiro, D. 1984. Voluntary control of systolic blood pressure during postural change. *Psychophysiology,* 21:673–680.

Vygotsky, L. S. 1962. *Thought and Language.* Cambridge, Mass.: MIT Press.

Wagstaff, G. F. 1981. *Hypnosis, Compliance and Belief.* New York: St. Martin's Press.

Waldrop, M. M. 1985. Machinations of thought. *Science 85,* 6 (March):38–45.

Walker, L. J. 1984. Sex differences in the development of moral reasoning: A critical review. *Child Development,* 55:677–691.

Walker, S. 1983. *Animal Thought.* London: Routledge & Kegan Paul.

Wallace, R. K. 1970. Physiological effects of Transcendental Meditation. *Science,* 167:1751–1754.

Wallach, M. A. 1970. Creativity. In Mussen, P. H., Ed., *Carmichael's Manual of Child Psychology.* 3rd ed. New York: Wiley.

———. 1971. *The Intelligence/Creativity Distinction.* New York: General Learning Press.

——— and Kogan, N. 1965. *Modes of Thinking in Young Children: A Study of the Creativity-Intelligence Distinction.* New York: Holt, Rinehart and Winston.

Wallston, B. S., Alagna, S. W., DeVellis, B. M., and DeVellis, R. F. 1984. Social support and health. *Health Psychology,* 4:367–391.

Walsh, E. J., and Warland, R. H. 1983. Social movement involvement in the wake of a nuclear accident: Activists and free riders in the TMI area. *American Sociological Review,* 48:764–780.

Walsh, J. 1983. Wide world of reports. *Science,* 220:804–805.

Walster, E., Aronson, V., and Abrahams, D. 1966. Importance of physical attractiveness in dating behavior. *Journal of Personality and Social Psychology,* 4:508–516.

——— and Walster, G. W. 1970. The matching hypothesis. Unpublished manuscript, University of Wisconsin.

——— and Walster, G. W. 1978. *A New Look at Love.* Reading, Mass.: Addison-Wesley.

Walters, G. C., and Grusec, J. E. 1977. *Punishment.* San Francisco: Freeman.

Waltz, D. L. 1982. Artificial intelligence. *Scientific American,* 247 (October):118–135.

Wanberg, K. W., and Horn, J. L. 1983. Assessment of alcohol use with multidimensional concepts and measures. *American Psychologist,* 38:1055–1069.

Warner, K. E. 1981. Cigarette smoking in the 1970s: The impact of the antismoking campaign on consumption. *Science,* 211 (February 13):729–730.

Warren, R. M. 1984. Perceptual restoration of obliterated sounds. *Psychological Bulletin,* 96:371–383.

Waterman, A. S. 1982. Identity development from adolescence to adulthood: An extension of theory and a review of research. *Developmental Psychology,* 18:341–358.

Watkins, L. R., and Mayer, D. J. 1982. Organization of endogenous opiate and nonopiate pain control systems. *Science,* 216:1185–1192.

Watkins, O. C., and Watkins, M. J. 1975. Buildup of proactive inhibition as a cue-overload effect. *Journal of Experimental Psychology: Human Learning and Memory,* 104:442–452.

Watson, J. B. 1924. *Behaviorism.* New York: Norton.

Waugh, N. C., and Norman, D. A. 1965. Primary memory. *Psychological Review,* 72:89–104.

Weatherley, D. 1964. Self-perceived rate of physical maturation and personality in late adolescence. *Child Development,* 35:1197–1210.

Weaver, W., Jr. 1981. Pollster detects "myths" about problems of aged. *New York Times* (November 19):15.

Webb, W. B. 1975. *Sleep: The Gentle Tyrant.* Englewood Cliffs, N.J.: Prentice-Hall.

———. 1985. A further analysis of age and sleep deprivation effects. *Psychophysiology,* 22:156–162.

Weber, E. H. 1834. *De Pulse, Resorptione, Audito et Tactu.* Leipzig: Kohler.

Webster, H. 1948. *Magic: A Sociological Study.* Stanford, Calif.: Stanford University Press.

Wechsler, D. 1958. *The Measurement and Appraisal of Adult Intelligence.* 14th ed. Baltimore: Williams & Wilkins.

———. 1975. Intelligence defined and undefined. *American Psychologist,* 30:135–139.

Weil, A. 1974a. Parapsychology: Andrew Weil's search for the true Geller. *Psychology Today,* 8 (June):45–50.

———. 1974b. Parapsychology: The letdown. *Psychology Today,* 8 (July):74–78+.

Weinberger, D. R., Torrey, E. F., Neophytides, A. N., and Wyatt, R. J. 1979. Lateral cerebral ventricular enlargement in chronic schizophrenia. *Archives of General Psychiatry,* 36:735–739.

Weingartner, H., Adefris, W., Eich, J. E., and Murphy, D. 1976. Encoding-imagery specificity in alcohol state-dependent learning. *Journal of Experimental Psychology: Human Learning and Memory,* 2:83–87.

———, Gold, P., Ballenger, J. C., Smallberg, S. A., Summers, R., Rubinow, D. R., Post, R. M., and Goodwin, F. K. 1981. Effects of vasopressin on human memory. *Science,* 211:601–603.

Weinraub, M., Brooks, J., and Lewis, M. 1977. The social network: A reconsideration of the concept of attachment. *Human Development*, 20:31–47.

Weisz, J. 1981. Learned helplessness in black and white children identified by their schools as retarded and nonretarded. Performance deterioration in response to failure. *Developmental Psychology*, 17:499–508.

Wender, P. H., and Klein, D. F. 1981. The promise of biological psychiatry. *Psychology Today*, 15 (February): 25–41.

West, S. 1985. Beyond the one-track mind. *Science 85*, 6 (November): 102–109.

Wetzel, C. G., and Insko, C. A. 1982. The similarity-attraction relationship: Is there an ideal one? *Journal of Experimental Social Psychology*, 18:253–276.

Whalen, R. E., and Simon, N. G. 1984. Biological motivation. *Annual Review of Psychology*, 35:257–276.

White, G. L. 1980. Physical attractiveness and courtship progress. *Journal of Personality and Social Psychology*, 39:660–668.

White, K., and Sloane, R. B. 1979. Drugs in brief psychotherapy. *Psychiatric Clinics of North America*, 2:171–187.

White, R. K., and Lippitt, R. 1960. *Autocracy and Democracy*. New York: Harper & Row.

White, R. T., and Gagné, R. M. 1976. Retention of related and unrelated sentences. *Journal of Educational Psychology*, 68:843–852.

White, R. W. 1959. Motivation reconsidered: The concept of competence. *Psychological Review*, 66:317–330.

Whitehead, A. N., and Russell, B. 1925. *Principia Mathematica*. 2nd ed. Cambridge, England: Cambridge University Press.

Whorf, B. L. 1956. *Language, Thought, and Reality*. Cambridge, Mass.: MIT Press.

Wilcoxon, H. C., Dragoin, W. B., and Kral, P. 1971. Illness-induced aversions in rat and quail: Relative salience of visual and gustatory cues. *Science*, 171:826–828.

Wilder, D. A., and Shapiro, P. N. 1984. Role of out-group cues in determining social identity. *Journal of Personality and Social Psychology*, 47:342–348.

Williams, B. M. 1974. Promise and caution. *Psychology Today*, 8 (November):126–127.

Williams, J. L. 1973. *Operant Learning: Procedures for Changing Behavior*. Monterey, Calif.: Brooks/Cole.

Williams, R. L., and Long, J. D. 1979. *Toward a Self-Managed Life Style*. 2nd ed. Boston: Houghton Mifflin.

Wilmer, H. A. 1982. Post-traumatic stress disorder. *Psychiatric Annals*, 12:995–1003.

Wilson, E. O. 1975. *Sociobiology: A New Synthesis*. Cambridge, Mass.: Harvard University Press.

Wilson, M., Crocker, J., Brown, C. E., Johnson, D., Liotta, R., and Konat, J. 1985. The attractive executive: Effects of sex of business associates on attributions of competence and social skills. *Basic and Applied Social Psychology*, 6:13–23.

———. and Daly, M. 1985. Competitiveness, risk taking, and violence: The young male syndrome. *Ethology and Sociobiology*, 6:59–73.

Wilson, R. S. 1983. The Louisville Twin Study: Developmental synchronies in behavior. *Child Development*, 54(2):298–316.

Winch, R. F. 1958. *Mate Selection: A Study of Complementary Needs*. New York: Harper & Row.

Winokur, G., Tsuang, M. T., and Crowe, R. R. 1982. The Iowa 500: Affective disorder in relatives of manic and depressed patients. *American Journal of Psychiatry*, 139:209–212.

Withey, S. B., and Abeles, R. P. 1980. *Television and Social Behavior: Beyond Violence and Children*. Hillsdale, N.J.: Erlbaum.

Wolfe, J. B. 1936. Effectiveness of token-rewards for chimpanzees. *Comparative Psychological Monographs*, 12:No. 5.

Wolfe, J. M. 1983. Hidden visual processes. *Scientific American*, 248 (February):94–102.

Wolpe, J. 1958. *Psychotherapy by Reciprocal Inhibition*. Stanford, Calif.: Stanford University Press.

———. 1969. *The Practice of Behavior Therapy*. Elmford, N.Y.: Pergamon.

Wood, W., Kallgren, C. A., and Preisler, R. M. 1985. Access to attitude-relevant information in memory as a determinant of persuasion: The role of message attributes. *Journal of Experimental Social Psychology*, 21:73–85.

Woodworth, R. S. 1918. *Dynamic Psychology*. New York: Columbia University Press.

———. 1941. *Heredity and Environment*. A report prepared for the Committee on Social Adjustment. New York: Social Science Research Council.

Woolfolk, R. L., and Richardson, F. C. 1984. Behavior therapy and the ideology of modernity. *American Psychologist*, 39:377–386.

Worchel, S., and Brown, E. H. 1984. The role of plausibility in influencing environmental attribution. *Journal of Experimental Social Psychology*, 20:86–96.

Wortman, C., and Silver, R. 1982. Coping with undesirable life events. Paper presented at the 90th annual convention of the American Psychological Association. Washington, D.C., August.

Wright, J. D., and Hamilton, R. F. 1978. Work satisfaction and age: Some evidence of the "job change" hypothesis. *Social Forces*, 56:1140–1158.

Wright, P. H., and Keple, T. W. 1981. Friends and parents of a sample of high school juniors: An exploratory study of relationship intensity and interpersonal rewards. *Journal of Marriage and the Family*, 43:559–570.

Wurtman, R. J. 1982. Nutrients that modify brain function. *Scientific American*, 246 (April):50–59.

———. 1985. Alzheimer's disease. *Scientific American*, 252 (January):62–74.

Wurtz, R. H., Goldberg, M. E., and Robinson, D. L. 1982. Brain mechanisms of visual attention. *Scientific American*, 246 (June):124–135.

Wyatt, R. J., Potkin, S. G., and Murphy, D. L. 1979. Platelet MAO activity in schizophrenia: A review of the data. *American Journal of Psychiatry*, 136:377–385.

Wyman, A. 1983. Animals sometimes seem human. *Columbus (Ohio) Dispatch* (October 30):1F.

Wynne, L. C., Singer, M. T., Bartko, J. J., and Toohey, M. L. 1977. Schizophrenics and their families: Research on parental communication. In Tanner, J. M., Ed., *Developments in Psychiatric Research*. London: Hodder and Stoughton.

Wyshak, G., and Frisch, R. E. 1982. Evidence for a secular trend in age of menarche. *New England Journal of Medicine*, 306:1033–1035.

Yankelovich, D. 1982. The work ethic is underemployed. *Psychology Today*, 16 (May):5–8.

Yarrow, M. R., Waxler, C. Z., and Scott, P. M. 1971. Child effects on adult behavior. *Developmental Psychology*, 5:300–311.

Yates, F. A. 1966. *The Art of Memory*. Chicago: University of Chicago Press.

Young, P. 1983. A conversation with Richard Jed Wyatt. *Psychology Today*, 17 (August):30–41.

Zachry, W. 1978. Originality and interdependence of representation and language development in infancy.

Child Development, 49:681–687.

Zahorik, D. M., and Bean, C. A. 1975. Resistance of "recovery" flavors to later association with illness. *Bulletin of the Psychonomic Society*, 6:309–312.

——, Maier, S. F., and Pies, R. W. 1974. Preferences for tastes paired with recovery from thiamine deficiency in rats: Appetitive conditioning or learned safety. *Journal of Comparative and Physiological Psychology*, 87:1083–1091.

Zajonc, R. B. 1980. Feeling and thinking. *American Psychologist*, 35:151–175.

Zamansky, H. S., and Bartis, S. P. 1985. The dissociation of an experience: The hidden observer observed. *Journal of Abnormal Psychology*, 94:243–248.

Zanna, M. P., and Hamilton, D. L. 1972. Attribute dimensions and patterns of trait inferences. *Psychonomic Science*, 27:353–354.

Zappert, L. T., and Weinstein, H. M. 1985. Sex differences in the impact of work on physical and psychological health. *American Journal of Psychiatry*, 142:1174–1178.

Zemian, F. P., Ritzemann, R. J., Hirschowitz, J., and Garver, D. L. 1985. Down-regulation of central dopamine receptors in schizophrenia. *American Journal of Psychiatry*, 142:1334–1337.

Zern, D. S. 1983. The relationship of certain group-oriented and individualistically oriented child-rearing dimensions to cultural complexity in a cross-cultural sample. *Genetic Psychological Monographs*, 108:3–20.

Zigli, B. 1985. Teens curb drug, alcohol use. *USA Today* (January 8):1A.

Zillmann, D. 1982. Television viewing and arousal. In Pearl, D., Bouthilet, L., and Lazar, J., Eds., *Television and Behavior. Vol. 2: Technical Reviews.* Washington, D.C.: U.S. Government Printing Office.

Zimbardo, P., Haney, C., and Banks, W. C. 1973. A Pirandellian prison. *New York Times Magazine* (April 8):38–40+.

—— and Ruch, F. L. 1975. *Psychology and Life.* 9th ed. Glenview, Ill.: Scott, Foresman.

Zimmer, J. 1984. Courting the gods of sport. *Psychology Today*, 18 (July):36–39.

Zimmerman, B. J. 1977. Modeling. In Hom, H. L., Jr., and Robinson, P. A., Eds., *Psychological Processes in Early Education.* New York: Academic Press.

—— and Ghozeil, F. S. 1974. Modeling as a teaching technique. *The Elementary School Journal*, 74:440–446.

—— and Koussa, R. 1979. Social influences on children's toy preferences: Effects of model rewardingness and affect. *Contemporary Educational Psychology*, 4:55–66.

Zimmerman, D. H., and West, C. 1975. Sex roles, interruptions and silences in conversation. In Thorne, B., and Henley, N., Eds., *Language and Sex Difference and Dominance.* Rowley, Mass.: Newbury House.

Zubeck, J. P. 1969. *Sensory Deprivation: Fifteen Years of Research.* New York: Appleton-Century-Crofts.

Zubin, J., and Spring, B. 1977. Vulnerability—A new view of schizophrenia. *Journal of Abnormal Psychology*, 86:103–126.

Zuckerman, M., Kernis, M. H., Guarnera, S. M., Murphy, J. F., and Rappoport, L. 1983. The egocentric bias: Seeing oneself as cause and target of others' behavior. *Journal of Personality*, 51:621–630.

Name Index

Subject Index

About the Authors

Sandra Scarr, who received her Ph.D. from Harvard University, is Commonwealth Professor of Psychology at the University of Virginia. From 1977 to 1983, she was Professor of Psychology at Yale University, and from 1970 to 1976, she was Professor of Child Psychology at the University of Minnesota. Her research on behavior genetics, intelligence, child development, day care, education, and intervention programs has been published in more than one hundred articles and books. She has been elected a Fellow of the American Psychological Association and the American Association for the Advancement of Science. She has also been elected by her colleagues to many posts in professional organizations, including the Presidency of the Division on Developmental Psychology of the American Psychological Association, the Governing Council of the Society for Research in Child Development, the Executive Committee of the Behavior Genetics Association, and the Membership Secretary of the International Society for the Study of Behavioral Development.

Professor Scarr is also the editor of the APA journal *Developmental Psychology* and serves on the editorial board of the series *Advances in Psychology*. In past years, she has served on the editorial boards of several psychology journals and as the editor of special issues for *American Psychologist*.

In addition to her academic activities, Professor Scarr has consulted with two dozen organizations to improve education and the ways in which families deal with their children. Her own family consists of four children—three daughters and a son—who range in age from 9 to 20; her husband, a pediatrician; and two cats.

James W. Vander Zanden is a professor in the College of Social and Behavioral Sciences at The Ohio State University and previously taught at Duke University. His Ph.D. degree is from the University of North Carolina. Professor Vander Zanden's published works include more than twenty professional articles, primarily in the area of race relations, and six other books.